EDMUND SPENSER'S

POETRY

SECOND EDITION

AUTHORITATIVE TEXTS

CRITICISM

A NORTON CRITICAL EDITION

EDMUND SPENSER'S

POETRY

SECOND EDITION

AUTHORITATIVE TEXTS
CRITICISM

Selected and Edited by

HUGH MACLEAN
STATE UNIVERSITY OF NEW YORK AT ALBANY

W · W · NORTON & COMPANY
New York   London

Since this page cannot legibly accommodate all of the copyright notices, the
page that follows constitutes an extension of the copyright page.

Library of Congress Cataloging in Publication Data
Spenser, Edmund, 1552?–1599.
   Edmund Spenser's poetry.
   (A Norton critical editon)
   Bibliography: p.
   Spenser, Edmund, 1552?–1599—Criticism and
interpretation—Addresses, essays, lectures.
   I. Maclean, Hugh, 1919–   . II. Title.
PR2352.M3   1981   821'.3   81–2601
                                      AACR2

Printed in the United States of America. All rights reserved.

W. W. Norton & Company, Inc., 500 Fifth Avenue,
New York, N.Y. 10110
W. W. Norton & Company Ltd. 37 Great Russell Street,
London WC1B 3NU

7 8 9 0

ISBN 0-393-95138-3

ACKNOWLEDGMENTS

Paul J. Alpers: "Narrative and Rhetoric in the *Faerie Queene*," *SEL*, Vol. 2 (1962), pp. 27–46. Reprinted by permission of *SEL*.

Harry Berger, Jr.: "Busirane and the War Between the Sexes: An Interpretation of *The Faerie Queene*, III,xi–xii," *English Literary Renaissance*, Vol. 1 (1971), pp. 99, 100, 111–12, 116–17. Copyright © 1971 *English Literary Renaissance*. Used by permission.

Douglas Bush: from *Mythology and the Renaissance Tradition in English Poetry*, rev. ed. (New York: W. W. Norton & Co., Inc., 1963), pp. 91–120. Copyright © 1963 by Douglas Bush. Reprinted by permission of The University of Minnesota Press.

Northrop Frye: "The Structure of Imagery in *The Faerie Queene*," *UTQ*, Vol. 30 (1961), pp. 109–127. Reprinted by permission of the University of Toronto Press.

Edwin Greenlaw: "Spenser's Fairy Mythology," *Studies in Phililogy*, Vol. 15 (1918), pp. 107–110, 116–121. Reprinted by permission of The University of North Carolina Press.

A. C. Hamilton: from *The Structure of Allegory in The Faerie Queene*. Copyright © 1961 Oxford University Press. Reprinted by permission of Oxford University Press.

S. K. Heninger, Jr.: from "The Orgoglio Episode in *The Faerie Queene*, *ELH*, Vol. 26 (1959), pp. 171–187. Reprinted by permission of The Johns Hopkins University Press.

A. Kent Hieatt: from *Chaucer, Spenser, Milton: Mythopoeic Continuities and Transformations* (Montreal: McGill-Queen's University Press, 1975), pp. 129–33. Copyright © 1975 A. Kent Hieatt. Reprinted by permission of the author and the publisher.

Graham Hough: from *A Preface to The Faerie Queene*. Copyright © 1962 by Graham Hough. Reprinted with the permission of W. W. Norton & Company, Inc. and Gerald Duckworth and Company Ltd.

J. W. Lever: from *The Elizabethan Love Sonnet* (London, 1956), pp. 99–136. Reprinted by permission of Methuen & Company, Ltd.

C. S. Lewis: from *The Allegory of Love* (Oxford University Press, 1936). Reprinted by permission of the publisher.

Isabel G. MacCaffrey: from "Allegory and Pastoral in *The Shepheardes Calender*," *ELH*, Vol. 36 (1969) pp. 88–96, 105–109. Reprinted by permission of The Johns Hopkins University Press and Wallace T. MacCaffrey, Executor of the Estate of Isabel G. MacCaffrey.

Louis Martz: from "The *Amoretti*: 'Most Goodly Temperature,'" in *Form and Convention in the Poetry of Edmund Spenser*, edited by W. Nelson (New York, 1961). Reprinted by permission of Columbia University Press.

William Nelson: from *The Poetry of Edmund Spenser* (New York, 1963). Reprinted by permission of Columbia University Press.

F. M. Padelford: "The Allegory of Chastity in *The Faerie Queene*," *Studies in Philology*, Vol. 24 (1924), p. 376. Reprinted by permission of The University of North Carolina Press.

Ricardo J. Quinones: from *The Renaissance Discovery of Time* (Cambridge, Mass.: Harvard University Press). Copyright © 1972 by the President and Fellows of Harvard College. Reprinted by permission of the publisher.

Thomas P. Roche, Jr.: from *The Kindly Flame: A Study of the Third and Fourth Books of Spenser's Faerie Queene*, pp. 7–84. Copyright © 1964 by Princeton University Press.

Hallett Smith: from "The Use of Conventions in Edmund Spenser's Minor Poems" in *Form and Convention in the Poetry of Edmund Spenser*, edited by W. Nelson (New York, 1961). Reprinted by permission of Columbia University Press.

Humphrey Tonkin: from *Spenser's Courteous Pastoral*. Copyright © 1972 Oxford University Press. Reprinted by permission of Oxford University Press.

Kathleen Williams: "Venus and Diana: Some Uses of Myth in *The Faerie Queene*," *ELH*, Vol. 28 (1961), pp. 103–117. Reprinted by permission of The Johns Hopkins University Press and J. B. Vickery, Executor of the Estate of Kathleen Williams.

Contents

Criticism

Preface to the Second Edition

Spenser . . . in what he sayth hath a way of expression peculiar to him-selfe; he bringeth downe the highest and deepest mysteries that are con-tained in humane learning, to an easie and gentle forme of delivery; which sheweth he is Master of what he treateth of: he can wield it as he pleaseth: And he hath done this so cunningly, that if one heede him not with great attention, rare and wonderful conceptions will unperceived slide by him that readeth his workes, and he will thinke he hath mett with nothing but familiar and easie discourses: But lett one dwell a while upon them, and he shall feele a strange fulness and roundness in all he sayth.
—SIR KENELM DIGBY (1603–1665)

Since the publication, in 1968, of the first edition of *Edmund Spen-ser's Poetry*, the volume of critical attention to virtually every aspect of Spenser's work has enormously increased; the size alone of the Selected Bibliography in this Second Edition gives some indication of the dazzling new worlds of profit and delight made available to students of Spenser's poetry in the last ten years or so. The quantita-tive growth of scholarship, of course, however luxuriant, need not guarantee a matching advance in critically subtle response to the varied challenges of the poetry; still, as an editor surveys the whole range of critical work on Spenser since 1968, he must be struck by both the sensitive penetration of these our new critics and by the extraordinary reach and scope of their endeavors. It is remarkable too that the vital and steadying influence of earlier scholarship continues to sound in the best recent criticism, which ignores no significant aspect of the poet's art, but which attends particularly to Books III and VI of *The Faerie Queene*, and to *The Shepheardes Calender*. Especially fruitful studies include those that focus upon Spenser's idea of the poet's social role, his narrative art, his creative treatment of myth; other important essays explore the principles informing Spenser's allegory and its manner of working. And an increasing number of interdisciplinary studies are opening new avenues in the green wood of Spenser's poetry: anthropological and psychological contexts (to say nothing of iconography) seem to promise especially glittering prizes for the student of this poet's art. The materials for this Second Edition have been assembled in the light of these critical developments, with a view to providing a considerably more generous selection of Spenser's poetry than that offered by the earlier edition, together with a selection of critical essays that indicate the expanding horizons of recent scholarship while not neglecting traditional ap-proaches to the poetry.

New selections from *The Faerie Queene* in this edition include Scudamour's account of his conquest of Amoret at the Temple of Venus (IV.x), the description of Britomart's experiences at Isis Church (V.vii.1–24), and the Proems to Books IV and V. Readers are thereby now enabled to compare and contrast the structural function and allegorical character of the "symbolic cores" in these Books with those of other Books in the poem, and also to weigh the shifting emphases of the poet's voice in his introductory stanzas to each of Books I–VI. To speak generally, these new selections from *The Faerie Queene* will make it possible for readers to form some conception of the poem as a whole, and in some measure to recognize the detailed and painstaking craft with which this poet works out his larger design: to acknowledge, at length, the aptness of Digby's estimate of Spenser, that "weight of matter, was never better joyned with propriety of language and with majesty and sweetnesse of verse, then by him."

As for the minor poetry, selections from *The Shepheardes Calender* now include the "June," "November," and "December" eclogues, as well as the "Januarye," "Aprill," and "October" eclogues, and the "Envoi" of the first edition. The inclusion of all four "plaintive" eclogues permits readers (more clearly than in the earlier edition) to experience and assess the force of Spenser's concern for the poet's aesthetic and social responsibilities, and, more generally, for the role of the artist in the stream of time. In particular, the inclusion of the two concluding eclogues of the *Calender* allows a reader to remark that gentle smile with which Spenser regards Colin's extravagant woe—and accordingly to recognize the more fully this poet's subtle command of his medium. The fifteen sonnets from *Amoretti* in the earlier edition have been increased by one, with the deletion of the thirteenth and thirty-fifth sonnets in favor of three others: the riddling celebration of "this continuall cruell civill warre" that informs Sonnet 44 may be regarded as pivotal to the thrust and movement of the entire sequence, while Sonnets 53 and 67 distinctively illustrate the poet's preference in this kind for a structural scheme that suits best his broadly conceived Christian humanism. Newly included, finally, are *Muiopotmos*, by one reading "Spenser's most original poem," and in any event an excellent introduction to the poet's work; and *Prothalamion*, which completes the series of progressively more accomplished odes that first appear in the "Aprill" and "November" eclogues. The new selections from Spenser's poetry, then, deepen or extend or complete structural and thematic movements that are indicated but somewhat less fully represented in the earlier edition.

The texts of poems are based on those of the early editions of

Spenser's poetry: selections from *The Faerie Queene* on the 1596 text, the minor poems on the texts of the first editions. The editor's aim is to deliver a text that closely follows the substantive form of the early edition in question, that reproduces the spelling and (essentially) the punctuation of that edition, and that introduces only those elements of modernization that are required to render the text accessible to modern readers. Unfamiliar words are glossed in the margins. The Textual Notes provide a list of (chiefly substantive) variants among the early editions of *The Faerie Queene* and the minor poems.

As in the first edition, an "Editor's Note" accompanies each poem or group of poems; since these serve a chiefly introductory purpose, dealing for the most part with such primary matters as the circumstances of composition, genre, and structure or plan, the original "Editor's Notes" have not been substantially revised. New "Editor's Notes," of course, are appended to *Muiopotmos* and *Prothalamion*. The original footnotes, on the other hand, have been carefully combed out to reflect editorial reconsiderations and a few second thoughts; and many have been revised with a view to drawing the reader's attention to those critical books or essays published since 1968 that the editor has found to be especially illuminating or incisive.

The editor's chief problem has been the selection of critical material for this edition from the wealth of newly available critical riches. Space limitations and the high quality of recent work have obliged the editor to delete, with sharp regret, most of the early criticism included in the first edition. Of the modern critical essays on *The Faerie Queene* collected there, those by Bush, Alpers, Frye, and Heninger have seemed to the editor much too useful to be abandoned; the essays by Hough and Kathleen Williams have been replaced by other examples of those critics' work. Similarly, the perceptive essays on *Amoretti* by Lever and Martz are retained, while Hallett Smith's wisdom is represented now by his thoughtful commentary on *Muiopotmos* and *Prothalamion*. In general terms, the essays on *The Faerie Queene* by Roche, Alpers, Frye, Hamilton, and Heninger might be said to deal essentially with the theory and practice, and the interpretation, of Spenser's allegory; those by Bush and Kathleen Williams with the poet's management (and creation) of myth; that by Greenlaw with some meanings of the term "faerie" and of Spenser's fairyland. The five distinctive critical readings of the House of Busirane, by Padelford, Lewis, Roche, Hieatt, and Berger reflect something of that special fascination Book III seems increasingly to hold for modern readers; they indicate too the steadily more sophisticated wit that critics bring to this episode. Tonkin's essay on the graceful centre of Book VI effectively epitomizes the quality and insight of much recent work on the Legend of Courtesy, while the essay by Quinones trenchantly sets the Cantos of Mutabilitie in the context of an awakening Renaissance awareness of time's power and meaning. And the selection from Isabel MacCaffrey's masterful account of *The Shepheardes Calender* will have special interest for readers concerned with the implications of Colin's plight and with Spenser's first exploration of "the imagined landscape of an allegorical country." The Selected Bibliography, considerably more extensive than that of the first edition, remains in fact a selected list of especially rewarding books and articles published since 1937.

The editor gratefully acknowledges his continuing debt to the materials brought together in *The Works of Edmund Spenser: A Variorum Edition,* ed. E. Greenlaw, C. G. Osgood, F. N. Padelford, and R. Heffner (Baltimore, 1932–49; 9 vols.). The Librarian and the staff of the University Library at the State University of New York at Albany, as always, have willingly assisted the editor throughout the course of his labors. The editor's colleagues in the Departments of English and of Classics have often helped him over rough places. Kate McLindon and Tom Bulger gave generously of their time in the preparation of the manuscript. Particular thanks are due to five scholars whose thoughtful suggestions have been in various ways incorporated in this edition: Judith Anderson, Donald Cheney, A. Kent Hieatt, Foster Provost, and David Richardson. Lastly, the editor wishes to thank his students at the State University of New York at Albany for their continuing enthusiasm, wit, and faith in Spenser's poetry: they have not been carried about with divers and strange doctrines. The cheerfully supportive assistance of all these persons is gratefully acknowledged by the editor, in the spirit of Hebrews xiii.1.

HUGH MACLEAN

A Chronology of Spenser's Life

1552   Probable date of his birth in London.

1561–1569 At the Merchant Taylors' School (founded in 1561), under its first headmaster, the famous educator Richard Mulcaster. Contributes a number of verse translations to Jan van der Noodt's *Theatre* [*of*] . . . *voluptuous Worldlings*, published in 1569.

1569–1576 At Cambridge as a "sizar" of Pembroke Hall; friendship with Gabriel Harvey. Graduates a Bachelor of Arts in 1573; a Master of Arts in 1576.

1578   Secretary to John Young (formerly Master of Pembroke), Bishop of Rochester, in Kent.

1579   First marriage, to Machabyas Chylde. Associated with Sir Philip Sidney and his circle; for a time in the employ of Robert Dudley, Earl of Leicester. Publication of *The Shepheardes Calender*.

1580   Publication of correspondence between Spenser and Harvey (five letters, two by Spenser). At work on *The Faerie Queene*. Appointed secretary to the Lord Deputy of Ireland, Lord Grey of Wilton, with whom he departs for Ireland in August.

1581   Awarded the post of Clerk in Chancery for Faculties, a sinecure previously held by Lodowick Bryskett, Clerk of the Council in Munster; retains the post until 1588.

1582   Leases the property of New Abbey, in County Kildare; a commissioner of muster for the County in 1583 and 1584.

1584   Appointed Deputy to Lodowick Bryskett.

1588   Occupies Kilcolman, an estate of some 3000 acres, situated between Limerick and Cork, in Munster.

1589   To England, and the court of Queen Elizabeth, with Sir Walter Raleigh (proprietor of Inchiquin, an estate of 42,000 acres thirty miles southeast of Kilcolman). *The Faerie Queene*, I–III, entered in the Stationers' Register, December.

1590   Publication of *The Faerie Queene*, I–III, together with the *Letter to Raleigh*.

1591   Grant from the Queen of an annual pension of £50, for life. Publication of *Daphnaida* and *Complaints*. Returns to Ireland, probably in the spring.

1594   Probable date of marriage to Elizabeth Boyle, in Cork.

1595   Publication of *Colin Clouts Come Home Againe*, and of *Amoretti* and *Epithalamion*.

1596   Publication of *The Faerie Queene*, I–VI; *Fowre Hymnes*; and *Prothalamion*. Probably in England to oversee the printing of at least the later Books of *The Faerie Queene*.

1598 The prose tract, *A Vewe of the present state of Irelande* (first published in 1633), entered in the Stationers' Register, April. Insurrection in northern and western Ireland spreads into Munster; Kilcolman sacked by the rebels. Spenser takes refuge in Cork, whence he carries letters from Sir Thomas Norris, Lord President of Munster, to the Privy Council in London (arriving on 24 December).

1599 Spenser dies in Westminster, 13 January; he is buried in Westminster Abbey.

1609 Publication of *The Faerie Queene* together with the *Cantos of Mutabilitie*.

The Texts of
The Poems

THE FAERIE
QVEENE.

Difpofed into twelue bookes,

Fashioning

XII. Morall vertues.

LONDON
Printed for VVilliam Ponfonbie.
1 5 9 6.

TO
THE MOST HIGH,
MIGHTIE
And
MAGNIFICENT
EMPRESSE RENOVV-
MED FOR PIETIE, VER-
TVE, AND ALL GRATIOVS
GOVERNMENT ELIZABETH BY
THE GRACE OF GOD QVEENE
OF ENGLAND FRAVNCE AND
IRELAND AND OF VIRGI-
NIA, DEFENDOVR OF THE
FAITH, &c. HER MOST
HVMBLE SERVAVNT
EDMVND SPENSER
DOTH IN ALL HV-
MILITIE DEDI-
CATE, PRE-
SENT
AND CONSECRATE THESE
HIS LABOVRS TO LIVE
VVITH THE ETERNI-
TIE OF HER
FAME.

A Letter of the Authors

EXPOUNDING HIS WHOLE INTENTION IN THE COURSE OF THIS WORKE:
WHICH FOR THAT IT GIVETH GREAT LIGHT TO THE READER, FOR THE
BETTER UNDERSTANDING IS HEREUNTO ANNEXED.[1]

*To the Right noble, and Valorous, Sir Walter Raleigh knight, Lo.
Wardein of the Stanneryes, and her Majesties liefetenaunt of the
County of Cornewayll.*

Sir knowing how doubtfully all Allegories may be construed, and
this booke of mine, which I have entituled the Faery Queene, being
a continued Allegory, or darke conceit, I have thought good aswell
for avoyding of gealous opinions and misconstructions, as also for
your better light in reading thereof, (being so by you commanded,)
to discover unto you the general intention and meaning, which in
the whole course thereof I have fashioned, without expressing of any
particular purposes or by-accidents[2] therein occasioned. The generall
end therefore of all the booke is to fashion[3] a gentleman or noble
person in vertuous and gentle discipline: Which for that I conceived
shoulde be most plausible[4] and pleasing, being coloured with an
historicall fiction, the which the most part of men delight to read,
rather for variety of matter, then for profite of the ensample: I chose
the historye of king Arthure, as most fitte for the excellency of his
person, being made famous by many mens former workes, and also
furthest from the daunger of envy, and suspition of present time.[5]
In which I have followed all the antique Poets historicall, first
Homere, who in the Persons of Agamemnon and Ulysses hath en-
sampled a good governour and a vertuous man, the one in his *Ilias*,
the other in his *Odysseis*: then Virgil, whose like intention was to
doe in the person of Aeneas: after him Ariosto comprised them both
in his Orlando: and lately Tasso dissevered them againe, and
formed both parts in two persons, namely that part which they in
Philosophy call Ethice, or vertues of a private man, coloured in his
Rinaldo: The other named Politice in his Godfredo.[6] By ensample

---

1. This "Letter" was appended to the
1590 edition of *The Faerie Queene*
(Books I–III). Such epistolary intro-
ductions were commonly employed by
Renaissance poets to explain or defend
their purpose and method; cf. Tasso's
account of the allegory in his epic poem
Gerusalemme Liberata, and Sir John
Harington's preface to his translation
of Ariosto's *Orlando Furioso* (1591),
not to mention the "Epistle" and
"Argument" prefixed to *The Shep-
heardes Calender*.
2. Side issues, secondary concerns.

3. I.e., to represent (in a secondary
sense only, to train or educate).
4. Acceptable, deserving of approval.
5. I.e., not subject to interpretation in
terms of contemporary political bias
or prejudice.
6. Lodovico Ariosto (1474–1533) was
author of the epic romance *Orlando
Furioso*, first published in complete
form in 1532; Torquato Tasso (1544–
1595) published his chivalric romance
Rinaldo in 1562 and the epic *Gerusa-
lemme Liberata* (centered on the heroic
figure of Count Godfredo) in 1581.

of which excellente Poets, I labour to pourtraict in Arthure, before he was king, the image of a brave knight, perfected in the twelve private morall vertues, as Aristotle hath devised,[7] the which is the purpose of these first twelve bookes: which if I finde to be well accepted, I may be perhaps encoraged, to frame the other part of polliticke vertues in his person, after that hee came to be king. To some I know this Methode will seeme displeasaunt, which had rather have good discipline delivered plainly in way of precepts, or sermoned at large, as they use, then thus clowdily enwrapped in Allegoricall devises. But such, me seeme, should be satisfide with the use of these dayes, seeing all things accounted by their showes, and nothing esteemed of, that is not delightfull and pleasing to commune sence. For this cause is Xenophon preferred before Plato, for that the one in the exquisite depth of his judgement, formed a Commune welth such as it should be, but the other in the person of Cyrus and the Persians fashioned a governement such as might best be: So much more profitable and gratious is doctrine by ensample, then by rule.[8] So have I laboured to doe in the person of Arthure: whome I conceive after his long education by Timon, to whom he was by Merlin delivered to be brought up, so soone as he was borne of the Lady Igrayne, to have seene in a dream or vision the Faery Queen, with whose excellent beauty ravished, he awaking resolved to seeke her out, and so being by Merlin armed, and by Timon throughly instructed, he went to seeke her forth in Faerye land. In that Faery Queene I meane glory in my generall intention, but in my particular I conceive the most excellent and glorious person of our soveraine the Queene, and her kingdome in Faery land. And yet in some places els, I doe otherwise shadow[9] her. For considering she beareth two persons, the one of a most royall Queene or Empresse, the other of a most vertuous and beautifull Lady, this latter part in some places I doe expresse in Belphoebe, fashioning her name according to your owne excellent conceipt of Cynthia,[1] (Phoebe and Cynthia being both names of Diana.) So in the person of Prince Arthure I sette forth magnificence in particular, which vertue for that (according to Aristotle and the rest)[2] it is

---

7. Aristotle does not actually distinguish twelve moral virtues in the *Nicomachaean Ethics,* but medieval and early sixteenth-century commentators, following Aquinas, had so divided them; Spenser's friend Lodowick Bryskett (influenced by the Italian commentator Piccolomini) speaks of twelve virtues in his *Discourse of Civill Life.*
8. This distinction between Xenophon's *Cyropaedia* and Plato's *Republic* recalls Sidney's praise of the poet (who "coupleth the generall notion with the particuler example") at the expense of the philosopher, whose "woordish de-

scription . . . dooth neyther strike, pierce, nor possesse the sight of the soule so much as that other dooth." Sidney calls the *Cyropaedia* "an absolute [i.e., complete, perfect] heroicall Poem."
9. I.e., portray.
1. Raleigh's poem *Cynthia* (of which only a fragment remains) celebrated the virtues of Queen Elizabeth.
2. I.e., notably, Cicero's *De inventione,* the *Somnium Scipionis* of Macrobius, and (among later commentators on the virtues) the pseudo-Senecan *Formula honestae vitae* written by Martin of Braga in the sixth century.

the perfection of all the rest, and conteineth in it them all, therefore in the whole course I mention the deedes of Arthure applyable to that vertue, which I write of in that booke. But of the xii. other vertues, I make xii. other knights the patrones, for the more variety of the history: Of which these three bookes contayn three, The first of the knight of the Redcrosse, in whome I expresse Holynes: The seconde of Sir Guyon, in whome I sette forth Temperaunce: The third of Britomartis a Lady knight, in whome I picture Chastity. But because the beginning of the whole worke seemeth abrupte and as depending upon other antecedents, it needs that ye know the occasion of these three knights severall adventures. For the Methode of a Poet historical is not such, as of an Historiographer.[3] For an Historiographer discourseth of affayres orderly as they were donne, accounting as well the times as the actions, but a Poet thrusteth into the middest, even where it most concerneth him, and there recoursing to the thinges forepaste, and divining of thinges to come, maketh a pleasing Analysis of all. The beginning therefore of my history, if it were to be told by an Historiographer, should be the twelfth booke, which is the last, where I devise that the Faery Queene kept her Annuall feaste xii. dayes, uppon which xii. severall dayes, the occasions of the xii. severall adventures hapned, which being undertaken by xii. severall knights, are in these xii books severally handled and discoursed. The first was this. In the beginning of the feast, there presented him selfe a tall clownishe[4] younge man, who falling before the Queen of Faries desired a boone (as the manner then was) which during that feast she might not refuse: which was that hee might have the atchievement of any adventure, which during that feaste should happen, that being graunted, he rested him on the floore, unfitte through his rusticity for a better place. Soone after entred a faire Ladye in mourning weedes, riding on a white Asse, with a dwarfe behind her leading a warlike steed, that bore the Armes of a knight, and his speare in the dwarfes hand. Shee falling before the Queene of Faeries, complayned[5] that her father and mother an ancient King and Queene, had bene by an huge dragon many years shut up in a brasen Castle, who thence suffred them not to yssew: and therefore besought the Faery Queene to assygne her some one of her knights to take on him that exployt. Presently that clownish person upstarting, desired that adventure: whereat the Queene much wondering, and the Lady much gainesaying, yet he earnestly importuned his desire. In the end the Lady told him that unlesse that armour which she brought, would serve him (that is the armour of a Christian man specified by Saint Paul

---

3. I.e., the method employed by an epic poet is not that of the historian.
4. I.e., of rustic appearance (appropriate to the man brought up in "ploughmans state," I. x. 66).
5. Lamented.

v. Ephes.)[6] that he could not succeed in that enterprise, which being forthwith put upon him with dewe furnitures[7] thereunto, he seemed the goodliest man in al that company, and was well liked of the Lady. And eftesoones[8] taking on him knighthood, and mounting on that straunge Courser, he went forth with her on that adventure: where beginneth the first booke, vz.

A gentle knight was pricking on the playne. &c.

The second day ther came in a Palmer bearing an Infant with bloody hands, whose Parents he complained to have bene slayn by an Enchaunteresse called Acrasia: and therfore craved of the Faery Queene, to appoint him some knight, to performe that adventure, which being assigned to Sir Guyon, he presently went forth with that same Palmer: which is the beginning of the second booke and the whole subject thereof. The third day there came in, a Groome who complained before the Faery Queene, that a vile Enchaunter called Busirane had in hand a most faire Lady called Amoretta, whom he kept in most grievous torment, because she would not yield him the pleasure of her body. Whereupon Sir Scudamour the lover of that Lady presently tooke on him that adventure. But being unable to performe it by reason of the hard Enchauntments, after long sorrow, in the end met with Britomartis, who succoured him, and reskewed his love.

But by occasion hereof, many other adventures are intermedled, but rather as Accidents, then intendments.[9] As the love of Britomart, the overthrow of Marinell, the misery of Florimell, the vertuousnes of Belphoebe, the lasciviousnes of Hellenora, and many the like.

Thus much Sir, I have briefly overronne to direct your understanding to the wel-head[1] of the History, that from thence gathering the whole intention of the conceit, ye may as in a handfull gripe al the discourse, which otherwise may happily[2] seeme tedious and confused. So humbly craving the continuaunce of your honorable favour towards me, and th'eternall establishment of your happines, I humbly take leave.

23. January. 1589.[3]
Yours most humbly affectionate.
Ed. Spenser.

---

6. Cf. the note on I. i. 1.
7. Suitable equipment.
8. Forthwith.
9. I.e., as matters relatively incidental to a central purpose.

1. Source, spring.
2. By chance.
3. I.e., 1590. In England (until 1753), the official year was reckoned from March 25.

The First Booke of The Faerie Queene

Contayning
The Legende of the Knight of the Red Crosse,
or
Of Holinesse

1

Lo I the man, whose Muse whilome° did maske,   *formerly*
   As time her taught, in lowly Shepheards weeds,[1]
Am now enforst a far unfitter taske,
For trumpets sterne to chaunge mine Oaten reeds,
And sing of Knights and Ladies gentle deeds;
Whose prayses having slept in silence long,
Me, all too meane, the sacred Muse areeds°   *counsels*
To blazon broad[2] amongst her learnéd throng:
Fierce warres and faithfull loves shall moralize my song.

2

Helpe then, O holy Virgin chiefe of nine,[3]
   Thy weaker° Novice to performe thy will,   *too weak*
   Lay forth out of thine everlasting scryne°   *chest for records*
The antique rolles, which there lye hidden still,
Of Faerie knights and fairest Tanaquill,[4]
Whom that most noble Briton Prince[5] so long
Sought through the world, and suffered so much ill,
That I must rue his undeservéd wrong:
O helpe thou my weake wit, and sharpen my dull tong.

3

And thou most dreaded impe[6] of highest Jove,
   Faire Venus sonne, that with thy cruell dart
   At that good knight so cunningly didst rove,°   *shoot*
That glorious fire it kindled in his hart,
Lay now thy deadly Heben° bow apart,   *ebony*
And with thy mother milde come to mine ayde:

1. These lines, recalling the verses prefixed to Virgil's *Aeneid,* associate Spenser and his poem with the traditions of classical epic, and announce his movement from the pastoral genre to the more elevated vein of heroic poetry; thus, "trumpets sterne" replace the shepherd's pipes ("Oaten reeds") appropriate for the poet of *The Shepheardes Calender.* For an account of Virgil's exemplary influence on Spenser's "idea of the poet," cf. the essay by Richard Neuse in *ELH,* XLV (1978), 606–639.
2. I.e., to proclaim.
3. Probably Clio, the Muse of history (in the light of I. xi. 5, and III. iii. 4).

Spenser refers to Clio as "eldest Sister of the crew" [of the nine Muses, daughters of Memory] in *The Teares of the Muses,* 53. An alternative, but less likely, identification is Calliope, the Muse of epic poetry.
4. Gloriana, i.e., Queen Elizabeth. "Caia Tanaquill," according to legend the Etruscan wife of a Roman king, L. Tarquinius Priscus, was considered by the Spanish humanist Vives (1492–1540) to be the exemplary pattern of a noble queen.
5. I.e., Arthur.
6. Child, i.e., Cupid, god of love.

Come both, and with you bring triumphant Mart,[7]
   In loves and gentle jollities arrayd,
After his murdrous spoiles and bloudy rage allayd.

4

And with them eke,° O Goddesse heavenly bright,[8]   *also*
   Mirrour of grace and Majestie divine,
   Great Lady of the greatest Isle, whose light
   Like Phoebus lampe throughout the world doth shine,
   Shed thy faire beames into my feeble eyne,
   And raise my thoughts too humble and too vile,°   *lowly*
   To thinke of that true glorious type° of thine,   *pattern*
   The argument of mine afflicted° stile: *humble*
The which to heare, vouchsafe, O dearest dred[9] a-while.

Canto I

The Patron of true Holinesse,
Foule Errour doth defeate:
Hypocrisie him to entrappe,
Doth to his home entreate.

1

A Gentle Knight was pricking° on the plaine,   *riding briskly*
   Y cladd in mightie armes and silver shielde,[1]
   Wherein old dints of deepe wounds did remaine,
   The cruell markes of many a bloudy fielde;
   Yet armes till that time did he never wield:
   His angry steede did chide his foming bitt,
   As much disdayning to the curbe to yield:
   Full jolly° knight he seemd, and faire did sitt,   *gallant*
As one for knightly giusts° and fierce encounters fitt.   *tourneys*

2

But on his brest a bloudie Crosse he bore,
   The deare remembrance of his dying Lord,
   For whose sweete sake that glorious badge he wore,
   And dead as living[2] ever him adored:
   Upon his shield the like was also scored,
   For soveraine hope, which in his helpe he had:
   Right faithfull true he was in deede and word,

---

7. Mars, god of war, and Venus's lover (Ovid, *Metamorphoses*, IV. 167–189).
8. I.e., Queen Elizabeth.
9. Object of reverence and awe.
1. Cf. Ephesians vi. 11–17: "Put on the whole armour of God, that ye may be able to stand against the wiles of the devil. . . . Above all, taking the shield of faith, wherewith ye shall be able to quench all the fiery darts of the wicked." Redcrosse's armor is that of every Christian in the conflict with evil.
2. Revelation i. 18: "I am he that liveth, and was dead; and, behold, I am alive for evermore."

But of his cheere° did seeme too solemne sad;°   *countenance/grave*
Yet nothing did he dread, but ever was ydrad.°   *dreaded*

3

Upon a great adventure he was bond,
    That greatest Gloriana to him gave,
    That greatest Glorious Queene of Faerie lond,
    To winne him worship,° and her grace to have,   *honor*
    Which of all earthly things he most did crave;
    And ever as he rode, his hart did earne°   *yearn*
    To prove his puissance in battell brave
Upon his foe, and his new force to learne;
Upon his foe, a Dragon[3] horrible and stearne.

4

A lovely Ladie[4] rode him faire beside,
    Upon a lowly Asse more white then snow,
    Yet she much whiter, but the same did hide
    Under a vele, that wimpled° was full low,   *folded*
    And over all a blacke stole she did throw,
    As one that inly mournd: so was she sad,
    And heavie sat upon her palfrey slow;
    Seeméd in heart some hidden care she had,
And by her in a line° a milke white lambe she lad.°   *leash/led*

5

So pure an innocent, as that same lambe,[5]
    She was in life and every vertuous lore,
    And by descent from Royall lynage came
    Of ancient Kings and Queenes, that had of yore
    Their scepters stretcht from East to Westerne shore,
    And all the world in their subjection held;
    Till that infernall feend with foule uprore
    Forwasted all their land, and them expeld:
Whom to avenge, she had this Knight from far compeld.°   *summoned*

6

Behind her farre away a Dwarfe[6] did lag,
    That lasie seemd in being ever last,
    Or weariéd with bearing of her bag
    Of needments at his backe. Thus as they past,
    The day with cloudes was suddeine overcast,
    And angry Jove an hideous storme of raine
    Did poure into his Lemans lap[7] so fast,

---

3. Cf. Revelation xx. 2: ". . . the dragon, that old serpent, which is the devil, and Satan . . ."
4. I.e., Una (first named in st. 45), representing Truth, in particular the true faith of Redcrosse. In this context, the "lowly Asse" is a symbol of humility.
5. The lamb indicates Una's Christian significance (cf. John i. 29), as well as her purity and innocence; for some at least among Spenser's readers, it would recall St. George's rescue (in *The Golden Legend*, Caxton's fifteenth-century translation of Jacobus de Voraigne's thirteenth-century *Legenda Aurea*) of the king's daughter, marked for sacrifice, with her accompanying lamb.
6. The dwarf may represent common sense, or practical understanding.
7. I.e., into the lap of his mistress, the earth.

That every wight° to shrowd° it did constrain,   *creature/cover*
And this faire couple eke to shroud themselves were fain.°   *eager*

7

Enforst to seeke some covert nigh at hand,
    A shadie grove not far away they spide,
    That promist ayde the tempest to withstand:
    Whose loftie trees yclad with sommers pride,
    Did spred so broad, that heavens light did hide,
    Not perceable with power of any starre:
    And all within were pathes and alleies wide,
    With footing worne, and leading inward farre:
Faire harbour° that them seemes; so in they entred arre.   *shelter*

8

And foorth they passe, with pleasure forward led,
    Joying to heare the birdes sweete harmony,
    Which therein shrouded from the tempest dred,
    Seemd in their song to scorne the cruell sky.
    Much can° they prayse the trees so straight and hy,[8]   *did*
    The sayling Pine, the Cedar proud and tall,
    The vine-prop Elme, the Poplar never dry,
    The builder Oake, sole king of forrests all,
The Aspine good for staves, the Cypresse funerall.

9

The Laurell, meed° of mightie Conquerours   *reward*
    And Poets sage, the Firre that weepeth still,
    The Willow worne of forlorne Paramours,
    The Eugh° obedient to the benders will,   *yew*
    The Birch for shaftes, the Sallow for the mill,
    The Mirrhe sweete bleeding in the bitter wound,[9]
    The warlike Beech, the Ash for nothing ill,
    The fruitfull Olive, and the Platane° round,   *plane-tree*
The carver Holme,° the Maple seeldom inward sound.   *holly*

10

Led with delight, they thus beguile the way,
    Untill the blustring storme is overblowne;
    When weening° to returne, whence they did stray,   *expecting*
    They cannot finde that path, which first was showne,
    But wander too and fro in wayes unknowne,
    Furthest from end then, when they neerest weene,
    That makes them doubt, their wits be not their owne:

---

8. Chaucer's *Parliament of Fowls*, 176–182, is the immediate source for this catalogue of trees; the literary convention has its roots in Ovid's *Metamorphoses*, X. 90–105. Spenser's epithets, for the most part referable to each tree's natural characteristics or uses, include scriptural and classical associations as well, e.g., "the Cedar proud and tall" recalls Isaiah ii. 13, while "the Cypresse funerall" glances at Ovid's story of Cyparissus (*Metamorphoses*, X. 106–142).

9. Perhaps merely an allusion to the sweet gum that flows from the tree when its bark is cut; but the associations of myrrh with Christ's birth and death (Matthew ii. 11; Mark xv. 23; and cf. the O.E.D.) suggest that the line recalls the trees in Paradise and also that other "tree" on which Christ was crucified.

So many pathes, so many turnings seene,
That which of them to take, in diverse° doubt they been.[1] *distracting*

11

At last resolving forward still to fare,
  Till that some end they finde or° in or out, *either*
  That path they take, that beaten seemd most bare,
  And like to lead the labyrinth about;° *out of*
  Which when by tract° they hunted had throughout, *track*
  At length it brought them to a hollow cave,
  Amid the thickest woods. The Champion stout
  Eftsoones° dismounted from his courser brave, *forthwith*
And to the Dwarfe a while his needlesse spere he gave.

12

"Be well aware," quoth then that Ladie milde,
  "Least suddaine mischiefe ye too rash provoke:
  The danger hid, the place unknowne and wilde,
  Breedes dreadfull doubts: Oft fire is without smoke,
  And perill without show: therefore your stroke
  Sir knight with-hold, till further triall made."
  "Ah Ladie," said he, "shame were to revoke
  The forward footing for° an hidden shade: *because of*
Vertue gives her selfe light, through darkenesse for to wade."

13

"Yea but," quoth she, "the perill of this place
  I better wot° then you, though now too late *know*
  To wish you backe returne with foule disgrace,
  Yet wisedome warnes, whilest foot is in the gate,
  To stay the steppe, ere forcéd to retrate.
  This is the wandring wood, this Errours den,
  A monster vile, whom God and man does hate:
  Therefore I read° beware." "Fly fly," quoth then *advise*
The fearefull Dwarfe: "this is no place for living men."

14

But full of fire and greedy hardiment,° *boldness*
  The youthfull knight could not for ought be staide,
  But forth unto the darksome hole he went,
  And lookéd in: his glistring armor made
  A litle glooming light, much like a shade,
  By which he saw the ugly monster plaine,
  Halfe like a serpent horribly displaide,
  But th'other halfe did womans shape retaine,[2]
Most lothsom, filthie, foule, and full of vile disdaine.

1. So at the outset of the *Inferno*, Dante has lost his way in a dark wood. The labyrinthine diversity of paths in this forest is analogous to the bewildering variety of choices open to mankind in life. For an extended account of Spenser's allegorical method in sts. 11–28, cf. the discussion by A. C. Hamilton in this edition.
2. The description of Errour combines elements from classical and Christian sources: specifically, the snake goddess in Hesiod, *Theogony*, 297–300, and (in Revelation ix. 7–10) the locusts with men's faces, "hair as the hair of women," and tails "like unto scorpions with stings in their tails." This first encounter with a monster of serpentine aspect points on to the climactic battle with "the dragon, that old serpent," in Canto xi.

15

And as she lay upon the durtie ground,
   Her huge long taile her den all overspred,
   Yet was in knots and many boughtes° upwound,   *coils*
   Pointed with mortall sting. Of her there bred
   A thousand yong ones, which she dayly fed,
   Sucking upon her poisonous dugs, eachone
   Of sundry shapes, yet all ill favoréd:
   Soone as that uncouth° light upon them shone,   *unaccustomed*
Into her mouth they crept, and suddain all were gone.

16

Their dam upstart, out of her den effraide,
   And rushéd forth, hurling her hideous taile
   About her curséd head, whose folds displaid
   Were stretcht now forth at length without entraile.°   *coiling*
   She lookt about, and seeing one in mayle
   Arméd to point,° sought backe to turne againe;   *completely*
   For light she hated as the deadly bale,°   *injury*
   Ay wont in desert darknesse to remaine,
Where plaine none might her see, nor she see any plaine.

17

Which when the valiant Elfe perceived, he lept
   As Lyon fierce upon the flying pray,
   And with his trenchand° blade her boldly kept   *sharp*
   From turning backe, and forcéd her to stay:
   Therewith enraged she loudly gan to bray,
   And turning fierce, her speckled taile advaunst,
   Threatning her angry sting, him to dismay:
   Who nought aghast, his mightie hand enhaunst:°   *raised*
The stroke down from her head unto her shoulder glaunst.

18

Much daunted with that dint, her sence was dazd,
   Yet kindling rage, her selfe she gathered round,
   And all attonce her beastly body raizd
   With doubled forces high above the ground:
   Tho° wrapping up her wrethéd sterne arownd,   *then*
   Lept fierce upon his shield, and her huge traine°   *tail*
   All suddenly about his body wound,
   That hand or foot to stirre he strove in vaine:
God helpe the man so wrapt in Errours endlesse traine.[3]

19

His Lady sad to see his sore constraint,
   Cride out, "Now now Sir knight, shew what ye bee,
   Add faith unto your force, and be not faint:
   Strangle her, else she sure will strangle thee."
   That when he heard, in great perplexitie,

3. An apt illustration of Spenser's "emblematic" manner, to which the Spenserian stanza is well suited: eight lines elaborate a striking visual image, and the Alexandrine adds a significant commentary.

His gall did grate[4] for griefe° and high disdaine,   *anger*
And knitting all his force got one hand free,
Wherewith he grypt her gorge° with so great paine,   *throat*
That soone to loose her wicked bands did her constraine.

20

Therewith she spewd out of her filthy maw
  A floud of poyson horrible and blacke,
  Full of great lumpes of flesh and gobbets raw,
  Which stunck so vildly, that it forst him slacke
  His grasping hold, and from her turne him backe:
  Her vomit full of bookes and papers[5] was,
  With loathly frogs and toades, which eyes did lacke,
  And creeping sought way in the weedy gras:
Her filthy parbreake° all the place defiléd has.[6]   *vomit*

21

As when old father Nilus gins to swell
  With timely° pride above the Aegyptian vale,   *seasonal*
  His fattie° waves do fertile slime outwell,   *rich*
  And overflow each plaine and lowly dale:
  But when his later spring gins to avale,°   *subside*
  Huge heapes of mudd he leaves, wherein there breed
  Ten thousand kindes of creatures,[7] partly male
  And partly female of his fruitfull seed;
Such ugly monstrous shapes elswhere may no man reed.°   *see*

22

The same so sore annoyéd has the knight,
  That welnigh chokéd with the deadly stinke,
  His forces faile, ne can no longer fight.
  Whose corage when the feend perceived to shrinke,
  She pouréd forth out of her hellish sinke
  Her fruitfull curséd spawne of serpents small,
  Deforméd monsters, fowle, and blacke as inke,
  Which swarming all about his legs did crall,
And him encombred sore, but could not hurt at all.

23

As gentle Shepheard in sweete even-tide,
  When ruddy Phoebus gins to welke° in west,   *fade, sink*
  High on an hill, his flocke to vewen wide,
  Markes which do byte their hasty supper best;
  A cloud of combrous gnattes do him molest,

---

4. I.e., his gall bladder (considered in Spenser's day to be the source of angry emotion) was violently disturbed.
5. Roman Catholic propaganda, directed against Queen Elizabeth and the Anglican Establishment; by extension, the literature of religious controversy generally, especially in its more virulent forms.
6. Revelation xvi. 13; "I saw three unclean spirits like frogs come out of the mouth of the dragon, and out of the mouth of the beast, and out of the mouth of the false prophet."
7. Ovid, *Metamorphoses,* I. 416–437, is the most likely source for Spenser's comments on spontaneous generation, although he could have drawn on numerous classical writers who refer to the special fertility of Nile mud, e.g., Plutarch and Diodorus Siculus.

All striving to infixe their feeble stings,
That from their noyance he no where can rest,
But with his clownish° hands their tender wings   *rustic*
He brusheth oft, and oft doth mar their murmurings.

24

Thus ill bestedd,° and fearefull more of shame,   *situated*
Then of the certaine perill he stood in,
Halfe furious unto his foe he came,
Resolved in minde all suddenly to win,
Or soone to lose, before he once would lin;°   *cease*
And strooke at her with more then manly force,
That from her body full of filthie sin
He raft° her hatefull head without remorse;   *cut away*
A streame of cole black bloud forth gushéd from her corse.

25

Her scattred brood, soone as their Parent deare
They saw so rudely falling to the ground,
Groning full deadly, all with troublous feare,
Gathred themselves about her body round,
Weening their wonted entrance to have found
At her wide mouth: but being there withstood
They flockéd all about her bleeding wound,
And suckéd up their dying mothers blood,
Making her death their life, and eke her hurt their good.

26

That detestable sight him much amazde,
To see th'unkindly Impes[8] of heaven accurst,
Devoure their dam; on whom while so he gazd,
Having all satisfide their bloudy thurst,
Their bellies swolne he saw with fulnesse burst,
And bowels gushing forth: well worthy end
Of such as drunke her life, the which them nurst;
Now needeth him no lenger labour spend,
His foes have slaine themselves, with whom he should contend.

27

His Ladie seeing all, that chaunst, from farre
Approcht in hast to greet his victorie,
And said, "Faire knight, borne under happy starre,
Who see your vanquisht foes before you lye:
Well worthy be you of that Armorie,°   *armor*
Wherein ye have great glory wonne this day,
And prooved your strength on a strong enimie,
Your first adventure: many such I pray,
And henceforth ever wish, that like succeed it may."

28

Then mounted he upon his Steede againe,

---

8. Unnatural offspring.

And with the Lady backward sought to wend;°   *turn, go*
  That path he kept, which beaten was most plaine,
  Ne ever would to any by-way bend,
  But still did follow one unto the end,
  The which at last out of the wood them brought.
  So forward on his way (with God to frend)°   *as a friend*
  He passéd forth, and new adventure sought;
Long way he travelléd, before he heard of ought.

29

At length they chaunst to meet upon the way
  An aged Sire, in long blacke weedes° yclad,   *garments*
  His feete all bare, his beard all hoarie gray,
  And by his belt his booke he hanging had;
  Sober he seemde, and very sagely sad,°   *grave*
  And to the ground his eyes were lowly bent,
  Simple in shew, and voyde of malice bad,
  And all the way he prayéd, as he went,
And often knockt his brest, as one that did repent.

30

He faire the knight saluted, louting° low,   *bowing*
  Who faire him quited,° as that courteous was: *responded in kind*
  And after askéd him, if he did know
  Of straunge adventures, which abroad did pas.
  "Ah my deare Sonne," quoth he, "how should, alas,
  Silly° old man, that lives in hidden cell,   *simple*
  Bidding° his beades all day for his trespas,   *telling*
  Tydings of warre and worldly trouble tell?
With holy father sits not with such things to mell.°   *meddle*

31

"But if of daunger which hereby doth dwell,
  And homebred evill ye desire to heare,
  Of a straunge man I can you tidings tell,
  That wasteth all this countrey farre and neare."
  "Of such," said he, "I chiefly do inquere,
  And shall you well reward to shew the place,
  In which that wicked wight his dayes doth weare:°   *spend*
  For to all knighthood it is foule disgrace,
That such a curséd creature lives so long a space."

32

"Far hence," quoth he, "in wastfull° wildernesse   *desolate*
  His dwelling is, by which no living wight
  May ever passe, but thorough great distresse."
  "Now," sayd the Lady, "draweth toward night,
  And well I wote,° that of your later° fight   *know/recent*
  Ye all forwearied be: for what so strong,
  But wanting rest will also want of might?
  The Sunne that measures heaven all day long,
At night doth baite° his steedes the Ocean waves emong. *refresh*

33

"Then with the Sunne take Sir, your timely rest,
  And with new day new worke at once begin:
  Untroubled night they say gives counsell best."
  "Right well Sir knight ye have adv iséd bin,"
  Quoth then that aged man; "the way to win
  Is wisely to advise: now day is spent;
  Therefore with me ye may take up your In°   *lodging*
  For this same night." The knight was well content:
So with that godly father to his home they went.

34

A little lowly Hermitage it was,
  Downe in a dale, hard by a forests side,
  Far from resort of people, that did pas
  In travell to and froe: a little wyde°   *apart*
  There was an holy Chappell edifyde,°   *built*
  Wherein the Hermite dewly wont° to say   *was accustomed*
  His holy things each morne and eventyde:
  Thereby a Christall streame did gently play,
Which from a sacred fountaine welléd forth alway.

35

Arrivéd there, the little house they fill,
  Ne looke for entertainement, where none was:
  Rest is their feast, and all things at their will;
  The noblest mind the best contentment has.
  With faire discourse the evening so they pas:
  For that old man of pleasing wordes had store,
  And well could file his tongue as smooth as glas;
  He told of Saintes and Popes, and evermore
He strowd° an Ave-Mary after and before.   *scattered*

36

The drouping Night thus creepeth on them fast,
  And the sad humour[9] loading their eye liddes,
  As messenger of Morpheus on them cast
  Sweet slombring deaw, the which to sleepe them biddes.
  Unto their lodgings then his guestes he riddes°:   *conducts*
  Where when all drownd in deadly° sleepe he findes,   *deathlike*
  He to his study goes, and there amiddes
  His Magick bookes and arts of sundry kindes,
He seekes out mighty charmes, to trouble sleepy mindes.

37

Then choosing out few wordes most horrible,
  (Let none them read) thereof did verses frame,
  With which and other spelles like terrible,
  He bad awake blacke Plutoes griesly Dame,[1]

9. Heavy moisture, i.e., the dew of   1. I.e., Proserpine.
sleep; Morpheus is the god of sleep.

And curséd heaven, and spake reprochfull shame
Of highest God, the Lord of life and light;
A bold bad man, that dared to call by name
Great Gorgon,[2] Prince of darknesse and dead night,
At which Cocytus quakes, and Styx[3] is put to flight.

38

And forth he cald out of deepe darknesse dred
Legions of Sprights, the which like little flyes
Fluttring about his ever damnéd hed,
A-waite whereto their service he applyes,
To aide his friends, or fray° his enimies: *frighten*
Of those he chose out two, the falsest twoo,
And fittest for to forge true-seeming lyes;
The one of them he gave a message too,
The other by him selfe staide other worke to doo.

39

He making speedy way through sperséd° ayre,   *dispersed*
And through the world of waters wide and deepe,
To Morpheus house[4] doth hastily repaire.
Amid the bowels of the earth full steepe,
And low, where dawning day doth never peepe,
His dwelling is; there Tethys[5] his wet bed
Doth ever wash, and Cynthia[6] still doth steepe
In silver deaw his ever-drouping hed,
Whiles sad Night over him her mantle black doth spred.

40

Whose double gates he findeth lockéd fast,
The one faire framed of burnisht Yvory,[7]
The other all with silver overcast;
And wakefull dogges before them farre do lye,
Watching to banish Care their enimy,
Who oft is wont to trouble gentle Sleepe.
By them the Sprite doth passe in quietly,
And unto Morpheus comes, whom drownéd deepe
In drowsie fit he findes: of nothing he takes keepe.°   *notice*

41

And more, to lulle him in his slumber soft,
A trickling streame from high rocke tumbling downe

2. I.e., Demogorgon, who "the hideous
Chaos keepes" (IV. ii. 47). Spenser's
conception of this figure as a mysterious
and terrible prince of darkness is prob-
ably based on relevant passages in
Boccaccio's allegorical mythography, *De
Genealogia Deorum Gentilium* (Venice,
1472; Basel, 1532), one of two such
works on which Spenser regularly de-
pends; the other is Natalis Comes's
Mythologiae . . . (Venice, 1551).
3. Styx, Cocytus, Acheron, Phlegethon,
and Lethe are the five rivers of hell.
4. Spenser's primary source for the
episode in the house of Morpheus is
Ovid, *Metamorphoses*, XI. 592–632.
5. The wife of Ocean, in classical
tradition; here synonymous with ocean.
6. Goddess of the moon.
7. Homer (*Odyssey*, XIX. 562–567)
and Virgil (*Aeneid*, VI. 893–896) refer
to the twin portals of Sleep: truthful
dreams pass through the gate of horn,
false dreams through that of ivory.

And ever-drizling raine upon the loft,
  Mixt with a murmuring winde, much like the sowne°   *sound*
  Of swarming Bees, did cast him in a swowne:°   *swoon*
  No other noyse, nor peoples troublous cryes,
  As still are wont t'annoy the walléd towne,
  Might there be heard: but carelesse Quiet lyes,
Wrapt in eternall silence farre from enemyes.

42

The messenger approching to him spake,
  But his wast° wordes returnd to him in vaine: *wasted*
  So sound he slept, that nought mought him awake.
  Then rudely he him thrust, and pusht with paine,
  Whereat he gan to stretch: but he againe
  Shooke him so hard, that forcéd him to speake.
  As one then in a dreame, whose dryer braine[8]
  Is tost with troubled sights and fancies weake,
He mumbled soft, but would not all his silence breake.

43

The Sprite then gan more boldly him to wake,
  And threatned unto him the dreaded name
  Of Hecate:[9] whereat he gan to quake,
  And lifting up his lumpish° head, with blame   *heavy*
  Halfe angry askéd him, for what he came.
  "Hither," quoth he, "me Archimago[1] sent,
  He that the stubborne Sprites can wisely tame,
  He bids thee to him send for his intent°   *purpose*
A fit false dreame, that can delude the sleepers sent."°   *senses*

44

The God obayde, and calling forth straight way
  A diverse° dreame out of his prison darke,   *distracting*
  Delivered it to him, and downe did lay
  His heavie head, devoide of carefull carke,°   *concerns*
  Whose sences all were straight benumbd and starke.°   *rigid*
  He backe returning by the Yvorie dore,
  Remounted up as light as chearefull Larke,
  And on his litle winges the dreame he bore
In hast unto his Lord, where he him left afore.

45

Who all this while with charmes and hidden artes,
  Had made a Lady of that other Spright,

---

8. I.e., too dry brain, not saturated with the dew of sleep.
9. The queen of Hades; in Natalis Comes, patroness of the black arts and goddess of dreams.
1. Archimago is primarily to be associated with hypocrisy, as the "Argument" to this Canto indicates; as "archmagus," he represents the power of black magic; as "arch-image" (for Spenser's Protestant audience), the idolatrous character of the Roman church. The black magician in hermit's disguise is regularly encountered in medieval romance, but specific features in the description of Archimago suggest that Spenser had in view the similarly disguised figure either of the hermit in Ariosto's *Orlando Furioso*, II. 12–13, or of the enchanter Malagigi in Tasso's *Rinaldo*, I. 31.

And framed of liquid ayre her tender partes
  So lively,° and so like in all mens sight,   *lifelike*
  That weaker° sence it could have ravisht quight:[2]   *too weak*
  The maker selfe for all his wondrous witt,
  Was nigh beguiléd with so goodly sight:
  Her all in white he clad, and over it
Cast a blacke stole, most like to seeme for Una fit.

46

Now when that ydle° dreame was to him brought,   *unsubstantial*
  Unto that Elfin knight he bad him fly,
  Where he slept soundly void of evill thought,
  And with false shewes abuse his fantasy,°   *imagination*
  In sort as he him schooléd privily:
  And that new creature borne without her dew,
  Full of the makers guile, with usage sly
He taught to imitate that Lady trew,
Whose semblance she did carrie under feignéd hew.°   *form*

47

Thus well instructed, to their worke they hast,
  And comming where the knight in slomber lay,
  The one upon his hardy head him plast,
  And made him dreame of loves and lustfull play,
  That nigh his manly hart did melt away,
  Bathéd in wanton blis and wicked joy:
  Then seeméd him his Lady by him lay,
  And to him playnd,° how that false wingéd boy   *complained*
Her chast hart had subdewd, to learne Dame pleasures toy.

48

And she her selfe of beautie soveraigne Queene,
  Faire Venus seemde unto his bed to bring
  Her, whom he waking evermore did weene
  To be the chastest flowre, that ay° did spring   *ever*
  On earthly braunch, the daughter of a king,
  Now a loose Leman° to vile service bound: *paramour*
  And eke the Graces[3] seeméd all to sing,
  Hymen iô Hymen, dauncing all around,
Whilst freshest Flora[4] her with Yvie girlond crownd.

49

In this great passion of unwonted° lust,   *unaccustomed*
  Or wonted feare of doing ought amis,

2. The creation of such figures by evil enchanters is a regular feature of medieval romance: Archimago's "new creature" is "borne without her dew," i.e., unnaturally. Spenser may also have recalled Apollo's creation (in the *Iliad*, V. 449–450) of a phantom resembling Aeneas, or the fashioning by Juno (in the *Aeneid*, X. 637–644) of a shadowy Aeneas, "like dreams that befool the sleeping senses."

3. The three Graces are Aglaìa, Thalia, and Euphrosyne, collectively the personification of grace and beauty. Cf. VI. x. 21–24.

4. Goddess of flowers and springtime. The context recalls E.K.'s Glosse to "March": "the Goddesse of flowres, but indede (as saith Tacitus) a famous harlot, which with the abuse of her body having gotten great riches, made the people of Rome her heyre. . . ."

He started up, as seeming to mistrust
Some secret ill, or hidden foe of his:
Lo there before his face his Lady is,
Under blake stole hyding her bayted hooke,
And as halfe blushing offred him to kis,
With gentle blandishment and lovely looke,
Most like that virgin true, which for her knight him took.

50

All cleane dismayd to see so uncouth° sight,   *unseemly*
  And halfe enragéd at her shameless guise,
  He thought have slaine her in his fierce despight:°   *indignation*
  But hasty heat tempring with sufferance wise,
  He stayde his hand, and gan himselfe advise
  To prove his sense, and tempt her faignéd truth.
  Wringing her hands in wemens pitteous wise,
  Tho can° she weepe, to stirre up gentle ruth,°   *did/pity*
Both for her noble bloud, and for her tender youth.

51

And said, "Ah Sir, my liege Lord and my love,
  Shall I accuse the hidden cruell fate,
  And mightie causes wrought in heaven above,
  Or the blind God, that doth me thus amate,°   *dismay*
  For° hopéd love to winne me certaine hate?   *instead of*
  Yet thus perforce he bids me do, or die.
  Die is my dew: yet rew my wretched state
  You,[5] whom my hard avenging destinie
Hath made judge of my life or death indifferently.

52

"Your owne deare sake forst me at first to leave
  My Fathers kingdome," There she stopt with teares;
  Her swollen hart her speach seemd to bereave,
  And then againe begun, "My weaker yeares
  Captived to fortune and frayle worldly feares,
  Fly to your faith for succour and sure ayde:
  Let me not dye in languor and long teares."
  "Why Dame," quoth he, "what hath ye thus dismayd?
What frayes° ye, that were wont to comfort me affrayd?"   *frightens*

53

"Love of your self," she said, "and deare° constraint   *dire*
  Lets me not sleepe, but wast the wearie night
  In secret anguish and unpittied plaint,
  Whiles you in carelesse sleepe are drownéd quight."
  Her doubtfull° words made that redoubted knight   *questionable*
  Suspect her truth: yet since no'untruth he knew,
  Her fawning love with foule disdainefull spight

---

5. The curious aural effect of lines 6–8 is deliberate on the part of Spenser, who often invites the reader to take note of the infelicitous expressions employed by evil or foolish figures: cf., for example, III. x. 31, and I. iv. 50.

He would not shend,° but said, "Deare dame I rew,   *reprove*
That for my sake unknowne such griefe unto you grew.

54

"Assure your selfe, it fell not all to ground;
 For all so deare as life is to my hart,
 I deeme your love, and hold me to you bound;
 Ne let vaine feares procure your needlesse smart,
 Where cause is none, but to your rest depart."
 Not all content, yet seemd she to appease°   *cease*
 Her mournefull plaintes, beguiléd of her art,
 And fed with words, that could not chuse but please,
So slyding softly forth, she turnd as to her ease.

55

Long after lay he musing at her mood,
 Much grieved to thinke that gentle Dame so light,° *frivolous*
 For whose defence he was to shed his blood.
 At last dull wearinesse of former fight
 Having yrockt a sleepe his irkesome spright,° *mind, spirit*
 That troublous dreame gan freshly tosse his braine,
 With bowres, and beds, and Ladies deare delight:
 But when he saw his labour all was vaine,
With that misforméd spright he backe returnd againe.

Canto II

*The guilefull great Enchaunter parts
The Redcrosse Knight from Truth:
Into whose stead faire falshood steps,
And workes him wofull ruth.°*   *harm*

1

By this the Northerne wagoner had set
 His sevenfold teme behind the stedfast starre,[1]
 That was in Ocean waves yet never wet,
 But firme is fixt, and sendeth light from farre
 To all, that in the wide deepe wandring arre:
 And chearefull Chaunticlere with his note shrill
 Had warnéd once, that Phoebus fiery carre[2]
 In hast was climbing up the Easterne hill,
Full envious that night so long his roome did fill.

2

When those accurséd messengers of hell,
 That feigning dreame, and that faire-forgéd Spright
 Came to their wicked maister, and gan tell
 Their bootelesse° paines, and ill succeeding night: *useless*
 Who all in rage to see his skilfull might
 Deluded so, gan threaten hellish paine

1. I.e., the constellation Boötes and the seven stars of the Big Dipper (or the Plough) had set behind the North Star.
2. The chariot of the sun.

And sad Prosérpines wrath, them to affright.
But when he saw his threatning was but vaine,
He cast about, and searcht his balefull° bookes againe.   *deadly*

3

Eftsoones he tooke that miscreated faire,
    And that false other Spright, on whom he spred
    A seeming body of the subtile aire,
    Like a young Squire, in loves and lusty-hed
    His wanton dayes that ever loosely led,
    Without regard of armes and dreaded fight:
    Those two he tooke, and in a secret bed,
    Covered with darknesse and misdeeming° night,   *misleading*
Them both together laid, to joy in vaine delight.

4

Forthwith he runnes with feignéd faithfull hast
    Unto his guest, who after troublous sights
    And dreames, gan now to take more sound repast,°   *repose*
    Whom suddenly he wakes with fearefull frights,
    As one aghast with feends or damnéd sprights,
    And to him cals, "Rise rise unhappy Swaine,
    That here wex° old in sleepe, whiles wicked wights   *grows*
    Have knit themselves in Venus shamefull chaine;
Come see, where your false Lady doth her honour staine."

5

All in amaze he suddenly up start
    With sword in hand, and with the old man went;
    Who soone him brought into a secret part,
    Where that false couple were full closely ment°   *joined*
    In wanton lust and lewd embracément:
    Which when he saw, he burnt with gealous fire,
    The eye of reason was with rage yblent,°   *blinded*
    And would have slaine them in his furious ire,
But hardly° was restreinéd of that aged sire.   *with difficulty*

6

Returning to his bed in torment great,
    And bitter anguish of his guiltie sight,
    He could not rest, but did his stout heart eat,
    And wast his inward gall with deepe despight,
    Yrkesome° of life, and too long lingring night.   *tired*
    At last faire Hesperus³ in highest skie
    Had spent his lampe, and brought forth dawning light,
    Then up he rose, and clad him hastily;
The Dwarfe him brought his steed: so both away do fly.⁴

7

Now when the rosy-fingred Morning faire,
    Weary of aged Tithones⁵ saffron bed,

---

3. The evening star; in this context a
herald of the morning.
4. That is, Holiness is separated from
Truth, through the pernicious influence

of indignation and lust (aggravated by
false dreams).
5. Husband of Aurora, goddess of the
dawn.

Had spred her purple robe through deawy aire,
And the high hils Titan[6] discoveréd,
The royall virgin shooke off drowsy-hed,
And rising forth out of her baser° bowre,   *humble*
Lookt for her knight, who far away was fled,
And for her Dwarfe, that wont to wait each houre;
Then gan she waile and weepe, to see that woefull stowre.°   *plight*

8

And after him she rode with so much speede
  As her slow beast could make; but all in vaine:
  For him so far had borne his light-foot steede,
  Prickéd with wrath and fiery fierce disdaine,
  That him to follow was but fruitlesse paine;
  Yet she her weary limbes would never rest,
  But every hill and dale, each wood and plaine
  Did search, sore grievéd in her gentle brest,
He so ungently left her, whom she lovéd best.

9

But subtill Archimago, when his guests
  He saw divided into double parts,
  And Una wandring in woods and forrests,
  Th'end of his drift,° he praisd his divelish arts,   *plot*
  That had such might over true meaning harts;
  Yet rests not so, but other meanes doth make,
  How he may worke unto her further smarts:
  For her he hated as the hissing snake,
And in her many troubles did most pleasure take.

10

He then devisde himselfe how to disguise;
  For by his mightie science° he could take   *knowledge*
  As many formes and shapes in seeming wise,°   *in appearance*
  As ever Proteus[7] to himselfe could make:
  Sometime a fowle, sometime a fish in lake,
  Now like a foxe, now like a dragon fell,°
  That of himselfe he oft for feare would quake,
  And oft would flie away. O who can tell
The hidden power of herbes, and might of Magicke spell?

11

But now seemde best, the person to put on
  Of that good knight, his late beguiléd guest:
  In mighty armes he was yclad anon,
  And silver shield: upon his coward brest
  A bloudy crosse, and on his craven crest
  A bounch of haires discolourd° diversly: *dyed*
  Full jolly knight he seemde, and well addrest,
  And when he sate upon his courser free,°   *noble*
Saint George himself ye would have deeméd him to be.

---

6. The sun.
7. A sea god who could change himself into many shapes, including that of water and fire (cf. *Odyssey*, IV. 398–

424). Spenser indicates the subtlety and terror of Archimago's magic; but he hints also, in these lines, at its ludicrous aspect, in the larger context of Book I.

12

But he the knight, whose semblaunt° he did beare,   *likeness*
  The true Saint George was wandred far away,
  Still flying from his thoughts and gealous feare;
  Will was his guide, and griefe led him astray.
  At last him chaunst to meete upon the way
  A faithlesse Sarazin° all armed to point,   *Saracen*
  In whose great shield was writ with letters gay
  Sans foy:[8] full large of limbe and every joint
He was, and caréd not for God or man a point.

13

He had a faire companion of his way,
  A goodly Lady clad in scarlot red,[9]
  Purfled° with gold and pearle of rich assay,   *decorated*
  And like a Persian mitre on her hed
  She wore, with crownes and owches° garnishéd,   *brooches*
  The which her lavish lovers to her gave;
  Her wanton palfrey all was overspred
  With tinsell trappings, woven like a wave,
Whose bridle rung with golden bels and bosses° brave.   *studs*

14

With faire disport° and courting dalliaunce   *diversion*
  She intertainde her lover all the way:
  But when she saw the knight his speare advaunce,
  She soone left off her mirth and wanton play,
  And bad her knight addresse him to the fray:
  His foe was nigh at hand. He prickt with pride
  And hope to winne his Ladies heart that day,
  Forth spurréd fast: adowne his coursers side
The red bloud trickling staind the way, as he did ride.

15

The knight of the Redcrosse when him he spide,
  Spurring so hote with rage dispiteous,°   *unpitying*
  Gan fairely couch° his speare, and towards ride: *lower*
  Soone meete they both, both fell and furious,
  That daunted with their forces hideous,
  Their steeds do stagger, and amazéd stand,
  And eke themselves too rudely rigorous,
  Astonied° with the stroke of their owne hand,   *stunned*
Do backe rebut,° and each to other yeeldeth land.   *recoil*

16

As when two rams stird with ambitious pride,
  Fight for the rule of the rich fleecéd flocke,

---

8. "Faithlessness," or false faith. Although Redcrosse has been separated from Una, and now follows the guidance of Sansfoy, his own "native vertue" (cf. st. 19) will suffice to overcome the furious brutality of Sansfoy.

9. Duessa, first explicitly identified in st. 44, recalls in particular "the purple clothed woman on the seven hills" of Revelation xvii. 4: "the woman was arrayed in purple and scarlet colour, and decked with gold and precious stones and pearls, having a golden cup in her hand full of abominations and filthiness of her fornication . . . ". Opposite to Una in name and attire, she represents false religion, especially (for Protestant readers) the pomp and hypocrisy of Rome.

Their hornéd fronts so fierce on either side
Do meete, that with the terrour of the shocke
Astonied both, stand sencelesse as a blocke,
Forgetfull of the hanging victory:
So stood these twaine, unmovéd as a rocke,
Both staring fierce, and holding idely
The broken reliques of their former cruelty.

17

The Sarazin sore daunted with the buffe
   Snatcheth his sword, and fiercely to him flies;
   Who well it wards, and quyteth° cuff with cuff: *returns*
   Each others equall puissaunce envies,
   And through their iron sides with cruell spies°   *glances*
   Does seeke to perce: repining° courage yields   *angry*
   No foote to foe. The flashing fier flies
   As from a forge out of their burning shields,
And streames of purple bloud new dies the verdant fields.

18

"Curse on that Crosse," quoth then the Sarazin,
   "That keepes thy body from the bitter fit;[1]
   Dead long ygoe I wote thou haddest bin,
   Had not that charme from thee forwarnéd° it: *guarded*
   But yet I warne thee now assuréd sitt,
   And hide thy head." Therewith upon his crest
   With rigour so outrageous he smitt,
   That a large share° it hewd out of the rest,   *piece*
And glauncing downe his shield, from blame°   *harm*
   him fairely blest.°   *preserved*

19

Who thereat wondrous wroth, the sleeping spark
   Of native vertue° gan eftsoones revive,   *power*
   And at his haughtie helmet making mark,
   So hugely stroke, that it the steele did rive,
   And cleft his head. He tumbling downe alive,
   With bloudy mouth his mother earth did kis,
   Greeting his grave: his grudging° ghost did strive   *complaining*
   With the fraile flesh: at last it flitted is,
Whither the soules do fly of men, that live amis.

20

The Lady when she saw her champion fall,
   Like the old ruines of a broken towre,
   Staid not to waile his woefull funerall,
   But from him fled away with all her powre;
   Who after her as hastily gan scowre,°   *run*
   Bidding the Dwarfe with him to bring away
   The Sarazins shield, signe of the conqueroure.
   Her soone he overtooke, and bad to stay,
For present cause was none of dread her to dismay.

---

1. I.e., the throes of death.

21

She turning backe with ruefull countenaunce,
  Cride, "Mercy mercy Sir vouchsafe to show
  On silly° Dame, subject to hard mischaunce,   *innocent*
  And to your mighty will." Her humblesse low
  In so ritch weedes and seeming glorious show,
  Did much emmove his stout heroicke heart,
  And said, "Deare dame, your suddein overthrow
  Much rueth° me; but now put feare apart,   *grieves*
And tell, both who ye be, and who that tooke your part."

22

Melting in teares, then gan she thus lament;
  "The wretched woman, whom unhappy howre
  Hath now made thrall to your commandément,
  Before that angry heavens list to lowre,°   *frown*
  And fortune false betraide me to your powre,
  Was (O what now availeth that I was!)
  Borne the sole daughter of an Emperour,
  He that the wide West under his rule has,
And high hath set his throne, where Tiberis[2] doth pas.

23

"He in the first flowre of my freshest age,
  Betrothéd me unto the onely haire°   *heir*
  Of a most mighty king, most rich and sage;
  Was never Prince so faithfull and so faire,
  Was never Prince so meeke and debonaire;°   *gracious*
  But ere my hopéd day of spousall shone,
  My dearest Lord fell from high honours staire,
  Into the hands of his accurséd fone,°   *foes*
And cruelly was slaine, that shall I ever mone.

24

"His blesséd body spoild of lively breath,[3]
  Was afterward, I know not how, convaid°   *removed*
  And fro me hid: of whose most innocent death
  When tidings came to me unhappy maid,
  O how great sorrow my sad soule assaid.°   *afflicted*
  Then forth I went his woefull corse to find,
  And many yeares throughout the world I straid,
  A virgin widow, whose deepe wounded mind
With love, long time did languish as the striken hind.

25

"At last it chauncéd this proud Sarazin
  To meete me wandring, who perforce me led
  With him away, but yet could never win

---

2. The river Tiber, in Rome. The claim
to dominion over "the wide West" con-
trasts with that of Una's lineage, whose
"scepters stretcht from East to West-
erne shore" (I. i. 5); Roman Catholic
power is partial and fragmentary in
comparison with the universal character
of Christian truth.

3. I.e., bereft of the breath of life.
Duessa's emphasis on inexplicable death
and loss reflects Spenser's association
of the church of Rome with Christ's
dead body. Cf. John xx. 2.

The Fort, that Ladies hold in soveraigne dread.
There lies he now with foule dishonour dead,
Who whiles he livde, was calléd proud Sans foy,
The eldest of three brethren, all three bred
Of one bad sire, whose youngest is Sans joy,
And twixt them both was borne the bloudy bold Sans loy.[4]

26

"In this sad plight, friendlesse, unfortunate,
  Now miserable I Fidessa dwell,
  Craving of you in pitty of my state,
  To do none° ill, if please ye not do well."   *no*
He in great passion all this while did dwell,
  More busying his quicke eyes, her face to view,
  Then his dull eares, to heare what she did tell;
  And said, "Faire Lady hart of flint would rew°   *pity*
The undeservéd woes and sorrowes, which ye shew.

27

"Henceforth in safe assuraunce may ye rest,
  Having both found a new friend you to aid,
  And lost an old foe, that did you molest:
  Better new friend then an old foe is° said."   *it is*
With chaunge of cheare the seeming simple maid
  Let fall her eyen, as shamefast to the earth,
  And yeelding soft, in that she nought gain-said,
  So forth they rode, he feining seemely merth,
And she coy lookes: so dainty they say maketh derth[5]

28

Long time they thus together traveiléd,
  Till weary of their way, they came at last,
  Where grew two goodly trees, that faire did spred
  Their armes abroad, with gray mosse overcast,
  And their greene leaves trembling with every blast,°   *breeze*
  Made a calme shadow far in compasse round:
  The fearefull Shepheard often there aghast
  Under them never sat, ne wont there sound
His mery oaten pipe, but shund th'unlucky ground.

29

But this good knight soone as he them can° spie,   *did*
  For the coole shade him thither hastly got:
  For golden Phoebus now ymounted hie,
  From fiery wheeles of his faire chariot
  Hurléd his beame so scorching cruell hot,
  That living creature mote it not abide;
  And his new Lady it enduréd not.
  There they alight, in hope themselves to hide
From the fierce heat, and rest their weary limbs a tide.°   *time*

4. The three brothers allegorically indicate the degeneration of man and his institutions progressively brought on by spiritual blindness.

5. A proverb: "fastidiousness brings poverty"; in this context, Duessa's coyness arouses the knight's desire.

30

Faire seemely pleasaunce each to other makes,
 With goodly purposes° there as they sit: *conversation*
 And in his falséd° fancy he her takes   *deceived*
 To be the fairest wight, that livéd yit;
 Which to expresse, he bends his gentle wit,
 And thinking of those braunches greene to frame
 A girlond for her dainty forehead fit,
He pluckt a bough; out of whose rift there came
Small drops of gory bloud, that trickled downe the same.[6]

31

Therewith a piteous yelling voyce was heard,
 Crying, "O spare with guilty hands to teare
 My tender sides in this rough rynd embard,°   *imprisoned*
 But fly, ah fly far hence away, for feare
 Least to you hap, that happened to me heare,
 And to this wretched Lady, my deare love,
 O too deare love, love bought with death too deare."
Astond he stood, and up his haire did hove,°   *rise*
And with that suddein horror could no member move.

32

At last whenas the dreadfull passion[7]
 Was overpast, and manhood well awake,
 Yet musing at the straunge occasion,
 And doubting much his sence, he thus bespake;
 "What voyce of damnéd Ghost from Limbo[8] lake,
 Or guilefull spright wandring in empty aire,
 Both which fraile men do oftentimes mistake,°   *mislead*
 Sends to my doubtfull eares these speaches rare,
And ruefull plaints, me bidding guiltlesse bloud to spare?"

33

Then groning deepe, "Nor damnéd Ghost," quoth he,
 Nor guilefull sprite to thee these wordes doth speake,
 But once a man Fradubio,[9] now a tree,
 Wretched man, wretched tree; whose nature weake,
 A cruell witch her curséd will to wreake,
 Hath thus transformd, and plast in open plaines,
 Where Boreas[1] doth blow full bitter bleake,
 And scorching Sunne does dry my secret vaines:
For though a tree I seeme, yet cold and heat me paines."

---

6. The ensuing episode combines elements from Virgil's account of Polydorus, who had been transformed into a tree from whose boughs black blood trickled down (*Aeneid*, III. 27–42), and from Ariosto's description of the exchange between Ruggiero and Astolfo, changed into a tree by the enchantress Alcina (*Orlando Furioso*, VI. 26–53). Cf. the detailed discussion of this episode by W. J. Kennedy in *ELR*, III (1973), 351–368.

7. Passion of dread.

8. The abode of lost spirits. The expression, "Limbo lake," seems to have been drawn from Thomas Phaer's translation of the *Aeneid* (published in 1584), and presumably does not indicate a specifically Christian Limbo.

9. "Brother Doubt."

1. The North Wind.

34

"Say on Fradubio then, or° man, or tree,"   *whether*
   Quoth then the knight, "by whose mischievous arts
   Art thou misshapéd thus, as now I see?
   He oft finds med'cine, who his griefe imparts;°   *makes known*
   But double griefs afflict concealing harts,
   As raging flames who striveth to suppresse."
   "The author then," said he, "of all my smarts,
   Is one Duessa[2] a false sorceresse,
That many errant° knights hath brought to wretchednesse. *wandering*

35

"In prime of youthly yeares, when corage hot
   The fire of love and joy of chevalree
   First kindled in my brest, it was my lot
   To love this gentle Lady, whom ye see,
   Now not a Lady, but a seeming tree;
   With whom as once I rode encompanyde,
   Me chauncéd of a knight encountred bee,
   That had a like° faire Lady by his syde,   *similarly*
Like a faire Lady, but did fowle Duessa hyde.

36

"Whose forgéd beauty he did take in hand,[3]
   All other Dames to have exceeded farre;
   I in defence of mine did likewise stand,
   Mine, that did then shine as the Morning starre:
   So both to battell fierce arraungéd arre,
   In which his harder° fortune was to fall   *hard*
   Under my speare: such is the dye° of warre: *hazard*
   His Lady left as a prise martiall,°   *spoil of battle*
Did yield her comely person, to be at my call.

37

"So doubly loved of Ladies unlike faire,
   Th'one seeming such, the other such indeede,
   One day in doubt I cast° for to compare,   *resolved*
   Whether° in beauties glorie did exceede;   *which one*
   A Rosy girlond was the victors meede:°   *reward*
   Both seemde to win, and both seemde won to bee,
   So hard the discord was to be agreede.
   Fraelissa° was as faire, as faire mote bee,   *Frailty*
And ever false Duessa seemde as faire as shee.

38

"The wicked witch now seeing all this while
   The doubtfull ballaunce equally to sway,
   What not by right, she cast to win by guile,
   And by her hellish science raisd streight way
   A foggy mist, that overcast the day,
   And a dull blast, that breathing on her face,
   Dimméd her former beauties shining ray,

2. I.e., of double nature; two-faced.   3. I.e., he maintained.

And with foule ugly forme did her disgrace:°   *disfigure*
Then was she faire alone, when none was faire in place.[4]

39

"Then cride she out, 'Fye, fye, deforméd wight,
  Whose borrowed beautie now appeareth plaine
  To have before bewitchéd all mens sight;
  O leave her soone, or let her soone be slaine.'
  Her loathly visage viewing with disdaine,
  Eftsoones I thought her such, as she me told,
  And would have kild her; but with faignéd paine,
  The false witch did my wrathfull hand withhold;
So left her, where she now is turnd to treén mould.[5]

40

"Thens forth I tooke Duessa for my Dame,
  And in the witch unweeting° joyd long time,   *unwittingly*
  Ne ever wist, but that she was the same,
  Till on a day (that day is every Prime,°   *spring*
  When Witches wont do penance for their crime)
  I chaunst to see her in her proper hew,°   *shape*
  Bathing her selfe in origane and thyme:[6]
  A filthy foule old woman I did vew,
That ever to have toucht her, I did deadly rew.

41

"Her neather partes misshapen, monstruous,
  Were hidd in water, that I could not see,
  But they did seeme more foule and hideous,
  Then womans shape man would beleeve to bee.
  Thens forth from her most beastly companie
  I gan refraine, in minde to slip away,
  Soone as appeard safe opportunitie:
  For danger great, if not assured decay°   *destruction*
I saw before mine eyes, if I were knowne to stray.

42

"The divelish hag by chaunges of my cheare°   *countenance*
  Perceived my thought, and drownd in sleepie night,
  With wicked herbes and ointments did besmeare
  My bodie all, through charmes and magicke might,
  That all my senses were bereavéd quight:
  Then brought she me into this desert waste,
  And by my wretched lovers side me pight,°   *placed*
  Where now enclosd in wooden wals full faste,
Banisht from living wights, our wearie dayes we waste."

43

"But how long time," said then the Elfin knight,
  "Are you in this misforméd house to dwell?"

---

4. I.e., when none present was fair; or,
perhaps, when none present was fair
in place of her.
5. Form of a tree.

6. Herbs valued for their powers of
healing skin disorders (such as
Duessa's, described in I. viii. 47).

"We may not chaunge," quoth he, "this evil plight,
Till we be bathéd in a living well;[7]
That is the terme prescribed by the spell."
"O how," said he, "mote I that well out find,
That may restore you to your wonted well?"°   *well-being*
"Time and suffiséd° fates to former kynd   *satisfied*
Shall us restore, none else from hence may us unbynd."

44

The false Duessa, now Fidessa hight,[8]
    Heard how in vaine Fradubio did lament,
    And knew well all was true. But the good knight
    Full of sad feare and ghastly dreriment,°   *gloom*
    When all this speech the living tree had spent,
    The bleeding bough did thrust into the ground,
    That from the bloud he might be innocent,
    And with fresh clay did close the wooden wound:
Then turning to his Lady, dead with feare her found.

45

Her seeming dead he found with feignéd feare,
    As all unweeting of that well she knew,[9]
    And paynd himselfe with busie care to reare
    Her out of carelesse° swowne. Her eylids blew   *unconscious*
    And dimméd sight with pale and deadly hew
    At last she up gan lift: with trembling cheare°   *demeanor*
    Her up he tooke, too simple and too trew,
    And oft her kist. At length all passéd feare,[1]
He set her on her steede, and forward forth did beare.

Canto III

Forsaken Truth long seekes her love,
And makes the Lyon mylde,
Marres blind Devotions mart,° and fals   *trade*
In hand of leachour vylde.

1

Nought is there under heav'ns wide hollownesse,
    That moves more deare compassion of mind,
    Then beautie brought t'unworthy° wretchednesse   *undeserved*
    Through envies snares or fortunes freakes unkind:
    I, whether lately through her brightnesse blind,
    Or through alleageance and fast fealtie,
    Which I do owe unto all woman kind,
    Feele my heart perst° with so great agonie,   *pierced*
When such I see, that all for pittie I could die.

---

7. I.e., the grace of God. "The water that I shall give him shall be in him a well of water springing up into everlasting life" (John iv. 14); "And he shewed me a pure river of water of life" (Revelation xxii. 1).
8. I.e., called Faith.
9. I.e., feigning ignorance of what she well knew.
1. I.e., having passed all fear.

2

And now it is empassionéd so deepe,
   For fairest Unaes sake, of whom I sing,
   That my fraile eyes these lines with teares do steepe,
   To thinke how she through guilefull handeling,°   *treatment*
   Though true as touch,[1] though daughter of a king,
   Though faire as ever living wight was faire,
   Though nor in word nor deede ill meriting,
   Is from her knight divorcéd in despaire
And her due loves derived° to that vile witches share.   *diverted*

3

Yet she most faithfull Ladie all this while
   Forsaken, wofull, solitarie mayd
   Farre from all peoples prease,° as in exile,   *press, gathering*
   In wildernesse and wastfull deserts strayd,
   To seeke her knight; who subtilly betrayd
   Through that late vision, which th'Enchaunter wrought,
   Had her abandond. She of nought affrayd,
   Through woods and wastnesse wide him daily sought;
Yet wishéd tydings none of him unto her brought.

4

One day nigh wearie of the yrkesome way,
   From her unhastie beast she did alight,
   And on the grasse her daintie limbes did lay
   In secret shadow, farre from all mens sight:
   From her faire head her fillet° she undight,°   *headband/unfastened*
   And laid her stole aside. Her angels face
   As the great eye of heaven shynéd bright,
   And made a sunshine in the shadie place;
Did never mortall eye behold such heavenly grace.

5

It fortunéd out of the thickest wood
   A ramping° Lyon rushéd suddainly,   *raging*
   Hunting full greedie after salvage° blood;   *wild*
   Soone as the royall virgin he did spy,
   With gaping mouth at her ran greedily,
   To have attonce devoured her tender corse:
   But to the pray when as he drew more ny,
   His bloudie rage asswagéd with remorse,
And with the sight amazd, forgat his furious forse.[2]

1. I.e., absolutely true, as the touchstone tests the quality of gold.
2. While lions in *The Faerie Queene* may represent irrational or ungoverned elements (as Wrath, in I. iv. 33, rides "a Lion, loth for to be led"), the actions of Una's lion recall those of lions in medieval romance, e.g., the lion which constantly attends the hero in *Guy of Warwick*, Sir Percival's lion in Malory's *Morte d'Arthur*, and particularly the lions who instinctively revere Josian, the virgin heroine in *Sir Bevis of Hamtoun*. As primate of the beasts, Una's lion allegorically represents the force of nature's law, supporting neglected or despised truth. William Nelson in *The Poetry of Edmund Spenser* . . . [N.Y., 1963], p. 156), has drawn attention to Richard Hooker's "Learned and Comfortable Sermon of . . . Faith in the Elect" (1585–1586), which puts matters in the context of Christian belief: "Lions, beasts ravenous by nature and keen with hunger, being set to devour, have as it were religiously adored the very flesh of the faithful man."

6

In stead thereof he kist her wearie feet,
 And lickt her lilly hands with fawning tong,
 As° he her wrongéd innocence did weet.°   *as though/know*
 O how can beautie maister the most strong,
 And simple truth subdue avenging wrong?
 Whose yeelded pride and proud submission,
 Still dreading death, when she had markéd long,
 Her hart gan melt in great compassion,
And drizling teares did shed for pure affection.

7

"The Lyon Lord of everie beast in field,"
 Quoth she, "his princely puissance doth abate,
 And mightie proud to humble weake does yield,
 Forgetfull of the hungry rage, which late
 Him prickt, in pittie of my sad estate:°   *condition*
 But he my Lyon, and my noble Lord,
 How does he find in cruell hart to hate
 Her that him loved, and ever most adord,
As the God of my life? why hath he me abhord?"

8

Redounding° teares did choke th'end of her plaint, *overflowing*
 Which softly ecchoed from the neighbour wood;
 And sad to see her sorrowfull constraint°   *distress*
 The kingly beast upon her gazing stood;
 With pittie calmd, downe fell his angry mood.
 At last in close hart shutting up her paine,
 Arose the virgin borne of heavenly brood,° *parentage*
 And to her snowy Palfrey got againe,
To seeke her strayéd Champion, if she might attaine.° *overtake*

9

The Lyon would not leave her desolate,
 But with her went along, as a strong gard
 Of her chast person, and a faithfull mate
 Of her sad troubles and misfortunes hard:
 Still° when she slept, he kept both watch and ward, *always*
 And when she wakt, he waited diligent,
 With humble service to her will prepard:
 From her faire eyes he tooke commaundément,
And ever by her lookes conceivéd her intent.

10

Long she thus traveiléd through deserts wyde,
 By which she thought her wandring knight shold pas,
 Yet never shew of living wight espyde;
 Till that at length she found the troden gras,
 In which the tract° of peoples footing was, *track*
 Under the steepe foot of a mountaine hore;° *grey*
 The same she followes, till at last she has
 A damzell spyde slow footing her before,
That on her shoulders sad° a pot of water bore. *heavy, bent down*

11

To whom approching she to her gan call,
  To weet, if dwelling place were nigh at hand;
  But the rude° wench her answered nought at all,   *ignorant*
  She could not heare, nor speake, nor understand;
  Till seeing by her side the Lyon stand,
  With suddaine feare her pitcher downe she threw,
  And fled away: for never in that land
  Face of faire Ladie she before did vew,
And that dread Lyons looke her cast in deadly hew.[3]

12

Full fast she fled, ne ever lookt behynd,
  As if her life upon the wager lay,[4]
  And home she came, whereas her mother blynd
  Sate in eternall night: nought could she say,
  But suddaine catching hold, did her dismay
  With quaking hands, and other signes of feare:
  Who full of ghastly fright and cold affray,°   *terror*
  Gan shut the dore. By this arrivéd there
Dame Una, wearie Dame, and entrance did requere.°   *request*

13

Which when none yeelded, her unruly Page
  With his rude clawes the wicket open rent,
  And let her in; where of his cruell rage
  Nigh dead with feare, and faint astonishment,[5]
  She found them both in darkesome corner pent;
  Where that old woman day and night did pray
  Upon her beades devoutly penitent;
  Nine hundred *Pater nosters* every day,
And thrise nine hundred *Aves* she was wont to say.

14

And to augment her painefull pennance more,
  Thrise every weeke in ashes she did sit,
  And next her wrinkled skin rough sackcloth wore,
  And thrise three times did fast from any bit:°   *bite (of food)*
  But now for feare her beads she did forget.
  Whose needlesse dread for to remove away,
  Faire Una framéd words and count'nance fit:
  Which hardly° doen, at length she gan them pray,   *with difficulty*
That in their cotage small, that night she rest her may.

15

The day is spent, and commeth drowsie night,
  When every creature shrowdéd is in sleepe;
  Sad Una downe her laies in wearie plight,
  And at her feet the Lyon watch doth keepe:
  In stead of rest, she does lament, and weepe
  For the late losse of her deare lovéd knight,

---

3. I.e., made her turn pale as death.
4. I.e., as if her life were at stake.

5. I.e., amazed and terrified to the point of fainting away.

And sighes, and grones, and evermore does steepe
  Her tender brest in bitter teares all night,
All night she thinks too long, and often lookes for light.

16

Now when Aldeboran was mounted hie
  Above the shynie Cassiopeias chaire,[6]
  And all in deadly sleepe did drownéd lie,
  One knockéd at the dore, and in would fare;
  He knockéd fast, and often curst, and sware,
  That readie entrance was not at his call:
  For on his backe a heavy load he bare
  Of nightly stelths and pillage severall,°   *of various kinds*
Which he had got abroad by purchase° criminall.   *acquisition*

17

He was to weete[7] a stout and sturdie thiefe,
  Wont to robbe Churches of their ornaments,
  And poore mens boxes° of their due reliefe,   *almsboxes*
  Which given was to them for good intents;
  The holy Saints of their rich vestiments
  He did disrobe, when all men carelesse slept,
  And spoild the Priests of their habiliments,°   *vestments*
  Whiles none the holy things in safety kept;
Then he by cunning sleights in at the window crept.

18

And all that he by right or wrong could find,
  Unto this house he brought, and did bestow
  Upon the daughter of this woman blind,
  Abessa daughter of Corceca slow,[8]
  With whom he whoredome usd, that few did know,
  And fed her fat with feast of offerings,
  And plentie, which in all the land did grow;
  Ne sparéd he to give her gold and rings:
And now he to her brought part of his stolen things.

19

Thus long the dore with rage and threats he bet,°   *beat*
  Yet of those fearefull women none durst rize,
  The Lyon frayéd° them, him in to let: *frightened*
  He would no longer stay him to advize,°   *consider*

6. Aldebaran is a star in the constellation Taurus. Cassiopeia, Andromeda's mother, foolishly boasted of her daughter's beauty, thus offending the Nereids; the gods ordained that Andromeda should be sacrificed to a sea monster (from which she was saved by Perseus). When Cassiopeia subsequently stirred up trouble anew, Poseidon placed her among the stars. Cf. Ovid, *Metamorphoses*, IV. 663–803, and Natalis Comes, *Mythologiae*, VIII. 6.
7. In fact.
8. Abessa's name (from *ab esse*, "[apart] from being," i.e., separate from the true Church; also, "abbess") associates her with monasticism; she is appropriately the daughter of Corceca ("blindness of heart"), whose name echoes Ephesians iv. 17–18: "Walk not as other Gentiles walk, in the vanity of their mind, Having the understanding darkened, being alienated from the life of God through the ignorance that is in them, because of the blindness of their heart." Corceca in particular is a type of superstitious fear and ignorance (cf. sts. 13–14). That Kirkrapine ("church robber") bestows his plunder on Abessa represents one kind of monastic abuse for which the Roman church was widely criticized.

But open breakes the dore in furious wize,
And entring is; when that disdainfull beast
Encountring fierce, him suddaine doth surprize,
And seizing cruell clawes on trembling brest,
Under his Lordly foot him proudly hath supprest.

20

Him booteth not resist,[9] nor succour call,
His bleeding hart is in the vengers° hand,   *avenger's*
Who streight him rent in thousand peeces small,
And quite dismembred hath: the thirstie land
Drunke up his life; his corse left on the strand.°   *ground*
His fearefull friends weare out the wofull night,
Ne dare to weepe, nor seeme to understand
The heavie hap,° which on them is alight,°   *lot/fallen*
Affraid, least to themselves the like mishappen might.

21

Now when broad day the world discovered° has,   *revealed*
Up Una rose, up rose the Lyon eke,
And on their former journey forward pas,
In wayes unknowne, her wandring knight to seeke,
With paines farre passing that long wandring Greeke,
That for his love refuséd deitie;[1]
Such were the labours of this Lady meeke,
Still seeking him, that from her still did flie,
Then furthest from her hope, when most she weened nie.°

                                                            believed near

22

Soone as she parted thence, the fearefull twaine,
That blind old woman and her daughter deare
Came forth, and finding Kirkrapine there slaine,
For anguish great they gan to rend their heare,
And beat their brests, and naked flesh to teare.
And when they both had wept and wayld their fill,
Then forth they ranne like two amazéd deare,
Halfe mad through malice, and revenging will,[2]
To follow her, that was the causer of their ill.

23

Whom overtaking, they gan loudly bray,
With hollow howling, and lamenting cry,
Shamefully at her rayling all the way,
And her accusing of dishonesty,°   *unchastity*
That was the flowre of faith and chastity;
And still amidst her rayling, she[3] did pray,
That plagues, and mischiefs, and long misery
Might fall on her, and follow all the way,
And that in endlesse error° she might ever stray.   *wandering*

---

9. I.e., it is useless for him to resist.
1. Odysseus, who preferred reunion with his wife Penelope to the immor-
tality offered him by Calypso.
2. Desire for revenge.
3. I.e., Corceca.

24

But when she saw her prayers nought prevaile,
  She backe returnéd with some labour lost;
  And in the way as she did weepe and waile,
  A knight her met in mighty armes embost,°   *encased*
  Yet knight was not for all his bragging bost,°   *boast*
  But subtill Archimag, that Una sought
  By traynes° into new troubles to have tost: *deceptive plots*
Of that old woman tydings he besought,
If that of such a Ladie she could tellen ought.

25

Therewith she gan her passion to renew,
  And cry, and curse, and raile, and rend her heare,
  Saying, that harlot she too lately knew,
  That causd her shed so many a bitter teare,
  And so forth told the story of her feare:
  Much seeméd he to mone her haplesse chaunce,
  And after for that Ladie did inquere;
  Which being taught, he forward gan advaunce
His fair enchaunted steed, and eke his charméd launce.

26

Ere long he came, where Una traveild slow,
  And that wilde Champion wayting her besyde:
  Whom seeing such, for dread he durst not show
  Himselfe too nigh at hand, but turnéd wyde°   *aside*
  Unto an hill; from whence when she him spyde,
  By his like seeming shield, her knight by name
  She weend it was,[4] and towards him gan ryde:
  Approching nigh, she wist° it was the same,   *believed*
And with faire fearefull humblesse° towards him shee came. *humility*

27

And weeping said, " Ah my long lackéd Lord,
  Where have ye bene thus long out of my sight?
  Much fearéd I to have been quite abhord,
  Or ought° have done, that ye displeasen might,   *aught*
  That should as death unto my deare hart light:[5]
  For since mine eye your joyous sight did mis,
  My chearefull day is turnd to chearelesse night,
  And eke my night of death the shadow is;
But welcome now my light, and shining lampe of blis."

28

He thereto meeting° said, "My dearest Dame,   *responding in kind*
  Farre be it from your thought, and fro my will,
  To thinke that knighthood I so much should shame,
  As you to leave, that have me lovéd still,
  And chose in Faery court of meere° goodwill,   *pure*

4. I.e., by his shield, which seemed to be that of Redcrosse, she supposed him to be her own particular knight.

5. I.e., that should be a deathlike blow to my sad heart.

Where noblest knights were to be found on earth:
The earth shall sooner leave her kindly° skill   *natural*
To bring forth fruit, and make eternall derth,
Then I leave you, my liefe,° yborne of heavenly berth.   *beloved*

29

"And sooth to say, why I left you so long,
Was for to seeke adventure in strange place,
Where Archimago said a felon strong
To many knights did daily worke disgrace;
But knight he now shall never more deface:°   *defame*
Good cause of mine excuse; that mote° ye please   *may*
Well to accept, and evermore embrace
My faithfull service, that by land and seas
Have vowd you to defend, now then your plaint appease."

30

His lovely° words her seemd due recompence   *loving*
Of all her passéd paines: one loving howre
For many yeares of sorrow can dispence:°   *make amends*
A dram of sweet is worth a pound of sowre:
She has forgot, how many a wofull stowre°   *peril*
For him she late endured; she speakes no more
Of past: true is, that true love hath no powre
To looken backe; his eyes be fixt before.
Before her stands her knight, for whom she toyld so sore.

31

Much like, as when the beaten marinere,
That long hath wandred in the Ocean wide,
Oft soust in swelling Tethys saltish teare,[6]
And long time having tand his tawney hide
With blustring breath of heaven, that none can bide,
And scorching flames of fierce Orions hound,[7]
Soone as the port from farre he has espide,
His chearefull whistle merrily doth sound,
And Nereus crownes with cups;[8] his mates him pledg around.

32

Such joy made Una, when her knight she found;
And eke th'enchaunter joyous seemd no lesse,
Then the glad marchant, that does vew from ground
His ship farre come from watrie wildernesse,
He hurles out vowes, and Neptune oft doth blesse:
So forth they past, and all the way they spent
Discoursing of her dreadfull late distresse,
In which he askt her, what the Lyon ment:
Who told her all that fell° in journey as she went.   *happened*

6. I.e., soaked by the ocean's waves; as in I. i. 39, Tethys, properly the consort of Oceanus, is identified with the ocean.

7. Sirius, the Dog Star, ascendant in July and August.

8. I.e., the mariners offer libations to Nereus, god of the Aegean Sea.

33

They had not ridden farre, when they might see
  One pricking towards them with hastie heat,
  Full strongly armd, and on a courser free,
  That through his fiercenesse foméd all with sweat,
  And the sharpe yron° did for anger eat,   *bit*
  When his hot ryder spurd his chtffféd° side;   *heated*
  His looke was sterne, and seeméd still to threat
  Cruell revenge, which he in hart did hyde,
And on his shield *Sans loy*[9] in bloudie lines was dyde.

34

When nigh he drew unto this gentle payre
  And saw the Red-crosse, which the knight did beare,
  He burnt in fire, and gan eftsoones prepare
  Himselfe to battell with his couchéd° speare.   *lowered*
  Loth was that other, and did faint through feare,
  To taste th'untryéd dint of deadly steele;
  But yet his Lady did so well him cheare,
  That hope of new good hap he gan to feele;
So bent° his speare, and spurnd his horse with yron heele.   *aimed*

35

But that proud Paynim° forward came so fierce,   *pagan*
  And full of wrath, that with his sharp-head speare
  Through vainely crosséd[1] shield he quite did pierce,
  And had his staggering steede not shrunke for feare,
  Through shield and bodie eke he should him beare:°   *thrust*
  Yet so great was the puissance of his push,
  That from his saddle quite he did him beare:
  He tombling rudely downe to ground did rush,
And from his goréd wound a well of bloud did gush.

36

Dismounting lightly from his loftie steed,
  He to him lept, in mind to reave° his life,   *take away*
  And proudly said, "Lo there the worthie meed
  Of him, that slew Sansfoy with bloudie knife;
  Henceforth his ghost freed from repining° strife,   *fretful*
  In peace may passen over Lethe lake,[2]
  When mourning altars purgd° with enemies life,   *cleansed*
  The blacke infernall Furies[3] doen aslake°:   *appease*
Life from Sansfoy thou tookst, Sansloy shall from thee take."

37

Therewith in haste his helmet gan unlace,
  Till Una cride, "O hold that heavie hand,

---

9. "Lawlessness"; this figure represents anarchical and even demonic opposition to all forms of man-made, natural, and divine law.
1. I.e., without the power inherent in the shield of Redcrosse.

2. The river of forgetfulness in the underworld.
3. Spirits of revenge and discord; E.K., in the Glosse to "November," calls them "the authours of all evill and mischiefe."

Deare Sir, what ever that thou be in place:[4]
Enough is, that thy foe doth vanquisht stand
Now at thy mercy: Mercie not withstand:°   *deny*
For he is one the truest knight[5] alive,
Though conquered now he lie on lowly land,
And whilest him fortune favour, faire did thrive
In bloudie field: therefore of life him not deprive."

38

Her piteous words might not abate his rage,
   But rudely rending up his helmet, would
   Have slaine him straight: but when he sees his age,
   And hoarie head of Archimago old,
   His hastie hand he doth amazéd hold,
   And halfe ashaméd, wondred at the sight:
   For that old man well knew he, though untold,
   In charmes and magicke to have wondrous might,
Ne ever wont in field, ne in round lists° to fight. *enclosures for jousting*

39

And said, "Why Archimago, lucklesse syre,
   What doe I see? what hard mishap is this,
   That hath thee hither brought to taste mine yre?
   Or thine the fault, or mine the error is,
   In stead of foe to wound my friend amis?"
   He answered nought, but in a traunce still lay,
   And on those guilefull dazéd eyes of his
   The cloud of death did sit. Which doen away,[6]
He left him lying so, ne would no lenger stay.

40

But to the virgin comes, who all this while
   Amaséd stands, her selfe so mockt° to see   *deceived*
   By him, who has the guerdon° of his guile,   *reward*
   For so misfeigning° her true knight to bee: *falsely pretending*
   Yet is she now in more perplexitie,
   Left in the hand of that same Paynim bold,
   From whom her booteth° not at all to flie;   *avails*
   Who by her cleanly garment catching hold,
Her from her Palfrey pluckt, her visage to behold.

41

But her fierce servant full of kingly awe
   And high disdaine, whenas his soveraine Dame
   So rudely handled by her foe he sawe,
   With gaping jawes full greedy at him came,
   And ramping on his shield, did weene the same
   Have reft away with his sharpe rending clawes:
   But he was stout, and lust did now inflame

4. I.e., whoever you are.   6. I.e., when he had recovered from
5. I.e., the one truest knight.   the swoon.

His corage more, that from his griping pawes
He hath his shield redeemed,° and foorth his swerd he drawes.

recovered

42

O then too weake and feeble was the forse
  Of salvage beast, his puissance to withstand:
  For he was strong, and of so mightie corse,
  As ever wielded speare in warlike hand,
  And feates of armes did wisely° understand.   *skilfully*
  Eftsoones he percéd through his chauféd chest
  With thrilling° point of deadly yron brand,°   *searching/sword*
  And launcht° his Lordly hart: with death opprest *pierced*
He roared aloud, whiles life forsooke his stubborne brest.[7]

43

Who now is left to keepe the forlorne maid
  From raging spoile of lawlesse victors will?
  Her faithfull gard removed, her hope dismaid,
  Her selfe a yeelded pray to save or spill.°   *destroy*
  He now Lord of the field, his pride to fill,
  With foule reproches, and disdainfull spight
  Her vildly entertaines,° and will or nill,   *deals with*
  Beares her away upon his courser light:
Her prayers nought prevaile, his rage is more of might.

44

And all the way, with great lamenting paine,
  And piteous plaints she filleth his dull° eares,   *deaf*
  That stony hart could riven have in twaine,
  And all the way she wets with flowing teares:
  But he enraged with rancor, nothing heares.
  Her servile beast yet would not leave her so,
  But followes her farre off, ne ought he feares,
  To be partaker of her wandring woe,
More mild in beastly kind,° then that her beastly foe.   *nature*

Canto IV

To sinfull house of Pride, Duessa
  guides the faithfull knight,
Where brothers death to wreak° Sansjoy   *avenge*
  doth chalenge him to fight.

1

Young knight, what ever that dost armes professe,
  And through long labours huntest after fame,
  Beware of fraud, beware of ficklenesse,
  In choice, and change of thy deare lovéd Dame,
  Least thou of her beleeve too lightly blame,

7. The force of nature's law is not itself sufficient to resist lawlessness in human society.

And rash misweening° doe thy hart remove: *misunderstanding*
  For unto knight there is no greater shame,
  Then lightnesse and inconstancie in love;
That doth this Redcrosse knights ensample plainly prove.

2

Who after that he had faire Una lorne,°   *left*
  Through light misdeeming° of her loialtie,   *misjudging*
  And false Duessa in her sted had borne,
  Calléd Fidess', and so supposd to bee;
  Long with her traveild, till at last they see
  A goodly building, bravely garnishéd,°   *adorned*
  The house of mightie Prince it seemd to bee:
  And towards it a broad high way that led,
All bare through peoples feet, which thither traveiléd.[1]

3

Great troupes of people traveild thitherward
  Both day and night, of each degree and place,°   *rank*
  But few returnéd, having scapéd hard,°   *with difficulty*
  With balefull beggerie, or foule disgrace,
  Which ever after in most wretched case,
  Like loathsome lazars,° by the hedges lay.   *lepers*
  Thither Duessa bad him bend his pace:
  For she is wearie of the toilesome way,
And also nigh consuméd is the lingring day.

4

A stately Pallace built of squaréd bricke,
  Which cunningly was without morter laid,
  Whose wals were high, but nothing strong, nor thick,
  And golden foile all over them displaid,
  That purest skye with brightnesse they dismaid:
  High lifted up were many loftie towres,
  And goodly galleries farre over laid°   *placed above*
  Full of faire windowes, and delightfull bowres;
And on the top a Diall told the timely° howres.[2]   *measured*

5

It was a goodly heape° for to behould,   *building*
  And spake the praises of the workmans wit;°   *skill*
  But full great pittie, that so faire a mould°   *structure*
  Did on so weake foundation ever sit:
  For on a sandie hill, that still did flit,°   *give way*

1. An indication of the true nature of this "goodly building"; cf. Matthew vii. 13: "For wide is the gate, and broad is the way, that leadeth to destruction, and many there be which go in thereat."
2. The castle's magnificence, in particular its surrounding wall covered with gold foil, recalls that of Alcina's residence in *Orlando Furioso*, VI. 59. That the building is surmounted by a clock indicates the destructive power of time over this edifice and its inhabitants, i.e., over man in a fallen world. Throughout this Canto, in his account of the House of Pride, its ruler and her attendants, and the eventual fate of its "noble crew," Spenser is preparing for the parallel but contrasting organization and significance of the House of Holiness, to be described in Canto x.

And fall away, it mounted was full hie,
That every breath of heaven shakéd it:
And all the hinder parts, that few could spie,
Were ruinous and old, but painted cunningly.[3]

6

Arrivéd there they passéd in forth right;
　For still to all the gates stood open wide,
　Yet charge of them was to a Porter hight°   *committed*
　Cald Malvenu,[4] who entrance none denide:
　Thence to the hall, which was on every side
　With rich array and costly arras dight:°   *decked*
　Infinite sorts of people did abide
　There waiting long, to win the wishéd sight
Of her, that was the Lady of that Pallace bright.

7

By them they passe, all gazing on them round, [5]
　And to the Presence° mount; whose glorious vew   *reception chamber*
　Their frayle amazéd senses did confound:
　In living Princes court none ever knew
　Such endlesse richesse, and so sumptuous shew;
　Ne Persia selfe, the nourse of pompous pride
　Like ever saw. And there a noble crew
　Of Lordes and Ladies stood on every side,
Which with their presence faire, the place much beautifide.

8

High above all a cloth of State was spred,
　And a rich throne, as bright as sunny day,
　On which there sate most brave embellishéd
　With royall robes and gorgeous array,
　A mayden Queene, that shone as Titans ray,[6]
　In glistring gold, and peerelesse pretious stone:
　Yet her bright blazing beautie did assay°   *attempt*
　To dim the brightnesse of her glorious throne,
As envying her selfe, that too exceeding shone.

3. The stanza may owe something to Chaucer's House of Fame, which is founded on ice ("a feble fundament / To bilden on a place hye," III. 1132–1133), and which has been partially eroded by the beams of the sun (1142–1150); but the primary reference is to Matthew vii. 26–27: " . . . every one that heareth these sayings of mine, and doeth them not, shall be likened unto a foolish man, which built his house upon the sand: And the rain descended, and the floods came, and the winds blew, and beat upon that house: and it fell: and great was the fall of it."
4. The court-of-love tradition, through the medium of moral allegory, influences Spenser's account both of the House of Pride and of the contrasting House of Holiness, in respect of setting, porter, presiding personage, and attendant counsellors. Malvenu's name, the opposite of *bienvenu* (welcome), and of *Bel-accueil*, a name often given to the porter in court-of-love allegories, suggests the essential inhospitality and lovelessness of the House of Pride, where self-love only reigns.
5. I.e., the crowd around gazing on them.
6. In this context, the expression "Titans ray" refers to the sun's brightness (as is usual in Spenser's work), but, more significantly, it recalls the Titans' wars, born of rebellious pride and hatred of the established order, against the rule of the Olympian gods (cf. Hesiod, *Theogony*, 617–735).

9

Exceeding shone, like Phoebus fairest child,[7]
    That did presume his fathers firie wayne,°   *chariot*
    And flaming mouthes of steedes unwonted° wilde   *unusually*
    Through highest heaven with weaker° hand to rayne;   *too weak*
    Proud of such glory and advancement vaine,
    While flashing beames do daze his feeble eyen,
    He leaves the welkin° way most beaten plaine,   *heavenly*
    And rapt° with whirling wheeles, inflames the skyen, *carried away*
With fire not made to burne, but fairely for to shyne.

10

So proud she shynéd in her Princely state,
    Looking to heaven; for earth she did disdayne,
    And sitting high; for lowly° she did hate: *lowliness*
    Lo underneath her scornefull feete, was layne
    A dreadfull Dragon with an hideous trayne,°   *tail*
    And in her hand she held a mirrhour bright,
    Wherein her face she often vewéd fayne,
    And in her selfe-loved semblance tooke delight;
For she was wondrous faire, as any living wight.[8]

11

Of griesly Pluto she the daughter was,
    And sad Proserpina the Queene of hell;
    Yet did she thinke her pearelesse worth to pas
    That parentage, with pride so did she swell,
    And thundring Jove, that high in heaven doth dwell,
    And wield the world, she clayméd for her syre,
    Or if that any else did Jove excell:
    For to the highest she did still aspyre,
Or if ought higher were then that, did it desyre.

12

And proud Lucifera[9] men did her call,
    That made her selfe a Queene, and crownd to be,
    Yet rightfull kingdome she had none at all,
    Ne heritage of native soveraintie,
    But did usurpe with wrong and tyrannie
    Upon the scepter, which she now did hold:
    Ne ruld her Realmes with lawes, but pollicie,° *political cunning*
    And strong advizement of six wisards old,
That with their counsels bad her kingdome did uphold.

7. Phaëthon, whose reckless driving of his father's chariot threatened to set the world on fire; Jove consequently destroyed him with a lightning bolt (Ovid, *Metamorphoses*, II. 1–400).
8. In common with other Renaissance figures, in literature and the visual arts, representing Pride, chief of the Seven Deadly Sins, the presiding personage in the House of Pride holds a looking glass, symbolic indication of her vain and worldly nature. The variety of such symbolic mirrors in Renaissance literature and art is discussed by S. C. Chew, *The Pilgrimage of Life* (New Haven, 1962).
9. Lucifera's name appropriately links her with Satan, called Lucifer in allusion to the tradition of his original brightness in heaven; this woman ruler (unlike Spenser's sovereign, Elizabeth) has seized power unlawfully, and holds her place by "policy" and magic, rather than by statesmanship supported by true religion.

13

Soone as the Elfin knight in presence came,
   And false Duessa seeming Lady faire,
   A gentle Husher,° Vanitie by name   *usher*
   Made rowme, and passage for them did prepaire:
   So goodly brought them to the lowest staire
   Of her high throne, where they on humble knee
   Making obeyssance, did the cause declare,
   Why they were come, her royall state to see,
To prove° the wide report of her great Majestee.   *confirm*

14

With loftie eyes, halfe loth to looke so low,
   She thankéd them in her disdainefull wise,
   Ne other grace vouchsaféd them to show
   Of Princesse worthy, scarse them bad arise.
   Her Lordes and Ladies all this while devise°   *make ready*
   Themselves to setten forth to straungers sight:
   Some frounce° their curléd haire in courtly guise, *arrange*
   Some prancke° their ruffes, and others trimly dight *display*
Their gay attire: each others greater pride does spight.

15

Goodly they all that knight do entertaine,
   Right glad with him to have increast their crew:
   But to Duess' each one himselfe did paine
   All kindnesse and faire courtesie to shew;
   For in that court whylome° her well they knew: *formerly*
   Yet the stout Faerie mongst the middest° crowd   *thickest*
   Thought all their glorie vaine in knightly vew,
   And that great Princesse too exceeding prowd,
That to strange knight no better countenance allowd.[1]

16

Suddein upriseth from her stately place
   The royall Dame, and for her coche doth call:
   All hurtlen° forth, and she with Princely pace,   *rush*
   As faire Aurora in her purple pall,°   *cloak*
   Out of the East the dawning day doth call:
   So forth she comes: her brightnesse brode° doth blaze; *abroad*
   The heapes of people thronging in the hall,
   Do ride each other, upon her to gaze:
Her glorious glitterand° light doth all mens eyes amaze. *glittering*

17

So forth she comes, and to her coche does clyme,
   Adornéd all with gold, and girlonds gay,
   That seemd as fresh as Flora in her prime,
   And strove to match, in royall rich array,
   Great Junoes golden chaire, the which they say
   The Gods stand gazing on, when she does ride

---

1. I.e., while Redcrosse is not taken in by the vanity of Lucifera and her court, he is himself in some degree vain.

To Joves high house through heavens bras-paved way
    Drawne of faire Pecocks, that excell in pride,
And full of Argus eyes their tailes dispredden wide.[2]

18

But this was drawne of six unequall beasts,[3]
    On which her six sage Counsellours did ryde,
    Taught to obay their bestiall beheasts,
    With like conditions to their kinds° applyde: *natures*
    Of which the first, that all the rest did guyde,
    Was sluggish Idlenesse the nourse of sin;
    Upon a slouthfull Asse he chose to ryde,
    Arayd in habit blacke, and amis° thin,   *hood*
Like to an holy Monck, the service to begin.

19

And in his hand his Portesse° still he bare,   *breviary*
    That much was worne, but therein little red,
    For of devotion he had little care,
    Still drownd in sleepe, and most of his dayes ded;
    Scarse could he once uphold his heavie hed,
    To looken, whether it were night or day:
    May seeme the wayne was very evill led,
    When such an one had guiding of the way,
That knew not, whether right he went, or else astray.

20

From worldly cares himselfe he did esloyne,°   *withdraw*
    And greatly shunnéd manly exercise,
    From every worke he chalengéd essoyne,[4]
    For contemplation sake: yet otherwise,
    His life he led in lawlesse riotise;
    By which he grew to grievous malady;
    For in his lustlesse° limbs through evill guise°   *feeble/living*
    A shaking fever raignd continually:
Such one was Idlenesse, first of this company.

21

And by his side rode loathsome Gluttony,
    Deforméd creature, on a filthie swyne,
    His belly was up-blowne with luxury,
    And eke with fatnesse swollen were his eyne,
    And like a Crane his necke was long and fyne,°   *scrawny*

2. The hundred eyes of Argus (who was killed by Mercury, at Jove's command) were set by Juno in the peacock's tail (Ovid, *Metamorphoses*, I. 590–726). On peacocks as symbols of pride in Renaissance art, cf. Chew, *op. cit.*, p. 96.

3. The counsellors ride in pairs, on mounts suited to the nature of each rider; but the beasts themselves are ill-matched and incongruous, as their differing gaits emphasize. Pictorial representations of the Seven Deadly Sins, in tapestries, woodcarving, and wall painting (not to mention emblem books like those of Alciati or Geoffrey Whitney), were sufficiently common in Spenser's day to make the identification of a single source for this passage unlikely. The poet may possibly have been indebted for some details to the procession of the Sins in John Gower's long didactic poem, *Mirour de l'Omme* (c. 1380).

4. Pleaded exemption.

With which he swallowd up excessive feast,
For want whereof poore people oft did pyne;°   *waste away*
And all the way, most like a brutish beast,
He spuéd up his gorge,[5] that all did him deteast.

22

In greene vine leaves he was right fitly clad;[6]
  For other clothes he could not weare for heat,
  And on his head an yvie girland had,
  From under which fast trickled downe the sweat:
  Still as he rode, he somewhat° still did eat,   *something*
  And in his hand did beare a bouzing can,[7]
  Of which he supt so oft, that on his seat
  His dronken corse he scarse upholden can,
In shape and life more like a monster, than a man.

23

Unfit he was for any worldly thing,
  And eke unhable once° to stirre or go°   *at all/walk*
  Not meet to be of counsell to a king,
  Whose mind in meat and drinke was drownéd so,
  That from his friend he seldome knew his fo:
  Full of diseases was his carcas blew,°   *livid*
  And a dry dropsie[8] through his flesh did flow:
  Which by misdiet daily greater grew:
Such one was Gluttony, the second of that crew.

24

And next to° him rode lustfull Lechery,   *after*
  Upon a bearded Goat, whose rugged haire,
  And whally° eyes (the signe of gelosy,)   *greenish*
  Was like the person selfe, whom he did beare:
  Who rough, and blacke, and filthy did appeare,
  Unseemely man to please faire Ladies eye;
  Yet he of Ladies oft was lovéd deare,
  When fairer faces were bid standen by:°   *away*
O who does know the bent of womens fantasy?

25

In a greene gowne he clothéd was full faire,
  Which underneath did hide his filthinesse,
  And in his hand a burning hart he bare,
  Full of vaine follies, and new fanglenesse:
  For he was false, and fraught° with ficklenesse,   *filled*
  And learnéd had to love with secret lookes,
  And well could daunce, and sing with ruefulnesse,
  And fortunes tell, and read in loving bookes,[9]
And thousand other wayes, to bait his fleshly hookes.

---

5. I.e., he vomited up what he had swallowed.
6. The portrait of Gluttony recalls that of Silenus in Ovid, *Metamorphoses,* IV. 26–27, XI. 90–93, and perhaps also in Virgil, *Eclogue VI;* both poets emphasize the senile grossness of one lost in the wild anarchy (or stupor) of drink.
7. Drinking cup.
8. I.e., a thirst-producing dropsy.
9. I.e., manuals dealing with the art of love (e.g., Ovid's *Ars Amatoria*); or, perhaps, erotic books.

26

Inconstant man, that lovéd all he saw,
　　And lusted after all, that he did love,
　　Ne would his looser life be tide to law,
　　But joyd weake wemens hearts to tempt and prove
　　If from their loyall loves he might them move;
　　Which lewdnesse fild him with reprochful paine
　　Of that fowle evill,[1] which all men reprove,
　　That rots the marrow, and consumes the braine:
Such one was Lecherie, the third of all this traine.

27

And greedy Avarice by him did ride,
　　Upon a Camell loaden all with gold;
　　Two iron coffers hong on either side,
　　With precious mettall full, as they might hold,
　　And in his lap an heape of coine he told;°   counted
　　For of his wicked pelfe° his God he made,   wealth
　　And unto hell him selfe for money sold;
　　Accurséd usurie was all his trade,
And right and wrong ylike in equall ballaunce waide.[2]

28

His life was nigh unto deaths doore yplast,
　　And thred-bare cote, and cobled shoes he ware,
　　Ne scarse good morsell all his life did tast,
　　But both from backe and belly still did spare,
　　To fill his bags, and richesse to compare;°   acquire
　　Yet chylde ne kinsman living had he none
　　To leave them to; but thorough daily care
　　To get, and nightly feare to lose his owne,
He led a wretched life unto him selfe unknowne.°   solitary

29

Most wretched wight, whom nothing might suffise,
　　Whose greedy lust° did lacke in greatest store,   desire
　　Whose need had end, but no end covetise,°   covetousness
　　Whose wealth was want, whose plenty made him pore,
　　Who had enough, yet wishéd ever more;
　　A vile disease, and eke in foote and hand
　　A grievous gout tormented him full sore,
　　That well he could not touch, nor go, nor stand:
Such one was Avarice, the fourth of this faire band.

30

And next to him malicious Envie rode,
　　Upon a ravenous wolfe, and still did chaw
　　Betweene his cankred° teeth a venemous tode,[3]   infected
　　That all the poison ran about his chaw;°   jaw

1. I.e., syphilis.
2. I.e., made no distinction between right and wrong.
3. In Ovid, *Metamorphoses*, II. 768– 769, the figure of Envy is described as "eating the flesh of snakes, proper food of her venom."

But inwardly he chawéd his owne maw°   *entrails*
At neighbours wealth, that made him ever sad;
For death it was, when any good he saw,
And wept, that cause of weeping none he had,
But when he heard of harme, he wexéd wondrous glad.

31

All in a kirtle of discolourd say[4]
 He clothéd was, ypainted full of eyes;
 And in his bosome secretly there lay
 An hatefull Snake, the which his taile uptyes° *coils*
 In many folds, and mortall sting implyes.°   *enfolds*
 Still as he rode, he gnasht his teeth, to see
 Those heapes of gold with griple° Covetyse,   *greedy*
 And grudgéd at the great felicitie
Of proud Lucifera, and his owne companie.

32

He hated all good workes and vertuous deeds,
 And him no lesse, that any like did use,°   *practice*
 And who with gracious bread the hungry feeds,[5]
 His almes for want of faith he doth accuse;
 So every good to bad he doth abuse:°   *pervert*
 And eke the verse of famous Poets witt
 He does backebite, and spightfull poison spues
 From leprous mouth on all, that ever writt:
Such one vile Envie was, that fifte in row did sitt.[6]

33

And him beside rides fierce revenging Wrath,
 Upon a Lion, loth for to be led;
 And in his hand a burning brond° he hath,   *sword*
 The which he brandisheth about his hed;
 His eyes did hurle forth sparkles fiery red,
 And staréd sterne on all, that him beheld,
 As ashes pale of hew and seeming ded;
 And on his dagger still his hand he held,
Trembling through hasty rage, when choler° in him sweld. *anger*

34

His ruffin° raiment all was staind with blood, *disarranged*
 Which he had spilt, and all to rags yrent,°   *torn*
 Through unadvizéd rashnesse woxen wood;° *mad*
 For of his hands he had no governement,°   *control*
 Ne cared for[7] bloud in his avengément:

4. In a variously colored woolen outer garment.
5. I.e., graciously feeds the hungry with bread.
6. Here merely one of Pride's attendants, Envy elsewhere in Spenser's work is a particularly threatening and insidious figure (or vice), notably the enemy of all true poets. In *The Faerie Queene*, VI. i. 8, the "Blatant Beast" is described as having been sent "Into this wicked world . . . To be the plague and scourge of wretched men: / Whom with vile tongue and venemous intent / He sore doth wound, and bite, and cruelly torment."
7. I.e., shrank from.

But when the furious fit was overpast,
  His cruell facts° he often would repent;   *deeds*
  Yet wilfull man he never would forecast,
How many mischieves should ensue his heedlesse hast.

35

Full many mischiefes follow cruell Wrath;
  Abhorréd bloudshed, and tumultuous strife,
  Unmanly° murder, and unthrifty scath,°   *inhuman/harm*
  Bitter despight, with rancours rusty knife,
  And fretting griefe the enemy of life;
  All these, and many evils moe° haunt ire,   *more*
  The swelling Splene,° and Frenzy raging rife,   *malice*
  The shaking Palsey, and Saint Fraunces fire:[8]
Such one was Wrath, the last of this ungodly tire.°   *procession*

36

And after all, upon the wagon beame
  Rode Sathan, with a smarting whip in hand,
  With which he forward lasht the laesie teme,
  So oft as Slowth still in the mire did stand.
  Huge routs° of people did about them band,   *crowds*
  Showting for joy, and still before their way
  A foggy mist had covered all the land;
  And underneath their feet, all scattered lay
Dead sculs and bones of men, whose life had gone astray.

37

So forth they marchen in this goodly sort,
  To take the solace° of the open aire,   *pleasure*
  And in fresh flowring fields themselves to sport;
  Emongst the rest rode that false Lady faire,
  The fowle Duessa, next unto the chaire
  Of proud Lucifera, as one of the traine:
  But that good knight would not so nigh repaire,°   *approach*
  Him selfe estraunging from their joyaunce vaine,
Whose fellowship seemd far unfit for warlike swaine.

38

So having solacéd themselves a space
  With pleasaunce of the breathing° fields yfed,   *fragrant*
  They backe returnéd to the Princely Place;
  Whereas an errant knight in armes ycled,°   *clad*
  And heathnish shield, wherein with letters red
  Was writ *Sans joy*, they new arrivéd find:
  Enflamed with fury and fiers hardy-hed,°   *audacity*
  He seemd in hart to harbour thoughts unkind,
And nourish bloudy vengeaunce in his bitter mind.[9]

---

8. Erysipelas, a disease causing acute inflammation of the skin.
9. Redcrosse, separated from Una, can resist the "joyaunce vaine" of Lucifera's court, but he is not proof against "joylessness," a condition akin to despair.

39

Who when the shaméd shield of slaine Sans foy
  He spide with that same Faery champions page,
  Bewraying° him, that did of late destroy   *revealing*
  His eldest brother, burning all with rage
  He to him leapt, and that same envious gage[1]
  Of victors glory from him snatcht away:
  But th'Elfin knight, which ought that warlike wage,[2]
  Disdaind to loose the meed he wonne in fray,
And him rencountring° fierce, reskewd the   *engaging in battle*
  noble pray.

40

Therewith they gan to hurtlen° greedily,   *rush together*
  Redoubted battaile ready to darrayne,°   *prepare*
  And clash their shields, and shake their swords on hy,
  That with their sturre they troubled all the traine;
  Till that great Queene upon eternall paine
  Of high displeasure, that ensewen might,
  Commaunded them their fury to refraine,
  And if that either to that shield had right,
In equall lists they should the morrow next it fight.

41

"Ah dearest Dame," quoth then the Paynim bold,
  "Pardon the errour of enragéd wight,
  Whom great griefe made forget the raines to hold
  Of reasons rule, to see this recreant knight,
  No knight, but treachour full of false despight
  And shamefull treason, who through guile hath slayn
  The prowest° knight, that ever field did fight,   *bravest*
  Even stout Sans foy (O who can then refrayn?)
Whose shield he beares renverst,° the more to heape disdayn. *reversed*

42

"And to augment the glorie of his guile,
  His dearest love the faire Fidessa loe
  Is there possesséd of the traytour vile,
  Who reapes the harvest sowen by his foe,
  Sowen in bloudy field, and bought with woe:
  That brothers hand shall dearely well requight
  So be, O Queene, you equall° favour showe."   *impartial*
  Him litle answerd th'angry Elfin knight;
He never meant with words, but swords to plead his right.

43

But threw his gauntlet as a sacred pledge,
  His cause in combat the next day to try:
  So been they parted both, with harts on edge,
  To be avenged each on his enimy.

1. Envied pledge.   2. I.e., who owned that shield.

That night they pas in joy and jollity,
Feasting and courting both in bowre and hall;
For Steward was excessive Gluttonie,
That of his plenty pouréd forth to all:
Which doen,° the Chamberlain Slowth did to rest them call.   done

44

Now whenas darkesome night had all displayd
Her coleblacke curtein over brightest skye,
The warlike youthes on dayntie couches layd,
Did chace away sweet sleepe from sluggish eye,
To muse on meanes of hopéd victory.
But whenas Morpheus had with leaden mace
Arrested all that courtly company,
Up-rose Duessa from her resting place,
And to the Paynims lodging comes with silent pace.

45

Whom broad awake she finds, in troublous fit,°   mood
Forecasting, how his foe he might annoy,
And him amoves° with speaches seeming fit: arouses
"Ah deare Sans joy, next dearest to Sans foy,
Cause of my new griefe, cause of my new joy,
Joyous, to see his ymage in mine eye,
And greeved, to thinke how foe did him destroy,
That was the flowre of grace and chevalrye;
Lo his Fidessa to thy secret faith I flye."

46

With gentle wordes he can° her fairely greet,   did
And bad say on the secret of her hart.
Then sighing soft, "I learne that litle sweet
Oft tempred is," quoth she, "with muchell° smart: much
For since my brest was launcht° with lovely dart   pierced
Of deare Sansfoy, I never joyéd howre,
But in eternall woes my weaker° hart   too weak
Have wasted, loving him with all my powre,
And for his sake have felt full many an heavie stowre.°   grief

47

"At last when perils all I weenéd past,
And hoped to reape the crop of all my care,
Into new woes unweeting I was cast,
By this false faytor,° who unworthy ware   impostor
His worthy shield, whom he with guilefull snare
Entrappéd slew, and brought to shamefull grave.
Me silly° maid away with him he bare,   innocent
And ever since hath kept in darksome cave,
For that° I would not yeeld, that° to Sans foy I gave.   because/what

48

"But since faire Sunne hath sperst° that lowring clowd,   dispersed
And to my loathéd life now shewes some light,

Under your beames I will me safely shrowd,
From dreaded storme of his disdainfull spight:
To you th'inheritance belongs by right
Of brothers prayse, to you eke longs° his love.   *belongs*
Let not his love, let not his restlesse spright
Be unrevenged, that calles to you above
From wandring Stygian shores,[3] where it doth endlesse move."

49

Thereto said he, "Faire Dame be nought dismaid
For sorrowes past; their griefe is with them gone:
Ne yet of present perill be affraid;
For needlesse feare did never vantage° none,   *aid*
And helplesse° hap it booteth not to mone.   *unavoidable*
Dead is Sans foy, his vitall paines are past,
Though greevéd ghost for vengeance deepe do grone:
He lives, that shall him pay his dewties° last,   *rites*
And guiltie Elfin bloud shall sacrifice in hast."

50

"O but I feare the fickle freakes,"° quoth shee,   *whims*
"Of fortune false, and oddes of armes in field."
"Why dame," quoth he, "what oddes can ever bee,
Where both do fight alike, to win or yield?"
"Yea but," quoth she, "he beares a charméd shield,
And eke enchaunted armes, that none can perce,
Ne none can wound the man, that does them wield."
"Charmd or enchaunted," answerd he then ferce,°   *fiercely*
"I no whit reck, ne you the like need to reherce."°   *recount*

51

"But faire Fidessa, sithens° fortunes guile,   *since*
Or enimies powre hath now captivéd you,
Returne from whence ye came, and rest a while
Till morrow next, that I the Elfe subdew,
And with Sans foyes dead dowry you endew."[4]
"Ay me, that is a double death," she said,
"With proud foes sight my sorrow to renew:
Where ever yet I be, my secrete aid
Shall follow you." So passing forth she him obaid.

Canto V

The faithfull knight in equall field
subdewes his faithlesse foe,
Whom false Duessa saves, and for
his cure to hell does goe.

1

The noble hart, that harbours vertuous thought,
And is with child of glorious great intent,

---

3. The banks of the river Styx, in the underworld.

4. I.e., endow you with the dowry of the dead Sansfoy.

Can never rest, untill it forth have brought
Th'eternall brood of glorie excellent:[1]
Such restlesse passion did all night torment
The flaming corage of that Faery knight,
Devizing, how that doughtie turnament
With greatest honour he atchieven might;
Still did he wake, and still did watch for dawning light.

2

At last the golden Orientall gate
    Of greatest heaven gan to open faire,
    And Phoebus fresh, as bridegrome to his mate,
    Came dauncing forth, shaking his deawie haire:
    And hurld his glistring beames through gloomy aire.
    Which when the wakeful Elfe perceived, streight way
    He started up, and did him selfe prepaire,
    In sun-bright armes, and battailous° array: *warlike*
For with that Pagan proud he combat will that day.

3

And forth he comes into the commune hall,
    Where earely waite him many a gazing eye,
    To weet° what end to straunger knights may fall.   *learn*
    There many Minstrales maken melody,
    To drive away the dull melancholy,
    And many Bardes, that to the trembling chord
    Can tune their timely° voyces cunningly,   *measured*
    And many Chroniclers, that can record
Old loves, and warres for Ladies doen by many a Lord.[2]

4

Soone after comes the cruell Sarazin,
    In woven maile all arméd warily,
    And sternly lookes at him, who not a pin
    Does care for looke of living creatures eye.
    They bring them wines of Greece and Araby,
    And daintie spices fetcht from furthest Ynd,
    To kindle heat of corage privily:°   *inwardly*
    And in the wine a solemne oth they bynd
T'observe the sacred lawes of armes, that are assynd.[3]

5

At last forth comes that far renowméd Queene,
    With royall pomp and Princely majestie;
    She is ybrought unto a paléd° greene,   *fenced*

---

1. The view that virtue must be ex-
pressed in action is regularly a mark
of Renaissance thought, from Castig-
lione's *Il Cortegiano* to Milton's
Areopagitica. Spenser's particular fig-
ure of speech recalls the expressions of
Plato's *Symposium,* 206c.
2. Spenser apparently does not dis-
tinguish among minstrels, bards, and
chroniclers: in the prose *Vewe of the*
Present State of Irelande, Irenius speaks
of his degree of reliance "uppon those
Bardes or Irishe Cronicles" (1205).
3. The setting of this encounter, to-
gether with these preliminaries to
battle, accords with established prece-
dent in medieval romance: proceedings
traditionally began with a ceremonial
oath to observe the laws of arms. Cf.
Shakespeare's *Richard II,* I. iii. 7–10.

And placéd under stately canapee,°   *canopy*
The warlike feates of both those knights to see.
On th'other side in all mens open vew
Duessa placéd is, and on a tree
Sans-foy his shield is hangd with bloudy hew:
Both those the lawrell girlonds to the victor dew.

6

A shrilling trompet sownded from on hye,
  And unto battaill bad them selves addresse:
  Their shining shieldes about their wrestes° they tye,   *wrists*
  And burning blades about their heads do blesse,°   *brandish*
  The instruments of wrath and heavinesse:
  With greedy force each other doth assayle,
  And strike so fiercely, that they do impresse
  Deepe dinted furrowes in the battred mayle;
The yron walles to ward their blowes are weake and fraile.

7

The Sarazin was stout, and wondrous strong,
  And heapéd blowes like yron hammers great:
  For after bloud and vengeance he did long.
  The knight was fiers, and full of youthly heat:
  And doubled strokes, like dreaded thunders threat:
  For all for prayse and honour he did fight.
  Both stricken strike, and beaten both do beat,
  That from their shields forth flyeth firie light,
And helmets hewen deepe, shew marks of eithers might.

8

So th'one for wrong, the other strives for right:
  As when a Gryfon⁴ seizéd° of his pray,   *in possession*
  A Dragon fiers encountreth in his flight,
  Through widest ayre making his ydle way,
  That would his rightfull ravine° rend away: *booty*
  With hideous horrour both together smight,
  And souce° so sore, that they the heavens affray: *strike*
  The wise Southsayer seeing so sad° sight,   *ominous*
Th'amazéd vulgar tels of warres and mortall fight.

9

So th'one for wrong, the other strives for right,
  And each to deadly shame would drive his foe:
  The cruell steele so greedily doth bight
  In tender flesh, that streames of bloud down flow,
  With which the armes, that earst° so bright did show,   *at first*
  Into a pure vermillion now are dyde:
  Great ruth in all the gazers harts did grow,

---

4. The griffon, referred to by Herodotus (*Histories*, III, 116) as guarding deposits of gold in the northern parts of Europe, is a legendary monster combining the body of a lion with the head and wings of an eagle; "but a griffoun" (as Sir John Mandeville wrote in the fourteenth century) hath a body greater than viii Lyons," and is stronger than 100 eagles (*Travels . . .* , ed. J. Bramont [London, 1928], p. 195).

Seeing the goréd woundes to gape so wyde,
That victory they dare not wish to either side.

10

At last the Paynim chaunst to cast his eye,
  His suddein° eye, flaming with wrathfull fyre,   *darting*
  Upon his brothers shield, which hong thereby:
  Therewith redoubled was his raging yre,
  And said, "Ah wretched sonne of wofull syre,
  Doest thou sit wayling by black Stygian lake,
  Whilest here thy shield is hangd for victors hyre,°   *reward*
  And sluggish german° doest thy forces slake,°   *brother/abate*
To after-send his foe, that him may overtake?⁵

11

"Goe caytive° Elfe, him quickly overtake,   *base*
  And soone redeeme from his long wandring woe;
  Goe guiltie ghost, to him my message make,
  That I his shield have quit° from dying foe."   *taken back*
  Therewith upon his crest he stroke him so,
  That twise he reeléd, readie twise to fall;
  End of the doubtfull battell deeméd tho°   *then*
  The lookers on, and lowd to him gan call
The false Duessa, "Thine the shield, and I, and all."

12

Soone as the Faerie heard his Ladie speake,
  Out of his swowning dreame he gan awake,
  And quickning° faith, that earst was woxen weake,   *vitalizing*
  The creeping deadly cold away did shake:
  Tho moved with wrath, and shame, and Ladies sake,
  Of all attonce he cast° avengd to bee,   *resolved*
  And with so'exceeding furie at him strake,
  That forcéd him to stoupe upon his knee;
Had he not stoupéd so, he should have cloven bee.

13

And to him said, "Goe now proud Miscreant,
  Thy selfe thy message doe° to german deare,   *give*
  Alone he wandring thee too long doth want:
  Goe say, his foe thy shield with his doth beare."
  Therewith his heavie hand he high gan reare,
  Him to have slaine; when loe a darkesome clowd
  Upon him fell: he no where doth appeare,
  But vanisht is. The Elfe him cals alowd,
But answer none receives: the darknes him does shrowd.⁶

14

In haste Duessa from her place arose,
  And to him running said, "O prowest° knight,   *bravest*
  That ever Ladie to her love did chose,

5. Sansjoy's reaction to the sight of his brother's shield recalls that of Aeneas, when, momentarily inclined to spare the defeated Turnus, he is once again roused to vengeful fury by the sight of the dead Pallas's sword belt on the shoulder of Turnus (*Aeneid,* XII. 941–949).

Let now abate the terror of your might,
And quench the flame of furious despight,
And bloudie vengeance; lo th'infernall powres
Covering your foe with cloud of deadly night,
Have borne him thence to Plutoes balefull bowres.
The conquest yours, I yours, the shield, and glory yours."

15

Not all so satisfide, with greedie eye
He sought all round about, his thirstie blade
To bath in bloud of faithlesse enemy;
Who all that while lay hid in secret shade:
He standes amazéd, how he thence should fade.
At last the trumpets Triumph sound on hie,
And running Heralds humble homage made,
Greeting him goodly with new victorie,
And to him brought the shield, the cause of enmitie.

16

Wherewith he goeth to that soveraine Queene,
And falling her before on lowly knee,
To her makes present of his service seene:°   proven
Which she accepts, with thankes, and goodly gree,°   favor
Greatly advauncing° his gay chevalree.   praising
So marcheth home, and by her takes the knight,
Whom all the people follow with great glee,
Shouting, and clapping all their hands on hight,
That all the aire it fils, and flyes to heaven bright.

17

Home is he brought, and laid in sumptuous bed:
Where many skilfull leaches° him abide,°   surgeons/attend
To salve his hurts, that yet still freshly bled.
In wine and oyle they wash his woundés wide,
And softly can embalme° on every side.   anoint
And all the while, most heavenly melody
About the bed sweet musicke did divide,°   descant
Him to beguile of griefe and agony:
And all the while Duessa wept full bitterly.

18

As when a wearie traveller that strayes
By muddy shore of broad seven-mouthéd Nile,
Unweeting of the perillous wandring wayes,
Doth meet a cruell craftie Crocodile,
Which in false griefe hyding his harmefull guile,
Doth weepe full sore, and sheddeth tender teares:
The foolish man, that pitties all this while

6. Here again Spenser might have drawn on Virgil (or Homer) for an account of similar measures taken by a god to protect his favorite (cf. *Aeneid*, V. 810–812; *Iliad*, III. 380); but it is more probable that the episode is based on Armida's protection of Rambaldo from the wrath of Tancred, in Tasso, *Gerusalemme Liberata* VII. 44–45.

His mournefull plight, is swallowed up unwares,
Forgetfull of his owne, that mindes anothers cares.[7]

19

So wept Duessa untill eventide,
   That° shyning lampes in Joves high house were light: *when*
   Then forth she rose, ne lenger would abide,
   But comes unto the place, where th'Hethen knight
   In slombring swownd° nigh voyd of vitall spright,   *swoon*
   Lay covered with inchaunted cloud all day:
   Whom when she found, as she him left in plight,
   To wayle his woefull case she would not stay,
But to the easterne coast of heaven makes speedy way.

20

Where griesly Night,[8] with visage deadly sad,
   That Phoebus chearefull face durst never vew,
   And in a foule blacke pitchie mantle clad,
   She findes forth comming from her darkesome mew,°   *cavern*
   Where she all day did hide her hated hew.
   Before the dore her yron charet stood,
   Alreadie harnesséd for journey new;
   And coleblacke steedes yborne of hellish brood,
That on their rustie bits did champ, as they were wood.°   *mad*

21

Who when she saw Duessa sunny bright,
   Adornd with gold and jewels shining cleare,
   She greatly grew amazéd at the sight,
   And th'unacquainted° light began to feare: *unfamiliar*
   For never did such brightnesse there appeare,
   And would have backe retyréd to her cave,
   Untill the witches speech she gan to heare,
   Saying, "Yet O thou dreaded Dame, I crave
Abide, till I have told the message, which I have."

22

She stayd, and foorth Duessa gan proceede,
   "O thou most auncient Grandmother of all,
   More old than Jove, whom thou at first didst breede,
   Or that great house of Gods caelestiall,
   Which wast begot in Daemogorgons hall,[9]
   And sawst the secrets of the world unmade,
   Why suffredst thou thy Nephewes° deare to fall   *grandsons*
   With Elfin sword, most shamefully betrade?
Lo where the stout Sansjoy doth sleepe in deadly shade.

7. The twelfth-century Latin bestiary translated by T. H. White observes that "hypocritical, dissolute and avaricious people have the same nature as [the crocodile]—also any people who are puffed up with the vice of pride, dirtied with the corruption of luxury, or haunted with the disease of avarice —even if they do make a show of falling in with the justifications of the Law, pretending in the sight of men to be upright and indeed very saintly" (*The Bestiary: A Book of Beasts*, T. H. White, trans. and ed. [New York, 1960], p. 50).
8. For his account of Night's origin, "age," and physical appearance, Spenser depends largely on the Renaissance mythographer, Natalis Comes (cf. *Mythologiae*, III. 12).
9. I.e., in Chaos.

23

"And him before, I saw with bitter eyes
  The bold Sansfoy shrinke underneath his speare;
  And now the pray of fowles in field he lyes,
  Nor wayld of friends, nor laid on groning beare,[1]
  That whylome was to me too dearely deare.
  O what of Gods then boots it to be borne,
  If old Aveugles sonnes so evill heare?[2]
  Or who shall not great Nightés children scorne,
When two of three her Nephews are so fowle forlorne?

24

"Up then, up dreary Dame, of darknesse Queene,
  Go gather up the reliques of thy race,
  Or else goe them avenge, and let be seene,
  That dreaded Night in brightest day hath place,
  And can the children of faire light deface.°"   *destroy*
  Her feeling speeches some compassion moved
  In hart, and chaunge in that great mothers face:
  Yet pittie in her hart was never proved°   *felt*
Till then: for evermore she hated, never loved.

25

And said, "Deare daughter rightly may I rew
  The fall of famous children borne of mee,
  And good successes, which their foes ensew:°   *attend*
  But who can turne the streame of destinee,
  Or breake the chayne of strong necessitee,
  Which fast is tyde to Joves eternall seat?[3]
  The sonnes of Day he favoureth, I see,
  And by my ruines thinkes to make them great:
To make one great by others losse, is bad excheat.°   *gain*

26

"Yet shall they not escape so freely all;
  For some shall pay the price of others guilt:
  And he the man that made Sansfoy to fall,
  Shall with his owne bloud price° that he hath split.   *pay for*
  But what art thou, that telst of Nephews kilt?"
  "I that do seeme not I, Duessa am,"
  Quoth she, "how ever now in garments gilt,
  And gorgeous gold arayd I to thee came;
Duessa I, the daughter of Deceipt and Shame."

27

Then bowing downe her agéd backe, she kist
  The wicked witch, saying; "In that faire face

1. I.e., on the bier attended by mourners.
2. I.e., if Aveugle's sons are so evilly treated. Aveugle ("blindness" or "darkness") is the son of Night.
3. Homer's is the first reference to the "golden rope" of Zeus, suspended from heaven, to which gods, men, and the entire universe are attached (*Iliad*, VIII. 18–27). Elsewhere in *The Faerie Queene*, Spenser employs the image to signify the harmonious order that informs the universe and links the actions of virtuous men (I. ix. 1), or, in an opposite sense, to represent the ambition motivating men to strive for position and power (II. vii. 46–47). Night's language hints at her misconception of the ordered design that informs the universe.

The false resemblance of Deceipt, I wist°   *knew*
Did closely lurke; yet so true-seeming grace
It carried, that I scarse in darkesome place
Could it discerne, though I the mother bee
Of falshood, and root of Duessaes race.
O welcome child, whom I have longd to see,
And now have seene unwares. Lo now I go with thee."

28

Then to her yron wagon she betakes,
And with her beares the fowle welfavourd° witch :   *attractive*
Through mirkesome° aire her readie way she makes. *murky, obscure*
Her twyfold° Teme, of which two blacke as pitch,   *twofold*
And two were browne, yet each to each unlich,°   *unlike*
Did softly swim away, ne ever stampe,
Unlesse she chaunst their stubborne mouths to twitch;
Then foming tarre,° their bridles they would champe, *black froth*
And trampling the fine element,[4] would fiercely rampe.

29

So well they sped, that they be come at length
Unto the place, whereas the Paynim lay,
Devoid of outward sense, and native strength,
Coverd with charméd cloud from vew of day,
And sight of men, since his late luckelesse fray.
His cruell wounds with cruddy° bloud congealed,   *clotted*
They binden up so wisely, as they may,
And handle softly, till they can be healed :
So lay him in her charet, close in night concealed.

30

And all the while she stood upon the ground,
The wakefull dogs did never cease to bay,
As giving warning of th'unwonted sound,
With which her yron wheeles did them affray,
And her darke griesly looke them much dismay;
The messenger of death, the ghastly Owle
With d
rearie shriekes did also her bewray;°   *reveal*
And hungry Wolves continually did howle,
At her abhorréd face, so filthy and so fowle.

31

Thence turning backe in silence soft they stole,
And brought the heavie corse with easie pace
To yawning gulfe of deepe Avernus hole.[5]
By that same hole an entrance darke and bace
With smoake and sulphure hiding all the place,
Descends to hell: there creature never past,
That backe returnéd without heavenly grace;

4. I.e., the air.
5. A lake near Naples, traditionally an entrance to hell; Virgil refers to it in terms like those employed here by Spenser (cf. *Aeneid*, VI. 200, 239–240). Sts. 31–35 owe much to Virgil's account of Aeneas's descent into Hades: even the assertion that "heavenly grace" alone assures return from hell has its classical counterpart in the *Aeneid*, VI. 129–131.

But dreadfull Furies, which their chaines have brast,°   *broken apart*
And damnéd sprights sent forth to make ill° men aghast.   *evil*

32

By that same way the direfull dames doe drive
  Their mournefull charet, fild with rusty blood,
  And downe to Plutoes house are come bilive:°   *quickly*
  Which passing through, on every side them stood
  The trembling ghosts with sad amazéd mood,
  Chattring their yron teeth, and staring wide
  With stonie eyes; and all the hellish brood
  Of feends infernall flockt on every side,
To gaze on earthly wight, that with the Night durst ride.

33

They pas the bitter waves of Acheron,[6]
  Where many soules sit wailing woefully,
  And come to fiery flood of Phlegeton,
  Whereas the damnéd ghosts in torments fry,
  And with sharpe shrilling shriekes doe bootlesse cry,
  Cursing high Jove, the which them thither sent.
  The house of endlesse paine is built thereby,
  In which ten thousand sorts of punishment
The curséd creatures doe eternally torment.

34

Before the threshold dreadfull Cerberus[7]
  His three deforméd heads did lay along,°   *at full length*
  Curléd with thousand adders venemous,
  And lilléd° forth his bloudie flaming tong: *lolled*
  At them he gan to reare his bristles strong,
  And felly gnarre,[8] untill dayes enemy
  Did him appease; then downe his taile he hong
  And suffered them to passen quietly:
For she in hell and heaven had power equally.

35

There was Ixion turnéd on a wheele,
  For daring tempt the Queene of heaven to sin;
  And Sisyphus an huge round stone did reele°   *roll*
  Against an hill, ne might from labour lin;°   *cease*
  There thirstie Tantalus hong by the chin;
  And Tityus fed a vulture on his maw;
  Typhoeus joynts were stretchéd on a gin,°   *rack*
  Theseus condemned to endlesse slouth by law,
And fifty sisters water in leake° vessels draw.[9]   *leaky*

6. Acheron ("stream of woe") and Phlegethon ("flaming") are two of the rivers of hell.
7. The three-headed hound that guards the entrance to hell.
8. I.e., fiercely snarl.
9. Ixion attempted to seduce Hera; Sisyphus was notorious for deceit and guile; Tantalus betrayed the gods' secrets; Tityus tried to rape Leto; Typhoeus rebelled against the gods; the fifty daughters of Danaus, forced to marry their cousins, killed their husbands on the wedding-night. For his account of these figures, Spenser relies on Natalis Comes; for the allusion to Theseus, cf. *Aeneid*, VI. 617–618.

36

They all beholding worldly wights in place,° *there*
    Leave off their worke, unmindfull of their smart,
    To gaze on them; who forth by them doe pace,
    Till they be come unto the furthest part:
    Where was a Cave ywrought by wondrous art,
    Deepe, darke, uneasie, dolefull, comfortlesse,
    In which sad Aesculapius farre a part
    Emprisond was in chaines remedilesse,
For that Hippolytus rent corse he did redresse.[1]

37

Hippolytus a jolly huntsman was,
    That wont in charet chace the foming Bore;
    He all his Peeres in beautie did surpas,
    But Ladies love as losse of time forbore:
    His wanton stepdame[2] lovéd him the more,
    But when she saw her offred sweets refused
    Her love she turnd to hate, and him before
    His father fierce of treason false accused,
And with her gealous termes his open° eares abused. *receptive*

38

Who all in rage his Sea-god syre[3] besought,
    Some curséd vengeance on his sonne to cast:
    From surging gulf two monsters straight were brought,
    With dread whereof his chasing steedes aghast,
    Both charet swift and huntsman overcast.
    His goodly corps on ragged cliffs yrent,
    Was quite dismembred, and his members chast
    Scattered on every mountaine, as he went,
That of Hippolytus was left no moniment.° *trace of identity*

39

His cruell stepdame seeing what was donne,
    Her wicked dayes with wretched knife did end,
    In death avowing th'innocence of her sonne.
    Which hearing his rash Syre, began to rend
    His haire, and hastie tongue, that did offend:
    Tho gathering up the relicks of his smart[4]
    By Dianes meanes, who was Hippolyts frend,
    Them brought to Aesculape, that by his art
Did heale them all againe, and joynéd every part.

40

Such wondrous science° in mans wit to raine *skill*
    When Jove avizd,° that could the dead revive, *perceived*

1. Aesculapius, the son of Apollo, was god of medical arts. For the following story of Hippolytus, Theseus's son, Spenser draws on *Metamorphoses*, XV. 497–550, and on *Aeneid*, VII. 765–769; but his primary authority, as is so often the case when he works with classical mythology, is that of a Renaissance mythographer, here Boccaccio, *De Genealogia Deorum*, X. 50.
2. Phaedra.
3. Neptune.
4. I.e., the remains of Hippolytus.

And fates expiréd⁵ could renew againe,
Of endlesse life he might him not deprive,
But unto hell did thrust him downe alive,
With flashing thunderbolt ywounded sore:
Where long remaining, he did alwaies strive
Himselfe with salves to health for to restore,
And slake the heavenly fire, that ragéd evermore.

41

There auncient Night arriving, did alight
From her nigh wearie waine, and in her armes
To Aesculapius brought the wounded knight:
Whom having softly disarayd of armes,
Tho gan to him discover° all his harmes,   reveal
Beseeching him with prayer, and with praise,
If either salves, or oyles, or herbes, or charmes
A fordonne° wight from dore of death mote raise,   undone
He would at her request prolong her nephews daies.

42

"Ah Dame," quoth he, "thou temptest me in vaine,
To dare the thing, which daily yet I rew,
And the old cause of my continued paine
With like attempt to like end to renew.
Is not enough, that thrust from heaven dew°   fitting
Here endlesse penance for one fault I pay,
But that redoubled crime with vengeance new
Thou biddest me to eeke°? Can Night defray°   augment/appease
The wrath of thundring Jove, that rules both night and day?"

43

"Not so," quoth she, "but sith that heavens king
From hope of heaven hath thee excluded quight,
Why fearest thou, that canst not hope for thing,
And fearest not, that more thee hurten might,
Now in the powre of everlasting Night?
Goe to then, O thou farre renowméd sonne
Of great Apollo, shew thy famous might
In medicine, that else° hath to thee wonne   already
Great paines, and greater praise, both never to be donne."°   ended

44

Her words prevaild: And then the learnéd leach
His cunning hand gan to his wounds to lay,
And all things else, the which his art did teach:
Which having seene, from thence arose away
The mother of dread darknesse, and let stay
Aveugles sonne there in the leaches cure,
And backe returning tooke her wonted way,
To runne her timely° race, whilst Phoebus pure   measured
In westerne waves his wearie wagon did recure.°   refresh

5. I.e., the completed term of life,
allotted by fate.

45

The false Duessa leaving noyous° Night,   *harmful*
  Returnd to stately pallace of dame Pride;
  Where when she came, she found the Faery knight
  Departed thence, albe° his woundés wide   *although*
  Not throughly heald, unreadie were to ride.
  Good cause he had to hasten thence away;
  For on a day his wary Dwarfe had spide,
  Where in a dongeon deepe huge numbers lay
Of caytive° wretched thrals,° that wayléd   *confined/slaves*
    night and day.

46

A ruefull sight, as could be seene with eie;
  Of whom he learnéd had in secret wise
  The hidden cause of their captivitie,
  How mortgaging their lives to Covetise,
  Through wastfull Pride, and wanton Riotise,
  They were by law of that proud Tyrannesse
  Provokt with Wrath, and Envies false surmise,
  Condemnéd to that Dongeon mercilesse,
Where they should live in woe, and die in wretchednesse.[6]

47

There was that great proud king of Babylon,[7]
  That would compell all nations to adore,
  And him as onely God to call upon,
  Till through celestiall doome° throwne out of dore,   *judgment*
  Into an Oxe he was transformed of yore:
  There also was king Croesus,[8] that enhaunst°   *exalted*
  His heart too high through his great riches store;
  And proud Antiochus,[9] the which advaunst°   *lifted*
His curséd hand gainst God, and on his altars daunst.

48

And them long time before, great Nimrod[1] was,
  That first the world with sword and fire warrayd;°   *made war on*
  And after him old Ninus[2] farre did pas°   *surpass*
  In princely pompe, of all the world obayd;
  There also was that mightie Monarch[3] layd

6. Many of the "wretched thrals" named in sts. 47–50 appear also in Chaucer's "Monk's Tale," which in turn was influenced by Boccaccio's extended account of the falls of princes, *De Casibus Illustrium Virorum*. But Spenser makes clear that all these figures, condemned by the law of "that proud Tyrannesse," Lucifera, have fallen as a consequence of pride or some other sin.
7. Nebuchadnezzar (cf. Daniel iii–iv).
8. A fabulously wealthy king of Lydia, in the sixth century B.C. Herodotus describes his career in the *Histories*, I. 26–30.
9. Antiochus IV, king of Syria in the second century B.C., who endeavored to extirpate the Jewish religion (cf. I Maccabees i. 20–24).
1. "A mighty hunter before the Lord" (Genesis x. 9); associated with the Tower of Babel, symbol of man's boundless pride.
2. Founder of Nineveh, "an exceeding great city"; its circumference was "a three days' journey" (Jonah iii. 3).
3. Alexander the Great, who from the time of his visit to the Libyan temple of Jupiter Ammon (in 331 B.C.) was worshipped in some quarters as the son of that deity. His biographer Arrian confirms the fact of his death after an extended drinking bout (*Life of Alexander the Great*, VII. 25–27).

Low under all, yet above all in pride,
    That name of native° syre did fowle upbrayd,   *natural*
    And would as Ammons sonne be magnifide,
Till scornd of God and man a shamefull death he dide.

49

All these together in one heape were throwne,
    Like carkases of beasts in butchers stall.
    And in another corner wide were strowne
    The antique ruines of the Romaines fall:
    Great Romulus the Grandsyre of them all,
    Proud Tarquin, and too lordly Lentulus,
    Stout Scipio, and stubborne Hanniball,
    Ambitious Sylla, and sterne Marius,
High Caesar, great Pompey, and fierce Antonius.[4]

50

Amongst these mighty men were wemen mixt,
    Proud wemen, vaine, forgetfull of their yoke:
    The bold Semiramis,[5] whose sides transfixt
    With sonnes owne blade, her fowle reproches spoke;
    Faire Sthenoboea,[6] that her selfe did choke
    With wilfull cord, for wanting° of her will;   *lacking*
    High minded Cleopatra, that with stroke
    Of Aspés sting her selfe did stoutly kill:
And thousands moe the like, that did that dongeon fill.

51

Besides the endlesse routs of wretched thralles,
    Which thither were assembled day by day,
    From all the world after their wofull falles,
    Through wicked pride, and wasted wealthes decay.
    But most of all, which in that Dongeon lay
    Fell from high Princes courts, or Ladies bowres,
    Where they in idle pompe, or wanton play,
    Consuméd had their goods, and thriftlesse howres,
And lastly throwne themselves into these heavy stowres.°   *violent ends*

52

Whose case whenas the carefull Dwarfe had tould,
    And made ensample of their mournefull sight
    Unto his maister, he no lenger would
    There dwell in perill of like painefull plight,
    But early rose, and ere that dawning light
    Discovered had the world to heaven wyde,
    He by a privie Posterne° tooke his flight,   *gate*
    That of no envious eyes he mote be spyde:
For doubtlesse death ensewd, if any him descryde.

53

Scarse could he footing find in that fowle way,
    For many corses, like a great Lay-stall°   *heap of trash*

4. The careers of these Roman leaders are described in Plutarch's *Lives of the Noble Grecians and Romans.*
5. The wife of Ninus.
6. The wife of Proetus, a king of Argos; her love for the younger Bellerophon led to her death.

Of murdred men which therein strowéd lay,
Without remorse,° or decent funerall: pity
Which all through that great Princesse pride did fall
And came to shamefull end. And them beside
Forth ryding underneath the castell wall,
A donghill of dead carkases he spide,
The dreadfull spectacle° of that sad house of Pride.   sign, example

Canto VI

From lawlesse lust by wondrous grace
    fayre Una is releast:
Whom salvage nation does adore,
    and learnes her wise beheast.°   bidding

1

As when a ship, that flyes faire under saile,
    An hidden rocke escapéd hath unwares,
    That lay in waite her wrack for to bewaile,[1]
The Marriner yet halfe amazéd stares
At perill past, and yet in doubt ne dares
To joy at his foole-happie° oversight: lucky
    So doubly is distrest twixt joy and cares
    The dreadlesse courage of this Elfin knight,
Having escapt so sad ensamples in his sight.

2

Yet sad he was that his too hastie speed
    The faire Duess had forst him leave behind;
    And yet more sad, that Una his deare dreed°   revered one
Her truth had staind with treason so unkind;°   unnatural
Yet crime in her could never creature find,
But for his love, and for her owne selfe sake,
    She wandred had° from one to other Ynd,   would have
    Him for to seeke, ne ever would forsake,
Till her unwares the fierce Sansloy did overtake.

3

Who after Archimagoes fowle defeat,
    Led her away into a forrest wilde,
    And turning wrathfull fire to lustfull heat,
With beastly sin thought her to have defilde,
And made the vassall of his pleasures vilde.°   vile
Yet first he cast by treatie,° and by traynes,°   entreaty/trickery
    Her to perswade, that stubborne fort to yilde:
    For greater conquest of hard love he gaynes,
That workes it to his will, then he that it constraines.

4

With fawning wordes he courted her a while,
    And looking lovely,° and oft sighing sore,   lovingly
    Her constant hart did tempt with diverse guile:

1. I.e., to cause her wreck (?). "Be-   Textual Notes.
waile" may be an error: see the

But wordes, and lookes, and sighes she did abhore,
As rocke of Diamond stedfast evermore.
Yet for to feed his fyrie lustfull eye,
He snatcht the vele, that hong her face before;
Then gan her beautie shine, as brightest skye,
And burnt his beastly hart t'efforce° her chastitye.   *violate*

5

So when he saw his flatt'ring arts to fayle,
And subtile engines bet from batteree,[2]
With greedy force he gan the fort assayle,
Whereof he weend possesséd soone to bee,
And win rich spoile of ransackt chastetee.
Ah heavens, that do this hideous act behold,
And heavenly virgin thus outragéd see,
How can ye vengeance just so long withhold,
And hurle not flashing flames upon that Paynim bold?

6

The pitteous maiden carefull° comfortlesse,   *full of care*
Does throw out thrilling shriekes, and shrieking cryes,
The last vaine helpe of womens great distresse,
And with loud plaints importuneth the skyes,
That molten starres do drop like weeping eyes;
And Phoebus flying so most shamefull sight,
His blushing face in foggy cloud implyes,°   *enwraps*
And hides for shame. What wit of mortall wight
Can now devise to quit a thrall[3] from such a plight?

7

Eternall providence exceeding° thought,   *transcending*
Where none appeares can make her selfe a way:
A wondrous way it for this Lady wrought,
From Lyons clawes to pluck the gripéd pray.
Her shrill outcryes and shriekes so loud did bray,
That all the woodes and forestes did resownd;
A troupe of Faunes and Satyres far away
Within the wood were dauncing in a rownd,
Whiles old Sylvanus slept in shady arber sownd.[4]

8

Who when they heard that pitteous strainéd voice,
In hast forsooke their rurall meriment,

2. I.e., his courtly wiles repulsed.
3. Free a slave.
4. The "woodgods" of Greek and Roman mythology, half man and half goat, are here engaged in "rurall meriment," appropriately for a context of English folklore; "Faunes or Sylvanes," according to E.K.'s Glosse to "July," "be of Poetes feigned to be Gods of the Woode." "Old Sylvanus," Roman god of fields and forests, was traditionally the lover of Pomona, divinity of fruit trees. Combining ignorance and idolatry with an instinct for natural goodness, these figures probably repre-
sent pre-Christian (or, perhaps, primitive Christian) religious belief and practice. That their appearance at once puts the "raging" Sansloy to flight supports the view that Spenser is indebted to Natalis Comes, who observes, with reference to the ancient belief that fauns and forest spirits watch over workers in field and forest, that nothing that happens in those areas escapes the attentive knowledge of God (*Mythologiae*, X). In other contexts, however, these figures take on a somewhat different significance (cf. III. x. 43–51).

And ran towards the far rebownded noyce,
To weet, what wight so loudly did lament.
Unto the place they come incontinent:°   *hastily*
Whom when the raging Sarazin espide,
A rude, misshapen, monstrous rablement,
Whose like he never saw, he durst not bide,
But got his ready steed, and fast away gan ride.

9

The wyld woodgods arrivéd in the place,
There find the virgin dolefull desolate,
With ruffled rayments, and faire blubbred° face,   *tear-stained*
As her outrageous foe had left her late,
And trembling yet through feare of former hate;
All stand amazéd at so uncouth° sight,   *strange*
And gin to pittie her unhappie state,
All stand astonied at her beautie bright,
In their rude eyes unworthie° of so wofull plight.   *undeserving*

10

She more amazed, in double dread doth dwell;
And every tender part for feare does shake:
As when a greedie Wolfe through hunger fell
A seely° Lambe farre from the flocke does take,   *innocent*
Of whom he meanes his bloudie feast to make,
A Lyon spyes fast running towards him,
The innocent pray in hast he does forsake,
Which quit° from death yet quakes in every lim   *saved*
With chaunge of feare, to see the Lyon looke so grim.

11

Such fearefull fit assaid° her trembling hart,   *afflicted*
Ne word to speake, ne joynt to move she had:
The salvage nation feele her secret smart,
And read her sorrow in her count'nance sad;
Their frowning forheads with rough hornes yclad,
And rusticke horror° all a side doe lay,   *roughness*
And gently grenning,° shew a semblance glad   *grinning*
To comfort her, and feare to put away,
Their backward bent knees teach her humbly to obay.[5]

12

The doubtfull Damzell dare not yet commit
Her single° person to their barbarous truth,°   *solitary/honesty*
But still twixt feare and hope amazd does sit,
Late learnd° what harme to hastie trust ensu'th,   *taught*
They in compassion of her tender youth,
And wonder of her beautie soveraine,
Are wonne with pitty and unwonted ruth,
And all prostrate upon the lowly plaine,
Do kisse her feete, and fawne on her with countenance faine.° *glad*

5. I.e., they teach their knees (bent   kneel in humble obedience to her.
backward like those of a goat) to

13

Their harts she ghesseth by their humble guise,°   *manner*
  And yieldes her to extremitie of time;[6]
  So from the ground she fearelesse doth arise,
  And walketh forth without suspect of crime:[7]
  They all as glad, as birdes of joyous Prime,°   *springtime*
  Thence lead her forth, about her dauncing round,
  Shouting, and singing all a shepheards ryme,
  And with greene braunches strowing all the ground,
Do worship her, as Queene, with olive girlond cround.[8]

14

And all the way their merry pipes they sound,
  That all the woods with doubled Eccho ring,
  And with their hornéd feet do weare° the ground,   *trample*
  Leaping like wanton kids in pleasant Spring.
  So towards old Sylvanus they her bring;
  Who with the noyse awakéd, commeth out,
  To weet the cause, his weake steps governing,
  And aged limbs on Cypresse stadle° stout,   *staff*
And with an yvie twyne his wast is girt about.

15

Far off he wonders, what them makes so glad,
  Or Bacchus merry fruit they did invent,[9]
  Or Cybeles franticke rites[1] have made them mad;
  They drawing nigh, unto their God present
  That flowre of faith and beautie excellent.
  The God himselfe vewing that mirrhour rare,[2]
  Stood long amazd, and burnt in his intent;°   *gaze*
  His owne faire Dryope now he thinkes not faire,
And Pholoe fowle, when her to this he doth compaire.[3]

16

The woodborne people fall before her flat,
  And worship her as Goddesse of the wood;
  And old Sylvanus selfe bethinkes° not, what   *concludes*
  To thinke of wight so faire, but gazing stood,
  In doubt to deeme her borne of earthly brood;
  Sometimes Dame Venus selfe he seemes to see,
  But Venus never had so sober mood;
  Sometimes Diana he her takes to bee,
But misseth bow, and shaftes, and buskins° to her knee.   *boots*

6. I.e., to present necessity.
7. I.e., without fear of reproach.
8. Una's beauty, as sts. 13–19 indicate, exerts a higher and qualitatively different power than that of merely natural beauty. But the satyrs' idolatrous worship of her reflects their inability to grasp fully the essential significance of her being.
9. I.e., whether they had found the grapes that, in the form of wine, make men merry.
1. Rhea, Greek goddess of the earth, was worshipped (as Cybele) throughout the Near Eastern world with rites led by priests who imitated madness and fury, and who performed orgiastic dances to the accompaniment of brass and percussion instruments.
2. I.e., that mirror of heavenly beauty.
3. Dryope was the wife of Faunus; Pholoe a nymph loved by Pan. Spenser's language indicates that the poet considered the names of Faunus, Pan, and Sylvanus to be interchangeable.

17

By vew of her he ginneth to revive
   His ancient love, and dearest Cyparisse,[4]
   And calles to mind his pourtraiture alive,[5]
   How faire he was, and yet not faire to this,
   And how he slew with glauncing dart amisse
   A gentle Hynd, the which the lovely boy
   Did love as life, above all worldly blisse;
   For griefe whereof the lad n'ould° after joy,   *would not*
But pynd away in anguish and selfe-wild annoy.°   *grief*

18

The wooddy Nymphes, faire Hamadryades[6]
   Her to behold do thither runne apace,
   And all the troupe of light-foot Naiades,[7]
   Flocke all about to see her lovely face:
   But when they vewéd have her heavenly grace,
   They envie her in their malitious mind,
   And fly away for feare of fowle disgrace:
   But all the Satyres scorne their woody kind,
And henceforth nothing faire, but her on earth they find.

19

Glad of such lucke, the luckelesse lucky maid,
   Did her content to please their feeble eyes,
   And long time with that salvage people staid,
   To gather breath in many miseries.
   During which time her gentle wit she plyes,
   To teach them truth, which worshipt her in vaine,°   *foolishly*
   And made her th'Image of Idolatryes;
   But when their bootlesse zeale she did restraine
From her own worship, they her Asse would worship fayn.° *eagerly*

20

It fortunéd a noble warlike knight[8]
   By just occasion to that forrest came,
   To seeke his kindred, and the lignage right,°   *true*
   From whence he tooke his well deservéd name:
   He had in armes abroad wonne muchell fame,
   And fild far landes with glorie of his might,
   Plaine, faithfull, true, and enimy of shame,
   And ever loved to fight for Ladies right,
But in vaine glorious frayes he litle did delight.

---

4. According to Ovid, Cyparissus, the beloved of Apollo, was changed by the god into a cypress (*Met.*, X. 106–142); in Natalis Comes's version, Cyparissus is associated rather with Sylvanus (*Mythologiae*, V. 10).
5. I.e., his appearance when he was alive.
6. Tree nymphs, whose lives did not outlast those of the trees they inhabited.
7. Nymphs of lakes and rivers, thought to have prophetic powers.

8. I.e., Satyrane (first named in st. 28), whose parentage recalls the theme, common in fairy lore, of a mortal's mating with an other-worldly being. He can tame wild beasts, resist the ferocious Sansloy (cf. sts. 43–47), and even subdue some kinds of monsters (III. vii. 29–36); but he is no match for the giantess Argante (III. vii. 42–43). His natural goodness enables him to protect Una more effectively than could the lion, but he cannot accomplish the task assigned to Redcrosse.

21

A Satyres sonne yborne in forrest wyld,
   By straunge adventure as it did betyde,°   *happen*
   And there begotten of a Lady myld,
   Faire Thyamis the daughter of Labryde,
   That was in sacred bands of wedlocke tyde
   To Therion, a loose unruly swayne;[9]
   Who had more joy to raunge the forrest wyde,
   And chase the salvage beast with busie payne,[1]
Then serve his Ladies love, and wast° in pleasures vayne.   *live idly*

22

The forlorne mayd did with loves longing burne,
   And could not lacke° her lovers company,   *be without*
   But to the wood she goes, to serve her turne,
   And seeke her spouse, that from her still does fly,
   And followes other game and venery:[2]
   A Satyre chaunst her wandring for to find,
   And kindling coles of lust in brutish eye,
   The loyall links of wedlocke did unbind,
And made her person thrall unto his beastly kind.

23

So long in secret cabin there he held
   Her captive to his sensuall desire,
   Till that with timely fruit her belly sweld,
   And bore a boy unto that salvage sire:
   Then home he suffred her for to retire,
   For ransome leaving him the late borne childe;
   Whom till to ryper yeares he gan aspire,°   *grow up*
   He noursled up in life and manners wilde,
Emongst wild beasts and woods, from lawes of men exilde.

24

For all he taught the tender ymp,° was but   *child*
   To banish cowardize and bastard° feare;   *base*
   His trembling hand he would him force to put
   Upon the Lyon and the rugged Beare,
   And from the she Beares teats her whelps to teare;
   And eke wyld roring Buls he would him make
   To tame, and ryde their backes not made to beare;
   And the Robuckes in flight to overtake,
That every beast for feare of him did fly and quake.[3]

25

Thereby so fearelesse, and so fell he grew,
   That his owne sire and maister of his guise°   *way of life*
   Did often tremble at his horrid vew,°   *appearance*

9. These names, by their Greek deriva-
tion, indicate the natures of each fig-
ure: Thyamis, "passion"; Labryde,
"turbulent," or "greedy"; Therion,
"wild beast."
1. I.e., with painstaking care.

2. The term means both "hunting" and
"sexual indulgence."
3. So Chiron the centaur, half man
and half horse, educated Achilles: cf.
Pindar's third Nemean Ode, 43 ff.

And oft for dread of hurt would him advise,
 The angry beasts not rashly to despise,
 Nor too much to provoke; for he would learne°   *teach*
 The Lyon stoup to him in lowly wise,
 (A lesson hard) and make the Libbard° sterne   *leopard*
Leave roaring, when in rage he for revenge did earne.°   *yearn*

26

And for to make his powre approvéd° more,   *established*
 Wyld beasts in yron yokes he would compell;
 The spotted Panther, and the tuskéd Bore,
 The Pardale° swift, and the Tigre cruell;   *panther*
 The Antelope, and Wolfe both fierce and fell;
 And them constraine in equall teme to draw.[4]
 Such joy he had, their stubborne harts to quell,
 And sturdie courage tame with dreadfull aw,
That his beheast they febaréd, as a tyrans law.

27

His loving mother came upon a day
 Unto the woods, to see her little sonne;
 And chaunst unwares to meet him in the way,
 After his sportes, and cruell pastime donne,
 When after him a Lyonesse did runne,
 That roaring all with rage, did lowd requere°   *demand*
 Her children deare, whom he away had wonne:
 The Lyon whelpes she saw how he did beare,
And lull in rugged armes, withouten childish feare.

28

The fearefull Dame all quakéd at the sight,
 And turning backe, gan fast to fly away,
 Until with love revokt° from vaine affright,   *restrained*
 She hardly° yet perswaded was to stay,   *with difficulty*
 And then to him these womanish words gan say;
 "Ah Satyrane, my dearling, and my joy,
 For love of me leave off this dreadfull play;
 To dally thus with death, is no fit toy,
Go find some other play-fellowes, mine own sweet boy."

29

In these and like delights of bloudy game
 He traynéd was, till ryper yeares he raught,°   *attained*
 And there abode, whilst any beast of name
 Walkt in that forest, whom he had not taught
 To feare his force: and then his courage haught°   *high*
 Desird of forreine foemen to be knowne,
 And far abroad for straunge adventures sought:
 In which his might was never overthrowne,
But through all Faery lond his famous worth was blown.

30

Yet evermore it was his manner faire,
 After long labours and adventures spent,

4. I.e., to draw evenly, in pairs.

Unto those native woods for to repaire,°   *return*
To see his sire and ofspring° auncient.   *origin*
And now he thither came for like intent;
Where he unwares the fairest Una found,
Straunge Lady, in so straunge habiliment,°   *attire*
Teaching the Satyres, which her sat around,
Trew sacred lore, which from her sweet lips did redound.°   *flow*

31

He wondred at her wisedome heavenly rare,
  Whose like in womens wit he never knew;
  And when her curteous deeds he did compare,
  Gan her admire, and her sad sorrowes rew,
  Blaming of Fortune, which such troubles threw,
  And joyd to make proofe of her crueltie
  On gentle Dame, so hurtlesse,° and so trew: *harmless*
  Thenceforth he kept her goodly company,
And learnd her discipline of faith and veritie.

32

But she all vowd unto the Redcrosse knight,
  His wandring perill closely° did lament,   *privately*
  Ne in this new acquaintaunce could delight,
  But her deare heart with anguish did torment,
  And all her wit in secret counsels spent,
  How to escape. At last in privie wise[5]
  To Satyrane she shewéd her intent;
  Who glad to gain such favour, gan devise,
How with that pensive Maid he best might thence arise.°   *depart*

33

So on a day when Satyres all were gone,
  To do their service to Sylvanus old,
  The gentle virgin left behind alone
  He led away with courage stout and bold.
  Too late it was, to Satyres to be told,
  Or ever hope recover her againe:
  In vaine he seekes that having cannot hold.
  So fast he carried her with carefull paine,°   *pains*
That they the woods are past, and come now to the plaine.[6]

34

The better part now of the lingring day,
  They traveild had, when as they farre espide
  A wearie wight forwandring° by the way,   *wandering along*
  And towards him they gan in hast to ride,
  To weet of newes, that did abroad betide,
  Or tydings of her knight of the Redcrosse.
  But he them spying, gan to turne aside,

5. I.e., secretly.
6. The episode that follows is based on the adventures of Angelica, Sacripante, and Rinaldo, in Ariosto, *Orlando Furioso*, I. 1–2. Spenser, however, substitutes for Ariosto's characteristically ironic and mocking tone one of high moral seriousness; further, he leaves unresolved the issue of the encounter between Satyrane (who reappears in Book III) and Sansloy (who appears again in II. ii).

For feare as seemd, or for some feignéd losse;°   *harm*
More greedy they of newes, fast towards him do crosse.

35

A silly° man, in simple weedes forworne,°   *simple/worn out*
  And soild with dust of the long driéd way;
  His sandales were with toilesome travell torne,
  And face all tand with scorching sunny ray,
  As he had traveild many a sommers day,
  Through boyling sands of Arabie and Ynde;
  And in his hand a Jacobs staffe,[7] to stay
  His wearie limbes upon: and eke behind,
His scrip° did hang, in which his needments he did bind.   *bag*

36

The knight approching nigh, of him inquerd
  Tydings of warre, and of adventures new;
  But warres, nor new adventures none he herd.
  Then Una gan to aske, if ought he knew,
  Or heard abroad of that her champion trew,
  That in his armour bare a croslet° red.   *small cross*
  "Aye me, Deare dame," quoth he, "well may I rew
  To tell the sad sight, which mine eies have red:°   *seen*
These eyes did see that knight both living and eke ded."

37

That cruell word her tender hart so thrild,°   *pierced*
  That suddein cold did runne through every vaine,
  And stony horrour all her sences fild
  With dying fit, that downe she fell for paine.
  The knight her lightly rearéd up againe,
  And comforted with curteous kind reliefe:
  Then wonne from death, she bad him tellen plaine
  The further processe° of her hidden griefe;   *account*
The lesser pangs can beare, who hath endured the chiefe.

38

Then gan the Pilgrim thus, "I chaunst this day,
  This fatall day, that shall I ever rew,
  To see two knights in travell on my way
  (A sory sight) arraunged in battell new,[8]
  Both breathing vengeaunce, both of wrathfull hew:
  My fearefull flesh did tremble at their strife,
  To see their blades so greedily imbrew,°   *thrust*
  That drunke with bloud, yet thristed after life:
What more? the Redcrosse knight was slaine with Paynim knife."

39

"Ah dearest Lord," quoth she, "how might that bee,
  And he the stoutest knight, that ever wonne?"°   *engaged in battle*
  "Ah dearest dame," quoth he, "how might I see
  The thing, that might not be, and yet was donne?"
  "Where is," said Satyrane, " that Paynims sonne,

---

7. I.e., a pilgrim's staff.   8. I.e., striking the first blows of their
                                      encounter.

That him of life, and us of joy hath reft?"
"Not far away," quoth he, " he hence doth wonne°   *remain*
Foreby a fountaine, where I late him left
Washing his bloudy wounds, that through the steele were cleft."

40

Therewith the knight thence marchéd forth in hast,
  Whiles Una with huge heavinesse° opprest,   *grief*
  Could not for sorrow follow him so fast;
  And soone he came, as he the place had ghest,
  Whereas that Pagan proud him selfe did rest,
  In secret shadow by a fountaine side:
  Even he it was, that earst would have supprest°   *ravished*
  Faire Una: whom when Satyrane espide,
With fowle reprochfull words he boldly him defide.

41

And said, "Arise thou curséd Miscreaunt,
  That hast with knightlesse guile and trecherous train°   *deceit*
  Faire knighthood fowly shaméd, and doest vaunt
  That good knight of the Redcrosse to have slain:
  Arise, and with like treason now maintain
  Thy guilty wrong, or else thee guilty yield."
  The Sarazin this hearing, rose amain,°   *at once*
  And catching up in hast his three square° shield,   *triangular*
And shining helmet, soone him buckled to the field.

42

And drawing nigh him said, "Ah misborne° Elfe,   *basely born*
  In evill houre thy foes thee hither sent,
  Anothers wrongs to wreake upon thy selfe:[9]
  Yet ill thou blamest me, for having blent°   *defiled*
  My name with guile and traiterous intent;
  That Redcrosse knight, perdie,° I never slew,   *truly*
  But had he beene, where earst his armes were lent,
  Th'enchaunter vaine his errour should not rew:
But thou his errour shalt, I hope now proven trew."[1]

43

Therewith they gan, both furious and fell,
  To thunder blowes, and fiersly to assaile
  Each other bent° his enimy to quell,   *determined*
  That with their force they perst both plate and maile,
  And made wide furrowes in their fleshes fraile,
  That it would pitty° any living eie.   *bring pity to*
  Large floods of bloud adowne their sides did raile:°   *flow*
  But floods of bloud could not them satisfie:
Both hungred after death: both chose to win, or die.

44

So long they fight, and fell revenge pursue,
  That fainting each, themselves to breathen let,
  And oft refreshéd, battell oft renue:

9. I.e., to draw upon yourself the consequences of another's wrongs.
1. I.e. [in reference to I. iii. 33–39], your experience at my hands shall now, I hope, confirm Archimago's foolishness in venturing to fight me.

As when two Bores with rancling malice met,
  Their gory sides fresh bleeding fiercely fret,°   *gnaw, tear*
  Til breathlesse both them selves aside retire,
  Where foming wrath, their cruell tuskes they whet,
  And trample th'earth, the whiles they may respire;
Then backe to fight againe, new breathéd and entire.°   *refreshed*

45

So fiersly, when these knights had breathéd once,
  They gan to fight returne, increasing more
  Their puissant force, and cruell rage attonce,
  With heapéd strokes more hugely, then before,
  That with their drerie° wounds and bloudy gore   *gory*
  They both deforméd, scarsely could be known.
  By this sad Una fraught with anguish sore,
  Led with their noise, which through the aire was thrown,
Arrived, where they in erth their fruitles bloud had sown.

46

Whom all so soone as that proud Sarazin
  Espide, he gan revive the memory
  Of his lewd lusts, and late attempted sin,
  And left the doubtfull° battell hastily,   *undecided*
  To catch her, newly offred to his eie:
  But Satyrane with strokes him turning, staid,
  And sternely bad him other businesse plie,
  Then hunt the steps of pure unspotted Maid:
Wherewith he all enraged, these bitter speaches said.

47

"O foolish faeries sonne, what furie mad
  Hath thee incenst, to hast thy dolefull fate?
  Were it not better, I that Lady had,
  Then that thou hadst repented it too late?
  Most sencelesse man he, that himselfe doth hate,
  To love another. Lo then for thine ayd
  Here take thy lovers token on thy pate."
  So they to fight; the whiles the royall Mayd
Fled farre away, of that proud Paynim sore afrayd.

48

But that false Pilgrim, which that leasing° told,   *falsehood*
  Being in deed old Archimage, did stay
  In secret shadow, all this to behold,
  And much rejoycéd in their bloudy fray:
  But when he saw the Damsell passe away
  He left his stond,° and her pursewd apace,   *place*
  In hope to bring her to her last decay.°   *destruction*
  But for to tell her lamentable cace,
And eke this battels end, will need another place.

Canto VII

The Redcrosse knight is captive made
By Gyaunt proud opprest,
Prince Arthur meets with Una great-
ly with those newes distrest.

1

What man so wise, what earthly wit so ware,°   *wary*
  As to descry° the crafty cunning traine,   *discover*
  By which deceipt doth maske in visour faire,
  And cast° her colours dyéd deepe in graine,   *dispose*
  To seeme like Truth, whose shape she well can faine,
  And fitting gestures to her purpose frame,
  The guiltlesse man with guile to entertaine?°   *receive*
  Great maistresse of her art was that false Dame,
The false Duessa, clokéd with Fidessaes name.

2

Who when returning from the drery Night,
  She fownd not in that perilous house of Pryde,
  Where she had left, the noble Redcrosse knight,
  Her hopéd pray, she would no lenger bide,
  But forth she went, to seeke him far and wide.
  Ere long she fownd, whereas he wearie sate,
  To rest him selfe, foreby° a fountaine side,   *near*
  Disarméd all of yron-coted Plate,[1]
And by his side his steed the grassy forage ate.

3

He feedes upon the cooling shade, and bayes°   *bathes*
  His sweatie forehead in the breathing wind,
  Which through the trembling leaves full gently playes
  Wherein the cherefull birds of sundry kind
  Do chaunt sweet musick, to delight his mind:
  The Witch approching gan him fairely greet,
  And with reproch of carelesnesse unkind
  Upbrayd, for leaving her in place unmeet,°   *unfitting*
With fowle words tempring faire, soure gall with hony sweet.

4

Unkindnesse past, they gan of solace treat,°   *speak*
  And bathe in pleasaunce of the joyous shade,
  Which shielded them against the boyling heat,
  And with greene boughes decking a gloomy glade,
  About the fountaine like a girlond made;
  Whose bubbling wave did ever freshly well,
  Ne ever would through fervent° sommer fade: *hot*

---

1. Having recognized something of the danger presented by worldly pride, Redcrosse has nonetheless been weakened by his struggle with Sansjoy; his "carelesnesse" (in a sense other than that signified by Duessa's language in st. 3) enthralls him to another form of pride.

The sacred Nymph, which therein wont to dwell,
Was out of Dianes favour, as it then befell.

5

The cause was this: one day when Phoebe[2] fayre
   With all her band was following the chace,
   This Nymph, quite tyred with heat of scorching ayre
   Sat downe to rest in middest of the race:
   The goddesse wroth gan fowly her disgrace,°   *scold, revile*
   And bad the waters, which from her did flow,
   Be such as she her selfe was then in place.°   *that place*
   Thenceforth her waters waxéd dull and slow,
And all that drunke thereof, did faint and feeble grow.

6

Hereof this gentle knight unweeting was,
   And lying downe upon the sandie graile,°   *gravel*
   Drunke of the streame, as cleare as cristall glas;
   Eftsoones his manly forces gan to faile,
   And mightie strong was turnd to feeble fraile.
   His chaungéd powres at first themselves not felt,
   Till crudled° cold his corage° gan assaile,   *congealing/vigor*
   And chearefull° bloud in faintnesse chill did melt,   *lively*
Which like a fever fit through all his body swelt.°   *raged*

7

Yet goodly court he made still to his Dame,
   Pourd out in loosnesse on the grassy grownd,
   Both carelesse of his health, and of his fame:
   Till at the last he heard a dreadfull sownd,
   Which through the wood loud bellowing, did rebownd,
   That all the earth for terrour seemd to shake,
   And trees did tremble. Th'Elfe therewith astownd,°   *amazed*
   Upstarted lightly from his looser make,°   *companion*
And his unready weapons gan in hand to take.

8

But ere he could his armour on him dight,°   *put*
   Or get his shield, his monstrous enimy
   With sturdie steps came stalking in his sight,
   An hideous Geant horrible and hye,[3]
   That with his talnesse seemd to threat the skye,
   The ground eke gronéd under him for dreed;
   His living like saw never living eye,
   Ne durst behold: his stature did exceed
The hight of three the tallest sonnes of mortall seed.

---

2. Diana, goddess of the moon. While the episode here described seems to be original with Spenser, lines 8–9 recall Ovid's account of the fountain of Salmacis, whose waters enfeebled persons bathing there (*Met.*, IV. 286–287).
3. For an extended account of the complex levels of meaning represented by the giant Orgoglio ("pride"), cf. the discussion by S. K. Heninger, Jr., in this volume. Orgoglio signifies that fleshly pride which is totally irrational and ungodly: "the basic and radical ur-sin of Pride, usurping Godhead" (Rosemond Tuve, *Allegorical Imagery* [Princeton, N.J., 1966], p. 106).

9

The greatest Earth his uncouth mother was,
   And blustring Aeolus[4] his boasted sire,
   Who with his breath, which through the world doth pas,
   Her hollow womb did secretly inspire,°   *breathe into*
   And fild her hidden caves with stormie yre,
   That she conceived; and trebling the dew time,
   In which the wombes of women do expire,°   *give birth*
   Brought forth this monstrous masse of earthly slime,
Puft up with emptie wind, and fild with sinfull crime.

10

So growen great through arrogant delight
   Of th'high descent, whereof he was yborne,
   And through presumption of his matchlesse might,
   All other powres and knighthood he did scorne.
   Such now he marcheth to this man forlorne,
   And left to losse:° his stalking steps are stayde   *dertruction*
   Upon a snaggy Oke, which he had torne
   Out of his mothers bowelles, and it made
His mortall mace, wherewith his foemen he dismayde.

11

That when the knight he spide, he gan advance
   With huge force and insupportable mayne,[5]
   And towardes him with dreadfull fury praunce;
   Who haplesse, and eke hopelesse, all in vaine
   Did to him pace, sad battaile to darrayne,°   *undertake*
   Disarmd, disgrast, and inwardly dismayde,
   And eke so faint in every joynt and vaine,
   Through that fraile° fountaine, which him feeble made, *weakening*
That scarsely could he weeld his bootlesse single blade.[6]

12

The Geaunt strooke so maynly° mercilesse,   *mightily*
   That could have overthrowne a stony towre,
   And were not heavenly grace, that him did blesse,° *preserve*
   He had beene pouldred° all, as thin as flowre: *crushed*
   But he was wary of that deadly stowre,°   *peril*
   And lightly lept from underneath the blow:
   Yet so exceeding was the villeins powre,
   That with the wind it did him overthrow,
And all his sences stound,° that still he lay full low. *stunned*

13

As when that divelish yron Engin[7] wrought
   In deepest Hell, and framd by Furies skill,
   With windy Nitre and quick° Sulphur fraught,° *inflammable/filled*
   And ramd with bullet round, ordaind to kill,
   Conceiveth fire, the heavens it doth fill
   With thundring noyse, and all the ayre doth choke,

4. God of the winds.
5. Irresistible strength.
6. I.e., sword alone, without the aid of armor or shield.
7. I.e., cannon.

That none can breath, nor see, nor heare at will,
Through smouldry cloud of duskish stincking smoke,
That th'onely breath[8] him daunts, who hath escapt the stroke.

14

So daunted when the Geaunt saw the knight,
His heavie hand he heavéd up on hye,
And him to dust thought to have battred quight,
Untill Duessa loud to him gan crye;
"O great Orgoglio, greatest under skye,
O hold thy mortall hand for Ladies sake,
Hold for my sake, and do him not to dye,
But vanquisht thine eternall bondslave make,
And me thy worthy meed unto thy Leman[9] take."

15

He hearkned, and did stay from further harmes,
To gayne so goodly guerdon,° as she spake: *reward*
So willingly she came into his armes,
Who her as willingly to grace° did take,   *favor*
And was posséssed of his new found make.°   *companion*
Then up he tooke the slombred sencelesse corse,
And ere he could out of his swowne awake,
Him to his castle brought with hastie forse,
And in a Dongeon deepe him threw without remorse.

16

From that day forth Duessa was his deare,
And highly honourd in his haughtie eye,
He gave her gold and purple pall° to weare,   *robe*
And triple crowne[1] set on her head full hye,
And her endowd with royall majestye:
Then for to make her dreaded more of men,
And peoples harts with awfull terrour tye,
A monstrous beast[2] ybred in filthy fen
He chose, which he had kept long time in darksome den.

17

Such one it was, as that renowméd Snake[3]
Which great Alcides in Stremona slew,
Long fostred in the filth of Lerna lake,
Whose many heads out budding ever new,
Did breed him endlesse labour to subdew:

8. I.e., the blast alone.
9. I.e., as your mistress.
1. Symbolic of Papal power.
2. The description of Duessa's beast echoes a number of passages in the Book of Revelation: "I saw a woman sit upon a scarlet coloured beast, full of names of blasphemy, having seven heads and ten horns" (xvii. 3), "behold a great red dragon, having seven heads and ten horns, and seven crowns upon his heads . . . [whose] tail drew the third part of the stars of heaven, and did cast them to the earth . . .

[he is] that old serpent, called the Devil, and Satan, which deceiveth the whole world" (xii. 3–4, 9). Spenser associates this figure of essential evil with the body of the corrupt Roman church. Pictures of the Beast of the Apocalypse regularly illustrate medieval literature on the vices and virtues (cf. Tuve, *op. cit.*, 102–108).
3. To destroy the Lernean hydra, a nine-headed beast of the swamps, was the second of twelve labors assigned to Hercules (also called Alcides).

But this same Monster much more ugly was;
  For seven great heads out of his body grew,
  An yron brest, and backe of scaly bras,
And all embrewd° in bloud, his eyes did shine as glas.   *stained, defiled*

18

His tayle was stretchéd out in wondrous length,
  That to the house of heavenly gods it raught,°   *reached*
  And with extorted powre, and borrowed strength,
  The ever-burning lamps from thence it brought,
  And prowdly threw to ground, as things of nought;
  And underneath his filthy feet did tread
  The sacred things, and holy heasts° foretaught.   *commandments*
Upon this dreadfull Beast with sevenfold head
He set the false Duessa, for more aw and dread.

19

The wofull Dwarfe, which saw his maisters fall,
  Whiles he had keeping of his grasing steed,
  And valiant knight become a caytive° thrall,   *captive*
  When all was past, tooke up his forlorne weed,°   *equipment*
  His mightie armour, missing most at need;
  His silver shield, now idle maisterlesse;
  His poynant° speare, that many made to bleed,   *sharp*
  The ruefull moniments° of heavinesse,   *memorials*
And with them all departes, to tell his great distresse.

20

He had not travaild long, when on the way
  He wofull Ladie, wofull Una met,
  Fast flying from the Paynims greedy pray,°   *clutch*
  Whilest Satyrane him from pursuit did let:°   *prevent*
  Who when her eyes she on the Dwarfe had set,
  And saw the signes, that deadly tydings spake,
  She fell to ground for sorrowfull regret,
  And lively breath her sad brest did forsake,
Yet might her pitteous hart be seene to pant and quake.

21

The messenger of so unhappie newes,
  Would faine have dyde: dead was his hart within,
  Yet outwardly some little comfort shewes:
  At last recovering hart, he does begin
  To rub her temples, and to chaufe her chin,
  And every tender part does tosse and turne:
  So hardly he the flitted life does win,°   *prevail upon*
  Unto her native prison[4] to retourne:
The gins her grievéd ghost° thus to lament and mourne.   *spirit*

22

"Ye dreary instruments of dolefull sight,[5]
  That doe this deadly spectacle behold,
  Why do ye lenger feed on loathéd light,

---

4. I.e., the body.   5. I.e., eyes.

Or liking find to gaze on earthly mould,°   *form*
 Sith cruell fates the carefull° threeds unfould, *full of care*
 The which my life and love together tyde?
 Now let the stony dart of senselesse cold
 Perce to my hart, and pas through every side,
And let eternall night so sad sight fro me hide.

23

"O lightsome day, the lampe of highest Jove,
 First made by him, mens wandring wayes to guyde,
 When darknesse he in deepest dongeon drove,
 Henceforth thy hated face for ever hyde,
 And shut up heavens windowes shyning wyde:
 For earthly sight can nought but sorrow breed,
 And late repentance, which shall long abyde.
 Mine eyes no more on vanitie shall feed,
But seeléd up with death, shall have their deadly meed.°" *reward*

24

Then downe againe she fell unto the ground;
 But he her quickly rearéd up againe:
 Thrise did she sinke adowne in deadly swownd,
 And thrise he her revived with busie paine:
 At last when life recovered had the raine,°   *rule*
 And over-wrestled his strong enemie,
 With foltring tong, and trembling every vaine,
 "Tell on," quoth she, "the wofull Tragedie,
The which these reliques sad present unto mine eie.

25

"Tempestuous fortune hath spent all her spight,
 And thrilling sorrow throwne his utmost dart;
 Thy sad tongue cannot tell more heavy plight,
 Then that I feele, and harbour in mine hart:
 Who hath endured the whole, can beare each part.
 If death it be, it is not the first wound,
 That launchéd° hath my brest with bleeding smart. *pierced*
 Begin, and end the bitter balefull stound;°   *sorrow*
If lesse, then that I feare, more favour I have found."

26

Then gan the Dwarfe the whole discourse declare,
 The subtill traines of Archimago old;
 The wanton loves of false Fidessa faire,
 Bought with the bloud of vanquisht Paynim bold:
 The wretched payre transformed to treen mould;[6]
 The house of Pride, and perils round about;
 The combat, which he with Sansjoy did hould;
 The lucklesse conflict with the Gyant stout,
Wherein captived, of life or death he stood in doubt.

27

She heard with patience all unto the end,
 And strove to maister sorrowfull assay,°   *affliction*

6. Form of a tree.

Which greater grew, the more she did contend,
And almost rent her tender hart in tway;
And love fresh coles unto her fire did lay:
For greater love, the greater is the losse.
Was never Ladie lovéd dearer day,
Then she did love the knight of the Redcrosse;
For whose deare sake so many troubles her did tosse.

28

At last when fervent sorrow slakéd was,
  She up arose, resolving him to find
  Alive or dead: and forward forth doth pas,
  All as the Dwarfe the way to her assynd:°   *indicated*
  And evermore in constant carefull mind
  She fed her wound with fresh renewéd bale;
  Long tost with stormes, and bet° with bitter wind,   *buffeted*
  High over hils, and low adowne the dale,
She wandred many a wood, and measurd many a vale.

29

At last she chauncéd by good hap to meet
  A goodly knight,[7] faire marching by the way
  Together with his Squire, arayéd meet:°   *properly*
  His glitterand° armour shinéd farre away,   *glittering*
  Like glauncing light of Phoebus brightest ray;
  From top to toe no place appearéd bare,
  That deadly dint of steele endanger may:
  Athwart his brest a bauldrick° brave he ware,   *shoulder belt*
That shynd, like twinkling stars, with stons most pretious rare.

30

And in the midst thereof one pretious stone
  Of wondrous worth, and eke of wondrous mights,
  Shapt like a Ladies head,[8] exceeding shone,
  Like Hesperus emongst the lesser lights,°   *stars*
  And strove for to amaze the weaker sights;
  Thereby his mortall blade full comely hong
  In yvory sheath, ycarved with curious slights;°   *patterns*
  Whose hilts were burnisht gold, and handle strong
Of mother pearle, and buckled with a golden tong.°   *pin*

31

His haughtie° helmet, horrid° all with gold,   *noble/bristling*
  Both glorious brightnesse, and great terrour bred;

7. I.e., Prince Arthur, the hero of *The Faerie Queene*, in whose person is "sette forth" (as the "Letter to Raleigh" states) "magnificence in particular, which vertue . . . (according to Aristotle and the rest) . . . is the perfection of all the rest, and conteineth in it them all . . .". Miss Tuve has shown (*op. cit.*, 57–143) that there was a long tradition of "Christian Magnificence," drawing on Cicero and Macrobius as well as Aristotle. In Book I, while Arthur's being and actions invite association with classical legend and British history, the Prince represents primarily the power of Christian grace to deliver exhausted man from the forces of evil, so that he may complete his earthly quest. Cf. viii. 1.

8. The Faerie Queene. Geoffrey of Monmouth (c. 1100–1154) observes that the inner side of Arthur's shield bore the image of the Virgin Mary (*Historia Regum Britanniae*, tr. S. Evans, rev. C. W. Dunn [N.Y., 1958], IX. 4). Cf. note to III. iii. 6.

For all the crest a Dragon[9] did enfold
With greedie pawes, and over all did spred
His golden wings: his dreadfull hideous hed
Close couchéd on the bever,° seemed to throw   *visor*
From flaming mouth bright sparkles fierie red,
That suddeine horror to faint harts did show;
And scaly tayle was stretcht adowne his backe full low.

32

Upon the top of all his loftie crest,
  A bunch of haires discolourd° diversly,   *dyed*
  With sprincled pearle, and gold full richly drest,
  Did shake, and seemed to daunce for jollity,
  Like to an Almond tree ymounted hye
  On top of greene Selinis[1] all alone,
  With blossomes brave bedeckéd daintily;
Whose tender locks do tremble every one
At every little breath, that under heaven is blowne.

33

His warlike shield[2] all closely covered was,
  Ne might of mortall eye be ever seene;
  Not made of steele, nor of enduring bras,
  Such earthly mettals soone consuméd bene:
  But all of Diamond perfect pure and cleene°   *clear*
  It framéd was, one massie entire mould,
  Hewen out of Adamant° rocke with engines keene,   *diamond-hard*
  That point of speare it never percen could,
Ne dint of direfull sword divide the substance would.

34

The same to wight he never wont disclose,
  But° when as monsters huge he would dismay,   *except*
  Or daunt unequall armies of his foes,
  Or when the flying heavens he would affray;°   *frighten*
  For so exceeding shone his glistring ray,
  That Phoebus golden face it did attaint,°   *dim, darken*
  As when a cloud his beames doth over-lay;
  And silver Cynthia wexéd pale and faint,
As when her face is staynd with magicke arts constraint.°   *force*

35

No magicke arts hereof had any might,
  Nor bloudie wordes of bold Enchaunters call,
  But all that was not such, as seemd in sight,

9. According to Geoffrey, a dragon was engraved upon Arthur's gold helmet. The dragon was also the ensign of Cadwallader, last king of the Britons. In the context of Book I, the dragon on Prince Arthur's helmet signifies primarily Arthur's power over the forces of evil symbolized by the "great red dragon" of Revelation.

1. Virgil refers to "the city of palms, Selinus," in Asia Minor (*Aeneid,* III. 705).
2. The description of Arthur's shield is closely patterned on that of Atlante's shield in Ariosto, *Orlando Furioso,* II. 55–56; but this shield, proof against the black arts of enchanters, is one of Christian faith (cf. Ephesians vi: 16).

Before that shield did fade, and suddeine fall:
And when him list the raskall routes° appall,   *crowds*
Men into stones therewith he could transmew,°   *change*
And stones to dust, and dust to nought at all;
And when him list the prouder lookes subdew,
He would them gazing blind, or turne to other hew.°   *form*

36

Ne let it seeme, that credence this exceedes,
For he that made the same, was knowne right well
To have done much more admirable deedes.
It Merlin was, which whylome° did excell   *formerly*
All living wightes in might of magicke spell:
Both shield, and sword, and armour all he wrought
For this young Prince, when first to armes he fell;°   *came*
But when he dyde, the Faerie Queene it brought
To Faerie lond, where yet it may be seene, if sought.[3]

37

A gentle youth, his dearely lovéd Squire[4]
His speare of heben° wood behind him bare,   *ebony*
Whose harmefull head, thrice heated in the fire,
Had riven many a brest with pikehead square;
A goodly person, and could menage° faire   *control*
His stubborne steed with curbéd canon bit,[5]
Who under him did trample as the aire,[6]
And chauft, that any on his backe should sit;
The yron rowels into frothy fome he bit.

38

When as this knight night to the Ladie drew,
With lovely° court he gan her entertaine;   *loving*
But when he heard her answeres loth, he knew
Some secret sorrow did her heart distraine:°   *oppress*
Which to allay, and calme her storming paine,
Faire feeling words he wisely gan display,
And for her humour fitting purpose faine,[7]
To tempt the cause it selfe for to bewray;
Wherewith emmoved, these bleeding words she gan to say.

39

"What worlds delight, or joy of living speach
Can heart, so plunged in sea of sorrowes deepe,
And heapéd with so huge misfortunes, reach?
The carefull° cold beginneth for to creepe,   *afflicting*
And in my heart his yron arrow steepe,
Soone as I thinke upon my bitter bale: *grief*
Such helplesse harmes yts better hidden keepe,

---

3. I.e., the virtue and faith figured in Arthur may still flourish in Spenser's England.
4. I.e., Timias ("honored").

5. Smooth round bit.
6. I.e., tread lightly and eagerly.
7. I.e., suited his speech and demeanor to her sorrowful mood.

Then rip up griefe, where it may not availe,
My last left comfort is, my woes to weepe and waile."

40

"Ah Ladie deare," quoth then the gentle knight,
    Well may I weene, your griefe is wondrous great;
    For wondrous great griefe groneth in my spright,
    Whiles thus I heare you of your sorrowes treat.
    But wofull Ladie let me you intrete,
    For to unfold the anguish of your hart:
    Mishaps are maistred by advice discrete,
    And counsell mittigates the greatest smart;
Found never helpe, who never would his hurts impart."

41

"O but," quoth she, "great griefe will not be tould,
    And can more easily be thought, then said."
    "Right so"; quoth he, "but he, that never would,
    Could never: will to might gives greatest aid."
    "But griefe," quoth she, "does greater grow displaid,
    If then it find not helpe, and breedes despaire."
    "Despaire breedes not," quoth he, "where faith is staid."°   *firm*
    "No faith so fast," quoth she, "but flesh does paire."°   *impair*
"Flesh may empaire," quoth he, "but reason can repaire."

42

His goodly reason, and well guided speach
    So deepe did settle in her gratious thought,
    That her perswaded to disclose the breach,
    Which love and fortune in her heart had wrought,
    And said; "Faire Sir, I hope good hap hath brought
    You to inquire the secrets of my griefe,
    Or that your wisedome will direct my thought,
    Or that your prowesse can me yield reliefe:
Then heare the storie sad, which I shall tell you briefe.

43

"The forlorne Maiden, whom your eyes have seene
    The laughing stocke of fortunes mockeries,
    Am th'only daughter of a King and Queene,
    Whose parents deare, whilest equall° destinies   *impartial*
    Did runne about,[8] and their felicities
    The favourable heavens did not envy,
    Did spread their rule through all the territories,
    Which Phison and Euphrates floweth by,
And Gehons golden waves doe wash continually.[9]

44

"Till that their cruell curséd enemy,
    An huge great Dragon horrible in sight,
    Bred in the loathly lakes of Tartary,°   *Tartarus (Hell)*
    With murdrous ravine,° and devouring might   *destruction*

8. I.e., did revolve.
9. Pison, Gihon, Hiddekel, and Eu- phrates are the four rivers of Paradise (Genesis ii. 10–14).

Their kingdome spoild, and countrey wasted quight:
Themselves, for feare into his jawes to fall,
He forst to castle strong to take their flight,
Where fast embard in mightie brasen wall,
He has them now foure yeres[1] besieged to make them thrall.

45

"Full many knights adventurous and stout
  Have enterprizd° that Monster to subdew;   *undertaken*
  From every coast that heaven walks about,
  Have thither come the noble Martiall crew,
  That famous hard atchievements still pursew,
  Yet never any could that girlond win,
  But all still shronke,° and still he greater grew: *quailed, fell back*
  All they for want of faith, or guilt of sin,
The pitteous pray of his fierce crueltie have bin.

46

"At last yledd with farre reported praise,
  Which flying fame throughout the world had spred,
  Of doughtie knights, whom Faery land did raise,
  That noble order hight° of Maidenhed,[2]   *called*
  Forthwith to court of Gloriane I sped,
  Of Gloriane great Queene of glory bright,
  Whose kingdomes seat Cleopolis[3] is red,°   *named*
  There to obtaine some such redoubted knight,
That Parents deare from tyrants powre deliver might.

47

"It was my chance (my chance was faire and good)
  There for to find a fresh unprovéd knight,
  Whose manly hands imbrewed° in guiltie blood *stained*
  Had never bene, ne ever by his might
  Had throwne to ground the unregarded° right: *unrespected*
  Yet of his prowesse proofe he since hath made
  (I witnesse am) in many a cruell fight;
  The groning ghosts of many one dismaide
Have felt the bitter dint of his avenging blade.

48

"And ye the forlorne reliques of his powre,
  His byting sword, and his devouring speare,
  Which have enduréd many a dreadfull stowre,° *conflict*
  Can speake his prowesse, that did earst you beare,
  And well could rule: now he hath left you heare,
  To be the record of his ruefull losse,
  And of my dolefull disaventurous deare:° *harm, loss*

1. The Book of Revelation refers to the dragon's persecution of "the woman clothed with the sun," who "fled into the wilderness, where she had a place prepared of God, that they should feed her there a thousand two hundred and threescore days" (xii. 1–6).

2. I.e., the Order of the Garter, whose members wore insignia including a figure of St. George slaying the dragon. Queen Elizabeth was head of the Order.
3. "Famed city"; in the historical allegory, the counterpart of Elizabethan London; but cf. the note to I. x. 58.

O heavie record of the good Redcrosse,
Where have you left your Lord, that could so well you tosse?°   *wield*

49

"Well hopéd I, and faire beginnings had,
  That he my captive languour should redeeme,[4]
  Till all unweeting, an Enchaunter bad
  His sence abusd, and made him to misdeeme
  My loyalty, not such as it did seeme;
  That rather death desire, then such despight.[5]
  Be judge ye heavens, that all things right esteeme,
  How I him loved, and love with all my might,
So thought I eke of him, and thinke I thought aright.

50

"Thenceforth me desolate he quite forsooke,
  To wander, where wilde fortune would me lead,
  And other bywaies he himselfe betooke,
  Where never foot of living wight did tread,
  That brought not backe the balefull body dead;[6]
  In which him chauncéd false Duessa meete,
  Mine onely° foe, mine onely deadly dread,   *particular*
  Who with her witchcraft and misseeming° sweete,   *deception*
Inveigled him to follow her desires unmeete.°   *improper*

51

"At last by subtill sleights she him betraid
  Unto his foe, a Gyant huge and tall,
  Who him disarméd, dissolute,° dismaid,   *enfeebled*
  Unwares surpriséd, and with mightie mall°   *club*
  The monster mercilesse him made to fall,
  Whose fall did never foe before behold;
  And now in darkesome dungeon, wretched thrall,
  Remedilesse, for aie° he doth him hold;   *ever*
This is my cause of griefe, more great, then may be told."

52

Ere she had ended all, she gan to faint:
  But he her comforted and faire bespake,
  "Certes, Madame, ye have great cause of plaint,
  That stoutest heart, I weene, could cause to quake.
  But be of cheare, and comfort to you take:
  For till I have acquit° your captive knight,   *set free*
  Assure your selfe, I will you not forsake."
His chearefull words revived her chearelesse spright,
So forth they went, the Dwarfe them guiding ever right.

4. I.e., that he should relieve my condition, captive to sadness (by freeing my parents from the grip of the dragon).
5. I.e., I would prefer death to the outrage of being thought disloyal.
6. I.e., that returned alive.

Canto VIII

Faire virgin to redeeme her deare
brings Arthur to the fight:
Who slayes the Gyant, wounds the beast,
and strips Duessa quight.

1

Ay me, how many perils doe enfold
   The righteous man, to make him daily fall?
   Were not, that heavenly grace doth him uphold,
   And stedfast truth acquite him out of all.
   Her love is firme, her care continuall,
   So oft as he through his owne foolish pride,
   Or weaknesse is to sinfull bands° made thrall: *bonds*
   Else should this Redcrosse knight in bands have dyde,
For whose deliverance she this Prince doth thither guide.

2

They sadly traveild thus, untill they came
   Nigh to a castle builded strong and hie:
   Then cryde the Dwarfe, "lo yonder is the same,
   In which my Lord my liege doth lucklesse lie,
   Thrall to that Gyants hatefull tyrannie:
   Therefore, deare Sir, your mightie powres assay."
   The noble knight alighted by and by[1]
   From loftie steede, and bad the Ladie stay,
To see what end of fight should him befall that day.

3

So with the Squire, th'admirer of his might,
   He marchéd forth towards that castle wall;
   Whose gates he found fast shut, ne living wight
   To ward the same, nor answere commers call.
   Then tooke that Squire an horne of bugle° small,   *wild ox*
   Which hong adowne his side in twisted gold,
   And tassels gay. Wyde wonders over all
   Of that same hornes great vertues weren told,
Which had approvéd° bene in uses manifold.   *demonstrated*

4

Was never wight, that heard that shrilling sound,
   But trembling feare did feele in every vaine;
   Three miles it might be easie heard around,
   And Ecchoes three answerd it selfe againe:
   No false enchauntment, nor deceiptfull traine
   Might once abide the terror of that blast,
   But presently° was voide and wholly vaine:[2]   *at once*

1. I.e., immediately.
2. The magic horn of Astolfo also struck evil doers with terror (*Orlando Furioso*, XV. 14); but the horn of Timias recalls rather the ram's horn of Joshua (Joshua vi. 5); further, it has the power of "them that preach . . . the word of God . . . their sound went into all the earth, and their words unto the ends of the world" (Romans x. 15–18).

No gate so strong, no locke so firme and fast,
But with that percing noise flew open quite, or brast.°   *burst*

5

The same before the Geants gate he blew,
  That all the castle quakéd from the ground,
  And every dore of freewill open flew.
  The Gyant selfe dismaiéd with that sownd,
  Where he with his Duessa dalliance° fownd,   *amorous play*
  In hast came rushing forth from inner bowre,
  With staring countenance sterne, as one astownd,
  And staggering steps, to weet, what suddein stowre°   *disturbance*
Had wrought that horror strange, and dared his dreaded powre.

6

And after him the proud Duessa came,
  High mounted on her manyheaded beast,
  And every head with fyrie tongue did flame,
  And every head was crownéd on his creast,
  And bloudie mouthéd with late cruell feast.
  That when the knight beheld, his mightie shild
  Upon his manly arme he soone addrest,°   *placed*
  And at him fiercely flew, with courage fild,
And eger greedinesse° through every member thrild.   *desire*

7

Therewith the Gyant buckled him to fight,[3]
  Inflamed with scornefull wrath and high disdaine,
  And lifting up his dreadfull club on hight,
  All armed with ragged snubbes° and knottie graine,   *snags*
  Him thought at first encounter to have slaine.
  But wise and warie was that noble Pere,
  And lightly leaping from so monstrous maine,°   *power*
  Did faire avoide the violence him nere;
It booted nought, to thinke, such thunderbolts to beare.

8

Ne shame he thought to shunne so hideous might:
  The idle° stroke, enforcing furious way,   *futile*
  Missing the marke of his misayméd sight
  Did fall to ground, and with his heavie sway°   *force*
  So deepely dinted in the driven clay,
  That three yardes deepe a furrow up did throw:
  The sad earth wounded with so sore assay,°   *assault*
  Did grone full grievous underneath the blow,
And trembling with strange feare, did like an earthquake show.

9

As when almightie Jove in wrathfull mood,
  To wreake° the guilt of mortall sins is bent,   *punish*

---

3. In terms of historical allegory, Arthur's encounter with Orgoglio represents Protestant victory over the Roman church; in a wider context, the battle shadows that of the Redeemer against the evil power of Antichrist. Arthur, in some sense a "Christ figure," is perhaps best described as "the channel for divine Christ-like power" (Tuve, *op. cit.*, p. 352n).

Hurles forth his thundring dart with deadly food,°   *feud*
  Enrold in flames, and smouldring dreriment,
  Through riven cloudes and molten firmament;
  The fierce threeforkéd engin° making way,   *weapon*
  Both loftie towres and highest trees hath rent,
  And all that might his angrie passage stay,
And shooting in the earth, casts up a mount of clay.

10

His boystrous° club, so buried in the ground,   *massive*
  He could not rearen up againe so light,°   *easily*
  But that the knight him at avantage found,
  And whiles he strove his combred clubbe to quight°   *free*
  Out of the earth, with blade all burning bright
  He smote off his left arme, which like a blocke
  Did fall to ground, deprived of native might;
  Large streames of bloud out of the trunckéd stocke
Forth gushéd, like fresh water streame from riven rocke.

11

Dismaiéd with so desperate deadly wound,
  And eke impatient of[4] unwonted paine,
  He loudly brayd with beastly yelling sound,
  That all the fields rebellowéd againe;
  As great a noyse, as when in Cymbrian plaine[5]
  An heard of Bulles, whom kindly rage[6] doth sting,
  Do for the milkie mothers want complaine,[7]
  And fill the fields with troublous bellowing,
The neighbour woods around with hollow murmur ring.

12

That when his deare Duessa heard, and saw
  The evill stownd,° that daungerd her estate,   *peril*
  Unto his aide she hastily did draw
  Her dreadfull beast, who swolne with bloud of late
  Came ramping forth with proud presumpteous gate,
  And threatned all his heads like flaming brands.
  But him the Squire made quickly to retrate,
  Encountring fierce with single° sword in hand,   *only*
And twixt him and his Lord did like a bulwarke stand.

13

The proud Duessa full of wrathfull spight,
  And fierce disdaine, to be affronted so,
  Enforst her purple beast with all her might
  That stop° out of the way to overthroe,   *obstacle*
  Scorning the let° of so unequall foe: *hindrance*
  But nathemore° would that courageous swayne *never the more*
  To her yeeld passage, gainst his Lord to goe,
  But with outrageous strokes did him restraine,
And with his bodie bard the way atwixt them twaine.

4. I.e., agonized by.   habitants.
5. Modern Jutland, formerly called the   6. I.e., natural passion.
Cimbric peninsula, after its original in-   7. I.e., lament the cows' absence.

14

Then tooke the angrie witch her golden cup,[8]
    Which still she bore, replete with magick artes;
    Death and despeyre did many thereof sup,
    And secret poyson through their inner parts,
    Th'eternall bale of heavie wounded harts;
    Which after charmes and some enchauntments said,
    She lightly sprinkled on his weaker° parts;   *too weak*
    Therewith his sturdie courage soone was quayd,°   *daunted*
And all his senses were with suddeine dread dismayd.

15

So downe he fell before the cruell beast,
    Who on his necke his bloudie clawes did seize,
    That life nigh crusht out of his panting brest:
    No powre he had to stirre, nor will to rize.
    That when the carefull° knight gan well avise,°   *watchful/notice*
    He lightly left the foe, with whom he fought,
    And to the beast gan turne his enterprise;
    For wondrous anguish in his hart it wrought,
To see his lovéd Squire into such thraldome brought.

16

And high advauncing his bloud-thirstie blade,
    Stroke one of those deforméd heads so sore,
    That of his puissance proud ensample made;[9]
    His monstrous scalpe° downe to his teeth it tore,   *skull*
    And that misforméd shape mis-shapéd more:
    A sea of bloud gusht from the gaping wound,
    That her gay garments staynd with filthy gore,
    And overflowéd all the field around;
That over shoes in bloud he waded on the ground.

17

Thereat he roaréd for exceeding paine,
    That to have heard, great horror would have bred,
    And scourging th'emptie ayre with his long traine,
    Through great impatience° of his grievéd hed   *agony*
    His gorgeous ryder from her loftie sted
    Would have cast downe, and trod in durtie myre,
    Had not the Gyant soone her succouréd;
    Who all enraged with smart and franticke yre,
Came hurtling in full fierce, and forst the knight retyre.

18

The force, which wont in two to be disperst,
    In one alone left° hand he new unites,   *remaining*

8. The golden cup of Revelation xvii. 4, here signifying the Roman Catholic doctrine of transubstantiation, as well as the employment of magic and the black arts by the powers of evil. Duessa's cup recalls that of Circe, whose drugs turned men into swine (*Odyssey*, X); it is to be contrasted with the chalice held by Fidelia (I. x. 13), and, within the larger structure of the poem, compared with other symbolically destructive cups, e.g., that of Acrasia (II. i. 55).
9. "And I saw one of his [the beast's] heads as it were wounded to death" (Revelation xiii. 3).

Which is through rage more strong then both were erst;
With which his hideous club aloft he dites,°   *raises*
And at his foe with furious rigour smites,
That strongest Oake might seeme to overthrow:
The stroke upon his shield so heavie lites,
That to the ground it doubleth him full low:
What mortall wight could ever beare so monstrous blow?

19

And in his fall his shield, that covered was,
    Did loose his vele by chaunce, and open flew:
    The light whereof, that heavens light did pas,°   *surpass*
    Such blazing brightnesse through the aier threw,
    That eye mote not the same endure to vew.
    Which when the Gyaunt spyde with staring eye,
    He downe let fall his arme, and soft withdrew
    His weapon huge, that heavéd was on hye
For to have slaine the man, that on the ground did lye.

20

And eke the fruitfull-headed° beast, amazed   *many-headed*
    At flashing beames of that sunshiny shield,
    Became starke blind, and all his senses dazed,
    That downe he tumbled on the durtie field,
    And seemed himselfe as conqueréd to yield.[1]
    Whom when his maistresse proud perceived to fall,
    Whiles yet his feeble feet for faintnesse reeld,
    Unto the Gyant loudly she gan call,
"O helpe Orgoglio, helpe, or else we perish all."

21

At her so pitteous cry was much amooved
    Her champion stout, and for to ayde his frend,
    Againe his wonted angry weapon prooved:°   *tried*
    But all in vaine: for he has read his end
    In that bright shield, and all their forces spend
    Themselves in vaine: for since that glauncing° sight,   *dazzling*
    He hath no powre to hurt, nor to defend;
    As where th'Almighties lightning brond does light,
It dimmes the dazéd eyen, and daunts the senses quight.

22

Whom when the Prince, to battell new addrest,
    And threatning high his dreadfull stroke did see,
    His sparkling blade about his head he blest,°   *brandished*
    And smote off quite his right leg by the knee,
    That downe he tombled; as an aged tree,[2]
    High growing on the top of rocky clift,
    Whose hartstrings with keene steele nigh hewen be,
    The mightie trunck halfe rent, with ragged rift
Doth roll adowne the rocks, and fall with fearefull drift.°   *force*

1. Similarly the brightness of Ruggiero's shield, suddenly displayed, overthrows his opponents (*Orlando Furioso*, XXII. 84–86).

2. The simile has many classical analogues; cf. in particular the *Aeneid*, II. 626–631.

23

Or as a Castle rearéd high and round,
   By subtile engins and malitious slight°   *trickery*
   Is underminéd from the lowest ground,
   And her foundation forst,° and feebled quight,   *shattered*
   At last downe falles, and with her heapéd hight
   Her hastie ruine does more heavie° make,   *forceful*
   And yields it selfe unto the victours might;
   Such was this Gyaunts fall, that seemd to shake
The stedfast globe of earth, as it for feare did quake.

24

The knight then lightly leaping to the pray,
   With mortall steele him smot againe so sore,
   That headlesse his unweldy bodie lay,
   All wallowd in his owne fowle bloudy gore,
   Which flowéd from his wounds in wondrous store.
   But soone as breath out of his breast did pas,
   That huge great body, which the Gyaunt bore,
   Was vanisht quite, and of that monstrous mas
Was nothing left, but like an emptie bladder was.

25

Whose grievous fall, when false Duessa spide,
   Her golden cup she cast unto the ground,
   And crownéd mitre rudely threw aside;
   Such percing griefe her stubborne hart did wound,
   That she could not endure that dolefull stound,°   *sorrow*
   But leaving all behind her, fled away:
   The light-foot Squire her quickly turnd around,
   And by hard meanes enforcing her to stay,
So brought unto his Lord, as his deservéd pray.

26

The royall Virgin, which beheld from farre,
   In pensive plight, and sad perplexitie,
   The whole atchievement° of this doubtfull warre,   *course*
   Came running fast to greet his victorie,
   With sober gladnesse, and myld modestie,
   And with sweet joyous cheare him thus bespake:
   "Faire braunch of noblesse, flowre of chevalrie,
   That with your worth the world amazéd make,
How shall I quite° the paines, ye suffer for my sake?   *requite*

27

"And you[3] fresh bud of vertue springing fast,
   Whom these sad eyes saw nigh unto deaths dore,
   What hath poore Virgin for such perill past,
   Wherewith you to reward? Accept therefore
   My simple selfe, and service evermore;
   And he that high does sit, and all things see
   With equall° eyes, their merites to restore,°   *impartial/reward*

3. I.e., the Squire.

Behold what ye this day have done for mee,
And what I cannot quite, requite with usuree.°   *interest*

28

"But sith the heavens, and your faire handeling°   *conduct*
  Have made you maister of the field this day,
  Your fortune maister eke with governing,°   *active control*
  And well begun end all so well, I pray,
  Ne let that wicked woman scape away;
  For she it is, that did my Lord bethrall,
  My dearest Lord, and deepe in dongeon lay,
  Where he his better dayes hath wasted all.
O heare, how piteous he to you for ayd does call."

29

Forthwith he gave in charge unto his Squire,
  That scarlot whore to keepen carefully;
  Whiles he himselfe with greedie° great desire   *eager*
  Into the Castle entred forcibly,
  Where living creature none he did espye;
  Then gan he lowdly through the house to call:
  But no man cared to answere to his crye.
  There raignd a solemne silence over all,
Nor voice was heard, nor wight was seene in bowre or hall.

30

At last with creeping crooked pace forth came
  An old old man, with beard as white as snow,
  That on a staffe his feeble steps did frame,°   *support*
  And guide his wearie gate both too and fro:
  For his eye sight him faileéd long ygo,
  And on his arme a bounch of keyes he bore,
  The which unuséd rust did overgrow:
  Those were the keyes of every inner dore,
But he could not them use, but kept them still in store.

31

But very uncouth sight was to behold,
  How he did fashion his untoward° pace,   *awkward*
  For as he forward mooved his footing old,
  So backward still was turnd his wrincled face,
  Unlike to men, who ever as they trace,°   *walk*
  Both feet and face one way are wont to lead.
  This was the auncient keeper of that place,
  And foster father of the Gyant dead;
His name Ignaro[4] did his nature right aread.°   *indicate*

32

His reverend haires and holy gravitie
  The knight much honord, as beseeméd well,[5]
  And gently askt, where all the people bee,

---

4. Ignorance; here particularly ignorance of the Gospel: his backward-turned countenance represents obsessive and invincible preoccupation with the Law of the Old Testament.
5. I.e., as was proper.

Which in that stately building wont to dwell.
Who answerd him full soft, he could not tell.
Againe he askt, where that same knight was layd,
Whom great Orgoglio with his puissaunce fell
Had made his caytive thrall; againe he sayde,
He could not tell: ne ever other answere made.

33

Then askéd he, which way he in might pas:
He could not tell, againe he answeréd.
Thereat the curteous knight displeaséd was,
And said, "Old sire, it seemes thou hast not red°   recognized
How ill it sits° with that same silver hed   accords
In vaine to mocke, or mockt in vaine to bee:
But if thou be, as thou art pourtrahéd
With natures pen, in ages grave degree,
Aread° in graver wise, what I demaund of thee."   tell

34

His answere likewise was, he could not tell.
Whose sencelesse speach, and doted° ignorance   senile
When as the noble Prince had markéd well,
He ghest his nature by his countenance,
And calmd his wrath with goodly temperance.
Then to him stepping, from his arme did reach
Those keyes, and made himselfe free enterance.
Each dore he opened without any breach;°   forcing
There was no barre to stop, nor foe him to empeach.°   oppose

35

There all within full rich arayd he found,
With royall arras° and resplendent gold.   tapestry
And did with store of every thing abound,
That greatest Princes presence° might behold.   person
But all the floore (too filthy to be told)
With bloud of guiltlesse babes, and innocents trew,
Which there were slaine, as sheepe out of the fold,
Defiléd was, that dreadfull was to vew,
And sacred° ashes over it was strowéd new.   accursed

36

And there beside of marble stone was built
An Altare, carved with cunning imagery,
On which true Christians bloud was often spilt,
And holy Martyrs often doen to dye,[6]
With cruell malice and strong tyranny:
Whose blessed sprites from underneath the stone
To God for vengeance cryde continually,
And with great griefe were often heard to grone,
That hardest heart would bleede, to heare their piteous mone.[7]

6. I.e., put to death.
7. "I saw under the altar the souls of them that were slain for the word of God, and for the testimony which they held: And they cried with a loud voice, saying, How long, O Lord, holy and true, dost thou not judge and avenge our blood on them that dwell on the earth?" (Revelation vi. 9–10). The scriptural recollections of this and the preceding stanza (cf. Matthew ii. 16) reinforce the association of Arthur with Christ.

37

Through every rowme he sought, and every bowr,
　　But no where could he find that wofull thrall:
　　At last he came unto an yron doore,
　　That fast was lockt, but key found not at all
　　Emongst that bounch, to open it withall;
　　But in the same a little grate was pight,°   *placed*
　　Through which he sent his voyce, and lowd did call
　　With all his powre, to weet, if living wight
Were houséd therewithin, whom he enlargen° might.   *free*

38

Therewith an hollow, dreary, murmuring voyce
　　These piteous plaints and dolours did resound;
　　"O who is that, which brings me happy choyce°   *chance*
　　Of death, that here lye dying every stound,°   *moment*
　　Yet live perforce in balefull darkenesse bound?
　　For now three Moones have changéd thrice their hew,°   *shape*
　　And have beene thrice hid underneath the ground,
　　Since I the heavens chearefull face did vew,
O welcome thou, that doest of death bring tydings trew."

39

Which when that Champion heard, with percing point
　　Of pitty deare° his hart was thrilléd sore,   *grievous*
　　And trembling horrour ran through every joynt,
　　For ruth of gentle knight so fowle forlore:°   *lost*
　　Which shaking off, he rent that yron dore,
　　With furious force, and indignation fell;
　　Where entred in, his foot could find no flore,
　　But all a deepe descent, as darke as hell,
That breathéd ever forth a filthie banefull smell.

40

But neither darkenesse fowle, nor filthy bands,
　　Nor noyous° smell his purpose could withhold,   *poisonous*
　　(Entire affection hateth nicer° hands)   *too fastidious*
　　But that with constant zeale, and courage bold,
　　After long paines and labours manifold,
　　He found the meanes that Prisoner up to reare;
　　Whose feeble thighes, unhable to uphold
　　His pinéd° corse, him scarse to light could beare,   *wasted*
A ruefull spectacle of death and ghastly drere.°   *wretchedness*

41

His sad dull eyes deepe sunck in hollow pits,
　　Could not endure th'unwonted sunne to view;
　　His bare thin cheekes for want of better bits,°   *food*
　　And empty sides deceivéd° of their dew,   *defrauded*
　　Could make a stony hart his hap to rew;
　　His rawbone armes, whose mighty brawnéd bowrs°   *muscles*
　　Were wont to rive steele plates, and helmets hew,
　　Were cleane consumed, and all his vitall powres
Decayd, and all his flesh shronk up like withered flowres.[8]

8. Sin has enfeebled and wasted the spirit of Holiness. Spenser's account of the knight's appearance (in sts. 40–41) may reflect his own impressions of

42

Whom when his Lady saw, to him she ran
  With hasty joy: to see him made her glad,
  And sad to view his visage pale and wan,
  Who earst in flowres of freshest youth was clad.
  Tho° when her well of teares she wasted had,   *then*
  She said, "Ah dearest Lord, what evill starre
  On you hath frownd, and pourd his influence bad,
  That of your selfe ye thus berobbéd arre,
And this misseeming hew[9] your manly looks doth marre?

43

"But welcome now my Lord, in wele or woe,
  Whose presence I have lackt too long a day;
  And fie on Fortune mine avowéd foe,
  Whose wrathfull wreakes° them selves do now alay.   *revenges*
  And for these wrongs shall treble penaunce pay
  Of treble good: good growes of evils priefe."°   *experience*
  The chearelesse man, whom sorrow did dismay,
  Had no delight to treaten° of his griefe;   *speak*
His long enduréd famine needed more reliefe.

44

"Faire Lady," then said that victorious knight,[1]
  "The things, that grievous were to do, or beare,
  Them to renew,° I wote, breeds no delight;   *recall*
  Best musicke breeds delight in loathing eare:
  But th'onely good, that growes of passéd feare,
  Is to be wise, and ware° of like agein.   *wary*
  This dayes ensample hath this lesson deare
  Deepe written in my heart with yron pen,
That blisse may not abide in state of mortall men.

45

"Henceforth sir knight, take to you wonted strength,
  And maister these mishaps with patient might;
  Loe where your foe lyes stretcht in monstrous length,
  And loe that wicked woman in your sight,
  The roote of all your care, and wretched plight,
  Now in your powre, to let her live, or dye."
  "To do her dye," quoth Una, "were despight,°   *spiteful*
  And shame t'avenge so weake an enimy;
But spoile° her of her scarlot robe, and let her fly."   *deprive*

46

So as she bad, that witch they disaraid,
  And robd of royall robes, and purple pall,

---

the Irish peasantry, reduced to misery by poverty and the ravages of continual war: "Out of everie corner of the woods and glinnes they came crepinge forthe uppon theire handes for their leggs coulde not beare them, they loked like Anotomies of deathe, they spake like ghostes cryinge out of theire graves . . ." (*A Vewe of the Present State of Irelande*, 3259–3262).
9. I.e., unseemly appearance.
1. I.e., Arthur, whose tactful manner of speech in this stanza reflects his courteous recognition of the humiliation felt by the exhausted and silent Redcrosse.

And ornaments that richly were displaid;
  Ne sparéd they to strip her naked all.
  Then when they had despoild her tire° and call,°   *attire/headdress*
  Such as she was, their eyes might her behold,
  That her misshapéd parts did them appall,
  A loathly, wrinckled hag, ill favoured, old,
Whose secret filth good manners biddeth not be told.[2]

47

Her craftie head was altogether bald,
  And as in hate of honorable eld,°   *age*
  Was overgrowne with scurfe and filthy scald;°   *scabby disease*
  Her teeth out of her rotten gummes were feld,°   *fallen*
  And her sowre breath abhominably smeld;
  Her driéd dugs, like bladders lacking wind,
  Hong downe, and filthy matter from them weld;
  Her wrizled° skin as rough, as maple rind,   *wrinkled*
So scabby was, that would have loathd all womankind.

48

Her neather parts, the shame of all her kind,
  My chaster° Muse for shame doth blush to write;   *too chaste*
  But at her rompe she growing had behind
  A foxes taile, with dong all fowly dight;°   *smeared*
  And eke her feet most monstrous were in sight;
  For one of them was like an Eagles claw,
  With griping talaunts° armd to greedy fight,   *talons*
  The other like a Beares uneven° paw:[3]   *rough*
More ugly shape yet never living creature saw.

49

Which when the knights beheld, amazd they were,
  And wondred at so fowle deforméd wight.
  "Such then," said Una, "as she seemeth here,
  Such is the face of falshood, such the sight
  Of fowle Duessa, when her borrowed light
  Is laid away, and counterfesaunce° knowne."   *deception*
  Thus when they had the witch disrobéd quight,
  And all her filthy feature° open showne,   *form*
They let her goe at will, and wander wayes unknowne.

50

She flying fast from heavens hated face,
  And from the world that her discovered wide,°   *widely*
  Fled to the wastfull wildernesse apace,
  From living eyes her open shame to hide,
  And lurkt in rocks and caves long unespide.

2. That Redcrosse, rescued by Arthur, now perceives Duessa's ugliness indicates the restored capacity of Holiness to recognize falsehood. The details of Duessa's appearance resemble those of Alcina's foul ugliness, revealed to the disenchanted Ruggiero in *Orlando Furioso*, VII. 71–73; but the ultimate source is Revelation xvii. 16: "these shall hate the whore, and shall make her desolate and naked."
3. "And the . . . feet [of the beast] were as the feet of a bear" (Revelation xiii. 2). Like the fox, falsehood is crafty; like eagle and bear, rapacious and brutal.

But that faire crew of knights, and Una faire
Did in that castle afterwards abide,
To rest them selves, and weary powres repaire,
Where store they found of all, that dainty was and rare.

Canto IX

His loves and lignage Arthur tells:
The knights knit friendly bands:
Sir Trevisan flies from Despayre,
Whom Redcrosse knight withstands.

1

O goodly golden chaine,[1] wherewith yfere°   *together*
 The vertues linkéd are in lovely wize:
 And noble minds of yore allyéd were,
 In brave poursuit of chevalrous emprize,°   *enterprise*
 That none did others saféty despize,
 Nor aid envy° to him, in need that stands,   *begrudge*
 But friendly each did others prayse devize
 How to advaunce with favourable hands,
As this good Prince redeemd the Redcrosse knight from bands.

2

Who when their powres, empaird through labour long,
 With dew repast they had recuréd° well,   *restored*
 And that weake captive wight now wexéd strong,
 Them list no lenger there at leasure dwell,
 But forward fare, as their adventures fell,°   *befell*
 But ere they parted, Una faire besought
 That straunger knight his name and nation tell;
 Least so great good, as he for her had wrought,
Should die unknown, and buried be in thanklesse thought.

3

"Faire virgin," said the Prince, "ye me require
 A thing without the compas° of my wit: *scope*
 For both the lignage and the certain Sire,
 From which I sprong, from me are hidden yit.
 For all so soone as life did me admit
 Into this world, and shewéd heavens light,
 From mothers pap I taken was unfit:°   *unsuitably*
 And streight delivered to a Faery knight,
To be upbrought in gentle thewes° and martiall might. *manners*

1. Cf. the note to I. v. 25. Chaucer, following Boethius, speaks of "the faire cheyne of love," with which "the Firste Moevere of the cause above" linked the elements ("Knightes Tale," 2987–2992); and also of the power of love, "that with an holsom alliaunce / Halt peples joyned, as hym lest hem gye, / Love, that knetteth lawe of compaignie, / And couples doth in vertue for to dwelle" (*Troilus and Criseyde*, III, 1746–1749).

4

"Unto old Timon[2] he me brought bylive,°   *immediately*
  Old Timon, who in youthly yeares hath beene
  In warlike feates th'expertest man alive,
  And is the wisest now on earth I weene;
  His dwelling is low in a valley greene,
  Under the foot of Rauran[3] mossy hore,°   *grey*
  From whence the river Dee as silver cleene°   *pure*
  His tombling billowes rolls with gentle rore:
There all my dayes he traind me up in vertuous lore.

5

"Thither the great Magicien Merlin came,
  As was his use, ofttimes to visit me:
  For he had charge my discipline to frame,
  And Tutours nouriture° to oversee.   *training*
  Him oft and oft I askt in privitie,
  Of what loines and what lignage I did spring:
  Whose aunswere bad me still assuréd bee,
  That I was sonne and heire unto a king,
As time in her just terme[4] the truth to light should bring."

6

"Well worthy impe,"° said then the Lady gent,°   *scion/gentle*
  "And Pupill fit for such a Tutours hand.
  But what adventure, or what high intent
  Hath brought you hither into Faery land,
  Aread° Prince Arthur, crowne of Martiall band?"   *tell*
  "Full hard it is," quoth he, "to read° aright   *discern*
  The course of heavenly cause, or understand
  The secret meaning of th'eternall might,
That rules mens wayes, and rules the thoughts of living wight.[5]

7

"For whither he through fatall° deepe foresight   *prophetic*
  Me hither sent, for cause to me unghest,
  Or that fresh bleeding wound, which day and night
  Whilome° doth rancle in my riven brest,   *incessantly*
  With forcéd fury following his° behest,   *its*
  Me hither brought by wayes yet never found,
  You to have helpt I hold my selfe yet blest."
  "Ah curteous knight," quoth she, "what secret wound
Could ever find,° to grieve the gentlest hart   *attain, succeed*
    on ground?"

8

"Deare Dame," quoth he, "you sleeping sparkes awake,
  Which troubled once, into huge flames will grow,

2. "Honor." Either the "Faery knight" of st. 3 (perhaps Malory's Sir Ector), or, more probably, Merlin brought the child to Timon.
3. A hill in western Wales. The Tudors were careful to associate their own Welsh beginnings with the semihistori-cal Arthurian legend, an association widely celebrated in Elizabethan literature.
4. I.e., in due course.
5. "How unsearchable are his judgments, and his ways past finding out" (Romans xi. 33).

Ne ever will their fervent fury slake,
  Till living moysture into smoke do flow,
  And wasted° life do lye in ashes low.   *consumed*
  Yet sithens° silence lesseneth not my fire,   *since*
  But told it flames, and hidden it does glow,
  I will revele, what ye so much desire:
Ah Love, lay downe thy bow, the whiles I may respire.°   *breathe*

9

"It was in freshest flowre of youthly yeares,
  When courage first does creepe in manly chest,
  Then first the coale of kindly° heat appeares   *natural*
  To kindle love in every living brest;
  But me had warnd old Timons wise behest,°   *bidding*
  Those creeping flames by reason to subdew,
  Before their rage grew to so great unrest,
  As miserable lovers use to rew,
Which still wex old in woe, whiles woe still wexeth new.

10

"That idle name of love, and lovers life,
  As losse of time, and vertues enimy
  I ever scornd, and joyd to stirre up strife,
  In middest of their mournfull Tragedy,
  Ay wont to laugh, when them I heard to cry,
  And blow the fire, which them to ashes brent:°   *burned*
  Their God himselfe,[6] grieved at my libertie,
  Shot many a dart at me with fiers intent,
But I them warded all with wary government.°   *self-discipline*

11

"But all in vaine: no fort can be so strong,
  Ne fleshly brest can arméd be so sound,
  But will at last be wonne with battrie long,
  Or unawares at disavantage found;
  Nothing is sure, that growes on earthly ground:
  And who most trustes in arme of fleshly might,
  And boasts, in beauties chaine not to be bound,
  Doth soonest fall in disaventrous° fight,   *disastrous*
And yeeldes his caytive neck to victours most despight.[7]

12

"Ensample make of him your haplesse joy,
  And of my selfe now mated,° as ye see;   *overcome*
  Whose prouder° vaunt that proud avenging boy   *too proud*
  Did soone pluck downe, and curbd my libertie.
  For on a day prickt° forth with jollitie   *urged*
  Of looser° life, and heat of hardiment,°   *too loose/boldness*
  Raunging the forest wide on courser free,
  The fields, the floods, the heavens with one consent
Did seeme to laugh on me, and favour mine intent.

6. I.e., Cupid.   7. I.e., greatest outrage.

13

"For-wearied with my sports, I did alight
    From loftie steed, and downe to sleepe me layd;
    The verdant gras my couch did goodly dight,°   *make*
    And pillow was my helmet faire displayd:
    Whiles every sence the humour sweet embayd,°   *pervaded*
    And slombring soft my hart did steale away,
    Me seeméd, by my side a royall Mayd
    Her daintie limbes full softly down did lay:
So faire a creature yet saw never sunny day.[8]

14

"Most goodly glee° and lovely blandishment°   *pleasure/flattery*
    She to me made, and bad me love her deare,
    For dearely sure her love was to me bent,
    As when just time expiréd should appeare.
    But whether dreames delude, or true it were,
    Was never hart so ravisht with delight,
    Ne living man like words did ever heare,
    As she to me delivered all that night;
And at her parting said, She Queene of Faeries hight.°   *was called*

15

"When I awoke, and found her place devoyd,°   *empty*
    And nought but presséd gras, where she had lyen,
    I sorrowed all so much, as earst I joyd,
    And washéd all her place with watry eyen.
    From that day forth I loved that face divine;
    From that day forth I cast° in carefull mind,   *resolved*
    To seeke her out with labour, and long tyne,°   *suffering*
    And never vow to rest, till her I find,
Nine monethes I seeke in vaine yet ni'll° that vow unbind."   *will not*

16

Thus as he spake, his visage wexéd pale,
    And chaunge of hew great passion did bewray;°   *reveal*
    Yet still he strove to cloke his inward bale,°   *grief*
    And hide the smoke, that did his fire display,
    Till gentle Una thus to him gan say;
    "O happy Queene of Faeries, that hast found
    Mongst many, one that with his prowesse may
    Defend thine honour, and thy foes confound:
True Loves are often sown, but seldom grow on ground."

17

"Thine, O then," said the gentle Redcrosse knight,
    "Next to that Ladies love, shalbe the place,
    O fairest virgin, full of heavenly light,
    Whose wondrous faith, exceeding earthly race,

8. Celtic folklore provided Spenser with the outlines of this episode, based on the liaison established by some elf or fairy with a mortal creature; cf. the essay by Edwin Greenlaw in this edition.

Was firmest fixt in mine extremest case.°   *plight*
And you, my Lord, the Patrone° of my life,   *protector*
Of that great Queene may well gaine worthy grace:
For onely worthy you through prowes priefe°   *trial*
Yf living man mote worthy be, to be her liefe.°"   *loved one*

18

So diversly discoursing of their loves,
   The golden Sunne his glistring head gan shew,
   And sad remembraunce now the Prince amoves,
   With fresh desire his voyage to pursew:
   Als° Una earnd° her traveill to renew.   *also/yearned*
   Then those two knights, fast friendship for to bynd,
   And love establish each to other trew,
    Gave goodly gifts, the signes of gratefull mynd,
And eke as pledges firme, right hands together joynd.

19

Prince Arthur gave a boxe of Diamond sure,°   *firm, perfect*
   Embowd° with gold and gorgeous ornament,   *clasped*
   Wherein were closd few drops of liquor pure,[9]
   Of wondrous worth, and vertue excellent,
   That any wound could heale incontinent:°   *forthwith*
   Which to requite, the Redcrosse knight him gave
   A booke, wherein his Saveours testament
    Was writ with golden letters rich and brave;
A worke of wondrous grace, and able soules to save.

20

Thus beene they parted, Arthur on his way
   To seeke his love, and th'other for to fight
   With Unaes foe, that all her realme did pray.°   *prey upon*
   But she now weighing the decayéd plight,
   And shrunken synewes of her chosen knight,
   Would not a while her forward course pursew,
   Ne bring him forth in face of dreadfull fight,
    Till he recovered had his former hew:
For him to be yet weake and wearie well she knew.

21

So as they traveild, lo they gan espy
   An arméd knight towards them gallop fast,
   That seeméd from some fearéd foe to fly,
   Or other griesly thing, that him agast.°   *terrified*
   Still as he fled, his eye was backward cast,
   As if his feare still followed him behind;
   Als flew his steed, as he his bands had brast,°   *burst*
    And with his wingéd heeles did tread the wind,
As he had beene a fole of Pegasus his kind.[1]

9. While medieval romances allude to such healing balms and cure-alls, these "drops of liquor pure" probably signify the Eucharist; Redcrosse presents Arthur with the New Testament.

1. Pegasus, the winged horse, stated by Hesiod (*Theogony*, 280–281) and Ovid (*Metamorphoses*, IV. 785–786) to have sprung from Medusa's blood.

22

Nigh as he drew, they might perceive his head
  To be unarmd, and curld uncombéd heares
  Upstaring° stiffe, dismayd with uncouth dread;   *bristling*
  Nor drop of bloud in all his face appeares
  Nor life in limbe: and to increase his feares,
  In fowle reproch of knighthoods faire degree,°   *condition, rank*
  About his neck an hempen rope he weares,
  That with his glistring armes does ill agree;
But he of rope or armes has now no memoree.

23

The Redcrosse knight toward him crosséd fast,
  To weet, what mister° wight was so dismayd: *kind of*
  There him he finds all sencelesse and aghast,
  That of him selfe he seemd to be afrayd;
  Whom hardly he from flying forward stayd,
  Till he these wordes to him deliver might;
  "Sir knight, aread who hath ye thus arayd,
  And eke from whom make ye this hasty flight:
For never knight I saw in such misseeming° plight."   *unseemly*

24

He answerd nought at all, but adding new
  Feare to his first amazment, staring wide
  With stony eyes, and hartlesse hollow hew,[2]
  Astonisht stood, as one that had aspide
  Infernall furies, with their chaines untide.
  Him yet againe, and yet againe bespake
  The gentle knight; who nought to him replide,
  But trembling every joynt did inly quake,
And foltring tongue at last these words seemd forth to shake.

25

"For Gods deare love, Sir knight, do me not stay;
  For loe he comes, he comes fast after mee."
  Eft° looking backe would faine have runne away;   *again*
  But he him forst to stay, and tellen free
  The secret cause of his perplexitie:
  Yet nathemore° by his bold hartie speach,   *not at all*
  Could his bloud-frosen hart emboldned bee,
  But through his boldnesse rather feare did reach,°   *penetrate*
Yet forst, at last he made through silence suddein breach.

26

"And am I now in safetie sure," quoth he,
  "From him, that would have forcéd me to dye?
  And is the point of death now turnd fro mee,
  That I may tell this haplesse history?"
  "Feare nought:" quoth he, "no daunger now is nye."
  "Then shall I you recount a ruefull cace,"
  Said he, "the which with this unlucky eye

2. I.e., despondent, vacant expression.

I late beheld, and had not greater grace
Me reft from it, had bene partaker of the place.[3]

27

"I lately chaunst (Would I had never chaunst)
  With a faire knight to keepen companee,
  Sir Terwin hight, that well himselfe advaunst
  In all affaires, and was both bold and free,
  But not so happie as mote happie bee:
  He loved, as was his lot, a Ladie gent,
  That him againe° loved in the least degree: *in return*
  For she was proud, and of too high intent,°   *aspiration*
And joyd to see her lover languish and lament.

28

"From whom returning sad and comfortlesse,
  As on the way together we did fare,
  We met that villen (God from him me blesse°)   *protect*
  That curséd wight, from whom I scapt why leare,°   *lately*
  A man of hell, that cals himselfe Despaire:[4]
  Who first us greets, and after faire areedes°   *tells*
  Of tydings strange, and of adventures rare:
  So creeping close, as Snake in hidden weedes,
Inquireth of our states, and of our knightly deedes.

29

"Which when he knew, and felt our feeble harts
  Embost° with bale,° and bitter byting griefe,   *exhausted/sorrow*
  Which love had launchéd with his deadly darts,
  With wounding words and termes of foule repriefe,°   *reproach*
  He pluckt from us all hope of due reliefe,
  That earst us held in love of lingring life;
  Then hopelesse hartlesse, gan the cunning thiefe
  Perswade us die, to stint° all further strife: *end*
To me he lent this rope, to him a rustie knife.

30

"With which sad instrument of hastie death,
  That wofull lover, loathing lenger light,
  A wide way made to let forth living breath.
  But I more fearefull, or more luckie wight,
  Dismayd with that deforméd dismall sight,

---

3. I.e., would have shared my companion's fate.
4. Redcrosse will now be tempted to despair of God's grace. The theme of Despair recurs in various forms of Renaissance literature, e.g., Skelton's *Magnyfycence,* and "The Legend of Cordelia" (in the 1574 edition of *A Mirror for Magistrates*), which may have contributed details to Spenser's personification of Despair. The "disease of desperation" was a subject for sermons and religious tracts as well as for medical works. In *The Anatomy of Mel-* *ancholy* (pub. 1621), Robert Burton describes the despair "which concerns God . . . [as] opposite to hope, and a most pernicious sin, wherewith the Devil seeks to entrap men . . . The part affected is the whole soul, and all the faculties of it" ("Religious Melancholy," II. ii). In his view, it is apt to overwhelm "poor distressed souls, especially if their bodies be predisposed by melancholy, they religiously given, and have tender consciences" (II. iii).

Fled fast away, halfe dead with dying feare:
Ne yet assured of life by you, Sir knight,
Whose like infirmitie like chaunce may beare:
But God you never let his charméd speeches heare."[5]

31

"How may a man," said he, "with idle speach
    Be wonne, to spoyle° the Castle of his health?"   deprive
"I wote," quoth he, "whom triall late did teach,
    That like would not[6] for all this worldés wealth:
    His subtill tongue, like dropping honny, mealt'th°   melts
    Into the hart, and searcheth every vaine,
    That ere one be aware, by secret stealth
    His powre is reft,° and weaknesse doth remaine.   taken away
O never Sir desire to try° his guilefull traine."   test

32

"Certes°," said he, "hence shall I never rest,   surely
    Till I that treachours art have heard and tride;
    And you Sir knight, whose name mote° I request,   might
    Of grace do me unto his cabin guide."
    "I that hight Trevisan," quoth he, "will ride
    Against my liking backe, to doe you grace:
    But nor for gold nor glee° will I abide   glitter
    By you, when ye arrive in that same place;
For lever° had I die, then see his deadly face."   rather

33

Ere long they come, where that same wicked wight
    His dwelling has, low in an hollow cave,
    Farre underneath a craggie clift ypight,°   placed
    Darke, dolefull, drearie, like a greedie grave,
    That still for carrion carcases doth crave:
    On top whereof aye dwelt the ghastly Owle,
    Shrieking his balefull note, which ever drave
    Farre from that haunt all other chearefull fowle;
And all about it wandring ghostes did waile and howle.

34

And all about old stockes° and stubs of trees,   stumps
    Whereon nor fruit, nor leafe was ever seene,
    Did hang upon the ragged rocky knees;°   crags
    On which had many wretches hangéd beene,
    Whose carcases were scattered on the greene,
    And throwne about the cliffs. Arrivéd there,
    That bare-head knight for dread and dolefull teene,°   grief
    Would faine have fled, ne durst approchen neare,
But th'other forst him stay, and comforted in feare.

35

That darkesome cave they enter, where they find
    That curséd man, low sitting on the ground,

5. I.e., may God keep you from ever   6. I.e., would not (again) do the like.
hearing his enchanted discourse.

Musing full sadly in his sullein mind;
 His griesie° lockes, long growen, and unbound,   *grey*
 Disordred hong about his shoulders round,
 And hid his face; through which his hollow eyne
 Lookt deadly dull, and staréd as astound;
 His raw-bone cheekes through penurie and pine,°   *inner torment*
Were shronke into his jawes, as° he did never dine.   *as if*

36

His garment nought but many ragged clouts,°   *shreds of clothing*
 With thornes together pind and patchéd was,
 The which his naked sides he wrapt abouts;
 And him beside there lay upon the gras
 A drearie corse, whose life away did pas,
 All wallowd in his owne yet luke-warme blood,
 That from his wound yet welléd fresh alas;
 In which a rustie knife fast fixéd stood,
And made an open passage for the gushing flood.

37

Which piteous spectacle, approving° trew   *confirming*
 The wofull tale that Trevisan had told,
 When as the gentle Redcrosse knight did vew,
 With firie zeale he burnt in courage bold,
 Him to avenge, before his bloud were cold,
 And to the villein said, "Thou damnéd wight,
 The author of this fact,° we here behold,   *deed*
 What justice can but judge against thee right,
With thine owne bloud to price° his bloud, here shed *pay for*
  in sight."

38

"What franticke fit," quoth he, "hath thus distraught
 Thee, foolish man, so rash a doome° to give?[7]   *judgment*
 What justice ever other judgement taught,
 But he should die, who merites not to live?
 None else to death this man despayring drive,
 But his owne guiltie mind deserving death.
 Is then unjust to each his due to give?
 Or let him die, that loatheth living breath?
Or let him die at ease, that liveth here uneath?°   *uneasily*

39

"Who travels by the wearie wandring way,
 To come unto his wishéd home in haste,
 And meetes a flood, that doth his passage stay,
 Is not great grace to helpe him over past,
 Or free his feet, that in the myre sticke fast?
 Most envious man, that grieves at neighbours good,

---

7. The arguments of Despair are drawn primarily from classical Stoicism and from precepts in the Old Testament bearing on the character of divine justice; allusions to God's mercy are conspicuously absent. That the arguments advanced by the tempter are by no means mutually supportive (cf. especially st. 42) demonstrates the essentially nonreasonable character of despair.

And fond,° that joyest in the woe thou hast,   *foolish*
 Why wilt not let him passe, that long hath stood
Upon the banke, yet wilt thy selfe not passe the flood?

40

"He there does now enjoy eternall rest
 And happie ease, which thou doest want and crave,
 And further from it daily wanderest:
 What if some litle paine the passage have,
 That makes fraile flesh to feare the bitter wave?
 Is not short paine well borne, that brings long ease,
 And layes the soule to sleepe in quiet grave?
 Sleepe after toyle, port after stormie seas,
Ease after warre, death after life does greatly please."

41

The knight much wondred at his suddeine° wit,   *quick*
 And said, "The terme of life is limited,
 Ne may a man prolong, nor shorten it;
 The souldier may not move from watchfull sted,° *position*
 Nor leave his stand, untill his Captaine bed."°   *directs*
 "Who life did limit by almightie doome,"
 Quoth he, "knowes best the termes establishéd;
 And he, that points the Centonell his roome,°   *station*
Doth license him depart at sound of morning droome.[8]

42

"Is not his deed, what ever thing is donne,
 In heaven and earth? did not he all create
 To die againe? all ends that was begonne.
 Their times in his eternall booke of fate
 Are written sure, and have their certaine date.
 Who then can strive with strong necessitie,
 That holds the world in his° still chaunging state, *its*
 Or shunne the death ordaynd by destinie?
When houre of death is come, let none aske whence, nor why.

43

"The lenger life, I wote the greater sin,
 The greater sin, the greater punishment:
 All those great battels, which thou boasts to win,
 Through strife, and bloud-shed, and avengément,
 Now praysd, hereafter deare thou shalt repent:
 For life must life, and bloud must bloud repay.[9]
 Is not enough thy evill life forespent?°   *already spent*
 For he, that once hath misséd the right way,
The further he doth goe, the further he doth stray.

44

"Then do no further goe, no further stray,
 But here lie downe, and to thy rest betake,

---

8. This response by Despair is a paraphrase of Cicero's allusion to the advice of Pythagoras (cf. *De Senectute*, XX).

9. "Whoso sheddeth man's blood, by man shall his blood be shed" (Genesis ix. 6).

Th'ill to prevent, that life ensewen may.[1]
For what hath life, that may it lovéd make,
And gives not rather cause it to forsake?
Feare, sicknesse, age, losse, labour, sorrow, strife,
Paine, hunger, cold, that makes the hart to quake;
And ever fickle fortune rageth rife,
All which, and thousands mo° do make a loathsome life.　　　*more*

45

"Thou wretched man, of death hast greatest need,
　If in true ballance thou wilt weigh thy state:
　For never knight, that daréd warlike deede,
　More lucklesse disaventures did amate:°　　　*daunt, cast down*
　Witnesse the dongeon deepe, wherein of late
　Thy life shut up, for death so oft did call;
　And though good lucke prolongéd hath thy date,°　　　*life span*
　Yet death then, would the like mishaps forestall,
Into the which hereafter thou maiest happen fall.

46

"Why then doest thou, O man of sin, desire
　To draw thy dayes forth to their last degree?
　Is not the measure of thy sinfull hire
　High heapéd up with huge iniquitie,
　Against the day of wrath,[2] to burden thee?
　Is not enough, that to this Ladie milde
　Thou falséd hast thy faith with perjurie,
　And sold thy selfe to serve Duessa vilde,°　　　*vile*
With whom in all abuse thou hast thy selfe defilde?

47

"Is not he just, that all this doth behold
　From highest heaven, and beares an equall° eye?　　　*impartial*
　Shall he thy sins up in his knowledge fold,
　And guiltie be of thine impietie?
　Is not his law, Let every sinner die:
　Die shall all flesh?[3] what then must needs be donne,
　Is it not better to doe willinglie,
　Then linger, till the glasse be all out ronne?
Death is the end of woes: die soone, O faeries sonne."

48

The knight was much enmovéd with his speach,
　That as a swords point through his hart did perse,
　And in his conscience made a secret breach,
　Well knowing true all, that he did reherse,°　　　*recount*
　And to his fresh remembrance did reverse°　　　*recall*
　The ugly vew of his deforméd crimes,
　That all his manly powres it did disperse,
　As he were charméd with inchaunted rimes,
That oftentimes he quakt, and fainted oftentimes.

1. I.e., that the remainder of your life
may bring.
2. I.e., Doomsday.
3. "All flesh shall perish together, and
man shall turn again into dust" (Job
xxxiv. 15).

49

In which amazement, when the Miscreant
  Perceivéd him to waver weake and fraile,
  Whiles trembling horror did his conscience dant,°   *daunt*
  And hellish anguish did his soule assaile,
  To drive him to despaire, and quite to quaile,°   *be dismayed*
  He shewed him painted in a table° plaine,   *picture*
  The damnéd ghosts, that doe in torments waile,
  And thousand feends that doe them endlesse paine
With fire and brimstone, which for ever shall remaine.[4]

50

The sight whereof so throughly him dismaid,
  That nought but death before his eyes he saw,
  And ever burning wrath before him laid,
  By righteous sentence of th'Almighties law:
  Then gan the villein him to overcraw,°   *exult over*
  And brought unto him swords, ropes, poison, fire,
  And all that might him to perdition draw;
  And bad him choose, what death he would desire:
For death was due to him, that had provokt Gods ire.

51

But when as none of them he saw him take,
  He to him raught° a dagger sharpe and keene,   *held out*
  And gave it him in hand: his hand did quake,
  And tremble like a leafe of Aspin greene,
  And troubled bloud through his pale face was seene
  To come, and goe with tydings from the hart,
  As it a running messenger had beene.
  At last resolved to worke his finall smart,
He lifted up his hand, that backe againe did start.

52

Which when as Una saw, through every vaine
  The crudled° cold ran to her well of life,[5]   *congealing*
  As in a swowne: but soone relived° againe,   *recovered*
  Out of his hand she snatcht the curséd knife,
  And threw it to the ground, enragéd rife,°   *deeply*
  And to him said, "Fie, fie, faint harted knight,
  What meanest thou by this reprochfull strife?
  Is this the battell, which thou vauntst to fight
With that fire-mouthéd Dragon, horrible and bright?

53

"Come, come away, fraile, feeble, fleshly wight,[6]
  Ne let vaine words bewitch thy manly hart,

---

4. The persuasive power of visual images (to which Spenser is always especially alert) caps and completes the sophistical rhetoric of the preceding stanzas.
5. I.e., her heart.
6. In contrast to the counsels of Despair, Una's appeal emphasizes the saving power of Christian grace: her language recalls the shield of faith by which "ye shall be able to quench all the fiery darts of the wicked" (Ephesians vi. 16), and the significance of Christ's death, "Blotting out the handwriting of ordinances that was against us" (Colossians ii. 14).

Ne divelish thoughts dismay thy constant spright.
In heavenly mercies hast thou not a part?
Why shouldst thou then despeire, that chosen art?
Where justice growes, there grows eke greater grace,
The which doth quench the brond of hellish smart,
And that accurst hand-writing doth deface.°   *blot out*
Arise, Sir knight arise, and leave this curséd place."

54

So up he rose, and thence amounted° streight.   *mounted (his horse)*
  Which when the carle° beheld, and saw his guest   *churl*
  Would safe depart, for all his subtill sleight,
  He chose an halter from among the rest,
  And with it hung himselfe, unbid° unblest.   *not prayed for*
  But death he could not worke himselfe thereby;
  For thousand times he so himselfe had drest,°   *made ready*
  Yet nathelesse it could not doe him die,
Till he should die his last, that is eternally.

Canto X

*Her faithfull knight faire Una brings
   to house of Holinesse,
Where he is taught repentance, and
   the way to heavenly blesse.°*   *bliss*

1

What man is he, that boasts of fleshly might,
  And vaine assurance of mortality,°   *mortal life*
  Which all so soone, as it doth come to fight,
  Against spirituall foes, yeelds by and by,[1]
  Or from the field most cowardly doth fly?
  Ne let the man ascribe it to his skill,
  That thorough grace hath gainéd victory.
  If any strength we have, it is to ill,
But all the good is Gods, both power and eke will.[2]

2

By that, which lately hapned, Una saw,
  That this her knight was feeble, and too faint;
  And all his sinews woxen weake and raw,°   *unready*
  Through long enprisonment, and hard constraint,
  Which he enduréd in his late restraint,
  That yet he was unfit for bloudie fight:
  Therefore to cherish him with diets daint,°   *dainty*
  She cast to bring him, where he chearen° might,   *be refreshed*
Till he recovered had his° late decayéd plight.   *from his*

1. I.e., at once.
2. "For by grace are ye saved through faith; and that not of yourselves: it is the gift of God: Not of works, lest any man should boast" (Ephesians ii. 8–9).

3

There was an auntient house[3] not farre away,
    Renowmd throughout the world for sacred lore,
    And pure unspotted life: so well they say
    It governd was, and guided evermore,
    Through wisedome of a matrone grave and hore;°   *grey-haired*
    Whose onely joy was to relieve the needes
    Of wretched soules, and helpe the helpelesse pore:
    All night she spent in bidding of her bedes,[4]
And all the day in doing good and godly deedes.

4

Dame Caelia[5] men did her call, as thought
    From heaven to come, or thither to arise,
    The mother of three daughters, well upbrought
    In goodly thewes,° and godly exercise: *discipline*
    The eldest two most sober, chast, and wise,
    Fidelia and Speranza virgins were,
    Though spousd,° yet wanting wedlocks solemnize;   *bethrothed*
    But faire Charissa to a lovely fere°   *mate*
Was linckéd, and by him had many pledges dere.[6]

5

Arrivéd there, the dore they find fast lockt;
    For it was warely watchéd night and day,
    For feare of many foes: but when they knockt,
    The Porter opened unto them streight way:
    He was an aged syre, all hory gray,
    With lookes full lowly cast, and gate full slow,
    Wont on a staffe his feeble steps to stay,
    Hight Humiltá.[7] They passe in stouping low;
For streight and narrow was the way, which he did show.[8]

6

Each goodly thing is hardest to begin,
    But entred in a spacious court they see,
    Both plaine, and pleasant to be walkéd in,
    Where them does meete a francklin° faire and free,
                                         freeman, landowner
    And entertaines with comely courteous glee,

3. In the House of Holiness, Redcrosse, having been brought by faith and hope to perceive and acknowledge his sinfulness, is cleansed by penance and repentance, and instructed in Christian love; at length, through contemplation irradiated by God's mercy, he is vouchsafed a vision of the New Jerusalem. Each significant detail of this Canto contrasts with its counterpart in Canto iv, as the House of Holiness, from which man perceives the Heavenly City, matches and counters the House of Pride, whose inhabitants fall at last into its grim dungeon, their "shameful end."
4. I.e., offering prayers.

5. "Heavenly."
6. I.e., many children. The daughters' names mean Faith, Hope, and Charity (or "spiritual love"). That Charissa is married (and has recently been delivered of a child) indicates the fruitfulness of this Christian virtue. "And now abideth faith, hope, charity, these three; but the greatest is charity" (I Corinthians xiii. 13).
7. Humility.
8. "Strait is the gate, and narrow is the way, which leadeth unto life, and few there be that find it" (Matthew vii. 14).

His name was Zele, that him right well became,
    For in his speeches and behaviour hee
    Did labour lively to expresse the same,
And gladly did them guide, till to the Hall they came.

7

There fairely them receives a gentle Squire,
    Of milde demeanure, and rare courtesie,
    Right cleanly clad in comely sad° attire;   *sober*
    In word and deede that shewed great modestie,
    And knew his good° to all of each degree,   *proper behavior*
    Hight Reverence. He them with speeches meet
    Does faire entreat; no courting nicetie,°   *affectation*
    But simple true, and eke unfainéd sweet,
As might become a Squire so great persons to greet.

8

And afterwards them to his Dame he leades,
    That aged Dame, the Ladie of the place:
    Who all this while was busie at her beades:
    Which doen, she up arose with seemely grace,
    And toward them full matronely did pace.
    Where when that fairest Una she beheld,
    Whom well she knew to spring from heavenly race,
    Her hart with joy unwonted inly sweld,
As feeling wondrous comfort in her weaker eld.°   *old age*

9

And her embracing said, "O happie earth,
    Whereon thy innocent feet doe ever tread,
    Most vertuous virgin borne of heavenly berth,
    That to redeeme thy woefull parents head,
    From tyrans rage, and ever-dying dread,[9]
    Hast wandred through the world now long a day;
    Yet ceasest not thy wearie soles to lead,
    What grace hath thee now hither brought this way?
Or doen thy feeble feet unweeting° hither stray?   *unwittingly*

10

"Strange thing it is an errant° knight to see   *wandering*
    Here in this place, or any other wight,
    That hither turnes his steps. So few there bee,
    That chose the narrow path, or seeke the right:
    All keepe the broad high way, and take delight
    With many rather for to go astray,
    And be partakers of their evill plight,
    Then with a few to walke the rightest way;
O foolish men, why haste ye to your owne decay?"

11

"Thy selfe to see, and tyred limbs to rest,
    "O matrone sage," quoth she, "I hither came,
    And this good knight his way with me addrest,°   *directed*

9. I.e., continual fear of death.

Led with thy prayses and broad-blazéd fame,
That up to heaven is blowne." The aunciant Dame
Him goodly greeted in her modest guise,
And entertaynd them both, as best became,
With all the court'sies, that she could devise,
Ne wanted ought, to shew her bounteous or wise.

12

Thus as they gan of sundry things devise,°   *discourse*
Loe two most goodly virgins came in place,
Ylinkéd arme in arme in lovely° wise,   *loving*
With countenance demure, and modest grace,
They numbred even steps and equall pace:
Of which the eldest, that Fidelia hight,
Like sunny beames threw from her Christall face,
That could have dazd the rash beholders sight,
And round about her head did shine like heavens light.

13

She was araiéd all in lilly white,
And in her right hand bore a cup of gold,
With wine and water fild up to the hight,
In which a Serpent did himselfe enfold,
That horrour made to all, that did behold;
But she no whit did chaunge her constant mood:°   *expression*
And in her other hand she fast did hold
A booke, that was both signd and seald with blood,
Wherein darke things were writ, hard to be understood.[1]

14

Her younger sister, that Speranza hight,
Was clad in blew, that her beseeméd well;
Not all so chearefull seeméd she of sight,[2]
As was her sister; whether dread did dwell,
Or anguish in her hart, is hard to tell:
Upon her arme a silver anchor lay,
Whereon she leanéd ever, as befell:
And ever up to heaven, as she did pray,
Her stedfast eyes were bent, ne swarvéd other way.[3]

15

They seeing Una, towards her gan wend,
Who them encounters with like courtesie;
Many kind speeches they betwene them spend,
And greatly joy each other well to see:

1. The details in Spenser's descriptions of Fidelia and Speranza reflect those of the emblematic and allegorical portraits of these figures in contemporary literature and art, notably emblem books like those of Ripa, Alciati, and Whitney. Fidelia's cup, contrasted to that held by Duessa, recalls the elevation by Moses of the brazen serpent (Numbers xxi. 8–9), which St. John interprets typologically as the lifting up of "the Son of man" (John iii. 14). Primarily her cup represents the sacrament of Holy Communion, encompassing both death and life. She holds the New Testament, "signd and seald" with Christ's blood. Cf. also II Peter iii. 16.
2. I.e., in appearance.
3. "Which hope we have as an anchor of the soul, both sure and stedfast, and which entereth into that within the veil" (Hebrews vi. 19).

Then to the knight with shamefast° modestie   *humble*
  They turne themselves, at Unaes meeke request,
  And him salute with well beseeming glee;
    Who faire them quites,° as him beseeméd best,   *responds to*
And goodly gan discourse of many a noble gest.°   *feat of arms*

16

Then Una thus; "But she your sister deare,
  The deare Charissa where is she become?[4]
  Or wants she health, or busie is elsewhere?"
    "Ah no," said they, "but forth she may not come:
  For she of late is lightned of her wombe,
  And hath encreast the world with one sonne more,
  That her to see should be but troublesome."
    "Indeede," quoth she, "that should her trouble sore,
But thankt be God, and her encrease so[5] evermore."

17

Then said the aged Caelia, "Deare dame,
  And you good Sir, I wote that of your toyle,
  And labours long, through which ye hither came,
    Ye both forwearied° be: therefore a whyle   *tired out*
  I read° you rest, and to your bowres recoyle.°"   *advise/retire*
  Then calléd she a Groome, that forth him led
  Into a goodly lodge, and gan despoile°   *disrobe*
  Of puissant armes, and laid in easie bed;
His name was meeke Obedience rightfully ared.°   *understood*

18

Now when their wearie limbes with kindly° rest,   *natural*
  And bodies were refresht with due repast,
  Faire Una gan Fidelia faire request,
    To have her knight into her schoolehouse plaste,
  That of her heavenly learning he might taste,
  And heare the wisedome of her words divine.
    She graunted, and that knight so much agraste,°   *favored*
  That she him taught celestiall discipline,[6]
And opened his dull eyes, that light mote in them shine.

19

And that her sacred Booke, with bloud[7] ywrit,
  That none could read, except she did them teach,
  She unto him discloséd every whit,
    And heavenly documents° thereout did preach,   *teaching*
  That weaker wit of man could never reach,
  Of God, of grace, of justice, of free will,
  That wonder was to heare her goodly speach:
    For she was able, with her words to kill,
And raise againe to life[8] the hart, that she did thrill.°   *pierce*

---

4. I.e., where is she?
5. I.e., may God increase her in that way.
6. I.e., holy laws.
7. I.e., Christ's blood.
8. "For the letter killeth, but the spirit giveth life" (II Corinthians iii. 6).

20

And when she list poure out her larger spright,[9]
  She would commaund the hastie Sunne to stay,
  Or backward turne his course from heavens hight;
  Sometimes great hostes of men she could dismay,
  Dry-shod to passe, she parts the flouds in tway;
  And eke huge mountaines from their native seat
  She would commaund, themselves to beare away,
  And throw in raging sea with roaring threat.
Almightie God her gave such powre, and puissance great.

21

The faithfull knight now grew in litle space,
  By hearing her, and by her sisters lore,
  To such perfection of all heavenly grace,
  That wretched world he gan for to abhore,
  And mortall life gan loath, as thing forlore,°   *abandoned*
  Greeved with remembrance of his wicked wayes,
  And prickt with anguish of his sinnes so sore,
  That he desirde to end his wretched dayes:
So much the dart of sinfull guilt the soule dismayes.

22

But wise Speranza gave him comfort sweet,
  And taught him how to take assuréd hold
  Upon her silver anchor, as was meet;
  Else had his sinnes so great, and manifold
  Made him forget all that Fidelia told.
  In this distresséd doubtfull agonie,
  When him his dearest Una did behold,
  Disdeining life, desiring leave to die,
She found her selfe assayld with great perplexitie.

23

And came to Caelia to declare her smart,
  Who well acquainted with that commune plight,
  Which sinfull horror[1] workes in wounded hart,
  Her wisely comforted all that she might,
  With goodly counsell and advisement right;
  And streightway sent with carefull diligence,
  To fetch a Leach,° the which had great insight   *physician*
  In that disease of grievéd conscience,
And well could cure the same; His name was Patience.

24

Who comming to that soule-diseaséd knight,
  Could hardly him intreat,° to tell his griefe: *persuade*
  Which knowne, and all that noyd° his heavie spright   *troubled*
  Well searcht, eftsoones he gan apply reliefe

9. I.e., higher power. The four allusions in this stanza to miraculous events described in the Old Testament (Joshua x. 12; II Kings xx. 10; Judges vii. 7; Exodus xiv. 21–31) are significantly climaxed by a more extended reference to Matthew xxi. 21: "Jesus answered and said unto them . . . if ye shall say unto this mountain, Be thou removed, and be thou cast into the sea; it shall be done."
1. I.e., horror of sin.

Of salves and med'cines, which had passing priefe,[2]
And thereto added words of wondrous might:[3]
By which to ease he him recuréd briefe,°   quickly
And much asswaged the passion° of his plight,   suffering
That he his paine endured, as seeming now more light.

25

But yet the cause and root of all his ill,
   Inward corruption, and infected sin,
   Not purged nor heald, behind remainéd still,
   And festring sore did rankle yet within,
   Close creeping twixt the marrow and the skin.
   Which to extirpe,° he laid him privily   root out
   Downe in a darkesome lowly place farre in,
   Whereas he meant his corrosives to apply,
And with streight° diet tame his stubborne malady.   strict

26

In ashes and sackcloth he did array
   His daintie corse, proud humors[4] to abate,
   And dieted with fasting every day,
   The swelling of his wounds to mitigate,
   And made him pray both earely and eke late:
   And ever as superfluous flesh did rot
   Amendment readie still at hand did wayt,
   To pluck it out with pincers firie whot,°   hot
That soone in him was left no one corrupted jot.

27

And bitter Penance with an yron whip,
   Was wont him once to disple° every day: discipline
   And sharpe Remorse his heart did pricke and nip,
   That drops of bloud thence like a well did play;
   And sad Repentance uséd to embay°   bathe
   His bodie in salt water smarting sore,
   The filthy blots of sinne to wash away.[5]
   So in short space they did to health restore
The man that would not live, but earst° lay at deathes dore.   formerly

28

In which his torment often was so great,
   That like a Lyon he would cry and rore,
   And rend his flesh, and his owne synewes eat.
   His owne deare Una hearing evermore
   His ruefull shriekes and gronings, often tore
   Her guiltlesse garments, and her golden heare,
   For pitty of his paine and anguish sore;
   Yet all with patience wisely she did beare;
For well she wist, his crime could else be never cleare.°   cleansed

29

Whom thus recovered by wise Patience,
   And trew Repentance they to Una brought:

---

2. I.e., surpassing power.
3. As absolution follows confession.
4. I.e., pride.

5. "Wash me throughly from mine iniquity, and cleanse me from my sin" (Psalms li. 2).

Who joyous of his curéd conscience,
Him dearely kist, and fairely eke besought
Himselfe to chearish, and consuming thought
To put away out of his carefull brest.
By this Charissa, late in child-bed brought,
Was woxen strong, and left her fruitfull nest;
To her faire Una brought this unacquainted guest.[6]

30

She was a woman in her freshest age,[7]
  Of wondrous beauty, and of bountie° rare,   *virtue*
  With goodly grace and comely personage,
  That was on earth not easie to compare;
  Full of great love, but Cupids wanton snare
  As hell she hated, chast in worke and will;
  Her necke and breasts were ever open bare,
  That ay thereof her babes might sucke their fill;
The rest was all in yellow robes arayéd still.

31

A multitude of babes about her hong,
  Playing their sports, that joyd her to behold,
  Whom still she fed, whiles they were weake and young,
  But thrust them forth still, as they wexéd old:
  And on her head she wore a tyre° of gold,   *headdress*
  Adornd with gemmes and owches° wondrous faire,   *jewels*
  Whose passing price uneath was to be told;[8]
  And by her side there sate a gentle paire
Of turtle doves, she sitting in an yvorie chaire.

32

The knight and Una entring, faire her greet,
  And bid her joy of that her happie brood;
  Who them requites with court'sies seeming meet,°   *appropriate*
  And entertaines with friendly chearefull mood.
  Then Una her besought, to be so good,
  As in her vertuous rules to schoole her knight,
  Now after all his torment well withstood,
  In that sad° house of Penaunce, where his spright   *grave*
Had past the paines of hell, and long enduring night.

33

She was right joyous of her just request,
  And taking by the hand that Faeries sonne,
  Gan him instruct in every good behest,
  Of love, and righteousnesse, and well to donne,[9]
  And wrath, and hatred warély to shonne,
  That drew on men Gods hatred, and his wrath,

6. "Though I have all faith, so that I could remove mountains, and have not charity, I am nothing" (I Corinthians xiii. 2).
7. The description of Charissa includes appropriate classical elements: Hymen, the god of marriage, was traditionally garbed in yellow (cf. *Metamorphoses,* X. 1); and doves were sacred to Venus. But the love figured in Charissa, "chast in worke and will," is essentially Christian in conception.
8. I.e., whose surpassing value might scarcely be estimated.
9. I.e., well-doing.

And many soules in dolours° had fordonne:°   *misery/ruined*
  In which when him she well instructed hath,
From thence to heaven she teacheth him the ready path.

34

Wherein his weaker° wandring steps to guide,   *too weak*
  An auncient matrone she to her does call,
  Whose sober lookes her wisedome well descride:°   *revealed*
  Her name was Mercie, well knowne over all,
  To be both gratious, and eke liberall:
  To whom the carefull charge of him she gave,
  To lead aright, that he should never fall
  In all his wayes through this wide worldés wave,
That Mercy in the end his righteous soule might save.

35

The godly Matrone by the hand him beares
  Forth from her presence, by a narrow way,
  Scattred with bushy thornes, and ragged breares,°   *briers.*
  Which still before him she removed away,
  That nothing might his ready passage stay:
  And ever when his feet encombred were,
  Or gan to shrinke, or from the right to stray,
  She held him fast, and firmely did upbeare,
As carefull Nourse her child from falling oft does reare.

36

Eftsoones unto an holy Hospitall,°   *retreat, sanctuary*
  That was fore° by the way, she did him bring,   *close*
  In which seven Bead-men[1] that had vowéd all
  Their life to service of high heavens king
  Did spend their dayes in doing godly thing:
  Their gates to all were open evermore,
  That by the wearie way were traveiling,
  And one sate wayting° ever them before,   *watching*
To call in commers-by, that needy were and pore.

37

The first of them that eldest was, and best,°   *chief*
  Of all the house had charge and governement,
  As Guardian and Steward of the rest:
  His office was to give entertainement
  And lodging, unto all that came, and went:
  Not unto such, as could him feast againe,
  And double quite,° for that he on them spent,   *repay*
  But such, as want of harbour° did constraine: *shelter*
Those for Gods sake his dewty was to entertaine.

38

The second was as Almner° of the place,   *distributor of alms*
  His office was, the hungry for to feed,

---

1. Properly men who pray for others' spiritual welfare, these "Bead-men" are dedicated to serving the corporal needs of other men; they are the counter-part in the House of Holiness of the Seven Deadly Sins in the House of Pride.

And thristy give to drinke, a worke of grace:
He feard not once him selfe to be in need,
Ne cared to hoord for those, whom he did breede:[2]
The grace of God he layd up still in store,
Which as a stocke° he left unto his seede;   *resource*
He had enough, what need him care for more?
And had he lesse, yet some he would give to the pore.

39

The third had of their wardrobe custodie,
In which were not rich tyres,° nor garments gay, *attire*
The plumes of pride, and wings of vanitie,
But clothés meet to keepe keene could° away,   *cold*
And naked nature seemely to aray;
With which bare wretched wights he dayly clad,
The images of God in earthly clay;
And if that no spare cloths to give he had,
His owne coate he would cut, and it distribute glad.

40

The fourth appointed by his office was,
Poore prisoners to relieve with gratious ayd,
And captives to redeeme with price of bras,°   *money*
From Turkes and Sarazins, which them had stayd;° *held captive*
And though they faultie were, yet well he wayd,
That God to us forgiveth every howre
Much more then that, why they in bands were layd, *for which*
And he that harrowd hell with heavie stowre,
The faultie soules from thence brought to his heavenly bowre.[3]

41

The fift had charge sicke persons to attend,
And comfort those, in point of death which lay;
For them most needeth comfort in the end,
When sin, and hell, and death do most dismay
The feeble soule departing hence away.
All is but lost, that living we bestow,°   *store up*
If not well ended at our dying day.
O man have mind of that last bitter throw;°   *throe*
For as the tree does fall, so lyes it ever low.

42

The sixt had charge of them now being dead,
In seemely sort their corses to engrave,°   *bury*
And deck with dainty flowres their bridall bed,
That to their heavenly spouse both sweet and brave° *fair*
They might appeare, when he their soules shall save.
The wondrous workemanship of Gods owne mould,° *image*

2. I.e., his own family.
3. An allusion to events described in the apocryphal Gospel of Nicodemus (cf. *The Apocryphal New Testament*, ed. and trans. M. R. James [Oxford, 1924], 94–146). This document, a composite account of the Passion and Resurrection and of Christ's descent into Hell, dates to the 4th or 5th century. The story of Christ's delivery of the righteous men who lived before his time is of earlier origin.

Whose face he made, all beasts to feare, and gave
All in his hand, even dead we honour should.
Ah dearest God me graunt, I dead be not defould.°   *defiled*

43

The seventh now after death and buriall done,
  Had charge the tender Orphans of the dead
  And widowes ayd, least they should be undone:°   *ruined*
  In face of judgement[4] he their right would plead,
  Ne ought the powre of mighty men did dread
  In their defence, nor would for gold or fee
  Be wonne their rightfull causes downe to tread:
  And when they stood in most necessitee,
He did supply their want, and gave them ever free.°   *freely*

44

There when the Elfin knight arrivéd was,
  The first and chiefest of the seven, whose care
  Was guests to welcome, towardes him did pas:
  Where seeing Mercie, that his steps up bare,°   *supported*
  And alwayes led, to her with reverence rare
  He humbly louted° in meeke lowlinesse,   *bowed*
  And seemely welcome for her did prepare:
  For of their order she was Patronesse,
Albe° Charissa were their chiefest founderesse.   *although*

45

There she awhile him stayes, him selfe to rest,
  That to the rest more able he might bee:
  During which time, in every good behest
  And godly worke of Almes and charitee
  She him instructed with great industree;
  Shortly therein so perfect he became,
  That from the first unto the last degree,
  His mortall life he learnéd had to frame
In holy righteousnesse, without rebuke or blame.

46

Thence forward by that painfull way they pas,
  Forth to an hill, that was both steepe and hy;
  On top whereof a sacred chappell was,
  And eke a litle Hermitage thereby,
  Wherein an aged holy man did lye,
  That day and night said his devotion,
  Ne other worldly busines did apply;°   *pursue*
  His name was heavenly Contemplation;
Of God and goodnesse was his meditation.[5]

47

Great grace that old man to him given had;
  For God he often saw from heavens hight,

4. I.e., in the court of law.
5. In the episode that follows, Spenser may have had in mind the moral refreshment and strength received by the hero of Ariosto's Rinaldo on the "Hill of Hope" (*Rinaldo*, **XI.** 56–65); but the encounter of Redcrosse and Contemplation is significant on a consistently higher plane.

All° were his earthly eyen both blunt° and bad,   *although/dim*
And through great age had lost their kindly° sight,   *natural*
Yet wondrous quick and persant° was his spright,   *piercing*
As Eagles eye, that can behold the Sunne:[6]
That hill they scale with all their powre and might,
That his frayle thighes nigh wearie and fordonne°   *exhausted*
Gan faile, but by her helpe the top at last he wonne.

48

There they do finde that godly aged Sire,
With snowy lockes adowne his shoulders shed,
As hoarie frost with spangles doth attire
The mossy braunches of an Oke halfe ded.
Each bone might through his body well be red,°   *seen*
And every sinew seene through° his long fast: *in consequence of*
For nought he cared his carcas long unfed;
His mind was full of spirituall repast,
And pyned° his flesh, to keepe his body low and chast.   *starved*

49

Who when these two approching he aspide,
At their first presence grew agrievéd sore,
That forst him lay his heavenly thoughts aside;
And had he not that Dame respected more,°   *greatly*
Whom highly he did reverence and adore,
He would not once have movéd for the knight.
They him saluted standing far afore;°   *before*
Who well them greeting, humbly did requight,
And askéd, to what end they clomb° that tedious height.   *had climbed*

50

"What end," quoth she, "should cause us take such paine,
But that same end, which every living wight
Should make his marke, high heaven to attaine?
Is not from hence the way, that leadeth right
To that most glorious house, that glistreth bright
With burning starres, and everliving fire,
Whereof the keyes are to thy hand behight°   *entrusted*
By wise Fidelia? she doth thee require,
To shew it to this knight, according° his desire."   *granting*

51

"Thrise happy man," said then the father grave,
"Whose staggering steps thy steady hand doth lead,
And shewes the way, his sinfull soule to save.
Who better can the way to heaven aread,°   *direct*
Then thou thy selfe, that was both borne and bred
In heavenly throne, where thousand Angels shine?
Thou doest the prayers of the righteous sead°   *offspring*
Present before the majestie divine,
And his avenging wrath to clemencie incline.

6. Commonly an attribute of eagles in medieval bestiaries; and cf. Chaucer, *Parliament of Fowls,* 330–1: "There myghte men the royal egle fynde, / That with his sharpe lok perseth the sonne . . ."

52

"Yet since thou bidst, thy pleasure shalbe donne.
Then come thou man of earth,[7] and see the way,
That never yet was seene of Faeries sonne,
That never leads the traveiler astray,
But after labours long, and sad delay,
Brings them to joyous rest and endlesse blis.
But first thou must a season fast and pray,
Till from her bands the spright assoiléd° is,   *set free*
And have her strength recured° from fraile infirmitis."   *recovered*

53

That done, he leads him to the highest Mount;[8]
Such one, as that same mighty man of God,
That bloud-red billowes like a walléd front
On either side disparted with his rod,
Till that his army dry-foot through them yod,°   *went*
Dwelt fortie dayes upon; where writ in stone
With bloudy letters by the hand of God,
The bitter doome of death and balefull mone°   *grief*
He did receive, whiles flashing fire about him shone.

54

Or like that sacred hill,[9] whose head full hie,
Adornd with fruitfull Olives all arownd,
Is, as it were for endlesse memory
Of that deare Lord, who oft thereon was fownd,
For ever with a flowring girlond crownd:
Or like that pleasant Mount,[1] that is for ay
Through famous Poets verse each where° renownd,   *everywhere*
On which the thrise three learnéd Ladies play
Their heavenly notes, and make full many a lovely lay.

55

From thence, far off he unto him did shew
A litle path, that was both steepe and long,
Which to a goodly Citie[2] led his vew;
Whose wals and towres were builded high and strong
Of perle and precious stone, that earthly tong
Cannot describe, nor wit of man can tell;

7. A hint of the knight's subsequent identification (in st. 61) as St. George (from Greek *georgos,* "farmer," or "ploughman").
8. Mt. Sinai (Exodus xxiv. 16–18); there is also a suggestion of that "great and high mountain" to which the angel carried John "in the spirit . . . and shewed [him] that great city, the holy Jerusalem, descending out of heaven from God" (Revelation xxi. 10).
9. The Mount of Olives.
1. Parnassus, the abode of the nine Muses, appropriately included here in view of Spenser's high opinion of the true poet's calling and insight; cf.

E. K.'s Argument to "October"; "Poetrie [is] a divine gift and heavenly instinct not to bee gotten by laboure and learning, but adorned with both: and poured into the witte by a certaine ενθουσιασμὸς and celestiall inspiration."
2. The New Jerusalem, whose "light was like unto a stone most precious, even like a jasper stone, clear as crystal; . . . and the twelve gates were twelve pearls; every several gate was of one pearl: and the street of the city was pure gold, as it were transparent glass" (Revelation xxi. 11, 21).

Too high a ditty° for my simple song;   *theme*
  The Citie of the great king hight it well,
Wherein eternall peace and happinesse doth dwell.

56

As he thereon stood gazing, he might see
  The blessed Angels to and fro descend
  From highest heaven, in gladsome companee,
  And with great joy into that Citie wend,
  As commonly° as friend does with his frend.   *sociably*
  Whereat he wondred much, and gan enquere,
  What stately building durst so high extend
  Her loftie towres unto the starry sphere,
And what unknowen nation there empeopled° were.   *settled*

57

"Faire knight," quoth he, "Hierusalem that is,
  The new Hierusalem, that God has built
  For those to dwell in, that are chosen his,
  His chosen people purged from sinfull guilt,
  With pretious bloud, which cruelly was spilt
  On curséd tree, of that unspotted lam,
  That for the sinnes of all the world was kilt:[3]
  Now are they Saints all in that Citie sam,°   *together*
More deare unto their God, then younglings to their dam."

58

"Till now," said then the knight, "I weenéd well,
  That great Cleopolis,[4] where I have beene,
  In which that fairest Faerie Queene doth dwell,
  The fairest Citie was, that might be seene;
  And that bright towre all built of christall cleene,°   *pure*
  Panthea,[5] seemd the brightest thing, that was:
  But now by proofe all otherwise I weene;
  For this great Citie that does far surpas,
And this bright Angels towre quite dims that towre of glas."

59

"Most trew," then said the holy aged man;
  "Yet is Cleopolis for earthly frame,°   *structure*
  The fairest peece, that eye beholdén can:
  And well beseemes all knights of noble name,
  That covet in th'immortall booke of fame
  To be eternizéd, that same to haunt,°   *frequent*
  And doen their service to that soveraigne Dame,
  That glorie does to them for guerdon° graunt: *reward*
For she is heavenly borne, and heaven may justly vaunt.[6]

3. "Behold the Lamb of God, which taketh away the sin of the world" (John i: 29).
4. The city of earthly glory; at once an ideal counterpart of Elizabeth's London and a symbolic image of the highest attainment within the reach of fallen man, unaided by direct divine intervention.
5. The ideal counterpart of either Westminister Abbey or one of Elizabeth's residences near London.
6. I.e., she may justly boast of her heavenly descent.

60

"And thou faire ymp, sprong out from English race,
  How ever now accompted° Elfins sonne, *accounted*
  Well worthy doest thy service for her grace,° *favor*
  To aide a virgin desolate foredonne.
  But when thou famous victorie hast wonne,
  And high emongst all knights hast hong thy shield,
  Thenceforth the suit° of earthly conquest shonne, *pursuit*
  And wash thy hands from guilt of bloudy field:
For bloud can nought but sin, and wars but sorrowes yield.

61

"Then seeke this path, that I to thee presage,° *point out*
  Which after all to heaven shall thee send;
  Then peaceably thy painefull pilgrimage
  To yonder same Hierusalem do bend,
  Where is for thee ordaind a blessed end:
  For thou emongst those Saints, whom thou doest see,
  Shalt be a Saint, and thine owne nations frend
  And Patrone: thou Saint George shalt callèd bee,
Saint George of mery England, the signe of victoree."[7]

62

"Unworthy wretch," quoth he, "of so great grace,
  How dare I thinke such glory to attaine?"
  "These that have it attaind, were in like cace,"
  Quoth he, "as wretched, and lived in like paine."
  "But deeds of armes must I at last be faine,° *willing*
  And Ladies love to leave so dearely bought?"
  "What need of armes, where peace doth ay remaine,"
  Said he, "and battailes none are to be fought?
As for loose loves are° vaine, and vanish into nought." *they are*

63

"O let me not," quoth he, "then turne againe
  Backe to the world, whose joyes so fruitlesse are;
  But let me here for aye in peace remaine,
  Or streight way on that last long voyage fare,
  That nothing may my present hope empare."° *impair*
  "That may not be," said he, "ne maist thou yit
  Forgo that royall maides bequeathèd care,° *charge*
  Who did her cause into thy hand commit,
Till from her cursèd foe thou have her freely quit."° *released*

64

"Then shall I soone," quoth he, "so God me grace,
  Abet° that virgins cause disconsolate, *maintain*

---

7. Although Aelfric's 9th-century *Lives of the Saints* includes a life of St. George, Spenser's conception of this figure, the patron saint of England, draws upon a literary tradition stemming from the *Legenda Aurea* (translated by Caxton in 1487), an allied pictorial tradition widely represented in painting and tapestry, and (with special reference to the birth of St. George) some hints in medieval folklore of the mysterious circumstances attending the infancy and youth of those mortals singled out by Providence for a glorious destiny.

And shortly backe returne unto this place,
To walke this way in Pilgrims poore estate.
But now aread, old father, why of late
Didst thou behight° me borne of English blood,   *call*
Whom all a Faeries sonne doen nominate?"°   *name, consider*
"That word shall I," said he, "avouchen° good,   *prove*
Sith to thee is unknowne the cradle of thy brood.

65

"For well I wote, thou springst from ancient race
Of Saxon kings, that have with mightie hand
And many bloudie battailes fought in place
High reard their royall throne in Britane land,
And vanquisht them, unable to withstand:
From thence a Faerie thee unweeting reft,°   *stole away*
There as thou slepst in tender swadling band,
And her base Elfin brood there for thee left.
Such men do Chaungelings call, so chaungd by Faeries theft.

66

"Thence she thee brought into this Faerie lond,
And in an heapéd furrow did thee hyde,
Where thee a Ploughman all unweeting fond,
As he his toylesome teme that way did guyde,
And brought thee up in ploughmans state to byde,°   *remain*
Whereof Georgos he thee gave to name;[8]
Till prickt with courage, and thy forces pryde,
To Faery court thou cam'st to seeke for fame,
And prove thy puissaunt armes, as seemes thee best became."°
    suited

67

"O holy Sire," quoth he, "how shall I quight°   *repay*
The many favours I with thee have found,
That hast my name and nation red° aright,   *told*
And taught the way that does to heaven bound?"°   *go*
This said, adowne he lookéd to the ground,
To have returnd, but dazéd were his eyne,
Through passing° brightnesse, which did quite confound
    surpassing
His feeble sence, and too exceeding shyne.
So darke are earthly things compard to things divine.

68

At last whenas himselfe he gan to find,°   *recover*
To Una back he cast him to retire;
Who him awaited still with pensive mind.
Great thankes and goodly meed° to that good syre,   *reward*
He thence departing gave for his paines hyre.[9]

8. Ovid describes the discovery, by an Etrurian ploughman, of Tages, son of the earth; Tages was destined to instruct his nation in the art of prophecy (*Metamorphoses*, XV. 558–559).

9. I.e., as recompense for his trouble.

So came to Una, who him joyed to see,
And after litle rest, gan him desire,
Of her adventure mindfull for to bee.
So leave they take of Caelia, and her daughters three.

Canto XI

*The knight with that old Dragon fights
two dayes incessantly:
The third him overthrowes, and gayns
most glorious victory.*[1]

1

High time now gan it wex° for Una faire,   *become*
    To thinke of those her captive Parents deare,
    And their forwasted kingdome to repaire:[2]
    Whereto whenas they now approchéd neare,
    With hartie words her knight she gan to cheare,
    And in her modest manner thus bespake;
    "Deare knight, as deare, as ever knight was deare,
    That all these sorrowes suffer for my sake,
High heaven behold the tedious toyle, ye for me take.

2

"Now are we come unto my native soyle,
    And to the place, where all our perils dwell;
    Here haunts that feend, and does his dayly spoyle,
    Therefore henceforth be at your keeping[3] well,
    And ever ready for your foeman fell.
    The sparke of noble courage now awake,
    And strive your excellent selfe to excell;
    That shall ye evermore renowméd make,
Above all knights on earth, that batteill undertake."

3

And pointing forth, "lo yonder is," said she,
    "The brasen towre in which my parents deare
    For dread of that huge feend emprisond be,
    Whom I from far see on the walles appeare,
    Whose sight my feeble soule doth greatly cheare:
    And on the top of all I do espye
    The watchman wayting tydings glad to heare,
    That O my parents might I happily
Unto you bring, to ease you of your misery."

4

With that they heard a roaring hideous sound,
    That all the ayre with terrour filléd wide,
    And seemd uneath° to shake the stedfast ground.   *almost*
    Eftsoones that dreadfull Dragon they espide,

1. For an extended account of the struc-
ture and allegory of Redcrosse's fight
with the dragon, cf. the essay by Carol
V. Kaske in *SP*, LXVI (1969), 609–638.

2. I.e., to restore to health their king-
dom, laid waste by "that old Dragon."
3. I.e., on your guard.

Where stretcht he lay upon the sunny side
Of a great hill, himselfe like a great hill.
But all so soone, as he from far descride
Those glistring armes, that heaven with light did fill,
He rousd himselfe full blith,° and hastned them untill.°

joyfully/toward

5

Then bad the knight his Lady yede° aloofe,   *go*
And to an hill her selfe with draw aside,
From whence she might behold that battailes proof°   *trial*
And eke be safe from daunger far descryde:
She him obayd, and turnd a little wyde.°   *aside*
Now O thou sacred Muse,[4] most learnéd Dame,
Faire ympe of Phoebus, and his aged bride,
The Nourse of time, and everlasting fame,
That warlike hands ennoblest with immortall name;

6

O gently come into my feeble brest,
Come gently, but not with that mighty rage,
Wherewith the martiall troupes thou doest infest,° *arouse, inspire*
And harts of great Heroës doest enrage,
That nought their kindled courage may aswage,
Soone as thy dreadfull trompe begins to sownd;
The God of warre with his fiers equipage°   *equipment*
Thou doest awake, sleepe never he so sownd,
And scaréd nations doest with horrour sterne astownd.° *appall*

7

Faire Goddesse lay that furious fit° aside,   *mood*
Till I of warres and bloudy Mars do sing,[5]
And Briton fields with Sarazin bloud bedyde,
Twixt that great faery Queene and Paynim king,
That with their horrour heaven and earth did ring,
A worke of labour long, and endlesse prayse:
But now a while let downe that haughtie° string, *lofty*
And to my tunes thy second tenor[6] rayse,
That I this man of God his godly armes may blaze.° *proclaim*

8

By this the dreadfull Beast[7] drew nigh to hand,
Halfe flying, and halfe footing in his hast,

---

4. Clio, Muse of history. Diverging from the traditional view that Jove and Memory were parents of the Muses (as in Hesiod, *Theogony*, 53–62), Spenser here follows Natalis Comes in making the Muses daughters of Apollo and Memory (cf. *Mythologiae*, IV. 10).
5. Possibly an allusion to Spenser's intended epic "of politicke vertues in [Arthur's] person, after that hee came to be king"; or the passage may anticipate later portions of *The Faerie Queene*, e.g., Book V.
6. I.e., lower strain; perhaps reflecting

Plato's distinction (in the *Republic*, III. 399) between the Phrygian mode, suited to courageous men in war, and the more restrained Dorian mode, befitting those preparing for battle.
7. Among the various references to such monstrous creatures in classical and medieval literature on which Spenser might have drawn for the description of this dragon (in sts. 8–15), he was most probably influenced by Ovid's detailed account of the "serpent sacred to Mars" which Cadmus overcame (*Metamorphoses*, III. 31–94).

That with his largenesse measuréd much land,
And made wide shadow under his huge wast;°   *girth*
As mountaine doth the valley overcast.
Approching nigh, he rearéd high afore°   *in front*
His body monstrous, horrible, and vast,
  Which to increase his wondrous greatnesse more,
Was swolne with wrath, and poyson, and with bloudy gore.

9

And over, all[8] with brasen scales was armd,
  Like plated coate of steele, so couchéd neare,[9]
  That nought mote perce, ne might his corse be harmd
  With dint of sword, nor push of pointed speare;
  Which as an Eagle, seeing pray appeare,
  His aery plumes doth rouze,° full rudely dight,°   *shake/arrayed*
  So shakéd he, that horrour was to heare,
  For as the clashing of an Armour bright,
Such noyse his rouzéd scales did send unto the knight.

10

His flaggy° wings when forth he did display,   *drooping*
  Were like two sayles, in which the hollow wynd
  Is gathered full, and worketh speedy way:
  And eke the pennes,° that did his pineons bynd,   *feathers, quills*
  Were like mayne-yards, with flying canvas lynd,
  With which whenas him list the ayre to beat,
  And there by force unwonted passage find,
  The cloudes before him fled for terrour great,
And all the heavens stood still amazéd with his threat.

11

His huge long tayle wound up in hundred foldes,
  Does overspred his long bras-scaly backe,
  Whose wreathéd boughts° when ever he unfoldes,   *coils*
  And thicke entangled knots adown does slacke,
  Bespotted as with shields of red and blacke,
  It sweepeth all the land behind him farre,
  And of three furlongs does but litle lacke;
  And at the point two stings in-fixéd arre,
Both deadly sharpe, that sharpest steele exceeden farre.

12

But stings and sharpest steele did far exceed[1]
  The sharpnesse of his cruell rending clawes;
  Dead was it sure, as sure as death in deed,
  What ever thing does touch his ravenous pawes,
  Or what within his reach he ever drawes.
  But his most hideous head my toung to tell
  Does tremble: for his deepe devouring jawes
  Wide gapéd, like the griesly mouth of hell,
Through which into his darke abisse all ravin° fell.[2]   *prey*

8. I.e., over the greater part of his body.
9. I.e., closely set.
1. I.e., were far exceeded by.

2. The stanza emphasizes the profound allegorical significance of this battle, which collects and encompasses all moral and historical interpretations.

13

And that° more wondrous was, in either jaw   *what*
    Three rancks of yron teeth enraungéd were,
    In which yet trickling bloud and gobbets raw
    Of late devouréd bodies did appeare,
    That sight thereof bred cold congealéd feare:
    Which to increase, and all atonce to kill,
    A cloud of smoothering smoke and sulphur seare°   *burning*
    Out of his stinking gorge° forth steeméd still,   *maw*
That all the ayre about with smoke and stench did fill.

14

His blazing eyes, like two bright shining shields,
    Did burne with wrath, and sparkled living fyre;
    As two broad Beacons, set in open fields,
    Send forth their flames farre off to every shyre,
    And warning give, that enemies conspyre,
    With fire and sword the region to invade;
    So flamed his eyne with rage and rancorous yre:
    But farre within, as in a hollow glade,
Those glaring lampes were set, that made a dreadfull shade.

15

So dreadfully he towards him did pas,°   *pace*
    Forelifting up aloft his speckled brest,
    And often bounding on the bruséd gras,
    As for great joyance of his newcome guest.
    Eftsoones he gan advance his haughtie crest,
    As ch',ufféd° Bore his bristles doth upreare,   *angry*
    And shoke his scales to battell readie drest;
    That made the Redcrosse knight nigh quake for feare,
As bidding bold defiance to his foeman neare.[3]

16

The knight gan fairely couch° his steadie speare,   *rest, aim*
    And fiercely ran at him with rigorous might:
    The pointed steele arriving rudely theare,
    His harder° hide would neither perce, nor bight,   *too hard*
    But glauncing by forth passéd forward right;
    Yet sore amovéd with so puissant push,
    The wrathfull beast about him turnéd light,°   *quickly*
    And him so rudely passing by, did brush
With his long tayle, that horse and man to ground did rush.

17

Both horse and man up lightly rose againe,
    And fresh encounter towards him addrest:
    But th'idle stroke yet backe recoyld in vaine,

The triumph of Redcrosse recalls and "re-creates" Christ's victory over sin; in another and lesser sense, it represents the triumph of Protestantism in England. But the contestants in this encounter are nothing less than Life and Death (cf. st. 49, 1–3); Redcrosse, then, becomes "man as Christ's Knight fighting evil pure" (Tuve, *op. cit.,* p. 107).
3. I.e., the dragon shook his scales as a sign of defiance.

And found no place his deadly point to rest.
Exceeding rage enflamed the furious beast,
To be avengéd of so great despight;°   *outrage*
For never felt his imperceable brest
So wondrous force, from hand of living wight;
Yet had he proved° the powre of many a puissant knight.   *tested*

18

Then with his waving wings displayéd wyde,
  Himselfe up high he lifted from the ground,
  And with strong flight did forcibly divide
  The yielding aire, which nigh too feeble found
  Her flitting partes, and element unsound,°   *weak*
  To beare so great a weight: he cutting way
  With his broad sayles, about him soaréd round:
  At last low stouping with unweldie sway,[4]
Snatcht up both horse and man, to beare them quite away.

19

Long he them bore above the subject plaine,[5]
  So farre as Ewghen° bow a shaft may send,   *yew*
  Till struggling strong did him at last constraine,
  To let them downe before his flightés end:
  As hagard° hauke presuming to contend   *wild*
  With hardie fowle, above his hable° might,   *powerful*
  His wearie pounces° all in vaine doth spend,   *talons*
  To trusse° the pray too heavie for his flight;   *seize*
Which comming downe to ground, does free it selfe by fight.

20

He so disseizéd of his gryping grosse,[6]
  The knight his thrillant° speare againe assayd   *piercing*
  In his bras-plated body to embosse,°   *plunge*
  And three mens strength unto the stroke he layd;
  Wherewith the stiffe beame quakéd, as affrayd,
  And glauncing from his scaly necke, did glyde
  Close under his left wing, then broad displayd.
  The percing steele there wrought a wound full wyde,
That with the uncouth smart the Monster lowdly cryde.

21

He cryde, as raging seas are wont to rore,
  When wintry storme his wrathfull wreck does threat,
  The rolling billowes beat the ragged shore,
  As they the earth would shoulder from her seat,
  And greedie gulfe does gape, as he would eat
  His neighbour element in his revenge:
  Then gin the blustring brethren[7] boldly threat,
  To move the world from off his stedfast henge,°   *axis*
And boystrous battell make, each other to avenge.

4. I.e., ponderous force.   6. I.e., heavy gripful.
5. I.e., the plain below.   7. I.e., the winds.

22

The steely head stucke fast still in his flesh,
   Till with his cruell clawes he snatcht the wood,
   And quite a sunder broke. Forth flowéd fresh
   A gushing river of blacke goarie blood,
   That drownéd all the land, whereon he stood;
   The streame thereof would drive a water-mill.
   Trebly augmented was his furious mood
   With bitter sense° of his deepe rooted ill,   *feeling*
That flames of fire he threw forth from his large nosethrill.

23

His hideous tayle then hurléd he about,
   And therewith all enwrapt the nimble thyes
   Of his froth-fomy steed, whose courage stout
   Striving to loose the knot, that fast him tyes,
   Himselfe in streighter bandes too rash implyes,[8]
   That to the ground he is perforce constraynd
   To throw his rider: who can° quickly ryse   *did*
   From off the earth, with durty bloud distaynd,°   *stained*
For that reprochfull fall right fowly he disdaynd.

24

And fiercely tooke his trenchand° blade in hand,   *sharp*
   With which he stroke so furious and so fell,
   That nothing seemd the puissance could withstand:
   Upon his crest the hardned yron fell,
   But his more hardned crest was armd so well,
   That deeper dint therein it would not make;
   Yet so extremely did the buffe him quell,°   *dismay*
   That from thenceforth he shund the like to take,
But when he saw them come, he did them still forsake.°   *avoid*

25

The knight was wrath to see his stroke beguyld,°   *foiled*
   And smote againe with more outrageous might;
   But backe againe the sparckling steele recoyld,
   And left not any marke, where it did light;
   As if in Adamant rocke it had bene pight.°   *struck*
   The beast impatient of his smarting wound,
   And of so fierce and forcible despight,°   *injury*
   Thought with his wings to stye° above the ground;   *rise*
But his late wounded wing unserviceable found.

26

Then full of griefe and anguish vehement,
   He lowdly brayd, that like was never heard,
   And from his wide devouring oven sent
   A flake° of fire, that flashing in his beard,   *flash*
   Him all amazd, and almost made affeard:
   The scorching flame sore swingéd° all his face,   *singed*
   And through his armour all his bodie seard,

8. I.e., too quickly entangles.

That he could not endure so cruell cace,
But thought his armes to leave, and helmet to unlace.

27

Not that great Champion of the antique world,[9]
 Whom famous Poetes verse so much doth vaunt,
 And hath for twelve huge labours high extold,
 So many furies and sharpe fits did haunt,
 When him the poysoned garment did enchaunt
 With Centaures bloud, and bloudie verses charmed,
 As did this knight twelve thousand dolours° daunt,   *sufferings*
 Whom fyrie steele now burnt, that earst° him armed,   *before*
That erst him goodly armed, now most of all him harmed.

28

Faint, wearie, sore, emboyléd, grievéd, brent°   *burned*
 With heat, toyle, wounds, armes, smart, and inward fire
 That never man such mischiefes did torment;
 Death better were, death did he oft desire,
 But death will never come, when needes require.
 Whom so dismayd when that his foe beheld,
 He cast to suffer him no more respire,°   *rest, take breath*
 But gan his sturdie sterne° about to weld,°   *tail/lash*
And him so strongly stroke, that to the ground him feld.

29

It fortunéd (as faire it then befell)
 Behind his backe unweeting,° where he stood,   *unnoticed*
 Of auncient time there was a springing well,
 From which fast trickled forth a silver flood,
 Full of great vertues, and for med'cine good.
 Whylome,° before that curséd Dragon got   *formerly*
 That happie land, and all with innocent blood
 Defyld those sacred waves, it rightly hot°   *was called*
The Well of Life,[1] ne yet his° vertues had forgot.   *its*

30

For unto life the dead it could restore,
 And guilt of sinfull crimes cleane wash away,
 Those that with sicknesse were infected sore,
 It could recure, and aged long decay
 Renew, as one were borne that very day.
 Both Silo[2] this, and Jordan did excell,

9. Hercules, who suffered terrible agony when he put on Nessus's robe, soaked in poisoned blood; and who, by the will of Jove, at last put off mortality and took his place in the stars (cf. *Metamorphoses*, IX. 134–270).

1. "And he shewed me a pure river of water of life, clear as crystal, proceeding out of the throne of God and of the Lamb. In the midst of the street of it, and on either side of the river, was there the tree of life, which bare twelve manner of fruits, and yielded her fruit every month; and the leaves of the tree were for the healing of the nations" (Revelation xxii. 1–2). Well and tree, narrowly interpreted, signify the sacraments of baptism and communion; in a larger sense, both symbolize the power of grace to free from sin and to renew man's strength in the spiritual conflict.

2. All these waters were known, either in scripture ("the pool of Siloam" in John ix. 7; the cleansing powers of Jordan, in II Kings v. 10–14), or in classical accounts (the river Cephissus, in Pliny, *Historia Naturalis*, II. cvi.

And th'English Bath, and eke the german Spau,
Ne can Cephise, nor Hebrus match this well:
Into the same the knight backe overthrowen, fell.

31

Now gan the golden Phoebus for to steepe
  His fierie face in billowes of the west,
  And his faint steedes watred in Ocean deepe,
  Whiles from their journall° labours they did rest,   *daily*
  When that infernall Monster, having kest°   *cast*
  His wearie foe into that living well,
  Can° high advance his broad discoloured brest,   *did*
  Above his wonted pitch,° with countenance fell,   *height*
And clapt his yron wings, as victor he did dwell.°   *remain*

32

Which when his pensive Ladie saw from farre,
  Great woe and sorrow did her soule assay,°   *assail*
  As weening that the sad end of the warre,
  And gan to highest God entirely° pray,   *earnestly*
  That feared chance from her to turne away;
  With folded hands and knees full lowly bent
  All night she watcht, ne once adowne would lay
  Her daintie limbs in her sad dreriment,
But praying still did wake, and waking did lament.

33

The morrow next gan early to appeare,
  That° Titan[3] rose to runne his daily race;   *when*
  But early ere the morrow next gan reare
  Out of the sea faire Titans deawy face,
  Up rose the gentle virgin from her place,
  And looked all about, if she might spy
  Her loved knight to move his manly pace:[4]
  For she had great doubt of his safety,
Since late she saw him fall before his enemy.

34

At last she saw, where he upstarted brave
  Out of the well, wherein he drenched lay;
  As Eagle fresh out of the Ocean wave,[5]
  Where he hath left his plumes all hoary gray,
  And deckt himselfe with feathers youthly gay,
  Like Eyas° hauke up mounts unto the skies,   *young*
  His newly budded pineons to assay,

230; the pure Hebrus, in Horace, *Epistles*, I. xvi. 13), or, in the case of Bath and Spa, in the Europe of Spenser's day, for their creative power or their purity.
3. The sun.
4. I.e., actively recovering.
5. "When the eagle grows old . . . then he goes in search of a fountain, and . . . he flies up to the height of heaven. . . . Then at length, diving down into the fountain, he dips himself three times in it, and instantly he is renewed with a great vigour of plumage and splendor of vision. Do the same thing, O man. . . . Seek for the spiritual fountain of the Lord and . . . then your youth will be renewed like the eagle's" (*The Bestiary, A Book of Beasts, ed. cit.,* 105–107.

And marveiles at himselfe, still as he flies:
So new this new-borne knight to battell new did rise.

35

Whom when the damnéd feend so fresh did spy,
 No wonder if he wondred at the sight,
 And doubted, whether his late enemy
 It were, or other new suppliéd knight.
 He, now to prove his late renewéd might,
 High brandishing his bright deaw-burning⁶ blade,
 Upon his crested scalpe so sore did smite,
 That to the scull a yawning wound it made:
The deadly dint his dulléd senses all dismaid.

36

I wote not, whether the revenging steele
 Were hardned with that holy water dew,
 Wherein he fell, or sharper edge did feele,
 Or his baptizéd hands now greater° grew;   *stronger*
 Or other secret vertue did ensew;
 Else never could the force of fleshly arme,
 Ne molten mettall in his bloud embrew:°   *plunge*
 For till that stownd° could never wight him harme, *moment*
By subtilty, nor slight,° nor might, nor mighty charme. *trickery*

37

The cruell wound enragéd him so sore,
 That loud he yelded° for exceeding paine;   *shrieked*
 As hundred ramping Lyons seemed to rore,
 Whom ravenous hunger did thereto constraine:
 Then gan he tosse aloft his stretchéd traine,
 And therewith scourge the buxome° aire so sore, *unresisting*
 That to his force to yeelden it was faine;°   *forced*
 Ne ought° his sturdie strokes might stand afore, *anything*
That high trees overthrew, and rocks in peeces tore.

38

The same advauncing high above his head,
 With sharpe intended° sting so rude him smot, *extended*
 That to the earth him drove, as stricken dead,
 Ne living wight would have him life behot:⁷
 The mortall sting his angry needle shot
 Quite through his shield, and in his shoulder seasd,
 Where fast it stucke, ne would there out be got:
 The griefe thereof him wondrous sore diseasd,° *troubled*
Ne might his ranckling paine with patience be appeasd.

39

But yet more mindfull of his honour deare,
 Then of the grievous smart, which him did wring,° *torment*
 From loathéd soile he can° him lightly reare, *did*
 And strove to loose the farre infixéd sting:
 Which when in vaine he tryde with struggeling,

6. I.e., gleaming with "that holy water 7. I.e., thought him alive.
dew" (st. 36).

Inflamed with wrath, his raging blade he heft,°   *raised*
And strooke so strongly, that the knotty string
    Of his huge taile he quite a sunder cleft,
Five joynts thereof he hewd, and but the stump him left.

40

Hart cannot thinke, what outrage, and what cryes,
    With foule enfouldred° smoake and flashing fire,
                           black as a thundercloud
    The hell-bred beast threw forth unto the skyes,
    That all was coveréd with darknesse dire:
    Then fraught with rancour, and engorgéd° ire,   *choking, congested*
    He cast at once him to avenge for all,
    And gathering up himselfe out of the mire,
    With his uneven wings did fiercely fall
Upon his sunne-bright shield, and gript it fast withall.

41

Much was the man encombred with his hold,
    In feare to lose his weapon in his paw,
    Ne wist yet, how his talants° to unfold;   *talons*
    Nor harder was from Cerberus[8] greedie jaw
    To plucke a bone, then from his cruell claw
    To reave° by strength the gripéd gage° away: *seize/prize*
    Thrise he assayd it from his foot to draw,
    And thrise in vaine to draw it did assay,
It booted nought to thinke, to robbe him of his pray.

42

Tho° when he saw no power might prevaile,   *then*
    His trustie sword he cald to his last aid,
    Wherewith he fiercely did his foe assaile,
    And double blowes about him stoutly laid,
    That glauncing fire out of the yron plaid;
    As sparckles from the Andvile° use to fly,   *anvil*
    When heavie hammers on the wedge are swaid;°   *struck*
    Therewith at last he forst him to unty°   *loosen*
One of his grasping feete, him to defend thereby.

43

The other foot, fast fixéd on his shield,
    Whenas no strength, nor stroks mote him constraine
    To loose, ne yet the warlike pledge to yield,
    He smot thereat with all his might and maine,
    That nought so wondrous puissance might sustaine;
    Upon the joynt the lucky steele did light,
    And made such way, that hewd it quite in twaine;
    The paw yet misséd not his minisht° might,   *lessened*
But hong still on the shield, as it at first was pight.°   *placed*

44

For griefe thereof, and divelish despight,
    From his infernall fournace forth he threw

8. Cf. I. v. 34 and note.

Huge flames, that dimméd all the heavens light,
Enrold in duskish smoke and brimstone blew;
As burning Aetna from his boyling stew°   *cauldron*
Doth belch out flames, and rockes in peeces broke,
And ragged ribs of mountaines molten new,
Enwrapt in coleblacke clouds and filthy smoke,
That all the land with stench, and heaven with horror choke.

45

The heate whereof, and harmefull pestilence
So sore him noyd,° that forst him to retire   *troubed*
A little backward for his best defence,
To save his bodie from the scorching fire,
Which he from hellish entrailes did expire.°   *breathe out*
It chaunst (eternall God that chaunce did guide)
As he recoyléd backward, in the mire
His nigh forwearied feeble feet did slide,
And downe he fell, with dread of shame sore terrifide.

46

There grew a goodly tree him faire beside,
Loaden with fruit and apples rosie red,
As they in pure vermilion had beene dide,
Whereof great vertues over all[9] were red°:   *known*
For happie life to all, which thereon fed,
And life eke everlasting did befall:
Great God it planted in that blessed sted°   *place*
With his almightie hand, and did it call
The Tree of Life, the crime of our first fathers fall.[1]

47

In all the world like was not to be found,
Save in that soile, where all good things did grow,
And freely sprong out of the fruitfull ground,
As incorrupted° Nature did them sow,   *untainted*
Till that dread Dragon all did overthrow.
Another like faire tree[2] eke grew thereby,
Whereof who so did eat, eftsoones did know
Both good and ill: O mornefull memory:
That tree through one mans fault hath doen us all to dy.

48

From that first tree forth flowd, as from a well,
A trickling streame of Balme[3], most soveraine
And daintie deare,[4] which on the ground still fell,
And overflowéd all the fertill plaine,

9. I.e., everywhere.
1. Adam was expelled from Paradise "lest he put forth his hand, and take also of the tree of life, and eat, and live for ever" (Genesis iii. 22); his "crime" is the responsibility for the consequent denial of this tree (which is mentioned again in Revelation xxii. 2) to his posterity, all mankind.
2. The tree of the knowledge of good and evil.

3. The sacrament of communion; more generally, the power of grace to heal and renew exhausted man. According to the Gospel of Nicodemus (*op. cit.*, 127–8), Seth restored his father Adam to health by the use of an "oil" flowing from "the tree of mercy"; so Christ's blood, in the fullness of time, would redeem mankind.
4. I.e., choicely precious.

As it had deawéd bene with timely° raine: *seasonable*
Life and long health that gratious° ointment gave,   *full of grace*
And deadly woundes could heale, and reare againe
The senselesse corse appointed° for the grave.   *made ready*
Into that same he fell: which did from death him save.

49

For nigh thereto the ever damnéd beast
  Durst not approch, for he was deadly made,[5]
  And all that life preservéd, did detest:
  Yet he it oft adventured° to invade.   *endeavored*
  By this the drouping day-light gan to fade,
  And yeeld his roome to sad succeeding night,
  Who with her sable mantle gan to shade
  The face of earth, and wayes of living wight,
And high her burning torch set up in heaven bright.

50

When gentle Una saw the second fall
  Of her deare knight, who wearie of long fight,
  And faint through losse of bloud, moved not at all,
  But lay as in a dreame of deepe delight,
  Besmeard with pretious Balme, whose vertuous° might   *efficacious*
  Did heale his wounds, and scorching heat alay,
  Againe she stricken was with sore affright,
  And for his safetie gan devoutly pray;
And watch the noyous° night, and wait for joyous day.   *harmful*

51

The joyous day gan early to appeare,
  And faire Aurora from the deawy bed
  Of aged Tithone gan her selfe to reare,
  With rosie cheekes, for shame as blushing red;
  Her golden lockes for haste were loosely shed
  About her eares, when Una her did marke
  Clymbe to her charet, all with flowers spred,
  From heaven high to chase the chearelesse darke;
With merry note her loud salutes the mounting larke.

52

Then freshly up arose the doughtie knight,
  All healéd of his hurts and woundés wide,
  And did himselfe to battell readie dight;
  Whose early foe awaiting him beside
  To have devourd, so soone as day he spyde,
  When now he saw himselfe so freshly reare,
  As if late fight had nought him damnifyde,°   *harmed*
  He woxe dismayd, and gan his fate to feare;
Nathlesse° with wonted rage he him advauncéd neare.   *nevertheless*

53

And in his first encounter, gaping wide,
  He thought attonce him to have swallowd quight,
  And rusht upon him with outragious pride;

5. I.e., death was his being and essence.

Who him r'encountring fierce, as hauke in flight,
Perforce rebutted° backe. The weapon bright   *drove*
Taking advantage of his open jaw,
Ran through his mouth with so importune° might,   *violent*
That deepe emperst his darksome hollow maw,
And back retyrd,° life bloud forth with all did draw.   *withdrawn*

54

So downe he fell, and forth his life did breath,
   That vanisht into smoke and cloudés swift;
So downe he fell, that th'earth him underneath
   Did grone, as feeble so great load to lift;
So downe he fell, as an huge rockie clift,
   Whose false° foundation waves have washt away,   *insecure*
With dreadfull poyse° is from the mayneland rift,   *force*
   And rolling downe, great Neptune doth dismay;
So downe he fell, and like an heapéd mountaine lay.[6]

55

The knight himselfe even trembled at his fall,
   So huge and horrible a masse it seemed;
And his deare Ladie, that beheld it all,
   Durst not approch for dread, which she misdeemed,°   *misjudged*
But yet at last, when as the direfull feend
   She saw not stirre, off-shaking vaine affright,
She nigher drew, and saw that joyous end:
   Then God she praysd, and thankt her faithfull knight,
That had atchieved so great a conquest by his[7] might.

Canto XII

Faire Una to the Redcrosse knight
betrouthéd is with joy:
Though false Duessa it to barre
her false sleights doe imploy.

1

Behold I see the haven nigh at hand,
   To which I meane my wearie course to bend;
Vere° the maine shete, and beare up with[1] the land,   *shift*
   The which afore is fairely to be kend,°   *seen*
And seemeth safe from stormes, that may offend;
   There this faire virgin wearie of her way
Must landed be, now at her journeyes end:
   There eke my feeble barke° a while may stay,   *ship*
'Till merry wind and weather call her thence away.[2]

6. That the imagery of fire and flame (dominant in earlier references to the dragon) is conspicuously absent from this stanza emphasizes the heroic character of the knight's victory.
7. I.e., God's might, exerted through Redcrosse; cf. II. i. 33.
1. Steer toward.

2. The nautical metaphor with which Spenser opens and concludes this Canto (and which recurs at the end of Book II) is a traditional introductory device; widely employed by classical authors, it appears also in Dante's *Paradiso*, II. 1–15, and in Chaucer's *Troilus and Criseyde*, II. 1–7.

2

Scarsely had Phoebus in the glooming East
 Yet harnesséd his firie-footed teeme,
 Ne reard above the earth his flaming creast,
 When the last deadly smoke aloft did steeme,
 That signe of last outbreathéd life did seeme
 Unto the watchman on the castle wall;
 Who thereby dead that balefull Beast did deeme,
 And to his Lord and Ladie lowd gan call,
To tell, how he had seene the Dragons fatall fall.

3

Uprose with hastie joy, and feeble speed
 That aged Sire, the Lord of all that land,
 And lookéd forth, to weet, if true indeede
 Those tydings were, as he did understand,
 Which whenas true by tryall he out fond,°   *found*
 He bad to open wyde his brazen gate,
 Which long time had bene shut, and out of hond[3]
 Proclayméd joy and peace through all his state;
For dead now was their foe, which them forrayéd° late. *ravaged*

4

Then gan triumphant Trompets sound on hie,
 That sent to heaven the ecchoéd report
 Of their new joy, and happie victorie
 Gainst him, that had them long opprest with tort,°   *wrong*
 And fast imprisonéd in siegéd fort.
 Then all the people, as in solemne feast,
 To him assembled with one full consort,°   *company*
 Rejoycing at the fall of that great beast,
From whose eternall bondage now they were releast.

5

Forth came that auncient Lord and aged Queene,
 Arayd in antique robes downe to the ground,
 And sad° habiliments right well beseene°; *sober/becoming*
 A noble crew about them waited round
 Of sage and sober Peres, all gravely gownd;
 Whom farre before did march a goodly band
 Of tall young men, all hable armes to sownd,[4]
 But now they laurell braunches bore in hand;
Glad signe of victorie and peace in all their land.

6

Unto that doughtie Conquerour they came,
 And him before themselves prostrating low,
 Their Lord and Patrone loud did him proclame,
 And at his feet their laurell boughes did throw.
 Soone after them all dauncing on a row
 The comely virgins came, with girlands dight,
 As fresh as flowres in medow greene do grow,
 When morning deaw upon their leaves doth light:
And in their hands sweet Timbrels° all upheld on hight. *tambourines*

3. I.e., at once.   4. I.e., clash in battle.

7

And them before, the fry° of children young
   Their wanton° sports and childish mirth did play,
   And to the Maydens sounding tymbrels sung
   In well attunéd notes, a joyous lay,
   And made delightfull musicke all the way,
   Untill they came, where that faire virgin stood;
   As faire Diana in fresh sommers day
   Beholds her Nymphes, enraunged in shadie wood,
Some wrestle, some do run, some bathe in christall flood.

      crowd
      frolicsome

8

So she beheld those maydens meriment
   With chearefull vew; who when to her they came,
   Themselves to ground with gratious humblesse bent,
   And her adored by honorable name,
   Lifting to heaven her everlasting fame:
   Then on her head they set a girland greene,
   And crownéd her twixt earnest and twixt game;°
   Who in her selfe-resemblance well beseene,[5]
Did seeme such, as she was, a goodly maiden Queene.

      jest, joke

9

And after, all the raskall many° ran,
   Heapéd together in rude rablement,°
   To see the face of that victorious man:
   Whom all admiréd, as from heaven sent,
   And gazd upon with gaping wonderment.
   But when they came, where that dead Dragon lay,
   Stretcht on the ground in monstrous large extent,
   The sight with idle° feare did them dismay,
Ne durst approch him nigh, to touch, or once assay.

      multitude
      confusion

      baseless

10

Some feard, and fled; some feard and well it faynd;°
   One that would wiser seeme, then all the rest,
   Warnd him not touch, for yet perhaps remaynd
   Some lingring life within his hollow brest,
   Or in his wombe might lurke some hidden nest
   Of many Dragonets, his fruitfull seed;
   Another said, that in his eyes did rest
   Yet sparckling fire, and bad thereof take heed;
Another said, he saw him move his eyes indeed.

      concealed

11

One mother, when as her foolehardie chyld
   Did come too neare, and with his talants play,
   Halfe dead through feare, her litle babe revyld,°
   And to her gossips° gan in counsell say;
   "How can I tell, but that his talants may
   Yet scratch my sonne, or rend his tender hand?"
   So diversly themeslves in vaine they fray;

      rebuked
      women friends

      frighten

5. I.e., attractively resembling her real self.

Whiles some more bold, to measure him nigh stand,
To prove° how many acres he did spread of land.   *determine*

12

Thus flockéd all the folke him round about,
  The whiles that hoarie° king, with all his traine,   *grey-haired*
  Being arrivéd, where that champion stout
  After his foes defeasance° did remaine,   *defeat*
  Him goodly greetes, and faire does entertaine,
  With princely gifts of yvorie and gold,
  And thousand thankes him yeelds for all his paine.
  Then when his daughter deare he does behold,
Her dearely doth imbrace, and kisseth manifold.°   *many times*

13

And after to his Pallace he them brings,
  With shaumes,° and trompets, and with Clarions sweet;   *oboes*
  And all the way the joyous people sings,
  And with their garments strowes the pavéd street:
  Whence mounting up, they find purveyance° meet   *provision*
  Of all, that royall Princes court became,°   *suited*
  And all the floore was underneath their feet
  Bespred with costly scarlot of great name,°   *quality*
On which they lowly sit, and fitting purpose° frame.   *discourse*

14

What needs me tell their feast and goodly guize,°   *behavior*
  In which was nothing riotous nor vaine?
  What needs of daintie dishes to devize,°   *talk*
  Of comely services, or courtly trayne?°   *assembly*
  My narrow leaves cannot in them containe
  The large discourse of royall Princes state.
  Yet was their manner then but bare and plaine:
  For th'antique world excesse and pride did hate;
Such proud luxurious pompe is swollen up but late.

15

Then when with meates and drinkes of every kinde
  Their fervent appetites they quenchéd had,
  That aunciént Lord gan fit occasion finde,
  Of straunge adventures, and of perils sad,
  Which in his travell him befallen had,
  For to demaund of his renowméd guest:
  Who then with utt'rance grave, and count'nance sad,
  From point to point, as is before exprest,
Discourst his voyage long, according his request.

16

Great pleasure mixt with pittifull° regard,   *sympathetic*
  That godly King and Queene did passionate,°   *express with feeling*
  Whiles they his pittifull adventures heard,
  That oft they did lament his lucklesse state,
  And often blame the too importune° fate,   *severe*
  That heapd on him so many wrathfull wreakes:°   *injuries*

For never gentle knight, as he of late,
So tosséd was in fortunes cruell freakes;
And all the while salt teares bedeawd the hearers cheaks.

17

Then said that royall Pere in sober wise;°   *manner*
  "Deare Sonne, great beene the evils, which ye bore
  From first to last in your late enterprise,
    That I note,° whether prayse, or pitty more: *know not*
  For never living man, I weene, so sore
  In sea of deadly daungers was distrest;
    But since now safe ye seiséd° have the shore,   *attained*
  And well arrivéd are, (high God be blest)
Let us devize of ease and everlasting rest."

18

"Ah dearest Lord," said then that doughty knight,
  "Of ease or rest I may not yet devize;
  For by the faith, which I to armes have plight,
    I bounden am streight after this emprize,°   *enterprise*
  As that your daughter can ye well advize,
  Backe to returne to that great Faerie Queene,
    And her to serve six yeares in warlike wize,
    Gainst that proud Paynim king, that workes her teene:°   *affliction*
Therefore I ought crave pardon, till I there have beene."[6]

19

"Unhappie falles that hard necessitie,"
  Quoth he, "the troubler of my happie peace,
  And vowéd foe of my felicitie;
    Ne I against the same can justly preace:°   *contend*
    But since that band° ye cannot now release,   *bond*
  Nor doen undo; (for vowes may not be vaine)
  Soone as the terme of those six yeares shall cease,
  Ye then shall hither backe returne againe,
The marriage to accomplish vowd betwixt you twain.

20

"Which for my part I covet to performe,
  In sort° as through the world I did proclame,   *manner*
  That who so kild that monster most deforme,
  And him in hardy battaile overcame,
    Should have mine onely daughter to his Dame,°   *wife*
  And of my kingdome heire apparaunt bee:
    Therefore since now to thee perteines° the same,   *belongs*
  By dew desert of noble chevalree,
Both daughter and eke kingdome, lo I yield to thee."

21

Then forth he calléd that his daughter faire,
  The fairest Un' his onely daughter deare,

---

6. That the marriage of Redcrosse and Una cannot be made final here and now signifies primarily that the final Christian triumph, the marriage of Christ and the true church, will be achieved only at the end of time, i.e., at the Day of Judgment. Meanwhile, the struggle against evil (and the Roman church) continues.

His onely daughter, and his onely heyre;
  Who forth proceeding with sad sober cheare,°   *countenance*
  As bright as doth the morning starre appeare
  Out of the East, with flaming lockes bedight,
  To tell that dawning day is drawing neare,
  And to the world does bring long wishéd light;
So faire and fresh that Lady shewd her selfe in sight.

22

So faire and fresh, as freshest flowre in May;
  For she had layd her mournefull stole aside,
  And widow-like sad wimple° throwne away,   *veil*
  Wherewith her heavenly beautie she did hide,
  Whiles on her wearie journey she did ride;
  And on her now a garment she did weare,
  All lilly white, withoutten spot, or pride,°   *ornament*
  That seemd like silke and silver woven neare,°   *closely*
But neither silke nor silver therein did appeare.[7]

23

The blazing brightnesse of her beauties beame,
  And glorious light of her sunshyny face
  To tell, were as to strive against the streame.
  My ragged rimes are all too rude and bace,
  Her heavenly lineaments for to enchace.°   *be a setting*
  Ne wonder; for her owne deare lovéd knight,
  All° were she dayly with himselfe in place,   *although*
  Did wonder much at her celestiall sight:
Oft had he seene her faire, but never so faire dight.°   *adorned*

24

So fairely dight, when she in presence came,
  She to her Sire made humble reverence,
  And bowéd low, that her right well became,
  And added grace unto her excellence:
  Who with great wisedome, and grave eloquence
  Thus gan to say. But eare he thus had said,
  With flying speede, and seeming great pretence,°   *pretension*
  Came running in, much like a man dismaid,
A Messenger with letters, which his message said.

25

All in the open hall amazéd stood,
  At suddeinnesse of that unwarie° sight,   *unexpected*
  And wondred at his breathlesse hastie mood.
  But he for nought would stay his passage right,°   *direct*
  Till fast° before the king he did alight;   *close*
  Where falling flat, great humblesse he did make,
  And kist the ground, whereon his foot was pight;°   *placed*

7. Una's appearance, presumably reflecting the victory of English Protestantism, certainly signifies the mystical union of Christ and the church: "the marriage of the Lamb is come, and his wife hath made herself ready. And to her was granted that she should be arrayed in fine linen, clean and white: for the fine linen is the righteousness of saints" (Revelation xix. 7–8). Cf. also Revelation xxi. 2, 11; and The Song of Solomon iv. 7: "Thou art all fair, my love; there is no spot in thee."

Then to his hands that writ° he did betake,°   *document/deliver*
Which he disclosing,° red thus, as the paper spake.   *unfolding*

26

"To thee, most mighty king of Eden faire,
  Her greeting sends in these sad lines addrest,
  The wofull daughter, and forsaken heire
  Of that great Emperour of all the West;
  And bids thee be advizéd for the best,
  Ere thou thy daughter linck in holy band
  Of wedlocke to that new unknowen guest:
For he already plighted his right hand
Unto another love, and to another land.

27

"To me sad mayd, or rather widow sad,
  He was affiauncéd long time before,
  And sacred pledges he both gave, and had,
  False erraunt knight, infamous, and forswore:
  Witnesse the burning Altars, which° he swore,   *by which*
  And guiltie heavens of[8] his bold perjury,
  Which though he hath polluted oft of yore,
Yet I to them for judgement just do fly,
And them conjure° t'avenge this shamefull injury.   *entreat*

28

"Therefore since mine he is, or° free or bond,   *whether*
  Or false or trew, or living or else dead,
  Withhold, O soveraine Prince, your hasty hond
  From knitting league with him, I you aread;°   *advise*
  Ne weene° my right with strength adowne to tread,   *think*
  Through weakenesse of my widowhed, or woe:
  For truth is strong, her rightfull cause to plead,
  And shall find friends, if need requireth soe,
So bids thee well to fare, Thy neither friend, nor foe, Fidessa."

29

When he these bitter byting words had red,
  The tydings straunge did him abashéd make,
  That still he sate long time astonishéd
  As in great muse, ne word to creature spake.
  At last his solemne silence thus he brake,
  With doubtfull eyes fast fixéd on his guest;
  "Redoubted knight, that for mine onely sake
Thy life and honour late adventurest,°   *hazarded*
Let nought be hid from me, that ought to be exprest.

30

"What meane these bloudy vowes, and idle threats,
  Throwne out from womanish impatient mind?
  What heavens? what altars? what enragéd heates
  Here heapéd up with termes of love unkind,°   *unnatural*
  My conscience cleare with guilty bands would bind?

---

8. I.e., heavens tainted by.

High God be witnesse, that I guiltlesse ame.
But if your selfe, Sir knight, ye faultie find,
Or wrappéd be in loves of former Dame,
With crime do not it cover, but disclose the same."

31

To whom the Redcrosse knight this answere sent,
  "My Lord, my King, be nought hereat dismayd,
  Till well ye wote by grave intendiment,°   *consideration*
  What woman, and wherefore doth me upbrayd
  With breach of love, and loyalty betrayd.
  It was in my mishaps, as hitherward
  I lately traveild, that unwares I strayd
  Out of my way, through perils straunge and hard;
That day should faile me, ere I had them all declard.

32

"There did I find, or rather I was found
  Of this false woman, that Fidessa hight,
  Fidessa hight the falsest Dame on ground,
  Most false Duessa, royall richly dight,
  That easie was t' invegle° weaker sight: *deceive*
  Who by her wicked arts, and wylie skill,
  Too false and strong for earthly skill or might,
  Unwares me wrought unto her wicked will,
And to my foe betrayd, when least I fearéd ill."

33

Then steppéd forth the goodly royall Mayd,
  And on the ground her selfe prostrating low,
  With sober countenaunce thus to him sayd;
  "O pardon me, my soveraigne Lord, to show
  The secret treasons, which of late I know
  To have bene wroght by that false sorceresse.
  She onely she it is, that earst did throw
  This gentle knight into so great distresse,
That death him did awaite in dayly wretchednesse.

34

"And now it seemes, that she subornéd hath
  This craftie messenger with letters vaine,
  To worke new woe and improvided scath,[9]
  By breaking of the band betwixt us twaine;
  Wherein she uséd hath the practicke paine[1]
  Of this false footman, clokt with simplenesse,
  Whom if ye please for to discover plaine,
  Ye shall him Archimago find, I ghesse,
The falsest man alive; who tries shall find no lesse."

35

The king was greatly movéd at her speach,
  And all with suddein indignation fraight,°   *filled*
  Bad on that Messenger rude hands to reach.

---

9. I.e., unforeseen harm.   1. I.e., cunning pains.

Eftsoones the Gard, which on his state did wait,
  Attacht° that faitor° false, and bound him strait: *seized/impostor*
Who seeming sorely chaufféd° at his band,   *angered*
As chainéd Beare, whom cruell dogs do bait,
  With idle force did faine them to withstand,
And often semblaunce made to scape out of their hand.

36

But they him layd full low in dungeon deepe,
  And bound him hand and foote with yron chains,
  And with continuall watch did warely keepe;
Who then would thinke, that by his subtile trains
He could escape fowle death or deadly paines?[2]
  Thus when that Princes wrath was pacifide,
  He gan renew the late forbidden banes,°   *banns of marriage*
And to the knight his daughter deare he tyde,
With sacred rites and vowes for ever to abyde.

37

His owne two hands the holy knots did knit,
  That none but death for ever can devide;
  His owne two hands, for such a turne° most fit,   *task*
The housling° fire did kindle and provide,   *sacramental*
And holy water thereon sprinckled wide;[3]
  At which the bushy Teade° a groome did light,   *torch*
  And sacred lampe in secret chamber hide,
Where it should not be quenchéd day nor night,
For feare of evill fates, but burnen ever bright.

38

Then gan they sprinckle all the posts with wine,
  And made great feast to solemnize that day;
  They all perfumde with frankencense divine,
And precious odours fetcht from far away,
That all the house did sweat with great aray:
  And all the while sweete Musicke did apply
  Her curious° skill, the warbling notes to play,   *elaborate, exquisite*
To drive away the dull Melancholy;
The whiles one sung a song of love and jollity.[4]

39

During the which there was an heavenly noise
  Heard sound through all the Pallace pleasantly,
  Like as it had bene many an Angels voice,

2. "And he laid hold on the dragon, that old serpent, which is the devil, and Satan, and bound him a thousand years. And cast him into the bottomless pit, and shut him up, and set a seal upon him, that he should deceive the nations no more, till the thousand years should be fulfilled: and after that he must be loosed a little season" (Revelation xx. 2–3).

3. Marriages in ancient times were solemnized with sacramental fire and water. Plutarch (*Roman Questions,* 1) explains the practice on four counts, of which two may especially have interested Spenser: (a) fire is masculine and active, water feminine and relatively passive; (b) as fire and water are most usefully productive in combination, so the joining of male and female in marriage (here anticipated by the betrothal of Redcrosse and Una) appropriately completes society.

4. Cf. *Epithalamion,* 242–260.

Singing before th'eternall majesty,
In their trinall triplicities on hye;[5]
Yet wist no creature, whence that heavenly sweet°   delight
Proceeded, yet each one felt secretly
Himselfe thereby reft of his sences meet,°   proper
And ravishéd with rare impression in his sprite.

40

Great joy was made that day of young and old,
And solemne feast proclaimd throughout the land,
That their exceeding merth may not be told:
Suffice it heare by signes to understand
The usuall joyes at knitting of loves band.
Thrise happy man the knight himselfe did hold,
Posséssed of his Ladies hart and hand,
And ever, when his eye did her behold,
His heart did seeme to melt in pleasures manifold.

41

Her joyous presence and sweet company
In full content he there did long enjoy,
Ne wicked envie, ne vile gealosy
His deare delights were able to annoy:
Yet swimming in that sea of blisfull joy,
He nought forgot, how he whilome had sworne,
In case he could that monstrous beast destroy,
Unto his Farie Queene backe to returne:
The which he shortly did, and Una left to mourne.

42

Now strike your sailes ye jolly Mariners,
For we be come unto a quiet rode,°   anchorage
Where we must land some of our passengers,
And light this wearie vessell of her lode.
Here she a while may make her safe abode,
Till she repairéd have her tackles spent,°   worn out
And wants supplide. And then againe abroad
On the long voyage whereto she is bent:
Well may she speede and fairely finish her intent.

5. The song is referable to that sung at the marriage of the Lamb (Revelation xix. 6). The "trinall triplicities" are the nine angelic orders, enumerated in Dante's *Paradiso*, XXVIII, and alluded to by Tasso, *Gerusalemme Liberata*, XVIII. 96. Cf. *An Hymne of Heavenly Beautie*, 85–98.

From The Second Booke of The Faerie Queene

Contayning
The Legend of Sir Guyon
or
Of Temperaunce

1

Right well I wote° most mighty Soveraine,   *know*
   That all this famous antique history,
   Of some th'aboundance of an idle braine
   Will judgéd be, and painted forgery,
   Rather then matter of just° memory,   *well-founded*
   Sith none, that breatheth living aire, does know,
   Where is that happy land of Faery,
   Which I so much do vaunt, yet no where show,
But vouch° antiquities, which no body can know.[1]   *affirm*

2

But let that man with better sence advize,°   *consider*
   That of the world least part to us is red:°   *known*
   And dayly how through hardy enterprize,
   Many great Regions are discoveréd,
   Which to late age[2] were never mentionéd.
   Who ever heard of th'Indian Peru?
   Or who in venturous vessell measuréd
   The Amazons huge river now found trew?
Or fruitfullest Virginia who did ever vew?[3]

3

Yet all these were, when no man did them know;
   Yet have from wisest ages hidden beene:
   And later times things more unknowne shall show.
   Why then should witlesse man so much misweene°   *misjudge*
   That nothing is, but that which he hath seene?
   What if within the Moones faire shining sphaere?
   What if in every other starre unseene
   Of other worldes he happily° should heare?   *by chance*
He wonder would much more: yet such to some appeare.

4

Of Faerie lond yet if he more inquire,
   By certaine signes here set in sundry place

1. The thought recalls that of Ariosto (in *Orlando Furioso*, VII. 1–2), who acknowledges that his story may not appeal to ignorant or foolish readers, and so directs the poem explicitly to an audience of relatively greater intelligence and insight.
2. I.e., to recent times.
3. Sir Walter Raleigh, to whom Elizabeth ("the Virgin Queen") in 1584 granted a patent to establish a "planta- tion" in America, twice attempted to settle a colony at Roanoke Island in Pamlico Sound. Although the Virginian project was not firmly established until 1607, the Dedication to the 1596 edition of *The Faerie Queene* adds the words "and of Virginia" to her title (which in the 1590 edition reads simply, "Queene of England, France and Ireland").

He may it find; ne let him then admire,°   *wonder*
But yield his sence to be too blunt and bace,
That no'te° without an hound fine footing° trace.   *cannot/tracks*
And thou, O fairest Princesse under sky,
In this faire mirrhour maist behold thy face,
And thine owne realmes in lond of Faery,
And in this antique Image thy great auncestry.[4]

5

The which O pardon me thus to enfold
  In covert° vele, and wrap in shadowes light,   *concealing*
  That feeble eyes your glory may behold,
  Which else could not endure those beamés bright,
  But would be dazled with exceeding light.
  O pardon, and vouchsafe with patient eare
  The brave adventures of this Faery knight
  The good Sir Guyon gratiously to heare,
In whom great rule of Temp'raunce goodly doth appeare.

Canto I

Guyon by Archimage abusd,°   *deceived*
  The Redcrosse knight awaytes,
Findes Mordant and Amavia slaine
  With pleasures poisoned baytes.

1

That cunning Architect[1] of cancred° guile,   *malignant*
  Whom Princes late displeasure left in bands,
  For falséd letters and subornéd wile,[2]
  Soone as the Redcrosse knight he understands,
  To beene departed out of Eden lands,
  To serve againe his soveraine Elfin Queene,
  His artes he moves, and out of caytives° hands   *menials'*
  Himselfe he frees by secret meanes unseene;
His shackles emptie left, him selfe escapéd cleene.

2

And forth he fares full of malicious mind,
  To worken mischiefe and avenging woe,
  Where ever he that godly knight may find,
  His onely hart sore, and his onely foe,
  Sith Una now he algates° must forgoe,   *entirely*
  Whom his victorious hands did earst restore
  To native crowne and kingdome late ygoe:[3]
  Where she enjoyes sure peace for evermore,
As weather-beaten ship arrived on happie shore.

---

4. That is, in Gloriana ("this faire mirrhour") is imaged Queen Elizabeth; the whole poem ("this antique Image") figures forth, in idealized terms, the character and achievements of Elizabethan England and the high lineage of its ruler.

1. I.e., Archimago, whose escape Spenser has foreshadowed in I. xii. 36.
2. I.e., forged letters and perjured deceitfulness.
3. I.e., lately.

3

Him therefore now the object of his spight
  And deadly food° he makes: him to offend   *feud*
  By forgéd treason, or by open fight
  He seekes, of all his drift° the ayméd end: *plotting*
  Thereto his subtile engins he does bend,
  His practick° wit, and his faire filéd° tong,   *crafty/smooth*
  With thousand other sleights: for well he kend,°   *knew*
  His credit now in doubtfull ballaunce hong;
For hardly could be hurt, who was already stong.

4

Still as he went, he craftie stales° did lay,   *snares*
  With cunning traines° him to entrap unwares,   *schemes*
  And privie° spials° plast in all his way,   *hidden/spies*
  To weete what course he takes, and how he fares;
  To ketch him at a vantage in his snares.
  But now so wise and warie was the knight
  By triall of his former harmes and cares,
  That he descride, and shonnéd still his slight:°   *trickery*
The fish that once was caught, new bait will hardly bite.

5

Nath'lesse° th'Enchaunter would not spare his paine,   *nevertheless*
  In hope to win occasion to his will;
  Which when he long awaited had in vaine,
  He chaungd his minde from one to other ill:
  For to all good he enimy was still.
  Upon the way him fortunéd to meet,
  Faire marching underneath a shady hill,
  A goodly knight[4] all armd in harnesse meete,°   *proper*
That from his head no place appearéd to his feete.

6

His carriage was full comely and upright,
  His countenaunce demure and temperate,
  But yet so sterne and terrible in sight,
  That cheard his friends, and did his foes amate:°   *dismay*
  He was an Elfin borne of noble state,
  And mickle worship[5] in his native land;
  Well could he tourney and in lists debate,°   *contend*
  And knighthood tooke of good Sir Huons hand,
When with king Oberon he came to Faerie land.[6]

---

4. I.e., Guyon, the knight of Temperance. In fact, Guyon does not quite personify Aristotle's temperate man, whose reason and emotions are so perfectly in balance that no temptation to emotional excess can move him; but rather the "continent" man, whose nature is apt to be tempted, and who must therefore impose continual restraint on his liability to emotional excess or defect. Such a man, according to Aristotle, will feel pleasure but will not be led by it (*Ethics*, VII. ix). Guyon's name may be derived from "Gihon,"

the river in Eden traditionally associated with the virtue of temperance (A. D. S. Fowler, "The River Guyon," *MLN*, LXXV [1960], 289–92); or it may reflect the equation of the term "gyon" with "wrestler" made in the *Legenda Aurea* (Susan Snyder, "Guyon the Wrestler," *RN*, XIV [1961], 249–252).
5. I.e., much honor.
6. Sir Huon, the hero of the thirteenth-century romance *Huon of Bordeaux*, was afforded particular favors by the fairy king Oberon.

7

Him als° accompanyd upon the way   *also*
  A comely° Palmer,[7] clad in blacke attire,   *seemly, sober*
  Of ripest yeares, and haires all hoarie gray,
  That with a staffe his feeble steps did stire,°   *steer*
  Least his long way his aged limbes should tire:
  And if by lookes one may the mind aread,
  He seemd to be a sage and sober sire,
And ever with slow pace the knight did lead,
Who taught his trampling steed with equall steps to tread.

8

Such whenas Archimago them did view,
  He weenéd well to worke some uncouth° wile,   *strange*
  Eftsoones untwisting his deceiptfull clew,[8]
  He gan to weave a web of wicked guile,
  And with faire countenance and flattring stile,
  To them approching, thus the knight bespake:
  "Faire sonne of Mars, that seeke with warlike spoile,
  And great atchievments great your selfe to make,
Vouchsafe to stay your steed for humble misers° sake."   *wretch's*

9

He stayd his steed for humble misers sake,
  And bad tell on the tenor of his plaint;
  Who feigning then in every limbe to quake,
  Through inward feare, and seeming pale and faint
  With piteous mone his percing speach gan paint;
  "Deare Lady how shall I declare thy cace,
  Whom late I left in langourous° constraint?   *sorrowful*
  Would God thy selfe now present were in place,
To tell this ruefull tale; thy sight could win thee grace.

10

"Or rather would, O would it had so chaunst,
  That you, most noble Sir, had present beene,
  When that lewd ribauld° with vile lust advaunst°   *ruffian/moved*
  Layd first his filthy hands on virgin cleene,°   *pure*
  To spoile her daintie corse so faire and sheene,°   *bright*
  As on the earth, great mother of us all,
  With living eye more faire was never seene,
  Of chastitie and honour virginall:
Witnesse ye heavens, whom she in vaine to helpe did call."

11

"How may it be," said then the knight halfe wroth,
  "That knight should knighthood ever so have shent?"°   *disgraced*
  "None but that saw," quoth he, "would weene for troth,
  How shamefully that Maid he did torment.
  Her looser° golden lockes he rudely rent,   *unbound*
  And drew her on the ground, and his sharpe sword,

---

7. The Palmer (a pilgrim who has visited the Holy Land) represents that enlightened reason which properly controls the passions in man; Guyon follows his companion's measured pace.
8. Ball of thread; i.e., preparing his deceptive plot.

Against her snowy brest he fiercely bent,
And threatned death with many a bloudie word;
Toung hates to tell the rest, that eye to see abhord."

12

Therewith amovéd from his sober mood,
  "And lives he yet," said he, "that wrought this act,
And doen the heavens afford him vitall food?"
"He lives," quoth he, "and boasteth of the fact,[9]
Ne yet hath any knight his courage crackt."
"Where may that treachour then," said he, "be found,
  Or by what meanes may I his footing tract?"°   *trace*
  "That shall I shew," said he, "as sure, as hound
The stricken Deare doth chalenge° by the bleeding wound."   *track*

13

He staid not lenger talke, but with fierce ire
  And zealous hast away is quickly gone
To seeke that knight, where him that craftie Squire
Supposd to be.[1] They do arrive anone,
Where sate a gentle Lady all alone,
  With garments rent, and haire discheveléd,
  Wringing her hands, and making piteous mone;
  Her swollen eyes were much disfiguréd,
And her faire face with teares was fowly blubberéd.

14

The knight approaching nigh, thus to her said,
  "Faire Ladie, through foule sorrow ill bedight,[2]
Great pittie is to see you thus dismaid,
And marre the blossome of your beautie bright:
For thy° appease your grief and heavie plight,   *therefore*
  And tell the cause of your conceivéd° paine.   *evident*
  For if he live, that hath you doen despight,°   *wrong*
  He shall you doe due recompence againe,
Or else his wrong with greater puissance maintaine."

15

Which when she heard, as in despightfull wise,[3]
  She wilfully her sorrow did augment,
And offred hope of comfort did despise:
Her golden lockes most cruelly she rent,
And scratcht her face with ghastly dreriment,°   *grief*
  Ne would she speake, ne see, ne yet be seene,
  But hid her visage, and her head downe bent,
  Either for grievous shame, or for great teene,°   *anguish*
As if her hart with sorrow had transfixéd beene.[4]

9. I.e., the rape of "that Maid."
1. As Guyon parts company with the Palmer, the knight's indignation, not itself blameworthy, flares into anger and overzealous haste, in consequence of his failure to retain rational control.
2. I.e., stricken.

3. I.e., in malicious fashion.
4. The behavior of Duessa (identified in st. 21) resembles that of the enchantress Ligridonia in Trissino's romance *L'Italia Liberata dai Goti* (1548), IV. 765 ff.

16

Till her that Squire bespake, "Madame my liefe,°   *dear*
  For Gods deare love be not so wilfull bent,
  But doe vouchsafe now to receive reliefe,
  The which good fortune doth to you present.
  For what bootes it to weepe and to wayment,°   *lament*
  When ill is chaunst, but doth the ill increase,
  And the weake mind with double woe torment?"
  When she her Squire heard speake, she gan appease
Her voluntarie° paine, and feele some secret ease.   *willful*

17

Eftsoone she said, "Ah gentle trustie Squire,
  What comfort can I wofull wretch conceave,
  Or why should ever I henceforth desire,
  To see faire heavens face, and life not leave,
  Sith that false Traytour did my honour reave?"°   *steal*
  "False traytour certes," said the Faerie knight,
  "I read° the man, that ever would deceave   *regard*
  A gentle Ladie, or her wrong through might:
Death were too little paine for such a foule despight.

18

"But now, faire Ladie, comfort to you make,
  And read,° who hath ye wrought this shamefull plight;   *tell*
  That short° revenge the man may overtake,   *speedy*
  Where so he be, and soone upon him light."
  "Certes," saide she, "I wote not how he hight,°   *is called*
  But under him a gray steede did he wield,°   *control*
  Whose sides with dapled circles weren dight;
  Upright he rode, and in his silver shield
He bore a bloudie Crosse, that quartred all the field."[5]

19

"Now by my head," said Guyon, "much I muse,°   *wonder*
  How that same knight should do so foule amis,
  Or ever gentle Damzell so abuse:
  For may I boldly say, he surely is
  A right good knight, and true of word ywis:°   *surely*
  I present was, and can it witnesse well,
  When armes he swore, and streight did enterpris°   *undertake*
  Th'adventure of the Errant damozell,[6]
In which he hath great glorie wonne, as I heare tell.

20

"Nathlesse he shortly shall againe be tryde,
  And fairely quite° him of th'imputed blame,   *acquit*
  Else be ye sure he dearely shall abyde,°   *suffer*
  Or make you good amendment for the same:
  All wrongs have mends, but no amends of shame.
  Now therefore Ladie, rise out of your paine,

5. I.e., divided the shield's surface   6. I.e., Una, the wandering maiden.
("field") into quarters.

And see the salving of your blotted name."[7]
Full loth she seemd thereto, but yet did faine;
For she was inly glad her purpose so to gaine.

21

Her purpose was not such, as she did faine,
  Ne yet her person such, as it was seene,
  But under simple shew and semblant plaine
  Lurckt false Duessa secretly unseene,
  As a chast Virgin, that had wrongéd beene:
  So had false Archimago her disguisd,
  To cloke her guile with sorrow and sad teene;
  And eke himselfe had craftily devised
To be her Squire, and do her service well aguised.°   *arrayed*

22

Her late forlorne and naked he had found,
  Where she did wander in waste wildernesse,
  Lurking in rockes and caves farre under ground,
  And with greene mosse covering her nakednesse,
  To hide her shame and loathly filthinesse;
  Sith her Prince Arthur of proud ornaments
  And borrowed beautie spoyld. Her nathelesse
  Th'enchaunter finding fit for his intents,
Did thus revest,° and deckt with due habiliments.°   *reclothe/attire*

23

For all he did, was to deceive good knights,
  And draw them from pursuit of praise and fame,
  To slug in slouth and sensuall delights,
  And end their daies with irrenowméd° shame.   *dishonorable*
  And now exceeding griefe him overcame,
  To see the Redcrosse thus advauncéd hye;[8]
  Therefore this craftie engine° he did frame,   *plot*
  Against his praise to stir up enmitye
Of such, as vertues like mote unto him allye.[9]

24

So now he Guyon guides an uncouth° way   *strange*
  Through woods and mountaines, till they came at last
  Into a pleasant dale, that lowly lay
  Betwixt two hils, whose high heads overplast,°   *looming above*
  The valley did with coole shade overcast;
  Through midst thereof a little river rold,
  By which there sate a knight with helme unlast,
  Himselfe refreshing with the liquid cold,
After his travell long, and labours manifold.

25

"Loe yonder he," cryde Archimage alowd,
  "That wrought the shamefull fact,° which I did shew;   *deed*

7. I.e., the vindication of your honor.
8. I.e., highly esteemed.
9. I.e., those of similarly virtuous na-
tures, likely to ally themselves with
Redcrosse.

And now he doth himselfe in secret shrowd,
To flie the vengeance for his outrage dew;
But vaine: for ye shall dearely do him rew,[1]
So God ye speed, and send you good successe;
Which we farre off will here abide to vew."
So they him left, inflamed with wrathfulnesse,
That streight against that knight his speare he did addresse.°   *direct*

26

Who seeing him from farre so fierce to pricke,
His warlike armes about him gan embrace,°   *put on*
And in the rest his readie speare did sticke;
Tho° when as still he saw him towards pace,   *then*
He gan rencounter him in equall race.
They bene ymet, both readie to affrap,°   *strike*
When suddenly that warriour[2] gan abace°   *lower*
His threatned speare, as if some new mishap
Had him betidde,° or hidden danger did entrap.   *befallen*

27

And cryde, "Mercie Sir knight, and mercie Lord,
For mine offence and heedlesse hardiment,°   *boldness*
That had almost committed crime abhord,
And with reprochfull shame mine honour shent,°   *disgraced*
Whiles curséd steele against that badge I bent,
The sacred badge of my Redeemers death,
Which on your shield is set for ornament:"
But his fierce foe his steede could stay uneath,°   *with difficulty*
Who prickt with courage kene, did cruell battell breath.

28

But when he heard him speake, streight way he knew
His error, and himselfe inclyning sayd;
"Ah deare Sir Guyon, well becommeth you,
But me behoveth rather to upbrayd,
Whose hastie hand so farre from reason strayd,
That almost it did haynous violence
On that faire image of that heavenly Mayd,[3]
That decks and armes your shield with faire defence:
Your court'sie takes on you anothers due offence."

29

So bene they both attone,° and doen upreare   *united*
Their bevers° bright, each other for to greete;   *visors*
Goodly comportance° each to other beare,   *behavior*
And entertaine themselves with court'sies meet.
Then said the Redcrosse knight, "Now mote I weet,[4]
Sir Guyon, why with so fierce saliaunce,°   *assault*

---

1. I.e., make him repent.
2. I.e., Guyon, whose character (if not perfectly temperate) inclines naturally to temperate conduct; his response to the "sacred badge" on the other's shield is an appropriate one, for faith and the temperance of reason are complementary (as the words of Redcrosse in st. 28 emphasize).
3. I.e., Gloriana.
4. I.e., may I know.

And fell intent ye did at earst me meet;
  For sith I know your goodly governaunce,°   *restraint*
Great cause, I weene, you guided, or some uncouth chaunce."

30

"Certes," said he, "well mote I shame to tell
  The fond encheason,° that me hither led.   *occasion*
  A false infamous faitour° late befell   *villain*
  Me for to meet, that seeméd ill bested,[5]
  And playnd of grievous outrage, which he red°   *said*
  A knight had wrought against a Ladie gent;
  Which to avenge, he to this place me led,
  Where you he made the marke of his intent,
And now is fled; foule shame him follow, where he went."

31

So can° he turne his earnest unto game,   *did*
  Through goodly handling and wise temperance.
  By this his aged guide in presence came;
  Who soone as on that knight his eye did glance,
  Eft soones of him had perfect cognizance,[6]
  Sith him in Faerie court he late avizd;°   *had seen*
  And said, "Faire sonne, God give you happie chance,
  And that deare Crosse upon your shield devizd,
Wherewith above all knights ye goodly seeme aguizd.°   *equipped*

32

"Joy may you have, and everlasting fame,
  Of late most hard atchiev'ment by you donne,
  For which enrolléd is your glorious name
  In heavenly Registers above the Sunne,
  Where you a Saint with Saints your seat have wonne:
  But wretched we, where ye have left your marke,
  Must now anew begin, like° race to runne;   *similar*
  God guide thee, Guyon, well to end thy warke,
And to the wishéd haven bring thy weary barke."

33

"Palmer," him answeréd the Redcrosse knight,
  "His be the praise, that this atchiev'ment wrought,
  Who made my hand the organ of his might;
  More then goodwill to me attribute nought:
  For all I did, I did but as I ought.
  But you, faire Sir, whose pageant[7] next ensewes,
  Well mote yee thee,° as well can wish your thought,   *thrive*
  That home ye may report thrise happie newes;
For well ye worthie bene for worth and gentle thewes."°   *manners*

34

So courteous congé° both did give and take,   *farewell*
  With right hands plighted, pledges of good will.

5. I.e., in difficulties.
6. Only with the Palmer's return is the allegiance of Redcrosse and Guyon "perfectly" confirmed.
7. I.e., role in life's drama.

Then Guyon forward gan his voyage make,
With his blacke Palmer, that him guided still.[8]
Still he him guided over dale and hill,
  And with his steedie° staffe did point his way: *steady*
His race° with reason, and with words his will,   *actions*
From foule intemperance he oft did stay,
And suffred not in wrath his hastie steps to stray.

[Although the specific assignment by Gloriana of Guyon's quest (to seek out and capture the enchantress Acrasia) is not described until the end of the second Canto, the remainder of Canto i dramatically illustrates Acrasia's terrible power over her victims. Guyon and the Palmer encounter the dying Amavia, who has stabbed herself for grief at the death of her husband, Mordant, a victim of Acrasia's evil magic; their child, Ruddymane, dabbles his hands in her blood. Having told her story, Amavia dies; Guyon, assisted by the Palmer, buries the couple, taking a sacred oath to avenge their deaths, but he is unable to cleanse the blood from the hands of Ruddymane. Allegorically, this episode emphasizes the destructive power of intemperate passion in fallen man. Leaving the child in the care of Medina, whose character and conduct exemplify the Aristotelian "Golden Mean" between extremes of "defect" and "excess" (represented by Medina's sisters, Elissa and Perissa), Guyon proceeds on his quest. After an interlude in Canto iii, during which the virgin huntress Belphoebe successfully resists the advances of Braggadocchio, a cowardly boaster, Cantos iv–vi are chiefly concerned with the struggles of Guyon against various representatives of the "irascible" element in man: Furor, Atin, and the brothers Cymochles and Pyrochles. Guyon subdues or successfully resists each of these figures; but he is not proof against the seductive persuasions of Acrasia's servant Phaedria (described by Spenser as "immodest Merth"), who conducts him across her "Idle lake." Guyon does not remain in her company; but he has now been deprived of the Palmer's guidance.]

Canto VII

   Guyon findes Mammon in a delve,°   *cave*
    Sunning his threasure hore:°   *ancient*
   Is by him tempted, and led downe,
    To see his secret store.[1]

1

As Pilot well expert in perilous wave,
  That to a stedfast starre his course hath bent,
  When foggy mistes, or cloudy tempests have
  The faithfull light of that faire lampe yblent,°   *obscured*
  And covered heaven with hideous dreriment,
  Upon his card° and compas firmes his eye,   *chart*
  The maisters of his long experiment,°   *experience*

8. Thus, the virtuous Guyon sets out on his quest, approved by faith and guided by enlightened reason.

1. For a critical overview of this Canto, cf. the essay by Humphrey Tonkin in *SEL*, XIII (1973), 1–13.

And to them does the steddy helme apply,
Bidding his wingéd vessell fairely forward fly:

2

So Guyon having lost his trusty guide,
   Late left beyond that Ydle lake, proceedes
   Yet on his way, of none accompanide;
   And evermore himselfe with comfort feedes,
   Of his owne vertues, and prayse-worthy deedes.
   So long he yode,° yet no adventure found,   *went*
   Which fame of her shrill trompet worthy reedes.°   *declares*
   For still he traveild through wide wastfull ground,
That nought but desert wildernesse shewed all around.

3

At last he came unto a gloomy glade,
   Covered with boughes and shrubs from heavens light,
   Whereas he sitting found in secret shade
   An uncouth, salvage,° and uncivile° wight,   *savage/wild*
   Of griesly hew, and fowle ill favoured sight;°   *appearance*
   His face with smoke was tand, and eyes were bleard,
   His head and beard with sout were ill bedight,°   *adorned*
   His cole-blacke hands did seeme to have beene seard
In smithes fire-spitting forge, and nayles like clawes appeard.

4

His yron coate all overgrowne with rust,
   Was underneath envelopéd with gold,
   Whose glistring glosse darkned with filthy dust,
   Well yet appearéd, to have beene of old
   A worke of rich entayle,° and curious° mould,   *carving/intricate*
   Woven with antickes° and wild Imagery: *fantastic figures*
   And in his lap a masse of coyne he told,°   *counted*
   And turnéd upsidowne, to feede his eye
And covetous desire with his huge threasury.

5

And round about him lay on every side
   Great heapes of gold, that never could be spent:
   Of which some were rude owre, not purifide
   Of Mulcibers devouring element;[2]
   Some others were new driven,° and distent°   *beaten/extended*
   Into great Ingoes,° and to wedges square;   *ingots*
   Some in round plates withouten moniment;°   *markings*
   But most were stampt, and in their metall bare
The antique shapes of kings and kesars° straunge and rare.   *emperors*

6

Soone as he Guyon saw, in great affright
   And hast he rose, for to remove aside
   Those pretious hils from straungers envious sight,
   And downe them pouréd through an hole full wide,
   Into the hollow earth, them there to hide.

2. I.e., the fire of which Mulciber
(Vulcan) was the god.

But Guyon lightly to him leaping, stayd
His hand, that trembled, as one terrifyde;
And though him selfe were at the sight dismayd,
Yet him perforce restraynd, and to him doubtfull sayd.[3]

7

"What are thou man, (if man at all thou art)
That here in desert hast thine habitaunce,
And these rich heapes of wealth doest hide apart
From the worldes eye, and from her right usaunce?"°   use
Thereat with staring eyes fixéd askaunce,[4]
In great disdaine, he answerd; "Hardy Elfe,
That darest vew my direfull countenaunce,
I read° thee rash, and heedlesse of thy selfe,   consider
To trouble my still seate, and heapes of pretious pelfe.

8

"God of the world and worldlings I me call,
Great Mammon,[5] greatest god below the skye,
That of my plenty poure out unto all,
And unto none my graces do envye:°   begrudge
Riches, renowme, and principality,
Honour, estate, and all this worldés good,
For which men swinck° and sweat incessantly,   toil
Fro me do flow into an ample flood,
And in the hollow earth have their eternall brood.°   breeding place

9

"Wherefore if me thou deigne to serve and sew,°   follow
At thy commaund lo all these mountaines bee;
Or if to thy great mind, or greedy vew
All these may not suffise, there shall to thee
Ten times so much be numbred francke and free."
"Mammon," said he, "thy godheades vaunt[6] is vaine,
And idle offers of thy golden fee;°   reward
To them, that covet such eye-glutting gaine,
Proffer thy giftes, and fitter servaunts entertaine.

10

"Me ill besits, that in der-doing armes,[7]
And honours suit° my vowéd dayes do spend,   pursuit

3. I.e., said to the apprehensive "wight of griesly hew."
4. I.e., with proudly averted eyes.
5. Mammon (from Syriac, "riches") is not simply the god of material wealth or the personification of its powerful attraction for men; he is a satanic figure, opposed to God as darkness is set against light in Matthew vi. 19–24. Cf. especially verse 24: "No man can serve two masters: for either he will hate the one, and love the other; or else he will hold to the one, and despise the other. Ye cannot serve God and mammon." The various temptations, of wealth (sts. 18, 32, 38), glory (st. 49), and, perhaps, knowledge (st. 63), are to be associated with the devil's temptations of Christ in the wilderness (Matthew iv. 1–11). Guyon, deprived of the Palmer's aid, and therefore dependent exclusively on "his owne vertues" (st. 2), after his successful but exhausting resistance to Mammon, is attended by an angel (viii. 5; cf. Matthew iv. 11). If he is not precisely a "Christ figure," his experience indicates the central relevance of Christ's temptations for those to which fallen man is subject.
6. I.e., boastful claim to godhead.
7. I.e., It is not fitting for me, engaged in daring deeds of arms.

Unto thy bounteous baytes, and pleasing charmes,
With which weake men thou witchest, to attend:
Regard of worldly mucke doth fowly blend,°   *defile*
And low abase the high heroicke spright,
That joyes for crownes and kingdomes to contend;
Faire shields, gay steedes, bright armes be my delight:
Those be the riches fit for an advent'rous knight."

11

"Vaine glorious Elfe," said he, "doest not thou weet,°   *know*
That money can thy wantes at will supply?
Shields, steeds, and armes, and all things for thee meet
It can purvay° in twinckling of an eye;   *provide*
And crownes and kingdomes to thee multiply.
Do not I kings create, and throw the crowne
Sometimes to him, that low in dust doth ly?
And him that raignd, into his rowme thrust downe,
And whom I lust,° do heape with glory and renowne?"   *choose*

12

"All otherwise," said he, "I riches read,°   *consider*
And deeme them roote of all disquietnesse;
First got with guile, and then preserved with dread,
And after spent with pride and lavishnesse,
Leaving behind them griefe and heavinesse.[8]
Infinite mischiefes of them do arize,
Strife, and debate, bloudshed, and bitternesse,
Outrageous wrong, and hellish covetize,
That noble heart as great dishonour doth despize.

13

"Ne thine be kingdomes, ne the scepters thine;
But realmes and rulers thou doest both confound,°   *destroy*
And loyall truth to treason doest incline;
Witnesse the guiltlesse bloud pourd oft on ground,
The crownéd often slaine, the slayer cround,
The sacred Diademe in peeces rent,
And purple robe goréd with many a wound;
Castles surprizd, great cities sackt and brent:°   *burned*
So mak'st thou kings, and gaynest wrongfull governement.

14

"Long were to tell the troublous stormes, that tosse
The private state,° and make the life unsweet: *condition*
Who° swelling sayles in Caspian sea doth crosse,   *he who with*
And in frayle wood on Adrian gulfe[9] doth fleet,
Doth not, I weene, so many evils meet."
Then Mammon wexing wroth, "And why then," said,
"Are mortall men so fond and undiscreet,

---

8. "But they that will be rich fall into temptation and a snare, and into many foolish and hurtful lusts, which drown men in destruction and perdition. For the love of money is the root of all evil . . . " (I Timothy vi. 9–10).

9. The Adriatic Sea, like the Caspian Sea notorious from ancient times for its storms.

So evill thing to seeke unto their ayd,
And having not complaine, and having it upbraid?"[1]

15

"Indeede," quoth he, "through fowle intemperaunce,
   Frayle men are oft captived to covetise:
   But would they thinke, with how small allowaunce
   Untroubled Nature doth her selfe suffise,
   Such superfluities they would despise,
   Which with sad cares empeach° our native joyes: *hinder*
   At the well head the purest streames arise:
   But mucky filth his braunching armes annoyes,
And with uncomely weedes the gentle wave accloyes.°   *clogs*

16

"The antique° world, in his first flowring youth,[2]   *ancient*
   Found no defect in his Creatours grace,
   But with glad thankes, and unreprovéd° truth,   *blameless*
   The gifts of soveraigne bountie did embrace:
   Like Angels life was then mens happy cace;
   But later ages pride, like corn-fed steed,
   Abusd her plenty, and fat swolne encreace
   To all licentious lust, and gan exceed
The measure of her meane,[3] and naturall first need.

17

"Then gan a curséd hand the quiet wombe
   Of his great Grandmother with steele to wound,
   And the hid treasures in her sacred tombe,
   With Sacriledge to dig. Therein he found
   Fountaines of gold and silver to abound,
   Of which the matter of his huge desire
   And pompous pride eftsoones he did compound;
   Then avarice gan through his veines inspire°   *breathe*
His greedy flames, and kindled life-devouring fire.

18

"Sonne," said he then, "let be thy bitter scorne,
   And leave the rudenesse of that antique age
   To them, that lived therein in state forlorne;
   Thou that doest live in later times, must wage°   *hire out*
   Thy workes for wealth, and life for gold engage.
   If then thee list my offred grace to use,
   Take what thou please of all this surplusage;
   If thee list not, leave have thou to refuse:
But thing refuséd, do not afterward accuse."

1. I.e., either (a) and, having, reproach
it, or (b) and, having it, reproach their
condition. Guyon's reply echoes the dis-
tinction between nature's requirements
and "the superfluity of Fortune" made
by Boethius (c. 475–525) in *De Con-
solatione Philosophiae*, II. Prose 5.
2. The myth of the Golden Age recurs
in every form of Elizabethan literature,
notably in pastoral poetry. Especially
influential treatments of the theme in
classical literature were those of Ovid
(*Metamorphoses*, I. 90–112) and Virgil
(*Eclogue IV*). Cf. also Boethius, *op.
cit.*, II. Metre 5.
3. I.e., her proper limits.

19

"Me list not," said the Elfin knight, "receave
　Thing offred, till I know it well be got,
　Ne wote° I, but thou didst these goods bereave　　　　*know*
　From rightfull owner by unrighteous lot,[4]
　Or that bloud guiltinesse or guile them blot."
　"Perdy°," quoth he, "yet never eye did vew,　　　　*truly*
　Ne toung did tell, ne hand these handled not,
　But safe I have them kept in secret mew,°　　　　*den*
From heavens sight, and powre of all which them pursew."

20

"What secret place," quoth he, "can safely hold
　So huge a masse, and hide from heavens eye?
　Or where hast thou thy wonne,° that so much gold　　　　*dwelling*
　Thou canst preserve from wrong and robbery?"
　"Come thou," quoth he, "and see." So by and by
　Through that thicke covert he him led, and found
　A darkesome way, which no man could descry,°　　　　*discover*
　That deepe descended through the hollow ground,
And was with dread and horrour compasséd around.

21

At length they came into a larger space,
　That stretcht it selfe into an ample plaine,
　Through which a beaten broad high way did trace,
　That streight did lead to Plutoes griesly raine:[5]
　By that wayes side, there sate infernall Payne,
　And fast beside him sat tumultuous Strife:
　The one in hand an yron whip did straine,°　　　　*wield*
　The other brandishéd a bloudy knife,
And both did gnash their teeth, and both did threaten life.

22

On thother side in one consort° there sate,　　　　*company*
　Cruell Revenge, and rancorous Despight,
　Disloyall Treason, and hart-burning Hate,
　But gnawing Gealosie out of their sight
　Sitting alone, his bitter lips did bight,
　And trembling Feare still to and fro did fly,
　And found no place, where safe he shroud him might,
　Lamenting Sorrow did in darknesse lye,
And Shame his ugly face did hide from living eye.

23

And over them sad Horrour with grim hew,°　　　　*aspect*
　Did alwayes sore, beating his yron wings;
　And after him Owles and Night-ravens flew,
　The hatefull messengers of heavy things,

4. I.e., by unjust division.
5. I.e., Pluto's horrible kingdom. Ultimately from Virgil's description of the gates of hell (*Aeneid*, VI. 267–281), Spenser's account of this region, es-pecially the personifications in st. 22, may reflect the influence of Sackville's "Induction" to *A Mirror for Magistrates.*

Of death and dolour telling sad tidings;
Whiles sad Celeno,[6] sitting on a clift,
A song of bale and bitter sorrow sings,
That hart of flint a sunder could have rift:°   *torn*
Which having ended, after him she flyeth swift.

24

All these before the gates of Pluto lay,
By whom they passing, spake unto them nought.
But th'Elfin knight with wonder all the way
Did feed his eyes, and fild his inner thought.
At last him to a litle dore he brought,
That to the gate of Hell, which gapéd wide,
Was next adjoyning, ne them parted ought:[7]
Betwixt them both was but a litle stride,
That did the house of Richesse from hell-mouth divide.

25

Before the dore sat selfe-consuming Care,
Day and night keeping wary watch and ward,
For feare least Force or Fraud should unaware
Breake in, and spoile° the treasure there in gard: *plunder*
Ne would he suffer Sleepe once thither-ward
Approch, albe° his drowsie den were next;   *although*
For next to death is Sleepe to be compard:[8]
Therefore his house is unto his annext;
Here Sleep, there Richesse, and Hel-gate them both betwext.

26

So soone as Mammon there arrived, the dore
To him did open, and affoorded way;
Him followed eke Sir Guyon evermore,
Ne darkenesse him, ne daunger might dismay.
Soone as he entred was, the dore streight way
Did shut, and from behind it forth there lept
An ugly feend, more fowle then dismall day,[9]
The which with monstrous stalke behind him stept,
And ever as he went, dew° watch upon him kept.[1]   *proper*

27

Well hopéd he, ere long that hardy guest,
If ever covetous hand, or lustfull eye,
Or lips he layd on thing, that likt° him best,   *pleased*
Or ever sleepe his eye-strings did untye,

6. Chief of the harpies, rapacious monsters of legend, who combined female face and torso with the wings and claws of a bird; in Spenser's time, the term "harpy" had already become associated with avarice and greed.
7. I.e., nor did anything separate them.
8. Death and Sleep were brothers, the offspring of Night (cf. Hesiod, *Theogony*, 211–212).
9. I.e., the day of death.
1. The fiend who follows Guyon during his sojourn in the underworld probably reflects Spenser's acquaintance (by way of Claudian's mythological epic poem, *De Raptu Proserpinae*, composed in the early fifth century A.D., and, perhaps, Pausanias's *Description of Greece*, written in the second century A.D.) with some features of the ancient Eleusinian festival and mysteries: initiates at these rites were followed by a "fury," to insure their strict observance of ritual procedures.

Should be his pray. And therefore still on hye
He over him did hold his cruell clawes,
Threatning with greedy gripe to do him dye
And rend in peeces with his ravenous pawes,
If ever he transgrest the fatall Stygian lawes.[2]

28

That houses forme within was rude and strong,
  Like an huge cave, hewne out of rocky clift,
  From whose rough vaut° the ragged breaches° hong,   *vault/fractures*
  Embost with massy gold of glorious gift,°   *quality*
  And with rich metall loaded every rift,
  That heavy ruine they did seeme to threat;
  And over them Arachne[3] high did lift
  Her cunning web, and spred her subtile° net,   *fine-spun*
Enwrappéd in fowle smoke and clouds more blacke then Jet.

29

Both roofe, and floore, and wals were all of gold,
  But overgrowne with dust and old decay,
  And hid in darkenesse, that none could behold
  The hew° thereof: for vew of chearefull day   *condition*
  Did never in that house it selfe display,
  But a faint shadow of uncertain light;
  Such as a lamp, whose life does fade away:
  Or as the Moone cloathéd with clowdy night,
Does shew to him, that walkes in feare and sad affright.

30

In all that rowme was nothing to be seene,
  But huge great yron chests and coffers strong,
  All bard with double bends,° that none could weene°   *bands/expect*
  Them to efforce° by violence or wrong;   *force open*
  On every side they placéd were along.
  But all the ground with sculs was scatteréd,
  And dead mens bones, which round about were flong,
  Whose lives, it seeméd, whilome° there were shed,   *formerly*
And their vile carcases now left unburiéd.

31

They forward passe, ne Guyon yet spoke word,
  Till that they came unto an yron dore,
  Which to them opened of his owne accord,
  And shewd of richesse such exceeding store,
  As eye of man did never see before;
  Ne ever could within one place be found,
  Though all the wealth, which is, or was of yore,
  Could gathered be through all the world around,
And that above were added to that under ground.

---

2. I.e., the laws of the underworld.
3. Ovid's account of Arachne, who engaged Minerva in a weaving contest, and who was subsequently transformed into a spider by the goddess (*Metamorphoses* VI. 1–145), is altered by Spenser, in his mock-heroic poem *Muiopotmos*, so that Arachne's own envy is identified as the cause of her change: the expressions of this stanza reflect that version of the myth.

32

The charge thereof unto a covetous Spright
  Commaunded was, who thereby did attend,
  And warily awaited day and night,
  From other covetous feends it to defend,
  Who it to rob and ransacke did intend.
  Then Mammon turning to that warriour, said;
  "Loe here the worldés blis, loe here the end,
  To which all men do ayme, rich to be made:
Such grace now to be happy, is before thee laid."

33

"Certes," said he, "I n'ill° thine offred grace,   *will not accept*
  Ne to be made so° happy do intend: *thus*
  Another blis before mine eyes I place,
  Another happinesse, another end.
  To them, that list, these base regardes° I lend: *concerns*
  But I in armes, and in atchievements brave,
  Do rather choose my flitting houres to spend,
  And to be Lord of those, that riches have,
Then them to have my selfe, and be their servile sclave."

34

Thereat the feend his gnashing teeth did grate,
  And grieved, so long to lacke his greedy pray:[4]
  For well he weenéd,° that so glorious bayte   *supposed*
  Would tempt his guest, to take thereof assay:°   *trial*
  Had he so doen, he had him snatcht away,
  More light then Culver° in the Faulcons fist.   *dove*
  Eternall God thee save from such decay.°   *ruin*
  But whenas Mammon saw his purpose mist,
Him to entrap unwares another way he wist.°   *knew*

35

Thence forward he him led, and shortly brought
  Unto another rowme, whose dore forthright,
  To him did open, as it had beene taught:
  Therein an hundred raunges weren pight,°   *placed*
  And hundred fornaces all burning bright;
  By every fornace many feends did bide,
  Deforméd creatures, horrible in sight,
  And every feend his busie paines applide,
To melt the golden metall, ready to be tride.°   *purified*

36

One with great bellowes gathered filling aire,
  And with forst wind the fewell did inflame;
  Another did the dying bronds° repaire   *embers*
  With yron toungs, and sprinckled oft the same
  With liquid waves, fiers Vulcans rage[5] to tame,

---

4. I.e., to be so long denied the prey he greedily desired.
5. I.e., the fire. Spenser's use of the god's name, by metonymy, for fire, here and elsewhere in *The Faerie Queene,* fol-lows Ovidian precedent (cf. *Metamorphoses,* VII. 104, IX. 263). Sts. 35–36 are based on Virgil's account of the Cyclopean forges beneath Mt. Etna (*Aeneid,* VIII. 417–454).

Who maistring them, renewd his former heat;
    Some scumd the drosse, that from the metall came;
    Some stird the molten owre with ladles great:
And every one did swincke,° and every one did sweat. *labor*

37

But when as earthly wight they present saw,
    Glistring in armes and battailous° aray, *warlike*
    From their whot worke they did themselves withdraw
    To wonder at the sight: for till that day,
    They never creature saw, that came that way.
    Their staring eyes sparckling with fervent fire,
    And ugly shapes did nigh the man dismay,
    That were it not for shame, he would retire,
Till that him thus bespake their soveraigne Lord and sire.

38

"Behold, thou Faeries sonne, with mortall eye,
    That living eye before did never see:
    The thing, that thou didst crave so earnestly,
    To weet, whence all the wealth late shewd by mee,
    Proceeded, lo now is reveald to thee.
    Here is the fountaine of the worldés good:
    Now therefore, if thou wilt enrichéd bee,
    Avise° thee well, and chaunge thy wilfull mood, *consider*
Least thou perhaps hereafter wish, and be withstood."

39

"Suffise it then, thou Money God," quoth hee,
    "That all thine idle offers I refuse.
    All that I need I have; what needeth mee
    To covet more, then I have cause to use?
    With such vaine shewes thy worldlings vile abuse:° *deceive*
    But give me leave to follow mine emprise."° *enterprise*
    Mammon was much displeasd, yet no'te° chuse, *could not*
    But beare the rigour of his bold mesprise,° *scorn*
And thence him forward led, him further to entise.

40

He brought him through a darksome narrow strait,
    To a broad gate, all built of beaten gold:
    The gate was open, but therein did wait
    A sturdy villein, striding stiffe and bold,
    As if that highest God defie he would;
    In his right hand an yron club he held,
    But he himselfe was all of golden mould,
    Yet had both life and sence, and well could weld° *wield*
That curséd weapon, when his cruell foes he queld.

41

Disdayne he calléd was, and did disdaine
    To be so cald, and who so did him call:
    Sterne was his looke, and full of stomacke° vaine, *arrogance*
    His portaunce° terrible, and stature tall, *bearing*

Far passing th'hight of men terrestriall;
Like an huge Gyant of the Titans race,
That made him scorne all creatures great and small,
And with his pride all others powre deface:°   *destroy*
More fit amongst blacke fiendes, then men to have his place.

42

Soone as those glitterand° armes he did espye,   *glittering*
  That with their brightnesse made that darknesse light,
  His harmefull club he gan to hurtle° hye,   *brandish*
  And threaten batteill to the Faery knight;
  Who likewise gan himselfe to batteill dight,°   *prepare*
  Till Mammon did his hasty hand withhold,
  And counseld him abstaine from perilous fight:
For nothing might abash the villein bold,
Ne mortall steele emperce his miscreated° mould.   *unnatural*

43

So having him with reason pacifide,
  And the fiers Carle° commaunding to forbeare,   *churl*
  He brought him in. The rowme was large and wide,
  As it some Gyeld° or solemne Temple weare: *guildhall*
  Many great golden pillours did upbeare
  The massy roofe, and riches huge sustayne,
  And every pillour deckéd was full deare°   *richly*
  With crownes and Diademes, and titles vaine,
Which mortall Princes wore, whiles they on earth did rayne.

44

A route° of people there assembled were,   *crowd*
  Of every sort and nation under skye,
  Which with great uprore preacéd° to draw nere   *pressed*
  To th'upper part, where was advauncéd hye
  A stately siege° of soveraigne majestye;   *throne*
  And thereon sat a woman gorgeous gay,[6]
  And richly clad in robes of royaltye,
  That never earthly Prince in such aray
His glory did enhaunce, and pompous pride display.

45

Her face right wondrous faire did seeme to bee,
  That her broad beauties beam great brightnes threw
  Through the dim shade, that all men might it see:
  Yet was not that same her owne native hew,°   *aspect*
  But wrought by art and counterfetted shew,
  Thereby more lovers unto her to call;
  Nath'lesse most heavenly faire in deed and vew

---

6. I.e., Philotime (from Greek, "love of honor"), identified in st. 49. Her appearance and situation recall those of Lucifera, described in I. iv. 6–8, 11, as the daughter of Pluto and Proserpina. Both figures, in differing contexts, represent perversions of the ideal exemplified by Gloriana: Lucifera has usurped her power "with wrong and tyrannie," while the fallen Philotime holds sway by pretense and artifice over the pushful mobs that crowd her court.

She by creation was, till she did fall;
Thenceforth she sought for helps, to cloke her crime withall.

46

There, as in glistring glory she did sit,
    She held a great gold chaine ylinckéd well,
    Whose upper end to highest heaven was knit,
    And lower part did reach to lowest Hell;
    And all that preace° did round about her swell,   *throng*
    To catchen hold of that long chaine, thereby
    To clime aloft, and others to excell:
    That was Ambition, rash desire to sty,°   *mount*
And every lincke thereof a step of dignity.[7]

47

Some thought to raise themselves to high degree,
    By riches and unrighteous reward,
    Some by close shouldring,° some by flatteree;   *thrusting aside*
    Others through friends, others for base regard;[8]
    And all by wrong wayes for themselves prepard.
    Those that were up themselves, kept others low,
    Those that were low themselves, held others hard,
    Ne suffred them to rise or greater grow,
But every one did strive his fellow downe to throw.

48

Which whenas Guyon saw, he gan inquire,
    What meant that preace about that Ladies throne,
    And what she was that did so high aspire.
    Him Mammon answeréd; "That goodly one,
    Whom all that folke with such contention,
    Do flocke about, my deare, my daughter is;
    Honour and dignitie from her alone,
    Derivéd are, and all this worldés blis
For which ye men do strive: few get, but many mis.

49

"And faire Philotimé she rightly hight,°   *is named*
    The fairest wight that wonneth° under skye,   *lives*
    But that this darksome neather world her light
    Doth dim with horrour and deformitie,
    Worthy of heaven and hye felicitie,
    From whence the gods have her for envy thrust:
    But sith thou hast found favour in mine eye,
    Thy spouse I will her make, if that thou lust,°   *desire*
That she may thee advance for workes and merites just."

50

"Gramercy° Mammon," said the gentle knight,   *thanks*
    "For so great grace and offred high estate;
    But I, that am fraile flesh and earthly wight,

7. Cf. I. v. 25 and note. Spenser's use of the image of the golden chain in this context reflects the opinion of Natalis Comes, who observes that it may occasionally signify avarice or ambition, which, though very powerful, cannot move a good man from his purposes (*Mythologiae*, II. 4).

8. I.e., bribes.

Unworthy match for such immortall mate
My selfe well wote, and mine unequall fate;
And were I not, yet is my trouth yplight,°   plighted
And love avowd to other Lady late,°   lately
That to remove the same I have no might:
To chaunge love causelesse is reproch to warlike knight."

51

Mammon emmovéd was with inward wrath;
    Yet forcing it to faine,[9] him forth thence led
    Through griesly shadowes by a beaten path,
    Into a gardin goodly garnishéd
    With hearbs and fruits, whose kinds mote not be red:° described
    Not such, as earth out of her fruitfull woomb
    Throwes forth to men, sweet and well savouréd,
    But direfull deadly blacke both leafe and bloom,
Fit to adorne the dead, and decke the drery toombe.[1]

52

There mournfull Cypresse grew in greatest store,
    And trees of bitter Gall, and Heben sad,
    Dead sleeping Poppy, and blacke Hellebore,
    Cold Coloquintida, and Tetra mad,
    Mortall Samnitis, and Cicuta bad,[2]
    With which th'unjust Atheniens made to dy
    Wise Socrates, who thereof quaffing glad
    Pourd out his life, and last Philosophy
To the faire Critias his dearest Belamy.°   intimate

53

The Gardin of Proserpina this hight;°   was named
    And in the midst thereof a silver seat,[3]
    With a thicke Arber goodly over dight,°   covered
    In which she often usd from open heat
    Her selfe to shroud, and pleasures to entreat.°   indulge in
    Next thereunto did grow a goodly tree,
    With braunches broad dispred° and body great,   spread out
    Clothéd with leaves, that none the wood mote see
And loaden all with fruit as thicke as it might bee.

54

Their fruit were golden apples[4] glistring bright,
    That goodly was their glory to behold,
    On earth like never grew, ne living wight

9. I.e., concealing his wrath.
1. Spenser's Garden of Proserpina combines elements from the *Odyssey* (the Grove of Persephone, X. 509–540), Claudian, *De Raptu Proserpinae* (the tree bearing golden fruit, II. 290–291), and Natalis Comes, *Mythologiae* (the identification of Proserpina with Hecate, goddess of poisons, III. 15).
2. These trees and plants either are commonly associated with death or are themselves poisonous; "Cicuta bad" is the hemlock (cf. *Phaedo*, 117–118).
3. On this seat (mentioned again in st. 63) Theseus was sentenced to remain forever, "condemned to endlesse slouth by law" (I. v. 35); it may also refer to the forbidden seat of the goddess Demeter, celebrated in the Eleusinian initiatory rites.
4. To fetch the golden apples of the Hesperides (the daughters of Atlas) was the eleventh of Hercules's twelve labors. For Spenser as for Natalis Comes (*Mythologiae*, VII. 7), the golden apples are symbols of avarice and discord.

Like ever saw, but° they from hence were sold;°   *unless/taken*
For those, which Hercules with conquest bold
Got from great Atlas daughters, hence began,
And planted there, did bring forth fruit of gold:
And those with which th'Euboean young man wan°   *won*
Swift Atalanta, when through craft he her out ran.[5]

55

Here also sprong that goodly golden fruit,
   With which Acontius got his lover trew,
   Whom he had long time sought with fruitlesse suit:
   Here eke that famous golden Apple grew,
   The which emongst the gods false Ate threw;
   For which th'Idaean Ladies disagreed,
   Till partiall Paris dempt° it Venus dew,   *adjudged*
   And had of her, faire Helen for his meed,°   *reward*
That many noble Greekes and Trojans made to bleed.[6]

56

The warlike Elfe much wondred at this tree,
   So faire and great, that shadowed all the ground,
   And his broad braunches, laden with rich fee,°   *wealth*
   Did stretch themselves without the utmost bound
   Of this great gardin, compast° with a mound,   *surrounded*
   Which over-hanging, they themselves did steepe,
   In a blacke flood which flowed about it round;
   That is the river of Cocytus deepe,[7]
In which full many soules do endlesse waile and weepe.

57

Which to behold, he clomb up to the banke
   And looking downe, saw many damnéd wights,
   In those sad waves, which direfull deadly stanke,
   Plongéd continually of° cruell Sprights,   *by*
   That with their pitteous cryes, and yelling shrights,°   *shrieks*
   They made the further shore resounden° wide: *echo*
   Emongst the rest of those same ruefull sights,
   One curséd creature[8] he by chaunce espide,
That drenchéd lay full deepe, under the Garden side.

5. Atalanta promised herself in marriage to that suitor who should defeat her in a foot race: those whom she defeated were condemned to death. Hippomenes (or, in another version of the story, Melanion of Euboea, an island near Boeotia) won the race and Atalanta's hand by casting down golden apples to intrigue and delay Atalanta, who turned aside to pick them up (Ovid, *Metamorphoses*, X. 560–680).
6. Spenser adapts the story of Acontius (who won his love, Cydippe, by the strategic use of an apple: cf. Ovid, *Heroides*, XX–XXI) to his theme by making the apple of that fable a golden one; and he identifies Ate, goddess of discord (rather than the Eris of Greek myth named by Hyginus, *Fabulae*, XCII), as the divinity who, angered at not having been invited to the marriage of Thetis and Peleus, threw among the invited goddesses a golden apple inscribed, "Let it be given to the fairest." The subsequent contest between Juno, Minerva, and Venus, on Mt. Ida, decided by Paris in favor of Venus (who had promised him Helen), led to the Trojan War.
7. One of the five rivers of hell, traditionally associated with tears and sorrow.
8. I.e., Tantalus, who was punished for revealing divine secrets to men, as well as for having killed his son Pelops and serving up the remains at a banquet for

58

Deepe was he drenchéd to the upmost chin,
     Yet gapéd still, as coveting to drinke
Of the cold liquor, which he waded in,
And stretching forth his hand, did often thinke
To reach the fruit, which grew upon the brincke:
But both the fruit from hand, and floud from mouth
Did flie abacke, and made him vainely swinke:
     The whiles he sterved° with hunger and with drouth°   *starved/thirst*
He daily dyde, yet never throughly dyen couth.[9]

59

The knight him seeing labour so in vaine,
     Askt who he was, and what he ment thereby:
Who groning deepe, thus answerd him againe;
"Most curséd of all creatures under skye,
Lo Tantalus, I here tormented lye:
Of whom high Jove wont whylome feasted bee,[1]
Lo here I now for want of food doe dye:
     But if that thou be such, as I thee see,
Of grace I pray thee, give to eat and drinke to mee."

60

"Nay, nay, thou greedie Tantalus," quoth he,
     "Abide the fortune of thy present fate,
And unto all that live in high degree,°   *place*
Ensample be of mind intemperate,
To teach them how to use their present state."
Then gan the curséd wretch aloud to cry,
Accusing highest Jove and gods ingrate,
     And eke blaspheming heaven bitterly,
As authour of unjustice, there to let him dye.

61

He lookt a little further, and espyde
     Another wretch, whose carkasse deepe was drent°   *immersed*
Within the river, which the same did hyde:
But both his hands most filthy feculent,°   *befouled*
Above the water were on high extent,°   *stretched*
And faynd° to wash themselves incessantly;   *tried*
Yet nothing cleaner were for such intent,
     But rather fowler seeméd to the eye;
So lost his labour vaine and idle° industry.   *futile*

62

The knight him calling, askéd who he was,
     Who lifting up his head, him answerd thus:
"I Pilate am the falsest Judge, alas,

_____

the gods; Spenser's account of his tor-
ment is based on the *Odyssey*, XI.
582–592. Both Boccaccio (*De Genea-
logia Deorum*, I. 14) and Natalis Comes
interpret this figure as a type of ava-

rice; Ovid (*Ars Amatoria*, II. 601–6)
and Pindar emphasize his arrogant pre-
sumption.
9. I.e., could never utterly die.
1. I.e., by whom Jove was formerly
feasted.

And most unjust, that by unrighteous
　And wicked doome,° to Jewes despiteous°　　　　　*judgment/malicious*
Delivered up the Lord of life to die,
　And did acquite a murdrer felonous;°　　　　　　　　　　　*wicked*
　The whiles my hands I washt in puritie,[2]
The whiles my soule was soyld with foule iniquitie."

63

Infinite moe,° tormented in like paine　　　　　　　　　　　*more*
　He there beheld, too long here to be told:
　Ne Mammon would there let him long remaine,
　For terrour of the tortures manifold,
　In which the damnéd soules he did behold,
　But roughly him bespake. "Thou fearefull foole,
　Why takest not of that same fruit of gold,
　Ne sittest downe on that same silver stoole,
To rest thy wearie person, in the shadow coole."[3]

64

All which he did, to doe him deadly fall
　In frayle intemperance through sinfull bayt;
　To which if he inclinéd had at all,
　That dreadfull feend, which did behind him wayt,
　Would him have rent in thousand peeces strayt:°　　　　　*immediately*
　But he was warie wise in all his way,
　And well perceivéd his deceiptfull sleight,
　Ne suffred lust his safetie to betray;
So goodly did beguile the Guyler° of the pray.　　　　　　　*deceiver*

65

And now he has so long remainéd there,
　That vitall powres gan wexe both weake and wan,°　　　　　*faint*
　For want of food, and sleepe, which two upbeare,
　Like mightie pillours, this fraile life of man,
　That none without the same endurén can.
　For now three dayes of men were full outwrought,°　　　　*completed*
　Since he this hardie enterprize began:
　For thy great Mammon fairely he besought,
Into the world to guide him backe, as he him brought.

66

The God, though loth, yet was constraind t'obay,
　For lenger time, then that, no living wight
　Below the earth, might suffred be to stay:
　So backe againe, him brought to living light.
　But all so soone as his enfeebled spright°　　　　　　　　*spirit*
　Gan sucke this vitall aire into his brest,

2. I.e., in token of purity. "Pilate . . . took water, and washed his hands before the multitude, saying, I am innocent of the blood of this just person . . ." (Matthew xxvii. 24).
3. Mammon invites Guyon to yield to sloth (and so to the punishment imposed on Theseus); to accept his offer is perhaps also, symbolically, to presume to probe into forbidden mysteries. Cf. F. Kermode, "The Cave of Mammon," in *Elizabethan Poetry:* Stratford-Upon-Avon Studies 2 (London, 1960), 151–174.

As overcome with too exceeding might,
The life did flit away out of her nest,
And all his senses were with deadly fit opprest.[4]

Canto VIII

*Sir Guyon laid in swowne is by
Acrates sonnes[1] despoyld,
Whom Arthur soone hath reskewéd
And Paynim brethren foyld.*

1

And is there care in heaven? and is there love
    In heavenly spirits to these creatures bace,
    That may compassion of their evils move?
    There is: else much more wretched were the cace
    Of men, then beasts. But O th'exceeding grace
    Of highest God, that loves his creatures so,
    And all his workes with mercy doth embrace,
    That blessed Angels, he sends to and fro,
To serve to wicked man, to serve his wicked foe.[2]

2

How oft do they, their silver bowers leave,
    To come to succour us, that succour want?°   need
    How oft do they with golden pineons, cleave
    The flitting skyes, like flying Pursuivant,°   messenger
    Against foule feends to aide us millitant?[3]
    They for us fight, they watch and dewly ward,
    And their bright Squadrons round about us plant,
    And all for love, and nothing for reward:
O why should heavenly God to men have such regard?

3

During the while, that Guyon did abide
    In Mammons house, the Palmer, whom whyleare°   earlier

4. Guyon's faint, in one sense, is the consequence of his having necessarily neglected the "vitall powres" of his nature: "food, and sleepe" have been denied throughout the course of his temptation, extending over a period of three days. The naturally temperate character of Guyon, further, as it were habituated to modesty and restraint, and confirmed in that course by continual resistance to the temptations of Mammon, has now been rendered virtually incapable of positively active expression: in parallel with the plight of Redcrosse, confined in the dungeon of Orgoglio, Guyon's condition requires the attentions of a higher power than his own. Analogies with Jonah's sojourn in the whale's belly and that of Jesus "in the heart of the earth" (Matthew xii. 40) are relevant too; but they need not obscure the fact that the action of Book II, expressed rather in terms of classical contexts and images than in those of scripture, takes place in a "fallen world." Cf. the essay by Roger Swearingen, in *SP*, LXXIV (1977), 165–185.

1. I.e., Pyrochles and Cymochles.

2. Cf. Hebrews i. 14: "Are [the angels] not all ministering spirits, sent forth to minister for them who shall be heirs of salvation?"; and, with special reference to the triple temptation of Jesus by Satan, Matthew iv. 11: "Then the devil leaveth him, and, behold, angels came and ministered unto him." In Book I, Arthur, the minister of grace, succoured the imprisoned Redcrosse; so here, an angel attends and guards the unconscious and helpless Guyon.

3. I.e., by warring on our behalf.

That wanton Mayd[4] of passage had denide,
By further search had passage found elsewhere,
And being on his way, approchéd neare,
Where Guyon lay in traunce, when suddenly
He heard a voice, that calléd loud and cleare,
"Come hither, come hither, O come hastily;"
That all the fields resounded with the ruefull cry.

4

The Palmer lent his eare unto the noyce,
  To weet, who calléd so importunely:°   *urgently*
  Againe he heard a more efforcéd° voyce,   *forceful*
  That bad him come in haste. He by and by[5]
  His feeble feet directed to the cry;
  Which to that shadie delve him brought at last,
  Where Mammon earst° did sunne his threasury: *formerly*
  There the good Guyon he found slumbring fast
In senselesse dreame; which sight at first him sore aghast.

5

Beside his head there sate a faire young man,
  Of wondrous beautie, and of freshest yeares,
  Whose tender bud to blossome new began,
  And flourish faire above his equall peares;[6]
  His snowy front° curléd with golden heares,   *forehead*
  Like Phoebus face adornd with sunny rayes,
  Divinely shone, and two sharpe wingéd sheares,°   *wings*
  Deckéd with diverse plumes, like painted Jayes,
Were fixéd at his backe, to cut his ayerie wayes.

6

Like as Cupido on Idaean hill,
  When having laid his cruell bow away,
  And mortall arrowes, wherewith he doth fill
  The world with murdrous spoiles and bloudie pray,
  With his faire mother he him dights° to play,   *prepares*
  And with his goodly sisters, Graces three;[7]
  The Goddesse pleaséd with his wanton play,
  Suffers her selfe through sleepe beguild to bee,
The whiles the other Ladies mind their merry glee.

7

Whom when the Palmer saw, abasht he was
  Through fear and wonder, that he nought could say,
  Till him the child bespoke, "Long lackt, alas,
  Hath bene thy faithfull aide in hard assay,°   *trial*
  Whiles deadly fit thy pupill doth dismay;°   *overcome*
  Behold this heavie sight, thou reverend Sire,
  But dread of death and dolour doe away;

4. I.e., Phaedria.
5. I.e., at once.
6. I.e., beyond that of other angels in his rank and station.
7. This view of the Graces as daughters of Venus (not merely her hand-maids, as in VI. x. 15) is probably derived from Boccaccio, *op. cit.*, III. 22, or Natalis Comes, *op. cit.*, IV. 13.

For life ere long shall to her home retire,
And he that breathlesse seemes, shal corage bold respire.[8]

8

"The charge, which God doth unto me arret,°   *entrust*
  Of his deare safetie, I to thee commend;°   *commit*
  Yet will I not forgoe, ne yet forget
  The care thereof my selfe unto the end,
  But evermore him succour, and defend
  Against his foe and mine: watch thou I pray;
  For evill is at hand him to offend."°   *harm*
  So having said, eftsoones he gan display°   *spread*
His painted nimble wings, and vanisht quite away.

9

The Palmer seeing his left empty place,
  And his slow eyes beguiléd of their sight,
  Woxe° sore affraid, and standing still a space,   *became*
  Gaz'd after him, as fowle escapt by flight;
  At last him turning to his charge behight,°   *entrusted*
  With trembling hand his troubled pulse gan try;
  Where finding life not yet dislodgéd quight,
  He much rejoyst, and courd° it tenderly,   *protected*
As chicken newly hatcht, from dreaded destiny.

[Directed to the scene by Archimago, Pyrochles and Cymochles are about to despatch the unconscious Guyon, but at this juncture Prince Arthur appears, and, after a fierce encounter with the brothers, kills them both. Allegorically, the episode recalls Arthur's deliverance of Redcrosse in Book I; but it is significant, and appropriate to the context of Book II, that in this engagement Arthur's shield remains covered, and that the final strokes in the battle are delivered with Guyon's sword. Having recovered consciousness, Guyon proceeds with the Prince to the House of Temperance, presided over by Alma; they gain entrance only after beating aside a ragged mob which is laying siege to the castle. This building represents the body, in its proper state of rationally controlled temperance, yet subject to continual attack by the Seven Deadly Sins together with those temptations to which the five senses are especially susceptible. Within the highest tower of this castle are the chambers of imagination, judgment, and memory; in this third room the two knights read about their respective ancestries in the chronicles of British and Elfin kings. On the following day, while Arthur remains behind to repel an attack on the castle by its besiegers (and eventually to destroy their leader, Maleger, who represents original sin as well as physical disease), Guyon departs with the Palmer to renew his quest.]

8. I.e., shall regain valiant spirit.

Canto XII

> Guyon, by Palmers governance,°   guidance
> passing through perils great,
> Doth overthrowe the Bowre of blisse,
> and Acrasie[1] defeat.

1

Now gins this goodly frame° of Temperance   structure
  Fairely to rise, and her adornéd hed
  To pricke° of highest praise forth to advance,   point
  Formerly grounded, and fast setteled
  On firme foundation of true bountihed;°   virtue
  And this brave knight, that for that vertue fights,
  Now comes to point of that same perilous sted,[2]
  Where Pleasure dwelles in sensuall delights,
Mongst thousand dangers, and ten thousand magick mights.

2

Two dayes now in that sea he sayléd has,
  Ne ever land beheld, ne living wight,
  Ne ought save perill, still as he did pas:
  Tho° when appearéd the third Morrow bright,   then
  Upon the waves to spred her trembling light,
  An hideous roaring farre away they heard,
  That all their senses filléd with affright,
  And streight they saw the raging surges reard
Up to the skyes, that them of drowning made affeard.[3]

3

Said then the Boteman, "Palmer stere aright,
  And keepe an even course; for yonder way
  We needes must passe (God to us well acquight,)°   preserve
  That is the Gulfe of Greedinesse, they say,
  That deepe engorgeth all this worldés pray:
  Which having swallowed up excessively,
  He soone in vomit up againe doth lay,°   cast
  And belcheth forth his superfluity,
That all the seas for feare do seeme away to fly.

4

"On th'other side an hideous Rocke is pight,
  Of mightie Magnes stone,[4] whose craggie clift

---

1. I.e., Acrasia (from Greek, "incontinence"; **disorder,** lack of harmony), a type of Circe, and the symbol of that self-indulgent sensuality which the continent man must steadfastly resist and control.
2. I.e., now directly approaches that dangerous place.
3. For the voyage of Guyon and the Palmer to the Bower of Bliss (sts. 2–38), Spenser draws primarily on

Homer's *Odyssey* and the *Mythologiae* of Natalis Comes; he makes use also of the voyage undertaken by Carlo and Ubaldo to Armida's bower, in Tasso, *Gerusalemme Liberata,* XV, and, perhaps, the medieval legend of St. Brandan, of which a version appears in the *Legenda Aurea.*
4. I.e., lodestone, supposed to be found in Magnesia (cf. Lucretius, *De Rerum Natura,* VI. 909–910).

Depending° from on high, dreadfull to sight,   *overhanging*
Over the waves his rugged armes doth lift,
And threatneth downe to throw his ragged rift°   *fragment*
On who so commeth nigh; yet nigh it drawes
All passengers, that none from it can shift:
For whiles they fly that Gulfes devouring jawes,
They on this rock are rent, and sunck in helplesse wawes."[5]

5

Forward they passe, and strongly he them rowes,
  Untill they nigh unto that Gulfe arrive,
  Where streame more violent and greedy growes:
  Then he with all his puissance doth strive
  To strike his oares, and mightily doth drive
  The hollow vessell through the threatfull wave,
  Which gaping wide, to swallow them alive,
  In th'huge abysse of his engulfing grave,
Doth rore at them in vaine, and with great terror rave.

6

They passing by, that griesly mouth did see,
  Sucking the seas into his entralles° deepe,   *inner depths*
  That seemed more horrible then hell to bee,
  Or that darke dreadfull hole of *Tartare*[6] steepe,
  Through which the damnéd ghosts doen often creepe
  Backe to the world, bad livers[7] to torment:
  But nought that falles into this direfull deepe,
  Ne that approcheth nigh the wide descent,
May backe returne, but is condemnéd to be drent.°   *drowned*

7

On th'other side, they saw that perilous Rocke,
  Threatning it selfe on them to ruinate,°   *fall crushingly*
  On whose sharpe clifts the ribs of vessels broke,
  And shivered ships, which had bene wreckéd late,
  Yet stuck, with carkasses exanimate°   *lifeless*
  Of such, as having all their substance spent
  In wanton joyes, and lustes intemperate,[8]
  Did afterwards make shipwracke violent,
Both of their life, and fame for ever fowly blent.°   *stained*

8

For thy, this hight The Rocke of vile Reproch,
  A daungerous and detestable place,
  To which nor fish nor fowle did once approch,
  But yelling Meawes,° with Seagulles hoarse and bace,   *gulls*
  And Cormoyrants, with birds of ravenous race,

5. I.e., helplessly sunk beneath the waves. The dangers described in sts. 3–8 are based on Homer's account of Scylla and Charybdis (*Odyssey*, XII).
6. I.e., the cavernous entrance to Tartarus (below Hades), where the rebel Titans were punished.
7. I.e., sinners.
8. Image and idea in lines 5–9 are paraphrased from **Natalis Comes**, *op. cit.*, VIII. 12.

Which still sate waiting on that wastfull clift,
For spoyle of wretches, whose unhappie cace,
After lost credite and consuméd thrift,
At last them driven hath to this despairefull drift.°   *end*

9

The Palmer seeing them in safetie past,
  Thus said; "Behold th'ensamples in our sights,
  Of lustfull luxurie and thriftlesse wast:
  What now is left of miserable wights,
  Which spent their looser daies in lewd delights,
  But shame and sad reproch, here to be red,°   *perceived*
  By these rent reliques, speaking their ill plights?
  Let all that live, hereby be counselléd,
To shunne Rocke of Reproch, and it as death to dred."

10

So forth they rowéd, and that Ferryman[9]
  With his stiffe oares did brush the sea so strong,
  That the hoare waters from his frigot° ran,   *swift vessel*
  And the light bubbles dauncéd all along,
  Whiles the salt brine out of the billowes sprong.
  At last farre off they many Islands spy,
  On every side floting the floods emong:
  Then said the knight, "Loe I the land descry,
Therefore old Syre thy course do thereunto apply."

11

"That may not be," said then the Ferryman,
  "Least we unweeting hap to be fordonne:°   *ruined*
  For those same Islands, seeming now and than,[1]
  Are not firme lande, nor any certein wonne,[2]
  But straggling plots, which to and fro do ronne
  In the wide waters: therefore are they hight
  The wandring Islands. Therefore doe them shonne;
  For they have oft drawne many a wandring wight
Into most deadly daunger and distresséd plight.

12

"Yet well they seeme to him, that farre doth vew,
  Both faire and fruitfull, and the ground dispred
  With grassie greene of delectable hew,
  And the tall trees with leaves apparelléd,
  Are deckt with blossomes dyde in white and red,
  That mote the passengers thereto allure;
  But whosoever once hath fastenéd
  His foot thereon, may never it recure,[3]
But wandreth ever more uncertain and unsure.

9. In the *Aeneid*, VI. 299, Charon, an aged and terrible figure, ferries the shades of the dead over the rivers of the underworld. Natalis Comes interprets this personage to signify confidence in God's mercy, sustaining the spirit of man near death (*op. cit.*, III. 4).
1. I.e., appearing here and there.
2. I.e., fixed place.
3. I.e., repair that error.

13

"As th'Isle of Delos whylome° men report — *formerly*
  Amid th' Aegaean sea long time did stray,
  Ne made for shipping any certaine port,
  Till that Latona⁴ traveiling that way,
  Flying from Junoes wrath and hard assay,° — *affliction*
  Of her faire twins was there deliveréd,
  Which afterwards did rule the night and day;
  Thenceforth it firmely was establishéd,
And for Apolloes honor highly herriéd."° — *praised*

14

They to him hearken, as beseemeth meete,
  And passe on forward: so their way does ly,
  That one of those same Islands, which doe fleet° — *float*
  In the wide sea, they needes must passen by,
  Which seemd so sweet and pleasant to the eye,
  That it would tempt a man to touchen there:
  Upon the banck they sitting did espy
  A daintie damzell, dressing of her heare,
By whom a litle skippet° floting did appeare. — *skiff*

15

She them espying, loud to them can° call, — *did*
  Bidding them nigher draw unto the shore;
  For she had cause to busie them withall;
  And therewith loudly laught: But nathemore
  Would they once turne, but kept on as afore:
  Which when she saw, she left her lockes undight,
  And running to her boat withouten ore,° — *oar*
  From the departing land it launchéd light,° — *quickly*
And after them did drive with all her power and might.

16

Whom overtaking, she in merry sort
  Them gan to bord, and purpose diversly,⁵
  Now faining dalliance and wanton sport,
  Now throwing forth lewd words immodestly;
  Till that the Palmer gan full bitterly
  Her to rebuke, for being loose and light:
  Which not abiding, but more scornefully
  Scoffing at him, that did her justly wite,° — *censure*
She turnd her bote about, and from them rowéd quite.

17

That was the wanton Phaedria, which late
  Did ferry him over the Idle lake:
  Whom nought regarding, they kept on their gate,° — *way*
  And all her vaine allurements did forsake,

4. For the story of Latona, cf. Ovid, *Metamorphoses*, VI. 184–218; but Spenser probably used Natalis Comes, who notes the instability of the island of Delos at that time (*op. cit.*, IX. 6). In Spenser's day, there was still a rather general belief in the existence of floating islands (for which Herodotus and Pliny also gave authority).
5. I.e., to accost, and chat of various things.

When them the wary Boateman thus bespake;
"Here now behoveth us well to avyse,°   *consider*
And of our safétie good heede to take;
For here before a perlous° passage lyes,   *dangerous*
Where many Mermayds haunt, making false melodies.

18

"But by the way, there is a great Quicksand,
And a whirlepoole of hidden jeopardy,
Therefore, Sir Palmer, keepe an even hand;
For twixt them both the narrow way doth ly."
Scarse had he said, when hard at hand they spy
That quicksand nigh with water coveréd;
But by the checkéd° wave they did descry   *checkered*
It plaine, and by the sea discolouréd:
It calléd was the quicksand of Unthriftyhed.

19

They passing by, a goodly Ship did see,
Laden from far with precious merchandize,
And bravely furnishéd, as ship might bee,
Which through great disaventure, or mesprize,°   *error*
Her selfe had runne into that hazardize;
Whose mariners and merchants with much toyle,
Laboured in vaine, to have recured° their prize,   *recovered*
And the rich wares to save from pitteous spoyle,
But neither toyle nor travell might her backe recoyle.°   *draw*

20

On th'other side they see that perilous Poole,
That calléd was the Whirlepoole of decay,
In which full many had with haplesse doole°   *grief*
Beene suncke, of whom no memorie did stay:
Whose circled waters rapt with whirling sway,[6]
Like to a restlesse wheele, still running round,
Did covet, as they passéd by that way,
To draw their boate within the utmost bound
Of his wide Labyrinth, and then to have them dround.

21

But th'heedfull Boateman strongly forth did stretch
His brawnie armes, and all his body straine,
That th'utmost sandy breach they shortly fetch,[7]
Whiles the dred daunger does behind remaine.
Suddeine they see from midst of all the Maine,
The surging waters like a mountaine rise,
And the great sea puft up with proud disdaine,
To swell above the measure of his guise,°   *custom*
As threatning to devoure all, that his powre despise.

22

The waves come rolling, and the billowes rore
Outragiously, as they enragéd were,

6. I.e., gripped by rapid whirling waters.   7. I.e., they soon reach the safety of the beach.

Or wrathfull Neptune did them drive before
  His whirling charet, for exceeding feare:
  For not one puffe of wind there did appeare,
  That all the three thereat woxe much afrayd,
  Unweeting, what such horrour straunge did reare.°   *cause*
  Eftsoones they saw an hideous hoast arrayd,
Of huge Sea monsters, such as living sence dismayd.[8]

23

Most ugly shapes, and horrible aspects,
  Such as Dame Nature selfe mote feare to see,
  Or shame, that ever should so fowle defects
  From her most cunning hand escapéd bee;
  All dreadfull pourtraicts of deformitee:
  Spring-headed Hydraes, and sea-shouldring Whales,
  Great whirlpooles, which all fishes make to flee,
  Bright Scolopendraes, armed with silver scales,
Mighty Monoceros, with immeasuréd° tayles.   *enormous*

24

The dreadfull Fish, that hath deserved the name
  Of Death, and like him lookes in dreadfull hew,
  The griesly Wasserman, that makes his game
  The flying ships with swiftnesse to pursew,
  The horrible Sea-satyre, that doth shew
  His fearefull face in time of greatest storme,
  Huge Ziffius, whom Mariners eschew°   *avoid*
  No lesse, then rockes, (as travellers informe,)
And greedy Rosmarines with visages deforme.

25

All these, and thousand thousands many more,
  And more deforméd Monsters thousand fold,
  With dreadfull noise, and hollow rombling rore,
  Came rushing in the fomy waves enrold,
  Which seemed to fly for feare, them to behold:
  Ne wonder, if these did the knight appall;
  For all that here on earth we dreadfull hold,
  Be but as bugs° to fearen babes withall,   *imaginary terrors*
Comparéd to the creatures in the seas entrall.°   *depths*

26

"Feare nought," then said the Palmer well avized;
  "For these same Monsters are not these in deed,
  But are into these fearefull shapes disguized
  By that same wicked witch, to worke us dreed,
  And draw from on this journey to proceede."

8. Most of the monsters named in sts. 23–24 are described in Pliny, *Historia Naturalis* (1st century A.D.) or in N. Gesner, *Historia Animalium* (1588); Spenser's catalogue includes creatures with especially strange or terrifying names. Thus, "whirlpooles," "Scolopendraes," "Monoceros," "Rosmarines" (and the "morse," named after Death), and "Ziffius," refer respectively to spouting whales, seagoing centipedes or annelid worms, narwhals, walruses, and swordfish. "Wasserman" and "Seasatyre" are perhaps referable to the dolphin and the seal; but Spenser was thinking first of mermen (described at length by Gesner).

Tho lifting up his vertuous staffe[9] on hye,
He smote the sea, which calméd was with speed,
And all that dreadfull Armie fast gan flye
Into great Tethys bosome,[1] where they hidden lye.

27

Quit° from that daunger, forth their course they kept,   *freed*
  And as they went, they heard a ruefull cry
  Of one, that wayld and pittifully wept,
  That through the sea the resounding plaints did fly:
  At last they in an Island did espy
  A seemely Maiden, sitting by the shore,
  That with great sorrow and sad agony,
  Seeméd some great misfortune to deplore,
And lowd to them for succour calléd evermore.

28

Which Guyon hearing, streight his Palmer bad,
  To stere the boate towards that dolefull Mayd,
  That he might know, and ease her sorrow sad:
  Who him avizing° better, to him sayd;   *counselling*
  "Faire Sir, be not displeasd, if disobayd:
  For ill it were to hearken to her cry;
  For she is inly nothing ill apayd,°   *pleased*
  But onely womanish fine forgery,
Your stubborne° hart t'affect with fraile infirmity.   *firm*

29

"To which when she your courage° hath inclind   *spirit*
  Through foolish pitty, then her guilefull bayt
  She will embosome° deeper in your mind,   *implant*
  And for your ruine at the last awayt."
  The knight was ruléd, and the Boateman strayt
  Held on his course with stayéd° stedfastnesse,   *constant*
  Ne ever shruncke, ne ever sought to bayt°   *rest*
  His tyréd armes for toylesome wearinesse,
But with his oares did sweepe the watry wildernesse.

30

And now they nigh approchéd to the sted,°   *place*
  Where as those Mermayds dwelt: it was a still
  And calmy bay, on th'one side shelteréd
  With the brode shadow of an hoarie hill,
  On th'other side an high rocke toured still,
  That twixt them both a pleasaunt port they made,
  And did like an halfe Theatre fulfill:
  There those five sisters[2] had continuall trade,°   *occupation*
And used to bath themselves in that deceiptfull shade.

9. Ubaldo, in Tasso's *Gerusalemme Liberata*, XIV. 73, bears a similar wand. Natalis Comes, remarking generally on the significance of Ulysses's voyage, observes that reason controls and restrains the baser impulses in man, as wild beasts must be held in check (*op. cit.*, VI. 6).

1. I.e., into the depths of the sea (cf. I. i. 39, and note).
2. The Sirens of Homer's *Odyssey*, XII, are the ultimate source for these figures, traditionally three in number; Spenser's reference to "five sisters" may indicate a correspondence with the five senses. Natalis Comes identifies the

31

They were faire Ladies, till they fondly° strived   *foolishly*
  With th'Heliconian maides³ for maistery;
  Of whom they over-comen, were deprived
  Of their proud beautie, and th'one moyity°   *half*
  Transformed to fish, for their bold surquedry,°   *presumption*
  But th'upper halfe their hew° retainéd still,   *form*
  And their sweet skill in wonted melody;
  Which ever after they abusd to ill,
T'allure weake travellers, whom gotten they did kill.

32

So now to Guyon, as he passéd by,
  Their pleasaunt tunes they sweetly thus applide;
  "O thou faire sonne of gentle Faery,
  That art in mighty armes most magnifide
  Above all knights, that ever battell tride,
  O turne thy rudder hither-ward a while:
  Here may thy storme-bet vessell safely ride;
  This is the Port of rest from troublous toyle,
The worlds sweet In, from paine and wearisome turmoyle."

33

With that the rolling sea resounding soft,
  In his big base them fitly answeréd,
  And on the rocke the waves breaking aloft,
  A solemne Meane° unto them measuréd,   *tenor*
  The whiles sweet Zephirus⁴ lowd whiteléd
  His treble, a straunge kinde of harmony;
  Which Guyons senses softly tickeléd,
  That he the boateman bad row easily,
And let him heare some part of their rare melody.

34

But him the Palmer from that vanity,
  With temperate advice discounselléd,
  That they it past, and shortly gan descry
  The land, to which their course they leveléd;°   *directed*
  When suddeinly a grosse fog over spred
  With his dull vapour all that desert has,
  And heavens chearefull face envelopéd,
  That all things one, and one as nothing was,
And this great Universe seemd one confuséd mas.

35

Thereat they greatly were dismayd, ne wist
  How to direct their way in darkenesse wide,
  But feard to wander in that wastfull mist,

Sirens and their song with the attractions of voluptuous desire, and more generally with the seductive powers that act on the irrational part of the soul (*op. cit.*, VII. 13).
3. I.e., the Muses. This contest is apparently Spenser's own invention.

4. The west wind, associated by Natalis Comes with the stimulation of sexual impulses (*op. cit.*, IV. 13). Cf. E. K.'s Glosse to "Aprill," which attributes to Zephyrus "the chiefedome and soveraigntye of al flowres and greene herbes, growing on earth."

For tombling into mischiefe unespide.
Worse is the daunger hidden, then descride.
Suddeinly an innumerable flight
Of harmefull fowles about them fluttering, cride,
And with their wicked wings them oft did smight,
And sore annoyéd, groping in that griesly night.

36

Even all the nation of unfortunate°   *ill-omened*
  And fatall birds about them flockéd were,
  Such as by nature men abhorre and hate,
  The ill-faste° Owle, deaths dreadfull messengere,   *ugly*
  The hoars Night-raven, trump of dolefull drere,
  The lether-wingéd Bat, dayes enimy,
  The ruefull Strich,° still waiting on the bere,   *screech owl*
  The Whistler° shrill, that who so heares, doth dy,   *plover*
The hellish Harpies, prophets of sad destiny.[5]

37

All those, and all that else does horrour breed,
  About them flew, and fild their sayles with feare:
  Yet stayd they not, but forward did proceed,
  Whiles th'one did row, and th'other stifly steare;
  Till that at last the weather gan to cleare,
  And the faire land it selfe did plainly show.
  Said then the Palmer, "Lo where does appeare
  The sacred° soile, where all our perils grow;   *cursed*
Therefore, Sir knight, your ready armes about you throw."

38

He hearkned, and his armes about him tooke,
  The whiles the nimble boate so well her sped,
  That with her crooked° keele the land she strooke,   *curved*
  Then forth the noble Guyon salliéd,
  And his sage Palmer, that him governéd;
  But th'other by his boate behind did stay.
  They marchéd fairly forth, of nought ydred,°   *afraid*
  Both firmely armd for every hard assay,
With constancy and care, gainst daunger and dismay.

39

Ere long they heard an hideous bellowing
  Of many beasts, that roard outrageously,
  As if that hungers point, or Venus sting
  Had them enragéd with fell surquedry;°   *arrogance*
  Yet nought they feard, but past on hardily,
  Untill they came in vew of those wild beasts:
  Who all attonce, gaping full greedily,
  And rearing fiercely their upstarting° crests,   *bristling*
Ran towards, to devoure those unexpected guests.

5. Celeno, the harpies' leader in Virgil's *Aeneid*, foretold the future in gloomy terms to Aeneas and his followers (III. 225–262).

40

But soone as they approcht with deadly threat,
   The Palmer over them his staffe upheld,
   His mighty staffe, that could all charmes defeat:
   Eftsoones their stubborne courages° were queld,   *spirits*
   And high advauncéd crests downe meekely feld,
   In stead of fraying,° they them selves did feare,   *terrifying*
   And trembled, as them passing they beheld:
   Such wondrous powre did in that staffe appeare,
All monsters to subdew to him, that did it beare.

41

Of that same wood it framed was cunningly,
   Of which Caduceus whilome was made,
   Caduceus the rod of Mercury,[6]
   With which he wonts° the Stygian realmes invade,   *is accustomed to*
   Through ghastly horrour, and eternall shade;
   Th' infernall feends with it he can asswage,
   And Orcus[7] tame, whom nothing can perswade,
   And rule the Furyes, when they most do rage:
Such vertue in his staffe had eke this Palmer sage.

42

Thence passing forth, they shortly do arrive,
   Whereas the Bowre of Blisse[8] was situate;
   A place pickt out by choice of best alive,
   That natures worke by art can imitate:[9]
   In which what ever in this worldly state
   Is sweet, and pleasing unto living sense,
   Or that may dayntiest fantasie aggrate,°   *gratify*
   Was pouréd forth with plentifull dispence,°   *liberality*
And made there to abound with lavish affluence.

43

Goodly it was encloséd round about,
   Aswell their entred guestes to keepe within,
   As those unruly beasts to hold without;
   Yet was the fence thereof but weake and thin;
   Nought feard their force, that fortilage° to win,   *fortress*
   But wisedomes powre, and temperaunces might,[1]
   By which the mightiest things efforcéd bin:[2]

6. Mercury's rod, the powers of which are described in the *Aeneid*, IV. 242–246, enables him to summon the shades of the dead from the underworld; in the view of Natalis Comes, Mercury represents the divine reason and wisdom of God (*op. cit.*, V. 5).
7. I.e., Pluto.
8. For his account of the Bower of Bliss, Spenser is indebted primarily to Tasso, *Gerusalemme Liberata*, XV–XVI (chiefly for descriptive detail), and to Trissino's romance, *L'Italia Liberata dai Goti* (for certain events and characters, including the name of the enchantress, "Acratia").
9. I.e., a place selected by the best living artists. In this physically lovely and seductive garden, however, art is characterized by excess (st. 50); nor does the beauty of the Bower reflect a condition in which art and nature are complementary, but rather one of mutual antagonism (st. 59).
1. I.e., that enclosure, proof against the physical force of Guyon or the beasts, was vulnerable to the power of wisdom and temperance.
2. I.e., are compelled.

And eke the gate was wrought of substaunce light,
Rather for pleasure, then for battery or fight.

44

Yt framéd was of precious yvory,
    That seemd a worke of admirable wit;
    And therein all the famous history
    Of Jason and Medaea was ywrit[3]
    Her mighty charmes, her furious loving fit,
    His goodly conquest of the golden fleece,
    His falséd faith, and love too lightly flit,
    The wondred° Argo, which in venturous peece[4]   *wonderful*
First through the Euxine seas bore all the flowr of Greece.

45

Ye might have seene the frothy billowes fry°   *foam*
    Under the ship, as thorough them she went,
    That seemd the waves were into yvory,
    Or yvory into the waves were sent;
    And other where the snowy substaunce sprent°   *sprinkled*
    With vermell,° like the boyes[5] bloud therein shed,   *vermilion*
    A piteous spectacle did represent,
    And otherwhiles° with gold besprinkeléd;   *elsewhere*
Yt seemd th'enchaunted flame, which did Creüsa[6] wed.

46

All this, and more might in that goodly gate
    Be red;° that ever open stood to all,   *seen*
    Which thither came: but in the Porch there sate
    A comely personage of stature tall,
    And semblaunce° pleasing, more then naturall,   *appearance*
    That travellers to him seemd to entize;
    His looser° garment to the ground did fall,   *too loose*
    And flew about his heeles in wanton wize,
Not fit for speedy pace, or manly exercize.

47

They in that place him Genius[7] did call:
    Not that celestiall powre, to whom the care
    Of life, and generation of all
    That lives, pertaines in charge particulare,

3. The ultimate source for the account of Jason's quest (in the ship Argo) for the Golden Fleece, and of his subsequent liaison with the sorceress Medea, is the *Argonautica*, by Apollonius of Rhodes (c. 200 B.C.), although the legend was known to Homer. That the gate is of ivory is an indication of the Bower's true nature; cf. the note on I. i. 40.
4. I.e., adventurous vessel.
5. Medea's younger brother Apsyrtus, killed by Jason at her instance, to delay pursuit of the Argonauts.
6. That he might be free to marry Creüsa, Creon's daughter, Jason deserted Medea; the sorceress subsequently destroyed Creüsa by sending her a poisoned robe, which burst into flames when she put it on.
7. Spenser depends primarily on Natalis Comes, *op. cit.*, IV. 3, for his account of Genius, god of birth and generation, for the evil spirits that oppose "Agdistes," and for the use of wine and flowers in ceremonial worship of Genius. The name "Agdistes" (or "Agdistis") is traditionally that of an androgynous deity, offspring of Zeus and Earth, connected with the Phrygian worship of Attis. But the figure here described as "Pleasures porter" (in sharp contrast to "Old Genius the porter" of the Garden of Adonis, in III. vi. 31) leads men by deceptive illusions into destructive lust.

Who wondrous things concerning our welfare,
And straunge phantomes doth let us oft forsee,
And oft of secret ill bids us beware:
That is our Selfe, whom though we do not see,
Yet each doth in him selfe it well perceive to bee.

48

Therefore a God him sage Antiquity
　Did wisely make, and good Agdistes call:
　But this same was to that quite contrary,
　The foe of life, that good envyes° to all,　　　　　*begrudges*
　That secretly doth us procure to fall,
　Through guilefull semblaunts,° which he makes us see.　*illusions*
　He of this Gardin had the governall,°　　　　　*management*
　And Pleasures porter was devizd° to bee,　　　　*considered*
Holding a staffe in hand for more formalitee.

49

With diverse flowres he daintily was deckt,
　And strowéd round about, and by his side
　A mighty Mazer° bowle of wine[8] was set,　　　*maple-wood*
　As if it had to him bene sacrifide;
　Wherewith all new-come guests he gratifide:
　So did he eke Sir Guyon passing by:
　But he his idle curtesie ℭefide,
　And overthrew his bowle disdainfully;
And broke his staffe, with which he charméd semblants sly.[9]

50

Thus being entred, they behold around
　A large and spacious plaine, on every side
　Strowéd with pleasauns, whose faire grassy ground
　Mantled with greene, and goodly beautifide
　With all the ornaments of Floraes pride,
　Wherewith her mother Art, as halfe in scorne
　Of niggard° Nature, like a pompous bride　　　　*miserly*
　Did decke her, and too lavishly adorne,
When forth from virgin bowre she comes in th'early morne.

51

Thereto the Heavens alwayes Joviall,°　　　　　*propitious*
　Lookt on them lovely,° still in stedfast state,　　*lovingly*
　Ne suffred storme nor frost on them to fall,
　Their tender buds or leaves to violate,
　Nor scorching heat, nor cold intemperate
　T'afflict the creatures, which therein did dwell,
　But the milde aire with season moderate
　Gently attempred, and disposd so well,
That still it breathéd forth sweet spirit° and holesome smell.　*breath*

8. The cup offered by Circe to Ulysses (*Odyssey*, X) is in one sense the model for this drinking bowl as well as for the golden cup held by Excess (in st. 56): to drink from either is to give way to sensual intemperance. The significance of the communion cup in Christian worship is parodied and perverted by both of these symbolic vessels.
9. I.e., raised deceitful illusions ("guilefull semblaunts").

52

More sweet and holesome, then the pleasant hill
   Of Rhodope,[1] on which the Nimphe, that bore
   A gyaunt babe, her selfe for griefe did kill;
   Or the Thessalian Tempe,[2] where of yore
   Faire Daphne Phoebus hart with love did gore;
   Or Ida, where the Gods loved to repaire,°   *resort*
   When ever they their heavenly bowres forlore;°   *deserted*
   Or sweet Parnasse, the haunt of Muses faire;
Or Eden selfe, if ought with Eden mote compaire.

53

Much wondred Guyon at the faire aspect
   Of that sweet place, yet suffred no delight
   To sincke into his sence, nor mind affect,
   But passéd forth, and lookt still forward right,°   *straight ahead*
   Bridling his will, and maistering his might:
   Till that he came unto another gate;
   No gate, but like one, being goodly dight
   With boughes and braunches, which did broad dilate° *spread out*
Their clasping armes, in wanton wreathings intricate.

54

So fashionéd a Porch with rare device,
   Archt over head with an embracing vine,
   Whose bounches hanging downe, seemed to entice
   All passers by, to tast their lushious wine,
   And did themselves into their hands incline,
   As freely offering to be gatheréd:
   Some deepe empurpled as the Hyacint,[3]
   Some as the Rubine,° laughing sweetly red,   *ruby*
Some like faire Emeraudes,° not yet well ripenéd.   *emeralds*

55

And them amongst, some were of burnisht gold,
   So made by art, to beautifie the rest,
   Which did themselves emongst the leaves enfold,
   As lurking from the vew of covetous guest,
   That the weake bowes, with so rich load opprest,
   Did bow adowne, as over-burdenéd.
   Under that Porch a comely dame did rest,
   Clad in faire weedes,° but fowle disorderéd,   *garments*
And garments loose, that seemd unmeet for womanhed.

56

In her left hand a Cup of gold she held,
   And with her right the riper° fruit did reach,   *overripe*
   Whose sappy liquor, that with fulnesse sweld,
   Into her cup she scruzd,° with daintie breach   *squeezed*
   Of her fine fingers, without fowle empeach,[4]

1. Jove turned Rhodope into a mountain as punishment for excessive pride (*Metamorphoses*, VI. 87–9).
2. The valley in Thessaly where Apollo pursued Daphne (*Metamor-* *phoses*, I. 452–567).
3. The jacinth, a gem of blue (or perhaps of reddish-orange) color.
4. I.e., crushing them daintily with her delicate fingers.

That so faire wine-presse made the wine more sweet:
   Thereof she usd to give to drinke to each,
   Whom passing by she happenéd to meet:
It was her guise,° all Straungers goodly so to greet.   *custom*

57

So she to Guyon offred it to tast;
   Who taking it out of her tender hond,
   The cup to ground did violently cast,
   That all in peeces it was broken fond,°   *found*
   And with the liquor stainéd all the lond:
   Whereat Excesse exceedingly was wroth,
   Yet no'te° the same amend, ne yet withstond,   *could not*
   But suffered him to passe, all° were she loth;   *although*
Who nought regarding her displeasure forward goth.

58

There the most daintie Paradise on ground,
   It selfe doth offer to his sober eye,
   In which all pleasures plenteously abound,
   And none does others happinesse envye:
   The painted flowres, the trees upshooting hye,
   The dales for shade, the hilles for breathing space,
   The trembling groves, the Christall[5] running by;
   And that, which all faire workes doth most aggrace,°   *add grace to*
The art, which all that wrought, appearéd in no place.[6]

59

One would have thought, (so cunningly, the rude,
   And scornéd parts were mingled with the fine,)
   That nature had for wantonesse ensude°   *imitated*
   Art, and that Art at nature did repine;°   *complain*
   So striving each th' other to undermine,
   Each did the others worke more beautifie;
   So diff'ring both in willes, agreed in fine:[7]
   So all agreed through sweete diversitie,
This Gardin to adorne with all varietie.

60

And in the midst of all, a fountaine[8] stood,
   Of richest substaunce, that on earth might bee,
   So pure and shiny, that the silver flood
   Through every channell running one might see;
   Most goodly it with curious imageree
   Was over-wrought, and shapes of naked boyes,
   Of which some seemd with lively jollitee,
   To fly about, playing their wanton toyes,°   *sports*
Whilest others did them selves embay° in liquid joyes.   *bathe*

5. I.e., the crystal stream.
6. The two final lines of st. 58, and most of st. 59, are based on Tasso, *Gerusalemme Liberata*, XVI. 9–10; Tasso's Garden of Armida is the primary model for many passages in sts. 58–88.
7. I.e., at last.
8. Fountain and bathing damsels are based on Tasso, *op. cit.*, XV. 55–66. In parallel with Archimago's seemingly pure fountain (I. i. 34), and the clear but enervating stream from which Redcrosse incautiously drinks (I. vii. 2–6), this fountain signifies the insidious attractions of intemperance, particularly in the form of sexual desire.

61

And over all, of purest gold was spred,
  A trayle of yvie in his native hew:
  For the rich mettall was so colouréd,
  That wight, who did not well avised it vew,
  Would surely deeme it to be yvie trew:
  Low his lascivious armes adown did creepe,
  That themselves dipping in the silver dew,
  Their fleecy flowres they tenderly did steepe,
Which° drops of Christall seemd for wantones to weepe.   *on which*

62

Infinit streames continually did well
  Out of this fountaine, sweet and faire to see,
  The which into an ample laver° fell,   *basin*
  And shortly grew to so great quantitie,
  That like a little lake it seemd to bee;
  Whose depth exceeded not three cubits hight,[9]
  That through the waves one might the bottom see,
  All paved beneath with Jaspar shining bright,
That seemd the fountaine in that sea did sayle upright.

63

And all the margent round about was set,
  With shady Laurell trees, thence to defend°   *ward off*
  The sunny beames, which on the billowes bet,°   *beat*
  And those which therein bathéd, mote offend.
  As Guyon hapned by the same to wend,
  Two naked Damzelles he therein espyde,
  Which therein bathing, seeméd to contend,
  And wrestle wantonly, ne cared to hyde,
Their dainty parts from vew of any, which them eyde.

64

Sometimes the one would lift the other quight
  Above the waters, and then downe againe
  Her plong, as over maisteréd by might,
  Where both awhile would coveréd remaine,
  And each the other from to rise restraine;
  The whiles their snowy limbes, as through a vele,
  So through the Christall waves appearéd plaine:
  Then suddeinly both would themselves unhele,°   *disclose*
And th'amarous sweet spoiles to greedy eyes revele.

65

As that faire Starre, the messenger of morne,
  His deawy face out of the sea doth reare:
  Or as the Cyprian goddesse,[1] newly borne
  Of th'Oceans fruitfull froth, did first appeare:
  Such seeméd they, and so their yellow heare
  Christalline humour° droppéd downe apace.   *moisture*

9. About 4½ feet.
1. Aphrodite, or Venus, who, according to Hesiod, sprang from sea foam (*Theogony*, 197); she was worshipped in ancient times principally on the islands of Cyprus and Cythera.

Whom such when Guyon saw, he drew him neare,
And somewhat gan relent° his earnest pace,   *slacken*
His stubborne brest gan secret pleasaunce to embrace.

66

The wanton Maidens him espying, stood
 Gazing a while at his unwonted guise:°   *manner*
 Then th'one her selfe low duckéd in the flood,
 Abasht, that her a straunger did avise:°   *regard*
 But th'other rather higher did arise,
 And her two lilly paps aloft displayd,
 And all, that might his melting hart entise
 To her delights, she unto him bewrayd:°   *revealed*
The rest hid underneath, him more desirous made.

67

With that, the other likewise up arose,
 And her faire lockes, which formerly were bownd
 Up in one knot, she low adowne did lose:°   *loosen*
 Which flowing long and thick, her clothed arownd,
 And th'yvorie in golden mantle gownd:
 So that faire spectacle from him was reft,°   *withdrawn*
 Yet that, which reft it, no lesse faire was fownd:
 So hid in lockes and waves from lookers theft,
Nought but her lovely face she for his looking left.

68

Withall she laughéd, and she blusht withall,
 That blushing to her laughter gave more grace,
 And laughter to her blushing, as did fall:
 Now when they spide the knight to slacke his pace,
 Them to behold, and in his sparkling face
 The secret signes of kindled lust appeare,
 Their wanton meriments they did encreace,
 And to him beckned, to approch more neare,
And shewd him many sights, that courage cold could reare.[2]

69

On which when gazing him the Palmer saw,
 He much rebukt those wandring eyes of his,
 And counseld well, him forward thence did draw.
 Now are they come nigh to the Bowre of blis
 Of her fond favorites so named amis:
 When thus the Palmer; "Now Sir, well avise;°   *take care*
 For here the end of all our travell° is: *arduous journey*
 Here wonnes° Acrasia, whom we must surprise,   *dwells*
Else she will slip away, and all our drift despise.[3]

70

Eftsoones they heard a most melodious sound,
 Of all that mote delight a daintie eare,
 Such as attonce might not on living ground,
 Save in this Paradise, be heard elswhere:
 Right hard it was, for wight, which did it heare,

2. I.e., that could excite sexual desire. 3. I.e., frustrate all our plans.

To read,° what manner musicke that mote bee: *tell*
    For all that pleasing is to living eare,
    Was there consorted° in one harmonee,   *joined*
Birdes, voyces, instruments, windes, waters, all agree.

71

The joyous birdes shrouded in chearefull shade,
    Their notes unto the voyce attempred° sweet;   *attuned*
    Th'Angelicall soft trembling voyces made
    To th'instruments divine respondence meet:°   *fitting*
    The silver sounding instruments did meet°   *join*
    With the base murmure of the waters fall:
    The waters fall with difference discreet,°   *suitable*
    Now soft, now loud, unto the wind did call:
The gentle warbling wind low answeréd to all.[4]

72

There, whence that Musick seeméd heard to bee,
    Was the faire Witch[5] her selfe now solacing,
    With a new Lover, whom through sorceree
    And witchcraft, she from farre did thither bring:
    There she had him now layd a slombering,
    In secret shade, after long wanton joyes:
    Whilst round about them pleasauntly did sing
    Many faire Ladies, and lascivious boyes,
That ever mixt their song with light licentious toyes.

73

And all that while, right over him she hong,
    With her false° eyes fast fixéd in his sight,   *deceitful*
    As seeking medicine, whence she was stong,
    Or greedily depasturing° delight: *feeding on*
    And oft inclining downe with kisses light,
    For feare of wakıng him, his lips bedewd,
    And through his humid eyes did sucke his spright,
    Quite molten into lust and pleasure lewd;
Wherewith she sighéd soft, as if his case she rewd.°   *pitied*

74

The whiles some one did chaunt this lovely lay;[6]
    "Ah see, who so faire thing doest faine° to see,   *delight*
    In springing flowre the image of thy day;
    Ah see the Virgin Rose, how sweetly shee
    Doth first peepe forth with bashfull modestee,
    That fairer seemes, the lesse ye see her may;
    Lo see soone after, how more bold and free

---

4. This stanza closely follows, but does not slavishly imitate, Tasso, *Gerusalemme Liberata*, XVI. 12; Spenser adds voices and instruments to the bird song and murmuring wind of his original.
5. I.e., Acrasia, whose seductive beauty masks and reinforces her power to destroy man's spiritual being (by inducing him to give way to sensual intemperance).
6. The theme of *carpe diem* ("take the day"), employed by Horace and the Latin elegiac poets, appears regularly in Renaissance verse; Spenser's song in sts. 74–75 is imitated from *Gerusalemme Liberata*, XVI. 14–15.

Her baréd bosome she doth broad display;
Loe see soone after, how she fades, and falles away.

75

"So passeth, in the passing of a day,
　　Of mortall life the leafe, the bud, the flowre,
　　Ne more doth flourish after first decay,
　　That earst was sought to decke both bed and bowre,
　　Of many a Ladie, and many a Paramowre:°   *lover*
　　Gather therefore the Rose, whilest yet is prime,
　　For soone comes age, that will her pride deflowre:
　　Gather the Rose of love, whilest yet is time,
Whilest loving thou mayst lovéd be with equall crime."°   *sin*

76

He ceast, and then gan all the quire of birdes
　　Their diverse notes t'attune unto his lay,
　　As in approvance of his pleasing words.
　　The constant paire heard all, that he did say,
　　Yet swarvéd not, but kept their forward way,
　　Through many covert groves, and thickets close,
　　In which they creeping did at last display°   *discover*
　　That wanton Ladie, with her lover lose,°   *wanton*
Whose sleepie head she in her lap did soft dispose.

77

Upon a bed of Roses she was layd,
　　As faint through heat, or dight to[7] pleasant sin,
　　And was arayd, or rather disarayd,
　　All in a vele of silke and silver thin,
　　That hid no whit her alablaster° skin,   *alabaster*
　　But rather shewd more white, if more might bee:
　　More subtile web Arachne[8] cannot spin,
　　Nor the fine nets, which oft we woven see
Of scorchéd deaw, do not in th'aire more lightly flee.°   *float*

78

Her snowy brest was bare to readie spoyle
　　Of hungry eies, which n'ote° therewith be fild,   *might not*
　　And yet through languour of her late sweet toyle,
　　Few drops, more cleare then Nectar, forth distild,
　　That like pure Orient perles adowne it trild,°   *trickled*
　　And her faire eyes sweet smyling in delight,
　　Moystened their fierie beames, with which she thrild
　　Fraile harts, yet quenchéd not; like starry light
Which sparckling on the silent waves, does seeme more bright.

79

The young man sleeping by her, seemd to bee
　　Some goodly swayne of honorable place,°   *rank*
　　That certes it great pittie was to see
　　Him his nobilitie so foule deface;°   *disgrace*
　　A sweet regard, and amiable grace,

7. I.e., prepared for.   8. Cf. II. vii. 28 and note.

Mixéd with manly sternnesse did appeare
Yet sleeping, in his well proportiond face,
And on his tender lips the downy heare
Did now but freshly spring, and silken blossomes beare.

80

His warlike armes, the idle instruments
 Of sleeping praise, were hong upon a tree,
 And his brave shield, full of old moniments,°   *knightly signs*
 Was fowly ra'st,° that none the signes might see;   *razed*
 Ne for them, ne for honour caréd hee,
 Ne ought, that did to his advauncement tend,[9]
 But in lewd loves, and wastfull luxuree,
 His dayes, his goods, his bodie he did spend:
O horrible enchantment, that him so did blend.°   *blind*

81

The noble Elfe, and carefull Palmer drew
 So nigh them, minding nought, but lustfull game,
 That suddein forth they on them rusht, and threw
 A subtile net,[1] which onely for the same
 The skilfull Palmer formally° did frame.   *in exact form*
 So held them under fast, the whiles the rest
 Fled all away for feare of fowler shame.
 The faire Enchauntresse, so unwares opprest,°   *surprised*
Tryde all her arts, and all her sleights, thence out to wrest.°   *twist*

82

And eke her lover strove: but all in vaine;
 For that same net so cunningly was wound,
 That neither guile, nor force might it distraine.°   *tear*
 They tooke them both, and both them strongly bound
 In captive bandes, which there they readie found:
 But her in chaines of adamant he tyde;
 For nothing else might keepe her safe and sound,
 But Verdant (so he hight) he soon untyde,
And counsell sage in steed thereof to him applyde.

83

But all those pleasant bowres and Pallace brave,°   *splendid*
 Guyon broke downe, with rigour pittilesse;
 Ne ought their goodly workmanship might save
 Them from the tempest of his wrathfulnesse,
 But that their blisse he turned to balefulnesse:
 Their groves he feld, their gardins did deface,
 Their arbers spoyle, their Cabinets° suppresse,   *bowers*
 Their banket houses burne, their buildings race,°   *raze*
And of the fairest late, now made the fowlest place.

9. By yielding to sensual intemperance, the youth has betrayed his knightly calling as well as his own potential for heroic action. Sir Philip Sidney touches on this theme in *Astrophel and Stella*: cf. esp. sonnets 18, 64.
1. With a net Vulcan trapped his wife Venus and her lover Mars (cf. *Metamorphoses*, IV. 169–189).

84

Then led they her away, and eke that knight
  They with them led, both sorrowfull and sad:
  The way they came, the same retourned they right,
  Till they arrivéd, where they lately had
  Charmed those wild-beasts, that raged with furie mad.
  Which now awaking, fierce at them gan fly,
  As in their mistresse reskew, whom they lad;°   *led*
  But them the Palmer soone did pacify.
Then Guyon askt, what meant those beastes, which there did ly.

85

Said he, "These seeming beasts are men indeed,
  Whom this Enchauntresse hath transforméd thus,
  Whylome her lovers, which her lusts did feed,
  Now turnéd into figures hideous,
  According to their mindes like° monstruous."[2]   *similarly*
  "Sad end," quoth he, "of life intemperate,
  And mournefull meed of joyes delicious:
  But Palmer, if it mote thee so aggrate,°   *please*
Let them returnéd be unto their former state."

86

Streight way he with his vertuous staffe them strooke,
  And streight of beasts they comely men became;
  Yet being men they did unmanly looke,
  And staréd ghastly, some for inward shame,
  And some for wrath, to see their captive Dame:
  But one above the rest in speciall,
  That had an hog beene late, hight Grille[3] by name,
  Repinéd greatly, and did him miscall,°   *abuse*
That had from hoggish forme him brought to naturall.

87

Said Guyon, "See the mind of beastly man,
  That hath so soone forgot the excellence
  Of his creation, when he life began,
  That now he chooseth, with vile difference,°   *change*
  To be a beast, and lacke intelligence."
  To whom the Palmer thus, "The donghill kind
  Delights in filth and foule incontinence:
  Let Grill be Grill, and have his hoggish mind,
But let us hence depart, whilest wether serves and wind."

---

2. Based on the account in Homer's *Odyssey*, X, of Circe's power to change men's shapes to those of swine, this episode also reflects Natalis Comes's observation on the Homeric story, that each man was changed into a beast appropriately matching the vice especially favored by him (*op. cit.*, VI. 6). 3. Plutarch's dialogue, *Whether the Beasts Have the Use of Reason*, is the ultimate source for this figure, who prefers (and deliberately chooses) the bestial condition to that of "naturall" form and being. Spenser probably knew of Grill from G. Gelli's *Circe* (1548), or Henry Iden's English translation of that work (1557).

The Third Booke of The Faerie Queene

Contayning
The Legend of Britomartis
or
Of Chastitie

1

It falles° me here to write of Chastity,   *befalls*
  That fairest vertue, farre above the rest;
  For which what needs me fetch from Faery
  Forreine ensamples, it to have exprest?
  Sith it is shrinéd in my Soveraines brest,
  And formed so lively° in each perfect part,   *lifelike*
  That to all Ladies, which have it profest,
  Need but behold the pourtraict° of her hart,   *image*
If pourtrayd it might be by any living art.

2

But living art may not least part expresse,
  Nor life-resembling pencill[1] it can paint,
  All were it Zeuxis or Praxiteles:[2]
  His daedale° hand would faile, and greatly faint,   *skillful*
  And her perfections with his error taint:
  Ne Poets wit, that passeth Painter farre
  In picturing the parts of beautie daint,°   *delicate*
  So hard a workmanship adventure darre,°   *dare*
For fear through want of words her excellence to marre.

3

How then shall I, Apprentice of the skill,
  That whylome° in divinest wits did raine,   *formerly*
  Presume so high to stretch mine humble quill?
  Yet now my lucklesse lot doth me constraine
  Hereto perforce. But O dred Soveraine
  Thus farre forth pardon, sith that choicest wit
  Cannot your glorious pourtraict figure plaine
  That I in colour showes may shadow° it,   *represent*
And antique° praises unto present persons fit.   *ancient*

4

But if in living colours, and right hew,°   *form*
  Your selfe you covet to see picturéd,
  Who can it doe more lively, or more trew,
  Then that sweet verse, with Nectar sprinckeléd,
  In which a gracious servant[3] picturéd

1. I.e., the artist's brush that creates "living art."
2. Zeuxis and Praxiteles, famous Greek artists of the fourth century B.C., epitomized excellence in painting and sculpture respectively.

3. I.e., Sir Walter Raleigh, whose poem *Cynthia* celebrated the virtues of Queen Elizabeth. He is represented in Book III, at one "level" of the allegory, by the figure of Timias, in his relations with Belphoebe.

His Cynthia, his heavens fairest light?
That with his melting sweetnesse ravishéd,
And with the wonder of her beamés bright,
My senses lulléd are in slomber of delight.

5

But let that same delitious° Poet lend   *pleasing*
  A little leave unto a rusticke Muse
  To sing his mistresse prayse, and let him mend,
  If ought amis her liking may abuse:°   *offend*
  Ne let his fairest Cynthia refuse,
  In mirrours more then one her selfe to see,
  But either Gloriana let her chuse,
  Or in Belphoebe fashionéd to bee:
In th'one her rule, in th'other her rare chastitee.[4]

Canto I

Guyon encountreth Britomart,
faire Florimell is chaced:
Duessaes traines[1] and Malecastaes
champions are defaced.°   *confounded*

1

The famous Briton Prince and Faerie knight,
  After long wayes and perilous paines endured,
  Having their wearie limbes to perfect plight°   *health*
  Restord, and sory° wounds right well recured,   *painful*
  Of the faire Alma greatly were procured,°   *urged*
  To make there lenger sojourne and abode;
  But when thereto they might not be allured,
  From seeking praise, and deeds of armes abrode,
They courteous congé° tooke, and forth together yode.°   *leave*
     went

2

But the captived Acrasia he sent,
  Because of travell long, a nigher way,
  With a strong gard, all reskew to prevent,
  And her to Faerie court safe to convay,
  That her for witnesse of his hard assay,°   *trial*
  Unto his Faerie Queene he might present:
  But he him selfe betooke another way,
  To make more triall of his hardiment,°   *courage*
And seeke adventures, as he with Prince Arthur went.

4. Cf. the "Letter to Raleigh," in which Spenser observes that [since] the Queen "beareth two persons, the one of a most royall Queene or Empresse, the other of a most vertuous and beautifull Lady, this latter part in some places I doe expresse in Belphoebe, fashioning her name according to your owne excellent conceipt of Cynthia." For a useful overview of Book III, cf. the essay by Harry Berger, Jr., in *Criticism*, XI (1969), 234–261.
1. The reference to Duessa probably reflects an earlier plan for Book III, in which she and Archimago were to have stirred up confusion and strife; cf. iv. 45.

3

Long so they travelléd through wastefull° wayes,   *desolate*
   Where daungers dwelt, and perils most did wonne,°   *abide*
   To hunt for glorie and renowméd praise;
   Full many Countries they did overronne,
   From the uprising to the setting Sunne,
   And many hard adventures did atchieve;
   Of all the which they honour ever wonne,
   Seeking the weake oppresséd to relieve,
And to recover right for such, as wrong did grieve.

4

At last as through an open plaine they yode,
   They spide a knight, that towards prickéd faire,[2]
   And him beside an aged Squire there rode,
   That seemed to couch° under his shield three-square,   *crouch*
   As if that age bad him that burden spare,
   And yield it those, that stouter could it wield:
   He them espying, gan himselfe prepare,
   And on his arme addresse° his goodly shield   *make ready*
That bore a Lion passant in a golden field.[3]

5

Which seeing good Sir Guyon, deare besought
   The Prince of grace, to let him runne that turne.
   He graunted: then the Faery quickly raught°   *took up*
   His poinant° speare, and sharpely gan to spurne°   *piercing/spur*
   His fomy steed, whose fierie feete did burne
   The verdant grasse, as he thereon did tread;
   Ne did the other backe his foot returne,
   But fiercely forward came withouten dread,
And bent° his dreadfull speare against the others head.   *aimed*

6

They bene ymet, and both their points arrived,
   But Guyon drove so furious and fell,°   *fiercely*
   That seemed both shield and plate it would have rived;°   *pierced*
   Nathelesse it bore his foe not from his sell,°   *saddle*
   But made him stagger, as he were not well:
   But Guyon selfe, ere well he was aware,   ·
   Nigh a speares length behind his crouper° fell,   *crupper*
   Yet in his fall so well him selfe he bare,
That mischievous mischance his life and limbes did spare.

7

Great shame and sorrow of that fall he tooke;
   For never yet, sith warlike armes he bore,
   And shivering[4] speare in bloudie field first shooke,

---

2. I.e., rode quickly and expertly.
3. I.e., (in heraldic terms), a lion walking, against a golden background. These were supposed to be the arms of Brute, legendary founder of the British race, and the ancestor of Britomart; cf. III. ix. 38–51.
4. I.e., quivering; or, perhaps, having the power to split and splinter whatever it strikes.

He found himselfe dishonoréd so sore.
Ah gentlest knight, that ever armour bore,
Let not thee grieve dismounted to have beene,
And brought to ground, that never wast before;
For not thy fault, but secret powre unseene,
That speare enchaunted was, which layd thee on the greene.[5]

8

But weenedst thou[6] what wight thee overthrew,
  Much greater griefe and shamefuller regret
  For thy hard fortune then thou wouldst renew,
  That of a single damzell thou wert met
  On equall plaine, and there so hard beset;
  Even the famous Britomart[7] it was,
  Whom straunge adventure did from Britaine fet,°   bring
To seeke her lover (love farre sought alas,)
Whose image she had seene in Venus looking glas.[8]

9

Full of disdainefull wrath, he fierce uprose,
  For to revenge that foule reprochfull shame,
  And snatching his bright sword began to close
  With her on foot, and stoutly forward came;
  Die rather would he, then endure that same.
  Which when his Palmer saw, he gan to feare
  His toward perill and untoward blame,[9]
  Which by that new rencounter he should reare:°   cause
For death sate on the point of that enchaunted speare.

10

And hasting towards him gan faire perswade,
  Not to provoke misfortune, nor to weene°   expect
  His speares default to mend with cruell blade;
  For by his mightie Science° he had seene   knowledge
  The secret vertue° of that weapon keene,   power
  That mortall puissance mote not withstond:

5. The spear, "made by Magick art of
yore" (iii. 60), recalls the enchanted
spear given by Astolfo to the warrior-
maiden Bradamante, in Ariosto, *Or-
lando Furioso*, XXIII. 15. Allegori-
cally, this encounter emphasizes the
power of chastity, which has strength
beyond that even of temperance or
continence.
6. I.e., if you knew.
7. Britomart (from Cretan, "sweet
maid") represents a human ideal of
chastity and, ultimately, of wedded love.
Described by Callimachus (in the third
century B.C.) as one of the nymphs in
Diana's retinue, "Britomartis" was also
known as Dictynna; in ancient Crete,
Diana was worshipped under the title of
Britomartis. The name of Spenser's
heroine also suggests Britain's warlike

might. In this figure are combined ele-
ments from several sources, e.g., the ad-
venturous course of her quest for Arthe-
gall parallels at many points that of
Bradamante for Ruggiero, in *Orlando
Furioso*; the dialogue between Brito-
mart and Glauce (in Canto ii) depends
closely on a similar scene in the pseudo-
Virgilian poem *Ciris*; and in general
conception Britomart may owe some-
thing to Camilla, the warrior-maiden
of Virgil's *Aeneid*, to whom Spenser
refers in iv. 2.
8. The "glassie globe," or crystal ball
(described in ii. 18–21), presented by
Merlin to King Ryence; it enabled the
viewer to foresee future events.
9. I.e., his imminent danger and un-
lucky injury.

Nothing on earth mote alwaies happie° beene.   *successful*
  Great hazard were it, and adventure fond,°   *foolish*
To loose long gotten honour with one evill hond.°   *action*

11

By such good meanes he him discounselléd,°   *dissuaded*
  From prosecuting his revenging rage;
  And eke the Prince like treaty handeléd,[1]
  His wrathfull will with reason to asswage,
  And laid the blame, not to his carriage,°   *conduct*
  But to his starting steed, that swarved asyde,
  And to the ill purveyance° of his page,   *preparation*
  That had his furnitures° not firmely tyde: *gear*
So is his angry courage fairely pacifyde.

12

Thus reconcilement was betweene them knit,
  Through goodly temperance, and affection chaste,
  And either vowd with all their power and wit,°   *knowledge*
  To let not others honour be defaste,°   *disgraced*
  Of friend or foe, who ever it embaste,°   *dishonored*
  Ne armes to beare against the others syde:
  In which accord the Prince was also plaste,
  And with that golden chaine of concord tyde.
So goodly all agreed, they forth yfere° did ryde.   *together*

13

O goodly usage of those antique times,[2]
  In which the sword was servant unto right;
  When not for malice and contentious crimes,
  But all for praise, and proofe of manly might,
  The martiall brood° accustoméd to fight: *race*
  Then honour was the meed° of victorie,   *reward*
  And yet the vanquishéd had no despight:
  Let later age that noble use envie,°   *imitate*
Vile rancour to avoid, and cruell surquedrie.°   *arrogance*

14

Long they thus travelléd in friendly wise,
  Through countries waste, and eke well edifyde,°   *built up*
  Seeking adventures hard, to exercise
  Their puissance, whylome full dernely° tryde: *grievously*
  At length they came into a forrest wyde,
  Whose hideous horror and sad trembling sound
  Full griesly° seemed: Therein they long did ryde,   *grim*
  Yet tract° of living creatures none they found,   *track*
Save Beares, Lions, and Buls, which roméd them around.

---

1. I.e., used similar appeals.
2. The placing of this stanza in the narrative recalls that of Ariosto's apostrophe to the virtues of ancient knighthood (*Orlando Furioso*, I. 22).

15

All suddenly out of the thickest brush,
    Upon a milk-white Palfrey° all alone,   *saddle horse*
    A goodly Ladie[3] did foreby° them rush,   *past*
    Whose face did seeme as cleare as Christall stone,
    And eke through feare as white as whalés bone:
    Her garments all were wrought of beaten gold,
    And all her steed with tinsell° trappings shone,   *glittering*
    Which fled so fast, that nothing mote° him hold,   *might*
And scarse them leasure gave, her passing to behold.

16

Still as she fled, her eye she backward threw,
    As fearing evill, that pursewd her fast;
    And her faire yellow locks behind her flew,
    Loosely disperst with puffe of every blast:
    All as a blazing starre[4] doth farre outcast
    His hearie° beames, and flaming lockes dispred,   *hairy*
    At sight whereof the people stand aghast:
    But the sage wisard telles, as he has red,°   *foreseen*
That it importunes° death and dolefull drerihed.° *portends/misery*

17

So as they gazéd after her a while,
    Lo where a griesly Foster° forth did rush,   *forester*
    Breathing out beastly lust her to defile:
    His tyreling jade[5] he fiercely forth did push,
    Through thicke and thin, both over banke and bush
    In hope her to attaine by hooke or crooke,
    That from his gorie sides the bloud did gush:
    Large were his limbes, and terrible his looke,
And in his clownish° hand a sharp bore speare he shooke. *rustic*

18

Which outrage when those gentle knights did see,
    Full of great envie° and fell gealosy,°   *indignation/anger*
    They stayd not to avise,° who first should bee,   *consider*
    But all spurd after fast, as they mote fly,
    To reskew her from shamefull villany.
    The Prince and Guyon equally bylive°   *speedily*
    Her selfe pursewd, in hope to win thereby

3. I.e., Florimell ("flower honey"), whose flight recalls that of the willful Angelica in *Orlando Furioso*, I. 33–35. In Spenser's allegory she represents primarily the evocative power of true beauty, forever the object of universal desire in all its varied forms. One "mythic" interpretation of Florimell's role in the poem is that of Northrop Frye, in "The Structure of Imagery in *The Faerie Queene*" (reprinted in this volume); by another view, the story of Florimell reflects "the alternate myth of Helen of Troy," i.e., the legend that Paris did not bring Helen herself, but an image of her, to Troy (T. P. Roche, Jr., *The Kindly Flame: A Study of the Third and Fourth Books of Spenser's Faerie Queene* [Princeton, N.J., 1964], 151–161).
4. I.e., a comet.
5. I.e., tired nag.

Most goodly meede, the fairest Dame alive:
But after the foule foster Timias did strive.

19

The whiles faire Britomart, whose constant mind,
  Would not so lightly follow beauties chace,
  Ne reckt° of Ladies Love, did stay behind,   *cared*
  And them awayted there a certaine space,
  To weet° if they would turne backe to that place: *know*
  But when she saw them gone, she forward went,
  As lay her journey, through that perlous Pace,°   *region*
  With stedfast courage and stout hardiment;
Ne evill thing she feared, ne evill thing she ment.°   *intended*

20

At last as nigh out of the wood she came,
  A stately Castle farre away she spyde,
  To which her steps directly she did frame.
  That Castle was most goodly edifyde,°   *built*
  And plaste for pleasure nigh that forrest syde:
  But faire before the gate a spatious plaine,
  Mantled with greene, itselfe did spredden wyde,
  On which she saw sixe knights, that did darraine°   *prepare*
Fierce battell against one,[6] with cruell might and maine.

21

Mainly° they all attonce upon him laid,   *violently*
  And sore beset on every side around,
  That nigh he breathlesse grew, yet nought dismaid,
  Ne ever to them yielded foot of ground
  All° had he lost much bloud through many a wound,   *although*
  But stoutly dealt his blowes, and every way
  To which he turnéd in his wrathfull stound,°   *assault*
  Made them recoile, and fly from dred decay,°   *destruction*
That none of all the sixe before, him durst assay.°   *engage*

22

Like dastard Curres, that having at a bay
  The salvage beast embost° in wearie chace,   *cornered*
  Dare not adventure° on the stubborne pray,   *rush in*
  Ne byte before, but rome from place to place,
  To get a snatch, when turnéd is his face.
  In such distresse and doubtfull° jeopardy,   *fearful*
  When Britomart him saw, she ran a pace°   *quickly*
  Unto his reskew, and with earnest cry,
Bad those same sixe forbeare that single enimy.

23

But to her cry they list° not lenden eare,   *cared*
  Ne ought the more their mightie strokes surceasse,
  But gathering him round about more neare,
  Their direfull rancour rather did encreasse;

6. I.e., Redcrosse. That Britomart aids
and effectively rescues him (cf. st. 29)
signifies primarily the necessity of chas-
tity to holiness. Cf. I Corinthians vi.
9–20.

Till that she rushing through the thickest preasse,
Perforce disparted their compacted gyre,°   circle
And soone compeld to hearken unto peace:
Tho° gan she myldly of them to inquyre   then
The cause of their dissention and outrageous yre.

24

Whereto that single knight did answere frame°;   make
  "These sixe would me enforce by oddes of might,
To chaunge my liefe,° and love another Dame,   beloved
That death me liefer were, then such despight,
So unto wrong to yield my wrested right:
For I love one, the truest one on ground,
Ne list me chaunge; she th'Errant Damzell hight,[7]
For whose deare sake full many a bitter stownd,°   attack
I have endured, and tasted many a bloudy wound."

25

"Certes,"° said she, "then bene ye sixe to blame,   surely
  To weene° your wrong by force to justifie: expect
For knight to leave his Ladie were great shame,
That faithfull is, and better were to die.
All losse is lesse, and lesse the infamie,
Then losse of love to him, that loves but one;
Ne may love be compeld by maisterie;°   superior force
For soone as maisterie comes, sweet love anone°   at once
Taketh his nimble wings, and soone away is gone."[8]

26

Then spake one of those sixe, "There dwelleth here
  Within this castle wall a Ladie faire,
Whose soveraine beautie hath no living pere,°   equal
Thereto so bounteous and so debonaire,
That never any mote with her compaire.
She hath ordaind this law, which we approve,°   make good
That every knight, which doth this way repaire,°   travel
In case he have no Ladie, nor no love,
Shall doe unto her service never to remove.

27

"But if he have a Ladie or a Love,
  Then must he her forgoe° with foule defame,   give up
Or else with us by dint of sword approve,°   prove
That she is fairer, then our fairest Dame,
As did this knight, before ye hither came."
"Perdie,"° said Britomart, "the choise is hard: indeed
But what reward had he, that overcame?"
"He should advauncéd be to high regard,"
Said they, "and have our Ladies love for his reward.[9]

7. I.e., Una, the wandering damsel.
8. Lines 7–9 are based on Chaucer's "The Franklin's Tale," 764–766.
9. The curious conditions enjoined by the Lady of Castle Joyeous anticipate her unrestrainedly sensual conduct in later stanzas of this Canto.

28

"Therefore aread° Sir, if thou have a love."   *tell*
  "Love have I sure," quoth she, "but Lady none;
  Yet will I not fro mine owne love remove,
  Ne to your Lady will I service done,
  But wreake° your wrongs wrought to this knight alone,   *avenge*
  And prove his cause." With that her mortall speare
  She mightily aventred° towards one,   *thrust*
  And downe him smot, ere well aware he weare,
Then to the next she rode, and downe the next did beare.

29

Ne did she stay, till three on ground she layd,
  That none of them himselfe could reare againe;
  The fourth was by that other knight dismayd,
  All° were he wearie of his former paine,   *although*
  That now there do but two of six remaine;
  Which two did yield, before she did them smight.
  "Ah," said she then, "now may ye all see plaine,
  That truth is strong, and trew love most of might,
That for his trusty servaunts doth so strongly fight."

30

"Too well we see," said they, "and prove° too well   *experience*
  Our faulty weaknesse, and your matchlesse might:
  For thy,[1] faire Sir, yours be the Damozell,
  Which by her owne law to your lot doth light,°   *fall*
  And we your liege men faith unto you plight."
  So underneath her feet their swords they mard,[2]
  And after her besought, well as they might,
  To enter in, and reape the dew reward:
She graunted, and then in they all together fared.

31

Long were it to describe the goodly frame,
  And stately port° of Castle Joyeous,   *appearance*
  (For so that Castle hight by commune name)
  Where they were entertaind with curteous
  And comely glee° of many gracious   *cheer*
  Faire Ladies, and of many a gentle knight,
  Who through a Chamber long and spacious,
  Eftsoones° them brought unto their Ladies sight,   *presently*
That of them cleepéd° was the Lady of delight.[3]   *called*

32

But for to tell the sumptuous aray
  Of that great chamber, should be labour lost:

1. I.e., therefore.
2. I.e., in token of defeat, they broke or hacked the blades of their swords, casting them at the feet of Britomart.
3. I.e., Malecasta ("badly chaste"), whose luxuriously ornate castle recalls similarly lavish dwellings in medieval romances of courtly love. Spenser's emphasis on extravagant excess indicates Malecasta's affinity with the destructively incontinent Acrasia of Book II; in this Castle, as in the Bower, the sexuality of the central figure is finally sterile.

For living wit, I weene, cannot display
The royall riches and exceeding cost,°   *value*
Of every pillour and of every post;
Which all of purest bullion framéd were,
And with great pearles and pretious stones embost,°   *adorned*
That the bright glister of their beamés cleare
Did sparckle forth great light, and glorious did appeare.

33

These straunger knights through passing, forth were led
   Into an inner rowme, whose royaltee
   And rich purveyance might uneath be red;[4]
   Mote Princes place beseeme so deckt to bee.
   Which stately manner when as they did see,
   The image of superfluous riotize,°   *extravagance*
   Exceeding much the state of meane degree,[5]
   They greatly wondred, whence so sumptuous guize°   *way of life*
Might be maintaynd, and each gan diversely devize.°   *guess*

34

The wals were round about apparelléd
   With costly clothes of Arras and of Toure,°   *Tours*
   In which with cunning hand was pourtrahéd
   The love of Venus and her Paramoure°   *lover*
   The faire Adonis, turnéd to a flowre,
   A worke of rare device, and wondrous wit.[6]
   First did it shew the bitter balefull stowre,°   *turmoil*
   Which her assayd with many a fervent fit,
When first her tender hart was with his beautie smit.

35

Then with what sleights and sweet allurements she
   Entyst the Boy, as well that art she knew,
   And wooéd him her Paramoure to be;
   Now making girlonds of each flowre that grew,
   To crowne his golden lockes with honour dew;°   *due*
   Now leading him into a secret shade
   From his Beauperes,° and from bright heavens vew,   *companions*
   Where him to sleepe she gently would perswade,
Or bathe him in a fountaine by some covert° glade.   *secret*

36

And whilst he slept, she over him would spred
   Her mantle, coloured like the starry skyes,
   And her soft arme lay underneath his hed,
   And with ambrosiall kisses bathe his eyes;

4. I.e., the luxurious richness of which might scarcely be described.

5. I.e., medium rank or class.

6. The myth of Venus and Adonis appears in Ovid, *Metamorphoses*, X. 519–739; Spenser drew on that source as well as on the version of Natalis Comes, the Renaissance mythographer (*Mythologiae*, V. 16). This myth is the operative symbol of Book III, which elaborates the various significances of the story in episode, character, and visual image. C. S. Lewis observes that these tapestries, appropriately in the setting of Castle Joyeous, present "a picture not of 'lust in action' but of lust suspended . . ." (*The Allegory of Love* [Oxford, 1936], p. 332).

And whilest he bathed, with her two crafty spyes,
 She secretly would search each daintie lim,
 And throw into the well sweet Rosemaryes,
 And fragrant violets, and Pances° trim,   *pansies*
And ever with sweet Nectar she did sprinkle him.

37

So did she steale his heedelesse hart away,
 And joyd his love in secret unespyde.
 But for she saw him bent to cruell play,
 To hunt the salvage beast in forrest wyde,
 Dreadfull of daunger, that mote him betyde,°   *befall*
 She oft and oft advized him to refraine
 From chase of greater° beasts, whose brutish pryde° *too great/spirit*
Mote breede° him scath° unwares: but all in vaine; *bring/harm*
For who can shun the chaunce, that dest'ny doth ordaine?

38

Lo, where beyond he lyeth languishing,°   *suffering*
 Deadly engoréd of a great wild Bore,
 And by his side the Goddesse groveling
 Makes for him endlesse mone, and evermore
 With her soft garment wipes away the gore,
 Which staines his snowy skin with hatefull hew:
 But when she saw no helpe might him restore,
 Him to a dainty flowre she did transmew,°   *transform*
Which in that cloth was wrought, as if it lively° grew. *actually*

39

So was that chamber clad in goodly wize,
 And round about it many beds were dight,[7]
 As whilome was the antique worldés guize,°   *custom*
 Some for untimely° ease, some for delight,   *unsuitable*
 As plebaséd them to use, that use it might:
 And all was full of Damzels, and of Squires,
 Dauncing and reveling both day and night,
And·swimming deepe in sensuall desires,
And Cupid still emongst them kindled lustfull fires.

40

And all the while sweet Musicke did divide°   *descant*
 Her looser° notes with Lydian[8] harmony;   *too loose*
 And all the while sweet birdes thereto applide
 Their daintie layes and dulcet melody,
 Ay° caroling of love and jollity,   *always*
 That wonder was to heare their trim consort.° *harmony*
 Which when those knights beheld, with scornefull eye,

---

7. I.e., many couches were arranged.
8. In Greek music, the Ionian and Lydian modes were considered to be soft, soothing, and suited to hospitable gatherings (Plato, *Republic*, III. 398); Spenser's near-contemporary Roger Ascham notes that the sweetness of the Lydian mode stimulates immoral thoughts and actions in young persons (*Toxophilus*, in *English Works of Roger Ascham*, ed. W. A. Wright [Cambridge, 1904], 4 vols., I, p. 12).

They sdeignéd° such lascivious disport,   *disdained*
And loathed the loose demeanure° of that wanton sort.   *conduct*

41

Thence they were brought to that great Ladies vew,
  Whom they found sitting on a sumptuous bed,
  That glistred all with gold and glorious shew,
  As the proud Persian Queenes accustoméd:[9]
  She seemd a woman of great bountihed,°   *virtue*
  And of rare beautie, saving that askaunce°   *sidewise*
  Her wanton eyes, ill signes of womanhed,
  Did roll too lightly, and too often glaunce,
Without regard of grace, or comely amenaunce.°   *behavior*

42

Long worke it were, and needlesse to devize°   *describe*
  Their goodly entertainement and great glee:
  She causéd them be led in curteous wize
  Into a bowre, disarméd for to bee,
  And chearéd well with wine and spiceree:°   *spiced refreshment*
  The Redcrosse Knight was soone disarméd there,
  But the brave Mayd would not disarméd bee,
  But onely vented up her umbriere,[1]
And so did let her goodly visage to appere.

43

As when faire Cynthia, in darkesome night,
  Is in a noyous° cloud envelopéd,   *noxious*
  Where she may find the substaunce thin and light,
  Breakes forth her silver beames, and her bright hed
  Discovers° to the world discomfited;°   *reveals/dejected*
  Of the poore traveller, that went astray,
  With thousand blessings she is heriéd;°   *praised*
  Such was the beautie and the shining ray,
With which faire Britomart gave light unto the day.[2]

44

And eke those six, which lately with her fought,
  Now were disarmd, and did them selves present
  Unto her vew, and company unsoght;
  For they all seeméd curteous and gent,
  And all sixe brethren, borne of one parent,
  Which had them traynd in all civilitee,°   *courtesy*
  And goodly taught to tilt and turnament;[3]
  Now were they liegemen to this Lady free,°   *noble*
And her knights service ought, to hold of her in fee.[4]

9. Duessa (I. ii. 13) and Lucifera (I. iv. 7) are described in similar terms.
1. I.e., raised the face guard of her helmet.
2. The stanza apparently glances at a similar episode in Ariosto, *Orlando Furioso*, when Bradamante removes her helmet (XXXII. 79–80); cf. the note on III. ix. 20.

3. A tilt is an encounter between two mounted knights, armed with spears; a tournament involves a number of knights, armed with spears and swords.
4. I.e., owed her knightly service, as their feudal homage.

45

The first of them by name Gardante hight, [5]
  A jolly person, and of comely vew;°   *appearance*
  The second was Parlante, a bold knight,
  And next to him Jocante did ensew;
  Basciante did him selfe most curteous shew;
  But fierce Bacchante seemd too fell and keene;
  And yet in armes Noctante greater grew:
    All were faire knights, and goodly well beseene, [6]
But to faire Britomart they all but shadowes beene.

46

For she was full of amiable° grace,   *pleasing*
  And manly terrour mixéd therewithall,
  That as the one stird up affections bace,
  So th'other did mens rash desires apall,
  And hold them backe, that would in errour fall; [7]
  As he, that hath espide a vermeill° Rose,   *vermilion*
  To which sharpe thornes and breres the way forstall,
  Dare not for dread his hardy hand expose,
But wishing it far off, his idle° wish doth lose.   *futile*

47

Whom when the Lady saw so faire a wight,
  All ignoraunt of her contrary sex,
  (For she her weend a fresh and lusty knight)
  She greatly gan enamouréd to wex,°   *grow*
  And with vaine thoughts her falséd° fancy vex: *deceived*
  Her fickle hart conceivéd hasty fire,
  Like sparkes of fire, which fall in sclender flex,°   *flax*
  That shortly brent° into extreme desire,   *burned*
And ransackt all her veines with passion entire.

48

Eftsoones she grew to great impatience
  And into termes of open outrage brust, [8]
  That plaine discovered° her incontinence,   *revealed*
  Ne reckt she, who had meaning did mistrust;
  For she was given all to fleshly lust,
  And pouréd forth in sensuall delight,
  That all regard of shame she had discust,°   *shaken off*
  And meet° respect of honour put to flight: *proper*
So shamelesse beauty soone becomes a loathly sight.

49

Faire Ladies, that to love captivéd arre,
  And chaste desires do nourish in your mind,

5. The knights' names (respectively, "watching," "speaking," "jesting," "kissing," "drinking," and, perhaps, "nocturnal activity") indicate their qualifications for attendance on Malecasta, the ruling personage of this court-of-love establishment. Similarly named figures appear in *The Romance of the Rose* and other medieval romances of courtly love by, e.g., Boccaccio and Machaut.
6. I.e., of good appearance.
7. Britomart is both woman and warrior; further, in her nature the attractive femininity associated with Venus is combined with the cool and virtuous strength of Diana.
8. I.e., broke into openly intemperate terms.

Let not her fault your sweet affections marre,
Ne blot the bounty° of all womankind;   *goodness*
'Mongst thousands good one wanton Dame to find:
Emongst the Roses grow some wicked weeds;
For this was not to love, but lust inclind;
For love does alwayes bring forth bounteous° deeds,   *virtuous*
And in each gentle hart desire of honour breeds.[9]

50

Nought so of love this looser° Dame did skill,°   *too loose/understand*
But as a coale to kindle fleshly flame,
Giving the bridle to her wanton will,
And treading under foote her honest name:
Such love is hate, and such desire is shame.
Still did she rove at her with crafty glaunce
Of her false eyes, that at her hart did ayme,
And told her meaning in her countenaunce;
But Britomart dissembled it with ignoraunce.[1]

51

Supper was shortly dight° and downe they sat,   *set out*
Where they were servéd with all sumptuous fare,
Whiles fruitfull Ceres, and Lyaeus fat[2]
Pourd out their plenty, without spight° or spare:°   *grudge/restraint*
Nought wanted there, that dainty was and rare;
And aye the cups their bancks did overflow,
And aye betweene the cups, she did prepare
Way to her love, and secret darts° did throw;   *glances*
But Britomart would not such guilfull message know.

52

So when they slakéd had the fervent heat
Of appetite with meates of every sort,
The Lady did faire Britomart entreat,
Her to disarme, and with delightfull sport
To loose her warlike limbs and strong effort,°   *power*
But when she mote not thereunto be wonne,
(For she her sexe under that straunge purport°   *appearance*
Did use to hide, and plaine apparaunce shonne:)
In plainer wise to tell her grievaunce she begonne.

53

And all attonce discovered her desire
With sighes, and sobs, and plaints, and piteous griefe,
The outward sparkes of her in burning fire;
Which spent in vaine, at last she told her briefe,
That but if[3] she did lend her short reliefe,
And do her comfort, she mote algates° dye.   *altogether*

9. This apostrophe to womankind is modeled on a similar passage in *Orlando Furioso*, XXVIII. 1.
1. I.e., pretended not to understand her meaning.
2. Ceres (Demeter) was the goddess of earth and its fruits, Lyaeus (Bacchus) the god of wine; thus (by metonymy), food and drink were plenteously provided.
3. I.e., unless.

But the chaste damzell, that had never priefe°   *experience*
Of such malengine° and fine forgerie,°   *guile/deceit*
Did easily beleeve her strong extremitie.[4]

54

Full easie was for her to have beliefe,
  Who by self-feeling of her feeble sexe,
  And by long triall of the inward griefe,
  Wherewith imperious love her hart did vexe,
  Could judge what paines do loving harts perplexe.°   *torment*
  Who meanes no guile, be guiléd soonest shall,
  And to faire semblaunce doth light faith annexe;°   *add*
  The bird, that knowes not the false fowlers call,
Into his hidden net full easily doth fall.

55

For thy she would not in discourteise wise,
  Scorne the faire offer of good will profest;
  For great rebuke° it is, love to despise,   *shame*
  Or rudely sdeigne a gentle harts request;
  But with faire countenaunce, as beseeméd best,
  Her entertaynd;° nath'lesse she inly deemd   *treated*
  Her love too light, to wooe a wandring guest:
  Which she misconstruing, thereby esteemd
That from like° inward fire that outward smoke had steemd. *matching*

56

Therewith a while she her flit° fancy fed,   *changeful*
  Till she mote winne fit time for her desire,
  But yet her wound still inward freshly bled,
  And through her bones the false instilléd fire
  Did spred it selfe, and venime close° inspire.   *secretly*
  Tho were the tables taken all away,
  And every knight, and every gentle Squire
  Gan choose his dame with Basciomani° gay,   *hand kissing*
With whom he meant to make his sport and courtly play.

57

Some fell to daunce, some fell to hazardry,°   *dicing*
  Some to make love, some to make meriment,
  As diverse wits to divers things apply;
  And all the while faire Malecasta bent
  Her crafty engins° to her close intent.   *wiles*
  By this th'eternall lampes, wherewith high Jove
  Doth light the lower world, were halfe yspent,
  And the moist daughters of huge Atlas[5] strove
Into the Ocean deepe to drive their weary drove.

58

High time it seeméd then for every wight
  Them to betake unto their kindly° rest;   *natural*

4. Because, although Britomart's chastity contrasts sharply with the incontinence of Malecasta, her innocent inexperience leads her to interpret Malecasta's conduct in the light of her own love (cf. Roche, *op. cit.*, p. 69).

5. The Hyades, or "rainers," seven stars in the constellation Taurus. Natalis Comes (*op. cit.*, IV. 7) calls them the daughters of Atlas.

Eftsoones long waxen torches weren light,
Unto their bowres° to guiden every guest: *chambers*
Tho when the Britonesse saw all the rest
Avoided° quite, she gan her selfe despoile,°   *departed/disrobe*
And safe commit to her soft fethered nest,
Where through long watch, and late dayes weary toile,
She soundly slept, and carefull thoughts did quite assoile.°   *dispel*

59

Now whenas all the world in silence deepe
   Yshrowded was, and every mortall wight
   Was drownéd in the depth of deadly° sleepe,   *deathlike*
   Faire Malecasta, whose engrievéd° spright   *afflicted*
   Could find no rest in such perplexéd plight,
   Lightly arose out of her wearie bed,[6]
   And under the blacke vele of guilty Night,[7]
   Her with a scarlot mantle coveréd,
That was with gold and Ermines faire envelopéd.

60

Then panting soft, and trembling everie joynt,
   Her fearfull feete towards the bowre she moved;
   Where she for secret purpose did appoynt
   To lodge the warlike mayd unwisely loved,
   And to her bed approching, first she prooved,°   *tested*
   Whether she slept or wakt, with her soft hand
   She softly felt, if any member mooved,
   And lent her wary eare to understand,
If any puffe of breath, or signe of sence she fond.

61

Which whenas none she fond, with easie shift,[8]
   For feare least her unwares she should abrayd,°   *awaken*
   Th'embroderd quilt she lightly up did lift,
   And by her side her selfe she softly layd,
   Of every finest° fingers touch affrayd;   *slightest*
   Ne any noise she made, ne word she spake,
   But inly sighed. At last the royall Mayd
   Out of her quiet slomber did awake,
And chaungd her weary side, the better ease to take.

62

Where feeling one close couchéd by her side,
   She lightly lept out of her filéd° bed,   *defiled*
   And to her weapon ran, in minde to gride°   *pierce*
   The loathéd leachour. But the Dame halfe ded
   Through suddein feare and ghastly drerihed,°   *horror*
   Did shrieke alowd, that through the house it rong,
   And the whole family therewith adred,°   *terrified*
   Rashly° out of their rouzéd couches sprong,   *hastily*
And to the troubled chamber all in armes did throng.

6. I.e., from the bed where she had restlessly lain.
7. Night is described as "guilty" because its black veil protectively conceals evil things; in Hesiod, *Theogony*, 224, Night is the mother of Deceit. Cf. III. iv. 55.
8. I.e., moving softly.

63

And those six Knights that Ladies Champions,
 And eke the Redcrosse knight ran to the stownd,°   *uproar*
 Halfe armed and halfe unarmd, with them attons:
 Where when confusedly they came, they fownd
 Their Lady lying on the sencelesse grownd; [9]
 On th'other side, they saw the warlike Mayd
 All in her snow-white smocke, with locks unbownd,
 Threatning the point of her avenging blade,
That with so troublous terrour they were all dismayde.

64

About their Lady first they flockt arownd,
 Whom having laid in comfortable couch,
 Shortly they reard out of her frosen swownd;°   *swoon*
 And afterwards they gan with fowle reproch
 To stirre up strife, and troublous contecke broch: [1]
 But by ensample of the last dayes losse,
 None of them rashly durst to her approch,
 Ne in so glorious spoile themselves embosse;°   *cover*
Her succourd eke the Champion of the bloudy Crosse.

65

But one of those six knights, Gardante hight,
 Drew out a deadly bow and arrow keene,
 Which forth he sent with felonous° despight,   *fierce*
 And fell intent against the virgin sheene:°   *fair*
 The mortall steele stayd not, till it was seene
 To gore her side, yet was the wound not deepe,
 But lightly raséd° her soft silken skin,   *grazed*
 That drops of purple bloud thereout did weepe,
Which did her lilly smock with staines of vermeil steppe. [2]

66

Wherewith enraged she fiercely at them flew,
 And with her flaming sword about her layd,
 That none of them foule mischiefe could eschew, [3]
 But with her dreadfull strokes were all dismayd:
 Here, there, and every where about her swayd°   *swung*
 Her wrathfull steele, that none mote it abide;°   *endure*
 And eke the Redcrosse knight gave her good aid,
 Ay joyning foot to foot, and side to side,
That in short space their foes they have quite terrifide.

67

Tho whenas all were put to shamefull flight,
 The noble Britomartis her arayd,
 And her bright armes about her body dight:°   *put on*
 For nothing would she lenger there be stayd,
 Where so loose life, and so ungentle trade°   *conduct*

9. I.e., lying senseless on the ground.
1. I.e., instigate troublesome discord.
2. In this Castle, even Britomart's chas-
tity is not altogether proof against the
ogling stares of lustful admirers.
3. I.e., none could avoid deadly danger.

Was usd of Knights and Ladies seeming gent:
So earely ere the grosse Earthes gryesy shade,[4]
Was all disperst out of the firmament,
They tooke their steeds, and forth upon their journey went.

Canto II

*The Redcrosse knight to Britomart
describeth Artegall:
The wondrous myrrhour, by which she
in love with him did fall.*

1

Here have I cause, in men just blame to find,
   That in their proper° prayse too partiall bee,   *own*
   And not indifferent° to woman kind,   *impartial*
   To whom no share in armes and chevalrie
   They do impart,° ne maken memorie   *allow*
   Of their brave gestes° and prowesse martiall;   *exploits*
   Scarse do they spare to one or two or three,
   Rowme in their writs; yet the same writing small
Does all their deeds deface,° and dims their glories all.   *obscure*

2

But by record of antique times I find,
   That women wont in warres to beare most sway,
   And to all great exploits them selves inclind:
   Of which they still the girlond bore away,
   Till envious Men fearing their rules decay,°   *destruction*
   Gan coyne streight° lawes to curb their liberty;   *strict*
   Yet sith they warlike armes have layd away,
   They have exceld in artes and pollicy,°   *statecraft*
That now we foolish men that prayse gin eke t'envy.[1]

3

Of warlike puissaunce in ages spent,
   Be thou faire Britomart, whose prayse I write,
   But of all wisedome be thou precedent,°   *model*
   O soveraigne Queene, whose prayse I would endite,° *proclaim*
   Endite I would as dewtie doth excite;°   *move*
   But ah my rimes too rude and rugged arre,
   When in so high an object they do lite,
   And striving, fit to make, I feare do marre:
Thy selfe thy prayses tell, and make them knowen farre.

4

She travelling with Guyon[2] by the way,
   Of sundry things faire purpose° gan to find,   *discourse*

---

4. I.e., the grim shades of night.
1. Spenser departs from Ariosto (e.g., *Orlando Furioso*, XX. 1) in that the English poet celebrates the martial and statesmanlike achievements of women in a vein of high seriousness.
2. Apparently a slip on Spenser's part; Redcrosse is meant (cf. st. 16).

T'abridg their journey long, and lingring day;
Mongst which it fell into that Faeries mind,
To aske this Briton Mayd, what uncouth° wind,   *strange*
Brought her into those parts, and what inquest°   *quest*
Made her dissemble her disguiséd kind:°   *nature*
Faire Lady she him seemd, like Lady drest,
But fairest knight alive, when arméd was her brest.

5

Thereat she sighing softly, had no powre
To speake a while, ne ready answere make,
But with hart-thrilling throbs and bitter stowre,°   *inward turmoil*
As if she had a fever fit, did quake,
And every daintie limbe with horrour shake;
And ever and anone the rosy red,
Flasht through her face, as it had been a flake°   *flash*
Of lightning, through bright heaven fulminéd;°   *shot forth*
At last the passion past she thus him answeréd.

6

"Faire Sir, I let you weete, that from the howre
I taken was from nourses tender pap,
I have beene trainéd up in warlike stowre,°   *combat*
To tossen° speare and shield, and to affrap°   *wield/strike*
The warlike ryder to his most mishap;
Sithence° I loathéd have my life to lead,   *since then*
As Ladies wont, in pleasures wanton lap,
To finger the fine needle and nyce° thread;   *delicate*
Me lever° were with point of foemans speare be dead.[3]   *rather*

7

"All my delight on deedes of armes is set,
To hunt out perils and adventures hard,
By sea, by land, where so they may be met,
Onely for honour and for high regard,°   *concerns*
Without respect° of richesse or reward.   *care*
For such intent into these parts I came,
Withouten compasse, or withouten card,°   *map*
Far fro my native soyle, that is by name
The greater Britaine,[4] here to seeke for prayse and fame.

8

"Fame blazéd° hath, that here in Faery lond   *proclaimed*
Do many famous Knightes and Ladies wonne,°   *dwell*
And many straunge adventures to be fond,
Of which great worth and worship° may be wonne;   *honor*
Which I to prove, this voyage have begonne.
But mote I weet of you, right curteous knight,

3. The warlike woman is a traditional literary type; for this account of Britomart's upbringing, however, Spenser may have drawn particularly on Tasso's account of the training regime that formed the character of the feminine warrior Clorinda (*Gerusalemme Liberata*, II. 39–40).
4. I.e., not the "lesser Britaine," or Brittany, in France.

Tydings of one, that hath unto me donne
Late foule dishonour and reprochfull spight,
The which I seeke to wreake,° and Arthegall he hight."[5]   *avenge*

9

The word gone out, she backe againe would call,
  As her repenting so to have missayd,[6]
  But that he it up-taking ere the fall,
  Her shortly answeréd; "Faire martiall Mayd
  Certes ye misaviséd° beene, t'upbrayd   *misinformed*
  A gentle knight with so unknightly blame:
  For weet ye well of all, that ever playd
  At tilt or tourney, or like warlike game,
The noble Arthegall hath ever borne the name.[7]

10

"For thy great wonder were it, if such shame
  Should ever enter in his bounteous° thought,   *virtuous*
  Or ever do, that mote deserven blame:
  The noble courage° never weeneth ought,   *spirit*
  That may unworthy of it selfe be thought.
  Therefore, faire Damzell, be ye well aware,°   *wary*
  Least that too farre ye have your sorrow sought:
  You and your countrey both I wish welfare,
And honour both; for each of other worthy are."

11

The royall Mayd woxe° inly wondrous glad,   *grew*
  To heare her Love so highly magnifide,
  And joyd that ever she affixéd had,
  Her hart on knight so goodly glorifide,
  How ever finely she it faind to hide:
  The loving mother, that nine monethes did beare,
  In the deare closet of her painefull side,
  Her tender babe, it seeing safe appeare,
Doth not so much rejoyce, as she rejoycéd theare.

12

But to occasion° him to further talke,   *induce*
  To feed her humour° with his pleasing stile,   *mood*
  Her list in strifull termes with him to balke,°   *dispute*
  And thus replide, "How ever, Sir, ye file
  Your curteous tongue, his prayses to compile,
  It ill beseemes a knight of gentle sort,
  Such as ye have him boasted, to beguile
  A simple mayd, and worke so haynous tort,°   *wrong*
In shame of knighthood, as I largely° can report.   *at length*

5. Arthegall, the destined mate of Britomart, is the hero of Book V ("The Legend of Justice") in *The Faerie Queene.* His name, which Spenser knew from Geoffrey of Monmouth's allusion to "Arthgal of Cargueir, that is now called Warwick" (*op. cit.,* IX. 12), invites association with that of Arthur, Lord Grey of Wilton, Spenser's chief in Ireland from 1580 to 1582, as well as with the Arthur of Welsh and British legend. See III. iii. 26 and note. For Geoffrey's *Historia,* cf. the note to III. iii. 6.

6. I.e., as if she repented having spoken thus wrongly.

7. I.e., has ever been most renowned.

13

"Let be[8] therefore my vengeaunce to disswade,
  And read,° where I that faytour° false may find."   *tell/villain*
"Ah, but if reason faire might you perswade,
  To slake your wrath, and mollifie° your mind,"   *soften*
Said he, "perhaps ye should it better find:
  For hardy° thing it is, to weene by might,   *bold*
  That man to hard conditions to bind,
  Or ever hope to match in equall fight,
Whose prowesse paragon[9] saw never living wight.

14

"Ne soothlich° is it easie for to read,°   *truly/know*
  Where now on earth, or how he may be found;
For he ne wonneth in one certaine stead,°   *place*
  But restlesse walketh all the world around,
  Ay° doing things, that to his fame redound,   *always*
  Defending Ladies cause, and Orphans right,
  Where so he heares, that any doth confound°   *persecute*
  Them comfortlesse,° through tyranny or might;   *helpless*
So is his soveraine honour raisde to heavens hight."

15

His feeling words her feeble sence much pleased,
  And softly sunck into her molten° hart;   *melting*
Hart that is inly hurt, is greatly eased
  With hope of thing, that may allegge° his smart;   *alleviate*
  For pleasing words are like to Magick art,
  That doth the charméd Snake in slomber lay:
  Such secret ease felt gentle Britomart,
  Yet list the same efforce with faind gainesay;[1]
So dischord oft in Musick makes the sweeter lay.

16

And said, "Sir knight, these idle termes forbeare,
  And sith it is uneath° to find his haunt,°   *difficult/abode*
Tell me some markes, by which he may appeare,
  If chaunce I him encounter paravaunt;°   *face to face*
  For perdie° one shall other slay, or daunt: *surely*
  What shape, what shield, what armes, what steed, what sted,
  And what so else his person most may vaunt?"°   *display*
  All which the Redcrosse knight to point ared,[2]
And him in every part before her fashionéd.

17

Yet him in every part before she knew,
  How ever list her now her knowledge faine,°   *hide*
Sith him whilome in Britaine she did vew,
  To her revealéd in a mirrhour plaine,

---

8. I.e., cease.
9. I.e., the equal of whose prowess.
1. I.e., yet was pleased to intensify
that sensation by pretended disagreement.
2. I.e., exactly described.

Whereof did grow her first engrafféd° paine;   *implanted*
Whose root and stalke so bitter yet did tast,
That but the fruit more sweetnesse did containe,
Her wretched dayes in dolour she mote wast,
And yield the pray of love to lothsome death at last.

18

By strange occasion she did him behold,
    And much more strangely gan to love his sight,
    As it in bookes hath written bene of old.
    In Deheubarth that now South-wales is hight,
    What time king Ryence raigned, and dealéd° right,   *dispensed*
    The great Magitian Merlin had devized,
    By his deepe science, and hell-dreaded might,
    A looking glasse,³ right wondrously aguized,°   *fashioned*
Whose vertues through the wyde world soone were solemnized.

19

It vertue° had, to shew in perfect sight,   *power*
    What ever thing was in the world contaynd,
    Betwixt the lowest earth and heavens hight,
    So that it to the looker appertaynd;
    What ever foe had wrought, or frend had faynd,
    Therein discovered was, ne ought mote pas,
    Ne ought in secret from the same remaynd;
    For thy it round and hollow shapéd was,
Like to the world it selfe, and seemed a world of glas.

20

Who wonders not, that reades° so wonderous worke?   *perceives*
    But who does wonder, that has red° the Towre,   *considered*
    Wherein th'Aegyptian Phao long did lurke
    From all mens vew, that none might her discoure,°   *discover*
    Yet she might all men vew out of her bowre?
    Great Ptolomae⁴ it for his lemans° sake   *lover's*
    Ybuilded all of glasse, by Magicke powre,
    And also it impregnable did make;
Yet when his love was false, he with a peaze° it brake.   *blow*

21

Such was the glassie globe that Merlin made,
    And gave unto king Ryence for his gard,°   *protection*
    That never foes his kingdome might invade,
    But he it knew at home before he hard
    Tydings thereof, and so them still debared.
    It was a famous Present for a Prince,
    And worthy worke of infinite reward,

3. I.e., a globe of glass, or crystal ball.
It was fashionable in Elizabethan times
to consult "speculators," who claimed
to foresee the future by crystal gazing.
Merlin's "mirror" recalls the "mirror
of glas" in Chaucer's "The Squire's
Tale," which assured the viewer's fore-
knowledge in matters of love or war.
4. Ptolemy II (308–246 B.C.), who
built the Pharos, Museum, and Library
at Alexandria; Arabian legend credited
him with particular abilities, amount-
ing to magical powers, in working with
glass.

That treasons could bewray, and foes convince;°   *conquer*
Happie this Realme, had it remainéd ever since.

22

One day it fortunéd, faire Britomart
   Into her fathers closet to repayre;°   *go*
   For nothing he from her reserved apart,
   Being his onely daughter and his hayre:°   *heir*
   Where when she had espyde that mirrhour fayre,
   Her selfe a while therein she vewd in vaine;
   Tho her avizing° of the vertues rare,   *thinking*
   Which thereof spoken were, she gan againe
Her to bethinke of, that mote to her selfe pertaine.

23

But as it falleth, in the gentlest harts
   Imperious Love hath highest set his throne,
   And tyrannizeth in the bitter smarts
   Of them, that to him buxome° are and prone:°   *yielding/submissive*
   So thought this Mayd (as maydens use to done)
   Whom fortune for her husband would allot,
   Not that she lusted after any one;
   For she was pure from blame of sinfull blot,
Yet wist° her life at last must lincke in that same knot.   *knew*

24

Eftsoones there was presented to her eye
   A comely knight, all armed in complete wize,
   Through whose bright ventayle° lifted up on hye   *visor*
   His manly face, that did his foes agrize,°   *terrify*
   And friends to termes of gentle truce entize,
   Lookt foorth, as Phoebus face out of the east,
   Betwixt two shadie mountaines doth arize;
   Portly° his person was, and much increast   *dignified*
Through his Heroicke grace, and honorable gest.°   *bearing*

25

His crest was covered with a couchant Hound,
   And all his armour seemed of antique mould,°   *form*
   But wondrous massie and assuréd sound,
   And round about yfretted° all with gold,   *adorned*
   In which there written was with cyphers° old,   *letters*
   Achilles armes, which Arthegall did win.
   And on his shield enveloped sevenfold
   He bore a crownéd litle Ermilin,°   *ermine*
That deckt the azure field with her faire pouldred° skin.[5]   *spotted*

26

The Damzell well did vew his personage,°   *image*
   And likéd well, ne further fastned° not,   *fixed on*

5. Arthegall's helmet displays a grey-hound lying down with head alertly raised; the crowned ermine on his shield is a symbol of royalty and of chastity. Ariosto alludes to the winning of Hector's arms by Mandricardo (*Or-lando Furioso*, XIV. 30–1); but that Arthegall should win the arms of Achilles is especially apt for this hero, given the legend that the British race was founded by the Trojan Brute. Cf. III. ix. 38–51.

But went her way; ne her unguilty age
Did weene, unwares, that her unlucky lot
Lay hidden in the bottome of the pot;
Of hurt unwist most daunger doth redound:°   result
But the false Archer, which that arrow shot
So slyly, that she did not feele the wound,
Did smyle full smoothly at her weetlesse wofull stound.

27

Thenceforth the feather in her loftie crest,
Rufféd of[6] love, gan lowly to availe,°   bow
And her proud portance,° and her princely gest,   bearing
With which she earst tryumphéd, now did quaile:° falter
Sad, solemne, sowre, and full of fancies fraile
She woxe; yet wist she neither how, nor why,
She wist not, silly° Mayd, what she did aile,   innocent
Yet wist, she was not well at ease perdy,°   certainly
Yet thought it was not love, but some melancholy.

28

So soone as Night had with her pallid hew
Defast° the beautie of the shining sky,   obscured
And reft from men the worlds desiréd vew,
She with her Nourse adowne to sleepe did lye;
But sleepe full farre away from her did fly:
In stead thereof sad sighes, and sorrowes deepe
Kept watch and ward about her warily,
That nought she did but wayle, and often steepe° stain
Her daintie couch with teares, which closely° she did weepe. secretly

29

And if that any drop of slombring rest
Did chaunce to still° into her wearie spright,   trickle
When feeble nature felt her selfe opprest,
Streight way with dreames, and with fantasticke sight
Of dreadfull things the same was put to flight,
That oft out of her bed she did astart,
As one with vew of ghastly feends affright:
Tho gan she to renew her former smart,
And thinke of that faire visage, written in her hart.

30

One night, when she was tost with such unrest,
Her aged Nurse, whose name was Glauce hight,[7]
Feeling her leape out of her loathéd nest,
Betwixt her feeble armes her quickly keight,°   caught
And downe againe in her warme bed her dight;°   placed
"Ah my deare daughter, ah my dearest dread,
What uncouth fit," said she, "what evil plight

6. I.e., ruffled by.
7. The episode that follows draws heavily on the pseudo-Virgilian *Ciris;* in particular, sts. 30, 32, 34–35, 40–41, and 50–51 echo the language of that poem. Spenser departs from his source chiefly in the allusion to the relations of reason and love (st. 36), and in sts. 43–44.

Hath thee opprest, and with sad drearyhead°   *grief*
Chaungéd thy lively cheare,° and living made thee dead?   *mood*

31

"For not of nought these suddeine ghastly feares
    All night afflict thy naturall repose,
    And all the day, when as thine equall peares
    Their fit disports with faire delight doe chose,
    Thou in dull corners doest thy selfe inclose,
    Ne tastest Princes pleasures, ne doest spred
    Abroad thy fresh youthes fairest flowre, but lose
    Both leafe and fruit, both too untimely shed,
As one in wilfull bale° for ever buriéd.   *grief*

32

"The time, that mortall men their weary cares
    Do lay away, and all wilde beastes do rest,
    And every river eke his course forbeares,
    Then doth this wicked evill thee infest,°   *attack*
    And rive with thousand throbs thy thrilléd° brest;   *pierced*
    Like an huge Aetn' of deepe engulféd griefe,
    Sorrow is heapéd in thy hollow chest,
    Whence forth it breakes in sighes and anguish rife,
As smoke and sulphure mingled with confuséd strife.

33

"Aye me, how much I feare, least love it bee;
    But if that love it be, as sure I read°   *perceive*
    By knowen signes and passions, which I see,
    Be it worthy of thy race and royall sead,
    Then I avow by this most sacred head
    Of my deare foster child, to ease thy griefe,
    And win thy will: Therefore away doe° dread;   *banish*
    For death nor daunger from thy dew reliefe
Shall me debarre, tell me therefore my liefest liefe."°   *beloved*

34

So having said, her twixt her armés twaine
    She straightly° straynd, and colléd° tenderly,   *closely/embraced*
    And every trembling joynt, and every vaine
    She softly felt, and rubbéd busily,
    To doe° the frosen cold away to fly;   *cause*
    And her faire deawy eies with kisses deare
    She oft did bath, and oft againe did dry;
    And ever her importund,° not to feare   *urged*
To let the secret of her hart to her appeare.

35

The Damzell pauzd, and then thus fearefully:
    "Ah Nurse, what needeth thee to eke° my paine?   *add to*
    Is not enough, that I alone doe dye,
    But it must doubled be with death of twaine?
    For nought for me but death there doth remaine."
    "O daughter deare," said she, "despaire no whit;

    For never sore, but might a salve obtaine:
    That blinded God, which hath ye blindly smit,
Another arrow hath your lovers hart to hit."

36

"But mine is not," quoth she, "like others wound;
    For which no reason can find remedy."
    "Was never such, but mote the like be found,"
    Said she, "and though no reason may apply
    Salve to your sore, yet love can higher stye,°   mount
    Then reasons reach, and oft hath wonders donne."
    "But neither God of love, nor God of sky
    Can doe," said she, "that, which cannot be donne."
"Things oft impossible," quoth she, "seeme, ere begonne."

37

"These idle words," said she, "doe nought asswage
    My stubborne smart, but more annoyance° breed,   grief
    For no no usuall fire, no usuall rage°   passion
    It is, O Nurse, which on my life doth feed,
    And suckes the bloud, which from my hart doth bleed.
    But since thy faithfull zeale lets me not hyde
    My crime, (if crime it be) I will it reed.°   tell
    Nor Prince, nor pere it is, whose love hath gryde°   pierced
My feeble brest of late, and launchéd° this wound wyde.   inflicted

38

"Nor man it is, nor other living wight;
    For then some hope I might unto me draw,
    But th'only shade and semblant° of a knight,   likeness
    Whose shape or person yet I never saw,
    Hath me subjected to loves cruell law:
    The same one day, as me misfortune led,
    I in my fathers wondrous mirrhour saw,
    And pleaséd with that seeming goodly-hed,°   good appearance
Unwares the hidden hooke with baite I swallowéd.

39

"Sithens° it hath infixéd faster hold   Since then
    Within my bleeding bowels, and so sore
    Now ranckleth in this same fraile fleshly mould,°   body
    That all mine entrailes flow with poysnous gore,
    And th'ulcer groweth daily more and more;
    Ne can my running sore find remedie,
    Other then my hard fortune to deplore,
    And languish as the leafe falne from the tree,
Till death make one end of my dayes and miserie."

40

"Daughter," said she, "what need ye be dismayd,
    Or why make ye such Monster of your mind?
    Of much more uncouth thing I was affrayd;
    Of filthy lust, contrarie unto kind:°   nature
    But this affection nothing straunge I find;

For who with reason can you aye° reprove,   *ever*
 To love the semblant pleasing most your mind, ·
 And yield your heart, whence ye cannot remove?
No guilt in you, but in the tyranny of love.[8]

41

"Not so th'Arabian Myrrhe[9] did set her mind;
 Nor so did Biblis spend her pining hart,
 But loved their native flesh against all kind,
 And to their purpose uséd wicked art:
 Yet playd Pasiphae a more monstrous part,
 That loved a Bull, and learnd a beast to bee;
 Such shamefull lusts who loaths not, which depart
 From course of nature and of modestie?
Sweet love such lewdnes bands° from his faire companie. *banishes*

42

"But thine my Deare (welfare thy heart my deare)
 Though strange beginning had, yet fixéd is
 On one, that worthy may perhaps appeare;
 And certes seemes bestowéd not amis:
 Joy thereof have thou and eternall blis."
 With that upleaning on her elbow weake,
 Her alablaster° brest she soft did kis,   *alabaster*
 Which all that while she felt to pant and quake,
As it an Earth-quake were; at last she thus bespake.

43

"Beldame,° your words doe worke me litle ease; *good mother*
 For though my love be not so lewdly bent,° *inclined*
 As those ye blame, yet may it nought appease
 My raging smart, ne ought my flame relent,° *abate*
 But rather doth my helpelesse griefe augment.
 For they, how ever shamefull and unkind,
 Yet did possesse° their horrible intent: *achieve*
 Short end of sorrowes they thereby did find;
So was their fortune good, though wicked were their mind.

44

"But wicked fortune mine, though mind be good,
 Can have no end, nor hope of my desire,
 But feed on shadowes, whiles I die for food,
 And like a shadow wexe,° whiles with entire *become*
 Affection, I doe languish and expire.
 I fonder, then Cephisus foolish child,[1]
 Who having vewéd in a fountaine shere°   *clear*
 His face, was with the love thereof beguild;
I fonder love a shade, the bodie farre exild."

8. Chaste love accords with reason; yet reason cannot match or control love's power (cf. st. 36).
9. Myrrha, consumed by passion for her father, Cinyras, consequently became the mother of Adonis (*Metamorphoses*, X. 312–518); for the stories of Biblis, who loved her brother, and of Pasiphae, who gave birth to the Minotaur, Spenser depended on Boccaccio, *De Genealogia Deorum*, IV. 9–10.
1. I.e., Narcissus.

45

"Nought like," quoth she, "for that same wretched boy
    Was of himselfe the idle Paramoure;
    Both love and lover, without hope of joy,
    For which he faded to a watry flowre.
    But better fortune thine, and better howre,°   *occasion*
    Which lov'st the shadow of a warlike knight;
    No shadow, but a bodie hath in powre:[2]
    That bodie, wheresoever that it light,°   *lodges*
May learnéd be by cyphers,° or by Magicke might.   *astrological signs*

46

"But if thou may with reason yet represse
    The growing evill, ere it strength have got,
    And thee abandond wholly doe possesse,
    Against it strongly strive, and yield thee not,
    Till thou in open field adowne be smot.
    But if the passion mayster thy fraile might,
    So that needs love or death must be thy lot,
    Then I avow to thee, by wrong or right
To compasse° thy desire, and find that lovéd knight."   *bring about*

47

Her chearefull words much cheard the feeble spright
    Of the sicke virgin, that her downe she layd
    In her warme bed to sleepe, if that she might;
    And the old-woman carefully displayd°   *arranged*
    The clothes about her round with busie ayd;
    So that at last a little creeping sleepe
    Surprisd her sense: She therewith well apayd,°   *pleased*
    The drunken lampe downe in the oyle did steepe,
And set her by to watch, and set her by to weepe.

48

Earely the morrow next, before that day
    His joyous face did to the world reveale,
    They both uprose and tooke their readie way
    Unto the Church, their prayers to appeale,°   *say*
    With great devotion, and with litle zeale:
    For the faire Damzell from the holy herse°   *ceremony*
    Her love-sicke hart to other thoughts did steale;
    And that old Dame said many an idle verse,
Out of her daughters hart fond fancies to reverse.

49

Returnéd home, the royall Infant[3] fell
    Into her former fit; for why, no powre
    Nor guidance of her selfe in her did dwell.
    But th'aged Nurse her calling to her bowre,°   *chamber*
    Had gathered Rew, and Savine, and the flowre
    Of Camphora, and Calamint, and Dill,

2. I.e., there is no shadow not cast by   3. I.e., noble maiden.
a body.

All which she in a earthen Pot did poure,
And to the brim with Colt wood did it fill,
And many drops of milke and bloud through it did spill.[4]

50

Then taking thrise three haires from off her head,
  Them trebly breaded° in a threefold lace,   *braided*
  And round about the pots mouth, bound the thread,
  And after having whisperéd a space
  Certaine sad words, with hollow voice and bace,
  She to the virgin said, thrise said she it;
  "Come daughter come, come; spit upon my face,
  Spit thrise upon me, thrise upon me spit;
Th'uneven number for this businesse is most fit."

51

That sayd, her round about she from her turnd,
  She turnéd her contrarie to the Sunne,
  Thrise she her turnd contrary, and returnd,
  All contrary, for she the right did shunne,
  And ever what she did, was streight° undonne.   *strictly*
  So thought she to undoe her daughters[5] love:
  But love, that is in gentle brest begonne,
  No idle charmes so lightly may remove,
That well can witnesse, who by triall it does prove.°   *test*

52

Ne ought it mote the noble Mayd avayle,
  Ne slake the furie of her cruell flame,
  But that she still did waste, and still did wayle,
  That through long languour, and hart-burning brame°   *longing*
  She shortly like a pynéd° ghost became,   *wasted*
  Which long hath waited by the Stygian strond.
  That when old Glauce saw, for feare least blame
  Of her miscarriage° should in her be fond,   *failure*
She wist not how t'amend, nor how it to withstand.

Canto III

Merlin bewrayes° to Britomart,   *reveals*
    the state of Artegall.
    And shewes the famous Progeny
      which from them springen shall.

1

Most sacred fire, that burnest mightily
  In living brests, ykindled first above,
  Emongst th'eternall spheres and lamping° sky,   *resplendent*
  And thence pourd into men, which men call Love;
  Not that same, which doth base affections move

---

4. The herbs gathered by Glauce were thought to cool love's ardor; milk and blood were intended to propitiate Hecate, patroness of black magic. Glauce's incantatory procedures reflect the practices of English witchcraft as well as ancient magical ceremonies.
5. I.e., her ward's.

In brutish minds, and filthy lust inflame,
But that sweet fit, that doth true beautie love,
And choseth vertue for his dearest Dame,
Whence spring all noble deeds and never dying fame:[1]

2

Well did Antiquitie a God thee deeme,
   That over mortall minds hast so great might,
   To order them, as best to thee doth seeme,
   And all their actions to direct aright;
   The fatall° purpose of divine foresight,   *fated*
   Thou doest effect in destinéd descents,°   *lineages*
   Through deepe impression of thy secret might,
   And stirredst up th'Heroes high intents,
Which the late world admyres for wondrous moniments.°   *memorials*

3

But thy dread darts in none doe triumph more,
   Ne braver° proofe in any, of thy powre   *finer*
   Shew'dst thou, then in this royall Maid of yore,
   Making her seeke an unknowne Paramoure,
   From the worlds end, through many a bitter stowre:°   *encounter*
   From whose two loynes thou afterwards did rayse
   Most famous fruits of matrimoniall bowre,
   Which through the earth have spred their living prayse,
That fame in trompe of gold eternally displayes.

4

Begin then, O my dearest sacred Dame,[2]
   Daughter of Phoebus and of Memorie,
   That doest ennoble with immortall name
   The warlike Worthies, from antiquitie,
   In thy great volume of Eternitie:
   Begin, O Clio, and recount from hence
   My glorious Soveraines goodly auncestrie,
   Till that by dew degrees and long protense,°   *extension*
Thou have it lastly brought unto her Excellence.

5

Full many wayes within her troubled mind,
   Old Glauce cast,° to cure this Ladies griefe: *considered*
   Full many waies she sought, but none could find,
   Nor herbes, nor charmes, nor counsell, that is chiefe
   And choisest med'cine for sicke harts reliefe:
   For thy great care she tooke,[3] and greater feare,
   Least that it should her turne to foule repriefe,°   *reproof*
   And sore reproch, when so her father deare
Should of his dearest daughters hard misfortune heare.

---

1. The distinction between lustful desire and that love which has "true beauty" for its object, glanced at in the "October" eclogue of *The Shepheardes Calender*, is developed at length by Spenser in *Fowre Hymnes*.
2. I.e., Clio, the Muse of *The Faerie Queene*. The nine "Worthies" were Hector, Alexander, Julius Caesar; Joshua, Daniel, Judas Maccabaeus; Arthur, Charlemagne, and Godfrey of Boulogne (cf. Caxton's "Preface" to *Le Morte d'Arthur*).
3. I.e., therefore she was much troubled.

6

At last she her avisd,° that he, which made   recalled
    That mirrhour, wherein the sicke Damosell
    So straungely vewéd her straunge lovers shade,
    To weet, the learnéd Merlin,[4] well could tell,
    Under what coast° of heaven the man did dwell,   region
    And by what meanes his love might best be wrought:
    For though beyond the Africk Ismaell,[5]
    Or th'Indian Peru he were, she thought
Him forth through infinite endevour to have sought.

7

Forthwith themselves disguising both in straunge
    And base attyre, that none might them bewray,
    To Maridunum, that is now by chaunge
    Of name Cayr-Merdin[6] cald, they tooke their way:
    There the wise Merlin whylome wont (they say)
    To make his wonne,° low underneath the ground,   dwelling
    In a deepe delve,° farre from the vew of day,   cave
    That of no living wight he mote be found,
When so he counseld with his sprights encompast round.

8

And if thou ever happen that same way
    To travell, goe to see that dreadfull place:
    It is an hideous hollow cave (they say)
    Under a rocke that lyes a little space
    From the swift Barry, tombling downe apace,
    Emongst the woodie hilles of Dynevowre:
    But dare thou not, I charge, in any cace,
    To enter into that same balefull Bowre,°   cavern
For fear the cruell Feends should thee unwares devowre.

9

But standing high aloft, low lay thine eare,
    And there such ghastly noise of yron chaines,
    And brasen Caudrons thou shalt rombling heare,
    Which thousand sprights with long enduring paines
    Do tosse,° that it will stonne thy feeble braines,   stir up

4. For the figure of Merlin, and his prophecies, Spenser draws chiefly on Geoffrey of Monmouth's *Historia Regum Britanniae* and on Holinshed's *Chronicles*, although for some details he used also Malory's *Le Morte d'Arthur* and Camden's *Britannic*. Geoffrey's *Historia* (c. 1139), an account of "the kings that dwelt in Britain before the Incarnation of Christ" and of "Arthur and the many others that did succeed him after the Incarnation" (I. 1), imaginatively combines British tradition and legend with the materials of early and contemporary histories (e.g., Bede's *Historia Ecclesiastica Gentis Anglorum* [731] and William of Malmesbury's *Gesta Regum Anglorum* [c. 1125]). The figure of Arthur as romantic hero is essentially Geoffrey's creation. The narrative design of this Canto is based on Ariosto's account of the visit made by Bradamante to Merlin's tomb, where the future is foretold to her (*Orlando Furioso*, III).

5. The African territories held by the Saracens, thought to be descendants of Ishmael.

6. I.e., Carmarthen, in Wales; Merlin's birthplace, according to Geoffrey (*Historia*, VI. 17). Dynevor Castle, near Carmarthen, was the seat of the princes of South Wales.

And oftentimes great grones, and grievous stounds,°   *outcries*
    When too huge toile and labour them constraines:
    And oftentimes loud strokes, and ringing sounds
From under that deepe Rocke most horribly rebounds.

10

The cause some say is this: A litle while
    Before that Merlin dyde, he did intend,
    A brasen wall in compas to compile°   *build*
    About Cairmardin, and did it commend°   *command*
    Unto these Sprights, to bring to perfect end.
    During which worke the Ladie of the Lake,[7]
    Whom long he loved, for him in hast did send,
    Who thereby forst his workemen to forsake,
Them bound till his returne, their labour not to slake.°   *slacken*

11

In the meane time through that false Ladies traine,°   *trickery*
    He was surprisd, and buried under beare,°   *tomb*
    Ne ever to his worke returnd againe:
    Nath'lesse those feends may not their worke forbeare,
    So greatly his commaundément they feare,
    But there doe toyle and travell day and night,
    Untill that brasen wall they up doe reare:°   *erect*
    For Merlin had in Magicke more insight,
Then ever him before or after living wight.

12

For he by words could call out of the sky
    Both Sunne and Moone, and make them him obay:
    The land to sea, and sea to maineland dry,
    And darkesome night he eke could turne to day:
    Huge hostes of men he could alone dismay,
    And hostes of men of meanest things could frame,
    When so him list his enimies to fray:°   *terrify*
    That to this day for terror of his fame,
The feends do quake, when any him to them does name.

13

And sooth,° men say that he was not the sonne   *truly*
    Of mortall Syre, or other living wight,
    But wondrously begotten, and begonne
    By false illusion of a guilefull Spright,
    On a faire Ladie Nonne, that whilome hight
    Matilda, daughter to Pubidius,
    Who was the Lord of Mathravall by right,
    And coosen° unto king Ambrosius.[8]   *kinsman*
Whence he induéd° was with skill so marvellous.   *endowed*

7. I.e., Nimue; the story of her relations with Merlin appears in Malory's *Le Morte d'Arthur*, IV. i.
8. Matraval was a town in Montgomeryshire, Wales; but the names of Matilda and Pubidius do not appear in Geoffrey's account, which identifies Merlin's sire only as an "incubus daemon" (VI. 18). This is also Ariosto's version (*Orlando Furioso*, XXXIII. 9).

14

They here ariving, staid a while without,
  Ne durst adventure rashly in to wend,°   go
  But of their first intent gan make new dout
  For dread of daunger, which it might portend:
  Untill the hardie° Mayd (with love to frend)   bold
  First entering, the dreadfull Mage° there found   magician
  Deepe busiéd bout worke of wondrous end,
  And writing strange characters in the ground,
With which the stubborn feends he to his service bound.

15

He nought was movéd at their entrance bold:
  For of their comming well he wist afore,
  Yet list them bid their businesse to unfold,
  As if ought in this world in secret store
  Were from him hidden, or unknowne of yore.
  Then Glauce thus, "Let not it thee offend,
  That we thus rashly through thy darkesome dore,
  Unwares° have prest: for either fatall end,[9]   suddenly
Or other mightie cause us two did hither send."

16

He bad tell on; And then she thus began:
  "Now have three Moones with borrowed brothers light,
  Thrice shinéd faire, and thrice seemed dim and wan,
  Sith° a sore evill, which this virgin bright   since
  Tormenteth, and doth plonge in dolefull plight,
  First rooting tooke; but what thing it mote bee,
  Or whence it sprong, I cannot read aright:
  But this I read, that but if[1] remedee
Thou her afford, full shortly I her dead shall see."

17

Therewith th'Enchaunter softly gan to smyle
  At her smooth speeches, weeting inly well,
  That she to him dissembled womanish guyle,
  And to her said, "Beldame, by that ye tell,
  More need of leach-craft° hath your Damozell,   medicine
  Then of my skill: who helpe may have elsewhere,
  In vaine seekes wonders out of Magicke spell."
  Th'old woman wox half blanck,[2] those words to heare;
And yet was loth to let her purpose plaine appeare.

18

And to him said, "If any leaches skill,
  Or other learnéd meanes could have redrest°   cured
  This my deare daughters deepe engrafféd° ill,   implanted
  Certes I should be loth thee to molest:
  But this sad evill, which doth her infest,
  Doth course of naturall cause farre exceed,

9. I.e., a purpose ordained by fate.   2. I.e., became somewhat disconcerted.
1. I.e., unless.

And houséd is within her hollow brest,
That either seemes some curséd witches deed,
Or evill spright, that in her doth such torment breed."

19

The wisard could no lenger beare her bord,°   *talk*
  But brusting° forth in laughter, to her sayd;   *bursting*
  "Glauce, what needs this colourable° word,   *deceptive*
  To cloke the cause, that hath it selfe bewrayd?
  Ne ye faire Britomartis, thus arayd,
  More hidden are, then Sunne in cloudy vele;
  Whom thy good fortune, having fate obayd,
  Hath hither brought, for succour to appele:
The which the powres to thee are pleaséd to revele."

20

The doubtfull° Mayd, seeing her selfe descryde,   *apprehensive*
  Was all abasht, and her pure yvory
  Into a cleare Carnation suddeine dyde;
  As faire Aurora rising hastily,
  Doth by her blushing tell, that she did lye
  All night in old Tithonus frosen bed,
  Whereof she seemes ashaméd inwardly.
  But her old Nourse was nought dishartenéd,
But vauntage made of that, which Merlin had ared.°   *said*

21

And sayd, "Sith then thou knowest all our griefe,
  (For what doest not thou know?) of grace I pray,
  Pitty our plaint, and yield us meet° reliefe."   *suitable*
  With that the Prophet still awhile did stay,
  And then his spirite thus gan forth display;°   *show*
  "Most noble Virgin, that by fatall lore[3]
  Hast learned to love, let no whit thee dismay
  The hard begin, that meets thee in the dore,
And with sharpe fits thy tender hart oppresseth sore.

22

"For so must all things excellent begin,
  And eke enrooted deepe must be that Tree,
  Whose big embodied braunches shall not lin,°   *cease*
  Till they to heavens hight forth stretchéd bee.
  For from thy wombe a famous Progenie
  Shall spring, out of the auncient Trojan blood,[4]
  Which shall revive the sleeping memorie
  Of those same antique Peres° the heavens brood,   *champions*
Which Greeke and Asian rivers stainéd with their blood.

3. I.e., fated knowledge.
4. The Elizabethans' belief, amounting virtually to religious conviction, in their descent, via Brute, from Aeneas and the Trojan race, echoes regularly in the literature of the age (e.g., in the "First Song" of Drayton's *Polyolbion*). Spenser twice recounts the legend in *The Faerie Queene:* in the opening stanzas of II. x, and again at III. ix. 38–51.

23

"Renowmèd kings, and sacred Emperours,
  Thy fruitfull Ofspring, shall from thee descend;
  Brave Captaines, and most mighty warriours,
  That shall their conquests through all lands extend,
  And their decayèd kingdomes shall amend:°   *restore*
  The feeble Britons, broken with long warre,
  They shall upreare, and mightily defend
  Against their forrein foe, that comes from farre,
Till universall peace compound° all civill jarre.   *settle*

24

"It was not, Britomart, thy wandring eye,
  Glauncing unwares in charmèd looking glas,
  But the streight° course of heavenly destiny,   *strict*
  Led with eternall providence, that has
  Guided thy glaunce, to bring his will to pas:
  Ne is thy fate, ne is thy fortune ill,
  To love the prowest° knight, that ever was.   *bravest*
  Therefore submit thy wayes unto his will,
And do by all dew meanes thy destiny fulfill."

25

"But read,"° said Glauce, "thou Magitian   *tell*
  What meanes shall she out seeke, or what wayes take?
  How shall she know, how shall she find the man?
  Or what needs her to toyle, sith fates can make
  Way for themselves, their purpose to partake?"°   *accomplish*
  Then Merlin thus; "Indeed the fates are firme,
  And may not shrinck, though all the world do shake:
  Yet ought mens good endevours them confirme,
And guide the heavenly causes to their constant terme.[5]

26

"The man whom heavens have ordaynd to bee
  The spouse of Britomart, is Arthegall:[6]
  He wonneth° in the land of Fayeree,   *dwells*
  Yet is no Fary borne, ne sib° at all   *related*
  To Elfes, but sprong of seed terrestriall,
  And whilome by false Faries stolne away,
  Whiles yet in infant cradle he did crall;°   *crawl*
  Ne other to himselfe is knowne this day,
But that he by an Elfe was gotten° of a Fay.   *begot*

5. I.e., fixed outcome. Merlin's words, together with his comments in sts. 21–22, emphasize Spenser's conviction that virtuous men and women play an active role in the Providential scheme that directs the universe. Britomart's love for Arthegall, demanding but formative as well, makes part of her divinely-appointed destiny.

6. Sts. 26–28 prepare for the alignment of the Tudor dynasty with the ancient rulers of Britain (culminating at st. 49) by indicating the connection of Arthegall with Arthur, who was the son of Uther Pendragon and Igerne (the wife of Gorlois). The circumstances of Arthegall's birth and upbringing also draw him into close association with Redcrosse (cf. I. x. 65–66). Arthur's quest for Gloriana is in some sense reflected and balanced by that of Britomart for Arthegall.

27

"But sooth he is the sonne of Gorlois,
 And brother unto Cador Cornish king,[7]
 And for his warlike feates renowméd is,
 From where the day out of the sea doth spring,
 Untill the closure° of the Evening.   *limit*
 From thence, him firmely bound with faithfull band,°   *bond*
 To this his native soyle thou backe shalt bring,
 Strongly to aide his countrey, to withstand
The powre of forrein Paynims,° which invade thy land.   *pagans*

28

"Great aid thereto his mighty puissaunce,
 And dreaded name shall give in that sad day:
 Where also proofe of thy prow° valiaunce   *courageous*
 Thou then shalt make, t'increase thy lovers pray.
 Long time ye both in armes shall beare great sway,
 Till thy wombes burden thee from them do call,
 And his last fate him from thee take away,
 Too rathe° cut off by practise criminall   *soon*
Of secret foes, that him shall make in mischiefe° fall. *misfortune*

29

"With thee yet shall he leave for memory
 Of his late puissaunce, his Image dead,[8]
 That living him in all activity
 To thee shall represent. He from the head
 Of his coosin Constantius without dread
 Shall take the crowne, that was his fathers right,
 And there with crowne himselfe in th'others stead:[9]
 Then shall he issew forth with dreadfull might,
Against his Saxon foes in bloudy field to fight.

30

"Like as a Lyon, that in drowsie cave
 Hath long time slept, himselfe so shall he shake,
 And comming forth, shall spred his banner brave
 Over the troubled South, that it shall make
 The warlike Mertians[1] for feare to quake:
 Thrise shall he fight with them, and twise shall win,
 But the third time shall faire accordaunce° make: *agreement*
 And if he then with victorie can lin,°   *cease*
He shall his dayes with peace bring to his earthly In.° *dwelling*

7. According to Geoffrey of Monmouth (*op. cit.*, IX. 1, 5), Cador assisted Arthur in the latter's battles against the Saxons.
8. I.e., Arthegall's son, the image of his deceased father.
9. Constantine, son of Cador, succeeded Arthur; not long after, he was killed by his nephew Conan (*Historia*, XI. 4–5). From this point to the end of the Canto, Spenser depends heavily on Geoffrey of Monmouth and on Holin-shed, diverging occasionally from their authority to take account of other chroniclers' narratives; now and then he departs altogether from these sources (e.g., Conan's wars with the Mercians, in st. 30; the Saxons' defeat by Careticus, in st. 33; and the manner of Pellite's death, in st. 36).
1. An Anglian tribe, who established the kingdom of Mercia, in south-central England, during the sixth century.

31

"His sonne, hight Vortipore, shall him succeede
  In kingdome, but not in felicity;
  Yet shall he long time warre with happy speed,°   *success*
  And with great honour many battels try:°   *undertake*
  But at the last to th'importunity
  Of froward° fortune shall be forst to yield.   *perverse*
  But his sonne Malgo shall full mightily
  Avenge his fathers losse, with speare and shield,
And his proud foes discomfit in victorious field.

32

"Behold the man, and tell me Britomart,
  If ay° more goodly creature thou didst see;   *ever*
  How like a Gyaunt in each manly part
  Beares he himselfe with portly° majestee,   *dignified*
  That one of th'old Heroés seemes to bee:
  He the six Islands,[2] comprovinciall
  In auncient times unto great Britainee,
  Shall to the same reduce,° and to him call   *restore*
Their sundry kings to do their homage severall.°   *diverse*

33

"All which his sonne Careticus awhile
  Shall well defend, and Saxons powre suppresse,
  Untill a straunger king from unknowne soyle
  Arriving, him with multitude oppresse;
  Great Gormond,[3] having with huge mightinesse
  Ireland subdewd, and therein fixt his throne,
  Like a swift Otter, fell° through emptinesse,   *fierce*
  Shall overswim the sea with many one
Of his Norveyses,° to assist the Britons fone.°   *Norwegians/foes*

34

"He in his furie all shall overrunne,
  And holy Church with faithlesse hands deface,
  That thy sad people utterly fordonne,°   *ruined*
  Shall to the utmost mountaines fly apace:
  Was never so great wast° in any place,   *destruction*
  Nor so fowle outrage doen by living men:
  For all thy Cities they shall sacke and race,°   *raze*
  And the greene grasse, that groweth, they shall bren,°   *burn*
That even the wild beast shall dy in starvéd den.

35

"Whiles thus thy Britons do in languour° pine,   *sorrow*
  Proud Etheldred[4] shall from the North arise,

2. I.e., Iceland, Norway, the Orkneys, Ireland, Gotland, and Dacia (Denmark).
3. Spenser here follows the *History of Ireland* (included in Holinshed's *Chronicles*, although composed by Richard Stanyhurst and Edward Campion) in his identification of Gormond as a Norwegian king, implicitly rejecting Geoffrey's allusion to "Gormond king of the Africans" (*op. cit.*, XI. 8).
4. In sts. 35–39 Spenser alters names and events in Geoffrey's narrative to conform with other Welsh and English source materials.

Serving th' ambitious will of Augustine,
And passing Dee with hardy enterprise,
Shall backe repulse the valiaunt Brockwell twise,
And Bangor with massacred Martyrs fill;
But the third time shall rew his foolhardise:°   *folly*
For Cadwan pittying his peoples ill,
Shall stoutly him defeat, and thousand Saxons kill.

36

"But after him, Cadwallin mightily
  On his sonne Edwin all those wrongs shall wreake;°   *avenge*
Ne shall availe the wicked sorcery
  Of false Pellite, his purposes to breake,
  But him shall slay, and on a gallowes bleake
Shall give th'enchaunter his unhappy hire;°   *reward*
  Then shall the Britons, late dismayd and weake,
  From their long vassalage gin to respire,°   *rest*
And on their Paynim foes avenge their ranckled° ire.   *embittered*

37

"Ne shall he yet his wrath so mitigate,
  Till both the sonnes of Edwin he have slaine,
Offricke and Osricke, twinnes unfortunate,
  Both slaine in battell upon Layburne plaine,
  Together with the king of Louthiane,
Hight Adin, and the king of Orkeny,
  Both joynt partakers of their fatall° paine: *fated*
  But Penda, fearefull of like desteny,
Shall yield him selfe his liegeman, and sweare fealty.

38

"Him shall he make his fatall Instrument,
  T'afflict the other Saxons unsubdewd;
He marching forth with fury insolent
  Against the good king Oswald, who indewd°   *invested*
  With heavenly powre, and by Angels reskewd,
All holding crosses in their hands on hye,
  Shall him defeate withouten bloud imbrewd:°   *spilt*
  Of which, that field for endlesse memory,
Shall Hevenfield be cald to all posterity.

39

"Where at Cadwallin wroth, shall forth issew,
  And an huge hoste into Northumber lead,
With which he godly Oswald shall subdew,
  And crowne with martyrdome his sacred head.
  Whose brother Oswin, daunted with like dread,
With price of silver shall his kingdome buy,°   *ransom*
  And Penda, seeking him adowne to tread,
  Shall tread adowne, and do him fowly dye,[5]
But shall with gifts his Lord Cadwallin pacify.

5. I.e., and Oswin shall defeat Penda   put him miserably to death.
(who sought to defeat Oswin), and

40

"Then shall Cadwallin dye, and then the raine
  Of Britons eke with him attonce° shall dye;   *forthwith*
  Ne shall the good Cadwallader with paine,
  Or powre, be hable it to remedy,
  When the full time prefixt by destiny,
  Shalbe expird of Britons regiment.°   *rule*
  For heaven it selfe shall their successe envy,
  And them with plagues and murrins° pestilent   *diseases*
Consume, till all their warlike puissaunce be spent.

41

"Yet after all these sorrowes, and huge hills
  Of dying people, during eight yeares space,
  Cadwallader not yielding to his ills,
  From Armoricke,[6] where long in wretched cace°   *state*
  He lived, returning[7] to his native place,
  Shalbe by vision staid from his intent:
  For th'heavens have decreéd, to displace
  The Britons, for their sinnes dew punishment,
And to the Saxons over-give° their government.   *give up*

42

"Then woe, and woe, and everlasting woe,
  Be to the Briton babe, that shalbe borne,
  To live in thraldome of° his fathers foe;   *to*
  Late King, now captive, late Lord, now forlorne,
  The worlds reproch, the cruell victors scorne,
  Banisht from Princely bowre° to wastfull° wood: *chamber/desolate*
  O who shall helpe me to lament, and mourne
  The royall seed, the antique Trojan blood,
Whose Empire lenger here, then ever any stood."[8]

43

The Damzell was full deepe empassionéd,°   *moved*
  Both for his griefe, and for her peoples sake,
  Whose future woes so plaine he fashionéd,
  And sighing sore, at length him thus bespake,
  "Ah but will heavens fury never slake,°   *slacken*
  Nor vengeaunce huge relent it selfe at last?
  Will not long misery late° mercy make,   *at length*
  But shall their name for ever be defast,°   *destroyed*
And quite from of the earth their memory be rast?"° *erased*

44

"Nay but the terme," said he, "is limited,
  That in this thraldome Britons shall abide,
  And the just revolution[9] measuréd,
  That they as Straungers shalbe notifide.°   *known*
  For twise foure hundreth yeares shalbe supplide,

6. Brittany, in northwestern France.   supposedly in 1132 B.C., to the death
7. I.e., expecting to return.   of Cadwallader, c. 690 A.D.
8. Reckoning from the arrival of Brute,   9. I.e., exact cycle.

Ere they to former rule restored shalbee,[1]
And their importune° fates all satisfide: *grievous*
Yet during this their most obscuritee,
Their beames shall oft breake forth, that men them faire may see.

45

"For Rhodoricke,[2] whose surname shalbe Great,
 Shall of him selfe a brave ensample shew,
 That Saxon kings his friendship shall intreat:
 And Howell Dha shall goodly well indew
 The salvage minds with skill of just and trew;
 Then Griffyth Conan also shall up reare
 His dreaded head, and the old sparkes renew
 Of native courage, that his foes shall feare,
Least backe againe the kingdome he from them should beare.° *take*

46

"Ne shall the Saxons selves all peaceably
 Enjoy the crowne, which they from Britons wonne
 First ill, and after ruléd wickedly:
 For ere two hundred yeares be full outronne,
 There shall a Raven[3] far from rising Sunne,
 With his wide wings upon them fiercely fly,
 And bid his faithlesse chickens overronne
 The fruitfull plaines, and with fell cruelty,
In their avenge, tread downe the victours surquedry.° *presumption*

47

"Yet shall a third both these, and thine subdew;
 There shall a Lyon[4] from the sea-bord wood
 Of Neustria come roring, with a crew
 Of hungry whelpes, his battailous° bold brood,   *warlike*
 Whose clawes were newly dipt in cruddy° blood,   *clotted*
 That from the Daniske Tyrants head shall rend
 Th'usurpéd crowne, as if that he were wood,°   *mad*
 And the spoile of the countrey conqueréd
Emongst his young ones shall divide with bountyhed.° *generosity*

48

"Tho when the terme is full accomplishid,
 There shall a sparke of fire,[5] which hath longwhile
 Bene in his ashes rakéd up, and hid,
 Be freshly kindled in the fruitfull Ile
 Of Mona, where it lurkéd in exile;
 Which shall breake forth into bright burning flame,
 And reach into the house, that beares the stile°   *title*

1. I.e., with the reign of Henry VII, who came to the throne in 1485, almost exactly eight hundred years after Cadwallader's death.
2. The Welsh rulers singled out here reigned within the period from 843 to 1136 A.D.
3. The (heathen) Danes, who first invaded England in 787 A.D.

4. William I of Normandy.
5. Henry VII was born in Anglesey (Mona), the last British territory remaining in the possession of the Welsh prince Llewelyn ap Griffith under the terms of his treaty with Edward I in 1283.

Of royall majesty and soveraigne name;°   *reputation*
So shall the Briton bloud their crowne againe reclame.

49

"Thenceforth eternall union shall be made
  Betweene the nations different afore,
  And sacred Peace shall lovingly perswade
  The warlike minds, to learne her goodly lore,°   *doctrine*
  And civile armes to exercise no more:
  Then shall a royall virgin[6] raine, which shall
  Stretch her white rod over the Belgicke shore,
  And the great Castle smite so sore with all,
That it shall make him shake, and shortly learne to fall.

50

"But yet the end is not." There Merlin stayd,°   *ceased*
  As° overcomen of the spirites powre,   *as if*
  Or other ghastly spectacle dismayd,
  That secretly he saw, yet note discoure:[7]
  Which suddein fit, and halfe extatick stoure°   *paroxysm*
  When the two fearefull women saw, they grew
  Greatly confuséd in behavioure;
  At last the fury° past, to former hew°   *seizure/appearance*
Hee turnd againe, and chearefull looks as earst° did shew.   *before*

51

Then, when them selves they well instructed had
  Of all, that needed them to be inquird,
  They both conceiving hope of comfort glad,
  With lighter hearts unto their home retird;
  Where they in secret counsell close conspird,
  How to effect so hard an enterprize,
  And to possesse° the purpose they desird: *achieve*
  Now this, now that twixt them they did devise,
And diverse plots did frame, to maske in strange disguise.

52

At last the Nourse in her foolhardy wit
  Conceived a bold devise,° and thus bespake;   *plan*
  "Daughter, I deeme that counsell aye most fit,
  That of the time doth dew advauntage take;
  Ye see that good king Uther now doth make
  Strong warre upon the Paynim brethren, hight
  Octa and Oza, whom he lately brake
  Beside Cayr Verolame, in victorious fight,
That now all Britanie doth burne in armés bright.[8]

53

"That therefore nought our passage may empeach,°   *hinder*
  Let us in feignéd armes our selves disguize,

6. Queen Elizabeth, whose navy turned back the galleons (or "great castles") of the Spanish Armada in 1588, and whose troops (from 1585 onward) were actively engaged in the Low Countries against those of Spain (Castile).
7. I.e., would not reveal.

8. These events, described in Geoffrey, *op. cit.*, VIII. 23, would have taken place about 470–480 A.D., i.e., approximately at the same time as the legendary emergence of Arthur.

And our weake hands (whom need new strength shall teach)
The dreadfull speare and shield to exercize:
Ne certes daughter that same warlike wize°   *manner*
I weene, would you misseme°; for ye bene tall,   *not be fitting*
And large of limbe, t'atchieve an hard emprize,
Ne ought ye want,° but skill, which practize small   *lack*
Will bring, and shortly make you a mayd Martiall.

54
"And sooth, it ought your courage much inflame,
  To heare so often, in that royall hous,
  From whence to none inferiour ye came,
  Bards tell of many women valorous
  Which have full many feats adventurous
  Performd, in paragone° of proudest men: *emulation*
  The bold Bunduca, whose victorious
  Exploits made Rome to quake, stout Guendolen,
Renowmèd Martia, and redoubted Emmilen.[9]

55
"And that, which more than all the rest may sway,°   *move*
  Late dayes ensample, which these eyes beheld,
  In the last field before Menevia[1]
  Which Uther with those forrein Pagans held,
  I saw a Saxon Virgin,[2] the which feld
  Great Ulfin thrise upon the bloudy plaine,
  And had not Carados her hand withheld
  From rash revenge, she had him surely slaine,
Yet Carados himselfe from her escapt with paine."°   *difficulty*

56
"Ah read," quoth Britomart, "how is she hight?"
  "Faire Angela," quoth she, "men do her call,
  No whit lesse faire, then terrible in fight:
  She hath the leading of a Martiall
  And mighty people, dreaded more then all
  The other Saxons, which do for her sake
  And love, themselves of her name Angles call.
  Therefore faire Infant her ensample make
Unto thy selfe, and equall courage to thee take."

57
Her harty° words so deepe into the mynd   *spirited*
  Of the young Damzell sunke, that great desire
  Of warlike armes in her forthwith they tynd,°   *kindled*
  And generous stout courage did inspire,

9. Boadicea, queen of the Iceni in southeastern England, led a revolt against the Romans in 61 A.D.; Gwendolen, the daughter of Corineus, slew her unfaithful husband in battle, and ruled Cornwall for fifteen years thereafter; Marcia, wife of the British king Guithelin, was renowned for her learning and statecraft; "Emmilen" perhaps refers to Charlemagne's daughter, but Spenser also gives the name to the mother of Sir Tristram (VI. ii. 29).
1. St. Davids; cf. Geoffrey, *op. cit.*, VIII. 16.
2. Angela, here identified with the Saxon queen for whom England was named; it is not known whether Spenser invented this account or based it on some lost source.

That she resolved, unweeting° to her Sire,   *unknown*
  Advent'rous knighthood on her selfe to don,
  And counseld with her Nourse, her Maides attire
  To turne into a massy habergeon,°   *coat of mail*
And bad her all things put in readinesse anon.

58

Th'old woman nought, that needed, did omit;
  But all things did conveniently purvay:°   *provide*
  It fortunéd (so time their turne did fit)[3]
  A band of Britons ryding on forray°   *a raid*
  Few dayes before, had gotten a great pray°   *booty*
  Of Saxon goods, emongst the which was seene
  A goodly Armour, and full rich aray,°   *equipment*
  Which longed to Angela, the Saxon Queene,
All fretted° round with gold, and goodly well beseene.   *adorned*

59

The same, with all the other ornaments,
  King Ryence causéd to be hangéd hy
  In his chiefe Church, for endlesse moniments°   *memorials*
  Of his successe and gladfull victory:
  Of which her selfe avising° readily,   *calling to mind*
  In th'evening late old Glauce thither led
  Faire Britomart, and that same Armory°   *armor*
  Downe taking, her therein appareléd,
Well as she might, and with brave bauldrick° garnishéd.   *shoulder belt*

60

Beside those armes there stood a mighty speare,
  Which Bladud[4] made by Magick art of yore,
  And usd the same in battell aye to beare;
  Sith which it had bin here preserved in store,
  For his great vertues° provéd long afore: *powers*
  For never wight so fast in sell° could sit,   *saddle*
  But him perforce unto the ground it bore:
  Both speare she tooke, and shield, which hong by it:
Both speare and shield of great powre, for her purpose fit.

61

Thus when she had the virgin all arayd,
  Another harnesse,° which did hang thereby,   *set of armor*
  About her selfe she dight, that the young Mayd
  She might in equall armes accompany,
  And as her Squire attend her carefully:
  Tho to their ready Steeds they clombe full light,°   *easily*
  And through back wayes, that none might them espy,
  Covered with secret cloud of silent night,
Themselves they forth convayd, and passéd forward right.

3. I.e., events fell out suitably for their needs.
4. A British king renowned for his powers in magic. Britomart's arms, Saxon and Celtic in origin, implicitly combine the strengths of both races; in them the powers of natural magic have been sanctified by a higher religious faith.

62

Ne rested they, till that to Faery lond
 They came, as Merlin them directed late:
 Where meeting with this Redcrosse knight, she fond
 Of diverse things discourses to dilate,°   *enlarge upon*
 But most of Arthegall, and his estate.°   *condition*
 At last their wayes so fell, that they mote part:
 Then each to other well affectionate,°   *disposed*
 Friendship professéd with unfainéd hart,
The Redcrosse knight diverst, but forth° rode Britomart.[5] *forward*

Canto IV

 Bold Marinell of Britomart,
   Is throwne on the Rich strond:°   *shore*
 Faire Florimell of Arthur is
   Long followed, but not fond.°   *found*

1

Where is the Antique glory now become,°   *gone*
 That whilome wont in women to appeare?
 Where be the brave atchievements doen by some?
 Where be the battels, where the shield and speare,
 And all the conquests, which them high did reare,
 That matter made for famous Poets verse,
 And boastfull men so oft abasht to heare?
 Bene they all dead, and laid in dolefull herse?
Or doen they onely sleepe, and shall againe reverse?° *return*

2

If they be dead, then woe is me therefore:
 But if they sleepe, O let them soone awake:
 For all too long I burne with envy° sore,   *longing*
 To heare the warlike feates, which Homere spake
 Of bold Penthesilee,[1] which made a lake
 Of Greekish bloud so oft in Trojan plaine;
 But when I read, how stout Debora strake
 Proud Sisera, and how Camill' hath slaine
The huge Orsilochus, I swell with great disdaine.° *indignation*

3

Yet these, and all that else had puissaunce,
 Cannot with noble Britomart compare,

---

5. So Britomart, supported by Glauce's "robust sense of reality," and instructed by Merlin's prophetic art (which has regularly indicated the directive power of divine will), rides forward on her quest, confidently aware "that her purpose contributes to a greater one which is God's" (Kathleen Williams, *Spenser's World of Glass, A Reading of The Faerie Queene* [Berkeley, 1966], p. 96).

1. Penthesilea, queen of the Amazons, is not mentioned by Homer, but she appears briefly in the *Aeneid* (I. 490–495); the encounter of Camilla and Orsilochus is also described in that epic (XI. 690–698). For the account of Sisera's destruction, which was brought to pass and celebrated by Deborah (although Sisera was actually killed by Jael), cf. Judges, iv.

Aswell for glory of great valiaunce,° valor
As for pure chastitie and vertue rare,
That all her goodly deeds do well declare.
Well worthy stock, from which the branches sprong,
That in late yeares so faire a blossome bare,
As thee, O Queene, the matter° of my song, theme
Whose lignage from this Lady I derive along.° throughout

4

Who when through speaches with the Redcrosse knight,
She learnéd had th'estate of Arthegall,
And in each point her selfe informd aright,
A friendly league of love perpetuall
She with him bound, and Congé° tooke withall. leave
Then he forth on his journey did proceede,
To seeke adventures, which mote him befall,
And win him worship° through his warlike deed, renown
Which alwayes of his paines he made the chiefest meed.° reward

5

But Britomart kept on her former course,
Ne ever dofte° her armes, but all the way took off
Grew pensive through that amorous discourse,
By which the Redcrosse knight did earst display° set forth
Her lovers shape, and chevalrous aray;
A thousand thoughts she fashioned in her mind,
And in her feigning fancie did pourtray
Him such, as fittest she for love could find,
Wise, warlike, personable, curteous, and kind.

6

With such selfe-pleasing thoughts her wound she fed,
And thought so to beguile° her grievous smart; charm away
But so her smart was much more grievous bred,
And the deepe wound more deepe engord her hart,
That nought but death her dolour mote depart.° remove
So forth she rode without repose or rest,
Searching all lands and each remotest part,
Following the guidance of her blinded guest,[2]
Till that to the sea-coast at length she her addrest.

7

There she alighted from her light-foot beast,
And sitting downe upon the rocky shore,
Bad her old Squire unlace her lofty creast;° helmet
Tho having vewd a while the surges hore,° grey
That gainst the craggy clifts did loudly rore,
And in their raging surquedry° disdaynd, arrogance
That the fast° earth affronted them so sore, firm
And their devouring covetize restraynd,
Thereat she sighéd deepe, and after thus complaynd.[3]

2. I.e., Cupid, god of love.
3. The central conceit of Britomart's "complaint" (the likening of a lover's condition to that of a ship in stormy seas) often appears in Renaissance love lyrics, e.g., in Petrarch's *Rime*, 189

8

"Huge sea of sorrow, and tempestuous griefe,
　　Wherein my feeble barke° is tosséd long,　　　　　　*vessel*
　　Far from the hopéd haven of reliefe,
　　Why do thy cruell billowes beat so strong,
　　And thy moyst mountaines each on others throng,
　　Threatning to swallow up my fearefull life?
　　O do thy cruell wrath and spightfull wrong
　　At length allay, and stint° thy stormy strife,　　　　　*cease*
Which in these troubled bowels raignes, and rageth rife.°　*strongly*

9

"For else my feeble vessell crazd,° and crackt　　　　　　*weakened*
　　Through thy strong buffets and outrageous blowes,
　　Cannot endure, but needs it must be wrackt
　　On the rough rocks, or on the sandy shallowes,
　　The whiles that love it steres, and fortune rowes;
　　Love my lewd° Pilot hath a restlesse mind　　　　　　*unskillful*
　　And fortune Boteswaine no assuraunce° knowes,　　　　*certainty*
　　But saile withouten starres gainst tide and wind:
How can they other do, sith both are bold and blind?

10

"Thou God of winds, that raignest in the seas,
　　That raignest also in the Continent,°　　　　　　　　　*land*
　　At last blow up some gentle gale of ease,
　　The which may bring my ship, ere it be rent,°　　　　　*torn apart*
　　Unto the gladsome port of her intent:°　　　　　　　　*purpose*
　　Then when I shall my selfe in safety see,
　　A table° for eternall moniment　　　　　　　　　　　*votive tablet*
　　Of thy great grace, and my great jeopardee,
Great Neptune, I avow to hallow unto thee."

11

Then sighing softly sore, and inly deepe,
　　She shut up all her plaint in privy° griefe;　　　　　　*secret*
　　For her great courage° would not let her weepe,　　　　*spirit*
　　Till that old Glauce gan with sharpe repriefe,°　　　　*reproof*
　　Her to restraine, and give her good reliefe,
　　Through hope of those, which Merlin had her told
　　Should of her name and nation be chiefe,
　　And fetch their being from the sacred mould°　　　　　*form*
Of her immortall wombe, to be in heaven enrold.

12

Thus as she her recomforted, she spyde,
　　Where farre away one all in armour bright,[4]

(in *Francesco Petrarca: Rime, Trionfi, e Poesie Latine*, ed. N. Sapegno [Milan, 1951]) and in Wyatt's translation of that sonnet, as well as in *Amoretti*, 34.
4. I.e., Marinell ("loves enimy," st. 26), for whom Florimell is searching (III.v.8–10). At one "level" of the allegory, Marinell (like Achilles the object of an over-solicitous mother's care) represents self-absorbed determination to ignore and so avoid love; the shock of Britomart's spear signifies the initial shattering of this "withdrawn" complacency, opening the way for an eventual acceptance of love's full meaning (Marinell and Florimell

With hastie gallop towards her did ryde;
Her dolour soone she ceast, and on her dight
Her Helmet, to her Courser mounting light:
Her former sorrow into suddein wrath,
Both coosen° passions of distroubled spright,   *kindred*
Converting, forth she beates the dustie path;
Love and despight° attonce her courage kindled hath.   *defiance*

13

As when a foggy mist hath overcast
The face of heaven, and the cleare aire engrost,°   *thickened*
The world in darkenesse dwels, till that at last
The watry Southwinde from the seabord cost
Upblowing, doth disperse the vapour lo'st,°   *released*
And poures it selfe forth in a stormy showre;
So the faire Britomart having disclo'st
Her clowdy care into a wrathfull stowre,[5]
The mist of griefe dissolved, did into vengeance powre.

14

Eftsoones her goodly shield addressing° faire,   *adjusting*
That mortall speare she in her hand did take,
And unto battell did her selfe prepaire.
The knight approching, sternely her bespake;
"Sir knight, that doest thy voyage rashly make
By this forbidden way in my despight,[6]
Ne doest by others death ensample take,
I read° thee soone retyre, whiles thou hast might,   *tell*
Least afterwards it be too late to take thy flight."

15

Ythrild° with deepe disdaine of his proud threat,   *deeply moved*
She shortly thus; "Fly they, that need to fly;
Words fearen babes. I meane not thee entreat
To passe; but maugre° thee will passe or dy."   *in spite of*
Ne lenger stayd for th'other to reply,
But with sharpe speare the rest made dearly° knowne.   *resolutely*
Strongly the straunge knight ran, and sturdily
Strooke her full on the brest, that made her downe
Decline her head, and touch her crouper with her crowne.[7]

16

But she againe° him in the shield did smite   *in return*
With so fierce furie and great puissaunce,

---

are finally united in Book V). It is relevant to note that, elsewhere in *The Faerie Queene,* Spenser identifies "Beautie, and money" as the two "engins" that threaten the "bulwarke of the Sight" in the House of Temperance (II.xi.9); Marinell, who guards his "Rich strond," is associated with material wealth, the rival of beauty as an object of human desire. While men are inclined to seek beauty, fair women seek the riches they desire:

"they for love of him would algates dy" (st. 26). In this sense, Marinell's opposition to the chaste Britomart signifies the obsessive care for riches that rejects love in every form save that of money.
5. I.e., having relieved her gloomy despondency by an outburst of anger.
6. I.e., in scorn of me.
7. I.e., that forced her backward so far that her head touched her horse's back (or crupper).

That through his threesquare scuchin° percing quite,   *shield*
And through his mayléd hauberque,° by mischaunce   *coat of mail*
The wicked steele through his left side did glaunce;
Him so transfixéd she before her bore
Beyond his croupe, the length of all her launce,
Till sadly soucing° on the sandie shore,   *falling*
He tombled on° an heape, and wallowd in his gore.   *in*

17

Like as the sacred Oxe, that carelesse stands,
  With gilden hornes, and flowry girlonds crownd,
  Proud of his dying honor and deare bands,°   *bonds*
  Whiles th' altars fume with frankincense arownd,
  All suddenly with mortall stroke astownd,°   *stunned*
  Doth groveling fall, and with his streaming gore
  Distaines° the pillours, and the holy grownd,   *stains*
  And the faire flowres, that deckéd him afore;
So fell proud Marinell upon the pretious shore.

18

The martiall Mayd stayd not him to lament,
  But forward rode, and kept her readie way
  Along the strond, which as she over-went,°   *traversed*
  She saw bestrowéd all with rich aray
  Of pearles and pretious stones of great assay,°   *worth*
  And all the gravell mixt with golden owre;°   *ore*
  Whereat she wondred much, but would not stay
  For gold, or perles, or pretious stones an howre,
But them despiséd all; for° all was in her powre.   *although*

19

Whiles thus he lay in deadly stonishment,°   *swoon*
  Tydings hereof came to his mothers eare;
  His mother was the blacke-browd Cymoent,[8]
  The daughter of great Nereus, which did beare
  This warlike sonne unto an earthly peare,°   *noble*
  The famous Dumarin; who on a day
  Finding the Nymph a sleepe in secret wheare,°   *place*
  As he by chaunce did wander that same way,
Was taken with her love, and by her closely lay.

20

There he this knight of her begot, whom borne
  She of his father Marinell did name,
  And in a rocky cave as wight forlorne,
  Long time she fostred up, till he became
  A mightie man at armes, and mickle° fame   *much*
  Did get through great adventures by him donne:

8. From Greek, "wave." Cymoent (also called Cymodoce, in Book IV) was one of the fifty Nereids, sea nymphs whose names and characteristics Spenser probably knew from Natalis Comes. The circumstances of Marinell's conception, and Cymoent's efforts to preserve him, recall Ovid's account of Thetis, Peleus, and Achilles (*Metamorphoses*, XI. 217–265; XIII. 162–170). As Thetis's device to protect her son Achilles proved futile, so Cymoent's efforts to control fate are unavailing (cf. st. 27).

For never man he suffred by that same
  Rich strond to travell, whereas he did wonne,°   *dwell*
But that he must do battell with the Sea-nymphes sonne.

21

An hundred knights of honorable name
  He had subdewed, and them his vassals made,
  That through all Farie lond his noble fame
  Now blazéd° was, and feare did invade,°   *proclaimed/afflict*
  That none durst passen through that perilous glade.
  And to advaunce° his name and glorie more,   *heighten*
  Her Sea-god syre she dearely° did perswade,°   *boldly/entreat*
  T'endow her sonne with threasure and rich store,
Bove all the sonnes, that were of earthly wombes ybore.

22

The God did graunt his daughters deare demaund,
  To doen° his Nephew in all riches flow;   *make*
  Eftsoones his heapéd waves he did commaund,
  Out of their hollow bosome forth to throw
  All the huge threasure, which the sea below
  Had in his greedie gulfe devouréd deepe,
  And him enrichéd through the overthrow
  And wreckes of many wretches, which did weepe,
And often waile their wealth, which he from them did keepe.

23

Shortly upon that shore there heapéd was,
  Exceeding riches and all pretious things,
  The spoyle of all the world, that it did pas
  The wealth of th'East, and pompe of Persian kings;
  Gold, amber, yvorie, perles, owches,° rings,   *brooches*
  And all that else was pretious and deare,°   *valuable*
  The sea unto him voluntary brings,
  That shortly he a great Lord did appeare,
As was in all the lond of Faery, or elsewheare.

24

Thereto he was a doughtie dreaded knight,
  Tryde often to the scath° of many deare,°   *harm/dearly*
  That none in equall armes him matchen might,
  The which his mother seeing, gan to feare
  Least his too haughtie hardines might reare°   *cause*
  Some hard mishap, in hazard of[9] his life:
  For thy she oft him counseld to forbeare
  The bloudie battell, and to stirre up strife,
But after all his warre, to rest his wearie knife.°   *sword*

25

And for his more assurance,° she inquired   *security*
  One day of Proteus[1] by his mightie spell,°   *magic charm*
  (For Proteus was with prophecie inspired)

---

9. I.e., to endanger.
1. A sea god who, traditionally, could foretell the future and change his shape at will: cf. Ovid, *Metamorphoses*, XI. 249–256, and Homer, *Odyssey*, IV. 384 ff.

Her deare sonnes destinie to her to tell,
  And the sad end of her sweet Marinell.
  Who through foresight of his eternall skill,°   *knowledge*
  Bad her from womankind to keepe him well:
  For of a woman he should have much ill,
A virgin strange and stout° him should dismay, or kill.   *bold*

26

For thy she gave him warning every day,
  The love of women not to entertaine;°   *accept*
  A lesson too too hard for living clay,
  From love in course of nature to refraine:
  Yet he his mothers lore did well retaine,
  And ever from faire Ladies love did fly;
  Yet many Ladies faire did oft complaine,
  That they for love of him would algates° dy: *entirely*
Dy, who so list for him, he was loves enimy.

27

But ah, who can deceive his destiny,
  Or weene by warning to avoyd his fate?
  That when he sleepes in most security,
  And safest seemes, him soonest doth amate,°   *dismay*
  And findeth dew effect or soone or late.
  So feeble is the powre of fleshly arme.
  His mother bad him womens love to hate,
  For she of womans force did feare no harme;
So weening to have armed him, she did quite disarme.

28

This was that woman, this that deadly wound,
  That Proteus prophecide should him dismay,
  The which his mother vainely° did expound,   *in vain*
  To be hart-wounding love, which should assay°   *assault*
  To bring her sonne unto his last decay.
  So tickle° be the termes of mortall state,°   *uncertain/condition*
  And full of subtile sophismes, which do play
  With double senses, and with false debate,
T'approve° the unknowen purpose of eternall fate.   *demonstrate*

29

Too true the famous Marinell it fownd,
  Who through late triall, on that wealthy Strond
  Inglorious now lies in senselesse swownd,
  Through heavy° stroke of Britomartis hond.   *grievous*
  Which when his mother deare did understond,
  And heavy tydings heard, whereas she playd
  Amongst her watry sisters by a pond,
  Gathering sweet daffadillyes, to have made
Gay girlonds, from the Sun their forheads faire to shade;

30

Eftsoones both flowres and girlonds farre away
  She flong, and her faire deawy lockes yrent,°   *tore*
  To sorrow huge she turnd her former play,

And gamesom merth to grievous dreriment:
She threw her selfe downe on the Continent,°   *ground*
Ne word did speake, but lay as in a swowne,
Whiles all her sisters did for her lament,
With yelling outcries, and with shrieking sowne;°   *sound*
And every one did teare her girlond from her crowne.

31

Soone as she up out of her deadly fit°   *swoon*
   Arose, she bad her charet° to be brought,   *chariot*
   And all her sisters, that with her did sit,
   Bad eke attonce their charets to be sought;
   Tho full of bitter griefe and pensive thought,
   She to her wagon clombe;° clombe all the rest,   *mounted*
   And forth together went, with sorrow fraught.
   The waves obedient to their beheast,°   *bidding*
Them yielded readie passage, and their rage surceast.

32

Great Neptune stood amazéd at their sight,
   Whiles on his broad round backe they softly slid
   And eke himselfe mournd at their mournfull plight,
   Yet wist not what their wailing ment, yet did
   For great compassion of their sorrow, bid
   His mightie waters to them buxome° bee: *yielding*
   Eftsoones the roaring billowes still abid,°   *remained*
   And all the griesly° Monsters of the See   *horrible*
Stood gaping at their gate, and wondred them to see.

33

A teme of Dolphins raungéd in aray,
   Drew the smooth charet of sad Cymoent;
   They were all taught by Triton, to obay
   To the long raynes, at her commaundément:
   As swift as swallowes, on the waves they went,
   That their broad flaggie° finnes no fome did reare,°   *drooping/raise*
   Ne bubbling roundell° they behind them sent;   *globule*
   The rest of° other fishes drawen weare,   *by*
Which with their finny oars the swelling sea did sheare.°   *cleave*

34

Soone as they bene arrived upon the brim°   *edge*
   Of the Rich strond, their charets they forlore,°   *left*
   And let their teméd fishes softly swim
   Along the margent of the fomy shore,
   Least they their finnes should bruze, and surbate° sore   *chafe*
   Their tender feet upon the stony ground:
   And comming to the place, where all in gore
   And cruddy bloud enwallowéd° they found   *tumbled*
The lucklesse Marinell, lying in deadly swound;

35

His mother swownéd thrise, and the third time
   Could scarce recovered be out of her paine;

Had she not bene devoyd of mortall slime,°   *clay*
She should not then have bene relived° againe,   *revived*
But soone as life recovered had the raine,
She made so piteous mone and deare wayment,°   *lamentation*
That the hard rocks could scarse from teares refraine,
And all her sister Nymphes with one consent°   *harmony*
Supplide her sobbing breaches[2] with sad complement.

36

"Deare image of my selfe," she said, "that is,
  The wretched sonne of wretched mother borne,
  Is this thine high advauncement, O is this
  Th'immortall name, with which thee yet unborne
  Thy Gransire Nereus promist to adorne?
  Now lyest thou of life and honor reft;°   *deprived*
  Now lyest thou a lumpe of earth forlorne,
  Ne of thy late life memory is left,
Ne can thy irrevocable destiny be weft?°   *avoided*

37

"Fond° Proteus, father of false prophecis,   *foolish*
  And they more fond, that credit to thee give,
  Not this the worke of womans hand ywis,°   *certainly*
  That so deepe wound through these deare members drive.
  I fearéd love: but they that love do live,
  But they that die, doe neither love nor hate.
  Nath'lesse to thee thy folly I forgive,
  And to my selfe, and to acccurséd fate
The guilt I doe ascribe: deare wisedome bought too late.

38

"O what availes it of immortall seed
  To beene ybred and never borne to die?
  Farre better I it deeme to die with speed,
  Then waste in woe and wailefull miserie.
  Who dyes the utmost dolour doth abye,°   *suffer*
  But who that lives, is left to waile his losse:
  So life is losse, and death felicitie.
  Sad life worse then glad death: and greater crosse
To see friends grave, then dead the grave selfe to engrosse.°   *fill*

39

"But if the heavens did his dayes envie,
  And my short blisse maligne,° yet mote they well   *grudge*
  Thus much afford me, ere that he did die
  That the dim eyes of my deare Marinell
  I mote have closéd, and him bed farewell,
  Sith other offices° for mother meet   *services*
  They would not graunt.
  Yet maulgre° them farewell, my sweetest sweet;   *in spite of*
Farewell my sweetest sonne, sith we no more shall meet."

---

2. I.e., the intervals between fits of sobbing.

40

Thus when they all had sorrowéd their fill,
    They softly gan to search his griesly wound:
    And that they might him handle more at will,
    They him disarmed, and spredding on the ground
    Their watchet° mantles frindgd with silver round,   *pale blue*
    They softly wipt away the gelly° blood   *clotted*
    From th'orifice; which having well upbound,
    They pourd in soveraine balme, and Nectar good,
Good both for earthly med'cine, and for heavenly food.

41

Tho when the lilly handed Liagore,[3]
    (This Liagore whylome had learnéd skill
    In leaches craft, by great Appolloes lore,°   *teaching*
    Sith her whylome upon high Pindus hill,
    He lovéd, and at last her wombe did fill
    With heavenly seed, whereof wise Paeon sprong)
    Did feele his pulse, she knew their staiéd still
    Some litle life his feeble sprites° emong;   *spirit*
Which to his mother told, despeire she from her flong.

42

Tho up him taking in their tender hands,
    They easily unto her charet beare:
    Her teme at her commaundement quiet stands,
    Whiles they the corse into her wagon reare,°   *raise*
    And strow with flowres the lamentable beare:[4]
    Then all the rest into their coches clim,°   *mount*
    And through the brackish waves their passage sheare;
    Upon great Neptunes necke they softly swim,
And to her watry chamber swiftly carry him.

43

Deepe in the bottome of the sea, her bowre
    Is built of hollow billowes heapéd hye,
    Like to thicke cloudes, that threat a stormy showre,
    And vauted° all within, like to the sky,   *arched*
    In which the Gods do dwell eternally:
    There they him laid in easie couch well dight;
    And sent in haste for Tryphon,[5] to apply
    Salves to his wounds, and medicines of might:
For Tryphon of sea gods the soveraine leach is hight.

44

The whiles the Nymphes sit all about him round,
    Lamenting his mishap and heavy° plight;   *sad*
    And oft his mother vewing his wide wound,

3. From Greek, "white-armed." Hesiod identifies Liagore as one of the Nereids (*Theogony*, 257); but Spenser's account of the birth of Paeon (the physician of the gods, in Homer, *Iliad*, V. 401–2, 899–901) is essentially his own invention.

4. I.e., the bier and its mournful burden.

5. A sea god skilled in healing; according to Boccaccio, he was the brother of Aesculapius (*De Genealogia Deorum*, VII. 36).

Curséd the hand, that did so deadly smight
Her dearest sonne, her dearest harts delight.[6]
But none of all those curses overtooke
The warlike Maid, th'ensample of that might,
But fairely well she thrived, and well did brooke°   *persist in*
Her noble deeds, ne her right course for ought forsooke.

45

Yet did false Archimage[7] her still pursew,
To bring to passe his mischievous intent,
Now that he had her singled° from the crew   *separated*
Of courteous knights, the Prince, and Faery gent,
Whom late in chace of beautie excellent
She left, pursewing that same foster strong;
Of whose foule outrage they impatient,°   *angered*
And full of fiery zeale, him followed long,
To reskew her from shame, and to revenge her wrong.

46

Through thick and thin, through mountaines and through plains,
Those two great champions did attonce° pursew   *together*
The fearefull damzell, with incessant paines:
Who from them fled, as light-foot hare from vew
Of hunter swift, and sent of houndés trew.
At last they came unto a double way,
Where, doubtfull which to take, her to reskew,
Themselves they did dispart,° each to assay,   *separate*
Whether more happie were, to win so goodly pray.

47

But Timias, the Princes gentle Squire,
That Ladies love unto his Lord forlent,°   *relinquished*
And with proud envy,° and indignant ire,   *indignation*
After that wicked foster fiercely went.
So beene they three three sundry wayes ybent.°   *turned*
But fairest fortune to the Prince befell,
Whose chaunce it was, that soone he did repent,°   *regret*
To take that way, in which that Damozell
Was fled afore, affraid of him, as feend of hell.

48

At last of her farre off he gainéd vew:
Then gan he freshly pricke his fomy steed,
And ever as he nigher to her drew,
So evermore he did increase his speed,
And of each turning still kept warie heed:
Aloud to her he oftentimes did call,
To doe° away vaine doubt, and needlesse dreed: *banish*

---

6. Thus Marinell (like Florimell in viii. 41–42) disappears from Book III, apparently "dead to the world" in the recesses of the wild salt sea. But he will eventually be cured by Tryphon (IV. xi. 7); shortly thereafter, in consequence of Cymoent's appeal to Neptune, he is united with Florimell; and their marriage is finally solemnized in V. iv. 3.
7. Cf. note to the "Argument" of III. i.

Full myld to her he spake, and oft let fall
Many meeke wordes, to stay and comfort her withall.

49

But nothing might relent° her hastie flight;   slacken
 So deepe the deadly feare of that foule swaine°   rustic
 Was earst impresséd in her gentle spright:
 Like as a fearefull Dove, which through the raine,°   domain
 Of the wide aire her way does cut amaine,   rapidly
 Having farre off espyde a Tassell gent,[8]
 Which after her his nimble wings doth straine,
 Doubleth her haste for feare to be for-hent,°   seized
And with her pineons cleaves the liquid firmament.

50

With no lesse haste, and eke with no lesse dreed,
 That fearefull Ladie fled from him, that ment
 To her no evill thought, nor evill deed;
 Yet former feare of being fowly shent,°   disgraced
 Carried her forward with her first intent:
 And though oft looking backward, well she vewd,
 Her selfe freed from that foster insolent,
 And that it was a knight, which now her sewd,°   pursued
Yet she no lesse the knight feard, then that villein rude.

51

His uncouth° shield and straunge armes her dismayd,   unusual
 Whose like in Faery lond were seldome seene,
 That fast she from him fled, no lesse affrayd,
 Then of wilde beastes if she had chaséd beene:
 Yet he her followd still with courage° keene,   spirit
 So long that now the golden Hesperus[9]
 Was mounted high in top of heaven sheene,°   bright
 And warned his other brethren joyeous,
To light their blesséd lamps in Joves eternall hous.

52

All suddenly dim woxe the dampish ayre,
 And griesly shadowes covered heaven bright,
 That now with thousand starres was deckéd fayre;
 Which when the Prince beheld, a lothfull sight,
 And that perforce, for want of lenger light,
 He mote surcease his suit,° and lose the hope   pursuit
 Of his long labour, he gan fowly wyte°   chide
 His wicked fortune, that had turnd aslope,°   awry
And curséd night, that reft from him so goodly scope.°   desired object

53

Tho when her wayes he could no more descry,
 But to and fro at disaventure° strayd;   random
 Like as a ship, whose Lodestarre suddenly
 Covered with cloudes, her Pilot hath dismayd;
 His wearisome pursuit perforce he stayd,

8. I.e., a male falcon.   9. The evening star.

And from his loftie steed dismounting low,
  Did let him forage. Downe himselfe he layd
  Upon the grassie ground, to sleepe a throw;°   *while*
The cold earth was his couch, the hard steele his pillow.

54
But gentle Sleepe envyde° him any rest;   *grudged*
  In stead thereof sad sorrow, and disdaine
  Of his hard hap° did vexe his noble brest,   *lot*
  And thousand fancies bet his idle braine
  With their light wings, the sights of semblants° vaine: *illusions*
  Oft did he wish, that Lady faire mote bee
  His Faery Queene, for whom he did complaine:°   *lament*
  Or that his Faery Queene were such, as shee:
And ever hastie Night he blaméd bitterlie.[1]

55
"Night thou foule Mother of annoyance° sad,   *grief*
  Sister of heavie death, and nourse of woe,
  Which wast begot in heaven, but for thy bad
  And brutish shape thrust downe to hell below,
  Where by the grim floud of Cocytus slow
  Thy dwelling is, in Herebus blacke house[2]
  (Blacke Herebus thy husband is the foe
  Of all the Gods) where thou ungratious,
Halfe of thy dayes doest lead in horrour hideous.

56
"What had th'eternall Maker need of thee,
  The world in his° continuall course to keepe,   *its*
  That doest all things deface,° ne lettest see   *obscure*
  The beautie of his worke? Indeed in sleepe
  The slouthfull bodie, that doth love to steepe
  His lustlesse° limbes, and drowne his baser° mind,   *feeble/too base*
  Doth praise thee oft, and oft from Stygian deepe
  Calles[3] thee, his goddesse in his error blind,
And great Dame Natures handmaide, chearing every kind.

57
"But well I wote, that to an heavy hart
  Thou art the root and nurse of bitter cares,
  Breeder of new, renewer of old smarts:
  In stead of rest thou lendest rayling° teares,   *bitter*
  In stead of sleepe thou sendest troublous feares,
  And dreadfull visions, in the which alive
  The drearie image of sad death appeares:

1. Arthur's lament, in sts. 55–60, is related to the genre of the Petrarchan lyric "complaint," often rendered at night by a forlorn lover (cf. also Dido's lament, *Aeneid*, IV. 522–554). The power of beauty may distract even the heroic mind; yet the scope and reach of Arthur's address to Night is appropriate to the heroic character of the Prince.

2. According to Hesiod, Chaos gave birth to Night and Erebus, whose abode was the underworld (*Theogony*, 123, 669–670).

3. I.e., summons thee from Stygian depths, and calls thee his goddess and the handmaid of Dame Nature.

So from the wearie spirit thou doest drive
Desiréd rest, and men of happinesse deprive.

58

"Under thy mantle blacke there hidden lye,
  Light-shonning theft, and traiterous intent,
  Abhorréd bloudshed, and vile felony,
  Shamefull deceipt, and daunger imminent;°   *threatening*
  Foule horror, and eke hellish dreriment:[4]
  All these I wote in thy protection bee,
  And light doe shonne, for feare of being shent:°   *put to shame*
  For light ylike° is lothed of them and thee,   *alike*
And all that lewdnesse° love, doe hate the light to see. *wickedness*

59

"For day discovers° all dishonest wayes,   *reveals*
  And sheweth each thing, as it is indeed:
  The prayses of high God he faire displayes
  And his large bountie rightly doth areed.°   *show*
  Dayes dearest children be the blesséd seed,
  Which darknesse shall subdew, and heaven win:
  Truth is his daughter; he her first did breed,
  Most sacred virgin, without spot of sin.
Our life is day, but death with darknesse doth begin.

60

"O when will day then turne to me againe,
  And bring with him his long expected light?
  O Titan, haste to reare thy joyous waine:[5]
  Speed thee to spred abroad thy beamés bright,
  And chase away this too long lingring night,
  Chase her away, from whence she came, to hell.
  She, she it is, that hath me done despight:°   *wrong*
  There let her with the damnéd spirits dwell,
And yeeld her roome to day, that can it governe well."

61

Thus did the Prince that wearie night outweare,°   *spend*
  In restlesse anguish and unquiet paine:
  And earely, ere the morrow did upreare
  His deawy head out of the Ocean maine,
  He up arose, as halfe in great disdaine,
  And clombe unto his steed. So forth he went,
  With heavie looke and lumpish° pace, that plaine   *dull*
  In him bewraid great grudge and maltalent:°   *ill will*
His steed eke seemed t'apply° his steps to his intent.° *suit/spirit*

---

4. The list of Night's offspring is based either on Hesiod, *Theogony*, 211–225, or on Natalis Comes, *Mythologiae*, III. 12.

5. I.e., may the sun soon rise.

Canto V

Prince Arthur heares of Florimell:
three fosters Timias wound,
Belphebe finds him almost dead,
and reareth out of sownd.°   *swoon*

1

Wonder it is to see, in diverse minds,
  How diversly love doth his pageants° play,   *roles*
  And shewes his powre in variable° kinds: *various*
  The baser wit,° whose idle thoughts alway   *mind*
  Are wont to cleave unto the lowly clay,
  It stirreth up to sensuall desire,
  And in lewd slouth to wast his carelesse day:
  But in brave sprite it kindles goodly fire,
That to all high desert° and honour doth aspire.[1]   *worth*

2

Ne suffereth it uncomely° idlenesse,   *unbecoming*
  In his free thought to build her sluggish nest:
  Ne suffereth it thought of ungentlenesse,
  Ever to creepe into his noble brest,
  But to the highest and the worthiest
  Lifteth it up, that else would lowly fall:
  It lets not fall, it lets it not to rest:
  It lets not scarse this Prince to breath at all,
But to his first poursuit him forward still doth call.

3

Who long time wandred through the forrest wyde,
  To finde some issue° thence, till that at last   *way out*
  He met a Dwarfe, that seeméd terrifyde
  With some late perill, which he hardly° past,   *with difficulty*
  Or other accident, which him aghast;°   *terrified*
  Of whom he askéd, whence he lately came,
  And whither now he travelléd so fast:
  For sore he swat,° and running through that same   *sweated*
Thicke forest, was bescratcht, and both his feet nigh lame.

4

Panting for breath, and almost out of hart,
  The Dwarfe him answerd, "Sir, ill mote I stay
  To tell the same. I lately did depart
  From Faery court, where I have many a day
  Servéd a gentle Lady of great sway,
  And high accompt° through out all Elfin land,   *reputation*
  Who lately left the same, and tooke this way:
  Her now I seeke, and if ye understand
Which way she faréd hath, good Sir tell out of hand."[2]

1. Cf. III. iii. 1, and note.   2. I.e., at once.

5

"What mister° wight," said he, "and how arayd?"   kind of
  "Royally clad," quoth he, "in cloth of gold,
  As meetest may beseeme a noble mayd;
  Her faire lockes in rich circlet be enrold,
  A fairer wight did never Sunne behold,
  And on a Palfrey rides more white then snow,
  Yet she her selfe is whiter manifold:
  The surest signe, whereby ye may her know,
Is, that she is the fairest wight alive, I trow."

6

"Now certes swaine," said he, "such one I weene,
  Fast flying through this forest from her fo,
  A foule ill favoured° foster, I have seene;   featured
  Her selfe, well as I might, I reskewd tho,
  But could not stay; so fast she did foregoe,°   go on before
  Carried away with wings of speedy feare."
  "Ah dearest God," quoth he, "that is great woe,
  And wondrous ruth° to all, that shall it heare.   grief
But can ye read Sir, how I may her find, or where?"

7

"Perdy me lever° were to weeten that,"   rather
  Said he, "then ransome of the richest knight,
  Or all the good that ever yet I gat:
  But froward° fortune, and too forward Night   perverse
  Such happinesse did, maulgre, to me spight,
  And fro me reft both life and light attone.°   together
  But Dwarfe aread, what is that Lady bright,
  That through this forest wandreth thus alone;
For of her errour° straunge I have great ruth and mone."   wandering

8

"That Lady is," quoth he, "where so she bee,
  The bountiest° virgin, and most debonaire,   most virtuous
  That ever living eye I weene did see;
  Lives none this day, that may with her compare
  In stedfast chastitie and vertue rare,
  The goodly ornaments of beautie bright;
  And is ycleped° Florimell the faire,   called
  Faire Florimell beloved of many a knight,
Yet she loves none but one, that Marinell is hight.

9

"A Sea-nymphes sonne, that Marinell is hight,
  Of my deare Dame is lovéd dearely well;
  In other none, but him, she sets delight,
  All her delight is set on Marinell;
  But he sets nought at all by Florimell:
  For Ladies love his mother long ygoe
  Did him, they say, forwarne° through sacred spell.   forbid
  But fame° now flies, that of a forreine foe   rumor
He is yslaine, which is the ground of all our woe.

10

"Five dayes there be, since he (they say) was slaine,
    And foure, since Florimell the Court for-went,°   *left*
    And vowéd never to returne againe,
    Till him alive or dead she did invent.°   *find*
    Therefore, faire Sir, for love of knighthood gent,
    And honour of trew Ladies, if ye may
    By your good counsell, or bold hardiment,
    Or° succour her, or me direct the way;   *either*
Do one, or other good, I you most humbly pray.³

11

"So may ye gaine to you full great renowme,
    Of all good Ladies through the world so wide,
    And haply in her hart find highest rowme,
    Of whom ye seeke to be most magnifide:
    At least eternall meede shall you abide."°   *await*
    To whom the Prince; "Dwarfe, comfort to thee take,
    For till thou tidings learne, what her betide,
    I here avow thee never to forsake.
Ill weares he armes, that nill° them use for Ladies sake."   *will not*

12

So with the Dwarfe he backe returned againe,
    To seeke his Lady, where he mote her find;
    But by the way he greatly gan complaine
    The want of his good Squire late left behind,
    For whom he wondrous pensive grew in mind,
    For doubt° of daunger, which mote him betide;   *fear*
    For him he lovéd above all mankind,
    Having him trew and faithfull ever tride,°   *proved*
And bold, as ever Squire that waited by knights side.

13

Who all this while full hardly was assayd
    Of deadly daunger, which to him betid;°   *befell*
    For whiles his Lord pursewd that noble Mayd,
    After that foster fowle he fiercely rid,
    To bene avengéd of the shame, he did
    To that faire Damzell: Him he chacéd long
    Through the thicke woods, wherein he would have hid
    His shamefull head from his avengement strong,
And oft him threatned death for his outrageous wrong.

14

Nathlesse the villen° sped him selfe so well,   *churl*
    Whether through swiftnesse of his speedy beast,
    Or knowledge of those woods, where he did dwell,
    That shortly he from daunger was releast,
    And out of sight escapéd at the least;°   *last*
    Yet not escapéd from the dew reward
    Of his bad deeds, which dayly he increast,

3. Spenser has neglected to correct the inconsistency between the Dwarfe's account of Florimell's departure from the Court and the glimpse (at III. i. 15–16) of Florimell in flight before Marinell's encounter with Britomart.

Ne ceaséd not, till him oppresséd hard
The heavy plague, that for such leachours is prepard.

15

For soone as he was vanisht out of sight,
His coward courage gan emboldned bee,
And cast° t'avenge him of that fowle despight,   *resolved*
Which he had borne of his bold enimee.
Tho to his brethren came: for they were three
Ungratious children of one gracelesse sire,[4]
And unto them complainéd, how that he
Had uséd bene of that foolehardy Squire;
So them with bitter words he stird to bloudy ire.

16

Forthwith themselves with their sad° instruments   *grievous*
Of spoyle and murder they gan arme bylive,°   *speedily*
And with him forth into the forest went,
To wreake the wrath, which he did earst revive
In their sterne brests, on him which late did drive
Their brother to reproch and shamefull flight:
For they had vowed, that never he alive
Out of that forest should escape their might;
Vile rancour their rude harts had fild with such despight.

17

Within that wood there was a covert glade,
Foreby° a narrow foord, to them well knowne,   *near*
Through which it was uneath° for wight to wade;   *difficult*
And now by fortune it was overflowne:
By that same way they knew that Squire unknowne
Mote algates° passe; for thy themselves they set   *necessarily*
There in await, with thicke woods over growne,
And all the while their malice they did whet
With cruell threats, his passage through the ford to let.°   *prevent*

18

It fortunéd, as they devizéd had,
The gentle Squire came ryding that same way,
Unweeting of their wile and treason bad,
And through the ford to passen did assay;
But that fierce foster, which late fled away,
Stoutly forth stepping on the further shore,
Him boldly bad his passage there to stay,
Till he had made amends, and full restore
For all the damage, which he had him doen afore.

19

With that at him a quiv'ring dart he threw,
With so fell force and villeinous despighte,
That through his haberjeon the forkehead flew,
And through the linkéd mayles° empiercéd quite,   *armor rings*
But had no powre in his soft flesh to bite:

---

4. Perhaps signifying the lusts variously of eye, ear, and touch.

That stroke the hardy Squire did sore displease,
  But more that him he could not come to smite;
  For by no meanes the high banke he could sease,°   *reach*
But laboured long in that deepe ford with vaine disease.°   *distress*

20

And still the foster with his long bore-speare
  Him kept from landing at his wishéd will;
  Anone one sent out of the thicket neare
  A cruell shaft, headed with deadly ill,
  And fetheréd with an unlucky quill;
  The wicked steele stayd not, till it did light
  In his left thigh, and deepely did it thrill:°   *pierce*
  Exceeding griefe that wound in him empight,°   *fixed*
But more that with his foes he could not come to fight.

21

At last through wrath and vengeaunce making way,
  He on the bancke arrived with mickle° paine,   *much*
  Where the third brother him did sore assay,
  And drove at him with all his might and maine
  A forrest bill,[5] which both his hands did straine;
  But warily he did avoide the blow,
  And with his speare requited him againe,
  That both his sides were thrilléd with the throw,°   *thrust*
And a large streame of bloud out of the wound did flow.

22

He tombling downe, with gnashing teeth did bite
  The bitter earth, and bad to let him in
  Into the balefull house of endlesse night,
  Where wicked ghosts do waile their former sin.
  Tho gan the battell freshly to begin;
  For nathemore for that spectacle bad,
  Did th'other two their cruell vengeaunce blin,°   *cease*
  But both attonce on both sides him bestad,°   *beset*
And load upon him layd,[6] his life for to have had.

23

Tho when that villain he avized,° which late   *perceived*
  Affrighted had the fairest Florimell,
  Full of fiers fury, and indignant hate,
  To him he turnéd, and with rigour° fell   *force*
  Smote him so rudely on the Pannikell,°   *brain pan*
  That to the chin he cleft his head in twaine:
  Downe on the ground his carkas groveling fell;
  His sinfull soule with desperate disdaine,
Out of her fleshly ferme° fled to the place of paine. *enclosure*

24

That seeing now the onely° last of three,   *solitary*
  Who with that wicked shaft him wounded had,
  Trembling with horrour, as° that did foresee   *as one*

5. A digging or pruning implement.   6. I.e., assailed him with blows.

The fearefull end of his avengement sad,
Through which he follow should his brethren bad,
His bootelesse bow in feeble hand upcaught,
And therewith shot an arrow at the lad;
Which faintly fluttring, scarce his helmet raught,°   *reached*
And glauncing fell to ground, but him annoyéd naught.

25

With that he would have fled into the wood;
But Timias him lightly overhent,°   *overtook*
Right as he entring was into the flood,
And strooke at him with force so violent,
That headlesse him into the foord he sent:
The carkas with the streame was carried downe,
But th'head fell backeward on the Continent.°   *ground*
So mischief fel upon the meaners crowne;[7]
They three be dead with shame, the Squire lives with renowne.

26

He lives, but takes small joy of his renowne;
For of that cruell wound he bled so sore,
That from his steed he fell in deadly swowne;
Yet still the bloud forth gusht in so great store,
That he lay wallowd all in his owne gore.
Now God thee keepe, thou gentlest Squire alive,
Else shall thy loving Lord thee see no more,
But both of comfort him thou shalt deprive,
And eke thy selfe of honour, which thou didst atchive.

27

Providence heavenly passeth living thought,
And doth for wretched mens reliefe make way;
For loe great grace or fortune thither brought
Comfort to him, that comfortlesse now lay.
In those same woods, ye well remember may,
How that a noble hunteresse did wonne,
She, that base Braggadochio did affray,°   *frighten*
And made him fast out of the forrest runne;
Belphoebe[8] was her name, as faire as Phoebus sunne.

28

She on a day, as she pursewd the chace
Of some wild beast, which with her arrowes keene
She wounded had, the same along did trace
By tract° of bloud, which she had freshly seene,   *trace*
To have besprinckled all the grassy greene;
By the great persue,° which she there perceaved,   *trail of blood*
Well hopéd she the beast engored had beene,

7. I.e., on those who intended mischief.
8. The "Letter to Raleigh" observes that Belphoebe "in some places" represents Queen Elizabeth in her character "of a most vertuous and beautifull Lady." More generally, as her name suggests, she is to be associated with Diana, worshipped originally as goddess of the forests and of the hunt. Belphoebe's is a natural chastity, virginal and pure, but limited in a way that the chastity of Britomart transcends, since the latter anticipates and requires its completion in wedded love.

And made more hast, the life to have bereaved:
But ah, her expectation greatly was deceaved.

29

Shortly she came, whereas that woefull Squire
  With bloud deforméd,° lay in deadly swownd: *made hideous*
  In whose faire eyes, like lamps of quenchéd fire,
  The Christall humour° stood congealéd rownd;   *fluid*
  His locks, like faded leaves fallen to grownd,
  Knotted with bloud, in bounches rudely ran,
  And his sweete lips, on which before that stownd°   *encounter*
  The bud of youth to blossome faire began,
Spoild of their rosie red, were woxen pale and wan.

30

Saw never living eye more heavy sight,
  That could have made a rocke of stone to rew,
  Or rive in twaine: which when that Lady bright
  Besides all hope[9] with melting eyes did vew,
  All suddeinly abasht she chaungéd hew,
  And with sterne horrour backward gan to start:
  But when she better him beheld, she grew
  Full of soft passion and unwonted smart:
The point of pitty percéd through her tender hart.[1]

31

Meekely she bowéd downe, to weete if life
  Yet in his frosen members did remaine,
  And feeling by his pulses beating rife,°   *strongly*
  That the weake soule her seat did yet retaine,
  She cast to comfort him with busie paine:
  His double folded necke she reard upright,
  And rubd his temples, and each trembling vaine;
  His mayléd haberjeon she did undight,°   *take off*
And from his head his heavy burganet did light.°   *remove*

32

Into the woods thenceforth in hast she went,
  To seeke for hearbes, that mote him remedy;
  For she of hearbes had great intendiment,°   *knowledge*
  Taught of the Nymphe, which from her infancy
  Her nourcéd had in trew Nobility:
  There, whether it divine Tobacco were,
  Or Panachaea, or Polygony,[2]
  She found, and brought it to her patient deare
Who al this while lay bleeding out his hartbloud neare.

9. I.e., contrary to expectation.
1. The remainder of this Canto is adapted from Ariosto's account of Angelica and Medoro (*Orlando Furioso*, XIX. 17–42). Spenser, however, alters the materials of his source to emphasize the special nature of Belphoebe's chastity: Angelica, wounded by love, at length allows Medoro to "gather the first rose"; but Belphoebe, by her nature unaware of the character of Timias's inner torment, gently reserves "that dainty Rose" (st. 51).
2. Raleigh introduced tobacco into England in 1584; "panachaea" refers to an herb with healing powers; polygony is an astringent root formerly used in medicine.

33

The soveraigne weede betwixt two marbles plaine°   smooth
  She pownded small, and did in peeces bruze,°   break
  And then atweene her lilly handés twaine,
  Into his wound the juyce thereof did scruze,°   squeeze
  And round about, as she could well it uze,
  The flesh therewith she suppled and did steepe,
  T'abate all spasme, and soke the swelling bruze,
  And after having searcht the intuse° deepe,   contusion
She with her scarfe did bind the wound from cold to keepe.

34

By this he had sweete life recured° againe,   recovered
  And groning inly deepe, at last his eyes,
  His watry eyes, drizling like deawy raine,
  He up gan lift toward the azure skies,
  From whence descend all hopelesse° remedies: unexpected
  Therewith he sighed, and turning him aside,
  The goodly Mayd full of divinities,
  And gifts of heavenly grace he by him spide,
Her bow and gilden quiver lying him beside.

35

"Mercy deare Lord," said he, "what grace is this,
  That thou hast shewéd to me sinfull wight,
  To send thine Angell from her bowre of blis,
  To comfort me in my distresséd plight?
  Angell, or Goddesse do I call thee right?
  What service may I do unto thee meete,
  That hast from darkenesse me returnd to light,
  And with thy heavenly salves and med'cines sweete,
Hast drest my sinfull wounds? I kisse thy blessed feete."

36

Thereat she blushing said, "Ah gentle Squire,
  Nor Goddesse I, nor Angell, but the Mayd,
  And daughter of a woody° Nymphe, desire   of the forest
  No service, but thy safety and ayd;
  Which if thou gaine, I shalbe well apayd.
  We mortall wights whose lives and fortunes bee
  To commun accidents still open layd,
  Are bound with commun bond of frailtee,
To succour wretched wights, whom we captivéd see."

37

By this her Damzels, which the former chace
  Had undertaken after her, arryved,
  As did Belphoebe, in the bloudy place,
  And thereby deemd the beast had bene deprived
  Of life, whom late their Ladies arrow ryved:°   pierced
  For thy the bloudy tract they follow fast,
  And every one to runne the swiftest stryved;
  But two of them the rest far overpast,
And where their Lady was, arrivéd at the last.

38

Where when they saw that goodly boy, with blood
  Defowléd, and their Lady dresse his wownd,
  They wondred much, and shortly understood,
  How him in deadly case° their Lady fownd,   *condition*
  And reskewéd out of the heavy stownd.°   *plight*
  Eftsoones his warlike courser, which was strayd
  Farre in the woods, while that he lay in swownd,
  She made those Damzels search, which being stayd,
They did him set thereon, and forth with them convayd.°   *removed*

39

Into that forest farre they thence him led,
  Where was their dwelling, in a pleasant glade,
  With mountaines round about environéd,
  And mighty woods, which did the valley shade,
  And like a stately Theatre it made,
  Spreading it selfe into a spatious plaine.
  And in the midst a little river plaide
  Emongst the pumy° stones, which seemd to plaine   *pumice*
With gentle murmure, that his course they did restraine.

40

Beside the same a dainty place there lay,
  Planted with mirtle trees and laurels greene,
  In which the birds song many a lovely lay
  Of gods high prayse, and of their loves sweet teene,°   *sorrow*
  As it an earthly Paradize had beene:
  In whose encloséd shadow there was pight
  A faire Pavilion, scarcely to be seene,
  The which was all within most richly dight,
That greatest Princes living it mote well delight.

41

Thither they brought that wounded Squire, and layd
  In easie couch his feeble limbes to rest,
  He rested him a while, and then the Mayd
  His ready wound with better salves new drest;
  Dayly she dresséd him, and did the best
  His grievous hurt to garish,° that she might,   *cure*
  That shortly she his dolour hath redrest,°   *healed*
  And his foule sore reducéd° to faire plight: *restored*
It she reducéd, but himselfe destroyéd quight.

42

O foolish Physick, and unfruitfull paine,
  That heales up one and makes another wound:
  She his hurt thigh to him recured againe,
  But hurt his hart, the which before was sound,
  Through an unwary dart, which did rebound°   *leap*
  From her faire eyes and gracious countenaunce.
  What bootes it him from death to be unbound,
  To be captivéd in endlesse duraunce°   *captivity*
Of sorrow and despaire without aleggeaunce?°   *alleviation*

43

Still as his wound did gather, and grow hole,
   So still his hart woxe sore, and health decayd:
   Madnesse to save a part, and lose the whole.
   Still whenas he beheld the heavenly Mayd,
   Whiles dayly plaisters to his wound she layd,
   So still his Malady the more increast,
   The whiles her matchlesse beautie him dismayd.
   Ah God, what other could he do at least,
But love so faire a Lady, that his life releast?°   *saved*

44

Long while he strove in his courageous brest,
   With reason dew the passion to subdew,
   And love for to dislodge out of his nest:
   Still when her excellencies he did vew,
   Her soveraigne bounty,° and celestiall hew,°   *goodness/form*
   The same to love he strongly was constraind:
   But when his meane estate he did revew,
   He from such hardy boldnesse was restraind,
And of his lucklesse lot and cruell love thus plaind.

45

"Unthankfull wretch," said he, "is this the meed,
   With which her soveraigne mercy thou doest quight?°   *repay*
   Thy life she savéd by her gracious deed,
   But thou doest weene with villeinous despight,°   *wrong*
   To blot her honour, and her heavenly light.
   Dye rather, dye, then so disloyally
   Deeme of her high desert,° or seeme so light: *worth*
   Faire death it is to shonne more shame, to dy:
Dye rather, dy, then ever love disloyally.

46

"But if to love disloyalty it bee,
   Shall I then hate her, that from deathés dore
   Me brought? ah farre be such reproch fro mee.
   What can I lesse do, then her love therefore,
   Sith I her dew reward cannot restore?
   Dye rather, dye, and dying do her serve,
   Dying her serve, and living her adore;
   Thy life she gave, thy life she doth deserve:
Dye rather, dye, then ever from her service swerve.

47

"But foolish boy, what bootes thy service bace
   To her, to whom the heavens do serve, and sew?
   Thou a meane Squire, of meeke and lowly place,
   She heavenly borne, and of celestiall hew.
   How then? of all love taketh equall vew:
   And doth not highest God vouchsafe to take
   The love and service of the basest crew?°   *company*

If she will not, dye meekly for her sake;
Dye rather, dye, then ever so faire love forsake."

48

Thus warreid° he long time against his will,   *struggled*
 Till that through weaknesse he was forst at last,
 To yield himselfe unto the mighty ill:
 Which as a victour proud, gan ransack fast
 His inward parts, and all his entrayles wast,
 That neither bloud in face, nor life in hart
 It left, but both did quite drye up, and blast;
 As percing levin,° which the inner part   *lightning*
Of every thing consumes, and calcineth° by art. *pulverizes*

49

Which seeing faire Belphoebe gan to feare,
 Least that his wound were inly well not healed,
 Or that the wicked steele empoysned were:
 Litle she weend, that love he close concealed;
 Yet still he wasted, as the snow congealed,
 When the bright sunne his beams thereon doth beat;
 Yet never he his hart to her revealed,
 But rather chose to dye for sorrow great,
Then with dishonorable termes her to entreat.

50

She gracious Lady, yet no paines did spare,
 To do him ease, or do him remedy:
 Many Restoratives of vertues° rare,   *powers*
 And costly Cordialles she did apply,
 To mitigate his stubborne mallady:
 But that sweet Cordiall, which can restore
 A love-sick hart, she did to him envy;°   *grudge*
 To him, and to all th'unworthy world forlore° *forlorn*
She did envy that soveraigne salve, in secret store.

51

That dainty Rose,[3] the daughter of her Morne,
 More deare then life she tenderéd, whose flowre
 The girlond of her honour did adorne:
 Ne suffred she the Middayes scorching powre,
 Ne the sharp Northerne wind thereon to showre,
 But lappéd° up her silken leaves most chaire,° *folded/dear*
 When so the froward skye began to lowre:
 But soone as calméd was the Christall aire,
She did it faire dispred, and let to florish faire.

52

Eternall God in his almighty powre,
 To make ensample of his heavenly grace,

3. Sts. 51–55 constitute an emblematic combination of the several aspects of that virginal chastity represented in Belphoebe: its natural beauty, its divine "root," and its mysterious power to control even the rulers of the earth as well as to resist evil. But cf. III. i. 46: Belphoebe lacks Britomart's passionate vigor. The story of Belphoebe and Timias is continued in IV. vii–viii.

In Paradize whilome did plant this flowre,
Whence he it fetcht out of her native place,
And did in stocke of earthly flesh enrace,°   *implant*
That mortall men her glory should admire:
In gentle Ladies brest, and bounteous race
Of woman kind it fairest flowre doth spire,°   *cause to spring*
And beareth fruit of honour and all chast desire.

53

Faire ympes° of beautie, whose bright shining beames *children*
  Adorne the world with like to heavenly light,
  And to your willes both royalties and Realmes
  Subdew, through conquest of your wondrous might,
  With this faire flowre your goodly girlonds dight,
  Of chastity and vertue virginall,
  That shall embellish more your beautie bright,
  And crowne your heades with heavenly coronall,
Such as the Angels weare before Gods tribunall.

54

To youre faire selves a faire ensample frame,
  Of this faire virgin, this Belphoebe faire,
  To whom in perfect love, and spotlesse fame
  Of chastitie, none living may compaire:
  Ne poysnous Envy justly can empaire
  The prayse of her fresh flowring Maidenhead;
  For thy she standeth on the highest staire
  Of th'honorable stage of womanhead,
That Ladies all may follow her ensample dead.

55

In so great prayse of stedfast chastity,
  Nathlesse she was so curteous and kind,
  Tempred with grace, and goodly modesty,
  That seeméd those two vertues strove to find
  The higher place in her Heroick mind:
  So striving each did other more augment,
  And both encreast the prayse of woman kind,
  And both encreast her beautie excellent;
So all did make in her a perfect complement.

Canto VI

The birth of faire Belphoebe and
Of Amoret is told.
The Gardins of Adonis fraught
With pleasures manifold.

1

Well may I weene,° faire Ladies, all this while   *expect*
  Ye wonder, how this noble Damozell
  So great perfections did in her compile,°   *heap up*
  Sith that in salvage forests she did dwell,

So farre from court and royall Citadell,
The great schoolmistresse of all curtesy:
Seemeth that such wild woods should far expell
All civill usage and gentility,
And gentle sprite deforme with rude rusticity.

2

But to this faire Belphoebe in her berth
   The heavens so favourable were and free,
   Looking with myld aspect upon the earth,
   In th'Horoscope of her nativitee,
   That all the gifts of grace and chastitee
   On her they pouréd forth of plenteous horne;
   Jove laught on Venus from his soveraigne see,°   *throne*
   And Phoebus with faire beames did her adorne,[1]
And all the Graces rockt her cradle being borne.

3

Her berth was of the wombe of Morning dew,[2]
   And her conception of the joyous Prime,°   *spring*
   And all her whole creation did her shew
   Pure and unspotted from all loathly crime,
   That is ingenerate in fleshly slime.°   *clay*
   So was this virgin borne, so was she bred,
   So was she traynéd up from time to time,[3]
   In all chast vertue, and true bounti-hed
Till to her dew perfection she was ripenéd.

4

Her mother was the faire Chrysogonee,[4]
   The daughter of Amphisa, who by race
   A Faerie was, yborne of high degree,
   She bore Belphoebe, she bore in like cace°   *condition*
   Faire Amoretta in the second place:
   These two were twinnes, and twixt them two did share
   The heritage of all celestiall grace.
   That all the rest it seemed they robbéd bare
Of bountie, and of beautie, and all vertues rare.

5

It were a goodly storie, to declare,
   By what straunge accident faire Chrysogone
   Conceived these infants, and how them she bare,
   In this wild forrest wandring all alone,

1. Spenser seems to imply that at Belphoebe's birth, Jupiter and Venus were "in trine," a particularly favorable astrological "aspect," thought to confer beauty, grace, fidelity, and honesty on persons born under the influence of that conjunction. While the "aspect" of the sun is not given, its influence was generally considered to be favorable to worldly fortune and high place.
2. "Thy people shall be willing in the day of thy power, in the beauties of holiness from the womb of the morning: thou hast the dew of thy youth" (Psalms cx. 3).
3. I.e., in each successive stage of her youth. While the stars were thought to influence the formation of character, they could not altogether take the place of virtuous education and training.
4. From Greek, "golden-born"; the name Amphisa also derives from Greek terms, signifying "of double nature."

After she had nine moneths fulfild and gone:
For not as other wemens commune brood,
They were enwombéd° in the sacred throne   *conceived*
Of her chaste bodie, nor with commune food,
As other wemens babes, they suckéd vitall blood.

6

But wondrously they were begot, and bred
    Through influence of th'heavens fruitfull ray,
    As it in antique bookes is mentionéd.[5]
    It was upon a Sommers shynie day,
    When Titan faire his beamés did display,
    In a fresh fountaine, farre from all mens vew, ← *proves her innocence*
    She bathed her brest, the boyling heat t' allay;
    She bathed with roses red, and violets blew,
And all the sweetest flowres, that in the forrest grew.

7

Till faint through irkesome wearinesse, adowne
    Upon the grassie ground her selfe she layd
    To sleepe, the whiles a gentle slombring swowne
    Upon her fell all naked bare displayd;
    The sunne-beames bright upon her body playd,
    Being through former bathing mollifide,°   *softened*
    And pierst into her wombe, where they embayd°   *suffused*
    With so sweet sence and secret power unspide,
That in her pregnant flesh they shortly fructifide.

8

Miraculous may seeme to him, that reades
    So straunge ensample of conception;
    But reason teacheth that the fruitfull seades
    Of all things living, through impression
    Of the sunbeames in moyst complexion,[6]
    Doe life conceive and quicknbd are by kynd:°   *nature*
    So after Nilus inundation,
    Infinite shapes of creatures men do fynd,
Informéd° in the mud, on which the Sunne hath shynd.[7]   *formed*

9

Great father he of generation
    Is rightly cald, th'author of life and light;
    And his faire sister[8] for creation
    Ministreth matter fit, which tempred right
    With heate and humour, breedes the living wight.
    So sprong these twinnes in wombe of Chrysogone,

5. Sts. 6–9, based on Ovid, *Metamorphoses*, I. 416–437, anticipate and prepare for Spenser's extended account of the life processes at work in the Garden of Adonis. The Renaissance mythographer Natalis Comes identifies Adonis with the sun, "sole author of all generation" (*Mythologiae*, IV. 13).

6. I.e., in a temperament, or physical constitution, predominantly "moist" in terms of its "humorous" character.
7. Cf. I. i. 21 and note.
8. I.e., the moon, whose light Plutarch considered favorable to the generation and growth of life in plants and animals (*Isis and Osiris*, 41).

Yet wist° she nought thereof, but sore affright,   *knew*
   Wondred to see her belly so upblone,
Which still increast, till she her terme had full outgone.°   *completed*

10

Whereof conceiving shame and foule disgrace,
   Albe her guiltlesse conscience her cleard,
   She fled into the wildernesse a space,
   Till that unweeldy burden she had reard,°   *brought forth*
   And shund dishonor, which as death she feard:
   Where wearie of long travell,° downe to rest   *labor*
   Her selfe she set, and comfortably cheard;
   There a sad cloud of sleepe her overkest,°   *covered*
And seizéd every sense with sorrow sore opprest.

11

It fortunéd, faire Venus having lost
   Her little sonne, the wingéd god of love,
   Who for some light displeasure, which him crost,
   Was from her fled, as flit° as ayerie Dove,   *swift*
   And left her blisfull bowre of joy above,
   (So from her often he had fled away,
   When she for ought him sharpely did reprove,
   And wandred in the world in strange aray,
Disguized in thousand shapes, that none might him bewray.)[9]

12

Him for to seeke, she left her heavenly hous,
   The house of goodly formes and faire aspects,
   Whence all the world derives the glorious
   Features of beautie, and all shapes select,
   With which high God his workmanship hath deckt;
   And searchéd every way, through which his wings
   Had borne him, or his tract° she mote detect: *track*
   She promist kisses sweet, and sweeter things
Unto the man, that of him tydings to her brings.

13

First she him sought in Court, where most he used
   Whylome to haunt, but there she found him not;
   But many there she found, which sore accused
   His falsehood, and with foule infamous blot
   His cruell deedes and wicked wyles did spot:
   Ladies and Lords she every where mote heare
   Complayning, how with his empoysned shot
   Their wofull harts he wounded had whyleare,
And so had left them languishing twixt hope and feare.

14

She then the Citties sought from gate to gate,
   And every one did aske, did he him see;

9. This episode is based on Tasso's version (in his pastoral drama *Aminta*) of the first *Idyl*, "Love the Runaway," by Moschus of Syracuse (fl. 250 B.C.). In his Glosse to "March," E. K. refers to "Moschus his Idyllion of wandering love."

And every one her answerd, that too late
He had him seene, and felt the crueltie
Of his sharpe darts and whot° artillerie;   *hot*
And every one threw forth reproches rife
Of his mischievous deedes, and said, That hee
Was the disturber of all civill life,
The enimy of peace, and author of all strife.

15

Then in the countrey she abroad him sought,
And in the rurall cottages inquired,
Where also many plaints to her were brought,
How he their heedlesse harts with love had fyred,
And his false venim through their veines inspyred;
And eke the gentle shepheard swaynes, which sat
Keeping their fleecie flockes, as they were hyred,
She sweetly heard complaine, both how and what
Her sonne had to them doen; yet she did smile thereat.

16

But when in none of all these she him got,
She gan avize,° where else he mote him hyde: *consider*
At last she her bethought, that she had not
Yet sought the salvage woods and forrests wyde,
In which full many lovely Nymphes abyde,
Mongst whom might be, that he did closely lye,[1]
Or that the love of some of them him tyde:
For thy she thither cast° her course t'apply,   *resolved*
To search the secret haunts of Dianes company.[2]

17

Shortly unto the wastefull° woods she came,   *wild*
Whereas she found the Goddesse with her crew,
After late chace of their embrewéd° game,   *blood-stained*
Sitting beside a fountaine in a rew,°   *row*
Some of them washing with the liquid dew
From off their dainty limbes the dustie sweat,
And soyle which did deforme their lively hew;
Others lay shaded from the scorching heat;
The rest upon her person gave attendance great.

18

She having hong upon a bough on high
Her bow and painted quiver, had unlaste
Her silver buskins° from her nimble thigh,   *high boots*
And her lancke° loynes ungirt, and brests unbraste, *slender*
After her heat the breathing cold to taste;
Her golden lockes, that late in tresses bright
Embreaded were for hindring of her haste,[3]
Now loose about her shoulders hong undight,
And were with sweet Ambrosia all besprinckled light.

---

1. I.e., that he was secretly hidden.
2. Spenser's management of structure, meaning, and mythology in Books III and IV, turning on the poet's presentment of Venus and Diana, is discussed by Kathleen Williams in her essay in this edition.
3. I.e., were braided up to prevent them from hindring her speed.

19

Soone as she Venus saw behind her backe,
  She was ashamed to be so loose surprized,
  And woxe halfe wroth against her damzels slacke,
  That had not her thereof before avized,°   *warned*
  But suffred her so carelesly disguized
  Be overtaken. Soone her garments loose
  Upgath'ring, in her bosome she comprized,°   *gathered*
  Well as she might, and to the Goddesse rose,
Whiles all her Nymphes did like a girlond her enclose.

20

Goodly she gan faire Cytherea[4] greet,
  And shortly askéd her, what cause her brought
  Into that wildernesse for her unmeet,
  From her sweete bowres, and beds with pleasures fraught:
  That suddein change she strange adventure thought.
  To whom halfe weeping, she thus answeréd,
  That she her dearest sonne Cupido sought,
  Who in his frowardnesse from her was fled;
That she repented sore, to have him angeréd.

21

Thereat Diana gan to smile, in scorne
  Of her vaine plaint, and to her scoffing sayd;
  "Great pittie sure, that ye be so forlorne
  Of your gay sonne, that gives ye so good ayd
  To your disports: ill mote ye bene apayd."[5]
  But she was more engrievéd, and replide;
  "Faire sister, ill beseemes it to upbrayd
  A dolefull heart with so disdainfull pride;
The like that mine, may be your paine another tide.°   *time*

22

"As you in woods and wanton wildernesse
  Your glory set, to chace the salvage beasts,
  So my delight is all in joyfulnesse,
  In beds, in bowres, in banckets, and in feasts:
  And ill becomes you with your loftie creasts,
  To scorne the joy, that Jove is glad to seeke;
  We both are bound to follow heavens beheasts,°   *commands*
  And tend our charges with obeisance meeke:
Spare, gentle sister, with reproch my paine to eeke.°   *increase*

23

"And tell me, if that ye my sonne have heard,
  To lurke emongst your Nymphes in secret wize;
  Or keepe their cabins: much I am affeard,
  Least he like one of them him selfe disguize,
  And turne his arrowes to their exercize:
  So may he long himselfe full easie hide:
  For he is faire and fresh in face and guize,

---

4. I.e., Venus, who according to tradition first emerged from the sea foam near the island of Cythera, off the southernmost point of Greece.
5. I.e., you are ill requited.

As any Nymph (let not it be envyde.)"°   *grudged*
So saying every Nymph full narrowly she eyde.

24

But Phoebe therewith sore was angeréd,
   And sharply said; "Goe Dame, goe seeke your boy,
   Where you him lately left, in Mars his bed;
   He comes not here, we scorne his foolish joy,
   Ne lend we leisure to his idle toy:°   *play*
   But if I catch him in this company,
   By Stygian lake I vow, whose sad annoy[6]
   The Gods doe dread, he dearely shall abye:°   *pay*
Ile clip his wanton wings, that he no more shall fly."

25

Whom when as Venus saw so sore displeased,
   She inly sory was, and gan relent,
   What she had said: so her she soone appeased,
   With sugred words and gentle blandishment,
   Which as a fountaine from her sweet lips went,
   And welléd goodly forth, that in short space
   She was well pleasd, and forth her damzels sent,
   Through all the woods, to search from place to place,
If any tract of him or tydings they mote trace.

26

To search the God of love, her Nymphes she sent
   Throughout the wandring forrest every where:
   And after them her selfe eke with her went
   To seeke the fugitive, both farre and nere.
   So long they sought, till they arrivéd were
   In that same shadie covert, whereas lay
   Faire Crysogone in slombry traunce whilere:°   *lately*
   Who in her sleepe (a wondrous thing to say)
Unwares had borne two babes, as faire as springing day.

27

Unwares she them conceived, unwares she bore:
   She bore withouten paine, that she conceived
   Withouten pleasure; ne her need implore
   Lucinaes[7] aide: which when they both perceived,
   They were through wonder nigh of sense bereaved,
   And gazing each on other, nought bespake:
   At last they both agreed, her seeming grieved
   Out of her heavy swowne not to awake,
But from her loving side the tender babes to take.

28

Up they them tooke, each one a babe uptooke,
   And with them carried, to be fosteréd;
   Dame Phoebe to a Nymph her babe betooke,
   To be upbrought in perfect Maydenhed,
   And of her selfe her name Belphoebe red:°   *called*

---

6. I.e., grievous affliction.   7. The goddess of childbirth.

But Venus hers thence farre away convayd,
To be upbrought in goodly womanhed,
And in her litle loves stead, which was strayd,
Her Amoretta cald, to comfort her dismayd.

29

She brought her to her joyous Paradize,
  Where most she wonnes, when she on earth does dwel.
So faire a place, as Nature can devize:
Whether in Paphos,[8] or Cytheron hill,
Or it in Gnidus be, I wote not well;
But well I wote by tryall, that this same
All other pleasant places doth excell,
And calléd is by her lost lovers name,
The Gardin of Adonis,[9] farre renowmd by fame.

30

In that same Gardin all the goodly flowres,
  Wherewith dame Nature doth her beautifie,
And decks the girlonds of her paramoures,
Are fetcht: there is the first seminarie°   *seed plot*
Of all things, that are borne to live and die,
According to their kindes.[1] Long worke it were,
Here to account° the endlesse progenie   *list*
Of all the weedes,° that bud and blossome there;   *plants*
But so much as doth need, must needs be counted° here. *recounted*

31

It sited was in fruitfull soyle of old,
  And girt in with two walles on either side;
The one of yron, the other of bright gold,[2] ← *pos, not imprisoning*

8. Important centers of the worship of Venus were those at Paphos, on the island of Cyprus, and at Cnidus, in Asia Minor. Spenser's allusion to "Cytheron hill" (instead of the island of Cythera) probably reflects his reading of Boccaccio, who notes that the goddess was worshipped also on Mt. Cytheron (*De Genealogia Deorum*, III. 22).
9. In ancient times, the term "garden of Adonis" referred in the first instance to a small pot of quick-growing herbs (cf. *Phaedrus*, 276b; Theocritus, *Idyl XV*. 113); but Spenser's Garden of Adonis takes its place in a long literary tradition of such earthly paradises, including Homer's Garden of Alcinous (*Odyssey*, VII. 112–134), Claudian's Cyprian Garden of Venus (*Epithalamium of Honoris and Maria*, 49–96), the Garden of Eden in Dante's *Purgatorio*, XXVIII, and the Garden of Nature in Chaucer's *Parliament of Fowls*, 120–308. Love allegories such as *The Romance of the Rose* and Boccaccio's *Teseide* contributed to the tradition as well. Spenser apparently drew on all these works in some degree; and

he also consulted Natalis Comes's discussion of Adonis (*Mythologiae*, V. 16).
1. The broadly neo-Platonic tenor of the philosophical ideas in sts. 30–50 reflects a number of classical and later sources, of which the Myth of Er in Plato's *Republic*, the *Enneads* of Plotinus (or Ficino's commentary on Plotinus), and Arthur Golding's Elizabethan translation of Ovid's *Metamorphoses* (together with Golding's "Prefatory Epistle"), are among the more significant.
  Spenser's account develops in four stages: sts. 30–35 describe, at first in symbolic terms, then more concretely, the cyclical process through which all life must pass; sts. 36–38 emphasize the indestructible character of that substance which persists through every vicissitude of the life cycle; sts. 39–42 sadly acknowledge the power of mutability even in this Garden, which might otherwise be perfect; sts. 43–50 couch a final account of the life process in mythological terms, centering on the figures of Venus and Adonis at the heart of the Garden.
2. Probably from Claudian, *op. cit.*, 56–57.

That none might thorough breake, nor overstride:
And double gates it had, which opened wide,
By which both in and out men moten° pas; could
Th'one faire and fresh, the other old and dride:
Old Genius³ the porter of them was,
Old Genius, the which a double nature has.

32

He letteth in, he letteth out to wend,
  All that to come into the world desire;
  A thousand thousand naked babes⁴ attend
  About him day and night, which doe require,
  That he with fleshly weedes° would them attire: clothes
  Such as him list, such as eternall fate
  Ordainéd hath, he clothes with sinfull mire,⁵
And sendeth forth to live in mortall state,
Till they againe returne backe by the hinder gate.

33

After that they againe returnéd beene,
  They in that Gardin planted be againe;
  And grow afresh, as they had never seene
  Fleshly corruption, nor mortall paine.
  Some thousand yeares so doen they there remaine;
  And then of him are clad with other hew,° form
  Or sent into the chaungefull world againe,
  Till thither they returne, where first they grew:
So like a wheele around they runne from old to new.⁶

34

Ne needs there Gardiner to set, or sow,
  To plant or prune: for of their owne accord
  All things, as they created were, doe grow,
  And yet remember well the mightie word,
  Which first was spoken by th'Almightie lord,
  That bad them to increase and multiply:⁷
  Ne doe they need with water of the ford,° stream
  Or of the clouds to moysten their roots dry;
For in themselves eternall moisture they imply.° contain

35

Infinite shapes of creatures there are bred,
  And uncouth° formes, which none yet ever knew, strange
  And every sort is in a sundry° bed separate
  Set by it selfe, and ranckt in comely rew:⁸
  Some fit for reasonable soules t'indew,° put on
  Some made for beasts, some made for birds to weare,

---

3. Cf. II. xii. 47 and note.
4. Possibly, souls in the pre-existent state; more probably, "seed principles" from which all natural life springs.
5. I.e., the flesh.
6. As in Plato's Myth of Er (*Republic*, X); and more generally in Ovid, *Metamorphoses*, XV. 165–172.
7. Genesis i. 22: "And God blessed them, saying, Be fruitful, and multiply."

Spenser's combination in this stanza of scriptural and Platonic materials probably reflects the influence of Golding's "Prefatory Epistle" to his translation of Ovid's *Metamorphoses*.
8. I Corinthians xv. 39: "All flesh is not the same flesh: but there is one kind of flesh of men, another flesh of beasts, and another of fishes, and another of birds."

And all the fruitfull spawne of fishes hew
  In endlesse rancks along enraungéd were,
That seemed the Ocean could not containe them there.

36

Daily they grow, and daily forth are sent
  Into the world, it to replenish more;
  Yet is the stocke not lessenéd, nor spent,
  But still remaines in everlasting store,
  As it at first created was of yore.
  For in the wide wombe of the world there lyes,
  In hatefull darkenesse and in deepe horrore,
  An huge eternall Chaos, which supplyes
The substances of natures fruitfull progenyes.[9]

37

All things from thence doe their first being fetch,
  And borrow matter, whereof they are made,
  Which when as forme and feature it does ketch,[1]
  Becomes a bodie, and doth then invade°   *enter*
  The state of life, out of the griesly shade.
  That substance is eterne, and bideth° so,   *remains*
  Ne when the life decayes, and forme does fade,
  Doth it consume, and into nothing go,
But chaungéd is, and often altred to and fro.

38

The substance is not chaunged, nor alteréd,
  But th'only forme and outward fashion;°   *appearance*
  For every substance is conditionéd°   *bound*
  To change her hew, and sundry formes to don,
  Meet for her temper and complexion:
  For formes are variable and decay,
  By course of kind,° and by occasion;   *nature*
  And that faire flowre of beautie fades away,
As doth the lilly fresh before the sunny ray.

39

Great enimy to it, and to all the rest,
  That in the Gardin of Adonis springs,
  Is wicked Time, who with his scyth addrest,°   *armed*
  Does mow the flowring herbes and goodly things,
  And all their glory to the ground downe flings,
  Where they doe wither, and are fowly mard:
  He flyes about, and with his flaggy° wings   *drooping*
  Beates downe both leaves and buds without regard,
Ne ever pittie may relent° his malice hard.   *soften*

40

Yet pittie often did the gods relent,
  To see so faire things mard, and spoyléd quight:
  And their great mother Venus did lament

9. Boccaccio refers to Chaos in strikingly similar terms (*op. cit.*, I. 2).
1. I.e., when it assumes shape and outline. Spenser's use of the term "forme" in sts. 37–38 contrasts with that in st. 35 (and, by extension, with the expressions of st. 32).

The losse of her deare brood, her deare delight:
Her hart was pierst with pittie at the sight,
When walking through the Gardin, them she spyde,
Yet no'te she find redresse for such despight.[2]
For all that lives, is subject to that law:
All things decay in time, and to their end do draw.

41

But were it not, that Time their troubler is,
All that in this delightfull Gardin growes,
Should happie be, and have immortall blis:
For here all plentie, and all pleasure flowes,
And sweet love gentle fits° emongst them throwes,   *impulses*
Without fell rancor, or fond gealosie;
Franckly each paramour his leman° knowes,   *lover*
Each bird his mate, ne any does envie
Their goodly meriment, and gay felicitie.

42

There is continuall spring, and harvest there
Continuall, both meeting at one time:[3]
For both the boughes doe laughing blossomes beare,
And with fresh colours decke the wanton Prime,[4]
And eke attonce the heavy trees they clime,
Which seeme to labour under their fruits lode:
The whiles the joyous birdes make their pastime
Emongst the shadie leaves, their sweet abode,
And their true loves without suspition tell abrode.

43

Right in the middest of that Paradise,
There stood a stately Mount,[5] on whose round top
A gloomy grove of mirtle trees did rise,
Whose shadie boughes sharpe steele did never lop,
Nor wicked beasts their tender buds did crop,
But like a girlond compasséd the hight,
And from their fruitfull sides sweet gum did drop,
That all the ground with precious deaw bedight,
Threw forth most dainty odours, and most sweet delight.

44

And in the thickest covert of that shade,
There was a pleasant arbour, not by art,
But of the trees owne inclination made,
Which knitting their rancke° braunches part to part,   *dense*

---

2. I.e., she could not repair that injury. The power of Time, however (as st. 42 makes clear), does not affect the Garden in quite the same fashion as it does the world of men.
3. A garden untroubled by seasonal change (as in Homer's Garden of Alcinous) is regularly the metaphor in medieval and Renaissance literature for that ideal world of which the present earthly world is an imperfect copy.
4. I.e., luxuriant spring.
5. The sexual symbolism of the Garden of Adonis should not be obscured: the Garden's essential health and productivity are in direct contrast to the côld and wasteful sexuality everywhere apparent in the Bower of Bliss.

With wanton yvie twyne entrayld° athwart,   *interlaced*
And Eglantine, and Caprifole° emong,   *honeysuckle*
Fashioned above within their inmost part,
    That nether Phoebus beams could through them throng,
Nor Aeolus sharp blast could worke them any wrong.

male eye can't penetrate here

45

And all about grew every sort of flowre,
    To which sad lovers were transformd of yore;
    Fresh Hyacinthus,[6] Phoebus paramoure,
    And dearest love,
    Foolish Narcisse, that likes the watry shore,
    Sad Amaranthus,[7] made a flowre but late,
    Sad Amaranthus, in whose purple gore
    Me seemes I see Amintas[8] wretched fate,
To whom sweet Poets verse hath given endlesse date.

46

There wont faire Venus often to enjoy   ← *female sexuality, undefined by maleness*
    Her deare Adonis joyous company,
    And reape sweet pleasure of the wanton boy;
    There yet, some say, in secret he does ly,   *Venus possessor / pursuer (but not Idea / relat)*
    Lappéd in flowres and pretious spycery,
    By her hid from the world, and from the skill°   *knowledge*
    Of Stygian Gods, which doe her love envy;
    But she her selfe, when ever that she will,
Possesseth him, and of his sweetnesse takes her fill.

47

And sooth it seemes they say: for he may not
    For ever die, and ever buried bee
    In balefull night, where all things are forgot;
    All° be he subject to mortalitie,   *although*
    Yet is eterne in mutabilitie,
    And by succession made perpetuall,
    Transforméd oft, and chaungéd diverslie:
    For him the Father of all formes[9] they call;
Therefore needs mote he live, that living gives to all.

48

There now he liveth in eternall blis,
    Joying his goddesse, and of her enjoyed:

6. Apollo, who had accidentally killed his friend Hyacinthus, ordained that the curiously marked hyacinth should thenceforth commemorate the dead youth (*Metamorphoses*, X. 163–219). For the story of Narcissus, cf. *ibid.*, III. 341–511.
7. From Greek, "unfading"; traditionally, the symbolic flower of eternity.
8. Probably an allusion to Sir Philip Sidney, or perhaps to *Amintae Gaudia*, a Latin pastoral by Thomas Watson. Originally, "Amyntas" refers to a shepherd in Virgil's *Eclogue X*.

9. Since Venus actively "possesseth" Adonis, her relationship to him is that of Form to Matter; yet in another sense, Adonis here represents the formal principle that endures through all the processes of change. But the symbolic values of this pair are not to be too narrowly confined, just as Spenser's philosophical ideas in the Canto resist efforts to relate them with narrow exactitude to specific sources, or to confine them within precise and closely logical bounds.

[handwritten: escapes the defining male gaze, but it's a male def. of femaleness]

Ne feareth he henceforth that foe of his,
Which with his cruell tuske him deadly cloyd:°   gored
For that wilde Bore,[1] the which him once annoyd,°   injured
She firmely hath emprisonéd for ay,
That her sweet love his malice mote avoyd,
In a strong rocky Cave, which is they say,
Hewen underneath that Mount, that none him losen° may.   set free

49

There now he lives in everlasting joy,
With many of the Gods in company,
Which thither haunt,° and with the wingéd boy   frequent
Sporting himselfe in safe felicity:
Who when he hath with spoiles and cruelty
Ransackt the world, and in the wofull harts
Of many wretches set his triumphes hye,
Thither resorts, and laying his sad darts
Aside, with faire Adonis playes his wanton parts.

50

And his true love faire Psyche[2] with him playes,
Faire Psyche to him lately reconcyld,   *[handwritten: Wanton desire]*
After long troubles and unmeet upbrayes,°   reproaches
With which his mother Venus her revyld,°   *[handwritten: reconciled]*   scolded
And eke himselfe her cruelly exyld: *[handwritten: w/the soul]*
But now in stedfast love and happy state
She with him lives, and hath him borne a chyld,
Pleasure, that doth both gods and men aggrate,°   gratify
Pleasure, the daughter of Cupid and Psyche late.

51

Hither great Venus brought this infant faire,
The younger daughter of Chrysogonee,[3]
And unto Psyche with great trust and care
Committed her, yfosteréd to bee,
And trainéd up in true feminitee:
Who no lesse carefully her tenderéd,°   cared for
Then her owne daughter Pleasure, to whom shee
Made her companion, and her lessonéd°   taught
In all the lore of love, and goodly womanhead.

52

In which when she to perfect ripenesse grew,
Of grace and beautie noble Paragone,°   model

---

1. Natalis Comes identifies the boar that wounded Adonis as winter, the threatening antagonist of spring, which nevertheless remains itself equally a part of the natural cycle (*op. cit.*, V. 16). Spenser may have meant his readers to understand by the boar that animal passion, violence, or instinct for disorder and chaos, which makes part of man's being and requires to be con-stantly controlled.
2. The story of Cupid and Psyche, representing the arduous purification, by trial and misfortune, of the human soul, is told by Apuleius in his Latin novel, *Metamorphoses* (commonly known as *The Golden Ass*), composed in the second century A.D.
3. I.e., Amoret.

She brought her forth into the worldés vew,
  To be th'ensample of true love alone,
  And Lodestarre of all chaste affectione,
  To all faire Ladies, that doe live on ground.
  To Faery court she came, where many one
  Admyrd her goodly haveour,° and found   *deportment*
His feeble hart wide launchéd° with loves cruell wound.   *pierced*

53

But she to none of them her love did cast,°   *grant*
  Save to the noble knight Sir Scudamore,
  To whom her loving hart she linkéd fast
  In faithfull love, t'abide for evermore,
  And for his dearest sake enduréd sore,°   *grievous*
  Sore trouble of an hainous enimy;
  Who her would forcéd have to have forlore
  Her former love, and stedfast loialty,
As ye may elsewhere read that ruefull history.

54

But well I weene, ye first desire to learne,
  What end unto that fearefull Damozell,
  Which fled so fast from that same foster stearne,
  Whom with his brethren Timias slew, befell:
  That was to weet, the goodly Florimell;·
  Who wandring for to seeke her lover deare,
  Her lover deare, her dearest Marinell,
  Into misfortune fell, as ye did heare,
And from Prince Arthur fled with wings of idle feare.

Canto VII

The witches sonne loves Florimell:
  she flyes, he faines° to die.   *desires*
Satyrane saves the Squire of Dames
  from Gyants tyrannie.

1

Like as an Hynd forth singled from the heard,
  That hath escapéd from a ravenous beast,
  Yet flyes away of her owne feet affeard,
  And every leafe, that shaketh with the least
  Murmure of winde, her terror hath encreast;
  So fled faire Florimell from her vaine feare,
  Long after she from perill was releast:
  Each shade she saw, and each noyse she did heare,
Did seeme to be the same, which she escapt whyleare.[1]

---

1. Florimell's flight is based on that of Angelica from Rinaldo, in Ariosto's *Orlando Furioso* (I. 33–34), which in turn has classical antecedents in Horace and Anacreon; but Florimell has none of the artful sophistication that recurrently marks Angelica's character (cf. *Orlando Furioso*, I. 50–51, 55–56): that is reserved by Spenser for the false Florimell, created by the witch (cf. viii. 5–8).

2

All that same evening she in flying spent,
 And all that night her course continewéd:
 Ne did she let dull sleepe once to relent,°   *slacken*
 Nor wearinesse to slacke her hast, but fled
 Ever alike, as if her former dred
 Were hard behind, her readie to arrest:°   *seize*
 And her white Palfrey having conqueréd
 The maistring raines out of her weary wrest,° *wrist*
Perforce her carriéd, where ever he thought best.

3

So long as breath, and hable° puissance   *sufficient*
 Did native courage unto him supply,
 His pace he freshly forward did advaunce,
 And carried her beyond all jeopardy,
 But nought that wanteth rest, can long aby.° *endure*
 He having through incessant travell spent
 His force, at last perforce a downe did ly,
 Ne foot could further move: The Lady gent° *gentle*
Thereat was suddein strooke with great astonishment.° *dismay*

4

And forst t'alight, on foot mote algates° fare, *entirely*
 A traveller unwonted to such way:
 Need teacheth her this lesson hard and rare,
 That fortune all in equall launce° doth sway, *balance*
 And mortall miseries doth make her play.
 So long she travelled, till at length she came
 To an hilles side, which did to her bewray
 A little valley, subject to² the same,
All covered with thick woods, that quite it overcame.° *spread over*

5

Through the tops of the high trees she did descry
 A litle smoke, whose vapour thin and light,
 Reeking° aloft, uprolléd to the sky: *smoking*
 Which chearefull signe did send unto her sight,
 That in the same did wonne some living wight.
 Eftsoones her steps she thereunto applyde,
 And came at last in weary wretched plight
 Unto the place, to which her hope did guyde,
To find some refuge there, and rest her weary syde.

6

There in a gloomy hollow glen she found
 A little cottage, built of stickes and reedes
 In homely wize, and wald with sods around,
 In which a witch did dwell, in loathly weedes,° *garments*
 And wilfull want, all carelesse of her needes;
 So choosing solitarie to abide,
 Far from all neighbours, that her devilish deedes

2. I.e., beneath.

And hellish arts from people she might hide,
And hurt far off unknowne, whom ever she envide.°   *hated*

7

The Damzell there arriving entred in;
    Where sitting on the flore the Hag she found,
    Busie (as seemed) about some wicked gin:°   *scheme*
    Who soone as she beheld that suddein stound,°   *surprising sight*
    Lightly upstarted from the dustie ground,
    And with fell looke and hollow deadly gaze
    Staréd on her awhile, as one astound,°   *stunned*
    Ne had one word to speake, for great amaze,
But shewd by outward signes, that dread her sence did daze.

8

At last turning her feare to foolish wrath,
    She askt, what devill had her thither brought,
    And who she was, and what unwonted° path   *unfamiliar*
    Had guided her, unwelcoméd, unsought?
    To which the Damzell full of doubtfull thought,
    Her mildly answered; "Beldame be not wroth
    With silly° Virgin by adventure brought   *innocent*
    Unto your dwelling, ignorant and loth,°   *reluctant*
That crave but rowme to rest, while tempest overblo'th."

9

With that adowne out of her Christall eyne
    Few trickling teares she softly forth let fall,
    That like two Orient pearles, did purely shyne
    Upon her snowy cheeke; and therewithall
    She sighéd soft, that none so bestiall,
    Nor salvage hart, but ruth° of her sad plight   *pity*
    Would make to melt, or pitteously appall;
    And that vile Hag, all° were her whole delight   *although*
In mischiefe, was much movéd at so pitteous sight.

10

And gan recomfort her in her rude wyse,
    With womanish compassion of her plaint,
    Wiping the teares from her suffuséd eyes,
    And bidding her sit downe, to rest her faint
    And wearie limbs a while. She nothing quaint°   *fastidious*
    Nor s'deignfull of so homely fashion,
    Sith brought she was now to so hard constraint,
    Sate downe upon the dusty ground anon,
As glad of that small rest, as Bird of tempest gon.°   *passed*

11

Tho gan she gather up her garments rent,°   *torn*
    And her loose lockes to dight in order dew,
    With golden wreath and gorgeous ornament;
    Whom such whenas the wicked Hag did vew,
    She was astonisht at her heavenly hew,°   *appearance*
    And doubted her to deeme an earthly wight,

But or° some Goddesse, or of Dianes crew,　　　　*either*
　　And thought her to adore with humble spright;
T'adore thing so divine as beauty, were but right.

12

This wicked woman had a wicked sonne,
　　The comfort of her age and weary dayes,
　　A laesie loord,° for nothing good to donne,[3]　　*lout*
　　But stretchéd forth in idlenesse alwayes,
　　Ne ever cast his mind to covet prayse,
　　Or ply him selfe to any honest trade,
　　But all the day before the sunny rayes
　　He used to slug,° or sleepe in slothfull shade:　　*idle*
Such laesinesse both lewd° and poore attonce him made.　*ignorant*

13

He comming home at undertime,° there found　　*noon*
　　The fairest creature, that he ever saw,
　　Sitting beside his mother on the ground;
　　The sight whereof did greatly him adaw,°　　*daunt*
　　And his base thought with terrour and with aw
　　So inly smot, that as one, which had gazed
　　On the bright Sunne unwares, doth soone withdraw
　　His feeble eyne, with too much brightnesse dazed,
So staréd he on her, and stood long while amazed.

14

Softly at last he gan his mother aske,
　　What mister° wight that was, and whence derived,　*kind of*
　　That in so straunge disguizement there did maske,
　　And by what accident she there arrived:
　　But she, as one nigh of her wits deprived,
　　With nought but ghastly lookes him answeréd,
　　Like to a ghost, that lately is revived
　　From Stygian shores, where late it wanderéd;
So both at her, and each at other wonderéd.

15

But the faire Virgin was so meeke and mild,
　　That she to them vouchsaféd to embace
　　Her goodly port,[4] and to their senses vild,°　　*vile*
　　Her gentle speach applide, that in short space
　　She grew familiare in that desert° place.　　*desolate*
　　During which time, the Chorle through her so kind
　　And curteise use° conceived affection bace,　　*demeanour*
　　And cast° to love her in his brutish mind;　　*resolved*
No love, but brutish lust, that was so beastly tind.°　*kindled*

16

Closely° the wicked flame his bowels brent,°　　*secretly/burned*
　　And shortly grew into outrageous fire;
　　Yet had he not the hart, nor hardiment,

---

3. I.e., good for nothing.　　4. I.e., she adopted a gently courteous manner toward them.

As unto her to utter his desire;
His caytive° thought durst not so high aspire,   *base*
But with soft sighes, and lovely semblaunces,°   *expressions*
He weened that his affection entire
She should aread; many resemblaunces°   *signs of love*
To her he made, and many kind remembraunces.

17

Oft from the forrest wildings° he did bring,   *crab apples*
   Whose sides empurpled were with smiling red,
   And oft young birds, which he had taught to sing
   His mistresse prayses, sweetly caroléd,
   Girlonds of flowres sometimes for her faire hed
   He fine would dight; sometimes the squirell wild
   He brought to her in bands, as conqueréd
   To be her thrall, his fellow servant vild;
All which, she of him tooke with countenance meeke and mild.

18

But past awhile, when she fit season° saw   *time*
   To leave that desert mansion, she cast
   In secret wize her selfe thence to withdraw,
   For feare of mischiefe, which she did forecast
   Might be by the witch or that her sonne compast:°   *contrived*
   Her wearie Palfrey closely, as she might,
   Now well recovered after long repast,
   In his proud furnitures° she freshly dight,   *trappings*
His late miswandred wayes now to remeasure° right.   *retrace*

19

And earely ere the dawning day appeard,
   She forth issewed, and on her journey went;
   She went in perill, of each noyse affeard,
   And of each shade, that did it selfe present;
   For still she fearéd to be overhent,°   *overtaken*
   Of that vile hag, or her uncivile sonne:
   Who when too late awaking, well they kent,°   *discovered*
   That their faire guest was gone, they both begonne
To make exceeding mone, as they had bene undonne.

20

But that lewd° lover did the most lament   *base*
   For her depart, that ever man did heare;
   He knockt his brest with desperate intent,
   And scratcht his face, and with his teeth did teare
   His rugged flesh, and rent his ragged heare:
   That his sad mother seeing his sore plight,
   Was greatly woe begon, and gan to feare,
   Least his fraile senses were emperisht° quight,   *enfeebled*
And love to frenzy turnd, sith love is franticke hight.

21

All wayes she sought, him to restore to plight,
   With herbs, with charms, with counsell, and with teares,

But tears, nor charms, nor herbs, nor counsell might
Asswage the fury, which his entrails teares:
So strong is passion, that no reason heares.
Tho when all other helpes she saw to faile,
She turnd her selfe backe to her wicked leares°   *lessons*
And by her devilish arts thought to prevaile,
To bring her backe againe, or worke her finall bale.°   *harm*

22

Eftsoones out of her hidden cave she cald
  An hideous beast,[5] of horrible aspect,
  That could the stoutest courage have appald;
  Monstrous mishapt, and all his backe was spect°   *speckled*
  With thousand spots of colours queint elect,[6]
  Thereto so swift, that it all beasts did pas:
  Like never yet did living eye detect;
  But likest it to an Hyena was,
That feeds on womens flesh, as others feede on gras.

23

It forth she cald, and gave it streight in charge,
  Through thicke and thin her to pursew apace,
  Ne once to stay to rest, or breath at large,
  Till her he had attaind, and brought in place,[7]
  Or quite devourd her beauties scornefull grace.
  The Monster swift as word, that from her went,
  Went forth in hast, and did her footing trace
  So sure and swiftly, through his perfect sent,°   *scent*
And passing speede, that shortly he her overhent.

24

Whom when the fearefull Damzell nigh espide,
  No need to bid her fast away to flie;
  That ugly shape so sore her terrifide,
  That it she shund no lesse, then dread to die,
  And her flit° Palfrey did so well apply°   *fleet/adapt*
  His nimble feet to her conceivéd feare,
  That whilest his breath did strength to him supply,
  From perill free he her away did beare:
But when his force gan faile, his pace gan wex areare.°   *slacken*

25

Which whenas she perceived, she was dismayd
  At that same last extremitie° full sore,   *adversity*
  And of her safetie greatly grew afrayd;
  And now she gan approch to the sea shore,
  As it befell, that she could flie no more,
  But yield her selfe to spoile of greedinesse.

5. Sts. 22–28 are based on the pursuit of Manricardo by a monstrous "orc," in Boiardo, *Orlando Innamorato* (III. iii. 24 ff.). Medieval bestiaries associate the hyena with changefulness, hypocrisy, sin, and death: "Those of you who serve wantonness and avarice are compared to this monster" (*The Bestiary*, ed. cit., p. 32). In particular, Spenser's beast represents the malicious slander that persistently pursues beauty, and undermines reputation.

6. I.e., strangely chosen.

7. I.e., back to the witch's abode.

Lightly she leapéd, as a wight forlore,
From her dull horse, in desperate distresse,
And to her feet betooke her doubtfull sickernesse.°   *safety*

26

Not halfe so fast the wicked Myrrha[8] fled
  From dread of her revenging fathers hond:
  Nor halfe so fast to save her maidenhed,
  Fled fearefull Daphne on th'Aegaean strond,
  As Florimell fled from that Monster yond,
  To reach the sea, ere she of him were raught:°   *seized*
  For in the sea to drowne her selfe she fond,°   *tried*
  Rather then of the tyrant to be caught:
Thereto feare gave her wings, and neede her courage taught.

27

It fortunéd (high God did so ordaine)
  As she arrivéd on the roring shore,
  In minde to leape into the mighty maine,
  A little boate lay hoving° her before,   *floating*
  In which there slept a fisher old and pore,
  The whiles his nets were drying on the sand:
  Into the same she leapt, and with the ore°   *oar*
  Did thrust the shallop from the floting strand:
So safetie found at sea, which she found not at land.

28

The Monster ready on the pray to sease,
  Was of his forward° hope deceivéd quight;   *eager*
  Ne durst assay to wade the perlous seas,
  But greedily long gaping at the sight,
  At last in vaine was forst to turne his flight,
  And tell the idle tidings to his Dame:
  Yet to avenge his devilish despight,°   *malice*
  He set upon her Palfrey tired lame,
And slew him cruelly, ere any reskew came.

29

And after having him embowelléd,
  To fill his hellish gorge,° it chaunst a knight   *maw*
  To passe that way, as forth he travelléd;
  It was a goodly Swaine, and of great might,
  As ever man that bloudy field did fight;
  But in vaine sheows,° that wont young knights bewitch,   *pretence*
  And courtly services tooke no delight,
  But rather joyd to be, then seemen sich:°   *such*
For both to be and seeme to him was labour lich.°   *like*

30

It was to weete the good Sir Satyrane,
  That raungd abroad to seeke adventures wilde,
  As was his wont in forrest, and in plaine;
  He was all armd in rugged steel unfilde,°   *unpolished*

8. For Myrrha, cf. the note on III. ii. 41; Daphne, fleeing from Apollo, was turned into a laurel tree (Ovid, *Metamorphoses*, I. 450–567).

As in the smoky forge it was compilde,°   *made*
And in his Scutchin° bore a Satyres hed: *shield*
   He comming present, where the Monster vilde
   Upon that milke-white Palfreyes carkas fed,
Unto his reskew ran, and greedily him sped.

31

There well perceived he, that it was the horse,
   Whereon faire Florimell was wont to ride,
   That of that feend was rent without remorse:
   Much fearéd he, least ought did ill betide
   To that faire Mayd, the flowre of womens pride;
   For her he dearely lovéd, and in all
   His famous conquests highly magnifide:°   *glorified*
   Besides her golden girdle, which did fall
From her in flight, he found, that did him sore apall.°   *dismay*

32

Full of sad feare, and doubtfull agony,
   Fiercely he flew upon that wicked feend,
   And with huge strokes, and cruell battery
   Him forst to leave his pray, for to attend
   Him selfe from deadly daunger to defend:
   Full many wounds in his corrupted flesh
   He did engrave,° and muchell bloud did spend,   *cut deeply*
   Yet might not do him dye, but aye more fresh
And fierce he still appeard, the more he did him thresh.°   *strike*

33

He wist not, how him to despoile of life,
   Ne how to win the wishéd victory,
   Sith him he saw still stronger grow through strife,
   And him selfe weaker through infirmity;
   Greatly he grew enraged, and furiously
   Hurling his sword away, he lightly lept
   Upon the beast, that with great cruelty°   *ferocity*
   Roréd, and ragéd to be under-kept:°   *held down*
Yet he perforce him held, and strokes upon him hept.

34

As he that strives to stop a suddein flood,
   And in strong banckes his violence enclose,
   Forceth it swell above his wonted mood,
   And largely overflow the fruitfull plaine,
   That all the countrey seemes to be a Maine,°   *sea*
   And the rich furrowes flote, all quite fordonne:°   *ruined*
   The wofull husbandman doth lowd complaine,
   To see his whole yeares labour lost so soone,
For which to God he made so many an idle boone.°   *prayer*

35

So him he held, and did through might amate:°   *subdue*
   So long he held him, and him bet so long,
   That at the last his fiercenesse gan abate,
   And meekely stoup unto the victour strong:

Who to avenge the implacable° wrong,   *irremediable*
    Which he supposéd donne to Florimell,
    Sought by all meanes his dolour° to prolong,   *pain*
    Sith dint of steele his carcas could not quell:
His maker with her charmes had framéd him so well.

36

The golden ribband, which that virgin wore
    About her sclender wast, he tooke in hand,
    And with it bound the beast, that lowd did rore
    For great despight of that unwonted band,
    Yet daréd not his victour to withstand,
    But trembled like a lambe, fled from the pray,
    And all the way him followd on the strand,
    As he had long bene learnéd to obay;
Yet never learnéd he such service, till that day.[9]

37

Thus as he led the Beast along the way,
    He spide far off a mighty Giauntesse,[1]
    Fast flying on a Courser dapled gray,
    From a bold knight, that with great hardinesse
    Her hard pursewd, and sought for to suppresse;
    She bore before her lap a dolefull Squire,
    Lying athwart° her horse in great distresse,   *across*
    Fast bounden hand and foote with cords of wire,
Whom she did meane to make the thrall of her desire.

38

Which whenas Satyrane beheld, in hast
    He left his captive Beast at liberty,
    And crost the nearest way, by which he cast°   *intended*
    Her to encounter, ere she passéd by:
    But she the way shund nathemore for thy,[2]
    But forward gallopt fast; which when he spyde,
    His mighty speare he couchéd warily,
    And at her ran: she having him descryde,
Her selfe to fight addrest,° and threw her lode aside.   *prepared*

39

Like as a Goshauke, that in foote doth beare
    A trembling Culver,° having spide on hight   *dove*
    An Egle, that with plumy wings doth sheare
    The subtile ayre, stouping° with all his might,   *plunging*
    The quarrey throwes to ground with fell despight,
    And to the battell doth her selfe prepare:
    So ran the Geauntesse unto the fight;
    Her firie eyes with furious sparkes did stare,°   *glitter*
And with blasphemous bannes° high God in peeces tare.   *oaths*

9. That Satyrane can bind the beast with Florimell's girdle (identified in IV. v. 3 as the symbol of chastity) indicates the capacity of courageously active virtue to control and restrain (but not to destroy) slander.

1. I.e., Argante, a type of unchastity, exemplifying the extremes of lust and sexual appetite in women, which male vigor alone cannot successfully resist.

2. I.e., but she did not turn aside on that account.

40

She caught in hand an huge great yron mace,
  Wherewith she many had of life deprived,
  But ere the stroke could seize° his ayméd place,   *attain*
  His speare amids her sun-broad shield arrived;
  Yet nathemore the steele a sunder rived,
  All were the beame° in bignesse like a mast,   *spear*
  Ne her out of the stedfast sadle drived,
  But glauncing on the tempred metall, brast°   *burst*
In thousand shivers, and so forth beside her past.

41

Her Steed did stagger with that puissaunt strooke;
  But she no more was movéd with that might,
  Then it had lighted° on an aged Oke,   *fallen*
  Or on the marble Pillour, that is pight
  Upon the top of Mount Olympus hight,
  For the brave youthly Champions to assay,
  With burning charet wheeles it nigh to smite:[3]
  But who that smites it, mars his joyous play,
And is the spectacle of ruinous decay.°   *destruction*

42

Yet therewith sore enraged, with sterne regard
  Her dreadfull weapon she to him addrest,°   *directed*
  Which on his helmet martelléd° so hard,   *hammered*
  That made him low incline his lofty crest,
  And bowd his battred visour to his brest:
  Wherewith he was so stund, that he n'ote° ryde,   *could not*
  But reeléd to and fro from East to West:
  Which when his cruel enimy espyde,
She lightly unto him adjoynéd side to syde;

43

And on his collar laying puissant hand,
  Out of his wavering seat him pluckt perforse,°   *forcibly*
  Perforse him pluckt, unable to withstand,
  Or helpe himselfe, and laying thwart her horse,
  In loathly wise like to a carion corse,°   *corpse*
  She bore him fast away. Which when the knight,
  That her pursewéd, saw, with great remorse
  He neare was touchéd in his noble spright,
And gan encrease his speed, as she encreast her flight.

44

Whom when as nigh approching she espyde,
  She threw away her burden angrily;
  For she list° not the battell to abide,   *cared*
  But made her selfe more light, away to fly:
  Yet her the hardy knight pursewd so nye,
  That almost in the backe he oft her strake:

3. The assumption that Mount Olympus was the site of the Olympic Games appears also in Sidney's *Apologie for Poetrie;* but Spenser may have been misled by the obscure language of the *Mythologiae* of Natalis Comes (V. 1).

But still when him at hand she did espy,
  She turnd, and semblaunce of faire fight did make;
But when he stayd, to flight againe she did her take.

45

By this the good Sir Satyrane gan wake
  Out of his dreame, that did him long entraunce,
  And seeing none in place, he gan to make
  Exceeding mone, and curst that cruell chaunce,
  Which reft from him so faire a chevisaunce:°   *enterprise*
  At length he spide, whereas that wofull Squire,
  Whom he had reskewéd from captivaunce
  Of his strong foe, lay tombled in the myre,
Unable to arise, or foot or hand to styre.°   *stir*

46

To whom approching, well he mote perceive
  In that foule plight a comely personage,
  And lovely° face, made fit for to deceive   *handsome*
  Fraile Ladies hart with loves consuming rage,
  Now in the blossome of his freshest age:
  He reard him up, and loosd his yron bands,
  And after gan inquire his parentage,
  And how he fell into that Gyaunts hands,
And who that was, which chacéd her along the lands.°   *countryside*

47

Then trembling yet through feare, the Squire bespake,
  "That Geauntesse Argante[4] is behight,
  A daughter of the Titans which did make
  Warre against heaven, and heapéd hils on hight,
  To scale the skyes, and put Jove from his right:
  Her sire Typhoeus was, who mad through merth,
  And drunke with bloud of men, slaine by his might,
  Through incest, her of his owne mother Earth
Whilome begot, being but halfe twin of that berth.

48

"For at that berth another Babe she bore,
  To weet the mighty Ollyphant,[5] that wrought
  Great wreake° to many errant knights of yore,   *destruction*
  And many hath to foule confusion° brought.   *ruin*
  These twinnes, men say, (a thing far passing thought)
  Whiles in their mothers wombe enclosd they were,
  Ere they into the lightsome° world were brought,   *bright*
  In fleshly lust were mingled both yfere,°   *together*
And in that monstrous wise did to the world appere.

49

"So lived they ever after in like sin,
  Gainst natures law, and good behavioure:°   *conduct*

4. The parentage of Argante and Ollyphant is essentially original with Spenser, who is concerned to emphasize their unnatural perversity and monstrous pride, and so links them with the Giants and Titans, traditionally rebels against established order (cf. Hesiod, *Theogony*, 664–735).

5. Literally, "elephant"; but Spenser's figure recalls Chaucer's *Tale of Sir Thopas*, 807–809: ". . . a greet geaunt,/ His name was Sire Olifaunt,/A perilous man of dede."

But greatest shame was to that maiden twin,
  Who not content so fowly to devoure°   *eagerly enjoy*
  Her native flesh, and staine her brothers bowre,
  Did wallow in all other fleshly myre,
  And suffred beasts her body to deflowre:
  So whot° she burnéd in that lustfull fyre,   *hot*
Yet all that might not slake her sensuall desyre.

50

"But over all the countrey she did raunge,
  To seeke young men, to quench her flaming thrust,°   *thirst*
  And feed her fancy with delightfull chaunge:
  Whom so she fittest finds to serve her lust,
  Through her maine° strength, in which she most doth trust,
                                      mighty
  She with her brings into a secret Ile,
  Where in eternall bondage dye he must,
  Or be the vassall of her pleasures vile,
And in all shamefull sort him selfe with her defile.

51

"Me seely° wretch she so at vauntage caught,   *simple*
  After she long in waite for me did lye,
  And meant unto her prison to have brought,
  Her lothsome pleasure there to satisfye;
  That thousand deathes me lever° were to dye,   *rather*
  Then breake the vow, that to faire Columbell
  I plighted have, and yet keepe stedfastly:
  As for my name, it mistreth° not to tell;   *needs*
Call me the Squyre of Dames,[6] that me beseemeth well.

52

"But that bold knight, whom ye pursuing saw
  That Geauntesse, is not such, as she seemed,
  But a faire virgin, that in martiall law,
  And deedes of armes above all Dames is deemed,
  And above many knights is eke esteemed,
  For her great worth; She Palladine is hight:
  She you from death, you me from dread redeemed.
  Ne any may that Monster match in fight,
But she, or such as she, that is so chaste a wight."[7]

53

"Her well beseemes that Quest," quoth Satyrane,
  "But read, thou Squyre of Dames, what vow is this,
  Which thou upon thy selfe hast lately ta'ne?"
  "That shall I you recount," quoth he, "ywis,°   *certainly*
  So be ye pleasd to pardon all amis.
  That gentle Lady, whom I love and serve,

6. The Squire of Dames exemplifies that bondage which the courtly love code imposes on its adherents; the cynical wastefulness and essential futility of his two "quests" are matched by the triviality of his lady's whimsical commands. The Squire's story is based on *Orlando Furioso*, XXVIII.

7. Only Palladine (and, presumably, Britomart herself) can put Argante to flight; i.e., true chastity alone effectively counters the force of perverted lust.

After long suit and weary servicis,
    Did aske me, how I could her love deserve,
And how she might be sure, that I would never swerve.

54

"I glad by any meanes her grace to gaine,
    Bad her commaund my life to save, or spill.°   *destroy*
    Eftsoones she bad me, with incessaunt paine
    To wander through the world abroad at will,
    And every where, where with my power or skill
    I might do service unto gentle Dames,
    That I the same should faithfully fulfill,
    And at the twelve monethes end should bring their names
And pledges; as the spoiles of my victorious games.

55

"So well I to faire Ladies service did,
    And found such favour in their loving hartes,
    That ere the yeare his course had compassid,°   *completed*
    Three hundred pledges for my good desartes,
    And thrise three hundred thanks for my good partes°   *conduct*
    I with me brought, and did to her present:
    Which when she saw, more bent to eke° my smartes,   *add to*
    Then to reward my trusty true intent,
She gan for me devise a grievous punishment.

56

"To weet, that I my travell should resume,
    And with like labour walke the world around,
    Ne ever to her presence should presume,
    Till I so many other Dames had found,
    The which, for all the suit I could propound,
    Would me refuse their pledges to afford,
    But did abide for ever chast and sound."
    "Ah gentle Squire," quoth he, "tell at one word,
How many foundst thou such to put in thy record?"

57

"In deed Sir knight," said he, "one word may tell
    All, that I ever found so wisely stayd;°   *constant*
    For onely three they were disposd so well,
    And yet three yeares I now abroad have strayd,
    To find them out." "Mote I," then laughing sayd
    The knight, "inquire of thee, what were those three,
    The which thy proffred curtesie denayd?°   *rejected*
    Or ill they seeméd sure avizd to bee, [8]
Or brutishly brought up, that nev'r did fashions see."

58

"The first which then refuséd me," said hee,
    "Certes was but a common Courtisane,
    Yet flat refusd to have a do with mee,
    Because I could not give her many a Jane."°   *coin*
    (Thereat full hartely laughed Satyrane).

8. I.e., either they were foolish.

"The second was an holy Nunne to chose,[9]
 Which would not let me be her Chappellane,°   *confessor*
 Because she knew, she said, I would disclose
Her counsell, if she should her trust in me repose.

59

"The third a Damzell was of low degree,
 Whom I in countrey cottage found by chaunce;
 Full little weenéd I, that chastitee
 Had lodging in so meane a maintenaunce,°   *condition*
 Yet was she faire, and in her countenance
 Dwelt simple truth in seemely fashion.
 Long thus I wooed her with dew observaunce,
 In hope unto my pleasure to have won;
But was as farre at last, as when I first begon.

60

"Safe her, I never any woman found,
 That chastity did for it selfe embrace,
 But were for other causes firme and sound;
 Either for want of handsome° time and place,   *suitable*
 Or else for feare of shame and fowle disgrace.
 Thus am I hopelesse ever to attaine
 My Ladies love, in such a desperate case.
 But all my dayes am like to wast in vaine,
Seeking to match the chaste with th'unchaste Ladies traine."°

61
                  company

"Perdy," said Satyrane, "thou Squire of Dames,
 Great labour fondly° hast thou hent° in hand,   *foolishly/taken*
 To get small thankes, and therewith many blames,
 That may emongst Alcides[1] labours stand."
 Thence backe returning to the former land,°   *place*
 Where late he left the Beast, he overcame,
 He found him not; for he had broke his band,
 And was returned againe unto his Dame,
To tell what tydings of faire Florimell became.

Canto VIII

  The Witch creates a snowy Lady,
    like to Florimell,
  Who wronged by Carle° by Proteus saved,   *churl*
    is sought by Paridell.

1

So oft as I this history record,
 My hart doth melt with meere° compassion,
 To thinke, how causelesse of her owne accord[1]
 This gentle Damzell, whom I write upon,   *pure*
 Should plongéd be in such affliction,

---

9. I.e., if you please.   1. I.e., through no culpable action on
1. Hercules.   her part.

Without all hope of comfort or reliefe,
   That sure I weene, the hardest hart of stone,
   Would hardly find° to aggravate her griefe;   *choose*
For misery craves rather mercie, then repriefe.°   *reproach*

2

But that accurséd Hag, her hostesse late,
   Had so enranckled her malitious hart,
   That she desyrd th'abridgement of her fate,[2]
   Or long enlargement° of her painefull smart.   *increase*
   Now when the Beast, which by her wicked art
   Late forth she sent, she backe returning spyde,
   Tyde with her broken girdle, it a part
   Of her rich spoyles, whom he had earst destroyd,
She weend,° and wondrous gladnesse to her hart applyde. *supposed*

3

And with it running hast'ly to her sonne,
   Thought with that sight him much to have relived;°   *restored*
   Who thereby deeming sure the thing as donne,
   His former griefe with furie fresh revived,
   Much more then earst, and would have algates rived[3]
   The hart out of his brest: for sith her ded
   He surely dempt,° himselfe he thought deprived   *thought*
   Quite of all hope, wherewith he long had fed
His foolish maladie, and long time had misled.

4

With thought whereof, exceeding mad° he grew,   *frenzied*
   And in his rage his mother would have slaine,
   Had she not fled into a secret mew,°   *hiding place*
   Where she was wont her Spights to entertaine
   The maisters of her art:[4] there was she faine°   *accustomed*
   To call them all in order to her ayde,
   And them conjure° upon eternall paine,   *charge*
   To counsell her so carefully° dismayd,   *grievously*
How she might heale her sonne, whose senses were decayd.° *destroyed*

5

By their advise, and her owne wicked wit,
   She there devized a wondrous worke to frame,°   *construct*
   Whose like on earth was never framéd yit,
   That even Nature selfe envide the same,
   And grudged to see the counterfet should shame
   The thing it selfe. In hand she boldly tooke
   To make another like the former Dame,
   Another Florimell, in shape and looke
So lively° and so like, that many it mistooke.   *lifelike*

6

The substance, whereof she the bodie made,
   Was purest snow in massie mould congeald,

2. I.e., to shorten the fated term of
her life.
3. I.e., entirely torn.
4. The evil spirits who enable the
witch to exert her magical powers; in
Macbeth, the witches refer to such
spirits as their "masters" (IV. i. 63).

Which she had gathered in a shadie glade
Of the Riphoean hils,[5] to her reveald
By errant Sprights, but from all men conceald:
The same she tempred with fine Mercury,
And virgin wex, that never yet was seald,
And mingled them with perfect vermily,°   *vermilion*
That like a lively sanguine° it seemed to the eye.   *blood-red*

7

In stead of eyes two burning lampes she set
  In silver sockets, shyning like the skyes,
  And a quicke moving Spirit did arret°   *assign*
  To stirre and roll them, like a womans eyes;
  In stead of yellow lockes she did devise,
  With golden wyre° to weave her curléd head;   *metallic thread*
  Yet golden wyre was not so yellow thrise°   *by a third*
  As Florimells faire haire: and in the stead
Of life, she put a Spright to rule the carkasse dead.

8

A wicked Spright yfraught° with fawning guile,   *filled*
  And faire resemblance above all the rest,
  Which with the Prince of Darknesse fell somewhile,
  From heavens blisse and everlasting rest;
  Him needed not instruct,[6] which way were best
  Himselfe to fashion likest Florimell,
  Ne how to speake, ne how to use his gest,°   *bearing*
  For he in counterfeisance° did excell,   *deception*
And all the wyles of wemens wits knew passing well.[7]

9

Him shapéd thus, she deckt in garments gay,
  Which Florimell had left behind her late,
  That who so then her saw, would surely say,
  It was her selfe, whom it did imitate,
  Or fairer then her selfe, it ought algate
  Might fairer be. And then she forth her brought
  Unto her sonne, that lay in feeble state;
  Who seeing her gan streight° upstart, and thought   *at once*
She was the Lady selfe, whom he so long had sought.

10

Tho fast her clipping twixt his armés twaine,
  Extremely joyéd in so happie sight,
  And soone forgot his former sickly paine;
  But she, the more to seeme such as she hight,
  Coyly rebutted° his embracement light;   *repelled*
  Yet still with gentle countenaunce retained,
  Enough to hold a foole in vaine delight:

---

5. The term was applied by ancient poets to the mountains supposed to exist in the wild northern parts of Europe and Asia.

6. I.e., he needed no instruction.
7. The appearance of chastity often cloaks immodesty and deceit. Cf. also I. i. 45 and note.

Him long she so with shadowes entertained,
As her Creatresse had in charge to her ordained.

11

Till on a day, as he disposéd was
  To walke the woods with that his Idole faire,
  Her to disport,° and idle time to pas,   *entertain*
  In th'open freshnesse of the gentle aire,
  A knight that way there chauncéd to repaire;°   *go*
  Yet knight he was not, but a boastfull swaine,
  That deedes of armes had ever in despaire,[8]
  Proud Braggadocchio, that in vaunting vaine
His glory did repose,° and credit did maintaine.   *establish*

12

He seeing with that Chorle so faire a wight,
  Deckéd with many a costly ornament,
  Much merveiléd thereat, as well he might,
  And thought that match a fowle disparagement:°   *disgrace*
  His bloudie speare eftsoones he boldly bent
  Against the silly clowne,° who dead through feare,   *rustic*
  Fell streight to ground in great astonishment;
  "Villein," said he, "this Ladie is my deare,
Dy, if thou it gainesay: I will away her beare."

13

The fearefull Chorle durst not gainesay, nor dooe,
  But trembling stood, and yielded him the pray;
  Who finding litle leasure her to wooe,
  On Tromparts steed her mounted without stay,°   *hindrance*
  And without reskew led her quite away.
  Proud man himselfe then Braggadocchio deemed,
  And next to none, after that happie day,
  Being possesséd of that spoyle, which seemed
The fairest wight on ground, and most of men esteemed.

14

But when he saw himselfe free from poursute,
  He gan make gentle purpose° to his Dame,   *discourse*
  With termes of love and lewdnesse dissolute;
  For he could well his glozing speaches frame
  To such vaine uses, that him best became:
  But she thereto would lend but light regard,
  As seeming sory, that she ever came
  Into his powre, that uséd her so hard,
To reave° her honor, which she more then life prefard.   *take away*

15

Thus as they two of kindnesse° treated long,   *love*
  There them by chaunce encountred on the way
  An arméd knight,[9] upon a courser strong,

---

8. I.e., from whom true feats of arms could never be expected. The boaster Braggadocchio and his squire Trompart have been introduced in II. iii; as their names indicate, they are knightly figures only in outward show.

9. I.e., Sir Ferraugh, who is not identified until IV. ii. 4.

Whose trampling feet upon the hollow lay°   ground
Seeméd to thunder, and did nigh affray
That Capons° courage: yet he lookéd grim,   coward
And fained to cheare his Ladie in dismay;
Who seemed for feare to quake in every lim,
And her to save from outrage, meekely prayéd him.

16

Fiercely that stranger forward came, and nigh
Approching, with bold words and bitter threat,
Bad that same boaster, as he mote, on high[1]
To leave to him that Lady for excheat,[2]
Or bide° him battell without further treat.°   endure/parley
That challenge did too peremptory seeme,
And fild his senses with abashment great;
Yet seeing nigh him jeopardy extreme,
He it dissembled well, and light seemed to esteeme.

17

Saying, "Thou foolish knight, that weenst with words
To steale away, that I with blowes have wonne,
And brought throgh points of many perilous swords:
But if thee list to see thy Courser ronne,
Or prove thy selfe, this sad° encounter shonne,   grievous
And seeke else° without hazard of thy hed."   elsewhere
At those proud words that other knight begonne
To wexe exceeding wroth, and him ared°   told
To turne his steede about, or sure he should be ded.

18

"Sith then," said Braggadocchio, "needes thou wilt
Thy dayes abridge, through proofe of puissance,
Turne we our steedes, that both in equall tilt°   mounted combat
May meet againe, and each take happie chance."
This said, they both a furlongs mountenance°   distance
Retyrd their steeds, to ronne in even race:
But Braggadocchio with his bloudie lance
Once having turnd, no more returnd his face,
But left his love to losse, and fled himselfe apace.

19

The knight him seeing fly, had no regard°   care
Him to poursew, but to the Ladie rode,
And having her from Trompart lightly reard,°   taken up
Upon his Courser set the lovely lode,
And with her fled away without abode.°   delay
Well weenéd he, that fairest Florimell
It was, with whom in company he yode,°   went
And so her selfe did alwaies to him tell;
So made him thinke him selfe in heaven, that was in hell.

20

But Florimell her selfe was farre away,
Driven to great distresse by Fortune straunge,

1. I.e., as loudly as he could.   2. I.e., as his property.

And taught the carefull° Mariner to play,   *full of care*
 Sith late mischaunce had her compeld to chaunge
 The land for sea, at randon° there to raunge: *random*
 Yet there that cruell Queene avengeresse,[3]
 Not satisfide so farre her to estraunge
 From courtly blisse and wonted happinesse,
Did heape on her new waves of weary wretchednesse.

21

For being fled into the fishers bote,
 For refuge from the Monsters crueltie,
 Long so she on the mightie maine did flote,
 And with the tide drove forward careleslie;
 For th'aire was milde, and clearéd was the skie,
 And all his windes Dan° Aeolus did keepe,   *Master*
 From stirring up their stormy enmitie,
 As pittying to see her waile and weepe;
But all the while the fisher did securely sleepe.

22

At last when droncke with drowsinesse, he woke,
 And saw his drover° drive along the streame,   *boat*
 He was dismayd, and thrise his breast he stroke,
 For marvell of that accident extreame;
 But when he saw that blazing beauties beame,
 Which with rare light his bote did beautifie,
 He marveild more, and thought he yet did dreame
 Not well awakt, or that some extasie°   *madness*
Assotted° had his sense, or dazéd was his eie. *bewildered*

23

But when her well avizing,° he perceived   *viewing*
 To be no vision, nor fantasticke sight,
 Great comfort of her presence he conceived,
 And felt in his old courage° new delight   *spirit*
 To gin awake, and stirre his frozen spright:
 Tho rudely askt her, how she thither came.
 "Ah," said she, "father, I note read[4] aright,
 What hard misfortune brought me to the same;
Yet am I glad that here I now in safety am.

24

"But thou good man, sith farre in sea we bee,
 And the great waters gin apace to swell,
 That now no more we can the maine-land see,
 Have care, I pray, to guide the cock-bote° well, *skiff*
 Least worse on sea then us on land befell."
 Thereat th'old man did nought but fondly° grin, *foolishly*
 And said, his boat the way could wisely tell:
 But his deceiptfull eyes did never lin,°   *cease*
To looke on her faire face, and marke her snowy skin.

3. I.e., the goddess Fortuna (Fortune). 4. I.e., cannot tell.

25

The sight whereof in his congealéd flesh,
 Infixt such secret sting of greedy lust,
 That the drie withered stocke it gan refresh,
 And kindled heat, that soone in flame forth brust:°   *burst*
 The driest wood is soonest burnt to dust.
 Rudely to her he lept, and his rough hand
 Where ill became him, rashly would have thrust,
 But she with angry scorne him did withstond,
And shamefully reprovéd for his rudeness fond.

26

But he, that never good nor maners knew,
 Her sharpe rebuke full litle did esteeme;
 Hard is to teach an old horse amble trew.
 The inward smoke, that did before but steeme,
 Broke into open fire and rage° extreme,   *passion*
 And now he strength gan adde unto his will,
 Forcing to doe, that did him fowle misseeme:°   *misbecome*
 Beastly he threw her downe, ne cared to spill[5]
Her garments gay with scales of fish, that all did fill.

27

The silly virgin strove him to withstand,
 All that she might, and him in vaine revild:°   *rebuked*
 She struggled strongly both with foot and hand,
 To save her honor from that villaine vild,
 And cride to heaven, from humane helpe exild.
 O ye brave knights, that boast this Ladies love,
 Where be ye now, when she is nigh defild
 Of filthy wretch? well may shee you reprove
Or falshood or of slouth, when most it may behove.[6]

28

But if that thou, Sir Satyran, didst weete,
 Or thou, Sir Peridure,[7] her sorie state,
 How soone would yee assemble many a fleete,
 To fetch from sea, that ye at land lost late;
 Towres, Cities, Kingdomes ye would ruinate,°   *ruin*
 In your avengement and dispiteous° rage,   *pitiless*
 Ne ought your burning fury mote abate;
 But if Sir Calidore[8] could it presage,°   *know of*
No living creature could his cruelty asswage.

29

But sith that none of all her knights is nye,
 See how the heavens of voluntary grace,
 And soveraine favour towards chastity,

---

5. I.e., nor cared if he stained. The
fisherman's attempt to rape Florimell
recalls Ariosto's account of an old
hermit's assault on Angelica (*Orlando
Furioso*, VIII. 30–50).
6. I.e., when it most behooves you to
aid her.

7. Geoffrey of Monmouth refers to Earl
Peredur, a knight of the Round Table
(*op. cit.*, IX. 12); Spenser may have
intended him to be the hero of a later
Book in *The Faerie Queene*.
8. The hero of Book VI ("The Legend
of Courtesie").

Doe succour send to her distresséd cace:
So much high God doth innocence embrace.°   *protect*
It fortunéd, whilest thus she stifly strove,
And the wide sea importunéd long space
With shrilling shriekes, Proteus[9] abroad did rove,
Along the fomy waves driving his finny drove.

30

Proteus is Shepheard of the seas of yore,
And hath the charge of Neptunes mightie heard;
An aged sire with head all frory° hore,   *frosty*
And sprinckled frost upon his deawy beard:
Who when those pittifull outcries he heard,
Through all the seas so ruefully resound,
His charet swift in haste he thither steard,
Which with a teeme of scaly Phocas° bound   *seals*
Was drawne upon the waves, that foméd him around.

31

And comming to that Fishers wandring bote,
That went at will, withouten carde° or sayle,   *chart*
He therein saw that yrkesome sight, which smote
Deepe indignation and compassion frayle°   *tender*
Into his hart attonce: streight did he hayle°   *drag*
The greedy villein from his hopéd pray,
Of which he now did very litle fayle,
And with his staffe, that drives his Heard astray,
Him bet so sore, that life and sense did much dismay.

32

The whiles the pitteous Ladie up did ryse,
Ruffled and fowly raid° with filthy soyle,   *smeared*
And blubbred face with teares of her faire eyes:
Her heart nigh broken was with weary toyle,
To save her selfe from that outrageous spoyle,
But when she lookéd up, to weet, what wight
Had her from so infamous fact assoyle,°   *freed*
For shame, but more for feare of his grim sight,
Downe in her lap she hid her face, and loudly shright.°   *shrieked*

33

Her selfe not savéd yet from daunger dred
She thought, but chaunged from one to other feare;
Like as a fearefull Partridge, that is fled
From the sharpe Hauke, which her attachéd neare,[1]
And fals to ground, to seeke for succour theare,
Whereas the hungry Spaniels she does spy,

9. At III. iv. 25 chiefly a prophet and seer, Proteus in sts. 29–41 is presented as shepherd of the seas and as shape shifter (echoing Homer, *Odyssey*, IV. 456–458, and Virgil, *Georgics*, IV. 387–395, 406–410). To Boccaccio (*op. cit.*, VII. 9), the various forms assumed by Proteus indicate the passions. Spenser has earlier in the poem indicated the association of changefulness with the forces opposed to order and harmonious unity, in his description of Archimago (I. ii. 10).

1. I.e., nearly seized.

With greedy jawes her readie for to teare;
In such distresse and sad perplexity
Was Florimell, when Proteus she did see thereby.

34

But he endevouréd with speeches milde
  Her to recomfort, and accourage bold,
  Bidding her feare no more her foeman vilde,
  Nor doubt himselfe; and who he was, her told.
  Yet all that could not from affright her hold,
  Ne to recomfort her at all prevayld;
  For her faint heart was with the frozen cold
  Benumbd so inly, that her wits nigh fayld,
And all her senses with abashment° quite   *fear*
    were quayld.°   *overcome*

35

Her up betwixt his rugged hands he reard,
  And with his frory lips full softly kist,
  Whiles the cold ysickles from his rough beard,
  Droppéd adowne upon her yvorie brest:
  Yet he himselfe so busily addrest,°   *applied*
  That her out of astonishment° he wrought.   *insensibility*
  And out of that same fishers filthy nest
  Removing her, into his charet brought,
And there with many gentle termes her faire besought.

36

But that old leachour, which with bold assault
  That beautie durst presume to violate,
  He cast° to punish for his hainous fault;   *resolved*
  Then tooke he him yet trembling sith of late,
  And tyde behind his charet, to aggrate°   *gratify*
  The virgin, whom he had abusde so sore:
  So draged him through the waves in scornefull state,
  And after cast him up, upon the shore;
But Florimell with him unto his bowre he bore.

37

His bowre is in the bottome of the maine,°   *ocean*
  Under a mightie rocke, gainst which do rave
  The roaring billowes in their proud disdaine,
  That with the angry working of the wave,
  Therein is eaten out an hollow cave,
  That seemes rough Masons hand with engines° keene   *tools*
  Had long while labouréd it to engrave:°   *dig out*
  There was his wonne, ne living wight was seene,
Save one old Nymph, hight Panope[2] to keepe it cleane.

38

Thither he brought the sory Florimell,
  And entertainéd her the best he might

2. From Greek, "all-seeing." Panope was traditionally one of the Nereids (Hesiod, *Theogony*, 250); but this homely figure is essentially Spenser's own creation.

And Panope her entertaind eke well,
As an immortall mote a mortall wight,
To winne her liking unto his delight:
With flattering words he sweetly wooéd her,
And offeréd faire gifts t'allure her sight,
But she both offers and the offerer
Despysde, and all the fawning of the flatterer.

39

Daily he tempted her with this or that,
And never suffred her to be at rest:
But evermore she him refuséd flat,
And all his fainéd kindnesse did detest,
So firmely she had sealéd up her brest.
Sometimes he boasted, that a God he hight:
But she a mortall creature lovéd best:
Then he would make himselfe a mortall wight;
But then she said she loved none, but a Faerie knight.

40

Then like a Faerie knight himselfe he drest;
For every shape on him he could endew:°   endow
Then like a king he was to her exprest,°   shown
And offred kingdomes unto her in vew,
To be his Leman° and his Ladie trew: lover
But when all this he nothing saw prevaile,
With harder meanes he cast her to subdew,
And with sharpe threates her often did assaile,
So thinking for to make her stubborne courage quaile.

41

To dreadfull shapes he did himselfe transforme,
Now like a Gyant, now like to a feend,
Then like a Centaure, then like to a storme,
Raging within the waves: thereby he weend
Her will to win unto his wishéd end.
But when with feare, nor favour, nor with all
He else could doe, he saw himselfe esteemd,
Downe in a Dongeon deepe he let her fall,
And threatned there to make her his eternall thrall.

42

Eternall thraldome was to her more liefe,°   dear
Then losse of chastitie, or chaunge of love:
Die had she rather in tormenting griefe,
Then any should of falsenesse her reprove,
Or loosenesse, that she lightly did remove.°   change
Most vertuous virgin, glory be thy meed,
And crowne of heavenly praise with Saints above,
Where most sweet hymmes of this thy famous deed
Are still emongst them song, that far my rymes exceed.[3]

3. "Florimell as Beauty is wooed by
Proteus, the mutable forms of this life,
but . . . beauty and love are above the
physical, mutable realm of Proteus"
(T. P. Roche, Jr., *op. cit.*, 161–162).

43

Fit song of Angels caroléd to bee;
    But yet what so my feeble Muse can frame,
    Shall be t'advaunce° thy goodly chastitee,   *praise*
    And to enroll thy memorable name,
    In th'heart of every honourable Dame,
    That they thy vertuous deedes may imitate,
    And be partakers of thy endlesse fame.
    It yrkes° me, leave thee in this wofull state,   *grieves*
To tell of Satyrane, where I him left of late.

44

Who having ended with that Squire of Dames
    A long discourse of his adventures vaine,
    The which himselfe, then° Ladies more defames,   *than*
    And finding not th' Hyena to be slaine,
    With that same Squire, returnéd backe againe
    To his first way. And as they forward went,
    They spyde a knight faire pricking on the plaine,
    As if he were on some adventure bent,
And in his port appearéd manly hardiment.

45

Sir Satyrane him towards did addresse,
    To weet, what wight he was, and what his quest:
    And comming nigh, eftsoones he gan to gesse
    Both by the burning hart, which on his brest
    He bare, and by the colours in his crest,
    That Paridell[4] it was. Tho to him yode,°   *went*
    And him saluting,° as beseeméd best,   *greeting*
    Gan first inquire of tydings farre abrode;
And afterwardes, on what adventure now he rode.

46

Who thereto answering, said; "The tydings bad,
    Which now in Faerie court all men do tell,
    Which turnéd hath great mirth, to mourning sad,
    Is the late ruine of proud Marinell,
    And suddein parture of faire Florimell,
    To find him forth: and after her are gone
    All the brave knights, that doen in armes excell,
    To savegard her, ywandred all alone;
Emongst the rest my lot (unworthy) is to be one."

47

"Ah gentle knight," said then Sir Satyrane,
    "Thy labour all is lost, I greatly dread,
    That hast a thanklesse service on thee ta'ne,
    And offrest sacrifice unto the dead:
    For dead, I surely doubt,° thou maist aread   *fear*

---

4. Paridell's name indicates his ancestral connection with the Trojan Paris; this relationship is outlined in ix. 36–37. The description of Paris by Natalis Comes is relevant: "Nature made him noble, but a little time joined him with lust" (*op. cit.*, VI. 23).

Henceforth for ever Florimell to be,
That all the noble knights of Maydenhead,
Which her adored, may sore repent° with me,   *grieve*
And all faire Ladies may for ever sory be."

48

Which words when Paridell had heard, his hew
Gan greatly chaunge, and seemed dismayd to bee;
Then said, "Faire Sir, how may I weene it trew,
That ye doe tell in such uncertaintee?
Or speake ye of report,° or did ye see   *rumor*
Just cause of dread, that makes ye doubt so sore?
For perdie else how mote it ever bee,
That ever hand should dare for to engore°   *shed*
Her noble bloud? the heavens such crueltie abhore."

49

"These eyes did see, that they will ever rew
T'have seene," quoth he, "when as a monstrous beast
The Palfrey, whereon she did travell, slew,
And of his bowels made his bloudie feast:
Which speaking token sheweth at the least
Her certaine losse, if not her sure decay:°   *destruction*
Besides, that more suspition encreast,
I found her golden girdle cast astray,°   *aside*
Distaynd with durt and bloud, as relique of the pray."

50

"Aye me," said Paridell, "the signes be sad,
And but God turne the same to good soothsay,°   *omen*
That Ladies safetie is sore to be drad:°   *feared*
Yet will I not forsake my forward way,
Till triall doe more certaine truth bewray."
"Faire Sir," quoth he, "well may it you succeed,
Ne long shall Satyrane behind you stay,
But to the rest, which in this Quest proceed
My labour adde, and be partaker of their speed."°   *fortune*

51

"Ye noble knights," said then the Squire of Dames,
"Well may ye speed in so praiseworthy paine:
But sith the Sunne now ginnes to slake his beames,
In deawy vapours of the westerne maine,
And lose° the teme out of his weary waine,   *release*
Mote not mislike° you also to abate   *ill please*
Your zealous hast, till morrow next againe
Both light of heaven, and strength of men relate:°   *bring back*
Which if ye please, to yonder castle turne your gate."°   *steps*

52

That counsell pleaséd well; so all yfere°   *together*
Forth marchéd to a Castle them before,
Where soone arriving, they restrainéd were
Of readie entrance, which ought evermore

To errant knights be commun: wondrous sore
Thereat displeasd they were, till that young Squire
Gan them informe the cause, why that same dore
Was shut to all, which lodging did desire:
The which to let you weet, will further time require.

Canto IX

Malbecco will no straunge knights host,
　For peevish gealosie:
Paridell giusts° with Britomart:　　　　　　　*jousts*
　Both shew their auncestrie.

1

Redoubted knights, and honorable Dames,[1]
　To whom I levell° all my labours end,　　　　*direct*
　Right sore I feare, least with unworthy blames
This odious argument my rimes should shend,°　　*disgrace*
　Or ought your goodly patience offend,
　Whiles of a wanton Lady I do write,
Which with her loose incontinence doth blend°　　*blemish*
　The shyning glory of your soveraigne light,
And knighthood fowle defacéd by a faithlesse knight.

2

But never let th'ensample of the bad
　Offend the good: for good by paragone°　　　*comparison*
　Of evill, may more notably be rad,°　　　　*perceived*
As white seemes fairer, matcht with blacke attone;°　*together*
　Ne all are shaméd by the fault of one:
　For lo in heaven, whereas all goodnesse is,
　Emongst the Angels, a whole legione
Of wicked Sprights did fall from happy blis;
What wonder then, if one of women all did mis?°　　*err*

3

Then listen Lordings, if ye list to weet
　The cause, why Satyrane and Paridell
　Mote not be entertaynd, as seeméd meet,
Into that Castle (as that Squire does tell.)
　"Therein a cancred° crabbéd Carle does dwell,　*malignant*
　That has no skill° of Court nor courtesie,　　*knowledge*
　Ne cares, what men say of him ill or well;
　For all his dayes he drownes in privitie,°　　*seclusion*
Yet has full large to live, and spend at libertie.

4

"But all his mind is set on mucky pelfe,°　　　*lucre*
　To hoord up heapes of evill gotten masse,°　　*wealth*
　For which he others wrongs, and wreckes° himselfe;　*harms*

---

1. Sts. 1–2 are based on the opening stanzas of Ariosto, *Orlando Furioso,* XXVIII.

Yet is he linckéd to a lovely lasse,
  Whose beauty doth her bounty° far surpasse,   *virtue*
  The which to him both far unequall yeares,
  And also far unlike conditions has;
  For she does joy to play emongst her peares,[2]
And to be free from hard restraint and gealous feares.

5

"But he is old, and witheréd like hay,
  Unfit faire Ladies service to supply;
  The privie° guilt whereof makes him alway   *secret*
  Suspect her truth, and keepe continuall spy
  Upon her with his other blinckéd° eye;   *dim*
  Ne suffreth he resort° of living wight   *visiting*
  Approch to her, ne keepe her company,
  But in close bowre her mewes° from all mens sight,   *shuts up*
Deprived of kindly° joy and naturall delight.   *natural*

6

"Malbecco he, and Hellenore she hight,
  Unfitly yokt together in one teeme,[3]
  That is the cause, why never any knight
  Is suffred here to enter, but he seeme
  Such, as no doubt of him he neede misdeeme."°   *suspect*
  Thereat Sir Satyrane gan smile, and say;
  "Extremely mad° the man I surely deeme,   *crazed*
  That weenes with watch and hard restraint to stay°   *restrain*
A womans will, which is disposd to go astray.

7

"In vaine he feares that, which he cannot shonne:
  For who wotes not, that womans subtiltyes
  Can guilen° Argus,[4] when she list misdonne?°   *deceive/misbehave*
  It is not yron bandes, nor hundred eyes,
  Nor brasen walls, nor many wakefull spyes,
  That can withhold her wilfull wandring feet;
  But fast° good will with gentle curtesyes,   *firm*
  And timely service to her pleasures meet
May her perhaps containe, that else would algates fleet."°   *fly*

8

"Then is he not more mad," said Paridell,
  "That hath himselfe unto such service sold,
  In dolefull thraldome all his dayes to dwell?
  For sure a foole I do him firmely hold,
  That loves his fetters, though they were of gold.

2. I.e., to take an active part in sophisticated society.

3. The aged and jealous husband, his bored young wife, and the gay sophisticate who turns matters to his own advantage, are familiar characters in literature from ancient times; cf. Chaucer, *The Merchant's Tale*. Spenser draws some details of his narrative from *Orlando Furioso*, XXXII; but the names of Malbecco (i.e., "cuckold") and his wife, together with that of Paridell, indicate the allegorical connection of these figures with Helen of Troy, her husband Menelaus, and her lover Paris.

4. The hundred-eyed monster ordered by Juno to watch Io, beloved by Jove (*Metamorphoses*, I. 626–721).

But why do we devise of others ill,
   Whiles thus we suffer this same dotard old,
   To keepe us out, in scorne of his owne will,
And rather do not ransack all, and him selfe kill?"

9

"Nay let us first," said Satyrane, "entreat
   The man by gentle meanes, to let us in,
   And afterwardes affray with cruell threat,
   Ere that we to efforce it do begin:
   Then if all fayle, we will by force it win,
   And eke reward the wretch for his mesprise,°   *insolence*
   As may be worthy of his haynous sin."
   That counsell pleasd: then Paridell did rise,
And to the Castle gate approcht in quiet wise.

10

Whereat soft knocking, entrance he desyrd.
   The good man selfe, which then the Porter playd,
   Him answeréd, that all were now retyrd
   Unto their rest, and all the keyes convayd
   Unto their maister, who in bed was layd,
   That none him durst awake out of his dreme;
   And therefore them of patience gently prayd.
   Then Paridell began to chaunge his theme,
And threatned him with force and punishment extreme.

11

But all in vaine; for nought mote him relent,
   And now so long before the wicket fast
   They wayted, that the night was forward spent,[5]
   And the faire welkin° fowly overcast,   *sky*
   Gan blowen up a bitter stormy blast,
   With shoure and hayle so horrible and dred,
   That this faire many° were compeld at last,   *company*
   To fly for succour to a little shed,
The which beside the gate for swine was orderéd.°   *prepared*

12

It fortunéd, soone after they were gone,
   Another knight,[6] whom tempest thither brought,
   Came to that Castle, and with earnest mone,°   *plea*
   Like as the rest, late entrance deare besought;
   But like so as the rest he prayd for nought,
   For flatly he of entrance was refusd,
   Sorely thereat he was displeasd, and thought
   How to avenge himselfe so sore abusd,
And evermore the Carle of curtesie[7] accusd.

5. I.e., well advanced. The episode described in sts. 11–18 is apparently based on a similar situation in the *Thebaid* (I. 401–481), an epic by the Roman poet Statius (61–c.96 A.D.); and on Bradamante's actions outside the Castle of Tristan in Ariosto, *Orlando Furioso*, XXXII.
6. I.e., Britomart.
7. I.e., of discourtesy.

13

But to avoyde th'intollerable stowre,°   *storm*
  He was compeld to seeke some refuge neare,
  And to that shed, to shrowd him from the showre,
  He came, which full of guests he found whyleare,°   *already*
  So as he was not let to enter there:
  Whereat he gan to wex exceeding wroth,
  And swore, that he would lodge with them yfere,
  Or them dislodge, all were they liefe or loth;[8]
And so defide them each, and so defide them both.

14

Both were full loth to leave that needfull tent,°   *shed*
  And both full loth in darkenesse to debate;
  Yet both full liefe him lodging to have lent,
  And both full liefe his boasting to abate;
  But chiefly Paridell his hart did grate,°   *fret*
  To heare him threaten so despightfully,
  As if he did a dogge to kenell rate,°   *scold*
  That durst not barke; and rather had he dy,
Then when he was defide, in coward corner ly.

15

Tho hastily remounting to his steed,
  He forth issewed; like as a boistrous wind,
  Which in th'earthes hollow caves hath long bin hid,
  And shut up fast within her prisons blind,°   *dark*
  Makes the huge element against her kind
  To move, and tremble as it were agast,
  Until that it an issew forth may find;
  Then forth it breakes, and with his furious blast
Confounds both land and seas, and skyes doth overcast.

16

Their steel-hed speares they strongly coucht, and met
  Together with impetuous rage and forse,
  That with the terrour of their fierce affret,°   *encounter*
  They rudely drove to ground both man and horse,
  That each awhile lay like a sencelesse corse.
  But Paridell sore bruséd with the blow,
  Could not arise, the counterchaunge to scorse,[9]
  Till that young Squire him rearéd from below;
Then drew he his bright sword, and gan about him throw.°   *brandish*

17

But Satyrane forth stepping, did them stay
  And with faire treatie° pacifide their ire,   *speech*
  Then when they were accorded° from the fray,   *reconciled*
  Against that Castles Lord they gan conspire,

8. I.e., whether they were willing or not.   9. I.e., to strike back by way of requital.

To heape on him dew vengeaunce for his hire.°   *reward*
They bene agreed, and to the gates they goe
To burne the same with unquenchable fire,
And that uncurteous Carle their commune foe
To do fowle death to dye, or wrap in grievous woe.

18

Malbecco seeing them resolved in deed
  To flame the gates, and hearing them to call
  For fire in earnest, ran with fearefull° speed,   *full of fear*
  And to them calling from the castle wall,
  Besought them humbly, him to beare with all,[1]
  As ignoraunt of servaunts bad abuse,
  And slacke attendaunce unto straungers call.
  The knights were willing all things to excuse,
Though nought beleved, and entraunce late did not refuse.

19

They bene ybrought into a comely bowre,°   *chamber*
  And served of all things that mote needfull bee;
  Yet secretly their hoste did on them lowre,°   *scowl*
  And welcomde more for feare, then charitee;
  But they dissembled, what they did not see,[2]
  And welcoméd themselves. Each gan undight
  Their garments wet, and weary armour free,
  To dry them selves by Vulcanes flaming light,
And eke their lately bruzéd parts to bring in plight.°   *health*

20

And eke that straunger knight emongst the rest
  Was for like need enforst to disaray:
  Tho whenas vailéd° was her loftie crest,   *lowered*
  Her golden locks, that were in tramels° gay   *plaits*
  Unbounden, did them selves adowne display,
  And raught° unto her heeles; like sunny beames,   *reached*
  That in a cloud their light did long time stay,
  Their vapour vaded,° shew their golden gleames,   *vanished*
And through the persant aire shoote forth their azure streames.[3]

21

She also dofte her heavy haberjeon,°   *coat of mail*
  Which the faire feature of her limbs did hyde,
  And her well plighted° frock, which she did won°   *folded/use*
  To tucke about her short, when she did ryde,
  She low let fall, that flowd from her lanck° syde   *slender*
  Downe to her foot, with carelesse° modestee.   *simple*
  Then of them all she plainly was espyde,
  To be a woman wight, unwist° to bee,   *unknown*
The fairest woman wight, that ever eye did see.

1. I.e., to bear with him.
2. I.e., they pretended not to notice his discourtesy.
3. The ultimate source for this simile, which appears also in Ariosto, *Orlando Furioso*, XXXII. 80, and in Tasso, *Gerusalemme Liberata*, IV. 29, is Ovid, *Metamorphoses*, XIV. 767–769. Cf. also III. i. 43.

22

Like as Minerva,[4] being late returnd
  From slaughter of the Giaunts conqueréd;
  Where proud Encelade, whose wide nosethrils burnd
  With breathéd flames, like to a furnace red,
  Transfixéd with the speare, downe tombled ded
  From top of Hemus, by him heapéd hye;
  Hath loosd her helmet from her lofty hed,
  And her Gorgonian[5] shield gins to untye
From her left arme, to rest in glorious victorye.

23

Which whenas they beheld, they smitten were
  With great amazement of so wondrous sight,
  And each on other, and they all on her
  Stood gazing, as if suddein great affright
  Had them surprised. At last avizing° right,   *perceiving*
  Her goodly personage and glorious hew,°   *form*
  Which they so much mistooke, they tooke delight
  In their first errour, and yet still anew
With wonder of her beauty fed their hungry vew.

24

Yet note° their hungry vew be satisfide,   *might not*
  But seeing still the more desired to see,
  And ever firmely fixéd did abide
  In contemplation of divinitie:
  But most they mervaild at her chevalree,
  And noble prowesse, which they had approved,°   *tested*
  That much they faynd to know, who she mote bee;
  Yet none of all them her thereof amoved,°   *stirred*
Yet every one her likte, and every one her loved.

25

And Paridell though partly discontent
  With his late fall, and fowle indignity,
  Yet was soone wonne his malice to relent,°   *soften*
  Through gracious regard of her faire eye,
  And knightly worth, which he too late did try,°   *experience*
  Yet triéd did adore. Supper was dight;°   *set out*
  Then they Malbecco prayd of curtesy,
  That of his Lady they might have the sight,
And company at meat, to do them more delight.

26

But he to shift their curious request,
  Gan causen,° why she could not come in place;   *explain*
  Her crased° health, her late° recourse to rest,   *infirm/recent*

4. "Bellona" in the 1590 edition. Cf.
E.K.'s Glosse to "October," where
Bellona is identified with "the goddesse
of battaile, that is Pallas [Athena]."
Enceladus, the giant son of Tartarus
and Earth, was destroyed by Zeus; but
it was Typhoeus whom Zeus overthrew
on Mt. Haemus, a mountain range in
Thrace.
5. Minerva wore the snaky-haired head
of Medusa, the Gorgon slain by
Perseus, in the "aegis" or breastplate
of her armour (*Metamorphoses*, IV.
803).

And humid evening ill for sicke folkes cace:
But none of those excuses could take place;[6]
Ne would they eate, till she in presence came.
She came in presence with right comely grace,
And fairely them saluted,° as became,   *greeted*
And shewd her selfe in all a gentle curteous Dame.

27

They sate to meat, and Satyrane his chaunce
  Was her before,[7] and Paridell besyde;
  But he him selfe sate looking still askaunce,°   *sidewise*
  Gainst Britomart, and ever closely eyde
  Sir Satyrane, that glaunces might not glyde:
  But his blind eye, that syded Paridell,
  All his demeasnure° from his sight did hyde: *behavior*
  On her faire face so did he feede his fill,
And sent close° messages of love to her at will.   *secret*

28

And ever and anone, when none was aware,
  With speaking lookes, that close embassage° bore,   *message*
  He roved° at her, and told his secret care: *darted*
  For all that art he learnéd had of yore.
  Ne was she ignoraunt of that lewd lore,
  But in his eye his meaning wisely red,
  And with the like him answerd evermore:
  She sent at him one firie dart, whose hed
Empoisned was with privy° lust, and gealous dred.   *secret*

29

He from that deadly throw° made no defence,   *thrust*
  But to the wound his weake hart opened wyde;
  The wicked engine° through false influence,   *device*
  Past through his eyes, and secretly did glyde
  Into his hart, which it did sorely gryde.°   *pierce*
  But nothing new to him was that same paine,
  Ne paine at all; for he so oft had tryde
  The powre thereof, and loved so oft in vaine,
That thing of course[8] he counted,° love to entertaine.   *regarded*

30

Thenceforth to her he sought to intimate
  His inward griefe, by meanes to him well knowne,
  Now Bacchus fruit[9] out of the silver plate°   *cup*
  He on the table dasht, as overthrowne,
  Or of the fruitfull liquor overflowne,
  And by the dauncing bubbles did divine,
  Or therein write to let his love be showne;

6. I.e., was acceptable.
7. I.e., was to sit opposite her.
8. I.e., as a usual occurrence.
9. I.e., the wine. This cup, like those held by Duessa (I. viii. 14) and Excess (II. xii. 56), signifies (in the particular context of love, lust, and chastity) the perversion or parody of a morally or spiritually healthful condition. Paridell's love hints are based on Ovid, *Heroides*, XVII. 75–90.

Which well she red out of the learnéd line,
A sacrament prophane in mistery of wine.

31

And when so of his hand the pledge she raught,[1]
   The guilty cup she fainéd to mistake,°   *let slip*
   And in her lap did shed her idle draught,
   Shewing desire her inward flame to slake:°   *relieve*
   By such close signes they secret way did make
   Unto their wils, and one eyes watch escape;
   Two eyes him needeth, for to watch and wake,
   Who lovers will deceive. Thus was the ape,
By their faire handling, put into Malbeccoes cape.[2]

32

Now when of meats and drinks they had their fill,
   Purpose° was movéd by that gentle Dame,   *proposal*
   Unto those knights adventurous, to tell
   Of deeds of armes, which unto them became,° *happened*
   And every one his kindred, and his name.
   Then Paridell, in whom a kindly° pryde   *natural*
   Of gracious speach, and skill his words to frame
   Abounded, being glad of so fit tyde°   *occasion*
Him to commend to her, thus spake, of all well eyde.

33

"Troy, that art now nought, but an idle name,
   And in thine ashes buried low dost lie,
   Though whilome far much greater then thy fame,
   Before that angry Gods, and cruell skye
   Upon thee heapt a direfull destinie,
   What boots it boast thy glorious descent,
   And fetch from heaven thy great Genealogie,
   Sith all thy worthy prayses being blent,°   *stained*
Their of-spring hath embaste, and later glory shent.° *disgraced*

34

"Most famous Worthy of the world, by whome
   That warre was kindled, which did Troy inflame,
   And stately towres of Ilion whilome
   Brought unto balefull ruine, was by name
   Sir Paris far renowmd through noble fame,
   Who through great prowesse and bold hardinesse,
   From Lacedaemon fetcht the fairest Dame,
   That ever Greece did boast, or knight possesse,
Whom Venus to him gave for meed of worthinesse.[3]

35

"Faire Helene, flowre of beautie excellent,
   And girlond of the mighty Conquerours,
   That madest many Ladies deare lament

---

1. I.e., when she reached to take the
cup from his hand.
2. I.e., they made a fool of him (as in

Chaucer, Introduction to "The Prior-
ess's Tale," 1630).
3. Cf. II. vii. 55 and note.

The heavie losse of their brave Paramours,
  Which they far off beheld from Trojan toures,
  And saw the fieldes of faire Scamander[4] strowne
  With carcases of noble warrioures,
  Whose fruitless lives were under furrow sowne,
And Xanthus sandy bankes with bloud all overflowne.

36

"From him my linage I derive aright,
  Who long before the ten yeares siege of Troy,
  Whiles yet on Ida he a shepheard hight,
  On faire Oenone got a lovely boy,
  Whom for remembraunce of her passéd joy,
  She of his Father Parius[5] did name;
  Who, after Greekes did Priams realme destroy,
  Gathred the Trojan reliques saved from flame,
And with them sayling thence, to th'Isle of Paros[6] came.

37

"That was by him cald Paros, which before
  Hight Nausa, there he many yeares did raine,
  And built Nausicle by the Pontick[7] shore,
  The which he dying left next in remaine
  To Paridas his sonne.
  From whom I Paridell by kin descend;
  But for faire Ladies love, and glories gaine,
  My native soile have left, my dayes to spend
In sewing° deeds of armes, my lives and labours end."   *following*

38

Whenas the noble Britomart heard tell
  Of Trojan warres, and Priams Citie sackt,
  The ruefull story of Sir Paridell,
  She was empassiond at that piteous act,
  With zelous envy° of Greekes cruell fact,°   *indignation/deed*
  Against that nation, from whose race of old
  She heard, that she was lineally extract:°   *descended*
  For noble Britons sprong from Trojans bold,
And Troynovant[8] was built of old Troyes ashes cold.

39

Then sighing soft awhile, at last she thus:
  "O lamentable fall of famous towne,
  Which raignd so many yeares victorious,
  And of all Asie bore the soveraigne crowne,
  In one sad night consumd, and throwen downe:
  What stony hart, that heares thy haplesse fate,
  Is not empierst with deepe compassiowne,
  And makes ensample of mans wretched state,
That floures so fresh at morne, and fades at evening late?

4. The river Scamander (also called
the Xanthus, after its river god) flowed
across the plains of Troy.
5. Spenser alters the name of Paris's
son by Oenone (actually Corythus) to
emphasize the direct line of descent
claimed by Paridell.
6. An island in the Aegean Sea.
7. The Black Sea.
8. I.e., London.

40

"Behold, Sir, how your pitifull complaint°   *lament*
  Hath found another partner of your payne:
  For nothing may impresse so deare constraint,°   *distress*
  As countries cause, and commune foes disdayne.
  But if it should not grieve you, backe agayne
  To turne your course, I would to heare desyre,
  What to Aeneas fell; sith that men sayne
  He was not in the Cities wofull fyre
Consumed, but did him selfe to safétie retyre."

41

"Anchyses sonne begot of Venus faire,"
  Said he, "out of the flames for safegard fled,
  And with a remnant did to sea repaire,
  Where he through fatall errour[9] long was led
  Full many yeares, and weetlesse° wanderéd   *at random*
  From shore to shore, emongst the Lybicke° sands,   *Lybian*
  Ere rest he found. Much there he sufferéd,
  And many perils past in forreine lands,
To save his people sad from victours vengefull hands.[1]

42

"At last in Latium[2] he did arrive,
  Where he with cruell warre was entertaind
  Of th'inland folke, which sought him backe to drive,
  Till he with old Latinus was constraind,
  To contract wedlock:[3] (so the fates ordaind.)
  Wedlock contract in bloud, and eke in blood
  Accomplishéd, that many deare complaind:
  The rivall slaine, the victour through the flood
Escapéd hardly, hardly praisd his wedlock good.

43

"Yet after all, he victour did survive,
  And with Latinus did the kingdome part.°   *divide*
  But after, when both nations gan to strive,
  Into their names the title to convart,[4]
  His sonne Iülus did from thence depart,
  With all the warlike youth of Trojans bloud,
  And in long Alba[5] plast his throne apart,
  Where faire it florishéd, and long time stoud,
Till Romulus renewing it, to Rome removd."

9. I.e., fated wandering.
1. Spenser passes rapidly over the earlier wanderings of Aeneas, omitting the encounter with Dido and the descent into the underworld, because he is chiefly concerned at this point to emphasize the Trojan ancestry of the British race.
2. Abode of the ancient Latins, whose king, Latinus, gave his daughter Lavinia in marriage to Aeneas (*Aeneid*, VII. 267–274); this precipitated war with the Rutulian leader Turnus, to whom Lavinia had previously been promised as his bride.
3. I.e., to ally himself through marriage with Lavinia.
4. I.e., to claim sole power.
5. Alba Longa, the most ancient town in Latium, situated on the slopes of Mt. Albanus, about 20 miles southeast of modern Rome. Spenser depends on Boccaccio (*op. cit.*, VI. 54) for his reference to the move of Iulus to Alba Longa.

44

"There there," said Britomart, "a fresh appeard
  The glory of the later world to spring,
  And Troy againe out of her dust was reard,
  To sit in second seat of soveraigne king,
  Of all the world under her governing.
  But a third kingdome yet is to arise,
  Out of the Trojans scatteréd of-spring,
  That in all glory and great enterprise,
Both first and second Troy shall dare to equalise.°   *equal*

45

"It Troynovant is hight, that with the waves
  Of wealthy Thamis[6] washéd is along,
  Upon whose stubborne neck, whereat he raves
  With roring rage, and sore him selfe does throng,°   *press*
  That all men feare to tempt his billowes strong,
  She fastned hath her foot, which standes so hy,
  That it a wonder of the world is song
  In forreine landes, and all which passen by,
Beholding it from far, do thinke it threates the skye.

46

"The Trojan Brute did first that Citie found,
  And Hygate made the meare° thereof by West,   *boundary*
  And Overt gate by North: that is the bound
  Toward the land; two rivers bound the rest.
  So huge a scope at first him seeméd best,
  To be the compasse of his kingdomes seat:
  So huge a mind could not in lesser rest,
  Ne in small meares containe his glory great,
That Albion[7] had conquered first by warlike feat."

47

"Ah fairest Lady knight," said Paridell,
  "Pardon I pray my heedlesse oversight,
  Who had forgot, that whilome I heard tell
  From aged Mnemon;[8] for my wits bene light.
  Indeed he said (if I remember right,)
  That of the antique Trojan stocke, there grew
  Another plant, that raught° to wondrous hight,   *reached*
  And far abroad his mighty branches threw,
Into the utmost Angle of the world he knew.

48

"For that same Brute, whom much he did advaunce°   *praise*
  In all his speach, was Sylvius his sonne,[9]
  Whom having slaine, through luckles arrowes glaunce

6. The river Thames, spanned by London Bridge.
7. The name of Britain at the time of Brute's arrival there (cf. Geoffrey of Monmouth, *op. cit.*, I. xvi).
8. From Greek, "memory."

9. I.e., the son of Sylvius. Sts. 48–51 are based on the account in Geoffrey of Monmouth, I. iii–xvii. Geoffrey, however, does not state that Brute founded Lincoln.

He fled for feare of that he had misdonne,
Or else for shame, so fowle reproch to shonne,
And with him led to sea an youthly trayne,°   *company*
Where wearie wandring they long time did wonne,
And many fortunes proved° in th'Ocean mayne,   *experienced*
And great adventures found, that now were long to sayne.

49

"At last by fatall° course they driven were   *fated*
   Into an Island spatious and brode,
   The furthest North, that did to them appeare:
   Which after rest they seeking far abrode,
   Found it the fittest soyle for their abode,
   Fruitfull of all things fit for living foode,
   But wholy wast, and void of peoples trode,°   *footstep*
   Save an huge nation of the Geaunts broode,
That fed on living flesh, and druncke mens vitall blood.

50

"Whom he through wearie wars and labours long,
   Subdewd with losse of many Britons bold:
   In which the great Goemagot of strong
   Corineus, and Coulin of Debon old
   Were overthrowne, and layd on th'earth full cold,
   Which quakéd under their so hideous masse,
   A famous history to be enrold
   In everlasting moniments of brasse,
That all the antique Worthies merits far did passe.

51

"His worke great Troynovant, his worke is eke
   Faire Lincolne, both renowméd far away,
   That who from East to West will endlong° seeke,   *from end to end*
   Cannot two fairer Cities find this day,
   Except Cleopolis: so heard I say
   Old Mnemon. Therefore Sir, I greet you well
   Your countrey kin,° and you entirely pray   *kinsman*
   Of pardon for the strife, which late befell
Betwixt us both unknowne." So ended Paridell.

52

But all the while, that he these speaches spent,
   Upon his lips hong faire Dame Hellenore,
   With vigilant regard, and dew attent,°   *attention*
   Fashioning worlds of fancies evermore
   In her fraile wit, that now her quite forlore:
   The whiles unwares away her wondring eye,
   And greedy eares her weake hart from her bore:
   Which he perceiving, ever privily
In speaking, many false belgardes° at her let fly.   *loving looks*

53

So long these knights discourséd diversly,
   Of straunge affaires, and noble hardiment,

Which they had past with mickle jeopardy,
That now the humid night was farforth spent,
And heavenly lampes were halfendeale ybrent:[1]
Which th'old man seeing well, who too long thought
Every discourse and every argument,
Which by the houres he measuréd, besought
Them go to rest. So all unto their bowres were brought.

Canto X

Paridell rapeth Hellenore:
Malbecco her pursewes:
Findes emongst Satyres, whence with him
To turne she doth refuse.

1

The morow next, so soone as Phoebus Lamp
  Bewrayéd had the world with early light,   *revealed*
  And fresh Aurora had the shady damp
  Out of the goodly heaven amovéd quight,
  Faire Britomart and that same Faerie knight[1]
  Uprose, forth on their journey for to wend:
  But Paridell complaynd, that his late fight
  With Britomart, so sore did him offend,°   *trouble*
That ryde he could not, till his hurts he did amend.

2

So forth they fared, but he behind them stayd,
  Maulgre his host, who grudgéd grievously,
  To house a guest, that would be needes obayd,
  And of his owne him left not liberty:
  Might wanting measure moveth surquedry.[2]
  Two things he fearéd, but the third was death;
  That fierce youngmans unruly maistery;
  His money, which he loved as living breath;
And his faire wife, whom honest long he kept uneath.°   *with difficulty*

3

But patience perforce he must abie,°   *endure*
  What fortune and his fate on him will lay,
  Fond° is the feare, that findes no remedie;   *foolish*
  Yet warily he watcheth every way,
  By which he feareth evill happen may:
  So th'evill thinkes by watching to prevent;
  Ne doth he suffer her, nor night, nor day,
  Out of his sight her selfe once to absent.
So doth he punish her and eke himselfe torment.

4

But Paridell kept better watch, then hee,
  A fit occasion for his turne to find:

---

1. I.e., half consumed.
1. I.e., Satyrane.

2. I.e., excessive power breeds arrogance.

False love, why do men say, thou canst not see,
   And in their foolish fancie feigne thee blind,
   That with thy charmes° the sharpest sight doest bind,   *spells*
   And to thy will abuse? Thou walkest free,
   And seest every secret of the mind;
   Thou seest all, yet none at all sees thee;
All that is by the working of thy Deitee.

5

So perfect in that art was Paridell,
   That he Malbeccoes halfen eye did wyle,[3]
   His halfen eye he wiléd wondrous well,
   And Hellenors both eyes did eke beguyle,
   Both eyes and hart attonce, during the whyle
   That he there sojournéd his wounds to heale;
   That Cupid selfe it seeing, close did smyle,
   To weet how he her love away did steale,
And bad, that none their joyous treason should reveale.

6

The learnéd lover lost no time nor tyde,
   That least avantage mote to him afford,
   Yet bore so faire a saile, that none espyde
   His secret drift,° till he her layd abord.   *aim*
   When so in open place, and commune bord,°   *table*
   He fortuned her to meet, with commune speach
   He courted her, yet bayted° every word,   *spoke softly*
   That his ungentle hoste n'ote him appeach
Of vile ungentlenesse, or hospitages breach.[4]

7

But when apart (if ever her apart)
   He found, then his false engins° fast he plyde,   *wiles*
   And all the sleights unbosomd in his hart;
   He sighed, he sobd, he swownd, he perdy° dyde,   *verily*
   And cast himselfe on ground her fast° besyde: *close*
   Tho when againe he him bethought to live,
   He wept, and wayld, and false laments belyde,°   *counterfeited*
   Saying, but if[5] she Mercie would him give
That he mote algates dye, yet did his death forgive.[6]

8

And otherwhiles with amorous delights,
   And pleasing toyes he would her entertaine,
   Now singing sweetly, to surprise her sprights,
   Now making layes of love and lovers paine,
   Bransles,° Ballads, virelayes,° and verses vaine;   *dances/songs*
   Oft purposes,° oft riddles he devysd,   *word games*
   And thousands like, which flowéd in his braine,

---

3. I.e., beguiled Malbecco's imperfect sight.
4. I.e., could not accuse him of discourtesy or of conduct unbecoming to a guest.
5. I.e., unless.
6. I.e., yet in fact gave up his "resolve" to die.

With which he fed her fancie, and entysd
To take to his new love, and leave her old despysd.

9

And every where he might, and every while
  He did her service dewtifull, and sewed°   *followed*
  At hand with humble pride, and pleasing guile,
  So closely yet, that none but she it vewed,
  Who well perceivéd all, and all indewed.°   *took in*
  Thus finely did he his false nets dispred,
  With which he many weake harts had subdewed
Of yore, and many had ylike misled:
What wonder then, if she were likewise carriéd?

10

No fort so fensible,° no wals so strong,   *fortified*
  But that continuall battery will rive,
  Or daily siege through dispurvayance° long, *lack of supplies*
  And lacke of reskewes will to parley drive;
  And Peece,° that unto parley eare will give,   *fortress*
  Will shortly yeeld it selfe, and will be made
  The vassall of the victors will bylive:°   *quickly*
  That stratageme had oftentimes assayd
This crafty Paramoure, and now it plaine displayd.

11

For through his traines° he her intrappéd hath,   *wiles*
  That she her love and hart hath wholy sold
  To him, without regard of gaine, or scath,°   *harm*
  Or care of credite, or of husband old,
  Whom she hath vowed to dub a faire Cucquold.
  Nought wants but time and place, which shortly shee
  Devizéd hath, and to her lover told.
  It pleaséd well. So well they both agree;
So readie rype to ill, ill wemens counsels bee.

12

Darke was the Evening, fit for lovers stealth,
  When chaunst Malbecco busie be elsewhere,
  She to his closet° went, where all his wealth *private room*
  Lay hid: thereof she countlesse summes did reare,° *take*
  The which she meant away with her to beare;
  The rest she fyred for sport, or for despight;°   *malice*
  As Hellene, when she saw aloft appeare
  The Trojane flames, and reach to heavens hight
Did clap her hands, and joyéd at that dolefull sight.[7]

13

This second Hellene, faire Dame Hellenore,
  The whiles her husband ranne with sory haste,
  To quench the flames, which she had tyned° before, *kindled*
  Laught at his foolish labour spent in waste;

7. Perhaps based on allusions in the   conduct at the time of Troy's fall.
Aeneid (e.g., VI. 517–519 to Helen's

And ranne into her lovers armes right fast;
Where streight embracéd, she to him did cry,
And call aloud for helpe, ere helpe were past;
For loe that Guest would beare her forcibly,
And meant to ravish her, that rather had to dy.

14

The wretched man hearing her call for ayd,
And readie seeing him with her to fly,
In his disquiet mind was much dismayd:
But when againe he backward cast his eye,
And saw the wicked fire so furiously
Consume his hart, and scorch his Idoles face,
He was therewith distresséd diversly,
Ne wist he how to turne, nor to what place;
Was never wretched man in such a wofull cace.

15

Ay° when to him she cryde, to her he turnd,   *always*
And left the fire; love money overcame:
But when he markéd, how his money burnd,
He left his wife; money did love disclame:°   *renounce*
Both was he loth to loose his lovéd Dame,
And loth to leave his liefest pelfe behind,
Yet sith he n'ote° save both, he saved that same,   *might not*
Which was the dearest to his donghill mind,
The God of his desire, the joy of misers blind.

16

Thus whilest all things in troublous uprore were,
And all men busie to suppresse the flame,
The loving couple need no reskew feare,
But leasure had, and libertie to frame
Their purpost flight, free from all mens reclame;°   *recall*
And Night, the patronesse of love-stealth faire,
Gave them safe conduct, till to end they came:
So bene they gone yfeare,° a wanton paire   *together*
Of lovers loosely knit, where list them to repaire.

17

Soone as the cruell flames yslakéd° were,   *abated*
Malbecco seeing, how his losse did lye,
Out of the flames, which he had quencht whylere
Into huge waves of griefe and gealosye
Full deepe emplongéd was, and drownéd nye,
Twixt inward doole° and felonous° despight;   *grief/fierce*
He raved, he wept, he stampt, he lowd did cry,
And all the passions, that in man may light,°   *occur*
Did him attonce oppresse, and vex his caytive spright.

18

Long thus he chawd the cud of inward griefe,
And did consume his gall with anguish sore,
Still when he muséd on his late mischiefe,

Then still the smart thereof increaséd more,
And seemed more grievous, then it was before:
At last when sorrow he saw booted nought,
Ne griefe might not his love to him restore,
He gan devise, how her he reskew mought,
Ten thousand wayes he cast in his confuséd thought.

19

At last resolving, like a pilgrim pore,
  To search her forth, where so she might be fond,
  And bearing with him treasure in close° store,   secret
  The rest he leaves in ground: So takes in hond
  To seeke her endlong, both by sea and lond.
  Long he her sought, he sought her farre and nere,
  And every where that he mote understond,
Of knights and ladies any meetings were,
And of eachone he met, he tydings did inquere.

20

But all in vaine, his woman was too wise,
  Ever to come into his clouch° againe,   grip
  And he too simple ever to surprise
  The jolly° Paridell, for all his paine.   gay
  One day, as he forpasséd by[8] the plaine
  With weary pace, he farre away espide
  A couple, seeming well to be his twaine,
  Which hovéd° close under a forrest side,   waited
As if they lay in wait, or else themselves did hide.

21

Well weenéd he, that those the same mote bee,
  And as he better did their shape avize,
  Him seeméd more their manner did agree;
  For th'one was arméd all in warlike wize,
  Whom, to be Paridell he did devize;°   guess
  And th'other all yclad in garments light,
  Discoloured° like to womanish disguise,   many colored
  He did resemble° to his Ladie bright;   liken
And ever his faint hart much earnéd° at the sight.   yearned

22

And ever faine° he towards them would goe,   eagerly
  But yet durst not for dread approchen nie,
  But stood aloofe, unweeting what to doe;
  Till that prickt forth with loves extremitie,
  That is the father of foule gealosy,
  He closely nearer crept, the truth to weet:
  But, as he nigher drew, he easily
  Might scerne,° that it was not his sweetest sweet,   discern
Ne yet her Belamour,° the partner of his sheet.   lover

23

But it was scornefull Braggadocchio,
  That with his servant Trompart hoverd there,

8. I.e., passed over.

Sith late he fled from his too earnest foe:
Whom such when as Malbecco spyéd clere,
He turnéd backe, and would have fled arere;°   *back*
Till Trompart ronning hastily, him did stay,
And bad before his soveraine Lord appere:
That was him loth, yet durst he not gainesay,
And comming him before, low louted° on the lay.°   *bowed/lea*

24

The Boaster at him sternely bent his browe,
   As if he could have kild him with his looke,
   That to the ground him meekely made to bowe,
   And awfull terror deepe into him strooke,
   That every member of his bodie quooke.°   *quaked*
   Said he, "Thou man of nought, what doest thou here,
   Unfitly furnisht with thy bag and booke,
   Where I expected one with shield and spere,
To prove° some deedes of armes upon an equall pere." *try*

25

The wretched man at his imperious speach,
   Was all abasht, and low prostrating, said;
   "Good Sir, let not my rudenesse be no breach
   Unto your patience, ne be ill ypaid;°   *pleased*
   For I unwares this way by fortune straid,
   A silly Pilgrim driven to distresse,
   That seeke a Lady," There he suddein staid,
   And did the rest with grievous sighes suppresse,
While teares stood in his eies, few drops of bitternesse.

26

"What Ladie, man?" said Trompart, "take good hart,
   And tell thy griefe, if any hidden lye;
   Was never better time to shew thy smart,
   Then now, that noble succour is thee by,
   That is the whole worlds commune remedy."
   That cheareful word his weake hart much did cheare,
   And with vaine hope his spirits faint supply,
   That bold he said; "O most redoubted Pere,
Vouchsafe with mild regard a wretches cace to heare."

27

Then sighing sore, "It is not long," said hee,
   "Sith I enjoyd the gentlest Dame alive;
   Of whom a knight, no knight at all perdee,
   But shame of all, that doe for honor strive,
   By treacherous deceipt did me deprive;
   Through open outrage he her bore away,
   And with fowle force unto his will did drive,
   Which all good knights, that armes do beare this day;
Are bound for to revenge, and punish if they may.

28

"And you most noble Lord, that can and dare
   Redresse the wrong of miserable wight,

Cannot employ your most victorious speare
In better quarrell, then defence of right,
And for a Ladie gainst a faithlesse knight;
So shall your glory be advauncéd° much,   *praised*
And all faire Ladies magnifie your might,
And eke my selfe, albe I simple such,[9]
Your worthy paine shall well reward with guerdon rich."

29

With that out of his bouget° forth he drew   *pouch*
Great store of treasure, therewith him to tempt;
But he on it lookt scornefully askew,°   *sidelong*
As much disdeigning to be so misdempt,°   *misjudged*
Or a war-monger° to be basely nempt;°   *mercenary/named*
And said, "Thy offers base I greatly loth,
And eke thy words uncourteous and unkempt;°   *unpolished*
I tread in dust thee and thy money both,
That, were it not for shame," So turnéd from him wroth.

30

But Trompart, that his maisters humor knew,
In lofty lookes to hide an humble mind,
Was inly tickled with that golden vew,
And in his eare him rounded° close behind: *whispered*
Yet stoupt he not, but lay still in the wind,[1]
Waiting advauntage on the pray to sease;
Till Trompart lowly to the ground inclind,
Besought him his great courage° to appease,   *anger*
And pardon simple man, that rash did him displease.

31

Bigge looking like a doughtie Doucepere,[2]
At last he thus; "Thou clod of vilest clay,
I pardon yield, and with thy rudenesse beare;
But weete henceforth, that all that golden pray,
And all that else the vaine world vaunten° may,   *boast of*
I loath as doung, ne deeme my dew reward:
Fame is my meed, and glory vertues pray.°   *booty*
But minds of mortall men are muchell mard,
And moved amisse with massie mucks unmeet regard.[3]

32

"And more, I graunt to thy great miserie
Gratious respect,° thy wife shall backe be sent,   *attention*
And that vile knight, who ever that he bee,
Which hath thy Lady reft, and knighthood shent,°   *disgraced*
By Sanglamort my sword, whose deadly dent°   *blow*

9. I.e., although I am so humble and lowly.
1. I.e., (in a hawking image), he did not swoop down on the prey, but hovered aloft.
2. One of Charlemagne's twelve peers ("les douze pairs").

3. I.e., men's minds are spoiled and turned away by unbecoming care for material wealth. The exaggerated alliteration is a Spenserian device to emphasize the pompous triviality of Braggadocchio's nature.

The bloud hath of so many thousands shed,
I sweare, ere long shall dearely it repent;
Ne he twixt heaven and earth shall hide his hed,
But soone he shall be found, and shortly doen be ded."

33

The foolish man thereat woxe wondrous blith,
   As if the word so spoken, were halfe donne,
   And humbly thankéd him a thousand sith,°   *times*
   That had from death to life him newly wonne.
   Tho forth the Boaster marching, brave begonne
   His stolen steed to thunder furiously,
   As if he heaven and hell would overronne,
   And all the world confound with cruelty,
That much Malbecco joyéd in his jollity.°   *gallant show*

34

Thus long they three together traveiléd,
   Through many a wood, and many an uncouth way,
   To seeke his wife, that was farre wanderéd:
   But those two sought nought, but the present pray,
   To weete the treasure, which he did bewray,°   *reveal*
   On which their eies and harts were wholly set,
   With purpose, how they might it best betray;
   For sith the houre, that first he did them let
The same behold, therewith their keene desires were whet.° *sharpened*

35

It fortunéd as they together fared,
   They spide, where Paridell came pricking fast
   Upon the plaine, the which himselfe prepared
   To giust with that brave straunger knight a cast,°   *bout*
   As on adventure by the way he past:
   Alone he rode without his Paragone;°   *companion*
   For having filcht her bels, her up he cast
   To the wide world, and let her fly alone,
He nould be clogd.[4] So had he servéd many one.

36

The gentle Lady, loose at randon left,
   The greene-wood long did walke, and wander wide
   At wilde adventure, like a forlorne weft,°   *waif*
   Till on a day the Satyres her espide
   Straying alone withouten groome° or guide;   *servant*
   Her up they tooke, and with them home her led,
   With them as housewife ever to abide,
   To milk their gotes, and make them cheese and bred,
And every one as commune good her handeléd.

37

That shortly she Malbecco has forgot,
   And eke Sir Paridell, all° were he deare;   *although*

---

4. I.e., (in a hawking image), having taken his pleasure, he abandoned her and went
his own way.

Who from her went to seeke another lot,
And now by fortune was arrivéd here,
Where those two guilers with Malbecco were:
Soone as the oldman saw Sir Paridell,
He fainted, and was almost dead with feare,
Ne word he had to speake, his griefe to tell,
But to him louted low, and greeted goodly well.

38

And after askéd him for Hellenore,
  "I take no keepe° of her," said Paridell,   *care*
  "She wonneth in the forrest there before."
So forth he rode, as his adventure fell;
  The whiles the Boaster from his loftie sell°   *saddle*
  Faynd to alight, something amisse to mend;
  But the fresh Swayne would not his leasure dwell,°   *await*
  But went his way; whom when he passéd kend,[5]
He up remounted light, and after fained to wend.

39

"Perdy nay," said Malbecco, "shall ye not:
  But let him passe as lightly, as he came:
  For litle good of him is to be got,
  And mickle perill to be put to shame.
  But let us go to seeke my dearest Dame,
  Whom he hath left in yonder forrest wyld:
  For of her safety in great doubt I am,
  Least salvage beastes her person have despoyld:
Then all the world is lost, and we in vaine have toyld."

40

They all agree, and forward them addrest:
  "Ah but," said craftie Trompart, "weete ye well,
  That yonder in that wastefull wildernesse
  Huge monsters haunt, and many dangers dwell;
  Dragons, and Minotaures, and feendes of hell,
  And many wilde woodmen, which robbe and rend
  All travellers; therefore advise ye well,
  Before ye enterprise that way to wend:
One may his journey bring too soone to evill end."

41

Malbecco stopt in great astonishment,°   *dismay*
  And with pale eyes fast fixéd on the rest,
  Their counsell craved, in daunger imminent.
  Said Trompart, "You that are the most opprest
  With burden of great treasure, I thinke best
  Here for to stay in safetie behind;
  My Lord and I will search the wide forrest."
  That counsell pleaséd not Malbeccoes mind;
For he was much affraid, himselfe alone to find.

5. I.e., when he was sure that Paridell had gone.

42

"Then is it best," said he, "that ye doe leave
  Your treasure here in some securitie,
  Either fast closéd in some hollow greave,°   *grove*
  Or buried in the ground from jeopardie,
  Till we returne againe in safetie:
  As for us two, least doubt of us ye have,
  Hence farre away we will blindfolded lie,
  Ne privie be unto your treasures grave."[6]
It pleaséd: so he did. Then they march forward brave.

43

Now when amid the thickest woods they were,
  They heard a noyse of many bagpipes shrill,
  And shrieking Hububs them approching nere,
  Which all the forrest did with horror fill:
  That dreadfull sound the boasters hart did thrill,°   *pierce*
  With such amazement, that in haste he fled,
  Ne ever lookéd backe for good or ill,
  And after him eke fearefull Trompart sped;
The old man could not fly, but fell to ground halfe ded.

44

Yet afterwards close creeping, as he might,
  He in a bush did hide his fearefull hed,
  The jolly Satyres full of fresh delight,
  Came dauncing forth, and with them nimbly led
  Faire Hellenore, with girlonds all bespred,
  Whom their May-lady they had newly made:
  She proud of that new honour, which they red,°   *declared*
  And of their lovely° fellowship full glade,   *loving*
Daunst lively, and her face did with a Lawrell shade.[7]

45

The silly man that in the thicket lay
  Saw all this goodly sport, and grievéd sore,
  Yet durst he not against it doe or say,
  But did his hart with bitter thoughts engore,
  To see th'unkindnesse° of his Hellenore.   *unnatural conduct*
  All day they dauncéd with great lustihed,
  And with their hornéd feet the greene grasse wore,
  The whiles their Gotes upon the brouzes° fed,   *twigs*
Till drouping Phoebus gan to hide his golden hed.

46

Tho up they gan their merry pypes to trusse,°   *pack*
  And all their goodly heards did gather round,
  But every Satyre first did give a busse°   *kiss*

6. I.e., and not know where your money
is hidden.
7. At I. vi. 7–19, appropriately for
that context, in which the satyrs' hos-
pitable reception of Una follows im-
mediately upon the flight of Sansloy,
they are represented as ignorant and
idolatrous, but also as inclined natu-
rally to the cause of virtue; their re-
ception and treatment of Hellenore is
marked primarily by their delight in
sensual pleasure.

To Hellenore: so busses did abound.
Now gan the humid vapour shed the ground
With perly deaw, and th'Earthés gloomy shade
Did dim the brightnesse of the welkin° round,   *heavens*
That every bird and beast awarnéd made,
To shrowd themselves, whiles sleepe their senses did invade.

47

Which when Malbecco saw, out of his bush
  Upon his hands and feete he crept full light,
  And like a Gote emongst the Gotes did rush,
  That through the helpe of his faire hornes[8] on hight,
  And misty dampe of misconceiving° night,   *misleading*
  And eke through likenesse of his gotish beard,
  He did the better counterfeite aright:
  So home he marcht emongst the hornéd heard,
That none of all the Satyres him espyde or heard.

48

At night, when all they went to sleepe, he vewd,
  Whereas his lovely wife emongst them lay,
  Embracéd of a Satyre rough and rude,
  Who all the night did minde° his joyous play: *attend to*
  Nine times he heard him come aloft ere day,
  That all his hart with gealosie did swell;
  But yet that nights ensample did bewray,
  That not for nought his wife them loved so well,
When one so oft a night did ring his matins bell.

49

So closely as he could, he to them crept,
  When wearie of their sport to sleepe they fell,
  And to his wife, that now full soundly slept,
  He whispered in her eare, and did her tell,
  That it was he, which by her side did dwell,
  And therefore prayd her wake, to heare him plaine.
  As one out of a dreame not wakéd well,
  She turned her, and returnéd backe againe:
Yet her for to awake he did the more constraine.

50

At last with irkesome trouble she abrayd;°   *awakened*
  And then perceiving, that it was indeed
  Her old Malbecco, which did her upbrayd,
  With loosenesse of her love, and loathly deed,
  She was astonisht with exceeding dreed,
  And would have wakt the Satyre by her syde;
  But he her prayd, for mercy, or for meed,
  To save his life, ne let him be descryde,
But hearken to his lore, and all his counsell hyde.

8. The horns of cuckoldry; they are the first physical sign of his gradual transformation into the monstrous figure of Jealousy. For a detailed discussion of Spenser's art in the remainder of this Canto, see Paul J. Alpers, *The Poetry of The Faerie Queene* (Princeton, N.J.), 215–228.

51

Tho gan he her perswade, to leave that lewd
 And loathsome life, of God and man abhord,
 And home returne, where all should be renewd
 With perfect peace, and bandes of fresh accord,
 And she received againe to bed and bord,
 As if no trespasse ever had bene donne:
 But she it all refuséd at one word,
 And by no meanes would to his will be wonne,
But chose emongst the jolly Satyres still to wonne.°   *dwell*

52

He wooéd her, till day spring he espyde;
 But all in vaine: and then turnd to the heard,
 Who butted him with hornes on every syde,
 And trode downe in the durt, where his hore° beard   *grey*
 Was fowly dight,° and he of death afeard.   *defiled*
 Early before the heavens fairest light
 Out of the ruddy East was fully reard,
 The heardes out of their foldes were looséd quight,
And he emongst the rest crept forth in sory plight.

53

So soone as he the Prison dore did pas,
 He ran as fast, as both his feete could beare,
 And never lookéd, who behind him was,
 Ne scarsely who before: like as a Beare
 That creeping close, amongst the hives to reare°   *carry off*
 An hony combe, the wakefull dogs espy,
 And him assayling, sore his carkasse teare,
 That hardly he with life away does fly,
Ne stayes, till safe himselfe he see from jeopardy.

54

Ne stayd he, till he came unto the place,
 Where late his treasure he entombéd had,
 Where when he found it not (for Trompart bace
 Had it purloynéd for his maister bad:)
 With extreme fury he became quite mad,
 And ran away, ran with himselfe away:
 That who so straungely had him seene bestad,°   *situated*
 With upstart haire, and staring eyes dismay,
From Limbo lake him late escapéd sure would say.

55

High over hilles and over dales he fled,
 As if the wind him on his winges had borne,
 Ne banck nor bush could stay him, when he sped
 His nimble feet, as treading still on thorne:
 Griefe, and despight, and gealosie, and scorne
 Did all the way him follow hard behind,
 And he himselfe himselfe loathed so forlorne,

So shamefully forlorne of womankind;
That as a Snake, still lurkéd in his wounded mind.

56

Still fled he forward, looking backward still,
    Ne stayd his flight, nor fearefull agony,
    Till that he came unto a rockie hill,
    Over the sea, suspended dreadfully,
    That living creature it would terrify,
    To looke adowne, or upward to the hight:
    From thence he threw himselfe dispiteously,°   *pitilessly*
    All desperate° of his fore-damnéd spright,   *despairing*
That seemed no helpe for him was left in living sight.

57

But through long anguish, and selfe-murdring thought
    He was so wasted and forpinéd° quight,   *enfeebled*
    That all his substance was consumed to nought,
    And nothing left, but like an aery Spright,
    That on the rockes he fell so flit and light,
    That he thereby received no hurt at all,
    But chauncéd on a craggy cliff to light;
    Whence he with crooked clawes so long did crall,
That at the last he found a cave with entrance small.

58

Into the same he creepes, and thenceforth there
    Resolved to build his balefull mansion,
    In drery darkenesse, and continuall feare
    Of that rockes fall, which ever and anon
    Threates with huge ruine him to fall upon,
    That he dare never sleepe, but that one eye
    Still ope he keepes for that occasion;
    Ne ever rests he in tranquillity,
The roring billowes beat his bowre so boystrously.

59

Ne ever is he wont on ought to feed,
    But toades and frogs, his pasture° poysonous,   *food*
    Which in his cold complexion° do breed   *constitution*
    A filthy bloud, or humour rancorous,
    Matter of doubt and dread suspitious,
    That doth with curelesse care consume the hart,
    Corrupts the stomacke with gall vitious,
    Croscuts the liver with internall smart,
And doth transfixe the soule with deathes eternall dart.

60

Yet can he never dye, but dying lives,
    And doth himselfe with sorrow new sustaine,
    That death and life attonce unto him gives.
    And painefull pleasure turnes to pleasing paine.
    There dwels he ever, miserable swaine,
    Hatefull both to him selfe, and every wight;
    Where he through privy griefe, and horrour vaine,

Is woxen so deformed, that he has quight
Forgot he was a man, and Gealosie is hight.

Canto XI

*Britomart chaceth Ollyphant,
findes Scudamour distrest:
Assayes the house of Busyrane,[1]
where Loves spoyles are exprest.*

1

O hatefull hellish Snake,[2] what furie furst
   Brought thee from balefull house of Proserpine,
   Where in her bosome she thee long had nurst,
   And fostred up with bitter milke of tine,°   *affliction*
   Fowle Gealosie, that turnest love divine
   To joylesse dread, and mak'st the loving hart
   With hatefull thoughts to languish and to pine,
   And feed it selfe with selfe-consuming smart?
Of all the passions in the mind thou vilest art.

2

O let him far be banishéd away,
   And in his stead let Love for ever dwell,
   Sweet Love, that doth his golden wings embay°   *bathe*
   In blesséd Nectar, and pure Pleasures well,
   Untroubled of vile feare, or bitter fell.°   *rancor*
   And ye faire Ladies, that your kingdomes make
   In th'harts of men, them governe wisely well,
   And of faire Britomart ensample take,
That was as trew in love, as Turtle° to her make.°   *dove/mate*

3

Who with Sir Satyrane, as earst ye red,
   Forth ryding from Malbeccoes hostlesse hous,
   Far off aspyde a young man, the which fled
   From an huge Geaunt, that with hideous
   And hatefull outrage long him chacéd thus;
   It was that Ollyphant, the brother deare
   Of that Argante vile and vitious,
   From whom the Squire of Dames was reft whylere;
This all as bad as she, and worse, if worse ought were.

4

For as the sister did in feminine
   And filthy lust exceede all woman kind,

1. The name is derived from that of
Busiris, a tyrannical Egyptian king,
who habitually sacrificed strangers to
Zeus, and who was eventually killed
by Hercules. The Busirane episode has
been variously interpreted; cf. the com-
ments by Padelford, Lewis, Roche,
Hieatt, and Berger in this edition.
2. The apostrophes of sts. 1–2, to the
snake of jealousy (probably echoing
Virgil's description of the frenzied
Alecto, in the *Aeneid*, VII. 342–355),
and to love, serve an appropriately
transitional function, as the chaste
warrior maiden Britomart once again
assumes central importance in the nar-
rative.

So he surpasséd his sex masculine,
In beastly use that I did ever find;°   *hear of*
Whom when as Britomart beheld behind
The fearefull boy so greedily pursew,
She was emmovéd in her noble mind,
T'employ her puissaunce to his reskew,
And prickéd fiercely forward, where she him did vew.

5

Ne was Sir Satyrane her far behinde,
But with like fiercenesse did ensew° the chace: *follow*
Whom when the Gyaunt saw, he soone resinde
His former suit, and from them fled apace;
They after both, and boldly bad him bace,[3]
And each did strive the other to out-goe,
But he them both outran a wondrous space,
For he was long, and swift as any Roe,°   *deer*
And now made better speed, t'escape his fearéd foe.

6

It was not Satyrane, whom he did feare,
But Britomart the flowre of chastity;
For he the powre of chast hands might not beare,
But alwayes did their dread encounter fly:
And now so fast his feet he did apply,
That he has gotten to a forrest neare,
Where he is shrowded in security.
The wood they enter, and search every where,
They searchéd diversely, so both divided were.

7

Faire Britomart so long him followéd,
That she at last came to a fountaine sheare,°   *clear*
By which there lay a knight[4] all wallowéd°   *grovelling*
Upon the grassy ground, and by him neare
His haberjeon, his helmet, and his speare;
A little off,° his shield was rudely throwne,   *aside*
On which the wingéd boy in colours cleare
Depeincted was, full easie to be knowne,
And he thereby, where ever it in field was showne.

8

His face upon the ground did groveling ly,
As if he had bene slombring in the shade,
That the brave Mayd would not for courtesy,
Out of his quiet slomber him abrade,°   *arouse*
Nor seeme too suddeinly him to invade:°   *intrude on*
Still as she stood, she heard with grievous throb
Him grone, as if his hart were peeces made,

3. I.e., challenged him.
4. I.e., Scudamour, whose shield bears Cupid's image; as Amoret's affianced lover, he is the courtly embodiment of male desire. The episode that follows is based primarily on similar events in Tasso, *Rinaldo*, V.

And with most painefull pangs to sigh and sob,
That pitty did the Virgins hart of patience rob.

9

At last forth breaking into bitter plaintes
   He said; "O soueraigne Lord that sit'st on hye,
   And raignst in blis emongst thy blesséd Saintes,
   How suffrest thou such shamefull cruelty,
   So long vnwreakéd° of thine enimy?   *unavenged*
   Or hast thou, Lord, of good mens cause no heed?
   Or doth thy iustice sleepe, and silent ly?
   What booteth then the good and righteous deed,
If goodnesse find no grace, nor righteousnesse no meed?

10

"If good find grace, and righteousnesse reward,
   Why then is Amoret in caytive band,[5]
   Sith that more bounteous creature neuer fared
   On foot, vpon the face of liuing land?
   Or if that heauenly iustice may withstand
   The wrongfull outrage of vnrighteous men,
   Why then is Busirane with wicked hand
   Suffred, these seuen monethes day in secret den
My Lady and my loue so cruelly to pen?

11

"My Lady and my loue is cruelly pend
   In dolefull darkenesse from the vew of day,
   Whilest deadly torments do her chast brest rend,
   And the sharpe steele doth riue her hart in tway,
   All for she Scudamore will not denay.°   *deny*
   Yet thou vile man, vile Scudamore art sound,
   Ne canst her ayde, ne canst her foe dismay;
   Vnworthy wretch to tread vpon the ground,
For whom so faire a Lady feeles so sore a wound."

12

There an huge heape of singultes° did oppresse   *sobs*
   His strugling soule, and swelling throbs empeach°   *hinder*
   His foltring toung with pangs of drerinesse,°   *grief*
   Choking the remnant of his plaintife speach,
   As if his dayes were come to their last reach.°   *end*
   Which when she heard, and saw the ghastly fit,
   Threatning into his life to make a breach,
   Both with great ruth and terrour she was smit,
Fearing least from her cage the wearie soule would flit.

13

Tho stooping downe she him amouéd light;
   Who therewith somewhat starting, vp gan looke,
   And seeing him behind a straunger knight,
   Whereas no liuing creature he mistooke,[6]

5. I.e., captive in bonds.

6. I.e., where he had mistakenly thought no one to be.

With great indignaunce he that sight forsooke,
And downe againe himselfe disdainefully
  Abjecting,° th'earth with his faire forhead strooke: *casting*
  Which the bold Virgin seeing, gan apply
Fit medcine to his griefe, and spake thus courtesly.

14

"Ah gentle knight, whose deepe conceivéd griefe
  Well seemes t'exceede the powre of patience,
  Yet if that heavenly grace some good reliefe
  You send, submit you to high providence,
  And ever in your noble hart prepense,°   *consider*
  That all the sorrow in the world is lesse,
  Then vertues might, and values° confidence,   *valor's*
  For who nill bide the burden of distresse,
Must not here thinke to live: for life is wretchednesse.

15

"Therefore, faire Sir, do comfort to you take,
  And freely read,° what wicked felon so   *tell*
  Hath outraged you, and thrald your gentle make.°   *mate*
  Perhaps this hand may helpe to ease your woe,
  And wreake your sorrow on your cruell foe,
  At least it faire endevour will apply."
  Those feeling wordes so neare the quicke did goe,
  That up his head he rearéd easily,
And leaning on his elbow, these few wordes let fly.

16

"What boots it plaine,° that cannot be redrest,   *to lament*
  And sow vaine sorrow in a fruitlesse eare,
  Sith powre of hand, nor skill of learnéd brest,
  Ne worldly price cannot redeeme my deare,
  Out of her thraldome and continuall feare?
  For he the tyraunt, which her hath in ward°   *control*
  By strong enchauntments and blacke Magicke leare,°   *lore*
  Hath in a dungeon deepe her close embard,
And many dreadfull feends hath pointed° to her gard.   *appointed*

17

"There he tormenteth her most terribly,
  And day and night afflicts with mortall paine,
  Because to yield him love she doth deny,
  Once to me yold,° not to be yold againe:[7]   *yielded*
  But yet by torture he would her constraine
  Love to conceive in her disdainfull brest;
  Till so she do, she must in doole° remaine,   *pain*
  Ne may by living meanes be thence relest:°   *released*
What boots it then to plaine, that cannot be redrest?"

7. In IV. x, Scudamour tells how he won the shield of Love, and subsequently Amoret herself (at the Temple of Venus); the account of the wedding feast, and of Busirane's abduction of Amoret on that occasion, appears in IV. i. 2–4.

18

With this sad hersall° of his heavy stresse,°   *account/distress*
  The warlike Damzell was empassiond sore,
  And said; "Sir knight, your cause is nothing lesse,
  Then is your sorrow, certes if not more;
  For nothing so much pitty doth implore,
  As gentle Ladies helplesse misery.
  But yet, if please ye listen to my lore,
  I will with proofe of last extremity,[8]
Deliver her fro thence, or with her for you dy."

19

"Ah gentlest knight alive," said Scudamore,
  "What huge heroicke magnanimity
  Dwels in thy bounteous brest? what couldst thou more,
  If she were thine, and thou as now am I?
  O spare thy happy dayes, and them apply
  To better boot,° but let me dye, that ought;   *advantage*
  More is more losse: one is enough to dy."
  "Life is not lost," said she, "for which is bought
Endlesse renowm, that more then death is to be sought."[9]

20

Thus she at length perswaded him to rise,
  And with her wend, to see what new successe°   *result*
  Mote him befall upon new enterprise;
  His armes, which he had vowed to disprofesse,°   *renounce*
  She gathered up and did about him dresse,
  And his forwandred steed unto him got:
  So forth they both yfere° make their progresse,   *together*
  And march not past the mountenaunce° of a shot,   *distance*
Till they arrived, whereas their purpose they did plot.

21

There they dismounting, drew their weapons bold
  And stoutly came unto the Castle gate;
  Whereas no gate they found, them to withhold,
  Nor ward° to wait at morne and evening late,   *porter*
  But in the Porch, that did them sore amate,°   *dismay*
  A flaming fire,[1] ymixt with smouldry smoke,
  And stinking Sulphure, that with griesly hate
  And dreadfull horrour did all entraunce choke,
Enforcéd them their forward footing to revoke.°   *withdraw*

22

Greatly thereat was Britomart dismayd,
  Ne in that stownd° wist, how her selfe to beare;   *crisis*

8. I.e., to the utmost of my strength and spirit.
9. I.e., that is to be sought even at the risk of death.
1. Sts. 21–25 are based on similar episodes in Tasso's *Rinaldo* (V. 58–61) and *Gerusalemme Liberata* (XIII. 34–35). Spenser may also have drawn on Richard Johnson's romance, *The Seven Champions of Christendom* (printed c. 1597), for some details, notably that of the fire barrier. That Britomart can pass unscathed through this "flaming fire" emphasizes the special power of her thoughtful chastity, which can cope successfully with challenges too demanding for Scudamour's proud and willful desire.

For daunger vaine it were, to have assayd
That cruell element, which all things feare,
Ne none can suffer to approchen neare:
And turning backe to Scudamour, thus sayd;
"What monstrous enmity provoke we heare,
Foolhardy as th'Earthes children, the which made
Battell against the Gods? so we a God invade.[2]

23

"Daunger without discretion to attempt,
   Inglorious and beastlike is: therefore Sir knight,
   Aread what course of you is safest dempt,°   *judged*
   And how we with our foe may come to fight."
   "This is," quoth he, "the dolorous despight,
   Which earst to you I playnd: for neither may
   This fire be quencht by any wit or might,
   Ne yet by any meanes removed away,
So mighty be th'enchauntments, which the same do stay.°   *support*

24

"What is there else, but cease these fruitlesse paines,
   And leave me to my former languishing?
   Faire Amoret must dwell in wicked chaines,
   And Scudamore here dye with sorrowing."
   "Perdy not so;" said she, "for shamefull thing
   It were t'abandon noble chevisaunce,°   *enterprise*
   For shew of perill, without venturing:
   Rather let try extremities of chaunce,
Then enterpriséd prayse for dread to disavaunce."[3]

25

Therewith resolved to prove her utmost might,
   Her ample shield she threw before her face,
   And her swords point directing forward right,
   Assayld the flame, the which eftsoones gave place,
   And did it selfe divide with equall space,
   That through she passéd; as a thunder bolt
   Perceth the yielding ayre, and doth displace
   The soring clouds into sad showres ymolt;°   *melted*
So to her yold the flames, and did their force revolt.°   *withdraw*

26

Whom whenas Scudamour saw past the fire,
   Safe and untoucht, he likewise gan assay,
   With greedy will, and envious desire,
   And bad the stubborne flames to yield him way:
   But cruell Mulciber would not obay
   His threatfull pride, but did the more augment
   His mighty rage, and with imperious sway
   Him forst (maulgre) his fiercenesse to relent,
And backe retire, all scorcht and pitifully brent.

2. I.e., similarly we attack the god of fire (cf. st. 26).

3. I.e., than to retreat fearfully from actions deserving praise.

27

With huge impatience he inly swelt,°   *burned*
  More for great sorrow, that he could not pas,
  Then for the burning torment, which he felt,
  That with fell woodnesse° he effiercéd° was,   *madness/enraged*
  And wilfully him throwing on the gras,
  Did beat and bounse his head and brest full sore;
  The whiles the Championesse now entred has
  The utmost° rowme, and past the formest dore,   *outermost*
The utmost rowme, abounding with all precious store.

28

For round about, the wals yclothéd were
  With goodly arras of great majesty,[4]
  Woven with gold and silke so close and nere,
  That the rich metall lurkéd privily,
  As faining to be hid from envious eye;
  Yet here, and there, and every where unwares
  It shewd it selfe, and shone unwillingly;
  Like a discolourd° Snake, whose hidden snares   *varicolored*
Through the greene gras his long bright burnisht backe declares.

29

And in those Tapets° weren fashionéd   *tapestries*
  Many faire pourtraicts, and many a faire feate,
  And all of love, and all of lusty-hed,
  As seeméd by their semblaunt did entreat;°   *concern*
  And eke all Cupids warres they did repeate,
  And cruell battels, which he whilome fought
  Gainst all the Gods, to make his empire great;
  Besides the huge massacres, which he wrought
On mighty kir.gs and kesars,° into thraldome brought.   *emperors*

30

Therein was writ, how often thundring Jove
  Had felt the point of his hart-percing dart,
  And leaving heavens kingdome, here did rove
  In straunge disguize, to slake his scalding smart;
  Now like a Ram, faire Helle to pervart,[5]
  Now like a Bull, Europa to withdraw:°   *carry off*

4. The chief literary source for sts. 28–46 is Ovid, *Metamorphoses*, VI. 103–128; but Spenser's elaboration of the stories alluded to in that passage reflects the influence of the Renaissance mythographers as well. The poet's art was also influenced by the wealth of mythological illustration in contemporary tapestry work and wall painting, as well as in the ceremonial pageantry of the court.
5. Boccaccio, following Ovid, *Fasti*, III. 851–876, tells the story of Helle and her brother Phrixus, whom their stepmother Ino meant to sacrifice to Zeus: they were saved by the intervention of Hermes (Mercury), who provided a ram with golden fleece to carry them through the air to safety (although Helle fell into the sea, subsequently called the Hellespont); the story is in *De Genealogia Deorum*, XIII. 68. Elsewhere in his commentary (IV. 68), Boccaccio associates the influence of the constellation Aries (of which the sign is a ram) with the characteristics of Jove as leader and lover. Spenser has apparently combined these elements to create his own myth.

Ah, how the fearefull Ladies tender hart
Did lively° seeme to tremble, when she saw   *actually*
The huge seas under her t'obay her servaunts law.

31

Soone after that into a golden showre
  Him selfe he chaunged faire Danaë to vew,
  And through the roofe of her strong brasen towre
  Did raine into her lap an hony dew,
  The whiles her foolish garde, that little knew
  Of such deceipt, kept th'yron dore fast bard,
  And watcht, that none should enter nor issew;
  Vaine was that watch, and bootlesse all the ward,°   *guard*
Whenas the God to golden hew° him selfe transfard.   *form*

32

Then was he turnd into a snowy Swan,
  To win faire Leda to his lovely° trade: *loving*
  O wondrous skill, and sweet wit of the man,
  That her in daffadillies sleeping made,
  From scorching heat her daintie limbes to shade:
  Whiles the proud Bird ruffing° his fethers wyde,   *ruffling*
  And brushing his faire brest, did her invade:
  She slept, yet twixt her eyelids closely spyde,
How towards her he rusht, and smiléd at his pryde.

33

Then shewd it, how the Thebane Semelee[6]
  Deceived of gealous Juno, did require
  To see him in his soveraigne majestee,
  Armd with his thunderbolts and lightning fire,
  Whence dearely she with death bought her desire.
  But faire Alcmena[7] better match did make,
  Joying his love, in likenesse more entire;°   *perfect*
  Three nights in one, they say, that for her sake
He then did put, her pleasures lenger to partake.

34

Twise was he seene in soaring Eagles shape,
  And with wide wings to beat the buxome° ayre,   *yielding*
  Once, when he with Asterie[8] did scape,
  Againe, when as the Trojane boy[9] so faire
  He snatcht from Ida hill, and with him bare:
  Wondrous delight it was, there to behould,
  How the rude Shepheards after him did stare,

6. Based on *Metamorphoses*, III. 253–309. Juno, jealous of Semele, took the form of her nurse, and suggested that she should request Jove to possess her as he customarily did Juno, i.e., in his full glory and radiance; in consequence, Semele was destroyed by the god's fire.
7. The mother of Hercules by Jove, who appeared to her in the guise of her husband Amphitryon. The compression of three nights into one probably reflects the comment of Natalis Comes, *op. cit.*, VI. 1.
8. Asterie, to escape the advances of Jove, took the form of a quail; but the god then appeared to her as an eagle.
9. I.e., Ganymede (cf. *Metamorphoses*, X. 155–162).

Trembling through feare, least down he fallen should,
And often to him calling, to take surer hould.

35

In Satyres shape Antiopa he snatcht:
   And like a fire, when he Aegin' assayd:
   A shepheard, when Mnemosyné he catcht:
   And like a Serpent to the Thracian mayd.[1]
   Whiles thus on earth great Jove these pageaunts° playd,   *scenes*
   The wingéd boy did thrust into his throne,
   And scoffing, thus unto his mother sayd,
   "Lo now the heavens obey to me alone,
And take me for their Jove, whiles Jove to earth is gone."

36

And thou, faire Phoebus, in thy colours bright
   Wast there enwoven, and the sad distresse,
   In which that boy thee plongéd, for despight,
   That thou bewrayedst his mothers wantonnesse,
   When she with Mars was meynt° in joyfulnesse: *mingled*
   For thy he thrild° thee with a leaden dart,   *pierced*
   To love faire Daphne, which thee lovéd lesse:[2]
   Lesse she thee loved, then was thy just desart,
Yet was thy love her death, and her death was thy smart.

37

So lovedst thou the lusty° Hyacinct,   *handsome*
   So lovedst thou the faire Coronis deare:[3]
   Yet both are of thy haplesse hand extinct,
   Yet both in flowres do live, and love thee beare,
   The one a Paunce,° the other a sweet breare: *pansy*
   For griefe whereof, ye mote have lively seene
   The God himselfe rending his golden heare,
   And breaking quite his gyrlond ever greene,
With other signes of sorrow and impatient teene.°   *woe*

38

Both for those two, and for his owne deare sonne,
   The sonne of Climene[4] he did repent,
   Who bold to guide the charet of the Sunne,
   Himselfe in thousand peeces fondly rent,
   And all the world with flashing fier brent;
   So like,° that all the walles did seeme to flame.   *lifelike*
   Yet cruell Cupid, not herewith content,

---

1. I.e., Proserpine, known to her Thracian worshippers as Cotytto.
2. For the story of Apollo and Daphne, cf. *Metamorphoses*, I. 450–567. Cupid's golden-tipped and lead-tipped arrows respectively symbolized success and failure in love (cf. st. 48); Spenser alters his original in the assertion that Apollo was struck by "a leaden dart."

3. For Apollo and Hyacinth, cf. *Metamorphoses*, X. 163–220. The story of Coronis, a victim of Apollo's jealous rage, appears in *ibid.*, II. 542–632, but the detail of her transformation into a sweetbriar is Spenser's own invention.
4. I.e., Phaethon; cf. *Metamorphoses*, II. 1–400.

Forst him eftsoones to follow other game,
And love a Shepheards daughter for his dearest Dame.

39

He lovéd Isse for his dearest Dame,[5]
    And for her sake her cattell fed a while,
    And for her sake a cowheard vile became,
    The servant of Admetus cowheard vile,
    Whiles that from heaven he sufferéd exile.
    Long were to tell each other lovely fit,°   *episode of love*
    Now like a Lyon, hunting after spoile,
    Now like a Stag, now like a faulcon flit:
All which in that faire arras was most lively writ.

40

Next unto him was Neptune picturéd,
    In his divine resemblance wondrous lyke:
    His face was rugged, and his hoarie hed
    Droppéd with brackish deaw; his three-forkt Pyke
    He stearnly shooke, and therewith fierce did stryke
    The raging billowes, that on every syde
    They trembling stood, and made a long broad dyke,
    That his swift charet might have passage wyde,
Which foure great Hippodames° did draw in   *sea horses*
    temewise tyde.

41

His sea-horses did seeme to snort amayne,°   *violently*
    And from their nosethrilles blow the brynie streame,
    That made the sparckling waves to smoke agayne,
    And flame with gold, but the white fomy creame,
    Did shine with silver, and shoot forth his beame.
    The God himselfe did pensive seeme and sad,
    And hong adowne his head, as he did dreame:
    For privy love his brest empiercéd had,
Ne ought but deare Bisaltis[6] ay could make him glad.

42

He lovéd eke Iphimedia deare,
    And Aeolus faire daughter Arne hight,
    For whom he turnd him selfe into a Steare,
    And fed on fodder, to beguile her sight.
    Also to win Deucalions daughter bright,[7]
    He turnd him selfe into a Dolphin fayre;
    And like a wingéd horse he tooke his flight,

5. Two separate myths are combined here: Apollo's appearance as a shepherd to Isse (*Metamorphoses*, VI. 124), and the story of Admetus, to whom Apollo was bound for nine years' service as a herdsman (cf. Hyginus, *Fabulae*, 50).
6. I.e., Theophane, changed by Neptune into a ewe that he might, in the form of a ram, outwit her suitors (cf. Hyginus, *Fabulae*, 88).
7. I.e., Melantho. For the allusions in this stanza Spenser depended on *Metamorphoses*, VI. 116–120, and the commentaries on the figures alluded to in that passage by Boccaccio and Natalis Comes.

To snaky-locke Medusa to repayre,
On whom he got faire Pegasus, that flitteth in the ayre.

43

Next Saturne[8] was, (but who would ever weene,
  That sullein Saturne ever weend to love?
  Yet love is sullein, and Saturnlike seene,
  As he did for Erigone it prove,)
  That to a Centaure did him selfe transmove.°   *transmute*
So prooved it eke that gracious God of wine,
  When for to compasse° Philliras hard love,   *achieve*
  He turnd himselfe into a fruitfull vine,
And into her faire bosome made his grapes decline.

44

Long were to tell the amorous assayes,
  And gentle pangues,° with which he makéd meeke   *pangs*
  The mighty Mars, to learne his wanton playes:
  How oft for Venus, and how often eek
  For many other Nymphes he sore did shreek,
  With womanish teares, and with unwarlike smarts,
  Privily moystening his horrid° cheek.   *rough*
  There was he painted full of burning darts,
And many wide woundes launchéd° through his inner parts.   *pierced*

45

Ne did he spare (so cruell was the Elfe)
  His owne deare mother, (ah why should he so?)
  Ne did he spare sometime to pricke himselfe,
  That he might tast the sweet consuming woe,
  Which he had wrought to many others moe.
  But to declare the mournfull Tragedyes,
  And spoiles, wherewith he all the ground did strow,
  More eath° to number, with how many eyes   *easy*
High heaven beholds sad lovers nightly theeveryes.

46

Kings Queenes, Lords Ladies, Knights and Damzels gent°   *gentle*
  Were heaped together with the vulgar sort,
  And mingled with the raskall rablement,
  Without respect of person or of port,°   *rank*
  To shew Dan° Cupids powre and great effort: *Master*
  And round about a border was entrayld,°   *entwined*
  Of broken bowes and arrowes shivered short,
  And a long bloudy river through them rayld,°   *flowed*
So lively and so like, that living sence it fayld.

8. In astrological tradition, the influence of Saturn was considered to be stern, ominous, and "crabbed" (cf. *Mutabilitie*, vii. 52). The stanza confuses Ovid's allusion to the seduction of Erigone by Bacchus with the reference to Saturn's deception of Philyra, who became the mother of Chiron the centaur (*Metamorphoses*, VI. 125–126). A scribal or printer's error may be responsible.

47

And at the upper end of that faire rowme,
   There was an Altar built of pretious stone,
   Of passing valew, and of great renowme,
   On which there stood an Image all alone,
   Of massy gold, which with his owne light shone;
   And wings it had with sundry colours dight,
   More sundry colours, then the proud Pavone[9]
   Beares in his boasted fan, or Iris bright,
When her discolourd° bow she spreds through   *many colored*
   heaven bright.

48

Blindfold he was, and in his cruell fist
   A mortall bow and arrowes keene did hold,
   With which he shot at randon, when him list,
   Some headed with sad lead, some with pure gold;
   (Ah man beware, how thou those darts behold)
   A wounded Dragon[1] under him did ly,
   Whose hideous tayle his left foot did enfold,
   And with a shaft was shot through either eye,
That no man forth might draw, ne no man remedye.

49

And underneath his feet was written thus,
   Unto the Victor of the Gods this bee:
   And all the people in that ample hous
   Did to that image bow their humble knee,
   And oft committed fowle Idolatree.
   That wondrous sight faire Britomart amazed,
   Ne seeing could her wonder satisfie,
   But ever more and more upon it gazed,
The whiles the passing° brightnes her fraile sences dazed.   *surpassing*

50

Tho as she backward cast her busie eye,
   To search each secret of that goodly sted,°   *place*
   Over the dore thus written she did spye
   Be bold: she oft it over-red,
   Yet could not find what sence it figuréd:
   But what so were therein or writ or ment,
   She was no whit thereby discouragéd
   From prosecuting of her first intent,
But forward with bold steps into the next roome went.

51

Much fairer, than the former, was that roome,
   And richlier by many partes° arayd: *degrees*
   For not with arras made in painefull° loome,   *painstaking*

9. I.e., the peacock. Iris is the goddess
of the rainbow. The combination of
images is probably based on a similar
passage in Tasso, *Gerusalemme Liber-
ata*, XVI. 24.
1. The hideous and blinded dragon is
an appropriate emblem for one aspect
of love, its cruelty and terror; in
Apuleius's *Metamorphoses* ("The
Golden Ass"), Psyche's evil sisters
persuade her that Cupid is a huge,
poisonous snake, reminding her also
that she is fated to wed a savage beast.

But with pure gold it all was overlayd,
 Wrought with wilde Antickes,° which their   *grotesque figures*
  follies playd,
 In the rich metall, as they living were:
 A thousand monstrous formes therein were made,
 Such as false love doth oft upon him weare,
For love in thousand monstrous formes doth oft appeare.

52

And all about, the glistring walles were hong
 With warlike spoiles, and with victorious prayes,°   *booty*
 Of mighty Conquerours and Captaines strong,
 Which were whilome captivéd in their dayes
 To cruell love, and wrought their owne decayes:
 Their swerds and speres were broke, and hauberques rent;
 And their proud girlonds of tryumphant bayes°   *laurels*
 Troden in dust with fury insolent,
To shew the victors might and mercilesse intent.

53

The warlike Mayde beholding earnestly
 The goodly ordinance° of this rich place,   *arrangement*
 Did greatly wonder, ne could satisfie
 Her greedy eyes with gazing a long space,
 But more she mervaild that no footings trace,
 Nor wight appeared, but wastefull emptinesse,
 And solemne silence over all that place:
 Straunge thing it seemed, that none was to possesse
So rich purveyance,° ne them keepe with carefulnesse. *provision*

54

And as she lookt about, she did behold,
 How over that same dore was likewise writ,
 Be bold, be bold, and every where *Be bold*,
 That much she muzed, yet could not construe it
 By any ridling skill, or commune wit.
 At last she spyde at that roomes upper end,
 Another yron dore, on which was writ,
 Be not too bold; whereto though she did bend
Her earnest mind, yet wist not what it might intend.[2]

55

Thus she there waited untill eventyde,
 Yet living creature none she saw appeare:
 And now sad shadowes gan the world to hyde,
 From mortall vew, and wrap in darkenesse dreare;
 Yet nould° she d'off her weary armes, for feare *would not*
 Of secret daunger, ne let sleepe oppresse
 Her heavy eyes with natures burdein deare,
 But drew her selfe aside in sickernesse,°   *safety*
And her welpointed° weapons did about her dresse.° *ready; arrange*

2. Britomart is as bold as Scudamour (cf. xii. 2, 29); but the fire that daunts his eager aggressiveness cannot resist the combined boldness and restraint that characterizes her chastity. The concluding lines of st. 55 draw attention to the judiciously tempered quality of Britomart's virtue.

Canto XII

The maske of Cupid,[1] *and th'enchaunted*
Chamber are displayd,
Whence Britomart redeemes faire
Amoret, through charmes decayd.°   weakened

1

'Tho when as chearelesse Night ycovered had
 Faire heaven with an universall cloud,
 That every wight dismayd with darknesse sad,°   heavy
 In silence and in sleepe themselves did shroud,
 She heard a shrilling Trompet sound aloud,
 Signe of nigh battell, or got victory;
 Nought therewith daunted was her courage proud,
 But rather stird to cruell enmity,
Expecting ever, when some foe she might descry.

2

With that, an hideous storme of winde arose,
 With dreadfull thunder and lightning atwixt,
 And an earth-quake, as if it streight would lose°   loosen
 The worlds foundations from his centre fixt;
 A direfull stench of smoke and sulphure mixt
 Ensewd, whose noyance fild the fearefull sted,°   place
 From the fourth houre of night untill the sixt;
 Yet the bold Britonesse was nought ydred,
Though much emmoved, but stedfast still perseveréd.

3

All suddenly a stormy whirlwind blew
 Throughout the house, that clappéd° every dore,   slammed
 With which that yron wicket[2] open flew,
 As it with mightie levers had bene tore:
 And forth issewd, as on the ready° flore   prepared
 Of some Theatre, a grave personage,
 That in his hand a branch of laurell bore,
 With comely haveour and count'nance sage,
Yclad in costly garments, fit for tragicke Stage.

4

Proceeding to the midst, he still did stand,
 As if in mind he somewhat had to say,
 And to the vulgar° beckning with his hand,   common people

1. This "maske" may be a revision of early work by Spenser, e.g., his "Court of Cupide," mentioned in the "Epistle" to *The Shepheardes Calender*, or the "Pageaunts" noted in the Glosse to "June." It is essentially a "disguising," or allegorical pageant making part of a wedding celebration; at IV.i.2–3, Spenser will allude again to the "mask of love" presented at the wedding of Scudamour and Amoret. Its personages, structure, and allegory reflect the influence of Tudor and Elizabethan courtly entertainments, in which elements from classical mythology, medieval romance, and court-of-love allegory had been fused. Specifically, the masque combines the court-of-love "procession of Cupid" (as in Andreas Capellanus's *De Amore*) with the presentation of Cupid as conqueror, riding in triumph with his adherents and victims (as in Petrarch's *Trionfo d'Amore*).

2. I.e., the "yron dore" in xi. 54.

In signe of silence, as to heare a play,
By lively actions he gan bewray
Some argument of matter passionéd;[3]
Which doen, he backe retyréd soft away,
And passing by, his name discoveréd,
Ease, on his robe in golden letters cypheréd.°   *written*

5

The noble Mayd, still standing all this vewd,
    And merveild at his strange intendiment;°   *purpose*
With that a joyous fellowship issewd
Of Minstrals, making goodly meriment,
With wanton Bardes, and Rymers impudent,
All which together sung full chearefully
A lay of loves delight, with sweet concent:°   *harmony*
After whom marcht a jolly company,
In manner of a maske, enrangéd orderly.

6

The whiles a most delitious harmony,
    In full straunge notes was sweetly heard to sound,
That the rare sweetnesse of the melody
The feeble senses wholly did confound,
And the fraile soule in deepe delight nigh dround:
And when it ceast, shrill trompets loud did bray,
That their report° did farre away rebound,   *echo*
And when they ceast, it gan againe to play,
The whiles the maskers marchéd forth in trim aray.

7

The first was Fancy, like a lovely boy,
    Of rare aspect, and beautie without peare;
Matchable either to that ympe of Troy,[4]
Whom Jove did love, and chose his cup to beare,
Or that same daintie lad, which was so deare
To great Alcides, that when as he dyde,
He wailéd womanlike with many a teare,
And every wood, and every valley wyde
He fild with Hylas name; the Nymphes eke Hylas cryde.[5]

8

His garment neither was of silke nor say,°   *fine wool*
    But painted plumes, in goodly order dight,
Like as the sunburnt Indians do aray
Their tawney bodies, in their proudest plight:°   *attire*
As those same plumes, so seemd he vaine and light,
That by his gate° might easily appeare;   *gait*

3. I.e., by expressive gestures, he re-
vealed the central theme to be pre-
sented in the masque. In Senecan
tragedies of the period, it was cus-
tomary to indicate the play's progres-
sive action by the presentation of
"dumb shows" between the acts.

4. I.e., Ganymede.
5. Spenser's allusion to the story of
Hercules and his youthful companion
Hylas (often repeated in classical liter-
ature) recalls particularly the version
of Theocritus, *Idyl XIII.*

For still he fared as dauncing in delight,
  And in his hand a windy fan[6] did beare,
That in the idle aire he moved still here and there.

9

And him beside marcht amorous Desyre,
  Who seemd of riper yeares, then th'other Swaine,
  Yet was that other swayne this elders syre,
  And gave him being, commune to them twaine:
  His garment was disguiséd very vaine,[7]
  And his embrodered Bonet sat awry;
  Twixt both his hands few sparkes he close did straine,°   *clasp*
  Which still he blew, and kindled busily,
That soone they life conceived, and forth in flames did fly.

10

Next after him went Doubt, who was yclad
  In a discoloured cote, of straunge disguyse,°   *fashion*
  That at his backe a brode Capuccio° had,   *hood*
  And sleeves dependant Albanese-wyse:[8]
  He lookt askew with his mistrustfull eyes,
  And nicely° trode, as thornes lay in his way,   *delicately*
  Or that the flore to shrinke he did avyse,°   *perceive*
  And on a broken reed he still did stay°   *support*
His feeble steps, which shrunke, when hard theron he lay.

11

With him went Daunger, clothed in ragged weed,°   *garment*
  Made of Beares skin, that him more dreadfull made,
  Yet his owne face was dreadfull, ne did need
  Straunge horrour, to deforme his griesly shade;
  A net in th'one hand, and a rustie blade
  In th'other was, this Mischiefe, that Mishap;
  With th'one his foes he threatned to invade,°   *assault*
  With th'other he his friends ment to enwrap:
For whom he could not kill, he practizd° to entrap.   *plotted*

12

Next him was Feare, all armed from top to toe,
  Yet thought himselfe not safe enough thereby,
  But feard each shadow moving to and fro,
  And his owne armes when glittering he did spy,
  Or clashing heard, he fast away did fly,
  As ashes pale of hew, and wingyheeld;
  And evermore on daunger fixt his eye,
  Gainst whom he alwaies bent° a brasen shield,   *directed*
Which his right hand unarméd fearefully did wield.

13

With him went Hope in rancke, a handsome Mayd,
  Of chearefull looke and lovely to behold;
  In silken samite° she was light arayd,   *rich cloth*
  And her faire lockes were woven up in gold;

---

6. I.e., a fan to stir the breeze.   8. Hanging down in the Albanian style.
7. I.e., unusually designed for the sake
of fashionable display.

She alway smyld, and in her hand did hold
An holy water Sprinckle,[9] dipt in deowe,°   *dew*
With which she sprinckled favours manifold,
On whom she list, and did great liking sheowe,
Great liking unto many, but true love to feowe.

14

And after them Dissemblance, and Suspect
  Marcht in one rancke, yet an unequall paire:
  For she was gentle, and of milde aspect,
  Courteous to all, and seeming debonaire,
  Goodly adornéd, and exceeding faire:
  Yet was that all but painted, and purloynd,
  And her bright browes were deckt with borrowed haire:
  Her deedes were forgéd, and her words false coynd,
And alwaies in her hand two clewes° of silke she twynd.   *balls*

15

But he was foule, ill favouréd, and grim,
  Under his eyebrowes looking still askaunce;°   *sideways*
  And ever as Dissemblance laught on him,
  He lowrd° on her with daungerous° eyeglaunce; *scowled/hard*
  Shewing his nature in his countenance;
  His rolling eyes did never rest in place,
  But walkt each° where, for feare of hid mischaunce,   *every*
  Holding a lattice[1] still before his face,
Through which he still did peepe, as forward he did pace.

16

Next him went Griefe, and Fury matcht yfere;°   *together*
  Griefe all in sable sorrowfully clad,
  Downe hanging his dull head with heavy chere,° *countenance*
  Yet inly being more, then seeming sad:
  A paire of Pincers in his hand he had,
  With which he pinchéd people to the hart,
  That from thenceforth a wretched life they lad,
  In wilfull languor and consuming smart,
Dying each day with inward wounds of dolours dart.

17

But Fury was full ill appareiléd
  In rags, that naked nigh she did appeare,
  With ghastly lookes and dreadfull drerihed;°   *horror*
  For from her backe her garments she did teare,
  And from her head oft rent her snarléd heare:
  In her right hand a firebrand she did tosse
  About her head, still roming here and there;
  As a dismayéd Deare in chace embost,°   *hard pressed*
Forgetfull of his safety, hath his right way lost.

18

After them went Displeasure and Pleasance,
  He looking lompish and full sullein sad,

---

9. An aspergillum, or brush for sprinkling holy water.

1. I.e., a small screen or vizard, permitting one to see while remaining unseen.

And hanging downe his heavy countenance;
 She chearefull fresh and full of joyance glad,
 As if no sorrow she ne felt ne drad;°   *feared*
 That evill matchéd paire they seemed to bee:
 An angry Waspe th'one in a viall had,
 Th'other in hers an hony-lady° Bee;   *honey-laden*
Thus marchéd these six couples forth in faire degree.° *order*

19

After all these there marcht a most faire Dame,
 Led of two grysie° villeins, th'one Despight,° *grim/outrage*
 The other clepéd° Cruelty by name: *called*
 She dolefull Lady, like a dreary Spright,
 Cald by strong charmes out of eternall night,
 Had deathes owne image figurd in her face,
 Full of sad signes, fearefull to living sight;
 Yet in that horror shewd a seemely grace,
And with her feeble feet did move a comely pace.

20

Her brest all naked, as net° ivory,   *pure*
 Without adorne of gold or silver bright,
 Wherewith the Craftesman wonts° it beautify, *is used to*
 Of her dew honour° was despoyléd quight, *covering*
 And a wide wound therein (O ruefull sight)
 Entrenchéd deepe with knife accurséd keene,
 Yet freshly bleeding forth her fainting spright,
 (The worke of cruell hand) was to be seene,
That dyde in sanguine red her skin all snowy cleene.

21

At that wide orifice her trembling hart
 Was drawne forth, and in silver basin layd,
 Quite through transfixéd with a deadly dart,
 And in her bloud yet steeming fresh embayd:° *bathed*
 And those two villeins, which her steps upstayd,
 When her weake feete could scarcely her sustaine,
 And fading vitall powers gan to fade,
 Her forward still with torture did constraine,
And evermore encreaséd her consuming paine.

22

Next after her the wingéd God himselfe[2]
 Came riding on a Lion ravenous,
 Taught to abay the menage° of that Elfe, *control*
 That man and beast with powre imperious
 Subdeweth to his kingdome tyrannous:
 His blindfold eyes he bad a while unbind,
 That his proud spoyle of that same dolorous
 Faire Dame he might behold in perfect kind;° *manner*
Which seene, he much rejoycéd in his cruell mind.

23

Of which full proud, himselfe up rearing hye,
 He lookéd round about with sterne disdaine;

2. I.e., Cupid.

And did survay his goodly company:
And marshalling the evill ordered traine,°   *assembly*
With that the darts which his right hand did straine,
Full dreadfully he shooke that all did quake,
And clapt on hie his coulourd wingés twaine,
That all his many° it affraide did make: *company*
Tho blinding him againe, his way he forth did take.

24

Behinde him was Reproch, Repentance, Shame;
Reproch the first, Shame next, Repent behind:
Repentance feeble, sorrowfull, and lame:
Reproch despightfull, carelesse, and unkind;
Shame most ill favour,° bestiall, and blind: *featured*
Shame lowrd, Repentance sighed, Reproch did scould;
Reproch sharpe stings, Repentance whips entwind,
Shame burning brond-yrons in her hand did hold:
All three to each° unlike, yet all made in one mould.   *each other*

25

And after them a rude confuséd rout°   *mob*
Of persons flockt, whose names is hard to read:°   *distinguish*
Emongst them was sterne Strife, and Anger stout,
Unquiet Care, and fond Unthriftihead,°   *wastefulness*
Lewd° Losse of Time, and Sorrow seeming dead,   *foolish*
Inconstant Chaunge, and false Disloyaltie,
Consuming Riotise,° and guilty Dread   *extravagance*
Of heavenly vengeance, faint Infirmitie,
Vile Povertie, and lastly Death with infamie.

26

There were full many moe like° maladies,   *similar*
Whose names and natures I note° readen well;   *cannot*
So many moe, as there be phantasies
In wavering wemens wit,° that none can tell,°   *mind/count*
Or paines in love, or punishments in hell;
All which disguizéd marcht in masking wise,
About the chamber with that Damozell,
And then returnéd, having marchéd thrise,
Into the inner roome, from whence they first did rise.°   *emerge*

27

So soone as they were in, the dore streight way
Fast lockéd, driven with that stormy blast,
Which first it opened; and bore all away.
Then the brave Maid, which all this while was plast
In secret shade, and saw both first and last,
Issewéd forth, and went unto the dore,
To enter in, but found it lockéd fast:
It vaine she thought with rigorous uprore
For to efforce,° when charmes had closéd it afore.   *force open*

28

Where force might not availe, there sleights and art
She cast° to use, both fit for hard emprize;   *purposed*

For thy from that same roome not to depart
Till morrow next, she did her selfe avize,°   *resolve*
When that same Maske againe should forth arize.
The morrow next appeard with joyous cheare,
Calling men to their daily exercize,
Then she, as morrow fresh, her selfe did reare°   *arouse*
Out of her secret stand, that day for to out weare.[3]

29

All that day she outwore in wandering,
  And gazing on that Chambers ornament,
  Till that againe the second evening
  Her covered with her sable vestiment,
  Wherewith the worlds faire beautie she hath blent:°   *obscured*
  Then when the second watch was almost past,[4]
  That brasen dore flew open, and in went
  Bold Britomart, as she had late forecast,°   *determined*
Neither of idle shewes, nor of false charmes aghast.

30

So soone as she was entred, round about
  She cast her eies, to see what was become
  Of all those persons, which she saw without:
  But lo, they streight were vanisht all and some,[5]
  Ne living wight she saw in all that roome,
  Save that same woefull Ladie,[6] both whose hands
  Were bounden fast, that did her ill become,
  And her small wast girt round with yron bands,
Unto a brasen pillour, by the which she stands.

31

And her before the vile Enchaunter[7] sate,
  Figuring° straunge characters of his art,   *drawing*
  With living bloud he those characters wrate,
  Dreadfully dropping from her dying hart,
  Seeming transfixéd with a cruell dart,
  And all perforce to make her him to love.
  Ah who can love the worker of her smart?
  A thousand charmes he formerly did prove;°   *try*
Yet thousand charmes could not her stedfast heart remove.

32

Soone as that virgin knight he saw in place,[8]
  His wicked bookes in hast he overthrew,
  Not caring his long labours to deface,[9]
  And fiercely ronning to that Lady trew,
  A murdrous kinfe out of his pocket drew,
  The which he thought, for villeinous despight,
  In her tormented bodie to embrew:°   *plunge*

3. I.e., to pass that day.
4. I.e., just before midnight. The "second watch" began at nine and ended at twelve.
5. I.e., one and all.
6. I.e., Amoret.
7. I.e., Busirane.
8. I.e., there.
9. I.e., not caring whether he destroyed his long labors.

But the stout Damzell to him leaping light,
His cursed hand withheld, and maisteréd his might.

33

From her, to whom his fury first he ment,°   *intended*
 The wicked weapon rashly° he did wrest,   *quickly*
 And turning to her selfe his fell intent,
 Unwares° it strooke into her snowie chest,   *suddenly*
 That little drops empurpled her faire brest.
 Exceeding wroth therewith the virgin grew,
 Albe the wound were nothing deepe imprest,
 And fiercely forth her mortall blade she drew,
To give him the reward for such vile outrage dew.

34

So mightily she smote him, that to ground
 He fell halfe dead; next stroke him should have slaine,
 Had not the Lady, which by him stood bound,
 Dernely° unto her calléd to abstaine,   *dismally*
 From doing him to dy. For else her paine
 Should be remedilesse, sith none but hee,
 Which wrought it, could the same recure againe.
 Therewith she stayd her hand, loth stayd to bee;
For life she him envyde,° and longed revenge to see. *begrudged*

35

And to him said, "Thou wicked man, whose meed
 For so huge mischiefe, and vile villany
 Is death, or if that ought do death exceed,
 Be sure, that nought may save thee from to dy,
 But if that[1] thou this Dame doe presently° *at once*
 Restore unto her health, and former state;
 This doe and live, else die undoubtedly."
 He glad of life, that lookt for death but late,
Did yield himselfe right willing to prolong his date.° *term of life*

36

And rising up, gan streight to overlooke°   *read*
 Those curséd leaves, his charmes backe to reverse;
 Full dreadfull things out of that balefull booke
 He red,° and measured° many a sad verse, *said/chanted*
 That horror gan the virgins hart to perse,
 And her faire locks up staréd stiffe on end,
 Hearing him those same bloudy lines reherse;° *recite*
 And all the while he red, she did extend
Her sword high over him, if ought° he did offend. *in any way*

37

Anon she gan perceive the house to quake,
 And all the dores to rattle round about;
 Yet all that did not her dismaiéd make,
 Nor slacke her threatfull hand for daungers dout,° *fear*

1. I.e., unless.

But still with stedfast eye and courage stout
Abode,° to weet what end would come of all.   *waited*
At last that mightie chaine, which round about
Her tender waste was wound, adowne gan fall,
And that great brasen pillour broke in peeces small.

38

The cruell steele, which thrild her dying hart,
Fell softly forth, as of his owne accord,
And the wyde wound, which lately did dispart°   *cleave*
Her bleeding brest, and riven bowels gored,[2]
Was closéd up, as it had not bene bored,
And every part to safety full sound,
As she were never hurt, was soone restored:
Tho when she felt her selfe to be unbound,
And perfect hole, prostrate she fell unto the ground.

39

Before faire Britomart, she fell prostrate,
Saying, "Ah noble knight, what worthy meed
Can wretched Lady, quit from wofull state,
Yield you in liew of this your gratious deed?
Your vertue selfe her owne reward shall breed,
Even immortall praise, and glory wyde,
Which I your vassall, by your prowesse freed,
Shall through the world make to be notifyde,°   *proclaimed*
And goodly well advance,° that goodly well was tryde."   *praise*

40

But Britomart uprearing her from ground,
Said, "Gentle Dame, reward enough I weene
For many labours more, then I have found,
This, that in safety now I have you seene,
And meane° of your deliverance have beene: *means*
Henceforth faire Lady comfort to you take,
And put away remembrance of late teene;°   *woe*
In stead thereof know, that your loving Make,°   *mate*
Hath no lesse griefe enduréd for your gentle sake."

41

She much was cheard to heare him mentiond,
Whom of all living wights she lovéd best.
Then laid the noble Championesse strong hond
Upon th'enchaunter, which had her distrest
So sore, and with foule outrages opprest:
With that great chaine, wherewith not long ygo
He bound that pitteous Lady prisoner, now relest,
Himselfe she bound, more worthy to be so,
And captive with her led to wretchednesse and wo.

42

Returning backe, those goodly roomes, which erst
She saw so rich and royally arayd,

2. I.e., pierced her torn inner parts.

Now vanisht utterly, and cleane subverst°   *overturned*
She found, and all their glory quite decayd,°   *destroyed*
That sight of such a chaunge her much dismayd.
Thence forth descending to that perlous° Porch, *perilous*
Those dreadfull flames she also found delayd,° *allayed*
And quenchéd quite, like a consuméd torch,
That erst all entrers wont so cruelly to scorch.

43

More easie issew now, then entrance late
She found: for now that fainéd° dreadfull flame, *false*
Which chokt the porch of that enchaunted gate,
And passage bard to all, that thither came,
Was vanisht quite, as it were not the same,
And gave her leave at pleasure forth to passe.
Th'Enchaunter selfe, which all that fraud did frame,
To have efforst° the love of that faire lasse, *compelled*
Seeing his worke now wasted deepe engrievéd was.

44

But when the victoresse arrivéd there,
Where late she left the pensife Scudamore,
With her owne trusty Squire, both full of feare,
Neither of them she found where she them lore:° *left*
Thereat her noble hart was stonisht sore;
But most faire Amoret, whose gentle spright
Now gan to feede on hope, which she before
Conceivéd had, to see her owne deare knight,
Being thereof beguyld was fild with new affright.

45

But he sad man, when he had long in drede
Awayted there for Britomarts returne,
Yet saw her not nor signe of her good speed,° *success*
His expectation to despaire did turne,
Misdeeming sure that her those flames did burne;
And therefore gan advize° with her old Squire, *consult*
Who her deare nourslings losse no lesse did mourne,
Thence to depart for further aide t'enquire:
Where let them wend at will, whilest here I doe respire.° *breathe*

[Sts. 43–45 first appear in the 1596 edition of *The Faerie Queene*. In the edition of 1590, the following stanzas conclude Book III].

At last she came unto the place, where late
She left Sir Scudamour in great distresse,
Twixt dolour and despight halfe desperate,
Of his loves succour, of his owne redresse,° *relief*
And of the hardie Britomarts successe:
There on the cold earth him now thrown she found,
In wilfull anguish, and dead heavinesse,° *grief*
And to him cald; whose voices knowen sound
Soon as he heard, himself he rearéd light from ground.

There did he see, that most on earth him joyd,
  His dearest love, the comfort of his dayes,
  Whose too long absence him had sore annoyd,°   *troubled*
  And weariéd his life with dull delayes:
  Straight he upstarted from the loathéd layes,°   *ground*
  And to her ran with hasty egernesse,
  Like as a Deare, that greedily embayes°   *bathes*
  In the coole soile,° after long thirstinesse,   *marsh*
Which he in chace enduréd hath, now nigh breathlesse.

Lightly he clipt her twixt his armes twaine,
  And streightly° did embrace her body bright,   *closely*
  Her body, late the prison of sad paine,
  Now the sweet lodge of love and deare delight:
  But she faire Lady overcommen quight
  Of huge affection, did in pleasure melt,
  And in sweete ravishment pourd out her spright:
  No word they spake, nor earthly thing they felt,
But like two senceles stocks in long embracement dwelt.

Had ye them seene, ye would have surely thought,
  That they had beene that faire Hermaphrodite,[3]
  Which that rich Romane of white marble wrought,
  And in his costly Bath causd to bee site:
  So seemd those two, as growne together quite,
  That Britomart halfe envying their blesse,°   *bliss*
  Was much empassiond° in her gentle sprite,   *moved*
  And to her selfe oft wisht like happinesse,
In vaine she wisht, that fate n'ould° let her yet possesse.   *would not*

Thus doe those lovers with sweet countervayle,°   *exchange*
  Each other of loves bitter fruit despoile.
  But now my teme begins to faint and fayle,
  All woxen weary of their journall° toyle: *daily*
  Therefore I will their sweatie yokes assoyle°   *release*
  At this same furrowes end, till a new day:
  And ye faire Swayns, after your long turmoyle,
  Now cease your worke, and at your pleasure play;
Now cease your worke; to morrow is an holy day.

3. Cf. Ovid, *Metamorphoses*, IV. 285–388. The gods granted the prayer of Salmacis that she and Hermaphroditus might never be parted, by fusing them into one creature. See also Edgar Wind, *Pagan Mysteries in the Renaissance* (New Haven, Conn., 1958), 164–165; also Donald Cheney, "Spenser's Hermaphrodite and the 1590 *Faerie Queene*," *PMLA*, LXXXVII (1972), 192–200.

From The Fourth Booke of the Faerie Queene

Containing
The Legend of Cambel and Telamond[1]
or
of Friendship

1

The rugged forhead that with grave foresight
  Welds° kingdomes causes, and affaires of state,[2]   *manages*
  My looser rimes (I wote) doth sharply wite,°   *blame*
  For praising love, as I have done of late,
  And magnifying lovers deare debate;
  By which fraile youth is oft to follie led,
  Through false allurement of that pleasing baite,
  That better were in vertues discipled,°   *instructed*
Then with vaine poemes weeds to have their fancies fed.

2

Such ones ill judge of love, that cannot love,
  Ne in their frosen hearts feele kindly° flame: *natural*
  For thy they ought not thing unknowne reprove,
  Ne naturall affection faultlesse blame,
  For fault of few that have abusd the same.
  For it of honor and all vertue is
  The roote, and brings forth glorious flowres of fame,
  That crowne true lovers with immortall blis,
The meed of them that love, and do not live amisse.

3

Which who so list looke backe to former ages,
  And call to count the things that then were donne,
  Shall find, that all the workes of those wise sages,
  And brave exploits which great Heroés wonne,
  In love were either ended or begunne:
  Witnesse the father of Philosophie,[3]
  Which to his Critias, shaded oft from sunne,
  Of love full manie lessons did apply,
The which these Stoicke censours cannot well deny.

---

1. No character named Telamond appears in the poem. Roche suggests that the name, "perfect world" (Greek *tereos*; Latin *mundus*) conflates those of the three brothers Priamond, Dyamond, and Triamond, whose story (in Cantos ii–iii) "constitutes an allegory of the harmony in the world" (*op. cit.*, 16–17; and cf. Edmund Spenser, *The Faerie Queene*, ed. Thomas P. Roche, Jr. [Harmondsworth, 1978], p. 1166).

2. These lines probably allude to the Queen's chief minister, William Cecil, Lord Burleigh, whose displeasure with some aspects of Spenser's earlier work the poet seems to notice in Book VI.xii.41.

3. I.e., Socrates, who discoursed on love to Phaedrus (not Critias) in the shadow of a plane tree (Plato, *Phaedrus*, 229a ff.).

4

To such therefore I do not sing at all,
  But to that sacred Saint my soveraigne Queene,
  In whose chast breast all bountie naturall,
  And treasures of true love enlockéd beene,
  Bove all her sexe that ever yet was seene;
  To her I sing of love, that loveth best,
  And best is loved of all alive I weene:
  To her this song most fitly is addrest,
The Queene of love, and Prince of peace from heaven blest.

5

Which that she may the better deigne to heare,
  Do thou dred infant,[4] Venus dearling dove,
  From her high spirit chase imperious feare,[5]
  And use of awfull Majestie remove:
  In sted thereof with drops of melting love,
  Deawd with ambrosiall kisses, by thee gotten
  From thy sweete smyling mother from above,
  Sprinckle her heart, and haughtie courage° soften,   *nature*
That she may hearke to love, and reade this lesson[6] often.

[The somewhat involved structure of Book IV in fact reflects Spenser's resolve to celebrate the full reach and scope of the traditional virtue of friendship. The first two Cantos are chiefly concerned with friendships true and false; in the third Canto, however, with the story of Cambel and the three sons of Agape, the larger role of friendship in human relationships is explored. Spenser's allegorical narrative thenceforth shows how friendship informs and steadies "lovers' deare debate," while it contributes to the establishment of social concord and natural harmony. For C.S. Lewis, Books III and IV constitute "a single book on the subject of love" (*op. cit.*, p. 338). Certainly Book IV carries forward the several narrative strands of Book III. Britomart and Arthegal meet, and pledge mutual love (Cantos iv, vi). Belphoebe and Timias are reconciled (Canto viii); in Cantos xi–xii, the marriage of Thames and Medway, magnificently celebrated by all the rivers, leads to the union of Florimell and Marinell, whose nuptials will be described in Book V. Scudamour's account of his "conquest . . . Of vertuous Amoret" in the Temple of Venus, finally, provides a "symbolic core" not merely for this Book but in some sense also for the subtly interwoven tapestry of love-relationships displayed in Books III and IV.]

4. I.e., Cupid.
5. I.e., the power to instill fear and awe.

6. I.e., the lesson not to fear love.

Canto X

Scudamour doth his conquest tell,
Of vertuous Amoret:
Great Venus Temple is described,
And lovers life forth set.

1

"True he it said, what ever man it sayd,
  That love with gall and hony doth abound,
  But if the one be with the other wayd,
  For every dram of hony therein found,
  A pound of gall doth over it redound.[1]
  That I too true by triall have approved:°   *proved*
  For since the day that first with deadly wound
  My heart was launcht,° and learnéd to have loved,   *pierced*
I never joyéd howre, but still with care was moved.

2

"And yet such grace is given them from above,
  That all the cares and evill which they meet,
  May nought at all their setled mindes remove,
  But seeme gainst common sence to them most sweet;
  As bosting in their martyrdome unmeet.°   *unseemly*
  So all that ever yet I have endured,
  I count as naught, and tread downe under feet,
  Since of my love at length I rest assured,
That to disloyalty she will not be allured.

3

"Long were to tell the travell° and long toile,   *travail*
  Through which this shield of love I late have wonne,
  And purchaséd this peerelesse beauties spoile,[2]
  That harder may be ended, then begonne.
  But since ye so desire, your will be donne.
  Then hearke ye gentle knights and Ladies free,
  My hard mishaps, that ye may learne to shonne;
  For though sweet love to conquer glorious bee,
Yet is the paine thereof much greater then the fee.°   *reward*

4

"What time the fame of this renowméd prise
  Flew first abroad, and all mens eares possest,
  I having armes then taken, gan avise[3]
  To winne me honour by some noble gest,°   *deed*
  And purchase me some place amongst the best.
  I boldly thought (so young mens thoughts are bold)[4]

---

1. I.e., doth excessively match it. Spenser employs this ancient adage (originally from Plautus, *Cistellaria*, I.i.70–71) also for Thomalin's "Embleme" to "March," in *The Shepheardes Calender*.
2. I.e., won Amoret as my reward.
3. I.e., resolved.
4. Cf. III.xi.54, and note.

That this same brave emprize° for me did rest,   *enterprise*
  And that both shield and she whom I behold,
Might be my lucky lot; sith all by lot we hold.

5

"So on that hard adventure forth I went,
  And to the place of perill shortly came.
  That was a temple faire and auncient,
  Which of great mother Venus bare the name,
  And farre renowméd through exceeding fame;
  Much more then that, which was in Paphos built,
  Or that in Cyprus,[5] both long since this same,
  Though all the pillours of the one were guilt,
And all the others pavement were with yvory spilt.°   *inlaid*

6

"And it was seated in an Island strong,
  Abounding all with delices° most rare,   *delights*
  And walled by nature gainst invaders wrong,
  That none mote have accesse, nor inward fare,°   *passage*
  But by one way, that passage did prepare.°   *provide*
  It was a bridge ybuilt in goodly wize,
  With curious Corbes° and pendants graven faire,   *corbels*
  And archéd all with porches, did arize
On stately pillours, framed after the Doricke guize.[6]

7

"And for defence thereof, on th'other end
  There rearéd was a castle faire and strong,
  That warded° all which in or out did wend,   *guarded*
  And flanckéd both the bridges sides along,
  Gainst all that would it faine to force or wrong.[7]
  And therein wonnéd° twenty valiant Knights;   *dwelt*
  All twenty tride in warres experience long;
  Whose office was, against all manner wights
By all meanes to maintaine that castels ancient rights.

8

"Before that Castle was an open plaine,
  And in the midst thereof a piller placed;
  On which this shield, of many sought in vaine,
  The shield of Love, whose guerdon me hath graced,
  Was hangd on high with golden ribbands laced;
  And in the marble stone was written this,
  With golden letters goodly well enchaced,
  Blesséd the man that well can use his blis:
Whose ever be the shield, faire Amoret be his.

9

"Which when I red, my heart did inly earne,°   *yearn*
  And pant with hope of that adventures hap.°   *(good) fortune*

5. Cf. III.vi.29, and note.
6. Of the Ionic, Doric, and Corinthian architectural orders, the Doric is the simplest.

7. The strength and purpose of this castle are to be contrasted with those of the "fence" enclosing the Bower of Bliss; cf. II.xii.43.

Ne stayéd further newes thereof to learne,
But with my speare upon the shield did rap,
That all the castle ringéd with the clap.
Streight forth issewd a Knight all armed to proofe,[8]
And bravely mounted to his most mishap
Who staying nought to question from aloofe,
Ran fierce at me, that fire glaunst from his horses hoofe.

10

"Whom boldly I encountered (as I could)[9]
And by good fortune shortly him unseated.
Eftsoones out sprung two more of equall mould;°   *stature*
But I them both with equall hap defeated:
So all the twenty I likewise entreated,°   *treated*
And left them groning there upon the plaine.
Then preacing to the pillour I repeated
The read° thereof for guerdon of my paine,   *inscription*
And taking downe the shield, with me did it retaine.

11

"So forth without impediment I past,
Till to the Bridges utter° gate I came: *outer*
The which I found sure lockt and chainéd fast.
I knockt, but no man aunswred me by name;
I cald, but no man answered to my clame.°   *call*
Yet I persevered still to knocke and call,
Till at the last I spide within the same,
Where one stood peeping through a crevis small,
To whom I cald aloud, halfe angry therewithall.

12

"That was to weet the Porter of the place,
Unto whose trust the charge thereof was lent
His name was Doubt, that had a double face,
Th'one forward looking, th'other backeward bent,
Therein resembling Janus auncient,
Which hath in charge the ingate° of the yeare: *entrance*
And evermore his eyes about him went,
As if some provéd perill he did feare,
Or did misdoubt° some ill, whose cause did not appeare.   *suspect*

13

"On th'one side he, on th'other sate Delay,
Behinde the gate, that none her might espy
Whose manner° was all passengers° to stay,   *custom/passers-by*
And entertaine with her occasions° sly,   *pretexts*
Through which some lost great hope unheedily,
Which never they recover might againe;
And others quite excluded forth,[1] did ly
Long languishing there in unpittied paine,
And seeking often entraunce, afterwards in vaine.

---

8. I.e., fully armed.   1. I.e., quite shut out.
9. I.e., as boldly as I knew how.

14

"Me when as he had privily° espide,   *secretly*
  Bearing the shield which I had conquerd late,
  He kend° it streight, and to me opened wide.   *recognized*
  So in I past, and streight he closd the gate.
  But being in, Delay in close await[2]
  Caught hold on me, and thought my steps to stay,
  Feigning full many a fond excuse to prate,
  And time to steale, the threasure of mans day,
Whose smallest minute lost no riches render° may.   *return*

15

"But by no meanes my way I would forslow,°   *delay*
  For ought that ever she could doe or say,
  But from my lofty steede dismounting low,
  Past forth on foote, beholding all the way
  The goodly workes, and stones of rich assay,°   *value*
  Cast into sundry shapes by wondrous skill,
  That like on earth no where I recken° may: *mention*
  And underneath, the river rolling still
With murmure soft, that seemed to serve the workmans will.

16

"Thence forth I passéd to the second gate,
  The Gate of good desert, whose goodly pride
  And costly frame, were long here to relate.
  The same to all stoode alwaies open wide:
  But in the Porch did evermore abide
  An hideous° Giant, dreadfull to behold,   *huge*
  That stopt the entraunce with his spacious stride,[3]
  And with the terrour of his countenance bold
Full many did affray, that else faine enter would.

17

"His name was Daunger[4] dreaded over all,
  Who day and night did watch and duely ward,
  From fearefull cowards, entrance to forstall,
  And faint-heart-fooles, whom shew of perill hard
  Could terrifie from Fortunes faire adward:°   *award*
  For oftentimes faint hearts at first espiall
  Of his grim face, were from approaching scard;
  Unworthy they of grace, whom one deniall
Excludes from fairest hope, withouten further triall.

18

"Yet many doughty warriours, often tride°   *proven*
  In greater perils to be stout and bold,
  Durst not the sternnesse of his looke abide,
  But soone as they his countenance did behold,
  Began to faint, and feele their corage cold.
  Againe some other, that in hard assaies°   *trials*

2. I.e., from ambush.
3. I.e., with his wide-straddling stance.
4. Here and at III.xii.11 the threatening appearance of this figure signifies chiefly the lady's reluctance, or refusal, to grant her love.

Were cowards knowne, and litle count did hold,[5]
  Either through gifts, or guile, or such like waies,
Crept in by stouping low, or stealing of the kaies.°   keys

19

"But I though meanest man of many moe,
  Yet much disdaining unto him to lout,°   bow
Or creepe betweene his legs, so in to goe,
  Resolved him to assault with manhood stout,
  And either beat him in, or drive him out.
Eftsoones advauncing that enchaunted shield,
  With all my might I gan to lay about:
  Which when he saw, the glaive° which he did wield   halberd
He gan forthwith t'avale,° and way unto me yield.   lower

20

"So as I entred, I did backeward looke,
  For feare of harme, that might lie hidden there;
And loe his hindparts, whereof heed I tooke,
  Much more deforméd fearefull ugly were,
  Then all his former parts did earst appere.
For hatred, murther, treason, and despight,
  With many moe lay in ambushment there,
  Awayting to entrap the warelesse° wight,   unwary
Which did not them prevent° with vigilant foresight.   anticipate

21

"Thus having past all perill, I was come
  Within the compasse of that Islands space;
The which did seeme unto my simple doome°   judgment
  The onely[6] pleasant and delightfull place,
  That ever troden was of footings trace.
For all that nature by her mother wit[7]
  Could frame in earth, and forme of substance base,
  Was there, and all that nature did omit,
Art playing second natures part, supplyéd it.

22

"No tree, that is of count,° in greenewood growes,   note
  From lowest Juniper to Cedar tall,
No flowre in field, that daintie odour throwes,
  And deckes his branch with blossomes over all,
  But there was planted, or grew naturall:
Nor sense of man so coy and curious nice,[8]
  But there mote find to please it selfe withall;
  Nor hart could wish for any queint° device,   elegant
But there it present was, and did fraile sense entice.

23

"In such luxurious plentie of all pleasure,
  It seemed a second paradise to ghesse,[9]
So lavishly enricht with natures threasure,

5. I.e., lightly regarded.
6. I.e., the unmatchably unique.
7. I.e., her (natural) ingenuity.

8. I.e., so exquisitely fastidious.
9. I.e., one might imagine it to be a
second paradise.

That if the happie soules, which doe possesse
Th'Elysian fields,[1] and live in lasting blesse,°   *bliss*
Should happen this with living eye to see,
They soone would loath their lesser happinesse,
And wish to life returned againe to bee,
That in this joyous place they mote have joyance free.

24

"Fresh shadowes, fit to shroud from sunny ray;
    Faire lawnds,° to take the sunne in season dew;   *glades*
    Sweet springs, in which a thousand Nymphs did play;
    Soft rombling° brookes, that gentle slomber drew;   *murmuring*
    High rearéd mounts, the lands about to vew;
    Low looking dales, disloignd° from common gaze;   *remote*
    Delightfull bowres, to solace lovers trew;
    False Labyrinthes,[2] fond runners eyes to daze;
All which by nature made did nature selfe amaze.

25

"And all without were walkes and alleyes dight
    With divers trees, enranged in even rankes;
    And here and there were pleasant arbors pight,
    And shadie seates, and sundry flowring bankes,
    To sit and rest the walkers wearie shankes,
    And therein thousand payres of lovers walkt,
    Praysing their god, and yeelding him great thankes,
    Ne ever ought but of their true loves talkt,
Ne ever for rebuke or blame of any balkt.°   *ceased*

26

"All these together by themselves did sport
    Their spotlesse pleasures, and sweet loves content.
    But farre away from these, another sort°   *company*
    Of lovers linckéd in true harts consent;
    Which lovéd not as these, for like intent,
    But on chast vertue grounded their desire,
    Farre from all fraud, or faynéd blandishment;
    Which in their spirits kindling zealous fire,
Brave thoughts and noble deedes did evermore aspire.°   *inspire*

27

"Such were great Hercules, and Hylas deare;
    Trew Jonathan, and David trustie tryde;
    Stout Theseus, and Pirithous his feare;°   *companion*
    Pylades and Orestes by his syde;
    Myld Titus and Gesippus without pryde;

---

1. In the classical underworld (cf, *Aeneid*, VI. 638 ff.), the spirits of those whose earthly lives were noble or admirable resided in the Elysian Fields.

2. I.e., mazes (such as that still in existence at Hampton Court Palace, near London).

Damon and Pythias whom death could not sever:[3]
All these and all that ever had bene tyde
In bands of friendship, there did live for ever,
Whose lives although decayed, yet loves decayéd never.

28

"Which when as I, that never tasted blis,
Nor happie howre, beheld with gazefull eye,
I thought there was none other heaven then this;
And gan their endlesse happinesse envye,
That being free from feare and gealosye,
Might frankely there their loves desire possesse;
Whilest I through paines and perlous jeopardie,
Was forst to seeke my lifes deare patronesse:
Much dearer be the things, which come through hard distresse.

29

"Yet all those sights, and all that else I saw,
Might not my steps withhold, but that forthright
Unto that purposd place I did me draw,
Where as my love was lodgéd day and night:
The temple of great Venus, that is hight
The Queene of beautie, and of love the mother,
There worshippéd of every living wight;
Whose goodly workmanship farre past all other
That ever were on earth, all were they set together.

30

"Not that same famous Temple of Diane,
Whose hight all Ephesus did oversee,
And which all Asia sought with vowes prophane,
One of the worlds seven wonders[4] sayd to bee,
Might match with this by many a degree:
Nor that, which that wise King of Jurie framed,
With endlesse cost, to be th'Almighties see;[5]
Nor all that else through all the world is named
To all the heathen Gods, might like to this be clamed.°   *proclaimed*

---

3. Spenser's immediate source for the stories of these famous pairs of friends (save David and Jonathan, for whom cf. I Samuel xviii.3; xx.17; xxiii.16–18) may well have been Lyly's *Euphues*: cf. the edition of M. W. Croll and H. Clemons (N.Y., 1964), p. 30. Cf. also (among a wealth of allusion in classical literature), for the story of Hercules' lost love, the beautiful youth Hylas, Theocritus, Idyl XIII; for the friendship of the warrior-kings Pirithous and Theseus, *Metamorphoses*, VIII. 303, 405–406; for the readiness of Pylades to die for Orestes, Euripides, *Orestes*, 802–803; for the tale of Damon and Pythias (universal touchstone of friendship), Cicero, *De Officiis*, III.45. The story of Titus and Gesippus appears in Boccaccio, *Decameron*, X.viii.
4. The Seven Wonders of the Ancient World were the Temple of Diana at Ephesus; the Great Pyramid of Cheops, at Gizeh; the Hanging Gardens of Babylon; the Mausoleum at Halicarnassus (modern Bodrum, in Turkey); the Colossus of Rhodes; the statue of Olympian Zeus by Phidias, in Athens; the Pharos, at Alexandria.
5. I.e., the Temple built by Solomon at Jerusalem: cf. I Kings vi.

31

"I much admyring that so goodly frame,
  Unto the porch approcht, which open stood;
  But therein sate an amiable° Dame,   *pleasant*
  That seemed to be of very sober mood,
  And in her semblant° shewed great womanhood: *demeanour*
  Strange was her tyre;° for on her head a crowne   *head-dress*
  She wore much like unto a Danisk° hood,   *Danish*
  Poudred with pearle and stone, and all her gowne
Enwoven was with gold, that raught full low a downe.

32

"On either side of her, two young men stood,
  Both strongly armed, as fearing one another;
  Yet were they brethren both of halfe the blood,
  Begotten by two fathers of one mother,
  Though of contrarie natures each to other:
  The one of them hight Love, the other Hate,
  Hate was the elder, Love the younger brother;
  Yet was the younger stronger in his state
Then th'elder, and him maystred still in all debate.°   *contention*

33

"Nathlesse that Dame so well them tempred° both,   *governed*
  That she them forcéd hand to joyne in hand,
  Albe that Hatred was thereto full loth,
  And turned his face away, as he did stand,
  Unwilling to behold that lovely band.[6]
  Yet she was of such grace and vertuous might,
  That her commaundment he could not withstand,
  But bit his lip for felonous° despight,   *fierce*
And gnasht his yron tuskes at that displeasing sight.

34

"Concord she cleepéd° was in common reed,°   *named/speech*
  Mother of blessed Peace, and Friendship trew;
  They both her twins, both borne of heavenly seed,
  And she her selfe likewise divinely grew;
  The which right well her workes divine did shew:
  For strength, and wealth, and happinesse she lends,
  And strife, and warre, and anger does subdew:
  Of litle much, of foes she maketh frends,
And to afflicted minds sweet rest and quiet sends.[7]

35

"By her the heaven is in his course contained,
  And all the world in state unmovéd stands,
  As their Almightie maker first ordained,
  And bound them with inviolable bands;

6. I.e., that loving bond.
7. That Dame Concord brings together the figures of Love and Hate recalls and symbolically represents the ancient metaphysical doctrine of *discordia concors,* i.e., the combination of discordant ele-ments brings forth concord. Cf., for example, Seneca, *Quaestiones Naturales,* VII. 27: "The whole harmony of the universe consists in discordancies." Cf. also Roche, *op. cit.,* pp. 17, 131.

Else would the waters overflow the lands,
    And fire devoure the ayre, and hell them quight,[8]
    But that she holds them with her blessèd hands.
    She is the nourse of pleasure and delight,
And unto Venus grace the gate doth open right.

36

"By her I entring halfe dismayèd was,
    But she in gentle wise me entertayned,°   *received*
    And twixt her selfe and Love did let me pas;
    But Hatred would my entrance have restrayned,
    And with his club me threatned to have brayned,
    Had not the Ladie with her powrefull speach
    Him from his wicked will uneath refrayned;[9]
    And th'other eke his malice did empeach,°   *prevent*
Till I was throughly past the perill of his reach.

37

"Into the inmost Temple thus I came,
    Which fuming all with frankensence I found,
    And odours rising from the altars flame.
    Upon an hundred marble pillors round
    The roofe up high was rearèd from the ground,
    All deckt with crownes, and chaynes, and girlands gay,
    And thousand pretious gifts worth many a pound,
    The which sad lovers for their vowes did pay;
And all the ground was strowed with flowres, as fresh as May.

38

"An hundred Altars round about were set,
    All flaming with their sacrifices fire,
    That with the steme thereof the Temple swet,
    Which rould in clouds to heaven did aspire,[1]
    And in them bore true lovers vowes entire:°   *unbroken*
    And eke an hundred brasen caudrons bright,
    To bath in joy and amorous desire,
    Every° of which was to a damzell hight;°   *each/assigned*
For all the Priests were damzels, in soft linnen dight.

39

"Right in the midst the Goddesse selfe did stand
    Upon an altar of some costly masse,
    Whose substance was uneath to understand:

---

8. I.e., and hell overwhelm them all in discord. The thought and expression of this stanza look ultimately to Boethius, *De Consolatione Philosophiae*, II. Metre 8: "That the world with stable feyth varieth accordable chaungynges; that the contrarious qualites of elementz holden among hemself allyaunce perdurable . . . al this accordaunce of thynges is bounde with love, that governeth erthe and see, and hath also comandement to the hevene. And yif this love slakede the bridelis, alle thynges that now loven hem

togidres wolden make batayle contynuely, and stryven to fordo the fassoun of this world, the which they now leden in accordable feith by feyre moevynges" (tr. Chaucer, *Boece*).
9. I.e., restrained with some difficulty.
1. The passage derives from Virgil's description of the Temple of Venus at Paphos: ". . . its hundred altars, warm with Sabaean incense, and constantly perfumed by garlands of fresh flowers" (*Aeneid*, I. 415–417).

For neither pretious stone, nor durefull° brasse,   *enduring*
Nor shining gold, nor mouldring clay it was;
But much more rare and pretious to esteeme,[2]
Pure° in aspect, and like to christall glasse,   *clear*
Yet glasse was not, if one did rightly deeme,
But being faire and brickle,° likest glasse did seeme.   *fragile*

40

"But it in shape and beautie did excell
All other Idoles, which the heathen adore,
Farre passing that, which by surpassing skill
Phidias did make in Paphos Isle of yore,
With which that wretched Greeke, that life forlore,°   *abandoned*
Did fall in love:[3] yet this much fairer shined,
But covered with a slender° veile afore;   *thin*
And both her feete and legs together twyned
Were with a snake, whose head and tail were fast combyned.[4]

41

"The cause why she was covered with a vele,
Was hard to know, for that her Priests the same
From peoples knowledge laboured to concele.
But sooth it was not sure for womanish shame,
Nor any blemish, which the worke mote blame;
But for, they say, she hath both kinds° in one,   *sexes*
Both male and female, both under one name:
She syre and mother is her selfe alone,
Begets and eke conceives, ne needeth other none.[5]

42

"And all about her necke and shoulders flew
A flocke of litle loves, and sports, and joyes,[6]
With nimble wings of gold and purple hew;
Whose shapes seemed not like to terrestriall boyes,
But like to Angels playing heavenly toyes;°   *games*
The whilest their eldest brother was away,
Cupid their eldest brother; he enjoyes
The wide kingdome of love with Lordly sway,
And to his law compels all creatures to obay.

2. I.e., and (more) precious in value.

3. Pliny mentions a youth who fell in love with Praxiteles' (not Phidias') statue of Venus at Cnidus (*Naturalis Historia*, XXXVI.v.21).

4. Since ancient times, a serpent swallowing its tail has symbolized the cyclical character of all life. Roche (*op. cit.*, 132) suggests that Spenser's image may look ultimately to *Hieroglyphica*, by the Alexandrian Horapollo Niliacus (fl. second or fourth cents. A.D.).

5. Virgil speaks of Venus as a god (not a goddess) who guides Aeneas safely out of burning Troy (*Aeneid*, II.632). The Roman scholar Macrobius (fl. c. 400 A.D.) comments approvingly on the learning that informs this passage, adding, "it would seem that the deity is both male and female" (*Saturnalia*, tr. P. V. Davies [N.Y., 1969], III.viii.1). Cf. also Catullus, *Carmina*, LXVIII. 51. Spenser alludes to an androgynous Venus also in *Colin Clouts Come Home Againe*: "For Venus selfe doth soly couples seeme,/ Both male and female, through commixture joynd" (801–802). For a learned discussion of ancient and Renaissance thought touching the androgynous nature of gods and mankind, cf. Wind, *op. cit.*, 211–215.

6. I.e., a group of playful "amor-etti," Cupid-like babies.

43

"And all about her altar scattered lay
  Great sorts° of lovers piteously complayning,   *companies*
  Some of their losse, some of their loves delay,
  Some of their pride,[7] some paragons disdayning,
  Some fearing fraud, some fraudulently fayning,
  As every one had cause of good or ill.
  Amongst the rest some one through loves constrayning,
  Tormented sore, could not containe it still,
But thus brake forth, that all the temple it did fill.[8]

44

" 'Great Venus, Queene of beautie and of grace,
  The joy of Gods and men, that under skie
  Doest fayrest shine, and most adorne thy place,
  That with thy smyling looke doest pacifie
  The raging seas, and makst the stormes to flie;
  Thee goddesse, thee the winds, the clouds doe feare,
  And when thou spredst thy mantle forth on hie,
  The waters play and pleasant lands appeare,
And heavens laugh, and al the world shews joyous cheare.

45

" 'Then doth the daedale° earth throw forth to thee   *fertile*
  Out of her fruitfull lap aboundant flowres,
  And then all living wights, soone as they see
  The spring breake forth out of his lusty° bowres,   *vigorous*
  They all doe learne to play the Paramours;
  First doe the merry birds, thy prety pages
  Privily° prickéd with thy lustfull powres,   *secretly*
  Chirpe loud to thee out of their leavy cages,
And thee their mother call to coole their kindly rages.[9]

46

" 'Then doe the salvage beasts begin to play
  Their pleasant friskes, and loath their wonted food;
  The Lyons rore, the Tygres loudly bray,°   *roar*
  The raging Buls rebellow through the wood,
  And breaking forth, dare tempt° the deepest flood,   *risk*
  To come where thou doest draw them with desire:
  So all things else, that nourish vitall blood,
  Soone as with fury° thou doest them inspire,   *lust*
In generation seeke to quench their inward fire.

47

" 'So all the world by thee at first was made,
  And dayly yet thou doest the same repayre:[1]
  Ne ought on earth that merry is and glad,
  Ne ought on earth that lovely is and fayre,

7. I.e., of their mistresses' disdain.
8. The hymn to Venus in sts. 44–47 derives from the invocation to Venus with which Lucretius (95–52/51 B.C.) opens his Epicurean treatise-poem, *De*

Rerum Natura.
9. I.e., their natural desires.
1. The view that Venus made the world is not Lucretian: it comes from Natalis Comes, *op. cit.*, IV. xiii.

But thou the same for pleasure didst prepayre.
  Thou art the root of all that joyous is,
  Great God of men and women, queene of th' ayre,
  Mother of laughter, and welspring of blisse,
O graunt that of my love at last I may not misse.'

48

"So did he say: but I with murmure° soft,   *lament*
  That none might heare the sorrow of my hart,
  Yet inly groning deepe and sighing oft,
  Besought her to graunt ease unto my smart,
  And to my wound her gratious help impart.
  Whilest thus I spake, behold with happy eye
  I spyde, where at the Idoles feet apart
  A bevie of fayre damsels close° did lye,   *hidden*
Wayting when as the Antheme should be sung on hye.

49

"The first of them did seeme of ryper yeares,
  And graver countenance then all the rest;
  Yet all the rest were eke her equall peares,
  Yet unto her obayéd all the best.[2]
  Her name was Womanhood, that she exprest
  By her sad semblant° and demeanure wyse: *countenance*
  For stedfast still her eyes did fixéd rest,
  Ne roved at randon after gazers guyse,°   *fashion*
Whose luring baytes oftimes doe heedlesse harts entyse.

50

"And next to her sate goodly Shamefastnesse,
  Ne ever durst her eyes from ground upreare,
  Ne ever once did looke up from her desse,°   *dais*
  As if some blame of evill she did feare,
  That in her cheekes made roses oft appeare.
  And her against[3] sweet Cherefulnesse was placed,
  Whose eyes like twinkling stars in evening cleare,
  Were deckt with smyles, that all sad humors chaced,
And darted forth delights, the which her goodly graced.

51

"And next to her sate sober Modestie,
  Holding her hand upon her gentle hart;
  And her against sate comely Curtesie,
  That unto every person knew her part;
  And her before was seated overthwart[4]
  Soft Silence, and submisse Obedience,
  Both linckt together never to dispart,°   *separate*
  Both gifts of God not gotten but from thence,
Both girlonds of his Saints against their foes offence.[5]

---

2. I.e., rendered her their best obedience.
3. I.e., directly opposite.
4. I.e., across from.

5. Save for Silence, the figures in sts. 50–51 regularly appear in medieval love-allegories.

52

"Thus sate they all a round in seemely rate:°   *manner*
   And in the midst of them a goodly mayd,
   Even in the lap of Womanhood there sate,
   The which was all in lilly white arayd,
   With silver streames amongst the linnen strayed;
   Like to the Morne, when first her shyning face
   Hath to the gloomy world it selfe bewrayed,°   *revealed*
   That same was fayrest Amoret in place,
Shyning with beauties light, and heavenly vertues grace.

53

"Whom soone as I beheld, my hart gan throb,
   And wade in doubt, what best were to be donne:
   For sacrilege me seemed the Church to rob,
   And folly seemed to leave the thing undonne,
   Which with so strong attempt I had begonne.
   Tho shaking off all doubt and shamefast feare,
   Which Ladies love I heard had never wonne
   Mongst men of worth, I to her steppéd neare,
And by the lilly hand her laboured up to reare.

54

"Thereat that formost matrone me did blame,
   And sharpe rebuke, for being over bold;
   Saying it was to Knight unseemely shame,
   Upon a recluse Virgin to lay hold,
   That unto Venus services was sold.°   *given*
   To whom I thus, 'Nay but it fitteth best,
   For Cupids man with Venus mayd to hold,
   For ill your goddesse services are drest
By virgins, and her sacrifices let to rest.'

55

"With that my shield I forth to her did show,
   Which all that while I closely had conceld;
   On which when Cupid with his killing bow
   And cruell shafts emblazond she beheld,
   At sight thereof she was with terror queld,
   And said no more: but I which all that while
   The pledge of faith, her hand engagéd held,
   Like warie hynd within the weedie soyle,[6]
For no intreatie would forgoe so glorious spoyle.

56

"And evermore upon the Goddesse face
   Mine eye was fixt, for feare of her offence,°   *displeasure*
   Whom when I saw with amiable grace
   To laugh at me, and favour my pretence,
   I was emboldned with more confidence,

6. I.e., the marshy ground.

And nought for nicenesse nor for envy sparing,
In presence of them all forth led her thence,
All looking on, and like° astonisht staring,   *alike*
Yet to lay hand on her, not one of all them daring.

57

"She often prayd, and often me besought,
    Sometime with tender teares to let her goe,
    Sometime with witching smyles: but yet for nought,
    That ever she to me could say or doe,
    Could she her wishéd freedome fro me wooe;
    But forth I led her through the Temple gate,
    By which I hardly past with much adoe:
    But that same Ladie[7] which me friended late
In entrance, did me also friend in my retrate.

58

"No lesse did Daunger threaten me with dread,
    When as he saw me, maugre all his powre,
    That glorious spoyle of beautie with me lead,
    Then Cerberus, when Orpheus did recoure°   *recover*
    His Leman° from the Stygian Princes boure.[8]   *lover*
    But evermore my shield did me defend,
    Against the storme of every dreadfull stoure:°   *encounter*
    Thus safely with my love I thence did wend."
So ended he his tale, where I this Canto end.

---

7. I.e., Concord.
8. Upon the death of his wife Eurydice, the divinely gifted musician Orpheus descended to Pluto's realm of Hades, through which flowed the river Styx; charming the ferryman Charon, the three-headed hound Cerberus, and the Judges of the Dead with his lyre, he won the right to bring Eurydice back to the upper world, on condition that he should not look behind him as he brought his bride back to light and life. As he emerged from the underworld, he looked back for Eurydice, and so lost her forever. Cf. *Metamorphoses*, X.1–63. For comment on the ironies attending Scudamour's comparison of himself to Orpheus, cf. the essay by Thomas H. Cain in *UTQ*, XII (1972), 24–47.

From The Fifth Booke of the Faerie Queene

Contayning
The Legend of Artegall
or
of Justice

1

So oft as I with state of present time,
    The image of the antique world compare,
    When as mans age was in his freshest prime,
    And the first blossome of faire vertue bare,
    Such oddes° I finde twixt those, and these which are,   *difference*
    As that, through long continuance of his course,
    Me seemes the world is runne quite out of square,[1]
    From the first point of his appointed sourse,
And being once amisse growes daily wourse and wourse.

2

For from the golden age, that first was named,
    It's now at earst[2] become a stonie one;
    And men themselves, the which at first were framed
    Of earthly mould, and formed of flesh and bone,
    Are now transforméd into hardest stone:
    Such as behind their backs (so backward bred)
    Were throwne by Pyrrha and Deucalione:[3]
    And if then those may any worse be red,°   *imagined*
They into that ere long will be degimenderéd.°   *degenerated*

3

Let none then blame me, if in discipline°   *instruction*
    Of vertue and of civill uses lore,
    I doe not forme them to the common line°   *standard*
    Of present dayes, which are corrupted sore,
    But to the antique use, which was of yore,

---

1. I.e., is careering away from its originally appointed and ordered course. Spenser's gloomy account, in this and the following seven stanzas, of the decay of the world, looks ultimately to Ovid's discussion (*Metamorphoses*, I. 89–151) of the progressive decline of all things from a first "golden" age, by way of silver and brazen ages, to a final age of "hard iron." But the English poet's dark mood is conditioned also by his own belief (shared by many contemporaries) in the deterioration of the physical universe, signalled by changes in the heavens and by religious and political upheaval in Europe. No doubt the poet's sensitive responsiveness to the wretched plight of Ireland (made worse by bad government) also contributed to his pessimistic view: cf. the prose *View of the Present State of Ireland*, written c. 1594–1597.

2. I.e., at length.

3. Ovid (*Metamorphoses*, I. 348–415) tells the story of Pyrrha and Deucalion, who, after a flood that destroyed all life, were divinely instructed to cast stones behind them, from which the world was miraculously repopulated. Spenser's addition of a "stonie" age to the traditional Ovidian catalogue reflects Natalis Comes (*op. cit.*, VIII.17), who recalls the story to account for the stony character of men since the Golden Age.

When good was onely for it selfe desyred,
    And all men sought their owne, and none no more;
    When Justice was not for most meed outhyred,[4]
But simple Truth did rayne, and was of all admyred.

4

For that which all men then did vertue call,
    Is now cald vice; and that which vice was hight,
    Is now hight vertue, and so used of all:
    Right now is wrong, and wrong that was is right,
    As all things else in time are chaungéd quight.
    Ne wonder; for the heavens revolution
    Is wandred farre from where it first was pight,
    And so doe make contrarie constitution
Of all this lower world, toward his dissolution.[5]

5

For who so list into the heavens looke,
    And search the courses of the rowling spheares,
    Shall find that from the point, where they first **tooke**
    Their setting forth, in these few thousand yeares
    They all are wandred much; that plaine appeares.
    For that same golden fleecy Ram, which bore
    Phrixus and Helle from their stepdames feares,
    Hath now forgot, where he was plast of yore,
And shouldred hath the Bull, which fayre Europa **bore**.[6]

6

And eke the Bull hath with his bow-bent horne
    So hardly butted those two twinnes of Jove,
    That they have crusht the Crab, and quite him **borne**
    Into the great Nemaean lions grove.[7]
    So now all range, and doe at randon rove
    Out of their proper places farre away,
    And all this world with them amisse doe move,
    And all his creatures from their course astray,
Till they arrive at their last ruinous decay.°   *destruction*

7

Ne is that same great glorious lampe of light,
    That doth enlumine all these lesser fyres,[8]

4. I.e., responsive to the largest bribes.
5. The poet associates changes in the heavens (consequent on the precession of the equinoxes) with moral degeneration and political upheaval in the world: "revolution," in 1. 6, is deliberately ambiguous. Cf. also *King Lear*, I.ii.103–117; and Donne's "First Anniversary," 201–219.
6. In the context of Ptolemaic cosmology, the signs of the zodiac no longer correspond to their originally matching constellations; e.g., the Ram, zodiacal sign for Aries, has strayed to the realm of the Bull (Taurus). Cf. F.R. Johnson, *Astronomical Thought in Renaissance England* (Baltimore, Md., 1937), p. 23n. For the story of Phrixus and Helle, cf. III.xi.30 and note. Jove assumed the

form of a bull to ravish Europa: cf. *Metamorphoses*, II.833–875.
7. That is, the zodiacal sign of Gemini ("the twinnes of Jove") has been thrust into the realm of the Crab (Cancer), which in turn has moved into the place of the Lion (Leo). Castor and Pollux were the twin offspring of Jove (in the guise of a swan) and Leda: cf. III.xii.32. To slay the Nemean Lion was the first of the twelve labors assigned to Hercules: cf. *Metamorphoses*, XI. 197.
8. I.e., the stars and other heavenly bodies, which were thought to derive their light from the sun. For an account of sixteenth-century views on solar declination, cf. A. Fowler, *Spenser and the Numbers of Time* (London, 1964), p. 194n.

In better case, ne keepes his course more right,
But is miscaried° with the other Spheres.   *strayed*
For since the terme of fourteene hundred yeres,
That learnéd Ptolomae his hight did take,
He is declynéd from that marke of theirs,
Nigh thirtie minutes to the Southerne lake;
That makes me feare in time he will us quite forsake.

8

And if to those Aegyptian wisards old,
Which in star-read° were wont have best insight,   *astronomy*
Faith may be given, it is by them told,
That since the time they first tooke the Sunnes hight,
Foure times his place he shifted hath in sight,
And twice hath risen, where he now doth West,
And wested twice, where he ought rise aright.
But most is Mars amisse of all the rest,
And next to him old Saturne, that was wont be best.[9]

9

For during Saturnes ancient raigne[1] it's sayd,
That all the world with goodnesse did abound:
All lovéd vertue, no man was affrayd
Of force, ne fraud in wight was to be found:
No warre was knowne, no dreadfull trompets sound,
Peace universall rayned mongst men and beasts,
And all things freely grew out of the ground:
Justice sate high adored with solemne feasts,
And to all people did divide° her dred beheasts.   *dispense*

10

Most sacred vertue she of all the rest,
Resembling God in his imperiall might;
Whose soveraine powre is herein most exprest,
That both to good and bad he dealeth right,
And all his workes with Justice hath bedight.°   *adorned*
That powre he also doth to Princes lend,
And makes them like himselfe in glorious sight,
To sit in his owne seate, his cause to end,°   *fulfill*
And rule his people right, as he doth recommend.[2]

11

Dread Soverayne Goddesse,[3] that doest highest sit
In seate of judgement, in th'Almighties stead,°   *place*
And with magnificke might and wondrous wit
Doest to thy people righteous doome aread,°   *proclaim*
That furthest Nations filles with awfull dread,
Pardon the boldnesse of thy basest thrall,
That dare discourse of so divine a read,°   *matter*

---

9. The authority for ll. 4–7 is Herodo-
tus, *Histories*, II. 142. In Spenser's day
planetary orbits were thought to be nor-
mally circular; contemporary observers
were therefore troubled by the relatively
eccentric orbits of Mars and Saturn.

1. I.e., the Golden Age.
2. Cf. Proverbs viii.15: "By me [i.e.,
God's wisdom] Kings reign, and princes
decree justice."
3. I.e., Queen Elizabeth.

As thy great justice prayséd over all:
The instrument whereof loe here thy Artegall.

[The association of justice with Queen Elizabeth, established in sts. 9–11
of the proem to Book V, leads aptly to the introduction, in Canto i, of
Arthegall, "Champion of true Justice," who has been taught "all the
discipline" of that virtue by Astraea, goddess of justice. The quest assigned
him by the Faerie Queene is the overthrow of the tyrant Grantorto ("great
wrong") and the restoration of the maiden Eirena to her kingdom, a task
duly accomplished in Canto xii (although, interestingly, in VI.i.4, Arthe-
gall is described as "returning yet halfe sad / From his late conquest which
he gotten had"). Structurally, Book V returns to the "linear" form of
Books I and II. Arthegall (aided by his squire Talus, "an yron man" pro-
vided by Astraea) in Cantos i–iv overcomes a succession of arrogant or
crass figures representing varieties of injustice. In Canto v, he is in turn
overcome by Radigund, beautiful Queen of the Amazons, who attires him
in women's clothing and sets him to work spinning flax (recalling the
servitude of Hercules to Omphale). Subsequently Britomart, heartened by
her vision in Isis Church (Canto vii), kills Radigund, frees Arthegall, and
restores order in the commonwealth. The remainder of Book V deals with
the further adventures of Arthegall, instructed by Queen Mercilla (the
mercy that tempers justice); and of Arthur, whose exploits in behalf of
justice are set out in Cantos viii, x, and xi. Earlier criticism was apt to
dwell on the relationship of Book V to Aristotle's analysis of justice in the
Nichomachaean Ethics, on Spenser's view of the measure of sovereignty ap-
propriate to women in political matters, and on the rather transparent his-
torical allegory of Cantos vi–xii. Since 1968, however, critics have focused
their attentions increasingly on Canto vii, showing how Britomart's sojourn
in Isis Church is central to the interwoven strands of moral, historical, and
psychological allegory in this Book.]

Canto VII

Britomart comes to Isis Church,
*   Where shee strange visions sees:*
She fights with Radigund, her slaies,
*   And Artegall thence frees.*

1

Nought is on earth more sacred or divine,
   That Gods and men doe equally adore,
   Then this same vertue, that doth right define:
   For th'hevens themselves, whence mortal men implore
   Right in their wrongs, are ruled by righteous lore
   Of highest Jove, who doth true justice deale
   To his inferiour Gods, and evermore
Therewith containes° his heavenly Common-weale: *controls*
The skill° whereof to Princes hearts he doth reveale.   *understanding*

2

Well therefore did the antique world invent,°   *feign*
 That Justice was a God of soveraine grace,
 And altars unto him, and temples lent,°   *gave*
 And heavenly honours in the highest place;
 Calling him great Osyris, of the race
 Of th'old Aegyptian Kings, that whylome were;
 With faynéd colours shading[1] a true case:
 For that Osyris, whilest he livéd here,
The justest man alive, and truest did appeare.[2]

3

His wife was Isis, whom they likewise made
 A Goddesse of great powre and soveraianty,
 And in her person cunningly did shade
 That part of Justice, which is Equity,[3]
 Whereof I have to treat here presently.°   *now*
 Unto whose temple when as Britomart
 Arrivéd, shee with great humility
 Did enter in, ne would that night depart;
But Talus mote not be admitted to her part.°   *side*

4

There she receivéd was in goodly wize
 Of many Priests, which duely did attend
 Uppon the rites and daily sacrifize,
 All clad in linnen robes with silver hemd;
 And on their heads with long locks comely kemd,° *combed*
 They wore rich Mitres shapéd like the Moone,
 To shew that Isis doth the Moone portend;° *signify*
 Like as Osyris signifies the Sunne.
For that they both like race in equall justice runne.[4]

5

The Championesse them greeting, as she could,[5]
 Was thence by them into the Temple led;
 Whose goodly building when she did behould,

1. I.e., (1) obscuring; (2) "shadowing forth."
2. Spenser's comments on Isis and Osiris depend primarily on Plutarch, *De Iside*, xiii, and on Diodorus Siculus, *Bibliotheca Historica*, I.xi–xxii; both authorities identify Osiris and Isis respectively with sun and moon, and both emphasize the justice that marked the reign of Osiris as King of Egypt. It appears also that Spenser's account of Britomart's sojourn in Isis Church reflects the experience of Lucius in the *Metamorphoses* of Apuleius, XI.iv–viii. For an intriguing discussion of the central role assigned to Isis and Osiris in "the cosmogonic myth running through the poem," cf. A. Fowler, *op. cit.*, 208–215.
3. James E. Phillips, writing in *HLQ*, XXXIII (1970), 103–120, observes that "Justice is the absolute, measure-for-measure equation of exact reward and punishment according to the letter of the law. . . . Equity is the taking into account of the individual circumstances in each case . . . Mercy or Clemency is the human and divine impulse to forgive." Cf. also the discussion by Frank Kermode of Elizabethan views of equity and their connection with Spenser's Isis Church, in *Shakespeare, Spenser, Donne: Renaissance Essays* (London, 1971), 50–59.
4. I.e., because the heavenly courses of sun and moon are equally precise and regular.
5. I.e., as she knew how to do (with decorum).

Borne uppon stately pillours, all dispred°   *overspread*
  With shining gold, and archéd over hed,
  She wondred at the workemans passing skill,
  Whose like before she never saw nor red;°   *imagined*
  And thereuppon long while stood gazing still,
But thought, that she thereon could never gaze her fill.

6

Thence forth unto the Idoll they her brought,
  The which was framéd all of silver fine,
  So well as could with cunning hand be wrought,
  And clothéd all in garments made of line,°   *linen*
  Hemd all about with fringe of silver twine.
  Uppon her head she wore a Crowne of gold,
  To shew that she had powre in things divine;
  And at her feete a Crocodile was rold,
That with her wreathéd taile her middle did enfold.[6]

7

One foote was set uppon the Crocodile,
  And on the ground the other fast did stand,
  So meaning to suppresse both forgéd guile,
  And open force:[7] and in her other hand
  She stretchéd forth a long white sclender wand.
  Such was the Goddesse; whom when Britomart
  Had long beheld, her selfe uppon the land
  She did prostrate, and with right humble hart,
Unto her selfe her silent prayers did impart.

8

To which the Idoll as it were inclining,
  Her wand did move with amiable looke,
  By outward shew her inward sence desining.°   *indicating*
  Who well perceiving, how her wand she shooke,
  It as a token of good fortune tooke.
  By this the day with dampe° was overcast,   *mist*
  And joyous light the house of Jove forsooke:
  Which when she saw, her helmet she unlaste,
And by the altars side her selfe to slumber plaste.

9

For other beds the Priests there uséd none,
  But on their mother Earths deare lap did lie,
  And bake° their sides upon the cold hard stone,   *harden*
  T'enure them selves to sufferaunce° thereby   *endurance*
  And proud rebellious flesh to mortify.°   *subject*
  For by the vow of their religion
  They tiéd were to stedfast chastity,

---

6. Cf. IV.x.40, and note. For an extended account of crocodiles in ancient and Renaissance iconography, cf. Jane Aptekar, *Icons of Justice: Iconography and Thematic Imagery in Book V of "The Faerie Queene"* (New York, 1967), Chapter VI.

7. Cf. I.v.18, and note; also Spenser's early *Visions of the Worlds Vanitie*, iii.1–6. "That the crocodile in this episode stands for both guile and force" is persuasively argued by Clifford Davidson in *SP*, LXVI (1969), 70–86.

And continence of life, that all forgon,°   *renounced*
They mote the better tend to their devotion.[8]

10

Therefore they mote not taste of fleshly food,
  Ne feed on ought, the which doth bloud containe,
  Ne drinke of wine, for wine they say is blood,
  Even the bloud of Gyants, which were slaine,
  By thundring Jove in the Phlegrean plaine.[9]
  For which the earth (as they the story tell)
  Wroth with the Gods, which to perpetuall paine
  Had damned her sonnes, which gainst them did rebell,
With inward griefe and malice did against them swell.

11

And of their vitall bloud, the which was shed
  Into her pregnant bosome, forth she brought
  The fruitfull vine, whose liquor blouddy red
  Having the mindes of men with fury fraught,
  Mote in them stirre up old rebellious thought,
  To make new warre against the Gods againe:
  Such is the powre of that same fruit, that nought
  The fell contagion may thereof restraine,
Ne within reasons rule, her madding mood containe.

12

There did the warlike Maide her selfe repose,
  Under the wings of Isis[1] all that night,
  And with sweete rest her heavy eyes did close,
  After that long daies toile and weary plight.
  Where whilest her earthly parts with soft delight
  Of sencelesse sleepe did deeply drownéd lie,
  There did appeare unto her heavenly spright
  A wondrous vision, which did close implie[2]
The course of all her fortune and posteritie.

13

Her seemed, as she was doing sacrifize
  To Isis, deckt with Mitre on her hed,
  And linnen stole after those Priestés guize,
  All sodainely she saw transfiguréd
  Her linnen stole to robe of scarlet red,[3]
  And Moone-like Mitre to a Crowne of gold,
  That even she her selfe much wonderéd
  At such a chaunge, and joyéd to behold
Her selfe, adorned with gems and jewels manifold.

---

8. This description of the priests' austere practice derives from Plutarch, *De Iside*, ii.
9. Spenser interestingly combines scriptural and classical materials in this passage. Ll.1–2 echo Genesis ix.4, "But flesh with the life thereof, which is the blood thereof, shall ye not eat"; the remainder of the stanza (together with st. 11) reflects *Metamorphoses* I. 151–162, and Plutarch, *De Iside*, vi.
1. Cf. Psalms lvii.1: "in the shadow of thy wings will I make my refuge."
2. I.e., secretly enfold.
3. I.e., "robed in imperial purple" (Kermode, *Spenser, Shakespeare, Donne*, p. 56). Yet the poet's choice particularly of "scarlet" looks on also to sts. 14–16.

14

And in the midst of her felicity,
    An hideous tempest seeméd from below,
    To rise through all the Temple sodainely,
    That from the Altar all about did blow
    The holy fire, and all the embers strow
    Uppon the ground, which kindled privily,
    Into outragious flames[4] unwares did grow,
    That all the Temple put in jeopardy
Of flaming, and her selfe in great perplexity.°   *concern*

15

With that the Crocodile, which sleeping lay
    Under the Idols feete in fearelesse bowre,[5]
    Seemed to awake in horrible dismay,
    As being troubled with that stormy stowre;°   *turmoil*
    And gaping greedy wide, did streight devoure
    Both flames and tempest:[6] with which growen great,
    And swolne with pride of his owne peerelesse powre,
    He gan to threaten her likewise to eat;
But that the Goddesse with her rod him backe did beat.

16

Tho turning all his pride to humblesse meeke,
    Him selfe before her feete he lowly threw,
    And gan for grace and love of her to seeke:
    Which she accepting, he so neare her drew,
    That of his game[7] she soone enwombéd grew,
    And forth did bring a Lion of great might;
    That shortly did did all other beasts subdew.
    With that she wakéd, full of fearefull fright,
And doubtfully dismayd through that so uncouth° sight.   *strange*

17

So thereuppon long while she musing lay,
    With thousand thoughts feeding her fantasie,
    Untill she spide the lampe of lightsome day,
    Up-lifted in the porch of heaven hie.
    Then up she rose fraught with melancholy,
    And forth into the lower parts did pas;
    Whereas the Priestes she found full busily
    About their holy things for morrow Mas:[8]
Whom she saluting° faire, faire resaluted was.   *greeting*

18

But by the change of her unchearefull looke,
    They might perceive, she was not well in plight;

---

4. I.e., the flames of love and desire. "The night before the consummation of her marriage," Olympias, mother of Alexander the Great, "dreamed that a thunderbolt fell upon her body, which kindled a great fire, whose divided flames dispersed themselves all about . . ." (Plutarch, *Lives*, tr. Dryden: "Alexander"). Plutarch adds that "once . . . a serpent was found lying by Olympias as she slept."
5. I.e., fearlessly lay sheltered under the idol's feet.
6. Cf. III.xi.48, and note.
7. I.e., his amorous play.
8. I.e., for the first religious observance next day.

Or that some pensivenesse to heart she tooke.
Therefore thus one of them, who seemed in sight
To be the greatest, and the gravest wight,
To her bespake; "Sir Knight it seemes to me,
That thorough evill rest of this last night,
Or ill apayd,° or much dismayd ye be,   *pleased*
That by your change of cheare is easie for to see."

19

"Certes," sayd she, "sith ye so well have spide
The troublous passion of my pensive mind,
I will not seeke the same from you to hide,
But will my cares unfolde, in hope to find
Your aide, to guide me out of errour blind."
"Say on," quoth he, "the secret of your hart:
For by the holy vow, which me doth bind,
I am adjured,° best counsell to impart   *sworn*
To all, that shall require my comfort in their smart."

20

Then gan she to declare the whole discourse°   *course*
Of all that vision, which to her appeard,
As well as to her minde it had recourse.[9]
All which when he unto the end had heard,
Like to a weake faint-hearted man he fared,°   *behaved*
Through great astonishment of that strange sight;
And with long locks up-standing, stifly stared
Like one adawéd° with some dreadfull spright.   *terrified*
So fild with heavenly fury,° thus he her behight.°   *frenzy/addressed*

21

"Magnificke Virgin, that in queint° disguise   *strange*
Of British armes doest maske thy royall blood,
So to pursue a perillous emprize,
How couldst thou weene, through that disguizéd hood,°   *covering*
To hide thy state from being understood?
Can from th'immortall Gods ought hidden bee?
They doe thy linage, and thy Lordly brood;°   *race*
They doe thy sire, lamenting sore for thee;
They doe thy love, forlorne in womens thraldome see.

22

"The end whereof, and all the long event,°   *outcome*
They doe to thee in this same dreame discover.
For that same Crocodile doth represent
The righteous Knight, that is thy faithfull lover,
Like to Osyris in all just endever.
For that same Crocodile Osyris is,
That under Isis feete doth sleepe for ever:
To shew that clemence oft in things amis,
Restraines those sterne behests, and cruell doomes of his.

9. I.e., as well as she could recall it.

23

"That Knight shall all the troublous stormes asswage,
  And raging flames, that many foes shall reare,
  To hinder thee from the just heritage
  Of thy sires Crowne, and from thy countrey deare.
  Then shalt thou take him to thy lovéd fere,°   *mate*
  And joyne in equall portion of thy realme.
  And afterwards a sonne to him shalt beare,
  That Lion-like shall shew his powre extreame:
So blesse thee God, and give thee joyance of thy dreame."[1]

24

All which when she unto the end had heard,
  She much was easéd in her troubles thought,
  And on those Priests bestowéd rich reward:
  And royall gifts of gold and silver wrought,
  She for a present to their Goddesse brought.
  Then taking leave of them, she forward went,
  To seeke her love, where he was to be sought;
  Ne rested till she came without relent°   *delay*
Unto the land of Amazons, as she was bent.[2]

---

1. By one reading, "Artegall, her 'faith-full lover,' is the Crocodile Osiris and [Britomart] is Isis. Together they represent justice and equity and will continue the British nation" (T.K. Dunseath, *Spenser's Allegory of Justice in Book Five of "The Faerie Queene"* [Princeton, N.J., 1968] p. 176.) By another, "The crocodile represents the energy (which resembles, and derives from, and in part *is* sexuality) which justice uses and abuses" (Aptekar, *op. cit.*, p. 107). Cf. also Angus Fletcher, *The Prophetic Moment: An Essay on Spenser* (Chicago, 1971), p. 277: "The episode in the temple shows Britomart passing through three stages of a female mystery: her initiation, her coronation, her marriage." 2. For further commentary on Britomart's experience at Isis Church, cf. the essays by Elizabeth Bieman (*UTQ*, XXXVII [1968], 156–174) and Alice Miskimin (*JEGP*, LXXVII [1978], 17–36).

From The Sixte Booke of the Faerie Queene

Contayning
The Legend of S. Calidore
or
of Courtesie

1

The waies, through which my weary steps I guyde,
   In this delightfull land of Faery,
   Are so exceeding spacious and wyde,
   And sprinckled with such sweet variety,
   Of all that pleasant is to eare or eye,
   That I nigh ravisht with rare thoughts delight,
   My tedious travell doe forget thereby;
   And when I gin to feele decay of might,
It strength to me supplies, and chears my dulléd spright.

2

Such secret comfort, and such heavenly pleasures,
   Ye sacred imps, that on Parnasso dwell,[1]
   And there the keeping have of learnings threasures,
   Which doe all worldly richos farre excell,
   Into the mindes of mortall men doe well,°   *flow*
   And goodly fury° into them infuse;   *inspiration*
   Guyde ye my footing, and conduct me well
   In these strange waies, where never foote did use,°   *go, frequent*
Ne none can find, but who was taught them by the Muse.[2]

3

Revele to me the sacred noursery
   Of vertue, which with you doth there remaine,
   Where it in silver bowre does hidden ly
   From view of men, and wicked worlds disdaine.
   Since it at first was by the Gods with paine
   Planted in earth, being derived at furst
   From heavenly seedes of bounty° soveraine,   *virtue*
   And by them long with carefull labour nurst,
Till it to ripenesse grew, and forth to honour burst.

4

Amongst them all growes not a fayrer flowre,
   Then is the bloosme of comely courtesie,[3]

1. I.e., the Muses.
2. Poetical claims of this kind are common from classical times onward (cf. Lucretius, *De Rerum Natura*, I. 925–926; Ariosto, *Orlando Furioso*, I. 1–2); in English poetry, the archetypal instance is Milton's allusion to his Muse's pursuit of "Things unattempted yet in prose or rhyme" (*Paradise Lost*, I. 16).

3. The "virtue" of courtesy celebrated by Spenser in Book VI owes something to Aristotle's discussion, in the *Nicomachaean Ethics*, of the man who is "concerned with the pleasures and pains of social life," and who "renders to each class what is befitting" (IV. 6), as well as to the doctrine (variously expressed by Chaucer and Roger Ascham) that virtuous conduct, not merely noble

Which though it on a lowly stalke doe bowre,°   *shelter*
Yet brancheth forth in brave nobilitie,
And spreds it selfe through all civilitie:°   *civilized life*
Of which though present age doe plenteous seeme,
Yet being matcht with plaine Antiquitie,
Ye will them all but faynéd showes esteeme,
Which carry colours° faire, that feeble eies misdeeme.°   *appearances*
                                              misjudge

5

But in the triall of true curtesie,
Its now so farre from that, which then it was,
That it indeed is nought but forgerie,
Fashioned to please the eies of them, that pas,
Which see not perfect things but in a glas:[4]
Yet is that glasse so gay,° that it can blynd   *brilliant*
The wisest sight, to thinke gold that is bras.
But vertues seat is deepe within the mynd,
And not in outward shows, but inward thoughts defynd.°   *determined*

6

But where shall I in all Antiquity
So faire a patterne finde, where may be seene
The goodly praise of Princely curtesie,
As in your selfe, O soveraine Lady Queene,
In whose pure minde, as in a mirrour sheene,°   *bright*
It showes, and with her brightnesse doth inflame°   *inspire*
The eyes of all, which thereon fixéd beene;[5]
But meriteth indeede an higher name:
Yet so from low to high uplifted is your name.

7

Then pardon me, most dreaded Soveraine,
That from your selfe I doe this vertue bring,
And to your selfe doe it returne againe:
So from the Ocean all rivers spring,
And tribute backe repay as to their King.
Right so from you all goodly vertues well
Into the rest, which round about you ring.
Faire Lords and Ladies, which about you dwell,
And doe adorne your Court, where courtesies excell.

---

or gentle blood, truly indicates "gentilesse" or "nobility." Calidore's conduct throughout the Book reflects also the influence of Castiglione's *Il Cortegiano:* Canto ix particularly well illustrates Castiglione's view of the bearing appropriate to a truly gentle person in a rural or "base" social environment. But more significant for Spenser than any outward expression of civility, or observance of the niceties of etiquette, is that inward quality of character (often but not always encountered in persons of noble blood) that gives rise to the courteous man's sensitive concern for his fellows.

4. Cf. I Corinthians xiii. 12: "For now we see through a glass, darkly; but then face to face . . .".

5. The image, a favorite with Spenser, who seems often to follow the expressions of Ficino's commentary on Plato's *Symposium* (cf. *HL*, 192–196; *HB*, 221–224), may also reflect II Corinthians iii. 18: "But we all, with open face beholding as in a glass the glory of the Lord, are changed into the same image from glory to glory, even as by the Spirit of the Lord."

[Sir Calidore's quest, which he describes early in Canto i as "an endlesse trace," is to find and subdue the Blatant Beast, a thousand-tongued monster that venomously afflicts men and women in every quarter of the world. That quest, however, is directly in view chiefly in Cantos i–iii (which present a series of episodes illustrating varieties of courtesy and discourtesy), and in Canto xii, at the conclusion of which the Beast, apparently tamed by Calidore, breaks his bonds, to range again through the world more terribly than before. Calidore does not appear at all in Cantos iv–viii, which illustrate the thematic virtue of Book III through the adventures of other personages, including Arthur and Timias. It is only in Canto xi that Calidore again assumes his properly active role, as he delivers Pastorella from a lawless band of forest brigands; soon thereafter, ashamed of having neglected his assigned task, he sets out once again on the quest which is destined to end in failure, "whether wicked fate so framed, / Or fault of men" VI. xii. 38).]

Canto IX

Calidore *hostes°* with Meliboe   *lodges*
and loves fayre Pastorell;
Coridon envies him, yet he
for ill rewards him well.

1

Now turne againe my teme thou jolly swayne,[1]
  Backe to the furrow which I lately left;
  I lately left a furrow, one or twayne
  Unploughed, the which my *coulter°* hath not cleft: *plowshare*
  Yet seemed the soyle both fayre and frutefull *eft,°*   *moreover*
  As I it past, that were too great a shame,
  That so rich frute should be from us bereft;
  Besides the great dishonour and defame,
Which should befall to Calidores immortall name.[2]

2

Great travell hath the gentle Calidore
  And toyle enduréd, sith I left him last
  Sewing° the Blatant beast,[3] which I forbore   *pursuing*

1. I.e., perhaps, Spenser's poetic powers, thus personified to accord with the setting of Calidore's sojourn with the shepherd.
2. Calidore (from Greek, "beautiful gift") may have been intended to represent, on one "level" of the allegory, Sir Philip Sidney, who is described as "the president Of noblesse and of chevalree" in "To His Booke," prefaced to *The Shepheardes Calender*. A persuasive case may also be made for the Earl of Essex.
3. Spenser's particular model for this monster is the curious "questing beast" of Malory's *Le Morte d'Arthur* (I. xix; X. xiii), derived in turn from medieval French romance; but the Blatant Beast incorporates also some features of Cerberus, the monstrous hound of classical poetry, with whom Spenser elsewhere in Book VI explicitly associates the Beast (i. 7–8; vi. 12). Ben Jonson understood that by the Blatant Beast "the Puritans" were signified; cf. *Ben Jonson: The Complete Poems*, ed. George Parfitt (Baltimore, Md., 1975), p. 465. Probably the poet had in view the extreme left wing of those concerned to reform the Anglican Establishment, but the Beast more generally represents shameful slander and calumny in every degree and condition of life.

To finish then, for other present hast.
Full many pathes and perils he hath past,
Through hils, through dales, throgh forests, and throgh plaines
In that same quest which fortune on him cast,[4]
Which he atchievéd to his owne great gaines,
Reaping eternall glorie of his restlesse° paines.   *unresting*

3

So sharply he the Monster did pursew,
 That day nor night he suffred him to rest,
 Ne rested he himselfe but natures dew,
 For dread of daunger, not to be redrest,
 If he for slouth forslackt° so famous quest.   *neglected*
 Him first from court he to the citties coursed,°   *chased*
 And from the citties to the townes him prest,
 And from the townes into the countrie forsed,
And from the country back to private farmes he scorsed.[5]

4

From thence into the open fields he fled,
 Whereas the Heardes° were keeping of their neat,° *herdsmen/cattle*
 And shepheards singing to their flockes, that fed,
 Layes of sweete love and youthes delightfull heat:
 Him thether eke for all his fearefull threat
 He followed fast, and chacéd him so nie,
 That to the folds, where sheepe at night doe seat,°   *rest*
 And to the litle cots,° where shepherds lie   *shelters*
In winters wrathfull time, he forcéd him to flie.

5

There on a day as he pursewed the chace,
 He chaunst to spy a sort of shepheard groomes,[6]
 Playing on pypes,° and caroling apace,   *bagpipes*
 The whyles their beasts there in the budded broomes° *broom plants*
 Beside them fed, and nipt the tender bloomes:
 For other worldly wealth they caréd nought.
 To whom Sir Calidore yet sweating comes,
 And them to tell him courteously besought,
If such a beast they saw, which he had thether brought.

6

They answered him, that no such beast they saw,
 Nor any wicked feend, that mote offend
 Their happie flockes, nor daunger to them draw:
 But if that such there were (as none they kend)
 They prayd high God him farre from them to send.
 Then one of them him seeing so to sweat,

4. In Book VI, the directive power of "fortune" is much more in evidence than in the first three Books of the poem; and while Calidore eventually manages to restrain the Blatant Beast for a time, by the end of Book VI the Beast has broken his bonds, and is once more ranging through the world (xii. 40).
5. I.e., forced the beast to exchange hoped-for refuge in the open country for that of private estates and farms.
6. I.e., a company of shepherds.

After his rusticke wise,° that well he weend,   *manner*
  Offred him drinke, to quench his thirstie heat,
And if he hungry were, him offred eke to eat.

7

The knight was nothing nice,° where was no need,   *fastidious*
  And tooke their gentle offer: so adowne
  They prayd him sit, and gave him for to feed
  Such homely what,° as serves the simple clowne,°   *thing/rustic*
  That doth despise the dainties of the towne.
  Tho having fed his fill, he there besyde
  Saw a faire damzell, which did weare a crowne
  Of sundry flowres, with silken ribbands tyde,
Yclad in home-made greene that her owne hands had dyde.

8

Upon a litle hillocke she was placed
  Higher then all the rest, and round about
  Environed with a girland, goodly graced,
  Of lovely lasses, and them all without[7]
  The lustie shepheard swaynes sate in a rout,°   *group*
  The which did pype and sing her prayses dew,
  And oft rejoyce, and oft for wonder shout,
  As if some miracle of heavenly hew°   *form*
Were downe to them descended in that earthly vew.

9

And soothly sure[8] she was full fayre of face,
  And perfectly well shapt in every lim,
  Which she did more augment with modest grace,
  And comely carriage of her count'nance° trim,   *demeanor*
  That all the rest like lesser lamps did dim:
  Who her admiring as some heavenly wight,
  Did for their soveraine goddesse her esteeme,
  And caroling her name both day and night,
The fayrest Pastorella her by name did hight.°   *call*

10

Ne was there heard, ne was there shepheards swayne
  But her did honour, and eke many a one
  Burnt in her love, and with sweet pleasing payne
  Full many a night for her did sigh and grone:
  But most of all the shepheard Coridon
  For her did languish, and his deare life spend;° *waste away*
  Yet neither she for him, nor other none
  Did care a whit, ne any liking lend:°   *give*
Though meane her lot, yet higher did her mind ascend.

11

Her whyles Sir Calidore there vewéd well,
  And markt her rare demeanure, which him seemed
  So farre the meane° of shepheards to excell,   *usual average*
  As that he in his mind her worthy deemed,

7. I.e., outside the ring of maidens.   8. I.e., truly.

To be a Princes Paragone° esteemed,   *consort*
He was unwares surprisd in subtile bands
Of the blynd boy,[9] ne thence could be redeemed
By any skill out of his cruell hands,
Caught like the bird, which gazing still on others stands.[1]

12

So stood he still long gazing thereupon,
  Ne any will had thence to move away,
  Although his quest[2] were farre afore him gon;
  But after he had fed, yet did he stay,
  And sate there still, untill the flying day
  Was farre forth spent, discoursing diversly
  Of sundry things, as fell,° to worke delay;   *befell*
  And evermore his speach he did apply
To th'heards, but meant them to the damzels fantazy.° *fancy*

13

By this the moystie° night approching fast,   *humid*
  Her deawy humour° gan on th'earth to shed,   *mist*
  That warned the shepheards to their homes to hast
  Their tender flocks, now being fully fed,
  For feare of wetting them before their bed;
  Then came to them a good old aged syre,
  Whose silver lockes bedeckt his beard and hed,
  With shepheards hooke in hand, and fit attyre,
That wild° the damzell rise; the day did now expyre. *bade*

14

He was to weet[3] by common voice esteemed
  The father of the fayrest Pastorell,
  And of her selfe in very deede so deemed;°   *considered*
  Yet was not so, but as old stories tell[4]
  Found her by fortune, which to him befell,
  In th'open fields an Infant left alone,
  And taking up brought home, and nourséd well
  As his owne chyld; for other he had none,
That she in tract° of time accompted was his owne.   *course*

15

She at his bidding meekely did arise,
  And streight unto her litle flocke did fare:
  Then all the rest about her rose likewise,
  And each his sundrie sheepe with severall° care   *separate*
  Gathered together, and them homeward bare:
  Whylest everie one with helping hands did strive

9. I.e., Cupid.
1. I.e., the lark, which in Elizabethan times was caught with a net while it stared in fascination at the hawk held by the fowler.
2. I.e., the object of his quest (the Blatant Beast).
3. I.e., in fact.
4. The figure of Pastorella (whose noble birth is revealed in xii. 14–22), and the Calidore-Pastorella episode with which Cantos ix–xii are centrally concerned, derive ultimately from Greek romance (e.g., *Daphnis and Chloe*, composed in the 3rd century A.D. by Longus), but these motifs had become literary commonplaces in the period of the Renaissance. Spenser made some use of Sidney's *Arcadia* for pastoral characters and the narrative outline of these Cantos.

Amongst themselves, and did their labours share,
  To helpe faire Pastorella, home to drive
Her fleecie flocke; but Coridon most helpe did give.

16

But Meliboe[5] (so hight that good old man)
  Now seeing Calidore left all alone,
  And night arrivéd hard at hand, began
  Him to invite unto his simple home;
  Which though it were a cottage clad with lome,°   *clay*
  And all things therein meane, yet better so
  To lodge, then in the salvage° fields to rome.   *wild*
  The knight full gladly soone agreed thereto,
Being his harts owne wish, and home with him did go.

17

There he was welcomed of that honest syre,
  And of his aged Beldame° homely well;   *wife*
  Who him besought himselfe to disattyre,°   *take off his armor*
  And rest himselfe, till supper time befell.
  By which home came the fayrest Pastorell,
  After her flocke she in their fold had tyde,
  And supper readie dight, they to it fell
  With small adoe, and nature satisfyde,
The which doth litle crave contented to abyde.[6]

18

Tho when they had their hunger slakéd well,
  And the fayre mayd the table° ta'ne away,   *food and drink*
  The gentle knight, as he that did excell
  In courtesie, and well could doe and say,
  For so great kindnesse as he found that day,
  Gan greatly thanke his host and his good wife;
  And drawing thence his speach another way,
  Gan highly to commend the happie life,
Which Shepheards lead, without debate° or bitter strife.   *contention*

19

"How much," sayd he, "more happie is the state,
  In which ye father here doe dwell at ease,
  Leading a life so free and fortunate,
  From all the tempests of these worldly seas,
  Which tosse the rest in daungerous disease;°   *distress*
  Where warres, and wreckes, and wicked enmitie
  Doe them afflict, which no man can appease,
  That certes° I your happinesse envie,   *surely*
And wish my lot were plast in such felicitie."

20

"Surely my sonne," then answered he againe,[7]
  "If happie, then it is in this intent,°   *respect*

5. From Greek, "honey-toned"; and cf.
st. 26.
6. I.e., nature needs little to be con-
tented.
7. Sts. 20–25 are based on a similar
passage, in which an aged shepherd
contrasts the futile magnificence and
show of city life with the natural
pleasures of rustic society, in Tasso,
Gerusalemme Liberata, VII. 8–13.

That having small, yet doe I not complaine
Of want, ne wish for more it to augment,
But doe my self, with that I have, content;
So taught of nature, which doth litle need
Of forreine helpes to lifes due nourishment:
The fields my food, my flocke my rayment breed;
No better doe I weare, no better doe I feed.

21

"Therefore I doe not any one envy,
 Nor am envyde of any one therefore;
 They that have much, feare much to loose thereby,
 And store of cares doth follow riches store.
 The litle that I have, growes dayly more
 Without my care,° but onely to attend it;   *worry*
 My lambes doe every yeare increase their score,
 And my flockes father daily doth amend° it.   *restore*
What have I, but to praise th'Almighty, that doth send it?

22

"To them, that list,° the worlds gay showes I leave,   *desire*
 And to great ones such follies doe forgive,°   *leave*
 Which oft through pride do their owne perill weave,
 And through ambition downe themselves doe drive
 To sad decay,° that might contented live.   *ruin*
 Me no such cares nor combrous thoughts offend,°   *disturb*
 Ne once my minds unmovéd quiet grieve,
 But all the night in silver sleepe[8] I spend,
And all the day, to what I list, I doe attend.

23

"Sometimes I hunt the Fox, the vowéd foe
 Unto my Lambes, and him dislodge away;
 Sometime the fawne I practise° from the Doe,   *plan*
 Or from the Goat her kidde how to convay;°   *steal away*
 Another while I baytes and nets display,
 The birds to catch, or fishes to beguyle:
 And when I wearie am, I downe doe lay
 My limbes in every° shade, to rest from toyle,   *any*
And drinke of every brooke, when thirst my throte doth boyle.

24

"The time was once, in my first prime of yeares,
 When pride of youth forth prickéd my desire,
 That I disdained amongst mine equall peares
 To follow sheepe, and shepheards base attire:
 For further fortune then I would inquire.°   *seek*
 And leaving home, to roiall court I sought;°   *went*
 Where I did sell my selfe for yearely hire,
 And in the Princes gardin daily wrought:
There I beheld such vainenesse, as I never thought.

8. I.e., soft and truly enriching sleep (aptly suggesting the moon's influence).

25

"With sight whereof soone cloyd, and long deluded
  With idle hopes, which them doe entertaine,
  After I had ten yeares my selfe excluded
  From native home, and spent my youth in vaine,
  I gan my follies to my selfe to plaine,°   *lament*
  And this sweet peace, whose lacke did then appeare.
  Tho backe returning to my sheepe againe,
  I from thenceforth have learned to love more deare
This lowly quiet life, which I inherite° here."   *possess*

26

Whylest thus he talkt, the knight with greedy eare
  Hong still upon his melting mouth attent;[9]
  Whose sensefull° words empierst his hart so neare,   *sensible*
  That he was rapt with double ravishment,
  Both of his speach that wrought him great content,
  And also of the object of his vew,[1]
  On which his hungry eye was alwayes bent;
  That twixt his pleasing tongue, and her faire hew,°   *form*
He lost himselfe, and like one halfe entrauncéd grew.

27

Yet to occasion meanes, to worke his mind,
  And to insinuate his harts desire,[2]
  He thus replyde; "Now surely syre, I find,
  That all this worlds gay showes, which we admire,
  Be but vaine shadowes to this safe retyre°   *retirement*
  Of life, which here in lowlinesse ye lead,
  Fearelesse of foes, or fortunes wrackfull° yre,   *destructive*
  Which tosseth states, and under foot doth tread
The mightie ones, affrayd of every chaunges dread.

28

"That even I which daily doe behold
  The glorie of the great, mongst whom I won,°   *dwell*
  And now have proved,° what happinesse ye hold   *experienced*
  In this small plot of your dominion,
  Now loath great Lordship and ambition;
  And wish the heavens so much had gracéd mee,
  As graunt me live in like condition;
  Or that my fortunes might transposéd bee
From pitch° of higher place, unto this low degree."   *height*

29

"In vaine," said then old Meliboe, "doe men
  The heavens of their fortunes fault accuse,
  Sith they know best, what is the best for them:
  For they to each such fortune doe diffuse,°   *distribute*
  As they doe know each can most aptly use.

9. I.e., attentively listened to his sweetly persuasive speech.
1. I.e., Pastorella.

2. I.e., to exercise reasoned thought, and, subtly, also to satisfy his emotional need.

For not that, which men covet most, is best,
Nor that thing worst, which men do most refuse;
But fittest is, that all contented rest
With that they hold: each hath his fortune in his brest.[3]

30

"It is the mynd, that maketh good or ill,
That maketh wretch or happie, rich or poore:
For some, that hath abundance at his will,
Hath not enough, but wants in greatest store;
And other, that hath litle, askes no more,
But in that litle is both rich and wise.
For wisedome is most riches; fooles therefore
They are, which fortunes doe by vowes devize,°   *plan to get*
Sith each unto himselfe his life may fortunize."°   *make fortunate*

31

"Since then in each mans self," said Calidore,
"It is, to fashion his owne lyfes estate,
Give leave awhyle, good father, in this shore
To rest my barcke, which hath bene beaten late
With stormes of fortune and tempestuous fate,
In seas of troubles and of toylesome paine,
That whether quite from them for to retrate
I shall resolve, or backe to turne againe,
I may here with your selfe some small repose obtaine.

32

"Not that the burden of so bold a guest
Shall chargefull° be, or chaunge to you at all;   *troublesome*
For your meane food shall be my daily feast,
And this your cabin both my bowre and hall.
Besides for recompence hereof, I shall
You well reward, and golden guerdon give,
That may perhaps you better much withall,
And in this quiet make you safer live."
So forth he drew much gold, and toward him it drive.°   *thrust*

33

But the good man, nought tempted with the offer
Of his rich mould,° did thrust it farre away,   *dross*
And thus bespake; "Sir knight, your bounteous proffer
Be farre fro me, to whom ye ill display
That mucky masse, the cause of mens decay,
That mote empaire my peace with daungers dread.
But if ye algates° covet to assay   *in any case*
This simple sort of life, that shepheards lead,
Be it your owne: our rudenesse to your selfe aread."°   *take*

34

So there that night Sir Calidore did dwell,
And long while after, whilest him list remaine,

3. The thought apparently derives from Juvenal, *Satire X*. 417–425, a passage to which Chaucer also al- ludes in *Troilus and Criseyde*, IV. 197– 201.

Dayly beholding the faire Pastorell,
And feeding on the bayt of his owne bane.°   *ruin*
During which time he did her entertaine
With all kind courtesies, he could invent;
And every day, her companie to gaine,
When to the field she went, he with her went:
So for to quench his fire, he did it more augment.

35

But she that never had acquainted beene
  With such queint° usage, fit for Queenes and Kings,   *elegant*
  Ne ever had such knightly service seene,
  But being bred under base shepheards wings,
  Had ever learned to love the lowly things,
  Did litle whit regard his courteous guize,°   *behavior*
  But caréd more for Colins[4] carolings
Then all that he could doe, or ever devize:
His layes, his loves, his lookes she did them all despize.

36

Which Calidore perceiving, thought it best
  To chaunge the manner of his loftie looke;°   *appearance*
  And doffing his bright armes, himself addrest°   *clothed*
  In shepheards weed, and in his hand he tooke,
  In stead of steelehead speare, a shepheards hooke,
  That who had seene him then, would have bethought
  On Phrygian Paris[5] by Plexippus brooke,
When he the love of fayre Oenone sought,
What time the golden apple was unto him brought.

37

So being clad, unto the fields he went
  With the faire Pastorella every day,
  And kept her sheepe with diligent attent,°   *attention*
  Watching to drive the ravenous Wolfe away,
  The whylest at pleasure she mote sport and play;
  And every evening helping them to fold:
  And otherwhiles for need, he did assay
  In his strong hand their rugged teats to hold,
And out of them to presse the milke: love so much could.

38

Which seeing Coridon, who her likewise
  Long time had loved, and hoped her love to gaine,
  He much was troubled at that straungers guize,
  And many gealous thoughts conceived in vaine,
  That this of all his labour and long paine
  Should reap the harvest, ere it ripened were,

---

4. I.e., Colin Clout, the shepherd poet, with whom Spenser associates himself; cf. E.K.'s Glosse to "Januarye," in *The Shepheardes Calendar*.
5. Cf. III. ix. 34, 36, and notes. "Plexippus brooke" is a term of Spenser's own invention, perhaps reflecting some unorthodox or mistaken etymology. That Spenser should, at this juncture, liken Calidore to Paris indicates the poet's larger purpose: while Calidore's abandonment of his quest is understandable (cf. x. 3), his calling is not that of the shepherd.

That made him scoule, and pout, and oft complaine
  Of Pastorell to all the shepheards there,
That she did love a stranger swayne then him more dere.

39

And ever when he came in companie,
  Where Calidore was present, he would loure,°   scowl
  And byte his lip, and even for gealousie
  Was readie oft his owne hart to devoure,
  Impatient of any paramoure:°   lover
  Who on the other side did seeme so farre
  From malicing, or grudging his good houre,[6]
  That all he could, he gracéd him with her,
Ne ever shewéd signe of rancour or of jarre.°   quarrelling

40

And oft, when Coridon unto her brought
  Or° litle sparrowes, stolen from their nest,   either
  Or wanton squirrels, in the woods farre sought,
  Or other daintie thing for her addrest,°   prepared
  He would commend his guift, and make the best.[7]
  Yet she no whit his presents did regard,
  Ne him could find to fancie in her brest:
  This newcome shepheard had his market mard.°   spoiled
Old love is litle worth when new is more prefard.

41

One day when as the shepheard swaynes together
  Were met, to make their sports and merrie glee,
  As they are wont in faire sunshynie weather,
  The whiles their flockes in shadowes shrouded bee,
  They fell to daunce: then did they all agree,
  That Colin Clout should pipe as one most fit;
  And Calidore should lead the ring, as hee
  That most in Pastorellaes grace did sit.
Thereat frowned Coridon, and his lip closely bit.

42

But Calidore of courteous inclination
  Tooke Coridon, and set him in his place,
  That he should lead the daunce, as was his fashion;
  For Coridon could daunce, and trimly trace.[8]
  And when as Pastorella, him to grace,
  Her flowry garlond tooke from her owne head,
  And plast on his, he did it soone displace,
  And did it put on Coridons in stead:
Then Coridon woxe° frollicke, that earst seeméd dead.   became

43

Another time, when as they did dispose°   incline
  To practise games, and maisteries° to try,   contests of strength
  They for their Judge did Pastorella chose;
  A garland was the meed of victory.

6. I.e., good fortune.   8. I.e., precisely execute the dance
7. I.e., praise it highly.   steps.

There Coridon forth stepping openly,
  Did chalenge Calidore to wrestling game:
  For he through long and perfect industry,
  Therein well practisd was, and in the same
Thought sure t'avenge his grudge, and worke his foe great shame.

44

But Calidore he greatly did mistake;
  For he was strong and mightily stiffe pight,[9]
  That with one fall his necke he almost brake,
  And had he not upon him fallen light,
  His dearest joynt[1] he sure had broken quight.
  Then was the oaken crowne by Pastorell
  Given to Calidore, as his due right;
  But he, that did in courtesie excell,
Gave it to Coridon, and said he wonne it well.

45

Thus did the gentle knight himselfe abeare°   conduct
  Amongst that rusticke rout in all his deeds,
  That even they, the which his rivals were,
  Could not maligne him, but commend him needs:
  For courtesie amongst the rudest breeds
  Good will and favour.[2] So it surely wrought
  With this faire Mayd, and in her mynde the seeds
  Of perfect love did sow, that last° forth brought   finally
The fruite of joy and blisse, though long time dearely bought.

46

Thus Calidore continued there long time,
  To winne the love of the faire Pastorell;
  Which having got, he uséd without crime°   sin
  Or blamefull blot, but menagéd so well,
  That he of all the rest, which there did dwell,
  Was favouréd, and to her grace commended.
  But what straunge fortunes unto him befell,
  Ere he attained the point by him intended,
Shall more conveniently in other place be ended.

Canto X

Calidore sees the Graces daunce,
  To Colins melody:
The whiles his Pastorell is led
  Into captivity.

1

Who now does follow the foule Blatant Beast,
  Whilest Calidore does follow that faire Mayd,
  Unmyndfull of his vow and high beheast,°   command
  Which by the Faery Queene was on him layd,

9. I.e., solidly built.
1. I.e., his neck.
2. Sts. 45–46 imply that Calidore's courtesy is motivated by a desire to gain the good will and approval of others (notably Pastorella). While this

That he should never leave, nor be delayd
From chacing him, till he had it attchieved?
But now entrapt of love, which him betrayd,
He mindeth more, how he may be relieved
With grace from her, whose love his heart hath sore engrieved.

2

That from henceforth he meanes no more to sew°   *pursue*
His former quest, so full of toile and paine;
Another quest, another game in vew
He hath, the guerdon of his love to gaine:
With whom he myndes° for ever to remaine,   *intends*
And set his rest[1] amongst the rusticke sort,
Rather then hunt still after shadowes vaine
Of courtly favour, fed with light report
Of every blaste, and sayling alwaies in the port.[2]

3

Ne certes mote he greatly blaméd be,
From so high step to stoupe unto so low.
For who had tasted once (as oft did he)
The happy peace, which there doth overflow,
And proved the perfect pleasures, which doe grow
Amongst poore hyndes, in hils, in woods, in dales,
Would never more delight in painted show
Of such false blisse, as there is set for stales,°   *snares*
T'entrap unwary fooles in their eternall bales.°   *woe*

4

For what hath all that goodly glorious gaze°   *spectacle*
Like to one sight, which Calidore did vew?
The glaunce whereof their dimméd eies would daze,°   *dazzle*
That never more they should endure the shew
Of that sunne-shine, that makes them looke askew.°   *asquint*
Ne ought in all that world of beauties rare,
(Save onely Glorianaes heavenly hew
To which what can compare?) can it compare;°   *rival*
The which as commeth now, by course[3] I will declare.

5

One day as he did raunge the fields abroad,
Whilest his faire Pastorella was elsewhere,
He chaunst to come, far from all peoples troad,°   *track*
Unto a place, whose pleasaunce did appere
To passe all others, on the earth which were:
For all that ever was by natures skill
Devized to worke delight, was gathered there,
And there by her were pouréd forth at fill,
As if this to adorne, she all the rest did pill.°   *ransack*

---

position does not as a rule make part of Spenser's conception of courtesy, many Renaissance writers on the subject admit the reasonable propriety for gentlemanly conduct of just such an attitude.

1. I.e., permanently remain.
2. I.e., never setting sail at all.
3. I.e., in due order, properly.

6

It was an hill plaste in an open plaine,
 That round about was bordered with a wood
 Of matchlesse hight, that seemed th'earth to disdaine,
 In which all trees of honour stately stood,
 And did all winter as in sommer bud,
 Spredding pavilions for the birds to bowre,°   *shelter*
 Which in their lower braunches sung aloud;
 And in their tops the soring hauke did towre,°   *perch*
Sitting like King of fowles in majesty and powre.

7

And at the foote thereof, a gentle flud°   *stream*
 His silver waves did softly tumble downe,
 Unmard with ragged mosse or filthy mud,
 Ne mote wylde beastes, ne mote the ruder clowne° *rustic*
 Thereto approch, ne filth mote therein drowne:°   *fall*
 But Nymphes and Faeries by the bancks did sit,
 In the woods shade, which did the waters crowne,
 Keeping all noysome° things away from it,   *harmful*
And to the waters fall tuning their accents fit.

8

And on the top thereof a spacious plaine
 Did spred it selfe, to serve to all delight,
 Either to daunce, when they to daunce would faine,° *desire*
 Or else to course about their bases light;[4]
 Ne ought there wanted, which for pleasure might
 Desiréd be, or thence to banish bale:°   *sorrow*
 So pleasauntly the hill with equall° hight,   *even*
 Did seeme to overlooke the lowly vale;
Therefore it rightly cleepéd° was mount Acidale.[5] *named*

9

They say that Venus, when she did dispose°   *incline*
 Her selfe to pleasaunce, uséd to resort
 Unto this place, and therein to repose
 And rest her selfe, as in a gladsome port,°   *manner*
 Or with the Graces[6] there to play and sport;
 That even her owne Cytheron,[7] though in it
 She uséd most to keepe her royall court,
 And in her soveraine Majesty to sit,
She in regard° hereof refusde and thought unfit. *comparison*

10

Unto this place when as the Elfin Knight
 Approcht, him seeméd that the merry sound

4. In the game of prisoner's base.
5. "Acidalia," a surname of Venus, referred to the Acidalian spring (in Boeotia) where the Graces, handmaids to the goddess, were reputed to bathe. The name may derive from ἀκηδής, "free from care."

6. "The Graces are the natural endowment of Calidore, as his name implies" (W. Nelson, *op. cit.*, 286). See also sts. 22–24 and note.
7. Perhaps Cythera is meant; but cf. the note on III. vi. 29.

Of a shrill pipe he playing heard on hight,°   *loudly*
And many feete fast thumping th'hollow ground,
That through the woods their Eccho did rebound.
He nigher drew, to weete what mote it be;
There he a troupe of Ladies dauncing found
Full merrily, and making gladfull glee,
And in the midst a Shepheard piping he did see.[8]

11

He durst not enter into th'open greene,
For dread of them unwares to be descryde,°   *observed*
For° breaking of their daunce, if he were seene;   *and for*
But in the covert of the wood did byde,
Beholding all, yet of them unespyde.
There he did see, that pleaséd much his sight,
That even he him selfe his eyes envyde,
An hundred naked maidens lilly white,
All raungéd in a ring, and dauncing in delight.

12

All they without were raungéd in a ring,
And dauncéd round; but in the midst of them
Three other Ladies did both daunce and sing,
The whilest the rest them round about did hemme,
And like a girlond did in compasse stemme:°   *encircle*
And in the middest of those same three, was placed
Another Damzell, as a precious gemme,
Amidst a ring most richly well enchaced,°   *adorned*
That with her goodly presence all the rest much graced.

13

Looke how the Crowne, which Ariadne[9] wore
Upon her yvory forehead that same day,
That Theseus her unto his bridale bore,
When the bold Centaures made that bloudy fray
With the fierce Lapithes, which did them dismay;°   *defeat*
Being now placéd in the firmament,
Through the bright heaven doth her beams display,
And is unto the starres an ornament,
Which round about her move in order excellent.

14

Such was the beauty of this goodly band,
Whose sundry parts were here too long to tell:
But she that in the midst of them did stand,
Seemed all the rest in beauty to excell,
Crownd with a rosie girlond, that right well

8. For an extended discussion of the Dance of the Graces, cf. the essay by Humphrey Tonkin in this edition.
9. Spenser here combines and rearranges two passages from Ovid's *Metamorphoses*. Ariadne, daughter of the Cretan king Minos, enabled Theseus to escape from the Labyrinth after he had killed the Minotaur that dwelt at its center; subsquently abandoned by him on the island of Naxos, she became the consort of Dionysus, who placed her bridal crown among the stars (VIII. 169–182). The battle of Centaurs and Lapithae (in which Theseus participated) took place at the wedding of Hippodamia to Pirithous (XII. 210–535).

Did her beseeme. And ever, as the crew°   *company*
   About her daunst, sweet flowres, that far did smell,
   And fragrant odours they uppon her threw;
But most of all, those three did her with gifts endew.

15

Those were the Graces, daughters of delight,
   Handmaides of Venus, which are wont to haunt
   Uppon this hill, and daunce there day and night:
   Those three to men all gifts of grace do graunt,
   And all, that Venus in her selfe doth vaunt,
   Is borrowéd of them. But that faire one,
   That in the midst was placéd paravaunt,°   *pre-eminently*
   Was she to whom that shepheard pypt alone,
That made him pipe so merrily, as never none.[1]

16

She was to weete that jolly Shepheards lasse,[2]
   Which pipéd there unto that merry rout,°   *company*
   That jolly shepheard, which there pipéd, was
   Poore Colin Clout (who knowes not Colin Clout?)
   He pypt apace,° whilest they him daunst about.   *briskly*
   Pype jolly shepheard, pype thou now apace
   Unto thy love, that made thee low to lout;°   *bow*
   Thy love is present there with thee in place,
Thy love is there advaunst° to be another Grace.   *raised*

17

Much wondred Calidore at this straunge sight
   Whose like before his eye had never seene,
   And standing long astonishéd in spright,
   And rapt with pleasaunce, wist not what to weene;°   *think*
   Whether it were the traine° of beauties Queene,   *assembly*
   Or Nymphes, or Faeries, or enchaunted show,
   With which his eyes mote have deluded beene.
   Therefore resolving, what it was, to know,
Out of the wood he rose, and toward them did go.

18

But soone as he appearéd to their vew,
   They vanisht all away out of his sight,
   And cleane were gone, which way he never knew;
   All save the shepheard, who for fell despight°   *anger*
   Of that displeasure, broke his bag-pipe quight,
   And made great mone for that unhappy° turne.   *unlucky*
   But Calidore, though no lesse sory wight,
   For that mishap, yet seeing him to mourne,
Drew neare, that he the truth of all by him mote learne.

---

1. I.e., as no one had ever piped.
2. In the "Aprill" eclogue of *The Shepheardes Calender* (113–117), Spenser had advanced the claims of "fayre Elisa, Queene of shepheardes all," to be a fourth Grace; but the figure here described, as sts. 25–28 indicate, is not too narrowly to be identified with a mysterious "Rosalind," or with Spenser's own bride, or with the Queen. As Colin's "love," she represents poetic inspiration as well as that ideal of human beauty which is divinely "graced."

19

And first him greeting, thus unto him spake,
  "Haile jolly shepheard, which thy joyous dayes
  Here leadest in this goodly merry make,°   *making*
  Frequented of these gentle Nymphes alwayes,
  Which to thee flocke, to heare thy lovely layes;
  Tell me, what mote these dainty Damzels be,
  Which here with thee doe make their pleasant playes?
  Right happy thou, that mayst them freely see:
But why when I them saw, fled they away from me?"

20

"Not I so happy," answerd then that swaine,
  "As thou unhappy, which them thence didst chace,
  Whom by no meanes thou canst recall againe,
  For being gone, none can them bring in place,
  But whom they of them selves list so to grace."
  "Right sory I," saide then Sir Calidore,
  "That my ill fortune did them hence displace.
  But since things passéd none may now restore,
Tell me, what were they all, whose lacke thee grieves so sore."

21

Tho gan that shepheard thus for to dilate;°   *discourse*
  "Then wote thou shepheard, whatsoever thou bee,
  That all those Ladies, which thou sawest late,
  Are Venus Damzels, all within her fee,°   *service*
  But differing in honour and degree:
  They all are Graces, which on her depend,[3]
  Besides a thousand more, which ready bee
  Her to adorne, when so she forth doth wend:
But those three in the midst, doe chiefe on her attend.

22

"They are the daughters of sky-ruling Jove,
  By him begot of faire Eurynome,[4]
  The Oceans daughter, in this pleasant grove,
  As he this way comming from feastfull glee,
  Of Thetis wedding with Aeacidee,
  In sommers shade him selfe here rested weary.
  The first of them hight mylde Euphrosyne,
  Next faire Aglaia, last Thalia merry:
Sweete Goddesses all three which me in mirth do cherry.°   *cheer*

23

"These three on men all gracious gifts bestow,
  Which decke the body or adorne the mynde,
  To make them lovely or well favoured show,
  As comely carriage, entertainement° kynde,   *manners*
  Sweete semblaunt,° friendly offices that bynde,   *demeanor*
  And all the complements° of curtesie: *accomplishments*

3. I.e., who belong to her and make part of her retinue.

4. Based on Hesiod, *Theogony*, 907–911. The suggestion that Jove sired the

They teach us, how to each degree and kynde
   We should our selves demeane, to low, to hie;
To friends, to foes, which skill men call Civility.

24

"Therefore they alwaies smoothly seeme to smile,
   That we likewise should mylde and gentle be,
   And also naked are, that without guile
   Or false dissemblaunce all them plaine may see,
   Simple and true from covert malice free:
   And eke them selves so in their daunce they bore,
   That two of them still froward° seemed to bee,   *turned away*
   But one still towards shewed her selfe afore;°   *in front*
That good should from us goe, then come in greater store.[5]

25

"Such were those Goddesses, which ye did see;
   But that fourth Mayd, which there amidst them traced,°   *danced*
   Who can aread,° what creature mote she bee,   *say*
   Whether a creature, or a goddesse graced
   With heavenly gifts from heven first enraced?°   *implanted*
   But what so sure she was, she worthy was,
   To be the fourth with those three other placed:
   Yet was she certes but a countrey lasse,
Yet she all other countrey lasses farre did passe.

26

"So farre as doth the daughter of the day,[6]
   All other lesser lights in light excell,
   So farre doth she in beautyfull array,
   Above all other lasses beare the bell,[7]
   Ne lesse in vertue that beseemes her well,
   Doth she exceede the rest of all her race,
   For which the Graces that here wont to dwell,
   Have for more honor brought her to this place,
And gracéd her so much to be another Grace.

27

"Another Grace she well deserves to be,
   In whom so many Graces gathered are,
   Excelling much the meane° of her degree;   *average*
   Divine resemblaunce, beauty soveraine rare,
   Firme Chastity, that spight ne blemish dare;[8]
   All which she with such courtesie doth grace,
   That all her peres cannot with her compare,
   But quite are dimméd, when she is in place.
She made me often pipe and now to pipe apace.

Graces after the marriage of Thetis to Peleus (the son of Aeacus) is Spenser's own.
5. Presumably based on Boccaccio, *De Genealogia Deorum*, V. 35. Cf. also the Glosse on "Aprill," 109.

6. I.e., the sun; cf. also III. iv. 59, where Truth is identified as the first daughter of Day.
7. I.e., take the prize.
8. I.e., that neither malice nor slur may injure.

28

"Sunne of the world, great glory of the sky,
  That all the earth doest lighten with thy rayes,
  Great Gloriana, greatest Majesty,
  Pardon thy shepheard, mongst so many layes,
  As he hath sung of thee in all his dayes,
  To make one minime° of thy poore handmayd,   *note in music*
  And underneath thy feete to place her prayse,
  That when thy glory shall be farre displayd
To future age of her this mention may be made."

29

When thus that shepheard ended had his speach,
  Sayd Calidore; "Now sure it yrketh° mee,   *pains*
  That to thy blisse I made this luckelesse breach,
  As now the author of thy bale° to be,   *grief*
  Thus to bereave thy loves deare sight from thee:
  But gentle Shepheard pardon thou my shame,
  Who rashly sought that, which I mote not see."
Thus did the courteous Knight excuse his blame,
And to recomfort him, all comely meanes did frame.

30

In such discourses they together spent
  Long time, as fit occasion forth them led;
  With which the Knight him selfe did much content,
  And with delight his greedy fancy fed,
  Both of his words, which he with reason red;°   *spoke*
  And also of the place, whose pleasures rare
  With such regard° his sences ravishéd,   *sight*
  That thence, he had no will away to fare,
But wisht, that with that shepheard he mote dwelling share.

Two Cantos of *Mutabilitie:*

WHICH, BOTH FOR FORME AND MATTER, APPEARE
TO BE PARCELL OF SOME FOLLOWING BOOKE OF THE
FAERIE QUEENE

(∵)

Under the Legend
of
Constancie.[1]

Canto VI

Proud Change (not pleasd, in mortall things,
  beneath the Moone, to raigne)
Pretends, as well of Gods, as Men,
  to be the Soveraine.

1

What man that sees the ever-whirling wheele
  Of Change, the which all mortall things doth sway,°   *rule*
But that therby doth find, and plainly feele,
How Mutability[2] in them doth play
Her cruell sports, to many mens decay?°   *destruction*
Which that to all may better yet appeare,
I will rehearse that whylome° I heard say,   *formerly*
How she at first her selfe began to reare,
Gainst all the Gods, and th'empire sought from
  them to beare.°   *take away*

2

But first, here falleth fittest to unfold
  Her antique race and linage ancient,
As I have found it registred of old,
In Faery Land mongst records permanent:
She was, to weet,[3] a daughter by descent
Of those old Titans,[4] that did whylome strive

---

1. It is not established that the *Cantos of Mutabilitie* were in fact intended to form part of *The Faerie Queene,* but that seems probable, given this statement by Matthew Lownes (publisher of the 1609 Folio), together with the metrical arrangement of stanzas, the division into Cantos, and particularly the expressions of Canto vi. 37. For an extended discussion of the Cantos in the context of Renaissance attitudes to time and change, see the essay by Ricardo Quinones in this edition. For W. Blissett, the Cantos are "a detached retrospective commentary on the poem as a whole": see "Spenser's Mutabilitie," in *Essays in English Literature from the Renaissance to the Victorian Age,* ed. M. Maclure and F. W. Watt (Toronto, 1964), pp. 26–42.
2. The power of change, personified in the cantos by the figure of Mutability, is not identical with that of time (cf. st. 8), which the poet imagines as itself subject to change (cf. vii. 47). The impact of astronomical science on Spenser's age reinforced the persuasive effect of classical expressions affirming the inevitability of change and decay (e.g., Ovid, *Metamorphoses,* XV. 237–251, and Lucretius, *De Rerum Natura,* V); "the ever-whirling wheele of Change" would be likely to suggest to readers in the early seventeenth century the image of Fortune's wheel.
3. I.e., in fact.
4. The Titans, offspring of Uranus, rebelled against him and made Saturn their ruler (Hesiod, *Theogony,* 137–210); subsequently he was deposed by his son, Jove (cf. the note on st. 27).

With Saturnes sonne for heavens regiment.°   rule
Whom, though high Jove of kingdome did deprive,
Yet many of their stemme° long after did survive.   race

3

And many of them, afterwards obtained
   Great power of Jove, and high authority;
   As Hecate,[5] in whose almighty hand,
   He plac't all rule and principality,
   To be by her disposéd diversly,
   To Gods, and men, as she them list° divide: chose to
   And drad° Bellona, that doth sound on hie   dreaded
   Warres and allarums unto Nations wide,
That makes both heaven and earth to tremble at her pride.

4

So likewise did this Titanesse aspire,
   Rule and dominion to her selfe to gaine;
   That as a Goddesse, men might her admire,°   wonder at
   And heavenly honours yield, as to them twaine.[6]
   And first, on earth she sought it to obtaine;
   Where she such proofe and sad° examples shewed   grievous
   Of her great power, to many ones great paine,
   That not men onely (whom she soone subdewed)
But eke all other creatures, her bad dooings rewed.

5

For, she the face of earthly things so changed,
   That all which Nature had establisht first
   In good estate, and in meet° order ranged,   fitting
   She did pervert, and all their statutes burst:
   And all the worlds faire frame (which none yet durst
   Of Gods or men to alter or misguide)
   She altered quite, and made them all accurst
   That God had blest; and did at first provide
In that still happy state for ever to abide.

6

Ne shee the lawes of Nature onely brake,
   But eke of Justice, and of Policie;°   government
   And wrong of right, and bad of good did make,
   And death for life exchangéd foolishlie:
   Since which, all living wights have learned to die,
   And all this world is woxen° daily worse.   grown
   O pittious worke of Mutabilitie!
   By which, we all are subject to that curse,
And death in stead of life have suckéd from our Nurse.[7]

---

5. According to Hesiod (*Theogony*, 411–453), Hecate, a Titaness by birth, was the only one of that race to be favored by Zeus (Jove); as the goddess of witches, she was associated in Renaissance mythography with Persephone and the underworld. Bellona (identified with Pallas Athena in E. K.'s Glosse to "October," 115) was the Roman goddess of war; a reference in Spenser's early translation, *The Visions of Bellay*, to the warlike figure of "Typhoeus sister," may account for this identification of Bellona as a descendant of the Titans.
6. I.e., Hecate and Bellona.
7. Sts. 5–6 summarize the physical, political, and moral consequences for the world of Mutability's ambition (allegorically, of the Fall).

7

And now, when all the earth she thus had brought
 To her behest,° and thrallèd to her might,   *bidding*
 She gan to cast° in her ambitious thought,   *resolve*
 T'attempt the empire of the heavens hight,
 And Jove himselfe to shoulder from his right.
 And first, she past the region of the ayre,
 And of the fire, whose substance thin and slight,
 Made no resistance, ne could her contraire,°   *withstand*
But ready passage to her pleasure did prepaire.

8

Thence, to the Circle of the Moone she clambe,[8]
 Where Cynthia[9] raignes in everlasting glory,
 To whose bright shining palace straight she came,
 All fairely deckt with heavens goodly story;°   *rows (of stars)*
 Whose silver gates (by which there sate an hory
 Old aged Sire, with hower-glasse in hand,
 Hight Tyme) she entred, were he liefe or sory:[1]
 Ne staide till she the highest stage° had scand,°   *level/mounted to*
Where Cynthia did sit, that never still did stand.

9

Her sitting on an Ivory throne shee found,
 Drawne of two steeds, th'one black, the other white,[2]
 Environd with tenne thousand starres around,
 That duly her attended day and night;
 And by her side, there ran her Page, that hight
 Vesper, whom we the Evening-starre intend:°   *call*
 That with his Torche, still twinkling like twylight,
 Her lightened all the way where she should wend,
And joy to weary wandring travailers did lend:

10

That when the hardy Titanesse beheld
 The goodly building of her Palace bright,
 Made of the heavens substance, and up-held
 With thousand Crystall pillors of huge hight,
 Shee gan to burne in her ambitious spright,
 And t'envie her that in such glorie raigned.
 Eftsoones she cast by force and tortious° might,   *wrongful*
 Her to displace; and to her selfe to have gained
The kingdome of the Night, and waters by her wained.°   *moved*

11

Boldly she bid the Goddesse downe descend,
 And let her selfe into that Ivory throne;
 For, shee her selfe more worthy thereof wend,°   *thought*

8. I.e., she climbed to the sphere of
the moon. Sts. 8–15 recall the disas-
trous consequences for universal order
of Phaethon's career across the heavens
in the chariot of his father Apollo, god
of the sun (Ovid, *Metamorphoses*, II.
1–400).
9. Goddess of the moon. The fact that
Queen Elizabeth was regularly identi-
fied with Cynthia by poets of the age
would render Mutability's threatening
conduct in sts. 8–13 particularly com-
pelling for English readers.
1. I.e., whether he were willing or not.
2. These steeds appear both in Boccac-
cio, *De Genealogia Deorum*, IV. 16, and
in Natalis Comes, *Mythologiae*, III. 17.

And better able it to guide alone:
Whether to men, whose fall she did bemone,
Or unto Gods, whose state she did maligne,°   *envy*
Or to th'infernall Powers, her need give lone[3]
Of her faire light, and bounty most benigne,
Her selfe of all that rule shee deeméd most condigne.°   *worthy*

12

But shee that had to her that soveraigne seat
    By highest Jove assigned, therein to beare
    Nights burning lamp, regarded not her threat,
    Ne yielded ought for favour or for feare;
    But with sterne countenaunce and disdainfull cheare,°   *aspect*
    Bending her hornéd browes, did put her back:
    And boldly blaming her for comming there,
    Bade her attonce from heavens coast to pack,
Or at her perill bide the wrathfull Thunders wrack.°   *destruction*

13

Yet nathemore° the Giantesse forbare: *not at all*
    But boldly preacing-on,° raught forth her hand   *advancing*
    To pluck her downe perforce° from off her chaire;   *by force*
    And there-with lifting up her golden wand,
    Threatned to strike her if she did with-stand.
    Where-at the starres, which round about her blazed,
    And eke the Moones bright wagon, still did stand,
All beeing with so bold attempt amazed,
And on her uncouth° habit and sterne looke still gazed.   *strange*

14

Meane-while, the lower World, which nothing knew
    Of all that chauncéd here, was darkned quite;
    And eke the heavens, and all the heavenly crew
    Of happy wights, now unpurvaide° of light,   *deprived*
    Were much afraid, and wondred at that sight;
    Fearing least Chaos broken had his chaine,
    And brought againe on them eternall night:
    But chiefely Mercury, that next doth raigne,[4]
Ran forth in haste, unto the king of Gods to plaine.°   *complain*

15

All ran together with a great out-cry,
    To Joves faire Palace, fixt in heavens hight;
    And beating at his gates full earnestly,
    Gan call to him aloud with all their might,
    To know what meant that suddaine lack of light.
    The father of the Gods when this he heard,
    Was troubled much at their so strange affright,
    Doubting least Typhon[5] were againe upreared,
Or other his old foes, that once him sorely feared.°   *frightened*

3. I.e., she must give.
4. Mercury was the son of Maia (cf. st. 16); in the Ptolemaic system of the universe, the sphere of the planet Mercury was next beyond that of the moon.
5. The giant Typhon, also called Typhoeus, rebelled against Zeus, who sub-

16

Eftsoones the sonne of Maia forth he sent
   Downe to the Circle of the Moone, to knowe
   The cause of this so strange astonishment,
   And why shee did her wonted course forslowe;°   *delay*
   And if that any were on earth belowe
   That did with charmes or Magick her molest,
   Him to attache,° and downe to hell to throwe: *seize*
   But, if from heaven it were, then to arrest
The Author, and him bring before his presence prest.°   *immediately*

17

The wingd-foot God, so fast his plumes did beat,
   That soone he came where-as the Titanesse
   Was striving with faire Cynthia for her seat:
   At whose strange sight, and haughty hardinesse,°   *boldness*
   He wondred much, and fearéd her no lesse.
   Yet laying feare aside to doe his charge,°   *assigned task*
   At last, he bade her (with bold stedfastnesse)
   Ceasse to molest the Moone to walke at large,[6]
Or come before high Jove, her dooings to discharge.°   *account for*

18

And there-with-all, he on her shoulder laid
   His snaky-wreathéd Mace,[7] whose awfull power
   Doth make both Gods and hellish fiends affraid:
   Where-at the Titanesse did sternely lower,°   *scowl*
   And stoutly answered, that in evill hower
   He from his Jove such message to her brought,
   To bid her leave faire Cynthias silver bower;
   Sith shee his Jove and him esteeméd nought,
No more then Cynthia's selfe; but all their kingdoms sought.

19

The Heavens Herald staid not to reply,
   But past away, his doings to relate
   Unto his Lord; who now in th'highest sky,
   Was placéd in his principall Estate,[8]
   With all the Gods about him congregate:
   To whom when Hermes had his message told,
   It did them all exceedingly amate,°   *dismay*
   Save Jove; who, changing nought his count'nance bold,
Did unto them at length these speeches wise unfold;

20

"Harken to mee awhile yee heavenly Powers;
   Ye may remember since th'Earths curséd seed[9]
   Sought to assaile the heavens eternall towers,

---

sequently confined him in the depths of
Tartarus (Hesiod, *Theogony*, 820–
868).
6. I.e., cease to hinder the moon's free
movement.

7. I.e., the caduceus. Cf. the note on
II. xii. 41.
8. I.e., was enthroned in his regal as-
pect.
9. I.e., the giants, whose rebellion Ovid
describes in *Metamorphoses*, I. 156–

And to us all exceeding feare did breed:
But how we then defeated all their deed,
Yee all doe knowe, and them destroiéd quite;
Yet not so quite, but that there did succeed
An off-spring of their bloud, which did alite
Upon the fruitfull earth, which doth us
      yet despite.°   *treat with contempt*

21

"Of that bad seed is this bold woman bred,
  That now with bold presumption doth aspire
  To thrust faire Phoebe from her silver bed,
  And eke our selves from heavens high Empire,
  If that her might were match to her desire:
  Wherefore, it now behoves us to advise°   *consider*
  What way is best to drive her to retire;
  Whether by open force, or counsell wise,
Areed° ye sonnes of God, as best ye can devise."   *advise*

22

So having said, he ceast; and with his brow
  (His black eye-brow, whose doomefull dreaded beck[1]
  Is wont to wield the world unto his vow,°   *will*
  And even the highest Powers of heaven to check)
  Made signe to them in their degrees to speake:
  Who straight gan cast° their counsell grave and wise.   *consider*
  Meane-while, th'Earths daughter, thogh she nought did reck
  Of Hermes message; yet gan now advise,
What course were best to take in this hot bold emprize.° *undertaking*

23

Eftsoones she thus resolved; that whil'st the Gods
  (After returne of Hermes Embassie)
  Were troubled, and amongst themselves at ods,
  Before they could new counsels re-allie,°   *form again*
  To set upon them in that extasie;°   *astonishment*
  And take what fortune time and place would lend:
  So, forth she rose, and through the purest sky
  To Joves high Palace straight cast° to ascend,   *resolved*
To prosecute her plot: Good on-set boads good end.

24

Shee there arriving, boldly in did pass;
  Where all the Gods she found in counsell close,°   *secret*
  All quite unarmed, as then their manner was.
  At sight of her they suddaine all arose,

---

162. Spenser does not usually distinguish between Titans and giants, considering them both representative of the rebellious spirit that seeks to challenge and overthrow established order in every sphere. The figure of Mutability, however, combines the will to violent rebellion (characteristic of the earthborn giants) with beauty (st. 31), intellectual poise, and a sense of pride more in keeping with the qualities appropriate for a descendant of the Titans, themselves gods, the offspring of heaven and earth.

1. I.e., his feared nod of command.

In great amaze, ne wist what way to chose.
But Jove, all fearelesse, forc't them to aby;°   *remain*
And in his soveraine throne, gan straight dispose°   *arrange*
  Himselfe more full of grace and Majestie,
That mote encheare° his friends, and foes mote terrifie.   *cheer*

25

That, when the haughty Titanesse beheld,
  All° were she fraught with pride and impudence,   *although*
  Yet with the sight thereof was almost queld;
  And inly quaking, seemed as reft of sense,
  And voyd of speech in that drad° audience;   *dread*
  Until that Jove himself, her selfe bespake:
  "Speake thou fraile woman, speake with confidence,
  Whence art thou, and what doost thou here now make?°   *intend*
What idle errand hast thou, earths mansion to forsake?"

26

Shee, halfe confuséd with his great commaund,
  Yet gathering spirit of her natures pride,
  Him boldly answered thus to his demaund:
  "I am a daughter, by the mothers side,
  Of her that is Grand-mother magnifide°   *glorified*
  Of all the Gods, great Earth, great Chaos child:[2]
  But by the fathers (be it not envide)
  I greater am in bloud (whereon I build)
Then all the Gods, though wrongfully from heaven exiled.

27

"For Titan (as ye all acknowledge must)
  Was Saturnes elder brother by birth-right;
  Both, sonnes of Uranus: but by unjust
  And guilefull meanes, through Corybantes slight,°   *trickery*
  The younger thrust the elder from his right:[3]
  Since which, thou Jove, injuriously hast held
  The Heavens rule from Titans sonnes by might;
  And them to hellish dungeons downe hast feld:
Witnesse ye Heavens the truth of all that I have teld."

28

Whilst she thus spake, the Gods that gave good eare
  To her bold words, and markéd well her grace,
  Beeing of stature tall as any there
  Of all the Gods, and beautifull of face,
  As any of the Goddesses in place,
  Stood all astonied, like a sort° of Steeres;   *herd*

2. Earth is the offspring of Chaos in Hesiod, *Theogony,* 116; Boccaccio terms her "great mother" in *De Genealogia Deorum,* I. 8.
3. According to Natalis Comes (VI. 20; II. 1), Titan agreed to abdicate his power in favor of Saturn on condition that the latter would kill all his children by swallowing them (thus assuring the eventual return of power to Titan); however, when Zeus was born to Saturn's consort Rhea, she gave Saturn a stone to swallow instead of the child, while her attendants, the Corybantes, beat on shields to prevent the child's cries from being heard. "The younger thrust the elder from his right," while applicable to Saturn and Titan, is primarily referable to the eventual overthrow of Saturn by Zeus.

Mongst whom, some beast of strange and forraine race,
    Unwares° is chaunc't, far straying from his peeres: *unexpectedly*
So did their ghastly gaze bewray° their hidden feares.   *reveal*

29

Till having pauzed awhile, Jove thus bespake;
    "Will never mortall thoughts ceasse to aspire,
    In this bold sort, to Heaven claime to make,
    And touch celestiall seates with earthly mire?
    I would have thought, that bold Procrustes[4] hire,°   *reward*
    Or Typhons fall, or proud Ixions paine,
    Or great Prometheus, tasting of our ire,
    Would have suffized, the rest for to restraine;
And warned all men by their example to refraine:

30

"But now, this off-scum of that curséd fry,[5]
    Dare to renew the like bold enterprize,
    And chalenge th'heritage of this our skie;
    Whom what should hinder, but that we likewise
    Should handle as the rest of her allies,
    And thunder-drive to hell?" With that, he shooke
    His Nectar-deawéd locks, with which the skyes
    And all the world beneath for terror quooke,°   *quaked*
And eft° his burning levin-brond° in hand   *then/lightning bolt*
    he tooke.

31

But, when he lookéd on her lovely face,
    In which, faire beames of beauty did appeare,
    That could the greatest wrath soone turne to grace
    (Such sway° doth beauty even in Heaven beare)   *power*
    He staide his hand: and having changed his cheare,°   *mood*
    He thus againe in milder wise began;
    "But ah! if Gods should strive with flesh yfere,°   *together*
    Then shortly should the progeny of Man
Be rooted out, if Jove should doe still° what he can:[6]   *always*

32

"But thee faire Titans child, I rather weene,°   *suppose*
    Through some vaine errour or inducement light,
    To see that° mortall eyes have never seene;   *that which*

4. The robber Procrustes ("the stretcher"), who killed his victims by cutting off or stretching their limbs to make them fit his bed, was eventually destroyed by Theseus. For Typhon, cf. the note to st. 15. Ixion, who attempted to ravish Hera (Juno), was punished by being bound to a continually revolving wheel of fire. Prometheus stole fire from heaven for the use of man; he was shackled to a cliff, where a vulture daily consumed his liver, which grew again by night. Cf. Ovid, *Metamorphoses*, VII. 438; III. 303; IV. 461; and Hesiod, *Theogony*, 521–

525. Procrustes is not inappropriately grouped with the other three figures, for in the context of Jove's mood and utterance, his story exemplifies the inexorable punishment in store for those who flout the authority of natural or divine law.
5. I.e., Mutability, this latest example of rebellious presumption.
6. Psalms lxxviii. 38–39: "Yea, many a time turned he his anger away, and did not stir up all his wrath. For he remembered that they were but flesh . . .".

Or through ensample of thy sisters might,
  Bellona; whose great glory thou doost spight,°   *envy*
  Since thou hast seene her dreadfull power belowe,
  Mongst wretched men (dismaide with her affright)[7]
  To bandie Crownes, and Kingdomes to bestowe:
And sure thy worth, no lesse then hers doth seem to showe.

33

"But wote° thou this, thou hardy Titanesse,   *know*
  That not the worth of any living wight
  May challenge ought in Heavens interesse;[8]
  Much lesse the Title of old Titans Right:
  For, we by Conquest of our soveraine might,
  And by eternall doome of Fates decree,
  Have wonne the Empire of the Heavens bright;
  Which to our selves we hold, and to whom wee
Shall worthy deeme partakers of our blisse to bee.

34

"Then ceasse thy idle claime thou foolish gerle,
  And seeke by grace and goodnesse to obtaine
  That place from which by folly Titan fell;
  There-to thou maist perhaps, if so thou faine°   *desire*
  Have Jove thy gratious Lord and Soveraigne."
  So, having said, she thus to him replide;
  "Ceasse Saturnes sonne, to seeke by proffers vaine
  Of idle hopes t'allure mee to thy side,
For to betray my Right, before I have it tride.

35

"But thee, O Jove, no equall° Judge I deeme   *impartial*
  Of my desert, or of my dewfull° Right;   *due*
  That in thine owne behalfe maist partiall seeme:
  But to the highest him, that is behight
  Father of Gods and men by equall might;[9]
  To weet, the God of Nature, I appeale."
  There-at Jove wexéd wroth, and in his spright
  Did inly grudge, yet did it well conceale;
And bade Dan Phoebus Scribe her Appellation° seale.   *appeal*

36

Eftsoones the time and place appointed were,
  Where all, both heavenly Powers, and earthly wights,
  Before great Natures presence should appeare,
  For triall of their Titles and best Rights:
  That was, to weet, upon the highest hights
  Of Arlo-hill[1] (Who knowes not Arlo-hill?)

7. I.e., terror of her.
8. I.e., may lay claim to any part of Heaven's dominion or title.
9. I.e., equally powerful over gods as over men. The god of nature, here described as masculine, appears in vii. 5, as Dame Nature; "Whether she man or woman inly were" must remain uncertain.
1. Galtymore, a peak in the Irish mountain range ("old father Mole") near which Spenser's estate of Kilcolman was situated; it overlooked the "Golden Vale" of Aherlow. In the char-

That is the highest head (in all mens sights)
Of my old father Mole, whom Shepheards quill
Renowméd hath with hymnes fit for a rurall skill.

37

And, were it not ill fitting for this file,°   *recital*
  To sing of hilles and woods, mongst warres and Knights,
  I would abate the sternenesse of my stile,
  Mongst these sterne stounds° to mingle soft delights;   *clashes*
  And tell how Arlo through Dianaes spights
  (Beeing of old the best and fairest Hill
  That was in all this holy-Islands hights)
  Was made the most unpleasant, and most ill.
Meane while, O Clio, lend Calliope thy quill.[2]

38

Whylome,° when Ireland florishéd in fame   *formerly*
  Of wealths and goodnesse, far above the rest
  Of all that beare the British Islands name,[3]
  The Gods then used (for pleasure and for rest)
  Oft to resort there-to, when seemed them best:
  But none of all there-in more pleasure found,
  Then Cynthia;[4] that is soveraine Queene profest°   *acknowledged*
  Of woods and forrests, which therein abound,
Sprinkled with wholsom waters, more then most on ground.

39

But mongst them all, as fittest for her game,°   *recreation*
  Either for chace of beasts with hound or boawe,
  Or for to shroude in shade from Phoebus flame,
  Or bathe in fountaines that doe freshly flowe,
  Or from high hilles, or from the dales belowe,
  She chose this Arlo; where shee did resort
  With all her Nymphes enrangéd on a rowe,
  With whom the woody Gods did oft consort:
For, with the Nymphes, the Satyres love to play and sport.

40

Amongst the which, there was a Nymph that hight
  Molanna;[5] daughter of old father Mole,
  And sister unto Mulla,[6] faire and bright:
  Unto whose bed false Bregog whylome stole,
  That Shepheard Colin dearely° did condole,   *earnestly*

---

acter of Colin Clout, the shepherd poet,
Spenser alludes to "Old father Mole . . .
that mountain gray," in *Colin Clouts
Come Home Againe,* 56–59, 104–115.
2. I.e., allow Calliope to tell the story
that follows. By an arguable alternative
reading, Calliope (Spenser's Muse,
throughout the poem) is now to employ
Clio's quill for the story of Faunus and
Molanna.
3. Spenser observes in *A Vewe of the
Present State of Irelande* that "it is
Certaine that Irelande hathe had the use

of lettres verye Ancientlye and longe
before Englande" (1246–1247).
4. I.e., Diana, goddess of the forest.
5. The river Behanna, which rises near
Galtymore and joins at length with the
Funsheon (Spenser's "Fanchin," in st.
44).
6. The river Awbeg; this stream and
the river Bregoge environed Spenser's
estate at Kilcolman. The tale of Mulla
and Bregog (Irish, "false") is told in
Colin Clouts Come Home Againe, 104–
155.

And made her lucklesse loves well knowne to be.
But this Molanna, were she not so shole,°   *shallow*
Were no lesse faire and beautifull then shee:
Yet as she is, a fairer flood may no man see.

41

For, first, she springs out of two marble Rocks,
  On which, a grove of Oakes high mounted growes,
  That as a girlond seemes to deck the locks
  Of som faire Bride, brought forth with pompous°   *magnificent*
    showes
  Out of her bowre,° that many flowers strowes: *chamber*
  So, through the flowry Dales she tumbling downe,
  Through many woods, and shady coverts° flowes   *thickets*
  (That on each side her silver channell crowne)
Till to the Plaine she come, whose Valleyes shee doth drowne.

42

In her sweet streames, Diana uséd oft
  (After her sweatie chace and toilesome play)
  To bathe her selfe; and after, on the soft
  And downy grasse, her dainty limbes to lay
  In covert° shade, where none behold her may: *secret*
  For, much she hated sight of living eye.
  Foolish God Faunus, though full many a day
  He saw her clad, yet longéd foolishly
To see her naked mongst her Nymphes in privity.[7]

43

No way he found to compasse° his desire.   *accomplish*
  But to corrupt Molanna, this her maid,
  Her to discover for some secret hire:°   *reward*
  So, her with flattering words he first assaid;
  And after, pleasing gifts for her purvaid,°   *provided*
  Queene-apples,[8] and red Cherries from the tree,
  With which he her alluréd and betraid,
  To tell what time he might her Lady see
When she her selfe did bathe, that he might secret° bee.   *hidden*

44

There-to hee promist, if she would him pleasure
  With this small boone, to quit° her with a better;   *repay*
  To weet, that where-as she had out of measure
  Long loved the Fanchin,[9] who by nought did set her,[1]

7. The episode that follows combines Irish folklore with classical materials, in particular the stories of Actaeon, who, having unexpectedly encountered Diana bathing with her nymphs, was changed by her into a stag and torn to pieces by his own hounds; and of Arethusa, changed by Diana into a fountain so that she might escape the river god Alpheus, who nevertheless continued to pursue her beneath the waves (Ovid, *Metamorphoses*, III.

138–252; V. 572–641). Natalis Comes understands this latter myth to refer allegorically to the pursuit of virtue by imperfection, form by matter: *op. cit.,* VI. 24.

8. A kind of apple colored red within; or possibly a quince. The temptation of Molanna by Faunus is to be associated with Satan's temptation of Eve in the Garden of Eden.

9. The river Funsheon.

1. I.e., who cared nothing for her.

That he would undertake, for this to get her
  To be his Love, and of him likéd well:
  Besides all which, he vowed to be her debter
  For many moe good turnes then he would tell;
The least of which, this little pleasure should excell.

45

The simple maid did yield to him anone;°   *at once*
  And eft him placéd where he close might view
  That° never any saw, save onely one;   *that which*
  Who, for his hire to so foole-hardy dew,
  Was of his hounds devoured in Hunters hew.[2]
  Tho,° as her manner was on sunny day,   *then*
  Diana, with her Nymphes about her, drew
  To this sweet spring; where, doffing her array,
She bathed her lovely limbes, for Jove a likely pray.

46

There Faunus saw that pleaséd much his eye,
  And made his hart to tickle in his brest,
  That for great joy of some-what he did spy,
  He could him not containe in silent rest;
  But breaking forth in laughter, loud profest
  His foolish thought. A foolish Faune indeed,
  That couldst not hold thy selfe so° hidden blest,   *thus*
  But wouldest needs thine owne conceit areed.°   *make known*
Babblers unworthy been of so divine a meed.°   *reward*

47

The Goddesse, all abashéd with that noise,
  In haste forth started from the guilty brooke;
  And running straight where-as she heard his voice,
  Enclosed the bush about, and there him tooke,
  Like darréd° Larke; not daring up to looke   *terrified*
  On her whose sight before so much he sought.
  Thence, forth they drew him by the hornes, and shooke
  Nigh all to peeces, that they left him nought;
And then into the open light they forth him brought.

48

Like as an huswife, that with busie care
  Thinks of her Dairie to make wondrous gaine,
  Finding where-as some wicked beast unware°   *unexpectedly*
  That breakes into her Dayr'house, there doth draine
  Her creaming pannes, and frustrate all her paine;
  Hath in some snare or gin° set close behind,   *trap*
  Entrappéd him, and caught into her traine,°   *snare*
  Then thinkes what punishment were best assigned,
And thousand deathes deviseth in her vengefull mind:

49

So did Diana and her maydens all
  Use silly Faunus, now within their baile:°   *custody*

2. I.e., who, deservedly rewarded for his foolhardiness, was devoured by his hounds in the slaughter that concludes the hunt.

They mocke and scorne him, and him foule miscall;
  Some by the nose him pluckt, some by the taile,
  And by his goatish beard some did him haile:°   pull
  Yet he (poore soule) with patience all did beare;
  For, nought against their wils might countervaile:°   resist
  Ne ought he said what ever he did heare;
But hanging downe his head, did like a Mome° appeare.   fool

50

At length, when they had flouted him their fill,
  They gan to cast what penaunce him to give.
  Some would have gelt° him, but that same   castrated
    would spill°   destroy
  The Wood-gods breed, which must for ever live:
  Others would through the river him have drive,
  And duckéd deepe: but that seemed penaunce light;
  But most agreed and did this sentence give,
  Him in Deares skin to clad; and in that plight,
To hunt him with their hounds, him selfe save how hee might.

51

But Cynthia's selfe, more angry then the rest,
  Thought not enough, to punish him in sport,
  And of her shame to make a gamesome jest;
  But gan examine him in straighter° sort,   stricter
  Which of her Nymphes, or other close consort,[3]
  Him thither brought, and her to him betraid?
  He, much affeard, to her confesséd short,°   soon
  That 'twas Molanna which her so bewraid.°   betrayed
Then all attonce their hands upon Molanna laid.

52

But him (according as they had decreed)
  With a Deeres-skin they covered, and then chast
  With all their hounds that after him did speed;
  But he more speedy, from them fled more fast
  Then any Deere: so sore him dread aghast.°   terrified
  They after followed all with shrill out-cry,
  Shouting as they the heavens would have brast:°   burst
  That all the woods and dales where he did flie,
Did ring againe, and loud reeccho to the skie.

53

So they him followed till they weary were;
  When, back returning to Molann' againe,
  They, by commaund'ment of Diana, there
  Her whelmed with stones.[4] Yet Faunus (for her paine)° trouble
  Of her beloved Fanchin did obtaine,
  That her he would receive unto his bed.
  So now her waves passe through a pleasant Plaine,
  Till with the Fanchin she her selfe doe wed,
And (both combined) themselves in one faire river spred.

---

3. I.e., secret companion.   4. Thus accounting for the shallowness
                              of the river (st. 40).

54

Nath'lesse,° Diana, full of indignation,   *nonetheless*
 Thence-forth abandoned her delicious brooke;
 In whose sweet streame, before that bad occasion,
 So much delight to bathe her limbes she tooke:
 Ne onely her, but also quite forsooke
 All those faire forrests about Arlo hid,
 And all that Mountaine, which doth over-looke
 The richest champian that may else be rid,[5]
And the faire Shure,[6] in which are thousand Salmons bred.

55

Them all, and all that she so deare did way,°   *esteem*
 Thence-forth she left; and parting from the place,
 There-on an heavy haplesse curse did lay,
 To weet, that Wolves, where she was wont to space,° *roam*
 Should harboured be, and all those Woods deface,
 And Thieves should rob and spoile that Coast around.
 Since which, those Woods, and all that
  goodly Chase,°   *hunting ground*
 Doth to this day with Wolves and Thieves abound:
Which too-too true that lands in-dwellers since have found.[7]

Canto VII

Pealing,° from Jove, to Natur's Bar,   *appealing*
 bold Alteration[1] pleades
Large Evidence: but Nature soone
 her righteous Doome° areads.° *judgment / delivers*

1

Ah! whither doost thou now thou greater Muse[2]
 Me from these woods and pleasing forrests bring?
 And my fraile spirit (that dooth oft refuse
 This too high flight, unfit for her weake wing)
 Lift up aloft, to tell of heavens King
 (Thy soveraine Sire) his fortunate successe,
 And victory, in bigger° noates to sing,   *louder*
 Which he obtained against that Titanesse,
That him of heavens Empire sought to dispossesse.

2

Yet sith I needs must follow thy behest,
 Doe thou my weaker° wit with skill inspire, *too weak*
 Fit for this turne; and in my feeble brest
 Kindle fresh sparks of that immortall fire,

5. I.e., the richest plain to be seen any-where.
6. The river Suir, which flows through the Vale of Aherlow.
7. Spenser employs similar terms to describe the miserable condition of Ire-land and its inhabitants in *Colin Clouts Come Home Againe*, 312–319.
1. I.e., Mutability.
2. Clio, who reassumes the central role temporarily assigned to Calliope at vi. 37.

Which learnéd minds inflameth with desire
Of heavenly things: for, who but thou alone,
That art yborne of heaven and heavenly Sire,
Can tell things doen in heaven so long ygone;
So farre past memory of man that may be knowne.

3

Now, at the time that was before agreed,
  The Gods assembled all on Arlo hill;
  As well those that are sprung of heavenly seed,
  As those that all the other world[3] doe fill,
  And rule both sea and land unto their will:
  Onely th'infernall Powers might not appeare;
  Aswell for horror of their count'naunce ill,
  As for th'unruly fiends which they did feare;°   *keep in awe*
Yet Pluto and Proserpina[4] were present there.

4

And thither also came all other creatures,
  What-ever life or motion doe retaine,
  According to their sundry kinds of features;
  That Arlo scarsly could them all containe;
  So full they filléd every hill and Plaine:
  And had not Natures Sergeant (that is Order)[5]
  Them well disposéd by his busie paine,°   *care*
  And raungéd farre abroad in every border,
They would have causéd much confusion and disorder.

5

Then forth issewed (great goddesse) great dame Nature,[6]
  With goodly port° and gracious Majesty;   *bearing*
  Being far greater and more tall of stature
  Then any of the gods or Powers on hie:
  Yet certes by her face and physnomy,°   *countenance*
  Whether she man or woman inly were,
  That could not any creature well descry:
  For, with a veile that wimpled° every where,   *covered in folds*
Her head and face was hid, that mote to none appeare.

3. I.e., the earth.
4. Rulers of the underworld.
5. The fact that Order is Nature's sergeant, or chief executive attendant, forcefully recalls the account of Mutability's changeful opposition to every law of ordered nature (vi. 5); but it is equally significant that the "times and seasons of the yeare" (together with Day and Night), when Mutability demands that they be called to support her case, appear in proper order and appropriate garb.
6. While Spenser's figure of "great dame Nature" (as st. 9 indicates) reflects his knowledge of Chaucer's allusions to the goddess Nature in *The Parliament of Fowls*, and perhaps also of "Natura" in Alain de Lille's twelfth-century *De Planctu Naturae*, he certainly drew on a wide range and variety of classical and medieval writings (e.g., Plutarch, Boethius, and Jean de Meun) for details of setting and of her appearance, as well as for the larger conception of her being. He is especially concerned (in sts. 5–6, and st. 13) to emphasize the power, the mystery, and the paradoxical inclusiveness of Nature. Thus, she is taller than the other gods; she is veiled (to protect mortals from the terror or the beauty of her visage); and she encompasses youth and age, being and becoming at once. These descriptive passages appropriately prepare for the succinct and inscrutable judgment on Mutability's plea, delivered in the final stanzas of this Canto.

6

That some doe say was so by skill devized,
   To hide the terror of her uncouth° hew,   *strange*
   From mortall eyes that should be sore agrized;°   *horrified*
   For that her face did like a Lion shew,
   That eye of wight could not indure to view:
   But others tell that it so beautious was,
   And round about such beames of splendor threw,
   That it the Sunne a thousand times did pass,°   *surpass*
Ne could be seene, but °like an image in a glass.   *except*

7

That well may seemen true: for, well I weene
   That this same day, when she on Arlo sat,
   Her garment was so bright and wondrous sheene,°   *fair*
   That my fraile wit cannot devize to what
   It to compare, nor finde like stuffe to that,
   As those three sacred Saints,[7] though else most wise,
   Yet on mount Thabor quite their wits forgat,
   When they their glorious Lord in strange disguise
Transfigured sawe; his garments so did daze their eyes.

8

In a fayre Plaine upon an equall° Hill,   *level*
   She placéd was in a pavilion;
   Not such as Craftes-men by their idle° skill   *vain*
   Are wont for Princes states° to fashion: *canopies*
   But th'earth her self of her owne motion,
   Out of her fruitfull bosome made to growe
   Most dainty trees; that, shooting up anon,
   Did seeme to bow their bloosming° heads full lowe,   *blossoming*
For homage unto her, and like a throne did shew.°   *appear*

9

So hard it is for any living wight,
   All her array and vestiments to tell,
   That old Dan Geffrey[8] (in whose gentle spright
   The pure well head of Poesie did dwell)
   In his *Foules parley* durst not with it mel,°   *meddle*
   But it transferd° to Alane,[9] who he thought   *referred*
   Had in his *Plaint of kindes* described it well:
   Which who will read set forth so as it ought,
Go seek he out that Alane where he may be sought.

10

And all the earth far underneath her feete
   Was dight with flowres, that voluntary grew

7. Peter, James, and John, to whom Jesus appeared in transfigured brightness: "his face did shine as the sun, and his raiment was white as the light" (Matthew xvii. 1–8).
8. Master Geoffrey Chaucer; in *The Parliament of Fowls,* 295–318, Chaucer briefly describes "this noble goddesse Nature," referring his readers to "Aleyn, in the Pleynt of Kynde," for a fuller account of Nature's "aray and face."
9. Alain de Lille, also known as Alanus de Insulis (1128–1208), author of *De Planctu Naturae,* a philosophical Latin poem celebrating the cosmic power of creative nature.

Out of the ground, and sent forth odours sweet,
Tenne thousand mores° of sundry sent and hew,   *plants*
That might delight the smell, or please the view:
The which, the Nymphes, from all the brooks thereby
Had gathered, which they at her foot-stoole threw;
That richer seemed then any tapestry,
That Princes bowres adorne with painted imagery.

11

And Mole himselfe, to honour her the more,
Did deck himself in freshest faire attire,
And his high head, that seemeth alwaies hore
With hardned frosts of former winters ire,
He with an Oaken girlond now did tire,°   *attire*
As if the love of some new Nymph late seene,
Had in him kindled youthfull fresh desire,
And made him change his gray attire to greene;
Ah gentle Mole! such joyance hath thee well beseene.°   *provided*

12

Was never so great joyance since the day,
That all the gods whylome assembled were,
On Haemus hill[1] in their divine array,
To celebrate the solemne bridall cheare,
Twixt Peleus, and dame Thetis pointed° there;   *appointed*
Where Phoebus self, that god of Poets hight,
They say did sing the spousall hymne full cleere,
That all the gods were ravisht with delight
Of his celestiall song, and Musicks wondrous might.

13

This great Grandmother of all creatures bred
Great Nature, ever young yet full of eld,°   *age*
Still mooving, yet unmovéd from her sted;°   *place*
Unseene of any, yet of all beheld;
Thus sitting in her throne as I have teld,
Before her came dame Mutabilitie;
And being lowe before her presence feld,°   *prostrated*
With meek obaysance and humilitie,
Thus gan her plaintif Plea, with words to amplifie;

14

"To thee O greatest goddesse, onely° great,   *uniquely*
An humble suppliant loe, I lowely fly
Seeking for Right, which I of thee entreat;
Who Right to all dost deale indifferently,°   *impartially*
Damning all Wrong and tortious° Injurie,   *wrongful*
Which any of thy creatures doe to other
(Oppressing them with power, unequally)°   *unjustly*
Sith of them all thou are the equall mother,
And knittest each to each, as brother unto brother.

1. The marriage of Peleus and Thetis took place on Mt. Pelion; the opening lines in Ovid's account of the lovers may have misled Spenser (cf. *Metamorphoses*, XI. 229–30).

15

"To thee therefore of this same Jove I plaine,
 And of his fellow gods that faine° to be,   *pretend*
 That challenge° to themselves the whole worlds raign;   *claim*
 Of which, the greatest part is due to me,
 And heaven it selfe by heritage in Fee:[2]
 For, heaven and earth I both alike do deeme,
 Sith heaven and earth are both alike to thee;
 And, gods no more then men thou doest esteeme:
For, even the gods to thee, as men to gods do seeme.

16

"Then weigh, O soveraigne goddesse, by what right
 These gods do claime the worlds whole soveraity;
 And that° is onely dew unto thy might   *that which*
 Arrogate to themselves ambitiously:
 As for the gods owne principality,°   *sovereignty*
 Which Jove usurpes unjustly; that to be
 My heritage, Jove's self cannot deny,
 From my great Grandsire Titan, unto mee,
Derived by dew descent; as is well knowen to thee.

17

"Yet mauger° Jove, and all his gods beside,   *despite*
 I doe possesse the worlds most regiment;°   *rule*
 As, if ye please it into parts divide,
 And every parts inholders° to convent,°   *tenants/convene*
 Shall to your eyes appeare incontinent.°   *at once*
 And first, the Earth (great mother of us all)
 That only seems unmoved and permanent,
 And unto Mutability not thrall;
Yet is she changed in part, and eeke in generall.[3]

18

"For, all that from her springs, and is ybredde,
 How-ever fayre it flourish for a time,
 Yet see we soone decay; and, being dead,
 To turne again unto their earthly slime:
 Yet, out of their decay and mortall crime,°   *corruption*
 We daily see new creatures to arize;
 And of their Winter spring another Prime,°   *spring*
 Unlike in forme, and changed by strange disguise:
So turne they still about, and change in restlesse wise.

19

"As for her tenants; that is, man and beasts,
 The beasts we daily see massacred dy,
 As thralls and vassalls unto mens beheasts:
 And men themselves doe change continually,
 From youth to eld, from wealth to poverty,
 From good to bad, from bad to worst of all.

2. I.e., in fee simple, conferring abso-
lute rule.
3. The arguments presented by Muta-
bility in sts. 17–25 reflect the influ-
ence, on thought and expression both,
of Lucretius's *De Rerum Natura*, V,
and (particularly) of Ovid's *Metamor-
phoses*, XV.

Ne doe their bodies only flit and fly:
But eeke their minds (which they immortall call)
Still change and vary thoughts, as new occasions fall.

20

"Ne is the water in more constant case;
 Whether those same on high, or these belowe.
 For, th'Ocean moveth stil, from place to place;
 And every River still doth ebbe and flowe:
 Ne any Lake, that seems most still and slowe,
 Ne Poole so small, that can his smoothnesse holde,
 When any winde doth under heaven blowe;
 With which, the clouds are also tost and rolled;
Now like great hills; and, streight,°   *immediately*
 like sluces, them unfold.°   *open*

21

"So likewise are all watry living wights
 Still tost, and turnéd, with continuall change,
 Never abyding in their stedfast plights.°   *conditions*
 The fish, still floting, doe at randon° range, *random*
 And never rest; but evermore exchange
 Their dwelling places, as the streames them carrie:
 Ne have the watry foules a certaine grange,° *abode*
 Wherein to rest, ne in one stead° do tarry; *place*
But flitting still doe flie, and still their places vary.

22

"Next is the Ayre: which who feeles not by sense
 (For, of all sense it is the middle meane)[4]
 To flit still? and, with subtill influence
 Of his thin spirit, all creatures to maintaine,
 In state of life? O weake life! that does leane
 On thing so tickle° as th'unsteady ayre;   *uncertain*
 Which every howre is changed, and altred cleane° *altogether*
 With every blast that bloweth fowle or faire:
The faire doth it prolong; the fowle doth it impaire.

23

"Therein the changes infinite beholde,
 Which to her creatures every minute chaunce;
 Now, boyling hot: streight, friezing deadly cold:
 Now, faire sun-shine, that makes all skip and daunce:
 Streight, bitter storms and balefull countenance,
 That makes them all to shiver and to shake:
 Rayne, hayle, and snowe do pay them sad penance,
 And dreadfull thunder-claps (that make them quake)
With flames and flashing lights that thousand changes make.

24

"Last is the fire: which, though it live for ever,
 Ne can be quenchéd quite; yet, every day,
 Wee see his parts, so soone as they do sever,
 To lose their heat, and shortly to decay;

4. I.e., the medium (for all the senses).

So, makes himself his owne consuming pray.
Ne any living creatures doth he breed:
But all, that are of others bredd, doth slay;
And, with their death, his cruell life dooth feed;
Nought leaving but their barren ashes, without seede.

25

"Thus, all these fower (the which the ground-work bee
Of all the world, and of all living wights)
To thousand sorts of Change we subject see:
Yet are they changed (by other wondrous slights)°   *devices*
Into themselves, and lose their native mights;
The Fire to Aire, and th' Ayre to Water sheere,°   *clear*
And Water into Earth: yet Water fights
With Fire, and Aire with Earth approaching neere:
Yet all are in one body, and as one appeare.[5]

26

"So, in them all raignes Mutabilitie;
How-ever these, that Gods themselves do call,
Of them doe claime the rule and soverainty:
As, Vesta, of the fire aethereall;[6]
Vulcan, of this, with us so usuall;
Ops,[7] of the earth; and Juno of the Ayre;
Neptune, of Seas; and Nymphes, of Rivers all.
For, all those Rivers to me subject are:
And all the rest, which they usurp, be all my share.

27

"Which to approven° true, as I have told,   *prove*
Vouchsafe, O goddesse, to thy presence call
The rest which doe the world in being hold:
As, times and seasons of the yeare that fall:
Of all the which, demand in generall,
Or judge thy selfe, by verdit° of thine eye,   *verdict*
Whether to me they are not subject all."
Nature did yeeld thereto; and by-and-by,°   *immediately*
Bade Order call them all, before her Majesty.

28

So, forth issewed the Seasons of the yeare;[8]
First, lusty Spring, all dight in leaves of flowres
That freshly budded and new bloosmes did beare
(In which a thousand birds had built their bowres
That sweetly sung, to call forth Paramours):
And in his hand a javelin he did beare,

5. These views are derived from Ovid's doctrine of the transmutation of elements (*Metamorphoses*, XV. 237–249), a position rejected by Lucretius (*De Rerum Natura*, I. 780–844).
6. I.e., of celestial fire. Vesta was Roman goddess of the hearth, and by extension of consecrated fire; traditionally, Aeneas was thought to have taken with him from Troy the eternal flame sacred to Vesta (*Aeneid*, II. 296).
7. Roman goddess of fertility and of the ground, identified by Boccaccio with Rhea, the consort of Saturn (*De Genealogia Deorum*, III. 2).
8. This description of the seasons may owe something to Ovid's personification of them in *Metamorphoses*, II. 25–30, and XV. 199–213; but the larger scope of the procession depicted in sts.

And on his head (as fit for warlike stoures)°   *encounters*
A guilt engraven morion° he did weare;   *helmet*
That as some did him love, so others did him feare.

29

Then came the jolly Sommer, being dight
  In a thin silken cassock° coloured greene,   *cloak*
  That was unlynéd all, to be more light:
  And on his head a girlond well beseene°   *ordered*
  He wore, from which as he had chifféd° been   *heated*
  The sweat did drop; and in his hand he bore
  A boawe and shaftes, as he in forrest greene
  Had hunted late the Libbard° or the Bore,   *leopard*
And now would bathe his limbes, with labor heated sore.

30

Then came the Autumne all in yellow clad,
  As though he joyéd in his plentious store,
  Laden with fruits that made him laugh, full glad
  That he had banisht hunger, which to-fore°   *formerly*
  Had by the belly oft him pinchéd sore.
  Upon his head a wreath that was enrold°   *enfolded*
  With eares of corne, of every sort he bore:
  And in his hand a sickle he did holde,
To reape the ripened fruits the which the earth had yold.°   *yielded*

31

Lastly, came Winter cloathéd all in frize,°   *rough cloth*
  Chattering his teeth for cold that did him chill,
  Whil'st on his hoary beard his breath did freese;
  And the dull drops that from his purpled bill°   *nose*
  As from a limbeck° did adown distill.   *alembic*
  In his right hand a tippéd staffe he held,
  With which his feeble steps he stayéd still:°   *continually*
  For, he was faint with cold, and weak with eld;
That scarse his looséd limbes he hable was to weld.°   *move*

32

These, marching softly, thus in order went,
  And after them, the Monthes all riding came;[9]
  First, sturdy March with brows full sternly bent,
  And arméd strongly, rode upon a Ram,
  The same which over Hellespontus swam:
  Yet in his hand a spade he also hent,°   *grasped*

28–46 reflects Spenser's awareness of medieval and Renaissance taste and expression in the various plastic arts as well as in literature.

9. In sts. 32–43, Spenser makes use especially of Ovid's *Fasti* and *Metamorphoses* for details bearing on the names, placement in the calendar, and mythological connections of the months. March leads because in England, until 1753, the year officially began on Lady Day, March 25th; although *The Shepheardes Calender* begins with January, "according to the simplicitie of commen understanding," as E.K. says in the "Argument." Each of the woodcuts accompanying individual eclogues in the *Calender* includes the zodiacal sign appropriate for that month; so here, March leads the procession, mounted on a ram, sign of the constellation Aries. Cf. the note on III. xi. 30.

And in a bag all sorts of seeds ysame,°   *together*
  Which on the earth he strowéd as he went,
And fild her womb with fruitfull hope of nourishment.

33

Next came fresh Aprill full of lustyhed,°   *vigor*
  And wanton as a Kid whose horne new buds:
  Upon a Bull[1] he rode, the same which led
  Europa floting through th'Argolick fluds:
  His hornes were gilden all with golden studs,
  And garnishéd with garlonds goodly dight
  Of all the fairest flowres and freshest buds
  Which th'earth brings forth, and wet he seemed in sight
With waves, through which he waded for his loves delight.

34

Then came faire May, the fayrest mayd on ground,
  Deckt all with dainties of her seasons pryde,
  And throwing flowres out of her lap around:
  Upon two brethrens shoulders she did ride,
  The twinnes of Leda;[2] which on eyther side
  Supported her like to their soveraine Queene.
  Lord! how all creatures laught, when her they spide,
  And leapt and daunc't as they had ravisht° beene!   *enraptured*
And Cupid selfe about her fluttred all in greene.

35

And after her, came jolly June, arrayd
  All in greene leaves, as he a Player were;[3]
  Yet in his time, he wrought as well as playd,
  That by his plough-yrons° mote right well appeare: *ploughshares*
  Upon a Crab[4] he rode, that him did beare
  With crooked crawling steps an uncouth pase,
  And backward yode,° as Bargemen wont to fare   *went*
  Bending their force contrary to their face,
Like that ungracious crew which faines demurest grace.[5]

36

Then came hot July boyling like to fire,
  That all his garments he had cast away:
  Upon a Lyon[6] raging yet with ire
  He boldly rode and made him to obay:
  It was the beast that whylome did forray
  The Nemaean forrest, till th'Amphytrionide
  Him slew, and with his hide did him array;
  Behinde his back a sithe,° and by his side   *scythe*
Under his belt he bore a sickle circling wide.

1. The constellation Taurus, here identified with the bull, in whose shape Jove abducted Europa, bearing her over the Argolic (i.e., Greek) waves.
2. Castor and Pollux, the Gemini.
3. I.e., like an actor garbed as a forest spirit, or as a "savage" man.
4. The constellation Cancer; cf. *Epithalamion*, 267–269.

5. I.e., like hypocritical courtiers whose affected fashion of leaving their lord's presence by walking backward (thus implying great respect) belies their true feelings.
6. The constellation Leo, here identified with the Nemean lion slain by Hercules, whose reputed father was Amphitryon.

37

The sixt was August, being rich arrayd
    In garment all of gold downe to the ground:
    Yet rode he not, but led a lovely Mayd[7]
    Forth by the lilly hand, the which was cround
    With eares of corne, and full her hand was found;
    That was the righteous Virgin, which of old
    Lived here on earth, and plenty made abound;
    But, after Wrong was loved and Justice solde,
She left th'unrighteous world and was to heaven extold.°   raised

38

Next him, September marchéd eeke on foote;
    Yet was he heavy laden with the spoyle
    Of harvests riches, which he made his boot,°   booty
    And him enricht with bounty of the soyle:
    In his one hand, as fit for harvests toyle,
    He held a knife-hook; and in th'other hand
    A paire of waights,[8] with which he did assoyle°   determine
    Both more and lesse, where it in doubt did stand,
And equall gave to each as Justice duly scanned.°   judged

39

Then came October full of merry glee:
    For, yet his noule was totty of the must,[9]
    Which he was treading in the wine-fats see,[1]
    And of the joyous oyle, whose gentle gust°   taste
    Made him so frollick and so full of lust:
    Upon a dreadfull Scorpion[2] he did ride,
    The same which by Dianaes doom unjust
    Slew great Orion: and eeke by his side
He had his ploughing share, and coulter ready tyde.

40

Next was November, he full grosse and fat,
    As fed with lard, and that right well might seeme;
    For, he had been a fatting° hogs of late,   fattening
    That yet his browes with sweat, did reek and steem,
    And yet the season was full sharp and breem;°   cold
    In planting eeke he took no small delight:
    Whereon he rode, not easie was to deeme;
    For it a dreadfull Centaure[3] was in sight,
The seed of Saturne, and faire Nais, Chiron hight.

7. The constellation Virgo; Astraea, Roman goddess of justice, was reputed to have left the earth when mankind first made war (Ovid, *Metamorphoses*, I. 127–150).
8. I.e., a pair of scales, sign of the constellation Libra.
9. I.e., his head was giddy from drinking new wine (cf. Chaucer, "The Reeve's Tale," 4253: "Myn heed is toty of my swynk to–nyght."
1. I.e., the liquorous "sea" of the wine vats.

2. The constellation Scorpio. Diana, jealous of Orion's boasted skill in hunting, sent a scorpion to kill him; subsequently regretting her action, she placed Orion and the scorpion among the stars (cf. Natalis Comes, *Mythologiae*, VIII. 22).
3. Chiron the centaur, whose parents were Saturn and Philyra the Naiad, was placed among the stars as Sagittarius, the Archer.

41

And after him, came next the chill December:
    Yet he through merry feasting which he made,
    And great bonfires, did not the cold remember;
    His Saviours birth his mind so much did glad:
    Upon a shaggy-bearded Goat[4] he rade,°   *rode*
    The same wherewith Dan Jove in tender yeares,
    They say, was nourisht by th'Idaean mayd;
    And in his hand a broad deepe boawle he beares;
Of which, he freely drinks an health to all his peeres.

42

Then came old January, wrappéd well
    In many weeds to keep the cold away;
    Yet did he quake and quiver like to quell,°   *perish*
    And blowe his nayles to warme them if he may:
    For, they were numbd with holding all the day
    An hatchet keene, with which he felléd wood,
    And from the trees did lop the needlesse spray:°   *branches*
    Upon an huge great Earth-pot steane[5] he stood;
From whose wide mouth, there flowéd forth the Romane floud.

43

And lastly, came cold February, sitting
    In an old wagon, for he could not ride;
    Drawne of two fishes[6] for the season fitting,
    Which through the flood before did softly slyde
    And swim away: yet had he by his side
    His plough and harnesse fit to till the ground,
    And tooles to prune the trees, before the pride
    Of hasting Prime did make them burgein° round: *bud*
So past the twelve Months forth, and their dew places found.

44

And after these, there came the Day, and Night,
    Riding together both with equall pase,
    Th'one on a Palfrey blacke, the other white;
    But Night had covered her uncomely face
    With a blacke veile, and held in hand a mace,
    On top whereof the moon and stars were pight,°   *placed*
    And sleep and darknesse round about did trace:°   *walk*
    But Day did beare, upon his scepters hight,
The goodly Sun, encompast all with beamés bright.

45

Then came the Howres, faire daughters of high Jove,[7]
    And timely Night, the which were all endewed

---

4. The infant Jove was cared for (on Mt. Ida) by Amalthea, who fed him goat's milk; the goat was stellified as the constellation Capricorn (Natalis Comes, *op. cit.*, VII. 2).

5. I.e., an earthen water jar, indicating the association of January with the constellation Aquarius, the water bearer.

6. The constellation Pisces.

7. Spenser follows Homer (*Iliad*, V. 749) and Ovid (*Fasti*, I. 125) in making the Hours attendants at the gates of Heaven; but he departs from Hesiod's identification of their parents as Zeus and Themis (*Theogony*, 900). Cf. *Epithalamion*, 98–102.

With wondrous beauty fit to kindle love;
  But they were Virgins all, and love eschewed,
  That might forslack° the charge to them foreshewed   *neglect*
  By mighty Jove; who did them Porters make
  Of heavens gate (whence all the gods issued)
  Which they did dayly watch, and nightly wake°   *guard*
By even turnes, ne ever did their charge forsake.

46

And after all came Life, and lastly Death;
  Death with most grim and griesly visage seene,
  Yet is he nought but parting of the breath;
  Ne ought to see, but like a shade to weene,°   *conceive*
  Unbodiéd, unsouled, unheard, unseene.
  But Life was like a faire young lusty boy,
  Such as they faine Dan Cupid to have beene,
  Full of delightfull health and lively joy,
Deckt all with flowres, and wings of gold fit to employ.

47

When these were past, thus gan the Titanesse;
  "Lo, mighty mother, now be judge and say,
  Whether in all thy creatures more or lesse
  Change doth not raign and beare the greatest sway:
  For, who sees not, that Time on all doth pray?°   *prey*
  But Times do change and move continually.
  So nothing here long standeth in one stay:
  Wherefore, this lower world who can deny
But to be subject still to Mutabilitie?"

48

Then thus gan Jove; "Right true it is, that these
  And all things else that under heaven dwell
  Are chaunged of Time, who doth them all disseise°   *deprive*
  Of being: But, who is it (to me tell)
  That Time himselfe doth move and still compell
  To keepe his course? Is not that namely wee[8]
  Which poure that vertue° from our heavenly cell,   *power*
  That moves them all, and makes them changéd be?
So them we gods doe rule, and in them also thee."

49

To whom, thus Mutability: "The things
  Which we see not how they are moved and swayd,
  Ye may attribute to your selves as Kings,
  And say they by your secret powre are made:
  But what we see not, who shall us perswade?
  But were they so, as ye them faine to be,
  Moved by your might, and ordred by your ayde;
  Yet what if I can prove, that even yee
Your selves are likewise changed, and subject unto mee?

8. I.e., only we.

50

"And first, concerning her that is the first,[9]
    Even you faire Cynthia, whom so much ye make
    Joves dearest darling, she was bred and nurst
    On Cynthus hill,[1] whence she her name did take:
    Then is she mortall borne, how-so ye crake;°   *brag*
    Besides, her face and countenance every day
    We changéd see, and sundry forms partake,
    Now hornd, now round, now bright, now brown and gray:
So that 'as changefull as the Moone' men use to say.

51

"Next, Mercury, who though he lesse appeare
    To change his hew, and alwayes seeme as one;
    Yet, he his course doth altar every yeare,
    And is of late far out of order gone:[2]
    So Venus eeke, that goodly Paragone,°   *model of excellence*
    Though faire all night, yet is she darke all day;
    And Phoebus self, who lightsome is alone,
    Yet is he oft eclipséd by the way,
And fills the darkned world with terror and dismay.

52

"Now Mars that valiant man is changéd most:
    For, he some times so far runs out of square,
    That he his way doth seem quite to have lost,
    And cleane without° his usuall sphere to fare;   *beyond*
    That even these Star-gazers stonisht are
    At sight thereof, and damne their lying bookes:
    So likewise, grim Sir Saturne oft doth spare°   *restrain*
    His sterne aspect, and calme his crabbéd lookes:
So many turning cranks° these have, so many crookes.   *twists*

53

"But you Dan Jove, that only constant are,
    And King of all the rest, as ye do clame,
    Are you not subject eeke to this misfare?°   *deviation*
    Then let me aske you this withouten blame,
    Where were ye borne? some say in Crete by name,
    Others in Thebes, and others other-where;
    But wheresoever they comment° the same,   *invent*
    They all consent that ye begotten were,
And borne here in this world, ne other can appeare.

54

"Then are ye mortall borne, and thrall to me,
    Unlesse the kingdome of the sky yee make
    Immortall, and unchangeable to bee;
    Besides, that power and vertue which ye spake,
    That ye here worke, doth many changes take,

9. I.e., according to the Ptolemaic system, the planet whose sphere is nearest to the earth.
1. Traditionally the birthplace of Diana and Apollo, on the island of Delos.

2. Astronomers in Spenser's time were increasingly troubled by the disparity between their observations and that regularity of the heavens assumed by traditional theory.

And your owne natures change: for, each of you
   That vertue have, or° this, or that to make,   *either*
   Is checkt and changéd from his nature trew,
By others opposition or obliquid view.[3]

55

"Besides, the sundry motions of your Spheares,
   So sundry waies and fashions as clerkes° faine,   *learned men*
   Some in short space, and some in longer yeares;
   What is the same but alteration plaine?
   Onely the starrie skie doth still remaine:
   Yet do the Starres and Signes therein still move,
   And even it self is moved, as wizards saine.[4]
   But all that moveth, doth mutation love:
Therefore both you and them to me I subject prove.

56

"Then since within this wide great Universe
   Nothing doth firme and permanent appeare,
   But all things tost and turnéd by transverse:[5]
   What then should let,° but I aloft should reare   *hinder*
   My Trophee, and from all, the triumph beare?
   Now judge then (O thou greatest goddesse trew!)
   According as thy selfe doest see and heare,
   And unto me addoom that[6] is my dew;
That is the rule of all, all being ruled by you."

57

So having ended, silence long ensewed,
   Ne Nature to or fro[7] spake for a space,
   But with firme eyes affixt, the ground still viewed.
   Meane while, all creatures, looking in her face,
   Expecting° th'end of this so doubtfull case,   *awaiting*
   Did hang in long suspence what would ensew,
   To whether side should fall the soveraigne place:
   At length, she looking up with chearefull view,
The silence brake, and gave her doome in speeches° few.   *phrases*

58

"I well consider all that ye have sayd,[8]
   And find that all things steadfastnes doe hate

3. I.e., the "influence" supposed to reside in each planet is affected and qualified by the relative position of other planets in the heavens.
4. I.e., as wise men say, even the sphere of the "fixed stars" is subject to change.
5. I.e., haphazardly.
6. I.e., adjudge that which.
7. I.e., for or against.
8. Nature's judgment acknowledges the fact of cosmic change, but in a sense altogether different from that suggested by "the ever-whirling wheele of Change" (vi. 1); recalling, rather, the account of the Garden of Adonis, and specifically that of Adonis in III. vi. 47, her words reflect the Neo-Platonic view that seeming change is in fact a "dilation," by which being fulfills itself according to Providential plan (cf. Plotinus, *Enneads*, III. vii. 4; Boethius, *De Consolatione*, IV. Meter 6). Boethius observes that the divine thought which controls and directs all being is properly called Providence; but that when it is "referred to things that it moves and regulates, then by men in ancient times it was called destiny [i.e., fate]" (Boethius, *op. cit.*, IV. Prose 6).

And changéd be: yet being rightly wayd°   *weighed*
They are not changéd from their first estate;
But by their change their being doe dilate:°   *extend*
And turning to themselves at length againe,
Doe worke their owne perfection so by fate:
Then over them Change doth not rule and raigne;
But they raigne over change, and doe their states maintaine.

59

"Cease therefore daughter further to aspire,
And thee content thus to be ruled by me:
For thy decay° thou seekst by thy desire;   *ruin*
But time shall come that all shall changéd bee,
And from thenceforth, none no more change shall see."
So was the Titaness put downe and whist,°   *silenced*
And Jove confirmed in his imperiall see.°   *throne*
Then was that whole assembly quite dismist,
And Natur's selfe did vanish, whither no man wist.°   *knew*

The VIII. Canto, unperfite.°   *unfinished*

1

When I bethinke me on that speech whyleare,°   *earlier*
Of Mutability, and well it way:°   *consider*
Me seemes, that though she all unworthy were
Of the Heav'ns Rule; yet very sooth to say,
In all things else she beares the greatest sway.
Which makes me loath this state of life so tickle,°   *uncertain*
And love of things so vaine to cast away;
Whose flowring pride, so fading and so fickle,
Short Time shall soon cut down with his consuming sickle.

2

Then gin I thinke on that which Nature sayd,
Of that same time when no more Change shall be,
But stedfast rest of all things firmely stayd
Upon the pillours of Eternity,
That is contrayr to Mutabilitie:
For, all that moveth, doth in Change delight:
But thence-forth all shall rest eternally
With Him that is the God of Sabbaoth hight:[9]
O that great Sabbaoth God, graunt me that Sabaoths sight.[1]

9. I.e., called the Lord of Hosts.
1. I.e., the sight of that day of eternal rest. It is probable that Spenser intended the word play implicit in the spelling of these terms. The response to Mutability made in this concluding stanza of *The Faerie Queene* is pitched at a level beyond that of Nature's judgment (which is given in terms of the process of change itself); yet the final appeal to a divine unmoved mover also recalls Boethius: "In so much is the thing more free from fate, as it holds the more closely to the center of things [i.e., to God]; and if the thing cleaves to the steadfastness of the thought of God, it is free from motion, and overcomes the necessity of fate" (Boethius, *op. cit.*, IV. Prose 6).

Editor's Note

On the evidence of the "Letter to Raleigh," *The Faerie Queene* was to have been a long epic poem, centered on the figure of Arthur, "before he was king," and divided into twelve Books, corresponding to "the twelve private morall vertues, as Aristotle hath devised"; Spenser further envisioned the composition of yet another substantial poem in which he might "frame the other part of polliticke vertues in [Arthur's] person, after that hee came to be king." That these expectations were not completely realized is scarcely surprising; nor does the fact that *The Faerie Queene* represents a portion only of the early plans mentioned in the "Letter" significantly reduce Spenser's achievement in this enormous poem. Some aspects of that achievement are discussed in the relevant critical essays reproduced in this edition. It may be helpful, however, to outline briefly the circumstances of the poem's composition, and, with initial reference to the "Letter to Raleigh," to comment on the poet's "end" and "Methode" in *The Faerie Queene*, noting some features of the poem's relationship to allegorical tradition and to the background of epic and romance.

Spenser probably began work on *The Faerie Queene* in 1579 or the early months of 1580. The earliest allusion to the poem occurs in a letter dated April 2nd, 1580, from Spenser to his Cambridge associate and friend, Gabriel Harvey: "Nowe, my *Dreames*, and *dying Pellicane*, being fully finished," the poet writes, "I wil in hande forthwith with my *Faery Queene*, whyche, I praye you hartily send me with al expedition: and your friendly Letters, and long expected Judgement wythal, whyche let not be shorte, but in all pointes suche, as you ordinarilye use, and I extraordinarily desire." In the fall of that year, Spenser (appointed secretary to Lord Grey) departed for Ireland; and for the next eight years, while he gradually improved his circumstances (acquiring the estate of Kilcolman in 1588 or early 1589), the poem developed under his hand. His colleague Lodowick Bryskett, in *A Discourse of Civill Life* (published in 1606), describes a social gathering which took place near Dublin, perhaps in 1582: Spenser, invited to discourse on moral philosophy (specifically, "whereby vertues are to be distinguished from vices"), declined, on the ground that he had already

> well entred into . . . a work tending to the same effect, which is in *heroical verse* under the title of a *Faerie Queene* to represent all the moral vertues, assigning to every vertue a Knight to be the patron and defender of the same, in whose actions and feates of arms and chivalry the operations of that vertue whereof he is the protector, are to be expressed, and the vices and unruly appetites that oppose themselves against the same, to be beaten down and overcome.

That some portions of the work were circulating in manuscript during the 1580's is certain, for Abraham Fraunce's *Arcadian Rhetorike*, published in 1588, quotes a stanza from the poem (II.iv.35) to exemplify "conceipted kindes of verses." Spenser's subsequent meeting with Sir Walter Raleigh (whose Irish estate lay next to Kilcolman), their voyage to England, and the audiences with an approving Queen Elizabeth, are recorded by the poet in *Colin Clouts Come Home Againe*. The first three Books of *The Faerie Queene* were registered with the Stationers' Company on December 1st, 1589, and published early in the following year, together with a dedication to the Queen, a number of sonnets addressed to influential persons, and the "Letter to Raleigh," perhaps composed while the volume was in press. Returning to Ireland in the early months of 1591 (as it appears), Spenser once more set to work on the poem: Sonnet 80 of the *Amoretti* indicates that he had managed to complete three more Books of *The Faerie Queene* before his marriage to Elizabeth Boyle, in the summer of 1594. Early in 1596, Books I–VI were published in London: for this edition, the three earlier Books underwent some changes, chiefly of punctuation and spelling, and the ending of Book III was altered to suit with the continuing narrative of Book IV. There is some evidence to suggest that Spenser was present during the printing of at least Books IV–VI.[1] As for the *Cantos of Mutabilitie* (first printed in the 1609 edition), while their numbering would suggest that they were intended to make part of the great poem, it is not possible to assign them certainly to a specific date; yet their substance and tone encourage the view that they were composed during the relatively troubled last years of the poet's life. It ought to be kept in mind that Spenser presumably did not compose his poem in sequence, beginning with Book I and working on through to the conclusion of Book III, and thence to Book VI and the *Cantos of Mutabilitie*: in particular (if the poet's correspondence with Gabriel Harvey may be relied on), the fact that Spenser at first set out to "emulate" and even "to overgo" Ariosto's *Orlando Furioso* has suggested to some scholars that passages now included in Books III and IV may have been composed at a very early stage in the development of the poem. Yet this would not at all rule out William Nelson's suggestion that Spenser assigned to each Book "a particular narrative flavor" (deriving from, e.g., Ariosto, Chaucer, Ovid, or Greek romance), in the interest of an artistic variety that should gracefully reflect the poet's awareness of epic tradition.

Although the "Letter to Raleigh" is not an altogether reliable guide to the poet's "whole intention" (particularly with respect to Spenser's account of Books II and III), it does provide an appropriate and generally helpful starting point for study of the poem. Of first importance is Spenser's statement that "the generall end . . . of all the booke is to fashion a gentleman or noble person in vertuous and gentle discipline." "To fashion" is the operative term here. In one sense, it means "to form, frame, make," as Spenser "the maker" creates his poem and its persons, notably the figure of Arthur, in whom is "sette forth magnificence in particular." In another sense, the term means "to present the form of, to represent": Spenser represents in Arthur (and in a relative way, also in those other knights whose several virtues are collected in him) an *exemplum* of that commanding ideal of manhood in which chivalric and ethical virtues combine. Finally, in accord with Spenser's conviction that "doctrine by ensample" is more effectively persuasive, ultimately more "profitable" than "good discipline delivered plainly in way of precepts," the pleasing history

---

1. F. B. Evans, "The Printing of Spenser's *Faerie Queene* in 1596," *SB*, XVIII (1965), 49–67.

of Arthur will effectively move those who read Spenser's poem, and draw them into the paths of "vertuous and gentle discipline." Especially in this latter sense, the poem may be called a "courtesy-book," although *The Faerie Queene* has less in common with (for example) Sir Thomas Elyot's *The Governour*, which outlines the details of a "governor's" education to show how the thing may be done, than with Castiglione's *Il Cortegiano*, which is concerned rather to describe the qualities that mark out the "gentle" man from his fellows. One might say that Spenser's "generall end" is twofold: to make a poem, and to persuade and move (even, perhaps, at length to remake) a society.

Spenser recognized that his "Methode," of "continued Allegory, or darke conceit . . . coloured with an historicall fiction," would displease some readers and confuse others; he persisted nonetheless, convinced that the poet must recognize the inclination of his audience to reject whatever "is not delightfull and pleasing to commune sence." "Methode," in another aspect, that of "a Poet historical," who begins *in medias res*, must also give attention to the artist who claims to have followed "all the antique Poets historicall," and the Italian masters of romantic epic besides. It must be admitted that to discuss these elements separately is to misrepresent in some measure the essential character of Spenser's "method" in *The Faerie Queene*, for the poem fully reflects the degree to which its author had accepted the Renaissance tendency to read the heroic fictions of epic poetry in allegorical terms: an epic poem all but demanded allegorical interpretation. Further, the particular interpenetration of epic and allegory in Spenser's *Faerie Queene* makes for a poem that does not in fact quite follow any of the works instanced by the "Letter," but virtually constitutes a moral, historical, and spiritual encyclopaedia for the English nation. Yet the modern reader needs to know something of the allegorical and the "epic" traditions if he is fully to appreciate the art of their combination in Spenser's poem.

In this context, to say that allegory is a metaphor continued through a whole discourse (or poem) may be a sufficiently accurate rhetorical description of the figure; but it is more important to recognize that the nature of allegory is to synthesize, to draw together and mutually relate various elements. The fictional narrative structure of an allegory may be said to support and reveal another, presumably more deeply significant, "level of meaning"; yet an allegorist is first of all an artist, and while didactic considerations may loom large in his work, that creation will, ideally, be characterized by an integrated unity of structure and meaning. Readers who allow themselves to become too exclusively concerned with the ramifications of one or another level of meaning in an allegory are apt to find that they are moving steadily away from the poem itself, and from the poem's conditioning literary tradition, toward those peripheral areas (e.g., philosophy, history, theology, etc.) on which the poem draws; at length, the poem may become no more than a repository of illustrative materials "pointing to" and supporting one or another nonliterary discipline. It is therefore of some importance to keep the poem itself firmly in view as an integrated artistic entity, and particularly to resist the separation of explicit statement from implicit meaning.

The allegorical interpretation of classical literature and mythology (notably Homer, Virgil, and Ovid), in moral and cosmological terms, had by Spenser's day become common throughout Europe. Dante, for instance, in the *Convivio* (referring to Ovid's account of Orpheus), distinguishes between a literal sense, "which does not go beyond the strict limits of the letter," and an allegorical sense, "which is a truth hidden under a beautiful fiction." Among writers whose work was especially influential in this regard, Giovanni Boccaccio (in the fourteenth century) and Natalis Comes (in the sixteenth) may be singled out here, for Spenser drew extensively on Boccaccio's *De Genealogia Deorum* and on the *Mythologiae* of Natalis Comes when he was making *The Faerie Queene*. For both of these "mythographers," the persons and episodes of classical mythology convey moral truths which are ultimately in accord with Christian faith: Natalis Comes is perhaps more concerned than is Boccaccio with the philosophical and scientific truths supposed to lie behind the veil of ancient myth, but his general approach does not significantly differ from that of his predecessor. The mythological exegesis undertaken by these men and others like them provided detailed interpretations of episode and extended narrative, and did much also to establish certain mythological figures as "types" of particular virtues or vices: thus, Hercules epitomized heroic valor; Marsyas, rash presumption; Midas, greed. By Spenser's time, the name alone of a given mythological personage might be expected to summon up for the instructed reader ("conditioned" by mythographical interpretation) an appropriate set of associative values. In painting and sculpture, and in the pageants and entertainments of Court and town, as well as in emblem books like those by Geoffrey Whitney, the allegorizing of classical mythology was everywhere in evidence; and Spenser was from an early age extraordinarily receptive to these influences.

Another kind of allegorical tradition reflected the influence of Biblical exegesis, gradually evolved by generations of patristic and lay commentators from the primitive Christian era. As early as the third century, Origen had considered that Holy Scripture included literal, moral, and mystical levels of meaning; by medieval times, there had developed the far more complex fourfold method of Biblical interpretation (described by Dante in the "Letter to Can Grande"), by which a literal or historical sense was to be distinguished from a spiritual sense (comprising allegorical, moral, and anagogical levels of meaning). In Spenser's age, Protestant churchmen, especially those sympathetic to Puritanism, were relatively insistent on the prime importance of the literal level; but the influence of fourfold interpretation continued to be pervasive. Further, according to typological interpretation of the Bible, events and persons in the Old Testament foreshadowed and gave promise (as anticipatory "types") of corresponding events and persons in the New: John Milton, who resisted efforts to interpret Scripture in more than one sense, could yet acknowledge that "in the Old Testament . . . this sense is sometimes a compound of the historical and typical."[2] Book I of *The Faerie Queene* provides the best evidence for the view that Spenser was deeply influenced by these assumptions and methods.

It is dangerous, of course, to bring to the reading of secular, nonallegorical literature the methods and expectations of Biblical exegesis, but the prob-

2. *De Doctrina Christiana*, I, xxx.

lem becomes more complex when one turns to *The Faerie Queene,* a poem explicitly described by its author as an allegory: the structure of imagery, especially in Book I, which continually recalls the expressions of Holy Scripture, invites interpretation in terms of a multileveled allegorical scheme. Again, since the poem as a whole evidently contains a good deal of historical (or topical), moral, and theological allegory, there is a strong temptation to search for consistent and continuing levels of allegory throughout the poem, and to wrest "significance" at each level from every character and episode. A difficulty with this approach is that it can lead to an obsessive concern with one or another level of meaning: topical allegory, perhaps, or, more insidiously, moral allegory. As Rosemond Tuve has said, "Of all authors, Spenser is done the most harm by translating all 'allegories' into 'moralizations'."[3] A sensible approach to the poem will be one that, first, refuses to glorify analysis at the expense of synthesis, and, secondly, recognizes that if the allegory is continued, it is also discontinuous: while the poet's use of allegory in *The Faerie Queene* reflects his debt to the traditions of mythological and Biblical interpretation, the allegory remains flexible, evocative, dependent to an important degree on context. Many episodes in Book I (but not all of them) are susceptible of rather formal multileveled interpretation; other Books will not so cheerfully yield to these methods. A lion comes to the aid of Una and acts as her protector for a time; but another lion is Anger's mount in the House of Pride. Rhodes Dunlap puts the matter succinctly: "most Renaissance allegory is not a firmly closed form, to which there is either overtly or deducibly a simple key, but rather an open form which sets up and dramatizes certain ideal patterns."[4] Spenser's *Faerie Queene* is a poem which reveals itself most fully to the reader who, recognizing that "equation is simply not the character of the allegorical relation,"[5] steadfastly resists the impulse to "impose" allegorical meanings, and responds with appropriate sensitivity to the subtly suggestive quality of Spenser's images.

If Spenser's allegory presents a demanding challenge to the reader who would know its nature, the relationship of *The Faerie Queene* to earlier heroic poetry is an issue no less complex. In the most broadly general terms, the poem is a romantic epic; more precisely, it is a heroic poem which has strong affinities with classical epic poetry, but which on the whole is most fruitfully to be associated with the characteristics of romance (and the Italian epic romances of the fifteenth and sixteenth centuries), and with symbolic patterns of imagery in the Bible. Of course, Spenser's debt to classical epic is by no means slight: the character of his classically oriented education insured close familiarity with the styles and conventions especially of Latin poetry, and *The Faerie Queene* reflects his considered regard for epic precedent. The thrust, after an appropriate invocation, "into the middest" of a twelve-part narrative to be centered (according to the "Letter") on a magnificently virtuous and active hero, clearly derives from the manner and broad design of classical epic. Spenser's particular emphasis in Book I on the role of Arthur as minister of divine grace (to say nothing of the "glory" explicitly associated with the "Faery

3. Rosemond Tuve, *Allegorical Imagery* . . . (Princeton, N.J., 1966), p. 333.
4. Rhodes Dunlap, "The Allegorical Interpretation of Renaissance Litera- ture," *PMLA,* LXXXII (1967), 39– 43.
5. R. Tuve, *op. cit.,* p. 404.

Queene") is primarily referable to the poet's Christian belief; yet it is worth recalling that the heroes of classical epic also are variously linked with divine power and knowledge in a fashion beyond the reach of ordinary men. Again, in so far as *The Faerie Queene* reminds a nation of its ancient traditions and points the way to an even more glorious future, the poem explicitly recalls the *Aeneid*; and one is regularly made aware (especially in Book III) of Spenser's commitment to the tradition, more or less subtly endorsed by the Tudor dynasty, of the British nation's Trojan origins. But Spenser does not follow slavishly in the track of Homer or Virgil: rather, he draws upon their achievements to the extent that these support and strengthen his own design.

"Fierce warres and faithfull loves shall moralize my song," the poet observes at the outset: the world of *The Faerie Queene* is in one sense primarily a world of medieval romance, in which knightly adventures, love in many forms, and every variety of the marvelous are dominant elements. The images in any given Book may also reflect the influence of other areas (as, for example, the imagery of Book I draws heavily on the Bible, while in Book II, classical images are much in evidence), but the landscape of the poem is regularly one in which knights, ladies, and magicians move against a background of forests, caverns, enchanted trees, giants, castles, and dragons: the appropriate environment, in fact, for a "historye of king Arthure." The pattern of narrative throughout (more or less completely realized in the several Books) is that of the knight's quest, traced through a series of arduous encounters, and an apparently conclusive defeat, to glorious and final victory. Thus in Book I, the Red Cross Knight overcomes a variety of unpleasant antagonists; when his own strength will no longer serve, he is enabled by the intervention of a power more than natural to establish his own identity, kill the dragon, and release his lady's parents from their long bondage. It is true, of course, as the "Letter" suggests, that Spenser was considerably influenced by the epic romance as that genre was developed in the Italian Renaissance, particularly by Ariosto and Tasso. Several characters and a number of episodes in *The Faerie Queene* evidently derive from *Orlando Furioso*, and Ariosto's narrative method, by which a number of stories proceed in parallel, is also that of Spenser, although the Italian's ironic manner is replaced in the English poem by a tone of moral earnestness. His debt to Tasso is of another sort: the Christian subject and emphasis of *Gerusalemme Liberata*, essentially the account of a quest to deliver a beleaguered city, must surely have appealed to Spenser, who could fully sympathize also with Tasso's view of love as a noble habit of the will, apt to inform and rouse the spirit of heroic aspiration in men. Spenser's affinities with Tasso, in fact, point to the heroic literature which for both poets constituted an influence more significant than any other: in the Bible (for the typologically oriented reader), the quest and travail of Moses prefigured that of Christ, through whose love men might expect at last to achieve the shining City of God, that "New Jerusalem" described in the concluding chapters of the Book of Revelation. The gardens and wildernesses, salt seas and crystal streams, heroes and monsters of romance, after all, reflect the symbolic patterns of Holy Scripture: Christ is the archetypal dragon killer. For Spenser as patriotic Englishman, all these "heroic" strands are collected in the figure of Queen Elizabeth: as leader of the British people, she recalls (and represents) the role and the achievement of Arthur; as leader of the English race, she carries forward the role of St. George; as "governor" of the Anglican Establishment, serving the good purposes of God, she directs a nation in the light of Christ's example. When Spenser speaks of "vertuous and gentle discipline," then, he means a discipline at once patriotic, traditional, humanistic, and religious, centered on an idealized conception of the sovereign. Symbolically, to serve the "Faery Queene" is to proceed out of darkness into light, to oppose chaotic disorder and espouse ordered harmony, to escape every kind of bondage and achieve real liberty.

As for the structural design of *The Faerie Queene*, the critical essays included in this volume indicate something of the range and character of those issues which have from an early date stimulated editors and scholars to praise or blame. Generations of critics have wrangled over the precise role assigned to Arthur, and the meaning of Spenser's allusion to "the twelve private morall vertues, as Aristotle hath devised"; but recent criticism has not, as a rule, insisted too fiercely on the need to discover detailed correspondences between the poem as we know it and those portions of the "Letter" which deal with the structure of *The Faerie Queene*. One may suppose that Spenser envisioned Book XII as a poetical unit which might in some sense match and balance Book I: with the descent of St. George from the Hill of Contemplation, the poem moves steadily along through a fallen world of space and time (as the opening stanzas of Book II make clear), and it is tempting to imagine that the final harmonious reunion at the court of Gloriana would have been symbolically linked with that entrance "through the gates into the city" promised by the concluding verses in the Book of Revelation. But this must remain conjectural. An inclination to read the poem primarily as an imaginative construct (with relatively slight emphasis on the description in the "Letter" of structural elements) informs the essays by Graham Hough and Northrop Frye: for both, the poem as it stands has its own artistic integrity. "If merely uncompleted," Frye observes, "then it still may be a unity, like a torso in sculpture." Whether or not the arrangement of Books I–VI corresponds to a structured pattern of relationships among the virtues (and the view that Book I "contains" the whole poem is a persuasive one), it is clear that Spenser has not constructed every Book on the same plan, although in at least five Books the quest of a particular knight is central in the narrative. The development of Books I and II, however, is linear, keyed to the progress of the Red Cross Knight and that of Guyon; that of Books III and IV, in contrast, unfolds spatially about the centrally symbolic myth of Venus and Adonis. In Books V and VI, narrative movement through time again assumes central importance. The structural pattern of Books III and IV radiates, so to speak, from the elaborately symbolic accounts of the Garden of Adonis and (in Book IV) the Temple of Venus; yet every Book is provided with its own "symbolic core," appropriately placed in the narrative: in Book I (for example), the House of Holiness; in Book VI, Mount Acidale.

The maintenance of unity through varied means extends, finally, to the basic structural element of the poem, the Spenserian stanza itself, so well suited to the emblematic method which the poet found congenial. In contrast with the continuous surge and forward progression of Milton's blank verse, or even with the lyrics of Donne, typically marshalled onward by a succession of logical connectives, Spenser's stanzas produce a spatial effect: they contribute to the development of an elaborate allegorical mosaic, and the rhymed stanzas help to emphasize this poet's affinity with medieval tradition. Individual stanzas often present a vividly realized visual description in the first eight lines, then comment on the meaning of that picture in the alexandrine: the most striking example occurs at I.i.18, but many other instances might be cited in Book I alone. This is not merely to say, with Pope's "old lady," that Spenser shows us a gallery of pictures: rather, the artist's instrument is appropriate to his poetic method and to the character of his imaginative outlook. And within the stanza, Spenser achieves an astonishing range of effect. He deliberately introduces exaggeratedly alliterative language, for example (cf. I.i.51, or III.x.31), to emphasize the "discordant" natures of evil or grotesque personages in the poem. The varied accents of his pentameter lines regularly accord with context: one thinks of the angel's summons to the Palmer (II.viii.3), or of the mesmeric rhythms in which Glauce's incantation is cast (III.ii.-50–51), or of the pitch and roll of Spenser's lines in almost any account of ships at sea, extending to the uneven metrical effects employed when shipwreck is in question (II.ii.24; III.iv.9).

For Hazlitt, Spenser is "the poet of our waking dreams," whose music lulls the senses. One sees the critic's point; yet the "generall end" of *The Faerie Queene*, after all, "is to fashion a gentleman or noble person in vertuous and gentle discipline." The poem, in fact, everywhere reminds its readers of "the jarring noises of the world," and Spenser contrives that each element in *The Faerie Queene* shall contribute to its vitality. "Art of a very complex kind," says Kathleen Williams, "creates the poem's sense of spontaneous life."[6] *The Faerie Queene* has been called "a dream-poem"; "but what the poet dreams of," as Northrop Frye observes, "is the strenuous effort, physical, mental, and moral, of waking up to one's true humanity."

6. Kathleen Williams, *Spenser's World of Glass: A Reading of The Faerie Queene* (Berkeley, Calif., 1966), p. 234.

From The Shepheardes Calender

To His Booke.

Goe little booke:[1] thy selfe present,
As child whose parent is unkent:°   *unknown*
To him that is the president°   *pattern*
Of noblesse and of chevalree,
5   And if that Envie barke at thee,
As sure it will, for succoure flee
     Under the shadow of his wing,[2]
And askéd, who thee forth did bring,
A shepheards swaine saye did thee sing,
10 All as his straying flocke he fedde:
And when his honor has thee redde,°   *seen*
Crave pardon for my hardyhedde.°   *boldness*
     But if that any aske thy name,
Say thou wert base° begot with blame: *lowly*
15 For thy[3] thereof thou takest shame.
And when thou art past jeopardee,
Come tell me, what was sayd of mee:
And I will send more after thee.

IMMERITO.[4]

Januarye

1. Spenser deliberately echoes Chaucer's expression in *Troilus and Criseyde*, V. 1786 ("Go, litel bok, go litel myn tragedye"), to indicate his sense of literary indebtedness to Chaucer, and to associate himself with the poet whom E.K. (who provided a "Glosse" for each division of the *Calender:* cf. Editor's Note) calls "the Loadestarre of our Language." At the conclusion of the *Calender*, Spenser again gracefully acknowledges Chaucer's mastery ("Envoy," 8–11). For a commentary directed especially to those portions of the

Argument

In *this fyrst Aeglogue* Colin cloute[1] *a shepheardes boy complaineth
him of his unfortunate love, being but newly (as semeth) enamoured
of a countrie lasse called* Rosalinde: *with which strong affection
being very sore traveled,*[2] *he compareth his carefull case*[3] *to the
sadde season of the yeare, to the frostie ground, to the frosen trees,
and to his owne winterbeaten flocke. And lastlye, fynding himselfe
robbed of all former pleasaunce and delights, hee breaketh his Pipe
in peeces, and casteth him selfe to the ground.*

COLIN CLOUTE

A Shepeheards boye (no better doe him call)	
When Winters wastful° spight was almost spent,	*devastating*
All in a sunneshine day, as did befall,	
Led forth his flock, that had bene long ypent.°	*pent up*
5 So faynt they woxe,° and feeble in the folde,	*grew*
That now unnethes° their feete could them uphold.	*scarcely*

All as the Sheepe, such was the shepeheards looke,	
For pale and wanne he was, (alas the while,)	
May seeme he lovd, or else some care he tooke:[4]	
10 Well couth° he tune his pipe, and frame his stile.	*could*
Tho° to a hill his faynting flocke he ledde,	*then*
And thus him playnd,° the while his shepe there fedde.	*lamented*

"Ye Gods of love, that pitie lovers payne,
(If any gods the paine of lovers pitie:)

Calender reproduced in this edition, cf.
the essay by Isabel MacCaffrey, in this
edition. The fullest discussion of the
Calender in its pastoral contexts is
Spenser, Marvell, and Renaissance Pastoral, by Patrick Cullen (Cambridge,
Mass., 1970).

2. I.e., the protective sponsorship of
Sir Philip Sidney, "the Noble and Vertuous Gentleman most worthy of all
titles both of learning and chevalrie"
to whom Spenser dedicates his poem.
Writing in October, 1579, Spenser remarked to Gabriel Harvey, "As for the
twoo worthy Gentlemen, Master *Sidney*,
and Master *Dyer*, they have me, I
thanke them, in some use of familiarity"; but the vein of self-conscious
diffidence in "To His Booke" indicates
the poet's awareness of the gulf dividing him from these men of affairs,
and of the need to guard against the
malicious envy in high places that
might easily bring down an aspiring
poet of relatively humble origins. The
fact that several eclogues in the *Calender* were potentially dangerous, by
virtue of their political or ecclesiastical
allegory, adds point to the cautious reserve of these lines.

3. I.e., therefore.
4. "The undeserving one."
1. "A name not greatly used, and yet
have I sene a Poesie of M. Skeltons
under that title. But indeede the word
Colin is Frenche, and used of the
French Poete Marot (if he be worthy
of the name of a Poete) in a certein
Aeglogue. Under which name this Poete
secretly shadoweth himself, as sometime did Virgil under the name of
Tityrus, thinking it much fitter, then
such Latine names, for the great unlikelyhoode of the language" [E.K.'s
Glosse]. E.K. thus emphasizes Spenser's
debt to three areas of pastoral tradition, with particular reference to Virgil's *Eclogue I*, to Clément Marot's
*Complaincte de ma Dame Loyse de
Savoye*, and to Skelton's *Colin Clout*.
Spenser is ordinarily associated also
with the figure of Colin in *Colin Clouts
Come Home Againe*, and (somewhat
less narrowly) with the "jolly shepheard" to whose piping the Graces
dance in *The Faerie Queene*, VI. x. 15–
16.

2. Troubled.
3. I.e., his sorrowful plight.
4. I.e., or else he was afflicted by some
sorrow.

15 Looke from above, where you in joyes remaine,
And bowe your eares unto my dolefull dittie.
And Pan thou shepheards God,[5] that once didst love,
Pitie the paines, that thou thy selfe didst prove.°   *experience*

"Thou barrein ground, whome winters wrath hath wasted,
20 Art made a myrrhour, to behold my plight:
Whilome° thy fresh spring flowrd, and after hasted   *formerly*
Thy sommer prowde with Daffadillies dight.°   *decked*
And now is come thy wynters stormy state,
Thy mantle mard, wherein thou maskedst late.

25 "Such rage as winters, reigneth in my heart,
My life bloud friesing with unkindly° cold: *unnatural*
Such stormy stoures° do breede my balefull° smart,   *tumults/painful*
As if my yeare were wast,° and woxen old.   *wasted*
And yet alas, but now my spring begonne,
30 And yet alas, yt is already donne.

"You naked trees, whose shady leaves are lost,
Wherein the byrds were wont to build their bowre:
And now are clothd with mosse and hoary frost,
Instede of bloosmes, wherwith your buds did flowre:
35 I see your teares, that from your boughes doe raine,
Whose drops in drery° ysicles remaine.   *dismal*

"All so my lustfull° leafe is drye and sere,   *vigorous*
My timely° buds with wayling all are wasted: *seasonable*
The blossome, which my braunch of youth did beare,
40 With breathéd sighes is blowne away, and blasted
And from mine eyes the drizling teares descend,
As on your boughes the ysicles depend.°   *hang*

"Thou feeble flocke, whose fleece is rough and rent,
Whose knees are weake through fast and evill fare:
45 Mayst witnesse well by thy ill governement,[6]
Thy maysters mind is overcome with care.
Thou weake, I wanne: thou leane, I quite forlorne:
With mourning pyne I, you with pyning mourne.

"A thousand sithes° I curse that carefull hower,   *times*
50 Wherein I longd the neighbour towne to see:
And eke tenne thousand sithes I blesse the stoure,°   *moment*
Wherein I sawe so fayre a sight, as shee.
Yet all for naught: such sight hath bred my bane.
Ah God, that love should breede both joy and payne.[7]

5. The wood nymph Syrinx, pursued by the amorous Pan, begged her sisters to change her shape that she might baffle his desire; she was consequently transformed into a reed (Ovid, *Metamor-*
phoses, I. 689–712). Cf. also "Aprill," 50–51, and note.
6. I.e., by being badly cared for.
7. The theme recurs throughout the *Calender*: cf. "June," 111–116; the

55 "It is not Hobbinol,[8] wherefore I plaine,
    Albee my love he seeke with dayly suit:
    His clownish° gifts and curtsies° I disdaine,   *rustic/courtesies*
    His kiddes, his cracknelles,° and his early fruit.   *biscuits*
    Ah foolish Hobbinol, thy gyfts bene vayne:
60 Colin them gives to Rosalind[9] againe.

    "I love thilke° lasse, (alas why doe I love?)   *this*
    And am forlorne, (alas why am I lorne?)[1]
    Shee deignes° not my good will, but doth reprove,   *accepts*
    And of my rurall musick holdeth scorne.
65 Shepheards devise° she hateth as the snake,   *invention*
    And laughes the songes, that Colin Clout doth make.

    "Wherefore my pype, albee° rude Pan thou please,   *although*
    Yet for thou pleasest not, where most I would:
    And thou unlucky Muse, that wontst to ease
70 My musing mynd, yet canst not, when thou should:
    Both pype and Muse, shall sore the while abye."[2]
    So broke his oaten pype, and downe dyd lye.

    By that, the welkéd Phoebus[3] gan availe,°   *lower*
    His weary waine,° and nowe the frosty Night   *wagon*
75 Her mantle black through heaven gan overhaile.°   *draw over*
    Which seene, the pensife boy halfe in despight
    Arose, and homeward drove his sonnéd° sheepe,   *sunned*
    Whose hanging heads did seeme his carefull case to weepe.

                        Colins Embleme.

                        Anchôra speme.[4]

---

conclusion of "December"; and, at a higher remove, "October," 91–99.

8. "A fained country name, whereby, it being so commune and usuall, seemeth to be hidden the person of some his very speciall and most familiar freend, whom he entirely and extraordinarily beloved, as peradventure shall be more largely declared hereafter" [E.K.'s Glosse]. In his Glosse to "September," 176, E.K. explicitly identifies Hobbinoll as "Mayster Gabriel Harvey."

9. "A feigned name, which being wel ordered, wil bewray the very name of hys love and mistresse, whom by that name he coloureth" [E.K.'s Glosse]. Citing classical and Renaissance instances, E.K. adds, "this generally hath bene a common custome of coun-

terfeicting the names of secret Personages."

1. "A prety Epanorthosis in these two verses, and withall a Paronomasia or playing with the word" [E.K.'s Glosse]. The rhetorical figure of epanorthosis "taketh away that that is said, and putteth a more meet word in the place" (Henry Peacham, *The Garden of Eloquence* [London, 1593], p. 172); paronomasia' is a form of pun.

2. I.e., shall dearly pay for that time of failure.

3. I.e., the setting sun.

4. "The meaning wherof is, that notwithstande his extreme passion and lucklesse love, yet leaning on hope, he is some what recomforted" [E.K.'s Glosse].

Aprill

Argument

This Aeglogue is purposely intended to the honor and prayse of our most gracious sovereigne, Queene Elizabeth. The speakers herein be Hobbinoll and Thenott,[1] two shepheardes: the which Hobbinoll being before mentioned, greatly to have loved Colin, is here set forth more largely, complayning[2] him of that boyes great misadventure in Love, whereby his mynd was alienate and with drawen not onely from him, who moste loved him, but also from all former delightes and studies, aswell in pleasaunt pyping, as conning[3] ryming and singing, and other his laudable exercises. Whereby he taketh occasion, for proofe of his more excellencie and skill in poetrie, to recorde a songe, which the sayd Colin sometime made in honor of her Majestie, whom abruptely he termeth Elysa.

| THENOT | HOBBINOLL |

Tell me good Hobbinoll, what garres° thee greete?°   *makes/weep*
What? hath some Wolfe thy tender Lambes ytorne?
Or is thy Bagpype broke, that soundes so sweete?
Or art thou of thy lovéd lasse forlorne?°   *deserted*

5 Or bene thine eyes attempred° to the yeare,   *attuned*
Quenching the gasping furrowes thirst with rayne?
Like April shoure, so stremes the trickling teares
Adowne thy cheeke, to quenche thy thristye° payne.   *thirsty*

1. The name is that of Colin's interlocutor in Marot's *Complaincte de ma Dame Loyse de Savoye;* elsewhere in the *Calender* (especially in "February"), Thenot seems to represent the wisdom of experience and mature years.
2. Lamenting.
3. Learning, studying.

HOBBINOLL

Nor thys, nor that, so muche doeth make me mourne,
10   But for° the ladde,[4] whome long I lovd so deare,   *that*
Nowe loves a lasse, that all his love doth scorne:
He plongd in payne, his tresséd° locks dooth teare.   *curled*

Shepheards delights he dooth them all forsweare,
Hys pleasaunt Pipe, whych made us meriment,
15   He wylfully hath broke, and doth forbeare
His wonted songs, wherein he all outwent.°   *surpassed*

THENOT

What is he for a Ladde,[5] you so lament?
Ys love such pinching payne to them, that prove?°   *feel (it)*
And hath he skill to make[6] so excellent,
20   Yet hath so little skill to brydle love?

HOBBINOLL

Colin thou kenst,° the Southerne shepheardes boye:[7]   *knowest*
Him Love hath wounded with a deadly darte.
Whilome on him was all my care and joye,
Forcing with gyfts to winne his wanton heart.

25   But now from me hys madding° mynd is starte,°   *foolish/broken away*
And woes° the Widdowes daughter of the glenne:[8]   *woos*
So nowe fayre Rosalind hath bredde° hys smart,   *caused*
So now his frend is chaungéd for a frenne.°   *stranger*

THENOT

But if hys ditties bene so trimly dight,[9]
30   I pray thee Hobbinoll, recorde° some one: *sing*
The whiles our flockes doe graze about in sight,
And we close shrowded in thys shade alone.

4. I.e., Colin, who loves the scornful Rosalind.
5. E.K. notes that the expression is "a straunge manner of speaking"; he renders it, "What maner of Ladde is he?" [Glosse].
6. "To rime and versifye. For in this word making, our olde Englishe Poetes were wont to comprehend all the skil of Poetrye, according to the Greeke woorde ποιεῖν, to make, whence commeth the name of Poetes" [E.K.'s Glosse].
7. "Seemeth hereby that Colin perteyneth to some Southern noble man . . ." [E.K.'s Glosse]. "The Southerne shephearde" may perhaps refer to the Earl of Leicester, but Spenser is more probably alluding to his own association with Bishop John Young.
8. "He calleth Rosalind the Widowes daughter of the glenne, that is, of a country Hamlet or borough, which I thinke is rather sayde to coloure and concele the person, then simply spoken. For it is well knowen, even in spighte of Colin and Hobbinoll, that shee is a Gentle woman of no meane house, nor endewed with anye vulgare and common gifts both of nature and manners:

HOBBINOLL

Contented I: then will I singe his laye[1]
Of fayre Elisa, Queene of shepheardes all:
35 Which once he made, as by a spring he laye,
And tunéd it unto the Waters fall.

"Ye dayntye Nymphs, that in this bless'd Brooke
    Doe bathe your brest,
Forsake your watry bowres, and hether looke,
40   At my request:
And eke you Virgins,[2] that on Parnasse dwell,
Whence floweth Helicon the learnéd well,
    Helpe me to blaze°   *proclaim, depict*
    Her worthy praise,
45 Which in her sexe doth all excell.

"Of fayre Elisa be your silver song,
    That bless'd wight:
The flowre of Virgins, may shee florish long,
    In princely plight.°   *condition*
50 For shee is Syrinx daughter without spotte,
Which Pan the shepheards God of her begot:[3]
    So sprong her grace
    Of heavenly race,
No mortall blemishe may her blotte.

---

but suche indeede, as neede nether Colin be ashamed to have her made knowne by his verses, nor Hobbinol be greved, that so she should be commended to immortalitie for her rare and singular Vertues" [E.K.'s Glosse]. E.K. mis-understands the meaning of "glenne" (a wooded mountain valley), which here appears for the first time in English.
9. I.e., neatly made.
1. "A songe. As Roundelayes and Vire-layes. In all this songe is not to be respected, what the worthinesse of her Majestie deserveth, nor what to the highnes of a Prince is agreeable, but what is moste comely for the meanesse of a shepheards witte, or to conceive, or to utter. And therefore he calleth her Elysa, as through rudenesse tripping in her name: and a shepheards daughter, it being very unfit, that a shepheards boy brought up in the shepefold, should know, or ever seme to have heard of a Queenes roialty" [E.K.'s Glosse].
2. I.e., the nine Muses, described by E.K. as "daughters of Apollo and Memorie, whose abode the Poets faine to be on Parnassus, a hill in Grece, for that in that countrye specially

florished the honor of all excellent studies" [Glosse]. Properly, Helicon was not a "well," but the mountain which harbored the springs called Hip-pocrene and Aganippe; medieval tradi-tion (as in Chaucer's *Hous of Fame*, 521–522, or *Troilus and Criseyde*, III. 1809) accounts for E.K.'s reference.
3. E.K., having briefly summarized Ovid's account of Pan and Syrinx, ob-serves that "here by Pan and Syrinx is not to bee thoughte, that the shephearde simplye meante those Poetical Gods: but rather supposing (as seemeth) her graces progenie to be divine and im-mortall . . . could devise no parents in his judgement so worthy for her, as Pan the shepheards God, and his best beloved Syrinx. So that by Pan is here meant the most famous and vic-torious King, her highnesse Father, late of worthy memorye K. Henry the eyght. And by that name, oftymes (as here-after appeareth) be noted kings and mighty Potentates: And in some place Christ himselfe, who is the verye Pan and god of Shepheardes" [Glosse]. Marot also had alluded to a monarch (Francis I) under the name of Pan.

55 "See, where she sits upon the grassie greene,
 (O seemely sight)
Yclad in Scarlot like a mayden Queene,
 And Ermines white.
Upon her head a Cremosin° coronet,   *crimson*
60 With Damaske roses and Daffadillies set:
 Bayleaves betweene,
 And Primroses greene
Embellish the sweete Violet.

"Tell me, have ye seene her angelick face,
65 Like Phoebe[4] fayre?
Her heavenly haveour,° her princely grace   *bearing*
 Can you well compare?°   *match*
The Redde rose medled° with the White yfere,° *combined/together*
In either cheeke depeincten° lively chere.[5]   *depict*
70 Her modest eye,
 Her Majestie,
Where have you seene the like, but there?

"I sawe Phoebus thrust out his golden hedde,
 Upon her to gaze:
75 But when he sawe, how broade her beames did spredde,
 It did him amaze.
He blusht to see another Sunne belowe,
Ne durst againe his fyrye face out showe:
 Let him, if he dare,
80 His brightnesse compare
With hers, to have the ouerthrowe.

"Shewe thy selfe Cynthia with thy silver rayes,
 And be not abasht:
When shee the beames of her beauty displayes,
85 O how art thou dasht?
But I will not match her with Latonaes seede,[6]
Such follie great sorow to Niobe did breede.°   *cause*
 Now she is a stone,
 And makes dayly mone,
90 Warning all other to take heede.

4. "The Moone, whom the Poets faine to be sister unto Phoebus, that is the Sunne" [E.K.'s Glosse]. Born on Cynthus Hill, in the island of Delos (according to legend), she was known also as Cynthia: cf. 82, below.
5. "By the mingling of the Redde rose and the White, is meant the uniting of the two principall houses of Lancaster and of Yorke: by whose longe discord and deadly debate, this realm many yeares was sore traveiled, and almost cleane decayed. Til the famous Henry the seventh, of the line of Lancaster, taking to wife the most vertuous Princesse Elisabeth, daughter to the fourth Edward of the house of Yorke, begat the most royal Henry the eyght aforesayde, in whom was the firste union of the Whyte Rose and the Redde" [E.K.'s Glosse].
6. Niobe, excessively proud of her fourteen children, presumed to scorn the Titaness Latona, who had given birth only to Apollo and Diana; these two consequently slew all of Niobe's offspring, and Zeus turned her into a stone, from which tears forever flow (cf. Ovid, *Metamorphoses*, VI. 148–312).

"Pan may be proud, that ever he begot
      Such a Bellibone,°   *fair maid*
And Syrinx rejoyse, that ever was her lot
      To beare such an one.
95 Soone as my younglings cryen for the dam,
To her will I offer a milkwhite Lamb:
      Shee is my goddesse plaine,°   *absolute*
      And I her shepherds swayne,
Albee forswonck and forswatt I am.[7]

100 "I see Calliope[8] speede her to the place,
      Where my Goddesse shines:
And after her the other Muses trace,°   *step*
      With their Violines.
Bene they not Bay braunches,[9] which they do beare,
105 All for Elisa in her hand to weare?
      So sweetely they play,
      And sing all the way,
That it a heaven is to heare.

"Lo how finely the graces[1] can it foote
110   To the Instrument:
They dauncen deffly,° and singen soote,°   *deftly/sweetly*
      In their meriment.
Wants not a fourth grace, to make the daunce even?
Let that rowme to my Lady be yeven:°   *given*
115   She shalbe a grace,
      To fyll the fourth place,
And reigne with the rest in heaven.[2]

"And whither rennes° this bevie of Ladies bright,   *runs*
      Raungéd in a rowe?
120 They bene all Ladyes of the lake[3] behight,°   *called*
      That unto her goe.

7. I.e., tired from work and bathed in sweat. The expression occurs also in "The Plowman's Tale," a lengthy satire on the clergy, thought at one time to be part of Chaucer's *Canterbury Tales.* Cf. "Envoy," 10, and note.
8. The Muse of epic poetry; "to whome they assigne the honor of al Poetical Invention, and the firste glorye of the Heroicall verse" [E.K.'s Glosse].
9. "The signe of honor and victory, and therfore of myghty Conquerors worn in theyr triumphes, and eke of famous Poets, as saith Petrarch in hys Sonets . . ." [E.K.'s Glosse].
1. "Three sisters, the daughters of Jupiter, whose names are Aglaia, Thalia, Euphrosyne. . . . Whom the Poetes feyned to be the Goddesses of al bountie and comelines, which therefore (as sayth Theodontius) they make three, to wete, that men first ought to

be gracious and bountiful to other freely, then to receive benefits at other mens hands curteously, and thirdly to requite them thankfully: which are three sundry Actions in liberalitye. And Boccace saith, that they be painted naked, (as they were indeede on the tombe of C. Julius Caesar) the one having her backe toward us, and her face fromwarde, as proceeding from us: the other two toward us, noting double thanke to be due to us for the benefit, we have done" [E.K.'s Glosse].
2. Cf. *The Faerie Queene,* VI. x. 16, and note.
3. "Ladyes of the lake be Nymphes. For it was an olde opinion amongste the Auncient Heathen, that of every spring and fountaine was a goddesse the Soveraigne. Whiche opinion stucke in the myndes of men not manye yeares sithence, by meanes of certain fine

Chloris,[4] that is the chiefest Nymph of al,
    Of Olive braunches beares a Coronall:°   *coronet*
        Olives bene for peace,
125   When wars doe surcease:
Such for a Princesse bene principall.°   *princely*

"Ye shepheards daughters, that dwell on the greene,
    Hye you there apace:°   *quickly*
Let none come there, but that Virgins bene,
130   To adorne her grace.
And when you come, whereas shee is in place,
See, that your rudenesse doe not you disgrace:
    Binde your fillets° faste,   *hair ribbons*
    And gird in your waste,
135 For more finesse, with a tawdrie lace.[5]

"Bring hether the Pincke and purple Cullambine,[6]
    With Gelliflowres:
Bring Coronations, and Sops in wine,
    Worne of Paramoures.°   *lovers*
140 Strowe me the ground with Daffadowndillies,
And Cowslips, and Kingcups, and lovéd Lillies:
    The pretie Pawnce,
    And the Chevisaunce,
Shall match with the fayre flowre Delice.

145 "Now ryse up Elisa, deckéd as thou art,
    In royall aray:
And now ye daintie Damsells may depart
    Echeone her way,
I feare, I have troubled your troupes to longe:
150 Let dame Eliza thanke you for her song.

---

fablers and lowd lyers, such as were the Authors of King Arthure the great and such like, who tell many an unlawfull leasing of the Ladyes of the Lake, that is, the Nymphes. For the word Nymphe in Greeke signifieth Well water, or otherwise a Spouse or Bryde" [E.K.'s Glosse]. A "Lady of the Lake" made part of the entertainment presented before Queen Elizabeth at Kenilworth in 1575; such a figure appears also in *Prince Henry's Barriers*, a masque by Ben Jonson presented before the court of King James I. Cf. also *The Faerie Queene*, III. iii. 10.

4. "The name of a Nymph, and signifieth greenesse, of whome is sayd, that Zephyrus the Westerne wind being in love with her, and coveting her to

wyfe, gave her for a dowrie, the chiefedome and soveraigntye of al flowres and greene herbes, growing on earth" [E.K.'s Glosse]. The name may also refer to a particular lady in the Queen's retinue.

5. I.e., to present a finer appearance, with a band of lace or silk (sold during the fair of St. Audrey).

6. Spenser's flower passage, deriving in some measure from Marot's *Complaincte de ma Dame Loyse de Savoye*, 229–236, in turn influenced Milton's *Lycidas*. "Coronations" are carnations, "sops in wine" clove pinks; the "Pawnce" is the pansy, and the "flowre Delice" a variety of iris. The "chevisaunce" has not been satisfactorily identified; it may be a species of wallflower.

And if you come hether,
  When Damsines° I gether,   *plums*
I will part them all you among."

THENOT

And was thilk same song of Colins owne making?
155 Ah foolish boy, that is with love yblent:°   *blinded*
Great pittie is, he be in such taking,°   *plight*
For naught caren, that bene so lewdly bent.[7]

HOBBINOL

Sicker° I hold him, for a greater fon,°   *surely/fool*
That loves the thing, he cannot purchase.
160 But let us homeward: for night draweth on,
And twincling starres the daylight hence chase.

Thenots Embleme.[8]

O quam te memorem virgo?

Hobbinols Embleme.

165   *O dea certe.*

---

7. I.e., for they that are so foolishly inclined are quite heedless.

8. "This Poesye is taken out of Virgile [*Aeneid*, I. 327–328], and there of him used in the person of Aeneas to his mother Venus, appearing to him in likenesse of one of Dianaes damosells: being there most divinely set forth. To which similitude of divinitie Hobbinoll comparing the excelency of Elisa, and being through the worthynes of Colins song, as it were, overcome with the hugenesse of his imagination, brusteth out in great admiration (O quam te memorem virgo?) being otherwise unhable, then by soddein silence, to expresse the worthinesse of his conceipt. Whom Thenot answereth with another part of the like verse, as confirming by his graunt and approvance, that Elisa is no whit inferiour to the Majestie of her, of whome that Poete so boldly pronounced, O dea certe" [E.K.'s Glosse].

June

Argument

This Aeglogue is wholly vowed[1] *to the complayning of Colins ill successe in his love. For being (as is aforesaid) enamoured of a Country lasse Rosalind, and having (as seemeth) founde place in her heart, he lamenteth to his deare frend Hobbinoll, that he is nowe forsaken unfaithfully, and in his steede Menalcas, another shepheard received disloyally. And this is the whole Argument of this Aeglogue.*

HOBBINOLL   **COLIN CLOUTE**

Lo Colin, here the place, whose pleasaunt syte
From other shades hath weand my wandring mynde.
Tell me, what wants me[2] here, to worke delyte?
The simple ayre, the gentle warbling wynde,
5 So calme, so coole, as no where else I fynde:
The grassye ground with daintye Daysies dight,°   *adorned*
The Bramble bush, where Byrds of every kynde
To the waters fall their tunes attemper° right.   *harmonize*

COLIN

O happy Hobbinoll, I blesse thy state,
10 That Paradise hast found, whych Adam lost.
Here wander may thy flock early or late,
Withouten dreade of Wolves to bene ytost:°   *disturbed*
Thy lovely layes here mayst thou freely boste.°   *display*

1. Devoted. But this eclogue also confronts "pastoral perspectives for the purpose of exploring their virtues and limitations" (Cullen, *op. cit.*, p. 84).
2. I.e., what do I lack.

But I unhappy man, whom cruell fate,
15 And angry Gods pursue from coste to coste,
Can nowhere fynd, to shroud my lucklesse pate.[3]

HOBBINOLL

Then if by me thou list adviséd be,
Forsake the soyle, that so doth the bewitch:[4]
Leave me those hilles, where harbrough° nis to see,   *shelter*
20 Nor holybush, nor brere, nor winding witche:[5]
And to the dales resort, where shepheards ritch,
And fruictfull flocks bene every where to see.
Here no night Ravens lodge more black then pitche,
Nor elvish ghosts, nor gastly owles doe flee.°   *flit*

25 But frendly Faeries, met with many Graces,[6]
And lightfote Nymphes can chace the lingring night,
With Heydeguyes,[7] and trimly trodden traces,°   *dances*
Whilst systers nyne, which dwell on Parnasse hight,
Doe make them musick, for their more delight:
30 And Pan himselfe to kisse their christall faces,
Will pype and daunce, when Phoebe shineth bright:
Such pierlesse pleasures have we in these places.

COLIN

And I, whylst youth, and course of carelesse yeeres
Did let me walke withouten lincks of love,
35 In such delights did joy amongst my peeres:
But ryper age such pleasures doth reprove,
My fancye eke from former follies move
To stayéd° steps: for time in passing weares   *sober*
(As garments doen, which wexen old above)[8]
40 And draweth newe delightes with hoary heares.

Tho couth° I sing of love, and tune my pype   *could*
Unto my plaintive pleas in verses made:

3. Ll. 1–16 recall the exchange between Meliboeus and Tityrus with which Virgil opens *Eclogue I*; but Spenser has subtly altered his original to suggest Colin's self-absorbed neglect of his responsibilities as poet.
4. "This is no poetical fiction, but unfeynedly spoken of the poete selfe, who for speciall occasion of private affayres, (as I have beene partly of himselfe informed) and for his more preferment, removing out of the Northparts, came into the South, as Hobbinol indeede advised him privately" [E.K.'s Glosse].
5. I.e., nor pliant ash (or wych elm).
6. E.K. has no time for fairies: "The opinion of faeries and elfes is very old, and yet sticketh very religiously in the myndes of some. But to roote that rancke opinion of elfes oute of mens hearts, the truth is, that there be no such thinges, nor yet the shadowes of the things, but onely by a sort of bald friers and knavish shavelings so feigned . . ." [Glosse]. But he can approve the allusion to "many Graces," for "Though there be indeede but three Graces or Charites . . . or at the utmost but foure, yet in respect of many gyftes of bounty, there may be sayde more. And so Musaeus sayth, that in Heroes eyther eye there satte a hundred Graces" [Glosse].
7. "A country daunce or round" [E.K.'s Glosse].
8. I.e., which take on the appearance of age.

Tho would I seeke for Queene apples[9] unrype,
To give my Rosalind, and in Sommer shade
45   Dight° gaudy Girlonds, was my comen trade,   *make*
To crowne her golden locks, but yeeres more rype,
And losse of her, whose love as lyfe I wayd,°   *esteemed*
Those weary wanton° toyes away dyd wype.   *playful*

HOBBINOLL

Colin, to heare thy rymes and roundelayes,
50   Which thou were wont on wastfull° hylls to singe,   *desolate*
I more delight, then larke in Sommer dayes:
Whose Echo made the neyghbour groves to ring,
And taught the byrds, which in the lower spring[1]
Did shroude in shady leaves from sonny rayes,
55   Frame to thy songe their cherefull cheriping,
Or hold theyr peace, for shame of thy swete layes.

I sawe Calliope[2] wyth Muses moe,
Soone as thy oaten pype began to sound,
Theyr yvory Luyts and Tamburins° forgoe,   *drums*
60   And from the fountaine, where they sat around,
Renne° after hastly thy silver sound.   *run*
But when they came, where thou thy skill didst showe,
They drewe abacke, as halfe with shame confound,°   *confounded*
Shepheard to see, them in theyr art outgoe.°   *surpass*

COLIN

65   Of Muses Hobbinoll, I conne no skill:[3]
For they bene daughters of the hyghest Jove,
And holden scorne of homely shepheards quill.[4]
For sith I heard, that Pan with Phoebus strove,
Which him to much rebuke and Daunger drove,[5]
70   I never lyst presume to Parnasse hyll,
But pyping lowe in shade of lowly grove,
I play to please my selfe, all be it ill.[6]

Nought weigh I, who my song doth prayse or blame,
Ne strive to winne renowne, or passe the rest:
75   With shepheard sittes not,[7] follow flying fame:

9. Cf. *Mutabilitie*, vi.43, and note.
1. I.e., the undergrowth.
2. Cf. "Aprill," 1. 100, and note. "Thys staffe is full of verie poetical invention" [E.K.'s Glosse].
3. I.e., I have no understanding.
4. Reed pipe.
5. "The tale is well knowne, howe that Pan and Apollo, striving for excellencye in musicke, chose Midas for their judge.

Who, being corrupted with partiall affection, gave the victorye to Pan undeserved: for which Phoebus sette a payre of asses eares upon hys head . . ." [E.K.'s Glosse]. Cf. *Metamorphoses*, XI. 146–193.
6. I.e., (1) although my music may be inferior; (2) although to do so may be wrong.
7. I.e., it is not suitable to.

But feede his flocke in fields, where falls hem best.[8]
I wote° my rymes bene rough, and rudely drest: *know*
The fytter they, my carefull case to frame:°   *express*
Enough is me to paint out my unrest,
80 And poore my piteous plaints out in the same.

The God of shepheards Tityrus[9] is dead,
Who taught me homely, as I can, to make.[1]
He, whilst he livéd, was the soveraigne head
Of shepheards all, that bene with love ytake:°   *seized*
85 Well couth he wayle hys Woes, and lightly slake
The flames, which love within his heart had bredd,
And tell us mery tales, to keepe us wake,
The while our sheepe about us safely fedde.

Nowe dead he is, and lyeth wrapt in lead,
90 (O why should death on hym such outrage showe?)
And all hys passing° skil with him is fledde,   *surpassing*
The fame whereof doth dayly greater growe.
But if on me some little drops would flowe,
Of that the spring was in his learnéd hedde,
95 I soone would learne° these woods to wayle my woe,   *teach*
And teache the trees their trickling teares to shedde.

Then should my plaints, causd of discurtesee,[2]
As messengers of all my painfull plight,
Flye to my love, where ever that she bee,
100 And pierce her heart with poynt of worthy wight:
As shee deserves, that wrought so deadly spight.
And thou Menalcas, that by trecheree
Didst underfong° my lasse, to wexe so light,[3]   *beguile*
Shouldest well be knowne for such thy villanee.

105 But since I am not, as I wish I were
Ye gentle shepheards, which your flocks do feede,
Whether on hylls, or dales, or other where,
Beare witnesse all of thys so wicked deede:
And tell the lasse, whose flowre is woxe° a weede,   *become*
110 And faultlesse fayth, is turned to faithlesse fere,°   *companion*
That she the truest shepheards hart made bleede,
That lyves on earth, and lovéd her most dere.

---

8. I.e., where best befalls them.
9. "That by Tityrus is meant Chaucer, hath bene already sufficiently sayde" [E.K.'s Glosse]. Of Thenot's allusion, in "Februarie," to Tityrus, E.K. observes, "I suppose he meanes Chaucer, whose prayse for pleasaunt tales cannot dye, so long as the memorie of hys name shal live, and the name of poetrie shal endure" [Glosse]. Cf. also E.K.'s Dedicatory Epistle to the *Calender*, in this edition.
1. I.e., who taught me to compose poetry in such homely fashion as I can.
2. "He meaneth the falsenesse of his lover Rosalinde, who, forsaking hym, hadde chosen another" [E.K.'s Glosse].
3. I.e., to behave so faithlessly.

HOBBINOLL

O carefull Colin, I lament thy case,
Thy teares would make the hardest flint to flowe.
115 Ah faithlesse Rosalind, and voide of grace,
That art the roote of all this ruthfull° woe.   *piteous*
But now is time, I gesse, homeward to goe:
Then ryse ye blesséd flocks, and home apace,
Least night with stealing steppes doe you forsloe,°   *hinder*
120 And wett your tender Lambes, that by you trace.°   *walk*

Colins Embleme.

Gia speme spenta.[4]

October[1]

Argument

In Cuddie[2] is set out the perfecte paterne of a Poete, whiche finding
no maintenaunce of his state and studies, complayneth of the con-

4. "All hope is lost." E.K. observes, "You remember that in the fyrst Aeglogue, Colins poesie was *Anchora speme*: for that as then there was hope of favour to be found in tyme. But nowe being cleane forlorne and rejected of her, as whose hope, that was, is cleane extinguished and turned into despeyre, he renounceth all comfort, and hope of good-

nesse to come . . ." [Glosse]. Cullen points out that "the moral issue involved in 'June' is not whether Colin does or does not have worldly ambition, but that he has the wrong ambition, to please only himself if he cannot please Rosalind" (*op. cit.*, p. 88).
1. "This Aeglogue is made in imitation of Theocritus his xvi. Idillion,

tempte of Poetrie, and the causes thereof: Specially having bene in all ages, and even amongst the most barbarous alwayes of singular accounpt[3] and honor, and being indede so worthy and commendable an arte: or rather no arte, but a divine gift and heavenly instinct not to bee gotten by laboure and learning, but adorned with both: and poured into the witte by a certaine ενθουσιασμòς.[4] *and celestiall inspiration, as the Author hereof els where at large discourseth, in his booke called the English Poete, which booke being lately come to my hands, I mynde also by Gods grace upon further advisement to publish.*

PIERS   CUDDIE

Cuddie, for shame hold up thy heavye head,	
And let us cast° with what delight to chace,	*devise*
And weary thys long lingring Phoebus race.[5]	
Whilome° thou wont the shepheards laddes to leade,	*formerly*
5 In rymes, in ridles, and in bydding base:[6]	
Now they in thee, and thou in sleepe art dead.	

CUDDIE

Piers, I have pypéd erst so long with payne,
That all mine Oten reedes[7] bene rent and wore:
And my poore Muse hath spent her sparéd store,
10   Yet little good hath got, and much lesse gayne.

---

wherein hee reproved the Tyranne Hiero of Syracuse for his nigardise towarde Poetes, in whome is the power to make men immortal for theyr good dedes, or shameful for their naughty lyfe. And the lyke also is in Mantuane, The style hereof as also that in Theocritus, is more loftye then the rest, and applyed to the heighte of Poeticall witte" [E.K.'s Glosse]. In fact, the influence of Theocritus on this eclogue is slight; Spenser's debt to the fifth eclogue of Mantuan (J. Baptista Spagnuoli, 1448–1516) is more significant, in structural outline as well as in detail. Mantuan's argument, however, bears chiefly on the avarice and sloth of the times; in Spenser's poem, these elements make part of a humanistic manifesto affirming the poet's directive role in society, and indicating his conviction of the high and ultimately sacred nature of true poetry. Cf. the essay by Richard Helgerson in *PMLA*, XCIII (1978), 893–911.

2. "I doubte whether by Cuddie be specified the authour selfe, or some other. For in the eyght Aeglogue the same person was brought in, singing a Cantion of Colins making, as he sayth. So that some doubt, that the

persons be different" [E.K.'s Glosse]. While Cuddie may be identified with one or another of Spenser's contemporaries, it is perhaps more rewarding to recognize the combination in Spenser's personality of elements represented by the frustrated Cuddie (who requires patronage in order to survive), and by the deeply confident Piers, whose idealism cannot be shaken by present trials (and whose promise of future reward appropriately concludes this eclogue).

3. Esteem.

4. "Enthousiasmos," or inspiration. Ultimately derived from Plato's *Ion*, 534, and *Phaedrus*, 245, the doctrine that poetry is "a divine gift and heavenly instinct" might have been found by E.K. in a number of Renaissance Italian works of literary criticism, e.g., Minturno's *De Poeta* (1559). The "English Poete" has not survived.

5. I.e., and pass this long day.

6. The game of prisoner's base; or, possibly, poetical contests.

7. E.K.'s Glosse refers to Virgil's term, "avena" (*Eclogue I*. 2); properly "oats," or "oat stalks," the term signifies in Virgil's (and Ovid's) usage a reed or pipe.

Such pleasaunce makes the Grashopper so poore,
And ligge so layd,[8] when Winter doth her straine.°   constrain

The dapper° ditties, that I wont devise,   pretty
To feede youthes fancie, and the flocking fry,[9]
15 Delighten much: what I the bett for thy?[1]
They han° the pleasure, I a sclender prise.   have
I beate the bush, the byrds to them doe flye:
What good thereof to Cuddie can arise?

PIERS

Cuddie, the prayse is better, then the price,
20 The glory eke much greater then the gayne:
O what an honor is it, to restraine
The lust of lawlesse youth with good advice:
Or pricke them forth with pleasaunce of thy vaine,°   poetic vein
Whereto thou list their traynéd° willes entice.[2]   allured

25 Soone as thou gynst to sette thy notes in frame,
O how the rurall routes° to thee doe cleave: crowds
Seemeth thou dost their soule of sence bereave,[3]
All as the shepheard,[4] that did fetch his dame
From Plutoes balefull bowre withouten leave:
30 His musicks might the hellish hound did tame.

---

8. "Lye so faynt and unlustie" [E.K.'s Glosse]; as in the fable of the ant and the grasshopper.
9. "Frye is a bold Metaphore, forced from the spawning fishes. For the multitude of young fish be called the frye" [E.K.'s Glosse].
1. I.e., in what way am I therefore the better?
2. "This place seemeth to conspyre with Plato, who in his first booke de Legibus sayth, that the first invention of Poetry was of very vertuous intent" [E.K.'s Glosse]. So in the "Letter to Raleigh," Spenser indicates his concern "to fashion a gentleman or noble person in vertuous and gentle discipline," referring to the pleasing force of "an historicall fiction, the which the most part of men delight to read, rather for variety of matter, then for profite of the ensample"; "doctrine by [fictional] ensample," in fact, is especially "profitable and gratious."
3. "What the secrete working of Musick is in the myndes of men, aswell appeareth, hereby, that some of the auncient Philosophers, and those the moste wise, as Plato and Pythagoras

held for opinion, that the mynd was made of a certaine harmonie and musicall nombers, for the great compassion and likenes of affection in thone and in the other as also by that memorable history of Alexander: to whom when as Timotheus the great Musitian playd the Phrygian melodie, it is said, that he was distraught with such unwonted fury, that streight way rysing from the table in great rage, he caused himselfe to be armed, as ready to goe to warre (for that musick is very war like:) And immediatly whenas the Musitian chaunged his stroke into the Lydian and Ionique harmony, he was so furr from warring, that he sat as styl, as if he had bene in matters of counsell. Such might is in musick" [E.K.'s Glosse].
4. "Orpheus: of whom is sayd, that by his excellent skil in Musick and Poetry, he recovered his wife Eurydice from hell" [E.K.'s Glosse]. The "hellish hound" referred to in line 30 is Cerberus, the three-headed hound guarding the gates of Hades (cf. Ovid, *Metamorphoses*, X. 22; Virgil, *Georgics IV*. 483).

CUDDIE

So praysen babes the Peacoks spotted traine,
And wondren at bright Argus blazing eye:[5]
But who rewards him ere the more for thy?[6]
Or feedes him once the fuller by a graine?
35 Sike° prayse is smoke, that sheddeth° in the skye,   *such/is dispersed*
Sike words bene wynd, and wasten soone in vayne.

PIERS

Abandon then the base and viler clowne,[7]
Lyft up thy selfe out of the lowly dust:
And sing of bloody Mars, of wars, of giusts,°   *jousts*
40 Turne thee to those, that weld° the awful crowne.   *bear*
To doubted° Knights, whose woundlesse armour[8] rusts,   *dreaded*
And helmes unbruzéd wexen° dayly browne.   *grow*

There may thy Muse display[9] her fluttryng wing,
And stretch her selfe at large from East to West:
45 Whither thou list in fayre Elisa rest,
Or if thee please in bigger notes to sing,
Advaunce° the worthy whome shee loveth best,[1]   *extol*
That first the white beare to the stake did bring.

And when the stubborne stroke of stronger stounds,°   *taxing efforts*
50 Has somewhat slackt the tenor of thy string:[2]
Of love and lustihead° tho mayst thou sing,   *pleasure*
And carrol lowde, and leade the Myllers rownde,[3]
All° were Elisa one of thilke same ring.   *although*
So mought our Cuddies name to Heaven sownde.

CUDDIE

55 Indeede the Romish Tityrus,[4] I heare,
Through his Mecaenas left his Oaten reede,

5. "Juno to [Argus] committed hir husband Jupiter his Paragon Io, because he had an hundred eyes: but afterwarde Mercury wyth hys Musick lulling Argus aslepe, slew him and brought Io away, whose eyes it is sayd that Juno for his eternall memory placed in her byrd the Peacocks tayle. For those coloured spots indeede resemble eyes" [E.K.'s Glosse]. Cf. Ovid, *Metamorphoses*, I. 622–723.
6. I.e., therefore.
7. I.e., too mean or low rustic. The stanza promises a movement to higher poetic "kinds," i.e., to the genres of tragedy and epic.
8. "Woundlesse armour," E.K. observes, "unwounded in warre, doe rust through long peace" [Glosse].
9. "A poeticall metaphore: whereof the meaning is, that if the Poet list showe his skill in matter of more dignitie,

then is the homely Aeglogue, good occasion is him offered of higher veyne and more Heroicall argument, in the person of our most gratious soveraign, whom (as before) he calleth Elisa. Or if mater of knighthoode and chevalrie please him better, that there be many Noble and valiaunt men, that are both worthy of his payne in theyr deserved prayses, and also favourers of hys skil and faculty" [E.K.'s Glosse].
1. I.e., the Earl of Leicester, whose heraldic device was a bear and "ragged" staff.
2. I.e., slackened the strings of your lyre, lowering its pitch; "that is when thou chaungest thy verse from stately discourse, to matter of more pleasaunce and delight" [E.K.'s Glosse].
3. "A kind of daunce" [E.K.'s Glosse].
4. "Wel knowen to be Virgile, who by Mecaenas means was brought into the

Whereon he earst° had taught his flocks to feede,   *formerly*
And laboured lands to yield the timely eare,
And eft did sing of warres and deadly drede,
60 So as the Heavens did quake his verse to here.[5]

But ah Mecaenas is yclad in claye,
And great Augustus long ygoe is dead:
And all the worthies liggen° wrapt in leade,   *lie*
That matter made for Poets on to play:
65 For ever, who in derring doe[6] were dreade,
The loftie verse of hem was lovéd aye.[7]

But after vertue gan for age to stoupe,
And mighty manhode brought a bedde of ease:[8]
The vaunting Poets found nought worth a pease,°   *pea*
70 To put in preace[9] among the learnéd troupe.
Tho gan the streames of flowing wittes to cease,
And sonnebright honour pend in shamefull coupe.[1]

And if that any buddes of Poesie,
Yet of the old stocke gan to shoote agayne:
75 Or° it mens follies mote be forst to fayne,   *either*
And rolle with rest in rymes of rybaudrye:
Or as it sprong, it wither must agayne:
Tom Piper makes us better melodie.[2]

---

favour of the Emperor Augustus, and by him moved to write in loftier kinde, then he erst had doen" [E.K.'s Glosse]. Cf. *The Faerie Queene*, I. Proem. 1–4.
5. "In these three verses are the three severall workes of Virgile intended. For in teaching his flocks to feede, is meant his Aeglogues. In labouring of lands, is hys Bucoliques. In singing of wars and deadly dreade, is his divine Aeneis figured" [E.K.'s Glosse].
6. I.e., daring deeds.
7. "He sheweth the cause, why Poetes were wont be had in such honor of noble men; that is, that by them their worthines and valor shold through theyr famous Posies be commended to al posterities. Wherfore it is sayd, that Achilles had never bene so famous, as he is, but for Homeres immortal verses. Which is the only advantage, which he had of Hector. . . . And that such account hath bene alwayes made of Poetes, aswell sheweth this that the worthy Scipio in all his warres against Carthage and Numantia had evermore in his company, and that in a most familiar sort the good olde Poet Ennius: as also that Alexander destroying Thebes, when he was enformed that the famous Lyrick Poet Pindarus was borne in that citie, not onely commaunded streightly, that no man should

upon payne of death do any violence to that house by fire or otherwise: but also specially spared most, and some highly rewarded, that were of hys kinne. So favoured he the only name of a Poete. Whych prayse otherwise was in the same man no lesse famous, that when he came to ransacking of king Darius coffers, whom he lately had overthrowen, he founde in a little coffer of silver the two bookes of Homers works, as layd up there for special jewells and richesse, which he taking thence, put one of them dayly in his bosome, and thother every night layde under his pillowe" [E.K.'s Glosse]. E.K. probably drew these materials from Plutarch's *Life of Alexander* or from Boccaccio.
8. I.e., brought into a passive and helpless state through love of luxurious ease; "he sheweth the cause of contempt of Poetry to be idlenesse and basenesse of mynd" [E.K.'s Glosse].
9. I.e., to present for competition.
1. " . . . shut up in slouth, as in a coupe or cage" [E.K.'s Glosse].
2. "An Ironicall Sarcasmus, spoken in derision of these rude wits, whych make more account of a ryming rybaud, then of skill grounded upon learning and judgment" [E.K.'s Glosse]. "Tom Piper" refers to the piper who accompanied the morris dancers.

PIERS

O pierlesse Poesye, where is then thy place?
80 If nor in Princes pallace thou doe sitt:
(And yet is Princes pallace the most fitt)
Ne brest of baser birth[3] doth thee embrace.
Then make thee winges of thine aspyring wit,
And, whence thou camst, flye backe to heaven apace.[4]

CUDDIE

85 Ah Percy it is all to weake and wanne,
So high to sore, and make so large a flight:
Her peecéd pyneons[5] bene not so in plight,°   condition
For Colin fittes[6] such famous flight to scanne:°   attempt
He, were he not with love so ill bedight,°   afflicted
90 Would mount as high, and sing as soote as Swanne.[7]

PIERS

Ah fon,° for love does teach him climbe so hie,   fool
And lyftes him up out of the loathsome myre:
Such immortall mirrhor,[8] as he doth admire,
Would rayse ones mynd above the starry skie.
95 And cause a caytive corage[9] to aspire,
For lofty love doth loath a lowly eye.

CUDDIE

All otherwise the state of Poet stands,
For lordly love is such a Tyranne fell:
That where he rules, all power he doth expell.[1]
100 The vaunted verse a vacant head demaundes,
Ne wont with crabbéd care the Muses dwell.
Unwisely weaves, that takes two webbes in hand.

Who ever casts to compasse° weightye prise,   attain
And thinks to throwe out thondring words of threate:

3. " . . . the meaner sort of men" [E.K.'s Glosse].
4. I.e., turn to a higher "kind" of poetry, inspired by divine love.
5. I.e., imperfect, patched wings: "unperfect skil" [E.K.'s Glosse].
6. I.e., it is proper for Colin.
7. "The comparison seemeth to be strange: for the swanne hath ever wonne small commendation for her swete singing: but it is sayd of the learned that the swan a little before hir death, singeth most pleasantly, as prophecying by a secrete instinct her neere destinie . . " [E.K.'s Glosse].
8. "Beauty, which is an excellent ob-

ject of Poeticall spirites . . . " [E.K.'s Glosse]. The lover, contemplating womanly beauty (which reflects immortal and heavenly beauty), is thereby enabled to rise above earthly concerns, and approach more nearly to divine beauty and love. Image and idea recur often in Spenser's work, notably in *Fowre Hymnes*.
9. " . . . a base and abject minde" [E.K.'s Glosse].
1. Many Elizabethan sonneteers make use of the conceit that love is an arbitrary tyrant, whose dictates the lover is powerless to resist: cf. *Amoretti*, 10.

105 Let powre in lavish cups and thriftie° bitts of meate,   *nourishing*
    For Bacchus fruite is frend to Phoebus wise.[2]
    And when with Wine the braine begins to sweate,
    The nombers flowe as fast as spring doth ryse.

    Thou kenst not Percie howe the ryme should rage.
110 O if my temples were distaind° with wine,[3]   *stained*
    And girt in girlonds of wild Yvie twine,
    How I could reare the Muse on stately stage,
    And teache her tread aloft in bus-kin[4] fine,
    With queint Bellona[5] in her equipage.

115 But ah my corage cooles ere it be warme,
    For thy, content us in thys humble shade:
    Where no such troublous tydes han vs assayde,°   *assailed*
    Here we our slender pipes may safely charme.[6]

PIERS

    And when my Gates shall han their bellies layd:[7]
120 Cuddie shall have a Kidde to store his farme.

Cuddies Embleme.

Agitante calescimus illo &c.[8]

2. Both Boccaccio (*De Genealogia Deorum*, V. 25) and Natalis Comes (*Mythologiae*, V. 13) note the power of wine to heighten poetic genius.
3. "He seemeth here to be ravished with a Poetical furie. For (if one rightly mark) the numbers rise so ful, and the verse groweth so big, that it seemeth he hath forgot the meanenesse of shepheards state and stile. . . . Wild yvie . . . is dedicated to Bacchus and therefore it is sayd that the Maenades (that is Bacchus franticke priests) used in theyr sacrifice to carry Thyrsos, which were pointed staves or Javelins, wrapped about with yvie" [E.K.'s Glosse].
4. The high boot traditionally worn by the actors of Greek tragedy.
5. "Strange Bellona; the goddesse of battaile, that is Pallas, which may therfore wel be called queint for that (as Lucian saith) when Jupiter hir father was in traveile of her, he caused his sonne Vulcane with his axe to hew his head. Out of which leaped forth lustely a valiant damsell armed at all poyntes . . . " [E.K.'s Glosse].

6. "Temper and order. For Charmes were wont to be made by verses as Ovid sayth" [E.K.'s Glosse]. The passage referred to may be *Amores*, III. vii. 27–30.
7. I.e., when my goats have been delivered of their young.
8. From Ovid, *Fasti*, VI. 5: *est deus in nobis; agitante calescimus illo* (There is a god in us, by whose movement we are kept warm). "Hereby is meant, as also in the whole course of this Aeglogue, that Poetry is a divine instinct and unnatural rage passing the reache of comen reason. Whom Piers answereth Epiphonematicos as admiring the excellencye of the skyll whereof in Cuddie hee hadde alreadye hadde a taste" [E.K.'s Glosse]. The rhetorical figure "epiphonema" is a brief moralizing summary of what has gone before. Spenser may have intended to assign part of the line from Ovid to Cuddie, the remainder to Piers.

November

Argument

In this xi. Aeglogue he bewayleth the death of some mayden of greate bloud, whom he calleth Dido.[1] The personage is secrete, and to me altogether unknowne, albe of him selfe I often required[2] the same. This Aeglogue is made in imitation of Marot his song, which he made upon the death of Loys the frenche Queene.[3] But farre passing his reache, and in myne opinion all other the Eglogues of this booke.

THENOT   **COLIN**

Colin my deare, when shall it please thee sing,
As thou were wont songs of some jouisaunce?°   *merriment*
Thy Muse to long slombreth in sorrowing,
Lulléd a sleepe through loves misgovernaunce.
5 Now somewhat sing, whose endles sovenaunce,°   *remembrance*
Emong the shepeheards swaines may aye remaine,
Whether thee list thy lovéd lasse advaunce,°   *praise*
Or honor Pan with hymnes of higher vaine.°   *vein*

1. By one reading, Dido represents Queen Elizabeth, "dead" to Leicester and England by virtue of her marriage negotiations with the French Duc d'Alencon (cf. Paul McLane, *Spenser's "Shepheardes Calender": A Study in Elizabethan Allegory* [Notre Dame, Ind., 1961], 47–60). By another, "Dido is . . . an image of Rosalind as Colin would have liked her to be"; further, the "real and therefore mortal . . . Dido's life and character are based" on the pattern of the relatively "ideal and mythic" Elisa [of "Aprill"]: cf. Cullen, *op. cit.*, 91–92n.
2. Requested.
3. Cf. "Januarye," Argument and note. In fact, the opening of this eclogue looks rather to Virgil, *Eclogue V*, the model for Marot's poem.

COLIN

Thenot, now nis the time of merimake.°   *festivity*
10 Nor Pan to herye,° nor with love to playe: *honor*
Sike myrth in May is meetest for to make,
Or summer shade under the cocked° haye.   *stacked*
But nowe sadde Winter welked[4] hath the day,
And Phoebus weary of his yerely taske,
15 Ystabled hath his steedes in lowlye laye,°   *meadow*
And taken up his ynne in Fishes haske.[5]
Thilke sollein° season sadder plight doth aske,°   *sullen/require*
And loatheth sike delightes, as thou doest prayse:
The mornefull Muse in myrth now list ne maske,
20 As shee was wont in youngth and sommer dayes.
But if thou algate lust light virelayes,[6]
And looser songs of love to underfong°   *undertake*
Who but thy selfe deserves sike Poetes prayse?
Relieve thy Oaten pypes,[7] that sleepen long.

THENOT

25 The Nightingale is sovereigne of song,
Before him sits the Titmose silent bee:[8]
And I unfitte to thrust in skilfull thronge,
Should Colin make judge of my fooleree.
Nay, better learne of hem, that learnéd bee,
30 And han be watered at the Muses well:[9]
The kindlye dewe drops from the higher tree,
And wets the little plants that lowly dwell.
But if sadde winters wrathe and season chill,
Accorde not with thy Muses meriment,
35 To sadder times thou mayst attune thy quill,°   *pipe*
And sing of sorrowe and deathes dreeriment.°   *grief*
For deade is Dido, dead alas and drent,°   *drowned*
Dido the great shepehearde[1] his daughter sheene:° *fair*
The fayrest May she was that ever went,[2]

---

4. "Shortned, or empayred. As the moone being in the waine is sayde of Lidgate to welk" [E.K.'s Glosse].

5. I.e., the sun's winter course appears to have sunk below the horizon. "A haske is a wicker pad, wherein they use to cary fish" [E.K.'s Glosse]. Although the zodiacal sign of Pisces corresponds to February, E.K. observes, "The sonne reigneth . . . in the signe Pisces all November" [Glosse]. Poet and glossator may intend some secret purpose by the allusion; or E.K. may simply have made a mistake.

6. "A light kind of song" [E.K.'s Glosse]; e.g., the rondeau.

7. I.e., take up your reed pipe again. Cf. "October," 1. 8 and note.

8. I.e., it is proper that the titmouse (a small bird not unlike the nuthatch) should be silent in the presence of the nightingale.

9. "For it is a saying of poetes, that they have dronk of the Muses well Castalias . . ." [E.K.'s Glosse]. The Castalian spring on Mt. Parnassus was sacred to Apollo and the Muses (hence called the Castalides).

1. ". . . some man of high degree, and not, as some vainely suppose, God Pan. The person both of the shepeharde and of Dido is unknowen, and closely buried in the authors conceipt. But out of doubt I am, that it is not Rosalind, as some imagin: for he speaketh soone after of her also" [E.K.'s Glosse].

2. I.e., the fairest maiden that ever walked.

40 Her like shee was not left behinde I weene.°   *believe*
    And if thou wilt bewayle my wofull tene,°   *grief*
    I shall thee give yond Cosset³ for thy payne:
    And if thy rymes as rownd and rufull bene,
    As those that did thy Rosalind complayne,
45 Much greater gyfts for guerdon thou shalt gayne,
    Then Kidde or Cosset, which I thee bynempt:°   *promised*
    Then up I say, thou jolly shepeheard swayne,
    Let not my small demaund be so contempt.°   *scorned*

                         COLIN

    Thenot to that I choose, thou doest me tempt,
50 But ah to well I wote my humble vaine,
    And howe my rymes bene rugged and unkempt:°   *rough*
    Yet as I conne, my conning I will strayne.⁴

    "Up then Melpomene thou mournefulst Muse of nyne,⁵
    Such cause of mourning never hadst afore:
55 Up grieslie ghostes⁶ and up my rufull ryme,
    Matter of myrth now shalt thou have no more.
    For dead shee is, that myrth thee made of yore.
        Dido my deare alas is dead,
        Dead and lyeth wrapt in lead:
60   O heavie herse,⁷
    Let streaming teares be pouréd out in store:
            O carefull verse.

    "Shepheards, that by your flocks on Kentish downes abyde,
    Waile ye this wofull waste° of natures warke: *devastation*
65 Waile we the wight, whose presence was our pryde:
    Waile we the wight, whose absence is our carke.°   *grief*
    The sonne of all the world is dimme and darke:
        The earth now lacks her wonted light,
        And all we dwell in deadly night,
70   O heavie herse.
    Breake we our pypes, that shrild as lowde as Larke,
            O careful verse.

    "Why doe we longer live, (ah why live we so long)
    Whose better dayes death hath shut up in woe?

---

3. "A lambe brought up without the dam" [E.K.'s Glosse].
4. I.e., yet as well as I know how, I will exert my skill.
5. An invocation to Melpomene, "the sadde and waylefull Muse, used of poets in honor of tragedies" [E.K.'s Glosse], suitably introduces the elaborately crafted elegy.
6. "The maner of tragicall poetes, to call for helpe of furies and damned ghostes: so is Hecuba of Euripides, and Tantalus brought in of Seneca" [E.K.'s Glosse]. E.K. is somewhat confused: the ghost of Tantalus appears in Seneca's *Thyestes*, but it is the ghost of Polydorus that appears in Euripides' *Hecuba*.
7. "The solemne obsequie in funeralles" [E.K.'s Glosse].

75 The fayrest floure our gyrlond all emong,
Is faded quite and into dust ygoe.° *gone*
Sing now ye shepheards daughters, sing no moe
    The songs that Colin made in her prayse,
    But into weeping turne your wanton° layes, *playful*
80   O heavie herse,
Now is time to dye. Nay time was long ygoe,
        O carefull verse.

"Whence is it, that the flouret of the field doth fade,
And lyeth buryed long in Winters bale:[8]
85 Yet soone as spring his mantle doth displaye,
It floureth fresh, as it should never fayle?
But thing on earth that is of most availe,° *worth*
    As vertues braunch and beauties budde,
    Reliven° not for any good. *revive*
90   O heavie herse,
The braunch once dead, the budde eke needes must quaile,° *wither*
        O carefull verse.[9]

"She while she was (that was, a woful word to sayne)
For beauties prayse and plesaunce had no pere:
95 So well she couth the shepherds entertayne,
With cakes and cracknells° and such country chere. *biscuits*
Ne would she scorne the simple shepheards swaine,
    For she would cal hem often heme° *home*
    And give hem curds and clouted° Creme. *clotted*
100   O heavie herse,
Als° Colin Cloute she would not once disdayne. *also*
        O carefull verse.

"But nowe sike happy cheere is turnd to heavie chaunce,
Such pleasaunce now displast by dolors dint:
105 All Musick sleepes, where death doth leade the daunce,
And shepherds wonted solace is extinct.
The blew in black, the greene in gray is tinct,° *dyed*
    The gaudie girlonds[1] deck her grave,
    The faded flowres her corse embrace.° *adorn*
110   O heavie herse,
Morne nowe my Muse, now morne with teares besprint.° *besprinkled*
        O carefull verse.

---

8. I.e., winter's harmful power.
9. While ll. 83–92 recall Moschus, Idyl III.99–104, there are scriptural echoes too: "For there is hope of a tree, if it be cut down, that it will sprout again, and that the tender branch thereof will not cease. Though the root thereof wax old in the earth, and the stock thereof die in the ground; yet through the scent of water it will bud, and bring forth boughs like a plant. But man dieth, and wasteth away: yea, man giveth up the ghost, and where is he?" (Job xiv.7–10).
1. "The meaning is, that the things which were the ornaments of her lyfe are made the honor of her funerall, as is used in burialls" [E.K.'s Glosse].

"O thou greate shepheard Lobbin,[2] how great is thy griefe,
Where bene the nosegays that she dight° for thee,   *made*
115 The coulourd chaplets wrought with a chiefe,
The knotted rushrings,[3] and gilte Rosemaree?
For shee deeméd nothing too deere for thee.
    Ah they bene all yclad in clay,
    One bitter blast blewe all away.
120   O heavie herse,
Thereof nought remaynes but the memoree.
     O carefull verse.

"Ay me that dreerie death should strike so mortall stroke,
That can undoe Dame Natures kindly° course: *natural*
125 The faded lockes[4] fall from the loftie oke,
The flouds° do gaspe, for dryéd is theyr sourse,   *streams*
And flouds of teares flowe in theyr stead perforse.
    The mantled medowes mourne,
    Theyr sondry colours tourne.
130   O heavie herse,
The heavens doe melt in teares without remorse.
     O carefull verse.

"The feeble flocks in field refuse their former foode,
And hang theyr heads, as they would learne to weepe:
135 The beastes in forest wayle as they were woode,°   *mad*
Except the Wolves, that chase the wandring sheepe:
Now she is gon that safely did hem keepe,
    The Turtle° on the baréd braunch,   *turtledove*
    Laments the wound, that death did launch.°   *inflict*
140   O heavie herse,
And Philomele[5] her song with teares doth steepe.
     O carefull verse.

"The water Nymphs, that wont with her to sing and daunce,
And for her girlond Olive braunches beare,

2. "The name of a shepherd, which seemeth to have bene the lover and deere frende of Dido" [E.K.'s Glosse]. If Dido is to be identified with Queen Elizabeth, "Lobbin" may well refer to her favorite Robert Dudley, Earl of Leicester (1531–1588), Spenser's patron in 1579–1580. "Lobbin," then, might be an anagram for "[R]obbin L."
3. "Agreeable for such base gyftes" [E.K.'s Glosse].
4. "Dryed leaves. As if Nature her selfe bewayled the death of the mayde" [E.K.'s Glosse]. Ll. 123–142 exemplify a traditional convention of pastoral elegy from the time of Theocritus, that "all nature mourns" the loved one's passing. In *Modern Painters* (5 vols., [London, 1843–1860], III.iv), John Ruskin describes the attribution of human capacities to inanimate objects as the "pathetic fallacy": "the extraordinary, or false appearances, when we are under the influence of emotion, or contemplative fancy."
5. "The nightingale: whome the poetes faine once to have bene a ladye of great beauty, till, being ravished by her sisters husbande, she desired to be turned into a byrd of her name" [E.K.'s Glosse]. Cf. *Metamorphoses*, VI. 424–674.

145 Now balefull boughes of Cypres[6] doen advaunce:°   *bring*
    The Muses, that were wont greene bayes° to weare,   *laurels*
    Now bringen bitter Eldre braunches seare,[7]
        The fatall sisters[8] eke repent,
        Her vitall threde so soone was spent.
150   O heavie herse,
    Morne now my Muse, now morne with heavie cheare.°   *mood*
        O carefull verse.

"O trustlesse[9] state of earthly things, and slipper° hope   *slippery*
    Of mortal men, that swincke° and sweate for nought,   *toil*
155 And shooting wide, doe misse the markéd scope:°   *target*
    Now have I learnd (a lesson derely bought)
    That nys on earth assuraunce to be sought:
        For what might be in earthlie mould,°   *form*
        That did her buried body hould,
160   O heavie herse,
    Yet saw I on the beare° when it was brought   *bier*
        O carefull verse.

"But maugre° death, and dreaded sisters deadly spight,   *in spite of*
    And gates of hel, and fyrie furies[1] forse,
165 She hath the bonds broke of eternall night,
    Her soule unbodied of the burdenous corpse.
    Why then weepes Lobbin so without remorse?°   *moderation*
        O Lobb, thy losse no longer lament,
        Dido nis dead, but into heaven hent.°   *taken*
170   O happye herse,
    Cease now my Muse, now cease thy sorrowes sourse,°   *flow*
        O joyfull verse.

"Why wayle we then? why weary we the Gods with playnts,
    As if some evill were to her betight?°   *befallen*
175 She raignes a goddesse now emong the saintes,
    That whilome was the saynt of shepheards light:°   *simple*
    And is enstalléd nowe in heavens hight.
        I see thee blessed soule, I see,[2]

---

6. "Used of the old paynims in the furnishing of their funerall pompe, and properly the signe of all sorow and heavinesse" [E.K.'s Glosse].

7. "So unlucky is the elder that in Langland's *Piers Plowman*, Judas is made to hang himself on an elder tree. . . . The elder is the tree of doom. . . ." (Robert Graves, *The White Goddess* [N.Y. 1958], 191–192).

8. I.e., the Fates: Clotho, who spins the thread of human life; Lachesis, who measures its length; Atropos, who cuts it with her shears.

9. "A gallant exclamation, moralised with great wisedom, and passionate with great affection" [E.K.'s Glosse]. The emphasis of ll. 153–162 on the "earthlie" context of Colin's dirge to this point dramatically prepares for the change of key, common to classical and Christian elegy, in the remainder of the poem.

1. The three Furies, Tisiphone, Alecto, and Megaera, daughters of Earth (or Night), dwelt in the depths of Tartarus; they punished men and women in life and after death. E.K. calls them "the authours of all evill and mischiefe" [Glosse]. Cf. *Aeneid*, VII. 324–326.

2. "A lively icon or respresentation, as if he saw her in heaven present" [E.K.'s Glosse].

Walke in Elisian fieldes[3] so free.
180 O happy herse,
Might I once come to thee (O that I might)
O joyfull verse.

"Unwise and wretched men to weete whats good or ill,
We deeme of Death as doome of ill desert:[4]
185 But knewe we fooles, what it us bringes until,°   to
Dye would we dayly, once it to expert.[5]
No daunger there the shepheard can astert:°   disturb
Fayre fieldes and pleasaunt layes° there bene,   meadows
The fieldes ay fresh, the grasse ay greene:
190 O happy herse,
Make hast ye shepheards, thether to revert,°   return
O joyfull verse.

"Dido is gone afore (whose turne shall be the next?)
There lives shee with the blessed Gods in blisse,
195 There drincks she Nectar with Ambrosia mixt,[6]
And joyes enjoyes, that mortall men doe misse.
The honor now of highest gods she is,
That whilome was poore shepheards pryde,
While here on earth she did abyde.
200 O happy herse,
Ceasse now my song, my woe now wasted° is.   spent
O joyfull verse."

THENOT

Ay francke shepheard, how bene thy verses meint°   mingled
With doolful pleasaunce, so as I ne wotte,°   know
205 Whether rejoyce or weepe for great constrainte?°   distress
Thyne be the cossette, well hast thow it gotte.
Up Colin up, ynough thou mornéd hast,
Now gynnes to mizzle,° hye we homeward fast.   drizzle

Colins Embleme.

La mort ny mord.[7]

3. Cf. *The Faerie Queene*, IV.x.23, and note.
4. I.e., as an appropriate recompense for an evil or ill-spent life.
5. I.e., to experience. E.K. calls attention to the similar thought in Plato, *Phaedo* (thinking perhaps of 68–69).
6. "Feigned to be the drink and food of the gods: ambrosia they liken to manna in Scripture, and nectar to be white like creme . . ." [E.K.'s Glosse].
7. "Which is as much to say as, *death biteth not*. For although by course of nature we be borne to dye, and being ripened with age, as with a timely harvest, we must be gathered in time, or els of our selves fall like rotted ripefruite

fro the tree: yet death is not to be counted for evill, nor (as the poete sayd a little before) as doome of ill desert. For though the trespasse of the first man brought death into the world, as the guerdon of sinne, yet being overcome by the death of one that dyed for al, it is now made (as Chaucer sayth) the grene path way to life. So that it agreeth well with that was sayd, that Death byteth not (that is) hurteth not at all" [E.K.'s Glosse]. Spenser acknowledges his debt to Marot, who called himself "Colin," by adopting the French poet's own motto for this eclogue which E.K. so much admires.

December

Argument

This Aeglogue (even as the first beganne) is ended with a complaynte of Colin to God Pan. Wherein as weary of his former wayes, he proportioneth his life to the foure seasons of the yeare, comparing hys youthe to the spring time, when he was fresh and free from loves follye. His manhoode to the sommer, which he sayth, was consumed with greate heate and excessive drouth caused throughe a Comet or blasinge starre, by which hee meaneth love, which passion is comenly compared to such flames and immoderate heate. His riper yeares hee resembleth to an unseasonable harveste wherein the fruites fall ere they be rype. His latter age to winters chyll and frostie season, now drawing neare to his last ende.

The gentle shepheard satte beside a springe,
All in the shadowe of a bushye brere,°   *briar*
That Colin hight, which wel could pype and singe,
For he of Tityrus[1] his songs did lere.°   *learn*
5   There as he satte in secreate shade alone,
    Thus gan he make of love his piteous mone.

"O soveraigne Pan thou God of shepheards all,
Which of our tender Lambkins takest keepe:
And when our flocks into mischaunce mought fall,
10 Doest save from mischiefe the unwary sheepe:
    Als° of their maisters hast no lesse regarde,   *also*
    Then of the flocks, which thou doest watch and ward:

---

1. Cf. "June," 1. 81, and note.

"I thee beseche (so be thou deigne to heare,
Rude ditties tund to shepheards Oaten reede,
15 Or if I ever sonet[2] song so cleare,
As it with pleasaunce mought thy fancie feede)
　　Hearken awhile from thy greene cabinet,°　　*bower*
　　The rurall song of carefull Colinet.

"Whilome in youth, when flowrd my joyfull spring,
20 Like Swallow swift I wandred here and there:
For heate of heedlesse lust me so did sting,
That I of doubted° daunger had no feare.　　*fearful*
　　I went° the wastefull woodes and forest wyde,　　*walked*
　　Withouten dreade of Wolves to bene espyed.

25 "I wont to raunge amydde the mazie thickette,
And gather nuttes to make me Christmas game:°　　*pleasure*
And joyéd oft to chace the trembling Pricket,°　　*young deer*
Or hunt the hartlesse° hare, til shee were tame.　　*timid*
　　What wreakéd° I of wintrye ages waste,　　*cared*
30 　　Tho deemed I, my spring would ever laste.

"How often have I scaled the craggie Oke,
All to dislodge the Raven of her neste:
Howe have I weariéd with many a stroke
The stately Walnut tree, the while the rest
35 　　Under the tree fell all for nuts at strife:
　　For ylike° to me was libertee and lyfe.　　*the same*

"And for I was in thilke same looser yeares,[3]
(Whether the Muse so wrought me from my birth,
Or I tomuch beleeved my shepherd peres)
40 Somedele° ybent to song and musicks[4] mirth.　　*somewhat*
　　A good olde shephearde, Wrenock[5] was his name,
　　Made me by arte more cunning in the same.

"Fro thence I durst in derring doe[6] compare
With shepheards swayne, what ever fedde in field:
And if that Hobbinol right judgement bare,°　　*held*
45 To Pan his owne selfe pype I neede not yield.
　　For if the flocking Nymphes did folow Pan,
　　The wiser Muses after Colin ranne.

"But ah such pryde at length was ill repayde,
50 The shepheards God (perdie God was he none)

2. A little poem or song.
3. I.e., since I was in those, my salad days.
4. "That is poetry, as Terence sayth, *Qui artem tractant musicam* ['those who follow poetic art,' Terence, *Phormio,* Prologue, 17], speaking of poetes" [E.K.'s Glosse].
5. Wrenock is thought to represent Richard Mulcaster (c.1530–1611), Spenser's headmaster at the Merchant Taylors' School in London.

My hurtlesse pleasaunce did me ill upbraide,
My freedome lorne, my life he lefte to mone.[7]
    Love they him calléd, that gave me checkmate,
    But better mought they have behote° him Hate.   *named*

55   "Tho gan my lovely Spring bid me farewel,
And Sommer season sped him to display
(For love then in the Lyons house[8] did dwell)
The raging fyre, that kindled at his ray.
    A comett stird up that unkindly heate,
60   That reigned (as men sayd) in Venus[9] seate.

"Forth was I ledde, not as I wont afore,
When choise I had to choose my wandring waye:
But whether luck and loves unbridled lore
Would leade me forth on Fancies bitte to playe,
65   The bush my bedde, the bramble was my bowre,
        The Woodes can witnesse many a wofull stowre.°   *affliction*

"Where I was[1] wont to seeke the honey Bee,
Working her formall rowmes[2] in Wexen frame:
The grieslie° Todestoole growne there mought I see   *ugly*
70 And loathéd Paddocks° lording on the same.   *toads*
    And where the chaunting birds luld me a sleepe,
    The ghastlie Owle her grievous° ynne doth keepe.   *dreary*

"Then as the springe gives place to elder time,
And bringeth forth the fruite of sommers pryde:
75 All° so my age now passéd youngthly pryme,   *even*
To thinges of ryper reason selfe° applyed.   *itself*
    And learnd of lighter timber cotes° to frame,   *shelters*
    Such as might save my sheepe and me from shame.°   *disaster*

"To make fine cages for the Nightingale,
80 And Baskets of bulrushes was my wont:
Who to entrappe the fish in winding sale°   *net*
Was better seene,° or hurtful beastes to hont?   *skilled*

---

6. I.e., daring deeds.
7. I.e., he did evilly abuse my harmless pleasure; my freedom was lost; he left me a life of lamentation.
8. "He imagineth simply that Cupid, which is Love, had his abode in the whote signe Leo, which is in middest of somer; a pretie allegory, whereof the meaning is that love in him wrought an extraordinarie heate of lust" [E.K.'s Glosse].
9. "The goddess of beauty or pleasure.

Also a signe in heaven, as it is here taken. So he meaneth that beautie, which hath alwayes aspect to Venus, was the cause of all his unquietnes in love" [E.K.'s Glosse].
1. "A fine description of the chaunge of hys lyfe and liking; for all things nowe seemed to hym to have altered their kindly [i.e., natural] course" [E.K.'s Glosse]. Cf. "November," l. 125, and note.
2. I.e., symmetrical compartments.

I learnéd als° the signes of heaven to ken,   *also*
How Phoebe fayles, where Venus sittes and when.[3]

85 "And tryéd time[4] yet taught me greater thinges,
The sodain rysing of the raging seas:
The soothe of byrds by beating of their wings,[5]
The power of herbs, both which can hurt and ease:[6]
 And which be wont t'enrage° the restlesse sheepe, *arouse*
90 An which be wont to worke eternall sleepe.

"But ah unwise and witlesse Colin Cloute,
That kydst° the hidden kinds of many a wede: *knew*
Yet kydst not ene° to cure thy sore hart roote,   *even*
Whose ranckling wound as yet does rifelye° bleede. *copiously*
95 Why livest thou stil, and yet hast thou deathes wound?
 Why dyest thou stil, and yet alive art founde?

"Thus is my sommer worne away and wasted,
Thus is my harvest hastened all to rathe:°   *soon*
The care that budded faire, is burnt and blasted,° *withered*
100 And all my hopéd gaine is turnd to scathe.°   *loss*
 Of all the seede, that in my youth was sowne,
 Was nought but brakes° and brambles to be mowne. *bracken*

"My boughes with bloosmes that crownéd were at firste,
And promiséd of timely fruite such store,
Are left both bare and barrein now at erst°   *length*
105 The flattring° fruite is fallen to grownd before, *promising*
 And rotted, ere they were halfe mellow ripe:
 My harvest wast, my hope away dyd wipe.

"The fragrant flowres,[7] that in my garden grewe,
110 Bene withered, as° they had bene gathered long. *as if*
Theyr rootes bene dryéd up for lacke of dewe,
Yet dewed with teares they han be ever among.[8]

---

3. Noting that "Phoebe fayles" refers to the eclipse of the moon, and that "Venus starre" is also called "Hesperus, and Vesper, and Lucifer," E.K. concludes, "All which skill in starres being convenient for shepheardes to knowe, Theocritus and the rest use" [Glosse].
4. I.e., life's experiences.
5. "A kind of sooth saying used in elder tymes, which they gathered by the flying of byrds: first (as is sayd) invented by the Thuscanes [i.e., the Etruscans], and from them derived to the Romanes . . ." [E.K.'s Glosse]. Cf. Cicero, *De Divinatione*, I.xli.

6. "That wonderous thinges be wrought by herbes, aswell appeareth by the common working of them in our bodies, as also by the wonderful enchauntments and sorceries that have bene wrought by them: insomuch that it is sayde that Circe, a famous sorceresse, turned men into sondry kinds of beastes and monsters, and onely by herbes . . ." [E.K.'s Glosse].
7. "Sundry studies and laudable partes of learning, wherein how our poete is seene, be thy witnesse, which are privie to his study" [E.K.'s Glosse].
8. I.e., have continually been.

Ah who has wrought my° Rosalind this spight,   *in my*
To spil° the flowres, that should her girlond dight?   *destroy*

115   "And I, that whilome wont to frame° my pype,   *direct*
Unto the shifting of the shepheards foote:
Sike follies nowe have gathered as too ripe
And cast hem out, as rotten and unsoote.°   *unsweet*
    The loser° Lasse I cast° to please nomore,   *fickle/resolve*
120   One⁹ if I please, enough is me therefore.

"And thus of all my harvest hope I have
Nought reapéd but a weedye crop of care:
Which, when I thought have thresht in swelling sheave,
Cockel° for corne, and chaffe for barley bare.°   *weeds/bore*
125   Soone as the chaffe should in the fan be fynd,¹
    All was blowne away of the wavering wynd.

"So now my yeare drawes to his latter terme,
My spring is spent, my sommer burnt up quite:
My harveste hasts to stirre up winter sterne,
130   And bids him clayme with rigorous rage hys right.
    So nowe he stormes with many a sturdy stoure,°   *blast*
    So now his blustring blast eche coste doth scoure.° *scourge*

"The carefull cold² hath nypt my rugged rynde,
And in my face deepe furrowes eld° hath pight:°   *age/placed*
135   My head besprent° with hoary frost I fynd,   *sprinkled*
And by myne eie the Crow his clawe dooth wright.
    Delight is layd abedde, and pleasure past,
    No sonne now shines, cloudes han all overcast.

"Now leave ye shepheards boyes your merry glee,
140   My Muse is hoarse and weary of thys stounde:°   *struggle*
Here will I hang my pype upon this tree,
Was never pype of reede did better sounde.
    Winter is come, that blowes the bitter blaste,
    And after Winter dreerie death does hast.

145   "Gather ye together my little flocke,
My little flock, that was to me so liefe:°   *dear*
Let me, ah lette me in your folds ye lock,
Ere the breme° Winter breede you greater griefe.   *fierce*
    Winter is come, that blowes the balefull breath,
150   And after Winter commeth timely death.

9. I.e., by one view, God; by another   2. "For care is sayd to coole the blood"
and more likely reading, Colin himself.   [E.K.'s Glosse].
1. I.e., be made fine; driven off.

"Adieu delightes,[3] that lulled me asleepe,
Adieu my deare, whose love I bought so deare:
Adieu my little Lambes and lovéd sheepe,
Adieu ye Woodes that oft my witnesse were:
155   Adieu good Hobbinol, that was so true,
       Tell Rosalind, her Colin bids her adieu."

Colins Embleme.

[*Vivitur ingenio: caetera mortis erunt.*][4]

[Envoy]

Loe I have made a Calender for every yeare,
That steele in strength, and time in durance shall outweare:
And if I marked well the starres revolution,
It shall continewe till the worlds dissolution.[1]
5 To teach the ruder shepheard how to feede his sheepe,
And from the falsers° fraud his folded flocke to keepe.   *deceiver's*
   Goe lyttle Calender, thou hast a free passeporte,
Goe but a lowly gate emongste the meaner sorte.
Dare not to match thy pype with Tityrus hys style,[2]
10   Nor with the Pilgrim that the Ploughman playde a whyle;[3]
But followed them farre off, and their high steppes adore,
The better please, the worse despise, I ask no more.
                     Merce non mercede.[4]

3. "A conclusion of all, where in sixe verses he comprehendeth briefly all that was touched in this booke. In the first verse his delights of youth generally; in the second, his love of Rosalind: in the thyrd, the keeping of sheepe, which is the argument of all Aeglogues: in the fourth, his complaints: and in the last two, his professed friendship and good will to his good friend Hobbinol" [E.K.'s Glosse].
4. Cf. Textual Notes. "The meaning whereof is, that all thinges perish and come to theyr last end, but workes of learned wits and monuments of poetry abide for ever . . ." [E.K.'s Glosse]. The passage is to be found in "Elegiae in Maecenatem," 37–38, part of the *Appendix Vergiliana*, a collection of minor poems attributed to Virgil in Spenser's time. Modern scholars are generally agreed that "Elegiae in Maecenatum" are not in fact Virgilian.
1. At the end of the *Metamorphoses,* Ovid observes that "neither fire nor sword nor consuming time can destroy" his work (XV. 871–872).
2. I.e., Chaucer's style or manner; probably also, by extension, the achievement of Virgil (cf. "October," 55).
3. I.e., either (1) with the Pilgrim, the role played for a time by the Ploughman, or, more probably, (2) with the Pilgrim, who played the role of a Ploughman for a time. If the latter is correct, l. 10 refers to William Langland (c. 1330–c. 1400), author of *The Vision of Piers Plowman.*
4. "For reward [in the sense of substantial and intelligent response] not for hire [or salary]."

Editor's Note

The Shepheardes Calender, first published in 1579, and four times reprinted
by 1597, consists of twelve pastoral eclogues, framed by the introductory
verses, "To His Booke," and by an envoy (or epilogue) of twelve lines in
couplets. The author is identified only as "Immerito," for Spenser's circum-
stances were by no means those of the privileged courtiers, "Master Sidney,
and Master Dyer": a note of cautious diffidence sounds also in "To His
Booke." Spenser's poem is provided with a preface (in the form of a letter
addressed to the poet's friend Gabriel Harvey) and a rambling introductory
note on the "generall argument," as well as with a "Glosse" or detailed com-
mentary on the language, imagery, and allegorical significance of each
eclogue: these elements were provided by one "E.K.," whose identity has not
been finally established. Among the various candidates proposed by scholars,
a relatively plausible case can be made for Edward Kirke, Spenser's colleague
at Cambridge; but it is also very possible that E.K. may have been Gabriel
Harvey or even the poet himself, either of whom might well have been in-
dulging in an elaborate literary game. The glosses are ordinarily printed in
full, together with Spenser's eclogues; in this edition, excerpts from the
glosses to "Januarye," "Aprill," "June," "October," "November" and "De-
cember" have been incorporated in the footnotes. E.K.'s comments are
often pedantic and occasionally inaccurate (e.g., his insistence on the term
"aeglogue"), but they regularly draw attention to the poet's learning and, in
particular, to his rhetorical skill; further, they emphasize, either directly or
by implication, the poet's serious attention to literary tradition, his loyalty
to the "best and most auncient Poetes," and his ability to bring something
new and peculiarly English to the genre of pastoral poetry. "So finally flyeth
this our new Poete, as a bird, whose principals be scarce growen out, but yet
as that in time shall be hable to keepe wing with the best."

Some critics might deplore Spenser's archaisms in the *Calender* (Dr.
Johnson's allusion, in 1750, to "studied barbarity," recalled the strictures
of Sidney and Ben Jonson); but from the time of the poem's first appear-
ance, while readers were attracted by its range of versification, intrigued by
its allegories, or impressed by the poet's vision of his role in society, the
most telling critical opinions emphasized Spenser's independent achieve-
ment within the context of poetical tradition, notably that of the pastoral
kind. Francis Meres, recalling Theocritus and Virgil, praised "Spencer their
imitator in his *Shepheardes Calender* . . . for fine Poeticall invention and
most exquisit wit" (*Palladis Tamia*, 1598); while Dryden, observing that
England had "produced a third poet in this kind, not inferior to [Theo-
critus and Virgil]," remarked also that Spenser was "master of our northern
dialect, and skilled in Chaucer's English."

One aspect of Spenser's particular relationship to literary tradition is
linguistic in character. The experiments with English quantitative verse, in
the company of Sidney and Dyer, had interested him; but at length he
would exclaim to Harvey, "Why a Gods name may not we, as else the
Greekes, have the kingdome of oure owne Language . . . ". In the *Calender*,
Spenser was consciously following literary precedent: not many years
before, the "Pléiade" (led by Du Bellay and Ronsard), impatient with the

continuing dependence of French poetry on an outworn and rigidly authoritative classicism, had encouraged the return to purer classical forms, together with an energetic and explorative use of the vernacular, in order to refresh and invigorate the language. Something of this linguistic nationalism, in an English context, informs Spenser's use of alliterative verse forms, archaic terms, and rustic names; in particular, Colin's name recalls the poetry of Skelton (as well as that of Clément Marot), while Virgil, "the Romish Tityrus," is gracefully drawn into association with an English Tityrus, Chaucer, the "God of shepheards" whom Spenser acknowledges for his master in the "June" eclogue. So the poet, consciously breaking new ground in his own time, takes care that the classical and English springs of his art shall not be neglected: his originality, never merely novel, truly returns to the sources and origins of relevant tradition.

In its formal aspect also, Spenser's way with traditional materials is neither to follow submissively after literary precedents nor to depart from them altogether, but rather to explore and develop their potential in a fashion appropriate to his circumstances and outlook. The name of his poem Spenser drew from a fifteenth-century French almanac and encyclopaedia, *Le Compost et Kalendrier des bergiers* (an English translation of which had been seven times reprinted before 1579); but this work did not otherwise influence *The Shepheardes Calender*, which represents a significant advance within the European development of the pastoral tradition. The pastoral eclogue, in its simplest original form (i.e., the Theocritean idyl of the third century B.C.), presents a dialogue between shepherds, who discourse and sing of love and death, while tending their flocks in a rustic setting. Under Virgil's hand, the thing became a carefully structured artistic creation, typically including disguised allusions to particular poets or leaders of the state; somewhat neglected in medieval times, the Virgilian eclogue was widely imitated by Italian and French Renaissance humanists, notably Petrarch, Boccaccio, and Mantuan, all of whom seized upon the genre as a vehicle for ecclesiastical satire (in the light of that peaceful repose which, in pastoral tradition, recalled the Golden Age, and also Eden), while they retained its conventional machinery. Spenser's immediate models were, in some particulars, the eclogues of Mantuan and Marot; yet he had Virgil's example in view when he chose the pastoral form for this first earnest of his poetical aspirations: "October" especially reflects his concern to combine a high Virgilian strain with the notes sounded in later vernacular versions of pastoral. For Spenser, fervently convinced that the poet, under divine guidance, serves a state by guiding its people in righteous ways, the tradition was peculiarly attractive and appropriate: its classical and Christian admixture enabled a poet to interweave natural, ecclesiastical, and moral elements about the figure of a central shepherd-pastor, whose expectations and problems should in some sense mirror those of the author himself.

The structure of the *Calender* bears on this matter. That Spenser brought artistic unity to a series of eclogues has often been singled out as his most significant contribution in the genre; but E.K.'s division of that series into four "plaintive," five "moral," and (by implication) three "recreative" eclogues does not account for the particular arrangement of these poems, nor does E.K. anywhere suggest that one thematic idea informs the

Calender. One critic regards the moral eclogues as the "heart" of the larger poem; another considers that "the love-story of Rosalinde and Colin Clout" is central. It may perhaps be suggested, however, that Spenser is most deeply concerned with the poet's acceptance of his responsibility, both to his craft and to his demanding role in society: to meet and master the challenge of "lordly love" is to recognize the power of that other "lofty love" to "rayse ones mynd above the starry skie." By this reading, the "moral" eclogues serve chiefly to illustrate, in terms of special interest for Spenser's age, the poet's struggle with himself; in that context, "Aprill" and the four "plaintive" eclogues are central. In "Aprill," with the aid of E.K.'s apparatus, the implications of irresponsibility are shown to be national in scope. "Januarye" describes Colin's plight; "June" is the "point of balance" for the comfortless shepherd-singer; and in "November" the poet, noting that Christ's sacrifice has given death new meaning, invites us to smile gently at this self-absorbed shepherd's woe. That Colin, in "December," abandons his art and relapses into self-pitying paralysis reminds the reader that Spenser is not too literally to be identified with the shepherd-poet, whose fate, however, may be that of any man.

Whatever interest of a linguistic, formal, or structural nature the *Calender* has held for its critics, there can be no doubt that the poem's continuing appeal for readers in every age derives in considerable measure from what James Russell Lowell in 1875 called "a variety, elasticity, and harmony of verse most grateful to the ears of man." To represent the *Calender* merely by selections is necessarily to obscure Spenser's extraordinary range of versification, which includes accentual alliterative verse, more than one kind of ballad stanza, quatrains, odes, and even an instance of the Italian sestina (employed also by Sidney in the *Arcadia*). Still, the eclogues selected for the present edition illustrate in some degree the variety of effect everywhere informing the *Calender*: the six-line stanza of "Januarye," for example (repeated, appropriately, in "December"), reappears in "October," but with an altered rhyme scheme; while the employment, in "Aprill," of linked quatrains to frame the emblematic ode that centers this eclogue, exemplifies the poet's delight in matching rhythmically contrasted forms within the separate eclogues. As for the lovely ode itself, its delicate interplay of metrical effects will reward close attention; and the unusual arrangement of long and short lines already gives promise of Spenser's *chef d'oeuvre* in this kind, *Epithalamion*.

The *Calender*, in fact, looks on to Spenser's later poetry, particularly *The Faerie Queene*, in more than one respect. The outline, in "October," of a prospective poetical career, does of course call to mind the themes of *The Faerie Queene* and the Platonic affinities of *Fowre Hymnes*. Again, Spenser's deep commitment to allegory and the "darke conceit," confirmed by the "Letter to Raleigh," is clearly in evidence, chiefly in those eclogues which glance at ecclesiastical differences, but also generally throughout the *Calender*, whatever one is to make of E.K.'s arch allusions to the poet's "secret meaning." Then too, the combination in each eclogue of woodcut, "argument," poem, and "Embleme," already indicates the poet's fondness for an emblematic manner that makes special allowance for the persuasive force of visual imagery: the ode in "Aprill" is really an elaborately multi-dimensional example of Spenser's art in this mode. Finally, the poet's concern with time and its meaning for men is continuously apparent in his work. In *The Ruines of Time*, the emphasis falls on time defeated, either through poetry, or, at a higher remove, by the mind's rejection of a sinful world; *Amoretti* and *Epithalamion* severally link the poet's courtship and marriage with the passage of earthly time, as if to imply an association of love and time (although the wedding song reaches on toward a heavenly home); then at last, after the steadily more gloomy musings that introduce Books II, V, and VI of *The Faerie Queene*, Time itself will be shouldered aside by the lovely and terrible Titaness of Change. But in 1579, the world lay before Spenser, and all things were possible:

> Loe I have made a Calender for every yeare,
> That steele in strength, and time in durance shall outweare:
> And if I markéd well the starres revolution,
>   It shall continewe till the worlds dissolution.

Muiopotmos[1]

or

The Fate of the Butterflie

To the right worthy and vertuous
Ladie; the La: Carey.[2]

Most brave and bountifull La: for so excellent favours as I have re-
ceived at your sweet handes, to offer these fewe leaves as in recom-
pence, should be as to offer flowers to the Gods for their divine
benefites. Therefore I have determined to give my selfe wholy to
you, as quite abandoned from my selfe,[3] and absolutely vowed to
your services: which in all right is ever held for full recompence of
debt or damage to have the person yeelded. My person I wot wel
how little worth it is. But the faithfull minde and humble zeale
which I beare unto your La: may perhaps be more of price, as may
please you to account and use the poore service thereof; which
taketh glory to advance your excellent partes and noble vertues, and
to spend it selfe in honouring you: not so much for your great
bounty to my self, which yet may not be unminded; nor for name
or kindreds sake by you vouchsafed, beeing also regardable; as for
that honorable name, which yee have by your brave deserts[4] purchast
to your self, and spred in the mouths of al men: with which I have
also presumed to grace my verses, and under your name to commend
to the world this smal Poeme, the which beseeching your La: to
take in worth,[5] and of all things therein according to your wonted
graciousnes to make a milde construction,[6] I humbly pray for your
happines.

> Your La: ever
> humbly;
> E. S.

1. From Greek *muia* ("fly"), *potmos* ("fate").
2. Lady Elizabeth Carey was the second daughter of Sir John Spencer of Althorpe; the poet praises her, as "Phyllis the floure of rare perfection," in *Colin Clouts Come Home Againe*, 541–547. One of Spenser's dedicatory sonnets to *The Faerie Queene* is addressed to Lady Carey; cf. Editor's Note.
3. I.e., as having given up all thought of self.
4. I.e., your admirable qualities.
5. I.e., to accept indulgently.
6. I.e., to interpret the poem with judicious reserve.

I sing of deadly dolorous debate,
Stired up through wrathfull Nemesis despight,°   *malice*
Betwixt two mightie ones of great estate,
Drawne into armes, and proofe° of mortall fight,   *trial*
5 Through prowd ambition, and hartswelling hate,
Whilest neither could the others greater might
And sdeignfull° scorne endure; that from small jarre° *haughty/discord*
Their wraths at length broke into open warre.[7]

The roote whereof and tragicall effect,
10 Vouchsafe, O thou the mournfulst Muse of nyne,[8]
That wontst° the tragick stage for to direct,   *are accustomed*
In funerall complaints and waylfull tyne,°   *sorrow*
Reveale to me, and all the meanes detect,°   *reveal*
Through which sad Clarion did at last declyne
15 To lowest wretchednes; And is there then
Such rancour in the harts of mightie men?[9]

Of all the race of silver-wingéd Flies°   *insects*
Which doo possesse the Empire of the aire,
Betwixt the centred earth, and azure skies,
20 Was none more favourable,° nor more faire,   *fortunate*
Whilst heaven did favour his felicities,
Then Clarion, the eldest sonne and haire
Of Muscaroll,[1] and in his fathers sight
Of all alive did seeme the fairest wight.°   *creature*

25 With fruitfull hope his aged breast he fed
Of future good, which his yong toward° yeares,   *promising*
Full of brave courage° and bold hardyhed,°   *spirit/courage*
Above th'ensample of his equall peares,
Did largely promise, and to him forered°   *presaged*
30 (Whilst oft his heart did melt in tender teares)
That he in time would sure prove such an one,
As should be worthie of his fathers throne.

The fresh yong flie, in whom the kindly° fire   *natural*
Of lustfull° youngth began to kindle fast,   *vigorous*
35 Did much disdaine to subject his desire
To loathsome sloth, or houres in ease to wast,
But joyed to range abroad in fresh attire;
Through the wide compas of the ayrie coast,°   *region*
And with unwearied wings each part t'inquire°   *explore*
40 Of the wide rule of his renownéd sire.

7. Ll. 1–8 recall the opening of the *Iliad*, in which Homer speaks of the wrathful enmity between Agamemnon, leader of the Greek armies besieging Troy, and Achilles, mightiest warrior in that host; the Greek poet identifies Apollo as the god who instigated their quarrel. The figure of Nemesis in Spenser's poem reflects that in *Metamorphoses*, XIV.694, or in Hesiod, *Theogony*, 223 ("Nemesis, who gives much pain to mortals"). 8. I.e., Melpomene, Muse of tragedy. 9. Cf. *Aeneid*, I.11: "Can the gods be capable of such vindictive rage?" 1. From Latin *musca* ("fly"). "Clarion" derives from Latin *clarus* ("brilliant," "illustrious").

For he so swift and nimble was of flight,
That from this lower tract° he dared to stie° *realm/mount*
Up to the clowdes, and thence with pineons light,
To mount aloft unto the Christall skie,
45 To vew the workmanship of heavens hight:
Whence downe descending he along would flie
Upon the streaming rivers, sport to finde;
And oft would dare to tempt° the troublous winde. *test*

So on a Summers day, when season milde
50 With gentle calme the world has quieted,
And high in heaven Hyperions fierie childe[2]
Ascending, did his beames abroad dispred,
Whiles all the heavens on lower creatures smilde;
Yong Clarion with vauntfull lustie head,[3]
55 After his guize° did cast° abroad to fare; *custom/resolve*
And theretoo gan his furnitures° prepare. *equipment*

His breastplate first, that was of substance pure,
Before his noble heart he firmely bound,
That mought his life from yron death assure,
60 And ward his gentle corpes° from cruell wound: *body*
For it by arte was framéd, to endure
The bit of balefull steele and bitter stownd,° *assault*
No lesse than that, which Vulcane made to shield
Achilles life from fate of Troyan field.[4]

65 And then about his shoulders broad he threw
An hairie hide of some wilde beast, whom hee
In salvage forrest by adventure° slew, *chance*
And reft° the spoyle his ornament to bee: *took*
Which spredding all his backe with dreadfull vew,° *appearance*
70 Made all that him so horrible did see,
Thinke him Alcides[5] with the Lyons skin,
When the Naemean Conquest he did win.

Upon his head his glistering Burganet,° *helmet*
The which was wrought by wonderous device,
75 And curiously engraven, he did set:
The mettall was of rare and passing price;° *value*
Not Bilbo[6] steele, nor brasse from Corinth fet,° *brought*
Nor costly Oricalche° from strange Phoenice; *brass*
But such as could both Phoebus arrowes ward,
80 And th'hayling darts of heaven beating hard.

---

2. I.e., Apollo.
3. I.e., with boastful eagerness.
4. The arming of the hero is a conventional feature of classical epic: cf. *Iliad*, XI.15–46, and *Aeneid*, XII.87–89. For the shield of Achilles, cf. *Iliad*, XVIII.

478–617.
5. Hercules. Cf. *The Faerie Queene*, V. Proem. 6, and note.
6. Bilbao, on the northern coast of Spain.

Therein two deadly weapons fixt he bore,
Strongly outlancéd° towards either side,   *out-thrust*
Like two sharpe speares, his enemies to gore:
Like as a warlike Brigandine, applyde°   *prepared*
85 To fight, layes forth her threatfull pikes[7] afore,
The engines° which in them sad death doo hyde: *weapons*
So did this flie outstretch his fearefull hornes,
Yet so as him their terrour more adornes.

Lastly his shinie wings as silver bright,
90 Painted with thousand colours, passing farre
All Painters skill, he did about him dight:°   *draw*
Not halfe so manie sundrie colours arre
In Iris[8] bowe, ne heaven doth shine so bright,
Distinguishéd with manie a twinckling starre,
95 Nor Junoes Bird[9] in her ey-spotted traine
So manie goodly colours doth containe.

Ne (may it be withouten perill spoken)
The Archer God, the sonne of Cytheree,[1]
That joyes on wretched lovers to be wroken,°   *avenged*
100 And heapéd spoyles of bleeding harts to see,
Beares in his wings so manie a changefull token.[2]
Ah my liege Lord, forgive it unto mee,
If ought against thine honour I have tolde;
Yet sure those wings were fairer manifolde.

105 Full manie a Ladie faire, in Court full oft
Beholding them, him secretly envide,
And wisht that two such fannes, so silken soft,
And golden faire, her Love would her provide;
Or that when them the gorgeous Flie had doft,
110 Some one that would with grace be gratifide,°   *rewarded*
From him would steale them privily° away,   *secretly*
And bring to her so precious a pray.

Report is that dame Venus on a day,
In spring when flowres doo clothe the fruitful **ground**,
115 Walking abroad with all her Nymphes to play,
Bad her faire damzels flocking her arownd,
To gather flowres, her forhead to array:
Emongst the rest a gentle Nymph was found,
Hight° Astery,[3] excelling all the crewe   *named*
120 In curteous usage,° and unstainéd hewe.   *behavior*

7. I.e., the rams with which such small galleys were equipped.
8. Goddess of the rainbow. Cf. *Aeneid*, IV.700–701.
9. I.e., the peacock.
1. I.e., Cupid, the son of Venus.
2. I.e., such various patternings.
3. Cf. *The Faerie Queene*, III.xi.34, and note. Arachne, challenging Pallas Athene's claim to mastery in weaving, made Asterie ("gripped by the struggling eagle") part of her tapestry; cf. *Metamorphoses*, VI.108. Spenser's account of the metamorphosis of Astery, essentially his own invention, owes much to the myth of Cupid and Psyche: cf. *The Faerie Queene*, III.vi.50, and note.

Who being nimbler joynted than the rest,
And more industrious, gatheréd more store
Of the fields honour, than the others best;
Which they in secret harts envying sore,
125 Tolde Venus, when her as the worthiest
She praisd, that Cupide (as they heard before)
Did lend her secret aide, in gathering
Into her lap the children of the spring.

Whereof the Goddesse gathering jealous feare,
130 Not yet unmindfull,° how not long agoe   *forgetful*
Her sonne to Psyche[4] secrete love did beare,
And long it close° concealed, till mickle° woe   *secretly/much*
Thereof arose, and manie a rufull teare;
Reason with sudden rage did overgoe,[5]
135 And giving hastie credit to th'accuser,
Was led away of° them that did abuse her.   *by*

Eftsoones° that Damzel by her heavenly might,   *forthwith*
She turned into a wingéd Butterflie,
In the wide aire to make her wandring flight;
140 And all those flowres, with which so plenteouslie
Her lap she filléd had, that bred her spight,
She placéd in her wings, for memorie
Of her pretended crime, though crime none were:
Since which that flie them in her wings doth beare.

145 Thus the fresh Clarion being readie dight,°   *attired*
Unto his journey did himselfe addresse,
And with good speed began to take his flight:
Over the fields in his franke° lustinesse,   *vigorous*
And all the champion° he soaréd light,   *plain*
150 And all the countrey wide he did possesse,
Feeding upon their pleasures bounteouslie,
That none gainsaid, nor none did him envie.

The woods, the rivers, and the medowes green,
With his aire-cutting wings he measured wide,
155 Ne did he leave the mountaines bare unseene,
Nor the ranke grassie fennes° delights untride.   *marshes*
But none of these, how ever sweete they beene,
Mote please his fancie, nor him cause t'abide:
His choicefull° sense with everie change doth flit.   *fickle*
160 No common things may please a wavering wit.°   *mind*

To the gay gardins his unstaid° desire   *shifting*
Him wholly caried, to refresh his sprights:
There lavish Nature in her best attire,
Powres forth sweete odors, and alluring sights;

---

4. In Greek, "psyche" means both "soul"   5. I.e., quick rage overcame reason.
and "butterfly."

165 And Arte with her contending, doth aspire
T'excell the naturall, with made delights:
And all that faire or pleasant may be found,
In riotous excesse doth there abound.

There he arriving, round about doth flie,
170 From bed to bed, from one to other border,
And takes survey with curious busie eye,
Of everie flowre and herbe there set in order;
Now this, now that he tasteth tenderly,
Yet none of them he rudely doth disorder,
175 Ne with his feete their silken leaves deface;°   *harm*
But pastures on the pleasures of each place.

And evermore with most varietie,
And change of sweetnesse (for all change is sweete)
He casts° his glutton sense to satisfie,   *seeks*
180 Now sucking of the sap of herbe most meete,°   *proper*
Or of the deaw, which yet on them does lie,
Now in the same bathing his tender feete:
And then he pearcheth on some braunch thereby,
To weather him, and his moyst wings to dry.

185 And then againe he turneth to his play,
To spoyle° the pleasures of that Paradise:[6]   *ravage*
The wholsome Saulge,° and Lavender still gray,   *sage*
Ranke smelling Rue, and Cummin good for eyes,
The Roses raigning in the pride of May,
190 Sharpe Isope,° good for greene wounds remedies,   *hyssop*
Faire Marigoldes, and Bees alluring Thime,
Sweete Marjoram, and Daysies decking prime.°   *spring*

Coole Violets, and Orpine growing still,[7]
Embathéd Balme, and chearfull Galingale,
195 Fresh Costmarie, and breathfull Camomill,
Dull Poppie, and drink-quickning Setuale,
Veyne-healing Verven, and hed-purging Dill,
Sound Savorie, and Bazill hartie-hale,
Fat Colworts, and comforting Perseline,
200 Colde Lettuce, and refreshing Rosmarine.[8]

And whatso else of vertue good or ill
Grewe in this Gardin, fetcht from farre away,
Of everie one he takes, and tastes at will,

6. The catalogue of plants that follows, in ll. 187–200, like that of trees in *The Faerie Queene*, I.i.8–9, is a literary convention, looking ultimately to *Metamorphoses*, X.90–104.
7. "Orpine" is commonly known in England as "live-long."
8. Among the less familiar plants named in this stanza, "galingale" was used as a condiment (e.g., by Chaucer's Cook: cf. *The Canterbury Tales*, "General Prologue," 381); costmary, camomile, and vervain are aromatic medicinal herbs; "setuale" is the modern valerian, used as a drug. Colewort is a kind of cabbage; purslane a succulent herb, in Spenser's day often used in salads.

And on their pleasures greedily doth pray.
205 Then when he hath both plaid, and fed his fill,
In the warme Sunne he doth himselfe embay,°   *bask*
And there him rests in riotous suffisaunce°   *abundance*
Of all his gladfulnes, and kingly joyaunce.

What more felicitie can fall to creature,
210 Than to enjoy delight with libertie,
And to be Lord of all the workes of Nature,
To raine in th'aire from earth to highest skie,
To feed on flowres, and weeds of glorious feature,
To take what ever thing doth please the eie?
215 Who rests not pleaséd with such happines,
Well worthie he to taste of wretchednes.

But what on earth can long abide in state?[9]
Or who can him assure of happie day;
Sith morning faire may bring fowle evening late,
220 And least mishap the most blisse alter may?
For thousand perills lie in close° awaite   *secret*
About us daylie, to worke our decay;°   *destruction*
That none, except a God, or God him guide,
May them avoyde, or remedie provide.

225 And whatso heavens in their secret doome°   *judgment*
Ordained have, how can fraile fleshly wight
Forecast, but it must needs to issue come?
The sea, the aire, the fire, the day, the night,
And th'armies of their creatures all and some[1]
230 Do serve to them ,and with importune° might   *grievous*
Warre against us the vassals of their will.
Who then can save, what they dispose to spill?[2]

Not thou, O Clarion, though fairest thou
Of all thy kinde, unhappie happie Flie,
235 Whose cruell fate is woven even now
Of° Joves owne hand, to worke thy miserie: *by*
Ne may thee helpe the manie hartie vow,
Which thy olde Sire with sacred pietie
Hath powred forth for thee, and th'altars sprent:°   *sprinkled*
240 Nought may thee save from heavens avengément.

It fortunéd (as heavens had behight)°   *ordained*
That in this gardin, where yong Clarion
Was wont to solace him,° a wicked wight   *himself*
The foe of faire things, th'author of confusion,
245 The shame of Nature, the bondslave of spight,
Had lately built his hatefull mansion,

9. I.e., can long remain secure.
1. I.e., one and all.
2. I.e., what they ordain to destruction.
For a discussion of the influence of Cal-
vinistic thought on *Muiopotmos* (perhaps
by way of Chaucer's "Nun's Priest's
Tale"), cf. the essay by Judith Ander-
son in *JMRS*, I (1971), 89–106.

And lurking closely, in awayte now lay,
How he might anie in his trap betray.

But when he spide the joyous Butterflie
250 In this faire plot dispacing° too and fro,   *moving*
Fearles of foes and hidden jeopardie,
Lord how he gan for to bestirre him tho,
And to his wicked worke each part applie:
His heart did earne° against his hated foe,   *rage*
255 And bowels so with ranckling poyson swelde,
That scarce the skin the strong contagion helde.

The cause why he this Flie so malicéd,
Was (as in stories it is written found)[3]
For that his mother which him bore and bred,
260 The most fine-fingred workwoman on ground,
Arachne, by his meanes was vanquishéd
Of Pallas, and in her owne skill confound,°   *overcome*
When she with her for excellence contended,
That wrought her shame, and sorrow never ended.

265 For the Tritonian Goddesse[4] having hard°   *heard*
Her blazéd° fame, which all the world had filled,   *proclaimed*
Came downe to prove° the truth, and due reward   *test*
For her prais-worthie workmanship to yeild;
But the presumptuous Damzel rashly dared
270 The Goddesse selfe to chalenge to the field,
And to compare° with her in curious° skill   *vie/intricate*
Of workes with loome, with needle, and with quill.°   *spool*

Minerva did the chalenge not refuse,
But deigned with her the paragon to make:[5]
275 So to their worke they sit, and each doth chuse
What storie she will for her tapet° take.   *tapestry*
Arachne figured° how Jove did abuse   *showed*
Europa like a Bull, and on his backe
Her through the sea did beare; so lively seene,
280 That it true Sea, and true Bull ye would weene.°   *suppose*

She seemed still backe unto the land to looke,
And her play-fellowes aide to call, and feare

<hr>

3. Spenser's account of the myth of Arachne differs significantly from that of Ovid (*Metamorphoses*, VI.1–145). In the Roman author's poem, Pallas Athene, outraged by the surpassing beauty of Arachne's tapestry, and by its truthful depiction of the gods' cheating tricks and riotous life, destroys the work; when wretched Arachne attempts suicide, the goddess, pitying yet stern, transforms the girl into a spider, "and as a spider she works on at her former art of weaving."

Spenser's version (ll. 259–352) differs chiefly in that a victorious Pallas Athene completes and crowns her tapestry by weaving in the exquisite butterfly that awakens Arachne's rancorous envy, leads to her self-transformation, and accounts for the spider's hatred for the butterfly since that time.
4. According to legend, Pallas Athene was reared by the sea-god Triton.
5. I.e., to accept the (challenge of) comparison.

The dashing of the waves, that° up she tooke   *so that*
Her daintie feete, and garments gathered neare:
285 But (Lord) how she in everie member shooke,
When as the land she saw no more appeare,
But a wilde wildernes of waters deepe:
Then gan she greatly to lament and weepe.

Before the Bull she pictured wingéd Love,
290 With his yong brother Sport, light fluttering
Upon the waves, as each had been a Dove;
The one his bowe and shafts, the other Spring°   *youth*
A burning Teade° about his head did move,   *torch*
As in their Syres new love both triumphing:°   *exulting*
295 And manie Nymphes about them flocking round,
And manie Tritons, which their hornes did sound.

And round about, her worke she did empale°   *enclose*
With a faire border wrought of sundrie flowres,
Enwoven with an Yvie winding trayle:
300 A goodly worke, full fit for Kingly bowres,
Such as Dame Pallas, such as Envie pale,
That al good things with venemous tooth devowres,
Could not accuse. Then gan the Goddesse bright
Her selfe likewise unto her worke to dight.°   *prepare*

305 She made the storie of the olde debate,
Which she with Neptune did for Athens trie:°   *engage in*
Twelve Gods doo sit around in royall state,
And Jove in midst with awfull Majestie,
To judge the strife betweene them stirréd late:
310 Each of the Gods by his like visnomie°   *visage*
Eathe° to be knowen; but Jove above them all,   *easy*
By his great lookes and power Imperiall.

Before them stands the God of Seas in place,
Clayming that sea-coast Citie as his right,
315 And strikes the rockes with his three-forkéd mace;
Whenceforth issues a warlike steed in sight,
The signe by which he chalengeth° the place,   *claims*
That° all the Gods, which saw his wondrous might   *so that*
Did surely deeme the victorie his due:
320 But seldome seene, forejudgment proveth true.

Then to her selfe she gives her Aegide shield,[6]
And steelhed speare, and morion° on her hedd,   *helmet*
Such as she oft is seene in warlicke field:
Then sets she forth, how with her weapon dredd
325 She smote the ground, the which streight foorth did yield
A fruitfull Olyve tree, with berries spredd,
That all the Gods admired; then all the storie
She compast° with a wreathe of Olyves hoarie.   *encircled*

6. I.e., her shield with the symbolic and protective device of the "aegis."

Emongst those leaves she made a Butterflie,
330 With excellent device and wondrous slight,°   *art*
Fluttring among the Olives wantonly,°   *playfully*
That seemed to live, so like it was in sight:
The velvet nap which on his wings doth lie,
The silken downe with which his backe is dight,
335 His broad outstretchéd hornes, his hayrie thies,
His glorious colours, and his glistering° eies.   *shining*

Which when Arachne saw, as overlaid,°   *overwhelmed*
And masteréd with workmanship so rare,
She stood astonied long, ne ought gainesaid,
340 And with fast fixéd eyes on her did stare,
And by her silence, signe of one dismaid,
The victorie did yeeld her as her share:
Yet did she inly fret, and felly° burne,   *fiercely*
And all her blood to poysonous rancor turne.

345 That shortly from the shape of womanhed
Such as she was, when Pallas she attempted,°   *challenged*
She grew to hideous shape of dryrihed,°   *horror*
Pinéd with griefe of follie late repented:
Eftsoones her white streight legs were alteréd
350 To crooked crawling shankes, of marrowe empted,
And her faire face to fowle and loathsome hewe,
And her fine corpes° to a bag of venim grewe.   *body*

This curséd creature, mindfull of that olde
Enfestred grudge, the which his mother felt,
355 So soone as Clarion he did beholde,
His heart with vengefull malice inly swelt,
And weaving straight a net with manie a folde
About the cave, in which he lurking dwelt,
With fine small cords about it stretchéd wide,
360 So finely sponne, that scarce they could be spide.

Not anie damzell, which her° vaunteth most   *herself*
In skilfull knitting of soft silken twyne;
Nor anie weaver, which his worke doth boast
In dieper,[7] in damaske, or in lyne;°   *linen*
365 Nor anie skiled in workmanship embost;[8]
Nor anie skiled in loupes of fingring fine,
Might in their divers cunning° ever dare,   *skill*
With this so curious networke to compare.

Ne doo I thinke, that that same subtil gin,°   *net*
370 The which the Lemnian God[9] framde craftilie,

---

7. A fabric patterned with small repeated designs.
8. I.e., in the art (in embroidery) of richly elaborate decoration.
9. I.e., Vulcan (Hephaestus), who was thrown down from Olympus by Jove; after falling for an entire day, he came to earth on the Aegean isle of Lemnos. For the story of his entrapment of Venus and her lover Mars, cf. *Metamorphoses*, IV.176–189.

Mars sleeping with his wife to compasse in,
That all the Gods with common mockerie
Might laugh at them, and scorne their shamefull sin,
Was like to this. This same he did applie,
375 For to entrap the careles Clarion,
That ranged each where without suspition.

Süspition of friend, nor feare of foe,
That hazarded° his health, had he at all,   *threatened*
But walkt at will, and wandred too and fro,
380 In the pride of his freedome principall:°   *princely*
Litle wist° he his fatall future woe,   *knew*
But was secure, the liker he to fall.
He likest is to fall into mischaunce,
That is regardles of his governaunce.°   *conduct*

385 Yet still Aragnoll[1] (so his foe was hight)
Lay lurking covertly him to surprise,
And all his gins that him entangle might,
Drest° in good order as he could devise.   *arranged*
At length the foolish Flie without foresight,
390 As he that did all daunger quite despise,
Toward those parts came flying careleslie,
Where hidden was his hatefull enemie.

Who seeing him, with secrete joy therefore
Did tickle inwardly in everie vaine,
395 And his false hart fraught with all treasons store,
Was filled with hope, his purpose to obtaine:
Himselfe he close upgathered more and more
Into his den, that his deceiptfull traine°   *snare*
By his there being might not be bewraid,°   *revealed*
400 Ne anie noyse, ne anie motion made.

Like as a wily Foxe, that having spide,
Where on a sunnie banke the Lambes doo play,
Full closely° creeping by the hinder side,   *secretly*
Lyes in ambushment of° his hopéd pray,   *for*
405 Ne stirreth limbe, till seeing readie tide,[2]
He rusheth forth, and snatcheth quite away
One of the litle yonglings unawares:
So to his worke Aragnoll him prepares.

Who now shall give unto my heavie eyes
410 A well of teares, that all may overflow?
Or where shall I finde lamentable cryes,
And mournfull tunes enough my griefe to show?
Helpe O thou Tragick Muse, me to devise
Notes sad enough, t'expresse this bitter throw:°   *throe*

---

1. From Latin *aranea*, "spider."   2. I.e., the right moment.

⁴¹⁵ For loe, the drerie stownd° is now arrived,   *moment*
That of all happines hath us deprived.

The luckles Clarion, whether cruell Fate,
Or wicked Fortune faultles him misled,
Or some ungracious blast out of the gate
⁴²⁰ Of Aeoles raine perforce him drove on hed,[3]
Was (O sad hap° and howre unfortunate)   *lot*
With violent swift flight forth cariéd
Into the curséd cobweb, which his foe
Had framéd for his finall overthroe.

⁴²⁵ There the fond Flie entangled, strugled long,
Himselfe to free thereout; but all in vaine.
For striving more, the more in laces strong
Himselfe he tide, and wrapt his wingés twaine
In lymie° snares the subtill loupes among;   *sticky*
⁴³⁰ That in the ende he breathelesse did remaine,
And all his yougthly forces idly spent,
Him to the mercie of th'avenger lent.°   *gave*

Which when the greisly° tyrant did espie,   *horrible*
Like a grimme Lyon rushing with fierce might
⁴³⁵ Out of his den, he seizéd greedelie
On the resistles pray, and with fell spight,
Under the left wing stroke° his weapon slie   *struck*
Into his heart, that his deepe groning spright
In bloodie streames foorth fled into the aire,
⁴⁴⁰ His bodie left the spectacle of care.[4]

Editor's Note

The greater number of those poems contained in Spenser's *Complaints*, published by Ponsonby in 1591, "are not" (as William Nelson observes) "the most attractive of his works." That five editions of *The Shepheardes Calender* had appeared by 1597 bears witness to the wide appeal of that brilliant *tour de force* by "this our new Poete." No such response was aroused by the *Complaints* volume, in which *Muiopotmos* keeps company with eight other "plaintive" poems or groups of poems that variously attend to the destructive impact of time and change on earthly glory, beauty, and virtue; and in that context often glance at the special position of the poet and his powerful art. A single edition evidently satisfied even those dour spirits avid after what Ponsonby termed "complaints and meditations of the worlds vanitie: verie grave and profitable"; it was not until 1612–13,

---

3. I.e., (some blast from the gate) of the kingdom of Aeolus [god of the winds] drove him headlong.
4. So Virgil concludes the *Aeneid*: "[Turnus's] limbs relax and grow cold;

and his moaning spirit flies resentfully into the shades" (XII.951–952). For a discussion of Spenser's handling of poetic conventions in *Muiopotmos*, cf. the essay by Hallett Smith in this edition.

with Matthew Lownes' folio edition of Spenser's *Works*, that all the poems in the first edition of *Complaints* were again in print. To be sure, the volume has particular interest for students of Spenser's developing command of his art, with special reference to the changes he rings on the genre of complaint, to his craft in translation (perhaps most interestingly on view in *The Ruines of Rome*), and, in *Mother Hubberds Tale*, to the attractions of medieval satire for a poet who found the medium of allegorical beast-fable apt for the expression of his own bitter disenchantment with a Court where expediency and self-interest often seemed to have driven "true courtesy" underground. Still, it is with a shock of real pleasure that most readers, tired with all these rather melancholy musings, come at length upon the enchanting and puzzling *Muiopotmos*, in Nelson's phrase "the lightest and most delicious of Spenser's poems."[1]

Muiopotmos was probably composed in 1590, perhaps fulfilling the commitment made in a dedicatory sonnet to Lady Carey included among seventeen such pieces addressed to influential persons at Queen Elizabeth's Court, and prefaced to *The Faerie Queene*. The poem has something in common with *Virgil's Gnat*, but Spenser's achievement in *Muiopotmos* is of another order of magnitude: conception, tone, and management of genre together reflect the poet's easy and innovative command of his craft. For Ralph Waldo Emerson, "Spenser seems to delight in his art for his own skill's sake";[2] and the view that *Muiopotmos* should in the first instance be regarded as a mock-heroic fancy, "a light, delicate *jeu d'esprit*,"[3] informs the work of a group of modern scholars who reserve their particular admiration for the poet's ability to employ poetic conventions in his own way, or to illuminate a central theme by the artful combination of seemingly disparate elements.

A different standpoint is variously represented by those who find in Spenser's remark that Lady Carey should "make a milde construction" of the poem an invitation to discover allegorical significance in the tale of Clarion and Aragnoll. James Russell Lowell had no doubt that "in Clarion the butterfly [Spenser] has symbolized himself,"[4] and a number of theories in this kind identify Aragnoll as William Cecil, Lord Burghley, whom the poet covertly criticizes elsewhere in his work. Other scholars prefer political allegory, accepting the identification of Aragnoll as Burghley, but matching Clarion with the Earl of Essex or the Earl of Oxford—both of whom, it may be added, have been cast as Aragnoll by still other critics, who propose Sir Walter Raleigh or Sir Philip Sidney for the role of Clarion.

Some at least of these views will never do. Yet one should not abandon the allegorists too dismissively, for that invitation "to make a milde construction" (not to mention the two intriguing stanzas with which the poem begins) indicates the presence of something more than delightful verse.

1. William Nelson, *The Poetry of Edmund Spenser* (New York, 1963), p. 71.
2. Ralph Waldo Emerson, *Works*, ed. E. W. Emerson and W. E. Forbes (Boston, 1846), VII, 229.
3. Hallett Smith, "The Use of Conventions in Spenser's Minor Poems," in *Form and Convention in the Poetry of Edmund Spenser: Selected Papers from the English Institute*, ed. William Nelson (New York, 1961), pp. 122–145.
4. James Russell Lowell, *Complete Writings* (New York, 1904), 16 vols., IV, 273.

"And is there then / Such rancour in the harts of mightie men?" calls to mind the agony of Lear in mid-passage: "Is there any cause in nature that makes these hard hearts?" For some, the "tragick" undersong of *Muiopotmos* serves a larger allegorical purpose. In 1833, John Wilson read the poem as an allegory of love and death; for D. C. Allen (writing in 1956), Clarion represents the rational soul, drawn down to destruction by the power, or the weakness, of the senses.[5] Other critics have been content to notice Spenser's harmonious blend of tragic and mock-heroic strains within a complaint for the cruel fate that may, by "secret doome," quite cancel earthly felicity. Perhaps the most succinctly persuasive reading of those keyed to the tragic element is that of William Nelson, who regards the poem as "a delightful teaching of the tragic lesson that on earth happiness is its own destruction, that only in heaven or by heavenly intervention is the fruitful olive victorious over chaos and death."[6]

Finally, the poet's skillful combination of genres, and of related tonal effects, is matched by his expert interweaving of mythological elements from, chiefly, Ovid and Apuleius (or Boccaccio's version of the story of Cupid and Psyche, based on Apuleius). That is not merely to say that Spenser everywhere follows his sources, for this poet delights to create his own myths. The story of Arachne is in Ovid; but Spenser's addition of the butterfly in Minerva's web makes new the transformation of an envious Arachne into Aragnoll's ancestor. As for Astery, if her name is Ovidian, and her literary antecedents connected with the Psyche myth, the nymph in *Muiopotmos* is Spenser's own creation; and the allusion to "her pretended crime, though crime none were," is altogether suited to the poem's larger concerns. Spenser's mythography in *The Faerie Queene* is more ambitious: one thinks of Florimell and Marinell, or of Faunus and Molanna. But the combination of exquisitely delicate artistry with sombre or haunting thematic undertones that informs those extended episodes is displayed with equal art in the microcosm of *Muiopotmos*. Renwick's judgment holds good still: "*Muiopotmos* is Spenser's most original poem."[7]

5. John Wilson, "Spenser," *Blackwood's Magazine*, XXXIV (1833), 824–856; D. C. Allen, "On Spenser's *Muiopotmos*," *SP*, LIII (1956), 141–158.
6. William Nelson, *The Poetry of Edmund Spenser*, p. 74.
7. W. L. Renwick, *Edmund Spenser: An Essay on Renaissance Poetry* (London, 1925), p. 57.

Amoretti and Epithalamion

From Amoretti

Sonnet 1

Happy ye leaves when as those lilly hands,
Which hold my life in their dead doing[1] might,
Shall handle you and hold in loves soft bands,
Lyke captives trembling at the victors sight.
5 And happy lines, on which with starry light,
Those lamping° eyes will deigne sometimes to look   *flashing*
And reade the sorrowes of my dying spright,°   *spirit*
Written with teares in harts close° bleeding book.   *secret*
And happy rymes bathed in the sacred brooke,
10 Of Helicon[2] whence she derivéd is,
When ye behold that Angels blesséd looke,
My soules long lackéd foode, my heavens blis.
Leaves, lines, and rymes, seeke her to please alone,
Whom if ye please, I care for other none.

Sonnet 10[3]

Unrighteous Lord of love, what law is this,
That me thou makest thus tormented be:
The whiles she lordeth in licentious blisse
Of her freewill, scorning both thee and me.
5 See how the Tyrannesse doth joy to see
The huge massacres which her eyes do make:
And humbled harts brings captives unto thee,
That thou of them mayst mightie vengeance take.
But her proud hart doe thou a little shake
10 And that high look, with which she doth comptroll
All this worlds pride, bow to a baser make,°   *mate*
And al her faults in thy black booke enroll.
That I may laugh at her in equall sort,[4]
As she doth laugh at me and makes my pain her sport.[5]

1. I.e., death-dealing.
2. Properly, the Hippocrene spring or fountain on Mt. Helicon; it was sacred to the nine Muses. "Helicon" represents the poet's inspiration; here it is also a metaphor for Heaven, whence his lady "derivéd is." Cf. *HB*, 106–'33, and "Aprill," 50–54, in the *Calender*.
3. Based on Petrarch, *Rime, ed. cit.,*

'21, which Wyatt had also imitated ("Behold, love, thy power how she despiseth"); but the description of the lady's tyrannical pride and power, and the concern to repair an essentially "unrighteous" situation in terms of appropriate justice, are Spenser's own.
4. I.e., in the same way.
5. An alexandrine; see also Sonnet 45.

Sonnet 22

This holy season[6] fit to fast and pray,
Men to devotion ought to be inclynd:
Therefore, I lykewise on so holy day,
For my sweet Saynt some service fit will find.[7]
5 Her temple fayre is built within my mind,
In which her glorious ymage placéd is,
On which my thoughts doo day and night attend
Lyke sacred priests that never thinke amisse.
There I to her as th'author of my blisse,
10 Will builde an altar to appease her yre:
And on the same my hart will sacrifise,
Burning in flames of pure and chast desyre:
The which vouchsafe O goddesse to accept,
Amongst thy deerest relicks to be kept.

Sonnet 28[8]

The laurell leafe, which you this day doe weare,
Gives me great hope of your relenting mynd:
For since it is the badg which I doe beare,[9]
Ye bearing it doe seeme to me inclind:
5 The powre thereof, which ofte in me I find,
Let it lykewise your gentle brest inspire
With sweet infusion, and put you in mind
Of that proud mayd, whom now those leaves attyre:
Proud Daphne scorning Phoebus lovely° fyre,   *loving*
10 On the Thessalian shore from him did flie:
For which the gods in theyr revengefull yre
Did her transforme into a laurell tree.
Then fly no more fayre love from Phoebus chace,
But in your brest his leafe and love embrace.

Sonnet 29

See how the stubborne damzell doth deprave°   *misinterpret*
My simple meaning with disdaynfull scorne:
And by the bay° which I unto her gave,   *laurel*
Accoumpts myselfe her captive quite forlorne.

6. I.e., the Lenten season.
7. The combination of religion and love has many precedents in Italian and (particularly) French love lyrics and sonnets, e.g., *Les Amours de Diane*, I. 43, by Philippe Desportes, and *Sonnets pour Helene*, II. 5, by Ronsard. Spenser, however, not content to compare his lady with a goddess, likens her particularly to a "Saynt," in keeping with his regard for spiritual beauty in woman. Cf. *Epithalamion*, 185–203.
8. This and the following sonnet combine elements from classical poetry and from that of the French Renaissance. Ovid tells how Daphne, seeking to escape from Apollo, was changed into a laurel tree (*Metamorphoses*, I. 452–567); Ronsard, fixing on Ovid's allusion to the laurel wreath accorded victorious generals, centers the eleventh of his *Sonnets . . . pour Astrée* on the connection of the laurel with his lady's pride.
9. I.e., the sign of the poet, of whose art Apollo was the patron.

5   "The bay," quoth she, "is of the victours borne,
    Yielded them by the vanquisht as theyr meeds,[1]
    And they therewith doe poetes heads adorne,
    To sing the glory of their famous deedes."
    But sith she will the conquest challeng needs,[2]
10   Let her accept me as her faithfull thrall,
    That her great triumph which my skill exceeds,
    I may in trump of fame blaze° over all.   *proclaim*
    Then would I decke her head with glorious bayes,
    And fill the world with her victorious prayse.

Sonnet 44

    When those renouméd noble Peres of Greece,
    Thrugh stubborn pride amongest themselves did jar°   *disagree*
    Forgetfull of the famous golden fleece,
    Then Orpheus[3] with his harp theyr strife did bar.°   *check*
5   But this continuall cruell civill warre,
    The which my selfe against my selfe doe make:
    Whilest my weak powres of passions warreid° arre,   *assailed*
    No skill can stint° nor reason can aslake.°   *stop/assuage*
    But when in hand my tunelesse harp I take,
10   Then doe I more augment my foes despight:°   *spite*
    And griefe renew, and passions doe awake
    To battaile, fresh against my selfe to fight.
    Mongst whome the more I seeke to settle peace,
    The more I fynd their malice to increase.

Sonnet 45

    Leave lady in your glasse of christall clene,°   *pure*
    Your goodly selfe for evermore to vew:
    And in my selfe, my inward selfe I meane,
    Most lively lyke behold your semblant °trew.   *likeness*
5   Within my hart, though hardly it can shew
    Thing so divine to vew of earthly eye,
    The fayre Idea[4] of your celestiall hew,°   *form*
    And every part remaines immortall:
    And were it not that through your cruelty,
10   With sorrow dimméd and deformd it were,

1. Rewards; cf. *Metamorphoses*, I. 560–561.
2. I.e., but since she must needs claim the victory.
3. Cf. *The Faerie Queene*, IV.x.58, and note. For the account of Orpheus's power to calm dissension among the Argonauts, Spenser probably relied on Natalis Comes, *op. cit.*, VII. 14.
4. I.e., mental image; not "Idea" in a specifically Platonic sense. While the octave is broadly Platonic in conception, mirror conceits of this type are often a feature of French and Italian sonnets and love lyrics. Lines 9–12 of the sestet may reflect the influence of Tasso, *Rime*, 169 (in Torquato Tasso, *Opere*, ed. B. Maier [Milan, 1963], 5 vols., I); but the conclusion is Spenser's own.

The goodly ymage of your visnomy,°   *countenance*
Clearer then christall would therein appere.
But if your selfe in me ye playne will see,
Remove the cause by which your fayre beames darkned be.

Sonnet 53

The Panther[5] knowing that his spotted hyde
Doth please all beasts, but that his looks them fray,°   *terrify*
Within a bush his dreadfull head doth hide,
To let them gaze whylest[6] he on them may pray.°   *prey*
5 Right so my cruell fayre with me doth play,
For with the goodly semblant° of her hew°   *appearance/form*
She doth allure me to mine owne decay,°   *ruin*
And then no mercy will unto me shew.
Great shame it is, thing so divine in view,
10 Made for to be the worlds most ornament,
To make the bayte her gazers to embrew,
Good shames to be to ill an instrument.
But mercy doth with beautie best agree,
As in theyr maker ye them beste may see.

Sonnet 54[7]

Of this worlds Theatre in which we stay,
My love lyke the Spectator ydly sits
Beholding me that all the pageants° play,   *roles*
Disguysing diversly my troubled wits.
5 Sometimes I joy when glad occasion fits,
And mask in myrth lyke to a Comedy:
Soone after when my joy to sorrow flits,
I waile and make my woes a Tragedy.
Yet she beholding me with constant eye,
10 Delights not in my merth nor rues° my smart: *pities*
But when I laugh she mocks, and when I cry
She laughes, and hardens evermore her hart.
What then can move her? if nor merth nor mone,
She is no woman, but a sencelesse stone.

Sonnet 67

Lyke as a huntsman after weary chace,
Seeing the game from him escapt away,
Sits downe to rest him in some shady place,

---

5. Ll. 1–4 derive substantially from Pliny, *op. cit.*, VIII. xxiii.
6. Until.

7. Cf. the comments of Louis Martz on this sonnet, in his essay in this edition.

With panting hounds beguiléd of their pray:
5   So after long pursuit and vaine assay,°   *attempt*
When I all weary had the chace forsooke,
The gentle deare returnd the selfe-same way,
Thinking to quench her thirst at the next brooke.
There she beholding me with mylder looke,
10 Sought not to fly, but fearelesse still did bide:
Till I in hand her yet halfe trembling tooke,
And with her owne goodwill hir fyrmely tyde.
Strange thing me seemd to see a beast so wyld,
So goodly wonne with her owne will beguyld.

Sonnet 68

Most glorious Lord of lyfe, that on this day,[8]
Didst make thy triumph over death and sin:
And having harrowd hell, didst bring away
Captivity thence captive us to win:[9]
5   This joyous day, deare Lord, with joy begin,
And grant that we for whom thou diddest dye
Being with thy deare blood clene washt from sin,[1]
May live for ever in felicity.
And that thy love we weighing worthily,
10 May likewise love thee for the same againe:
And for thy sake that all lyke deare didst buy,
With love may one another entertayne.[2]
So let us love, deare love, lyke as we ought,
Love is the lesson which the Lord us taught.

Sonnet 71

I joy to see how in your drawen work,[3]
Your selfe unto the Bee ye doe compare;
And me unto the Spyder that doth lurke,
In close awayt[4] to catch her unaware.
5   Right so your selfe were caught in cunning snare
Of a deare foe, and thralléd to his love:
In whose streight° bands ye now captivéd are   *strict*
So firmely, that ye never may remove.
But as your worke is woven all about,[5]

---

8. Easter Sunday.
9. Before the resurrection, Christ descended into hell and brought away those deserving salvation: "When he ascended up on high, he led captivity captive. . . . he also descended first into the lower parts of the earth . . . He that descended is the same also that ascended up far above all heavens, that he might fill all things . . . " (Ephesians iv. 8–10).

1. "Jesus Christ . . . that loved us, and washed us from our sins in his own blood" (Revelation i. 5).
2. "This is my commandment, That ye love one another, as I have loved you" (John xv. 12).
3. Tapestry work, done by drawing out the threads of warp and woof to form patterns.
4. I.e., secret ambush.
5. Cf. Textual Notes.

10 With woodbynd flowers and fragrant Eglantine:
So sweet your prison you in time shall prove,°   *find*
With many deare delights bedeckéd fyne.
And all thensforth eternall peace shall see,
Betweene the Spyder and the gentle Bee.

Sonnet 72[6]

Oft when my spirit doth spred her bolder winges,
In mind to mount up to the purest sky:
It down is weighd with thoght of earthly things
And clogd° with burden of mortality,   *encumbered*
5 Where when that soverayne beauty it doth spy,
Resembling heavens glory in her light:
Drawne with sweet pleasures bayt, it back doth fly,
And unto heaven forgets her former flight.
There my fraile fancy fed with full delight,
10 Doth bath in blisse and mantleth[7] most at ease:
Ne thinks of other heaven, but how it might
Her harts desire with most contentment please.
Hart need not wish none other happinesse,
But here on earth to have such hevens blisse.

Sonnet 75

One day I wrote her name upon the strand,°   *beach*
But came the waves and washéd it away:
Agayne I wrote it with a second hand,
But came the tyde, and made my paynes his pray.°   *prey*
5 "Vayne man," sayd she, "that doest in vaine assay,
A mortall thing so to immortalize,
For I my selve shall lyke to this decay,
And eek my name bee wypéd out lykewize."
"Not so," quod° I, "let baser things devize°   *quoth/contrive*
10 To dy in dust, but you shall live by fame:
My verse your vertues rare shall eternize,
And in the hevens wryte your glorious name.
Where whenas death shall all the world subdew,
Our love shall live, and later life renew."

Sonnet 79

Men call you fayre, and you doe credit° it,   *believe*
For that your selfe ye dayly such doe see:
But the trew fayre,° that is the gentle wit,   *beauty*

6. Although the first five lines of this sonnet appear to be based on Tasso, *Rime, ed. cit.,* 67, the thought and imagery of Spenser's poem are thereafter steadily more independent of the Italian model; and the "anti-Platonic" conclusion is Spenser's own.
7. I.e., (in a term from hawking), stretches wings and legs, to ease them.

And vertuous mind, is much more praysd of me.
5 For all the rest, how ever fayre it be,
Shall turne to nought and loose that glorious hew:°   *form*
But onely that is permanent and free
From frayle corruption, that doth flesh ensew.°   *pursue*
That is true beautie: that doth argue you
10 To be divine and borne of heavenly seed:
Derived from that fayre Spirit, from whom al true
And perfect beauty did at first proceed.[8]
He onely fayre, and what he fayre hath made,
All other fayre lyke flowres untymely fade.

Sonnet 89[9]

Lyke as the Culver° on the baréd bough,   *dove*
Sits mourning for the absence of her mate:
And in her songs sends many a wishfull vow,
For his returne that seemes to linger late;
5 So I alone now left disconsolate,
Mourne to my selfe the absence of my love:
And wandring here and there all desolate,
Seek with my playnts to match that mournful dove:
Ne joy of ought that under heaven doth hove,°   *abide*
10 Can comfort me, but her owne joyous sight:
Whose sweet aspect both God and man can move,
In her unspotted pleasauns° to delight.   *pleasantness*
Dark is my day, whyles her fayre light I mis,
And dead my life that wants° such lively blis.   *lacks*

Epithalamion[1]

Ye learned sisters[2] which have oftentimes
Beene to me ayding, others to adorne:
Whom ye thought worthy of your gracefull rymes,
That even the greatest did not greatly scorne
5 To heare theyr names sung in your simple layes,
But joyéd in theyr prayse.[3]
And when ye list your owne mishaps to mourne,
Which death, or love, or fortunes wreck did rayse,
Your string could soone to sadder tenor° turne,   *mood*
10 And teach the woods and waters to lament
Your dolefull dreriment.°   *grief*

---

8. I.e., the Holy Spirit, from which
Heavenly Beauty itself is derived. Cf.
HHB, 13.
9. Sonnet 88 in some editions.
1. "On the bed chamber," from Latin
and Greek; the first use of the term
in English.
2. The nine Muses.

3. For example, the "Aprill" eclogue
in *The Shepheardes Calender;* much of
The Faerie Queene (especially the in-
troductory stanzas to each Book) might
also be cited. Lines 7–11 may refer to
poems in Spenser's *Complaints,* e.g.,
The Teares of the Muses and *The
Ruines of Time.*

Now lay those sorrowfull complaints aside,
And having all your heads with girland crownd,
Helpe me mine owne loves prayses to resound,°   celebrate
15 Ne let the same of° any be envide: by
So Orpheus[4] did for his owne bride,
So I unto my selfe alone will sing,
The woods shall to me answer and my Eccho ring.

Early before the worlds light giving lampe,
20 His golden beame upon the hils doth spred,
Having disperst the nights unchearefull dampe,
Doe ye awake, and with fresh lusty hed,[5]
Go to the bowre° of my belovéd love,   chamber
My truest turtle dove,
25 Bid her awake; for Hymen[6] is awake,
And long since ready forth his maske to move,
With his bright Tead° that flames with many a flake,°   torch/spark
And many a bachelor to waite on him,
In theyr fresh garments trim.
30 Bid her awake therefore and soone her dight,°   dress
For lo the wishéd day is come at last,
That shall for al the paynes and sorrowes past,
Pay to her usury of long delight:
And whylest she doth her dight,
35 Doe ye to her of joy and solace° sing,   pleasure
That all the woods may answer and your eccho ring.

Bring with you all the Nymphes that you can heare[7]
Both of the rivers and the forrests greene:
And of the sea that neighbours to her neare,
40 Al with gay girlands goodly wel beseene.[8]
And let them also with them bring in hand,
Another gay girland
For my fayre love of lillyes and of roses,
Bound truelove wise with a blew silke riband.[9]
45 And let them make great store of bridale poses,°   posies
And let them eeke° bring store of other flowers   also
To deck the bridale bowers.
And let the ground whereas her foot shall tread,
For feare the stones her tender foot should wrong
50 Be strewed with fragrant flowers all along,
And diapred lyke the discolored mead.[1]
Which done, doe at her chamber dore awayt,

4. Cf. *The Faerie Queene*, IV.x.58, and note.
5. I.e., vigor.
6. The god of marriage, and the presiding deity at wedding processions (or "maskes"); traditionally, he bore a flaming torch; cf. Catullus, *Ode 61*, 1–15.

7. I.e., that can hear you.
8. I.e., attractively adorned.
9. Symbolizing the fidelity of true love.
1. I.e., diversely adorned like the vari-colored meadows.

For she will waken strayt,°   *straightway*
The whiles doe ye this song unto her sing,
55   The woods shall to you answer and your Eccho ring.

Ye Nymphes of Mulla[2] which with carefull heed,
The silver scaly trouts doe tend full well,
And greedy pikes which use therein to feed,
(Those trouts and pikes all others doo excell)
60   And ye likewise which keepe the rushy lake,
Where none doo fishes take,
Bynd up the locks the which hang scatterd light,
And in his waters which your mirror make,
Behold your faces as the christall bright,
65   That when you come whereas my love doth lie,
No blemish she may spie.
And eke ye lightfoot mayds which keepe the deere,[3]
That on the hoary mountayne use to towre,[4]
And the wylde wolves which seeke them to devoure,[5]
70   With your steele darts doo chace from comming neer
Be also present heere,
To helpe to decke her and to help to sing,
That all the woods may answer and your eccho ring.

Wake, now my love, awake;[6] for it is time,
75   The Rosy Morne long since left Tithones[7] bed,
All ready to her silver coche to clyme,
And Phoebus gins to shew his glorious hed.
Hark how the cheerefull birds do chaunt theyr laies
And carroll of loves praise.
80   The merry Larke hir mattins° sings aloft,   *morning song*
The thrush replyes, the Mavis descant playes,[8]
The Ouzell° shrills, the Ruddock° warbles soft,   *blackbird/robin*
So goodly all agree with sweet consent,
To this dayes merriment.
85   Ah my deere love why doe ye sleepe thus long,
When meeter° were that ye should now awake,   *more fitting*
T'awayt the comming of your joyous make,°   *mate*
And hearken to the birds lovelearnéd song,
The deawy leaves among.
90   For they of joy and pleasance to you sing,
That all the woods them answer and theyr eccho ring.

2. The river Awbeg, near Spenser's Irish estate of Kilcolman; cf. the note on *Mutabilitie*, vi. 41.
3. Cf. Textual Notes.
4. A term from hawking, meaning "to soar or sail aloft"; here, "to frequent high places."
5. Cf. *Mutabilitie*, vi. 55, and note.

6. Cf. The Song of Solomon ii. 10–13.
7. The husband of Aurora, goddess of the dawn; cf. Homer, *Iliad*, XI. 1–2.
8. I.e., the thrush carols the melody. Such bird consorts were conventional in medieval poetry; cf. Chaucer's *Romance of the Rose*, 655–668.

My love is now awake out of her dreame,
And her fayre eyes like stars that dimméd were
With darksome cloud, now shew theyr goodly beams
95 More bright then Hesperus[9] his head doth rere.
Come now ye damzels, daughters of delight,
Helpe quickly her to dight,
But first come ye fayre houres[1] which were begot
In Joves sweet paradice, of Day and Night,
100 Which doe the seasons of the yeare allot,
And al that ever in this world is fayre
Doe make and still° repayre.   *continually*
And ye three handmayds of the Cyprian Queene,[2]
The which doe still adorne her beauties pride,
105 Helpe to addorne my beautifullest bride:
And as ye her array, still throw betweene°   *at intervals*
Some graces to be seene,
And as ye use to Venus, to her sing,
The whiles the woods shal answer and your eccho ring.

110 Now is my love all ready forth to come,
Let all the virgins therefore well awayt,
And ye fresh boyes that tend upon her groome
Prepare your selves; for he is comming strayt.
Set all your things in seemely good aray
115 Fit for so joyfull day,
The joyfulst day that ever sunne did see.
Faire Sun, shew forth thy favourable ray,
And let thy lifull° heat not fervent be   *life-giving*
For feare of burning her sunshyny face,
120 Her beauty to disgrace.°   *mar*
O fayrest Phoebus, father of the Muse,[3]
If ever I did honour thee aright,
Or sing the thing, that mote° thy mind delight,   *might*
Doe not thy servants simple boone° refuse,   *request*
125 But let this day let this one day be myne,
Let all the rest be thine.
Then I thy soverayne prayses loud wil sing,
That all the woods shal answer and theyr eccho ring.

Harke how the Minstrels gin to shrill aloud
130 Their merry Musick that resounds from far,

9. The evening star.
1. For the birth and parentage of the Hours, cf. the note on *Mutabilitie*, vii. 45; Spenser drew on Natalis Comes (*Mythologiae*, IV. 16) for the assertion that the Hours control the seasons and preserve natural beauty in every form. Cf. also A. Kent Hieatt, *Short Time's Endless Monument* . . . (New York, 1960), 32–41.
2. I.e., the Graces (Aglaia, Euphrosyne, and Thalia), attendant on Venus, who was worshipped in the ancient world principally on the islands of Cyprus and Cytherea.
3. Spenser usually follows Hesiod (*Theogony*, 77) in making the Muses daughters of Jove; but the assertion that Apollo was their sire, while it may reflect another authority or commentary, is quite characteristic of the poet's willingness to invent his own mythology, or freely elaborate upon established myth.

The pipe, the tabor, and the trembling Croud,[4]
That well agree withouten breach or jar.°   *discord*
But most of all the Damzels doe delite,
When they their tymbrels° smyte,   *tambourines*
135 And thereunto doe daunce and carrol sweet,
That all the sences they doe ravish quite,
The whyles the boyes run up and downe the street,
Crying aloud with strong confuséd noyce,
As if it were one voyce.
140 *Hymen iô Hymen, Hymen*[5] they do shout,
That even to the heavens theyr shouting shrill
Doth reach, and all the firmament doth fill,
To which the people standing all about,
As in approvance doe thereto applaud
145 And loud advaunce her laud,[6]
And evermore they *Hymen Hymen* sing,
That al the woods them answer and theyr eccho ring.

Loe where she comes along with portly° pace,   *stately*
Lyke Phoebe[7] from her chamber of the East,
150 Arysing forth to run her mighty race,[8]
Clad all in white, that seemes° a virgin best.   *suits*
So well it her beseemes that ye would weene
Some angell she had beene.
Her long loose yellow locks lyke golden wyre,
155 Sprinckled with perle, and perling[9] flowres a tweene,
Doe lyke a golden mantle her attyre,
And being crownéd with a girland greene,
Seeme lyke some mayden Queene.[1]
Her modest eyes abashéd to behold
160 So many gazers, as on her do stare,
Upon the lowly ground affixéd are.
Ne dare lift up her countenance too bold,
But blush to heare her prayses sung so loud,
So farre from being proud.[2]
165 Nathlesse° doe ye still loud her prayses sing.   *nevertheless*
That all the woods may answer and your eccho ring.

---

4. I.e., bagpipe (probably, in view of *The Faerie Queene*, VI. x. 18), drum, and fiddle, the instruments of Irish popular music.
5. The ritual cry at weddings; cf. the recurrent refrain in Catullus, *Ode 61.*
6. I.e., sing her praises.
7. Diana, the virginal goddess of the moon.
8. Cf. Psalms xix. 5: "Which is as a bridegroom coming out of his chamber, and rejoiceth as a strong man to run a race." But Spenser, as in *The Faerie Queene*, III, is concerned primarily to emphasize the mysterious power of

virginity, particularly of female chastity.
9. Winding; or, possibly, lacework flowers.
1. An aptly graceful allusion to Queen Elizabeth. In *Amoretti*, 74, Spenser pays court to the significant influence on his life and career exerted by "three Elizabeths": his mothèr, the Queen, and his future bride.
2. Perhaps an allusion to earlier stages of the poet's courtship, recorded in the first sixty sonnets of *Amoretti*, in which the lover recurrently complains of his lady's cruel pride.

Tell me ye merchants daughters did ye see
So fayre a creature in your towne before,
So sweet, so lovely, and so mild as she,
170 Adornd with beautyes grace and vertues store,°   *wealth*
Her goodly eyes lyke Saphyres shining bright,
Her forehead yvory white,
Her cheekes lyke apples which the sun hath rudded,° *reddened*
Her lips lyke cherryes charming men to byte,
175 Her brest like to a bowle of creame uncrudded,° *uncurdled*
Her paps lyke lyllies budded,
Her snowie necke lyke to a marble towre,[3]
And all her body like a pallace fayre,
Ascending uppe with many a stately stayre,
180 To honors seat and chastities sweet bowre.[4]
Why stand ye still ye virgins in amaze,
Upon her so to gaze,
Whiles ye forget your former lay to sing,
To which the woods did answer and your eccho ring.

185 But if ye saw that which no eyes can see,
The inward beauty of her lively spright,[5]
Garnisht with heavenly guifts of high degree,
Much more then would ye wonder at that sight,
And stand astonisht lyke to those which red°   *saw*
190 Medusaes mazeful hed.[6]
There dwels sweet love and constant chastity,
Unspotted fayth and comely womanhood,
Regard of honour and mild modesty,
There vertue raynes as Queene in royal throne,
195 And giveth lawes alone.
The which the base affections[7] doe obay,
And yeeld theyr services unto her will,
Ne thought of thing uncomely° ever may   *unbecoming*
Thereto approch to tempt her mind to ill.
200 Had ye once seene these her celestial threasures,
And unrevealéd pleasures,
Then would ye wonder and her prayses sing,
That al the woods should answer and your echo ring.

Open the temple gates unto my love,
205 Open them wide that she may enter in,[8]

3. "Thy neck is as a tower of ivory"
(Song of Solomon vii. 4). The scrip-
tural allusion is appropriately placed,
concluding the catalogue of physical
attractions (for which Spenser draws
on the conventions of classical and
Renaissance precedents), and looking
on to the account of a beauty far more
significantly powerful and directive.
4. I.e., to the head, seat of reason and
of the "higher faculties" generally.

5. I.e., living spirit; soul.
6. All who looked directly on the
Gorgon Medusa (whose hair had been
changed into serpents by Pallas Athena)
were turned to stone: cf. Ovid, *Meta-
morphoses*, IV. 780–781.
7. I.e., the lower emotions; the pas-
sions.
8. "Open yee the gates, that the
righteous nation which keepeth the truth
may enter in" (Isaiah xxvi. 2).

And all the postes adorne as doth behove,[9]
And all the pillours deck with girlands trim,
For to recyve this Saynt with honour dew,
That commeth in to you.
210 With trembling steps and humble reverence,
She commeth in, before th'almighties vew,
Of her ye virgins learne obedience,
When so ye come into those holy places,
To humble your proud faces;
215 Bring her up to th'high altar, that she may
The sacred ceremonies there partake,
The which do endlesse matrimony make,
And let the roring Organs loudly play
The praises of the Lord in lively notes,
220 The whiles with hollow throates
The Choristers the joyous Antheme sing,
That al the woods may answere and their eccho ring.

Behold whiles she before the altar stands
Hearing the holy priest that to her speakes
225 And blesseth her with his two happy hands,[1]
How the red roses flush up in her cheekes,
And the pure snow with goodly vermill° stayne,   *vermilion*
Like crimsin dyde in grayne,[2]
That even th'Angels which continually,
230 About the sacred Altare doe remaine,
Forget their service and about her fly,
Ofte peeping in her face that seemes more fayre,
The more they on it stare.
But her sad° eyes still fastened on the ground,   *grave*
235 Are governéd with goodly modesty,
That suffers not one looke to glaunce awry,
Which may let in a little thought unsownd.°   *immodest*
Why blush ye love to give to me your hand,
The pledge of all our band?°   *bond*
240 Sing ye sweet Angels, Alleluya sing,
That all the woods may answere and your eccho ring.

Now al is done; bring home the bride againe,
Bring home the triumph of our victory,
Bring home with you the glory of her gaine,[3]

9. I.e., adorn the doorposts, as is fitting. The symbolic decoration of doorposts (for example, with the myrtle, sacred to Venus) was a feature of nuptial ceremonies in ancient times. The scriptural echoes of lines 204–205 are, it seems, deliberately juxtaposed with the poet's frank acceptance of "pagan" customs as appropriately conjoined with this Christian occasion:

Epithalamion, permeated with Spenser's Christian humanism, furnishes many such instances of the poet's willingness to entertain classical and Christian elements in concert. Cf. esp. 242–260, 409–426.
1. I.e., hands which bestow happiness by virtue of the priest's blessing.
2. I.e., thoroughly; fast.
3. I.e., the glory of having gained her.

245 With joyance bring her and with jollity.
Never had man more joyfull day then this,
Whom heaven would heape with blis.
Make feast therefore now all this live long day,
This day for ever to me holy is,
250 Poure out the wine without restraint or stay,
Poure not by cups, but by the belly full,
Poure out to all that wull,°   *will*
And sprinkle all the postes and wals with wine,[4]
That they may sweat, and drunken be withall.
255 Crowne ye God Bacchus with a coronall,°   *garland*
And Hymen also crowne with wreathes of vine,
And let the Graces daunce unto the rest;
For they can doo it best:
The whiles the maydens doe theyr carroll sing,
260 To which the woods shal answer and theyr eccho ring.

Ring ye the bels,[5] ye yong men of the towne,
And leave your wonted° labors for this day: *usual*
This day is holy; doe ye write it downe,
That ye for ever it remember may.
265 This day the sunne is in his chiefest hight,
With Barnaby the bright,[6]
From whence declining daily by degrees,
He somewhat loseth of his heat and light,
When once the Crab behind his back he sees.[7]
270 But for this time it ill ordainéd was,
To chose the longest day in all the yeare,
And shortest night, when longest fitter weare:
Yet never day so long, but late° would passe.   *at last*
Ring ye the bels, to make it weare away,
275 And bonefiers make all day,
And daunce about them, and about them sing
That all the woods may answer, and your eccho ring.

Ah when will this long weary day have end,
And lende me leave to come unto my love?
280 How slowly do the houres theyr numbers spend?
How slowly does sad Time his feathers move?[8]
Hast thee O fayrest Planet[9] to thy home

4. A traditional practice at Roman weddings.
5. Perhaps a reference to the arduous and controlled practice (or art) of "change ringing," distinct from bell ringing of a merely random and enthusiastic nature. If so, the passage is appropriately placed in the structure of the poem, which from this point becomes steadily more calm and quiet in tone.
6. St. Barnabas's Day (June 11, Old Style), the longest day of the year.
7. In mid-June, the sun moves from the astrological "house" of Cancer, the Crab, to that of Leo, the Lion.
8. The consonantal arrangement of lines 280–281 adds special force to their content.
9. I.e., the sun, in the Ptolemaic system one of the planets circling about the earth.

Within the Westerne fome:
Thy tyred steedes long since have need of rest.
285 Long though it be, at last I see it gloome,°   grow dark
And the bright evening star with golden creast
Appeare out of the East.
Fayre childe of beauty, glorious lampe of love
That all the host of heaven in rankes doost lead,
290 And guydest lovers through the nightés dread,
How chearefully thou lookest from above,
And seemst to laugh atweene thy twinkling light
As joying in the sight
Of these glad many which for joy doe sing,
295 That all the woods them answer and their echo ring.

Now ceasse ye damsels your delights forepast;
Enough is it, that all the day was youres:
Now day is doen, and night is nighing fast:
Now bring the Bryde into the brydall boures.
300 Now night is come, now soone her disaray,
And in her bed her lay;
Lay her in lillies and in violets,
And silken courteins over her display,
And odourd sheetes, and Arras coverlets.[1]
305 Behold how goodly my faire love does ly
In proud humility;
Like unto Maia,[2] when as Jove her tooke,
In Tempe, lying on the flowry gras,
Twixt sleepe and wake, after she weary was,
310 With bathing in the Acidalian brooke.
Now it is night, ye damsels may be gon,
And leave my love alone,
And leave likewise your former lay to sing:
The woods no more shal answere, nor your echo ring.

315 Now welcome night, thou night so long expected,
That long daies labour doest at last defray,°   pay for
And all my cares, which cruell love collected,
Hast sumd in one, and cancelléd for aye:
Spread thy broad wing over my love and me,
320 That no man may us see,
And in thy sable mantle us enwrap,
From feare of perrill and foule horror free.
Let no false treason seeke us to entrap,
Nor any dread disquiet once annoy

1. Especially fine tapestry spreads.
2. The most beautiful of Atlas's seven daughters (who were subsequently stellified as the Pleiades), Maia became the mother of Mercury (Hermes) by Jove, according to the Homeric *Hymn to Hermes*. Spenser's allusions to Tempe and "the Acidalian brooke" are his own, although he may have been influenced by a hint in Natalis Comes's version of the story (*Mythologiae*, V. 5).

325   The safety of our joy:
     But let the night be calme and quietsome,
     Without tempestuous storms or sad afray:°   *fear*
     Lyke as when Jove with fayre Alcmena lay,
     When he begot the great Tirynthian groome:
330   Or lyke as when he with thy selfe did lie,
     And begot Majesty.[3]
     And let the mayds and yongmen cease to sing:
     Ne let the woods them answer, nor theyr eccho ring.

     Let no lamenting cryes, nor dolefull teares,
335   Be heard all night within nor yet without:
     Ne let false whispers, breeding hidden feares,
     Breake gentle sleepe with misconceivéd dout.°   *fear*
     Let no deluding dreames, nor dreadful sights
     Make sudden sad affrights;
340   Ne let housefyres, nor lightnings helpelesse harmes,
     Ne let the Pouke,[4] nor other evill sprights,
     Ne let mischivous witches with theyr charmes,
     Ne let hob Goblins, names whose sence we see not,
     Fray° us with things that be not.   *terrify*
345   Let not the shriech Oule,[5] nor the Storke be heard:
     Nor the night Raven that still° deadly yels,   *continually*
     Nor damnéd ghosts cald up with mighty spels,
     Nor griesly vultures make us once affeard:
     Ne let th'unpleasant Quyre of Frogs still croking
350   Make us to wish theyr choking.
     Let none of these theyr drery accents sing;
     Ne let the woods them answer, nor theyr eccho ring.

     But let stil Silence trew night watches keepe,
     That sacred peace may in assurance rayne,
355   And tymely sleep, when it is tyme to sleepe,
     May poure his limbs forth on your pleasant playne,
     The whiles an hundred little wingéd loves,[6]
     Like divers fethered doves,
     Shall fly and flutter round about your bed,
360   And in the secret darke, that none reproves,
     Their prety stealthes shal worke, and snares shal spread

3. According to classical tradition, Hercules (who dwelt at Tiryns, in Argolis) was the son of Jove and Alcmena: cf. Ovid, *Metamorphoses*, IX. 23–26. The assertion that Jove and Night begot Majesty is Spenser's own; Ovid identifies the parents of Majesty as Honor and Reverence (*Fasti*, V. 23).
4. Puck, in general terms to be identified with the Robin Goodfellow of English fairy lore, but here essentially a malicious spirit of evil.
5. The screech owl, like the raven a bird of ill omen. The stork is catalogued with these and other "unclean" birds in Deuteronomy xiv. 12–18; while Ovid speaks of the bird as one that "claps its rattling bill" (*Metamorphoses*, VI. 97).
6. I.e., cupids. Such playfully mischievous figures, reflecting the influence of "Anacreontic" poetry, often appear in Elizabethan sonnets and love lyrics. Spenser may have had his eye on Du Bellay's *Epithalame*, 307–310.

To filch away sweet snatches of delight,
Conceald through covert night.
Ye sonnes of Venus, play your sports at will,
365 For greedy pleasure, carelesse of your toyes,°   amorous dallying
Thinks more upon her paradise of joyes,
Then what ye do, albe it good or ill.
All night therefore attend your merry play,
For it will soone be day:
370 Now none doth hinder you, that say or sing,
Ne will the woods now answer, nor your Eccho ring.

Who is the same, which at my window peepes?
Or whose is that faire face, that shines so bright,
Is it not Cinthia,[7] she that never sleepes,
375 But walkes about high heaven al the night?
O fayrest goddesse, do thou not envy
My love with me to spy:
For thou likewise didst love, though now unthought,[8]
And for a fleece of woll,° which privily,   wool
380 The Latmian shephard once unto thee brought,
His pleasures with thee wrought.
Therefore to us be favorable now;
And sith of wemens labours thou hast charge,[9]
And generation goodly dost enlarge,
385 Encline thy will t'effect our wishfull vow,
And the chast wombe informe with timely seed,
That may our comfort breed:
Till which we cease our hopefull hap[1] to sing,
Ne let the woods us answere, nor our Eccho ring.

390 And thou great Juno, which with awful might   awe-inspiring
The lawes of wedlock still dost patronize,
And the religion° of the faith first plight   sanctity
With sacred rites hast taught to solemnize:
And eeke for comfort often callèd art
395 Of women in their smart,°   pains
Eternally bind thou this lovely° band,   loving
And all thy blessings unto us impart.
And thou glad Genius,[2] in whose gentle hand,
The bridale bowre and geniall bed[3] remaine,
400 Without blemish or staine,

7. Goddess of the moon, who took as her lover Endymion, a shepherd tending his flocks on the slopes of Mt. Latmus, in Asia Minor. Virgil names Pan as the goddess's lover (*Georgics*, III. 391–393); but Spenser in this instance is following the fifth-century commentary on Virgil compiled by Servius, a Latin grammarian.
8. I.e., though not thought of now.

9. Both Diana and Juno were invoked under the name of Lucina, goddess who "brings to light," and therefore presides over childbirth.
1. I.e., the lot for which we hope.
2. The god of birth and generation; cf. *The Faerie Queene*, II. xii. 47 and note.
3. I.e., generative as well as pleasant bed (with a play on the god's name).

And the sweet pleasures of theyr loves delight
With secret ayde doest succour and supply,
Till they bring forth the fruitfull progeny,
Send us the timely fruit of this same night.
405 And thou fayre Hebe,[4] and thou Hymen free,
Grant that it may so be.
Til which we cease your further prayse to sing,
Ne any woods shal answer, nor your Eccho ring.

And ye high heavens, the temple of the gods,
410 In which a thousand torches flaming bright
Doe burne, that to us wretched earthly clods,
In dreadful darknesse lend desiréd light;
And all ye powers which in the same[5] remayne,
More then we men can fayne,°   imagine
415 Poure out your blessing on us plentiously,
And happy influence upon us raine,
That we may raise a large posterity,
Which from the earth, which they may long possesse,
With lasting happinesse,
420 Up to your haughty pallaces may mount,
And for the guerdon° of theyr glorious merit   reward
May heavenly tabernacles there inherit,
Of blessed Saints for to increase the count.
So let us rest, sweet love, in hope of this,[6]
425 And cease till then our tymely joyes to sing,
The woods no more us answer, nor our eccho ring.

Song made in lieu of many ornaments,
With which my love should duly have bene dect,°   adorned
Which cutting off through hasty accidents,[7]
430 Ye would not stay your dew time to expect,°   await
But promist both to recompens,
Be unto her a goodly ornament,
And for short time an endlesse moniment.°   memorial

4. Daughter of Juno, and cup-bearer to the gods; Spenser, following Ovid as well as the Renaissance mythographers, regards her primarily as the goddess of youth and rejuvenation (cf. *Metamorphoses*, IX. 397–401).
5. I.e., in the heavens. "Powers" apparently refers both to the ninefold hierarchy of heavenly beings (cf. *HHB*, 85–98) and to the various "influences" exerted by the stars on the lives of men.
6. Cf. Textual Notes.
7. Perhaps merely an allusion to some unexpected change in plan touching the date of Spenser's marriage; but cf. A. Kent Hieatt, *op. cit.*, for an ingenious alternative explanation in terms of the poem's structure.

Editor's Note

The sonnet sequence *Amoretti* and the marriage ode *Epithalamion* were published together in 1595: this circumstance, given the fact that Spenser's view of love and marriage in these poems is generally agreeable to that set out in Book III of *The Faerie Queene*, has encouraged some readers to assume that the poems refer specifically and consistently to Spenser's courtship of Elizabeth Boyle, a courtship culminating in their marriage, at Cork, during the summer of 1594. In fact, a number of sonnets in the *Amoretti* were very probably written at a much earlier period (one or two, perhaps, even before 1580); the marriage, after all, was Spenser's second; nor is it unlikely that the sonnet sequence includes poems originally composed to honor other ladies (e.g., Elizabeth, Lady Carey, whom Spenser had on several occasions complimented in verse). Further, there is no allusion in the sequence to marriage, which concludes with four sonnets lamenting the lady's absence, and which is followed, rather curiously, by four brief pieces in the light Anacreontic manner (i.e., the style and mood characteristic of lyrics by the Greek poet Anacreon [c. 563–478 B.C.], and by his imitators). To question a narrowly biographical reading of the *Amoretti*, of course, is not to deny that the sonnets in their published form steadily emphasize the spiritual and physical attributes of one lady (who is at once a more central and a more elaborately portrayed figure than the lady of Sidney's *Astrophel and Stella*), or that Spenser has artfully combined the conventions of Petrarchan practice with a structural time scheme based on the seasonal cycle: the movement from New Year's Day on to spring and to the Lenten season (Sonnet 22), and thence to another year's beginning and to a second Eastertide (Sonnet 68), may possibly glance at the period of Spenser's own courtship, but it is more probably a device to create an effect of verisimilitude. Again, while the four "complaining" sonnets that bring the *Amoretti* to a close perhaps refer to actual events, literary convention might equally account for their position at the end of the sequence. In short, as Northrop Frye observes, regarding the persistent efforts to link "Shakespeare the man" with his sonnets, "we should be better advised to start with the assumption that the sonnets are poetry, therefore written within a specific literary tradition and a specific literary genre."[1]

It has been said that, "as a professed poet in the 1590's, Spenser was almost bound to write a sonnet-sequence; and, by the same token, to write it in a certain way."[2] The influence of Petrarch's songs and sonnets had of course touched English poetry some years before Spenser's time, notably in the sonnets and love lyrics of Wyatt and Surrey; and the appearance in 1582 of Thomas Watson's *Hekatompathia* gave some indication of a renewed interest in Petrarchan modes by the younger English poets. But the Petrarchan sonnet cycle in English became truly "fashionable" with the appearance, in 1591, of a pirated edition of Sidney's *Astrophel and Stella* (which had existed in manuscript since 1582): Daniel's *Delia*, Constable's *Diana*, and Drayton's *Idea's Mirror* are merely the most notable among the considerable number of sequences published before 1595. To speak generally, these

1. "How True A Twain," *Fables of Identity* (New York, 1963), p. 91.

2. *Daphnaida and Other Poems*, ed. W. L. Renwick (London, 1929), p. 192.

English poets (in common with such figures as Desportes and Ronsard) were struck by Petrarch's linked arrangement of economically rhymed sonnets, by his delicate fusing of Neo-Platonic elements with frank recognition of the lady's sensual attraction, and by his varied and dramatic employment of the "conceit" (an ingenious and elaborate metaphor central in the structure of a poem) as an instrument with which to explore the paradoxical nature of love. In their turn, each of the more gifted English sonneteers developed an individual manner: Sidney adapted Petrarchan materials with particular subtlety, preferring rhyme schemes that retained something of the Italian discipline, demonstrating everywhere his concern for different kinds of dramatic effect, and, in substance, pressing beyond Petrarch to analyze the stress and conflict informing human love. It is remarkable that Spenser, especially in the light of his early associations with Sidney, should have produced a sonnet sequence that owes relatively little to the versification, general presentation of love, and structural arrangement of *Astrophel and Stella*.

Critics of the *Amoretti*, dazzled by the achievements of Shakespeare and Sidney in this medium, have generally been quicker to praise Spenser's sequence as a whole than to admire the force or intensity of individual sonnets. That was to be expected, in view of the poet's attention to structural design: the movement of the turning year and the lover's effort to apprehend truly the nature of his lady's pride make two such threads, but within these larger patterns smaller groupings (e.g., Sonnets 28 and 29) reinforce and illustrate the central thrust of the sequence. And another reading, keyed to Sonnets 13 and 54, discovers yet more structural complexity in these poems (cf. the essay by Louis Martz, on p. 723 of this edition). But Spenser's achievement is not limited to his structural invention. While he probably drew the device of linked quatrains from Marot, his consistently skillful employment of these verse forms together with a closing couplet in the manner of Surrey (and Shakespeare), all within the five rhymes of Italian tradition, provided English poetry with a compact sonnet form well suited to the extended expression of a single idea (in the first twelve lines), followed by an epigrammatic concluding couplet. The Spenserian sonnet is also sufficiently flexible to permit the development of thought in three quatrains (cf. Sonnet 1), and even, on occasion, in the traditional octave-sestet structure generally favored by Sidney (as in Sonnet 10). In another regard, his use of the conceit, Spenser is not strikingly original, although he employs traditional conventions with easy mastery: Anacreontic "legions of loves with little wings" are here, together with the arbitrary "Lord of love" familiar in Ovidian tradition, and Sonnet 22 is cast in the terms of love-as-religion that appealed also to Ronsard and Desportes. Somewhat more individual is the poet's preference for analogies between various wild creatures (e.g., panther, tiger, deer) and his lady, in contexts which, at first rather ominous and limiting, eventually give promise of that higher reach of peaceful concord into which love's power may free men and women: Sonnet 71 is perhaps Spenser's most remarkable essay in this kind. The concern with three progressively higher realms of being is characteristic of Spenser's Christian humanism, recurrently in evidence throughout the *Amoretti*: convinced that the order of nature is not denied or ultimately cancelled by heavenly order, but that it reflects that higher order and directs man thence, the poet employs Neo-

Platonic as well as Christian terms to express his vision of love's force and meaning: in Sonnet 79 particularly, the two traditions seem to combine and fuse. The *Amoretti*, in fact, are significantly related to *Fowre Hymnes* (cf. the essay by William Nelson in this edition), as well as to the noble marriage ode with which they are usually associated.

The relationship of Spenser's *Epithalamion* to classical and Renaissance examples of the "epithalamic" convention (most influentially represented by the sixty-first and sixty-fourth odes of the Latin elegiac poet Catullus) has been definitively discussed by Thomas M. Greene, who draws attention also to Spenser's departure from conventional precedent in respect of versification, imagery, and structural design.[3] It remains chiefly to notice the structural analysis of *Epithalamion* set out in 1960 by A. Kent Hieatt.[4] In brief, he argues that the poem is structured in terms of time and its divisions: the twenty-four stanzas "in some fashion represent hours and are associated with the personified Hours who attend the bride"; the refrain, consistently positive for sixteen stanzas, is put negatively thereafter, an arrangement corresponding to the hours of light and darkness in southern Ireland at the summer solstice; there are 365 "long lines" (i.e., lines of five feet or more) in the poem. Perhaps the most intriguing aspect of this critic's proposal bears on the curious seven-line "envoy," ordinarily explained away on one or another biographical hypothesis, and the fact that the regular pattern of Spenser's rhyme scheme appears to be marred by the omission of a short line following line 424. By Hieatt's reading, these features are deliberately introduced by the poet, who recognized that (by the Ptolemaic system) when the sphere of the fixed stars completes its orbit of 360 degrees, that of the sun still falls short by one degree: "Spenser ostensibly ends his poem in its 359th long line [i.e., line 426], symbolizing in one way the incomplete circle of the sun at the time when the heavenly hours and the celestial sphere are completing theirs, but . . . the envoy, adding six more long lines, expresses symbolically what this daily incompleteness of the sun entails: the creation of the measure of the solar years of 365 days, symbolized by the 365 long lines of the poem including its [envoy]" (p. 46). As for the irregularity after line 424, there are sixty-eight short lines in the poem (corresponding to the total of seasons, months, and weeks); just as the "symbolic lack at the annual level" is made good by the six long lines of the envoy, so the short 431st line, "But promist both to recompens," dramatically makes Spenser's poetic circle just. These proposals may surprise some: yet one cannot too lightly pass over the evidence (chiefly in early poems) of Spenser's concern with numerically organized poetical structure, not to mention the pervasive and continuing influence of medieval number symbolism in the Renaissance. However that may be, *Epithalamion* seems at length to tower most delightfully above the attentions of all the the most sensitive critics; and W. L. Renwick may reasonably have the last word: "In the hands of the born master and trained craftsman the Humanist method of teaching is vindicated by this perfect reconciliation of Italian form, Roman matter, Irish landscape, literary tradition and personal emotion . . ."[5]

3. "Spenser and the Epithalamic Convention," *CL*, IX (1957), 215–228.
4. Cf. esp. 8–16, 31–59.

5. *Daphnaida and Other Poems*, 204–205.

Fowre Hymnes

To the Right Honorable and Most Vertuous Ladies, the Ladie Margaret Countesse of Cumberland, and the Ladie Marie Countesse of Warwicke.[1]

Having in the greener times of my youth, composed these former two Hymnes in the praise of Love and beautie, and finding that the same too much pleased those of like age and disposition, which being too vehemently caried with that kind of affection, do rather sucke out poyson to their strong passion, then hony to their honest delight, I was moved by the one of you two most excellent Ladies, to call in the same. But being unable so to doe, by reason that many copies thereof were formerly scattered abroad, I resolved at least to amend, and by way of retractation to reforme them, making in stead of those two Hymnes of earthly or naturall love and beautie, two others of heavenly and celestiall. The which I doe dedicate joyntly unto you two honorable sisters, as to the most excellent and rare ornaments of all true love and beautie, both in the one and the other kinde, humbly beseeching you to vouchsafe the patronage of them, and to accept this my humble service, in lieu of the great graces and honourable favours which ye dayly shew unto me, untill such time as I may by better meanes yeeld you some more notable testimonie of my thankfull mind and dutifull devotion.

And even so I pray for your happinesse. Greenwich this first of September. 1596.

Your Honors most bounden ever in all humble service.

Ed. Sp.

An Hymne in Honour of Love

> Love, that long since hast to thy mighty powre,
> Perforce subdude my poore captivéd hart,
> And raging now therein with restlesse stowre,°   *tumult*
> Doest tyrannize in everie weaker part;[2]

---

1. Spenser had previously praised both of these ladies in *Colin Clouts Come Home Againe*, 492–507; he had complimented Anne (not Mary), Countess of Warwick, in *The Ruines of Time*, 244–245. The view that Lady War- wick's Puritan sympathies significantly influenced Spenser's "retractation" is not now accorded much scholarly support: cf. the Editor's Note.
2. In lines 1–49, Spenser follows classical and Renaissance practice in his

5   Faine would I seeke to ease my bitter smart,
     By any service I might do to thee,
     Or ought that else might to thee pleasing bee.

     And now t'asswage the force of this new flame,
     And make thee more propitious in my need,
10   I meane to sing the praises of thy name,
     And thy victorious conquests to areed;°   *proclaim*
     By which thou madest many harts to bleed
     Of mighty Victors, with wyde wounds embrewed,°   *stained*
     And by thy cruell darts to thee subdewed.

15   Onely I feare my wits enfeebled late,
     Through the sharpe sorrowes, which thou hast me bred,° *caused*
     Should faint, and words should faile me, to relate
     The wondrous triumphs of thy great godhed.
     But if thou wouldst vouchsafe to overspred
20   Me with the shadow of thy gentle wing,
     I should enabled be thy actes to sing.

     Come then, O come, thou mightie God of love,
     Out of thy silver bowres and secret blisse,
     Where thou doest sit in Venus lap above,
25   Bathing thy wings in her ambrosiall kisse,
     That sweeter farre then any Nectar is;
     Come softly, and my feeble breast inspire
     With gentle furie,° kindled of thy fire.   *poetical rapture*

     And ye sweet Muses, which have often proved°   *felt*
30   The piercing points of his avengefull darts;
     And ye faire Nimphs, which oftentimes have loved
     The cruell worker of your kindly° smarts,   *natural*
     Prepare your selves, and open wide your harts,
     For to receive the triumph of your glorie,
35   That made you merie oft, when ye were sorie.

     And ye faire blossomes of youths wanton° breed, *unrestrained*
     Which in the conquests of your beautie bost,
     Wherewith your lovers feeble eyes you feed,
     But sterve° their harts, that needeth nourture most, *starve*
40   Prepare your selves, to march amongst his host,
     And all the way this sacred hymne do sing,
     Made in the honor of your Soveraigne king.

     Great god of might, that reignest in the mynd,
     And all the bodie to thy hest° doest frame,   *command*

---

apostrophe to and invocation of Cupid, the god of love, presented here as a cruel tyrant proudly triumphing over his abject captives. The theme, central in Ovid's *Amores*, I. ii, is elaborately developed by Petrarch in his *Trionfi.* Cf. *The Faerie Queene,* III. xii, and the note to the Argument of that Canto.

45 Victor of gods, subduer of mankynd,[3]
  That doest the Lions and fell° Tigers tame,   *fierce*
  Making their cruell rage thy scornefull game,
  And in their roring taking great delight;
  Who can expresse the glorie of thy might?

50 Or who alive can perfectly declare,
  The wondrous cradle of thine infancie?[4]
  When thy great mother Venus first thee bare,
  Begot of Plentie and of Penurie,
  Though elder then thine owne nativitie;
55 And yet a chyld, renewing still thy yeares
  And yet the eldest of the heavenly Peares.[5]

  For ere this worlds still° moving mightie masse,   *continually*
  Out of great Chaos ugly prison crept,[6]
  In which his goodly face long hidden was
60 From heavens view, and in deepe darknesse kept,
  Love, that had now long time securely slept
  In Venus lap, unarméd then and naked,
  Gan reare his head, by Clotho[7] being wakéd.

  And taking to him wings of his owne heate,
65 Kindled at first from heavens life-giving fyre,
  He gan to move out of his idle seate,
  Weakely at first, but after with desyre
  Lifted aloft, he gan to mount up hyre,
  And like fresh Eagle, make his hardie° flight   *bold*
70 Through all that great wide wast, yet wanting° light. *lacking*

  Yet wanting light to guide his wandring way,
  His owne faire mother, for all creatures sake,
  Did lend him light from her owne goodly ray:[8]

3. Although Plato is ultimately the source for this idea (cf. *Symposium*, 178a), Spenser probably drew directly on the widely influential *Commentary on Plato's Symposium*, by Marsilio Ficino (1433–1499): "Certainly He is great to whose rule men and gods they say are all subject: for according to the ancients, the gods love like men, which is what Orpheus and Hesiod mean when they say that the minds of mortals and immortals alike are ruled over by Love" (I. 2). The translation quoted in these notes is that by Sears Jayne (Columbia, Mo., 1944).
4. The account, in lines 50–98, of creation and of the created universe, relates to the account presented in *HB*, 29–56, somewhat as material cause to formal cause.
5. I.e., the gods. The myth of Love's begetting by Plenty and Penury appears in Plato's *Symposium*, 203b–c;

for the paradox of Love's age, Spenser probably drew on Ficino's *Commentary*, V. 10, rather than on the *Symposium*, 178b, 195c. Like Natalis Comes (*Mythologiae*, IV. 14), he is quite willing to combine the relatively "orthodox" view that Venus was Cupid's mother with the logically incompatible account given by the *Symposium*.
6. Ficino discusses the sources of this idea (e.g., in Hesiod, *Theogony*, 116–122), and the subsequent "nourishing" and "completion" of love, in the *Commentary*, I. 3.
7. Clotho, one of the three Fates; while Lachesis is concerned with the past, and Atropos with the future, Clotho's concern is with "the things that are" (*Republic*, 617c).
8. Ficino describes the "infusion of the divine light" [into formless substance] as "the nourishing of love" (*Commentary*, I. 3).

Then through the world his way he gan to take,
75 The world that was not till he did it make;
Whose sundrie parts he from them selves did sever,
The which before had lyen confuséd ever.[9]

The earth, the ayre, the water, and the fyre,
Then gan to raunge them selves in huge array,[1]
80 And with contrary forces to conspyre
Each against other, by all meanes they may,
Threatning their owne confusion and decay:
Ayre hated earth, and water hated fyre,
Till Love relented° their rebellious yre.   *abated*

85 He then them tooke, and tempering goodly well
Their contrary dislikes with lovéd meanes,
Did place them all in order, and compell
To keepe them selves within their sundrie raines,°   *domains*
Together linkt with Adamantine chaines;
90 Yet so, as that in every living wight
They mixe themselves, and shew their kindly° might.[2]   *natural*

So ever since they firmely have remained,
And duly well observéd his beheast;
Through which now all these things that are contained
95 Within this goodly cope,° both most and least   *canopy*
Their being have, and dayly are increast,
Through secret sparks of his infuséd fyre,
Which in the barraine cold he doth inspyre.°   *breathe into*

Thereby they all do live, and movéd are
100 To multiply the likenesse of their kynd,
Whilest they seeke onely, without further care,
To quench the flame, which they in burning fynd:
But man, that breathes a more immortall mynd,
Not for lusts sake, but for eternitie,
105 Seekes to enlarge his lasting progenie.[3]

For having yet in his deducted° spright,   *reduced*
Some sparks remaining of that heavenly fyre,

9. Lines 76–84 recall the opening of Ovid's *Metamorphoses*, especially I. 18–25.
1. I.e., formidable martial order.
2. "Wherefore, all the parts of the world . . . are bound to each other by a certain mutual affection so that it may justly be said that love is a perpetual knot and binder of the world . . . " (Ficino, *Commentary*, III. 3).
3. The thought of lines 103–112 recalls that of Plato in the *Symposium*, 208b: "This is how every mortal creature perpetuates itself. It cannot, like the divine, be still the same throughout eternity; it can only leave behind new life to fill the vacancy that is left in its species by obsolescence. This . . . is how the body and all else that is temporal partakes of the eternal: there is no other way. And so it is no wonder that every creature prizes its own issue, since the whole creation is inspired by this love, this passion for immortality" (trans. M. Joyce, in *Collected Dialogues* . . . , ed. Edith Hamilton and H. Cairns [New York, 1961]. Cf. also Ficino, *Commentary*, VI. 11.

He is enlumind with that goodly light,
Unto like goodly semblant° to aspyre: *likeness*
110 Therefore in choice of love, he doth desyre
That° seemes on earth most heavenly, to embrace,   *that which*
That same is Beautie, borne of heavenly race.

For sure of all, that in this mortall frame
Containéd is, nought more divine doth seeme,
115 Or that resembleth more th'immortall flame
Of heavenly light, then Beauties glorious beame.[4]
What wonder then, if with such rage° extreme   *passion*
Fraile men, whose eyes seek heavenly things to see,
At sight thereof so much enravisht bee?

120 Which well perceiving, that imperious boy,
Doth therwith tip his sharp empoisnéd darts;[5]
Which glancing through the eyes with countenance coy,
Rest not, till they have pierst the trembling harts,
And kindled flame in all their inner parts,
125 Which suckes the blood, and drinketh up the lyfe
Of carefull° wretches with consuming griefe.   *careworn*

Thenceforth they playne,° and make ful piteous mone   *complain*
Unto the author of their balefull bane;[6]
The daies they waste, the nights they grieve and grone,
130 Their lives they loath, and heavens light disdaine;
No light but that, whose lampe doth yet remaine
Fresh burning in the image of their eye,
They deigne to see, and seeing it still° dye.   *continually*

The whylst thou tyrant Love doest laugh and scorne
135 At their complaints, making their paine thy play;
Whylest they lye languishing like thrals forlorne,
The whyles thou doest triumph in their decay,°   *destruction*
And otherwhyles, their dying to delay,
Thou doest emmarble° the proud hart of her,   *turn to marble*
140 Whose love before their life they doe prefer.

So hast thou often done (ay me the more)
To me thy vassall, whose yet bleeding hart,
With thousand wounds thou mangled hast so sore

4. Cf. Ficino, *Commentary*, VI. 9.
5. The account in lines 120–133 of the role played in love by the eyes is close to that in Sir Thomas Hoby's translation (pub. 1561) of Castiglione's *Il Cortegiano* (1528): cf. *Three Renaissance Classics* . . . , ed. B. A. Milligan (N.Y., 1953), 524–525. However, by Spenser's time such descriptions of the lover's plight were characteristic of love poetry in the Petrarchan manner. For those concerned to establish more narrowly the Platonic character of *Fowre Hymnes*, this passage corresponds to the lover's attraction to the beauty of one individual body (*Symposium,* 210), and to the first stage of the Neo-Platonic "ladder" of love discussed by the fifteenth-century humanists Benivieni (in his *Canzona della Amore celeste et divino*) and Pico della Mirandola (in his commentary on Benivieni's poem).
6. I.e., deadly ruin.

That whole remaines scarse any little part,
145 Yet to augment the anguish of my smart,
Thou hast enfrosen her disdainefull brest,
That no one drop of pitie there doth rest.

Why then do I this honor unto thee,
Thus to ennoble thy victorious name,
150 Since thou doest shew no favour unto mee,
Ne once move ruth° in that rebellious Dame,   *pity*
Somewhat to slacke the rigour of my flame?
Certes° small glory doest thou winne hereby,   *surely*
To let her live thus free, and me to dy.

155 But if thou be indeede, as men thee call,
The worlds great Parent, the most kind preserver
Of living wights, the soveraine Lord of all,[7]
How falles it then, that with thy furious fervour,
Thou doest afflict as well the not deserver,
160 As him that doeth thy lovely heasts[8] despize,
And on thy subjects most doest tyrannize?

Yet herein eke° thy glory seemeth more,[9]   *also*
By so hard handling those which best thee serve,
That ere thou doest them unto grace restore,
165 Thou mayest well trie if they will ever swerve,
And mayest them make it better to deserve;
And having got it, may it more esteeme.
For things hard gotten, men more dearely deeme.

So hard those heavenly beauties be enfyred,°   *hardened by fire*
170 As things divine, least passions doe impresse,[1]
The more of stedfast mynds to be admyred,
The more they stayéd° be on stedfastnesse: *fixed*
But baseborne mynds such lamps regard the lesse,
Which at first blowing take not hastie fyre,
175 Such fancies feele no love, but loose desyre.[2]

For love is Lord of truth and loialtie,
Lifting himselfe out of the lowly dust,

7. "But if Love creates everything, He also preserves everything, for the functions of creation and preservation always belong together" (Ficino, *Commentary*, III. 2).
8. I.e., commands to love.
9. Lines 162–244 in some degree counterbalance the emphasis of lines 120–161: distinguishing initially between true love and "loose desyre," Spenser places particular stress on the power of "that sweet passion" to refine and inspire the lover.

1. I.e., as things divine are least affected or influenced by passion.
2. Cf. the distinction drawn by Ficino between the man who is "too eager for procreation and gives up contemplation, or is immoderately desirous of copulation with women," and he who "praises, of course, the beauty of the body, but through it . . . contemplates the more excellent beauty of the soul, the mind, and God . . . " (*Commentary*, II. 7).

On golden plumes up to the purest skie,
Above the reach of loathly sinfull lust,
180 Whose base affect° through cowardly distrust   *passion*
Of his weake wings, dare not to heaven fly,
But like a moldwarpe° in the earth doth ly.   *mole*

His dunghill thoughts, which do themselves enure°   *accustom*
To dirtie drosse, no higher dare aspyre,
185 Ne can his feeble earthly eyes endure
The flaming light of that celestiall fyre,
Which kindleth love in generous desyre,
And makes him mount above the native might
Of heavie earth, up to the heavens hight.

190 Such is the powre of that sweet passion,
That it all sordid basenesse doth expell,
And the refynéd mynd doth newly fashion
Unto a fairer forme, which now doth dwell
In his high thought, that would it selfe excell;
195 Which he beholding still with constant sight,
Admires the mirrour of so heavenly light.[3]

Whose image printing in his deepest wit,
He thereon feeds his hungrie fantasy,°   *imagination*
Still full, yet never satisfyde with it,
200 Like Tantale, that in store doth stervéd ly:[4]
So doth he pine in most satiety,
For nought may quench his infinite desyre,
Once kindled through that first conceivéd fyre.

Thereon his mynd affixéd wholly is,
205 Ne thinks on ought, but how it to attaine;
His care, his joy, his hope is all on this,
That seemes in it all blisses to containe,
In sight whereof, all other blisse seemes vaine.
Thrise happie man, might he the same possesse;
210 He faines° himselfe, and doth his fortune blesse.   *imagines*

And though he do not win his wish to end,[5]
Yet thus farre happie he him selfe doth weene,
That heavens such happie grace did to him lend,

3. "A lover imprints a likeness of the loved one upon his soul and so the soul of the lover becomes a mirror in which is reflected the image of the loved one" (Ficino, *Commentary*, II. 8). For some readers, this stanza marks a distinctly second stage of the "Platonic ascent," corresponding to that indicated by Benivieni and Pico; yet Spenser may have meant merely that the lover, in whose mind his mis-tress's image firmly rests, no longer requires the actual presence of the loved one, although he continues to love her individual beauty.
4. I.e., that starves in the midst of plenty. For the figure of Tantalus, cf. *The Faerie Queene*, II. vii. 57, and note.
5. I.e., although he does not achieve his desire.

As thing on earth so heavenly, to have seene,
215 His harts enshrinéd saint, his heavens queene,
Fairer then° fairest, in his fayning° eye,   *than/longing*
Whose sole aspect[6] he counts felicitye.

Then forth he casts° in his unquiet thought,   *considers*
What he may do, her favour to obtaine;[7]
220 What brave exploit, what perill hardly° wrought,   *with difficulty*
What puissant conquest, what adventurous paine,
May please her best, and grace unto him gaine:
He dreads no danger, nor misfortune feares,
His faith, his fortune, in his breast he beares.

225 Thou art his god, thou art his mightie guyde,
Thou being blind, letst him not see his feares,
But cariest him to that which he hath eyde,
Through seas, through flames, through thousand swords and speares:
Ne ought so strong that may his force withstand,
230 With which thou armest his resistlesse° hand.   *irresistible*

Witnesse Leander, in the Euxine waves,
And stout Aeneas in the Trojane fyre,
Achilles preassing through the Phrygian glaives,°   *swords*
And Orpheus daring to provoke the yre
235 Of damnéd fiends, to get his love retyre:[8]
For both through heaven and hell thou makest way,
To win them worship which to thee obay.

And if by all these perils and these paynes,
He may but purchase lyking in her eye,
240 What heavens of joy, then to himselfe he faynes,°   *fashions*
Eftsoones° he wypes quite out of memory,   *at once*
What ever ill before he did aby:°   *suffer*
Had it bene death, yet would he die againe,
To live thus happie as her grace to gaine.

245 Yet when he hath found favour to his will,
He nathemore° can so contented rest,   *never the more*
But forceth further on, and striveth still
T'approch more neare, till in her inmost brest,
He may embosomd bee, and lovéd best;

6. I.e., the mere sight of whom.
7. Lines 218–237 may reflect the influence of Phaedrus's eulogy of love in the *Symposium*, 178–180, or of Ficino's *Commentary*, I. 4; the passage also seems to echo Castiglione's recurrent reference, in *Il Cortegiano*, to the fierce courage that characterizes lovers generally.
8. I.e., to get his love (Eurydice) returned to him from the underworld.

Spenser significantly alters the list of classical lovers given in Plato and Ficino: he substitutes Leander and Aeneas for Alcestis, silently passes over the nature of Achilles's love for Patroclus, and reverses Plato's judgment on the conduct of Orpheus, reserving the final and climactic place for his allusion to that poet and musician.

₂₅₀ And yet not best, but to be loved alone:
For love can not endure a Paragone.°   *rival*

The feare whereof, O how doth it torment
His troubled mynd with more then hellish paine![9]
And to his fayning fansie represent
₂₅₅ Sights never seene, and thousand shadowes vaine,
To breake his sleepe, and waste his ydle braine;
Thou that hast never loved canst not beleeve,
Least part of th'evils which poore lovers greeve.

The gnawing envie, the hart-fretting feare,
₂₆₀ The vaine surmizes, the distrustfull showes,°   *appearances*
The false reports that flying tales doe beare,
The doubts, the daungers, the delayes, the woes,
The faynéd friends, the unassuréd foes,[1]
With thousands more then any tongue can tell,
₂₆₅ Doe make a lovers life a wretches hell.

Yet is there one more curséd then they all,
That cancker worme, that monster Gelosie,
Which eates the hart, and feedes upon the gall,
Turning all loves delight to miserie,
₂₇₀ Through feare of loosing his felicitie.
Ah Gods, that ever ye that monster placed
In gentle love, that all his joyes defaceth.°   *eclipsed*

By these, O Love, thou doest thy entrance make,
Unto thy heaven, and doest the more endeere,
₂₇₅ Thy pleasures unto those which them partake,
As after stormes when clouds begin to cleare,
The Sunne more bright and glorious doth appeare;
So thou thy folke, through paines of Purgatorie,
Dost beare unto thy blisse, and heavens glorie.

₂₈₀ There thou them placest in a Paradize
Of all delight, and joyous happie rest,
Where they doe feede on Nectar heavenly wize,[2]
With Hercules and Hebe,[3] and the rest
Of Venus dearlings,° through her bountie blest,   *darlings*
₂₈₅ And lie like Gods in yvorie beds arayd,
With rose and lillies over them displayd.°   *spread out*

9. The renewed emphasis of lines 245–272 on those subtle terrors that afflict the lover (while stemming directly from the very intensity of his ardor) reaches a climax with the monstrous image of Jealousy: the movement from "a wretches hell" to the "Paradize / Of all delight" is thereby given emphatically dramatic force.

1. I.e., those not certainly known to be foes.
2. I.e., in heavenly fashion.
3. Hebe became the wife of Hercules after the latter took his place among the gods (cf. Hesiod, *Theogony*, 950–953).

There with thy daughter Pleasure they doe play
Their hurtlesse sports, without rebuke or blame,
And in her snowy bosome boldly lay
290 Their quiet heads, devoyd of guilty shame,
After full joyance of their gentle game,
Then her they crowne their Goddesse and their Queene,
And decke with floures thy altars well beseene.

Ay me, deare Lord,[4] that ever I might hope,
295 For all the paines and woes that I endure,
To come at length unto the wishéd scope°   object
Of my desire; or might my selfe assure,
That happie port for ever to recure.°   recover
Then would I thinke these paines no paines at all,
300 And all my woes to be but penance small.

Then would I sing of thine immortall praise
An heavenly Hymne, such as the Angels sing,
And thy triumphant name then would I raise
Bove all the gods, thee onely honoring,
305 My guide, my God, my victor, and my king;
Till then, dread Lord, vouchsafe to take of me
This simple song, thus framed in praise of thee.

An Hymne in Honour of Beautie

Ah whither, Love, wilt thou now carrie mee?
What wontlesse° fury dost thou now inspire   unaccustomed
Into my feeble breast, too full of thee?[1]
Whylest seeking to aslake° thy raging fyre,   assuage
5 Thou in me kindlest much more great desyre,
And up aloft above my strength doest rayse
The wondrous matter[2] of my fyre to prayse.

That as I earst° in praise of thine owne name,   lately
So now in honour of thy Mother deare,[3]
10 An honourable Hymne I eke° should frame;   also
And with the brightnesse of her beautie cleare,
The ravisht harts of gazefull° men might reare,   gazing intently
To admiration of that heavenly light,
From whence proceeds such soule enchaunting might.

4. I.e., Cupid, to whom the expressions of line 305 (and the opening apostrophe and invocation of this *Hymne*) also refer.
1. This is that "form of possession or madness" which, according to Plato, stimulates the soul to "rapt passionate expression, especially in lyric poetry" (*Phaedrus*, 245a, trans. R. Hackforth, *ed. cit.*); according to Ficino, "by di-

vine madness, man is raised above the nature of man and passes over into God" (*Commentary*, VII. 13). As in *HL*, the opening section of this *Hymne* (lines 1–28) combines apostrophe and invocation, directed now to Venus, goddess of love.
2. I.e., beauty.
3. I.e., Venus.

15   Therto do thou great Goddesse, queene of Beauty,
      Mother of love, and of all worlds delight,
      Without whose soverayne grace and kindly dewty,
      Nothing on earth seems fayre to fleshly sight,
      Doe thou vouchsafe with thy love-kindling light
20   T'illuminate my dim and dulléd eyne,°   *eyes*
      And beautifie this sacred hymne of thyne.

      That both to thee, to whom I meane it most,
      And eke to her, whose faire immortall beame,
      Hath darted fyre into my feeble ghost,°   *spirit*
25   That now it wasted is with woes extreame,
      It may so please that she at length will streame
      Some deaw of grace, into my withered hart,
      After long sorrow and consuming smart.

      What time[4] this worlds great workmaister did cast°   *resolve*
30   To make al things, such as we now behold,
      It seemes that he before his eyes had plast
      A goodly Paterne, to whose perfect mould
      He fashioned them as comely as he could;
      That now so faire and seemely they appeare,
35   As nought may be amended any wheare.[5]

      The wondrous Paterne wheresoere it bee,
      Whether in earth layd up in secret store,°   *place*
      Or else in heaven, that no man may it see
      With sinfull eyes, for feare it to deflore,°   *desecrate*
40   Is perfect Beautie which all men adore,[6]
      Whose face and feature doth so much excell
      All mortal sence, that none the same may tell.

      Thereof as every earthly thing partakes,
      Or° more or lesse by influence divine,   *either*
45   So it more faire accordingly it makes,
      And the grosse matter of this earthly myne,[7]

4. I.e., when. In parallel with the structural arrangement of *HL*, lines 29–63 present a second, "formal," account of creation.
5. "The work of the creator, whenever he looks to the unchangeable and fashions the form and nature of his work after an unchangeable pattern, must necessarily be made fair and perfect" (*Timaeus*, 28 a–b; trans. B. Jowett, *ed. cit.*).
6. According to the Platonic "doctrine of reminiscence," they adore it because they had seen it while in a higher condition of being, before their imprisonment in the body (*Phaedrus*, 250a–c). Spenser does not subscribe to this theory, so that his position is logically contradictory; but the observation that "no man may it see / With sinfull eyes" illustrates his characteristic concern with moral virtue. Cf. line 166, and note.
7. So described because its darkness contrasts with heavenly light, and also because "celestiall powre" works upon the materials of "duller earth." Spenser may have drawn on Castiglione: "Beautie is the true monument and spoile of the victory of the soule, when she with heavenly influence beareth rule over martiall and grosse nature, and with her light overcommeth the darkenesse of the bodie" (*ed. cit.*, p. 601).

Which clotheth it, thereafter doth refyne,
Doing away the drosse which dims the light
Of that faire beame, which therein is empight.°   *implanted*

50 For through infusion of celestiall powre,
The duller earth it quickneth with delight,
And life-full spirits privily doth powre
Through all the parts, that to the lookers sight
They seeme to please.[8] That is thy soveraine might,
55 O Cyprian Queene,[9] which flowing from the beame
Of thy bright starre, thou into them doest streame.

That is the thing which giveth pleasant grace
To all things faire, that kindleth lively fyre,
Light of thy lampe, which shyning in the face,
60 Thence to the soule darts amorous desyre,
And robs the harts of those which it admyre,
Therewith thou pointest thy Sons poysned arrow,
That wounds the life, and wastes° the inmost marrow.   *devastates*

How vainely then doe ydle wits invent,[1]
65 That beautie is nought else, but mixture made
Of colours faire, and goodly temp'rament
Of pure complexions,[2] that shall quickly fade
And passe away, like to a sommers shade,
Or that it is but comely composition
70 Of parts well measurd, with meet° disposition.   *proper*

Hath white and red in it such wondrous powre,
That it can pierce through th'eyes unto the hart,
And therein stirre such rage and restlesse stowre,°   *tumult*
As nought but death can stint° his dolours smart?   *end*
75 Or can proportion of the outward part,
Move such affection in the inward mynd,
That it can rob both sense and reason blynd?

Why doe not then the blossomes of the field,
Which are arayd with much more orient° hew,   *brilliant*
80 And to the sense most daintie odours yield,

8. "Beauty is a kind of force or light, shining from Him through everything, first through the Angelic Mind, second through the World-Soul and the rest of the souls, third through Nature, and fourth through corporeal Matter. . . . the entire charm of the divine countenance, which is called universal beauty, is incorporeal, not only in the Angelic Mind and in the World-Soul, but also in the sight of the eyes. Nor do we love only this whole beauty all at once; but moved by our admiration, we love also its parts" (Ficino, *Commentary*, II. 5; V. 5).

9. I.e., Venus.
1. "There are some who think that beauty consists in a disposition of parts, or, to use their own language, size and proportion together with a certain agreeableness of colors. We do not agree with their opinion" (Ficino, *Commentary*, V. 3). Drawing significantly on Ficino, but glancing occasionally also at Castiglione, Spenser now proceeds to distinguish between what beauty is not and what it truly is (lines 64–140).
2. I.e., a perfectly matched bodily combination of the four "humours"; Spen-

Worke like° impression in the lookers vew?   *similar*
Or why doe not faire pictures like powre shew,
In which oftimes, we Nature see of° Art   *by*
Exceld, in perfect limming° every part.   *painting*

85 But ah, beleeve me, there is more then so
That workes such wonders in the minds of men.
I that have often proved,° too well it know;   *experienced*
And who so list the like assayes to ken,[3]
Shall find by tryall, and confesse it then,
90 That Beautie is not, as fond men misdeeme,°   *misjudge*
An outward shew of things, that onely seeme.

For that same goodly hew of white and red,
With which the cheekes are sprinckled, shal decay,
And those sweete rosy leaves so fairely spred
95 Upon the lips, shall fade and fall away
To that they were, even to corrupted clay.
That golden wyre, those sparckling stars so bright
Shall turne to dust, and loose their goodly light.

But that faire lampe,[4] from whose celestiall ray
100 That light proceedes, which kindleth lovers fire,
Shall never be extinguisht nor decay,
But when the vitall spirits doe expyre,
Unto her native planet shall retyre,[5]
For it is heavenly borne and can not die,
105 Being a parcell° of the purest skie.   *part*

For when the soule, the which derivéd was
At first, out of that great immortall Spright,[6]
By whom all live to love, whilome° did pas   *formerly*
Downe from the top of purest heavens hight,
110 To be embodied here, it then tooke light
And lively spirits from that fayrest starre,[7]
Which lights the world forth from his firie carre.

Which powre retayning still or° more or lesse,   *either*
When she in fleshly seede is eft enraced,[8]
115 Through every part she doth the same impresse,

---

ser is drawing on Ficino's allusion to "a temperate combination of the four elements" (*Commentary*, V. 6).
3. I.e., and whoever wishes to make the same trials.
4. I.e., that true beauty (which resides in the immortal soul).
5. According to Neo-Platonic doctrine, when the soul descends from heaven to assume a body, it receives "vitall spirits" from the sun. "Soul and body, naturally very different from each other,

are joined by the median, spirit, which is a certain very thin and clear vapor, created through the heat of the heart from the purest part of the blood; and thence diffused through all the parts. This spirit receives the powers of the soul and transfers them into the body" (Ficino, *Commentary*, VI. 6).
6. I.e., God.
7. I.e., the sun (Phoebus Apollo, whose fiery chariot daily traverses the sky: cf. Ovid, *Metamorphoses*, II. 58–73).
8. I.e., again implanted.

According as the heavens have her graced,
And frames her house, in which she will be placed,
Fit for her selfe, adorning it with spoyle
Of th'heavenly riches, which she robd erewhyle.

120 Therof it comes, that these faire soules, which have
The most resemblance of that heavenly light,
Frame to themselves most beautifull and brave°   *splendid*
Their fleshly bowre, most fit for their delight,
And the grosse matter by a soveraine might
125 Tempers so trim,° that it may well be seene,   *neatly*
A pallace fit for such a virgin Queene.[9]

So every spirit, as it is most pure,
And hath in it the more of heavenly light,
So it the fairer bodie doth procure
130 To habit° in, and it more fairely dight°   *dwell/adorn*
With chearefull grace and amiable sight.°   *appearance*
For of the soule the bodie forme doth take:
For soule is forme, and doth the bodie make.

Therefore where ever that thou doest behold
135 A comely corpse,° with beautie faire endewed,   *body*
Know this for certaine, that the same doth hold
A beauteous soule, with faire conditions thewed,[1]
Fit to receive the seede of vertue strewed.°   *scattered*
For all that faire is, is by nature good;
140 That is a signe to know the gentle blood.

Yet oft it falles,° that many a gentle mynd   *occurs*
Dwels in deforméd tabernacle drownd,
Either by chaunce, against the course of kynd,°   *nature*
Or through unaptnesse° in the substance fownd,   *inaptitude*
145 Which it assuméd of some stubborne grownd,
That will not yield unto her formes direction,
But is performed° with some foule imperfection.[2]   *made*

And oft it falles (ay me the more to rew)
That goodly beautie, albe° heavenly borne,   *although*

9. "The body is most like heaven, whose substance is temperate, and does not interfere by any excess of humors, with the soul's work of incarnation" (Ficino, *Commentary,* V. 6). Cf. also note to line 46.
1. I.e., conditioned with fair qualities.
2. Ficino observes that while one soul, "finding a suitable seed on the earth, may have shaped out" an appropriate body, another "may likewise even have begun a work, but because of the unsuitability of its material, its body will not have been carried out with such great fidelity to its pattern" (*Com-*

mentary, VI. 6). Castiglione, noting "the affinitie that beautie hath with goodnesse," accounts for the unchastity of some beautiful women by "ill bringing up, the continuall provocations of lovers, tokens, povertie, hope, deceites, feare, and a thousand other matters" (*ed. cit.,* p. 602); cf. lines 155–158. Somewhat as in *HL,* 173–189, a central concern of the poet in lines 141–189 is the contrast between lust, "that hellish fierbrand," and "gentle Love," with which "that celestiall ray" of beauty is appropriately matched.

150 Is foule abusd, and that celestiall hew,°   *form*
 Which doth the world with her delight adorne
 Made but the bait of sinne, and sinners scorne;
 Whilest every one doth seeke and sew° to have it, *entreat*
 But every one doth seeke, but to deprave it.

155 Yet nathemore° is that faire beauties blame, *never the more*
 But theirs that do abuse it unto ill:
 Nothing so good, but that through guilty shame
 May be corrupt, and wrested unto will.
 Nathelesse° the soule is faire and beauteous still, *nonetheless*
160 How ever fleshes fault it filthy make:
 For things immortall no corruption take.

 But ye faire Dames, the worlds deare ornaments,
 And lively images of heavens light,
 Let not your beames with such disparagements° *disgraceful actions*
165 Be dimd, and your bright glorie darkned quight;
 But mindfull still of your first countries sight,[3]
 Doe still preserve your first informéd° grace, *imparted*
 Whose shadow yet shynes in your beauteous face.

 Loath that foule blot, that hellish fierbrand,
170 Disloiall lust, faire beauties foulest blame,° *fault*
 That base affections, which your eares would bland,° *flatter*
 Commend to you by loves abuséd name;
 But is indeede the bondslave of defame,° *disgrace*
 Which will the garland of your glorie marre,
175 And quench the light of your bright shyning starre.

 But gentle Love, that loiall is and trew,
 Will more illumine your resplendent ray,
 And adde more brightnesse to your goodly hew,
 From light of his pure fire, which by like way
180 Kindled of yours, your likenesse doth display,
 Like as two mirrours by opposd reflexion,
 Doe both expresse the faces first impression.[4]

 Therefore to make your beautie more appeare,
 It you behoves to love, and forth to lay
185 That heavenly riches, which in you ye beare,
 That men the more admyre their fountaine may,
 For else what booteth° that celestiall ray, *avails*
 If it in darknesse be enshrinéd ever,
 That it of loving eyes be vewéd never?

3. I.e., the heavenly vision once theirs, now lost (cf. *Phaedrus*, 250a–c). Strictly speaking, however, Spenser does not concur with Plato in this regard.
4. "[The lover] loves, yet knows not what he loves . . . not realizing that his lover is as it were a mirror in which he beholds himself" (*Phaedrus*, 255d); "a lover imprints a likeness of the loved one upon his soul, and so the soul of the lover becomes a mirror in which is reflected the image of the loved one" (Ficino, *Commentary*, II. 8).

190 But in your choice of Loves, this well advize,°   *consider*
    That likest to your selves ye them select,
    The which your forms first sourse may sympathize,[5]
    And with like beauties parts be inly deckt:
    For if you loosely love without respect,°   *care*
195 It is no love, but a discordant warre,
    Whose unlike parts amongst themselves do jarre.°   *quarrel*

    For Love is a celestiall harmonie,
    Of likely harts composd of starres concent,[6]
    Which joyne together in sweete sympathie,
200 To worke ech others joy and true content,
    Which they have harbourd since their first descent
    Out of their heavenly bowres, where they did see
    And know ech other here beloved to bee.

    Then wrong it were that any other twaine
205 Should in loves gentle band° combynéd bee,   *bond*
    But those whom heaven did at first ordaine,
    And made out of one mould the more t'agree:
    For all that like the beautie which they see,
    Streight° do not love: for love is not so light,   *immediately*
210 As streight to burne at first beholders sight.[7]

    But they which love indeede, looke otherwise,
    With pure regard and spotlesse true intent,
    Drawing out of the object of their eyes,
    A more refynéd forme, which they present
215 Unto their mind, voide of all blemishment;
    Which it reducing to her first perfection,[8]
    Beholdeth free from fleshes frayle infection.

    And then conforming it unto the light,
    Which in it selfe it hath remaining still
220 Of that first Sunne, yet sparckling in his sight,
    Thereof he fashions in his higher skill,°   *understanding*
    An heavenly beautie to his fancies will,

5. I.e., may be in harmony with. Lines 190–259 describe, first in Neo-Platonic, then in more narrowly Petrarchan terms, the harmonious character of that true love foreordained in heaven.

6. I.e., of similar hearts brought together by the harmony of the stars. "Those who . . . are born under the same star, are so constituted, that the image of the more beautiful of the two flowing through the eyes into the soul of the other, corresponds to and agrees completely with a like image formed from its very generation both in the celestial body and in the inner part of the soul" (Ficino, *Commentary*, VI. 6).

7. Contrast Marlowe, *Hero and Leander*, I. 176: "Who ever lov'd, that lov'd not at first sight?"

8. I.e., restoring it (the form) to its pristine perfection. "The soul . . . compares the image [i.e., the image of the beloved's soul, transmitted through the eyes] with its own interior Idea, and if anything is lacking to the image to be a perfect representation of the . . . body, the soul restores it by reforming, and then loves the reformed image itself as its own work" (Ficino, *Commentary*, VI. 6). The thought of this stanza is substantially comparable with that of *HL*, 190–196.

And it embracing in his mind entyre,°   *inward*
The mirrour of his owne thought doth admyre.[9]

225 Which seeing now so inly faire to be,
As outward it appeareth to the eye,
And with his spirits proportion to agree,
He thereon fixeth all his fantasie,
And fully setteth° his felicitie,   *establishes*
230 Counting it fairer, then it is indeede,[1]
And yet indeede her fairenesse doth exceede.

For lovers eyes more sharply sighted bee
Then other mens, and in deare loves delight
See more then any other eyes can see,
235 Through mutuall receipt of beamés bright,
Which carrie privie° message to the spright,   *secret*
And to their eyes that inmost faire° display,   *beauty*
As plaine as light discovers dawning day.

Therein they see through amorous eye-glaunces,
240 Armies of loves[2] still flying too and fro,
Which dart at them their litle fierie launces,
Whom having wounded, backe againe they go,
Carrying compassion to their lovely foe;
Who seeing her faire eyes so sharpe effect,
245 Cures all their sorrowes with one sweete aspect.°   *look*

In which how many wonders doe they reede°   *perceive*
To their conceipt,° that others never see,   *fancy*
Now of her smiles, with which their soules they feede,
Like Gods with Nectar in their bankets free,
250 Now of her lookes, which like to Cordials bee;
But when her words embassade° forth she sends,   *on an embassy*
Lord how sweete musicke that unto them lends.°   *affords*

Sometimes upon her forhead they behold
A thousand Graces masking in delight,

9. "In the course of time, [lovers] do not see the loved one in his true image received through the senses, but they see him in an image already remade by the soul according to the likeness of its own Idea, an image which is more beautiful than the body itself. Moreover, they wish to see continuously that body whence the image first came . . . to the eye and spirit, which like a mirror receive images when the body is present and lose them when it is absent, the presence of the beautiful body itself is necessary for them to shine continuously with its brilliance and be charmed and pleased . . . and the soul, being very compliant with them, is led to desire the same thing" (Ficino, *Commentary*, VI. 6). These stanzas recall the earlier stages of that "stayre of love" described by Castiglione (*ed. cit.*, 610–613); but the parallel need not be too fervently pressed.
1. "Lovers are so deceived that they think a person is more beautiful than he is" (Ficino, *Commentary*, VI. 6); "through the vertue of imagination [the lover] shall fashion with himselfe that beautie much more faire than it is in deede" (*Il Cortegiano, ed. cit.*, p. 610).
2. I.e., cupids. The extended Petrarchan fancy of lines 232–245 may have been based on a broadly similar passage in *Il Cortegiano* (*ed. cit.*, 524–525).

255 Sometimes within her eye-lids they unfold
Ten thousand sweet belgards,° which to their sight   *loving glances*
Doe seeme like twinckling starres in frostie night:
But on her lips, like rosy buds in May,
So many millions of chaste pleasures play.

260 All those, O Cytherea,[3] and thousands more
Thy handmaides be, which do on thee attend
To decke thy beautie with their dainties store,
That may it more to mortall eyes commend,
And make it more admyred of foe and frend;
265 That in mens harts thou mayst thy throne enstall
And spred thy lovely kingdome[4] over all.

Then *Iö tryumph*,[5] O great beauties Queene,
Advaunce° the banner of thy conquest hie,   *raise*
That all this world, the which thy vassals beene,
270 May draw to thee, and with dew fealtie,
Adore the powre of thy great Majestie,
Singing this Hymne in honour of thy name,
Compyld by me, which thy poore liegeman° am.   *vassal*

In lieu° whereof graunt, O great Soveraine,   *return*
275 That she whose conquering beautie doth captive
My trembling hart in her eternall chaine,
One drop of grace at length will to me give,
That I her bounden thrall by her may live,
And this same life, which first fro me she reaved,°   *took away*
280 May owe to her, of whom I it received.

And you faire Venus dearling, my deare dread,[6]
Fresh flowre of grace, great Goddesse of my life,
When your faire eyes these fearefull lines shal read,
Deigne to let fall one drop of dew reliefe,
285 That may recure° my harts long pyning griefe,   *cure*
And shew what wondrous powre your beauty hath,
That can restore a damnéd wight from death.

An Hymne of Heavenly Love

Love, lift me up upon thy golden wings,
From this base world unto thy heavens hight,
Where I may see those admirable things,
Which there thou workest by thy soveraine might,

3. I.e., Venus. In the final stanzas of this *Hymne*, as in its opening passages, the poet praises the goddess of love and (significantly) the particular beauty of that lady to whom his love is given.
4. I.e., kingdom of love.

5. The chant of those captives who tremble submissively before the God of Love (cf. Ovid, *Amores*, I. ii. 34).
6. I.e., sovereign mistress (who inspires reverence and awe).

5 Farre above feeble reach of earthly sight,
That I thereof an heavenly Hymne may sing
Unto the god of Love, high heavens king.[1]

Many lewd layes (ah woe is me the more)
In praise of that mad fit, which fooles call love,
10 I have in th'heat of youth made heretofore,
That in light wits did loose affection° move.[2]   *passion*
But all those follies now I do reprove,
And turnéd have the tenor of my string,[3]
The heavenly prayses of true love to sing.

15 And ye that wont with greedy vaine desire
To reade° my fault, and wondring° at my flame,   *regard/marveling*
To warme your selves at my wide sparckling fire,
Sith° now that heat is quenchéd, quench my blame,   *since*
And in her ashes shrowd my dying shame:
20 For who my passéd follies now pursewes,
Beginnes his owne, and my old fault renewes.

Before this worlds great frame, in which al things
Are now containd, found any being place
Ere flitting Time could wag his eyas° wings   *newly fledged*
25 About that mightie bound,[4] which doth embrace
The rolling Spheres, and parts their houres by space,
That high eternall powre, which now doth move
In all these things, moved in it selfe by love.[5]

It loved it selfe, because it selfe was faire;
30 (For faire is loved;) and of it selfe begot

1. I.e., Christ. Spenser probably intended these lines to recall but also to correct the emphasis of *HL*, 301–305. While the language of *HHL* often recalls that of Neo-Platonic thought, the substance of this *Hymne* is essentially Christian. Cf. the notes to line 107 and line 284. Structurally, the opening of the *Hymne* (lines 1–21) diverges from those of *HL* and *HB* in that it is largely taken up with the "retractation" of 8–21; the invocation proper is reserved for a later stanza (43–49).
2. While lines 8–14 may be read as a "retractation" of earlier work, such formal recantations (following Petrarchan precedent) were often no more than a literary convention.
3. I.e., have altered the pitch of my instrument.
4. I.e., the sphere of the fixed stars, which encloses the spheres of the planets; by its degrees the "planetary" (or "unequal") hours were measured.

5. Structurally parallel to earlier accounts, in *HL* and *HB*, of the creative process, this third passage (22–126) is substantially more inclusive, dealing with the initial creation, the fall of Lucifer and his legions, and the subsequent creation and fall of man. Spenser may perhaps be thinking of creation in terms of "efficient" cause, defined by Aristotle as "the primary source of the change or coming to rest; e.g. . . . the father is cause of the child, and generally what makes of what is made and what causes change of what is changed" (*Physics*, II. 3; in *The Basic Works of Aristotle*, ed. R. McKeon [New York, 1941], p. 241). Lines 27–31 combine the Christian view of God as love with the Platonic doctrine that "Love is . . . a longing not for the beautiful itself, but for the conception and generation that the beautiful effects. . . . To love is to bring forth upon the beautiful" (*Symposium*, 206b–e).

Like to it selfe his eldest sonne and heire,
Eternall, pure, and voide of sinfull blot,
The firstling of his joy, in whom no jot
Of loves dislike, or pride was to be found,
35 Whom he therefore with equall honour crownd.[6]

With him he raignd, before all time prescribed,°   *ordained*
In endlesse glorie and immortall might,
Together with that third from them derived,[7]
Most wise, most holy, most almightie Spright,
40 Whose kingdomes throne no thought of earthly wight
Can comprehend, much lesse my trembling verse
With equall° words can hope it to reherse.°   *suitable/recount*

Yet O most blessed Spirit, pure lampe of light,
Eternall spring of grace and wisedome trew,[8]
45 Vouchsafe to shed into my barren spright,
Some little drop of thy celestiall dew,
That may my rymes with sweet infuse embrew,[9]
And give me words equall unto my thought,
To tell the marveiles by thy mercie wrought.

50 Yet being pregnant still with powrefull grace,
And full of fruitfull love, that loves to get°   *beget*
Things like himselfe, and to enlarge his race,
His second brood though not in powre so great,
Yet full of beautie, next he did beget
55 An infinite increase of Angels bright,
All glistring glorious in their Makers light.

To them the heavens illimitable hight,
Not this round heaven,[1] which we from hence behold,
Adornd with thousand lamps of burning light,
60 And with ten thousand gemmes of shyning gold,
He gave as their inheritance to hold,
That they might serve him in eternall blis,
And be partakers of those joyes of his.

There they in their trinall triplicities[2]
65 About him wait, and on his will depend,

6. In spite of the expression, "Like to it selfe" (31), Spenser seems to consider the Son as essentially coequal with God the Father: cf. lines 127–128.
7. I.e., the Holy Ghost.
8. "God hath revealed [the things which God hath prepared for them that love him] unto us by his Spirit. . . . the things of God knoweth no man, but the Spirit of God. . . . Which things also we speak, not in the words which man's wisdom teacheth, but which the Holy Ghost teacheth" (I Corinthians ii. 9–13).
9. I.e., permeate or imbue with sweet infusion.
1. I.e., that part of the universe within the sphere of the fixed stars (cf. line 25).
2. The nine orders of angels, subdivided into three "hierarchies," viz. (in ascending order), Angels, Archangels,

He downe descended, like a most demisse°   submissive
And abject thrall, in fleshes fraile attyre,[9]
That he for him might pay sinnes deadly hyre,°   wages
And him restore unto that happie state,
140   In which he stood before his haplesse fate.

In flesh at first the guilt committed was,
Therefore in flesh it must be satisfyde:
Nor spirit, nor Angell, though they man surpas,
Could make amends to God for mans misguyde,°   wrongdoing
145   But onely man himselfe, who selfe did slyde.
So taking flesh of sacred virgins wombe,
For mans deare sake he did a man become.[1]

And that most blessed bodie, which was borne
Without all blemish or reprochfull blame,
150   He freely gave to be both rent and torne
Of cruell hands, who with despightfull shame
Revyling him, that them most vile became,[2]
At length him nayléd on a gallow tree,
And slew the just, by most unjust decree.

155   O huge and most unspeakeable impression[3]
Of loves deepe wound, that pierst the piteous hart
Of that deare Lord with so entyre affection,
And sharply launching° every inner part,   piercing
Dolours of death into his soule did dart;
160   Doing him die,[4] that never it deserved,
To free his foes, that from his heast° had swerved.   command

What hart can feele least touch of so sore launch,
Or thought can think the depth of so deare wound?
Whose bleeding sourse their streames yet never staunch,
165   But stil do flow, and freshly still redound,°   overflow
To heale the sores of sinfull soules unsound,
And clense the guilt of that infected cryme,
Which was enrooted in all fleshly slyme.

O blessed well of love,[5] O floure of grace,
170   O glorious Morning starre, O lampe of light,
Most lively image of thy fathers face,

9. "[Christ Jesus] . . . made himself of no reputation, and took upon him the form of a servant, and was made in the likeness of men: And being found in fashion as a man, he humbled himself, and became obedient unto death, even the death of the cross" (Philippians ii. 7–8).
1. "God sending his own Son in the likeness of sinful flesh, and for sin, condemned sin in the flesh" (Romans viii. 3).

2. I.e., that became them most vilely.
3. The somewhat awkward phrasing may be deliberate; cf. A. N. Satterthwaite, *Spenser, Ronsard, and Du Bellay: A Renaissance Comparison* (Princeton, N.J., 1960), p. 205.
4. I.e., killing him.
5. "The water that I shall give him shall be in him a well of water springing up into everlasting life" (John iv. 14). Cf. also *The Faerie Queene*, I. xi. 29, and note.

Eternall King of glorie, Lord of might,
Meeke lambe of God before all worlds behight,°   *ordained*
How can we thee requite for all this good?
175 Or what can prize° that thy most precious blood?   *pay for*

Yet nought thou ask'st in lieu of all this love,
But love of° us for guerdon of thy paine.   *from*
Ay me; what can us lesse then that behove?°   *befit*
Had he requiréd life of us againe,
180 Had it beene wrong to aske his owne with gaine?°   *advantage*
He gave us life, he it restoréd lost;
Then life were least, that us so litle cost.

But he our life hath left unto us free,
Free that was thrall, and blessed that was band;[6]
185 Ne ought demaunds, but that we loving bee,
As he himselfe hath loved us afore hand,
And bound therto with an eternall band,°   *bond*
Him first to love, that us so dearely bought,
And next, our brethren to his image wrought.[7]

190 Him first to love, great right and reason is,
Who first to us our life and being gave;
And after when we faréd had amisse,
Us wretches from the second death[8] did save;
And last the food of life, which now we have,
195 Even himselfe in his deare sacrament,
To feede our hungry soules unto us lent.°   *gave*

Then next to love our brethren, that were made
Of that selfe mould, and that selfe makers hand,
That° we, and to the same againe shall fade,   *as*
200 Where they shall have like heritage of land,
How ever here on higher steps we stand;
Which also were with selfe same price redeemed
That we, how ever of us light esteemed.

And were they not, yet since that loving Lord
205 Commaunded us to love them for his sake,[9]
Even for his sake, and for his sacred word,
Which in his last bequest he to us spake,
We should them love, and with their needs partake;°   *share*
Knowing that whatsoere to them we give,
210 We give to him, by whom we all doe live.

6. I.e., cursed; in a secondary sense, bound.
7. "Thou shalt love the Lord thy God with all thy heart, and with all thy soul, and with all thy mind. . . . Thou shalt love thy neighbor as thyself" (Matthew xxii. 37–39).
8. I.e., damnation; the consequence of Adam's fall.
9. "A new commandment I give unto you, That ye love one another; as I have loved you, that ye also love one another" (John xiii. 34).

Such mercy he by his most holy reede°   *precept*
Unto us taught, and to approve° it trew,   *prove*
Ensampled it by his most righteous deede,
Shewing us mercie, miserable crew,
215 That we the like should to the wretches shew,[1]
And love our brethren; thereby to approve,
How much himselfe that lovéd us, we love.

Then rouze thy selfe, O earth, out of thy soyle,[2]
In which thou wallowest like to filthy swyne
220 And doest thy mynd in durty pleasures moyle,°   *defile*
Unmindfull of that dearest Lord of thyne;
Lift up to him thy heavie clouded eyne,°   *eyes*
That thou his soveraine bountie mayst behold,
And read° through love his mercies manifold.   *perceive*

225 Beginne from first, where he encradled was
In simple cratch,° wrapt in a wad° of hay, *manger/bundle*
Betweene the toylefull Oxe and humble Asse,
And in what rags, and in how base aray,
The glory of our heavenly riches lay,
230 When him the silly° Shepheards came to see,   *simple*
Whom greatest Princes sought on lowest knee.

From thence reade on the storie of his life,
His humble carriage,° his unfaulty wayes,   *bearing*
His cancred° foes, his fights, his toyle, his strife, *malignant*
235 His paines, his povertie, his sharpe assayes,°   *trials*
Through which he past his miserable dayes,
Offending none, and doing good to all,
Yet being malist° both of great and small.   *hated*

And looke at last how of° most wretched wights,   *by*
240 He taken was, betrayd, and false accused,
How with most scornefull taunts, and fell despights
He was revyld, disgrast, and foule abused,
How scourgd, how crownd, how buffeted, how brused;
And lastly how twixt robbers crucifyde,
245 With bitter wounds through hands, through feet and syde.

Then let thy flinty hart that feeles no paine,
Empiercéd be with pittifull remorse,
And let thy bowels bleede in every vaine,
At sight of his most sacred heavenly corse,°   *body*
250 So torne and mangled with malicious forse,

1. "Be ye therefore merciful, as your Father also is merciful" (Luke vi. 36). 2. "[The Lord] . . . raiseth up the poor out of the dust, and lifteth up the beggar from the dunghill . . . to make them inherit the throne of glory" (I Samuel ii. 8); cf. also Psalms cxiii. 7–8. Cf. *HL*, 176–189.

And let thy soule, whose sins his sorrows wrought,
Melt into teares, and grone in grievéd thought.

With sence whereof whilest so thy softened spirit
Is inly toucht, and humbled with meeke zeale,
255 Through meditation of his endlesse merit,
Lift up thy mind to th'author of thy weale,°   *welfare*
And to his soveraine mercie doe appeale;
Learne him to love, that lovéd thee so deare,
And in thy brest his blessed image beare.

260 With all thy hart, with all thy soule and mind,
Thou must him love, and his beheasts embrace;
All other loves, with which the world doth blind
Weake fancies, and stirre up affections° base,   *passions*
Thou must renounce, and utterly displace,
265 And give thy selfe unto him full and free,
That full and freely gave himselfe to thee.[3]

Then shalt thou feele thy spirit so possest,
And ravisht with devouring great desire
Of his deare selfe, that shall thy feeble brest
270 Inflame with love, and set thee all on fire
With burning zeale, through every part entire,°   *inward*
That in no earthly thing thou shalt delight,
But in his sweet and amiable° sight.   *lovely*

Thenceforth all worlds desire will in thee dye,[4]
275 And all earthes glorie on which men do gaze,
Seeme durt and drosse in thy pure sighted eye,
Compared to that celestiall beauties blaze,
Whose glorious beames all fleshly sense doth daze
With admiration of their passing° light,   *surpassing*
280 Blinding the eyes and lumining the spright.

Then shall thy ravisht soule inspiréd bee
With heavenly thoughts, farre above humane skil,°   *understanding*
And thy bright radiant eyes shall plainely see
Th'Idee[5] of his pure glorie, present still°   *constantly*
285 Before thy face, that all thy spirits shall fill
With sweete enragement° of celestiall love,   *rapture*
Kindled through sight of those faire things above.

---

3. "We love him, because he first loved us" (I John iv. 19).
4. Cf. *HL*, 183–192.
5. I.e., idea; signifying here the heavenly glory of God. Recurrently through-
out this *Hymne*, but especially in these concluding stanzas, Spenser employs Neo-Platonic expressions to describe an essentially Christian vision.

An Hymne of Heavenly Beautie

Rapt with the rage° of mine own ravisht thought,   *fervent passion*
Through contemplation of those goodly sights,
And glorious images in heaven wrought,
Whose wondrous beauty breathing sweet delights,
5 Do kindle love in high conceipted° sprights: *minded*
I faine° to tell the things that I behold,   *long*
But feele my wits to faile, and tongue to fold.[1]

Vouchsafe then, O thou most almightie Spright,[2]
From whom all guifts of wit and knowledge flow,
10 To shed into my breast some sparkling light
Of thine eternall Truth, that I may show
Some litle beames to mortall eyes below,
Of that immortall beautie, there with thee,
Which in my weake distraughted° mynd I see.   *distracted*

15 That with the glorie of so goodly sight,
The hearts of men, which fondly° here admyre   *foolishly*
Faire seeming shewes, and feed on vaine delight,
Transported with celestiall desyre
Of those faire formes, may lift themselves up hyer,
20 And learne to love with zealous humble dewty
Th'eternall fountaine of that heavenly beauty.

Beginning then below,[3] with th'easie vew
Of this base world, subject to fleshly eye,
From thence to mount aloft by order dew,
25 To contemplation of th'immortall sky,
Of the soare faulcon[4] so I learne to fly,
That flags° awhile her fluttering wings beneath,   *droops*
Till she her selfe for stronger flight can breath.°   *take breath*

1. Throughout this *Hymne*, Spenser draws heavily on the Bible and on apocryphal literature; at the same time, he regularly employs the language of Platonic and Neo-Platonic thought. Thus, while the figure addressed in lines 8–21 may be identified with the "Spirit of truth. . . . which is the Holy Ghost" (John xiv. 17, 26), the language and imagery of lines 1–28 generally recall those of Plato "touching the fourth sort of madness . . . the best of all forms of divine possession, both in itself and in its sources . . . when he that loves beauty is touched by such madness he is called a lover. Such a one, as soon as he beholds the beauty of this world, is reminded of true beauty, and his wings begin to grow; then is he fain to lift his wings and fly upward . . ." (*Phaedrus*, 249e).

2. I.e., the Holy Spirit.
3. In each of the preceding *Hymnes*, an introductory passage is followed by an account of creation; here, the poet (in lines 22–105) deals rather with the ordered arrangement of the created universe, moving progressively from lower to higher stages of being, and thence to the creator himself, in a fashion that balances and matches the contrary movement of *HB*. Perhaps Spenser had in mind the Aristotelian concept of "final cause": cause "in the sense of end or 'that for the sake of which' a thing is done. . . . 'that for the sake of which' means what is best and the end of the things that lead up to it" (*Physics*, II. 3).
4. I.e., a young falcon in its first plumage.

Then looke who list, thy gazefull eyes to feed
30 With sight of that is faire, looke on the frame
Of this wyde universe, and therein reed°   perceive
The endlesse kinds of creatures, which by name
Thou canst not count, much lesse their natures aime:°   guess
All which are made with wondrous wise respect,°   care
35 And all with admirable beautie deckt.

First th'Earth, on adamantine° pillers founded,   unbreakable
Amid the Sea engirt with brasen bands;[5]
Then th'Aire still flitting, but yet firmely bounded
On everie side, with pyles of flaming brands,[6]
40 Never consumed nor quencht with mortall hands;
And last, that mightie shining christall wall,[7]
Wherewith he hath encompésséd this All.

By view whereof, it plainly may appeare,
That still as every thing doth upward tend,
45 And further is from earth, so still more cleare
And faire it growes, till to his perfect end
Of purest beautie, it at last ascend:
Ayre more then water, fire much more than ayre,
And heaven then fire appeares more pure and fayre.

50 Looke thou no further, but affixe thine eye
On that bright shynie round still° moving Masse,   constantly
The house of blessed Gods,[8] which men call Skye,
All sowd with glistring stars more thicke then grasse,
Whereof each other doth in brightnesse passe;°   surpass
55 But those two most, which ruling night and day,
As King and Queene, the heavens Empire sway.°   rule

And tell me then, what hast thou ever seene,
That to their beautie may comparéd bee,
Or can the sight that is most sharpe and keene,
60 Endure their Captains flaming head[9] to see?
How much lesse those, much higher in degree,[1]
And so much fairer, and much more then these,
As these are fairer then the land and seas?

5. "The pillars of the earth are the Lord's, and he hath set the world upon them" (I Samuel ii. 8); "He hath compassed the waters with bounds, until the day and night come to an end" (Job xxvi. 10).
6. I.e., the region of fire between that of air and the sphere of the moon; but line 40 suggests that Spenser is not precisely distinguishing this region from that of "aether," purer than the element of fire, and presumed to fill all space beyond the sphere of the moon.

7. The crystalline sphere beyond that of the fixed stars.
8. I.e., the planets. Cf. The Wisdom of Solomon, xiii. 2: " . . . the heavenly luminaries, the rulers of the world, [men] considered gods. . . . through delight in their beauty" (*The Apocrypha*, trans. E. J. Goodspeed [New York, 1959], p. 202).
9. I.e., the light of the sun.
1. I.e., how much less can one endure the sight of those other heavens above these?

For farre above these heavens which here we see,
65 Be others farre exceeding these in light,
Not bounded, not corrupt, as these same bee,
But infinite in largenesse and in hight,
Unmoving, uncorrupt, and spotlesse bright,
That need no Sunne t'illuminate their spheres,
70 But their owne native light farre passing theirs.[2]

And as these heavens still by degrees arize,
Untill they come to their first Movers bound,[3]
That in his mightie compasse doth comprize,°   enclose
And carrie all the rest with him around,
75 So those likewise doe by degrees redound,°   surge upward
And rise more faire, till they at last arive
To the most faire, whereto they all do strive.

Faire is the heaven, where happy soules have place,
In full enjoyment of felicitie,
80 Whence they doe still behold the glorious face
Of the divine eternall Majestie;
More faire is that, where those Idees on hie,
Enraungéd be, which Plato so admyred,
And pure Intelligences from God inspyred.[4]

85 Yet fairer is that heaven,[5] in which doe raine
The soveraine Powres and mightie Potentates,
Which in their high protections doe containe
All mortall Princes, and imperiall States;
And fayrer yet, whereas the royall Seates
90 And heavenly Dominations are set,
From whom all earthly governance is fet.°   drawn

Yet farre more faire be those bright Cherubins,
Which all with golden wings are overdight,°   overspread
And those eternall burning Seraphins,
95 Which from their faces dart out fierie light;[6]
Yet fairer then they both, and much more bright
Be th'Angels and Archangels, which attend
On Gods owne person, without rest or end.

2. "And there shall be no night there; and they need no candle, neither light of the sun; for the Lord God giveth them light" (Revelation xxii. 5).
3. I.e., the sphere of the *primum mobile.*
4. Plato distinguishes between the heavenly region in which "souls that are called immortal" properly reside, and those "regions without" where "true being dwells," i.e., the ideas of justice, temperance, knowledge, etc. (*Phaedrus,* 247c–e). "Intelligences" may refer to angelic being in a general sense: cf. Dante, *Paradiso,* XXVIII. 75–77; and Aquinas, *Summa Theologica,* I. Q. 79, Art. 10 ("in some works translated from the Arabic, the separate substances, which we call angels, are called intelligences" (*Basic Writings of St. Thomas Aquinas,* ed. A. C. Pegis [New York, 1945], 2 vols., I, p. 762).
5. Cf. *HHL,* 64, and note.
6. Spenser conforms only in part to the traditional color symbolism of medieval art, by which scarlet (the

These thus in faire each other farre excelling,
100 As to the Highest they approch more neare,
Yet is that Highest farre beyond all telling,
Fairer than all the rest which there appeare,
Though all their beauties joyned together were:
How then can mortall tongue hope to expresse,
105 The image of such endlesse perfectnesse?

Cease then my tongue,[7] and lend unto my mynd
Leave to bethinke how great that beautie is,
Whose utmost° parts so beautifull I fynd,   outermost
How much more those essentiall parts of his,
110 His truth, his love, his wisedome, and his blis,
His grace, his doome,° his mercy and his might,   judgment
By which he lends us of himselfe a sight.

Those unto all he daily doth display,
And shew himselfe in th'image of his grace,
115 As in a looking glasse,[8] through which he may
Be seene, of all his creatures vile and base,
That are unable else to see his face,
His glorious face which glistereth else so bright,
That th'Angels selves can not endure his sight.

120 But we fraile wights, whose sight cannot sustaine
The Suns bright beames, when he on us doth shyne,
But that their points rebutted backe againe
Are duld, how can we see with feeble eyne,°   eyes
The glory of that Majestie divine,
125 In sight of whom both Sun and Moone are darke,
Compared to his least resplendent sparke?

The meanes therefore which unto us is lent,
Him to behold, is on his workes to looke,[9]
Which he hath made in beauty excellent,
130 And in the same, as in a brasen booke,
To reade enregistred in every nooke

color of flame) was considered appropriate for the Seraphim, blue for the contemplative Cherubim.
7. Having considered the "utmost parts" of the Heavenly Beauty that is God, the poet moves on (in lines 106–182) to the "essential" attributes of Deity.
8. The metaphor appears regularly in Platonic and Neo-Platonic writings; but in this context cf. particularly I Corinthians xiii. 12: "For now we see through a glass, darkly; but then face to face . . . ". Spenser's language is close to that of Jean Calvin, who observes, with reference to Hebrews xi. 3,

that "this skillful ordering of the universe is for us a sort of mirror in which we can contemplate God, who is otherwise invisible" (*Institutes of the Christian Religion*, ed. J. T. McNeil, trans. F. L. Battles [Philadelphia, 1960], I. v. 1).
9. "For the invisible things of him from the creation of the world are clearly seen, being understood by the things that are made" (Romans i. 20). Calvin writes that "the most perfect way of seeking God . . . is . . . for us to contemplate him in his works whereby he renders himself near and familiar to us, and in some manner communicates himself" *ibid.*, I. v. 9).

His goodnesse, which his beautie doth declare,
For all thats good, is beautifull and faire.

Thence gathering plumes of perfect speculation,°   *vision*
135   To impe[1] the wings of thy high flying mynd,
Mount up aloft through heavenly contemplation,
From this darke world, whose damps° the soule do blynd, *noxious fogs*
And like the native brood of Eagles kynd,[2]
On that bright Sunne of glorie fixe thine eyes,
140   Cleared from grosse mists of fraile infirmities.

Humbled with feare and awfull reverence,
Before the footestoole of his Majestie,
Throw thy selfe downe with trembling innocence,
Ne dare looke up with corruptible eye
145   On the dred face of that great Deity,
For feare, lest if he chaunce to looke on thee,
Thou turne to nought, and quite confounded be.

But lowly fall before his mercie seate,
Close covered with the Lambes integrity,[3]
150   From the just wrath of his avengefull threate,
That sits upon the righteous throne on hy:
His throne is built upon Eternity,
More firme and durable then steele or brasse,
Or the hard diamond, which them both doth passe.°   *surpass*

155   His scepter is the rod of Righteousnesse,[4]
With which he bruseth° all his foes to dust,   *crushes*
And the great Dragon strongly doth represse,
Under the rigour of his judgement just;
His seate is Truth, to which the faithfull trust;
160   From whence proceed her beames so pure and bright,
That all about him sheddeth glorious light.

Light farre exceeding that bright blazing sparke,
Which darted is from Titans flaming head,
That with his beames enlumineth the darke
165   And dampish aire, whereby al things are red:°   *seen*
Whose nature yet so much is marvelléd°   *wondered at*
Of mortall wits, that it doth much amaze°   *bewilder*
The greatest wisards, which thereon do gaze.

1. I.e., (as in hawking), to improve the capacity for flight by engrafting feathers.
2. I.e., like young eagles (traditionally thought capable of gazing steadily at the sun).
3. "The Lamb which is in the midst of the throne shall feed them, and shall lead them into living fountains of waters" (Revelation vii. 17).
4. "Thy throne, O God, is for ever and ever: the sceptre of thy kingdom is a right sceptre" (Psalms xlv. 6); "And the great dragon was cast out, that old serpent, called the Devil, and Satan, which deceiveth the whole world" (Revelation xii. 9).

But that immortall light which there doth shine,
170 Is many thousand times more bright, more cleare,
More excellent, more glorious, more divine,[5]
Through which to God all mortall actions here,
And even the thoughts of men, do plaine appeare:
For from th'eternall Truth it doth proceed,
175 Through heavenly vertue, which her beames doe breed.

With the great glorie of that wondrous light,
His throne is all encompasséd around,
And hid in his owne brightnesse from the sight
Of all that looke thereon with eyes unsound:
180 And underneath his feet are to be found
Thunder, and lightning, and tempestuous fyre,
The instruments of his avenging yre.[6]

There in his bosome Sapience[7] doth sit,
The soveraine dearling of the Deity,
185 Clad like a Queene in royall robes, most fit
For so great powre and peerelesse majesty.
And all with gemmes and jewels gorgeously
Adornd, that brighter then the starres appeare,
And make her native brightnes seem more cleare.

190 And on her head a crowne of purest gold
Is set, in signe of highest soveraignty,
And in her hand a scepter she doth hold,
With which she rules the house of God on hy,
And menageth° the ever-moving sky,   *controls*
195 And in the same[8] these lower creatures all,
Subjected to her powre imperiall.

5. "The beauty of God . . . certainly excels the rest of the beauties as much as the true light of the sun in itself, pure, single, and inviolate, surpasses the splendor of the sun, which is split up, divided, adulterated, and obscured through the cloudy air" (Ficino, *Commentary*, VI. 17).

6. "And out of the throne proceeded lightnings and thunderings and voices: and there were seven lamps of fire burning before the throne" (Revelation iv. 5).

7. The figure of Sapience (central in lines 183–259) is dramatically opposed to that of Venus in *HB;* in another and essential aspect, this figure parallels that of Christ in *HHL*. Although Sapience has been associated by scholars with a variety of Christian and pre-Christian concepts, it is reasonably well established that by this symbolic personage Spenser refers to Christ, the second person of the Trinity, from early Christian times regularly identified with the figure (or attribute) of Wisdom in the Old Testament and in apocryphal literature. Perhaps the most striking allusion is that of I Corinthians i. 22–24: "For the Jews require a sign, and the Greeks seek after wisdom: But we preach Christ crucified, unto the Jews a stumblingblock, and unto the Greeks foolishness; But unto them which are called, both Jews and Greeks, Christ the power of God, and the wisdom of God." In "wisdom literature," three passages are especially relevant to lines 182–189: Proverbs viii. 30 ("I [Wisdom] was by him, as one brought up with him: and I was daily his delight, rejoicing always before him"), and The Wisdom of Solomon ix. 4 ("the wisdom that sits by [God's] throne"), and vii. 29 ("For she is fairer than the sun, Or any group of stars; Compared with light, she is found superior").

8. I.e., by the same power, simultaneously. "For she reaches in strength from one end of the earth to the other, And conducts everything well" (Wisdom of Solomon, viii. 1).

Both heaven and earth obey unto her will,
And all the creatures which they both containe:
For of her fulnesse which the world doth fill,
200 They all partake, and do in state remaine,
As their great Maker did at first ordaine,
Through observation of her high beheast,
By which they first were made, and still increast.[9]

The fairenesse of her face no tongue can tell,
205 For she the daughters of all wemens race,
And Angels eke,° in beautie doth excell,   *also*
Sparkled on her from Gods owne glorious face,
And more increast by her owne goodly grace,
That it doth farre exceed all humane thought,
210 Ne can on earth compared be to ought.

Ne could that Painter[1] (had he lived yet)
Which pictured Venus with so curious° quill,   *ingenious*
That all posteritie admyréd it,
Have purtrayd this, for all his maistring skill;
215 Ne she her selfe, had she remainéd still,
And were as faire, as fabling wits do fayne,°   *imagine*
Could once come neare this beauty soverayne.

But had those wits the wonders of their dayes,
Or that sweete Teian Poet[2] which did spend
220 His plenteous vaine° in setting forth her prayse,   *vein*
Seene but a glims of this, which I pretend,°   *present*
How wondrously would he her face commend,
Above that Idole of his fayning° thought,   *imaginative*
That all the world shold with his rimes be fraught?°   *filled*

225 How then dare I, the novice of his Art,
Presume to picture so divine a wight,
Or hope t'expresse her least perfections part,
Whose beautie filles the heavens with her light,
And darkes the earth with shadow of her sight?
230 Ah gentle Muse thou art too weake and faint,
The pourtraict of so heavenly hew° to paint.   *form*

Let Angels which her goodly face behold
And see at will, her soveraigne praises sing,
And those most sacred mysteries unfold,
235 Of that faire love of mightie heavens king.

9. I.e., and are continually brought
forth. "Though she is one, she can do
all things, And while remaining in her-
self, she makes everything new" (Wis-
dom, vii. 27). Cf. also Wisdom i. 7:
"For the spirit of the Lord fills the
world"; and Proverbs iii. 19: "The
Lord by wisdom hath founded the
earth; by understanding hath he estab-
lished the heavens."
1. Probably the Greek painter Apelles,
who lived in the fourth century B.C. His
most famous picture showed Aphrodite
(Venus) rising from the sea foam.
2. Anacreon, who was born about
550 B.C. at Teos, in Asia Minor.

Enough is me t'admyre so heavenly thing,
And being thus with her huge love possest,
In th'only wonder of her selfe to rest.

But who so may, thrise happie man him hold,
240 Of all on earth, whom God so much doth grace,
And lets his owne Belovéd to behold:
For in the view of her celestiall face,
All joy, all blisse, all happinesse have place,
Ne ought on earth can want unto the wight,
245 Who of her selfe can win the wishfull° sight.   *desired*

For she out of her secret threasury,
Plentie of riches forth on him will powre,[3]
Even heavenly riches, which there hidden ly
Within the closet of her chastest bowre,
250 Th'eternall portion of her precious dowre,°   *dowry*
Which mighty God hath given to her free,
And to all those which thereof worthy bee.[4]

None thereof worthy be, but those whom shee
Vouchsafeth to her presence to receave,
255 And letteth them her lovely face to see,
Wherof such wondrous pleasures they conceave,
And sweete contentment, that it doth bereave°   *steal away*
Their soule of sense, through infinite delight,
And them transport from flesh into the spright.

260 In which they see such admirable things,
As carries them into an extasy,[5]
And heare such heavenly notes, and carolings,
Of Gods high praise, that filles the brasen sky,
And feele such joy and pleasure inwardly,
265 That maketh them all worldly cares forget,
And onely thinke on that before them set.

Ne from thenceforth doth any fleshly sense,
Or idle thought of earthly things remaine:
But all that earst° seemd sweet, seemes now offense,   *formerly*
270 And all that pleaséd earst, now seemes to paine.
Their joy, their comfort, their desire, their gaine,
Is fixéd all on that which now they see,
All other sights but faynéd° shadowes bee.   *illusory*

3. "But all blessings came to me along with her, And uncounted wealth is in her hands. . . . I will not hide her wealth away, For it is an unfailing treasure for men, And those who get it make friends with God" (Wisdom vii. 11–14).
4. Probably an allusion to the doctrine of predestination, although Spenser might have drawn on Wisdom vi. 16: " . . . she goes about in search of those who are worthy of her, and she graciously appears to them in their paths, And meets them in every thought."
5. The final stanzas of this *Hymne*, describing the glorious rapture of the heavenly vision, parallel the concluding movement of *HHL*.

And that faire lampe, which useth to enflame
275 The hearts of men with selfe consuming fyre,
Thenceforth seemes fowle, and full of sinfull blame;°   *fault*
And all that pompe, to which proud minds aspyre
By name of honor, and so much desyre,
Seemes to them basenesse, and all riches drosse,
280 And all mirth sadnesse, and all lucre losse.[6]

So full their eyes are of that glorious sight,
And senses fraught with such satietie,
That in nought else on earth they can delight,
But in th'aspect of that felicitie,
285 Which they have written in their inward ey;
On which they feed, and in their fastened° mynd   *fixed*
All happie joy and full contentment fynd.

Ah then my hungry soule, which long hast fed
On idle fancies of thy foolish thought,
290 And with false beauties flattring bait misled,
Hast after vaine deceiptfull shadowes sought,
Which all are fled, and now have left thee nought,
But late repentance through thy follies prief;°   *experience*
Ah ceasse to gaze on matter of thy grief.

295 And looke at last up to that soveraine light,
From whose pure beams al perfect beauty springs,[7]
That kindleth love in every godly spright,
Even the love of God, which loathing brings
Of this vile world, and these gay seeming things;
300 With whose sweete pleasures being so possest,
Thy straying thoughts henceforth for ever rest.

Editor's Note

The dedicatory epistle prefixed to *Fowre Hymnes*, like others among Spenser's efforts in this kind, presents the reader with some problems of interpretation. For those who take the epistle at face value, "the greener times of my youth" refers to Spenser's Cambridge years or to the period of the *Calender*: it is argued that, whatever one makes of the hints that two early poems were somehow revised, the seriously inclined Countess of Warwick persuaded the poet, considerably later in his career, to compose two other *Hymnes* that should offset and in a manner compensate for the expressions of the earlier poems. It would follow that the allusions (in *An Hymne of Heavenly Love*, 8–21) to "lewd layes" composed in youth are to be taken quite seriously, a conclusion not without some difficulties. Others hold that Spenser did in fact revise early work to make the first

6. "I preferred her to scepters and thrones, And I thought wealth of no account compared with her" (Wisdom, vii. 8). Cf. also Job xxviii. 12–19.

7. "So the light and beauty of God, which is pure, freed from all other things, is called . . . infinite beauty" (Ficino, *Commentary*, VI. 18).

two *Hymnes*, but that these revisions were undertaken in 1595–1596; the "retractation" is a conventional gesture, while the *Fowre Hymnes* are, in fact, "a single, carefully constructed poem, in four parts."[1] Others again, including those for whom the poet's Christian humanism is a prime consideration, note that Spenser calls his patrons "most excellent and rare ornaments of all true love and beautie, both in the one and the other kinde . . ."; in this light (so runs the argument), an emphasis on earthly love and beauty in the two earlier poems, probably not much revised for the 1596 volume, is not really contradicted or denied in the later *Hymnes*, which as it were complement and complete those youthful works by a mature and essentially meditative affirmation of the higher power that rests in heavenly love and beauty. Finally, Robert Ellrodt argues, in his study of the Platonic elements in Spenser's poetry, that the first two *Hymnes* "in all likelihood were written or rewritten after the publication of *Colin Clout* in 1595."[2]

It is of interest that Spenser should have called the poems "hymns," since the term collects classical as well as scriptural associations: Milton, deliberating on the choice of a form into which the great poem might best be cast, would seriously consider "those magnific odes and hymns, wherein Pindarus and Callimachus are in most things worthy" and "those frequent songs throughout the law and prophets beyond all these."[3] The term (in Greek usage signifying a song in praise of a god or hero) was especially associated in ancient times with the "Orphic Hymns," initiatory lyric chants making part of the ceremonies of Hellenic "mystery" religion. In form and "kind," Renaissance Neo-Platonic thought assuredly provided Spenser with precedents and to spare for his undertaking in *Fowre Hymnes*. Verbal and ideological resemblances between the *Hymnes* and Benivieni's *Canzona della Amore celeste et divino*, for instance, have suggested to some that this Italian ode might have had an important, even direct, influence on Spenser; but the trend of recent criticism (in this aspect of Spenser's poetry) is to acknowledge the influence of Ficino, and perhaps also of Plotinus, while emphasizing the poet's kinship with Leone Ebreo and Louis Le Roy. To attempt a measured estimate of the character and extent of Spenser's Neo-Platonism in *Fowre Hymnes* is certainly beyond the scope of this Note; it is perhaps possible to say, however, that critics are no longer much inclined to read the *Hymnes* primarily in terms of their relationship to one or another Neo-Platonic rendering of the Platonic "ladder" or "ascent" (e.g., in Benivieni's ode, the commentary on that ode by Pico della Mirandola, or Castiglione's *Il Cortegiano*). That the first two *Hymnes* illustrate the application of Platonic doctrine to a conventional Petrarchan manner may still be generally granted; but recent critics of these poems have drawn attention rather to the centrally Christian cast of Spenser's thought, permeated however thoroughly with Platonic elements more or less adaptable to Christian belief. In this context, one extreme position

1. Josephine W. Bennett, "The Theme of Spenser's *Fowre Hymnes*," *SP*, XXXVII (1931), p. 48.

2. R. Ellrodt, *Neoplatonism in the Poetry of Spenser* (Geneva, 1960), p. 211.

3. *The Reason of Church Government Urged Against Prelaty*, Preface to Book II.

would place all four poems within the traditions of Christian mysticism; another and more recent study, which acknowledges the close affinity of Christian and Platonic thought, firmly holds that "in all of the *Fowre Hymnes* the creed is a consistent Protestant Christianity, while the Platonism and Neo-Platonism are adventitious."[4] William Nelson's summary remarks (in this edition) are of particular interest in this regard.

In any event, and whatever critical path one may follow among the thickety controversies that have sprung up about these poems, structural balance and pattern are everywhere present in *Fowre Hymnes*. The footnotes to this edition give some indication of progressive stages in the movement of Spenser's thought within each *Hymne*: while one would not wish to advance too pressingly the case for parallel design, it does appear that all four poems are developed in terms of a broadly similar structural scheme, in four parts. The introductory stanzas ordinarily include an "apostrophe" to the appropriate god or divine power, together with an invocation to that authority; only in the third *Hymne* is the invocation (*not* in this case precisely addressed to the divine person central in the poem) slightly delayed. There follows a description of creation, variously imagined in each poem. The final *Hymne* apparently diverges from this scheme, to present instead an account of the ordered universe; yet it is tempting to believe that Spenser, with Aristotle's theory of causes in view, may be completing a series referable successively to material, formal, and efficient cause with a passage corresponding to Aristotle's final cause, "in the sense of end." The third section of each *Hymne*, generally the most substantial and extensive, comprises the "argument" proper, which is expressed in dualistic terms. In the first two *Hymnes*, appearance is everywhere matched with reality, illusion with truth: thus, the "loose desyre" that "baseborne mynds" take for love is countered by "that sweet passion" in the "high thought" of the true lover; as for beauty, mere "proportion of the outward part" is no more than an indication of the "inward mynd," and of the pure spirit irradiated by "that heavenly light"—which nevertheless can be made "the bait of sinne" in a fallen world. If the pattern of these earlier poems emphasizes contrast and opposition, that of the two later *Hymnes* develops rather in terms of partial and complete truth: an account of Christ's entry into history introduces the discussion of that event's significance for mankind, while in the fourth *Hymne*, a vision of God's power and glory is completed by the symbolic figure of Sapience, who bestows "heavenly riches" on those who are worthy. The concluding stanzas of each poem, finally, describe a "Paradise," or a comparable spiritual condition, appropriate to the context of each *Hymne*.

In the area of imagery as well, the variety of matching elements is very rich: one might single out Spenser's careful use of mirror imagery, which accords with shifting thematic contexts. Then too, the complex and far-ranging patterns of light imagery are artfully interwoven with various perceptual modes: the normal vision of natural eyesight; the "sharply sighted" eyes of lovers, who perceive what is "inly faire"; and that higher vision

---

4. A. W. Satterthwaite, *op. cit.*, p. 169.

vouchsafed to the enraptured soul. In fact, for readers who are troubled by the uncertainties attending the composition of these poems, or discontented with Spenser's philosophical expression in them, the poet's command of structure and image may well constitute his most impressively persuasive achievement. As one of the most astute critics of *Fowre Hymnes* has remarked, "In attempting to pierce through to a complete understanding of Spenser, it is well to keep in mind that we are working with a piece of renaissance art, not a philosophical treatise."[5]

5. C. G. Osgood, in *The Works of Edmund Spenser*, ed. E. Greenlaw, C. G. Osgood, F. M. Padelford, R. Heffner (Baltimore, Md., 1932–1949), 10 vols., v. 7, p. 681.

Prothalamion[1]

1

Calme was the day, and through the trembling ayre,
Sweete breathing Zephyrus did softly play,
A gentle spirit, that lightly did delay°   *temper*
Hot Titans beames, which then did glyster° fayre: *shine*
5   When I whom sullein care,
Through discontent of my long fruitlesse stay
In Princes Court, and expectation vayne
Of idle hopes, which still doe fly away,
Like empty shaddowes, did aflict my brayne,[2]
10   Walkt forth to ease my payne
Along the shoare of silver streaming Themmes,
Whose rutty° Bancke, the which his River hemmes,   *rooty*
Was paynted all with variable° flowers,   *various*
And all the meades adornd with daintie gemmes,
15   Fit to decke maydens bowres,
And crowne their Paramours,°   *lovers*
Against the Brydale day, which is not long:[3]
   Sweete Themmes runne softly, till I end my song.

2

There, in a Meadow, by the Rivers side,
20   A Flocke of Nymphes I chauncéd to espy,
All lovely Daughters of the Flood° thereby,   *river*
With goodly greenish locks all loose untyde,
As each had bene a Bryde,[4]
And each one had a little wicker basket,
25   Made of fine twigs entrayléd° curiously,   *interlaced*
In which they gathered flowers to fill their flasket:°   *basket*
And with fine Fingers, cropt full feateously[5]
The tender stalkes on hye.
Of every sort, which in that Meadow grew,

1. The term, which signifies "a preliminary nuptial song," is invented by Spenser, who subtitles his poem, "a spousall verse." For an account of the tradition informing such verses, cf. the essay by Dan S. Norton in *English Studies in Honor of James Southall Wilson* (Charlottesville, Va., 1951), 223–241; for commentary on Spenser's use of poetic conventions in the poem, cf. the essay by Hallett Smith in this edition.
2. The acquisition of an estate, and a certain social standing, in Ireland scarcely alleviated Spenser's continued longing for advancement at the court of Queen Elizabeth, in Westminster.
3. I.e., in anticipation of the bridal day, which is not far off. But the line incorporates other suggestions as well, in the context chiefly of the movement of time. Cf. the essay by Harry Berger, Jr., in *EIC*, XV (1965), 363–380.
4. It was customary in Spenser's day for brides to let their hair hang free at the marriage ceremony.
5. I.e., and with a delicate touch, plucked most dextrously.

30 They gathered some; the Violet pallid blew,
The little Dazie, that at evening closes,
The virgin Lillie, and the Primrose trew,
With store° of vermeil° Roses,   *abundance/vermilion*
To decke their Bridegromes posies,°   *bouquets*
35 Against the Brydale day, which was not long:
    Sweete Themmes runne softly, till I end my song.

3

With that, I saw two Swannes of goodly hewe,°   *appearance*
Come softly swimming downe along the Lee;[6]
Two fairer Birds I yet did never see:
40 The snow which doth the top of Pindus[7] strew,
Did never whiter shew,
Nor Jove himselfe when he a Swan would be
For love of Leda, whiter did appeare:[8]
Yet Leda was they say as white as he,
45 Yet not so white as these, nor nothing neare;
So purely white they were,
That even the gentle streame, the which them bare,
Seemed foule to[9] them, and bad his billowes spare°   *forbear*
To wet their silken feathers, least they might
50 Soyle their fayre plumes with water not so fayre
And marre their beauties bright,
That shone as heavens light,
Against their Brydale day, which was not long:
    Sweete Themmes runne softly, till I end my song.

4

55 Eftsoones° the Nymphes, which now had Flowers their fill,   *presently*
Ran all in haste, to see that silver brood,[1]
As they came floating on the Christal Flood.
Whom when they sawe, they stood amazéd still,
Their wondring eyes to fill,
60 Them seemed they never saw a sight so fayre,
Of Fowles so lovely, that they sure did deeme
Them heavenly borne, or to be that same payre
Which through the Skie draw Venus silver Teeme,[2]
For sure they did not seeme
65 To be begot of any earthly Seede,
But rather Angels or of Angels breede:°   *race*

6. I.e., probably, down the stream [of the Thames], bordered by meadowlands or leas. That "Lee," here and at l. 115, refers to the river Lea (which enters the Thames at Greenwich) is unlikely. Flocks of swans were regularly to be seen on the Thames in Spenser's time. Allegorically, these two represent the brides-to-be, Elizabeth and Catherine Somerset, daughters of Edward Somerset, Earl of Worcester.
7. "Pindus" properly refers to the mountain range constituting the western boundary of the Thessalian plain, in Greece. Ovid often alludes to Pindus' height (e.g., *Metamorphoses*, II.225); for Spenser, the mountain has mythical associations as well. Cf. *The Faerie Queene*, III.iv.41.
8. Cf. *Metamorphoses*, VI.109; and *The Faerie Queene*, III.xi.32.
9. I.e., compared with.
1. I.e., that silvery pair of noble lineage.
2. Traditionally, the chariot of Venus was drawn through the air by swans; cf. *Metamorphoses*, X.717–718.

Yet were they bred of Somers-heat[3] they say,
In sweetest Season, when each Flower and weede°   *plant*
The earth did fresh aray,
70 So fresh they seemed as day,
Even as their Brydale day, which was not long:
    Sweete Themmes runne softly, till I end my song.

5

Then forth they all out of their baskets drew,
Great store of Flowers, the honour° of the field,   *glory*
75 That to the sense did fragrant odours yeild,
All which upon those goodly Birds they threw,
And all the Waves did strew,
That like old Peneus Waters they did seeme,
When downe along by pleasant Tempes shore
80 Scattred with Flowres, through Thessaly they streeme,
That they appeare through Lillies plenteous store,
Like a Brydes Chamber flore:[4]
Two of those Nymphes, meane while, two Garlands bound,
Of freshest Flowres which in that Mead° they found,   *meadow*
85 The which presenting all in trim Array,
Their snowie Foreheads[5] therewithall they crownd,
Whil'st one did sing this Lay,
Prepared against that Day,
Against their Brydale day, which was not long:
90   Sweete Themmes runne softly, till I end my song.

6

"Ye gentle Birdes, the worlds faire ornament,
And heavens glorie, whom this happie hower
Doth leade unto your lovers blisfull bower,
Joy may you have and gentle hearts content
95 Of your loves couplement:°   *union*
And let faire Venus, that is Queene of love,
With her heart-quelling Sonne upon you smile,
Whose smile they say, hath vertue° to remove   *power*
All Loves dislike, and friendships faultie guile
100 For ever to assoile.[6]
Let endlesse Peace your steadfast hearts accord,°   *harmonize*
And blesséd Plentie wait upon your bord,°   *table*
And let your bed with pleasures chast abound,
That fruitfull issue may to you afford,[7]
105 Which may your foes confound,
And make your joyes redound,°   *overflow*

3. Spenser puns on the ladies' surname.
4. The Peneus river flows through the vale of Tempe, in Thessaly, between Mt. Ossa and Mt. Olympus to the sea; Spenser probably recalls Catullus, *Odes*, 64. 278–288.
5. I.e., those of the swans.
6. I.e., has power to remove all cause for aversion in love, and to dispel forever the offensive guile that may undermine friendship. Venus appears as beneficent overseer of marriage in Statius, *Silvae*, I.ii.162–193, and in Claudian, *Epithalamium de Nuptiis Honorii Augusti*, 190–287.
7. I.e., be given.

Upon your Brydale day, which is not long:
   Sweete Themmes run softlie, till I end my Song."

7

So ended she; and all the rest around
110 To her redoubled that her undersong,[8]
Which said, their bridale daye should not be long.
And gentle Eccho from the neighbour ground,
Their accents did resound.
So forth those joyous Birdes did passe along,
115 Adowne the Lee, that to them murmurde low,
As he would speake, but that he lackt a tong,
Yet did by signes his glad affection show,
Making his streame run slow.
And all the foule which in his flood did dwell
120 Gan flock about these twaine, that did excell
The rest, so far, as Cynthia[9] doth shend°   *surpass*
The lesser starres. So they enrangéd° well,   *ordered*
Did on those two attend,
And their best service lend,°   *give*
125 Against their wedding day, which was not long:
   Sweete Themmes run softly, till I end my song.

8

At length they all to mery London came,
To mery London, my most kyndly Nurse,
That to me gave this Lifes first native sourse:
130 Though from another place I take my name,
An house of auncient fame.[1]
There when they came, whereas those bricky towres,[2]
The which on Themmes brode aged backe doe ryde,
Where now the studious Lawyers have their bowers
135 There whylome° wont the Templer Knights to byde,   *formerly*
Till they decayd[3] through pride:
Next whereunto there standes a stately place,[4]
Where oft I gaynéd giftes and goodly grace
Of that great Lord, which therein wont to dwell,
140 Whose want too well now feeles my freendles case:
But Ah here fits° not well   *suits*
Olde woes but joyes to tell

---

8. I.e., re-echoed the refrain of her song.
9. I.e., Diana, goddess of the moon, called Cynthia from Mt. Cynthus (on the island of Delos), her birthplace. The customary allusion to Queen Elizabeth is implicit here also.
1. Born and bred in London, Spenser associates himself with the Spencers of Althorp in Northamptonshire (cf. also *Colin Clouts Come Home Againe*, 536–555), who claimed descent from the ancient house of Despencer.
2. I.e., the Temple, between Fleet Street and the north bank of the Thames; originally the London residence of the Knights Templar. When that order was suppressed by Edward II, the property passed to the Knights of St. John, and was subsequently leased to the students of English common law. The estate was formally granted to the lawyers by James I.
3. I.e., until their downfall.
4. I.e., Leicester House, London residence of "that great Lord" the Earl of Leicester, Spenser's patron in 1579–1580. When, after the Earl's death in 1588, the estate passed into the possession of Robert Devereux, 2nd Earl of Essex, the building was called Essex House.

Against the bridale daye, which is not long:
  Sweete Themmes runne softly, till I end my song.

9

145 Yet therein now doth lodge a noble Peer,[5]
Great Englands glory and the Worlds wide wonder,
Whose dreadfull name, late through all Spaine did thunder,
And Hercules two pillors standing neere,
Did make to quake and feare:
150 Faire branch of Honor, flower of Chevalrie,
That fillest England with thy triumphs fame,
Joy have thou of thy noble victorie,
And endlesse happinesse of thine owne name
That promiseth the same:[6]
155 That through thy prowesse and victorious armes,
Thy country may be freed from forraine harmes:
And great Elisaes glorious name may ring
Through al the world, filled with thy wide Alarmes,
Which some brave muse may sing
160 To ages following,[7]
Upon the Brydale day, which is not long:
  Sweete Themmes runne softly, till I end my song.

10

From those high Towers, this noble Lord issuing,
Like Radiant Hesper[8] when his golden hayre
165 In th'Ocean billowes he hath Bathéd fayre,
Descended to the Rivers open viewing,
With a great traine ensuing.[9]
Above the rest were goodly to bee seene
Two gentle Knights[1] of lovely face and feature
170 Beseeming well the bower of anie Queene,
With gifts of wit and ornaments of nature,
Fit for so goodly stature:
That like the twins of Jove[2] they seemed in sight,
Which decke the Bauldricke of the Heavens bright.[3]
175 They two forth pacing to the Rivers side,
Received those two faire Brides, their Loves delight,
Which at th'appointed tyde,°   *time*
Each one did make his Bryde,
Against their Brydale day, which is not long:
180   Sweete Themmes runne softly, till I end my song.

5. I.e., the Earl of Essex, who (together with Sir Walter Raleigh) had in June, 1596, overwhelmed a Spanish fleet at Cadiz, plundered the city, and forced the destruction of forty-odd merchantmen together with their enormously valuable cargoes. Cadiz lies some fifty miles northwest from the Straits of Gibraltar, anciently known as the Pillars of Hercules.
6. I.e., punningly, that promises to be happy ("heureux") and glorious.
7. I.e., through all the world, every-where touched by expressions of your active and wide-ranging spirit, which some gifted poet [e.g., Spenser] may celebrate for the benefit of future ages.
8. I.e., Hesperus, the morning star in this context.
9. I.e., attended by an extensive retinue.
1. The bridegrooms-to-be, Henry Gilford and William Petre.
2. I.e., Castor and Pollux, the Gemini.
3. I.e., the zodiac (regarded as a belt studded with stars).

Editor's Note

Early and late, rivers run through the poetic landscape of Spenser's verse, watering and refreshing all that country. One thinks first, perhaps, of the magnificent concourse of streams from all the world, gathered for the wedding of Medway and Thames, and celebrated in *The Faerie Queene*, IV.xi; yet the earliest poems of the *Complaints* volume abound in riverine allusion, and Spenser takes care that Colin's ode to Elisa in the "Aprill" eclogue of *The Shepheardes Calender* should be "tuned [to] the waters fall" of streams and springs in nature as well as those derived from classical sources. The tale of Mulla and Bregog, in *Colin Clouts Come Home Againe*, and the related account of Faunus and Molanna, in the *Mutabilitie Cantos*, bear witness to the poet's continuing fascination with river lore. But pride of place in this context must be granted to the "spousall verse" that celebrates "silver streaming Themmes" as surely as it pays court to the social occasion for which *Prothalamion* was composed.

On November 8, 1596, Elizabeth and Catherine Somerset, the daughters of Edward Somerset, fourth Earl of Worcester, were married to (respectively) Henry Guildford and William Petre. The wedding took place at Essex House, in the Strand, in London. The poet may have been acquainted with relatives of the brides' family; but his sponsorship by the Earl of Essex (who was linked to the Somersets by blood and amity) probably explains how Spenser came to write *Prothalamion*. There were plenty of precedents for such a poem. Spenser seems to have known two Latin poems, William Leland's *Cygnea Cantio*, published in 1545, and William Camden's *De Connubio Tamis et Isis*, published in 1586; as well as an English poem by one W. Vallans, *A Tale of Two Swannes*, which appeared in 1590. In a letter of 1580, Spenser speaks to Gabriel Harvey of his intention "to sette forth a booke . . . whyche I entitle *Epithalamion Thamesis*"; this was to have been a topographic and antiquarian poem, describing "the marriage of the Thames," together with an account of "all the rivers throughout Englande, whyche came to the wedding."[1] Vallans, in his preface to *A Tale of Two Swannes*, states that he has "seen [*Epithalamion Thamesis*] in Latine verse";[2] but that poem now is lost. Nor has an independent English version survived. Presumably the original project was subsumed by the larger plan of *The Faerie Queene*, emerging triumphantly in the fourth Book.

But if *Prothalamion* has something in common with the poems by Camden and Vallans, it is of course much more than a further instance of a relatively minor poetic kind. As Hallett Smith observes, its individualized employment of conventions that mark other river poems at once extends and focuses the compass of the genre. The opening stanza places this poet in his own landscape; subsequently, with quiet decorum, Spenser establishes his right to celebrate just these events, these personages. Metrical form and versification may be thought to represent the final and most

1. *Three proper and wittie familiar Letters* . . . (London, 1580).
2. W. Vallans, Preface, "A Tale of Two Swannes" [1590], in John Leland, *Itinerary*, ed. Thomas Hearne (London, 1744), 9 vols.; Vol. V, vi–vii.

assured stage in a progression of experiments in the ode that (looking to the Italian *canzone*) began with the "Aprill" and "November" eclogues of *The Shepheardes Calender*, took flight in the rapturous *Epithalamion*, and concluded with what Coleridge called "the swan-like movement of his exquisite *Prothalamion*."[3] Recent criticism, finally, has drawn attention to the ways by which Spenser subtly matches the flow of London's river to that of time. Every human act is subject at last to time's power; still, the character and quality of mankind's occasions in some sense confer significant purpose on time's movement, and so make it more than a meaningless and terrifying onward surge. That the actions of men and women in time may be at once poignant and nobly in accord with larger patterns of order is the humanistic thought that informs such expressions as "Against the bridale daye, which is not long," as well as the reminder that these four young lovers are to be joined together "at th' appointed tyde." Even the sardonic and threatening contexts of T. S. Eliot's "The Fire Sermon," after all, do not altogether silence the timeless beauty of that lovely refrain: "Sweete Themmes, runne softly, till I end my song."

3. S. T. Coleridge, *Table Talk and Omnia* (London, 1917), p. 64.

Textual Notes

In this edition, the text of *The Faerie Queene* is based on that of the
1596 edition, in a microfilm copy of the volume (STC 23082) in the Hunt-
ington Library; the text of the *Cantos of Mutabilitie* is based on that of the
1609 edition, in a microfilm copy of the *Cantos* in the Newberry Library
copy. Texts of the minor poems are based on the first editions of each work
in microfilm copies of the volumes in the Huntington Library. References
to other editions in the list of variants are made to copies of the 1590 and
1609 editions of *The Faerie Queene* in the New York Public Library; to a
microfilm copy of the 1611 edition of Spenser's *Works* in the Library of
the University of Washington; and to microfilm copies of the 1581, 1586,
1591, and 1597 editions of *The Shepheardes Calender* in the Huntington
Library. A very few variants from the 1617 edition of Spenser's *Works* are
noted: these are drawn from the relevant lists of variants in the Variorum
edition.

The text of Spenser's poetry in this edition has been "updated" as fol-
lows: (1) italicized proper names are given in roman type; (2) the use of
"i," "u," and "v," is regularized to conform with modern practice; (3) the
ampersand is replaced by "and"; (4) diphthongs are replaced by separate
characters; (5) quotations are punctuated in accord with modern practice;
(6) the silent "e" is substituted for the apostrophe in such words as
"ador'd" and "perceiv'd"; (7) accents are inserted over final "ed" and "es"
to indicate the sounding of the extra syllable. Some textual peculiarities of
the minor poems (e.g., the combination of upper and lower case type for
the names of characters in *The Shepheardes Calender*, and at line begin-
nings throughout the *Amoretti*) have also been regularized.

The problem of deciding on an authoritative text for *The Faerie Queene*
is complicated by the fact that Books I–III in the edition of 1596 differ
considerably, in respect of substantives as well as accidentals, from the text
of the 1590 edition. Further, some of the corrections noted in the list of
"Faults Escaped" ("F.E.") appended to the 1590 edition were made
part of subsequent editions, but others were not incorporated into the
text in any of the early editions. While a number of substantive re-
visions seem certainly to reflect Spenser's hand, it is difficult to be sure
of the degree to which the punctuation and spelling of 1596 reflect the
poet's own preferences. Spenser's editors have responded variously to
this challenge: Morris, for example (in his edition of 1869), adheres

552

to the 1590 text, while Dodge (in 1908) retains the spelling of that edition but considers the substantive readings of the 1596 text to be "generally authoritative." The greater number of modern editors, however, base their texts on that of 1596: as the Variorum editors observe, "the text of 1596 shows sufficient alteration for the better to justify the opinion that Spenser was responsible for an incidental revision," and further, "the 1596 quarto has the authority of the last edition in Spenser's lifetime." It has seemed to the present editor that the purposes of this Norton Critical Edition will be best served by a text based on that of 1596.

In view particularly of the "updating" of quotational punctuation in this edition, the textual notes are confined chiefly to substantive departures from the basic texts and significant substantive variants in the early quartos, the 1609 folio of *The Faerie Queene*, and the 1611 volume of Spenser's *Works*. The first reading given for each entry in the textual notes is that which has been adopted for the text of this edition. In the list of variants, "1590 *etc*." indicates an identical reading in all four of the early editions of *The Faerie Queene*; "1596 *etc*." an identical reading in the editions of 1596, 1609, and 1611. With a few exceptions, substantive variants appearing only in the edition of 1611 are not included in these textual notes. Whether or not a correction indicated in "F.E." is made in one or more of these early editions, the present edition excludes those corrections which are not clearly of substantive significance, or which evidently refer to a compositor's error in the edition of 1590. Thus, the correction of "sire" to "fire," in I.v.40.9, is excluded; that of "seene" to "seeme," in I.vii.36.1, is also excluded; that of "murmuring" to "murmur ring," in I.viii.11.9, is included in the list of variants. Errors clearly resulting from a compositor's mistake, such as the inversion of a letter, or the omission of a letter (where the meaning is not affected) are excluded. Save for a very few of the most helpful substantive emendations proposed by scholars and editors from the time of John Hughes, no attempt is made in the list of variants to take account of the wide range of conjectural readings, for which the student is referred to the various textual appendices of the Variorum edition.

The punctuation and spelling of *The Faerie Queene* in the present edition closely follow the text of the 1596 edition (given those alterations imposed by the "updating" of quotational punctuation). Occasionally the punctuation of another among the early editions is silently substituted for the punctuation of 1596, where the clarity of Spenser's text is thereby helped on without substantive alteration of the meaning of the passage in question. The textual notes in the present edition do not, as a rule, take account of the large number of variants in punctuation and spelling between 1590 and 1596. However, several of the more significant punctuational variants among the four early editions which bear substantively upon the text are included (e.g., I.xi.6.5–6; III.v.37.2). The textual notes also include a few spelling variants of particular interest, such as the preference of the 1596 text (e.g., at I.v.15.2) for "thirstie" to the "thristy" of 1590, the substitution in 1596 of "am" for the eye-rhyme "ame" of 1590 (e.g., at I.v.26.6), or the consequences for the text of the failure, in 1609, to recognize syllabic "es" (e.g., at I.v.23.8, or I.x.34.8). In the case of the minor poems, finally, for which textual problems are generally less challenging than they are where *The Faerie Queene* is concerned, departures of punctuation or spelling (other than obvious compositorial errors, or the "crowding off" of punctuation, as in the *Amoretti* and *Epithalamion* of 1595) from the texts of the first editions, together with significant variants in later editions, are included in the notes. Quotational punctuation has been supplied for Sonnets 29 and 75 in the *Amoretti*. The aim throughout has been to clarify the text for modern readers without significantly altering the meaning and character of Spenser's text.

THE FAERIE QUEENE

A Letter of the Authors . . .

Line 8. by accidents *1590.*

Dedication
The dedication to the edition of 1590 reads: TO THE MOST MIGHTIE AND MAGNIFICENT EMPRESSE ELIZABETH, BY THE GRACE OF GOD QUEENE OF ENGLAND, FRANCE AND IRELAND DEFENDER OF THE FAITH &c. Her most humble Servant: *Ed. Spenser.*

Book I
Proem 1.2. taught, *1590, 1609, 1611;* taught *1596.*
Proem 4.5. my *1596 etc.;* mine *1590.*
i.Arg.3. entrappe *1590; entrape 1596; entrap 1609, 1611.*
i.2.1. But *1596 etc.;* And *1590.*
i.5.1. an innocent *1596;* and innocent *1590;* an Innocent *1609, 1611.*
i.9.6. sweete bleeding *1590, 1596;* sweet, bleeding *1609, 1611.*
i.10.4. They *1590, 1609, 1611;* The *1596.*
i.12.5. stroke *F.E.;* hardy stroke *1590 etc.*
i.15.6. poisonous *1596 etc.;* poisnous *1590.*
i.21.5. spring *F.E.;* ebbe *1590 etc.;* to avale *F.E., 1596 etc.;* t'avale *1590.*
i.28.8 passed *1590;* passeth *1596 etc.*
i.30.9. sits *1590, 1596;* fits *1609, 1611.*
i.31.6. you *1596 etc.;* thee *1590.*
i.42.8. sights *F.E., 1596 etc.;* sighes *1590.*
i.46.7. usage *1590, 1596;* visage *1609, 1611.*
i.48.9. her with Yvie *1590;* her Yvie *1596 etc.*
i.50.3. thought have *1590, 1596;* thought t'have *1609, 1611.*
i.53.6. since no'untruth *1590, 1596;* sith n'untruth *1609, 1611.*
ii.6.2. his guiltie sight *1590 etc.;* this guiltie sight *1758 conj. Upton.*

ii.8.9. loved *1590, 1609, 1611;* lovest *1596.*
ii.16.5. Astonied both *1590, 1596;* Astonied, both *1609, 1611.*
ii.16.8. idely *1590, 1596;* idlely *1609, 1611.*
ii.17.5. cruell spies *F.E.;* cruelties *1590 etc.*
ii.17.9. dies *1590, 1596;* die *1609, 1611.*
ii.22.5. your *1596 etc.;* thy *1590.*
ii.27.9. so dainty *1590, 1596;* so, Dainty *1609, 1611.*
ii.29.1. can *1590, 1596;* gan *1609, 1611.*
ii.29.2. shade him thither hastly *1590;* shade thither hastly *1596;* shadow thither hast'ly *1609, 1611.*
ii.29.3. ymounted *F.E.;* that mounted *1590 etc.*
ii.40.1. Thens *F.E., 1609, 1611;* Then *1590, 1596.*
ii.40.2. unweeting *1590;* unweening *1596 etc.*
ii.41.5. Thens *F.E., 1609, 1611;* Then *1590, 1596.*
ii.45.6. up gan lift *1590, 1596;* gan up-lift *1609, 1611.*
iii.1.4. Through *1590, 1596;* By *1609, 1611.*
iii.28.9. liefe *1590, 1596;* life *1609, 1611.*
iii.29.9. defend, now *1596 etc.;* defend. Now *1590.*
iii.34.9. spurnd *1596 etc.;* spurd *1590.*
iii.36.7. mourning *1590, 1609, 1611;* morning *1596.*
iii.38.7. that *F.E.;* the *1590 etc.*
iii.44.7. feares, *1590, 1596;* feares *1609, 1611.*
iv.3.5. case *F.E., 1596 etc.;* care *1590.*
iv.11.3. worth *1590, 1609, 1611;* wroth *1596.*
iv.12.2. a Queene *1590, 1609, 1611;* Queene *1596.*
iv.12.7. Realmes *1596 etc.;* Realme *1590.*
iv.16.3. hurtlen *1590, 1596;* hurlen *1609, 1611.*

iv.16.9. glitterand *1590;* glitter and *1596 etc.*

iv.20.3 From *1590;* For *1596 etc.*

iv.22.8. corse *F.E., 1596 etc.;* course *1590.*

iv.23.7. dry dropsie *1590 etc.;* dire dropsie *1758 conj. Upton.*

iv.27.4. mettall full, *1590, 1596;* mettall, full *1609, 1611.*

iv.30.4 chaw *1590, 1596;* jaw *1609, 1611.*

iv.32.9. fifte *F.E.;* first *1590 etc.*

iv.45.5. of my new joy *F.E., 1609, 1611;* of new joy *1590, 1596.*

v.1.9. did he wake *1590, 1609, 1611;* did wake *1596.*

v.2.5. hurld *F.E.;* hurls *1590 etc.*

v.7.9. helmets hewen deepe *1596 etc.;* hewen helmets deepe *1590.*

v.15.2. thirstie *1596 etc.;* thristy *1590.*

v.17.4. wash his woundes *1590, 1596;* washen his wounds *1609, 1611.*

v.23.8 Nightes *1590, 1596;* Nights drad *1609, 1611.*

v.24.9. for *1590;* and *1596 etc.*

v.26.6. am *1596 etc.;* ame *1590.*

v.35.5. thirstie *1596 etc.;* thristy *1590.*

v.35.9. leake *F.E., 1596 etc.;* lete *1590.*

v.38.6. cliffs *F.E.;* clifts *1590 etc.*

v.41.2. nigh *1590;* high *1596 etc.*

v.51.5. that *F.E.;* the *1590 etc.*

vi.1.3. "The use of 'bewaile' is either very forced (? suggested by the consequences of a wreck), or it is a mere error" *(O.E.D.). Church, in 1758, proposed* assayle.

vi.1.5. in *F.E.;* it *1590 etc.*

vi.5.5. win *1590;* with *1596 etc.*

vi.8.7. misshapen *1609, 1611;* mishappen *1590;* mishapen *1596.*

vi.12.3. twixt *1590, 1596;* through *1609, 1611.*

vi.14.2. doubled *1590, 1596;* double *1609, 1611.*

vi.15.2. Or *1590;* Of *1596 etc.*

vi.23.8. noursled *1596 etc.;* nousled *1590.*

vi.25.9. earne *1590, 1596;* yearne *1609, 1611.*

vi.26.5. fierce and fell *F.E., 1596 etc.;* swift and cruell *1590.*

vi.26.9. as a tyrans *1590;* as tyrans *1596;* as proud tyrants *1609, 1611.*

vi.38.8 thristed *1590, 1596;* thirsted *1609, 1611.*

vi.39.7. quoth he *1596 etc.;* qd. she *1590.*

vi.44.1. fell *1596 etc.;* full *1590.*

vi.47.8. they to *1590;* they two *1596 etc.*

vii.5.9. drunke thereof, did *1596 etc.;* drinke thereof, do *1590.*

vii.18.4. brought *1596 etc.;* braught *1590.*

vii.18.5. nought *1596 etc.;* naught *1590.*

vii.20.3. the *1596 etc.;* that *1590.*

vii.22.9. sad sight fro *1596 etc.;* sad fro *1590.*

vii.32.8. Whose *1596 etc.;* Her *1590.*

vii.37.7. trample *1596 etc.;* amble *1590.*

vii.43.4. whilest *1596;* whiles *1590;* whil'st *1609, 1611.*

vii.43.5. runne *F.E., 1596 etc.;* come *1590.*

vii.47.3. hands *F.E., 1596 etc.;* hand *1590.*

vii.48.9. have you *1596 etc.;* have yee *1590.*

viii.Arg. 3. the *F.E.;* that *1590 etc.*

viii.3.1. the *1596 etc.;* his *1590.*

viii.10.3. avantage *1596 etc.;* advantage *1590.*

viii.11.9. murmur ring *F.E.;* murmuring *1590 etc.*

viii.14.4. inner *1590, 1596;* inward *1609, 1611.*

viii.21.5. their *1590 etc.;* his *1758 conj. Church.*

viii.24.6. his *1596 etc.;* her *1590.*

viii.27.7. eyes *1596 etc.;* eye *1590.*

viii.33.5. sits *1590;* fits *1596 etc.*

viii.41.7. and helmets *1590, 1609, 1611;* helmets *1596.*

viii.44.4. delight *1590 etc.;* dislike *1734 conj. Jortin.*

ix.Arg.2. bands *F.E., 1596 etc.;* hands *1590.*

ix.8.9. the *F.E., 1596 etc.;* that *1590.*

ix.9.5. Timons *F.E., 1596 etc.;* Cleons *1590.*

ix.12.9. on *F.E., 1609, 1611;* at *1590, 1596.*

ix.13.1. For-wearied *1596;* For wearied *1590;* Fore-wearied *1609, 1611.*

ix.15.8. vow *1596 etc.;* vowd *1590.*

ix.18.9. as *1590;* the *1596 etc.*

ix.19.7. his *F.E., 1596 etc.;* this *1590.*

ix.33.3. ypight *1596 etc.;* yplight *1590.*

ix.34.6. cliffs *F.E.;* clifts *1590 etc.*

ix.46.7. falsed *1596 etc.;* falsest *1590.*

ix.52.1. saw *1596 etc.;* heard *1590.*

ix.53.1. feeble *1590;* seely *1596;* silly *1609, 1611.*

x.15.4. well *1596 etc.;* for *1590.*

x.15.9. gan *1590, 1596;* can *1609, 1611.*

x.16.8. her *F.E.;* be *1590 etc.*

x.20.5. This line, omitted in 1590 and 1596, appears first in 1609.

x.27.6. His bodie in salt water smarting sore *1596 etc.;* His blamefull body in salt water sore *1590.*

x.34.8. worldes *1590, 1596;* worlds *1609, 1611.*

x.36.6. Their *1609, 1611;* There *1590, 1596.*

x.36.9. in commers-by *1609, 1611;* in-commers by *1590, 1596.*

x.38.1. as *1590, 1596, 1611;* an *1609.*

x.50.1 she *1590, 1609, 1611;* he *1596.*

x.52.1. since *1590, 1596;* sith *1609, 1611.*

x.52.6. Brings *1609, 1611;* Bring *1590, 1596.*

x.57.5. pretious *F.E.;* piteous *1590 etc.*

x.59.2. frame *F.E.;* fame *1590 etc.*

x.61.3. thy *1590, 1609, 1611;* to thy *1596.*

x.62.4. (Quoth he) as wretched, and liv'd in like paine *1596 etc.;* As wretched men, and lived in like paine *1590.*

x.62.8. and battailes none are to be fought *1596 etc.;* and bitter battailes all are fought *1590.*

x.62.9. are vaine *1596 etc.;* they' are vaine *1590.*

x.64.7. doen *1590, 1609, 1611;* doen then *1596.*

x.65.3. place *1596 etc.;* face *1590.*

xi.2.4. at *F.E., 1596 etc.;* it *1590.*

xi.3. *This stanza first appears in 1596.*

xi.5.1. his *F.E.;* this *1590 etc.*

xi.6.5. aswage, *1590, 1596;* aswage; *1609, 1611.*

xi.6.6. sownd; *1590, 1596;* sound, *1609, 1611.*

xi.6.9. scared *F.E.;* feared *1590 etc.*

xi.8.7. vast *1609, 1611;* vaste *1590;* wast *1596.*

xi.11.5. as *F.E.;* all *1590 etc.*

xi.26.6. swinged *1590, 1596;* singed *1609, 1611.*

xi.27.2. vaunt *1590;* daunt *1596 etc.*

xi.30.5. one *F.E.;* it *1590 etc.*

xi.37.2. yelded *1590, 1596;* yelled *1609, 1611.*

xi.39.4. sting *1590;* string *1596 etc.*

xi.39.7 string *1590;* sting *1596 etc.*

xi.39.8. a *1590, 1596;* in *1609, 1611.*

xi.41.4. Nor *1609, 1611;* For *1590, 1596.*

xi.51.2. the *1590;* her *1596 etc.*

xi.51.7. spred, *1758 conj. Church;* spred; *1590 etc.*

xi.51.8. darke; *1758 conj. Church;* darke, *1590 etc.*

xii.3.5. fond *1590;* found *1596 etc.*

xii.7.3. sung *1596 etc.;* song *1590.*

xii.11.5. talants *F.E., 1611;* talents *1590, 1596, 1609.*

xii.16.1. pleasure *1590;* pleasures *1596 etc.*

xii.17.1. that *1590;* the *1596 etc.*

xii.21.7. that dawning day is drawing neare *1590;* the dawning day is dawning neare *1596 etc.*

xii.27.7. of *1590;* and *1596 etc.*

xii.28.7. her *1590;* his *1596 etc.*

xii.32.5. t'invegle *F.E.;* to invegle *1590 etc.*

xii.34.2. vaine *F.E., 1596 etc.;* faine *1590.*

xii.37.6. the *1590, 1596;* a *1609, 1611.*

xii.38.3. frankencense *1596 etc.;* frankincense *1590.*

xii.40.9. His *1590;* Her *1596 etc.*

Book II

i.1.7. caytives *1590, 1596;* caytive *1609, 1611.*

i.2.7. native *1590;* natives *1596 etc.*

i.3.2. food *1590, 1596;* feud *1609;* feude *1611.*

i.3.9 be *1590, 1596;* he *1609, 1611.*

i.8.5. faire *1590, 1609, 1611;* a faire *1596.*

i.10.5. corse *1596 etc.;* corps *1590.*

i.16.1. liefe *1596 etc.;* life *1590.*

i.18.6. did he *1596 etc.;* he did *1590.*

i.29.1. attone *1596 etc.;* at one *1590.*

i.31.2. handling *1590, 1609, 1611;* handing *1596.*

i.33.8. thrise *F.E.;* these *1590 etc.*

vii.4.4. yet *1590;* it *1596 etc.*

vii.4.8. upsidowne *1596 etc.;* upside downe *1590.*

vii.7.3. heapes *1596 etc.;* hils *1590.*

vii.10.1. besits *1590, 1596;* befits *1609, 1611.*

vii.12.9. as *1596 etc.;* in *1590.*

vii.18.2. that antique *1590, 1609, 1611;* antique *1596.*

vii.21.5. infernall *1596 etc.;* internall *1590.*

vii.24.7. ought *1596 etc.;* nought *1590.*

vii.37.1. as *1596 etc.;* an *1590.*

vii.40.5. As if *1590, 1609, 1611;* As *1596./* that *F.E.;* the *1590 etc.*

vii.40.7. But *1596 etc.;* And *1590./* golden *1596 etc.;* yron *1590.*

vii.41.3. his *1590;* to *1596 etc.*

vii.52.6. With which *1734 conj. Jortin;* Which with *1590, 1596;* Which-with *1609, 1611.*

vii.60.4. intemperate *1596 etc.;* more temperate *1590.*

vii.64.9. of the *1596 etc.;* of his *1590.*

viii.3.8. Come hither, come hither *1596;* Come hether, come hether *1590;* Come hither, hither *1609, 1611.*

xii.Arg.1. by *1596 etc.;* through *1590.*

xii.Arg.2. passing through *1596 etc.;* through passing *1590.*

xii.1.6. for that *F.E.;* for this *1590 etc.*

xii.13.9. honor *1596 etc.;* temple *1590.*

xii.15.1. can *1590, 1596;* gan *1609, 1611.*

xii.20.8. their *1590;* the *1596 etc.*

xii.21.1. th'heedfull *1596 etc.;* th'earnest *1590.*

xii.27.4. the resounding *1590, 1596;* resounding *1609, 1611.*

xii.32.4. That *1590, 1609, 1611;* Thou *1596.*

xii.39.8. upstarting *1596 etc.;* upstaring *1590.*

xii.48.7. of this *1596 etc.;* oft his *1590.*

xii.51.1. Thereto *1596 etc.;* Therewith *1590.*

xii.52.9. *Eden* selfe, if *1590; Eden,* if *1596; Eden,* if that *1609, 1611.*

xii.57.9. nought *1590;* not *1596 etc.*

xii.60.5. curious *1590, 1596;* pure *1609, 1611.*

xii.61.8. tenderly *1596 etc.;* fearefully *1590.*

xii.73.1. that *1590, 1596;* the *1609, 1611.*

xii.81.4. the *1596 etc.;* that *1590.*

xii.83.7. spoyle *1590;* spoyld *1596 etc.*

Book III

Proem 1.2. That *1596 etc.;* The *1590.*

Proem 4.2. Your selfe you *1596 etc.;* Thy selfe thou *1590.*

i.Arg.3. *Malecastaes F.E.; Materastaes 1590 etc.*

i.7.2. sith *1590, 1596;* since *1609, 1611.*

i.14.8. creatures *1596 etc.;* creature *1590.*

i.21.9. sixe before, *1590, 1596;* sixe, before *1609, 1611.*

i.30.6. mard *F.E.;* shard *1590 etc.*

i.31.6. of many *1590;* many *1596 etc.*

i.41.8. lightly *1609, 1611;* highly *1590, 1596.*

i.47.7. which *1596 etc.;* that *1590.*

i.56.8. *Basciomani 1596 etc.; Bascimano 1590.*

i.60.8. wary *1609, 1611;* weary *1590, 1596.*

i.60.9. fond *1590, 1596;* fand *1609, 1611.*

ii.4.1. Guyon *should read* Redcrosse.

ii.8.5. Which I to prove, *1596 etc.;* Which to prove, I *1590.*

ii.9.7. well of all, *1590, 1596;* well, of all *1609, 1611.*

ii.30.5. in her warme bed her dight *1596 etc.;* her in her warme bed dight *1590.*

ii.36.1. others *1596 etc.;* other *1590.*

ii.37.2. For no *1590 etc.;* For know *1758 conj. Upton.*

ii.49.7. a earthen *1590, 1596;* an earthen *1609, 1611.*

iii.1.1. Most *1590, 1596;* Oh *1609, 1611.*

iii.4.8. protense *1590;* pretence *1596 etc.*

iii.15.3. to unfold *1590, 1596;* unfold *1609, 1611.*

iii.22.9. *Greeke 1590; Greece 1596 etc.*

iii.29.1. With *1590;* Where *1596 etc.*

iii.35.1. thy *1590;* the *1596 etc.*

iii.37.7. their *1590;* the *1596 etc.*

iii.43.9. of the earth *F.E.;* th'earth *1590 etc.*

iii.44.5. yeares shalbe *1590;* shalbe *1596;* shall be full *1609, 1611.*

iii.44.6. to *1596 etc.;* unto their *1590.*

iii.50.9. Hee *F.E.;* Shee *1590;* She *1596 etc./* looks as earst *1609;* looks *1590, 1596.*

iii.51.9. disguise *1590;* devise *1596 etc.*

iii.53.3. (whom need new strength shall teach) *1596 etc.;* (need makes good schollers) teach *1590.*

iv.6.9. her *1590, 1596;* had *1609, 1611.*

iv.8.4. Why *1590;* Who *1596 etc.*

iv.8.9. these *1596 etc.;* thy *1590.*

iv.15.6. speare *1609, 1611;* speares *1590, 1596.*

iv.33.4. raynes *1590;* traines *1596 etc.*

iv.39.9. sith we no more shall meet *1596 etc.;* till we againe may meet *1590.*

iv.59.5. Dayes dearest children *1596 etc.;* The children of day *1590.*

v.Arg.4. sownd *1590, 1596;* swound *1609, 1611.*

v.3.2. that at *1590, 1596;* at the *1609, 1611.*

v.5.5. A *1590;* And *1596 etc.*

v.11.1. ye *1590;* you *1596 etc.*

v.37.2. undertaken after her, *1590;* undertaken after her *1596;* undertaken, after her *1609, 1611.*

v.37.6. follow *1596 etc.;* followd *1590.*

v.38.9. forth with *1590, 1609, 1611;* forthwith *1596.*

v.39.9. his *1596 etc.;* their *1590.*

v.40.4. loves sweet *1596 etc.;* sweet loves *1590.*

v.40.9. living *1596 etc.;* liking *1590.*

v.44.7. revew *1590;* renew *1596 etc.*

v.52.6. admire: *1609, 1611;* admyre *1590;* admire *1596.*

vi.3.9. was *1596 etc.;* were *1590.*

vi.6.5. his *1590, 1596;* his hot *1609, 1611.*

vi.12.4. beautie *1590;* beauties *1596 etc.*

vi.25.5. Which as *1609, 1611;* From which *1590, 1596.*

vi.26.4. To seeke the fugitive, both farre and nere. *1609;* To seeke the fugitive. *1590;* To seeke the fugitive, both farre and nere, *1596.*

vi.28.6. thence *1590;* hence *1596 etc.*

vi.40.6. spyde *1590 etc.;* saw *1758 conj. Church.*

vi.42.5. heavy *1596 etc.;* heavenly *1590.*

vi.45.4. *This half-line first appears in 1609.*

vii.9.3. two *1590 etc.;* to *1715 conj. Hughes.*

vii.13.6. had *1596 etc.;* hath *1590.*

vii.18.5. be by the witch or that *1908 conj. Dodge;* by the witch or by *1590;* be the witch or that *1596 etc.*

vii.19.6. her *1590, 1596;* that *1609, 1611.*

vii.22.4. Monstrous mishapt *1596 etc.;* Monstrous, mishapt *1590.*

vii.34.2. enclose *1590 etc.;* constraine *1758 conj. Church;* containe *1908 conj. Dodge.*

vii.43.7. saw, with great remorse *1609, 1611;* saw with great remorse, *1590, 1596.*

vii.45.1. the good *1590;* good *1596 etc./* wake *1590, 1596;* awake *1609, 1611.*

vii.48.4. And many hath to foule *1596 etc.;* Till him Chylde *Thopas* to *1590.*

vii.49.5. staine *1590;* straine *1596 etc.*

vii.50.2. thrust *1590;* thurst *1596 etc.*

vii.58.3. a do *1596;* adoe *1590;* a-do *1609, 1611.*

viii.2.7. broken *1596 etc.;* golden *1590.*

viii.5.1. advise *1596 etc.;* device *1590.*

viii.7.4. a womans *1596 etc.;* to womens *1590.*

viii.20.2. Fortune *1596;* fortune *1590, 1609, 1611.*

viii.23.9. am *1596 etc.;* ame *1590.*

viii.30.3. frory *1590, 1596;* frowy *1590, 1596.*

viii.33.9. thereby *1596 etc.;* her by *1590.*

viii.49.4. his *1590, 1596;* a *1609, 1611.*

ix.4.5. her *1590, 1596;* his *1609, 1611.*

ix.13.9. And so defide them each *1590;* And defide them each *1596;* And them defied each *1609, 1611.*

ix.14.7. to kenell *1596 etc.;* in kenell *1590.*

ix.22.1. *Minerva 1596 etc.; Bellona 1590.*

ix.24.5. But most *1590, 1609, 1611;* But *1596.*

ix.27.5. that *1596 etc.;* with *1590.*

ix.48.6. to sea *1590, 1609, 1611;* to the sea *1596.*

x.8.9. take to *1596 etc.;* take with *1590.*

x.13.8. would beare *1596 etc.;* did beare *1590.*

x.18.4. Then *1596 etc.;* So *1590.*

x.27.2. Sith *1590, 1596;* Since *1609, 1611.*

x.31.3. with thy *1596 etc.;* that with *1590.*

x.31.7. vertues pray *1596;* vertuous pray *1590;* vertues pay *1609, 1611.*

x.39.7. am *1596 etc.;* ame *1590.*

x.40.3. wastefull *1596 etc.;* faithfull *1590.*

x.46.6. th' Earthes *1590, 1596;* the Earthes *1609, 1611.*

x.53.8. with life away *1590, 1596;* away with life *1609, 1611.*

xi.2.3. golden *1609, 1611;* golding *1590, 1596.*

xi.4.4. that I did ever *1596 etc.;* all, that I ever *1590.*

xi.4.9. him did *1596 etc.;* did him *1590.*

xi.9.6. hast thou, *1609, 1611;* hast, thou *1590, 1596.*

xi.12.1. singultes *1609, 1611;* singulfes *1590, 1596.*

xi.19.9. death *1590 etc.;* life *1734 conj. Jortin.*

xi.22.8. Foolhardy as th'Earthes children, the which made *1596;* Foolhardy, as the Earthes children, which made *1590;* Foole-hardy, as th' Earthes children, the which made *1609, 1611.*

xi.23.5. This is *1590, 1609, 1611;* This *1596.*

xi.26.7. with imperious sway *1590;* imperious sway *1596;* his imperious sway *1609, 1611.*

xi.27.7. entred *1596 etc.;* decked *1590.*

xi.28.8. Like a *1596 etc.;* Like to a *1590.*

xi.33.9. her *1590, 1596;* his *1609, 1611.*

xi.39.6. each *1596 etc.;* his *1590.*

xi.39.8. Stag *1734 conj. Jortin;* Hag *1590 etc.*

xi.49.8. ever more *1609, 1611;* evermore *1590, 1596.*

xii.5.7. concent *1590, 1609, 1611;* consent *1596.*

xii.7.8 wood *1596 etc.;* word *1590.*

xii.9.3. other *1609, 1611;* others *1590, 1596.*

xii.12.3. and *1596 etc.;* or *1590.*

xii.12.6. wingyheeld *1596 etc.;* winged heeld *1590.*

xii.18.8. hony-lady *1590 etc.;* honyladen *1758 conj. Upton.*

xii.23.5. his right hand *F.E., 1609, 1611;* his right *1590, 1596.*

xii.26.6. All *1590;* And *1596 etc.*

xii.26.7. with that *1596 etc.;* by the *1590.*

xii.27.3. and bore all away *1596 etc.;* nothing did remayne *1590.*

xii.33.3. her selfe *1596 etc.;* the next *1590.*

xii.34.4. her *1609, 1611;* him *1590, 1596.*

xii.41.7. *The line as it stands is an alexandrine: Church (1758) suggested that* prisoner *should be omitted; Upton (1758) proposed to eliminate either* prisoner *or* Lady.

xii.42.2. She *1596 etc.;* He *1590.*

xii.42.4. She *F.E., 1596 etc.;* He *1590.*

xii.42.5. her *F.E., 1596 etc.;* him *1590.*

Book IV

Proem 1.2 Welds *1596;* Wields *1609, 1611*

x.1.8 launcht *1596;* launc't *1609, 1611*

x.2.8 Since *1596;* Sith *1609, 1611*

x.9.1 earne *1596;* yearne *1609, 1611*

x.17.5 adward *1596;* award *1609, 1611*

x.19.1 meanest *1609, 1611;* nearest *1596*

x.26.9 aspire *1596, 1609;* inspire *1611, 1715 Hughes*

x.37.9 May *1609, 1611;* may *1596*

x.42.6 eldest *1596;* elder *1609, 1611*

x.56.4 at *1596;* on *1609, 1611*

Book V

Proem 2.2 at *1596, 1609;* as *1611, 1715 Hughes*

Proem 11.2 stead *1609, 1611;* place *1596*

vii.6.9 with her *1596, 1609, 1611;* with his *1855 conj. Child*

vii.20.7 up-standing, stifly *1596, 1609, 1611;* upstanding stifly *1758 conj. Upton*

Book VI

ix.6.5. him *1609, 1611;* them *1596.*

ix.26.1. eare *1596;* care *1609, 1611.*

ix.26.4. rapt *1596, 1611;* wrapt *1609.*

ix.36.8. Oenone *1715 corr. Hughes;* Benone *1596 etc.*

ix.46.5. dwell *1611;* well *1596, 1609.*

x.2.9. in the port *1609, 1611;* on the port *1596.*

x.4.9. now, by course *1596;* now by course, *1609, 1611.*

x.24.7. froward *1611;* forward *1596, 1609.*

Cantos of Mutabilitie

vi.4.5. And *1609;* At *1909 conj. Smith.*

vi.10.1. That *1609;* Tho *1715 conj. Hughes.*

vi.38.2. wealths *1609;* wealth *1715 conj. Hughes.*

vii.2.3. feeble *1715 conj. Hughes;* sable *1609 etc.*

vii.9.7 kindes *1609;* kinde *1758 conj. Upton.*

vii.10.4. mores *1609;* more *1715 conj. Hughes.*

vii.16.3. thy *1609;* my *1611.*

vii.28.3. did beare *1609;* beare *1611.*

vii.41.5. rade; rode *1609, 1611. The spelling adopted is warranted by the O.E.D.*

vii.55.7. saine *1609;* faine *1611.*

viii.2.8. Sabbaoth *1609;* Sabaoth *1611.*

viii.2.9. Sabbaoth *1609;* Sabaoth *1611./*Sabaoths *1609, 1611;* Sabbath's *1758 conj. Upton.*

THE SHEPHEARDES CALENDER

To His Booke

12. my *1579, 1581, 1586, 1591, 1597;* thy *1611.*

Januarye

28. yeare *1579, 1581, 1586, 1591;* yeares *1597, 1611.*

34. bloosmes *1579;* blosomes *1581;* blossomes *1586 etc.*

37. All so *1579, 1581;* Also *1586 etc.*

49. hower, *1581 etc.;* hower. *1579.*

April

8. thristye *1579;* thirstie *1581 etc.*

36. tuned *1579, 1581, 1611;* turned *1586, 1591, 1597.*

39. Forsake *1581 etc.;* For sake *1579.*

64. angelick *1579;* angelike *1581, 1586, 1591;* angellike *1597;* angel-like *1611.*

135. finesse *1579, 1581, 1586, 1591;* finenesse *1597, 1611.*

143. Chevisaunce, *1597, 1611;* Chevisaunce. *1579, 1581, 1586, 1591.*

144. Delice. *1611;* Delice, *1579, 1581, 1586, 1591, 1597.*

June

1. syte *1579, 1581;* sight *1586 etc.*

16. shroud *1611, 1617;* shouder *1579, 1581, 1586, 1591, 1597*

18. the soyle *1579, 1581, 1586, 1591;* thy soyle *1597 etc.*

58. thy *1579; 1611 etc.;* the *1581, 1586, 1591, 1597*

80. poore *1579, 1581;* poure *1586 etc.*

98. painfull *1579, 1597, 1611, 1617;* plaineful *1581, 1586, 1591*

October

Arg.[p.448]. *whiche* 1581 *etc.*; *whishe* 1579.

Arg.[p. 449]. ἐνθουσιασμὸς 1579; Kithousiasmos 1581, 1586, 1591, 1597; Enthousiasmos 1611.

2. chace, 1597, 1611; chace: 1579, 1581, 1586, 1591.

6. dead. 1597, 1611; dead? 1579, 1581, 1586, 1591.

39-40. giusts, . . . crowne. 1579; guists, . . . crowne. 1581, 1586, 1591; gusts, . . . crowne, 1611.

79. thy 1586 *etc.*; the 1579, 1581.

96a. CUDDIE. *omitted* 1579, 1581.

100. demaundes, . . . dwell. 1910 *Sélincourt*; demaundes. . . . dwell, 1579, 1581, 1586, 1591, 1597; demands, . . . dwell: 1611.

November

15. Ystabled 1579, 1581, 1586, 1591; Ystablished 1597; Ystablisht 1611 *etc.*

23. sike 1579, 1581, 1586, 1591; like 1597, 1611 *etc.*

53. mourn(e)fulst 1579, 1581, 1586, 1591; mournful(l) 1597, 1611 *etc.*

178. thee 1579, 1581, 1586, 1591; the 1597, 1611 *etc.*

December

Arg. [p. 462] riper 1579, 1581, 1586, 1591; ripest 1597, 1611 *etc.*

18. rurall 1579, 1581; laurell 1586, 1591; lawrell 1597, 1611 *etc.*

29. wreaked 1579, 1581, 1586, 1591, 1597; recked 1611 *etc.*

43. derring doe 1908 *conj. Dodge;* derring to 1579 *etc.*

75. All so 1586 *etc.;* Also 1579, 1581

84. Phoebe 1579, 1581, 1586, 1591; Phoebus 1597, 1611 *etc.*

98. to 1579, 1581, 1586, 1597, 1617; too 1591, 1611

103. with 1579, 1581; and 1586 *etc.*

127. his 1579, 1581, 1586, 1591; my 1597, 1611 *etc.*

146. so 1579, 1581, 1586, 1591; most 1597,⟨1611 *etc.*

157. *The emblem is omitted in all texts before 1715: "J. Hughes brilliantly restored the missing Emblem from the Gloss" (Var.).*

MUIOPOTMOS

34. youngth 1910 *Selincourt;* yonght 1591; youth 1611, 1617

149. champion he 1591; champaine o're he 1611, 1617

254. earne 1591; yearne 1611, 1617

299. Yvie winding 1591; Iviewinding 1611, 1617

335. hayrie 1591; ayrie 1611, 1617

392. hatefull 1591; fatal 1611, 1617

420. Of 1591; On 1611, 1617

AMORETTI

Sonnet 1

2. might, 1611; might 1595.

Sonnet 10

1. love, 1611; love 1595.

2. be: 1595; be? 1611.

11. pride, 1910 *Sélincourt;* pride 1595, 1611.

Sonnet 28

9. Phoebus 1611; Phaebus 1595.

13. Phoebus 1611; Phebus 1595.

Sonnet 29

4. forlorne. 1910 *Sélincourt;* forlorne, 1595, 1611.

Sonnet 35

1-3. covetize, . . . paine, . . . suffize: 1910 *Sélincourt;* covetize, . . . paine: . . . suffize, 1595; covetice . . . paine, . . . suffice: 1611.

14. shadowes, 1910 *Sélincourt;* shadowes 1595, 1611.

Sonnet 44

5. continuall cruell 1595; continuall, cruell, 1611, 1617

7. arre, 1611, 1617; arre. 1595

Sonnet 45

5. shew 1611; shew, 1595.

6. eye, 1617; eye: 1595, 1611.

10. were: 1595; were, 1611.

Sonnet 53

5-6. play, . . . hew 1595; play . . . . hew, 1611, 1617

6. semblant 1595; semblance 1611, 1617

10. ornament, 1617; ornament: 1595, 1611

Sonnet 67

2. escapt away, 1805 *Todd;* escapt away: 1595; escape away, 1611, 1617

4. pray: 1611, 1617; pray. 1595; Prey: 1715 *Hughes*

Sonnet 68
1. lyfe, *1910 Sélincourt;* lyfe *1595, 1611.*
3. hell, *1611;* hell *1595./* away *1611;* away, *1595.*
4. win: *1611;* win. *1595.*

Sonnet 71
3. lurke, *1595;* lurke *1611.*
9. about, *1595, 1611;* above *1862 conj. Collier.*
13. see, *1611;* see. *1595.*

Sonnet 75
2. away *1611;* a way *1595.*
6. immortalize, *1611;* immortalize. *1595.*
9. devize *1611;* devize, *1595.*

Sonnet 79
4. mind, *1910 Sélincourt;* mind *1595, 1611.*

Sonnet 89
3. vow *1617;* vew *1595, 1611.*

EPITHALAMION

15. envide: *1611;* envide, *1595.*
22. awake, *1611;* awake *1595.*
33. delight: *1611;* delight, *1595.*
61. take, *1611;* take. *1595.*
67. deere *1910 conj. Sélincourt;* dore *1595, 1611.*
92. dreame *1595, 1611;* dreames *1869 conj. Morris.*
105. bride: *1611;* bride *1595.*
116. see. *1611;* see *1595.*
129. aloud *1611;* aloud, *1595.*
158. Queene. *1611;* Queene, *1595.*
209. you. *1611;* you, *1595.*
214. faces; *1611;* faces *1595.*
215. may *1611;* may, *1595.*
218. play *1617;* play; *1595;* play, *1611.*
220. throates *1611;* throates. *1595.*
237. unsownd. *1611;* unsownd, *1595.*

239. band? *1617;* band, *1595;* band. *1611.*
290. nightes *1715 conj. Hughes;* nights *1595;* nights sad *1611.*
304. coverlets. *1611;* coverlets, *1595.*
310. brooke. *1611;* brooke *1595.*
341. Pouke *1862 corr. Collier;* Ponke *1595, 1611.*
385. thy *1611;* they *1595.*
411. clods, *1611;* clods: *1595.*
424. *The short line that should properly have followed line 424 (to maintain the rhyme scheme) may have dropped out through the compositor's fault; but cf. the alternative explanation advanced by A. Kent Hieatt,* Short Time's Endless Monument . . . *(New York, 1960).*

FOWRE HYMNES

An Hymne in Honour of Love
120. perceiving, . . . boy, *1611;* perceiving . . . boy, *1596.*
166–167. deserve: . . . esteeme. *1910 Sélincourt;* deserve, . . . esteeme, *1596;* deserve: . . . esteeme. *1611.*
228a. *The fifth line of this stanza may have dropped out through a compositor's error.*
242. aby: *1617;* aby, *1596;* aby *1611.*
250. alone: *1611;* alone, *1596.*
297. desire; *1611;* desire, *1596.*

An Hymne in Honour of Beautie
10. frame; *1611;* frame, *1596.*
14. soule enchaunting *1862 corr. Collier;* foule enchaunting *1596, 1611.*
32! Paterne, . . . mould *1805 Todd;* Paterne . . . mould, *1596;* Pattern . . . mould *1611.*

33. could; *1611;* could, *1596.*
47. clotheth *1595;* closeth *1611.*
165. quight: *1617;* quight, *1596;* quight; *1611.*
195. no love *1595;* not love *1611.*
235. of beames *1595;* the beames *1611.*
258. lips, *1611;* lips *1596.*

An Hymne of Heavenly Love
53. in powre *1596;* of powre *1611.*
72. still to them *1596;* unto them *1611.*
80. increase *1611;* increase, *1596.*
83. light, *1611;* light *1596.*
94. hate, *1611;* hate *1596.*
112. heavenly, rare *1596;* heavenly rare *1611.*
123. death, *1611;* death *1596.*
214. mercie, miserable crew, *1910 Sélincourt;* mercie miserable

crew, *1596;* mercy (miserable crew) *1611.*

245. feet and syde *1596;* feet, throgh side *1611.*

261. embrace; *1805 Todd;* embrace, *1596;* embrace: *1611.*

266. to thee *1596;* for thee *1611.*

284. glorie, present still *1611;* glorie present still *1596.*

An Hymne of Heavenly Beautie

50. eye *1715 conj. Hughes;* eye, *1596, 1611.*

80. behold *1611;* behold, *1596.*

108. fynd: *1611;* fynd, *1596.*

121. Suns bright *1596;* Sun-bright *1611.*

132. declare. *1611;* declare, *1596.*

165. And dampish *1715 Hughes;* The dark and dampish *1596;* The darke damp *1611.*

170. times more bright, more cleare *1611;* times more cleare *1596.*

180. found *1611;* found, *1596.*

205. she *1596;* she, *1611.*

268. remaine: *1611;* remaine, *1596.*

270. to paine. *1715 Hughes;* to paine, *1596;* a paine. *1611.*

PROTHALAMION

3. delay *1596, 1611, 1617;* allay *1715 conj. Hughes*

102. your *1611, 1617;* you *1596*

175. pacing *1596;* pasing *1611, 1617;* passing *1679, 1715 Hughes*

Criticism

Early Critical Views

"E.K."

Dedicatory Epistle to *The Shepheardes Calender*

*To the most excellent and learned both orator and poete, MAYSTER
GABRIELL HARVEY,*[1] *his verie special and singular good frend
E. K. commendeth the good lyking of this his labour, and the
patronage of the new Poete.*

Uncouthe unkiste, sayde the olde famous Poete Chaucer:[2] whom
for his excellencie and wonderfull skil in making, his scholler Lid-
gate, a worthy scholler of so excellent a maister, calleth the Loade-
starre of our Language:[3] and whom our Colin clout in his Aeglogue[4]
calleth Tityrus the God of shepheards, comparing hym to the worthi-
nes of the Roman Tityrus Virgile. Which proverbe, myne owne
good friend Ma. Harvey, as in that good old Poete it served well
Pandares purpose, for the bolstering of his baudy brocage,[5] so very
well taketh place in this our new Poete, who for that he is uncouthe
(as said Chaucer) is unkist, and unknown to most men, is regarded
but of few. But I dout not, so soone as his name shall come into the
knowledg of men, and his worthines be sounded in the tromp of
fame, but that he shall be not onely kiste, but also beloved of all,

---

1. Gabriel Harvey (c. 1545–1630),
temperamentally disputatious, but an
able rhetorician, was a Fellow of Pem-
broke Hall; he became Spenser's friend
at Cambridge. The "Spenser-Harvey
correspondence," published in 1580,
throws light on Spenser's early interest
in quantitative versification in English,
and gives some indication of his literary
aspirations [*Editor*].
2. Cf. Chaucer, *Troilus and Criseyde*,
I, 809; "Unknowe, unkist, and lost,
that is unsought" [*Editor*].
3. John Lydgate (c. 1370–c. 1451), in
his long didactic poem, *The Fall of
Princes*, l. 252 [*Editor*].
4. I.e., eclogue (from Greek, "selec-
tion"), in this context signifying a
formal pastoral poem in the classical
tradition. The spelling adopted by E. K.
reflects a mistaken etymology [*Editor*].
5. Pandering [*Editor*].

embraced of the most, and wondred at of the best. No lesse I thinke, deserveth his wittinesse[6] in devising, his pithinesse in uttering, his complaints of love so lovely, his discourses of pleasure so pleasantly, his pastorall rudenesse,[7] his morall wisenesse, his dewe observing of Decorum[8] everye where, in personages, in seasons, in matter, in speach, and generally in al seemely simplycitie of handeling his matter, and framing his words: the which of many thinges which in him be straunge, I know will seeme the straungest, the words them selves being so auncient, the knitting of them so short and intricate, and the whole Periode and compasse of speache so delightsome for the roundnesse, and so grave for the straungenesse. And firste of the wordes to speake, I graunt they be something hard, and of most men unused, yet both English, and also used of most excellent Authors and most famous Poetes. In whom whenas this our Poet hath bene much traveiled and throughly redd,[9] how could it be, (as that worthy Oratour[1] sayde) but that walking in the sonne although for other cause he walked, yet needes he mought be sunburnt; and having the sound of those auncient Poetes still ringing in his eares, he mought needes in singing hit out some of theyr tunes. But whether he useth them by such casualtye[2] and custome, or of set purpose and choyse, as thinking them fittest for such rusticall rudenesse of shepheards, eyther for that theyr rough sounde would make his rymes more ragged and rustical, or els because such olde and obsolete wordes are most used of country folke, sure I think, and think I think not amisse, that they bring great grace and, as one would say, auctoritie to the verse. For albe amongst many other faultes it specially be objected of Valla against Livie, and of other against Saluste,[3] that with over much studie they affect antiquitie, as coveting thereby credence and honor of elder yeeres, yet I am of opinion, and eke the best learned are of the lyke, that those auncient solemne wordes are a great ornament both in the one and in the other; the one labouring to set forth in hys worke an eternall image of antiquitie, and the other carefully discoursing matters of gravitie and importaunce. For if my memory fayle not, Tullie[4] in that booke, wherein he endevoureth to set forth the paterne of a perfect Oratour,

6. Intelligence, skill [*Editor*].
7. I.e., his deliberately unpolished rustic style (which appropriately matches the setting and persons of these poems) [*Editor*].
8. I.e., his concern for what is fitting and proper in this pastoral context [*Editor*].
9. I.e., inasmuch as our poet has become widely and thoroughly acquainted (with "those auncient Poetes") [*Editor*].

1. I.e., Cicero; cf. *De Oratore*, II. xiv. 60 [*Editor*].
2. Chance [*Editor*].
3. Lorenzo Valla (1405–1457) emended the text of *Annales*, by the Roman historian Titus Livius (59 B.C.–A.D. 17); Sir John Cheke (1514–1557), Edward VI's tutor, and professor of Greek at Cambridge, criticized the use of archaic terms by the Roman historian Sallust (86–34 B.C.) [*Editor*].
4. I.e., Cicero; cf. *De Oratore*, III. xxxviii. 153 [*Editor*].

sayth that' ofttimes an auncient worde maketh the style seeme grave, and as it were reverend: no otherwise then we honour and reverence gray heares for a certein religious regard, which we have of old age. Yet nether every where must old words be stuffed in, nor the commen Dialecte and maner of speaking so corrupted therby, that as in old buildings it seme disorderly and ruinous. But all as in most exquisite pictures they use to blaze[5] and portraict not onely the daintie lineaments of beautye, but also rounde about it to shadow the rude thickets and craggy clifts, that by the basenesse of such parts, more excellency may accrew to the principall; for oftimes we fynde ourselves, I knowe not how, singularly delighted with the shewe of such naturall rudenesse, and take great pleasure in that disorderly order. Even so doe those rough and harsh termes enlumine and make more clearly to appeare the brightnesse of brave and glorious words. So ofentimes a dischorde in Musick maketh a comely concordaunce:[6] so great delight tooke the worthy Poete Alceus[7] to behold a blemish in the joynt of a wel shaped body. But if any will rashly blame such his purpose in choyse of old and unwonted[8] words, him may I more justly blame and condemne, or[9] of witlesse headinesse[1] in judging, or of heedelesse hardinesse in condemning; for not marking the compasse of hys bent, he wil judge of the length of his cast.[2] For in my opinion it is one special prayse, of many whych are dew to this Poete, that he hath laboured to restore, as to theyr rightfull heritage such good and naturall English words, as have ben long time out of use and almost cleare disherited. Which is the onely cause, that our Mother tonge, which truely of it self is both ful enough for prose and stately enough for verse, hath long time ben counted most bare and barrein of both. Which default when as some endevoured to salve and recure, they patched up the holes with peces and rags of other languages, borrowing here of the french, there of the Italian, every where of the Latine, not weighing how il, those tongues accorde with themselves, but much worse with ours: So now they have made our English tongue, a gallimaufray or hodgepodge of al other speches.[3] Other some not so wel seene[4] in the English tonge as perhaps in other languages, if them happen to here an olde word albeit very naturall and significant, crye out streight way, that we

---

5. Depict [*Editor*].
6. Cf. *The Faerie Queene*, III.ii.15: "So dischord oft in Musick makes the sweeter lay" [*Editor*].
7. Alcaeus, a Greek lyric poet of the seventh century B.C.; cf. Cicero, *De Natura Deorum*, I. xxviii. 79 [*Editor*].
8. Unfamiliar [*Editor*].
9. Either [*Editor*].
1. Rashness [*Editor*].
2. I.e., not noting the extent of the artist's purpose, the rash critic foolishly presumes to judge the other's achievement [*Editor*].
3. E.K.'s position recalls that of Sir John Cheke, who observes (in a letter to Sir Thomas Hoby), "our own tongue should be written clean and pure, unmixed and unmangled with borrowing of other tongues" [*Editor*].
4. I.e., skilled [*Editor*].

speak no English, but gibbrish, or rather such, as in old time Evanders mother spake.[5] Whose first shame is, that they are not ashamed, in their own mother tonge straungers to be counted and alienes. The second shame no lesse then the first, that what so they understand not, they streight way deeme to be sencelesse, and not at al to be understode. Much like to the Mole in Aesopes fable, that being blynd her selfe, would in no wise be perswaded, that any beast could see. The last more shameful then both, that of their owne country and natural speach, which together with their Nources milk they sucked, they have so base regard and bastard judgement, that they will not onely themselves not labor to garnish and beautifie it, but also repine, that of [6] other it shold be embellished. Like to the dogge in the maunger, that him selfe can eate no hay, and yet barketh at the hungry bullock, that so faine would feede: whose currish kind though cannot be kept from barking, yet I conne[7] them thanke that they refraine from byting.

Now for the knitting of sentences, whych they[8] call the joynts and members therof, and for al the compasse of the speach, it is round without roughnesse, and learned wythout hardnes, such indeede as may be perceived of the leaste, understoode of the moste, but judged onely of the learned. For what in most English wryters useth to be loose, and as it were ungyrt, in this Authour is well grounded, finely framed, and strongly trussed up together. In regard whereof, I scorne and spue out the rakehellye route of our ragged rymers (for so themselves use to hunt the letter)[9] which without learning boste, without judgement jangle, without reason rage and fome, as if some instinct of Poeticall spirite had newly ravished them above the meanenesse of commen capacitie. And being in the middest of all theyr bravery, sodenly eyther for want of matter, or of ryme, or having forgotten theyr former conceipt, they seeme to be so pained and traveiled in theyr remembrance, as it were a woman in childebirth or as that same Pythia, when the traunce came upon her.

Os rabidum fera corda domans &c.[1]

Nethelesse[2] let them a Gods name feede on theyr owne folly, so they seeke not to darken the beames of others glory. As for Colin, under whose person the Authour selfe is shadowed, how furre he is from such vaunted titles and glorious showes, both him selfe sheweth, where he sayth.

5. Cf. the anecdote in Aulus Gellius (a Latin grammarian of the second century A.D.), *Noctes Atticae*, I. x. 2 [*Editor*].
6. By [*Editor*].
7. Can [*Editor*].
8. I.e., rhetoricians [*Editor*].
9. E.K. thrusts at the excessive alliteration which characterized the work of many Elizabethan versifiers; cf. Sidney's allusion (in *An Apologie for Poetrie*) to "coursing of a Letter, as if they were bound to followe the method of a Dictionary" [*Editor*].
1. "Taming the frenzied mouth and savage heart"; cf. Virgil, *Aeneid*, VI. 80 [*Editor*].
2. Nevertheless [*Editor*].

Of Muses Hobbin. I conne no skill.   And,
Enough is me to paint out my unrest, &c.[3]

And also appeareth by the basenesse of the name, wherein, it semeth, he chose rather to unfold great matter of argument covertly, then professing it, not suffice thereto accordingly. Which moved him rather in Aeglogues, then other wise to write, doubting perhaps his habilitie, which he little needed, or mynding to furnish our tongue with this kinde, wherein it faulteth,[4] or following the example of the best and most auncient Poetes, which devised this kind of wryting, being both so base[5] for the matter, and homely for the manner, at the first to trye theyr habilities; and as young birdes, that be newly crept out of the nest, by little first to prove theyr tender wyngs, before they make a greater flyght. So flew Theocritus,[6] as you may perceive he was all ready full fledged. So flew Virgile, as not yet well feeling his winges. So flew Mantuane, as being not full somd.[7] So Petrarque. So Boccace; So Marot, Sanazarus, and also divers other excellent both Italian and French Poetes, whose foting this Author every where followeth, yet so as few, but they be wel sented can trace him out. So finally flyeth this our new Poete, as a bird, whose principals[8] be scarce growen out, but yet as that in time shall be hable to keepe wing with the best.

Now as touching the generall dryft and purpose of his Aeglogues, I mind not to say much, him selfe labouring to conceale it. Onely this appeareth, that his unstayed[9] yougth had long wandred in the common Labyrinth of Love, in which time to mitigate and allay the heate of his passion, or els to warne (as he sayth) the young shepheards .s.[1] his equalls and companions of his unfortunate folly, he compiled these xii. Aeglogues, which for that they be proportioned to the state of the xii. monethes, he termeth the SHEP-HEARDS CALENDAR, applying an olde name[2] to a new worke. Hereunto have I added a certain Glosse or scholion for thexposition of old wordes and harder phrases: which maner of glosing and commenting, well I wote, wil seeme straunge and rare in our tongue: yet for somuch as I knew many excellent and proper devises both in wordes and matter would passe in the speedy course of reading, either as unknowen, or as not marked, and that in this kind, as in other we might be equal to the learned of other nations, I thought

---

3. These verses occur in "June," 65, 79 [*Editor*].
4. Is deficient [*Editor*].
5. Humble, low [*Editor*].
6. Theocritus of Syracuse, Greek lyric poet of the third century B.C., whose "Idyls" initiated the genre of pastoral poetry, subsequently developed and elaborated by Virgil, Mantuan (Baptista Spagnuoli, 1448–1516, born in Mantua), Petrarch, Boccaccio, Clément Marot (1497–1544), and Jacopo Sannazaro (1458–1530) [*Editor*].

7. Fledged [*Editor*].
8. The first two primary feathers of a hawk's wing [*Editor*].
9. Unsteady [*Editor*].
1. *Scilicet*, i.e., namely [*Editor*].
2. I.e., that of *Le Compost et Kalendrier des bergiers*, first published at Paris in 1493; an English translation of the work had been often reprinted by Spenser's time [*Editor*].

good to take the paines upon me, the rather for that by meanes of some familiar acquaintaunce I was made privie to his counsell and secret meaning in them, as also in sundry other works of his. Which albeit I know he nothing so much hateth, as to promulgate, yet thus much have I adventured upon his frendship, him selfe being for long time furre estraunged, hoping that this will the rather occasion him, to put forth divers other excellent works of his, which slepe in silence, as his Dreames, his Legendes, his Court of Cupide, and sondry others;[3] whose commendations to set out, were verye vayne; the thinges though worthy of many, yet being knowen to few. These my present paynes if to any they be pleasurable or profitable, be you judge, mine own good Maister Harvey, to whom I have both in respect of your worthinesse generally, and otherwyse upon some particular and special considerations voued this my labour, and the maydenhead of this our commen frends Poetrie, himselfe having already in the beginning dedicated it to the Noble and worthy Gentleman, the right worshipfull Ma. Phi. Sidney, a special favourer and maintainer of all kind of learning. Whose cause I pray you Sir, yf Envie shall stur up any wrongful accusasion, defend with your mighty Rhetorick and other your rare gifts of learning, as you can, and shield with your good wil, as you ought, against the malice and outrage of so many enemies, as I know wilbe set on fire with the sparks of his kindled glory. And thus recommending the Author unto you, as unto his most special good frend, and my selfe unto you both, as one making singuler account of two so very good and so choise frends, I bid you both most hartely farwel, and commit you and your most commendable studies to the tuicion of the greatest.

Your owne assuredly to be commaunded
E. K.

JOHN HUGHES

[Remarks on *The Faerie Queene* and *The Shepheardes Calender*]†

By what has been offer'd in the foregoing Discourse on Allegorical Poetry, we may be able, not only to discover many Beauties in the *Fairy Queen*, but likewise to excuse some of its Irregularities. The chief Merit of this Poem consists in that surprizing Vein of fabulous

3. These poems are lost, although it has been suggested that some part of *The Court of Cupid* may survive in *The Faerie Queene*, III. xii [*Editor*].
† From Hughes's "Remarks on the *Fairy Queen*," and "Remarks on the *Shepherd's Calendar*," in Volume I of his edition of Spenser's *Works* (London, 1715: 5 vols.).

Invention, which runs thro it, and enriches it every where with Imagery and Descriptions more than we meet with in any other modern Poem. The Author seems to be possess'd of a kind of Poetical Magick; and the Figures he calls up to our View rise so thick upon us, that we are at once pleased and distracted by the exhaustless Variety of them; so that his Faults may in a manner be imputed to his Excellencies: His Abundance betrays him into Excess, and his Judgment is overborne by the Torrent of his Imagination.

That which seems the most liable to Exception in this Work, is the Model of it, and the Choice the Author has made of so romantick a Story. The several Books appear rather like so many several Poems, than one entire Fable: Each of them has its peculiar Knight, and is independent of the rest; and tho some of the Persons make their Appearance in different Books, yet this has very little Effect in connecting them. Prince Arthur is indeed the principal Person, and has therefore a share given him in every Legend; but his Part is not considerable enough in any one of them: He appears and vanishes again like a Spirit; and we lose sight of him too soon, to consider him as the Hero of the Poem.

These are the most obvious Defects in the Fable of the *Fairy Queen*. The want of Unity in the Story makes it difficult for the Reader to carry it in his Mind, and distracts too much his Attention to the several Parts of it; and indeed the whole Frame of it wou'd appear monstrous, if it were to be examin'd by the Rules of Epick Poetry, as they have been drawn from the Practice of Homer and Virgil. But as it is plain the Author never design'd it by those Rules, I think it ought rather to be consider'd as a Poem of a particular kind, describing in a Series of Allegorical Adventures or Episodes the most noted Virtues and Vices: to compare it therefore with the Models of Antiquity, wou'd be like drawing a Parallel between the Roman and the Gothick Architecture. In the first there is doubtless a more natural Grandeur and Simplicity: in the latter, we find great Mixtures of Beauty and Barbarism, yet assisted by the Invention of a Variety of inferior Ornaments; and tho the former is more majestick in the whole, the latter may be very surprizing and agreeable in its Parts.

It may seem strange indeed, since Spenser appears to have been well acquainted with the best Writers of Antiquity, that he has not imitated them in the Structure of his Story. Two Reasons may be given for this: The first is, That at the time when he wrote, the Italian Poets, whom he has chiefly imitated, and who were the first Revivers of this Art among the Moderns, were in the highest vogue, and were universally read and admir'd. But the chief Reason was probably, that he chose to frame his Fable after a Model which might give the greatest Scope to that Range of Fancy which was so remarkably his Talent. There is a Bent in Nature, which is apt to determine Men that particular way in which they are most capable of excelling; and tho it is certain he might have form'd a better Plan, it is to be question'd whether he cou'd have executed any other so well.

It is probably for the same reason, that among the Italian Poets, he rather follow'd Ariosto, whom he found more agreeable to his Genius, than Tasso, who had form'd a better Plan, and from whom he has only borrow'd some particular Ornaments; yet it is but Justice to say, that his Plan is much more regular than that of Ariosto. In the *Orlando Furioso*, we every where meet with an exuberant Invention, join'd with great Liveliness and Facility of Description, yet debas'd by frequent Mixtures of the comick Genius, as well as many shocking Indecorums. Besides, in the Huddle and Distraction of the Adventures, we are for the most part only amus'd with extravagant Stories, without being instructed in any Moral. On the other hand, Spenser's Fable, tho often wild, is, as I have observ'd, always emblematical: And this may very much excuse likewise that Air of Romance in which he has follow'd the Italian Author. The perpetual Stories of Knights, Giants, Castles, and Enchantments, and all that Train of Legendary Adventures, wou'd indeed appear very trifling, if Spenser had not found a way to turn them all into Allegory, or if a less masterly Hand had fill'd up his Draught. But it is surprizing to observe how much the Strength of the Painting is superior to the Design. It ought to be consider'd too, that at the time when our Author wrote, the Remains of the old Gothick Chivalry were not quite abolish'd: It was not many Years before, that the famous Earl of Surry, remarkable for his Wit and Poetry in the Reign of King Henry the Eighth, took a romantick Journey to Florence, the Place of his Mistress's Birth, and publish'd there a Challenge against all Nations in Defence of her Beauty. Justs and Turnaments were held in England in the Time of Queen Elizabeth. Sir Philip Sidney tilted at one of these Entertainments, which was made for the French Ambassador, when the Treaty of Marriage was on foot with the Duke of Anjou: and some of our Historians have given us a very particular and formal Account of Preparations, by marking out Lists, and appointing Judges, for a Tryal by Combat, in the same Reign, which was to have decided the Title to a considerable Estate; and in which the whole Ceremony was perfectly agreeable to the fabulous Descriptions in Books of Knight-Errantry. This might render his Story more familiar to his first Readers; tho Knights in Armour, and Ladies Errant are as antiquated Figures to us, as the Court of that time wou'd appear, if we cou'd see them now in their Ruffs and Fardingales.

There are two other Objections to the Plan of the *Fairy Queen*, which, I confess, I am more at a loss to answer. I need not, I think, be scrupulous in mentioning freely the Defects of a Poem, which, tho it was never suppos'd to be perfect, has always been allow'd to be admirable.

The first is, that the Scene is laid in Fairy-Land, and the chief Actors are Fairies. The Reader may see their imaginary Race and History in the Second Book, at the end of the Tenth Canto: but if he is not prepar'd before-hand, he may expect to find them acting agreeably to the common Stories and Traditions about such fancy'd Beings. Thus Shakespear, who has introduc'd them in his *Midsummer-Night's Dream*, has made them speak and act in a manner perfectly adapted to their suppos'd Characters; but the Fairies in this Poem are not distinguish'd from other Persons. There is this Misfortune likewise attends the Choice of such Actors, that having been accustom'd to conceive of them in a diminutive way, we find it difficult to raise our Ideas, and to imagine a Fairy encountring with a Monster or a Giant. Homer has pursu'd a contrary Method, and represented his Heroes above the Size and Strength of ordinary Men; and it is certain that the Actions of the *Iliad* wou'd have appear'd but ill proportion'd to the Characters, if we were to have imagin'd them all perform'd by Pigmies.

But as the Actors our Author has chosen, are only fancy'd Beings, he might possibly think himself at liberty to give them what Stature, Customs and Manners he pleas'd. I will not say he was in the right in this: but it is plain that by the literal Sense of Fairy-Land, he only design'd an Utopia, an imaginary Place; and by his Fairies, Persons of whom he might invent any Action proper to human Kind, without being restrain'd, as he must have been, if he had chosen a real Scene and historical Characters. As for the mystical Sense, it appears both by the Work it self, and by the Author's Explanation of it, that his Fairy-Land is England, and his Fairy-Queen, Queen Elizabeth; at whose Command the Adventure of every Legend is suppos'd to be undertaken.

The other Objection is, that having chosen an historical Person, Prince Arthur, for his principal Hero; who is no Fairy, yet is mingled with them: he has not however represented any part of his History. He appears here indeed only in his Minority, and performs his Exercises in Fairy-Land, as a private Gentleman; but we might at least have expected, that the fabulous Accounts of him, and of his Victories over the Saxons, shou'd have been work'd into some beautiful Vision or Prophecy: and I cannot think Spenser wou'd wholly omit this, but am apt to believe he had done it in some of the following Books which were lost.

* * *

I have not yet said any thing concerning Spenser's Versification; in which, tho he is not always equal to himself, it may be affirm'd, that he is superior to all his Cotemporaries, and even to those that follow'd him for some time, except Fairfax,[1] the applauded Translator of Tasso. In this he commendably study'd the Italians, and must be allow'd to have been a great Improver of our English Numbers: Before his time, Musick seems to have been so much a Stranger to our Poetry, that, excepting the Earl of Surry's Lyricks, we have very few Examples of Verses that had any tolerable Cadence. In Chaucer there is so little of this, that many of his Lines are not even restrain'd to a certain Number of Syllables. Instances of this loose Verse are likewise to be found in our Author, but it is only in such Places where he has purposely imitated Chaucer, as in the second Eclogue, and some others. This great Defect of Harmony put the Wits in Queen Elizabeth's Reign upon a Design of totally changing our Numbers, not only by banishing Rhime, but by new moulding our Language into the Feet and Measures of the Latin Poetry. Sir Philip Sidney was at the Head of this Project, and has accordingly given us some Hexameter and Pentameter Verses in his *Arcadia*. But the Experiment soon fail'd; and tho our Author, by some Passages in his Letters to Mr. Harvey, seems not to have disapprov'd it, yet it does not appear by those Poems of his, which are preserv'd, that he gave it any Authority by his Example.

As to the Stanza in which the *Fairy Queen* is written, tho the Author cannot be commended for his Choice of it, yet it is much more harmonious in its kind than the Heroick Verse of that Age. It is almost the same with what the Italians call their *Ottave Rime*, which is us'd both by Ariosto and Tasso, but improv'd by Spenser, with the Addition of a Line more in the Close, of the Length of our Alexandrines. The Defect of it, in long or narrative Poems, is apparent. The same Measure, closed always by a full Stop, in the same Place, by which every Stanza is made as it were a distinct Paragraph, grows tiresom by continual Repetition, and frequently breaks the Sense, when it ought to be carry'd on without Interruption. With this Exception, the Reader will however find it harmonious, full of well-sounding Epithets, and of such elegant Turns on the Thought and Words, that Dryden himself owns he learn'd these Graces of Verse chiefly from our Author; and does not scruple to say, that in this Particular *only Virgil surpass'd him among the Romans, and only Mr. Waller among the English.*

* * *

1. Edward Fairfax (c. 1575–1635) translated Tasso's *Gerusalemme Liber-* *ata* in 1600 (under the title "Godfrey of Bulloigne") [*Editor*].

In the Remarks on the *Fairy Queen*, I have chiefly consider'd our
Author as an Allegorical Writer; and his Poem as fram'd after a
Model of a particular kind. In some of his other Writings, we find
more Regularity, tho less Invention. There seems to be the same
difference between the *Fairy Queen* and the *Shepherd's Calendar*, as
between a Royal Palace and a little Country Seat. The first strikes
the Eye with more Magnificence; but the latter may perhaps give
the greatest Pleasure. In this Work the Author has not been misled
by the Italians; tho Tasso's *Aminta*[2] might have been at least of as
good Authority to him in the Pastoral, as Ariosto in the greater kind
of Poetry. But Spenser rather chose to follow Nature it self, and to
paint the Life and Sentiments of Shepherds after a more simple and
unaffected manner.

The two things which seem the most essential to Pastoral, are
Love, and the Images of a Country Life: and to represent these, our
Author had little more to do, than to examine his own Heart, and
to copy the Scene about him; for at the time when he wrote the
Shepherd's Calendar, he was a passionate Lover of his Rosalind:
and it appears that the greatest part of it, if not the whole, was
compos'd in the Country on his first leaving the University; and
before he had engag'd in Business, or fill'd his Mind with the
Thoughts of Preferment in a Life at Court. Perhaps too there is a
certain Age most proper for Pastoral Writing; and tho the same
Genius shou'd arise afterwards to greater Excellencies, it may grow
less capable of this. Accordingly in the Poem call'd *Colin Clout's
come home again*, which was written a considerable time after, we
find him less a Shepherd than at first: He had then been drawn out
of his Retirement, had appear'd at Court, and been engag'd in an
Employment which brought him into a Variety of Business and
Acquaintance, and gave him a quite different Sett of Ideas. And
tho this Poem is not without its Beauties; yet what I wou'd here
observe is, that in the Pastoral Kind it is not so simple and unmix'd,
and consequently not so perfect as the *Eclogues*, of which I have
perhaps given the Reason.

But I am sensible that what I have mention'd as a Beauty in
Spenser's Pastorals, will not seem so to all Readers; and that the
Simplicity which appears in them may be thought to have too much
of the *Merum Rus*.[3] If our Author has err'd in this, he has at least
err'd on the right hand. The true Model of Pastoral Writing seems
indeed not to be yet fix'd by the Criticks; and there is room for the
best Judges to differ in their Opinions about it: Those who wou'd
argue for the Simplicity of Pastoral, may say, That the very Idea
of this kind of Writing is the Representation of a Life of Retire-

2. A pastoral drama composed in 1573
[*Editor*].

3. "Real country" (in the sense of
mere, absolute rusticity) [*Editor*].

ment and Innocence, made agreeable by all those Pleasures and
Amusements, which the Fields, the Woods, and the various Seasons
of the Year afford to Men, who live according to the first Dictates
of Nature, and without the artificial Cares and Refinements, which
Wealth, Luxury, and Ambition, by multiplying both our Wants and
Enjoyments, have introduc'd among the Rich and the Polite: That
therefore as the Images, Similies, and Allusions are to be drawn
from the Scene; so the Sentiments and Expressions ought no where
to taste of the City, or the Court, but to have such a kind of plain
Elegance only, as may appear proper to the Life and Characters of
the Persons introduc'd in such Poems: That this Simplicity, skilfully
drawn, will make the Picture more natural, and consequently more
pleasing: That even the low Images in such a Representation are
amusing, as they contribute to deceive the Reader, and make him
fancy himself really in such a Place, and among such Persons as are
describ'd; the Pleasure in this case being like that express'd by
Milton of one walking out into the Fields:

> ————Who long in populous Cities pent,
> Where Houses thick, and Sewers annoy the Air,
> Forth issuing on a Summer's Morn to breathe
> Among the pleasant Villages and Farms
> Adjoin'd, from each thing met conceives Delight;
> The Smell of Grain, or tedded Grass, or Kine,
> Or Dairy, each rural Sight, each rural Sound.[4]

This indeed seems to be the true Reason of the Entertainment
which Pastoral Poetry gives to its Readers: for as Mankind is de-
parted from the Simplicity, as well as the Innocence, of a State of
Nature, and is immers'd in Cares and Pursuits of a very different
kind; it is a wonderful Amusement to the Imagination, to be some-
times transported, as it were, out of modern Life, and to wander in
these pleasant Scenes which the Pastoral Poets provide for us, and
in which we are apt to fancy our selves reinstated for a time in our
first Innocence and Happiness.

Those who argue against the strict Simplicity of Pastoral Writing,
think there is something too low in the Characters and Sentiments
of mere Shepherds, to support this kind of Poetry, if not rais'd and
improv'd by the Assistance of Art; or at least that we ought to dis-
tinguish between what is simple, and what is rustick, and take care
that while we represent Shepherds, we do not make them Clowns:
That it is a Mistake to imagine that the Life of Shepherds is in-
capable of any Refinement, or that their Sentiments may not some-
times rise above the Country. To justify this, they tell us, that we
conceive too low an Idea of this kind of Life, by taking it from that
of modern Shepherds, who are the meanest and poorest sort of

4. *Paradise Lost,* IX. 445–451 [*Editor*].

People among us. But in the first Ages of the World it was otherwise; that Persons of Rank and Dignity honour'd this Employment; that Shepherds were the Owners of their own Flocks; and that David was once a Shepherd, who became afterwards a King, and was himself too the most sublime of Poets. Those who argue for the first kind of Pastoral, recommend Theocritus as the best Model; and those who are for the latter, think that Virgil, by raising it to a higher Pitch, has improv'd it. I shall not determine this Controversy, but only observe, that the Pastorals of Spenser are of the former kind.

It is for the same Reason that the Language of the *Shepherd's Calendar*, which is design'd to be rural, is older than that of his other Poems. Sir Philip Sidney however, tho he commends this Work in his *Apology for Poetry*, censures the Rusticity of the Stile as an Affectation not to be allow'd. The Author's profess'd Veneration for Chaucer partly led him into this; yet there is a difference among the Pastorals, and the Reader will observe, that the Language of the Fifth and Eighth is more obsolete than that of some others; the reason of which might be, that the Design of those two Eclogues being Allegorical Satire, he chose a more antiquated Dress, as more proper to his Purpose. But however faulty he may be in the Excess of this, it is certain that a sprinkling of the rural Phrase, as it humours the Scene and Characters, has a very great Beauty in Pastoral Poetry; and of this any one may be convinc'd, by reading the Pastorals of Mr. Philips,[5] which are written with great Delicacy of Taste, in the very Spirit and Manner of Spenser.

Having said that Spenser has mingled Satire in some of his Eclogues, I know not whether this may not be another Objection to them: it may be doubted whether any thing of this kind shou'd be admitted to disturb the Tranquillity and Pleasure which shou'd every where reign in Pastoral Poems; or at least nothing shou'd be introduc'd more than the light and pleasant Railleries or Contentions of Shepherds about their Flocks, their Mistresses, or their Skill in piping and singing. I cannot wholly justify my Author in this, yet must say that the Excellency of the Moral in those Pastorals does in a great measure excuse his trangressing the strict Rules of Criticism. Besides, as he design'd under an Allegory to censure the vicious Lives of bad Priests, and to expose their Usurpation of Pomp and Dominion, nothing cou'd be more proper to this purpose than the Allegory he has chosen; the Author of our Holy Religion having himself dignify'd the Parable of a good Shepherd; and the natural Innocence, Simplicity, Vigilance, and Freedom from Ambition, which are the Characters of that kind of Life, being a very good Contrast to the Vices and Luxury, and to that Degeneracy from their first Pattern, which the Poet wou'd there reprehend. * * *

5. Ambrose Philips (c. 1675–1749) [*Editor*].

SAMUEL TAYLOR COLERIDGE

[Spenser's Art]†

There is this difference, among many others, between Shakspeare and Spenser:—Shakspeare is never colored by the customs of his age; what appears of contemporary character in him is merely negative; it is just not something else. He has none of the fictitious realities of the classics, none of the grotesquenesses of chivalry, none of the allegory of the middle ages; there is no sectarianism either of politics or religion, no miser, no witch,—no common witch,—no astrology—nothing impermanent of however long duration; but he stands like the yew-tree in Lorton vale, which has known so many ages that it belongs to none in particular; a living image of endless self-reproduction, like the immortal tree of Malabar. In Spenser the spirit of chivalry is entirely predominant, although with a much greater infusion of the poet's own individual self into it than is found in any other writer. He has the wit of the southern with the deeper inwardness of the northern genius.

No one can appreciate Spenser without some reflection on the nature of allegorical writing. The mere etymological meaning of the word, allegory,—to talk of one thing and thereby convey another,—is too wide. The true sense is this,—the employment of one set of agents and images to convey in disguise a moral meaning, with a likeness to the imagination, but with a difference to the understanding,—those agents and images being so combined as to form a homogeneous whole. This distinguishes it from metaphor, which is part of an allegory. But allegory is not properly distinguishable from fable, otherwise than as the first includes the second, as a genus its species; for in a fable there must be nothing but what is universally known and acknowledged, but in an allegory there may be that which is new and not previously admitted. The pictures of the great masters, especially of the Italian schools, are genuine allegories. Amongst the classics, the multitude of their gods either precluded allegory altogether, or else made every thing allegory, as in the Hesiodic Theogonia; for you can scarcely distinguish between power and the personification of power. The Cupid and Psyche of, or found in, Apuleius, is a phenomenon. It is the Platonic mode of accounting for the fall of man. The Battle of the Soul by Prudentius[1] is an early instance of Christian allegory.

† From the third in "A Course of Lectures" (1818); the published versions of these lectures are based on notes arranged by H. N. Coleridge. Cf. *Coleridge's Miscellaneous Criticism*, ed. T. M. Raysor (Cambridge, Mass., 1936), 32–38.
1. Latin (Christian) poet of the fourth century A.D. [*Editor*].

Narrative allegory is distinguished from mythology as reality from symbol; it is, in short, the proper intermedium between person and personification. Where it is too strongly individualized, it ceases to be allegory; this is often felt in the Pilgrim's Progress, where the characters are real persons with nicknames. Perhaps one of the most curious warnings against another attempt at narrative allegory on a great scale, may be found in Tasso's account of what he himself intended in and by his Jerusalem Delivered.

As characteristic of Spenser, I would call your particular attention in the first place to the indescribable sweetness and fluent projection of his verse, very clearly distinguishable from the deeper and more interwoven harmonies of Shakspeare and Milton. This stanza is a good instance of what I mean:—

> Yet she, most faithfull ladie, all this while
> Forsaken, wofull, solitarie mayd,
> Far from all peoples preace, as in exile,
> In wildernesse and wastfull deserts strayd
> To seeke her knight; who, subtily betrayd
> Through that late vision which th' enchaunter wrought,
> Had her abandond; she, of nought affrayd,
> Through woods and wastnes wide him daily sought,
> Yet wished tydinges none of him unto her brought.
> *[F.Q.*, I.iii.3]

2. Combined with this sweetness and fluency, the scientific construction of the metre of the Faery Queene is very noticeable. One of Spenser's arts is that of alliteration, and he uses it with great effect in doubling the impression of an image:—

> In *w*ildernesse and *w*astful deserts—
> Through *w*oods and *w*astnes *w*ilde,—
> They passe the bitter *w*aves of Acheron,
> Where many soules sit *w*ailing *w*oefully,
> And come to *f*iery *f*lood of *Ph*legeton,
> Whereas the damned ghosts in torments fry,
> And with *sh*arp *sh*rilling *sh*rieks doth bootlesse cry,—&c.
> *[F.Q.*, I.v.33]

He is particularly given to an alternate alliteration, which is, perhaps, when well used, a great secret in melody:—

> A *r*amping lyon *r*ushed suddenly,—
> And *s*ad to *s*ee her *s*orrowful constraint,—
> And on the grasse her *d*aintie *l*imbes *d*id *l*ay,—&c.
> *[F.Q.*, I.iii.5]

You can not read a page of the Faery Queene, if you read for that purpose, without perceiving the intentional alliterativeness of the words; and yet so skilfully is this managed, that it never strikes any unwarned ear as artificial, or other than the result of the necessary movement of the verse.

3. Spenser displays great skill in harmonizing his descriptions of external nature and actual incidents with the allegorical character and epic activity of the poem. Take these two beautiful passages as illustrations of what I mean:—[Quotes from I.ii.1–2, and I.v.2].

Observe also the exceeding vividness of Spenser's descriptions. They are not, in the true sense of the word, picturesque; but are composed of a wondrous series of images, as in our dreams. Compare the following passage with any thing you may remember in *pari materia*[2] in Milton or Shakspeare:—[Quotes I.vii.31–32].

4. You will take especial note of the marvellous independence and true imaginative absence of all particular space or time in the Faery Queene. It is in the domains neither of history or geography; it is ignorant of all artificial boundary, all material obstacles; it is truly in land of Faery, that is, of mental space. The poet has placed you in a dream, a charmed sleep, and you neither wish, nor have the power, to inquire where you are, or how you got there. It reminds me of some lines of my own:—

> Oh ! would to Alla !
> The raven or the sea-mew were appointed
> To bring me food !—or rather that my soul
> Might draw in life from the universal air !
> It were a lot divine in some small skiff
> Along some ocean's boundless solitude
> To float forever with a careless course
> And think myself the only being alive ![3]

Indeed Spenser himself, in the conduct of his great poem, may be represented under the same image, his symbolizing purpose being his mariner's compass:—

> As pilot well expert in perilous wave,
> That to a stedfast starre his course hath bent,
> When foggy mistes or cloudy tempests have
> The faithfull light of that faire lampe yblent,
> And coverd Heaven with hideous dreriment;
> Upon his card and compas firmes his eye,
> The maysters of his long experiment,
> And to them does the steddy helme apply,
> Bidding his winged vessell fairely forward fly.
>
> [II.vii.1]

So the poet through the realms of allegory.

2. I.e., "in similar vein" [*Editor*].   3. From Coleridge's drama, *Remorse,* IV. iii [*Editor*].

5. You should note the quintessential character of Christian chivalry in all his characters, but more especially in his women. The Greeks, except, perhaps, in Homer, seem to have had no way of making their women interesting, but by unsexing them, as in the instances of the tragic Medea, Electra, &c. Contrast such characters with Spenser's Una, who exhibits no prominent feature, has no particularization, but produces the same feeling that a statue does, when contemplated at a distance:—

> From her fayre head her fillet she undight,
> And layd her stole aside : her angels face,
> As the great eye of Heaven, shyned bright,
> And made a sunshine in the shady place ;
> Did never mortal eye behold such heavenly grace.
>
> [I.iii.4]

6. In Spenser we see the brightest and purest form of that nationality which was so common a characteristic of our elder poets. There is nothing unamiable, nothing contemptuous of others, in it. To glorify their country—to elevate England into a queen, an empress of the heart—this was their passion and object; and how dear and important an object it was or may be, let Spain, in the recollection of her Cid,[4] declare! There is a great magic in national names. What a damper to all interest is a list of native East Indian merchants! Unknown names are non-conductors; they stop all sympathy. No one of our poets has touched this string more exquisitely than Spenser; especially in his chronicle of the British Kings,[5] and the marriage of the Thames with the Medway,[6] in both which passages the mere names constitute half the pleasure we receive. To the same feeling we must in particular attribute Spenser's sweet reference to Ireland:—

> Ne thence the Irishe rivers absent were ;
> Sith no lesse famous than the rest they be, &c.
>
> *　　*　　*　　*　　*　　*　　*　　*
>
> And Mulla mine, whose waves I whilom taught to weep.
>
> [IV.xi.40–41]

And there is a beautiful passage of the same sort in the Colin Clout's Come Home Again:—

> " One day," quoth he, " I sat, as was my trade,
> Under the foot of Mole," &c.　　　　[56–57]

Lastly, the great and prevailing character of Spenser's mind is fancy under the conditions of imagination, as an ever-present but

4. Rodrigo Diaz de Bivar, "el Cid" (c. 1030–1099), national hero of Spain [*Editor*].
5. *The Faerie Queene*, II. x [*Editor*].
6. *The Faerie Queene*, IV. xi [*Editor*].

not always active power. He has an imaginative fancy, but he has not imagination, in kind or degree, as Shakspeare and Milton have; the boldest effort of his powers in this way is the character of Talus.[7] Add to this a feminine tenderness and almost maidenly purity of feeling, and above all, a deep moral earnestness which produces a believing sympathy and acquiescence in the reader, and you have a tolerably adequate view of Spenser's intellectual being.

7. Arthegall's servant, "made of yron mould," in *The Faerie Queene*, V [*Editor*].

Twentieth-Century Criticism

EDWIN GREENLAW

[Spenser's Fairy Mythology]†

* * *

The realm of Gloriana is two-fold: England, in the historical allegory; the Celtic Otherworld in the fairy aspect. In the proem to Book II, both senses are found in clear connection. Spenser asks where is "that happy land of Faery," only to remind the reader that every day great regions are being discovered that always have existed though men were unaware. "Certein signes" will reveal this land to the one who seeks; by which he means, of course, such signs as are familiar in Celtic folklore. But he goes on at once to say that Elizabeth may find her own realm to be this "lond of Faery." This double sense is kept throughout the poem, with a variety of effects. Arthur has had a vision of the Fairy Queen, but has sought vainly for her realm. Yet with Guyon he is in Fairy Land all the time. Guyon visits the Celtic Otherworld three times: it is on Phaedria's island; in the Underworld of Mammon; and in Acrasia's Bower of Bliss. On the other hand, Britomart says that she has come from her native soil, "the greater Britaine," to "Faery lond" because she has heard of famous knights and ladies that inhabit that realm. It would be easy to multiply illustrations of this double geography; the one point that I wish to make, as a basis for what is to follow, is that Spenser fuses the well known romance and folklore conception of a land of enchantment, difficult of access, with a quite arbitrary and literal conception of England as the scene in which the action of his poem takes place.

* * *

Celtic originals and analogues of certain parts of the *Faerie Queene* are more frequent than has been supposed. The subject is too broad for complete study here; it merits a thorough investiga-

---

† From "Spenser's Fairy Mythology," by Edwin Greenlaw, *SP*, XV (1918), 105– 122. (The original footnotes have been slightly edited.)

tion by a specialist in Celtic who also knows Spenser's work well enough to be aware of certain peculiarities in his method. My purpose is merely to indicate several characteristics of Spenser's use of his fairy magic, which differs from his employment of ordinary romance conventions, in order to make clear a special definition of the fairy *dramatis personae* in his poem.

Sometimes a similarity between one of Spenser's stories and one by Ariosto or Tasso conceals the ultimate sources. Britomart is like Bradamante in many respects; her name and some details Spenser takes from the pseudo-Vergilian *Ciris*; yet the most important fact about her is something quite distinct from either the Italian or the Latin source. It is as though one should identify the story of the Lady of the Lake, cited above, with some classical source because Triton and Arion figure in it. Spenser's method is composite; a brief incident, even a stanza, may reflect many elements. For this reason, the study of his sources is fraught with peculiar perils. Thus, Artegal's captivity by Radigund is thoroughly rationalized, yet it is unquestionably related to the large number of legends in which a mortal is captured by a *fée* who offers him her love, with imprisonment as a penalty for refusal. Of clearer significance is the episode in which Calidore comes upon Colin piping while the three Graces, with Rosalind in addition, are dancing (VI. x). This scene is filled, after Spenser's wont, with reminiscences of the classics; there is also the pastoral setting of the shepherd piping to his lass; there is the compliment contained in her inclusion among the Graces, and the reminiscence, comparatively late in the life of the poet, of the Rosalind of his youth. But underneath is a thread of pure Celtic folklore, as the following analysis of the incident will show.

Calidore, separated from Pastorella for a time, wanders into a place that is "far from all people's troad." The scene passes all others on earth in beauty,—a hill in the midst of a plain bordered about with woods of matchless height, so that the trees seem to disdain the earth. At the foot of the hill a gentle stream flows; to its pure waters no beast or clown may come near. By the banks, guarding the stream and the hill, are Nymphs and Fairies; they sing to the accompaniment of the water's fall. As Calidore approaches the hill, he hears sweet music and the sound of dancing feet. He does not venture into the open, but peeping from the covert of the woods has a sight of a hundred maidens dancing; in the midst are three others, who in turn surround a damsel like the precious gem in the midst of a ring. This damsel is crowned with a rose garland, and is continually pelted by flowers thrown upon her by the dancers. Calidore gazes long at the sight, uncertain whether it is a company of Venus' followers, or nymphs, or fairies, or an "enchanted show." At length he approaches, to test the reality of what he sees, but all vanish save the shepherd Colin.

Despite the classical myth and the pastoral conventions in this passage, the foundation is that of the fairy vision, widely known in folklore. Colin, a mortal in love with a *fée*, has become an inhabitant of her world. His life is so happy that Calidore, momentarily forgetting his own love

> had no will away to fare,
> But wisht that with that shepheard he mote dwelling share.

All the details,—the fairy hill, far-off from human pathway, guarded by fairies against the approach of anything unclean; the fairy music, heard from a great distance; the hundred dancers, the *fée* herself in the center of the group; the disappearance at the approach of a mortal not initiated into the mysteries of the fairy folk,—all these are commonplaces in folk tradition. Even today in Ireland, peasants tell of the music of the "good people," of the sacred hills, of the dancers.[1]

The incident just analyzed gives pretty clear proof of Spenser's acquaintance with the fairy traditions of the folk. There are good reasons for believing that he must have known many such traditions. His friendship with the Sidneys (Sir Henry was for a time Lord President of Wales); his antiquarian instincts, manifested not only in his prolonged study of many ancient chronicles in preparation for writing the chronicle passages in the *Faerie Queene*, but also in his prose tract on Ireland, in which he shows no little knowledge of folk customs and belief; the fact that he lived in Ireland for ten years before publishing the first part of the poem, to say nothing of the relation between the subject-matter of that poem and the stuff with which folk tradition deals,—are all reasons for expecting that in so long a poem, written by a man of wide learning and interests, we should find materials of this nature. It may also be noted that he introduces Welsh words into his chronicle, and that he recognizes in the tract on Ireland the affinity among the languages spoken in Ireland, Cornwall, and Wales. Most, if not all, of the *Faerie Queene* as we have it was written in Ireland; Spenser could not but have heard many tales about the *Sidhe* folk; his poem reflects this kind of learning as well as classical philosophy and the thousand other things with which it is filled.

*   *   *

The significance of the vision of the Fairy Queen is that by this device Spenser is able to establish the basis on which his poem rests. The traditional Arthur was a British king about whose birth many mysterious legends clustered, and who, at the end of his life, was

1. For illustrations recently taken down from the lips of peasants see Wentz, *Fairy Faith in Celtic Countries*, pp. 31– 32; 79–80; 296ff. See also Paton, *Fairy Mythology*, pp. 90–91, and the index.

received in *Faerie*, after that last great battle in the West, to be healed of his grievous wound by Morgain, or *La Dame du Lac*, or by these and other powerful fays together. After a long sojourn in *Faerie*, he was to come again and rule Britain. This belief is extant in parts of Wales today, as it was in Layamon's time. Lydgate phrases it compactly:

> He [Arthur] is a king y-crowned in Fairye;
> With sceptre and pall, and with his regalty,
> Shall he resort, as lord and soveraigne
> Out of Fairye, and reigne in Britaine.
>
> *(Falls of Princes*, VIII, 24.)

Spenser's use of this tradition about the fairy sovereign gives the clue to the idea on which the entire poem rests. The interpretation is to be found in the return, through the Welsh house of Tudor, of the old British line to the throne of England, now long occupied by strangers. To state the proposition concisely: *Spenser conceives the Tudor rule as a return of the old British line; he conceives Elizabeth Tudor as the particular sovereign, coming out of Faerie, whose return fulfils the old prophecy*. That is to say, the poem is at once a glorification of Elizabeth's ancestry and a glorification of the Queen as an individual. Had England's greatness in the last two decades of the sixteenth century, Spenser's time, an era which the poet recognized as not only putting the realm on a new footing of prosperity and power but also as marking the beginning of a far-reaching imperial policy,—had this greatness come during the rule of a Tudor king, Spenser would have figured that king under the name of Prince Arthur. But his sovereign was a woman. The prophecy, then, is fulfilled through personifying, in Arthur, the spirit of Great Britain, now united to the Faerie Queene herself. This is not only an excellent poetical device; it is also a most interesting development of the Arthurian legend, true to the spirit of that legend if not to its letter. It is also quite in keeping with Spenser's method of complex allegory, a method by which different qualities and forces, different attributes of perfection, are, like Plato's *ideas*, embodied now in one concrete form and now in another.

These statements are, I think, capable of nearly formal proof. To begin with, there is a sharp distinction, throughout the *Faerie Queene*, between *fairy* knight and British. Thus, Artegal is a changeling, not a fairy:

> He wonneth in the land of Fayeree,
> Yet is no fairy borne, ne sib at all
> To Elfes, but sprong of seed terrestriall,
> And whylom by false fairies stolen away.
>
> (III, iii, 26.)

Guyon, on the other hand, is "elfin borne"; he was of noble state and "mickle worship in his native land"; he had been knighted by Huon (II. i. 6). Amphisa was a fairy "by race" (III. vi. 4). Priamond and his brothers were born of a fay (IV. ii. 44). Redcross, however, was "sprong out from English race, However now accompted Elfins sonne." The Hermit goes on to explain that he came from the ancient race of Saxon kings, but was stolen as a child by a fairy who left her own child and took Redcross to fairy land where he was brought up by a ploughman.[2] Furthermore, Prince Arthur, not a fairy but a "Briton knight," seeks Gloriana, the Fairy Queen, whom he has seen in a vision. Her image he bears on his shield. Guyon, a Fairy knight, promises to aid him in his quest, and they are companions throughout the second book. In the House of Alma they read with delight ancient chronicles that set forth the origin of each: Arthur reads *Briton Moniments* and Guyon *Antiquitee of Faery Lond*.

Summarizing the evidence thus far, we note: (1) the careful distinction between the two classes of knights, a distinction that is preserved both for the great knights and for the lesser figures as well. (2) The hero of Book I is a Briton; of Book II is a Fairy. Yet there is no distinction in appearance, size or personal character, the distinction is of race. Both classes of knights perform valorous deeds against enchantment; the Fairy possesses no supernatural power, for example, as against the Briton. (3) Arthur, contrary to certain folk traditions, is not a fairy sovereign; Gloriana is.

We come now to a consideration of the place of the chronicles in the *Faerie Queene*. These are found in II. x., in which is given a rhymed chronicle of British kings from Brutus to Uther, and in III. iii., where the history is continued in the form of Merlin's prophecy to Britomart concerning her descendants as far as Cadwallader, last of the kings. Only Arthur and his son are omitted. Miss Carrie M. Harper, in her excellent study of the sources of Spenser's history, has suggested that the British point of view and the interest in Welsh tradition, "may be partly accounted for by the Welsh blood of the Tudors."[3] It is safe to go much farther than this. Far from being mere episodes, these chronicles are important structurally. This is indicated by the elaborate invocations prefixed to the cantos containing the historical material, and also by Spenser's repeated statements that in this poem he is celebrating the ancestry of the Queen.[4] Moreover, while Spenser's chronicle deals only with British kings and is thus a recognition of Elizabeth's British ancestry, the

---

2. I, x, 60–67. Compare the "Birth of St. George," in Percy, and the story of the "weird ladye of the woods." The Hermit tells Redcross that he is to be known as "Saint George of mery England."

3. *Sources of the British Chronicle History in Spenser's Faerie Queene*, p. 181.

4. Compare, for example, II., Prologue, st. IV, where the English realm is called the "lond of Faery" and in this "antique ymage" the Queen is asked to see her "great auncestry." See also the invocations to II. x. and III. iii.

point is driven home by means of the fairy chronicle, which is definitely referred to the Tudor house. Most of the fairy monarchs have the word *elf* incorporated in their names, from Elfe, the founder of the dynasty, who wedded a fay, through Elfin,[5] Elfinan, Elfiline, Elfinell, Elfant, Elfar, Elfinor, down to Elficleos, who is identified with Henry VII. Oberon (Henry VIII) succeeded, since Elferon (Prince Arthur) died before his father, and the last reigning monarch is Tanaquil (Gloriana), by whom Spenser means Elizabeth.[6]

By this means Spenser is able to bridge the gap in chronology necessary to his design; he omits all reference to Saxon or Norman kings, or to kings of England prior to Henry VII. The past, both near and remote, is blended with the present. Arthur and Gloriana are in one sense the ancestors of Elizabeth; in another sense they are now living, rulers of England.[7] This fact may be plainly seen if we add to these two chronicles the relevation of Britomart's descendants as given to her by Merlin (III. iii. 26 ff.). Artegal, whom Britomart is to wed, is not a fairy, though he thinks he was born from the union of an elf with a fay. In truth, Merlin says, he is son of Gorlois and brother of the Cornish king, Cador. The name Artegal comes from the chronicles and, as Miss Harper observes (pp. 143–144), the device makes up for the omission of the historical Arthur here and in Book II. At the end of Merlin's list of kings we are told that the Britons will be driven out first by a Raven (the Danes) and then by the Lion of Neustria (William of Normandy), but that "when the term is full accomplished . . . a sparke of fire" shall break forth from Mona and

> So shall the Briton blood their crowne agayn reclame.

Thus Spenser once more covers the period from 1228 when Llewellyn, the last British prince, gave up Wales and retired to Anglesey (Mona), where Henry VII was afterwards born. By this means the chronological interim is bridged, as by the device of the fairy genealogy in II, x, and we are once more brought to the Tudor regime.

Preparatory to an interpretation of these facts it is necessary to recall the various aspects under which Elizabeth appears. As Gloriana, she typifies not only the glory but the "rule" of England.[8] As Belphoebe and, to a certain extent, as Britomart, she typifies chas-

---

5. The name Elphin is often met in Welsh folk tales. One hero of that name was the finder of the bard Taliessin. See *Mabinogion*, ed. Guest, p. 325.

6. The passage is in II. x. 70 ff. The Welsh word for Elves is *Ellyllon*, a point not without significance here.

7. Thus, for example, in II. x. 4 Spenser says that Elizabeth's name, realm, and race come from Prince Arthur. Here he is thinking of the historical Arthur, ancestor of Elizabeth in the literal sense.

8. See the *Letter*, the proem to II, stanzas 4 and 5, and the proem to III., st. 5.

tity. But as Britomart she is primarily representative of British power, the warlike might of England.[9] As Mercilla, she is Elizabeth the merciful, the poet's interpretation of her unwillingness to sentence Mary of Scotland to death. She is also, of course, Cynthia, a conception parallel to that of Belphoebe; and Tanaquil, the daughter of Henry VIII. Of all these conceptions, that of Gloriana *plus* Britomart is by far the most constant and important. The union between Arthur and Gloriana and that between Artegal and Britomart then become significant of Spenser's fundamental conception in the structure of the poem. How closely knit the two stories are is indicated by the facts, already pointed out, that Artegal parallels Arthur in an important sense in the chronicles, and that Britomart, in Book III at least, plays Arthur's rôle. The full significance of this conception it is now possible to define.

By *Fairy* Spenser means *Welsh*, or, more accurately, *Tudor*, as distinguished from the general term British. He looks on England as Britain, ignoring, for the purpose of his poem, post-Conquest history.[1] The Tudor dynasty, therefore, brings back the ancient British line, and one purpose of the poem is to celebrate this fact in compliment to the Queen. But Gloriana, the Faerie Queene, is *Elizabeth Tudor*. The old British spirit, the real England, represented in Prince Arthur, finds in her "glory," in the rich connotation given that term in the Renaissance, and also the powerful government ("rule"—see the proem to III, stanza 5) that was making England a great European power and was the prophecy of the coming British imperialism. Thus the epic celebrates both the ancestry of Elizabeth, the return of the old British strain, and also her greatness as an individual. The title that Spenser chooses for his poem takes on new significance.

It remains only to add that the Britomart-Artegal story relates primarily to Great Britain. The deeds of Artegal, for example, as I have pointed out elsewhere,[2] reflect the international relations of Elizabeth's government, especially the conflict with Philip of Spain. But the Arthur-Gloriana story, complementary to this, is concerned with the return of the native British race to power. Spenser has left

---

9. Strictly speaking, the third book deals with the rescue of Amoret. Scudamore, the knight who should be the hero of the book, does not succeed in accomplishing his "adventure," so Britomart comes to his assistance. Thus Britomart is the counterpart of Arthur in the other books, with the difference that while Arthur renders assistance to Redcross and Guyon in their hour of need, each of the titular heroes of the first two books achieves his final "adventure" without any aid from the "greatest knight in the world." It is this well-known romance convention

that Spenser makes use of in his poem, not the idea that no one virtue is sufficient but that Magnificence includes them all.

1. The words "England" and "English" occur only a few times in the entire *F.Q.* St. George (Redcross) belongs to "mery England"; he is sprung from "English race," born of "English blood" (I.x.60–64). The only other examples of the use of the word have nothing to do with what is discussed in this paper.

2. "Spenser and British Imperialism," *Modern Philology*, January, 1912.

evidence of this distinction in the passage (III, ii, 7–8) in which Britomart says that she has come from her "native soyle, that is by name The greater Britaine," to "Faery lond," where she has heard that many famous knights and ladies dwell. That is, fairy land, for the moment, is Wales, the last stronghold of Britain. This is quite in agreement with the entire conception. Avalon, Fairy Land, Wales, is ruled by a *fée* who became the protector of Arthur, healed his wound, and preserved him until the time for his return, in the Tudor house, to worldly empire. The only addition that Spenser makes is that the great *fée*, in the person of Elizabeth, herself assumes the rule of Great Britain.

* * *

DOUGLAS BUSH

[Spenser's Treatment of Classical Myth]†

Although it is a textbook commonplace that Spenser's poetry gathers many-colored threads from ancient, medieval, and modern worlds into one shimmering web, scholars nowadays speak less certainly than they once did of his familiarity with ancient literature. While his acquaintance with medieval and Renaissance writing has been extended, his supposed classical learning has been reduced here and there. We do not speak of Spenser's Platonism as if it came from the fountainhead, for there is hardly any evidence that he knew Plato at first hand. Doubtless, like most men of his time, he read Ficino and similar authors, and slighted the Greek. At any rate the so-called Platonism which runs through so much of his work, and constantly kindles his idealistic nature, is thoroughly of the Renaissance.[1] It has been proved that the ethical scheme of *The Faerie Queene* is based directly upon Aristotle; it has also been proved that it is not based upon Aristotle. Again, for Spenser as for most men of his age, Aristotle meant not so much the body of writings that we know as the numerous strata of medieval and Renaissance commentary; and his name might be attached to pagan doctrines of morality implicit in the Christian tradition.

Or there is *The Shepheardes Calender*. A critical legend, started by E. K. and repeated with embellishments by later generations, has found Greek influence in Spenser's pastorals. But it has been conclusively shown that "direct Greek influence on the *Calender*,

† From *Mythology and the Renaissance Tradition in English Poetry*, rev. ed. (W. W. Norton & Co., Inc., New York, 1963), 91–120. The original footnotes have been slightly edited.
1. The latest and fullest study of the whole subject is Robert Ellrodt, *Neoplatonism in the Poetry of Spenser* (Geneva, 1960). Cf. M. Evans, "Platonic Allegory in *The Faerie Queene*," *RES*, XII (1961), 132–143.

if it existed at all, was negligible"; that Spenser's chief models were Marot and the poets of the Pléiade, along with Chaucer and Mantuan; and that even Virgil's influence "seems to have been slight, indirect, and distorted."[2]

These are some instances of the way in which Spenser's direct debt to classical, especially Greek, literature has been shrinking. Few modern readers have brought to Spenser the classical equipment of J. W. Mackail, and Mackail has said that "even for traces of any influence on him from Homer, from the Greek lyrists, or from Attic tragedians we may search through him in vain."[3] The exceptions that can be lodged against that statement seem to be relatively few.

On the other hand, as I have remarked, Spenser's debt to medieval and Renaissance literature has been steadily illuminated and extended. Such facts are no reflection upon the genuineness of the poet's wide culture, but they do involve a shift of emphasis. The process of investigation, still far from complete, has not been mere barren source-hunting; it has helped to clarify our understanding of Spenser's art and thought, to root him more solidly in his own age. Closer scrutiny of dozens of Renaissance figures, along with fuller knowledge of the Middle Ages and the medieval tradition, has exploded the older conception of the Renaissance as a sudden awakening, a complete break with the medieval past. The Elizabethan author, as we have frequent occasion to observe, was, in his treatment of mythology and his general mental habit, nearer 1400 than 1700. Spenser would have been more at ease with Chaucer than with Dryden.

* * *

The Elizabethans, despite their generally superior knowledge of Latin and sometimes Greek authors, were very often content, like their medieval predecessors, to gather their mythological nosegays from the nearest conservatory. What was much more important, the mythographers * * * were not merely convenient dictionaries of reference; their allegorical interpretations, their conception of myth as the root of all poetry, were of prime attractiveness and value, not least to an imagination so richly creative and strongly ethical as Spenser's. His desk evidently held well-thumbed copies of Boccaccio's *De Genealogia Deorum* and Natalis Comes.

* * *

We have met already [i.e., in Bush's discussion of Spenser's use of Homer, Virgil, and Ovid, not reproduced here] some mixing of

2. M. Y. Hughes, "Spenser and the Greek Pastoral Triad," *SP*, XX, 187; *Virgil and Spenser* (1929), p. 307.

3. *The Springs of Helicon* (1909), p. 98.

classical and non-classical elements, but this is so typical of the Renaissance imagination and of Spenser in particular that we may look at a wider range of examples.

One familiar but often arresting kind of fusion brings together the classical and the Biblical. Within the compass of the *Shepheardes Calender* Pan is at various times Henry VIII, the pope, and Christ (as in Marot's pastoral poems he is both God and Francis I); if the mixture casts back to Petrarch's allegorical eclogues, it also looks forward to Hippotades, Camus, and the Pilot of the Galilean lake.[4] Of course such things are a commonplace in Renaissance art of all kinds; the comprehensive unity of all truth and beauty permits the most diverse and flexible combinations. Thus Spenser's loveliest description of the dawn blends classical myth and the imagery and language of the nineteenth Psalm:

> At last the golden Orientall gate
>> Of greatest heaven gan to open faire,
>> And Phoebus fresh, as bridegrome to his mate,
>> Came dauncing forth, shaking his deawie haire:
>> And hurld his glistring beames through gloomy aire.
>> Which when the wakeful Elfe perceiv'd, streight way
>> He started up, and did him selfe prepaire,
>> In sun-bright armes, and battailous array:
>> For with that Pagan proud he combat will that day.[5]

Here there is no incongruity; Hebraic and classical images are fused in the alembic of a Renaissance imagination. And the pure natural light of the sun dawns above the false glitter of the House of Pride to which, forgetful of his quest, the knight of holiness has been led. Everywhere Spenser freely mingles fictitious and historical, Hebraic and classical. The well of life which renewed the strength of the Red Cross Knight—that is, the sacrament of baptism—excels, as well it may, "Silo" and Jordan, Bath, "the german Spau," Cephisus and Hebrus. The hill from which the same Christian soldier surveys "the new Hierusalem" is

> like that sacred hill, whose head full hie,
> Adornd with fruitfull Olives all arownd,

4. I.e., it looks forward to Milton's allusions, in *Lycidas,* to Hippotades (Aeolus, son of Hippotas), Camus (the god of the river Cam, in Cambridge), and "the Pilot of the Galilean lake" (St. Peter; cf. Luke, v. 2–4) [*Editor*].

5. *F.Q.,* I.v.2. Cf. Psalm xix.5; "In them hath he set a tabernacle for the sun: which cometh forth as a bridegroom out of his chamber, and rejoiceth as a giant to run his course." The same combination appears in

another place where the decorative impulse subserves the poet's deepest personal ardor and reverence (though the necessary shift from Phoebus to Phoebe mars the astronomical logic):

> Loe where she comes along with portly pace
> Lyke Phoebe from her chamber of the East,
> Arysing forth to run her mighty race. . . .

Cf. *Comus,* 95–101.

Is, as it were for endlesse memory
Of that deare Lord, who oft thereon was fownd,
For ever with a flowring girlond crownd:
Or like that pleasaunt Mount, that is for ay
Through famous Poets verse each where renownd,
On which the thrise three learned Ladies play
Their heavenly notes, and make full many a lovely lay.[6]

This instinctive fusing of apparently alien elements is not a mere matter of random or irreverent allusion, it is central in Spenser's sensibility and artistry.

To the casual reader *The Faerie Queene* may seem a tissue of decorative episodes and quite often, without closer scrutiny, we may think that the poet has forgotten his serious purpose in the elaboration of sensuous detail. In the account of Mammon's temptations of Guyon, Spenser has in mind the familiar three tests of folk-lore and Satan's three temptations of Christ; this is one of the two passages Milton referred to when he called Spenser "sage and serious," "a better teacher than Scotus or Aquinas." Here if anywhere Spenser is in a soberly didactic mood, and this is the scene of the final temptation: [Quotes II.vii.53–55]. After these lines, laden with glamorous images of beauty, we may not remember that the knight of temperance is winning a hard victory over avarice and ambition and we may have no ear for the groans of Tantalus and Pilate. But such a reaction would miss the subtle and pervasive suggestion that these are images of specious beauty or at best of earthly love and vanity.

The *locus classicus* is of course the Bower of Bliss (Milton's other passage). The groundwork of the whole second book is the ethical psychology of Plato and Aristotle and Christian writers. The groundwork of this final episode is the story of Circe, though there is far less of Homer than of the allegorical tradition that interpreted the myth as the battle between flesh and spirit. Spenser, like Milton in *Comus,* is showing the conquest of sensual appetite by the virtuous will; but while Milton's Lady is invulnerable, Spenser's hero is not quite so. When the sirens sing

O turne thy rudder hither-ward a while:
Here may thy storme-bet vessell safely ride;
This is the Port of rest from troublous toyle,
The worlds sweet In, from paine and wearisome turmoyle,

it is no wonder that Guyon's senses are "softly tickeled," and that a little later he slackens his pace to gaze at the wanton damsels in the pool. But these are only realistic admissions of human frailty.

6. *F.Q.*, I.x.54.

Critics in the romantic tradition, misled by inadequate apprehension of appearances, could see Spenser letting a really voluptuous imagination have free rein. This wholly mistaken notion was happily killed by C. S. Lewis in his *Allegory of Love*. He showed with what subtlety Spenser worked cumulative variations on two main motives: the contrast between the simple purity of nature and the diseased luxuriance of artifice, and the contrast between healthy love and the insatiable lust of the eye. The interweaving of these motives makes the Bower a beautiful nursery of sterile corruption. In destroying it Guyon is no rigorous puritan; it is not the kind of place that could be "reopened under new management."

This is not to say that Spenser's senses are not richly responsive to physical beauty, but his tone varies with his purpose. In the first canto of the third book he wishes to suggest the sensuality of the Castle Joyous and gives five luscious stanzas to tapestries in which Venus, like Acrasia, gluts her eyes on Adonis; in the Gardens of Adonis, the scene of wholesome fecundity, the love of Venus and Adonis is the union of matter and form. Once in a while the distinction between good and evil may seem less clear-cut. We touched before on Spenser's expansion of Ovid in the mythological tapestries which "shew Dan Cupids powre and great effort." These pictures hang in the mansion of the evil enchanter, Busyrane, that foe of chastity; but profane love may seem to lose half its evil by losing all its grossness when it appears in tapestries depicting Europa on the bull's back, Danae in her tower, and many more. [Quotes *F. Q.*, III.xi.32] Never on Olympus did Jove's exploits receive such mild censure. But Spenser is not escaping from the *utile* into the *dulce*; the conception of love in such a picture is judged and placed by the tone and the context and by our recollection of Britomart or Una or *Epithalamion*.

One very different, indeed unique, item must be mentioned, Sir Calidore's vision of the Graces. Wandering one day beyond the pastoral community, he hears "a shrill pipe" and "many feete fast thumping th' hollow ground"—Spenser's natural magic does not forbid homely realism—and then the knight, who is no example of the lust of the eye, beholds such a sight

> That even he him selfe his eyes envyde,
> An hundred naked maidens lilly white,
> All raunged in a ring, and dauncing in delight.[7]

This is pure, unearthly beauty; the dancing maidens are as sexless as lilies waving in the wind. In the center of the ring are the three

---

7. *F.Q.*, VI.x.10 ff. See the Variorum commentary and Edgar Wind, *Pagan Mysteries in the Renaissance* (New Haven, 1958).

classical Graces, and Colin Clout's Rosalind, and the symbolic relation of the Graces to Courtesy is duly expounded.

This item leads into a world or otherworld traditionally blended with that of classical myth, the Celtic (if the word may be used in a broad sense). We remember the medieval *Sir Orfeo* and the *Merchant's Tale,* in which Pluto and Proserpine are the king and queen "of Fayerye." In such blending of the classical and the fairy world Spenser is pre-eminent over his contemporaries in degree, not in kind. Philomela, says Ovid, was more beautiful than *naidas et dryadas,* and Golding renders "fairies."[8] Nashe as a matter of course links the sprites of English folklore with the woodland divinities of "idolatrous former daies and the fantasticall world of Greece."[9] Reginald Scot catalogues all kinds of "bugs" ranging from centaurs to Tom Thumb, and quotes a decree of a General Council about women who profess to "ride abroad with Diana, the goddess of the Pagans, or else with Herodias."[1] But we need only think of the name of Oberon's wife, Titania, who fell in love with Bully Bottom.

Naturally, then, in *The Faerie Queene* we find Celtic motives woven into the narrative texture and into the allegory. Sometimes they proclaim their origin, sometimes they have become almost unrecognizable through combination with other material; yet always they contribute their peculiar quality of strangeness added to beauty. Spenser's second book draws more from the classics than any other, and expounds the classical virtue of temperance in terms of the classical divisions of the soul, but even here the three chief adventures involve Celtic elements. The wanton Phaedria is a lady of the lake and not merely an adaptation of Tasso's Armida (who belongs anyhow to the same romantic sisterhood). The *Odyssey* is romantic enough, but it is not such a repository of wonders, such an *omnium gatherum,* as Spenser's twelfth canto. Here we have matter from modern books of travel, from Celtic *imrama,* from Mandeville and possibly Lucian's *True History;* Ovidian and Homeric myths and an apparent recollection of Christ calming the waters; strange beasts from Gesner and from Plutarch the hoggish Grill (to whose stubborn individuality the irrational part of one's soul accords a degree of respect); the guide Reason from Ariosto, music and enticing damsels from Tasso. . . . Or, if we think of the Cave of Mammon mainly in terms of Spenser's *chiaroscuro* effects, or of the ethical psychology of Aristotle and Plato, we may remind ourselves of other elements:

8. *Metam.* vi.452–453; Golding, ed. Rouse, p. 130, line 579.
9. *Works,* ed. McKerrow, I, 347.
1. *The Discovery of Witchcraft* (ed. 1665), bk. vii, c. 15, p. 85: bk. iii,

c. 16, p. 36 (on Herodias, cf. Chambers, *The Mediaeval Stage,* I, 109). Scot expatiates on the text that "the gods of the Gentiles are Devils."

The old man who guards a fairy hill is a stock character; sometimes he is a *leprechaun*, who guards a treasure that he tries to hide when he is caught by a mortal; sometimes he is a fairy king. Again, the idea that to touch any object in the Underworld will necessitate remaining in the power of the fairy owner is not only a part of the Proserpina myth, but of Celtic folk tradition generally. The very nature of Guyon's temptation: the offer of riches, love, fame, is in the story of Murrough. Guyon's sight of souls suffering the tortures of hell, which seems to owe something to Dante, is analogous to the legends about magic islands converted into places of eternal punishment. But the most significant detail is that of the apples. Since Warton's time the relation between Spenser's account of the Garden of Proserpina and Claudian's *De Raptu Proserpinae* has been recognized. In this we have the famous golden bough. But while Warton sees in the silver stool "a new circumstance of temptation," he does not explain it. In Celtic tradition resting beneath an apple tree subjected one to danger from fays. Lancelot, for example, is sleeping under an apple tree when he is seized by fays and carried into captivity. Ogier comes to an orchard, eats an apple, and is soon in the power of Morgain. Avalon is "apple land."[2]

Spenser's Celtic lore may not have embraced all these items but he must have known some.

In the "Gardens of Adonis," and on a larger scale in the *Cantos of Mutability*, Spenser employs classical myth in a way that is more symbolic than allegorical, though it springs from the allegorical or "parabolic" habit of mind. The earlier passage, the sixth canto of the third book, begins with the miraculous conception of Belphoebe and Amoret. Then we have Venus searching for Cupid, a theme that Renaissance poets loved to play with.[3] Venus encounters Diana, who is in that extreme dishabille so common among Spenserian ladies. During the hunt for Cupid the two infants, Belphoebe and Amoret, are found, and one is taken by each goddess, to be reared according to their respective standards.

Then comes the "scientific" part of the canto, the description of the Gardens of Adonis where Venus dwells. "A thousand thousand naked babes" are in this garden; some are clothed in flesh and sent to live in the world; after a time they return to be "planted" in the garden, and, in forgetfulness of their mortal life, they grow again during "some thousand yeares." These souls grow in the same way as animals and plants, under the care of nature and the porter, "Old Genius." In the wide womb of the world there lies

2. E. Greenlaw, *SP*, XV, 111.

3. Spenser's handling of the theme again illustrates his taste. He had probably read Moschus at some time (see E. K.'s gloss on *March*), but he follows rather the embroidering of Moschus in the prologue of Tasso's *Aminta* (J. D. Bruce, *MLN*, XXVII, 183–185).

> An huge eternal Chaos, which supplyes
> The substances of natures fruitfull progenyes.
>
> All things from thence doe their first being fetch,
>   And borrow matter, whereof they are made,
>   Which when as forme and feature it does ketch,
> Becomes a bodie, and doth then invade
> The state of life, out of the griesly shade.
> That substance is eterne, and bideth so,
> Ne when the life decayes, and forme does fade,
> Doth it consume, and into nothing go,
> But chaunged is, and often altred to and fro.
>
> The substance is not chaunged, nor altered,
>   But th' only forme and outward fashion . . .

Even here Spenser has Ovid in mind, though it is Ovid versifying Platonic ideas.[4]

Of this continual renewing of life the great enemy is Time, who mows down "the flowring herbes and goodly things"; but for Time the garden would be a cloudless paradise. Yet even Time cannot destroy a covert on a hill where Venus lives eternally with Adonis . . . [Quotes *F. Q.*, III.vi.47–8].

Thus Spenser sets forth the idea of permanence underlying eternal flux. The theme is presented first in the concrete manner of a Platonic myth, then generalized in abstract terms, and finally embodied in the myth of Venus and Adonis. The myth which, in connection with the Castle Joyous, had been erotic here becomes metaphysical: Venus is matter, Adonis is form, and their perpetual love represents the perpetuity of life.[5] In this canto Spenser does not seem to be greatly troubled—apart from the activities of Time—since he has found at least an imaginative reconciliation between the fact of change and the desire for stability; and, though as a whole the myth is given in naturalistic terms, there is a reminder (stanza 34) that the great process has divine sanction.

For a still more elaborate and a more deeply troubled answer to the question of change and permanence we must turn to the *Cantos of Mutability*, which were first published in 1609 and were evidently Spenser's last composition.

* * *

4. *Metam.* xv. 252–260. See J. W. Bennett, "Spenser's Garden of Adonis," *PMLA*, XLVII, 66–67.

5. For one illustration of Spenser's symbolism one might quote Pico della Mirandola: "Venus is said to be born of the Sea; Matter the Inform Nature, whereof every Creature is compounded, is represented by Water, continually flowing, easily receptible of any form" (*A Platonick Discourse upon Love*, tr. Thomas Stanley, II.xiii, *Poems*, 1651; *Poems and Translations of Thomas Stanley*, ed. G. M. Crump (Clarendon Press, 1962), p. 211. Cf. Leo Hebraeus, *Dialoghi d'Amore*, ed. Caramella, pp. 131–132.

For his answer to the question of the one and the many, the question whether unity lies behind the eternal flux, Spenser, in the true vein of Renaissance reconcilers, seeks a compromise. That compromise is half "scientific," half Christian. All things work out the law of their being, not in the naturalistic sense but under divine control; and then will come eternity when all shall be changed for the last time. Yet the doctrine of evolution under Providence, however traditional, does not seem to have wholly quieted Spenser's distress, however devout a Christian he was. After Nature's orthodox verdict comes a personal reaction, in two stanzas that are the voice of an infant crying in the night: [Quotes viii.1–2]. Keats, writing in an era of Revolutionary optimism, made the defeat of the Titans by the gods a symbol of progress (though his main theme was more personal and less cheering); but in the late sixteenth century the theory of progress was only coming to birth. From a world of medieval fixities Spenser contemplates the spectacle of ceaseless change and he cannot suppress the instinctive and age-old feeling of *contemptus mundi*. For all the differences in substance and manner, there is a general parallel between *Mutability* and Donne's *Anniversaries*. Though Spenser has not lost his awareness of beauty, he longs for release from the fallen world.

A partly similar dichotomy appears elsewhere in Spenser, for example, in the *Fowre Hymnes*. Although the Renaissance religion of beauty achieved its culmination in mystical union with the divine essence, most adherents lingered on the lower rungs of the Platonic ladder, satisfying their sense of poetry with mystical rhapsodies and their other senses with mundane mistresses. Scholars have disagreed on whether Spenser's two later hymns are a continuation or a repudiation of the first two. In the first two, following Castiglione in part, Spenser touched two or three of the orthodox stages in the Platonic ascent from the love of woman to absolute love and beauty. But those two could never lead on to Spenser's third hymn with its devout account of Christ and the redemption of man, which belongs to a different order of vision and experience. Spenser was neither a mystic nor a pseudomystic but an evangelical Christian with a Platonic ethical strain. So in the eighth canto of the second book of *The Faerie Queene* there is a point beyond which the moral reason cannot go, and Guyon is protected, when the palmer is helpless, first by an angel and then by Arthur, the instrument of God's providence.[6] And in *Mutability*, as we have seen, the metaphysical doctrine of permanence behind the flux is inadequate reassurance, and Spenser turns away from earth to the hope of heaven.

6. On this and many related questions, see A. S. P. Woodhouse, "Nature and Grace in the *Faerie Queene*," *ELH*, XVI (1949), 194–228.

It is at such moments, surely, that Spenser's inmost self is stirred. The mood may be more intelligible if we remember Chaucer's recoil not merely from the passions he had so subtly delineated in *Troilus* but from all earthly love. Or there is Sidney's "Leave me, O love which reachest but to dust. . . ." It does not mean that Chaucer and Sidney and Spenser can permanently renounce the joys of earth, can deny for good the rights of half their nature, but that, in moments of profound revulsion, all things seem dross except God. Such moments of course are rare; these poets' names suggest delight in all that the world can give. But we are in no doubt concerning the orthodox normality of Chaucer's religious faith and that of Sidney and Spenser was more active and intense. Yet only in a Renaissance poet, and only in Spenser among English poets, could we have a poem about the government of the universe based on a classical myth, in the setting of a medieval court of love in Ireland, including the mishaps of a mythological Peeping Tom, and ending with a heartfelt prayer to "that great Sabbaoth God."

It would be hard to find in *The Faerie Queene* two consecutive cantos that give a wider and finer display of Spenser's particular gifts. Few readers are likely to dissent from Courthope's judgment that *Mutability* is "both in conception and execution, the most sublime part" of the poem. It is, to be sure, the Elizabethan, not the Miltonic, sublime. When sources range from Ovid to Alanus de Insulis, and mood and style from the celestial to the earthy, when the poet pauses in his search for unity to paint gorgeous pictures of diversity, the total effect is almost kaleidoscopic.

* * * Spenser without the classics would be different, but his main outlines would be little changed; Spenser without medieval and modern literature would be inconceivable. To borrow a paragraph from Courthope:

> Spenser's genius is inspired almost exclusively by the Middle Ages. The chivalrous matter of his poems is mediaeval: so is his allegorical spirit: so is his quasi-archaic diction. Enthusiastic admirer of the classics as he is, all that he really draws from them is a frequent allusion to the tales of Greek mythology, and a certain concinnity in the metrical combination of words and phrases, which he imitates from the style of the Latin poets. The structure of his composition is in every sense of the word "romantic."[7]

There are very few passages in Spenser's work of which one can say, "Here he is writing like a classical ancient." Classical influence on him is much more indirect than direct. In the main it reaches him as already transmogrified, romanticized, by medieval, Italian, and

7. *History of English Poetry*, III, 134.

French writers. Such classical "impurity" is of course the note of his age.

Spenser's treatment of myth, then, is largely colored by the medievalism apparent in his fable, in his narrative and descriptive technique, in his own thought and feeling, and by the theory and practice of continental literature of the sixteenth century. Myths are retold with Italian sensuousness, and allegorized with medieval seriousness. Spenser's romantic-didactic conception of poetry led him, as it led others, to borrow material from some ancients, to alter its form and spirit for his own purposes. "He shows no suspicion of Malherbe's rule, that if you borrow from the classics you must adhere rigidly to the traditional story or characteristics; that a dead mythology admits of no development; that to add new stories or new features only emphasizes the decorative, fantastic character of your material."[8] Nor did his borrowings from the classics teach him, any more than they taught most of his fellows, the lessons of form, selection, precision, restraint. It is needless to add that if he had learned those lessons he could not have written *The Faerie Queene*.

THOMAS P. ROCHE, JR.

[The Elizabethan Idea of Allegory] †

Allegorical reading (or more simply allegory) is a form of literary criticism with a metaphysical basis. It postulates a verbal universe at every point correspondent with the physical world in which we live, that is, a Realistic view of language. The history of allegorical interpretation of the Bible and secular literature is too long and complicated to relate here, but by the time of the sixteenth century allegory had attached itself firmly to the image of the universe created by Ptolemy and Dionysius the Areopagite and familiarly known as the "Elizabethan world picture." According to this theory there are in reality three worlds: the *sublunary*, the fallen world in which we live, subject to change and decay; the *celestial*, the unchanging world of the planets and stars; the *supercelestial*, the dwelling of angels and the Godhead. These three worlds are held together by God's Love and are analogically correspondent. Thus, in the sublunary world fire burns, while in the celestial world its analogue the sun not only burns but by its burning nourishes life,

8. Sir H. J. C. Grierson, *The Background of English Literature* (London, 1925), p. 17. See Ferdinand Brunot, *La doctrine de Malherbe* (Paris, 1891), pp. 168–170.

† From *The Kindly Flame: A Study of the Third and Fourth Books of Spenser's "Faerie Queene,"* by Thomas P. Roche, Jr. (Princeton, N.J., 1964), Introduction.

and in the supercelestial world the seraphim burn with love for their Creator.[1] The three worlds are a progression away from the material and toward the spiritual, and just as our image of the purely spiritual seraphim is drawn from our knowledge of the visible fire and sun, so too is our knowledge of universal truths drawn (in part) from our reading of the imitation of the visible worlds. Pico makes this quite clear in the introduction to his *Heptaplus*:

> For euen as the . . . three worlds being girt and buckled with the bands of concord doe by reciprocall libertie, interchange their natures; the like do they also by their appellations. And this is the principle from whence springeth & groweth the discipline of allegoricall sense. For it is certaine that the ancient fathers could not conueniently haue represented one thing by other figures, but that they had first learned the secret amity and affinitie of all nature. Otherwise there could bee no reason, why they should represent this thing by this forme, and that by that, rather then otherwise. But hauing the knowledge of the vniuersall world, and of euery part thereof, and being inspired with the same spirit, that not onely knoweth all things: but did also make all things: they haue oftentimes, and very fitly figured the natures of the one world, by that which they knew to bee correspondent thereto in the others.[2]

The basis of allegorical reading is this analogical nature of the universe. In an hierarchical universe where each thing has a fixed place the relationship of any two things in the same world or sphere may adumbrate the relationship of two other things in another world or sphere. The original pair do not lose their identity or relationship by such adumbration; they simply call attention to other possible relationships through the fact that they themselves are related in such a way. The analogies are validated by the fact that the whole hierarchical structure with its often unseen web of interrelationships is contained within the mind of God, Who sees the relationship of all things one to another. In allegorical reading a further step is taken: since words represent things, words must represent this basic analogical relationship.

The whole matter will be made clearer by returning to Harington's *Apology for Poetry*. Immediately following his definition of allegory is an example: "*Perseus* sonne of *Iupiter* is fained by the

1. *Iohannis Pici Mirandvlae . . . omnia . . . opera*, Venice, 1557, sig. **4. "Elemetaris urit: coelestis uiuificat: supercoelestis amat." The quotation may also be found on p. 188 of *De Hominis Dignitate, Heptaplus, De Ente et Uno*, ed. Eugenio Garin, Florence, 1942.
2. The translation is that of the English translator of Pierre de la Primaudaye, *The French Academie*, London, 1618, p.

671. De la Primaudaye in his discussion of the division of the universal world simply translates the second proemium to Pico's *Heptaplus*. The original Latin text is on sig. **4 of the Venice, 1557, edition and on p. 192 of the Garin edition. The passage also occurs in Fornari's *Della Espositione Sopra L'Orlando furioso Parte Seconda*, Florence, 1550, vol. 2, p. 3.

Poets to haue slaine *Gorgon*, and after that conquest atchieued, to haue flowen vp to heauen." Harington gives an euhemeristic interpretation as the "Historicall sence" and continues with several more senses:

> Morally it signifieth thus much, *Perseus* a wise man, sonne of *Iupiter* endewed with vertue from aboue, slayeth sinne and vice, a thing base & earthly; signified by *Gorgon*, and so mounteth vp to the skie of vertue: It signifies in one kinde of Allegorie thus much; the mind of man being gotten by God, and so the childe of God killing and vanquishing the earthlinesse of this Gorgonicall nature, ascendeth vp to the vnderstanding of heauenly things, of high things, of eternal things; in which cõtemplacion cõsisteth the perfection of man: this is the natural allegory, because mã [is] one of the chiefe works of nature: It hath also a more high and heauenly Allegorie, that the heauenly nature, daughter of *Iupiter*, procuring with her continuall motion, corruption and mortality in the inferiour bodies, seuered it selfe at last from these earthly bodies, and flew vp on high, and there remaineth for euer. It hath also another Theological Allegorie; that the angelicall nature, daughter of the most high God the creator of all things; killing & ouercomming al bodily substance, signified by *Gorgon*, ascended into heauen: the like infinite Allegories I could pike out of other Poeticall fictions, saue that I would auoid tediousnes.[3]

The final, almost parenthetical comment is worth the consideration of any one piecing out the Elizabethan idea of allegory. Many poetical fictions adumbrate more than one allegorical meaning, and these meanings, as the Perseus example shows, need not conform totally with every detail in the narrative (vehicle of the continued metaphor). Perseus, the son of Jupiter, may become in an allegorical reading the *daughter* of God, as in the "more high and heauenly Allegorie." Perseus is not the name or personification of the heavenly or the angelical natures; he is an allegorical representation of these beings because in his narrative he is the offspring (not son or daughter) of Jupiter, and hence because of the poetic statement of this particular adventure the whole statement may adumbrate these and any other heavenly mysteries that follow this particular pattern. There is no relation between narrative statement and allegorical meaning except the "secret amity and affinitie of all nature." When the structural patterns of the narrative coincide with the structural patterns of any other events of nature or supernature, we as readers are entitled to view the conformity or analogy as an allegorical meaning.

* * *

3. Harington, *Orlando Furioso*, 1591, sig. Piiij–Piiij^v. Reprinted in Smith, vol. 2, pp. 202–203. For an earlier interpretation of the Perseus myth that follows the method employed by Harington but finds different meanings see Giovanni Boccaccio, *Genealogie Deorum Gentilium*, ed. Vincenzo Romano, 2 vols., Bari, 1951, vol. I, p. 19 (Book I, chap. 3).

PAUL J. ALPERS

Narrative and Rhetoric in the *Faerie Queene*†

Whenever we interpret a narrative poem, we must decide how narrative action reveals poetic meaning. In this essay, I want to propose a new way of seeing the relation between poetic meaning and narrative events in the *Faerie Queene*. The usual view of this relation is based on what I would call a confusion between narrative materials and poetic narration. Spenser's narrative materials are stories, settings, and characters, while his poetic narration is a sequence of stanzas. Confusing the two produces interpretations like Ruskin's analysis of Book I—one of the first reactions against the romantic tendency to dismiss or minimize Spenser's allegory:

> [Holiness], in the opening of the book, has Truth (or Una) at its side, but presently enters the Wandering Wood, and encounters the serpent Error; that is to say, Error in her universal form, the first enemy of Reverence and Holiness. . . . Having vanquished this first open and palpable form of Error, as Reverence and Religion must always vanquish it, the Knight encounters Hypocrisy, or Archimagus: Holiness cannot detect Hypocrisy, but believes him, and goes home with him; whereupon, Hypocrisy succeeds in separating Holiness from Truth; and the Knight (Holiness) and Lady (Truth) go forth separately from the house of Archimagus. Now observe; the moment Godly Fear, or Holiness, is separated from Truth, he meets Infidelity, or the Knight sans Foy. . . .[1]

Ruskin simply translates the narrative materials of Book I into abstract terms. Characters and settings are given consistent symbolic identifications, and the narrative action indicates their conceptual relations. Ruskin makes what is still the fundamental assumption of Spenserian criticism—that the sequence of stanzas in the *Faerie Queene* is equivalent to the narrative materials of the poem. Since "narrative materials" is too bulky a term for frequent use, I shall refer to the stories, settings, and characters of the *Faerie Queene* as Spenser's *fiction*—that which is feigned to exist and happen.

Ruskin's method of interpretation is still accepted as valid for allegorical passages in the *Faerie Queene*; it is usually qualified by saying that some episodes are not allegorical, but are to be considered as exemplary or dramatic narrative. All recent critics define Spenser's technique by the poles of narrative and allegory.[2] As exemplary or

† From "Narrative and Rhetoric in the *Faerie Queene*," *SEL*, II (1962), 27–46. The original footnotes have been slightly edited.
1. *The Stones of Venice*, Appendix 2

("Theology of Spenser"), in *Works*, ed. E. T. Cook and A. Wedderburn (London, 1904), XI, 251–252.
2. See W. B. C. Watkins, *Shakespeare and Spenser* (Princeton, 1950), p. 130;

dramatic narrative, Spenser's fiction is taken to be real, according to the conventional suspension of disbelief we grant to any romance or novel. As allegory, the fiction is understood to be less real than its conceptual translation, but it nevertheless provides both the terms and the syntax of the translation. "What happens" poetically is taken to be identical with, or at least determined by, "what happens" fictionally. Whatever the specific content or meaning, it is expressed by the characters and settings that constitute and the events that take place in the putative reality of the poem.

However, when we read the poem on this assumption, we find numerous inconsistencies, some of which produce major interpretive difficulties. We find inconsistencies, I suggest, because our criterion of consistency is not valid. In turning narrative materials into stanzas of poetry, Spenser's attention is focused on the reader's mind and feelings and not on what is happening within his fiction. His poetic motive in any given stanza is to elicit a response—to modify or complicate feelings and attitudes. His stanzas, then, are modes of address by the poet to the reader. For this reason, I call his use of narrative materials *rhetorical*.

The most striking instance in which this approach resolves a fictional inconsistency is the problem of why the figure of Time is in the Garden of Adonis. According to Spenser's myth, the flowers in the garden are souls or forms that are sent out into the world; having lived and died on earth, they return to the Garden of Adonis to be replanted and reborn. The garden itself is a spontaneously flowering paradise and projects the idea that nature is permanent because its change is orderly. Literally, then, it is simply a mistake to place wicked Time with his scythe in the Garden of Adonis: the realm he rules is the earth below, and he represents a principle of sudden and final death that is presumably resolved by the orderly cycles of the garden.[3]

C. S. Lewis, *The Allegory of Love* (Oxford, 1936), p. 334, and *English Literature in the Sixteenth Century* (Oxford, 1954), p. 381; Hallett Smith, *Elizabethan Poetry* (Cambridge, Mass., 1952), p. 335.
3. Brents Stirling maintains that "there is nothing inconsistent in Time mowing down the 'flowring herbes and goodly things,'" "The Philosophy of Spenser's 'Garden of Adonis,'" *PMLA*, XLIX (1934), 526. Stirling is primarily concerned with charges that Spenser inconsistently places Time in a changeless garden, and he is entirely correct in pointing out that Spenser never represents the Garden of Adonis as changeless. But it is still necessary to explain how the figure of Time is compatible with the depiction of "continuall spring, and harvest . . . both meeting at one time" three stanzas later. The problem is not that Spenser places a figure named Time in the Garden, but that he depicts Time as a destroyer, an agent of death not of change. The words that describe Time's actions—"mow," "flings," "wither," "fowly mard," and "beates downe"—all suggest final destruction; there is a sharp contrast with the terms of preceding stanzas, all of which suggest a process—"chaungefull" (stanza 33, which ends, "so like a wheele around they runne from old to new") and "decayes" and "fade," which appear jointly in both stanzas 37 and 38. Stirling's argument, as it stands, depends on identifying change and death. But the depiction of Time will not support, as the rest of the canto will, the formula used of Adonis, "eterne in mutabilitie" (III, vi, 47).

Yet poetically Time's presence is perfectly valid. The potency of the image of a natural paradise depends on our understanding the idea of change that it corrects and resolves. In order to make us aware of earthly mutability, Spenser is willing to neglect both his fable and its philosophic coherence. He sets these aside in order to introduce a concept or feeling that is relevant to our understanding of the Garden of Adonis. In the stanza preceding the description of Time, Spenser explains the continuity of matter. "The substance is not chaunged," he says, but forms are:

> For formes are variable and decay,
> By course of kind, and by occasion;
> And that faire flowre of beautie fades away,
> As doth the lilly fresh before the sunny ray.
>
> (III.vi.38)

Spenser returns to the flowers of the garden by means of an image developed in the course of direct address to the reader. In the next four stanzas, he lays out the double suggestion of the image of the lily—on the one hand the inevitability of decay, and on the other the sense of benignity and naturalness given by "sunny ray."

The first of these stanzas is the presentation of earthly time:

> Great enimy to it, and to all the rest,
> That in the Gardin of Adonis springs,
> Is wicked Time, who with his scyth addrest,
> Does mow the flowring herbes and goodly things,
> And all their glory to the ground downe flings,
> Where they doe wither, and are fowly mard:
> He flyes about, and with his flaggy wings
> Beates downe both leaves and buds without regard,
> Ne ever pittie may relent his malice hard.
>
> (III.vi.39)

Time is more the activated abstraction of a sonnet than a fictional personage. The striking details of the stanza impress us primarily as emphatic diction, and not as the attributes of an emblematic character, "Wicked," "mow," "to the ground downe flings," "wither," "fowly mard," "beates downe," "malice hard"—this series runs through the stanza and is juxtaposed with the language of delicate pastoral—"flowring herbes," "glory," "leaves and buds." Spenser is multiplying statements about the action of earthly time. But the stanza, although more like a sonnet than a mythical narrative, is not exactly like a sonnet. In accordance with his rhetorical aim—to give a comprehensive sense of earthly time—Spenser presents Time as both mower and winged. These two versions are quite distinct, but Spenser accommodates them by turning Time's wings, which ordinarily represent swiftness of flight, into instruments of destruction. He thus creates a quasi-fiction that gives continuity and move-

ment to his statements: fictional action is in the service of direct
address to the reader.

The stanza that follows is also organized and developed as an
address to the reader:

> Yet pittie often did the gods relent,
> To see so faire things mard, and spoyled quight:
> And their great mother Venus did lament
> The losse of her deare brood, her deare delight:
> Her hart was pierst with pittie at the sight,
> When walking through the Gardin, them she spyde,
> Yet no'te she find redresse for such despight.
> For all that lives, is subject to that law:
> All things decay in time, and to their end do draw.
>
> (III.vi.40)

The first line directly echoes the last line of the stanza on Time and
produces an important shift of tone. "Ne ever pittie may relent his
malice hard" has a note of finality and rigor. "Yet pittie often did
the gods relent" conveys tender solicitude for Time's victims. In
other words, Spenser presents Venus's mourning for her flowers
within the framework of our responses to his diction and verse
rhythms. Between the image of the lily and this stanza we have
undergone a cumulative verbal experience, so that Spenser now re-
turns to the pathos of the lily with increased command and weight.
At the end of this stanza, he elicits from Venus's fictional tenderness
a tone of direct address that is both delicate and grave. His explana-
tion of the goddess's helplessness is really a summary statement of
Time's dominion over nature. It is from this rhetorical point that
he presents the garden as a paradise (III.vi.41–2). And even here
he begins by saying, "But were it not, that Time their troubler is."
In a strict philosophical sense, this concession is absurd, but poeti-
cally it places the vision of "continuall spring, and harvest . . . both
meeting at one time" in a wider context of human feeling about
time.

The poetic coherence of the *Faerie Queene* is usually described in
terms of fictional consistency; but it is rather to be found in the co-
herence of the reader's feelings and attitudes. One of the great
puzzles of the poem is the ending of Book I, when the Red Cross
Knight leaves Una. Spenser does not explicitly address the reader,
but we can solve the interpretive dilemma only by recognizing that
the mode of his narration is rhetorical:

> Yet swimming in that sea of blisfull joy,
> He nought forgot, how he whilome had sworne,
> In case he could that monstrous beast destroy,

Unto his Farie Queene backe to returne:
The which he shortly did, and Una left to mourne.
(I.xii.41)

If the knight's separation from Una does not mean separation from
Truth, as it did earlier in the book, then what does it mean? The
question is unanswerable if we assume that Spenser's fiction is the
main vehicle of his meaning. But surely Spenser's intention is clear
enough. The holy knight still bears his burden of flesh, and there-
fore must resume a life of heroic action. Marriage to Una symboli-
cally tells us about the knight's election and his moral condition,
but it is not the literal truth about his human experience. As literal
experience, the marriage is a "sea of blisfull joy" and suggests perma-
nent earthly happiness—precisely what is not possible for man
since the Fall. Una's mourning suggests the pathos of the fact that
the servant of God does not enjoy the eternal bliss of the saints in
heaven. It would be absurd to say that Truth mourns: both the mar-
riage and Una have simply their literal meanings, human marriage
and human wife. But although they are demoted to non-allegorical
status, Spenser uses them to modify the reader's understanding of
issues that have been presented allegorically.

There is a further fictional inconsistency in the departure of the
Red Cross Knight. He has already promised the hermit Contempla-
tion that he will forsake arms and take up a "Pilgrims poore estate"
(I.x.64), and this vow is directly contradicted by the vow to return
to the Fairy Queen. Yet both vows serve the same poetic purpose:
each in its context enlarges the reader's sense of the conflicting im-
peratives that involve the elected man. The vow to the Fairy Queen,
which is not mentioned until the last canto, is introduced simply to
be used as a poetic device in the conclusion of Book I. In fictional
terms, this conclusion must seem clumsy and almost meaningless.
But it is entirely true to the reader's sense of Spenser's central con-
cern—human experience seen under the aspect of man's relation
to God.

When we assume that Una retains a specific identity and is there-
fore always Truth, or that Spenser holds a mirror up to a putatively
real garden that is external to him, we assume that the narrative
poem is a world. This idea underlies the interpretive assumptions
that I have been questioning. For our purposes, the most pertinent
statement of it is by Tasso:

> As in this wonderful realm of God, which is called the world,
> one sees the sky scattered or highlighted with such a variety of
> stars, and the air and sea full of birds and fish, and so many ani-
> mals, both fierce and gentle, inhabiting the earth, in which we are

accustomed to wonder at brooks and fountains and lakes and fields and meadows and woods and mountains; . . . for all that, the world is single which holds in its lap so many and so diveɪse things, its form and essence are single, the knot is single with which its parts are brought together and bound in discordant concord; and, with nothing lacking in it, yet there is nothing there which does not serve for either necessity or ornament: so by the same token I judge that an excellent poet (who is called divine for no other reason than that making himself like the supreme maker in his workings [*al supremo artefice nelle sue operazioni assomigliandosi*], he comes to participate in his divinity) can make a poem in which, as in a little world, here we read of armies drawn up, here of battles on land and sea, here of sieges of cities, . . . there deeds of cruelty, of boldness, of courtesy, of magnanimity, there the events of love, now happy now unhappy, now joyous now pitiful: but that nonetheless the poem is single that contains so much variety of material, its form and its soul are single; and that all these things are composed in such a way that one thing looks to another, one thing corresponds to another, one thing depends on another either necessarily or plausibly, so that if one single part is taken away or has its place changed, the whole is destroyed.[4]

Interpretations of the *Faerie Queene* characteristically assume that Spenser's poem is a world in Tasso's sense. All the narrative materials are selected and developed in order to make the poem an ordered creation that is obedient to its own laws. My argument, on the other hand, is that Spenser's poetic motive is consistently to elicit responses. In the *Faerie Queene*, poetic meaning is defined with reference to the reader's awareness and not to the coherence of a self-contained and internally consistent fiction.

* * *

The *Apology for Poetry* provides considerable support for our view of the *Faerie Queene* as a continual address to the reader rather than as a fictional world. Sidney justifies the poet's use of fiction, but he does not describe or analyze poetic fictions. For example, he does not raise what is, for Tasso, a central question— whether the narrative of a heroic poem should be historically true. Sidney's criterion of truth is not the nature of the fiction in itself, but its didactic efficacy. He consistently describes poetry as a moral influence operating on the reader's mind. Hence his golden world is entirely different from the world of the poem that Tasso describes.

---

4. [Translated from] *Discorsi del Poema Eroico* in *Le Prose Diverse*, ed. Cesare Guasti (Florence, 1875), I, 154–155. For a penetrating history of the idea of "the poem as heterocosm," see M. H. Abrams, *The Mirror and the Lamp* (New York, 1953), pp. 272–285.

At first "golden world" refers to poetic landscape and is really a metaphor for the attractiveness of poetry ("Nature never set forth the earth in so rich tapistry as divers Poets have done"). Sidney then goes on to say that Nature never produced such excellent men as the heroes of epic poetry:

> Neither let this be jestingly conceived, because the works of the one be essentiall, the other, in imitation or fiction; for any understanding knoweth the skil of the Artificer standeth in that Idea or fore-conceite of the work, and not in the work it selfe. And that the Poet hath that Idea is manifest, by delivering them forth in such excellencie as hee hath imagined them. Which delivering forth also is not wholie imaginative, as we are wont to say by them that build Castles in the ayre: but so farre substantially it worketh, not onely to make a Cyrus, which had been but a particuler excellencie, as Nature might have done, but to bestow a Cyrus upon the worlde, to make many Cyrus's, if they wil learne aright why and how that Maker made him.[5]

For Tasso, the poet resembles "il supremo artefice nelle sue operazioni"[6] because he creates his own little world, the poem. For Sidney, the poet "substantially worketh" by creating virtuous men. If this defines a golden world, it is a world of heroic readers.

I call the mode of narration in the *Faerie Queene* rhetorical, because each stanza is an address to the reader. But we do not feel, as we do in *Paradise Lost*, that a decisive voice speaks to us. Spenser's manner of address is much more self-effacing than Milton's—so much so that C. S. Lewis finds it possible to claim that "outside the proems to the books and cantos he scarcely writes a line that is not for the story's sake."[7] Nevertheless, Spenser's style is not, as Mr. Lewis proposes, "to be judged as the style of a story-teller"; it makes sense only as a rhetorical instrument, a means of modifying the reader's feelings. Without attempting a comprehensive discussion of Spenser's style, I want to examine a crucial phenomenon in his poetry—the pictorial effects in which his well-known verbal sensuousness seems to be in the service of fictional narration.

It has always been assumed that in his pictorial stanzas, Spenser's purpose is primarily imitative or descriptive: his language is chosen to suggest a "real" object, which of course can be symbolic or emblematic.[8] But we often find that a striking pictorial effect is not identical with visual description:

5. *An Apologie for Poetrie*, in *Elizabethan Critical Essays*, ed. G. G. Smith (Oxford, 1904), I, 156–157.
6. "The supreme maker in his workings" [*Editor*].

7. *English Literature in the Sixteenth Century*, p. 389.
8. The most extreme statement of this view is Joseph B. Dallett, "Ideas of Sight in *The Faerie Queene*," *ELH*, XXVII (1960), 87–121.

For round about, the wals yclothed were
With goodly arras of great majesty,
Woven with gold and silke so close and nere,
That the rich metall lurked privily,
As faining to be hid from envious eye;
Yet here, and there, and every where unwares
It shewd it selfe, and shone unwillingly;
Like a discoloured Snake, whose hidden snares
Through the greene gras his long bright burnisht backe declares.

(III.xi.28)

Several words and phrases that support a pictorial effect are not at all
descriptive—for example, "unwares," "unwillingly," and most not-
ably "faining to be hid from envious eye," where Spenser directly
suggests the kind of feeling that Busyrane's tapestries induce. Other
phrases that do have a visual reference are persuasive because they
are suggestive moral formulas—"close and nere," "lurked privily,"
"hidden snares." A great deal of quasi-visual effect is achieved
through verse rhythms, particularly in the sixth and ninth lines.
Spenser is using all the verbal resources of his poetry; our sense of
physical immediacy comes specifically from our experience of words
and their poetic disposition, and not from any optical illusion. The
last line is the most distinctly pictorial, yet we are not meant to see
the color green at all. The effect of the line comes from the rhythmic
crowding of words, and we are to hear the alliterated formula
"greene gras." Literally, the "long bright burnisht backe" of the
snake is like a fitfully gleaming golden thread. But through allitera-
tion, rhythm, and the concluding "declares" with its strong rhyme,
Spenser makes us feel we are dazzled, our field of vision filled—nor
do we remember that the snake is "discoloured." The stanza has a
pictorial effect because Spenser wants to achieve a certain psycho-
logical impact, not because he wants to render real visual experi-
ence. He impresses upon us, as if it were a direct sensation, the
sinister moral atmosphere of Busyrane's palace.

This stanza is not a description, but a "speaking picture" in Sid-
ney's sense:

Whatsoever the Philosopher sayth shoulde be doone, hee [the
poet] giveth a perfect picture of it in some one, by whom hee
presupposeth it was doone. . . . A perfect picture I say, for hee
yeeldeth to the powers of the minde an image of that whereof
the Philosopher bestoweth but a woordish description: which
dooth neyther strike, pierce, nor possesse the sight of the soule
so much as that other dooth. . . . No doubt the Philosopher with
his learned definition, bee it of vertue, vices, matters of publick
policie or privat government, replenisheth the memory with many
infallible grounds of wisdom, which, notwithstanding, lye darke

before the imaginative and judging powre, if they bee not illu-
minated or figured foorth by the speaking picture of Poesie.[9]

We ordinarily understand "speaking picture" to mean "a picture
that speaks." But Sidney does not attribute to poetry any formal
analogies with painting, nor does he think poetry is vivid because it
imitates the visual experience of external objects. He is speaking of
the psychological effect of poetry. The poem enables the reader's
imagination to function properly: he can, as Sidney says elsewhere
in this passage, "satisfie his inward conceits with being witnes to it
selfe of a true lively knowledge." Poetry immediately implants in
the mind images that the completely sound and regenerate man
would produce by his ordinary psychological activity.[1] Observe that
Sidney does not limit the resources of poetry in order to make it
pictorial. All that he says assumes the full exploitation of the verbal
resources that specifically belong to poetry and have nothing to do
with painting. "Speaking picture," then, means "speaking that is so
vivid, has so much of its own life, that it gives immediacy and clarity
to its subject matter." In using the traditional phrase as a metaphor
for the psychological effect of poetry, Sidney deals with the crucial
problem in any didactic theory—to show that the knowledge con-
veyed by poetry is necessarily dependent on the emotional force
and quasi-sensory immediacy of verse.

The relation between Spenser's pictorial language and his rhetori-
cal use of narrative materials becomes very clear in Calidore's vision
of the Graces, where pictorial experience is part of the fictional
action. Spenser attempts neither a real description nor a dramatiza-
tion of the hero's visual experience, but rather directly conveys the
vision and its significance to the reader. Hence at the climax of the
passage, the observing hero and what he sees vanish into a heroic
simile. The vision begins when Calidore comes to an open green on
the top of Mount Acidale:

> There he did see, that pleased much his sight,
> That even he him selfe his eyes envyde,
> An hundred naked maidens lilly white,
> All raunged in a ring, and dauncing in delight.
> (VI.x.11)

Spenser does not paint a picture or portray Calidore as first seeing,
then responding. Descriptive elements are absorbed into a rendering

9. *Elizabethan Critical Essays*, I, 164–
165.
1. For an excellent account of Renais-
sance psychological ideas that are rele-
vant to this passage, see Perry Miller,
The New England Mind: The Seven-
teenth Century (Cambridge, Mass.,
1939), chs. ix and x. For another ex-
ample of a "speaking picture" as it is
defined here, see the presentation of
Time in the Garden of Adonis (dis-
cussed above).

of Calidore's response, which is completely identified with our experience in reading the passage. Thus two clauses that render quality of response intervene between the verb "see" and its object "naked maidens"; feeling and rhythm are dammed up so that the release will imitate Calidore's surprise and delight. This rhythmic effect and the shift of tone it produces in the next to last line account for the extraordinary impression the word "naked" makes on most readers. From the remarks of critics, we would gather that the vision of the Graces is the healthy analogue of the long erotic description of Acrasia's damsels (II.xii. 63–68).[2] Not at all—this single line is almost all we see of the dancing maidens. There are, after all, a hundred of them, and we are not meant to see a naked human body any more than Wordsworth meant to describe, or meant us to see, the leaves and petals of the ten thousand daffodils that danced in the breeze. Pictorial description renders real visual experience, while Spenser's diction uses visual suggestions to make us experience the words themselves.

The next stanza decisively shows the difference between pictorial description and the rhetorical use of pictorial diction:

> All they without were raunged in a ring,
> And daunced round; but in the midst of them
> Three other Ladies did both daunce and sing,
> The whilest the rest them round about did hemme,
> And like a girlond did in compasse stemme:
> And in the middest of those same three, was placed
> Another Damzell, as a precious gemme,
> Amidst a ring most richly well enchaced,
> That with her goodly presence all the rest much graced.
>
> (VI.x.12)

Clearly there is no pictorial equivalence between the two images in this stanza: if the lady is in the center of a ring of dancing maidens, she cannot be described as the jewel set into a ring for the finger. But it would be absurd to complain that Spenser is visually confusing, for he has no desire to be visually convincing. He uses sensory suggestions in order to give a quasi-physical presence to images and words that express value.

The rationale of Spenser's sensuousness is exceptionally clear in the profound and breath-taking stanza that concludes the vision.

2. Lewis contrasts "the naked damsels in Acrasia's fountain and the equally naked (in fact rather more naked) damsels who dance round Colin Clout" (*Allegory of Love*, p. 331). Similarly, Maurice Evans says, "The symbol [Spenser] chooses in Book VI for supreme perfection is that of naked maidens dancing without shame" (*En-glish Poetry in the Sixteenth Century* [London, 1955], p. 147). H. J. C. Grierson praises Spenser's "flowery meadows of irrelevance—pageants and processions and the marriage of rivers and Colins piping to their naked loves" (*Cross Currents in English Literature of the XVIIth Century* [London, 1929], p. 60).

Although it is a heroic simile, it is not announced by the usual "like" or "as": the modification of the poet's voice does not suggest that he is turning from the narration of action (which scarcely exists at this point) in order to state an analogy, Spenser begins with "Looke," and his simile continues and intensifies our experience of the preceding stanza:

> Looke how the Crowne, which Ariadne wore
> Upon her yvory forehead that same day,
> That Theseus her unto his bridale bore,
> When the bold Centaures made that bloudy fray,
> With the fierce Lapithes, which did them dismay;
> Being now placed in the firmament,
> Through the bright heaven doth her beams display,
> And is unto the starres an ornament,
> Which round about her move in order excellent.
> (VI.x.13)

The significance of the Graces is not expressed by the hero's fictional experience, nor by a symbolic vision that we see within a fictional framework. We understand the Graces' dance by responding to a simile that develops our previous responses to imagery and diction. What Spenser makes us "see" is not a fixed image, an emblem in the usual sense, but a sacramental transformation of turbulence and fury into order and beauty. Our experience is specifically an experience of words and is modulated and developed in the very act of reading. The process is quite explicit in this stanza, for the crux of the simile has no iconographic or fictional reason for being there. The Centaurs and the Lapithes are not at all necessary to Ariadne's crown—they belong to another myth—nor does their bloody fray correspond to any part of the Graces' dance. Yet once there, the bloody fray is both relevant and necessary—as the syntax, which directs our reading, makes us recognize.

There is a temporal dimension in our reading of any poem, and in a narrative poem it is conventionally identified with a sequence of fictional events. But in the *Faerie Queene*, as our last example shows, time is the dimension of verbal events—the lines and stanzas that create and modify the reader's responses. An episode in the *Faerie Queene*, then, is best described as a developing psychological experience within the reader, rather than as an action to be observed by him.

*   *   *

Ruskin's corrective to romantic criticism was perfectly just, but he was simply pointing to the obvious. Allegorical encounters and emblematic figures were simply the raw material of story to Spenser.[3] In its general outlines, Spenser's allegory is usually plain enough; confusion sets in when we try to elaborate its significance by treating poetic details as if they were fictional details. It is perfectly clear what Spenser means by Guyon's resistance to Mammon and his destruction of the Bower of Bliss. But we should not be content with dull and simple meanings in episodes of such impressiveness and length. In all the climactic episodes of the *Faerie Queene*, Spenser brings us into extraordinarily close, almost physical contact with his verse, in order that our psychological experience be identified as closely as possible with the direct experience of language in the activity of reading. The immediacy of the reader's psychological experience is the sign of all these episodes—the Red Cross Knight's misery in the Cave of Despair, the menacing glitter of Busyrane's palace, the oppressiveness of Mammon's cave, the seductive *otium* of the Bower of Bliss. Simply to recall what is surely a general feeling about the high points of the poem does not in itself prove that Spenser's narration is rhetorical in its mode—a continuous address to the reader, rather than an internally consistent fictional narration. But I submit that when we examine these or any other episodes in detail, we shall find that their symbolic material serves to enrich our responses in the way I have described, and not to complicate the significance of a translated or rationalized fiction.

3. The phrase "continued allegory, or dark conceit" in the Letter to Raleigh refers to the symbolic nature of Spenser's materials, but it does not guarantee or even imply that a fiction with a continuous double significance is the main vehicle of poetic meaning in the *Faerie Queene*. Spenser would have found exactly this notion of allegory in Tasso's preface to *Gerusalemme Liberata*, which he certainly knew but from which he borrows nothing in his own prefatory letter. Spenser's formula "dark conceit" is based on the rhetoricians' definition of allegory as the local device of continued metaphor ("dark" is the stock epithet for the figure in rhetorical handbooks). Furthermore, in his remarks on *Gerusalemme Liberata*, Spenser does not follow the allegorical interpretation of the heroes that Tasso develops by rationalizing the fiction of his poem. The only possible conclusion is that Tasso's division of a heroic poem into the imitation of actions and the allegory hidden beneath this surface (*Prose*, I, 301) meant very little to Spenser.

GRAHAM HOUGH

[The Unity of *The Faerie Queene*] †

I

The essence of the romantic epic is in its material. This is the material of chivalric romance, but re-handled in an age when chivalry has become a remote legend. Yet it is a legend still in a sense in touch with the life of the day. In this Spenser is entirely at one with his Italian predecessors. At the court of Queen Elizabeth as at the court of Ferrara chivalric manners still constitute an aristocratic social ideal, and the adventures of knight-errantry are still a source of literary delight. There is the fusion of a deliberate and indulged archaism with a surviving or a revived ideal of conduct, and the poles between which the romantic epic moves are at one extreme an imaginative game, at the other the fashioning of a noble person in virtuous and gentle discipline. The emphasis naturally varies in different writers. Spenser is least close in spirit to Ariosto, for whom the whole machinery was a matter of ironic and sometimes burlesque artistry. In some ways he is nearest to Boiardo, who shares with him a genuine homesickness for a knightly past. In others he is nearer to Tasso, who reforms his historic and legendary material according to the religious pressures of his own age. But all are alike in using their knights, ladies and magicians, their military encounters and enchanted gardens with a sophisticated awareness of their obsolete quality and a deliberate turning of the material to various contemporary ends. Their matter is not given, like that of the primary epic, nor even dictated by an overriding national tradition; it is to some extent arbitrarily chosen, playfully or gravely eclectic, at the same time popular and literary. We should hardly call the romantic epic an artificial form, in the sense of something mechanically contrived; it has grown in response to a real taste. But the taste is not one of the primary human needs; it is the result of a great deal of secondary elaboration.

The immense attraction of this kind of material to the writer was that it permitted so much variety and freedom of treatment. The stock of romance motifs was so large and it had had so many accretions from history, from classical epic and from mythology that almost any kind of fiction, from the pious apologue to the erotic novella, can find a place within the boundaries. Spenser has availed himself of all the freedom that he met with in his predeces-

† From *A Preface to "The Faerie Queene,"* by Graham Hough (New York, 1962), Chapter XIV.

sors. It is worth emphasizing this for it is often suggested that he gives us a spare and Protestant version of his luxuriant Italian exemplars. I have tried to indicate throughout the variety of Spenser's tone and manner, and there is no need to recapitulate. I believe he has suffered from an excessive stress on his religious and didactic purpose; and a current tendency to insist on his community of spirit with Milton is also overworked.[1] He is not really very like Milton; the sparsely-furnished grandeurs of Milton's epic belong to a very different world from the crowded and infinitely varied pageant of *The Faerie Queene*. Spenser shares with the Italian writers the tendency to become encyclopedic in scope, to include extremes of experience and feeling, to reduce to the same picture-plane images drawn from very different depths and different levels.

In one respect he is like Ariosto and Tasso but has surpassed them. This is the pictorial element. We are continually haunted in reading the Italian writers by reminiscences and suggestions of Renaissance painting, but these elusive parallels are far stronger in Spenser. There is a paradox in this, for Spenser can have seen very little, if any, of the great Italian pictorial art; such acquaintance as he had with the visual mythology and the iconographical symbolism of his time must have been almost entirely from emblem-books, tapestries and court pageantry. Yet Botticelli's *Primavera* and *Birth of Venus* seem far closer to Calidore's vision on Mount Acidale than to the elegant verses of Politian with which they are really connected. Bellini's *Allegory* in the Uffizi might be taking place on the outskirts of Spenser's Temple of Venus; Giorgione's *Tempestà* surely occurred in some corner of Spenser's forest. Una among the satyrs should have been illustrated by Piero di Cosimo, the Garden of Adonis by the Bellini of *The Feast of Gods*, and the marriage of Thames and Medway by the Raphael of the *Triumph of Galatea*. These no doubt are fanciful or personal associations; they are made only in order to suggest how fully, for all his Englishness, Spenser shared in the general spirit of Renaissance art.

To return to the conventions of the romantic epic—there is much in Spenser's organization of his material that is quite new. The internal structure of the books is capricious—sometimes continuous, more or less episodic narrative, sometimes Ariostan interweaving. But the self-contained character of each book (except for III and IV which partly run together) has no parallel in the Italian poems. At first sight this looks like a merely external device of construction, but on a closer acquaintance it is seen to give a very different quality to the whole poem. In Ariosto there are no real internal divisions; it is a long breathless gallop from first to last. In

1. E.g. "Blake is a poet in the tradition of Spenser and Milton." H. Bloom, *The Visionary Company*, 1962, p. 1.

Tasso all (or nearly all) is subordinated to the needs of a unified epic structure. Spenser's poem is composed of parts each with a certain unity of its own. This offers the opportunity for a real sequence and development of thematic interest, as I shall try to suggest in a moment. For it is of course by its thematic content that each book is given its separate integrity. As far as material and incident are concerned, much would be interchangeable between one part and another; but however loosely or intermittently the allegory may be pursued, the idea of Temperance, or Justice, or Courtesy or whatever it may be, does control and dominate each book. This thematic arrangement makes it possible to organize the medley of motifs and episodes in large blocks, each with its distinctive tone and colouring. And this is something quite different from either the Ariostan or the Tassonian form. In spite of incompletenesses and loose ends *The Faerie Queene* does by this means arrive at an authentic form of its own. It is characteristic of Spenser that this formal principle is given by his theme, not by the sequence of his images. Without implying any lack of invention or narrative vitality it is true to say that Spenser is a more thoughtful poet than either Ariosto or Tasso. Not because he has serious moral intentions that extend outside his poem (though of course he has), but because it is his thought that dictates the real form of his work; dianoia, not the demands of narrative sprightliness or neo-classic convention.

II

The unifying factor among the books—Arthur's quest of Gloriana—is largely ineffective as a narrative device. The loves of Artegall and Britomart provide a stronger narrative thread than those of Arthur and the Faerie Queene. We cannot tell how far this is due to the incomplete state of the design. If we had the reunion in Cleopolis, above all if we had Cleopolis itself and not merely a few scattered allusions to it, no doubt the whole sequence of adventures would be seen in different proportions. We can only deal with what we have, and in what we have the figure of Gloriana does not appear at all and that of Arthur only in an intermittent and inorganic way. That is in the narrative, on the plane of presented images. If we look behind the image to the thematic content Arthur and Gloriana have a fuller and more continuous significance. The allegorical meaning announced in the Letter is not particularly plausible, nor very well borne out by the development of the poem itself. It is safe to say that nobody actually reading *The Faerie Queene* ever thinks of Magnificence in search of Glory, and as the idea is so faint and uninsistent it hardly seems worth while to inquire whether the glory referred to is earthly or heavenly fame. The real significance of Arthur and Gloriana is that they are the main vehicles of that glorification of Britain that is the great thematic groundswell beneath the diverse surface movements of the poem. But the 'glorification' of Britain is perhaps an unfortunate phrase. It suggests a patriotic trumpet-blowing which is only a very small part of Spenser's intention. 'Idealization' would be better, except that that suggests a sort of discarnate abstraction that is equally un-Spenserian.

The element of dynastic celebration is already present in the Italian epics. Both Ariosto and Tasso offer their works as part of the mythical history of the Estensi, the ducal house of Ferrara, just as Spenser offers his as part of the mythical history of the Tudors. In the primary epic no doubt such historical and genealogical motifs are still living and currently felt realities. In the romantic epics they are a deliberate reconstruction, fancy rather than imagination, half-way between legend and made-up courtly compliment. Ariosto makes his Ruggiero and Bradamante, Tasso his Rinaldo, the mythical ancestors of the house of Este; and no one of course was expected to believe this. And it does not in any sense constitute a national celebration. The duchy of Ferrara was not coterminous with Italy—we cannot say the Italian nation for there was no Italian nation. Ariosto has a deep feeling for Italy, as we can see when he laments her exposure to foreign invaders; but Italy is a geographical or cultural concept, not a nation. Spenser in celebrating Britain has something far more actual and self-aware to deal with. The long-established sense of English nationality, powerfully reinforced by the Tudor settlement and the successes against Spain, gave Spenser a much stronger historical foundation for his poem. And by a happy chance, the mythical genealogy on which the romantic epic relies for its link with a legendary past in his case already existed; it had a status outside his poem. The descent of the Tudors from the ancient British kings, of Elizabeth from Arthur, was attached to a tradition going back to Geoffrey of Monmouth, and was already, as we have seen, part of the political mythology of the age. So that what is mere flattery or complimentary fancy in the Italian epics is something more in Spenser; it is already a real element in the imaginative consciousness of the poet and his contemporaries.

By building on this, by adorning his verse with English and Irish geography and historical allusion, Spenser is going some way towards providing a British mythology, and giving *The Faerie Queene* at least a chance of occupying the ideal epic situation in the tradition of his own country. I do not think that he has completely succeeded. French, British or Celtic in origin, largely translated as it may be, it is the Arthurian legend that is the real British mythology, and it is Malory who has established it. Spenser's Arthur is aside from the central tradition; Spenser is describing the *enfances* of the king that we know, and they are merely his own invention. One does not invent a mythology; and Spenser's Arthur remains a personal imaginative creation, not a true part of the national consciousness. But the effect of having this Arthurian link between the past and the present is to make his poem a more serious and more firmly grounded conception than its Italian predecessors. And it is serious in a way that goes deeper than mere national pride.

The English have always been inclined to see their history as a microcosm of the history of humanity. This may be dangerous—at its worst it can lead to provincialism or *folie de grandeur*. At its best it is ennobling. The real disaster is to see a national history not as a microcosm of the human situation but as the actual historic centre of the human situation. This is the German error, and we have seen its consequences. The English may have come some way towards it at the close of the nineteenth century, but in Spenser's day this was neither spiritually nor historically a danger. Christendom was already torn in two, but the concept of Christendom still existed; and the great spiritual and historical current that carries *The Faerie Queene* along is directed towards conforming the idea of Britain with the idea of a Christian kingdom. Arthur represents both a historic ancestor and a spiritual ideal. The situation that both the great Italian epics inherited from the *chansons de geste*—Christendom embattled against the infidel—has disappeared from *The Faerie Queene*. Its place is taken by the less contingent and more comprehensive warfare of good against evil in every relation of life. Yet the protagonist in this war is a British prince. It is in this subtler and profounder way that Spenser inherits the tradition of the Christian epic, and without chauvinism or special pleading integrates it with the intention of his national heroic poem.

We seem for the moment to have forgotten Gloriana. If Arthur is the bearer of the historic national consciousness, what of the Faerie Queene herself? Britain and Fairyland both appear in the poem, yet Fairyland is also Britain. Is this a mere duplication and confusion, or can we distinguish between them? I think we can. Queen Elizabeth, as we have seen, is given two ancestries—one which links her with Arthur and the ancient British kings, and one with the purely fanciful history of the realm of Fairyland. They serve two different ends. The one embodies the destiny of the historical Britain, culminating in the actual Tudor rule. The other embodies the destiny of an ideal Britain, the kingdom of love, of chivalry, of true devotion, culminating in that idealized version of queenliness that was so powerful a factor in the Elizabethan imagination. The glorification of the Queen is sometimes court flattery; but it is also something quite different—a dedication to an embodied ideal in which the actual Queen becomes the cynosure of a complex range of erotic, patriotic and quasi-religious feelings that is now almost impossible for us to realize fully. *Iam redit et virgo, redeunt Saturnia regna. . . .*[2] The roots of this feeling go very deep into the mythological past, where ideas of divine monarchy, the great goddess, the virgin and the destined bride are seen faintly moving in a remote and shadowy distance. I have never yet seen a satisfying account of the way this mythic substratum affects individual poetic creation, though nowadays everybody talks about it. We should not demand more precision than the situation allows; and clearly we miss much of the power of much of our greatest poetry if we remain wholly unaware of this ancestral presence. The Faerie Queene both is and is not Queen Elizabeth; Cleopolis both is and is not London. It is London and its court as they ought to be and are not (Spenser is quite clear that they are not). It is also London and its court (the heart of an England seen as the type of all humanity) as they really are in some ultimate depth of the imagination.

III

One thing that is clear is that Cleopolis is not the Heavenly City. It is sharply distinguished from the Heavenly City, the New Jerusalem, in the episode on the Mount of Contemplation (I. x. 57 seq.) "Yet is Cleopolis for earthly frame, / The fairest peece that eyes beholden can". It follows then that "that soveraigne Dame" who rules it, though spoken of as "heavenly borne", is an earthly governor; and the scene of the whole action is on earth. There is a tendency to make *The Faerie Queene* a more other-worldly poem than it really is. It is a religious poem in the sense that its earthly action is suffused with Christian thought and feeling, but not in the sense that it is occupied with a supernatural quest. It is no *Pilgrim's Progress* and has little affinity with *Paradise Lost*. It is only near the beginning, in the Red Cross Knight's vision of the New Jerusalem just referred to, and at the close, in the aspiration towards the eternal Sabbath, that man's last end enters directly into the theme. Its field is the world and its theme the conduct of life in the sublunary sphere. Its dilemmas and oppositions are ethical, social and erotic. When it engages with cosmology the explanations offered are naturalistic. Of course Spenser is a Christian, of course his whole view of life is contained and bounded by a Christian consciousness, but the sphere of his artistic operation is the natural world, and even his ethics, though their ultimate sanction is outside nature, tend to assume a naturalistic colouring. We can if we will draw a contrast with Dante. The sins punished in Hell or refined away in Purgatory are sins because they are forbidden, and they are equally sins and equally forbidden even when they are steeped in every

2. "Now the virgin comes back, and the rule of Saturn is restored" (Vergil, 4th Eclogue) [*Editor*].

imaginable human sweetness, as were those of Paolo and Francesca. Spenser rarely exposes himself to this cruel dilemma. The evil in his world is as a rule clearly recognizable by its ugliness. If not it is a deliberate imposture and ultimately unmasked, like the false Flori-mell. In the case of beauty and sensuous delight we feel (or at least I feel) a struggle to accommodate the naturalistic ethic to the demands of an absolute morality; and poetically speaking the abso-lute morality wins no more than a doubtful victory. The unutterably clear and poignant human sympathy confronted with an inexorable law that is ultimately beyond human sympathy—that is what Dante shows us in his colloquy with Francesca. Spenser avoids this and wishes to avoid it; his tendency is to show that every true human sympathy can be accommodated to eternal law. But it is the right management and direction of human sympathy that he is mainly concerned with. Eternal law does not find any very clear definition in his pages.

No one in Spenser gives all his heart to an earthly love and then has to laugh at it as unworthy and unimportant in the end, like Chaucer's Troilus. No one in Spenser has to reject or deny the passion that he has lived for, like Malory's Lancelot. And no one in Spenser transmutes his earthly love into a love of a different order, like Dante. This is to say that Spenser has overcome, or is striving to overcome, the desperate medieval split between *amour courtois* and the severity of the Christian scheme of redemption. But this is the theme of Professor Lewis's *Allegory of Love*, and there is no need to repeat what he has expounded so brilliantly. He sees Spen-ser as the inaugurator of the romance of marriage, against the medieval romance of illicit love. We might add however that except for Artegall and Britomart it is their status as lovers that is impor-tant with Spenser's characters, not their status as potential married people. A tender, chivalrous love is the highest human value in Spenser's world; and it is always an uncomplicated unwavering love that looks to its "right true end", to a human and earthly fruition. The delays and deviations in reaching that consummation are the substance of romantic narrative, and Spenser retains much of the procedure of the medieval romance of courtship; but there is never any suspicion of that lingering pleasure in frustration for its own sake that M. de Rougemont has found characteristic of love in the Western world.[3]

It follows from this that there cannot be much of Platonism, either of the original or the neo-variety in Spenser's love-morality. Although "Spenser and Renaissance Platonism" is one of the stan-dard themes for commentary I have said little about it for I have

3. Denis de Rougemont, *L'Amour et l'Occident*, 1939 (revised 1956).

found little of the platonic spirit in *The Faerie Queene*. Love may have a heavenly birth, but there is never the slightest suggestion that love of an earthly object should be the stepping-stone to heavenly love. Indeed there is very little about heavenly love in the poem. So much I could see for myself; but there is another reason for keeping away from the subject of Spenser's 'Platonism'. It has recently been studied with such exhaustive learning by M. Ellrodt[4] that to do other than cite him would be an impertinence. It is not possible to summarize his extremely detailed investigation, but the following are the points that are most to our purpose here. There is a large body of diffused Platonism in the literature at Spenser's disposal—dilute philosophical Platonism in Boethius, literary and poetical Platonism in Petrarch, a social and gallant version of Platonism in Castiglione. But there is no evidence that Spenser's acquaintance with Plato himself was more than very moderate, or that he had any acquaintance at all with Plotinus or the Italian neo-Platonic writers, Ficino, Benevieni or Pico—except perhaps in the last of the *Four Hymns*. Platonic-looking expressions are often poetic adornments without real philosophical content, and the superficially Platonic character of many passages in *The Faerie Queene* is not confirmed by real examination. Take for example the invocation of love in III. iii. 1:

> Most Sacred fire, that burnest mightily
> In living brests, ykindled first above,
> Emongst th'eternall spheres and lamping sky,
> And thence pourd into men, which men call Love;
> Not that same, which doth base affections move
> In brutish minds, and filthy lust inflame,
> But that sweet fit, that doth true beautie love,
> And chooseth vertue for his dearest Dame,
> Whence spring all noble deeds and never dying fame.

M. Ellrodt comments on this passage:

The opening lines raise an expectation of the Neo-Platonic contrast between love as a desire of contemplation kindled by intellectual beauty, and love as a desire of generation excited by earthly beauty. But from the closing lines it appears that the higher love is conceived as a spur to virtuous action on earth rather than an invitation to fly back to heaven. . . . The love that sent Britomart on her quest for a husband, the love that "afterwards did raise most famous fruites of matrimonialle bowre" is obviously not a desire of intellectual beauty. Yet that same love has been described as "ykindled first above" and contrasted with brutish love. The distinction therefore was not drawn on the metaphysical level, be-

4. Robert Ellrodt, *Neoplatonism in the Poetry of Spenser*, Geneva, 1960.

tween the earthly and the heavenly Venus, but on the earthly—
and Christian—level, between virtuous love and "filthy lust". . . .
It is characteristic of Spenser that his conception of love, whenever
he echoes the Platonists, should remain either purely ethical when
human love is concerned, or purely natural when cosmic love is
discussed. To both human and cosmic love he ascribes a heavenly
origin, but in *The Faerie Queene* he has no place for "heavenly
love" as conceived by the Platonists, love "ad divinam pluchri-
tudinem cogitandam".[5]

To his ethical and natural conceptions of love we must add all
that Spenser inherited from the romance tradition of love-poetry and
all that he found about him in the English lyric tradition—that
tender idealization of sensuousness, the loving appreciation of the
unity of soul and body that is one of the great secular legacies of
the Middle Ages. A sense of preciousness and fragility in this feeling
is perhaps a part of its essence. This often arises in medieval poetry
because the love itself is a stolen thing; in Spenser from a different
cause. Though love and happiness can be reconciled and both are at
home in the natural world there is something in the world that is
against them. The Blatant Beast, the brigands and Mutability are
always at large; and if Spenser is the great poet of natural happiness
he also knows its limits and its lack. Otherwise he could not make it
so poignantly beautiful.

IV

In discussing *The Faerie Queene* we always tend to speak of it as
a whole poem, and it is continually necessary in the course of
special arguments to pull oneself up and recall that it is a fragment.
Of course it is a fragment—six books and the chance survival of
part of a seventh out of what should have been twelve. Yet our
unguarded way of speaking of it is not mere carelessness; it does
correspond to a genuine experience. When we become familiar with
the poem we do feel it as a whole. And I do not think that this is
merely because we have got used to our half loaf and decide to
make the best of it. The poem is unfinished because Spenser died.
But I suspect he must have known for some time that his vast
project was not likely to be completed. It sometimes happens that a
man's life and work tends to round itself off, even when death
comes prematurely, according to some plan that was not premedi-
tated and is never consciously entertained. It is perhaps a fantasy,
but I cannot help feeling that something of this sort must have
happened with Spenser. At all events it is possible to experience a
sense of completeness in the poem as it stands.

It begins with the book of Holiness, because for Spenser this is

5. Op. cit., pp. 34–35.

the necessary ground of all human development. A Catholic poet might have put it at the end; Spenser's placing of it as he does corresponds to the Protestant theology of prevenient grace—without it all other activity is worthless. Next comes Temperance, as the first condition of any possible human integrity. It is what divides man from the beasts—the moral control of passion that distinguishes him from the natural world while still leaving him a part of it. These books are self-contained, complete within themselves; they have perhaps greater density and complexity of organization than all the others; yet they are in a sense preliminary to Spenser's main preoccupations.

Then we have Books III and IV, called the legends of Chastity and Friendship, but really to be taken together as the poem's great central area, concerned with Love. It is primarily love between men and women, love in the ideal romantic sense. Whatever Spenser's ostensible subject this is the theme to which he continually returns. The celebration of love, the distinction of its different tempers and varieties, the portrayal of the conditions which foster it, and of its enemies in the heart and in the outer world—it is this that forms the main substance of *The Faerie Queene*. Other human qualities are there as its environment and its support. Love is the active source of value. It is in human life and human relations that Spenser sees the quintessence of love; but it is a quintessence distilled from the force of love pervading the whole universe; the Lucretian Venus or the power of concord that keeps the whole creation together. The Temple of Venus with its romance of courtship and the Garden of Adonis with its life-giving cosmic power are the two allegorical poles on which this central part of the poem turns.

Since man is a political animal the force of concord must be prolonged into the social and political sphere. This is the function of the book of Justice, and it is perhaps the one grave fault in *The Faerie Queene* that the repressive function of Justice is so much more evident than its socially harmonizing power. By now the main lines of Spenser's view of life are laid down. There remains the final enhancement of a spontaneous natural grace. This is celebrated in the book of Courtesy. It is a natural flowering that crowns the whole with loveliness. But the scene of the poem is the world, and no achievement of virtue or beauty in the world is lasting. Everything is subject to change, and this seems at first subversive of all happiness and all good. By submitting to the judgement of nature it is just possible to see this change as life-giving and re-creative. But man can never fully see it so; the weight of mutability presses too heavily upon him. It is only by projecting his mind outside the created world, by seeing it for a moment in its eternal setting, that a resting-place can be found. This takes us a step beyond the ideal naturalism that is the normal temper of Spenser's mind. If the two closing stanzas are the chance breaking-off point of an unfinished poem, there can never have been a happier chance.

This is not the formal design at one time projected. It is not a formal design of any sort. But it is an organic growth with its own kind of wholeness. The legend of St. George is the perfect beginning; Courtesy is the perfect end; the great continued narratives have a mutual coherence of theme, and are grouped as they should be in the middle. Mutability is the perfect epilogue. The real meaning of a form is usually hidden from its creator; and still less can we know by what imperceptible inspiration the poem assumed the form it has. It is not even easy to see the work in its entirety, for we are distracted by the richness of detail. I suspect however that all who come to know it well end by feeling that in spite of a grandiose plan cut short *The Faerie Queene* in its actual state fulfils the law of its being.

NORTHROP FRYE

The Structure of Imagery in *The Faerie Queene*†

* * *

To demonstrate a unity in *The Faerie Queene*, we have to examine the imagery of the poem rather than its allegory. It is Spenser's habitual technique, developing as it did out of the emblematic visions he wrote in his nonage, to start with the image, not the allegorical translation of it, and when he says at the beginning of the final canto of Book II:

> Now ginnes this goodly frame of Temperaunce
> Fayrely to rise

one feels that the "frame" is built out of the characters and places that are clearly announced to be what they are, not out of their moral or historical shadows. Spenser prefaces the whole poem with sonnets to possible patrons, telling several of them that they are in the poem somewhere, not specifying where: the implication is that for such readers the allegory is to be read more or less *ad libitum*. Spenser's own language about allegory, "darke conceit," "clowdily enwrapped," emphasizes its deliberate vagueness. We know that Belphoebe refers to Elizabeth: therefore, when Timias speaks of "her, whom the hevens doe serve and sew," is there, as one edition suggests, a reference to the storm that wrecked the Armada? I cite this

† From "The Structure of Imagery in *The Faerie Queene*," *UTQ*, XXX (1961), 109–127.

only as an example of how subjective an allegorical reading can be. Allegory is not only often uncertain, however, but in the work of one of our greatest allegorical poets it can even be addled, as it is in *Mother Hubberds Tale*, where the fox and the ape argue over which of them is more like a man, and hence more worthy to wear the skin of a lion. In such episodes as the legal decisions of Artegall, too, we can see that Spenser, unlike Milton, is a poet of very limited conceptual powers, and is helpless without some kind of visualization to start him thinking. I am far from urging that we should "let the allegory go" in reading Spenser, but it is self-evident that the imagery is prior in importance to it. One cannot begin to discuss the allegory without using the imagery, but one could work out an exhaustive analysis of the imagery without ever mentioning the allegory.

Our first step is to find a general structure of imagery in the poem as a whole, and with so public a poet as Spenser we should hardly expect to find this in Spenser's private possession, as we might with Blake or Shelley or Keats. We should be better advised to look for it in the axioms and assumptions which Spenser and his public shared, and which form the basis of its imaginative communication.[1] Perhaps the *Mutabilitie Cantos*, which give us so many clues to the sense of *The Faerie Queene* as a whole, will help us here also.

The action of the *Mutabilitie Cantos* embraces four distinguishable levels of existence. First is that of Mutability herself, the level of death, corruption, and dissolution, which would also be, if this poem were using moral categories, the level of sin. Next comes the world of ordinary experience, the nature of the four elements, over which Mutability is also dominant. Its central symbol is the cycle, the round of days, months, and hours which Mutability brings forth as evidence of her supremacy. In the cycle there are two elements: becoming or change, which is certainly Mutability's, and a principle of order or recurrence within which the change occurs. Hence Mutability's evidence is not conclusive, but could just as easily be turned against her. Above our world is upper nature, the stars in their courses, a world still cyclical but immortal and unchanged in essence. This upper world is all that is now left of nature as God originally created it, the state described in the Biblical story of Eden and the Classical myth of the Golden Age. Its regent is Jove, armed with the power which, in a world struggling against chaos and evil, is "the right hand of justice truly hight." But Jove, however he may bluster and threaten, has no authority over Mutability; that authority belongs to the goddess Nature, whose viceroy he is. If Mutability could be cast out of the world of ordinary experience, lower and

1. In what follows the debt is obvious to A. S. P. Woodhouse, "Nature and Grace in *The Faerie Queene*," *ELH* (Sept. 1949), but there are some differences of emphasis owing to the fact that I am looking for a structure of images rather than of concepts.

upper nature would be reunited, man would re-enter the Golden Age, and the reign of "Saturn's son" would be replaced by that of Saturn. Above Nature is the real God, to whom Mutability appeals when she brushes Jove out of her way, who is invoked in the last stanza of the poem, and who appears in the reference to the Transfiguration of Christ like a mirage behind the assembly of lower gods.

Man is born into the third of these worlds, the order of physical nature which is theologically "fallen" and under the sway of Mutability. But though in this world he is not of it: he really belongs to the upper nature of which he formed part before his fall. The order of physical nature, the world of animals and plants, is morally neutral: man is confronted from his birth with a moral dialectic, and must either sink below it into sin or rise above it into his proper human home. This latter he may reach by the practice of virtue and through education, which includes law, religion, and everything the Elizabethans meant by art. The question whether this "art" included what we mean by art, poetry, painting, and music, was much debated in Spenser's day, and explains why so much of the criticism of the period took the form of apologetic. As a poet, Spenser believed in the moral reality of poetry and in its effectiveness as an educating agent; as a Puritan, he was sensitive to the abuse and perversion of art which had raised the question of its moral value in the first place, and he shows his sense of the importance of the question in his description of the Bower of Bliss.

Spenser means by "Faerie" primarily the world of realized human nature. It is an "antique" world, extending backward to Eden and the Golden Age, and its central figure of Prince Arthur was chosen, Spenser tells us, as "furthest from the daunger of envy, and suspition of present time." It occupies the same space as the ordinary physical world, a fact which makes contemporary allusions possible, but its time sequence is different. It is not timeless: we hear of months or years passing, but time seems curiously foreshortened, as though it followed instead of establishing the rhythm of conscious life. Such foreshortening of time suggests a world of dream and wishfulfilment, like the fairylands of Shakespeare's comedies. But Spenser, with his uneasy political feeling that the price of authority is eternal vigilance, will hardly allow his virtuous characters even to sleep, much less dream, and the drowsy narcotic passages which have so impressed his imitators are associated with spiritual peril. He tells us that sleep is one of the three divisions of the lowest world, the other two being death and hell; and Prince Arthur's long tirade against night (III. iv) would be out of proportion if night, like its seasonal counterpart winter, did not symbolize a lower world than Faerie. The vision of Faerie may be the *author's* dream, as the pilgrimage of Christian is presented as a dream of Bunyan, but what the poet dreams of is the strenuous effort, physical, mental, and moral, of waking up to one's true humanity.

In the ordinary physical world good and evil are inextricably confused; the use and the abuse of natural energies are hard to distinguish, motives are mixed and behaviour inconsistent. The perspective of Faerie, the achieved quest of virtue, clarifies this view. What we now see is a completed moral dialectic. The mixed-up physical world separates out into a human moral world and a demonic one. In this perspective heroes and villains are purely and simply heroic and villainous; characters are either white or black, for the quest or against it; right always has superior might in the long run, for we are looking at reality from the perspective of man as he was originally made in the image of God, unconfused about the difference between heaven and hell. We can now see that physical nature is a source of energy, but that this energy can run only in either of two opposing directions: toward its own fulfilment or towards its own destruction. Nature says to Mutability: "For thy decay thou seekst by thy desire," and contrasts her with those who, struggling out of the natural cycle, "Doe worke their owne perfection so by fate."

Spenser, in Hamlet's language, has no interest in holding the mirror up to nature unless he can thereby show virtue her own feature and scorn her own image. His evil characters are rarely converted to good, and while there is one virtuous character who comes to a bad end, Sir Terpine in Book V, this exception proves the rule, as his fate makes an allegorical point about justice. Sometimes the fiction writer clashes with the moralist in Spenser, though never for long. When Malbecco offers to take Hellenore back from the satyrs, he becomes a figure of some dignity as well as pathos; but Spenser cannot let his dramatic sympathy with Malbecco evolve. Complicated behaviour, mixed motives, or the kind of driving energy of character which makes moral considerations seem less important, as it does in all Shakespeare's heroes, and even in Milton's Satan—none of this could be contained in Spenser's framework.

The Faerie Queene in consequence is necessarily a romance, for romance is the genre of simplified or black and white characterization. The imagery of this romance is organized on two major principles. One is that of the natural cycle, the progression of days and seasons. The other is that of the moral dialectic, in which symbols of virtue are parodied by their vicious or demonic counterparts. Any symbol may be used ambivalently, and may be virtuous or demonic according to its context, an obvious example being the symbolism of gold. Cyclical symbols are subordinated to dialectical ones; in other words the upward turn from darkness to dawn or from winter to spring usually symbolizes the lift in perspective from physical to human nature. Ordinary experience, the morally neutral world of physical nature, never appears as such in *The Faerie Queene*, but its place in Spenser's scheme is symbolized by nymphs and other elemental spirits, or by the satyrs, who may be tamed and awed by the sight of Una or more habitually stimulated by the sight of Hellenore. Satyrane, as his name indicates, is, with several puns intended, a good-natured man, and two of the chief heroes, Redcrosse and Artegall, are explicitly said to be natives of this world and not, like Guyon, natives of Faerie. What this means in practice is that their quests include a good deal of historical allegory.

In the letter to Raleigh Spenser speaks of a possible twenty-four books, twelve to deal with the private virtues of Prince Arthur and the other twelve with the public ones manifested after he was crowned king. But this appalling spectre must have been exorcized very quickly. If we look at the six virtues he did treat, we can see that the first three, holiness, temperance, and chastity, are essentially private virtues, and that the next three, friendship, justice, and courtesy, are public ones. Further, that both sets seem to run in a sort of Hegelian progression. Of all public virtues, friendship is the most private and personal; justice the most public and impersonal, and courtesy seems to combine the two, Calidore being notable for his capacity for friendship and yet able to capture the Blatant Beast that eluded Artegall. Similarly, of all private virtues, holiness is most dependent on grace and revelation, hence the imagery of Book I is Biblical and apocalyptic, and introduces the theological virtues. Temperance, in contrast, is a virtue shared by the enlightened heathen, a prerequisite and somewhat pedestrian virtue (Guyon loses his horse early in the book and does not get it back until Book V), hence the imagery of Book II is classical, with much drawn from the *Odyssey* and from Platonic and Aristotelian ethics. Chastity, a virtue described by Spenser as "farre above the rest," seems to combine something of both. The encounter of Redcrosse and Guyon is indecisive, but Britomart, by virtue of her enchanted spear, is clearly stronger than Guyon, and hardly seems to need Redcrosse's assistance in Castle Joyeous.

We note that in Spenser, as in Milton's *Comus*, the supreme private virtue appears to be chastity rather than charity. Charity, in the sense of Christian love, does not fit the scheme of *The Faerie Queene*: for Spenser it would primarily mean, not man's love for God, but God's love for man, as depicted in the *Hymn of Heavenly Love*. Charissa appears in Book I, but her main connexions are with the kindliness that we associate with "giving to charity"; Agape appears in Book IV, but is so minor and so dim-witted a character that one wonders whether Spenser knew the connotations of the word. Hence, though Book I is the only book that deals explicitly with

Christian imagery, it does not follow that holiness is the supreme virtue. Spenser is not dealing with what God gives to man, but with what man does with his gifts, and Redcrosse's grip on holiness is humanly uncertain.

In one of its aspects *The Faerie Queene* is an educational treatise, based, like other treatises of its time, on the two essential social facts of the Renaissance, the prince and the courtier. The most important person in Renaissance society to educate was the prince, and the next most important was the courtier, the servant of the prince. Spenser's heroes are courtiers who serve the Faerie Queene and who metaphorically make up the body and mind of Prince Arthur. To demonstrate the moral reality of poetry Spenser had to assume a connexion between the educational treatise and the highest forms of literature. For Spenser, as for most Elizabethan writers, the highest form of poetry would be either epic or tragedy, and the epic for him deals essentially with the actions of the heroic prince or leader. The highest form of prose, similarly, would be either a Utopian vision outlined in a Platonic dialogue or in a romance like Sidney's *Arcadia*, or a description of an ideal prince's ideal education, for which the classical model was Xenophon's *Cyropaedia*. Spenser's preference of Xenophon's form to Plato's is explicit in the letter to Raleigh. This high view of education is inseparable from Spenser's view of the relation between nature and art. For Spenser, as for Burke centuries later, art is man's nature. Art is nature on the human plane, or what Sidney calls a second nature, a "golden" world, to use another phrase of Sidney's, because essentially the same world as that of the Golden Age, and in contrast to the "brazen" world of physical nature. Hence art is no less natural than physical nature—the art itself is nature, as Polixenes says in *The Winter's Tale*—but it is the civilized nature appropriate to human life.

Private and public education, then, are the central themes of *The Faerie Queene*. If we had to find a single word for the virtue underlying all private education, the best word would perhaps be fidelity: that unswerving loyalty to an ideal which is virtue, to a single lady which is love, and to the demands of one's calling which is courage. Fidelity on the specifically human plane of endeavour is faith, the vision of holiness by which one lives; on the natural plane it is temperance, or the ability to live humanely in the physical world. The corresponding term for the virtue of public education is, perhaps, concord or harmony. On the physical plane concord is friendship, again the ability to achieve a human community in ordinary life; on the specifically human plane it is justice and equity, the foundation of society.

In the first two books the symbolism comes to a climax in what we may call a "house of recognition," the House of Holiness in

Book I and the House of Alma in Book II. In the third the climax is the vision of the order of nature in the Gardens of Adonis. The second part repeats the same scheme: we have houses of recognition in the Temple of Venus in Book IV and the Palace of Mercilla in Book V, and a second *locus amoenus* vision in the Mount Acidale canto of Book VI, where the poet himself appears with the Graces. The sequence runs roughly as follows: fidelity in the context of human nature; fidelity in the context of physical nature; fidelity in the context of nature as a whole; concord in the context of physical nature; concord in the context of human nature; concord in the context of nature as a whole. Or, abbreviated: human fidelity, natural fidelity, nature; natural concord, human concord, art. Obviously, such a summary is unacceptable as it stands, but it may give some notion of how the books are related and of how the symbolism flows out of one book into the next one.

The conception of the four levels of existence and the symbols used to represent it come from Spenser's cultural tradition in general and from the Bible in particular. The Bible, as Spenser read it for his purposes, describes how man originally inhabited his own human world, the Garden of Eden, and fell out of it into the present physical world, which fell with him. By his fall he lost the tree and water of life. Below him is hell, represented on earth by the kingdoms of bondage, Egypt, Babylon, and Rome, and symbolized by the serpent of Eden, otherwise Satan, otherwise the huge water-monster called Leviathan or the dragon by the prophets. Man is redeemed by the quest of Christ, who after overcoming the world descended to hell and in three days conquered it too. His descent is usually symbolized in art as walking into the open mouth of a dragon, and when he returns in triumph he carries a banner of a red cross on a white ground, the colours typifying his blood and flesh. At the end of time the dragon of death is finally destroyed, man is restored to Eden, and gets back the water and tree of life. In Christianity these last are symbolized by the two sacraments accepted by the Reformed Church, baptism and the Eucharist.

The quest of the Redcross knight in Book I follows the symbolism of the quest of Christ. He carries the same emblem of a red cross on a white ground; the monster he has to kill is "that old dragon" (quatrain to Canto xi; cf. Rev. xii, 9) who is identical with the Biblical Satan, Leviathan, and serpent of Eden, and the object of killing him is to restore Una's parents, who are Adam and Eve, to their kingdom of Eden, which includes the entire world, now usurped by the dragon. The tyranny of Egypt, Babylon, and the Roman Empire continues in the tyranny of the Roman Church, and the Book of Revelation, as Spenser read it, prophesies the future ascendancy of that church and its ultimate defeat in its vision of the dragon and Great Whore, the latter identified with his Duessa. St. George fights the dragon for three days in the garden of Eden, refreshed by the water and tree of life on the first two days respectively.

But Eden is not heaven: in Spenser, as in Dante, it is rather the summit of purgatory, which St. George goes through in the House of Holiness. It is the world of recovered human nature, as it originally was and still can be when sin is removed. St. George similarly is not Christ, but only the English people trying to be Christian, and the dragon, while he may be part of Satan, is considerably less Satanic than Archimago or Duessa, who survive the book. No monster, however loathsome, can really be evil: for evil there must be a perversion of intelligence, and Spenser drew his dragon with some appreciation of the fact mentioned in an essay of Valéry, that in poetry the most frightful creatures always have something rather childlike about them:

> So dreadfully he towards him did pas,
>   Forelifting up aloft his speckled brest,
>   And often bounding on the brused gras,
>   As for great joyance of his newcome guest.   (I, xi, 15)

Hence the theatre of operations in the first book is still a human world. The real heaven appears only in the vision of Jerusalem at the end of the tenth canto and in a few other traces, like the invisible husband of Charissa and the heavenly music heard in the background of the final betrothal. Eden is within the order of nature but it is a new earth turned upward, or sacramentally aligned with a new heaven. The main direction of the imagery is also upward: this upward movement is the theme of the House of Holiness, of the final quest, and of various subordinate themes like the worship of Una by the satyrs.

We have spoken of the principle of symbolic parody, which we meet in all books of *The Faerie Queene*. Virtues are contrasted not only with their vicious opposites, but with vices that have similar names and appearances. Thus the golden mean of temperance is parodied by the golden means provided by Mammon; "That part of justice, which is equity" in Book V is parodied by the anarchistic equality preached by the giant in the second canto, and so on. As the main theme of Book I is really faith, or spiritual fidelity, the sharpest parody of this sort is between Fidelia, or true faith, and Duessa, who calls herself Fidessa. Fidelia holds a golden cup of wine and water (which in other romance patterns would be the Holy Grail, though Spenser's one reference to the Grail shows that he has no interest in it); Duessa holds the golden cup of the Whore of Babylon. Fidelia's cup also contains a serpent (the redeeming brazen serpent of Moses typifying the Crucifixion); Duessa sits on the dragon of the Apocalypse who is metaphorically the same beast as the serpent of Eden. Fidelia's power to raise the dead is stressed; Duessa raises Sansjoy from the dead by the power of Aesculapius, whose emblem is the serpent. Of all such parodies in the first book the most important for the imagery of the poem as a whole is the parody of the tree and water of life in Eden. These symbols have their demonic counterparts in the paralysed trees of Fradubio and Fraelissa and in the paralysing fountain from which St. George drinks in the seventh canto.

Thus the first book shows very clearly what we have called the subordinating of cyclical symbols to dialectical ones: the tree and water of life, originally symbols of the rebirth of spring, are here symbols of resurrection, or a permanent change from a life in physical nature above the animals to life in human nature under God. The main interest of the second book is also dialectical, but in the reverse direction, concerned with human life in the ordinary physical world, and with its separation from the demonic world below. The Bower of Bliss is a parody of Eden, and just as the climax of Book I is St. George's three-day battle with the dragon of death, so the narrative climax of Book II is Guyon's three-day endurance in the underworld. It is the climax at least as far as Guyon's heroism is concerned, for it is Arthur who defeats Maleger and it is really the Palmer who catches Acrasia. * * *

Having outlined the dialectical extremes of his imagery, Spenser moves on to consider the order of nature on its two main levels in the remaining books. Temperance steers a middle course between care and carelessness, jealousy and wantonness, miserliness and prodigality, Mammon's cave and Acrasia's bower. Acrasia is a kind of sinister Venus, and her victims, Mordant wallowing in his blood, Cymochles, Verdant, have something of a dead, wasted, or frustrated Adonis about them. Mammon is an old man with a daughter, Philotime. Much of the symbolism of the third book is based on these two archetypes. The first half leads up to the description of the Gardens of Adonis in Canto vi by at least three repetitions of the theme of Venus and Adonis. First we have the tapestry in the Castle Joyeous representing the story, with a longish description attached. Then comes the wounding of Marinell on his "precious shore" by Britomart (surely the most irritable heroine known to romance), where the sacrificial imagery, the laments of the nymphs, the strewing of flowers on the bier are all conventional images of Adonis. Next is Timias, discovered by Belphoebe wounded in the thigh with a boar-spear. Both Belphoebe and Marinell's mother Cymoent have pleasant retreats closely analogous to the Gardens of Adonis. In the second half of the book we have three examples of

the old man and young woman relationships: Malbecco and Hellen-
ore, Proteus and Florimell, Busirane and Amoret. All these are evil:
there is no idealized version of this theme. The reason is that the
idealized version would be the counterpart to the vision of charity
in the *Hymn of Heavenly Love*. That is, it would be the vision of
the female Sapience sitting in the bosom of the Deity that we meet
at the end of the *Hymn to Heavenly Beauty*, and this would take
us outside the scope of *The Faerie Queene*, or at any rate of its
third book.

The central figure in the third book and the fourth is Venus,
flanked on either side by Cupid and Adonis, or what a modern poet
would call Eros and Thanatos. Cupid and Venus are gods of natural
love, and form, not a demonic parody, but a simple analogy of
Christian love, an analogy which is the symbolic basis of the *Fowre
Hymnes*. Cupid, like Jesus, is lord of gods and creator of the cosmos,
and simultaneously an infant, Venus' relation to him being that of
an erotic Madonna, as her relation to Adonis is that of an erotic
Pièta. Being androgynous, she brings forth Cupid without male
assistance;[2] she loses him and goes in search of him, and he returns
in triumph in the great masque at the end as lord of all creation.

The Garden of Adonis, with its Genius and its temperate climate,
is so carefully paralleled to the Bower of Bliss that it clearly repre-
sents the reality of which the Bower is a mirage. It presents the
order of nature as a cyclical process of death and renewal, in itself
morally innocent, but still within the realm of Mutability, as the
presence of Time shows. Like Eden, it is a paradise: it is nature
as nature would be if man could live in his proper human world,
the "antique" Golden Age. It is a world where substance is constant
but where "Forms are variable and decay"; and hence it is closely
connected with the theme of metamorphosis, which is the central
symbol of divine love as the pagans conceived it.

* * *

Just as Book III deals with the secular and natural counterpart of
love, so Book VI deals with the secular and natural counterpart of
grace. The word grace itself in all its human manifestations is a
thematic word in this book, and when the Graces themselves appear
on Mount Acidale we find ourselves in a world that transcends the
world of Venus:

> These three to men all gifts of grace do graunt,
> And all that Venus in herself doth vaunt
> Is borrowed of them   (VI.x.15)

2. This detail is not in *The Faerie Queene:* see *Colin Clouts Come Home
Againe*, 800 ff.

The Graces, we are told, were begotten by Jove when he returned from the wedding of Peleus and Thetis. This wedding is referred to again in the *Mutabilitie Cantos* as the most festive occasion the gods had held before the lawsuit of Mutability. For it was at this wedding that Jove was originally "confirmed in his imperial see": the marriage to Peleus removed the threat to Jove's power coming from the son of Thetis, a threat the secret of which only Prometheus knew, and which Prometheus was crucified on a rock for not revealing. Thus the wedding also led, though Spenser does not tell us this, to the reconciling of Jove and Prometheus, and it was Prometheus, whose name traditionally means forethought or wisdom, who, according to Book II, was the originator of Elves and Fays —that is, of man's moral and conscious nature. There are still many demonic symbols in Book VI, especially the attempt to sacrifice Serena, where the custom of eating the flesh and giving the blood to the priests has obvious overtones of parody. But the centre of symbolic gravity, so to speak, in Book VI is a pastoral Arcadian world, where we seem almost to be entering into the original home of man where, as in the child's world of Dylan Thomas's *Fern Hill*, it was all Adam and maiden. It is no longer the world of Eros; yet the sixth book is the most erotic, in the best sense, of all the books in the poem, full of innocent nakedness and copulation, the surprising of which is so acid a test of courtesy, and with many symbols of the state of innocence and of possible regeneration like the Salvage Man and the recognition scene in which Pastorella is reunited to her parents.

Such a world is a world in which the distinction between art and nature is disappearing because nature is taking on a human form. In the Bower of Bliss the *mixing* of art and nature is what is stressed: on Mount Acidale the art itself is nature, to quote Polixenes again. Yet art, especially poetry, has a central place in the legend of courtesy. Grace in religion implies revelation by the Word, and human grace depends much on good human words. All through the second part of *The Faerie Queene*, slander is portrayed as the worst enemy of the human community: we have Ate and Sclaunder herself in Book IV, Malfont with his tongue nailed to a post in Mercilla's court, as an allegory of what ought to be done to *other* poets; and finally the Blatant Beast, the voice of rumour full of tongues. The dependence of courtesy on reasonable speech is emphasized at every turn, and just as the legend of justice leads us to the figure of the Queen, as set forth in Mercilla, who manifests the order of society, so the legend of courtesy leads us to the figure of the poet himself, who manifests the order of words.

When Calidore commits his one discourteous act and interrupts

Colin Clout, all the figures dancing to his pipe vanish. In Elizabethan English a common meaning of art was magic, and Spenser's Colin Clout, like Shakespeare's Prospero, has the magical power of summoning spirits to enact his present fancies, spirits who disappear if anyone speaks and breaks the spell. Nature similarly vanishes mysteriously at the end of the *Mutabilitie Cantos*, just as the counterpart to Prospero's revels is his subsequent speech on the disappearance of all created things. Colin Clout, understandably annoyed at being suddenly deprived of the company of a hundred and four naked maidens, destroys his pipe, as Prospero drowns his book. Poetry works by suggestion and indirection, and conveys meanings out of all proportion to its words; but in magic the impulse to complete a pattern is very strong. If a spirit is being conjured by the seventy-two names of God as set forth in the *Schemhamphoras*, it will not do if the magician can remember only seventy-one of them. At the end of the sixth book the magician in Spenser had completed half of his gigantic design, and was ready to start on the other half. But the poet in Spenser was satisfied: he had done his work, and his vision was complete.

A. C. HAMILTON

[The Cosmic Image: Spenser and Dante]†

* * *

* * * I shall analyse an episode from Spenser's poem, the most obvious choice being the opening episode in which the Red Cross Knight defeats Error. I shall compare it, since we have been considering the art of reading allegory, to the opening episode of Dante's *Commedia*. These are the only two major classics in modern literature which were conceived by their authors as allegories; yet, strangely enough, they have never been brought into any significant relationship.

* * *

Unless these poets write a common language of allegory, there is little we may ever understand about the genre; but if they do, comparison of the opening episodes of each poem should be mutually illuminating. At first the differences in matter and method may seem too striking. Dante's Wood is nasty, brutish, rough (to adapt Hobbes's relevant phrase), and fills his heart with fear; Spenser's is

† From *The Structure of Allegory in "The Faerie Queene,"* by A. C. Hamilton (Oxford, 1961), Chapter I. (The original footnotes have been slightly edited.)

a pleasant Wood where the knight and his lady are beguiled with delight. Dante describes in concrete and very real terms a man of flesh and blood who is defeated by fear and doubt until Virgil aids him; Spenser uses allegorical devices of a chivalric combat between an armed knight and a monster which personifies Error. But such differences are not essential. Spenser's Wood is also dark, for the enshrouding trees 'heauens light did hide, / Not perceable with power of any starre' and leads to the monster's 'darksome hole'.[1] That Beatrice sends Virgil to aid Dante, and that Una accompanies her knight, reflect rather differences of religious faith than of poetical method. (The differences of method are more apparent than real, but I leave this point until later.) Moreover, these differences do not rule out striking similarities. In larger terms each episode presents an image of one lost in a Wood where he confronts certain monsters (Dante's three beasts, Spenser's threefold enemy in the woman-serpent with her brood) and is overcome by error and doubt. Dante is driven back into the dark pass where he struggles with death until Beatrice aids him: Spenser's knight wanders until he comes to the dark den where he is almost slain before Una aids him. (The *donna . . . beata e bella* and the 'louely Ladie' clearly suggest God's grace.) Then both begin their Exodus—the one treading that pass which had allowed none to go alive ('che non lasciò già mai persona viva') and the other taking by-ways 'where neuer foot of liuing wight did tread' (i. vii. 50)—until they are restored to the heavenly Jerusalem. Essentially, then, each episode is an initiation: the candidate wanders in a labyrinth or maze which prepares him for his salvation. It initiates the poet also by committing him to his kind of allegory. Further, it initiates the reader by offering a brief allegory of what is to come, and by teaching him the art of reading allegory.

The literal level of an allegory seems the most difficult to read properly. Does the fiction exist in its own right, or is it a veil which must be torn aside to reach the allegorical levels beneath? The latter has been the usual fashion in which to read not only Spenser, as we have seen, but also Dante. Modern Dante criticism recognizes, however, that the *Commedia* does not respond to such allegorizing. On this subject Professor Hatzfeld writes:

> In passages where . . . the allegorical sense *is* the literal one, the reader is even less entitled to ask extratextual and biographical questions, such as whether the dark wood means heresy, or fornication, or pursuit of worldly honors in Dante's life, or whether the leopard means Florence and the lion Charles of Valois. These

1. All references are to the opening episode of each poem, unless indicated otherwise. For Dante, I cite the edition of *La Divina Commedia*, ed. C. H. Grandgent (New York, rev. ed., 1933).

questions refer only to potentialities, namely, Dante's life as raw material, and abandon the actually achieved world of Dante's poetical symbolism. In other words, the new Dante interpretation makes a strong point of the fact that Dante in his poetry (not in his prose) overcomes the usual mediaeval allegorism and fuses personal, theological, political, moral, even astronomical elements into symbols of a decidedly poetical and not didactic quality.[2]

But not modern Spenser criticism where, as we have seen, the poem's literal level is still translated into moral precept and historical example. We are told that in the episode of the Wandering Wood, the knight is Holiness, Una is Truth, Error is obvious error: *ergo*, the episode means that Holiness defeats Error with the aid of Truth. We are told this by the critics, not by Spenser who does not name the knight, nor the lady, and describes the monster in very real terms. Again without support from the text, we are told that the knight is England, Una is the true Church, Error is the Church of Rome: *ergo*, the episode means that England passed successfully through the dangers of Reformation.[3] Since both poems share a similar critical history—contemporary praise for their profound meaning, the neo-classical eclipse, the romantic age's rejection of the allegory for lyrical beauty (Livingston Lowes on Spenser, Croce on Dante), and yesterday's search for hidden meanings—probably Spenser criticism needs to catch up.

What seems so perverse about translating the literal level is that Spenser, like Dante, labours to render the fiction in its own right. It is an image presented in realistic and visual detail. There is the precise physical detail of the monster's huge tail wound about the knight's body, his strangling her gorge, her filthy vomit, the serpents swarming about his legs, and the final gruesome beheading. There is the exact rendering of the monster 'vpon the durtie ground', her brood 'sucking vpon her poisonous dugs', her vomit 'full of great lumpes of flesh and gobbets raw'. The details are immediately repulsive to all the senses: to the *sight* with the monster half-serpent, half-woman, and her deformed brood sucking up her blood; to the *hearing* with the monster's loud braying and her brood 'groning full deadly'; to the *smell* with the 'deadly stinke' of her vomit; to the *taste* with the violent spewing of the flood of poison; and to the *touch* with the monster's tail strangling him. The realism of the episode is enforced by its dramatic action: the monster's brood creeping into her mouth 'and suddain all were gone', her rushing forth and retreating before the knight, the brilliant chiaroscuro effect of the knight's armour which casts 'a litle glooming light,

2. Helmut Hatzfeld, 'Modern Dante Criticism', *Comparative Literature*, iii (1951), 297–298.

3. See *Var. Sp.* i. 422 f., 449 f.

much like a shade' into Error's dark hole, the brood with 'bowels gushing forth'. This monster has all the terrible reality of a nightmare, and even Fuseli who saw the nightmare could complain that 'when Spenser dragged into light the entrails of the serpent slain by the Red Knight, he dreamt a butcher's dream and not a poet's'.[4] Clearly the poet labours to make us see. His whole effort is to render a clearly-defined, exact, and visual image. No less than with Dante, Spenser's reader must respect the primacy and integrity of the poem's literal level.

Whatever the differences of their critical traditions, both poets clearly demand that the reader focus upon this literal level. For Dante it may be enough to point * * * to Holy Scripture with its insistence upon the literal level. For the Renaissance poet there is the classically-derived doctrine that the poet gathers precept and example into a poetic image which he makes us see; and behind this doctrine is the neo-Platonic faith that if man once sees virtues and vices, he will embrace the one and shun the other. For the Protestant poet there is also the renewed emphasis upon the Bible's literal sense. But they may share a simpler basis for insisting upon the literal level of their poems. Ever since Plato, poets have recognized that they deliver fiction rather than truth or morality. In the *Convivio* Dante claims that 'the literal sense ought always to come first, as being that sense in the expression of which the others are all included, and without which it would be impossible and irrational to give attention to the other meanings, and most of all to the allegorical'. Further, the highest allegorical sense, the anagogic, sustains and illuminates the literal by seeing in it the poem's total meaning: 'this occurs when a writing is spiritually expounded, which even in the literal sense by the things signified likewise gives intimation of higher matters belonging to the eternal glory'.[5] The corresponding Renaissance claim is Sidney's doctrine that 'in Poesie, looking but for fiction [that is, *only* for fiction and not allegorical truth], they [the readers] shal vse the narration but as an imaginatiue groundplot of a profitable inuention'.[6] Since the fiction is the groundplot for readers of both Dante and Spenser, to strip it away leaves the poem barren. As readers we must respect what they have given us. To read their allegories we must accept as given that Dante's matter is a history of what happened to him, and that Spenser's 'History' (he insists upon the term) is 'matter of iust memory' (II. Pr. 1).

4. See E. C. Mason, *The Mind of Henry Fuseli* (London, 1951), p. 217.
5. *Convivio*, trans. W. W. Jackson (Oxford, 1909), p. 74. See also his letter to Can Grande in *The Letters of Dante*, trans. Paget Toynbee (Oxford, 1920).
6. See the Ponsonby edition (ed. A. S. Cook [Boston, 1890], p. 36) whose version is here less elegant but more explicit.

But how may we understand their opening episodes? Not according to the usual medieval or Renaissance theories of allegory: these, with their stresss upon levels of allegorical meaning, only distract. If we seek more clear authority for the art of reading than the *Letter to Can Grande* and the *Apology for Poetry* provide, we must begin with the poems themselves, with the fact that each within its tradition is a separate kind of allegory which demands its own kind of reading. And this provides the clue we need. The opening episode of each poem defines the art of reading the allegory. The initiation which is described here both separates and joins: it separates the candidate from us, from our way of life, and enters him upon a pilgrimage which is treated in the rest of the poem. It follows that there are two ways of understanding. The first is outward, that extrinsic meaning which relates the episode (and the poem) to our world; the second is intrinsic, that inner coherence which binds all parts of the poem. Allegory's unique power is achieved through the contrapuntal relationship between the poem's world and our world, and by the centripetal relationship of its parts. More comprehensively and significantly than other genres, it points beyond itself and also to itself. The brazen world of fallen nature and the poem's golden world, reality and the ideal, fact and fiction become united in our reading.

In their opening episodes both poets exploit the metaphor of the labyrinth or maze, of one wandering lost in a Wood where he encounters beasts. Dante's source has been found in Horace's *Satires*,[7] Spenser's in medieval romance; but the more likely source is Holy Scripture. There we learn that Wisdom (with whom Beatrice and Una are identified) 'wil walke with him [her lover] by crooked waies, and bring him vnto feare, and dread, and torment him with her discipline vntill shee haue tried his soule, and haue proued him by her iudgementes. Then will she returne the streight way vnto him, and comfort him, and shew him her secrets.'[8] But the metaphor is universal, too centrally archetypal to be traced to any source. Or if any, it is that of Christ who, after His baptism, entered the Wilderness where He was with the wild beasts during his initiation into the role of Redeemer. (Dante's baptism is signified by the metaphor of the lake in which he struggles, the knight's baptism by

---

7. J. H. Whitfield, *Dante and Virgil* (Oxford, 1949), p. 74. Cf. Upton: 'what are these trees and labyrinths [of the Wandering Wood], but the various amusements and errors of human life? So Horace and Dante apply the similitude' (*Spenser's 'Faerie Queene'*, ii. 339).

8. Eccles. iv. 17–18. The Genevan version (London, 1580) which I cite throughout this study. The tropological signifi-cance of Spenser's episode, then, is that given by Fulke Greville to Sidney's *Arcadia*: 'his end in them was not vanishing pleasure alone, but morall Images, and Examples, (as directing threds) to guide every man through the confused *Labyrinth* of his own desires, and life' (*Life of Sir Philip Sidney*, ed. Nowell Smith [Oxford, 1907], p. 223).

the spiritual armour which he dons.) The Renaissance poet may mingle classical myth with Scripture: the labyrinthine wood with the monster in the middle invokes the myth of Theseus who enters the labyrinth to slay the Minotaur in the middle, and is guided out by Ariadne's thread. He may do so because Christ is the true Theseus who slew monsters, and the Word is 'the thread that will direct us through the winding and intricate labyrinths of this life'.[9]

Singleton has shown Dante's complex use of this metaphor, how it is designed to locate us by showing the way of our life.[1] It is *our* life, as Dante's opening line suggests, but his experience in the Wood is unique. He becomes lost only when he separates himself from the common herd, from our life, through love of Beatrice. As Christian alone in the City of Destruction knows that he bears upon his back the burden which plunges him deeper into hell, Dante in the Dark Wood is forced by the beasts back into the darkness.[2] In the beginning when he is with us, he is nameless; he may begin to find himself only by losing himself, that is, by finding himself lost; and finally Beatrice will restore him to himself, and name him Dante. As in Bunyan where the pilgrim in our city is anonymous— after he enters the way of salvation he is named Christian—and in Spenser where the knight is not named until after he endures the first test. We may say, then, that Dante's poem arises out of its opening episode: once he realizes the horror of our way of life, he is prepared to be initiated into a new way of life.

Spenser also exploits the metaphor in order to locate us within our world. When the knight has been chosen by Una and the Faery Queen, he goes out 'to winne him worship, and her grace to haue' until the tempest drives every one into hiding: 'euery wight to shrowd it did constrain, / And this faire couple eke to shroud themselues were fain.' All seek the shady grove where 'all within were pathes and alleies wide, / With footing worne, and leading inward farre.' The ominous phrase, 'so in they entred arre', announces the beginning of his initiation (literally, *inire*, to enter in). Within the Wood they no longer lead their way, but passively are led: 'led with delight' they 'wander too and fro in wayes vnknowne':

> That path they take, that beaten seemd most bare,
> And like to lead the labyrinth about;
> Which when by tract they hunted had throughout,
> At length it brought them to a hollow caue,
> Amid the thickest woods.

9. Alexander Ross, *Mystagogus Poeticus* (London, 1647), p. 254.
1. C. S. Singleton, *Dante Studies*, I (Cambridge, Mass., 1954), p. 7.
2. Francis Fergusson acutely remarks of Dante's experience: 'once in the terror of the Dark Wood, he had to explore the full import of that experience before his spirit was free to take another direction'. *Dante's Drama of the Mind* (Princeton, 1953), p. 5.

This is the path which 'euery wight' takes, but none returns. In the first stage of the initiation the candidates (both Dante and Spenser's knight) wander as we do in our life.

In the second stage they are proven worthy of being chosen. To pass this test separates them from us. In Canto II Dante's spirit is so overwhelmed by cowardice that he withdraws from what he has begun. Virgil abjures him:

> L'anima tua è da viltate offesa,
> La qual molte fïate l'omo ingombra,
> Sì che d'onrata impresa lo rivolve,
> Come falso veder bestia, quand' ombra.

Dante is freed from all doubts of his worthiness only after he is told by Virgil how Beatrice cares for him. Only through faith in her compassion may he enter upon his journey. (These doubts recur at the beginning of his final ascent, the 'dubbi' of *Paradiso* IV, but Beatrice herself is there to resolve them.) In Spenser the knight wanders lost (that is, he is overcome by Error) and in doubt—'the place vnknowne and wilde, / Breedes dreadfull doubts'—until he so persists that he sees Error herself. The battle with this monster is described in terms of her labyrinthine tail which 'her den all ouer-spred, / Yet was in knots and many boughtes vpwound, / Pointed with mortall sting', for this is the labyrinth which he must over-come. In the encounter his courage is first overcome—l'anima tua è da viltate offesa—and he retreats. Only when the lady intercedes with the injunction: 'add faith vnto your force, and be not faint', does he slay the monster. Then the brood, the doubts bred by the earlier experience in the Wood, 'him encombred sore'—la qual molte fïate l'omo ingombra—but with the death of Error they cannot hurt him and only destroy themselves. Spenser's remark during the battle, 'God helpe the man so wrapt in *Errours* endlesse traine', points to our life here: this monster will devour us, as she devours all who take the beaten path to her den, unless God helps us. But when God intercedes through the Lady, the knight may go 'forward on his way (with God to frend)'. Then he is no longer led by the path, but keeps it:

> That path he kept, which beaten was most plaine,
> Ne euer would to any by-way bend,
> But still did follow one vnto the end.

(The straight march of the concluding line demonstrates his vic-tory over the labyrinth.) In Una's address to him:

> Well worthy be you of that Armorie,
> Wherein ye haue great glory wonne this day,
> And proou'd your strength on a strong enimie,
> Your first aduenture,

the repetition of 'you' and 'your' emphasizes that the battle proves him worthy his armour.[3] (Yet worthy only within his armour: 'that Armorie, / *Wherein* ye haue great glory wonne': at first he uses 'all his force' to free himself from the monster, but defeats her only when he 'strooke at her with *more then manly force*'.) His worthiness which is sealed by his faith sets him apart from us, even as Dante is commended by the Virgin as 'il tuo fedele'. Through this victory over the world, that is, over our way of life, both Dante and Spenser's knight are initiated into their pilgrimage.

Dante's poetic method may seem to differ radically from Spenser's. Dante renders the experience directly as his own; he describes dramatically and concretely the fear and agony which he suffers in the Wood. In contrast, Spenser leaves the given for the less real: rather than describe a man in error and doubt, he shows a wandering knight battling with Error. These are the terms in which C. S. Lewis has taught us to regard allegory.[4] And such abstract personification, we say, is alien to the reality of Dante's poem. But what, in fact, does Spenser do? In similarly dramatic and concrete terms, he shows a man confronting a monster; and in the immediate visual terms which we have noted earlier, he describes the physical impact of the battle. His 'Allegoricall deuices' serve to sharpen the sense of reality; they add to it; and render it more 'real'. Spenser's metaphor is overt: to yield to the world is to wander in an enchanting Wood; to seek the way out—how difficult it is to avoid metaphor!—is to battle a woman serpent. Dante's metaphor is half-submerged, but it is no less present. Beatrice sees Dante struggling with death: 'non vedi tu la morte che 'l combatte / Su la fiumana ove 'l mar non ha vanto.' This is the sea which Dante struggles to leave:

> E come quei che, con lena affannata,
> Uscito fuor del pelago a la riva,
> Si volge a l'acqua perigliosa e guata;

and Virgil, in the lines quoted previously, sees Dante's spirit *encumbered* with cowardice, *stricken* by doubts. Once Dante accepts Virgil as his guide, the beast no longer forces him back into the dolorous pass. In effect he has 'slain' the beast. Metaphorically? yes. But it is

3. It is evident that the episode also proves Spenser worthy of his role as England's heroic poet. The catalogue of trees which he so carefully elaborates in stanzas 8 and 9 imitates Chaucer's *Parlement of Foules*, 169–82. It indicates that he now wears the mantle as England's poet. Behind both poets' use of the catalogue is Ovid's account of Orpheus, the archetype of the inspired poet, moving trees with his music. The power of Orpheus descends now to Spenser as he begins to create his faery land. Spenser's imitation of Chaucer is all the more apt since the poet in the *Parlement* enters a delightful Wandering Wood where he is overcome by error: 'no wit hadde I, for errour, for to chese, / To entre or flen, or me to save or lese' (146–7). Cf. Affrican's rebuke in 155–6. Since Chaucer is indebted to Dante's opening episode (see J. A. W. Bennett, *The Parlement of Foules* [Oxford, 1957], pp. 63–65), there is a nice historical connexion between Spenser and Dante.

4. *The Allegory of Love* (Oxford, 1936), pp. 44f.

all metaphor: the Dark Wood, the beasts, even (though in a different way) Hell itself, the Wandering Wood, the monster with her brood, the dungeon of Orgoglio. Dante's three beasts are emblems of the three stages of his journey through Hell. Spenser's monster is an emblem of Error; but what does Error signify? Not vice, nor any simple psychological state such as we meet in the personifications of other poets. Error is all that which stands between the knight and his entering upon his salvation, that is, Hell itself and the death which he must suffer before he may be reborn. The dragon-figure suggests this all-encompassing significance, as it does again in the knight's final antagonist. More simply, Error is what Dante means by the Dark Wood and the three beasts.

Spenser's treatment is more sophisticated largely because his age allowed him to be.[5] For one thing, his knight is more obviously an ideal pattern of what man should be. His entrance into the enchanting wood where he slays the woman-serpent invokes the analogy to Adam who, at the beginning of his quest, entered the Garden of Eden where the enchantress Eve joined with the serpent conspired his fall. (Eden was traditionally linked with the labyrinth,[6] and in medieval-Renaissance iconography the woman-serpent is the common emblem for Satan.) As Adam was tempted by the fruit of the knowledge of good and evil, the knight is first overcome by the serpent's vomit 'full of bookes and papers'. Through faith, however, the knight defeats the serpent-Eve and enters the path which leads to his salvation. But in one way Spenser's treatment is more primitive than Dante's. He uses the symbol of the cave which traditionally signifies rebirth. Yet surely Dante's metaphor of the struggle in the water suggests another primitive metaphor, such as that used in *Beowulf* where the hero grapples with the sea monster.

---

5. His elaborate personification follows Renaissance convention, and in this matter it is pertinent to refer to Harington's preference for Ariosto's personification over Dante's. 'This description of the monster of covetousnesse, is (in my fancy) very well handled by mine Author, far beyond the like in *Dant* who maketh her onely like a Wolfe, pined with famine; But *Ariosto* goeth farder, and more significantly, describing her first to be ugly, because of all vices it is the most hatefull; eares of an asse, being for the most part ignorant, or at the least carelesse of other mens good opinions; a Wolfe in head and breast, namely ravenous and never satisfied; a Lions grisly jaw, terrible and devouring; a Foxe in all the rest, wyly and craftie, and timerous of those that are stronger then himselfe; all which applications are so proper and so plaine, as it is needlesse to stand upon them.' *Orlando Furi-*

oso (London, 1634), p. 213.
6. Cf. Bartas' account of Adam in the Garden of Eden: 'musing, anon through crooked Walks he wanders, / Round-winding rings, and intricate Meanders, / False-guiding paths, doubtfull beguiling strays, / And right-wrong errors of an end-less Maze' (*Diuine Weeks and Workes,* trans. Sylvester (London, 1633), p. 86). Milton's Adam relates how he 'stray'd I knew not whither' at his creation until in vision God comes as his 'Guide / To the Garden of bliss'. Once in the garden he is so overcome by its delight that 'here had new begun / My wandring, had not hee who was my Guide / Up hither, from among the Trees appeer'd / Presence Divine' (*Paradise Lost,* viii. 283, 298–9, 311–14). This is the Red Cross Knight's state of innocence in which he conquers the labyrinth 'with God to frend'.

Besides this significant pointing to our world, the initiation described in the opening episode of each poem points inward to the poem's world. In Dante, as Mr. Singleton has shown, it serves as prologue.[7] The three beasts represent the three stages of descent into Hell, Beatrice reveals the role which the poem fulfils, and Dante's journey here corresponds to his journey through Hell. Thus it stands by itself as a brief epic, a 'dumb show' revealing the argument of the drama which will unfold. Virgil saves Dante from the beasts, as later he will guide him through Hell. It is Beatrice who persuades him to begin his journey, as later she brings him to his final salvation. Spenser's opening episode points inward in the same significant way to the world of his poem. The woman-serpent is later revealed as Duessa, the 'goodly Lady' with 'her neather partes misshapen, monstruous', and by the composite symbol of Duessa upon the Dragon. The knight's victory over Error is an emblem, then, of his final victory over Duessa and the Dragon. Here Una reveals the role which the poem fulfils, as later she prepares the knight to battle the Dragon by leading him to the house of Holiness where he is confirmed in faith. As Dante leaves the labyrinth to enter the descending circles of Hell, the knight leaves the Wood only to lose faith in Una through Archimago's false vison, and to wander lost, 'all in amaze' upon that path which leads him into Orgoglio's dungeon. After his rescue by Arthur, as he girds himself for the second stage of his journey—it is also an ascent through Purgatory—he meets Despair. By using the same allegorical language, Spenser places the two scenes in close correspondence. As Error is 'a monster vile, whom God and man does hate', Despair is 'a man of hell', a 'Snake in hidden weedes'. The one lives in a 'darksome hole' in the thickest woods, the other in a 'darkesome caue' among 'old stockes and stubs of trees'.[8] Again the knight must enter the cave and fight the monster. But while the first struggle was outward and physical, this is inward and spiritual. It takes place within his conscience; therefore the labyrinth he treads is intellectual. Error's vomit of books and papers appears in Despair's learning. Earlier he wanders in a maze until Error's 'huge traine / All suddenly about his body wound', now he wonders in amazement until Despair's arguments charm him in 'his guilefull traine'. Against Error Una urges him to 'shew what ye bee': now she reminds him what he is, one chosen by God. As before, she offers faith, that is, faith in God's mercy. Each encounter tests the knight: the earlier proves him worthy his armour, the later to be worthy as one chosen by God.

More than this, we may say, in Singleton's phrase, that Spenser's

7. *Dante Studies*, pp. 5–6.
8. Cf. I. i. 13 and I. ix. 28; I. i. 14 and I. ix. 34, 35. After the knight defeats Error, 'then mounted he vpon his Steede againe': after he defeats Despair, 'vp he rose, and thence amounted streight' (I. i. 28; I. ix. 54).

opening scene also 'figured and forecast, as well as any single scene might do, the whole configuration of the journey beyond'. The knight's token entrance into the cave—he only looks in—is fulfilled later when he descends into the dark depths of Orgoglio's dungeon. Through Una's intercession again, he is redeemed when Arthur makes his deep descent to restore him to light. Later he pays tribute to her 'whose wondrous faith, exceeding earthly race, / Was firmest fixt in mine extremest case.' Then in his last battle he 'descends' into the cave: his sword plunges into the Dragon's mouth which 'wide gaped, like the griesly mouth of hell'. As he slays Error by adding faith to his force, here his 'baptized hands' wielding 'his godly armes' defeat the Dragon. The first battle against the Dragon initiates his fall: this last battle initiates him to that restored state signified by his marriage to Una. In the cycle of fall and ascent he progresses from light to darkness to light. But with this difference: that 'his glistring armor made / A litle glooming light, much like a shade' as he peers into Error's cave, while at the end 'those glistring armes . . . heauen with light did fill' (i. xi. 4). The opening episode which shows his primal state of innocence becomes a measure of his later descent into sin, and a promise of his final ascent.

The two kinds of reading which we have applied to Dante and Spenser, the one pointing outward to our world, and the other turning inward to the poem's world focus in our single vision of the poem as fiction. That fiction is 'an ideal space', as Curtius terms Dante's poem,[9] or a 'golden world' in Sidney's phrase. Though allegory usually suggests a way of writing in which one thing is said but another is meant, our poets tell 'of Forests, and inchantments drear, / Where *more* is meant then meets the ear.'[1] We read the fiction not by translating, but by retaining the fiction as metaphor. Earlier poets had written fiction, but for Dante and Spenser both the matter and form of their poetry were transformed by Holy Scripture. Mr. Singleton has convinced us that Dante imitates Scripture: 'the literal sense is given as an historical sense standing in its own right, like Milton's, say—Not devised in order to convey a hidden truth, but given in the focus of single vision'.[2] Here Spenser's kind of allegory may seem antithetical to Dante's. Dante moves towards greater reality as his poem proceeds: Spenser moves in an unreal world of giants and dragons where Dr. Johnson would never stub his toe. But what does this difference amount to? Dante's fiction is that his matter is fact; Spenser's fiction is that his matter is

9. *European Literature and the Latin Middle Ages*, trans. Trask (New York, 1953), p. 18.

1. *Il Penseroso*, 119–20.
2. *Dante Studies*, p. 15.

romance. The one establishes the illusion of historical reality, the other of faery land. For both poets, their fiction is a metaphor of Holy Scripture. Dante's position is clear; but what of Spenser? To consider briefly the knight's final battle against the Dragon. We say that here Spenser exploits the allegorical devices of the armed knight facing a fire-breathing Dragon while his lady retires to a hill. But where is the truth of this fiction? It is not the moral truth that Holiness defeats Sin or Death, or the historical fact that England defeats the powers of Antichrist. Its truth is given by Holy Scripture. The knight's three-day battle in Eden against the Dragon in order to release Una's parents, Adam and Eve, imitates Christ's harrowing hell, His three-day descent through which mankind is restored to the Tree and Well of Life. The fiction of both poets, then, whether it is given as an historical sense or as romance, is a metaphor of Holy Scripture. Once we see that each poet writes metaphor, then one poem becomes a metaphor of the other. And it is this fact which allows them to be compared.

Once we allow that in reading Spenser's poem we should focus upon the image, rather than upon some idea behind the image, our understanding gathers around our response to the poem's literal level because it arises from it. Our sense of that other reality to which the poem points, by first pointing to itself, grows from our sense of the poem's reality. We may be said to understand—literally to under-stand—the poem because we bear the whole poem in our response. That response is integrated because the intense delight given by the poem determines, at the same time, our understanding of its meaning. Our delight and understanding being integrated, our awareness of the literal and allegorical levels is continuous and simultaneous, and our vision of the poem whole. This simple, yet radical, alteration of focus may be achieved by reading the poem not for its hidden truth but rather for its fiction. Instead of treating the narration as a veil to be torn aside for the hidden meaning, we should allow Sidney's art of reading poetry by using the narration 'but as an imaginatiue groundplot of a profitable inuention'. Once we allow this art of reading, then Spenser's allegory need not be read as a complicated puzzle concealing riddles which confuse the reader in labyrinths of error, but as an unfolding drama revealing more and greater significance as it brings the reader full understanding of its complex vision.

S. K. HENINGER, JR.

[Orgoglio] †

The modern tendency to dissociate the "historical" and the "moral" allegory in *The Faerie Queene* can easily lead to a perversion of Spenser's purpose. Any dichotomy between history and morality would have been offensive to Elizabethans, whose very reason for studying the past was the hope of finding some ethical norm. As Richard Harvey flatly stated, "the most morals [is] the best History."[1] Protestants especially stressed this moralistic view of history, and furthermore argued that the future would unfold in strict accord with the prophecies set down in the Revelation of St. John. Therefore future events would also be largely determined by the ethical insight which the Apocalypse provided. Spenser adhered to this prevailing attitude, and in *The Faerie Queene* he hoped to produce convincing testimony that history and morality are indeed but different statements of the same truth. He is explicit on this point in the Proem to Book I; drawing from "the antique rolles" of England (I. proem. 2. 4), he promises that "fierce warres and faithfull loves shall moralize my song" (I. proem. 1. 9).

At his best, Spenser succeeds in contriving poetry which satisfies the special function of the poet to synthesize history and morality —to provide a "continued Allegory," as Spenser says in his letter to Raleigh. And Spenser is at his best in describing the capture of the Red Crosse Knight by the Giant Orgoglio. Although the meaning is complex, each of the intricate details subsists within the same allegorical continuum. Since this episode is the nadir of Red Crosse's fortunes and the turning-point of Book I, it is a stringent test for the coadunating faculty of Spenser's imagination.

Most readers begin their interpretation of Orgoglio by following the linguistic clue that he must be an embodiment of pride. The name would be most immediately meaningful as the Italian word for "pride, disdaine, haughtines,"[2] closely related to Spanish *orgullo* and French *orgueil*. Since the root is common to the Romance Languages, the appellation would associate the Giant with Rome and Catholicism. We must note, however, that the Giant is not specifically called "Orgoglio" until after he has overcome Red Crosse.

† From "The Orgoglio Episode in *The Faerie Queene*, by S. K. Heninger, Jr., *ELH*, XXVI (1959), 171–187. The original footnotes have been slightly edited.

1. *Philadelphus, or A Defence of Brutes, and the Brutans History* (London, 1593), G 3.

2. Giovanni Florio, *A worlde of Wordes, or dictionarie in Italian and English* (London, 1598), p. 248.

We hear the name only when Duessa approaches him with the proposition that he make Red Crosse his bondslave and take her for his paramour (I. vii. 14. 4–9). Therefore the starting-point for an interpretation of this episode does not lie in the meaning of the name "Orgoglio."

A more fundamental point-of-beginning will be found in the genealogical mythus which Spenser provides for the Giant. Here, as he often does, Spenser first suggests the significance of the char-

> The greatest Earth his uncouth mother was,
>   And blustring Aeolus his boasted sire,
>   Who with his breath, which through the world doth pas,
>   Her hollow womb did secretly inspire,
>   And fild her hidden caves with stormie yre,
>   That she conceiv'd.   (I. vii. 9. 1–6)

acter. When Orgoglio interrupts the dalliance of Red Crosse and Duessa beside the magic fountain, Spenser devotes one stanza to physical description of the Giant, and then carefully relates his parentage:

Spenser expressly states that Orgoglio has been generated by a boisterous wind blowing through caves in the earth. By the principles of Renaissance meteorology, this origin identifies him as an earthquake. Gabriel Harvey had cited this scientific theory in a letter to Spenser:

> The Materiall Cause of Earthquakes . . . is no doubt great abóun-dance of wynde, or stoare of grosse and drye vapors, and spirites, fast shut up, & as a man would saye, emprysoned in the Caves, and Dungeons of the Earth.[3]

No Elizabethan would have missed the transparent mythologizing, the obvious implication that Orgoglio is the mythical embodiment of an earthquake.

This conclusion is supported by much of Orgoglio's physical description. His entrance is heralded by "a dreadfull sownd":

> Which through the wood loud bellowing, did rebownd,
>   That all the earth for terrour seemd to shake,
>   And trees did tremble.   (I. vii. 7. 5–7)

And when he walks, "the ground eke groned under him for dreed" (I. vii. 8. 6). During the battle with Red Crosse, "the Geaunt strooke so maynly mercilesse,/That could have overthrowne a stony towre" (I. vii. 12. 1–2). In the next canto, when Prince Arthur comes to liberate Red Crosse, the Giant's club misses the Prince and digs into the ground:

3. *Three proper, and wittie, familiar Letters* (London, 1580), B4v.

The sad earth wounded with so sore assay,
Did grone full grievous underneath the blow,
And trembling with strange feare, did like an earthquake show.

(I. viii. 8. 7–9)

After a violent battle, Prince Arthur finally slays Orgoglio, whose fall "seemd to shake/The stedfast globe of earth, as it for feare did quake" (I. viii. 23. 8–9).

Since Orgoglio is the personification of an earthquake, what significance would this have for Spenser's audience? The occasion of Gabriel Harvey's long letter to Spenser was the terrifying earthquake of 6 April 1580, and this was an event which few Englishmen forgot. It was so frightening that a special order of prayer was decreed "upon Wednesdayes and Frydayes, to avert and turne Gods wrath from us, threatned by the late terrible earthquake, to be used in all parish churches."[4] Sermons for a long time thereafter cited the earthquake as an admonition "to amende our evill life, to reforme our wicked conversation, to be renewed in the spirite of the inwarde man, and to be heavenly minded."[5] Here is a vivid example of moral instruction derived from historical incident.

When Orgoglio is seen as an earthquake, and therefore as a visitation of God's wrath to warn man to repentance, this gives allegorical meaning to the opening stanzas of Canto VII. There the Dwarf has just led Red Crosse from the House of Pride, and the Knight is resting beside a spring when Duessa arrives. Cajoled by her, the Knight relaxes in the physical pleasantness of the glade and indulges his sensual appetites. When he quenches his thirst from the stream, which has magical powers to enervate any man who drinks of it, "mightie strong was turnd to feeble fraile" (I. vii. 6. 5). But the Knight continues his sinful relations with Duessa (I. vii.7. 1–3); and in this weakened condition, unready in the midst of sensual pleasure, the Knight is attacked by Orgoglio and easily captured.

This spring with its magical properties is a truncated version of the Salmacis story that Ovid had related in the *Metamorphoses* (IV. 285 ff.). Salmacis was the nymph of a fountain in Caria, a vain and slothful girl who never joined her sister-nymphs in the sylvan activities led by Diana. When youthful Hermaphroditus bathed himself in her waters, Salmacis was so undone by passion that she intertwined her body with his and prayed to the gods "that this same wilfull boy and I may never parted bee."[6] The gods capriciously consented to this unusual request, as Ovidian gods so often do, and their bodies were fused as one. When Hermaphroditus

4. *Liturgies and Occasional Forms of Prayer Set Forth in the Reign of Queen Elizabeth* (Parker Society, 1847), p. 464.
5. Abraham Fleming, *A Bright Burning Beacon* (London, 1580), E1–E1ᵛ.
6. I quote from the translation of Arthur Golding (1567) reprinted as *Shakespeare's Ovid*, ed. W. H. D. Rouse (London, 1904), p. 91, line 461.

realized that his masculinity had been diluted to half its former strength, he also prayed for a boon:

> That whoso commes within this Well may so bee weakened there,
> That of a man but halfe a man he may fro thence retire.[7]

The gods were again compliant, and thenceforth whoever drank from Salmacis' spring lost his strength.

Spenser has used only so much of Ovid's legend as he needs. He has eliminated Hermaphroditus completely, and attributes the enervating properties of the water solely to the displeasure of Diana when the indolent Salmacis showed indifference to the chase (I. vii. 5. 1–9). Ovid has never had more ardent disciples than the Elizabethans, however, and to Spenser's audience this enchanted spring would inevitably recall Salmacis.

Since myth was a form of history, it also was subject to moral interpretation; and the venerated tradition of moralizing Ovid would bring with Salmacis' story a moralized meaning. As Golding summarized it in the epistle preceding his translation of the *Metamorphoses*:

> Hermaphrodite and Salmacis declare that idlenesse
> Is cheefest nurce and cherisher of all volupteousnesse,
> And that voluptuous lyfe breedes sin: which linking all toogither
> Make men too bee effeminate, unweeldy, weake and lither.[8]

The interlude beside the fountain shows Red Crosse being both idle and voluptuous, and Spenser focuses the moral significance of this episode by connecting it with the history of Salmacis. The sinfulness of this dalliance with Duessa makes Red Crosse a proper victim for the Giant, the agent of God's wrath, that inevitably follows. Orgoglio wages battle "as when almightie Jove in wrathfull mood,/ To wreake the guilt of mortall sins is bent" (I. viii. 9. 1–2).

The interpretation of an earthquake as a warning to repentance was of course based on the Holy Scriptures. Often in the Bible the anger of God descends upon sinful men in the form of an earthquake, but nowhere more terrifyingly than in the Revelation of St. John. The Book of Revelation provided many of the central doctrines for the new militant Protestantism, and recent scholarship has shown its formative influence on Book I of *The Faerie Queene*.[9] Therefore by turning to it we can perhaps fit the Orgoglio

7. *Ibid.*, p. 91, lines 477–478.
8. P. 3, lines 113–116.
9. See particularly Josephine W. Bennett, *The Evolution of "The Faerie Queene"* (Univ. of Chicago Press, 1942), pp. 109–119; and John E. Hankins, "Spenser and the Revelation of St. John," *PMLA*, LX (1945), 364–381.

episode into the larger framework of allegory based on the Apocalypse.

In the Book of Revelation earthquakes occur as visitations upon the wicked most prominently as the climaxes of three separate but interrelated series of prophecies leading up to the final Day of Judgment: the opening of the seven seals on the book of God (vi. 1–viii. 1), the trumpetings of the seven angels (viii. 2–xi. 19), and the vials poured by seven angels into the air (xvi. 1–xvi. 21). These key passages agree that the Last Judgment will be heralded by an earthquake destroying the world. Moreover, Protestant scholiasts derived their theories of damnation and redemption from the Book of Revelation. With this gloss, for example, Heinrich Bullinger amplified the meaning of the seven seals:

> In the opening of the seven seales, there is severally accompted and reckned up, what and how great evils should come upon men from the which not somuch as the faithfull living in this world, should be free. Wares, slaughters, famine, pestilences are recyted, and such other lyke plagues: Agayne persecutions, seditions, and (a great deale worse then all these) ye seducyng, and distroying of men through corrupt doctryne. . . .
> . . . In the calamities, troubles, evils, and corruptions declared hitherto, the Aungel of God is brought in, who marketh the elect of God, in theyr foreheades: and all they through the goodnes and custodye of God, are saved from perdition.[1]

Doomsday will engulf all men, the righteous with the wicked; but the elect shall be saved by the Angel of God and brought to Heaven.

The process of Red Crosse's redemption can be easily traced in the Orgoglio episode. Through his relations with Duessa, the Knight has been guilty of carnality; and even worse, as Bullinger said, he has been seduced by "corrupt doctryne." When Orgoglio brings in Judgment Day, the Knight therefore finds himself helpless in the dungeon beneath the afflictions of his sins. During the battle with the Giant, however, we have been told that Red Crosse is blessed with "heavenly grace" (I. vii. 12. 3); he is one of the elect. So now that he has felt the wrathful hand of God, the Knight is ready for his spiritual rebirth. The Squire's magic horn which automatically opens the gates of Orgoglio's stronghold is a clear-cut analogue to the archangel's trumpet which will open graves on Doomsday. Prince Arthur then enters as the Angel of God who has come to mark the elect and save him from damnation. When the

1. *A hundred sermons vpon the Apocalipse* (2nd ed.; London, 1573), A6v–A7. See also Franciscus Junius, *The apocalyps . . . With a briefe and methodical exposition* (Cambridge, 1596), p. 76; and *The Bible* (London, 1603), with comm. of Junius on Revelation [STC 2190], fol. 113.

Prince finds Red Crosse, he is "a ruefull spectacle of death" (I. viii. 40. 9). Spenser graphically describes him as a long-dead corpse: "His sad dull eyes [are] deepe sunck in hollow pits"; he has "bare thin cheekes" and "rawbone armes"; "all his vitall powres/ [Are] Decayd, and all his flesh shronk up like withered flowers" (I. viii. 41. 1–9). Nevertheless, Arthur retrieves Red Crosse from the perdition of the dungeon (which had "no flore,/ But [was] all a deepe descent, as darke as hell" [I. viii. 39. 7–8]), and brings the Knight back to Una.

When we read Orgoglio as the earthquake heralding the Last Judgment, the significance of the Giant's falling upon Red Crosse becomes evident. The Knight has succumbed to fleshly temptation, for which he must be punished. The wages of sin are death, and so in Orgoglio's tomb-like dungeon the Knight undergoes a literal mortification of the flesh. There he lies helpless, until Divine grace lifts the soul and reunites it with Divinity. In Spenser's words, "This good Prince [Arthur] redeemd the *Redcrosse* knight from bands" (I. ix. 1. 9), where "redeemd" should be read with Christian connotations.

Now the introductory stanza of Canto VIII becomes intelligible as an explication of the allegory:

> Ay me, how many perils doe enfold
>> The righteous man, to make him daily fall?
>> Were not, that heavenly grace doth him uphold,
>> And stedfast truth acquite him out of all.
>> Her love is firme, her care continuall,
>> So oft as he through his owne foolish pride,
>> Or weaknesse is to sinfull bands made thrall.
>>> (I. viii. 1. 1–7)

Red Crosse, "the righteous man" before us, has been shown beset by temptation in the grove of Salmacis, which exemplifies the "many perils" which daily surround us; and he has "fallen," re-enacting the drama of Original Sin. He is not lost, however: Red Crosse is rescued from eternal damnation in the dungeon of Orgoglio by Prince Arthur, or "heavenly grace," and reunited with Una, or "stedfast truth." She is constant even though he is led into sin by "his owne foolish pride, / Or weaknesse." Orgogolio, of course, must be equated with the "sinful bands" which have enthralled the Knight, just as "bands" = Orgoglio in I. ix. 1. 9.

Prince Arthur properly interprets Red Crosse's capture as a warning to reform his sinful ways: Arthur knows that "th'only good, that growes of passed feare, / Is to be wise, and ware of like again" (I. viii. 44. 5–6). From this experience he also draws the conclusion "that blisse may not abide in state of mortall men" (I. viii. 44. 9), presumably because all men are touched with Original Sin. But Red Crosse is now eligible for bliss because he no longer exists as a "mortal" man. He has undergone the mortification of Orgoglio's dungeon. This episode is indeed the turning-point of Book I, because from his experience with Orgoglio the Knight emerges as a soul that has subordinated the flesh. In consequence, he is no longer tempted by sins induced by the senses. He still must battle the intellectual crime of hopelessness, though;[2] so in Canto IX the Knight encounters Despair, a sin of the soul, who almost succeeds in having him commit self-murder. But Una dramatically stops the suicide, and then leads Red Crosse to the House of Holiness, where after the proper instruction and repentance he is shown the New Jerusalem.

In this allegory which outlines the steps to salvation, Orgoglio is an earthquake serving to chastise Red Crosse for his sinfulness, epitomized by his idleness and lechery beside the magic spring. And simultaneously he serves a closely related strand of allegory by representing the destruction of the world on Judgment Day, when only the elect of God will be retrieved from perdition.

This is but one facet of the Giant's allegorical function, however; and when Red Crosse first lies vanquished and Duessa calls the Giant by name, "Orgoglio," a wholly new complex of associations is brought in. Spenser shifts gears, as it were, changing the emphasis from religio-moral to religio-political instruction. There is no discontinuity at this point, because the new phase grows smoothly out of what has gone before. The Revelation of St. John is still the basic text. Now, however, an exposé of Catholic corruption becomes the predominant occupation of the allegory. Protestants had read the Revelation not only as a guide-book along the narrow path to Heaven, but also as a prophecy of world-wide misery propagated by Catholic emperors and prelates. They were the Antichrist. The afflictions disclosed beneath the seven seals and contained in the seven vials of plague—the "wares, slaughters, famine, pestilences . . . persecutions, seditions and . . . distroying of men through corrupt doctryne"—all this suffering was directly attributable to the Pope and his viceroys. More precisely, Mary's marriage to Philip had oppressed England as tyrannously as Orgoglio had imprisoned Red Crosse. So at this point in his narrative Spenser speaks with the indignant voice of an anti-Catholic propagandist.

Now not only the meaning, but the imagery itself derives from the Book of Revelation. Duessa is clearly labelled as the Whore of Babylon, and she triumphantly rides upon the seven-headed Beast. At this point Orgoglio, as Duessa's consort, does become

2. This allegory is explicated in the introductory stanza of Canto X (I. x. 1. 1–5).

an embodiment of pride—the pride of Catholic despots, of the Pope, of Antichrist.[3]

In addition to leading the Christian toward the New Jerusalem, St. John's Apocalypse was also intended to encourage the faithful in their resistance to the pagan tyranny of Rome. It therefore had political implications. A blasphemous government, because of its efforts to eliminate godliness from the individual heart, was inevitably damned; in view of the promised Armageddon, it was just as inevitably doomed to destruction. And since the Apocalypse does not deal with what God in Christ has already done, but with what is yet to come to insure the establishment of His kingdom, each generation rightly interprets the Revelation according to its own milieu. To St. John writing in Patmos, Babylon was classical Rome in its hedonistic power, and the Revelation was a promise of its demolition. To Spenser and his contemporaries, Babylon was figured in the Church at Rome, and the Revelation was a promise of the overthrow of Catholic might. In our own times, the number of the Beast has been found to fit Hitler.

Certainly in Spenser's day it was common to correlate St. John's Revelation with current events. When Franciscus Junius' commentary on the apocalypse was printed in English, the titlepage advertised it as "a little treatise, applying the words of S. John to our last times that are full of spirituall and corporall troubles and divisions in Christendom." Sir John Napier in his *Plaine discouery of the whole Reuelation of S. Iohn* (1593) printed in parallel columns (1) the text of the Apocalypse, (2) a prose paraphrase of the text, and (3) historical information that supported his interpretation.

When viewed in the light of contemporary history, the victory of Prince Arthur over Orgoglio becomes the victory of pious Protestantism over corrupt Catholicism. The Giant is finally overthrown by the God-given brightness of Arthur's visage and armor (I. viii. 19. 1 ff.), the sight of which leaves Orgoglio powerless: "for he has read his end / In that bright shield" (I. viii. 21. 4–5). God in this way expresses His incontrovertible will. At this point Duessa throws aside her golden cup and mitre, and attempts to escape (I. viii. 25. 1–3)—symbolically announcing the defeat of the

3. Many details of Cantos VII and VIII identify Orgoglio with the Antichrist as conceived by Protestants. He dresses Duessa in the gold and purple of the Babylonian Whore (I. vii. 16. 3), he sets the triple crown of the hated Papacy upon her head (I. vii. 16. 4), and he provides her with the seven-headed scarlet-colored Beast (I. vii. 16. 6–9 ff.). The gorgeous trappings of his palace (I. viii. 35. 1–4) suggest the decadent splendor of Babylon and Rome. The floor is covered "with bloud of guiltlesse babes, and innocents trew" (I. viii. 35. 6); and the souls of martyrs are discovered beneath a sacrificial altar (I. viii. 36. 1–9). These evidently are the same victims of Antichrist revealed beneath the fifth seal in the Book of Revelation (vi. 9–11). See Hankins, "Spenser and Revelation of St. John," pp. 365, 378.

Babylonian Whore, the consort of Antichrist, the personification of the Church at Rome. She is brought to triumphant Prince Arthur (I. viii. 25. 9), and in the presence of all, her true vile nature is exposed (I. viii. 46. 1 ff.). As a perfect gloss on this action, we may note Bullinger's explanation of God's purpose in transmitting the Apocalypse:

> Especially he sheweth the judgement (that is to witte, yᵉ pun-
> ishement) of the harlot in purple, (I meane of the Pope and the
> beast) to be seene. First he brought foorth an honest & noble
> matrone, to weete, the very spouse of Christ. Now as it were by
> opposition he setteth against her a proude whore, that false new
> start up Romishe Church, who extolling her selfe braggeth more
> of her outwarde apparence then of inward furniture. And he
> affirmeth yᵗ she shall perish for her great offences.[4]

The intended contrast between Una and Duessa is equally obvious. One of Spenser's intentions was, therefore, a confident re-statement of the Apocalypse in his own terms. Orgoglio is the incarnation of Catholic pride and tyranny, which in the end will be overcome and completely destroyed by Prince Arthur, the allegorical complex representing English Protestantism. When Red Crosse succumbs to the power of Orgoglio, Spenser reveals the incapacity of the individual soul if it succumbs to the sensuality and materialism of popish Rome.

We must not forget, however, that Spenser's vehicle was Italian romance. He was not attempting to imitate the Bible nor a polemical pamphlet. And so perhaps by concentrating on Orgoglio's significance we have distorted the Giant's true character—that is, we have dealt with his meaning to the detriment of his actual appearance in the story. In fact, Spenser has done an admirable job of sublimating the serious argument so that on the level of simple narrative-plot Orgoglio is quite convincing in his role of giant in a fairy-tale. He carries his heavy allegorical burden without impairing the childlike wonder and excitement which attends the adventure.

When creating a fairy-tale villain such as Orgoglio, Spenser of course had a rich tradition to draw upon, a tradition which had flourished in folklore, classical mythology, and romance. Here properly we look for Orgoglio's literary antecedents. Spenser labelled him a "Giant," and this would place him under the onus of numerous myths about Giants and Titans related most prominently by Hesiod[5] and Ovid.[6] These malicious superhumans were the off-spring of Uranus (Heaven) and Ge (Earth), and they were most

---

4. *Hundred Sermons*, B1ᵛ.
5. *Theogony*, 133 ff., 183 ff., 617 ff.

6. *Metamorphoses*, tr. Golding, p. 24, lines 171 ff. [I. 151 ff.].

infamous for the battles which they had waged against the rightful gods.[7]

As C. W. Lemmi has noted,[8] Orgoglio shows a striking resemblance to the Giants described by Natalis Comes. Springing from the basest Element, Earth, the Giants were not accustomed to the virtues of moderation and justice. Instead, they were partial to sensuality and anger, and they dared attack even Jove himself. Natalis Comes asserts that the Giants were no different from rash men who, driven by a craze for wealth and power, flout all Divinity and attempt to take religion into their own hands. So in the Giants, Spenser happily found an embodiment for the Antichrist which would nonetheless accord with his mise en scène of Italian romance. Orgoglio, by being a Giant, is automatically endowed with the vices that Protestant England attributed to Catholic despots; and yet, on the non-allegorical level he convincingly performs in the romance as the wicked ogre who imprisons the hero.

* * *

Spenser has crowded much into this episode. He had looked into three areas of history—into classical mythology, the Book of Revelation, and recent politics—and in each he found the same archetypal pattern of evil predominating for awhile, but finally being overcome by Divine beneficence. Spenser thought (perhaps wishfully) that he had found an ethical norm, and this moral provides the theme for the Orgoglio episode.

Spenser presents his theme by progressively augmenting the initial statement that Orgoglio is an earthquake. He becomes a warning to repentance, the destruction of the world heralding the Last Judgment, physical death preparing for the resurrection, the Antichrist who brings misery to mankind, the embodiment of Catholic tyranny. In the Giants of mythology Spenser found a solvent to fuse all these constituent meanings into a single unified character, so that as the episode proceeds they function simultaneously and consistently. As Spenser controls the conditions, various properties of Orgoglio are activated at different moments —but the total Orgoglio is always present at least latently. Therefore when Prince Arthur releases Red Crosse from Orgoglio's dungeon, the complex of meaning must include the simple fairy-

---

7. Spenser makes numerous references to "the *Titans*, that whylome rebelled/ Gainst highest heauen" (V. i. 9. 6–7), and he presents many of his vicious and villainous characters in this form: Lucifera (I. iv. 8. 5 ff.), Disdaine (II. vii. 41. 6–8, VI. vii. 41. 1 ff.), Argante (III. vii. 47. 2 ff.) and Ollyphant (III. xi. 3. 3 ff.), Care (IV. v. 37. 1–2), Ge-ryoneo (V. x. 8. 6. ff.), Grantorto (V. xii. 15. 1–9), and Change (VII. vi. 2. 5 ff.).

8. "The Symbolism of the Classical Episodes in *The Faerie Queene*," *PQ*, VIII (1929), 275–276. See Natalis Comes, *Mythologiae* (Padua, 1616), p. 344 [VI. xxi].

tale rescue of the hero from the villain's den, the religio-moral salvation of the elect on Doomsday, and the religio-political deliverance of mankind from Spanish bigotry. To isolate historical or moral allegory is to decompose Spenser's compound.

KATHLEEN WILLIAMS

[Myth and Character in Books III and IV of *The Faerie Queene*] †

* * *

* * * The first two books have, from the nature of their subjects, a kind of precision which in general it is not too difficult to tabulate. Structure and meaning are interdependent, and illustrative or enriching mythological material can be seen as exact in its primary function, so far as that can be differentiated from the aura of indefinable association which necessarily accompanies and develops it. In the third and fourth books this is, I believe, still true; but the structure, unsupported by a traditional or logical series of temptations and a final victory over dragon or enchantress, is of a different kind, and mythology is used more pervasively and perhaps with more complication. Indeed myth here is itself, in a sense, an element of structure, in that the meanings are in part built up by connections between a few mythological situations and, especially, mythological or legendary personages, who appear in some cases as themselves and also as elements in the characters of Spenser's invention. Thus the characters are inter-related by their relation to a common centre, and the shaping of the material depends to a considerable degree upon this common reference.

In such an arrangement, the myths and legends have to work rather harder, and must often have more than one such central and definable function. One of their tasks approximates to that of the Ulysses story in Book Two. Marinell recalls very clearly certain episodes in the life of Achilles, while Artegall no less clearly recalls both Achilles and Hercules. But even here the use of mythology is less straightforward. As a type of the just hero, using his strength to overthrow injustice and inhumanity, Hercules is relevant to Artegall as was Ulysses to Guyon. But whereas in the second book other aspects of Ulysses's character are not relevant, and we are given no opportunity to consider them—his reputation for craftiness, or for the betrayal of his comrades—in Artegall's case we are led, by the

† From "Venus and Diana: Some Uses of Myth in *The Faerie Queene*," by Kathleen Williams, *ELH*, XXVIII (1961), 101–120. (The original footnotes have been slightly edited.)

choice of incidents, to remember that Hercules had other charac-
teristics as well as an unusual facility in destroying monsters. His
labours as a whole properly represented the exercise of justice, but
he was known also for his uncontrolled temper and for his readiness
to submit to the feminine tyranny of Omphale, or as Spenser has it
of Iole, who showed her power over the hero by making him sit at
her spinning wheel. Similarly the fierce and wrathful warrior
Achilles possessed a streak of feminine softness which in the cen-
turies after Homer had been more fully treated by the narrators of
new versions of the fall of Troy. The moralization of myth here
takes second place to the paradoxical elements in the figures of
classical story; different aspects are developed which establish mean-
ings through their relation either within one character or between
two characters. Spenser's attitude to the myths and legends is,
rightly, arbitrary; as Diodorus Siculus advises, he 'takes out of them
that which is to the purpose, and is in the form of a similitude.'
Arbitrary, but never, I think, unjustifiable. The use he makes of
them is always genuinely, if embryonically, present in the myth, is
usually traditional, and is pointed to in Spenser's text. And through
the deliberate playing of these 'similitudes' against one another, a
considerable complexity of meaning is established in perhaps the
most economical of all possible ways, that of contrast.

That Spenser makes much use of contrast within likeness has of
course long been recognized, and parallelism between two complete
books, Holiness and Temperance, has lately been rewardingly ex-
plored by Mr. A. C. Hamilton.[1] But in the books which I propose
to consider, the method is especially marked and works in a particu-
lar way. The figures of myth constitute a firm centre of reference,
and the paradoxical quality suggested by a character such as
Achilles can then be developed through similarities within differ-
ence, and differences within similarity, in a series of related persons.
The structure and the meaning which is inseparable from structure
here depend chiefly upon such relationships and not upon a progres-
sive narrative. The contrasts, moreover, are now arranged so as to
establish the meaning of characters rather than of events. Both, of
course, are still important; but whereas in the preceding books one
main figure has to encounter a number of different situations, here
several more or less main figures have to encounter rather similar
situations, and the most important point of differentiation is in their
varying reactions. In the first and second books, it is important to
know as exactly as we can what the cave of Mammon or the
dungeons of Orgoglio are. In the third and fourth, it is at least as
important to differentiate between the main figures themselves,

---

1. " 'Like Race to Runne': The Parallel
Structure of *The Faerie Queene*, Books I
and II," *PMLA*, LXXIII (1958), 327–
334. [*Editor*].

within the context suggested by their relation to Achilles, Diana, and the rest, as it is to differentiate between the hyaenas, giants, wild men or foul fosters who throng their paths. Certain places, indeed, are in themselves important, as are the houses of Malecasta and Busyrane, the Temple of Venus, or Isis Church, which though it occurs in the fifth book has relevance to preceding stories. But even these contribute to the system of parallel and contrast between persons: implicit in them as an unavoidable comparison in behavior.

The stories of the chief invented characters, therefore, have a certain rough similarity. Of Amoret, Florimell, and Britomart, each is separated from or searching for a particular knight, but in every case the behavior of the characters is different. Arthur, seeking Gloriana, is another parallel with a difference, and he here serves to bring out further aspects of the theme. Belphoebe, as twin sister of Amoret, is an important part of the whole system of comparison. But Britomart, being both a knight and a woman in search of a knight, is related by likeness and difference to most of the others. They are the faulty attempts at solving the problems set by the figures of myth: she is the complete success. In this sense Britomart dominates the third book as fully as Red Crosse and Guyon do theirs. In Book Four she takes part, and powerfully, in the action, but there is here no one dominant knight. Instead we have, appropriately to the theme, a dominant group of knights, Cambel and the three sons of Agape, set in symmetrical relationship and forming, in themselves, a unity; a unity which is emphasised by another tournament which stands over against theirs, the tournament for Florimell's girdle, a scene of pointless and chaotic strife. As Britomart presents the theme of Book Three in its aspect of success and of completeness, so does this close-knit group present the theme of Book Four. But the themes are two aspects of the same thing, and to speak of the books as one is usual and, I think, legitimate. Technically entitled the Legends of Chastity and of Friendship, they examine the same subject, love, with slightly differing emphasis; love is a kind of friendship, friendship a kind of love. For this reason, the troubled adventures of Amoret and Scudamour, Florimell and Marinell, Britomart and Artegall, are continued in the book Of Friendship and indeed beyond that book.

The series of relationships which builds up both books is repeated in little, and in much more schematic form, within the dominant group of Book Four. First, the three sons of Agape unfold, it has been said, the nature of Agape itself. The differences between the three warrior brothers are real, but complementary, and contribute to a common unity:

> Like three faire branches budding farre and wide,
> That from one roote deriv'd their vitall sap.
>
> (IV.ii.43)

When two brothers are killed by Cambel, the third, Triamond, possesses both their souls, and all is knit together by a marriage between the two pairs of brother and sister. Thus the group presents an example of the workings of strife and friendship, and of love as an aspect of friendship; an example of concord, schematically shown through the relations not only of two warriors but of the two warriors and the ladies who restrain and accord them, the wedding of force with gentleness, enmity with love. This is a dominant theme of both books; both might be called the Legend of Concord, for the idea of concord in its Renaissance signification underlies the whole structure of likeness and difference, of inadequacy overcome by the conjunction of opposites which, when alone, are useless or even harmful. The subjects of chastity and of friendship are both developed in relation to true and false *concordia*.

The most precise and particular statement of the nature of concord is that given in Scudamour's description of the Temple of Venus. Outside the Temple stand two young men,

> Both strongly arm'd, as fearing one another;
> Yet were they brethren both of halfe the blood,
> Begotten by two fathers of one mother,
> Though of contrarie natures each to other:
> The one of them hight Love, the other Hate.
>
> (IV.x.32)

Between them stands Concord, tempering them so well that she forces them to join hands, just as she keeps the world steady by holding 'with her blessed hands' air and fire, lands and waters. Concord involves opposition accorded, an equilibrium of opposing principles expressed, in another familiar version of the same conception, by the birth of Harmonia from the union of Mars and Venus. This Renaissance commonplace possessed both profundity and adaptability, and could be applied cosmically, politically, or socially; to friendships and loves, or to the completion of the individual human personality. By taking such a conception as the central idea of his books on love Spenser is able to include a very great deal, for relationships and cross-relationships like those suggested in the true concord of Cambel, Triamond, Canacee and Cambina, or in the imperfect concord of Venus and Diana, can be economically suggested. The idea of discords tempered was not only familiar to Spenser—it could not have failed to be that—but seems far more than an accepted commonplace. It is present elsewhere in *The*

Faerie Queene and elsewhere in the poems. In cosmic terms, *An Hymne of Love* tells how love at the creation of the world set the elements in order,

> tempering goodly well
> Their contrary dislikes with loved meanes,

while in the human terms of the *Amoretti* the warring lovers are bound at last in a league that no discord can spill. It is through divine or human love that concord was most readily presented.

So in the two central books of *The Faerie Queene* the discords, discords incompletely or falsely resolved, and discords properly tempered in concord, are displayed through the behavior of different characters in similar situations, the characters being elucidated by their common reference to figures of classical myth; and these figures are themselves capable of considerable manipulation, since their attributes or their stories had already been seen as giving them a certain ambiguity of meaning. The two on whom I propose to concentrate by way of example, Venus and Diana, make an appearance in the poem in their own persons. Together, they form one point of reference for several of the characters: the problem of relationship, of concord, which they pose is developed in a series of variations.

Venus and Diana make their very spirited joint personal appearance in the third book, and are closely connected there with their respective wards, Amoret and Belphoebe. They are introduced, indeed, by way of explaining the nature of Belphoebe and, later, of Amoret. Their encounter takes place because Venus, searching for her lost child Cupid, enlists Diana's aid in finding him, and their conversation on the subject strikes a rather curious note. It has been described as a débat through which the two unfriendly goddesses reach a reconciliation, but one might more accurately term it a rather suspect alliance in which the two opposing principles are ready surreptitiously to borrow each others' functions, a false imitation of concord. Each is spiteful and jealous, but it is Venus who comes off best in the encounter with her suggestion that Diana's train of nymphs may not be quite what it seems. Here, she hints, is precisely the place for her to start looking for Cupid. The nymphs may well be hiding him; he may even now be present, disguised as one of them. The quarrel is smoothed over, but the suggestion that a hidden relationship exists between Diana's followers and Cupid is firmly established. It emerges into the next stage of the story, where the goddesses, searching for Cupid, instead find and adopt the twin children born without inherited sin,

> Pure and unspotted from all loathly crime,
> That is ingenerate in fleshly slime.   (III.vi.3)

Why these two, who never know each other during the course of the existing poem, are presented as twin sisters, has often been considered. One modern scholar dismisses the relationship as a caprice on Spenser's part, but more usually it is suggested that their virtues are of equal value, or are complementary. It is also possible that the sisters, offspring of a single birth, are complementary in the sense that they should not have been parted, and that their relationship underlines, or is underlined by, that of Venus and Diana, who stand opposed to each other and yet have a devious and hidden kind of kinship.

The kinship had been hinted at often enough, in art and in literature, and it could have various meanings, serious or frivolous, sound or suspect, according as emphasis was placed. It survived vigorously until the early eighteenth century, when that understanding Spenserian Matthew Prior used it in his *Cloe Hunting,* and it occurs in a stanza, translated from Marot, which was printed following the *Amoretti*:

> As Diane hunted on a day,
> She chaunst to come where Cupid lay,
>   his quiver by his head:
> One of his shafts she stole away,
> And one of hers did close convay,
>   into the others stead:
>   With that love wounded my loves hart,
>   but Diane beasts with Cupids dart.

Cupid shoots with the arrows of Diana, Diana with the arrows of Cupid; a kind of complicated interchange is set up in which chastity becomes a weapon of love, or uses love as a weapon. That arrows were used by both Cupid and Diana made an appropriate hinge on which such relationships could turn. And Diana's ward Belphoebe the huntress grows up to wound Timias

> Through an unwary dart, which did rebound
> From her faire eyes and gracious countenance
> (III.v.42)

even as she tries to cure the wound he has already received from the cruel shaft of the foster. Indeed there is in the remote and radiant figure of Belphoebe something of the strangeness of the Venus/Diana exchanges. In the course of her pursuit of a wounded beast she is led straight to the wounded Timias, one quarry replacing another. So in Book Two, where she first and briefly appears, the same pursuit leads her to Trompart and the hidden Braggadocchio, whom she almost shoots in mistake for her rightful quarry, the wounded hind.

In that earlier appearance Belphoebe is, of course, modelled on the appearance of Venus, in the guise of a huntress nymph, to Aeneas in Virgil's first book. Spenser's is an intricately beautiful passage in which both the Venus aspect and the Diana aspect suggested by the Virgilian parallel are emphasized and enriched. The long description is full of the sensuous imagery of the Canticles, while Belphoebe's clothes are an elaborately decorative and gorgeous version of the simple robe and buskin of the huntress. The analogy with Venus/Diana here is usually seen as relating to the allegorical meanings which were attributed to Virgil's Venus by neoplatonic commentators, Venus Urania manifesting herself in active life, 'the beauty of moral ideals.' Some such meaning is certainly applicable to the Belphoebe of Book Two, and indeed remains applicable to her appearance in Book Three, for throughout there is attached to her a splendour, a suggestion of the rarefied and ideal. But in the third book, where she takes a much greater part in the action, this does not quite account for her. She is here not only the embodiment of an ideal, momentarily revealed; she is rather a person seen as, and behaving as, an ideal. Her remote and not quite human aspiration is seen in relation to another theme, her innocence is considered in its effects upon ordinary fallen humanity. When Timias wakes from his faint to see her, we are referred back to Book Two by his speech,

> Angell, or Goddesse do I call thee right?
> What service may I do unto thee meete,
>
> (III.v.35)

which echoes the speech of Trompart and, with differences, that of Aeneas before him. We are still to remember Belphoebe as Venus/Diana, and still to appreciate her fineness. But the reminder is straightway followed, here, by the débat of the two goddesses, suggesting that in this book a further aspect of the Venus/Diana connection is to be explored, though without negating the first. Belphoebe acts out her story with Timias, and in doing so she shows her self from another point of view, that of human relationships. She accepts the love of Timias as the adoration due to her, and as requiring no return. As Diana's huntress, she can be loved, but the love must be manifested as worship; yet it is not clearly distinguished from Timias's tenderness to the wounded Amoret, her unknown complement and twin, which is regarded as a breach of faith. 'Is this the faith, she said, and said no more.' And Timias is returned to her grace through the agency of a dove, bird of Venus as well as of peace, with her present to him tied around its neck, a jewel like a bleeding heart. But in or out of favour the situation is at no point presented as a true good for Timias, for by it he is not inspired to greatness but is kept from his proper task, the quest, as Arthur's squire, for glory. Refusing to make himself known to Arthur, who is wasting time in looking for him, he lives uselessly and ignobly, 'all mindlesse of his owne deare Lord.' His devotion, it seems, should be to something else.

Spenser is here showing us, I think, not the result of worship of an ideal, but the result of worship of the lady *as* an ideal, and he regards it with sympathy and with scepticism. What Belphoebe demands, and Timias attempts, is shown in action as a very uneasy thing. Her excellence remains, but it is too simple and one-sided an excellence for a complicated world. Genuine in itself, it yet produces a confusion of effects it never intends, when Belphoebe emerges from her own isolated 'earthly paradise' in the midst of the forest of the passions. In the real world, the arrows of Diana can have an effect hard to be distinguished from that of the arrows of Cupid; the chase of honor can turn, however unintentionally, into the chase of love. Belphoebe, set apart by her innocent birth and by Diana's training, and at home in her own paradise, seems never fully to comprehend the people she meets; her behavior is not quite adapted to a fallen and a complex state. The non-human nobleness which is a tribute to a queen operates a little differently in the moral world of the poem as a whole.

Like Belphoebe, Amoret is brought up in a highly specialized environment, and again like her sister she demonstrates the problems raised, in the real world, by the simplifications which are in place in an earthly paradise. But where Belphoebe is martial and fiercely aspiring, Amoret is wholly submissive, for she is reared by Venus in 'true feminitee,' 'In all the lore of love, and goodly womanhead.' As a child she is brought up in the Garden of Adonis, for which in a sense her innocent birth fits her. The Garden, one knows, is a complicated place, but so far as it concerns Amoret it is simple enough, Venus's joyous earthly paradise,

> the first seminarie
> Of all things, that are borne to live and die,
> According to their kindes. (III.vi.30)

There

> of their owne accord
> All things, as they created were, doe grow,
> And yet remember well the mightie word,
> Which first was spoken by th'Almightie lord,
> That bad them to increase and multiply. (vi.34)

As a place of natural generation, it is like the Golden Age—'There is continuall spring, and harvest there / Continuall'—or more precisely the paradisal images suggest that it is a kind of Eden, where sensuality is spontaneous, frank, and blameless as in the prelapsarian garden. An etymological connection was of course made.

The Garden is walled, protected, but threatened: time the destroyer is already within the wall, Adonis's boar is imprisoned but alive. Here as in Eden is potential disaster, and the innocent joy of the Garden is as precarious as Amoret's is soon seen to be. It exists only by the rigorous exclusion of whatever may bring harshness and pain. The Cupid who is allowed to enter is not the annoying child or the hostile tyrant, but the benevolent husband of Psyche and father of Pleasure. He must lay his sad darts aside and leave the 'spoiles and cruelty' with which he has ransacked the 'world,' the real and painful and fallen world, and here Psyche, her troubles over, brings up Amoret with the child Pleasure. In this aspect, the Garden is essentially the same as Love's heaven or paradise in *An Hymne of Love,* the dream of the miserable lover in the real world, a place free from 'the gnawing envie, the hart-fretting feare.' This paradise, like the Garden, is the home of Pleasure, and she dwells there without pain and without blame. A similar distance from painful reality is suggested in the reference to the Garden of Adonis in Book Two, where it occurs as the equivalent of Eden in the Elfin History, the place where the first Elfe, newly created by Prometheus, finds the first Fay. Again the parallel is with innocence, with love and indeed with life itself as natural, simple, and protected, lacking all fierceness or self-assertion. To attain concord, here, is made unnecessary, for the discord which it should surmount is not allowed to intrude. Instead of Mars, Adonis, an Adonis who hunts no longer; and even Cupid's weapons must be left outside the walls.

From this protected happiness Amoret has to go into the 'world' of 'spoiles and cruelty,' of strife and inherited sin, where even love is also war; into Venus's other domain, denoted by her Temple, guarded as it is by Hate and Love, their hands forcibly linked by Concord. In the 'world,' the meaning of Amoret's mythological background as Venus's ward is developed and defined by its relation to the tradition of courtly love. This is itself used metaphorically to express a certain attitude to human relationships which has its classical and its modern, as well as its medieval, forms, and which owes its enduring power to its expression (though its distorted expression) of a truth: that in personal relationships, and in love as the most intense and so most representative of such relationships, there is always an element of hostility. The truth as realistically and maturely interpreted can be found in the *Amoretti,* which are built up partly through variations on this theme. The lady is warrior, tyrant, even traitor, the lover is huntsman, and both fear the prison of love, the loss of liberty to the other. Yet at the close of the sequence the hostility is resolved, the prisoned birds sing, the spider and the bee live in eternal peace. But there are other handlings of the theme in which love stops eternally short of concord, in which the warfare and the chase are perpetual and mutual, in which each feels and inflicts pain, and endless revenge is disguised as affection. And of course the distortion is itself equally true to human life, and is portrayed by Spenser with equal insight.

It is this which the submissive and feminine Amoret, reared in a place from which all hostility is barred, and wholly lacking in the aggressive self-reliance which characterizes her huntress sister, has now to face. All assertion of self she sees as menacing and terrible, and what to Scudamour is a mere convention of behavior becomes to her an obsessive reality. Scudamour fights twenty knights, enters the Temple of Venus, and terrifies Amoret's guardians with his shield, on which, since he is 'Cupid's man,' the sincere but conventional courtly lover, is emblazoned the cruel Cupid excluded from the Garden of Adonis, 'Cupid with his killing bow / And cruell shafts.' He then leads out the protesting Amoret as the prize of his prowess, while the statue of Venus, with the doubtful quality she possesses in the human world, laughs her approval of the desecration of her Temple. Cupid may be shut out of the Temple, replaced by his small and harmless brothers; yet Scudamour his representative is, as he himself suggests, drawn in to that same Temple by its appurtenances, the danger, the parade of modesty, the white-robed virgin priestesses, the exclusive femininity. Venus, the great natural creative power of the universe, is ready to depend for the fulfillment of her purpose in the human world upon hostility, the weapons of Diana and the spoils of Cupid, upon exclusiveness set as a snare for violence. Human happiness, after all, is no part of her concern.

This, at least, is how Amoret comes to see her situation, when she has been taken from the Temple as Eurydice was taken from the underworld. The comparison is Scudamour's, proud of an enterprise as dangerous as that of Orpheus; the irony is Spenser's, for as Eurydice was lost again from the threshold of the living world, so is Amoret, on the day of her wedding, lost to the deathlike enchantments of Busyrane, and imprisoned in her own obsession. The shadowy Maske of Cupid which conveys her away contains some of the conventional denizens of the Temple of Venus and of the courtly tradition, Danger, and Doubt; but now their traditional function is changed, and from the lady's devices against the lover they have become the torturers of the lady herself. Of them there are as many

> as there be phantasies
> In wavering wemens wit, that none can tell,
> Of paines in love, or punishments in hell.
>
> (III.xii.26)

Busyrane, who sacrifices Amoret to the destructive Cupid, is presumably named from Busiris, who made human sacrifices to his own god in Egypt. He appears in the mythological commentators and in Diodorus and Apollodorus, but most relevantly in the *Ars Amatoria*,[2] where he is directly related to the Ovidian (and in part courtly) conception of love as hostility and deceit, a perpetual strife in which *concordia* is seen as no more than the momentary defeat of one cruelty by another. Ovid's Busiris is an illustration of the theme that love is the result of deceit, which should be avenged by deceit. 'Let them fall into the snares they have set.' The victim is equally the hunter and should, as victim, suffer, so Amoret's Doubt and Danger are turned in more terrible form against her. Busyrane's house is decorated everywhere with the predatory and treacherous loves of the gods: gods as bulls or serpents, love which kills as Semele and Daphne were killed.

> Yet was thy love her death, and her death was thy smart.
>
> (III. xi. 36)

Everywhere is portrayed the mutual horror of a situation in which each punishes and is punished, 'all Cupids warres they did repeate.' Amoret is freed by Britomart, through whom she unthinks her obsession as Busyrane is made to unread his spells, but she is still not free from the cause of the obsession, the fear of assertion as necessarily destructive. Still 'His will she feard.' Her lack is explained or typified in her past history, and she will not be free until her own soft submissiveness is joined with its opposing principle, gentleness with self-assertive 'will' or, in one of Spenser's figures in Book Four, the dove with the falcon. The incompleteness and consequent distortion suggested by the separation of the sisters must be overcome, as it is, in the first version of the poem, in the union of Amoret and Scudamour. The hermaphrodite image there used is a symbol of marriage, but of marriage as itself a symbol of the necessary concord of opposites on which the world depends, and individual human welfare also.

In the second version of the poem, this union is displayed not in Amoret's story but in Britomart's. Britomart stands between the separated sisters as an example of completed and integrated human nature, 'aimable grace and manly terror' both, the great champion who can help knights and ladies alike because in her are united the masculine and the feminine, the self-sufficient and the dependent, passion and chastity. In her Venus and Diana, Venus and Mars, are in true and unsurreptitious relation. She is accepted on her own terms as knight and as lady, neither potential destroyer nor potential victim; and, herself an example of concord, she achieves a further concord in her connection with Artegall.

How Britomart has become the invincible knight, strong because loving, loving because strong, we are shown after her first appear-

2. Cf. the discussion of the House of Busyrane by Thomas P. Roche, Jr., in this edition [*Editor*].

ance in the poem, in the account of her love for Artegall. She has seen him first, and uncomprehendingly, in the magic mirror, and her immediate response has something of Amoret's confused horror. She hints of it to her old nurse Glauce as if it were a brutal and destructive visitation, love for a shadow, unnatural and leading to death. The passage is based on the Virgilian *Ciris*, but it echoes also the talk of Ovid's Myrrha and her nurse in the *Metamorphoses*, and it is related to Scylla, Biblis, Pasiphae, and the whole Ovidian context of perversity and pain. But through the commonsense wisdom represented by Glauce, and through the sense of personal responsibility represented by Merlin, Britomart learns that human affections are guided by divine purpose, that her eyes were led to the mirror by a higher power than Venus, and that her vision of Artegall will lead to the fulfilling of heavenly destiny for centuries to come. The looking-glass has shown her not a shadow, an illusion, but a fuller truth than she could otherwise see, for it is a little image of the world, a glass globe

> Like to the world it selfe, and seem'd a world of glas.
> (III.ii.19)

Its virtue is to 'shew in perfect sight, / What ever thing was in the world contaynd,' 'What ever foe had wrought, a frend had faynd.' For Britomart love is a mirror of truth, a means to fulfillment through the concord of necessary opposites in herself, in her union with Artegall, and in the history of her race. For Merlin's account of the future history of Britain, where she and Artegall and their descendants are to rule, is more than a compliment worked in for the benefit of Elizabeth Tudor. It serves to convince Britomart that no personal situation is merely personal, but may have results that go far beyond ourselves. For her love becomes an instrument of divine providence, and she accepts completely the responsibility of the fully human being for its fellows. Her part, Merlin tells her, is to fit herself to cooperate actively with a creative and purposeful destiny:

> Therefore submit thy wayes unto his will,
> And do by all dew meanes thy destiny fulfill.
> (III.iii.24)

Merlin's prophecy is throughout in terms of the divine, and just, will, which deals with the Britons as did Jehovah with the Hebrews, supporting, checking, punishing; and in this process the union of Artegall with Britomart, of impulsive force with restraining wisdom, of justice with equity, is to play an essential part, culminating in the reconciliation of Briton and Saxon under the house of Tudor, mingling the blood and the attributes of each. In Britomart's story, the theme of concord is taken beyond the realm of the personal; what the others cannot attain is for her only a first step. Throughout, her sense of destiny and responsibility keeps her on her quest where the others, even Arthur, can be distracted, and always what is stressed is her constancy, courage, and perfect balance of qualities. She is, in the phrase of the moralizers of the myths, the true Venus/Diana, or Venus armata, as even her name may suggest: Britomartis, the nymph whose apotheosis as the moon-goddess Diana Dictynna is told in the *Ciris*. Later, in the prophetic dream of Book Five, Britomart becomes Isis the Queen, the power in whom, as Plutarch and Apuleius would show, all the goddesses are made one, Cybele, Minerva, Venus, Diana Dictynna. In the union of Isis with Osiris is the true justice which sustains the universe.

* * *

Readings of The House of Busyrane
(*The Faerie Queene,* III. xi–xii)

F. M. PADELFORD

[The Spiritual Values of Matrimony]†

* * *

The allegory of Amoret is handled with such subtlety that it is likely to be unnoticed. What the poet aims to imply is that her susceptibility to the wiles of Busyrane—lust—was the natural result of her training for, as opposed to Britomart who early devoted herself to a life of worthy activity, Amoret was reared in the garden of Adonis, under the tutelage of Psyche who tendered her no less carefully than her own daughter Pleasure, and lessoned her in all the lore of love. Thus reared in the midst of luxury and ease and social largesse, she was not prepared—any more than was Scuda-more, her lover—to place the spiritual values of matrimony upper-most. Rather, she could not refrain from surrendering herself to physical delight when once it enjoyed the conventional sanction of marriage. Amoret, and not the heroine of the book, is the character who is chosen for discipline in chastity. Seemingly Spenser later came to feel that he had not made the office of this character in the allegory sufficiently clear, for in a later book he was at pains to introduce the story of the separation of Scudamore and Amoret, and to relate how at the marriage feast, the evil enchanter stole the

† From "The Allegory of Chastity in *The Faerie Queene*," by F. M. Padelford, *SP*, XXI (1924), 367–381.

bride away. Only such chastity as was exemplified in Britomart, who kept all of the claims of life in equipoise, could accomplish the true marriage of souls for these charming lovers.

* * *

C. S. LEWIS

[Chastity Vs. Courtly Love]†

* * *

* * * To find the real foe of Chastity, the real portrait of false love, we must turn to Malecasta and Busirane. The moment we do so, we find that Malecasta and Busirane are nothing else than the main subject of this study—Courtly Love; and that Courtly Love is in Spenser's view the chief opponent of Chastity. But Chastity for him means Britomart, married love. The story he tells is therefore part of my story: the final struggle between the romance of marriage and the romance of adultery.

Malecasta lives in Castle Joyeous amid the 'courteous and comely glee' of gracious ladies and gentle knights.[1] Somebody must be paying for it all, but one cannot find out who. The Venus in her tapestries entices Adonis 'as well that art she knew': we are back in the world of the Vekke[2] and the commandments of Love. In the rooms of the castle there is 'dauncing and reveling both day and night', and 'Cupid still emongst them kindles lustfull fyres'. The six knights with whom Britomart contends at its gate (Gardante, Parlante, and the rest) might have stepped straight out of the *Roman de la Rose*, and in the very next stanza the simile of the rose itself occurs. The place is dangerous to spirits who would have gone through the Bower of Bliss without noticing its existence. Britomart gets a flesh wound there, and Holiness himself is glad to be helped in his fight against Malecasta's champions by Britomart; by which the honest poet intends, no doubt, to let us know that even a religious man need not disdain the support which a happy marriage will give him against fashionable gallantry. For Britomart is married love.

Malecasta clearly represents the dangerous attractions of courtly love—the attractions that drew a Surrey or a Sidney. Hers is the face that it shows to us at first. But the House of Busirane is the

† From *The Allegory of Love*, by C. S. Lewis (New York, 1958), Chapter VII. (The original footnotes have been slightly edited.)
1. *F.Q.* III.i.31.

2. The name (in the Middle English version) of a character in the French allegorical love poem *Le Roman de la Rose* [*Editor*].

bitter ending of it. In these vast, silent rooms, dazzling with snake-like gold, and endlessly pictured with 'Cupid's warres and cruell battailes', scrawled over with 'a thousand monstrous formes' of false love, where Britomart awaits her hidden enemy for a day and a night, shut in, entombed, cut off from the dawn which comes outside 'calling men to their daily exercize', Spenser has painted for us an unforgettable picture not of lust but of love—love as understood by the traditional French novel or by Guillaume de Lorris[3]— in all its heartbreaking glitter, its sterility, its suffocating monotony. And when at last the ominous door opens and the Mask of Cupid comes out, what is this but a picture of the deep human suffering which underlies such loves?

> Unquiet care and fond Unthriftyhead;
> Lewd Losse of Time, and Sorrow seeming dead,
> Inconstant Chaunge, and false Disloyalty;
> Consuming Riotise, and guilty Dread
> Of heavenly vengeaunce: faint Infirmity;
> Vile Poverty; and, lastly, Death with infamy.[4]

The Mask, in fact, embodies all the sorrows of Isoud among the lepers, and Launcelot mad in the woods, of Guinevere at the stake or Guinevere made nun and penitent, of Troilus waiting on the wall, of Petrarch writing *vergogna è 'l frutto*[5] and Sidney rejecting the love that reaches but to dust; or of Donne writing his fierce poems *from* the house of Busirane soon after Spenser had written *of* it. When Britomart rescues Amoret from this place of death she is ending some five centuries of human experience, predominantly painful. The only thing Spenser does not know is that Britomart is the daughter of Busirane—that his ideal of married love grew out of courtly love.

Who, then, is Amoret? She is the twin sister of Belphoebe and both were begotten by the Sun,

> pure and unspotted from all loathly crime
> That is ingenerate in fleshly slime,[6]

the meaning of which is best understood by comparison with Spenser's sonnet,

> More then most faire, full of the living fire,
> Kindled above unto the maker neare.[7]

And we know that the Sun is an image of the Good for Plato,[8] and therefore of God for Spenser. The first important event in the life of

3. Author (d. 1235) of the first part of *Le Roman de la Rose* [*Editor*].
4. *F.Q.* III.xii.25.
5. "The fruit [of my frenzied love] is shame"; Petrarch, *Rima, ed. cit.,* 3 [*Editor*].

6. *F.Q.* III.vi.3.
7. *Amoretti*, viii.
8. *Republic*, 507 d. et seq.

these twins was their adoption by Venus and Diana: Diana the goddess of virginity, and Venus from whose house 'all the world derives the glorious features of beautie'.[9] Now the circumstances which led up to this adoption are related in one of the most me- dieval passages in the whole *Faerie Queene*—a *débat* between Venus and Diana; but this *débat* has two remarkable features. In the first place, the Venus who takes part in it is a Venus severed from Cupid, and Cupid, as we have already seen, is associated with courtly love. I say 'associated' because we are dealing with what was merely a feeling in Spenser's mind, not a piece of intellectual and historical knowledge, as it is to us. There is therefore no consistent and conscious identification of Cupid with courtly love, but Cupid tends to appear in one kind of context and to be absent from another kind. And when he does appear in contexts approved by our domestic poet, he usually appears with some kind of reserva- tion. He is allowed into the Garden of Adonis on condition of his 'laying his sad dartes asyde': in the Temple of Venus it is only his younger brothers who flutter round the neck of the goddess. We are therefore fully justified in stressing the fact that Venus finds Amoret only because she has lost Cupid, and finally adopts Amoret *instead of* Cupid. The other important novelty is that this *débat* ends with a reconciliation; Spenser is claiming to have settled the old quarrel between Venus and Diana, and that after a singularly frank state- ment of the claims of each. And when the two goddesses have agreed, their young wards

> twixt them two did share
> The heritage of all celestiall grace;
> That all the rest it seemd they robbed bare,

and one of them, Amoret, became

> th'ensample of true love alone
> And Lodestarre of all chaste affection.

She was taken by Venus to be reared in the Garden of Adonis, guarded by Genius the lord of generation, among happy lovers and flowers (the two are here indistinguishable) whose fecundity never ceases to obey the Divine Command. This was her nursery: her school or university was the Temple of Venus. This is a region neither purely natural, like the Garden, nor artificial in the bad sense, like the Bower of Bliss: a region where,

> all that nature did omit,
> Art, playing second natures part, supplyed it.[1]

Here Amoret no longer grows like a plant, but is committed to the

---

care of Womanhood; the innocent sensuousness of the garden is replaced by 'sober Modestie', 'comely Curtesie',

> Soft Silence and submisse Obedience,

which are gifts of God and protect His saints 'against their foes offence'. Indeed the whole island is strongly protected, partly by Nature, and partly by such immemorial champions of maidenhead in the Rose tradition, as Doubt, Delay, and Daunger. But when the lover comes he defeats all these and plucks Amoret from her place among the modest virtues. The struggle in his own mind before he does so, his sense of 'Beauty too rich for use, for earth too dear', is a beautiful gift made by the humilities of medieval love poetry to Spenser at the very moment of his victory over the medieval tradition:

> my hart gan throb
> And wade in doubt what best were to be donne;
> For sacrilege me seem'd the Church to rob,
> And folly seem'd to leave the thing undonne.

Amoret, however, cannot withdraw her hand, and the conclusion of the adventure may be given in the words of the poet who has studied most deeply this part of *The Faerie Queene*:

> she what was Honour knew,
> And with obsequious Majestie approv'd
> My pleaded reason.[2]

The natural conclusion is marriage, but Busirane for centuries has stood in the way. That is why it is from the marriage feast that Busirane carries Amoret away, to pine for an indefinite period in his tomblike house. When once Britomart has rescued her thence, the two lovers become one flesh—for that is the meaning of the daring simile of the Hermaphrodite in the original conclusion of Book III. But even after this, Amoret is in danger if she strays from Britomart's side; she will then fall into a world of wild beasts where she has no comfort or guide, and may even become the victim of monsters who live on the 'spoile of women'.[3]

* * *

---

2. *Paradise Lost*, VIII. 508–510 [*Editor*].   3. *F.Q.* IV. vii. 2, 12.

THOMAS P. ROCHE, JR.

[Love, Lust, and Sexuality]†

* * *

Busyrane is trying to transfer Amoret's love for Scudamour to himself by charms, but the conventional romance structure of this episode should not blind us to its real meaning. He is literally trying to kill Amoret. His love is not sexual but destructive—destructive of the will to love within Amoret herself. Amoret is afraid of the physical surrender which her marriage to Scudamour must entail. The wedding mask crystallizes this fear, and she turns from a joyful acceptance to a cold rejection of the claims of the physical. This is why Busyrane is the great enemy to chastity; he represents a negative force of which chastity is the positive ideal. He represents the negation of chastity, and this for Spenser did not mean lust.

Although Spenser gives no iconographical details to identify his Busyrane, we may learn much from the etymology of his name. Warton suggested long ago that Busyrane is derived from Busiris, "The king of Egypt, famous for his cruelty and inhospitality."[1] Warton, I believe, is correct. The history of Busiris is too complicated to relate. It must suffice to say that Busiris originally was the location of the chief tomb of Osiris, and that in later writers Busiris became the king of the place where Osiris was killed. The complicated traditions agree that Busiris is a location or an agent of sacrificial destruction and is associated with the sacrifice of Osiris.[2] The connection may seem remote, but we must recall the identification of Britomart and Arthegall with Isis and Osiris in Book V and remember that Britomart triumphs over Busyrane before she encounters Arthegall. Even more important is Ovid's retelling of the Busiris legend in the first book of the *Ars Amatoria*. This relates Busiris to the qualities I have been trying to establish as the traits of Busyrane:

"If you are wise, cheat women only, and avoid trouble; keep faith save for this one deceitfulness. Deceive the deceivers; they are mostly an unrighteous sort; let them fall into the snare which they

† From *The Kindly Flame: A Study of the Third and Fourth Books of Spenser's "Faerie Queene,"* by Thomas Roche, Jr. (Princeton, N.J., 1964), Chapter I.

1. *Var.*, 3.287.
2. See Sir Ernest A. T. Wallis Budge, *Osiris and the Egyptian Resurrection*, 2 vols., London, 1911. Ancient writers who deal with this story include Plutarch, Diodorus Siculus, Apollodorus, Isocrates, Herodotus, and Ovid. See also Heywood's dumbshow in *The Brazen Age, Dramatic Works of Thomas Heywood*, ed. John Pearson, 6 vols., London, 1874, vol. 3, p. 183; Ralegh, *The History of the World*, London, 1614, sig. S2ᵛ; *Paradise Lost*, 1. 307, and Isabel Rathborne, *The Meaning of Spenser's Fairyland*, pp. 86–90. Professor Rosemond Tuve has kindly pointed out to me the significant appearance of Busiris in Christine de Pisan, *The Epistle of Othea to Hector*, ed. James D. Gordon, Philadelphia, 1942, pp. 68–69.

have laid. Egypt is said to have lacked the rains that bless its fields, and to have been parched for nine years, when Thrasius approached Busiris, and showed that Jove could be propitiated by the outpoured blood of a stranger. To him said Busiris, 'Thou shalt be Jove's first victim, and as a stranger give water unto Egypt.' Phalaris too roasted in his fierce bull the limbs of Perillus, its maker first made trial of his ill-omened work. Both were just; for there is no juster law than that contrivers of death should perish by their own contrivances. Therefore, that perjuries may rightly cheat the perjured, let the woman feel the smart of a wound she first inflicted."[3]

Ovid's ironic advice to his hypothetical lover throws a new light on the Busiris legend and brings us back to Warton's suggested etymology. These lines betray an attitude toward love and women; it is the same attitude that underlies the conceit of love as war, and it is of particular interest that the well-known Ovidian treatise should link this attitude with the figure of Busiris. Here, it would appear, is the nexus between the conventional figure of Busiris and Spenser's Busyrane; here is the deceit, the sadism, and the destruction, which we associate with Amoret's plight.

But there are further possibilities in Busyrane's name, possibilities that suggest the sixteenth century usage of the word *abuse* as imposture, ill-usage, delusion. For example, Sidney's sentence from the *Arcadia* quoted in the OED is entirely appropriate: "Was it not enough for him to have deceived me, and through the deceit abused me, and after the abuse forsaken me?" or we might use the obsolete form *abusion*, which the OED defines as "perversion of the truth, deceit, deception, imposture," giving as an example Spenser's lines, "Foolish delights and fond Abusions, Which do that sence besiege with fond illusions." All of these meanings are implicit in the etymology of Busyrane—the illusion, the deceit, the sadism, the destruction.

What then does this make of Busyrane? Is he not the abuse of marriage just as his house is the objectification of Amoret's fears of marriage? He is the abuse of marriage because his mask of Cupid presents an image of marriage as a sacrifice just as Busiris was a place of sacrifice. He is an abuse of marriage because the mind he possesses cannot distinguish between the act of marriage and adulterous love. He is an abuse of marriage because the falsity of his view of love can lead only to lust or death. His power is derived from the *abusion* of the mind in distorting the image of love. The meaning he presents to the wedding guests is trivial, at the most, lust; the meaning he presents to Amoret is the sacrifice of personal integrity. Lust is the least complex of his perversions; he is the image of love distorted in the mind, distorted by lascivious anticipa-

3. Ovid, *Ars Amatoria*, Book I. 643–658.

tion or horrified withdrawal. He becomes the denial of the unity of body and soul in true love. And in all these respects he is the chief adversary of Britomart as the knight of chastity. Britomart's response to the mask and to Busyrane is that of the intelligent moral reader, who can detect the difference between true and false love.

This interpretation of Busyrane and his power over Amoret explains why Scudamour cannot rescue her. Amoret's fears are based on moral and physical grounds. Scudamour can dispel neither. Unwillingly he is the cause of these fears, and any attempt on his part to dispel them would be self-defeating since it would mean her eventual surrender, the basis of her fears. Britomart, on the other hand, can attack these fears on both the moral and physical grounds. As a woman she understands Amoret's attitude toward the physical side of love, and as the exemplar of chastity she is able to make the moral distinction between marriage and adulterous love. Her entry through the wall of flame gives her an intimate knowledge of the House of Busyrane, and her understanding finally allows her to release Amoret from her fears.

* * *

A. KENT HIEATT

[Sexual Adventurism] †

* * *

Most centrally * * * this Masque of Cupid as it relates to Amoret marshals the temptations and horrors of the life of loose sexual commitments, of frequent passion, and of angling for domination of a lover and for deception of a husband or other lovers, as these activities would be seen by a chaste woman, fully committed to one man but tortured by his jealous and insistent dominance over her, as over a sexual prize—a woman, that is, with whom he should have gently and gradually created an entirely different kind of relationship. Such love * * * is really hate, close to the state of the Knight's Tale's Cupid, 'out of alle charitee'. The adulterous temptations begin for Amoret in the fancy and the artificially stoked desire of a life of ease and leisure. They progress through the doubt, dangers, and fearful delights of secret assignations and amours. Such love dangles hopes, but less often satisfactions, before its victims. All of these concepts, personified, pass before us in turn in the Masque of Cupid. Dissemblance and Suspect, Grief and Fury,

† From *Chaucer Spenser Milton: Mythopoeic Continuities and Transformations*, by A. Kent Hieatt (Montreal and London, 1975), Chapter VIII.

Displeasure and Pleasure, attend on an unfaithful beloved and a jealous lover. Despite and Cruelty are the lot of an unfaithful wife as conceived by Amoret but also of Amoret herself, a chaste woman, who insists on maintaining her chastity in spite of all temptations and the provocations of a jealous and dominating lover: her heart is taken from her body and bedevilled, yet she will not surrender her love. Like Florimell, she reamins love's martyr. As for the remaining figures of the Masque, a woman's ultimate fate in a life of superficial adultery, is, in Amoret's vision, not orgasmic bliss among lusty satyrs but rather something belonging to middle-class ideas, like the final stages of Hogarth's 'Marriage à la Mode', or, less familiarly but more accurately, like what is warned against in certain Continental and English morality plays and interludes:[1] Reproach, Repentance, Shame, Strife, Anger, Care, Unthriftihead, Loss of Time, Sorrow, Change, Disloyalty, Riotise, Dread, Infirmity, Poverty, and Death with Infamy.

All, or almost all, the figures in the Masque exist in Amoret's imagination, but this imagination is one that bodies forth the real consequences of a certain course of action for a chaste woman to whom frivolous surrender has for the first time become a live option, so that she knows what it is to waver ('wavering' being equivocally applied to both 'wemen' and 'wit'):

> There were full many moe like maladies,
>> Whose names and natures I note readen well;
>> So many moe, as there be phantasies
>> In wavering wemens wit, that none can tell,
>> Or paines in love, or punishments in hell.
>
> [xii. 26]

These are quite different from the images of Hellenore's mind, facilely submitting to the Love God's pains and fashioning worlds of fancies 'In her fraile wit' (ix. 52). They are also different from the counterfeits which are the stock-in-trade of the spirit who had fallen with the Prince of Darkness and who animates the body of the false Florimell: he 'all the wyles of wemens wits knew passing well' (viii. 8).

Amoret's torturer, an element in Scudamour himself, is a destroyer of the concord between man and wife. The most advanced embodiment of this concord in *The Faerie Queene* is the relation in V.vii between Britomart-Isis-moon and Artegall-Osiris-crocodile-sun

---

1. John Rastell's *Calisto and Melebea* is an English example. Jean Bretog, *Trage-die françoise à huict personnages: traictant de l'amour d'un serviteur envers sa maitress, et de tout ce qui en advint* (Lyon, 1571; Chartres, 1831) is closer to what is meant here, although of little literary significance. Less to the point but far better than either of these, and well worth translating into English, is the work published as *De Spiegel der Minnen door Colijn van Rijssele*, ed. Margaretha W. Immink (Utrecht, 1913).

in the Temple of Isis, running 'in equal justice' and achieving a freely offered and freely accepted love and friendship * * *. Certainly then, the explanation of this torturer's name—Busirane—suggested by Professor Roche,[2] is the most apposite one. The key to Roche's etymological explanation is the association of 'Busiris' with the death of Osiris. In the light of Spenser's usual masterful way with mythology, the partly contradictory late Classical and post-Classical lore concerning these two figures, the town of Busiris, and Typhon * * * would have easily permitted him to identify the murderer of Osiris as Busiris. 'Busiris' in this sense, then, furnishes the root of the name 'Busirane', although this name no doubt embodies other phonetic felicities.

* * *

One further reason for believing that in the House of Busirane Amoret is being importuned unintentionally by the masterful practices of her husband to turn from her constant love of him to the life of sexual adventurism is that a kind of reduplicative allegory overtakes Amoret in Book IV. While Britomart sleeps, Amoret is captured by Lust himself—Lust who 'could awhape an hardy hart' (vii. 5): that is, who ostensibly is powerful enough to stupefy a strong heart with fear but in fact (considering the singularity of this image) is strong enough to snatch the strongest hearts, just as the Love God joys to see Amoret's heart removed from her bosom and carried before her in the Masque of Cupid. * * * Amoret, like Aemylia, is not simply preyed on by a lustful being, but is herself in some fashion invaded by desire, although she will not perform the acts which desire calls for. She successfully resists both importunities—those of Busirane and Lust—and is finally rescued by the chaste amity of Britomart in the one case and by Belphoebe's virginity in the other.

* * * It is probably true that this episode of Amoret, Timias, and Belphoebe in Book IV is required by Spenser's emergency measures in squaring the accounts of his friend Ralegh with the Queen after the revelation of Ralegh's relations with Elizabeth Throgmorton, but it is equally true that Spenser would not have chosen Amoret for this ambiguous role unless she had been suitable for it. She is readied for pleasure, not overpudicity. Spenser is apparently saying to the Queen that her maid of honour and her favourite Ralegh were touched, but not dominated by, Lust. So with Amoret. In the House of Busirane she is being driven by her lover to become part of the usual courtly round of love that Spenser so strongly condemns elsewhere:

2. Thomas P. Roche, Jr., *The Kindly Flame* (Princeton, 1964), p. 81.

And is love then (said *Corylas*) once knowne
In Court, and his sweet lore professed there?
I weened sure he was our God alone:
And only wonned in fields and forests here,
  Not so (quoth he) love most aboundeth there.
For all the walls and windows there are writ,
All full of love, and love, and love my deare,
And all their talke and studie is of it,
Ne any there doth brave or valiant seeme,
Unlesse that some gay Mistresse badge he beares:
Ne any one himselfe doth ought esteeme,
Unlesse he swim in love up to the eares.
But they of love and of his sacred lere,
(As it should be) all otherwise devise,
Then we poore shepheards are accustomd here,
And him do sue and serve all otherwise,
For with lewd speeches and licentious deeds,
His mightie mysteries they do prophane,
And use his ydle name to other needs,
But as a complement for courting vaine,
So him they do not serve as they professe,
But make him serve to them for sordid uses,
Ah my dread Lord, that doest liege hearts possesse,
Avenge thy selfe on them for their abuses.
    [*Colin Clouts Come Home Againe*, 771–94]

The allegory of Lust in Book IV is simply an intensification of what
we have already seen in the House of Busirane. For purposes of
Spenser's defending his friend and patron, and Elizabeth Throg-
morton, and of maintaining the allegorical locus of Amoret, it was
not intended that Timias and Amoret should be punished, but that
the unclean cleaving thing, amorous desire without constancy to
one lover, should be extirpated.

The friendship which Britomart brings to Amoret is what reverses
the charms of Busirane, so that Amoret's wound becomes whole
and the chains drop from her body, in the inner room where the
magician had held her in thrall. Busirane must not be destroyed
(III.xii. 34) because he is a part of Scudamour. As a masterful
principle of hate, he is ready to destroy Amoret finally (xii. 32),
and he wounds Britomart superficially as the masterful principle of
Malecasta had done in canto i. In Book IV Britomart and Amoret
now go forth in amity, in spite of Amoret's suspicions of what she
takes to be a male's intentions—suspicions which are soon allayed
in the formation of the first four-group of that book, with Britomart
as knight to Amoret and as lady to another knight, so that they may
all be lodged in a castle with a custom. * * *

HARRY BERGER, JR.

[War Between the Sexes]†

The masculine mind wounded first by desire and then by jealousy and envy: this is the center of the emotional and psychological experience visualized by Spenser as Busirane's house and depicted in the concluding two cantos of Book III of *The Faerie Queene.* * * *

Burisrane, in addition to the meanings suggested by Nelson, Roche, and Williams,[1] is simply *Busy-reign*: the male imagination trying busily (because unsuccessfully) to dominate and possess woman's will by art, by magic, by sensory illusions and threats—by all the instruments of culture except the normal means of persuasion. In a vastly more subtle manner than Paridell, Busirane displays before Britomart a slanted history, articulated into three rooms or phases—his phases. His message is that erotic experience must inevitably terminate in torment and breakdown; he charts the psycho-cultural development of this process from the mythic past of the first room to the latest and most immediate moment in the third room. Tapestry, sculpture, relief, theater, music, poetry, and magic are all put into play to convince Britomart of *Busy-reign's* power and to impress on her the sad range of possibilities offered male and female psyches by the centuries of erotic experience crystallized in pagan, medieval, and Renaissance institutions, as in the literature in which Spenser finds them reflected. "When Britomart rescues Amoret from this place of death she is ending . . . centuries of human experience, predominantly painful."[2]

* * *

* * * From tapestries to icon to reliefs to masque, and from the beginning to the end of the masque, there is increasing inwardness, compression, and complication, correlated with increasing activity and motion, and, above all, with increasing proximity to the present moment of narrative.

That the masquers returned to "the inner roome, from whence they first did rise" (xii.26.9) prepares us for their connection to the final episode. When Britomart gains entry into that room, she looks about expecting to see "all those persons, which she saw without: / But lo, they streight were vanisht all and some, / Ne living wight

---

† From "Busirane and the War Between the Sexes: An Interpretation of *The Faerie Queene* III.xi–xii," by Harry Berger, Jr., *ELR*, I (1971), 99–121. (The original footnotes have been slightly edited.)
1. William Nelson, *The Poetry of Ed-* *mund Spenser: A Study* (New York, 1963), pp. 229–30; Roche, pp. 81–83; Kathleen Williams, *Spenser's World of Glass* (Berkeley and Los Angeles, 1966), pp. 109–10; also Fowler, pp. 20*n.*, 150*n*.
2. C. S. Lewis, *The Allegory of Love* (London, 1936), p. 341.

she saw in all that roome" (xii.30.3–5), save Amoret, bound by an iron chain to a brazen pillar, and sitting before her "the vile Enchaunter,"

> Figuring straunge characters of his art,
> With living bloud he those characters wrate,
> Dreadfully dropping from her dying hart,
> Seeming transfixed with a cruell dart,
> And all perforce to make her him to love.
> Ah who can love the worker of her smart?
> A thousand charmes he formerly did prove;
> Yet thousand charmes could not her stedfast heart remove. (xii.31)

The substitution of this more condensed and dramatic scene for the expected masque strengthens the connection between them; and one is tempted to read the masque as an explication of what is happening here—or, conversely, to read this scene as the dramatic situation, previously unarticulated, which anchors the masque in the story of Britomart, Amoret, and Scudamour. The "straunge characters" of Busirane's art allude to the symbolic figures of the masque. Amoret's bleeding heart—her desire for Scudamour—is at once the medium through which he works his charms and the source of her resistance to the charms. Since the cruel dart may refer both to her passion for Scudamour and to the torment Busirane inflicts, the two male figures tend momentarily to converge, most explicitly in the stale lovers' paradox, "who can love the worker of her smart?" If the dropping blood symbolizes what her painful wound costs her in terms of psychic energy and well-being, either or both male figures may be the cause.[3]

This transaction between Busirane and Amoret, and involving Britomart and Scudamour in ways which are not yet articulated, radically alters the meaning of the masque. Prior to this, its reference had been retrospective: the first two rooms had recapitulated in generalized form not only the past history of lust and false love, but also many of the motifs, characters, and incidents of the preceding ten cantos: the masque furnished the decadent end and the climax of this history. But the final episode changes the direction of reference to the future. The masque is now resituated in the beginning of the experience of true love and friendship, where it points toward the threats which will materialize in Books iv and v.

* * *

By itself, Busirane's masque of Cupid does not deal either with true love or with the personal problems which afflict lovers who have

---

3. Busirane dips his pen in the wound of love to inscribe the charms that bind Amoret: I read this as an iconographic echo of the influence of bards and rhymers in the masque, an influence she was apparently protected from in the Garden of Adonis and which is therefore all the more terrifying now.

presumably become friends. Except in the most oblique manner, and in a very few symbolic details, its pageant gives us no information about the reason for Amoret's imprisonment, nor about the particular problems she and Scudamour face. We know she is being tortured because she will not transfer her love to Busirane, but the role forced on Amoret in the masque is that neither of a true lover nor of a truly beloved. She is in fact miscast: the feminine personifications preceding her—Hope, Dissemblance, Fury, and Pleasance—display modes of behavior and feeling which have little to do with her, though much to do with the conventional sonnet figure Spenser later epitomizes as Mirabella in Book vi (vii.28–viii.27), much also with the carryings-on of False Florimell and Hellenore. Cupid punishes her as if she were Mirabella because her effect on men is superficially the same: "To Faery court she came, where many one / Admyrd her goodly haveour, and found / His feeble hart wide launched with loves cruell wound" (vi.52.7–9). As an object of hate and revenge, it is irrelevant to the logic of the masque that she refuses love *because* she will not deny Scudamour; the refusal itself is all that matters.

Busirane's motives extend beyond revenge, beyond the masque's archaic presentation of false love, and beyond the merely generalized or symbolic treatment of Amoret as a scapegoat in man's war on women. What he does in the third room is related not only to Scudamour but also to Britomart. This complex network of relationships is not spelled out for us in Book iii; it remains problematical. But this much seems clear: in showing Britomart what and how Amoret suffers, Busirane tries to dissuade both from their promised futures. The masque refers indifferently to relations in courtship and in marriage, the latter because of the echoes of the Malbecco episode. Either or both are presented as dramatic rituals in which the woman's role is determined by the male mind, rituals refined through centuries of practice and soured by centuries of hate. Busirane has already abused Amoret's mind by forcing on it an anticipatory image of herself as doomed by the very strength of her chaste affection, and this *abusion* is displayed as an exemplum before Britomart. His rooms depict the phases leading up to the advanced stage of disaffection which his house as a whole represents, and depict them so as to suggest that the sequence of erotic phases is grounded *in* potential jealousy—the jealousy inherent in infinite desire—not merely productive *of* jealousy. He thus plays on the conflict in the loving virgin between her chastity and her desire, using the intensity of the latter to push the former toward fear, panic, and frigidity. He encourages her fear of losing independence, her dread of male possession, by flaunting the evil power of art and magic whereby masculine eros masters the world and woman.

* * *

* * * The House of Busirane is by no means a picture of Scuda-mour's "unconscious mind" (whatever that means), yet it does suggest a developed and traditional structure of male presupposi-tions about courtship which tacitly influence him so that he tends to see his relationship to Amoret as one of assault and conquest rather than one of persuasion, protection, and companionship.[4] Brito-mart's tour through the house is her formal initiation into this structure (the elements of which she had previously experienced and seen throughout Book III), while the very change signified by the tour, her replacing Scudamour, renders the existing form of the structure obsolete.

At the same time, something of that structure is symbolically introjected at xii.33.4, when Busirane communicates his influence inside Britomart on the blade of his knife. Though the wound is superficial, she responds with a ferocity which turns out to be excessive and to jeopardize Amoret's freedom: Amoret, who knows more than Britomart about Busirane, warns her not to kill him,

> else her paine
> Should be remedilesse, sith none but hee,
> Which wrought it, could the same recure againe.
> Therewith she stayd her hand, loth stayd to bee;
> For life she him envyde, and long'd revenge to see. (xii.34.5–9)

Britomart's wound is at once a miniature of Amoret's and the antithesis of a wound of Cupid's. It arouses feelings of hate and revenge toward the male mind, feelings which jeopardize the capac-ity for chaste affection. Britomart is to be bold but not too bold, for then she would too violently inhibit her "true feminitee . . . and goodly womanhead" (III.vi.51.5–9), her ability to open herself to Artegal. Hence in Book IV she has to get to know Amoret better, and her patronage of Amoret brings her together with Artegal in IV.vi. The sequence of events suggests the following allegory: chaste affection was prematurely bestowed on, or won by, the masculine lover before either the man or the woman was prepared for the communion of true love. It has therefore to be withdrawn into feminine safekeeping, to be guided and husbanded by the feminine mind until a later and more appropriate moment.[5] Britomart's sub-

---

4. Cf. A. Kent Hieatt, "Scudamour's Practice of *Maistrye* upon Amoret," *PMLA*, LXXVII, 4 (September, 1962), 509–10; Graham Hough, *A Preface to "The Faerie Queene"* (New York, 1963), pp. 175–76; Nelson, pp. 230–31; Roche, pp. 83, 128ff.; Williams, p. 105ff.

5. Having been wounded by Busirane, Britomart hides her womanhood in IV.i–vi and becomes more martial; Amoret becomes concerned, as if she fears Brito-mart may violate and destroy (her)

chaste affection. Amoret's virtues, de-veloped as defenses against such dangers as Florimell encounters, are built up so that woman may court and draw the male in security, may arouse desire and still remain aloof, independent, and chaste. The word *womanhead*, applied to Amoret in III.vi.51.9, fuses *maiden-head* and *womanhood*: in Amoret the two are fused, and this is what defines and causes her particular range of prob-lems and virtues.

sequent separation from Amoret in Book IV is intimately connected to the effect on her of her encounters with Artegal. It is not only desire, but also a deeper, more troubling emotion of "secret feare" which she feels again on seeing Artegal in person (IV.vi.29): the nightmare fear of her own lust as well as his, the fear of being captured and possessed in mind and heart as well as in body, the fear of collaborating with the male enemy in yielding control of herself and her destiny. To some extent, this fear is blatantly acted out in the rape of Amoret by the figure Lust, who appears as a nightmare version of Artegal in the primitive guise that marked his appearance at Satyrane's tourney. Thus Britomart has not yet gained full control over the femininity embodied as Amoret—she has not yet, that is, fully internalized Amoret. And Spenser's technique of personification suggests that she will not, until Amoret as a separate figure has been discarded: true love must ultimately be liberated from its *ensample*, chaste affection from its *lodestarre*, the psychic disposition from its Faerie model. What Amoret stands for is jeopardized by the pure, exclusive, and separated figure of Amoret through which that particular psychic complex is exhibited.

HUMPHREY TONKIN

[Pastorella and the Graces]†

* * *

The Dance of the Graces is the intellectual and poetic centre of the Legend of Courtesy. We have already traced the gradual 'rarefication' of Spenser's story—from the cruelties of the outside world, to the shepherds' country, to the Golden World. Within this Golden World, we move swiftly from fairy dance, to Dance of the Graces, to the central, all-important figure of the shepherd maid who is both Colin Clout's mistress and also has the appearance and the substance of a goddess. Everything in Spenser's poetic repertoire contributes to make this almost schizophrenic vision credible. Even the dance itself does not exist in isolation, but at the top of an ascending series. Early in Canto ix, Pastorella sits in the centre of the shepherds' 'rout' just as the central figure of the Dance of the Graces is surrounded by the circling dancers. In both cases the ladies surrounding the central figure are likened to a garland. Later, the shepherds dance to Colin Clout's pipe and again Pastorella is the foremost dancer. While it may be illegitimate categorically to asso-

† From *Spenser's Courteous Pastoral: Book Six of "The Faerie Queene,"* by Humphrey Tonkin (Oxford, 1972), Chapter V.

ciate the figure of Pastorella with the figure in the centre of the circling dancers on Mount Acidale, such parallels make the Dance of the Graces an all-inclusive vision which embraces and contains these lesser emblems of order. The range of association which the Dance embodies is well expressed in the stanzas describing the Graces and explaining Colin Clout's role.

> Those were the Graces, daughters of delight,
> Handmaides of *Venus*, which are wont to haunt
> Uppon this hill, and daunce there day and night:
> Those three to men all gifts of grace do graunt,
> And all, that *Venus* in her selfe doth vaunt,
> Is borrowed of them. But that faire one,
> That in the midst was placed paravaunt,
> Was she to whom that shepheard pypt alone,
> That made him pipe so merrily, as never none.
>
> She was to weete that jolly Shepheards lasse,
> Which piped there unto that merry rout,
> That jolly shepheard, which there piped, was
> Poore *Colin Clout* (who knowes not *Colin Clout*?)
> He pypt apace, whilest they him daunst about.
> Pype jolly shepheard, pype thou now apace
> Unto thy love, that made thee low to lout;
> Thy love is present there with thee in place,
> Thy love is there advaunst to be another Grace.
>
> (VI. X. 15–16)

The introduction of the author's own *persona* into the world he creates is of course a convention of pastoral. Even in its simplest form the convention has a far-reaching effect on the relation of author and reader to the work, since it blurs the distinction between the poet and his own creation much as the comments of a character on the play he is a part of change the relationship between audience and play. Sometimes (as in Sidney's *Arcadia,* for instance) the author's *persona* plays only a very minor role. But in Spenser's poem the poet's fictional self is piping not for some minor shepherds' dance but for the dance which sums up and epitomizes many of the principal themes of the work—just *how* principal we shall see as this study progresses. The dancers dance to Colin's music: it is he who orders and controls them. In a sense, the relation of the dance to Colin is like the relation of the poem to Spenser. We are confronted in this beautiful scene with the spectacle of the poet creating, the poem coming into being. But, paradoxically, the poem which here comes into being is the poem which contains that poem: the whole is contained in the part.

This, though, is not the end of the complexity. Colin does not pipe to an abstraction or a vision, but to an earthly girl, to his own mistress. She and the shepherd are the two static figures amidst, or beside, the swirling dancers. While we are told that she is an earthly girl, she is nevertheless as ethereal as the other dancers: she disappears as they do, thereby suggesting not only that poetic inspiration is elusive and obscure, but that love, too, is uncertain and fleeting. Or perhaps just as Colin is a fictional Spenser, Colin's love for the girl is a fictional representation of the poet's relation to the controlling idea of his poem, round which he shapes and orders the subsidiary images and themes. If this is so, then the girl in the centre of the dance is the flower of courtesy itself.

The final line of the passage, 'Thy love is there advaunst to be another Grace', introduces another dimension to the paradox. Not only does the dance revolve round the central figure, the poem round the central emblem, but there is also a mysterious relationship between the various revolving circles. This was suggested to us in the stanzas immediately preceding those I have just quoted. Somehow, we know not how (but we believe it), a simple shepherd girl *is* another Grace, *is* the flower of courtesy. Spenser deliberately keeps her position ambiguous (the whole dance depends on such ambiguity): she is another Grace and more than another Grace and worthy to be another Grace. The remark 'And all, that Venus in her selfe doth vaunt / Is borrowed of them' has, I think, an intentional double meaning: either Venus borrows her grace from the Graces, or we borrow from Venus grace *through* the Graces. In other words, we are either watching a dance of four Graces (who epitomize the grace of Venus, since Venus borrows grace from them) or watching a dance of three Graces with Venus in the centre (in which event Venus's grace is passed down to us through the three Graces who surround her).

This ambiguity is mirrored in the visual ambiguities which confront us early on in the episode. I asserted that we see the Dance through Calidore's eyes. Calidore is able to follow and understand the pattern of the hundred maidens who hem the central dancers, but the precise configuration of these central damsels escapes him. When we are told that Colin's mistress was 'as a precious gemme, / Amidst a ring most richly well enchaced', what precisely does this mean in visual terms? Are the three Graces smaller stones surrounding the greater (in which event Colin's mistress is in the centre) or do they correspond to the circle of the ring (in which event Colin's mistress is a fourth member of the same circle)? Is she, in other words, Venus or a fourth Grace? The ambiguity is visual as well as conceptual. By associating Colin's mistress with Venus, Spenser makes the Graces (emblems of courtesy, according to Colin) her handmaids; by associating her with a fourth Grace, he makes her the means by which Venus's powers descend to us. She is thus both the epitome of courtesy and the source of courtesy; and the dance becomes the dance of courtesy, bound together by the love which emanates from Venus.

At stanza 17 the enchantment evaporates. Calidore steps into the ring and the dancers vanish 'all away out of his sight'. This is the climax of Calidore's intrusions—the third and most cataclysmic. One would like to think that Calidore had learned from his previous intrusions. But at first there is precious little evidence that he has. His manner is inappropriately hearty: 'Haile jolly shepheard, which thy joyous dayes / Here leadest in this goodly merry make, / Frequented of these gentle Nymphes always.' As Colin Clout, recovering his composure, explains, regrettably things are not quite as simple as that: the Graces only come when they, and not we, choose. You can't have miracles to order.

Calidore's reaction is again curiously inappropriate. As with Calepine and Serena, he blames the whole incident on 'my ill fortune', and presses Colin for an explanation. The figures Calidore has seen, says Colin, are the Graces, who 'on men all gracious gifts bestow/ Which decke the body or adorne the mynde'—

> As comely carriage, entertainement kynde,
> Sweete semblaunt, friendly offices that bynde,
> And all the complements of curtesie:
> They teach us, how to each degree and kynde
> We should our selves demeane, to low, to hie;
> To friends, to foes, which skill men call Civility.
>
> (VI. x. 23)

All this has been made clear to us in the preceding sections of the book, especially in those episodes involving Calidore. But Colin's attention now shifts to the central figure. Again Spenser avoids precise definition:

> So farre as doth the daughter of the day,
> All other lesser lights in light excell,
> So farre doth she in beautyfull array,
> Above all other lasses beare the bell. . . .
>
> Another Grace she well deserves to be,
> In whom so many Graces gathered are,
> Excelling much the meane of her degree;
> Divine resemblance, beauty soveraine rare,
> Firme Chastity, that spight ne blemish dare;
> All which she with such courtesie doth grace,
> That all her peres cannot with her compare,
> But quite are dimmed, when she is in place.
> She made me often pipe and now to pipe apace.
>
> (VI. x. 26–7)

The final line is both a comment on the poem and a suggestion about its inspiration. The romantic reader, anxious to read the poem as a kind of confessional, might choose to call this 'Grace' Spenser's own Elizabeth Boyle. Others, taking their cue from the *Shepheardes Calender*, may call her Rosalind. But perhaps it would be both truer to the spirit of the poem and more immediately relevant to its theme to call her that inspiration which brought the poem into being, the '*Idea* or fore-conceit' out of which the poet fashioned the work of art.

Almost in the same breath, Spenser turns to the Queen. Perhaps (he seems to say), even so all-embracing and transcendent a vision as this might be misconstrued in a poem ostensibly in praise of the Queen herself. The central figure of the dance, an all-inclusive symbol of virtue, has usurped the position normally allotted the sovereign, who cannot by any stretch of the imagination be incorporated into the dance as Spenser has described it. In turning to the Queen, the poet employs the traditional idea that thus Gloriana's handmaid will be eternized in verse. If Colin's mistress is indeed another Grace, then the Queen is her Venus.

Calidore's reply to Colin's explanation is both illuminating and perplexing. For the first time, he is driven to an admission not simply of 'lucklessness' but of imperfection. He has, he says, 'rashly sought that, which I mote not see'. What is this thing which Calidore 'mote not see', and what effect will it have upon him? Colin's explanation of the significance of the Graces may only be a kind of rationalization of a vision essentially irrational, a quality which somehow lies outside the range of the questing knight, the man of action. If so, then there remains a further question, ultimately the most important. Can this vision be translated into action? To this question we must return.

In the presence of such strange knowledge, and overcome by the beauty of the place in which it was vouchsafed him, Calidore is reluctant to leave—'Thence, he had no will away to fare / But wisht, that with the shepheard he mote dwelling share.' This chance remark reminds us that it was actually the sight of beauty that kept Calidore among the shepherds: he saw Pastorella and he elected to stay. Soon the shepherds' world will disappear as the vision of the Graces disappeared. In each case Calidore stands before these creations of the imagination much as the reader stands before the work of art. If Colin is the poet and the dance is his poetry, Calidore represents ourselves, the readers, in our fumbling efforts to understand the incomprehensible and our insistence on pat answers.

The perceptive reader will recognize that this puts Spenser's audience uncomfortably close to Mirabella and the Salvage Nation, or to Amoret in the House of Busyrane. Like Calidore, these characters did not understand the nature of poetic truth. Their inability to understand metaphor is linked with Calidore's inability to comprehend the nature of the dance. Thus, not only is Spenser's own *persona*, Colin Clout, brought within the scope of the poem, but so are we. The Dance of the Graces is the most important statement of a persistent theme in Book vi, the relation between poetry and society. Behind that stand two other related themes: the nature of fiction and our response to art. Book vi is a poem talking about itself.

Though Calidore does appear to learn from his conversation with Colin Clout, his incursion on the Golden World of Mount Acidale destroys the vision. Not only must we recognize the limitations of Calidore in ourselves, but we must also understand that Calidore, all unwittingly, repeatedly does what the Beast does intentionally: he breaks in and destroys. Book vi is the only book the object of whose quest is all around us. We must travel to Canto xii to meet Acrasia or Grantorto, but the Blatant Beast races through the world of the Legend of Courtesy like an ever-present and vulgar philistinism—not merely outside us but within us all.

* * *

RICARDO QUINONES

[The *Mutabilitie Cantos*] †

* * *

* * * the point of the poem is not the distant first Fall, with its curse, its conversion of life processes into death processes, and its attendant sense of historical decline, but the later assault upon the heavens, a threatened second fall, which is taking place in Spenser's own life time. An older order, to which Spenser committed his faith and from which he derived his hope, is threatened by a newer order, which he regards as morally dangerous. Emulation, replacement—those processes which were heretofore largely absent—now force themselves upon his consciousness. *The Two Cantos of Mutabilitie* represent the eruption of deeply experienced history on what had been Spenser's ideal landscape. Former faiths and aspirations, promising a degree of security and continuity, are radically challenged. Whatever might be said of the poem's connection with the Tyrone rebellion in Ireland, and with Spenser's forced evacuation and bitter end, it is clearly not the work of an administrator who sees some future open to him.[1] There is certainly more than usual significance

† From *The Renaissance Discovery of Time*, by Ricardo Quinones (Cambridge, Mass., 1972), Chapter VII. (The origi- nal footnotes have been slightly edited.)
1. See Raymond Jenkins, "Spenser and Ireland," *ELH*, XIX (1952), 131–142.

in the report (unverified) that a newborn child of the writer of the Garden of Adonis and the *Epithalamion* perished in the Irish uprising.

Mutabilitie's associations with the first Fall are extremely important, both in larger intellectual import and in their revelation of Spenser's preoccupations. In Spenser's concept of trial we noted the persistence of sin and evil. Archimago returns to deprive Guyon's victory of its total satisfaction; Grylle remains unredeemed. While legacies from the past are sources of inspiration for Spenser, as we have seen, and while he once planned to write a poem in praise of the *stemmata dudleiana*[2] (which was partially achieved in the *Complaints*), he was nevertheless aware of other unregenerate continuities. Mutabilitie is the recurrent and damaging remnant from the first assault on the heaven. Although Jove seemed to defeat the Titans, "Yet many of their stemme long after did survive." The earth in conjunction with chaos has produced these rebellious powers which never seem to be completely mastered and periodically return to overextend their power. Though defeated for a time, they too have their perseverance, so that the battle is never entirely ended. The earth, we remember, is fruitful, and chaos lent substance to the great creative processes of the Garden of Adonis. Jove explains that while he destroyed his assailants,

> Yet not so quite, but that there did succeed
> An off-spring of their bloud, which did alite
> Upon the fruitful earth, which doth us yet despite.
>
> (VII.vi.20)

Beyond this Spenserian proclivity for genealogies, Mutabilitie's connection with the first Fall helps to place this new phase of Spenser's work in Renaissance developments.

If there is any meaning to the progressive enlightenment of the neo-Platonism that helped to promote the greater optimism of the high Renaissance, it was in its faith that somehow the lapse of the first parents had not been as all-destructive as was traditionally supposed. As Cassirer has shown in his *Platonic Renaissance in England*, Plato's meliorism replaced Augustine's rigor.[3] Similar to the introduction of Thomistic Aristotelianism in the thirteenth century, this later touch of Hellenism reinvigorated the human spirit. Upon the ashes of the first ruin, a more optimistic Christian philosophical and social edifice was constructed which gave man some possibility of communicating with divinity, of having an integrated view of the cosmos and an important position in the scheme of things. Spenser's world view, his vision of history and love and

2. I.e., genealogy of the Dudleys [*Editor*].
3. Quinones refers to Ernst Cassirer, *The Platonic Renaissance in England*, tr. J. P. Pettegrove (New York, 1970), "esp. pp. 88–96" [*Editor*].

children, is an important endorsement of these possibilities. Although in the sublunary world all was change and confusion, in the spheres above the moon there was constancy and rest, and true directing order and spiritual light. The physical heavens in their imputed immutability and unchanging perfection were the symbols of more permanent values which continued to serve as guides and standards for men. But now in Spenser's time these apparently enduring values and man's capacity to know them are challenged. Into this world of graduated mediation intrudes another principle, regarded as a second historical fall (Dante's "twice-robbed tree"), that calls into question the order and direction of the universe, and plunges man into the darker world of *chorismos*.[4]

Mutabilitie is more than change. Her attempt to become a cosmic principle—that is, a principle by which men should direct their actions and in which they should place their faiths—symbolizes Renaissance developments in science and in moral and political philosophy which, Spenser feared, tended to kill man's prior sense of rapport with the spiritual forces of the universe and his own hopes for continuity. Her endorsement of change and her own aggressive behavior plunges man into brute conflict and emulative struggle. A root irrationality inheres in the working out of things; the order of history is not continuity, but change based on power. Although Spenser's style and method of presentation might still be part of what Danby has called Great House literature, his present vision of the world shows the unmistakable influence of the stage, and particularly that genre which first began to deal with vital Renaissance energies, the history play. Behind Mutabilitie's ascensionism is the emulative spirit of Tamburlaine:

> The thirst of reign and sweetness of a crown,
> That caused the eldest son of heavenly Ops
> To thrust his doting father from his chair,
> And place himself in the imperial heaven,
> Moved me to manage arms against thy state.
> What better precedent than mighty Jove?
>
> (II.vii.12–17)

The cosmic and natural precedent that Tambulaine claims for his thrusting out of the older order is dramatically duplicated in Mutabilitie's attempt to wrest control of the heavens. In each, broader Renaissance developments are more specifically embodied in this new sense of struggle and emulation within the processes of succession.

She is a descendant of the Titans "that did whylome strive"; like Bellona, so did she "aspire." But unsatisfied with control of the earth,

4. I.e., a fragmented universe [*Editor*].

> She gan to cast in her ambitious thought,
> T'attempt the empire of the heavens hight,
> And Jove himselfe to shoulder from his right.
>
> (VII.vi.7)

She boldly ascends to the circle of the moon, whose splendor she admires and envies:

> Shee gan to burne in her ambitious spright,
> And t'envie her that in such glorie raigned.
> Eftsoones she cast by force and tortious might,
> Her to displace; and to her selfe to have gained
> The kingdome of the Night, and waters by her wained.
>
> (10)

Like Tamburlaine in front of Mycetes or Richard of York with Henry VI, she feels herself "more worthy" of the ivory throne. Undaunted by any threats, Mutabilitie presses forward to expel Cynthia from her throne: "boldly preacing-on raught forth her hand / To pluck her downe perforce from off her chaire." (13) Spenser, as we have seen, like Shakespeare, particpates in the general Renaissance *carpe florem* and *carpe diem* themes. It is legitimate for man to reach out his hand, provided, these English writers insist, such action is within a broader frame of religious or social sanction. Mutabilitie represents single, isolated seizure without any larger concerns. Her endorsement of change, similar to that of the Richards in Shakespeare's first tetralogy, leads to no larger good. Milton, too, in highly dramatic comment, would qualify this act of reaching out the hand to take. We see Eve: "forth reaching to the fruit, she plucked, she eat." But her hand is "rash," and the hour "evil."

Mutabilitie's intellectual parentage and relations are further clarified when she decides, in the manner of many of the opportunists of the history play, to take occasion by the forelock and force her way into Jove's court, rather than wait for his leave. Before the gods can rally themselves she resolves to set upon them, "And take what fortune, time, and place would lend." Up she marches, armed with the proverb of political expediency that echoes throughout Shakespeare, particularly among his villains, "good on-set boads good end." (23)

Mutabilitie's boldness is electric. Jove's functionaries are more than unsettled by her brashness: they are somewhat astounded and abashed by her vitality. She crashes through the older conceptions. The conventional image of time, "hory / Old aged Sire, with hower glasse in hand," seems decrepit and clearly passé in contrast with her energy: "she entred, were he liefe or sory." (8) The stars, witnessing the struggle between Cynthia and Mutabilitie,

> still did stand,
> All beeng with so bold attempt amazed,

> And on her uncouth habit and sterne look still gazed.
> (13)

Mercury, too, is at first taken back by the sight of Mutabilitie:

> At whose strange sight, and haughty hardinesse,
> He wondred much, and feared her no lesse.
> (17)

Into the counsel of the gods she barges, uninvited, and finds them

> All quite unarm'd, as then their manner was.
> At sight of her they sudaine all arose,
> In great amaze, ne wist what way to chose.
> (24)

And after she speaks and literally challenges Jove's birthright, the gods

> Stood all astonied, like a sort of steeres;
> Mongst whom, some beast of strange and forraine race,
> Unwares is chauns't . . .
>
> (28)

It must be said that the members of Jove's court suffer from a malady most incident to long-continuing civilizations. The whetstone of ambition has been worn smooth; they have been domesticated, and their air of defenselessness reveals their shock at Mutabilitie's bold challenge. The woods have been cleared for them and they no longer remember the primitive struggle. They themselves have been victimized by the very order and continuity of their regime. The emotions they feel are not unlike those of a son who, abiding within the overarching parental control, suddenly witnesses those figures on whom he depended challenged by another son on equal ground. No little envy and self-blame enters into their combined fear and admiration of the challenger.

Jove's courtiers, however, like their lord, are sturdy and recover. And in a way, there had been cosmic justification for their admiration. The gods are moved by Mutabilitie's beauty, as Jove will later be in allowing her to speak:

> (Being of stature tall as any there
> Of all the Gods, and beautifull of face
> As any of the Goddesses in place . . .)
> (28)

And this is as it should be, when we consider how much Spenser admires and participates in the role of change within the universe. Time is ideally the image of eternity, and Spenser will always detect the presence of divinity and spiritual order behind the moving pageants of seasons and months and hours. Mutabilitie's attractiveness also has its prototype in Christian myth. Lucifer was, after all, the brightest angel, the Child of Light. In *Paradise Lost* he is ignorant of how much he is diminished, but in Spenser's poem Mutabilitie still enjoys the beauty she has as God's means of bringing his creation to fulfillment. We can measure then the difference between her attractiveness and that of Shakespeare's villains, a Richard III or an Edmund. Theirs lies in the sexual appeal of arrogant will itself, of brutal cunning and enforcement. Shakespeare has a much more human sense of evil and of passion. But in Spenser, Mutabilitie is more a principle of cosmic proportions—however far-reaching and painful her practical ramifications might be—and as such she still enjoys divine favor, shown in her beauty.

Mutabilitie's person does not challenge the gods as much as the content of her speech. Not only is she a goddess in appearance and spirit (*de facto*, we might say) but *de jure*, too, she has some rightful claim to sovereignty. And it is here that Spenser's Tudor myth encounters Tudor reality. The established order has not always been so. At its beginning violent change and guile helped to usher in the new order. By what right is peaceful succession urged on Mutabilitie when the establishment itself was born in violence and revolution? What Mutabilitie is practicing she has merely learned from her betters. In dramatizing this fundamental problem of history—the problem of original sin—Spenser's mythic treatment covers the contemporary American scene as well, where the explosive demands of the unjustly deprived challenge the order of a beleaguered establishment.

As the Mortimers will haunt the Lancasters, and eventually topple the weak Henry VI in Shakespeare's first tetralogy, so Mutabilitie is up on her genealogy when she shows that Jove's father, Saturn, obtained power by displacing an elder brother. For Mutabilitie, as it was for Tamburlaine, emulation is indeed a cosmic process, with divine precedent:

> For, Titan (as ye all acknowledge must)
>   Was Saturnes elder brother by birth-right;
>   Both, sonnes of Uranus: but by unjust
>   And guilefull meanes, through Corybantes slight,
>   The younger thrust the elder from his right:
>   Since which, thou Jove, injuriously hast held
>   The Heavens rule from Titans sonnes by might.
>   (27)

Mutabilitie's challenge carries with it the implication that at the heart of the historical process are emulation and blood beginnings. Consequently, a vision of history akin to the Augustinian view would be confirmed, if not by the Cain-Abel motif, then by Jacob-Esau. Man can not redeem himself in time, and rather than enjoying continuity he is exposed to a series of replacements. In the historical vision of man's struggle with time, the concept of original sin is a recurring obstacle, a force that must be overcome. Wherever original sin predominates, the earthly city is an invalid locus of redemption. So Augustine looks to the heavenly city—precisely because of this process; so Dante abandons the city of his youth, beset by the contentious waves of struggle and exile and the fratricidal desolations of civil war. So, in Shakespeare's first and second tetralogies, the fundamental issue will be to redeem the original curse, which is almost synonymous with redeeming time. In Dante's temporal realm, the *Purgatorio*, the pattern also exists: redemption proceeds against the stain of original sin. But rather than being an antagonist, original sin is the essential memory—a kind of viaticum —that Dante must carry with him on his ascent before he reaches his deliverance. But in a later age, in the presence of the Platonic optimism of the high Renaissance and the Elizabethan faith in succession and the ideals of continuity, the original fault radically challenges these hopes with the inescapable facts of replacement and emulation.

Jove does not answer this deep argument with Tudor myth, but rather with Tudor reality. Unlike Henry VI he does not consider his title weak, but rather as secured by conquest. But it is a conquest that is destined, and part of the order of things. A *View of the Present State of Ireland* shows that Spenser is not being ironic in giving Jove the tyrant's plea. The Elizabethans, as E. W. Talbert has argued, considered necessity to be a highly valid argument.[5] This is Spenser's defense:

> For, we by Conquest or of our soveraine might,
> And by eternall doome of Fates decree,
> Have wonne the Empire of the Heavens bright . . .
> (33)

An awesomeness in great rule links it with the powers that be in the universe. Spenser, ever the poetic idealist, or one might say Hellenist, confers upon the nature of things the dread power of fate and necessity. Whatever his origins in time, Jove is better deserving to be a higher principle than Mutabilitie. In fact, as with the other devotees of emulation, say, a Richard III or an Edmund, there is something self-destructive in Mutabilitie's plea. In embracing her program men foolishly exchange death for life. And nature warns her in her final judgment, "thy decay thou seekest by thy desire." For Shakespeare, as for Spenser, to advocate change and to resist the possibilities of continuity is to go against basic life forces. This is sufficient proof of unworthiness for rule.

5. *The Problem of Order* (Chapel Hill, N.C., 1962), pp. 55–56, 116–117.

If thus far Mutabilitie's arguments, touching the complexities and ambiguities of politics and history, derive from Machiavelli, her further and terrible insights into change could derive from Montaigne. When she informs the assemblage (vii. 18) that all earthly things are involved in the processes of birth and decay, this is not new. Even the next stanza, which traces the progress of man's pilgrimage, is still conventional up to a point:

> And men themselves do change continually,
> From youth to eld, from wealth to poverty,
> From good to bad, from bad to worst of all.

The language even echoes Thenot's earlier piece of consolation. But what follows gives it an essentially different flavor. Thenot encountered the world of change with an essential inner equilibrium and stability, which was typical of the simpler type of being that the men of the Renaissance, with their great strivings to overcome time, abandoned. They did not recommend acquiescence, but rather effort. Spenser in his notion of heroic trial combined both of these approaches. But Mutabilitie undoes both possibilities when she describes not only external change but a new awareness of inner change:

> Ne doe their bodies only flit and fly:
> But eeke their minds (which they immortall call)
> Still change and vary thoughts, as new occasions fall.
>
> (vii.19)

As the Player King in *Hamlet* will see it: " 'tis a question left us yet to prove / Whether love lead fortune, or else fortune love." For the newer Renaissance idealism, this skepticism had disastrous consequences. Mutabilitie's claims, or Hamlet's own increased awareness of her powers, imply an end to any sense of man as a creature of rational choice and heroic determinations. Discourse, looking before and after, enjoying historical connection and extension, is ruled out by the present pressures. Any conception of heroism or fidelity is impossible, and achievement is robbed of heroic distinction when it becomes merely a product of adrenalin. Ideal considerations are lost under the force of matter.

As with man's mind, so with his institutions and his beliefs: "Nothing doth firme and permanent appeare." Tudor myth must finally encounter cosmic reality. The reign of Mutabilitie suggests the end of the era of Elizabethan glory and accomplishment to which Spenser had dedicated himself and which he had celebrated. Mutabilitie's lesson of time is clear:

> who sees not, that Time on all doth pray?
> But Times do change and move continually.

So nothing here long standeth in one stay.
(47)

History itself is negated as a source of repair for Spenser; those thrilling consolations experience their own twilight, and man is forced more and more to seek an individual recovery for his existence in time.

Mutabilitie's assault further robs man of any immortal pretensions, any communication with divinity. The lights are hid that shone with such fragile reassurance in a dark world. Jove might claim that spiritual direction exists and controls the processes of change, but in a brash, young, rationalistic way (anticipatory of Edmund's iconoclastic scoffs, partially justified, at Gloucester's notion of heavenly influence) Mutabilitie wonders who has seen these powers:

> The things,
> Which we see not how they are mov'd and swayd,
> Ye may attribute to your selves as Kings,
> And say they by your secret powre are made:
> But what we see not, who shall us perswade?

(49)

In a scientific manner, is she not insisting that things, in order to have existence, must have location in space and time? Such are the implications for the development of the modern world that Mutabilitie represents. The Gods themselves are subject to change. Far from being a universal principle, Jove himself was born in time, although some might say his birthplace was Crete, some Thebes, and others elsewhere. (53) Cultural anthropology and comparative religion combine to shatter any absolute basis for existing belief. In a world of mutability, Spenserian man is cut adrift, facing only the isolation of the historical moment and the horizons of birth and death in time.

To be sure, nature corrects the picture. Mutabilitie's presentation of the progress of the months and the seasons works against her own argument. Change occurs, but there is greater continuity. Nature's presiding sergeant is Order, and the rich pageants of the seasonal calender scenically reveal the beauty of multiplicity, where life's continuities predominate over its terminations. Old senile February, drawn by fishes because he cannot walk, still looks ahead to ploughing and pruning. The dead and the dying look to the duties of the season. And while it is Death that concludes the parade, it is Life that is finally described. Spenser's own inner faith in an outward directing order shines through the actual natural process of Mutabilitie. Time, rather than the enemy of the organism, is actually the arena of his development. Inherent formal principles are brought out through time; consequently, time is not a determining principle, but rather a subordinate one: it works a higher purpose. Nature's summary judgment is that, while all things hate steadfastness,

> yet being rightly wayd
> They are not changed from their first estate;
> But by their change their being doe dilate:
> And turning to themselves at length againe,
> Do worke their owne perfection so by fate:
> Then over them Change doth not rule and raigne;
> But they raigne over change, and do their states maintaine.
>
> (58)

A Swiss theologian, Theodor Bovet, provides a useful modern gloss on this thought. In his short essay, *Have Time and Be Free*, he senses the larger possibilities of fulfillment triumphing over the pressures of time: "Time also is not an inexorable, austere pacemaker governed by the swing of a clock pendulum, hurrying us through our life, demolishing our previous work, and finally conducting us to our death. It is much more our framework, according to which we unfold, and realize ourselves, and which finally guides us to another aspect and another time."[6] But despite Spenser's reliance on the presiding order of continuity and his participation in the large cosmic processes, the cry of individual loss and replacement is not muted. In the first stanza, in the last, and even in the interlude, the suffering of men is too plainly felt to be ignored:

> What man that sees the ever-whirling wheele
> Of Change, the which all mortall things doth sway,
> But that thereby doth find, and plainly feele,
> How Mutability in them doth play
> Her cruell sports to many mens decay?
>
> (vi.1)

Even the delightful interlude of mythologized geography is used to explain why wolves and thieves flourish in what was once a pleasant place. Diana abandoned it and afflicted it with a curse:

> Since which, those Woods, and all that goodly Chase,
> Doth to this day with Wolves and Thieves abound:
> Which too-too true the lands in-dwellers since have found.
>
> (vi.55)

In keeping with the thrust of these cantos, events are seen through the image of an original offense that continues to have consequences. But it is in the two stanzas from the eighth canto of the unfinished book of Constancy that Spenser's individual voice most painfully cries out. The heroic consonance between "here" and "there" is shattered, as Spenser returns to the vanity literature of his

6. Tr. A. J. Ungersma (Richmond, Va.: John Knox Press, 1964), p. 22.

youthful translations. Here, it is not unfair to remark, Spenser for once speaks what he feels, not what he ought to say. The power of Mutabilitie persuades him to

> loath this state of life so tickle,
> And love of things so vaine to cast away;
> Whose flowring pride, so fading and so fickle,
> Short Time shall soon cut down with his consuming sickle.

Short Time does not yield endless monuments. The consolations of perpetuation through process or achievement no longer hold true, and Spenser yearns for an individual redemption. In the second stanza he requires an eternity that is "contrayr to Mutabilitie," not a continuity that is "eterne in mutabilitie." If the *Two Cantos of Mutabilitie* represent the triumph of time, the added two stanzas pray for the triumph of eternity. The restless condition of mankind, which he so manfully and dutifully shouldered in his heroic conception of trial, is now unbearable, and his final plea is for rest and steadfastness.

* * *

ISABEL MACCAFFREY

[The Shepheardes Calender]†

To read the large-scale masterpieces of Elizabethan literature with something of the agility they assume and demand is an art which must be self-consciously cultivated by us today. *The Shepheardes Calender*, an early, relatively brief essay in a complex mode, provides exercise for our wit in smaller compass. We ought, I believe, to bring to it something of the same resources that we bring to Spenser's larger work. As Ernest de Selincourt wrote, "It lies along the high-road that leads him to Faery land."[1] It is the product of the same sensibility, and in it we can discern the special proclivities of the poet's imagination: the preference for radical allegory and "iconographical ambiguity";[2] the search for a form that will contain variety and unify it without violating its subtle life-patterns; the exploitation of a setting that can also serve as a complex con-

† From "Allegory and Pastoral in *The Shepheardes Calender*," by Isabel G. MacCaffrey, *ELH*, XXXVI (1969), 88–109. (The original footnotes have been slightly edited.)

1. "Introduction," *The Poetical Works of Edmund Spenser*, ed. J. C. Smith and E. de Selincourt (Oxford Standard Authors, London, 1961), p. xx.

2. C. S. Lewis's useful term for the Renaissance way of reading images, *Studies in Medieval and Renaissance Literature* (Cambridge, 1966), p. 160.

trolling metaphor. The great invention of Faerie Land is anticipated by Spenser's evocation of the archetypal hills, valleys, woods, and pastures of the *Calender*.

Early critics tended to read the work as a kind of anthology, a series of experiments in various verse-forms; Spenser's themes, conceived as subordinate to his forms, could be subsumed under E.K.'s categories, plaintive, moral, and recreative.[3] The poem's reputation has taken an upward turn in the past few years, accompanied by a critical tendency to stress the unifying power of its metaphors, and there have been several attempts to reduce its pattern to a single thematic statement. The reconstruction of the poem's composition by Paul McLane suggests the difficulties of determining the history of Spenser's intention; but McLane's conclusion supports the inclination of modern readers to see the *Calender* as the product of a unified design, eventually more or less explicit in the poet's imagination.[4]

While it is, I believe, essential to assume that *The Shepheardes Calender* makes sense as a whole, many readings of it, though subtly argued, in the end ignore certain of its elements that may not conform to the proposed pattern. A. C. Hamilton's discussion of the poet's "effort to find himself," R. A. Durr's distinction "between the flesh and the spirit, *amor carnis* and *amor spiritus*," M. C. Bradbrook's thesis that Spenser deals with "the pursuit of honour, surveyed from what was traditionally the lowest of human occupations"—all of these accounts and others, offer us valuable perspectives on Spenser's themes.[5] But all underestimate the power of the poet's imagination, its world-making energy, its drive toward comprehensiveness, its urge to include rather than to exclude meanings.

This energy is visible at the start in Spenser's very choice of forms. His "originality" lay in combining a group of eclogues with a calendar framework, that is, variety with unity.[6] It is a typically Spenserian invention: the two forms neutralize each other's disadvantages and cooperate to produce a structure that uniquely combines symbolic range and resonance with the most fundamental ordering pattern in our experience, the life-cycle itself. The etymol-

3. See comments in the *Variorum* (*The Minor Poems*, Vol. I, ed. C. G. Osgood and H. G. Lotspeich, Baltimore, 1943) by Herford (p. 581) and Mackail (pp. 584–85) and W. L. Renwick's suggestions on the composition of the poem in his edition, *The Shepherd's Calendar* (London, 1930), p. 167.

4. Spenser's *"Shepheardes Calender"*: A *Study in Elizabethan Allegory* (Notre Dame, 1961), p. 326.

5. Essays cited are, *seriatim*: A. C. Hamilton, "The Argument of Spenser's *Shepheardes Calender*," *ELH*, XXIII (1956), 171–82; R. A. Durr, "Spenser's Calendar of Christian Time," *ELH*, XXIV (1957), 269–95; M. C. Bradbrook, "No Room at the Top: Spenser's Pursuit of Fame," *Elizabethan Poetry*, ed. J. R. Brown and Bernard Harris (London, 1960), pp. 91–109.

6. The generic traditions are outlined by S. K. Heninger, Jr., "The Implications of Form for *The Shepheardes Calender*," *SR*, IX (1962), 309–21.

ogy of *eclogue* encourages us to view the separate poems as independent "selections"; the calendar offers the limitation of a circumscribing frame at once linear and cyclical. In consequence, the *Calender* already exhibits the formal paradoxes that confront us in infinite recombination in *The Faerie Queene*: discontinuous continuity, multiple reference, analogical relationships that point simultaneously to likeness and to unlikeness.

These paradoxes are set in motion and contained by the pastoral paradigm, which is to some degree implied by both of the poem's formal components, eclogue and calendar. Development of the implications of pastoral in the early Renaissance had brought it to a point of relative sophistication which was exploited and then notably extended in Spenser's poem. It is important to realize that by the 1570's, the paradigm was not confined exclusively to idyllic themes. Originating in the impulse to criticize artificial and corrupt urban civilization, the pastoral "world" itself was soon infected by that corruption and became in turn the object of critical scrutiny. In the eclogues of Mantuan and Barnabe Googe, the pastoral metaphor is microcosmic, and the preoccupations of fallen man, as well as his vision of unfallen bliss, can be accommodated within it. So, in the *Calender*, Spenser's imagined world includes storms and sunshine, friendly and hostile landscapes, benevolent and ravenous animals, good and bad shepherds, high and low personages. The poet has chosen not to limit himself to the merely idyllic version of pastoral. This choice is reflected in the formal range of the *Calender*. The decorum of the convention dictated that it move, stylistically, in a temperate zone between the heights of epic and tragedy, and the depths of satirical comedy; the range was wide enough, however, to permit excursions into both these extreme borderlands, as the *Maye* and *October* eclogues demonstrate. The twin concepts of the calendar, with its changing seasons and months, and of the eclogue-group, with its changing metrical and tonal patterns, thus combine with the multiple references of sophisticated pastoral to compose a design of rich potentiality. Above all, this complex literary paradigm offers a context hospitable to allegory; as A. C. Hamilton has said, "the most obvious parallel between the *Calender* and [*The Faerie Queene*] is that each is radically allegorical."[7]

We have to ask, then, what the nature and concern of the allegory may be; and the answer must resemble the answers we devise in commenting on the much more complex allegory of the later poem. Paul McLane has observed that Colin Clout's career is like that of "the main characters of the *Faerie Queene*, most of whom lead a double or triple life on the various levels of the poem."[8]

7. The *Structure of Allegory in "The Faerie Queene"* (Oxford, 1961), p. 47.

8. *Spenser's "Shepheardes Calender,"* p. 322.

Though the metaphor of "levels" is, I believe, one that we ought to discard in speaking of allegory, McLane's point concerning the multiple life of Colin can be extended to all the major images of the *Calender*. An obvious example is provided by the avatars of Pan, who figures as Henry VIII, as the "God of shepheards all," and as Christ, "the onely and very Pan, then suffering for his flock."[9] These meanings are not equally valid or ultimate, metaphysically, but they are equally potent in the poem, and they imply each other. We lose something by insisting on any single meaning of a Spenserian image, for the reason that all the meanings are related to and shed light on each other. The "statement" incarnate in each thus includes a comment on the relationship of a particular imagining to congruent ones. The *Calender*, like *The Faerie Queene*, is encyclopedic in its design, for Spenser's imagination (like Milton's) is most at home when it is working in a context that can include, or at least allude to, the entire cosmic order. The poem's concern is the nature of human life—our life's shape and quality, its form, its content or "feel," and ultimately its relation to the one life outside and beyond it.

It is this effort at comprehensiveness that makes us uneasy with any single formula for the *Calender*'s meaning, whether religious, social, or metaphysical. Boccaccio's defense of the poet's fictions includes the remark that images are used to "make truths . . . the object of strong intellectual effort and various interpretation."[1] Pope, who thought *The Shepheardes Calender* "sometimes too allegorical," praised the poem's basic metaphor because it allowed Spenser to expose "to his readers a view of the great and little worlds, and their various changes and aspects."[2] He is speaking of the pastoral which, like the calendar frame, encourages, indeed demands, variety of reference; in Puttenham's famous phrase, it was devised "to insinuate and glaunce at greater matters," which, as W. L. Renwick pointed out in the commentary to his edition, could refer to several kinds of subject. "Since all personal and contemporary affairs were proper subject for Pastoral, the interpretation of the simple allegory is various: the shepherds are poets, scholars, governors, ecclesiastics, by a series of easy allusions."[3] All of these matters, in Spenser's imagination, involved each other; each area of "meaning" overlaps with the others, and each alone can offer only an incomplete statement concerning human life.

Renaissance and medieval ontology provided, of course, a ration-

9. The text of *The Shepheardes Calender* quoted in this essay is that of the Oxford one-volume edition, cited in Note 1. Citations will be to line numbers for the poem, page numbers for prose and gloss. References to Pan are in *Aprill*, p. 434; *December*, 7; *Maye*, p. 439.

1. *Boccaccio on Poetry*, ed. C. G. Osgood (Library of Liberal Arts, New York, 1956), p. 60.
2. *Discourse on Pastoral Poetry; Variorum*, p. 574.
3. *The Shepherd's Calendar*, pp. 164–165.

ale for a literature of multiple significances. In a world of concentric realities, a single metaphor could touch several circumferences in one trajectory; intersecting a number of different but analogous worlds, it could speak of church, of state, of poetry, of the individual soul's destiny, of divine providence as manifested in the cosmic pattern. It is well to remind ourselves of this relationship between the literature and the "world picture" of the Elizabethans, for although it has now become a cliché, it lends point to the choice of allegory as the vehicle for major works by Spenser and others, as well as to the development of a drama with broad symbolic resources. For Spenser, the interlocking complexities of reality could only be rendered accurately in a sequence of metaphors susceptible of simultaneous reference—that is, the continued metaphor of allegory.

The Shepheardes Calender, then, as Spenser's first attempt to devise a "visionary geography,"[4] must be read as an anticipation of his greatest work. The formal differences between the two poems are, of course, obvious. The continuousness of the metaphor in the *Calender* is not that of narrative; the poem "has a situation but no plot."[5] The ground-metaphor of *The Faerie Queene* is the chivalric world of Faerie Land, a place where lives unfold and journeys are traced. Time dominates the *Calender* not as the medium of narrative, but as a geometric pattern which may be described schematically as a circle intersected by linear tracks. The space of the poem is an imagined space whose emblematic features conform to the particular circumstances of each eclogue and are related to those of other eclogues, both adjacent and remote. All of them are drawn from the body of images loosely contained within the pastoral paradigm, but spatial continuity, like narrative line, is not to be insisted upon. The description of the structure by W. W. Greg is still the most comprehensive and objective:

> The architectonic basis of Spenser's design consists of the three Colin eclogues standing respectively at the beginning, in the middle, and at the close of the year. These are symmetrically arranged . . . [and supported] by two subsidiary eclogues, those of April and August, in both of which another shepherd sings one of Colin's lays. . . . It is upon this framework that are woven the various moral, polemical, and idyllic themes which Spenser introduces.[6]

In this geometrical structure, the poem's meaning is figured. As almost every recent critic has said, that meaning somehow concerns

4. C. S. Lewis, *The Allegory of Love* (Oxford, 1948), p. 260. Lewis points out the necessity of an imagined "world" for fully developed allegory.

5. Durr, "Spenser's Calendar of Christian Time," p. 284.
6. *Pastoral Poetry and Pastoral Drama* (London, 1906), p. 91.

man's relation to the cycle of nature.[7] Spenser is considering the degree to which "natural" terms must enter into a definition of what man is; we are made aware of the pattern of human life as biologically cyclical, but also as spiritually transcendent in various directions: hence the design of linear or vertically oriented images intersecting the circular ground-plan. "Man is part of nature, but this world's brief beauty gives him less than he asks, and though he loves it he needs to look beyond it. . . . For us the natural cycle is in itself the way of death, and we will gain life only by looking to the cycle's source."[8]

The character whose life is defined by these patterns, as Greg's description properly points out, is Colin Clout. Yet exclusive concentration on Colin may obscure Spenser's purpose; if this hero is a pilgrim, he never attains the Heavenly City, and it is left to other voices to define for us the alternatives to the life within "nature" figured by Colin's career. His life is congruent with the circle's movement toward "experience" and imminent death. He is an anti-hero, his unredeemed existence tracing a movement which defines the failure of man to realize his *own* nature. Colin recognizes that submission to the seasonal round has led only to death: "So now my yeare drawes to his latter terme" (*Dec.* 127); his life has passed like a dream, and bidding adieu to the "delightes, that lulled me asleepe" (151), he is left alone in a winter landscape.

Colin's uncompleted quest for understanding is expressed in the poem by a sequence of changes in the relationship between nature and man, devised with a good deal of subtlety by Spenser to provide simultaneously a commentary upon and a critique of the macrocosm / microcosm analogy at the root of the pastoral paradigm. The *Calender* begins in January, principally so that Spenser may stress the circular pattern by framing his poem with "winter" eclogues.[9] Since *Januarye* is also the first stage in Spenser's critique of his analogical base, we must see man and nature in it as congruent. Hence, when the poem begins, the protagonist has already suffered disillusionment as the result of love-longing; "his carefull case" resembles "the sadde season of the yeare," as the Argument painstakingly indicates. In fact, we are to see Colin in unwounded innocence only through the reminiscences of other shepherds. The Colin of *Januarye*, however, is still a *literary* innocent; in making his comparison between careful case and sad sea-

7. See Durr, "Spenser's Calendar," pp. 290–99; and Hamilton's discussion of the theme of "the dedicated life where man does not live according to Nature but seeks escape out of Nature," "The Argument," pp. 175–76.

8. Kathleen Williams, *Spenser's World of Glass* (Berkeley and Los Angeles, 1966), p. 203. Miss Williams' succinct pages on the *Calender* in this book outline a view of the poem close to the one I am arguing in many respects.

9. Heninger discusses this aspect of the structure, "a pattern repeated endlessly throughout eternity," in "The Implications of Form," p. 317.

son, he uses the metaphor of the mirror,[1] indicating that for him the macrocosm still reflects accurately the little world of man, offering valid analogies for his inner state:

> And from mine eyes the drizling teares descend,
> As on your boughes the ysicles depend.   (41–42)

In *Iune*, however, as Greg points out, Spenser devises "a specific inversion of the 'pathetic fallacy' "[2] in order to express Colin's literary disillusionment. The insights of experience include the recognition that a naive version of the pastoral metaphor inadequately expresses reality. It is no accident that in *Iune* Colin explicitly renounces the "rymes and roundelayes" of his youth, thus described by Hobbinol:

> Whose Echo made the neyghbour groues to ring,
> And taught the byrds, which in the lower spring
> Did shroude in shady leaues from sonny rayes,
> Frame to thy songe their chereful cheriping.   (52–55)

The relationship of sound to echo, a version of the mirror-image of *Januarye*, is shown to be invalid in June when the harmonies of nature clash with the disharmony of Colin's suffering. He is exiled from Paradise, and those songs now seem to him "weary wanton toyes" (48).

In *December*, Colin reflects on life and death, finally recognizing, and despairingly accepting, the fundamental incongruity of man and nature. His Muse is "hoarse and weary"; his pipe is hung up on a tree (140–41).

> And I, that whilome wont to frame my pype,
> Vnto the shifting of the shepheards foote:
> Sike follies nowe haue gathered as too ripe
> And cast hem out, as rotten and vnsoote.   (115–18)

Those aspects of his life which indicate its congruence with nature are unsatisfying or inadequate to the demands made upon them. The old Colin is wise in nature's ways; he has learned "the soothe of byrds" and "the power of herbs," yet this knowledge is of no avail in curing his "ranckling wound."

> But ah vnwise and witlesse *Colin cloute*,
> That kydst the hidden kinds of many a wede:
> Yet kydst not ene to cure thy sore hart roote,
> Whose ranckling wound as yet does rifelye bleede.
> (91–4)

The metaphor of unripeness, which Milton was later to develop in

---

1. For an excellent analysis of these stanzas of *Januarye*, see Hallett Smith, *Elizabethan Poetry* (Cambridge, Mass., 1952), p. 35.
2. *Pastoral Poetry*, p. 93.

the opening lines of *Lycidas*, insists that fulfilment for man cannot be looked for within the cycle.

> The flatring fruite is fallen to grownd before,
> And rotted, ere they were halfe mellow ripe.
>
> (106–7)

The life of Colin Clout, then, traces for us the line of human life as it diverges psychologically from the life of nature, while remaining physically bound to it. The event which allows this divergence to manifest itself is a familiar one in pastoral poetry from Theocritus to Marvell. It is love, the disturber of pastoral harmony, a metaphor for the troubling of human life which we call sin—that is, the dominance of passion. It is, as Colin says, the result of pride: "But ah such pryde at length was ill repayde" by Cupid (*Dec.* 49). In consequence the orderly cycle of human life is turned awry, its promise blasted. This melancholy situation is depicted in Theocritus' eighth Idyll, as rendered by an anonymous translator of 1588:

> A tempest marreth trees; and drought, a spring:
> Snares unto foules, to beastes, netts are a smarte;
> Love spoiles a man.

Mantuan's *Ecologue II* (Turberville's translation) describes the pains of the "unlucky lad" Amyntas:

> Forgetful he of former flocke, and damage done with knaves,
> Was all inraged with this flash; at night he nought but raves.
> The season that for quiet sleepe by nature poynted was,
> In bitter plaintes and cruell cries, this burning Boy did passe.[3]

And Marvell's Mower, in the century after Spenser, complains of the "unusual Heats" that accompany Juliana:

> This heat the Sun could never raise,
> Nor Dog-star so inflame's the dayes.
> It from an higher Beauty grow'th,
> Which burns the Fields and Mower both:
> Which mads the Dog, and makes the Sun
> Hotter than his own *Phaeton*.
> Not *July* causeth these extremes,
> But *Juliana's* scorching beams.[4]

The interesting feature of all these descriptions of love lies in their stress on the disruption of macrocosmic harmony. Images of tempest, drought, insomnia, and withered grass became appropriate figures for man's fallen state, the seasons' difference that signifies the penalty of Adam. In the Argument to *December* Colin's "summer"

3. The quotations are from the texts printed in Frank Kermode, ed., *English Pastoral Poetry* (London, 1952), pp. 63, 77.

4. "Damon the Mower," ll. 17–24, *The Poems of Andrew Marvell*, ed. Hugh Macdonald (The Muses' Library, London, 1956), p. 44.

is meteorologically described: "which he sayth, was consumed with greate heate and excessiue drouth caused throughe a Comet or blasinge starre, by which he meaneth 'loue, which passion is comenly compared to such flames and immoderate heate." Colin himself repeats the point:

> A comett stird vp that vnkindly heate,
> That reigned (as men sayd) in *Venus seate*. (59–60)

The congruence between man's nature and external nature is violently reestablished in a baleful conjunction of planets and passions; the analogy becomes a kind of parody upon the harmonious prelapsarian unity.

* * *

The lay of *Aprill*, the third of Colin's songs, is designed, like those in *August* and *Nouember*, to confirm Piers' claim in *October* that love, seconded by imagination, can lift us out of the cycle of death. All three poems offer visions of a world in which reality corresponds to human desires. All are elaborate in form, their higher mood surpassing the reach of ordinary shepherds' wit. In celebrating Eliza, Rosalind, and Dido, Colin must keep decorum with themes that transcend the natural order as he observes it in "reality" in many of the other eclogues. The fox of *Maye*, the wolf of *September*, the "Ambitious brere" of *Februarye*, the lowly pastors of *Iulye*, the disharmonies of *Iune*—all these manifest the nature of fallen being. But *Aprill* and *August* offer visions of possibility, and *Nouember* a glimpse of actuality that transcends all human potentiality. Bacon was later to disparage poets for submitting "the shows of things to the desires of the mind," but as both Sidney and Spenser affirm, those desires themselves bear witness to the presence of a realm of being inadequately figured by the shows of things.

All three of Colin Clout's songs are monuments of wit and demonstrations of its capacities; the *Aprill* lay is, in addition, Spenser's most eloquent depiction of a monument of power, a model that refers to our life on earth. It is a vision of perfection within fallen nature that can be effected by exercising another kind of art. Once our world has become the prey of sin, nature can be restored to something like its original purity only with the aid of civilization, that "nurture" regularly opposed in Elizabethan debates to unaltered "nature." The arts of government can unite antagonists and create another Eden, at least a demi-paradise—the garden of the world, as Elizabeth's poets were fond of calling her kingdom. This world is presented in *Aprill*, where the lay's formal artifice can be taken as a symbol of all the artful patterns that bring order out of chaos. *Aprill* speaks of the work of art, be it a commonwealth, a dance, or a poem; *October* speaks of the maker, "the perfect paterne of a Poete" (p. 456). He can create on earth a mirror, fragile but exact, of the world not as it is but as it might be. The making of golden worlds is the chief function assigned to poetry by Sidney; and it lies behind Piers' description of the poet's heavenly goal in *October*:

> Then make thee winges of thine aspyring wit,
> And, whence thou camst, flye backe to heaven apace.
>
> (83–4)

In *Nouember* we contemplate the true heavenly garden; in *Aprill* we see a fictive version of its earthly counterpart, transient but potent, created by poet and queen.[5] Colin's art cooperates with that of "our most gracious souereigne" to produce a golden world in imagination; and this world is capable, as the Envoy to the *Calender* insists, of surviving every catastrophe except the final one: "It shall continewe till the worlds disolution" (p. 467).

The microcosmic character of the lay of *Aprill* hardly requires elaboration. The images create a comprehensive harmony that extends from the flowers on the green to golden Phoebus and silver Cynthia, removed from their "natural" orbits, like the Sun in Donne's *The Sunne Rising*, to circle this little cosmos and do homage to its sustaining power. Here, as in Eden, spring and autumn dance hand in hand and flowers of all seasons blossom together to deck Eliza, whose complexion predictably unites "the Redde rose medled with the White yfere" (68). Joining classical and native strains, as later they were to be joined in *Epithalamion*, nymphs of Helicon dance beside Ladies of the Lake and "shepheards daughters, that dwell on the greene" (127)—the two latter groups figuring, it has been suggested, a union of the spirits of water and land.[6] The "chiefest Nymph" brings the final tribute: a coronal of olive branches, signifying the surcease of war, Eliza's establishment of the Peaceable Kingdom, the Golden Age restored. The *Aprill* lay, though not composed in the heroic mode prescribed by Piers in *October*, speaks of the subjects there recommended, and is presided over by Calliope (100). The epic poet is to turn to

> those, that weld the awful crowne,
> To doubted Knights, whose woundlesse armour rusts,
> And helmes vnbruzed wexen dayly browne.
>
> (*Oct.*, 40–42)

Another incarnation of Elizabeth, Mercilla in *Faerie Queene* V, is also a peaceable ruler; at her feet is a sword "Whose long rest rusted the bright steely brand" (V. ix. 30). The sterner style of epic de-

---

5. "Colin's two songs in the *Calender*, the praise of Elisa and the lament for Dido, give between them the whole situation." Williams, *idem*.

6. W. F. Staton, Jr., "Spenser's 'April' Lay as a Dramatic Chorus," *SP*, LIX (1962), 115. Warton was the first to note the similarity between *Aprill* and the royal entertainments; *Variorum*, pp. 284–85.

mands images like those of the rusted armour or sword; and those images, too, remind us that epic treats of life in a harsh and threatened fallen world, where the sword may at any moment be drawn. For the homely yet courtly vision of high pastoral, the coronal of olive is more decorous. Yet both images project an ideal that was often referred to by writers on the arts of government. Spenser's version of it in *Aprill* is a world of possibility created by poetry; Castiglione celebrates princely virtue in *The Courtier* in a congruent allusion:

That vertue, which perhaps among all the matters that belong unto man is the chiefest and rarest, that is to say, the manner and way to rule and to raigne in the right kinde. Which alone were sufficient to make men happie, and to bring once againe into the world the golden age, which is written to have beene when Saturnus raigned in the olde time.[7]

Pastoral imagery finds a new sanction in figuring this happy state, as in *Nouember* its validity was to be confirmed in another direction. The more one reads *The Shepheardes Calender*, the more one is struck by the force of Hallett Smith's judgment that "the pastoral idea, in its various ramifications, *is* the *Calender*."[8] The pastoral paradigm, in the service of a potent and resourceful imagination, proves itself to be a flexible expressive instrument. The serious use of pastoral in the Renaissance, by Spenser and others, received, of course, support from its presence in the Bible and from the central paradox of Christianity where low degree is exalted. So the humblest genre can figure the highest matters. This paradox is exploited by Spenser in a secular context in *Aprill*, where the greatest personage of the land enters the shepherds' country world and hallows it. In turn, that world itself provides emblems supremely apt for figuring the special graces of her reign. There is a union of estates, a little mirror of Gloriana's England—appropriately enough, if we recall that on the twenty-third of the month was celebrated the feast of England's patron saint.

Having tested for himself the resources of one of the basic metaphors of his tradition, Spenser laid aside his pastoral pipe for a time. Already, the queen of shepherds was being metamorphosed into the queen of faerie. Yet pastoral was not abandoned for good; it is absorbed into Faerie Land itself, making an essential contribution to the vast landscape of *The Faerie Queene*. And in one of his last poems, *Colin Clouts Come Home Againe*, Spenser produced a classic example of the pastoral paradigm. Yet in the end, the interest for us of *The Shepheardes Calender* lies not in the pastoral "matter," but in the mode of its handling. De Selincourt's view of the poem as embodying "a world of Spenser's own" strikes the most

7. *The Book of the Courtier*, tr. Thomas Hoby (Everyman's Library, London, 1943), p. 273.
8. *Elizabethan Poetry*, p. 46.

relevant note.[9] Formally and thematically, it stands as a character-istic product of this poet's imagination, which from the beginning was a maker of worlds. The *Calender* is an ambitious, encyclopedic allegory, controlled by a metaphor that is capable of sustaining a complex *significatio*. Spenser's powers were to develop far beyond the point which they had attained in 1579; particularly in the matter of inventing a narrative, he had much to learn. Yet this early work, especially as it offered an opportunity to explore the imagined land-scape of an allegorical country, can be seen as an essential prologue to the bold inventions of *The Faerie Queene*, where the romantic world of the medieval storytellers is transformed into a visionary geography of unsurpassed flexibility, enchantment, and expressive power.

HALLETT SMITH

[*Muiopotmos* and *Prothalamion*]†

* * *

* * * In approaching these poems I will assume my conclusions based upon *The Shepheardes Calender* and the *Amoretti*—that Spenser was a conscious artist, well aware of the conventions and interested in using them in English to demonstrate the marvelous possibilities of that language, but fundamentally independent and experimental. Whether he succeeds or fails artistically, Spenser seems always insistent upon handling a convention in such a way as to leave upon it the unmistakable stamp of his own mind and style.

* * *

Muiopotmos, or The Fate of the Butterflie was published in the volume called *Complaints* (1591), but it has its own title page dated 1590. It was presumably written not long before. It is dedicated to Lady Carey, in an epistle signed by Spenser, full of the usual Eliza-bethan flattery and self-deprecation but interesting because the poet beseeches her to take his gift in worth, and in all things therein *to make a mild construction*, according to her wonted graciousness. I suppose this means that she is to read no more into the poem than is there, and perhaps more specifically, not to suppose it to be a

9. "Introduction," p. xx.
† From "The Use of Conventions in Spenser's Minor Poems," by Hallett Smith, in *Form and Convention in the*

Poetry of Edmund Spenser, ed. William Nelson (New York, 1961), pp. 122–145. (The original footnotes have been slightly edited.)

satire or topical poem, like *Mother Hubberds Tale* and *Virgil's Gnat*, which preceded *Muiopotmos* in the *Complaints* volume.

Muiopotmos contains many puzzles, and the scholarly commentary on the poem has largely concerned itself with suggesting answers to these puzzles, the authors often forgetting Spenser's admonition to make a mild construction. The poem begins as if it were to be a mock epic:

> I sing of deadly dolorous debate,
> Stir'd vp through wrathfull Nemesis despight,
> Betwixt two mightie ones of great estate,
> Drawne into armes, and proofe of mortall fight,
> Through prowd ambition, and hartswelling hate,
> Whilest neither could the others greater might
> And sdeignfull scorne endure; that from small iarre
> Their wraths at length broke into open warre.

One expects something like the battle of the frogs and the mice, and the second stanza continues with an invocation to the muse Melpomene, "the mournfulst Muse of nine." But then the poem proceeds to tell of Clarion, the butterfly, how he, a fresh and lusty youth, put on his armor and sallied forth, surveying delectable gardens, only to be caught in the web of the sinister spider, Aragnoll, and killed. There is no "deadly dolorous debate," no "open warre," unless a single stroke by the spider be so considered, no epic battle. However, Spenser does revive the appropriate rhetoric in a stanza just preceding the catastrophe, and Melpomene is again invoked; the final line in its abruptness suggests the ending of the Aeneid.

Most of the 440 lines of the poem, however, are devoted to description of the garden and to the elaboration of two Ovidian myths which are standard and conventional digressions in an epyllion. One is the metamorphosis of Astery, to explain the flowerlike designs in the wings of butterflies; the other is the metamorphosis of Arachne, to explain the notorious malice of spiders: Arachne was the mother of Aragnoll.

The poem has obvious relationships with Chaucer—the mock heroics of *Sir Thopas* and *The Nun's Priest's Tale* hover vaguely in the background, and there is a Chaucerian catalogue of flowers. In style and tone *Muiopotmos* somewhat resembles *Virgil's Gnat*, that translation of the *Culex* which Spenser had done ten years before, in the "raw conceipt" of his youth, to use the terms Spenser applied to the time when he was twenty-seven or twenty-eight years of age. But the most clearly conventional parts of the poem are the two Ovidian digressions.

In the first one Spenser accounts for the beautiful markings in a butterfly's wing by inventing a small and charming metamorphosis.

His pretense is that it is legendary, but actually he invents it on the pattern of the story of Cupid and Psyche. One of Venus's nymphs, named Astery, is the most successful of all in gathering flowers; she arouses the envy of the other nymphs, who report falsely that Cupid has been helping her. Venus, afraid of having her son involved in another love affair like that with Psyche which caused so much trouble, changes the nymph Astery into a butterfly, and places on her wings those flowers which had caused her downfall, since when all butterflies carry these designs on their wings.

The legend provides a pleasant prologue to Spenser's elaborate description of the garden; it associates the action with an Ovidian mythological world, and it supplies a kind of mirror-image of the main plot of the poem. It is Astery's fate, through no fault of her own, to be transformed into a butterfly; it is Clarion the butterfly's fate, through no fault of his own, to get caught in the spider's web and be slain.

The second metamorphosis tells the story of Minerva and Arachne from Book Six of Ovid's Metamorphoses. It is introduced to explain the malice of Aragnoll the spider, since he is Arachne's son. Spenser greatly abbreviates Ovid's narrative. In the weaving contest he has Arachne portray only the rape of Europa instead of the twenty-one amours of the gods in Ovid's account. But he adds to the story of Minerva's weaving a detail which is invented to make the mythological digression more relevant. Minerva weaves a butterfly into her picture, and it is the butterfly which is the final triumph of her art. Spenser also changes the ending of the legend; in his version Arachne turns into a spider from envy and grief, whereas Ovid had made the metamorphosis a gift of the goddess to prevent the mortal woman from committing suicide. Spenser by his change relates the legend more closely to his main plot as he uses it to account for Aragnoll's hatred of butterflies.

To Spenser the convention he was using was not a fully fixed and rigid one. It was generally defined by the example of *Virgil's Gnat,* influenced by Chaucer and Ovid, traditional enough to be recognized, but not so fixed in form as the pastoral eclogue. Its trivial subject and light tone gave freedom for pictorial and descriptive effects. The serious episodes are seen in miniature, and the effect is more playful and less satirical than the mock heroic. The poem is a delicate artifact, suitable for presentation to a lady. Its theme is the romantic one so dear to Spenser's heart—the theme of joy and delight which fades and dies as an exemplification of mutability.

> What more felicitie can fall to creature
> Than to enjoy delight with libertie,
> And to be Lord of all the works of Nature,
> To raine in th'aire from earth to highest skie,

> To feed on flowres, and weeds of glorious feature,
> To take what euer thing doth please the eie?
> Who rests not pleased with such happines,
> Well worthie he to taste of wretchednes.
>
> But what on earth can long abide in state?
> Or who can him assure of happie day;
> Sith morning faire may bring fowle euening late,
> And most mishap the most blisse alter may?
> For thousand perills lie in close awaite
> About vs daylie, to worke our decay;
> That none, except a God, or God him guide,
> May them auoyde, or remedie prouide.   (ll. 209–224)

The first two lines were chosen by John Keats to stand on the title page of his first book of poems in 1817, together with a portrait of Spenser.

Because of some puzzles in the poem and because *Virgil's Gnat* is a topical poem, many modern commentators have been tempted to read *Muiopotmos* as an allegory. The interpretations vary. We have been told that the poem is about Spenser and Lady Carey, Ralegh and Essex, Spenser and Burghley, Sidney and Oxford, Burghley and Essex, the defeat of the Armada,[1] and, most recently, The Soul Caught in the Eternal War between Reason and Sensuality.[2] If I were to add to this formidable list, I would be tempted to suggest that *Muiopotmos* is a *prophetic* allegory: that the butterfly represents the scholarly critic who gets caught in the spider-web of extraneous antiquarian, historical, and philosophical learning. But I shall refrain. The tone of the poem, which most of the learned allegorical interpreters ignore, is the first and most important clue to the interpretation, and that tone would almost certainly rule out any heavy philosophical, military, or political allegory. The second clue, I think, comes from Sonnet 71 of *Amoretti*, in which the poet describes his lady's embroidery or "drawen work" as portraying a spider and a bee. It may be that Lady Carey also was interested in sewing; she is the patroness of the poem and Professor Strathmann noticed that there is a record of presenting Queen Elizabeth with a highly embroidered satin garment.[3] I think it is clear that the poem is a light, delicate, *jeu d'esprit* in which Spenser combines elements from Ovid, from a Chaucerian tradition, and from *Virgil's Gnat*. Renwick considered *Muiopotmos* to be "Spenser's most original poem, and that because the 'kind' is simply that of 'minor poetry' and allows a freedom impossible in most of his other works."[4] It seems to me that in *Muiopotmos* we have an example of Spenser's

1. *The Works of Edmund Spenser: A Variorum Edition*, ed. E. Greenlaw, C. G. Osgood, F. M. Padelford, and R. Heffner; 9 vols. (Baltimore, Md., 1932–1949), VIII, 599–608.

2. D. C. Allen, *Image and Meaning: Metaphoric Traditions in Renaissance Poetry* (Baltimore, Md., 1960), 20–41.
3. *Works*, VIII, 403.
4. *Works*, VIII, 603.

eclectic use of several conventions, and particularly his ability to invent in the manner of the Ovidian metamorphosis and to impress upon conventional elements something of his own style. Lotspeich compares with his success here the Faunus and Molanna interlude in the Mutability Cantos, "in that vein of playful pleasantry, with just a touch of seriousness, which the Elizabethans controlled supremely well."[5]

* * *

Prothalamion is even more completely lyric than the *Epithalamion*. It is a spousal or betrothal song for the two daughters of the Earl of Worcester; its date in the autumn of 1596 may thus be established with some exactness. The name *Prothalamion* seems to be a coinage of Spenser's. No other Elizabethan uses it except Drayton, who was clearly influenced by Spenser. There was, however, a convention of such poems. Dan Norton,[6] who has traced the tradition most fully, shows that betrothal ceremonies, in life and in fiction, encouraged the composition of poems, but that the authors of them derived their motifs largely from the convention of the epithalamion.

Spenser, however, makes use of another tradition—one in which he himself had already experimented. It is the tradition of river poems. Sixteen years before the *Prothalamion* Spenser had composed, in Latin, a poem called *Epithalamion Thamensis*. It was never published and is now unknown, but one can guess what it was like from other examples of the genre. Later on, Spenser composed an elaborate account of the marriage of the Thames and the Medway for the eleventh canto of Book IV of *The Faerie Queene*. And in the very personal and topical poem *Colin Clouts Come Home Againe* (1591) he inserted a passage of 55 lines describing the marriage of two Irish rivers. As worked out by Osgood forty years ago,[7] the principal themes or motifs of river poems, as practised by Camden, Leland, Vallans, and Spenser, were three: (1) a journey of some swans, (2) a marriage of two rivers, and (3) some topographic, antiquarian review of places on the banks of the two rivers.

The obvious qualities of such a poem are learning, especially of an antiquarian sort, facility at mythical invention or adaptation, and copiousness of description. It is the kind of thing for which the talents of Michael Drayton later turned out to be appropriate.

Spenser, in writing the *Prothalamion*, modified the convention in two ways: he returned, as he was so prone to do, to Chaucer and

5. H. G. Lotspeich, *Classical Mythology in the Poetry of Edmund Spenser* (Princeton, N.J., 1932), p. 12.
6. "The Tradition of Prothalamia," in *English Studies in Honor of James Southall Wilson* (Charlottesville, Va.,

1951), pp. 223–241.
7. "Spenser's English Rivers," *Transactions of the Connecticut Academy of Arts and Sciences*, XXIII (1920), 65–108.

introduced some elements of the dream vision and complaint. The poet opens with a description of the calm, pleasant day, which contrasts with his own mood of "sullein care, / Through discontent of my long fruitlesse stay / In prince's court, and expectation vayne / Of idle hopes, which still do fly away." He sees the water-nymphs gathering flowers; two beautiful swans appear, and the nymphs strew flowers before them and one of them sings a congratulatory lay. Then he reverts to his personal associations by mentioning London as his birthplace, his "most kindly nurse," and recalling that at Essex House, formerly the palace of his patron Leicester, "Oft I gayned giftes and goodly grace / Of that great lord, which therein wont to dwell, / Whose want too well now feedes my freendles case."

The other modification is to extend the allusiveness of the poem not into antiquarian or topographical lore, but to lively current matters of interest. There are puns on the names of Somerset and Devereux. The studious lawyers who now inhabit the Temple are mentioned as well as the ancient Knights Templar. A whole stanza is devoted to the Earl of Essex,

> Great Englands glory and the Worlds wide wonder,
> Whose dreadfull name, late through all Spaine did thunder,
> And Hercules two pillors standing neere,
> Did make to quake and feare.   (ll. 145–149)

The rather cold conventional elements of the river song have been relieved by the reflective, somewhat melancholy tone of the poet—a tone which contrasts with the happiness of the occasion. As he says,

> But Ah here fits not well
> Olde woes but ioyes to tell
> Against the bridale daye, which is not long:
>   Sweet *Themmes* runne softly, till I end my Song.

Furthermore, the journalistic allusiveness of the poem balances the artifice of the nymphs and the symbolic swans.

No novelties of structure mark the *Prothalamion*; it is less formal than the *Epithalamion*, and, perhaps for that reason, only half as long. The movement of the stanzas has been much admired, and the versification in general, as well as Spenser's deftness in manipulating the stanza toward the refrain. That refrain has paid the price of its popularity by serving as ironic contrast in that other poem which uses events on the Thames as reflections of the values of contemporary life. I mean of course *The Waste Land*.

If we try to generalize about Spenser's use of conventions in the minor poems I think we must make at least the following observations. Spenser was a poet to whom the conventions were still alive.

He saw them used by contemporary French and Italian writers as well as by the ancients. In fact, I do not think that he felt there was as much chronological difference between the ancients and the moderns as do we. In some sense Eliot's famous remark can be applied to Spenser, that for him the whole of European literature from Homer to the present day had a contemporaneous existence.

To be sure, Spenser adapted the conventions to his own use. In doing this he was following in the footsteps of his master Chaucer and showing the way to his disciple Milton. Like them he felt that the personal element in poetry, the reflection of the mind and temper of the individual writer, is expressed most vividly when it is embedded in a convention. Like them also, he saw to it that his work was distinctively English, that it displayed an instinctive and intimate love of English rivers and flowers and trees, and an artist's pride in the English language.

J. W. LEVER

[The *Amoretti*] †

[In the *Amoretti*] we have to face not merely unevenness in quality, or hesitation between a "conventional" and a "lover-like" approach, but an attempted blending of two collections of sonnets, differing in subject-matter, characterization, and general conception. * * * What probably happened with *Amoretti* was that round about 1594 Spenser felt the urge to make his own contribution in the sonnet medium. He had by him a fair number of individual sonnets, some dating back a few years, others written in recent months during the pause following the completion of Part II of *The Faerie Queene* which is mentioned in sonnet LXXX. To make up a sequence, convention required him to recount the story of his courtship from its inception onwards, providing an adequate record of the lovers' moods and encounters. At this stage of his literary development, however—and perhaps at this point in his private life —he was no longer imaginatively concerned with the wide range of erotic experience that had already been explored on the level of allegory. His interest lay in a single, resolved state of love: the condition of assured courtship awaiting its consecration in marriage. A large number of the recent sonnets would tend to celebrate betrothal, and relatively few would probe its antecedent anxieties. To redress the balance, the simplest expedient would be to take up

† From *The Elizabethan Love Sonnet* by J.W. Lever (London, 1956), 99–136.

some earlier sonnets on the vicissitudes of *amour courtois*, written experimentally as off-shoots of the main allegorical work, and attach as many as were needed to the opening and middle portions of *Amoretti*. It was not uncommon for Elizabethan poets to adapt old verse to new purposes—Spenser's own treatment of the verse in der Noodt's tract is an obvious example—and this would explain, though not artistically condone, the presence of sonnets that jarred with the dominant tone of the sequence. * * *

There would seem to be only one way of doing justice to Spenser's sequence, and that is by setting apart those sonnets which evidently belong to an earlier phase and run counter to the general stream of Thought and feeling. * * * There are at least some eighteen sonnets best considered apart from the main group. All these relate to the experience of the scorned lover. * * *[1]

The remaining seventy-one sonnets make up the solid core of the *Amoretti* sequence. In considering Renaissance poetry, the first step must always be to determine 'the nature of the imitation'—in other words, to ascertain the distinctive qualities of a work by comparison with its models. While Spenser's sonnets were products of a lifetime's development and drew their ideas and inspiration from many sources, it is easy to distinguish certain immediate influences. For the general conception of the sequence we may look to the famous discourse of Bembo on *amor razionale* which ends the fourth book of Castiglione's *Il Cortegiano*. Widely known to English readers through Hoby's translation *The Courtier*, this popular work was certainly not the only channel through which a poet of Spenser's learning might discover the attitude of sixteenth-century Neoplatonism towards sexual love. But its mode of presentation made it especially suitable as a model. Instead of a formal dissertation of experience as shaped by circumstance, he would not have found it hard to incorporate such incidents. But the preconceived doctrines on which both *Amoretti* and *The Faerie Queene* were built involved him, it seems, in major difficulties. The ending of the sequence is a flaw in the artistic design, and its full implications must necessarily affect one's final estimate of Spenser as a poet of the sonnet.

In *Amoretti* the use of imagery is almost as distinctive as the handling of content. Little need be said of the sonnets that have been set apart from the main body. Their technique, fashioned after the allegorical style, is based on calculated exaggeration, and the images employed, neither metaphors nor genuine similes, may perhaps be described as emblematic. * * *

1. Lever's list includes   Sonnets 10 and   54, of those reproduced in this edition [*Editor*].

Spenser abandoned these methods in the sequence proper, but his characteristic treatment of courtship led to other peculiarities. Sidney had excelled in the use of personification and conceit to express subjective problems and emotional conflicts. For Spenser, there was no question of dramatizing sense-perception; and it followed that the Anacreontic fables and classical myths, with their personified eroticism, played no important part in *Amoretti*. Here the lady's eyes harboured no 'winged guest', and the angels who took Cupid's place were not susceptible to mythological treatment. Conceits are indeed to be found in these sonnets, but they are of minor importance in relation to the central issue. That of LXXI, with its spider and bee analogies, appears only after the real problem of the betrothed lady's position has been settled, and amounts to little more than affectionate banter. The old tale of the sickness of the lady and the lover's impatience with her physicians had inspired the impassioned sonnet CII of *Astrophel and Stella*. It was borrowed again for sonnet L of *Amoretti*; but by giving the illness to the lover instead of his lady, Spenser transposed the conceit to a minor key. In general, personification and conceit, with their functions of introspection and self-analysis, become subordinate or merely decorative devices.

If conceit furthered the intellectual assessment of experience, metaphor involved an intuitive sense of affinities between nature and spirit more congenial to the Latin imagination than the English. The Italian writers who supplied Spenser with his models maintained in their imagery a continuity of outlook that went back to the pagan world. The myths of the classics became the personifications of romance allegory and the metaphors of the Renaissance sonnet. But the English tradition militated against such expressions of affinity. Mythological allusions often became ornamental embellishments or intellectual symbols, and the metaphors of Italian literature were usually rendered as similes or conceits. In writing his great allegorical poem Spenser had necessarily created superb myths of his own,[2] though subjecting them to a distinctly individual treatment: but in the personal medium of the sonnet the national tradition reasserted itself. LXXVI and LXXVII of *Amoretti* differed from their model in Tasso's poem by relegating myth to a minor place and dissociating the idea of the lady's physical maturity from that of inanimate growth and fruition. * * * The metaphors of the sequence have a special character, and serve to relate the lovers' mental states to observed cases of purposeful activity. * * *

Simile, however, is the most usual type of imagery in *Amoretti*. The direct sensuous apprehension of likeness requires no deep com-

---

2. An admirable account of Spenser's treatment of allegorical myths is given in C. S. Lewis's *The Allegory of Love*, Chapter VII.

mitments of intellect or imagination. Even so, it will commonly be found that the evocations of Spenser's similes are less perceptual than they at first appear.

> For loe my love doth in her selfe containe
>   all this worlds riches that may farre be found,
>   if Saphyres, loe her eies be Saphyres plaine,
>   if Rubies, loe her lips be Rubies sound:
> If Pearles, her teeth be pearles both pure and round . . . (xv)

Precious jewels exercise an immemorial fascination upon the mind. Traditionally they were the repositories of various virtues, so that mention of them suggested not so much any definite physical properties of colour and shape as the ideal qualities they embodied. Often, by placing his sensuous images in apposition to spiritual concepts or abstract states of being, Spenser invested them by association with a similar ideality:

> Fayre bosome fraught with vertues richest treasure,
>   The neast of love, the lodging of delight:
>   the bowre of blisse, the paradice of pleasure,
>   the sacred harbour of that hevenly spright. (LXXVI)

At the same time, the extremer forms of spiritualization were generally avoided. Thus in sonnet LXIV the exotic aromas described in Canticles, symbolizing for the church the mystic rapture of the soul possessed by divine love, were replaced, not indeed by the sensualities of wild nature, but by the variegated scents of an English garden, the perfect expression of nature under the control and purposeful direction of mankind.[3] By such means the sensuous aspects of love were neither hypostatized, nor completely abstracted from themselves, but given their due subordinate place in the hierarchy of psychic values.

In the choice of words it had been, since Wyatt's time, the constant care of English poets to free the language from medieval encumbrances and to establish a contemporary diction. On the basis of Tudor achievements Sidney had evolved his flexible speech-rhythms, his colloquialisms and neologisms, which gave effect to every turn of the alert, quick-witted Elizabethan mind. Spenser, however, stood aside from this development and sought instead to incorporate in his diction the obsolete or obsolescent language of a bygone age. 'It was his aim,' wrote De Selincourt, 'to perfect for himself an instrument from which he could extract a music as subtle as Chaucer's, and by means of which he could create around his

---

3. The same biblical cadences return in *Epithalamion*, ll. 167–184, but the imagery now shows the fragrant flowers of courtship changed into the ripe fruits of marriage.

subject the atmosphere of an ideal antique world.'[4] The comment was made with reference to *The Faerie Queene* but it is also applicable to *Amoretti*. There is hardly a sonnet which does not contain words deliberately chosen for their strangeness. Medievalisms fast passing out of current use were revived and liberally introduced. We find 'mote' for 'might have', 'eke' for 'also', 'sith' for 'since', etc. Completely antiquated, almost forgotten words reappear, such as 'beseene', 'assoyle', 'stoures', 'amearst'. Side by side with these, Spenser introduced foreign loan-words, taking pains, when they had already been assimilated, to restore the marks of their alien origin. Such romance forms as 'semblant', 'pleasance', and 'richesse' replaced their familiar, anglicized variants. He chose, likewise, the romance spelling for 'ensample', 'pourtraict', 'noyous' and 'approch', applied the French stress to 'massacre', and French pronunciation to 'sacrifise'. Chaucer and the fifteenth-century allegorists showed precedents for many of these usages; but in their time the words were newcomers to the language and unavoidably conveyed an exotic flavour. Spenser's mannerisms, on the other hand, were a deliberate retrogression, aiming to associate with his treatment of courtship a sense of remoteness from the everyday world. From similar motives, he frequently departed from the customary sentence-order and used alien constructions, even at the risk of obscuring his meaning. A certain latitude in this respect has commonly been granted to poets; but Spenser made of it a regular practice and virtually disregarded the word-order of his own language. Such constructions as

> But they that skill not of so heavenly matter,
> all that they know not, envy or admyre,
> rather than envy let them wonder at her,
> but not to deeme of her desert aspyre (LXXXV)

almost justify Jonson's quip that 'in affecting the ancients . . . he writ no language'. In company with the 'aged accents and untimely words', they assist in estranging the diction of Spenser's sonnets from that of his time.

* * *

Invented in his earlier experiments at sonnet-writing, [Spenser's distinctive verse form] was essentially a system of interlacing rhymes suitable for a fourteen-line narrative or meditative stanza. Hitherto English poets had sought to escape from the narrative tradition in their sonnets, and to aim instead at a verse-form that would promote concise, inferential thinking based upon particular experiences. Spenser, however, deliberately weakened the capacity

4. The *Oxford* Spenser (1912), Introduction, p. lxi.

of his verse-form to suggest apposition, contrast, or logical correlation. His interlacing rhymes knit the whole sonnet into a seamless texture of sound, overlaying all verse divisions that correspond with separate links in a chain of logic, and setting up fourteen lines of unhalting, melodious exposition. The demonstrative exception was sonnet VIII, which, adopting the pure Surrey form, gave admirable expression to a moment of objective self-examination. But in general Spenser, on conscious philosophical grounds, rejected this approach. He would not accept the intrinsic validity of sense perception, and therefore could not admit logical inferences from perception as the informing principle of his love sonnets. True, courtship with its psychic discipline necessitated a measure of reflection and analysis of motives; true, too, that betrothal legitimately brought senses and affections into play. But these remained subordinate to a divinely appointed scheme, whose operations were independent of the fallible human faculties. The poet's task, as Spenser saw it, was not so much to shape through his art an ordered pattern from the flux of actuality, as to demonstrate a preordained design; not to hold the mirror up to life, but to justify the ways of God to men. Spenser's attempt to perform this task through the sonnet medium is implicit in all aspects of his formal technique.

* * *

An ancient, instinctive dualism in the English consciousness, tending to the view that nature and spirit were fundamentally opposed, distinguished the love poetry of this country from that of Mediterranean lands. Its stamp is set upon the Elizabethan treatment of the sonnet, as appears frequently when comparison is made between a French or Italian original and its English rendering. This dualism shapes the whole character of Sidney's sequence, where a romance pattern of experience is re-lived by an outstanding representative of sixteenth-century English values. Spenser, approaching the dilemma on a far more speculative plane, evolved his own solution in terms of Neoplatonist metaphysics. While his philosophical theories were derived from a general European school of thought, their application to creative literature necessarily involved a treatment modified by specifically English intuitions. Consequently Spenser's poetry laid particular stress upon psychic volition and practical virtue as the integrative factors capable of reconciling nature and spirit, rather than upon the transcendental powers of the soul as celebrated by Italian poets. Confirmation of this attitude was afforded by Protestant teaching, with its emphasis upon the individual conscience and on the merit of sacramental marriage. Thus Spenser's poetry was largely concerned with a denigration of the romance cult of courtly love and the substitution of a new theme: the triumph of virtuous courtship in betrothal and holy matrimony. It was an undertaking of great significance for the whole future of English literature; and no small part of Spenser's achievement was to have found expression for it through the personal medium of the sonnet sequence. *Amoretti* celebrated, often with striking beauty and delicacy, a courtship in which spiritual aspiration and natural desire were happily reconciled through a willed discipline of the psyche. Instead of conflict in the soul, pangs of conscience, and a final call for the renunciation of the flesh, love in these sonnets induced a growing measure of physical and spiritual ease. In this respect Spenser's sequence amply vindicates his right to be considered as one of the great masters of the English sonnet.

* * *

LOUIS MARTZ

[The *Amoretti*] †

But what of the other alleged disproportions and inconsistencies in the sequence [e.g., in particular, J. W. Lever's opinion that "the sonnets show irreconcilable inconsistencies in the presentation of the heroine"]? These too, I feel, tend to disappear within a dominant tone of assurance and poise and mutual understanding that controls the series. This peculiar and highly original relationship between the lover and his lady may be our best key to the whole sequence. It involves a variety of closely related issues: how does the lover characterize himself? what attitudes does he adopt toward the lady? what sort of audience does she provide? how does she receive his addresses? It is worth while to examine first the nature of this lady, for she talks and acts more than most of these heroines do. Most Petrarchan ladies, as Pope might say, "have no characters at all"; and even Sidney's Stella, though she comes to display considerable adroitness in damping her lover's ardors, remains for most of the sequence a black-eyed effigy around which Astrophel performs his brilliant Portrait of the Lover as a very young dog.

But Spenser's lady has a very decided and a very attractive character.[1] First of all, it is clear that the lover's tributes to "her mind

---

† From "The *Amoretti:* 'Most Goodly Temperature,' " in *Form and Convention in the Poetry of Edmund Spenser,* ed. W. Nelson (New York, 1961), 146–168.

1. See Hallett Smith, *Elizabethan Poetry* (Cambridge: Harvard Univ. Press, 1952), 166–167.

adornd with vertues manifold" (Sonnet 15), her "deep wit" (Sonnet 43), her "gentle wit, and vertuous mind" (Sonnet 79), her "words so wise," "the message of her gentle spright" (Sonnet 81) —it is clear that all these tributes to her mental powers are very well deserved. Quite early in the sequence, in the paired Sonnets 28 and 29, we find the lady wittily turning the tables on her lover in a dialogue that throws a bright light on their peculiar relationship. In Sonnet 28 the lover has noticed that she is wearing a laurel leaf, and this sign, he says, "gives me great hope of your relenting mynd," since it is the poet's own symbol; he goes on to warn her of the fate that befell proud Daphne when she fled from the god of poetry, and he ends with the witty turn:

> Then fly no more fayre love from Phebus chace,
> but in your brest his leafe and love embrace.

Then in Sonnet 29 the lady pertly carries on this play of wit:

> See how the stubborne damzell doth deprave
> my simple meaning with disdaynfull scorne:
> and by the bay which I unto her gave,
> accoumpts my selfe her captive quite forlorne.
> The bay (quoth she) is of the victours borne,
> yielded them by the vanquisht as theyr meeds,
> and they therewith doe poetes heads adorne,
> to sing the glory of their famous deedes.

All right, he says, since she claims the conquest, "let her accept me as her faithfull thrall":

> Then would I decke her head with glorious bayes,
> and fill the world with her victorious prayse.

I do not see how this interchange can be taken as anything but smiling and good-humored, yes, even humorous, in our sense of the word. The phrase "stubborne damzell" tells us a great deal about the poet's tone here: it is intimate, smiling, affectionate, respectful, reproachful, and courtly, all at once: it strikes exactly the tone that an older man, of experience and wisdom (someone a bit like Emma's Mr. Knightley) might adopt toward a bright and beautiful and willful young lady for whom he feels, not awe, but deep admiration and affection. It is an attitude that also implies considerable hope and confidence that his suit will in time be rewarded. It is an attitude that finds a fulfillment and perfect counterpart later on, after his acceptance, in the gentle wit of Sonnet 71, which even Mr. Lever takes as "affectionate banter" (p. 130). This is the sonnet where the lady, in a witty reversal of the poet's complaints, has woven into her embroidery a fable of the Bee and the Spyder; the poet picks up the imagery with joy and develops it with a deeply affectionate humor. Indeed, throughout the sequence she is certainly one of the most smiling and "chearefull" ladies to appear in any English sequence, and I doubt that her smiles are outdone anywhere on the Continent. Sonnets 39 and 40, wholly devoted to her smiling and her "amiable cheare," are only the most sustained of many indications of her "sweet eye-glaunces" and her "charming smiles" (Sonnet 17). In view of this it is hard to see why readers have insisted upon taking the whole sequence so solemnly. Sonnet 16, very early in the game, is enough in itself to tell us otherwise, with its playful, deliberately hyperbolic, and clearly smiling use of the Alexandrian Cupid:

> One day as I unwarily did gaze
>   on those fayre eyes my loves immortall light:
>   the whiles my stonisht hart stood in amaze,
>   through sweet illusion of her lookes delight;
> I mote perceive how in her glauncing sight,
>   legions of loves with little wings did fly:
>   darting their deadly arrowes fyry bright,
>   at every rash beholder passing by.
> One of those archers closely I did spy,
>   ayming his arrow at my very hart:
>   when suddenly with twincle of her eye,
>   the Damzell broke his misintended dart.
> Had she not so doon, sure I had bene slayne,
>   yet as it was, I hardly scap't with paine.

Now the meaning of "twincle" as a wink, a nod, a hint, was current in Elizabethan usage; a damsel with a twinkle would seem to hold here every modern connotation. At the same time, the strong colloquialism of the last two lines seems to warn us with a similar twinkle not to take this lover's professions of grief too solemnly.

But what then shall we make of Mr. Lever's eighteen excommunicated sonnets, along with others of this kind, where the lady commits those "huge massacres" with her eyes, and as a "cruell warriour"

> greedily her fell intent poursewth,
> Of my poore life to make unpittied spoile.

(Sonnet 11)

Many of these are done with such extravagant exaggeration of the conventional poses that they strike me as close to mock-heroic. These are the conventions of love, the poet seems to say; these are the usual rituals of courtship; he will gladly pay these tributes, and even overpay them, since this is what his delightful damsel seems to expect, and she thoroughly deserves this state; at the same time a girl of her deep wit will know exactly how to take them, in the spirit offered. She can be expected to respond with a smile and a witty rejoinder, as she does in Sonnet 18, herself outdoing the Petrarchan poses:

> But when I pleade, she bids me play my part,
>   and when I weep, she sayes teares are but water:
>   and when I sigh, she sayes I know the art,
>   and when I waile, she turnes hir selfe to laughter.

We can begin to see, then, the kind of relationship in which these charges of cruelty are uttered; we can begin to anticipate the sort of tone that the lover will tend to adopt in paying his conventional tributes.

Spenser's title is in itself a clue: *Amoretti*, the diminutive form, implying a relationship of intimate affection; it might be translated as: "intimate little tokens of love."[2] At the same time, the Italian title seems to draw a special attention to the great Continental tradition from which the sequence takes its themes, its imagery, its form. A complete definition might read: *Amoretti*, "intimate little tokens of love made out of ancient materials deriving, primarily, from Italy."

And so we have: [Quotes Sonnet 10].

The tone here is very hard to describe. It would be too much to call it parody, and yet the postures seem to be deliberately judged by the presence of some degree of smiling. It would be too much to call the sonnet comic, and yet, if we temper the term rightly, there is an element of comedy here, though not so broad as in the sonnet with the "twincle." At the same time, of course, a great many of these sonnets of complaint are delivered in a straightforward manner, and others allow little more than the glimmer of a smile to break through in the last line or two. I am arguing only that the series is frequently touched with an element that we might call humor, parody, or comedy; it is a light touch, but it is, I think, sovereign. Among the sixty sonnets that comes within the first year of courtship, it is possible to single out at least fifteen that seem clearly to display this transforming humor (for example: Sonnets 10, 12, 16, 18, 20, 24, 26, 28, 29, 30, 32, 33, 37, 43, 46, 48, 50, 57); and their presence is bound to have considerable effect upon our reading of all the other sonnets of complaint. As prime examples I would instance Sonnet 30, where Spenser drives into absurdity the old Petrarchan cliché: "My love is lyke to yse, and I to fyre"; or Sonnet 32, where the homely image of the "paynefull smith" beating the iron with "his heavy sledge" prepares the way for an account of how the lover's "playnts and prayers" beat futilely "on th'andvyle of her stubberne wit";

2. This translation was suggested by my friend Thomas Bergin.

What then remaines but I to ashes burne,
and she to stones at length all frosen turne?

Lines such as these, so close to parody, need not be taken as utterly inconsistent with those other sonnets, such as 7, 8, and 9, where the poet praises his lady's angelic virtue, with that famous tribute to her eyes:

Then to the Maker selfe they likest be,
whose light doth lighten all that here we see.

(Sonnet 9)

Does the opening line of the next sonnet (10)—"Unrighteous Lord of love what law is this, / That me thou makest thus tormented be?"—conflict with that exalted view of the lady? On the contrary, the poet seems to be making a clear distinction between those essential qualities deriving from the heavenly Maker, and those "cruelties" demanded by conventional Cupid, the unrighteous Lord of love, the adversary of the "glorious Lord of lyfe" who in Sonnet 68 teaches the lovers that devout lesson of love.

* * *

In Sonnet 45 we have, fully developed, the view that her essential being is belied by her proud and tyrannic aspects; here the lover, with a tone of excessive courtesy, urges the lady to stop looking in her mirror, "Your goodly selfe for evermore to vew," and instead to seek within her lover's "inward selfe" the image of her "semblant trew": [Quotes the remainder of the sonnet].

In still other sonnets the lover attempts to make a virtue of necessity by converting her twofold aspect into an example of "most goodly temperature": "Myld humblesse mixt with awfull majesty" (Sonnet 13):

Was it the worke of nature or of Art,
which tempred so the feature of her face,
that pride and meeknesse mixt by equall part,
doe both appeare t'adorne her beauties grace?

(Sonnet 21)

In short, the sonnets that deal with the proud and cruel fair form an indispensable part of the series; they represent the due and proper acknowledgment of all the usual forms of tribute:

Bring therefore all the forces that ye may,
and lay incessant battery to her heart,
playnts, prayers, vowes, ruth, sorrow, and dismay,
those engins can the proudest love convert.
And if those fayle fall downe and dy before her,
so dying live, and living do adore her.

Sonnet 14 thus foretells the use of every possible mode of Petrarchan approach, and the series thoroughly fulfills the promise, in many various modes: exalted, solemn, tender, touched with the edge of a smile, tinged with a hint of wit, or broadly comic.

Then, as we come close to the point where the lover discovers his acceptance, we find the rich variety of all the earlier sonnets summed up for us in Sonnet 54, which is perhaps more important than any other individual sonnet for an understanding of the sequence:

> Of this worlds Theatre in which we stay,
>   My love lyke the Spectator ydly sits
>   beholding me that all the pageants play,
>   disguysing diversly my troubled wits
> Sometimes I joy when glad occasion fits,
>   and mask in myrth lyke to a Comedy:
>   soone after when my joy to sorrow flits,
>   I waile and make my woes a Tragedy.

Those lines provide the best possible answer to any who might doubt the presence of mirth and comedy in the sequence; but more important is the way in which this sonnet indicates the complete recognition of the lover that he is deliberately playing many parts, staging "all the pageants" in an ancient festival of courtship, adopting all the masks that may catch his lady's eye and prove his devotion.

> Yet she beholding me with constant eye,
>   delights not in my merth nor rues my smart:
>   but when I laugh she mocks, and when I cry
>   she laughes, and hardens evermore her hart.
> What then can move her? if nor merth nor mone,
>   she is no woman, but a sencelesse stone.

* * *

Most goodly temperature indeed: in that one phrase Spenser has given us the best possible account of the *Amoretti*, as he leads us back to the ancient roots and affiliations of the word *temperature*: *temperatura, temperatus, temperatio*; signifying, in the terms of my Latin dictionary: a due mingling, fit proportion, proper combination, symmetry, a regulating power, an organizing principle.

WILLIAM NELSON

[Fowre Hymnes]†

In the *Fowre Hymnes* Spenser undertakes to expound his philosophy of love. There is a kind of preliminary sketch of this philosophy in Colin's rhapsody in *Colin Clouts Come Home Againe*, and the theme of generation, in particular, is the principal subject of the Garden of Adonis episode in the third book of *The Faerie Queene*. As a work devoted wholly to the philosophy of love the *Fowre Hymnes* stands alone, I think, in English literature of its time, though it belongs to a numerous company of such essays written in Renaissance Italy and France. The genre derives principally from the *Vita Nuova* and from Ficino's translations of Plato and Plotinus and his commentaries on them, especially his exposition *De amore* of Plato's *Symposium*. Some of the literary treatments of this kind are in prose, like Bembo's *Gli Asolani*, the speech which Castiglione attributes to Bembo in *Il Cortegiano*, the *Dialoghi d'Amore* of Leone Ebreo, and *Le Sympose de Platon de l'Amour et de Beauté . . . avec trois livres de Commentaires* of Louis Le Roy; others are in verse, like Benivieni's *Canzona dello Amore celeste et divino* which was published with a commentary by Pico della Mirandola.[1] Each of these works undertakes by Platonic or neo-Platonic means to discover the relationship between earthly and heavenly love.

Two of the sonnets of the *Amoretti* bear directly on this problem, one of them in Christian terms, the other in Platonic. In the first of these (LXVIII) the poet draws an earthly lesson from a contemplation of the surpassing love of Christ for mankind:

> So let us love, deare love, lyke as we ought,
> love is the lesson which the Lord us taught.

The second (LXXII) must be quoted in full: [Quotes Sonnet 72].
The object of both poems is to justify the earthly as an illustration or reflection of the heavenly. When Sidney treats this theme he writes wittily rather than seriously, and not only his manner but his meaning contrasts with Spenser's. Astrophel's love for Stella directly opposes reason and philosophy:

> Plato I have read for nought, but if he tame
> Such coltish yeeres

† From *The Poetry of Edmund Spenser* by William Nelson (New York, 1963), 97–115. The original footnotes have been slightly edited.

1. See John Charles Nelson, *Renaissance Theory of Love* (New York, 1958).

> With what strange checkes I in my selfe am shent,
> When into Reasons Audit I doe goe:
> And by such counts my selfe a Banckerowt know
>
> Reason, in faith thou art well serv'd, that still
> Would'st brabling be, with sence and love in me[2] . . .

And the lesson of Christ teaches Sidney not to love his dear love but to turn away from that which reaches but to dust to "Eternall Love."[3] For Italian Platonists like Benivieni and Castiglione human love is not indeed antithetic to reason; it is rather a first step to be left behind as the true lover rises to a truer love, "grade by grade to the uncreated sphere/ . . . whence fashioned were/ All beauties in the loved one manifest."[4] But Spenser neither declares the earthly incompatible with the heavenly, as Sidney does, nor does he envision an unbroken ascent which spurns earth in its aspiration for heaven. He would have both loves, the one infinitely good, the other good too because, though finite, it imitates the infinite.

These are the two goods of the earthly and the heavenly hymns. In his dedication Spenser explains that the former hymns were written "in the greener times" of his youth, and since they "too much pleased those of like age and disposition," feeding their strong passions, he was moved to add the hymns of "celestiall" love and beauty "by way of retractation." Some scholars have argued that this account is a fiction designed to preserve decorum by associating sexual love with youth and contemplative love with maturity. They may indeed be right, for I find it hard to believe that even in his greenest times Spenser would have thought his paean of love complete without reference to a realm transcending the mundane.

As the poet says, the hymns of heavenly love and heavenly beauty constitute a palinode for the earthly pair:

> But all those follies now I do reprove,
> And turned have the tenor of my string,
> The heavenly prayses of true love to sing.   (*HHL*, 12–14)

A palinode makes little sense unless one knows what it is opposed to, and it is evident that the two later hymns are designed to gain strength and meaning from the two former. The method is a complex system of parallels and contrasts. Each hymn begins with an invocation and ends with a paradisal vision. The two hymns of love are linked by their common concern with motive; the hymns of

2. *The Complete Works of Sir Philip Sidney*, ed. A. Feuillerat (Cambridge, 1912–26), I, 246, 250, 251.
3. *Ibid.*, p. 322.

4. Girolamo Benivieni, "Ode of Love," tr. J. B. Fletcher, *Literature of the Italian Renaissance* (New York, 1934), p. 340.

beauty by their common concern with the goal toward which that motive drives. But between earth and heaven there lies a great gulf.

Both hymns of love invoke the god, but the home of earthly love is Venus' lap while that of heavenly love is "heavens hight." Earthly love is the son of Venus and at the same time "Begot of Plentie and of Penurie"—the Plenty of Beauty and the Penury which is the hunger for Beauty. In *Colin Clouts Come Home Againe* Love's genealogy is explained differently: he is the child of the hermaphrodite Venus, born pure and spotless of a beautiful conjunction of opposites. Heavenly love is Christ, derived not from a desire for something lacking nor from a mixture of contraries but from single Plenty alone, for the "high eternall powre"

> lov'd it selfe, because it selfe was faire;
> (For faire is lov'd;) and of it selfe begot
> Like to it selfe his eldest sonne and heire. . . .   (*HHL*, 29–31)

The creation of the mutable world is a history of the works of earthly love: Love reconciled the warring elements of chaos, binding together contraries "with adamantine chains," setting bounds to the things so created, dividing the heavens and the earth, the land and the sea. The Almighty, too, is described as the generative force,

> that loves to get
> Things like himselfe, and to enlarge his race   (*HHL*, 51–52)

and it is He who created the angels and their dwelling place, "the heavens illimitable hight,/ Not this round heaven." And after the fall of Lucifer He made man "of clay, base, vile, and next to nought,"

> and breathd a living spright
> Into his face most beautifull and fayre,
> Endewd with wisdomes riches, heavenly, rare. (*HHL*, 110–12)

But apart from man, nothing is said of His creation of "this round heaven" and the living world within it, so that there is no direct contradiction of the earlier hymn by the later.

As Cupid generates the world so he inspires in its creatures the desire for generation. Beasts seek their mates blindly, unaware of the nature of the force that urges them and ignorant, too, of its procreative purpose. But man, who occupies a special and exalted place within the animate world, retains within his spirit some trace of "that heavenly fire" which is defined in *Colin Clouts Come Home Againe* as "the sparke of reasons might." He therefore knowingly seeks Beauty "borne of heavenly race," and

> Not for lusts sake, but for eternitie,
> Seekes to enlarge his lasting progenie.   (*HL*, 104–5)

His search is terribly difficult, for Love "enmarbles" the lady's proud heart and makes her pitiless so that the lover suffers anguish. This suffering tests the validity of the lover's passion. "Baseborne mynds" which feel only "loose desyre" will not endure it. The high distance of the lady cleanses the lover's soul of "dunghill thoughts" and spurs him to great deeds in the hope of winning her favor. Even when the victory is in sight, however, the purgation continues, for the lover can be satisfied only by the knowledge that he alone is loved in return. Until that time he suffers from countless fears, surmises, envies, rumors, delays, and worst of all, from jealousy. But after purgatory comes paradise—an earthly paradise, for it rewards an earthly love, a paradise of nectar and ivory beds arrayed with roses and lilies:

> There with thy daughter Pleasure they doe play
> Their hurtlesse sports, without rebuke or blame,
> And in her snowy bosome boldly lay
> Their quiet heads, devoyd of guilty shame,
> After full joyance of their gentle game. . . .   (HL, 287–91)

Point for point, the nature of this earthly love is compared with that of the realm of heaven. There, "pride and love may ill agree"; Lucifer falls through pride but in Christ "no jot/ Of loves dislike, or pride was to be found." The parallel to the lover's anguish is that of Jesus, caused by the

> huge and most unspeakeable impression
> Of loves deepe wound, that pierst the piteous hart. . . .
> (HHL, 155–56)

If earthly love lifts himself "out of the lowly dust,/ On golden plumes up to the purest skie," heavenly love descends, "Out of the bosome of eternall blisse"

> like a most demisse
> And abject thrall, in fleshes fraile attyre. . . .   (HHL, 136–37)

For the "brave exploits" of the one there is the "humble carriage" of the other. The earthly lover demands to be loved alone; Christ asks us to love Him and also "our brethren to his image wrought." Yet the jealous exclusiveness of human love has its counterpart in heaven:

> With all thy hart, with all thy soule and mind,
> Thou must him love, and his beheasts embrace:
> All other loves, with which the world doth blind
> Weake fancies, and stirre up affections base,
> Thou must renounce. . . .   (HHL, 260–64)

And with renunciation and purification the lover of Christ attains a vision, not of ivory beds, but of "Th'Idee of his pure glorie."

The search for true Beauty discloses similar contrasts. The movement of the earthly hymn is down, beginning with the aboriginal "wondrous Paterne" according to which "the worlds great workmaister" fashioned all things "as comely as he could," and descending with the soul to be embodied past the sphere of the sun to the living lady, fair in spirit and therefore in body. The movement of the heavenly hymn is up,

> Beginning then below, with th'easie vew
> Of this base world, subject to fleshly eye . . .　　(HHB, 22–23)

and rising through the elements and the spheres of the mutable world to the "Unmoving, uncorrupt" heaven beyond, organized like this one in nine degrees of increasing beauty.[5] The discovery of mundane beauty demands the distinction between essence and appearance. It must be identified not with features, colors, proportions that fade and die but with the source of which these appearances are the reflection, the inward beauty of the soul which is divinely derived and therefore immortal. Similarly, even the intelligible aspects of the universe offer only a hint of the celestial beauty from which they arise:

> Cease then, my tongue, and lend unto my mynd
> Leave to bethinke how great that beautie is,
> Whose utmost parts so beautifull I fynd,
>
> How much more those essentiall parts of his,
> His truth, his love, his wisedome, and his blis,
> His grace, his doome, his mercy, and his might,
> By which he lends us of himselfe a sight.　　(HHB, 106–12)

In the realm of the earthly hymn, beauty manifests itself to those who love. Spenser does not say with Marlowe (and Shakespeare), "Who ever lov'd that lov'd not at first sight?" Beauty of appearance may stir the beholder—so fancy is bred—but

> all that like the beautie which they see,
> Streight do not love: for love is not so light,
> As streight to burne at first beholders sight.　　(HB, 208–10)

In *Colin Clouts Come Home Againe* the shepherds are taught that when Beauty darts her beams into the mind of man he seeks cure

5. Spenser's account of the celestial hierarchy has puzzled his commentators because it corresponds to none of the usual descriptions (see C. A. Patrides, "Renaissance Thoughts on the Celestial Hierarchy," *JHI*, XX [1959], 161. But there is a close analogue to Spenser's list in *Discorsi del Conte Annibal Romei* (Venice, 1585), pp. 6–7, and it may be that both derive from a common source. * * *

for his pain from her that wounded him. In the hymn, the poet makes it clear that only when the lover-to-be apprehends essential rather than apparent beauty does he truly fall in love. The first step is liberation of the sensible image from "fleshes frayle infection." Next, this purer form is "conformed" to the sun-derived light of his own spirit, the result being a heavenly beauty which is the "mirrour of his owne thought." This is "fairer, then it is indeede" when "indeede" refers to the lady's appearance, "And yet indeede her fairenesse doth exceede" when "indeede" refers to that more profound beauty which even the sharp-sighted lover cannot fully see. With this achievement, the lover perceives beauty at its earthly summit:

> Sometimes upon her forhead they behold
> A thousand Graces masking in delight,
> Sometimes within her eye-lids they unfold
> Ten thousand sweet belgards, which to their sight
> Doe seeme like twinckling starres in frostie night:
> But on her lips like rosy buds in May,
> So many millions of chaste pleasures play.   (HB, 253–59)

These are the attributes of Beauty, the "handmaides" of Venus.

The way to a vision of Heavenly Beauty begins, like the path to Venus, with beautiful appearance in this world, but Spenser distinguishes the two journeys by beginning the one with a fair countenance and the other with the fair world of sense. The rise to the celestial is accomplished through heavenly contemplation of the "high flying mynd." At the pinnacle of heaven is the Highest, bathed in light so brilliant that the sun, source of beauty for the lower universe, seems dark. Neither men nor angels can look directly at those bright beams, but some happy mortals "whom God so much doth grace" may, like the angels themselves, see God's "owne Beloved" Sapience who sits in His bosom, dimming the beauty of Venus.

As the earthly hymns, then, distinguish love from lust and essential from superficial beauty, so the heavenly hymns oppose Christ to Cupid and Sapience to Venus. At the same time, these oppositions declare the relationship, however distant, between the blind generative passion of beasts and the love of Christ, between the beauty of mundane creation and the unimaginable splendor of God.

This fabric of love is a weaving of Spenser's own. The strands which compose it are diverse, indeed incompatible by philosophic standards. They derive from the *fin amor* of Provence, from the ancient conception of Nature as a generative force, from Christian doctrine and Christian mysticism, and from what must loosely be called Platonism. In full accord with the spirit of most Renaissance thinking Spenser's effort in the *Fowre Hymnes*, as in his other poems, is to discover common direction in the traditions which he inherited, even at the cost of blurring distinctions logically necessary. The very diversity of the traditions which enter into it is therefore essential to the conception of the work.

The language and thought of the hymns insistently echoes that of the amorists of the Middle Ages. Like Spenser, they make much of the distinction between true love and beastly lust, of the play of the eyes, the haughtiness of the lady, the monomania and suffering of the lover, the sickness of jealousy, the stimulation to noble deeds and poetic utterance, and the purification of the lover's spirit. The goal of the lover is sexual union, whether in the form of a token smile or kiss or in physical consummation, and it is conceived of as a "joy" or ecstasy beyond the experience of ordinary mortals. By Chaucer's time, at least, even marriage can be accommodated to the convention, for if Troilus has no thought of wedding, the prize of the *Knight's Tale* is not merely Emily's heart but her hand as well, and it is essential to the *Franklin's Tale* that the true union of Dorigen and Arveragus is the consequence of a most courtly courtship. While this love of the troubadours and their followers is at base sensual, it is not without its links to heaven. If Andrew the Chaplain retracts his art of courtly love in a concluding book of divine love he by the same token associates the two. The love language of the Provençal poets becomes the language in which nuns are taught to express their adoration of Christ. With Dante, the lady herself becomes an angel and the final ecstasy of love the divine vision.

Despite these resemblances, Spenser's understanding of the nature of love differs significantly from that of the courtly amorists. When the writer of the medieval tradition distinguishes between love and lust he does so on the basis of the involvement of the heart rather than the body, his touchstone being the gentility of the enamored spirits. Spenser says this too, but his distinction depends primarily upon man's "more immortal mind," his "sparke of reasons might." For the troubadour and his heirs, reason characterizes a heavenly love, not an earthly. Indeed, it is the enemy of earthly love, however "gentle." Dante, it is true, asserts that Beatrice's image was of such virtue "that no time did it suffer Love to rule over me without the faithful counsel of reason, in those things where such counsel were useful to hear,"[6] but even this is to make reason love's handmaid, not love's guide.

Although Dante and the courtly amorists speak of love as a creative force they do not concern themselves with the kind of creation represented by the bearing of children and the peopling of the earth.

6. *La Vita Nuova*, ii (tr. P. H. Wicksteed, the Temple Classics).

For this aspect of his philosophy Spenser drew upon the ancient conception of Nature as a beneficent and fecund power. Ovid's account of the making of the world closely resembles that of Spenser in the *Hymne of Love*; both tell of an original Chaos of antagonistic and unlimited elements drawn into harmony and set in bounds by the creator. Ovid is not sure whether this power is Nature or some other god; Claudian identifies her with Nature, governor of marriage and generation. The twelfth-century philosophical poets Bernard Silvestris and Alain de Lille find a place for *Natura* between God and the world, associating her both with the creation and ordering of the cosmos and with childbearing. Jean de Meun's *Romance of the Rose* assigns to Nature and her high priest Genius (the Roman god of generation) the final victory of the lover, and it is Nature who presides over the marriage contest of Chaucer's *Parlement of Foules*. Spenser's familiarity with this tradition is made evident by his description of Genius as the porter in the Garden of Adonis and by his choice of the goddess as the arbiter of Mutabilitie's claim to dominion over the world.

* * *

Inextricably mixed with these strains in Spenser's thinking is the Platonic. The teaching of Plato came to the poet and his contemporaries along a tangle of paths: from the philosopher himself and from his followers Porphyry and Plotinus; from Greek and Latin moralists like Plutarch, Vergil, Cicero, Macrobius, and Boethius; from St. Augustine and other fathers of the Christian church; from philosophers and poets of the high Middle Ages; and from the revivified Platonism of the Italian Renaissance. *Fin amor* was itself influenced by Platonic notions and Italian Platonism was in turn indebted to *fin amor*. It is only rarely possible, therefore, to assert of an aspect of Spenser's philosophy that it derives, let us say, from Ficino and not from Plotinus, Vergil, or Chaucer. But the connections between Spenser's ideas and the Platonic grand scheme of things are clear enough.

* * *

Spenser was of course first of all a Christian. There is nothing in Plato or Plotinus that corresponds to the descent of God into the flesh and His sacrifice for mankind. But it is idle to ask whether Spenser was a Christian Platonist or a Platonic Christian. From the time of the Fathers, Christianity had itself been Platonic, and St. Augustine's admiration for Plato and his debt to Plotinus are well known. Medieval theologians adapted to Christian uses whatever they could of classical philosophy, sometimes stretching the literal sense of the Bible in order to make it consonant with pagan teaching, sometimes reinterpreting pagan teaching to fit it to the Bible. By appropriate changes in form and function even the ancient gods were made to serve true religion. Furthermore, classical writers and philosophers were themselves turned almost Christian in the sense that their morality and striving for truth were thought to arise from some apprehension of the as yet unrevealed verity of Christ. Some Platonic tenets, such as the belief in the eternity of the world and in metempsychosis, proved difficult to accommodate to Christianity; others, like the complex series of hypostases between the One and the realm of matter, held little interest for most Christians. But both Platonists and Christians identify the highest with ultimate good and ultimate beauty, both find material existence in comparison shadowy and poor, both urge man to break from the bounds of earth toward the celestial. The Sapience who sits in God's bosom in the *Hymne of Heavenly Beautie* has been variously interpreted as the Holy Ghost, Christ, the Sapience of the Book of Wisdom, and the Platonic Heavenly Venus, and she has qualities of each of these. Since Spenser does not tell us specifically which she is, he no doubt intends what is common to all, a wealth and wisdom of which this world's riches and knowledge are only a token, an entity associated with God yet not altogether beyond the apprehension of the purified human soul. The high "Ideas . . . which Plato so admyred" are ranged in the celestial realm between the souls of the happy and the Powers and Dominations of the Bible. The Hill of Contemplation from which the Red Cross Knight sees the New Jerusalem is likened to Sinai, the Mount of Olives, and Parnassus.

Spenser's system of love, as even so cursory a study shows, reaches upward from this world but keeps foothold within it. Examined as a logical construct, it disintegrates at once into a conglomeration of inconsistencies and even absurdities. But it has a coherence of another kind. The poet was attempting to justify by the authority of literature, the wisdom of the ancients, and revealed religion his deep feelings about the relationships of man and woman and man and God. He saw a likeness between the love that draws the sexes together, producing noble deeds and perpetuating the race, and the love that draws man to God and fills the world with beauty. To testify to this likeness he summoned his cloud of witnesses.

Selected Bibliography

The Works of Edmund Spenser: A Variorum Edition, ed. E. Greenlaw, C. G. Osgood, F. M. Padelford, et al., 9 vols. (Baltimore, 1932–1949) takes account of textual variants in the early editions, notes preferred readings and emendations in later editions, and provides extensive selections from the whole range of criticism of Spenser's poetry. The most significant early edition of Spenser's complete works is that edited by John Hughes (London, 1715). Important later editions of the works are those edited by R. E. N. Dodge (Boston, 1908) and by J. C. Smith and E. de Selincourt (Oxford, 1909–1910). Important editions of The Faerie Queene include those of Ralph Church (London, 1758), John Upton (London, 1758), and A. C. Hamilton (London and N.Y., 1977). Among editions of the minor works, Lilian Winstanley's edition of Fowre Hymnes (Cambridge, 1907), W. L. Renwick's editions of The Shepherd's Calendar (London, 1930), Complaints (London, 1928), and Daphnaida and Other Poems (London, 1929), and S. P. Zitner's edition of The Mutabilitie Cantos (London, 1968) are notable.

Bibliographies include F. I. Carpenter, A Reference Guide to Edmund Spenser (Chicago, 1923; reprint ed., Gloucester, Mass., 1950); Dorothy R. Atkinson, Edmund Spenser: A Bibliographical Supplement [covering the period from 1923 to 1937] (Baltimore, 1937); and Waldo F. McNeir and Foster Provost, Edmund Spenser: An Annotated Bibliography 1937–1972 (Pittsburgh, 1975). C. G. Osgood has compiled a Concordance to the Poems of Edmund Spenser (Washington, D.C., 1915). Jewel Wurtsbaugh, Two Centuries of Spenserian Scholarship (Baltimore, 1936), provides a useful survey of early scholarship.

The fullest biography is that by A. C. Judson, The Life of Edmund Spenser (Baltimore, 1945).

Spenser Studies: A Renaissance Poetry Annual (Pittsburgh, 1980–) includes essays on Spenser and related Renaissance subjects. Spenser Newsletter, published thrice yearly, includes reviews, abstracts, and reports on Spenser scholarship and criticism.

The book lists below do not include criticism published before 1937, periodical articles reprinted in this edition, or critical studies primarily concerned with works by Spenser not included in this edition.

GENERAL STUDIES

Barney, Stephen A. Allegories of History, Allegories of Love. Hamden, Conn., 1979.

Bush, Douglas. Mythology and the Renaissance Tradition in English Poetry. Revised edition. New York, 1963.

Caldwell, Mark. "Allegory: The Renaissance Mode." ELH, XLIV (1977), 580–600.

Chew, Samuel. The Pilgrimage of Life. New Haven, Conn., 1962.

Comito, Terry. The Idea of the Garden in the Renaissance. New Brunswick, N.J., 1978.

Cooper, Helen. Pastoral: Mediaeval into Renaissance. Totowa, N.J., 1977.

Crampton, Georgia Ronan. The Condition of Creatures: Suffering and Action in Chaucer and Spenser. New Haven, Conn., 1974.

Curtius, Ernst Robert. European Literature and the Latin Middle Ages. Trans. Willard R. Trask. New York, 1953.

Dundas, Judith. "Allegory as a Form of Wit." SRen, XI (1964), 223–233.

Durling, Robert. The Figure of the Poet in Renaissance Epic. Cambridge, Mass., 1965.

Fletcher, Angus. Allegory, the Theory of a Symbolic Mode. Ithaca, N.Y., 1964.

Fowler, Alastair, ed. Silent Poetry: Essays in Numerological Analysis. New York, 1970.

Fowler, Alastair. Triumphal Forms: Structural Patterns in Elizabethan Poetry. Cambridge, 1970.

Freeman, Rosemary. *English Emblem Books.* London, 1948.

Frye, Northrop. *Anatomy of Criticism: Four Essays.* Princeton, N.J., 1957.

Frye, Northrop. *Spiritus Mundi: Essays on Literature, Myth, and Society.* Bloomington, Indiana, 1976.

Giamatti, A. Bartlett. *The Earthly Paradise and the Renaissance Epic.* Princeton, N.J., 1966.

Gombrich, E. H. *Symbolic Images.* London, 1972.

Grant, Patrick. *Images and Ideas in Literature of the English Renaissance.* Amherst, Mass., 1979.

Heninger, S. K., Jr. *The Cosmograpical Glass: Renaissance Diagrams of the Universe.* San Marino, Calif., 1977.

Heninger, S. K., Jr. *Touches of Sweet Harmony: Pythagorean Cosmology and Renaissance Poetics.* San Marino, Calif., 1974.

Honig, Edwin. *Dark Conceit: The Making of Allegory.* Evanston, Ill., 1959.

Javitch, Daniel. *Poetry and Courtliness in Renaissance England.* Princeton, N.J., 1978.

Johnson, Francis R. *Astronomical Thought in Renaissance England.* Baltimore, 1937.

Keach, William. *Elizabethan Erotic Narratives: Irony and Pathos in the Ovidian Poetry of Shakespeare, Marlowe, and their Contemporaries.* New Brunswick, N.J., 1977.

Lanham, Richard A. *The Motives of Eloquence: Literary Rhetoric in the Renaissance.* New Haven, Conn., 1976.

Levin, Harry. *The Myth of the Golden Age in the Renaissance.* Bloomington, Indiana, 1969.

Lewis, C. S. *The Allegory of Love.* Oxford, 1936.

Lewis, C. S. *The Discarded Image: An Introduction to Medieval and Renaissance Literature.* Cambridge, 1964.

Lewis, C. S. *English Literature in the Sixteenth Century Excluding Drama.* Oxford, 1954.

Lewis, C. S. *Studies in Medieval and Renaissance Literature.* Ed. Walter Hooper. Cambridge, 1966.

Merivale, Patricia. *Pan the Goat-God: His Myth in Modern Times.* Cambridge, Mass., 1969.

Miskimin, Alice S. *The Renaissance Chaucer.* New Haven, Conn., 1975.

Murrin, Michael. *The Allegorical Epic: Essays in its Rise and Decline.* Chicago, 1980.

Murrin, Michael. *The Veil of Allegory.* Chicago, 1969.

Nelson, William. "From 'Listen Lordlings', to 'Dear Reader'." *UTQ,* XLVI (1976), 110–125.

Panofsky, Erwin. *Studies in Iconology: Humanistic Themes in the Art of the Renaissance.* London, 1962.

Parker, Patricia A. *Inescapable Romance: Studies in the Poetics of a Mode.* Princeton, N.J., 1979.

Peterson, Douglas L. *The English Lyric from Wyatt to Donne: A History of the Plain and Eloquent Styles.* Princeton, N.J., 1967.

Quinones, Ricardo. *The Renaissance Discovery of Time.* Cambridge, Mass., 1972.

Rossky, William. "Imagination in the English Renaissance: Psychology and Poetic." *SRen,* V (1958), 49–73.

Seznec, Jean. *The Survival of the Pagan Gods.* Trans. Barbara F. Sessions. New York, 1953.

Smith, Hallett. *Elizabethan Poetry: A Study in Conventions, Meaning, and Expression.* Cambridge, Mass., 1952.

Starnes, D. T., and Talbert, E. W. *Classical Myth and Legend in Renaissance Dictionaries.* Chapel Hill, N.C., 1955.

Steadman, John M. *Nature Into Myth: Medieval and Renaissance Moral Symbols.* Pittsburgh, Pa., 1979.

Tayler, E. W. *Nature and Art in Renaissance Literature.* New York, 1964.

Tuve, Rosemond. *Allegorical Imagery: Some Mediaeval Books and Their Posterity.* Princeton, N.J., 1966.

Tuve, Rosemond. *Elizabethan and Metaphysical Imagery.* Chicago, 1947.

Wilson, F. P. *Elizabethan and Jacobean.* Oxford, 1945.

Wind, Edgar. *Pagan Mysteries in the Renaissance.* New Haven, Conn., 1958.

Winny, James, ed. *The Frame of Order: An Outline of Elizabethan Belief taken from Treatises of the Late Sixteenth Century.* London, 1957.

Woodhouse, A. S. P. *The Poet and His Faith: Religion and Poetry in England from Spenser to Eliot and Auden.* Chicago, 1965.

Yates, Frances R. *The Occult Philosophy in the Elizabethan Age.* London, 1979.

SPENSER'S POETRY: COLLECTIONS OF CRITICISM

Alpers, Paul J., ed. *Elizabethan Poetry: Modern Essays in Criticism.* New York, 1967.

Atchity, K. J., ed. *Eterne In Mutabilitie: The Unity of "The Faerie Queene": Essays Published in Memory of Davis Philoon Harding, 1914–1970.* Hamden, Conn., 1972.

Cummings, R. M., ed. *Spenser: The Critical Heritage.* London, 1971.

Elliott, John R., Jr., ed. *The Prince of Poets: Essays on Edmund Spenser.* New York, 1968.

Frushell, Richard C., and Vondersmith, Bernard J., eds. *Contemporary Thought on Edmund Spenser.* Carbondale, Ill., 1975.

Hamilton, A. C., ed. *Essential Articles for the Study of Edmund Spenser.* Hamden, Conn., 1972.

Kennedy, Judith M., and Reither, James A., eds. *A Theatre for Spenserians.* Toronto, 1973.

Mueller, W. R., ed. *Spenser's Critics: Changing Currents in Literary Taste.* Syracuse, N.Y., 1959.

Mueller, W. R., and Allen, D. C., eds. *That Soveraine Light: Essays in Honor of Edmund Spenser 1552–1952.* Baltimore, 1952.

Nelson, William, ed. *Form and Convention in the Poetry of Edmund Spenser: Selected Papers from the English Institute* [1959–1960]. New York, 1961.

Richardson, David, ed. *Spenser and the Middle Ages.* Cleveland, 1976 [microfiche].

Richardson, David, ed. *Spenser: Classical, Medieval, Renaissance, and Modern.* Cleveland, 1977 [microfiche].

Richardson, David, ed. *Spenser at Kalamazoo.* Cleveland, 1978 [microfiche].

Richardson, David, ed. *Spenser at Kalamazoo, 1979.* Cleveland, 1979 [(microfiche].

SPENSER'S POETRY: GENERAL

Arthos, John. *On the Poetry of Spenser and the Form of Romances.* London, 1956.

Bender, John B. *Spenser and Literary Pictorialism.* Princeton, N.J., 1972.

Bennett, Josephine W. "Genre, Milieu, and the 'Epic-Romance.' " In *English Institute Essays, 1951.* New York, 1952.

Berger, Harry, Jr. "The Spenserian Dynamics." *SEL,* VIII (1968), 1–18.

Bradbrook, M. C. "No Room at the Top: Spenser's Pursuit of Fame." In *Elizabethan Poetry.* Stratford-upon-Avon Studies, 2. Ed. J. R. Brown and B. Harris. London, 1960.

Ellrodt, Robert. *Neoplatonism in the Poetry of Spenser.* Geneva, 1960.

Helgerson, Richard. "The Elizabethan Laureate: Self-Presentation and the Literary System." *ELH,* XLVI (1979), 193–220.

Helgerson, Richard. "The New Poet Presents Himself: Spenser and the Idea of a Literary Career." *PMLA,* XCIII (1978), 893–911.

Hollander, John. "Spenser and the Mingled Measure." *ELR,* I (1971), 226–238.

Lotspeich, Henry G. *Classical Mythology in the Poetry of Edmund Spenser.* Princeton, N.J., 1932. Reprinted, New York, 1965.

Nelson, William. *The Poety of Spenser: A Study.* New York, 1963.

Patrides, C. A. "The Achievement of Edmund Spenser," *YR,* Spring 1980, 427–443.

Richardson, David. "Duality in Spenser's Archaisms." *Studies in the Literary Imagination* (Atlanta, Ga.), XI (1978), 81–98.

Rix, H. D. *Rhetoric in Spenser's Poetry.* University Park, Pa., 1940.

Satterthwaite, A. W. *Spenser, Ronsard, and Du Bellay: A Renaissance Comparison.* Princeton, N.J., 1960.

Smith, Charles G. *Spenser's Proverb Lore.* Cambridge, Mass., 1970.

Starnes, D. T. "Spenser and the Graces." *PQ,* XXI (1942), 268–282.

Starnes, D. T. "Spenser and the Muses." *TSE,* XXII (1942), 31–58.

Watkins, W. B. C. *Shakespeare and Spenser.* Princton, N.J., 1950.

Witaker, Virgil K. *The Religious Basis of Spenser's Thought.* Stanford, Calif., 1950.

Wilson, Rawdon. "Images and 'Allegoremes' of Time in the Poetry of Spenser." *ELR,* IV (1974), 56–82.

THE FAERIE QUEENE: GENERAL STUDIES

Alpers, Paul J. "How to Read *The Faerie Queene.*" *EIC,* XVIII (1968), 429–443.

Alpers, Paul J. "Narration in *The Faerie Queene*." *ELH*, XLIV (1977), 19–39.
Alpers, Paul J. *The Poetry of "The Faerie Queene*." Princeton, N.J., 1967.
Anderson, Judith H. *The Growth of a Personal Voice: "Piers Plowman" and "The Faerie Queene*." New Haven, 1976.
Baybak, Michael, Delany, Paul, and Hieatt, A. Kent. "Placement 'in the Middest' in *The Faerie Queene*." *PLL*, V (1969), 227–234.
Bennett, Josephine W. *The Evolution of "The Faerie Queene*." Chicago, 1942.
Bradner, Leicester. *Edmund Spenser and "The Faerie Queene*." Chicago, 1948.
Brand, C. P. "Tasso, Spenser, and the *Orlando Furioso*." In *Petrarch to Pirandello: Studies in Italian Literature in Honour of Beatrice Corrigan*, edited by J. A. Molinaro, pp. 95–110. Toronto, 1973.
Brown, James Neil. "The Unity of *The Faerie Queene*, Books I–V." *Southern Review* [Australia], X (1977), 3–21.
Cain, Thomas H. *Praise in "The Faerie Queene*." Lincoln, Nebraska, 1978.
Cheney, Donald. *Spenser's Image of Nature: Wild Man and Shepherd in "The Faerie Queene*." New Haven, Conn., 1966.
Cosman, Madeleine P. "Spenser's Ark of Animals: Animal Imagery in *The Faerie Queene*." *SEL*, III (1963), 85–107.
Craig, Joanne. "The Image of Mortality: Myth and History in *The Faerie Queene*." *ELH*, XXXIX (1972), 520–544.
Craig, Martha. "The Secret Wit of Spenser's Language." In *Elizabethan Poetry: Modern Essays in Criticism*, edited by Paul Alpers, pp. 447–472. New York, 1967.
Cullen, Patrick. *Infernal Triad: The Flesh, the World, and the Devil in Spenser and Milton*. Princeton, N.J., 1974.
Dees, Jerome S. "The Narrator of *The Faerie Queene*: Patterns of Response." *TSLL*, XII (1971), 537–568.
Dundas, Judith. "The Rhetorical Basis of Spenser's Imagery." *SEL*, VIII (1968), 59–75.
Dundas, Judith. "*The Faerie Queene*: The Incomplete Poem and the Whole Meaning." *MP*, LXXI (1974), 257–265.
Evans, Maurice. *Spenser's Anatomy of Heroism: A Commentary on "The Faerie Queene*." Cambridge, 1970.
Fletcher, Angus. *The Prophetic Moment: An Essay on Spenser*. Chicago, 1971.
Fowler, Alastair. *Spenser and the Numbers of Time*. London, 1964.
Freeman, Rosemary. *"The Faerie Queene": A Companion for Readers*. London, 1970.
Giamatti, A. Bartlett. *Play of Double Senses: Spenser's "Faerie Queene*." Englewood Cliffs, N.J., 1975.
Giamatti, A. Bartlett. "Primitivism and the Process of Civility in Spenser's *Faerie Queene*." In *First Images of America: The Impact of the New World on the Old*, edited by F. Chiappelli. 2 vols., I, 71–82. Berkeley, Calif., 1976.
Giamatti, A. Bartlett. "Spenser: From Magic to Miracle." In *Four Essays in Romance*, edited by Herschel Baker, pp. 17–31. Cambridge, Mass., 1971.
Glazier, Lyle. "The Nature of Spenser's Imagery." *MLQ*, XVI (1955), 300–310.
Gray, J. C. "Bondage and Deliverance in *The Faerie Queene*: Varieties of a Moral Imperative." *MLR*, LXX (1975), 1–12.
Guth, Hans P. "Allegorical Implications of Artifice in Spenser's *Faerie Queene*." *PMLA*, LXXVI (1961), 474–479.
Hamilton, A. C. "Spenser's Treatment of Myth." *ELH*, XXVI (1959), 335–354.
Hamilton, A. C. *The Structure of Allegory in "The Faerie Queene*." Oxford, 1961.
Hankins, John E. *Source and Meaning in Spenser's Allegory: A Study of "The Faerie Queene*." Oxford, 1971.
Hill, R. F. "Spenser's Allegorical 'Houses.' " *MLR*, LXV (1970), 721–733.
Hinton, Stan. "The Poet and His Narrator: Spenser's Epic Voice." *ELH*, XLI (1974), 165–181.
Holleran, James V. "A View of Comedy in *The Faerie Queene*." In *Essays in Honor of Esmond Linworth Marilla*, edited by Thomas A. Kirby and William J. Olive, pp. 101–114. Baton Rouge, La., 1970.
Horton, Ronald A. *The Unity of "The Faerie Queene*." Athens, Ga., 1978.
Hough, Graham. *A Preface to "The Faerie Queene*." London, 1962.
Hughes, M. Y. "The Arthurs of *The Faerie Queene*." *Etudes Anglaises*, VI (1953), 193–213.
Klein, Joan L. "From Errour to Acrasia." *HLQ*, XLI (1978), 173–199.
Lewis, C. S. *Spenser's Images of Life*. Ed. Alastair Fowler. Cambridge, 1967.
MacCaffrey, Isabel G. *Spenser's Allegory: The Anatomy of Imagination*. Princeton, N.J., 1976.
MacLachlan, Hugh. " 'In the Person of Prince Arthur': Spenserian *Magnificence* and the Ciceronian Tradition." *UTQ*, XLVI (1976), 125–146.

MacLure, Millar. "Nature and Art in *The Faerie Queene*." *ELH*, XXVIII (1961), 1–20.

Miller, Milton. "Nature in *The Faerie Queene*." *ELH*, XVIII (1951), 191–200.

Murrin, Michael. "The Rhetoric of Fairyland." In *The Rhetoric of Renaissance Poetry from Wyatt to Milton*, edited by Thomas O. Sloan and Raymond B. Waddington, pp. 73–95. Berkeley, Calif., 1974.

Nelson, William. "Spenser *ludens*." In *A Theatre for Spenserians*. Ed. Judith M. Kennedy and James A. Reither.

Neuse, Richard. "Milton and Spenser: The Virgilian Triad Revisited." *ELH*, XLV (1978), 606–639.

Nohrnberg, James. *The Analogy of "The Faerie Queene."* Princeton, New Jersey, 1976.

O'Connell, Michael. *Mirror and Veil: The Historical Dimension of Spenser's "Faerie Queene."* Chapel Hill, N.C., 1977.

Orange, Linwood E. " 'All Bent to Mirth': Spenser's Humorous Wordplay." *SAQ*, LXXI (1972), 539–547.

Owen, W. J. B. "Narrative Logic and Imitation in *The Faerie Queene*." *CL*, VII (1955), 324–337.

Owen, W. J. B. "The Structure of *The Faerie Queene*." *PMLA*, LXVIII (1953), 1079–1100.

Paglia, Camille A. "The Apollonian Androgyne and *The Faerie Queene*." *ELR*, IX (1979), 42–63.

Phillips, James E. "Spenser's Syncretistic Religious Imagery." *ELH*, XXXVI (1969), 110–130.

Potts, Abbie Findlay. *Shakespeare and "The Faerie Queene."* Ithaca, N.Y., 1958.

Rose, Mark. *Heroic Love: Studies in Sidney and Spenser*. Cambridge, Mass., 1968.

Sale, Roger. *Reading Spenser: An Introduction to "The Faerie Queene."* New York, 1968.

Sessions, William A. "Spenser's Georgics," *ELR*, X (1980), 202–238.

Shaheen, Naseeb. *Biblical References in "The Faerie Queene."* Memphis, Tenn., 1977.

Sonn, Carl. "Spenser's Imagery." *ELH*, XXVI (1959), 156–170.

Tonkin, Humphrey. "Some Notes on Myth and Allegory in *The Faerie Queene*." *MP*, LXX (1973), 291–301.

Tonkin, Humphrey. "Theme and Emblem in Spenser's *Faerie Queene*." *ELH*, XL (1973), 221–230.

Tuve, Rosemond. *Essays: Spenser, Herbert, Milton*. Ed. Thomas P. Roche, Jr. Princeton, 1970.

Walter, J. H. "*The Faerie Queene*: Alterations and Structure." *MLR*, XXXVI (1941), 37–58.

Webster, John. "Oral Form and Written Craft in Spenser's *Faerie Queene*." *SEL*, XVI (1976), 75–93.

West, Michael. "Spenser and the Renaissance Ideal of Christian Heroism." *PMLA*, LXXXVIII (1973), 1013–1032.

Williams, Kathleen. "Spenser and the Metaphor of Sight." In *Renaissance Studies in Honor of Carroll Camden*, edited by J. A. Ward, pp. 153–169. *Rice University Studies*, 60, ii. Houston, 1974.

Williams, Kathleen. "Vision and Rhetoric: The Poet's Voice in *The Faerie Queene*." *ELH*, XXXVI (1969), 131–144.

Williams, Kathleen. *Spenser's "Faerie Queene": The World of Glass*. Berkeley, Calif., 1966.

Wilson, Robert R. "The Deformation of Narrative Time in *The Faerie Queene*." *UTQ*, XLI (1971), 48–62.

Woodhouse, A. S. P. "Nature and Grace in *The Faerie Queene*." *ELH*, XVI (1949), 194–228.

Woods, Susanne. "Aesthetic and Mimetic Rhythms in the Versification of Gascoigne, Sidney, and Spenser." *Studies in the Literary Imagination*, XI (1978), 31–44.

THE FAERIE QUEENE: BOOK I

Allen, D. C. "Arthur's Diamond Shield in *The Faerie Queene*." *JEGP*, XXXVI (1937), 234–243.

Allen, Margaret J. "The Harlot and the Mourning Bride." In *The Practical Vision: Essays in English Literature in Honour of Flora Roy*. Ed. Jane Campbell and James Doyle, pp. 13–28. Waterloo, Canada, 1978.

Berger, Harry, Jr. "Spenser's *Faerie Queene*, Book I: Prelude to Interpretation." *Southern Review* [Australia] II (1966), 18–49.

Blythe, Joan H. "Spenser and the Seven Deadly Sins: Book I, Cantos iv and v." *ELH*, XXXIX (1972), 342–352.

Brooks-Davies, Douglas, ed. *Spenser's "Faerie Queene": A Critical Commentary on Books I and II.* Manchester, 1977.

Davis, Walter R. "Arthur, Partial Exegesis, and the Reader." *TSLL*, XVIII (1977), 553–576.

Hamilton, A. C. "'Like Race to Runne': The Parallel Structure of *The Faerie Queene*, Books I and II." *PMLA*, LXXIII (1958), 327–334.

Hankins, John E. "Spenser and the Revelation of St. John." *PMLA*, LX (1945), 364–381.

Jordan, Richard D. "Una Among the Satyrs: *The Faerie Queene*, 1.6." *MLQ*, XXXVIII (1977), 123–131.

Kaske, Carol V. "The Dragon's Spark and Sting and the Structure of Red Cross's Dragon-fight: *The Faerie Queene*, I. xi–xii." *SP*, LXVI (1969), 609–638.

Kennedy, William J. "Rhetoric, Allegory, and Dramatic Modality in Spenser's Fradubio Episode." *ELR*, III (1973), 351–368.

Koller, Katherine. "Art, Rhetoric, and Holy Dying in *The Faerie Queene*, With Special Reference to the Despair Canto." *SP*, LXI (1964), 128–139.

Miller, Lewis H., Jr. "The Ironic Mode in Books I and II of *The Faerie Queene*." *PLL*, VII (1971), 133–149.

Mounts, Charles E. "Spenser's Seven Bead-Men and the Corporal Works of Mercy." *PMLA*, LIV (1939), 974–980.

Neill, Kerby. "The Degradation of the Red Cross Knight." *ELH*, XIX (1952), 173–190.

Orange, Linwood E. "Sensual Beauty in Book I of *The Faerie Queene*." *JEGP*, LXI (1962), 555–561.

Rose, Mark. *Spenser's Art: A Companion to Book I of "The Faerie Queene."* Cambridge, Mass., 1975.

Rusche, Harry. "Pride, Humility, and Grace in Book I of *The Faerie Queene*." *SEL*, VII (1967), 29–39.

Shroeder, John W. "Spenser's Erotic Drama: the Orgoglio Episide." *ELH*, XXIX (1962), 140–159.

Skulsky, Harold. "Spenser's Despair Episode and the Theology of Doubt," *MP*, LXXVIII (1981), 227–242.

Steadman, John M. "Spenser's *Errour* and the Renaissance Allegorical Tradition." *NM*, LXII (1961), 22–38.

Steadman, John M. "Una and the Clergy: the Ass Symbol in *The Faerie Queene*." *JWCI*, XXI (1958), 134–137.

Waters, D. Douglas. *Duessa As Theological Satire*. Columbia, Mo., 1970.

Waters, D. Douglas. "Prince Arthur as Christian Magnanimity in Book One of *The Faerie Queene*." *SEL*, IX (1969), 53–62.

Weiner, Andrew D. "'Fierce Warres and Faithful Loues': Pattern as Structure in *The Faerie Queene* I." *HLQ*, XXXVII (1974), 33–57.

Wells, R. Headlam. "Spenser's Christian Knight: Erasmian Theology in *The Faerie Queene*, Book I," *Anglia*, XCVII (1979), 350–366.

Whitaker, Virgil K. "The Theological Structure of *The Faerie Queene*, Book I." *ELH*, XIX (1952), 151–164.

See also Cullen (listed under *The Faerie Queene*: General Studies).

THE FAERIE QUEENE: BOOK II

Berger, Harry, Jr. *The Allegorical Temper: Vision and Reality in Book II of Spenser's "Faerie Queene."* New Haven, Conn., 1957.

Carscallen, James. "The Goodly Frame of Temperance: the Metaphor of Cosmos in *The Faerie Queene*, Book II." *UTQ*, XXXVII (1968), 136–155.

Doran, Madeleine. "On Elizabethan 'Credulity,' with Some Questions Concerning the Use of the Marvelous in Literature." *JHI*, I (1940), 151–176.

Durling, Robert. "The Bower of Bliss and Armida's Palace." *CL*, VI (1954), 335–347.

Evans, Maurice. "The Fall of Guyon." *ELH*, XXVIII (1961), 215–224.

Fowler, Alastair. "The River Guyon." *MLN*, LXXV (1960), 289–292.

Gohlke, Madelon S. "Embattled Allegory: Book II of *The Faerie Queene*." *ELR*, VIII (1978), 123–140.

Hamilton, A. C. "A Theological Reading of *The Faerie Queene*, Book II." *ELH*, XXV (1958), 155–162.

Hieatt, A. Kent. "Milton's Comus and Spenser's False Genius." *UTQ*, XXXVIII (1969), 313–318.

Hoopes, Robert. "'God Guide Thee, Guyon': Nature and Grace Reconciled in *The Faerie Queene*, Book II." *RES*, V (1954), 14–24.

Hughes, M. Y. "Spenser's Acrasia and the Circe of the Renaissance." *JHI*, IV (1943), 381–399.

Kaske, Carol. " 'Religious Reuerence Doth Buriall Teene': Christian and Pagan in *The Faerie Queene*, II.i–ii.," *RES*, XXX (1979), 129–143.

Kermode, Frank. "The Cave of Mammon." In *Elizabethan Poetry*. Stratford-upon-Avon Studies, 2, ed. J. R. Brown and B. Harris, pp. 151–173. London, 1960.

Miller, Lewis H., Jr. "A Secular Reading of *The Faerie Queene*, Book II." *ELH*, XXXIII (1966), 154–169.

Moore, Geoffrey A. "The Cave of Mammon: Ethics and Metaphysics in Secular and Christian Perspective." *ELH*, XLII (1975), 157–170.

Neill, Kerby. "Spenser's Acrasia and Mary Queen of Scots." *PMLA*, LX (1945), 632–638.

Nellish, B. "The Allegory of Guyon's Voyage: An Interpretation." *ELH*, XXX (1963), 89–106.

Okerlund, Arlene N. "Spenser's Wanton Maidens: Reader Psychology and the Bower of Bliss." *PMLA*, LXXXVIII (1973), 62–68.

Pollock, Zaidig. "Concupiscence and Intemperance in the Bower of Bliss." *SEL*, XX (1980), 43–58.

Snyder, Susan. "Guyon the Wrestler." *RN*, XIV (1961), 249–252.

Sonn, Carl. "Sir Guyon in the Cave of Mammon." *SEL*, I (1961), 17–30.

Swearingen, Roger. "Guyon's Faint." *SP*, LXXIV (1977), 165–185.

Tonkin, Humphrey. "Discussing Spenser's Cave of Mammon." *SEL*, XIII (1973), 1–13.

Wright, Lloyd. "Guyon's Heroism in the Bower of Bliss," *TSLL*, XV (1974), 597–603.

See also Cullen (listed under *The Faerie Queene*: General Studies); and Brooks-Davies, Hamilton, and Miller (listed under *The Faerie Queene*: Book I).

THE FAERIE QUEENE: BOOKS III AND IV

Bean, John C. "Making the Daimonic Personal: Britomart and Love's Assault in *The Faerie Queene*." *MLQ*, XL (1979), 237–255.

Berger, Harry, Jr. "*The Faerie Queene*, Book III: A General Description." *Criticism*, XI (1969), 234–261.

Berger, Harry, Jr. "The Discarding of Malbecco: Conspicuous Allusion and Cultural Exhaustion in *The Faerie Queene*, III, ix–x." *SP*, LXVI (1969), 135–154.

Berger, Harry, Jr. "Two Spenserian Retrospects: The Antique Temple of Venus and the Primitive Marriage of Rivers." *TSLL*, X (1968), 5–25.

Blackburn, William. "Spenser's Merlin," *Renaissance and Reformation*, N.S. IV (1980), 179–193.

Blissett, William. "Florimell and Marinell." *SEL*, V (1965), 87–104.

Burchmore, David. "The Unfolding of Britomart: Mythic Iconography in *The Faerie Queene*." In *Renaissance Papers 1977*. Ed. Dennis G. Donovan and A. Leigh DeNeef. Durham, N.C., 1978.

Brill, Lesley. " 'Battles That Need Not Be Fought': *The Faerie Queene*, III.i." *ELR*, V (1975), 198–211.

Brill, Lesley. "Chastity as Ideal Sexuality in the Third Book of *The Faerie Queene*." *SEL*, XI (1971), 15–26.

Cheney, Donald. "Spenser's Hermaphrodite and the 1590 *Faerie Queene*." *PMLA*, LXXXVII (1972), 192–200.

Crampton, Georgia R. "Spenser's Lyric Theodicy: The Complaints of *The Faerie Queene*, III.iv." *ELH*, XLIV (1977), 205–221.

DeNeef, A. Leigh. "Spenser's *Amor Fuggitivo* and the Transfixed Heart." *ELH*, XLVI (1979), 1–20.

Edwards, Calvin. "The Narcissus Myth in Spenser's Poetry." *SP*, LXXIV (1977), 63–88.

Geller, Lila. "Venus and the Three Graces: A Neoplatonic Paradigm for Book III of *The Faerie Queene*." *JEGP*, LXXV (1976), 56–74.

Gilde, Helen C. " 'The sweet lodge of love and deare delight': The Problem of Amoret." *PQ*, L (1971), 63–74.

Hieatt, A. Kent. *Chaucer, Spenser, Milton: Mythopoeic Continuities and Transformations*. Montreal. 1975.

Hill, Iris T. "Britomart and 'Be bold, Be not too bold'." *ELH*, XXXVIII (1971), 173–187.

Hughes, Felicity A. "Psychological Allegory in *The Faerie Queene* III.xi–xii." *RES*, XXIX (1978), 129–146.

Huston, J. Dennis. "The Function of the Mock Hero in Spenser's *Faerie Queene*." *MP*, LXVI (1969), 212–217.

Lanham, Richard A. "The Literal Britomart." *MLQ*, XXVIII (1967), 426–445.

Maclean, Hugh. " 'Restless anguish and unquiet paine': Spenser and the Complaint, 1579–1590." In *The Practical Vision: Essays in English Literature in*

Honour of Flora Roy. Ed. Jane Campbell and James Doyle, pp. 29–48. Waterloo, Canada, 1978.

McNeir, Waldo F. "Ariosto's Sospetto, Gascoigne's Suspicion, and Spenser's Malbecco." In *Festschrift für Walther Fischer*, pp. 34–48. Heidelberg, 1959.

Mills, Jerry Leath. "Spenser and the Numbers of History: A Note on the British and Elfin Chronicles in *The Faerie Queene.*" *PQ*, LV (1976), 281–287.

Murtaugh, Daniel M. "The Garden and the Sea: The Topography of *The Faerie Queene*, Book III." *ELH*, XL (1973), 325–338.

Nestrick, William V. "Spenser and the Renaissance Mythology of Love." *Literary Monographs*, VI (1975), 37–50.

Quilligan, Maureen. "Words and Sex: The Language of Allegory in the *De planctu naturae*, the *Roman de la Rose*, and Book III of *The Faerie Queene.*" *Allegorica*, II (1977), 195–216.

Ramsay, Judith C. "The Garden of Adonis and the Garden of Forms." *UTQ*, XXXV (1966), 188–206.

Roche, Thomas P., Jr. *The Kindly Flame: A Study of the Third and Fourth Books of Spenser's "Faerie Queene."* Princeton, N.J., 1964.

Sims, Dwight. "Cosmological Structure in *The Faerie Queene*, Book III." *HLQ*, XL (1977), 99–116.

Sims, Dwight. "The Syncretic Myth of Venus in Spenser's Legend of Chastity." *SP*, LXXI (1974), 427–450.

Thompson, Claud A. "Spenser's 'Many Faire Pourtraicts, and Many a Faire Feate.' " *SEL*, XII (1972), 21–32.

Tonkin, Humphrey. "Spenser's Garden of Adonis and Britomart's Quest." *PMLA*, LXXXVIII (1973), 408–417.

Weld, J. S. "The Complaint of Britomart: Wordplay and Symbolism." *PMLA*, LXVI (1951), 548–551.

THE FAERIE QUEENE: BOOK V

Aptekar, Jane. *Icons of Justice: Iconography and Thematic Imagery in Book V of "The Faerie Queene."* New York, 1969.

Bieman, Elizabeth. "Britomart in Book V of *The Faerie Queene.*" *UTQ*, XXXVII (1968), 156–174.

Davidson, Clifford. "The Idol of Isis Church." *SP*, LXVI (1969), 70–86.

Dunseath, T. K. *Spenser's Allegory of Justice in Book Five of "The Faerie Queene."* Princeton, N.J., 1968.

Graziani, Rene. "Elizabeth at Isis Church." *PMLA*, LXXIX (1964), 376–389.

Knight, W. Nicholas. "The Narrative Unity of Book V of *The Faerie Queene*: 'That Part of Justice Which is Equity.' " *RES*, XXI (1970), 267–294.

Lievsay, John L. "An Immediate Source for *Faerie Queene*, Book V, Proem." *MLN*, LIX (1944), 469–472.

Miskimin, Alice. "Britomart's Crocodile and the Legends of Chastity." *JEGP*, LXXVII (1978), 17–36.

Phillips, James E. "Renaissance Concepts of Justice and the Structure of *The Faerie Queene*, Book V." *HLQ*, XXXIV (1970), 103–120.

Waters, D. Douglas. "Spenser and the 'Mas' at the Temple of Isis." *SEL*, XIX (1979), 43–54.

See also Fletcher (listed under *The Faerie Queene*: General Studies).

THE FAERIE QUEENE: BOOK VI

Atkinson, Dorothy F. "The Pastorella Episode in *The Faerie Queene.*" *PMLA*, LIX (1944), 361–372.

Berger, Harry, Jr. "The Prospect of Imagination: Spenser and the Limits of Poetry." *SEL*, I (1961), 93–120.

Berger, Harry, Jr. "A Secret Discipline: *The Faerie Queene*, Book VI." In *Form and Convention in the Poetry of Edmund Spenser*, edited by William Nelson; pp. 35–75. New York, 1961.

Culp, Dorothy W. "Courtesy and Fortune's Chance in Book VI of *The Faerie Queene.*" *MP*, LXVIII (1971), 254–259.

Culp, Dorothy. "Courtesy and Moral Virtue." *SEL*, XI (1971), 37–51.

Geller, Lila. "The Acidalian Vision: Spenser's Graces in Book VI of *The Faerie Queene.*" *RES*, XXIII (1972), 267–277.

Geller, Lila. "Spenser's Theory of Nobility in Book VI of *The Faerie Queene.*" *ELR*, V (1975), 49–57.

Mallette, Richard. "Poet and Hero in Book VI of *The Faerie Queene.*" *MLR*, LXXII (1977), 257–267.

Maxwell, J. C. "The Truancy of Calidore." *ELH*, XIX (1952), 143–149.

Miller, David. "Abandoning the Quest." *ELH*, XLVI (1979), 173–192.

Nestrick, William V. "The Virtuous and Gentle Discipline of Gentlemen and Poets." *ELH*, XXIX (1962), 357–371.

Neuse, Richard. "Book VI as Conclusion to *The Faerie Queene.*" *ELH*, XXXV (1968), 329–353.

Rusche, Harry. "The Lesson of Calidore's Truancy," *SP*, LXXVI (1979), 149–161.

Snare, Gerald. "The Poetics of Vision: Patterns of Grace and Courtesy in *The Faerie Queene*, VI." In *Renaissance Papers 1974*. Ed. Dennis G. Donovan and A. Leigh DeNeef. Durham, N.C., 1975.

Snare, Gerald. "Spenser's Fourth Grace." *JWCI*, XXXIV (1971), 350–355.

Tonkin, Humphrey. *Spenser's Courteous Pastoral: Book VI of "The Faerie Queene."* Oxford, 1972.

Wells, Robin. "Spenser and the Courtesy Tradition: Form and Meaning in the Sixth Book of *The Faerie Queene.*" *ES*, LVIII (1977), 221–229.

Williams, Arnold. *Flower on a Lowly Stalk: The Sixth Book of "The Faerie Queene."* East Lansing, Mich., 1967.

Williams, Kathleen. "Courtesy and Pastoral in *The Faerie Queene*, Book VI." *RES*, XIII (1962), 337–346.

Woods, Susanne. "Closure in *The Fairie Queene.*" *JEGP*, LXXVI (1977), 195–216.

See also Javitch (listed under General Studies) and Cheney (listed under *The Faerie Queene*: General Studies).

THE FAERIE QUEENE: MUTABILITIE CANTOS

Allen, D. C. "On the Closing Lines of *The Faerie Queene.*" *MLN*, LXIV (1949), 93–94.

Blissett, William. "Spenser's Mutabilitie." In *Essays in English Literature from the Renaissance to the Victorian Age Presented to A. S. P. Woodhouse.* Ed. Millar MacLure and F. W. Watt, pp. 26–42. Toronto, 1964.

Friedland, Louis S. "Spenser's Sabaoth's Rest." *MLQ*, XVII (1956), 199–203.

Hawkins, Sherman. "Mutabilitie and the Cycle of the Months." In *Form and Convention in the Poetry of Edmund Spenser*, edited by William Nelson, pp. 76–102. New York, 1961.

Holahan, Michael. "*Iamque Opus Exegi*: Ovid's Changes and Spenser's Brief Epic of Mutability." *ELR*, VI (1976), 244–270.

Holland, Joanne F. "The Cantos of Mutabilitie and the Form of *The Faerie Queene.*" *ELH*, XXXV (1968), 21–31.

Owen, Lewis J. "Mutable in Eternity: Spenser's Despair and the Multiple Forms of Mutabilitie." *JMRS*, II (1972), 49–68.

Ringler, R. N. "The Faunus Episode." *MP*, LXIII (1965), 12–19.

Wells, Robin. "Semper Eadem: Spenser's 'Legend of Constancie,'" *MLR*, LXXIII (1978), 250–255.

THE SHEPHEARDES CALENDER

Alpers, Paul. "The Eclogue Tradition and the Nature of Pastoral." *CE*, XXXIV (1972), 352–371.

Berger, Harry, Jr. "Mode and Diction in *The Shepheardes Calender.*" *MP*, LXVII (1969), 140–149.

Brown, James N. "Stasis and Art in *The Shepheardes Calender.*" *Massachusetts Studies in English*, III (1971), 7–16.

Cain, Thomas H. "The Strategy of Praise in Spenser's 'Aprill.'" *SEL*, VIII (1968), 45–58.

Cullen, Patrick. *Spenser, Marvell, and Renaissance Pastoral.* Cambridge, Mass., 1970.

Dixon, Michael F. "Rhetorical Patterns and Methods of Advocacy in Spenser's *Shepheardes Calender.*" *ELR*, VII (1977), 131–154.

Durr, R. A. "Spenser's Calendar of Christian Time." *ELH*, XXIV (1957), 269–295.

Fujii, Haruhiko. "*Lycidas* and Spenser's Pastorals." *Hiroshima Studies in English Language and Literature*, XIX (1972), 34–50.

Fujii, Haruhiko. *Time, Landscape, and the Ideal Life: Studies in the Pastoral Poetry of Spenser and Milton.* Kyoto, 1974.

Hamilton, A. C. "The Argument of Spenser's *Shepheardes Calender.*" *ELH*, XXIII (1956), 171–182.

Hardin, Richard F. "The Resolved Debate of Spenser's 'October.'" *MP*, LXXIII (1976), 257–263.

Heninger, S. K., Jr. "The Implications of Form for *The Shepheardes Calender.*" *SRen*, IX (1962), 309–321.

Hoffman, Nancy. *Spenser's Pastorals: "The Shepheardes Calender" and "Colin Clouts Come Home Againe."* Baltimore, 1977.
Jenkins, Raymond. "Who Is E.K.?" *SAB*, XIX (1944), 147–160; XX (1945), 22–38, 82–94.
McLane, Paul E. *Spenser's Shepheardes Calender: A Study in Elizabethan Allegory.* Notre Dame, Ind., 1961.
McNeir, Waldo. "The Drama of Spenser's *Shepheardes Calender.*" *Anglia,* XCV (1977), 34–59.
Mallette, Richard. "Spenser's Portrait of the Artist in *The Shepheardes Calender* and *Colin Clouts Come Home Againe.*" *SEL*, XIX (1979), 19–42.
Miller, David L. "Authorship, Anonymity, and *The Shepheardes Calender.*" *MLQ*, XL (1979), 219–236.
Montrose, Louis A. " 'Eliza, Queene of shepheardes,' and the Pastoral of Power," *ELR*, X (1980), 153–182.
Montrose, Louis A. " 'The perfecte paterne of a Poete': The Poetics of Courtship in *The Shepheardes Calender.*" *TSLL*, XXI (1979), 34–67.
Moore, John W., Jr. "Colin Breaks His Pipe: A Reading of the 'January' Eclogue." *ELR*, V (1975), 3–24.
Röstvig, Maren-Sofie. "*The Shepheardes Calender*: A Structural Analysis." *Renaissance and Modern Studies* [Nottingham], XIII (1969), 49–75.
Shore, David R. "Colin and Rosalind: Love and Poetry in *The Shepheardes Calender.*" *SP*, LXXIII (1976), 176–188.
Staton, W. F., Jr. "Spenser's 'Aprill' Lay as a Dramatic Chorus." *SP*, LIX (1962), 111–118.
Walker, Steven. " 'Poetry Is/Is Not a Cure for Love': The Conflict of Theocritean and Petrarchan *Topoi* in *The Shepheardes Calender.*" *SP*, LXXVI (1979), 353–365.
Waters, D. Douglas. "Spenser and Symbolic Witchcraft in *The Shepheardes Calender.*" *SEL*, XIV (1974), 3–15.
See also Cooper, Merivale, and Smith (listed under General Studies), and Helgerson (listed under Spenser's Poetry: General).

MUIOPOTMOS

Allen, D. C. "On Spenser's *Muiopotmos.*" *SP*, LIII (1956), 141–158.
Anderson, Judith. " 'Nat worth a boterflye': *Muiopotmos* and *The Nun's Priest's Tale.*" *JMRS*, I (1971), 89–106.
Court, Franklin E. "The Theme and Structure of Spenser's *Muiopotmos.*" *SEL*, X (1970), 1–15.
Dundas, Judith. "*Muiopotmos*: A World of Art." *YES*, V (1975), 30–38.
Wells, William. " 'To Make a Milde Construction': The Significance of the Opening Stanzas of *Muiopotmos.*" *SP*, XLII (1945), 544–554.

AMORETTI

Bernard, John. "Spenserian Pastoral and the *Amoretti,*" *ELH*, XLVII (1980), 419–432.
Cummings, Peter M. "Spenser's *Amoretti* as an Allegory of Love." *TSLL*, XII (1970), 163–179.
Dunlop, Alexander. "The Unity of Spenser's *Amoretti.*" In *Silent Poetry: Essays in Numerological Analysis.* Ed. Alastair Fowler.
Hardison, O. B., Jr. "*Amoretti* and the *Dolce Stil Novo.*" *ELR*, II (1972), 208–216.
Hunter, G. K. "Spenser's *Amoretti* and the English Sonnet Tradition." In *A Theatre for Spenserians.* Ed. Judith M. Kennedy and James A. Reither.
John, Lisle C. *The Elizabethan Sonnet Sequences: Studies in Conventional Conceits.* Columbia University Studies in English and Comparative Literature, #133. New York, 1938.
Johnson, William C. "Spenser's *Amoretti* and the Art of the Liturgy." *SEL*, XIV (1974), 47–61.
Kaske, Carol V. "Spenser's *Amoretti* and *Epithalamion* of 1595: Structure, Genre, and Numerology." *ELR*, VIII (1978), 271–295.
Kellogg, Robert. "Thought's Astonishment and the Dark Conceits of Spenser's *Amoretti.*" In *Renaissance Papers 1965.* Ed. George Walton Williams and Peter G. Phialas. Durham, N.C., 1966.
Lever, J. W. *The Elizabethan Love Sonnet.* London, 1956.
McNeir, Waldo. "An Apology for Spenser's 'Amoretti.' " *Die Neueren Sprachen,* XIV (1965), 1–9.
Miller, Jacqueline T. " 'Love Doth Hold My Hand': Writing and Wooing in the Sonnets of Sidney and Spenser." *ELH,* XLVI (1979), 541–548.

748 · Bibliography

Neely, Carol. "The Structure of English Renaissance Sonnet Sequences." *ELH*, XLV (1978), 359–389.

See also Peterson and Smith (listed under General Studies).

EPITHALAMION

Cirillo, Albert R. "Spenser's *Epithalamion*: The Harmonious Universe of Love." *SEL*, VIII (1968), 19–34.
Clemen, Wolfgang. "The Uniqueness of Spenser's *Epithalamion*." In *The Poetic Tradition: Essays on Greek, Latin, and English Poetry*. Ed. D. C. Allen and Henry T. Rowell. Baltimore, 1968.
Greene, Thomas M. "Spenser and the Epithalamic Convention." *CL*, IX (1957), 215–228.
Hieatt, A. Kent. "The Daughters of Horus: Order in the Stanzas of *Epithalamion*." In *Form and Convention in the Poetry of Edmund Spenser*. Ed. William Nelson.
Hieatt, A. Kent. *Short Time's Endless Monument: The Symbolism of the Numbers in Edmund Spenser's "Epithalamion."* New York, 1960.
Hill, W. Speed. "Order and Joy in Spenser's *Epithalamion*." *Southern Humanities Review*, VI (1972), 81–90.
Hyman, L. W. "Structure and Meaning in Spenser's *Epithalamion*." *Tennessee Studies in Literature*, III (1958), 37–42.
Miller, Paul W. "The Decline of the English Epithalamion." *TSLL*, XII (1970), 405–416.
Mulryan, John. "The Function of Ritual in the Marriage Songs of Catullus, Spenser, and Ronsard." *Illinois Quarterly*, XXXV (1972), 50–64.
Neuse, Richard. "The Triumph Over Hasty Accidents: A Note on the Symbolic Mode of the *Epithalamion*." *MLR*, LXI (1966), 163–174.
Stevenson, W. H. "The Spaciousness of Spenser's *Epithalamion*." *REL*, V (1964), 61–69.
Tufte, Virginia. "'High Wedlock Then be Honored': Rhetoric and the Epithalamium." *Pacific Coast Philology*, I (1966), 32–41.
Wickert, Max A. "Structure and Ceremony in Spenser's *Epithalamion*." *ELH*, XXXV (1968), 135–157.
See also Fowler, *Triumphal Forms*, and Smith (listed under General Studies); and Kaske (listed under *Amoretti*).

FOWRE HYMNES

Comito, Terry. "A Dialectic of Images in Spenser's *Fowre Hymnes*." *SP*, LXXIV (1977), 301–321.
Jayne, Sears. "Ficino and the Platonism of the English Renaissance." *CL*, IV (1952), 214–238.
Quitslund, Jon A. "Spenser's Image of Sapience." *SRen*, XVI (1969), 181–213.
Rollinson, Philip. "A Generic View of Spenser's *Fowre Hymnes*." *SP*, LXVIII (1971), 292–304.
Stewart, James T. "Renaissance Psychology and the Ladder of Love in Castiglione and Spenser." *JEGP*, LVI (1957), 225–230.

PROTHALAMION

Berger, Harry, Jr. "Spenser's 'Prothalamion': An Interpretation." *EIC*, XV (1965), 363–380.
Fowler, Alastair. "*Prothalamion*," in *Conceitful Thought: The Interpretation of English Renaissance Poems*. Edinburgh, 1975.
Norton, Dan S. "The Tradition of Prothalamia." In *English Studies in Honor of James Southall Wilson*. University of Virginia Studies, #4. Charlottesville, Va., 1951.
Patterson, Sandra. "Spenser's *Prothalamion* and the Catullan Epithalamic Tradition." *Comitatus*, X (1979–80), 97–106.
Prager, Carolyn. "Emblem and Motion in Spenser's *Prothalamion*." *Studies in Iconography*, II (1976), 114–120.
Wine, M. L. "Spenser's 'sweete Themmes': Of Time and the River." *SEL*, II (1962), 111–117.
Woodward, Daniel H. "Some Themes in Spenser's 'Prothalamion.'" *ELH*, XXIX (1962), 34–46.